UNTEEN

WITHDRAWN

Sourcebook on Labor

SOURCEBOOK ON LABOR

Neil W. Chamberlain
Professor of Economics
Graduate School of Business
Columbia University

McGRAW-HILL BOOK COMPANY, INC.
New York   Toronto   London
1958

Preface

This book is an effort to bring together some of the raw materials of the subject of industrial relations. It includes documents such as union constitutions, collective agreements, company statements of labor policy, laws and court decisions, arbitration awards, and reports of governmental inquiries. It is sprinkled with excerpts from congressional hearings on a variety of topics such as labor monopoly, union political activity, minimum wages, and strike control. It contains portions of speeches made by labor officials and management representatives. The student is offered the views of partisans expressed in their own words, the decisions of governmental bodies free of interpretative gloss, and accounts of incidents as reported at the time of occurrence.

There are two purposes to be served by a collection of this kind. One is to provide readier access to fugitive materials which are often difficult to locate even in the best organized and best stocked libraries. A student should ideally see and handle these documents in their original form, but in view of the difficulties involved in making this possible, their assembly in one volume is a convenient and acceptable substitute.

The second purpose is to afford the student greater opportunity to make an informed judgment for himself on the debatable issues of labor relations and to appraise for himself the plausibility of judgments made by those who write his textbooks. It is not satisfactory to ask students to accept the conclusions of "experts," however cogently argued. Where points of view differ it is preferable to permit him to evaluate for himself the source material out of which "expert" opinions are formed. Different interpretations of the same problem are here presented in the words and arguments of those who would convince others of the rightness of their views. The student is exposed to unfiltered bias, often persuasively reasoned, of the sort to which he will continue to be exposed for the rest of his life, and asked to examine it critically.

It has not been an easy task to compile this volume. With few exceptions, the problem has been one of a surplus of riches. Keeping the total length to something which would not shock even a tolerant publisher has been a condition not easy to meet. At the same time, the necessity had to be faced of including enough materials to give a semblance of adequate and provocative treatment of the topics covered. Others would not always have selected as I have, I know; I would welcome from them suggestions for exclusion, inclusion, and substitution.

This volume is designed to stand on its own feet, as something usable independent of a text. It has, however, also been designed to parallel my own text, *Labor,* with the chapter organization here closely following the organization of subject matter in that book.

Neil W. Chamberlain

Contents

Contents

Contents

Contents

1: Labor Force and Labor Market

The following BLS summary of a paper presented before the American Statistical Association in 1955 has significance for students of industrial relations problems. As industries and occupations expand or decline, they present problems to unions as well as to business establishments. The changing composition of the labor force likewise suggests areas in which the unions will have to seek new members if they are to maintain even their present relative strength in the economy.

CHANGING PATTERNS OF INDUSTRIAL EMPLOYMENT

By Seymour L. Wolfbein, Bureau of Labor Statistics

CHANGES IN INDUSTRIAL STRUCTURE OF FACTORY EMPLOYMENT

The manufacturing segment of the nonagricultural economy is at one and the same time the most volatile sector, moving sharply up or down in employment in response to changing levels of economic activity and war and peace; by far the largest industry division in the U.S.; and, perhaps paradoxically, very stable in the proporton of nonagricultural employment it accounts for throughout the period since 1919.

Thus, manufacturing employment shows a greater amplitude of change throughout this period than any other employment division. Factory employment fell from about 10½ million in 1929 to 6¾ million in 1932, then rose to 17⅓ million by the peak war year of 1943. It rose by more than 70 percent in the few years between 1939 and 1943. As a result of these movements, manufacturing employment has accounted for as much as 41 percent of all nonfarm jobs during World War II and as little as 29 percent at the bottom of the depression. Aside from these abnormal periods, however, manufacturing as a percent of total nonfarm employment has been quite stable—accounting for about one out of every three nonfarm jobs. . . .

From many points of view, some of the most important structural changes in American industry have occurred within the manufacturing division. A substantial part of the upward shift in earnings since 1939, the growth of trade unionism, the changing geography of American industry, alterations in the job structure, etc. can be traced to the industrial changes in factory employment in the U.S.A. Some of these . . . can be highlighted as follows:

1

1. Between 1939 and 1955 the durable and nondurable goods industries reversed positions. In 1939, the nondurables employed about 55 percent of all manufacturing employees; by 1955, they were employing 2½ million less than the durables and accounted for only about 43 percent of the total.

2. As against an increase in total manufacturing employment of about 65 percent during this period of time, the hard goods industries rose by more than 100 percent. Most of the structural increase was concentrated within three industry groups: electrical and nonelectrical machinery and transportation equipment (mostly autos and aircraft). In fact, these three industries now account for more than one out of every four factory workers in the U.S.— almost double the proportion of a decade ago.

3. Just the opposite story must be told for the nondurables segment, which rose only 30 percent between 1939 and 1955. Here, too, three industries played a major role in the downward shift in industrial structure in the light goods industries—textiles, apparel and food. These three groups used to account for one out of three factory workers in 1939, but failed to keep pace with general employment increases since that time. In fact, the textile industry alone, which used to be the single most important employer within manufacturing, actually declined between 1939 and 1955—this in the face of the tremendous employment advances in practically every other segment.

Every other major industry division of nonagricultural employment experienced changes of comparable importance in their employment structures. The following discussion illustrates some of these changes in a few of the divisions, summarized briefly and rather starkly in order to conserve time and space:

THE DECLINE IN EXTRACTIVE INDUSTRIES

The only major industry division showing an absolute decline in employment since 1919 was mining. In the face of an increase in nonfarm employment of almost 85 percent since 1919, employment in mining *declined* by one-third since that time. This decline has been regular and persistent over the 35 year

Employment Trends in Mining, 1939–1955

	1939	1955 [1]	Change 1939–1955
All mining	845	747	−12%
Metal mining	102	96	([2])
Anthracite	90	36	−60
Bituminous	388	209	−46
Petroleum and gas	189	300	+59
Nonmetallic mining	76	106	+40

[1] 11 month average.

[2] Less than 1%.

period and has brought the proportion that mining accounts of total employment down from a little over 4 percent to 1½ percent.

However, the overall trend for mining masks a series of major changes in
the internal structure of employment in the extractive industries in this country.
As a matter of fact, the overall decline is a compound of contrasting trends
among the individual industries in this division:

Thus, in 1939, employment in the bituminous coal industry alone out-
numbered employment in petroleum and gas by more than 2 to 1; today
petroleum and gas operations employ more workers than bituminous *and* anthracite mining put together.

DIFFERENTIAL TRENDS IN TRANSPORTATION AND PUBLIC UTILITIES

Just as the changes in use and market demand for different sources of fuel
and power have reflected themselves in major changes in the industrial structure of extractive operations, so have the differential trends in demand for
various modes of travelling and shipping shown their effects on the employment
picture in the transportation segment of the nonfarm economy.

Since 1919, the transportation and public utilities field has afforded about
the same number of jobs to nonfarm workers—approximately 4 millions. In
addition to mining, however, this is the only other major industry division
which has declined—and declined substantially—in the *proportion* it bears to
the total nonagricultural economy. During the 1920's, the segment accounted
for between 13 and 14 percent of all employees in nonagricultural establishments. Since that time, the proportion has declined steadily during the thirties
and forties and through the present decade, and now stands at about 8½
percent.

The comparative stability of employment levels in the field in the face of substantial increases in output and service during this period reflects not only a
rise in productivity but also the relative increases and declines in importance
of the different individual industries in the group. Thus, employment by rail-

Employment Trends in Transportation, 1947–1955, in Thousands

	1947	1955 [1]	Change 1947–1955
All transportation..........................	2,984	2,714	− 9%
Interstate railroads......................	1,557	1,203	−23
Local railways and bus lines.............	185	118	−36
Bus lines, exc. local....................	63	44	−30
Trucking................................	551	764	+39
Air transportation......................	82	113	+38
All other transportation.................	546	473	−13

[1] 11 month average.

roads, still the biggest component of the transportation field, declined during the past decade; declines also took place in such areas as local and even interstate bus lines. The increases, as expected, came in the newer forms of transportation, especially by air and truck.

THE GROWTH OF TRADE AND THE SERVICES

Between 1919 and 1955 nonagricultural employment changed as follows:

All nonagricultural employment.....	+ 83%
Service.........................	177
Government..	158
Construction....................	146
Trade	129
Finance..	108
Manufacturing.................	57
Transportation and public utilities	9
Mining.......................	− 34

The major areas of secular growth are represented by trade, service, and government activities, most of the latter being in State and local government, most of which, in turn, involves community services such as teaching and police and fire protection (more than a million teachers are classified in this government division). It is not surprising to find, by the same token, that the major areas of growth occupationally are found in the professions and clerical and sales jobs, which, in turn, employ large proportions of women whose labor market participation rates have risen substantially during this period of time.

Throughout this time, these three industry divisions have contributed the major share of employment growth in the nonfarm sector of the economy. Even during the decade 1929 to 1939, when nonagricultural employment declined, only three industry divisions increased their employment: trade, service, and government. The employment growth in these three areas continues right up to the present. For example, nonfarm employment fell significantly (by about 1½ million) between 1953 and 1954. But trade employment fell only fractionally and government and service actually increased. The only other segment to gain in employment was finance and insurance, also basically a service activity. An exactly similar story can be told for the current year. Nonfarm employment, in very recent months, has exceeded the 1953 peak—but only because trade, service, government and its allied finance and insurance divisions are up over two years ago. All the rest are still below 1953 levels.

As a result of these trends, the three divisions of trade, service and government now account for almost half of all nonfarm employment in the U.S. (47 percent) in contrast to a little over one-third (35.1 percent) back in 1919.

THE SHIFT FROM GOODS TO SERVICES

The significant growth in some of the trade and service areas just described points toward one of the really fundamental changes in industrial structure:

the gradual but persistent shift in employment from the goods-producing sectors to the service-producing sectors of the American economy.

Taking annual average 1955 (estimated) as an example, we find the following situation:

Employed in the production of goods (in thousands)		Employed in the production of services (in thousands)	
Mining.....................	747	Trade......................	10 631
Construction................	2,513	Transp. & Public Utilities......	4,049
Manufacturing..............	16,511	Finance, insurance...........	2,188
Agriculture.................	8,200[1]	Service....................	5,697
		Government	6,886
	27,971		29,451

[1] Estimated annual figure from Dept. of Agriculture data on farm employment

This summary table assigns to the goods-producing segment of the economy all of the extractive industries—the coal, oil, gas, lead, zinc, etc., all of construction—the building of homes, highways, factories, offices, etc., all of manufacturing—the steel, clothing, machinery, autos, chemicals, etc. and all of agriculture —the feed, food and fibers. These comprise practically all of the *goods* we produce. To the service-producing segment are assigned all of the activities which involve buying, selling, financing, transporting, servicing, teaching, etc. These comprise the services produced by workers in each of the assigned industries. With the exception of farming, where the distinction is often difficult to make, all the categories are confined to wage and salary workers only. Excluded are the nonagricultural self-employed, domestics and unpaid family workers, the great majority of whom, of course, would appear under the service-producing segment if counted.

Even with these exclusions we find that there are now in the U.S. more persons engaged in the production of services than in the production of goods. Although this situation was only recently attained, we have been moving toward it in a continuous and persistent manner ever since the end of World War I. (See the chart on page 6.)

The fact that we now have more workers engaged in the production of services rather than goods is an important hallmark in the evolution of our standard of living. Generally speaking, this evolution—in other countries of the world as well as in prior civilizations—has proceeded something like the following: In the beginning—and this was particularly true in primitive times—practically all of the population is found to be in what we now call "the labor force." Not only do all men work, but so do practically all women and even the very young. Furthermore, practically all of the workers are engaged in the production of "goods," i.e. in providing the basic necessities of food, clothing, and

Employment in Goods Producing Industries Compared with Employment in Service Industries Annual Averages, 1919–1955

SOURCE: Nonfarm wage and salary employment from the U.S. Bureau of Labor Statistics. Agricultural employment including proprietors, family workers, and hired workers from the Bureau of Agricultural Economics, U.S. Depatment of Agriculture.

shelter. As technical advances are made, two developments apparently occur. In the first place, the proportion of the population in the labor force declines. Women can withdraw from the working population to the home; the young can take more time for education and training; the old can withdraw into "retirement." In the second place, more and more of those remaining in the labor force can be engaged in the production of "services"—and we see the growth of what we now call the professional, clerical, and service occupations.

The gradual shift in employment from the goods to service-producing sectors reflects much the same kind of evolution in this country. In the first fifty years of the century in the U.S., for example, we have *doubled* the gross national product per capita (adjusted for price change). We have done this with a labor force as a percent of population which has remained practically unchanged between 1900 and 1950—and with a labor force working many less hours now than at the turn of the century. The tremendous gain in output (or standard of living) has been attained mostly through major advances in productivity which have prevailed so dramatically in some of the key goods-producing sectors of the economy, especially in agriculture and manufacturing. These gains have made possible the enormous increase in the production of goods with only modest employment increases and made possible the employment of significantly increasing numbers of workers for jobs in the growing service industries.

WORKING PEOPLE IN THE NEXT TWENTY YEARS

By Arthur Larson, Under Secretary of Labor; an address at the Annual Convention of the International Association of Industrial Editors, Los Angeles, June 20, 1956

We know, if recent trends are sustained that the population of the United States in 1975 will be about 220 million—which would be the equivalent of adding to our present population the entire population of Great Britain. We can tell with reasonable certainty, also, that the growth in the various age brackets will be uneven and will distort present proportions somewhat. For example, in the first ten years we shall see a rapid jump in the number of teen-agers, who will increase by about 11½ million, and a considerable increase in the 45–64 group, amounting to nearly 6 million. Meanwhile, the number of people in the 20–44 group will increase by only 2 million!

You don't need the gift of prophecy—only a little elementary arithmetic—to draw a number of obvious conclusions.

One is that this flood of teen-agers had better have good schools to go to, or we shall not only miss a superb opportunity to bring up a well-educated well-trained generation of crucial importance, but we shall positively compound many times over our problems of juvenile delinquency and maladjustment.

Another is that, with the 20–44 age group failing to increase in this period by anything like enough to meet the demands of the rapidly growing population, there will be severe temptation for the teen-agers to drop out of school and take the jobs that may open up as a result. This would be a double misfortune, because it would probably detract from the use of the older workers who are the logical source of supply to meet this need, and especially because it would deprive the young people of a proper education at the very time when an education is becoming almost indispensable in the labor market. In this future day we are thinking about, a person without a high school education will be a distinctly disadvantaged minority group. In 1910, the percentage of young people of high school graduating age who actually graduated from high school was only 9%; in 1940 this was 48%; in 1955 it was 62%. Just as we now have special programs for disadvantaged groups, such as older workers or the physically handicapped, it would not be surprising to read, in 1976, about how the Department of Labor is to launch a special new program—for the Educationally Handicapped!

The problem posed by the disproportionate rise in the number of people in the middle and older brackets is well known. By 1975, the 45–64 group will have increased by 10 million. . . . By 1975 also our population over age 65 will have grown by 6½ million to 20 million, up almost 50 percent from now, and will amount to 9% of the total population. . . .

While the total population is increasing to 220 million, and the work force is increasing by about 21 million, it is quite possible that the total gross national product may double, in the opinion of some reputable economists. This would mean, per capita, an increase of about 50 percent. This projected increase, although it may seem large, is really not unrealistic; in fact, it is not much more than the increase which took place between 1929 and 1956. . . .

As to the welfare of working people, the happy message contained in these cold G.N.P. figures is that these higher incomes should make possible the alleviation of many everyday problems. . . .

While this rapid rise in living standards and level of education is going on, there is also a rapid rise in the skill level of workers. In 1910 unskilled workers accounted for 36 percent of the work force; by 1950 this was down to 19 percent. In the same period the percentage of semi-skilled workers rose from 15 to 23. This process is relentlessly going on at all levels. What this may mean for greater regularity of employment can be seen today in our new figures on characteristics of the unemployed. Unskilled workers, although they now make up only about a tenth of the insured employed, accounted for a third of the insured unemployed. Simultaneously, we are experiencing acute shortages of engineers and some highly skilled workers. Our employment service May inventory of job openings, for which local applicants could not be found, ran as follows: professional and managerial, 13,900; clerical and sales, 4,699; service, 2,020; skilled, 9,319; semiskilled, 2,175; unskilled, 399.

From these figures, which reflect only such shortages as turn up in the Employment Service, it is clear that the acuteness of demand of the present and of the future is in proportion to the degree of skill involved. We have 35 times as many openings for professional and managerial people as for unskilled laborers, and 23 times as many for skilled as for unskilled.

What all this adds up to is one single resounding new fact about working people: labor is not a class, and by 1976 there probably will have disappeared almost all vestiges of the concept of "labor" as a sort of minority set apart from other people, having its own special interests and point of view. Working people must be thought of as average middle-income Americans, making up practically the entire population.

A lot of mistakes have been made in the past, and are still being made, because too many of us carry about in our minds an obsolete stereotype of the kind of person we think of when we hear the word "labor." Perhaps it is the result of hundreds of cartoons and W.P.A. murals, in which Labor is depicted as a clean-cut young man in denim overalls and heavy work shoes; his neatly rolled-up sleeves reveal bronzed muscular forearms slightly tensed as he grasps his trowel or hammer; his jaw is square, his gaze is clear, he never smokes, he is never bald, he never has a mustache, and he never ever wears glasses.

But how about assistant editors? Aren't they "labor"? How about the frail little man with thick glasses who tunes the piano? How about the girl on television with the cute lisp who simultaneously sprays wave-set on her hair and gives you the good news that you no longer need to use pin-curlers?

They all work for a living. They are just as much "labor" as the man with bulging muscles and a shovel. They all have social security. They all suffer if they don't have workmen's compensation when injured. And they certainly all have in common that universal ambition: to get a raise.

The key to understanding the future of "labor," then, is full and prompt appreciation of the fact that "labor" is practically everybody, that "labor's" wants are those of everybody, and that "labor's" problems will be those of everybody.

What are the implications of this new picture of "labor" for the future of labor unions? One cannot, of course, predict the future growth of union membership in the same way as general population growth, since it depends so heavily on such matters as union policy, intensity and direction of organizing efforts, and economic conditions. If the rate of growth over the past ten years were simply to continue, the proportion of union members to total nonagricultural employment would remain about what it is now—roughly one-third.

The extent to which union expansion may improve that proportion, and, indeed, the extent to which organized labor increases its contribution in our society over the next twenty years, will depend heavily on how successfully it adapts itself to the new concept of labor I have just described. Since the age of automatic technology is rapidly raising the relative proportion of white-collar —or at least sport-shirt—employees in the work force, much will turn upon the degree to which union organizing policy emphasizes the unionization of clerks, engineers and salaried employees, and upon the degree to which these workers embrace unionization as a means of advancing their interests.

FOR DISCUSSION AND ANALYSIS

1. Seymour Wolfbein has presented some significant data on "Changing Patterns of Industrial Employment" in the first reading of this chapter.

(a) On the basis of your own *a priori* reasoning, what would you expect to have been the impact on union organization and the labor movement of the changes he describes?

(b) Now check the facts to see if the actual changes in union organization have accorded with your expectations.

2. If the concept of "labor" which Arthur Larson urges were adopted by the labor movement and labor unions, how might it affect organizing strategy, bargaining tactics, public relations, political activity?

3. Within the past twenty-five years there has been an expanding interest in the reasons why a worker may prefer one job over another, or why he may like one job and dislike another. There has been a veritable avalanche of studies of workers' job satisfaction, some by university researchers and a great many more by company industrial relations departments. Obviously such material is of interest to the student of industrial relations since it casts light on the motivation of workers—in their conduct towards management, in their conduct towards the union, and in their own interpersonal relations.

A variety of techniques have been employed in conducting such studies. Most commonly, the investigation of worker attitudes towards jobs proceeds by interview and questionnaire.

Below is reprinted a portion of an interview schedule used in one investigation of worker views on what makes a "good" and a "bad" job.

1. Introduction
   a. What kind of work are you doing now, where?
   b. How long have you been there?
   c. Have you done the same kind of work ever since you came to the company? If not, specify changes.
2. Employment history
3. Factors in job satisfaction
   a. Do you expect to stay with the company?
      What makes you feel that way?
      If the answer is "No," are you looking around for other work now?
      If so, how? If not, why not?
   b. Do you think you are getting a fair wage for what you are doing?
      What makes you feel that way?
      How much do you think you should get?
   c. Is there any other job in the company which you would rather have than your present job?
      If so, why? If not, why not?
      Do you think you could do this job?
      What do you think are your chances of getting it?
   d. What do you think are the main things a job should have to make it a good job?
   e. If you had your choice, what would you most like to do? Why?
4. Choice of first job
   a. When did you go to work?
      How did you happen to start work at that time?
   b. What was your first regular job?
      How did you get it?
   c. Did you look around for any other jobs?
      If "Yes," why did you pick this one?
      If "No," why not?
   d. How did it work out?
      Would you pick the same job if you had it to do over again? Why?
   e. When you were in school, what did you want to do? Why?
      What did your parents want you to do? Why?
5. Questions for unemployed workers
   a. Are you looking for a job now? If so, how? What kind of job? Why this particular kind?
   b. Have you found any jobs that you did not take? If so, why did you not take them? How did you find them?
   c. Have you found the State Employment Service helpful or not? Why?

Suppose you were working as assistant to the vice president in charge of personnel in a company, the characteristics of which (industry, location, number of employees, etc.) you may specify. He calls you in one day and tells you that he is considering some kind of survey to find out how the workers in your company like their jobs and what things about their jobs they dislike. He asks you to draft the plans for such a survey. Outline in some detail a program which you think would serve the purpose, including the drafting of a questionnaire or interview schedule if you should make use of either. To what uses might such a survey be put?

4. The following advertisement was placed in many of the nation's daily newspapers early in 1956 by the American Iron and Steel Institute.

STEELWORKERS LIKE THEIR JOBS

. . . AND PAY DAY IS ONLY ONE OF MANY REASONS

How long does the average worker stay on the job in the steel companies the country over?

One answer is—thousands of them spend an entire working lifetime in steel. A more detailed answer is . . .

> 4 years or less on the job . . . . . 28% of all workers
> 5–9 years on the job . . . . 23% of all workers
> 10–14 years on the job . . . . 16% of all workers
> 15–24 years on the job . . . . 17% of all workers
> 25–34 years on the job . . . . 13% of all workers
> 35 and more years on the job . . 3% of all workers

Men don't stay on jobs in our free country unless they like their jobs. *And steelworkers stay.* Their average length of service with present employers is more than twelve years.

Pay day is pleasant because wage levels in the industry place steelworkers among the top 10 per cent of all industrial workers. . . . And, since 1950, steelworkers' average hourly earnings have increased about four times as fast as the cost of living.

Steelworkers are safer at work than at home. In steel, safety is almost a religion. Accident frequency in steel is half the average for all manufacturing.

Among other benefits steelworkers enjoy are good working conditions . . . most modern tools, processes and equipment . . . insurance benefits . . . vacations . . . pensions.

There are more than half a million of these steady-going workers in the industry. The vast expansion under way right now to increase the country's steelmaking capacity by 15 million tons in just three years will create thousands of new jobs—good jobs, with good futures.

Steel is a rapidly growing industry. Production capacity increased 40 per cent just since World War II. Today, expanding even more rapidly, steel is constantly requiring new skills and offering greater incentive and opportunity for advancement.

No wonder steelworkers stay on the job. . . . They know that *America and Steel Must Grow Together.*

If steelworkers stay on their jobs because they like their jobs, as the above ad suggests, why have they formed a strong and militant union?

2: Background on Unionism

The readings for this chapter have been selected with a view to providing some appreciation of the road that unions have traveled to win public acceptance. It is obviously impossible to convey in so short a space any feeling of the attitudes of all segments of society towards unionism over a period of 150 years. Nevertheless, the reader should come away with an impressionistic feel of the changes in the attitudes of the parties themselves and of the public over the years, along with a sense of the strife and turmoil which were part of the process by which attitudes were changed.

A CITIZEN ON LABOR ORGANIZATIONS, 1795

Notice inserted by "A.B." in the New York Daily Advertiser for March 30, 1795

The carpenters and masons of this city, having combined and raised their wages two shillings a day beyond the price of last season, it behooves the citizens in general, but particularly those who intend to build the present year, to oppose designs as unjust as they are impolitic. An acquiescence on the part of the citizens on this occasion will in all probability not only excite similar attempts among all other descriptions of persons who live by manual labor, but induce reiterated efforts to increase their wages at seasons when they find their services most wanted. That a trifling addition to their former wages may by some be deemed proper will not be disputed, but when a combination is formed to extort an unreasonable advance every man will deem it an imposition and set his face against the measure. Those who conceive themselves affected by the present combination are requested to meet at Batten's Tavern, near the theatre, on Wednesday evening at 7 o'clock to consider the means that ought to be adopted on this occasion.

A JUDGE ON LABOR ORGANIZATIONS, 1867

The case below, decided by the New Jersey Supreme Court in 1867, involved a charge brought against a body of workmen that they had conspired unlawfully against their employer by threatening to strike if he did not discharge certain of his employees who had presumably re-

12

fused to join their organization. Chief Justice Beasley rendered the opinion, part of which is here reproduced.

State v. Donaldson, 32 NJL 151, 1867

It appears to me that it is not to be denied, that the alleged aim of this combination was unlawful; the effort was to dictate to this employer whom he should discharge from his employ. This was an unwarrantable interference with the conduct of his business, and it seems impossible that such acts should not be, in their usual effects, highly injurious. How far is this mode of dictation to be held lawful? If the manufacturer can be compelled in this way to discharge two or more hands, he can, by similar means, be coerced to retain such workmen as the conspirators may choose to designate. So his customers may be proscribed, and his business in other respects controlled. I cannot regard such a course of conduct as lawful. It is no answer to the above consideration to say, that the employer is not compelled to submit to the demand of his employes; that the penalty of refusal is simply that they will leave his service. There is this coercion: the men agree to leave simultaneously, in large numbers and by preconcerted action. We cannot close our eyes to the fact, that the threat of workmen to quit the manufacturer, under these circumstances, is equivalent to a threat, that unless he yield to their unjustifiable demand, they will derange his business, and thus cast a heavy loss upon him. The workmen who make this threat understand it in this sense, and so does their employer. In such a condition of affairs, it is idle to suggest that the manufacturer is free to reject the terms which the confederates offer. In the natural position of things, each man acting as an individual, there would be no coercion; if a single employe should demand the discharge of a co-employe, the employer would retain his freedom, for he could entertain or repel the requisition without embarrassment to his concern; but in the presence of a coalition of his employes, it would be but a waste of time to pause to prove that, in most cases, he must submit, under pain of often the most ruinous losses, to the conditions imposed on his necessities. It is difficult to believe that a right exists in law, which we can scarcely conceive can produce, in any posture of affairs, other than injurious results. It is simply the right of workmen, by concert of action, and by taking advantage of their position, to control the business of another. I am unwilling to hold that a right which cannot, in any event, be advantageous to the employe, and which must be always hurtful to the employer, exists in law. In my opinion, this indictment sufficiently shows that the force of the confederates was brought to bear upon their employer for the purpose of oppression and mischief. and that this amounts to a conspiracy.

A CLERGYMAN ON LABOR ORGANIZATIONS, 1887

The following paragraphs are taken from a 355-page account of the Scranton City Guard, a citizens' militia which was organized for the protection of life and property during the violent strikes which swept the nation during the depression year of 1877. The author of this history of

the disorders in the rail and coal industries of the Lackawanna Valley
was a minister who served as Chaplain of the Guard. The passage below
has been extracted to provide some indication of the outlook on labor
of a "wearer of the cloth," an outlook which he shared with many of his
colleagues.

A City's Danger and Defense, by Samuel C. Logan, D.D., 1887, pp. 326–327

The right of any man to cease working, or to determine for whom, and for what wages, he shall work, no man of intelligence ever questioned. The right of any number of men to associate and fix a value upon their labor, and to refuse to work until they can secure the price which is established is equally unquestioned. But the right of one man, or of any number of men, to attempt to prevent from working those who set a lower price upon their services; or skill, or whose condition demands that they shall work even for inadequate wages, is a direct infringement of the first principles of personal liberty. This is a plan of Co-operation and labor Association which enlightened law defines as a wicked "conspiracy," which true manhood must forever resist. It is an oppression which is blind and destructive of all the rights of the individual man —a mere monarchy of the mob.

The whole matter of "Combination," for the purpose of limiting business, and of controlling industry, to the end of aggrandizing particular parties, is essentially, at war with the best interests of mankind; whether it be undertaken in the interest of Capital or of Labor. It can only end in injustice, oppression and abuse. The vital idea upon which the progress of commerce and true civilization must ever depend is that of JUST AND HEALTHY COMPETITION. Every man, waiting for work, must expect to be hired at his own true value; and not at the valuation of a class or an Association with which he may be connected. Unless he shall first sell himself to his Association, this is impossible. Every corporation and association, for the purpose of manufacturing, or for the conducting of trade, or for the prosecution of any industry, must expect only the rewards of the true values, which they may be able to present in the open markets of the world. "Co-operation," for the control of values upon the mere selfish basis, is a legal iniquity. It is an attempted obstruction of the march of that civilization whose life, power and blessing, to the world, are to be found only in the true appreciation of the individual man. Business is never to be conceived of as a scheme of benevolence, or a direct system of philanthropy. Fair competition and an open market are the demands of a free humanity; and every scheme of co-operation or association which brings the workingman to the doors of the shop, seeking for a place, upon any other ground than, that of his own personal worth to his employer, must be false in principle, and therefore degrading to manhood. COMPETITION, AND NOT SELFISH COMBINATION, IS THE ESSENTIAL FOUNDATION UPON WHICH THE WHOLE STRUCTURE OF INDUSTRIAL SOCIETY MUST STAND, IN A FREE COUNTRY, AND UNDER TRUE CHRISTIAN CIVILIZATION.

The demand that men should be employed because they are members of a league or association; or that they shall work, or cease working at the order of such an association; is simply an attempt to place free men, and free labor, under a bondage, degrading and unendurable to true manhood. It is the inauguration of a system which will necessarily belittle humanity itself, and place barriers to the advancement and elevation of society. It is a scheme which is contrary to the whole spirit of our modern institutions. Its essential principle is, *that communism which leads to anarchy,* under which society or associated industry are alike impossible. In opposition to this whole scheme of evil, whether undertaken by a league of capitalists, and business companies in order to control production, and restrict the supply and demand of the market; or by the workmen, to their own aggrandizement, to secure that which they have not honestly earned, every virtuous, patriotic and worthy citizen should give his protest.

CAUSES OF LABOR UNREST, 1918

Concern that some major and specific sore spots of labor unrest might have an adverse effect on needed production during World War I prompted President Wilson to appoint a special "Mediation Commission," under the chairmanship of the Secretary of Labor. A part of their report follows.

Report of President's Mediation Commission to the President of the United States, January 9, 1918

An accumulation of industrial disturbances west of the Mississippi gave rise to national concern and pressed for an understanding of its causes, with a view to the correction of disclosed evils. The immediate anxiety of the Government was the dangerous diminution of the copper supply available for ammunition, due particularly to the strikes in Arizona, and the hampering of the war program, both as to ships and aircraft, because of the disturbed labor conditions in the Pacific Northwest. . . .

Amidst all the diversity of conditions in the four copper districts there were three basic claims urged by the men and resisted by the companies:

(a) While not expressed in so many words, the dominant feeling of protest was that the industry was conducted upon an autocratic basis. The workers did not have representation in determining those conditions of their employment which vitally affected their lives as well as the company's output. Many complaints were, in fact, found by the commission to be unfounded, but there was no safeguard against injustice except the say-so of one side to the controversy. In none of the mines was there direct dealing between companies and unions. In some mines grievance committees had been recently established, but they were distrusted by the workers as subject to company control, and, in any event, because the final determination of every issue was left with the company. In place of orderly processes of adjustment, workers were given the alternative of submission or strike.

(b) The men sought the power to secure industrial justice in matters of vital concern to them. The power they sought would in no way impinge on the correlative power which must reside in management. Only by a proper balance of adequate power on each side can just equilibrium in industry be attained. In the minds of the workers only the right to organize secured them an equality of bargaining power and protection against abuses. There was no demand for a closed shop. There was a demand for security against discrimination directed at union membership. The companies denied discrimination, but refused to put the denial to the reasonable test of disinterested adjustment.

(c) The men demanded the removal of certain existing grievances as to wages, hours, and working conditions, but the specific grievances were, on the whole, of relatively minor importance. The crux of the conflict was the insistence of the men that the right and the power to obtain just treatment were in themselves basic conditions of employment, and that they should not be compelled to depend for such just treatment on the benevolence or uncontrolled will of the employers. . . .

CAUSES OF LABOR DIFFICULTIES

1. The commission had wide opportunities, both as to the extent of territory and the variety of industries investigated, to inquire into industrial conditions in war time. The commission visited Arizona, the Pacific coast, Minneapolis and St. Paul, and Chicago; studied the situation in the copper mines, the telephone industry, the Northwest lumber industry, the meat-packing industry as centered in Chicago, the rapid-transit situation and the related industrial condition in the Twin Cities, and observed as well other industries in the States adjacent to those visited. All relevant sources of information were tapped, for close contact was had with workmen on strike and at work; employers and professional men, and Federal and State officials who are brought particularly in touch with labor matters; and in addition, the voluminous official files of Federal and State authorities furnished much knowledge. While undoubtedly each industry presents its own peculiarities, certain underlying general factors applicable to all industry emerge from the three months' work of the commission.

2. Throughout its inquiry and in all its work the commission kept steadily in mind the war needs of the country. The conclusion cannot be escaped that the available man power of the Nation, serving as the industrial arm of war, is not employed to its full capacity nor wisely directed to the energies of war.

3. The effective conduct of the war suffers needlessly because of (a) interruption of work due to actual or threatened strikes, (b) purposed decrease in efficiency through the "strike on the job," (c) decrease in efficiency due to labor unrest, and (d) dislocation of the labor supply.

4. These are not new conditions in American industry, nor are their causes new. The conditions and their causes have long been familiar and long uncorrected. War has only served to intensify the old derangements by making greater demands upon industry and by affording the occasion for new disturbing factors.

5. Among the causes of unrest, familiar to students of industry, the following stand out with special significance to the industrial needs of war:

in negotiations and adjustments with employers in respect to wages, hours of labor, and relations and conditions of employment is recognized.

After discussion, which occupied two sessions, the resolution was rejected. The groups representing the public and labor, respectively, voted unanimously in its favor, but the employers group, by a divided vote, rejected it. Although an overwhelming majority of the delegates were in favor of this proposal, it was, nevertheless, not adopted, since the rules already adopted by the conference required . . . a majority of each group to declare the judgment of the conference.

The issue over which the conference had thus broken up was whether employees were entitled to representation by national trade unions, if they so desired, or whether representation might be restricted to employees of the individual firm, if the employer so desired.

This issue was reexamined by a second industrial conference, composed solely of public representatives, which was convened by the President soon after the dissolution of the first one. The Secretary of Labor served as chairman, with Herbert Hoover as vice chairman. The excerpt from their report, reprinted below, deals with this issue.

Report of the Industrial Conference called by the President, Washington, D.C., March 6, 1920, pp. 30–32

Two of the most highly controversial questions which have come before the Conference are collective bargaining and the obligation to carry out the collective bargain when made.

The term "collective bargaining," as herein used, means negotiation between an employer or an association of employers on the one side and the employees acting as a group, on the other. There are two types of collective bargaining as thus defined; one in which the employees act as a group through the trade or labor union; the other in which they act as a group through some other plan of employee representation.

An analysis of the heated controversies that are current with reference to collective bargaining indicates that the employees place the emphasis on the *right* of wage-earners to bargain collectively, and that the employers place the emphasis on the *right* of employers to bargain or refuse to bargain collectively at their discretion.

The Conference believes that the matter is not advanced materially by the assertion of the right, on the one side, to bargain collectively, or on the other side, of the right to refuse to bargain collectively; as abstract rights both undoubtedly exist. The real question, however, is whether, as a matter of policy, better relationships between employers and employees will be promoted, and a more effective industrial organization for the nation will be brought about, if a system of collective bargaining is adopted.

On the question of policy, the principal difference relates to the machinery through which the collective bargaining is carried out. While there are some employers who still insist upon the policy of dealing with their employees individually, and not as a group, we think their number is diminishing. Many employers, however, object to collective bargaining through the trade union, on the ground that its agents are often not truly representative of their employees, that they are often uninformed in regard to the technical details of the business involved, and that, instead of feeling concern for the success of this business upon which the welfare of the employees as well as of the employers vitally depends, they care primarily for the success of the unions which they represent.

On the other hand, employees often object to collective bargaining through employee representatives, on the ground that such spokesmen, because themselves employees, are too dependent upon the employer, and too much under his influence to be good negotiators.

The Conference is in favor of the policy of collective bargaining. It sees in a frank acceptance of this principle the most helpful approach to industrial peace. It believes that the great body of the employers of the country accept this principle. The difference of opinion appears in regard to the method of representation. In the plan proposed by the Conference for the adjustment of disputes, provision is made for the unrestricted selection of representatives by employees, and at the same time provision is also made to insure that the representatives of employees in fact represent the majority of the employees, in order that they may be able to bind them in good faith. The Conference believes that the difficulties can be overcome and the advantages of collective bargaining secured if employers and employees will honestly attempt to substitute for an unyielding, contentious attitude, a spirit of co-operation with reference to those aspects of the employment relation where their interests are not really opposed but mutual.

Essential to the success of collective bargaining is a clear realization by both sides, of the obligations which it imposes, and of the limitations of these obligations. The collective bargain usually relates to standards only, such as the rate of wages to be paid, the hours to constitute a day's work, and the conditions under which the work is to be performed. There is also usually a specified time during which the agreed standards are to be maintained. The agreement imposes on the employer the obligation to observe these standards if he provides work. It does not bind him to provide work. Similarly, it imposes on employees the obligation to accept the agreed standards so long as they remain at work. It does not bind them to continue in employment. . . .

The Conference has given a great deal of consideration to the whole question of enforcement of collective bargains once entered upon. As shown above, bargains of this character do not lend themselves readily to legal enforcement. The social and legal forces that surround the problem are of the most complex order and must be a matter of development in the community. The Conference believes that for the present at least, enforcement [of collective bargains] must rest substantially upon good faith. It is obvious that the essence of success in collective bargaining lies in the fidelity of both sides to agreements.

EMPLOYEE REPRESENTATION PLANS

Statement of Thomas M. Girdler, Chairman and President, Republic Steel Co., Cleveland, Ohio, in To Create a National Labor Board, hearings before the Senate Committee on Education and Labor, 73d Cong., 2d Sess., 1934, part 3, pp. 774–777

I began work in a steel plant at Pittsburgh in 1902, and was presently made a foreman. Since then I have been continuously in charge of labor. My experience covers work at various plants, including 7 years in the mills of the Atlantic Steel Co. at Atlanta, Ga. I spent 16 years with the Jones & Laughlin Steel Corporation at Pittsburgh, beginning as assistant superintendent in one of its plants and concluding as president of the corporation in charge of 25,000 employees.

For a number of years I was superintendent of the Aliquippa plant of the Jones & Laughlin Co., located on the Ohio River. This employed anywhere from 5,000 to 10,000 men, according to the condition of business.

All of the plants of that company were operated on the open-shop basis. We did not have any labor union to tell us what to do, but I made it my business to know the needs of my men. I previously had personal experience working in steel plants, and I thought then and I think now, that I know something about how the workers in steel plants feel about these matters.

My door was open for employees to come to me at any time if they had anything to say, and they did come, singly and in groups. I became acquainted with them and could call hundreds of them by name. I kept in close touch with the work of the plant and impressed upon my staff and all our superintendents and foremen the necessity and the importance of keeping alive to the needs and wishes of our employees. We never had labor troubles of any consequence, even though they were sometimes occurring in the plants of other companies, especially in 1919. I attribute this result to the direct personal contact between our management and our men. . . .

I know something about the way labor unions work, and the business agents whom they put forward to deal with employers are certainly not economists or lawyers. The arguments which they use are not such as are found in books. They undoubtedly represent national labor organizations, but this is a disadvantage to the workers, as these business agents are acting under the direction of men who are much more interested in the development of their national organization than they are in solving the problems of any particular plant.

The employee-representation plans that have been adopted since the passage of the National Recovery Act provide generally for the selection of individual representatives as required by the act. They are not company unions or unions in any sense of the word. These plans provide a method of collective bargaining on wages, hours, and working conditions, between management and employees through their own elected representatives, and are so designed to provide a means for collective expression of opinion for negotiation. . . .

Anyone who thinks that these representatives, chosen by secret vote to represent their fellow workers would be overawed in dealing with their foreman, superintendent, or even the president of the company, certainly does not understand the independence of steel-plant workers. These representatives handle matters referred to them by the men in the group they represent. They meet by themselves and then after that meeting join with the company representatives in a meeting in which they discuss the matters presented by their constituents.

In connection with these meetings, 785 meetings were held and the total attendance at these meetings was 6,968. The total amount of money paid by the company on account of time spent at these meetings by representatives averaged approximately 43 cents per employee for 8 months. If the employees were required to pay dues to the American Federation of Labor during these 8 months, it would have cost each employee $8, or a total cost to all employees of $272,000.

These figures clearly indicate that any law which makes it impossible for the company to pay wages to employee representatives for time lost on account of attendance at meetings, immediately imposes a burden of expense on employees if they act through a union. . . .

The best way to test the success of any plan is by the results obtained. I have here a summarized statement of the volume of cases handled under our representation plan during the first 8 months, and I am going to give you these figures in totals, which will speak for themselves.

From June 16, 1933, to March 1, 1934, a period of 8½ months, our employee representatives handled 1,222 cases through the plan. Of this number 886 cases, or 72 percent of the total cases handled, were settled in favor of the workmen and to their satisfaction.

Only 7 percent of the total cases presented by the employee representatives were pending settlement as of March 1, 1934, and the remaining 21 percent were either voluntarily withdrawn by the workmen, compromised, or settled in the negative.

The employee-representation plan is simply a continuation and further development of the principle of direct contact between management and employees, which, as I have told you, constitutes in my opinion the correct way of dealing with labor problems.

I understand that it has been repeatedly stated before your committee that many employees who wanted to join the American Federation of Labor or some of its subsidiary unions have been discharged by employers. I desire to state that, although I have always known that there have been more or less union men working in plants in my charge, I have never fired an employee, either before or since the adoption of the act, simply because he was a labor union man. Some times labor union men who were neglecting their work have been discharged, and this neglect has in some instances been because they were wasting their time and wasting the time of other employees in working hours by talking about labor union matters. Also, employees who were not labor union men have been discharged when they were neglecting their work or interfering with the work of their fellow employees.

You cannot direct successfully the operations of many thousands of men without maintaining proper plant discipline, and I say without qualification that workers generally have a higher regard for an executive who possesses both fairness and firmness than they have for one whose acts are characterized by weakness.

Statement of Frank Purnell, President, The Youngstown Sheet & Tube Co., speaking of the Youngstown employee-representation plan in To Create a National Labor Board, hearings before the Senate Committee on Education and Labor, 73d Cong., 2d Sess., 1934, part 3, p. 791

The real object of any plan of industrial relationship between employees and employers should be to bring about a feeling of confidence and mutual respect, to allay suspicion, to guarantee freedom of action, and to encourage hearty cooperation. Kindness toward and consideration for each other are constantly stressed. The fact that in the main interests of employers and employees are common and mostly identical is brought out by frank discussion of all matters.

Statement of W. C. Sutherland, Vice President, Pittsburgh Steel Co., Pittsburgh, Pa., in National Labor Relations Board, hearings before the Senate Committee on Education and Labor, 74th Cong., 1st Sess., 1935, part 3, pp. 377–378

Mr. Chairman, members of the committee, and gentlemen, my experience in the steel industry covers a period of 34 years, during which time I have worked in nearly every branch of the industry and have, during most of the time, had direct supervision over large numbers of men.

My first experience was in a mill where all the skilled steel workers were members of a union. It was at this time a local organization which had formerly been dissatisfied with the rulings of the national organization, had severed all affiliations with that institution, and functioned absolutely independently as an organization through which there was a direct contact between employer and employees, and all matters concerning either of these groups were always negotiated through this collective bargaining agency. Harmony always prevailed, which can be attributed to the fact that the negotiations were always between groups with a common interest and no outsiders or noninterested persons ever participated in any way. This arrangement of 34 years ago was at that time, what the present employees' representation plan, in successful operations in the steel plants today is—a successful means for collective bargaining.

My experience has always found a decidedly friendly and cooperative attitude between the men and the management of those engaged in the steel industry, and I am sure that that condition would prevail in all cases today were it not for the fact that disinterested persons have set out to establish the fact that because one person is an employer and another an employee, they must for that reason be enemies and that legislation must be enacted to provide a means of settling disputes which should never arise and would never arise if the third or disinterested party was not legislated into something where his interests were only of a selfish kind. . . .

The management's door has always been and still is open to receive any employees who have anything to say for themselves or their fellow workmen, and they do come in in groups and individually, and are always given a courteous hearing and an honest answer, and reasonable requests where conditions permit are granted or adjusted. Some requests have been made which the management could not in fairness grant, and the refusal in these cases, when thoroughly explained, has always been accepted in the spirit in which the decision was made.

Statement of John L. Lewis, President, United Mine Workers of America, in To Create a National Labor Board, *hearings before the Senate Committee on Education and Labor, 73d Cong., 2d Sess., 1934, part 1, pp. 142–145*

The iron and steel industry from time to time fulminates about its desire to maintain and protect and perpetuate the sacred principle of the open shop in that industry. Time after time it makes these pronouncements in public places and the public press. The term "open shop" implies that the shop is open to the workers to join any form of organization that they may desire or elect, and yet the contrary is true, and the steel industry within the lifetimes of most of us has never been open to the workers to join a union except that form of union foisted upon the workers through so-called "plans of employee representation" in the various units of the steel industry.

In proof sufficient of this statement I point out that in all of the plants of the Carnegie Steel Co., a subsidiary of the United States Steel Corporation, there are no legitimate union men. In the plants of the American Bridge Co., a subsidiary of the Steel Corporation, there are no members of legitimate unions. The same is true of the National Tube Co. The same is true in all of the subsidiary plants of that company with the exception of their coal properties, and there are union men in the coal properties of the United States Steel Corporation because the United States Steel Corporation, with all of its power and influence, has not been able to prevent it, and that is the only reason.

In their steel plants they have an espionage system that reports and rapidly weeds out any man who joins a union or who talks as if he wanted to join a union or who attends a meeting of a labor organization or who is seen conferring with representatives of organized labor, and the only union to which he can belong is the so-called "union" promoted by the steel corporations and set forth in their plans of employee representation.

I do not know why a corporation thinks it has the right to organize, administer, regulate, operate, conduct, and finance a labor union of its employees. From the sheer standpoint of ethics I do not know why the United States Steel Corporation or the automobile industry, or any other industry would say to itself, "We will prevent our workers from having the kind of an organization which they desire to represent them, and we will prevent them from employing the kind of agents, the type of agents that they desire to represent them, and we will so arrange it that they can only have the kind of an organization that we wish to give them and they can only employ the type and character of an individual to represent them which is pleasing to us."

There is not even an element of sportsmanship in that sort of a policy. Our British cousins would say that it is not even cricket. . . .

I wish the Senators could have sat in on the hearings held this week in Washington before the National Labor Board on the conditions in the automobile industry. It was developed there from evidence that in the automobile industry in Detroit and other cities since the enactment of the Recovery Act, to which, in August and September of 1933, the automobile industry did by coercion and by intimidation form company unions; that the automobile industry did discriminate against numerous individuals and discharge them and deprive them of their employment, some of them after many years of service, for joining other unions than company unions and for talking of joining other unions than the company unions; that it did discharge certain of the elected representatives by company unions, elected in their shop unions, after those men found through experience that the company unions were but hollow mockeries and did join other unions; that the automobile industry, since the organization of the company unions, did deny the rights of collective bargaining to workers who had organized themselves into other groups and other unions by refusing to meet them in conference except under such conditions, such stipulations that they found they could not accede to, for instance, turning over the list of their membership to the company without any guaranty that their members would not be discriminated against or discharged.

What was the formula for organizing the company unions in one of the plants of the General Motors? On a certain day the foreman of the shop, or a shop foreman, would go to the men of strong character in his shop, men of personality, with some elements of leadership, and tell them they were called at a meeting in the office that afternoon. The meeting would assemble that afternoon in the company office and they would be addressed by a representative of the company, they would be told that the company wanted to form a company union, that the company expected these people to help them, that these men would be paid their regular hourly rates for such help by the company. They were then given copies of the constitution and bylaws of such company union, they were told that an election would be held, that the company would fix the date of an election, that the company would supervise the election, that the election would be held in the plant, that ballot boxes would be provided, that the watchers would be designated, and they were asked to help, and they were asked under such conditions and under such circumstances that they testified that their refusal to participate or their refusal to help would in their judgment have jeopardized their standing with the company, and their jobs.

The arrangements were thus made, the notices of the election were posted, each individual in the shop was canvassed by his foreman or his subforeman, and each of them was told that the foreman desired to have a 100 percent record in his shop and he insisted that he go and vote and that the act of voting in the company-held election would make them members in good standing of this newly formed company union. They had no investment in it, they had no duty in the matter to perform except the dropping of a ballot in the box under the eye of the foreman or shop representative, and that made them members in good standing of this form of company union.

Witnesses testified that they resisted voting, that they were opposed to such participation, that they explained to the foreman they did not believe in that form of union, but they were asked to vote anyhow, and, against their will, they voted, and the returns were published that so many thousand men in this shop and this plant participated in the election and that they elected such representatives as were designated. The company fixed the requirements of representatives to be elected. It designated how many should be elected, or regulated the election and threw all manner of restrictions around it, and, in addition to that, the company financed it. They paid for the printing, they paid for the time of those key men in forming this organization, and it was testified that they pay the regular hourly rates to all of the representatives of this union in carrying out the business of the union and in taking up the grievances of individuals that arise in the ordinary course of its operation.

In other words, the company unions in the automobile industry are merely subsidiary organizations to the General Motors and other corporations engaged in that industry. They are subsidiary organizations just as much as a subsidiary sales company in another city. They are subsidiary organizations just as much as a captive coal company operating a captive mine for the Wheeling Steel Co. is to that company, and yet they seek to impose upon the workers this form of economic repression and they seek to chide those who would undertake to change that condition in this modern year of 1934.

VIOLATIONS OF FREE SPEECH AND RIGHTS OF LABOR

Report of the Senate Committee on Education and Labor, 77th Cong., 1st Sess., 1941, part 4, pp. 88–98

. . . The employee representation plan at the Berger plant [of Republic Steel] in Canton, Ohio, was not an effective means of collective bargaining. The employees, therefore, formed a Federal union, the Loyalty Local, which was chartered by the A. F. of L. in 1933. Of the 450 production employees at Berger, 300 joined the Loyalty Local. The local attempted to bargain with the corporation and presented a 7-point program to govern their relations. The company declined the program in its entirety. The matter was then brought before the Labor Board established by the N.R.A. The board's opinion details the negotiations and describes the meeting between the Loyalty Local and the company as follows: "The meeting culminated with a remark by the company that it was not its 'policy' to sign such agreements." The board found that the company by its failure to bargain collectively had violated section 7 (a) of the N.I.R.A. Its order was that unless the company recognized the Loyalty Local within 7 days the case would be transferred to the Enforcement Division. The company then filed suit for an injunction against the Board, which was granted by the Supreme Court of the District of Columbia on May 8, 1935.

The union took a strike vote and then had a final and unsatisfactory conference with the company on or about the 22d of May. The company was then informed of the proposed strike which was called on Monday, May 27, 1935, the day on which the Supreme Court held the N.R.A. unconstitutional.

The activities of Republic Steel Corporation in preparation for this strike and during its conduct form a fitting prologue to the activities during the strike of 1937. A study of the Berger strike indicates that Republic has pursued a consistent antiunion policy which essentially has not been modified by Federal labor legislation.

The strike was called on the 27th of May. On the same day Federal Laboratories, Inc., delivered $8,804.30 worth of munitions to the corporation. . . . After the strike was called, on the 28th or 29th of May, 63 men were transported from Buffalo to Canton. These men, according to Williams, chief of Republic police, were not in the Buffalo police department. "These men were sent in there for the purpose of taking over jobs in the plant." . . . In less euphemistic language, Republic was importing strikebreakers. Mr. White's explanation of this conduct is most ingenious:

MR. WHITE: They were to take the places of the men who could not get into the plants on account of the streets being barricaded.

SENATOR LA FOLLETTE: How could these men get in any better than your own men?

MR. WHITE: These men—in America we have some men who don't require too much formality to—in other words, they take care of their own civil rights.

The union established picket lines a block from the plant the night before the strike. The next day the pickets moved up to the entrances of the plants. Mr. White was on the street addressing the men and urging them to leave the "radicals" and return to work. The company guards on the street were carrying wooden billy clubs and iron bolts. Those remaining on company property carried sidearms. This situation immediately precipitated considerable violence. Fourteen people were hospitalized as a result of injuries sustained from attacks by the guards on this day.

Violence continued during the following days. Innocent bystanders, school children, and women who happened to be in the path of the private police were mercilessly beaten and shot. According to the account of Mr. Smith, an eyewitness not involved in the strike, "there were about 200 people trapped between 2 advancing contingents of Republic police, 'who were just mowing them down.'"

SENATOR LA FOLLETTE: Describe what happened next.

MR. SMITH: It is almost beyond description, Senator. It was just about the bloodiest scene possible of enactment in America, I believe; at least in peace times. It would be hard, I believe, for anyone who witnessed that scene to describe it with any degree of justice at all.

I saw women struck with those iron bars just as mercilessly as though they were men. I saw a group of school children across the street running around in a panic, scared, crying at the top of their lungs because they were frightened out of their wits by this tear-gas shooting that was going on all around them. These guards were rushing around the people, and beating the people to the brick pavement, and then beating them after they were down.

The Republic officials assumed full responsibility for this onslaught, which they had authorized. One of the company policemen testified that he and his fellows had used, on this occasion, long-range gas guns, short-range gas guns, revolvers, gas bombs and steel pipes. He was one of 40 guards who went out so armed in an armored truck. He testified that Superintendent Williams' comment on these activities was, "Good job." Vice President White said that he did not know how these things were to be "avoided entirely unless there is maintenance of law and order." Republic's conception of law and order apparently was the use of public police protection for armed Republic guards whenever the latter went outside of the plants. A request for such protection was not made until after the repeated riots of the first 3 days of the strike. As a result of these assaults by Republic police, 28 people were hospitalized with serious injuries, including fractured skulls, a fractured jaw bone, a broken arm, contusions of the face, gunshot and buckshot wounds, and lacerations. In addition, numerous people were indiscriminately gassed with tear and sickening gas. Republic Steel Corporation paid $42,448.25 in claims to persons injured during the strike. Zurich Insurance Co. also paid $2,152.20 and made a cash settlement of $15,700. With this appalling record of violence, Mr. Girdler admitted in a prepared statement before the committee that—

. . . some mistakes were made by Republic employees.

Details of occasions where our men have erred have been developed at length before this Committee. On one occasion in 1935 at our Canton, Ohio plant, after a complete breakdown in all local law enforcement, our guards escorted workers through the streets of Canton in going to and from work. They did that because absolutely no protection was to be had from the civil authorities. The outcome, in the heat and excitement of the moment, was a regrettable riot.

As a result of that unfortunate experience, our guards learned it was wrong to leave company property. The breakdown of law enforcement in any community rests upon the heads of the law enforcement officials. No private interest should attempt to assume that responsibility. My orders are that during any period of labor trouble or excitement, company guards are not to leave company property and are strictly to avoid violence of every kind.

The emergence of a citizens' committee and back-to-work movement, which became a pattern of the strikes of 1936–37, appeared early in the Berger strike. . . . On Tuesday, the second day of the strike, there was a luncheon meeting of businessmen who "agreed to use our influence with the public officials to enforce the law in the strike zone and bring things to a peaceful conclusion as soon as possible." This committee met with the mayor and the sheriff. They then went to the commissioners who promised to furnish the mayor with money to employ as many men as necessary.

A back-to-work vote was taken by the company in which the alloy plant workers, who had struck in sympathy, voted while the Berger men were excluded from the vote. Foremen and other supervisors were present at the poll and the ballots were so arranged that it was possible to see at a distance of 15 or 16 feet whether a man was voting to work or to strike. No distinction was made between the Berger and Alloy strikes. After the results of the vote were announced as being overwhelmingly in favor of a return to work, the strike was broken. . . .

Prior to and during the strike, Republic had spies fraternizing with the men and holding key positions in the union. They were given large sums of money under an extremely loose financial arrangement. One spy was paid over $2,435 on blind vouchers for his expenses. The spies used their union positions not only to obtain information but also to initiate a back-to-work movement.

The height of spy activity was reached after the beginning of the organizing drive by the S.W.O.C. [Steel Workers' Organizing Committee] in June 1936. Regardless of Mr. Williams' attempt to sidestep the issue, when the evidence in the committee's record accumulated beyond the possibility of impeachment or dismissal as exceptional aberrations, he finally capitulated and admitted that espionage was conducted regularly by his department. . . .

The Subcommittee of the Committee on Education and Labor questioned many spies and undercover men hired by Republic. The existence of spies other than those examined by the committee was admitted by Superintendent Williams and his captains of police. The spies, like the industrial police, learned about the availability of jobs from the "grapevine." Two of these men, Harold Frederick Vargo, alias Ira Albert, alias Richard Brooks, and Joseph Vamos were professional strikeguards of long experience. These men were put in the Youngstown plant with instructions from Captain Butler to let him know "if any rumors went around about labor or anything like that."

Mr. Vargo ran the whole gamut of a labor spy's experiences. He was a volunteer organizer for the union, recruited membership for the C.I.O., spoke at the union meetings, and was present at secret organizing meetings. Mr. Vargo maneuvered until he was elected to the office of financial secretary of the union. This position gave him custody of all the records of membership and dues. He mailed his reports to Captain Butler addressed to a post-office box. These accounts were corroborated by Captain Butler. When the union officials realized that Mr. Vargo was a spy and he, therefore, became useless to the company in Youngstown, he was sent to Buffalo to be a uniformed Republic patrolman. His compensation was indefinite. He received more than a mill worker, the position for which he was listed on the payroll. In addition he had an expense account. As to its size Mr. Vargo testified:

> Well, whatever was necessary for me; whatever I could get. That was it. If you have got an expense account, I know that I get as much as I can out of it.

Mr. Vargo was paid in cash by Captain Butler who likewise was paid in cash by Mr. Williams.

Captain Butler testified that he also had men from the regular Republic police force on the streets to report on the activities of union organizers. The information thus gathered was sent to Mr. Williams at Cleveland. . . .

Mr. Williams explained that most of the espionage reports were made orally to him, on the basis of which certain memoranda were drawn and issued as the dittoed reports. These indicate that Republic spies were present at union meetings and made a record of attendance despite the union's desire for secrecy as to the people present. Labor contracts and financial reports are found in these detailed accounts of union meetings. The names, addresses, and activities of union men are carefully recorded. Many of those men were later dismissed by Republic Steel Corporation. The National Labor Relations Board found that those discharges were for union activity. Another listed as a union man was shadowed and even beaten. . . .

One of the most important factors in the conduct of a union organization drive is the distribution of leaflets, pamphlets, and other literature. In and around the Republic plants efforts were made by the company police to prevent the distribution of union literature. In Youngstown the organizers attempted to distribute literature at every gate on every shift. But the men were easily intimidated by the company police. Boys were then employed to distribute the literature. They were offered bribes to leave their papers and go home. Testimony to this effect was not refuted by Captain Butler. Stronger methods were used in Buffalo. Organizer Doyle testified:

This policeman, every time that we gave a worker a paper, as soon as the worker stepped into the doorway he would take it from him. When we saw this we began to fold the papers up small so that the workers who wanted to keep them would be able to put them in their pockets so the policemen would not be able to have a chance to take it away from them.

When we done this, the policeman deliberately put his hands in their pockets and took the papers off of them. After we were there a little while, the captain of the Republic police force, Mr. Todd, who was supervising the work of the policemen there, sent four of them across the street where the workers coming out of the plant would have to wait for a streetcar to go to get their automobiles, and the same thing was going on across the street, taking the papers away from the men that were coming out.

An identified Republic policeman, Mr. Sodders, dressed in workers' clothes and wearing brass knuckles, struck and injured one of the men distributing leaflets. Mr. Sodders had been active in espionage work during the Berger strike. Republic's accounts show numerous payments of large sums to Mr. Sodders over a period of years. There were similar assaults on persons distributing literature in Cleveland. Paul Castman, a union man, described an attack on him by Republic Police Sergeant Brown:

MR. CASTMAN: . . . as I was handing him this stub of the card back, a man shoved him out of the way and swung at me with a blackjack, which I could not get out of the way of, and it hit me in the side of the face on the jaw, breaking one of my teeth and also the partial plate that I wore in my mouth.

It staggered me and I stumbled backward off the curb and fell to the ground in between these two parked automobiles, whereupon that man with the blackjack jumped on me with his knees and proceeded to keep beating me around the head and the arms and the hands with this blackjack, breaking my arm, cutting my head in a couple of places which neces-

sitated quite a few stitches to sew up. Also on my left elbow; they had
to sew my elbow up.

All of these assaults took place on public streets not company property.

STATEMENT OF PUBLIC POLICY

National Labor Relations Act, 1935, Sec. 1

Experience has proved that protection by law of the right of employes to
organize and bargain collectively safeguards commerce from injury, impairment, or interruption, and promotes the flow of commerce by removing certain
recognized sources of industrial strife and unrest, by encouraging practices
fundamental to the friendly adjustment of industrial disputes arising out of
differences as to wages, hours, or other working conditions, and by restoring
equality of bargaining power between employers and employes.

It is hereby declared to be the policy of the United States to eliminate the
causes of certain substantial obstructions to the free flow of commerce and to
mitigate and eliminate these obstructions when they have occurred by encouraging the practice and procedure of collective bargaining and by protecting the
exercise by workers of full freedom of association, self-organization, and designation of representatives of their own choosing, for the purpose of negotiating
the terms and conditions of their employment or other mutual aid or protection.

UNION RECOGNITION

*In the succession of turbulent events on the labor scene during the
decade of the thirties, one that stood out in calm contrast was the recognition by United States Steel of the incipient Steelworkers' Union. The fact
that this recognition could have excited such public interest that it was
given banner headlines in the newspapers of the day is indicative of the
existing labor-management strife in the industry. For what was headlined
as a great union victory was actually less than the union was entitled to
under the National Labor Relations Act, passed two years previously.
United States Steel recognized the Steelworkers' Union as the bargaining
agent for its members only, whereas its majority status (as yet not proved,
however) under the Act gave it exclusive bargaining rights. This was,
however, just a way-station briefly occupied on the road to full recognition not only in big steel but in other major industries, as the "practice
and procedure of collective bargaining," which it was now public policy
to encourage, became less strange to managements which for years had
been free to ignore them. United States Steel's recognition of the union
was important in that tense decade, since it symbolized that the new
dispensation was here to stay. If even Steel, which had so bitterly con-
tested the unions since before the turn of the century, now accepted
unionism as inevitable, other managements too had to learn to face the
new order.*

Fortune, May, 1937, pp. 91–94, 176, 179–180 *

IT HAPPENED IN STEEL

On June 27, 1936, Myron Charles Taylor, Chairman of the Board of U.S. Steel Corp., set sail for Europe. This was no unusual move for him, for besides his obvious interest in international affairs he owns a former Medici property outside of Florence and he likes to wander solemnly through museums and cathedrals. But Mr. Taylor sailed for Europe in 1936 in a peculiarly philosophical mood. Lesser men than he could see the handwriting that John Llewellyn Lewis had written on the forbidding walls of the Corporation's mills. It was evident to Mr. Taylor that a great change had come over the face of U.S. industry. The blood and brimstone labor philosophy of his predecessor, Judge Elbert H. Gary, was out of tune with the times. So was the covering material under which the Judge had sought to hide its worst horrors (perhaps even from himself); the idea of the big steel "family," for instance, and good will toward the worker, and social welfare. Labor was in arms. What FORTUNE later described (in October) as "the irrepressible conflict of the twentieth century" had broken out. The industrial problem had become a social problem, and unless something were done about it, the social problem would presently generate chaos.

But what was to be done? To give in to labor spinelessly meant to lose control over the business one had been hired to manage. To fight labor adamantly meant, for a long time, no business at all. In its unhurried course Mr. Taylor's mind explored the various angles—possible, probable, past, and future. And after he had reached the ancient enclosure of his Florentine villa he felt that he had made enough progress to sit down and write himself a memorandum. This he did. He wrote it and tore it up and rewrote it and revised it and rewrote it again. And at length there emerged a dozen crystal lines, remarkable not so much for the originality of their substance as for their unambiguous expression of a fundamental compromise. So terse were those lines that they cannot properly be defined as a memorandum. They constitute a formula—the Myron Taylor formula for industrial peace. Hitherto this document has been known only to a limited circle of friends, to whom Mr. Taylor showed it when he returned to the U.S. But a few copies do exist outside of Mr. Taylor's private file. And this is what they say:

The Company recognizes the right of its employees to bargain collectively through representatives freely chosen by them without dictation, coercion or intimidation in any form or from any source. It will negotiate and contract with the representatives of any group of its employees so chosen and with any organization as the representative of its members, subject to the recognition of the principle that the right to work is not dependent on membership or non-membership in any organization and subject to the right of every employee freely to bargain in such manner and through such representatives, if any, as he chooses.

That was all. Whether by coincidence or design, the statement is exactly 100 words long, and these 100 words represent a summer's work. But they packed more dynamite than any 100 words ever written by a U.S. industrialist. Superficially they inject no new principle, and hence do not shriek from the housetops. Fundamentally, however, they bring forth and formulate what was previously only inchoate; and in this sense they achieve the dignity of statesmanship. For reasons best known to himself, Mr. Taylor never gave these words to the world. As a result of his reticence no one outside of his most intimate acquaintances has understood what the Chairman has been up to. The greatest news story of the day—his settlement on March 1, 1937, with John L. Lewis and the C.I.O.—followed logically from the formula and incorporated its every point. But since no one has known about the formula, no one has been able to explain that spectacular event.

A body of rumor and legend has therefore grown up around the Taylor-Lewis agreement, and the process has been encouraged by the fact that the two men worked in the most incredible secrecy. The nation's most potent industrialist and the nation's most dramatic laborite, the latter making front-page news almost every day in the General Motors strike, succeeded in meeting each other ten or twelve times during a period of fifty days without arousing the suspicions of the most alert newshawks in the world. But the real story is neither complicated nor mysterious. Shorn of analysis and of a few intimate passages that must await the publication of somebody's memoirs, it goes like this.

Shortly after one o'clock, in the big dining room of Washington's Mayflower Hotel, the business of eating lunch was halted. There had entered the room at that moment a tall and austere man and a handsome woman, known to most persons present as Mr. and Mrs. Myron C. Taylor. But as Mr. and Mrs. Taylor advanced, who should be seated in their path, halfway through lunch, but Pennsylvania's Senator Joseph F. Guffey and C.I.O.'s rugged Chairman, John L. Lewis. As he passed this pair of laborites Mr. Taylor bowed. And having seated his wife at a nearby table, he conspicuously returned to Senator Guffey's table, where he held out his hand, first to the Senator and next to Mr. Lewis. The three men then stood chatting for almost a minute, whereupon Mr. Taylor, having delivered himself of a pleasantry, turned and rejoined his wife.

If the Mayflower dining room had not been the nation's No. 1 meeting place frequented by political sophisticates, the shock of this encounter might not have been so general; but as it was, both the waiters and the luncheoners lost all interest in lunch. Moreover, the poise of the room was broken all over again some minutes later when Senator Guffey and Mr. Lewis finished eating. This pair now crossed over to Mr. Taylor's table, where they greeted Mrs. Taylor, Mr. Lewis meeting her for the first time. Senator Guffey then hurried on; but the inspirator of the C.I.O. sat down and remained seated for more than twenty minutes, carrying on an animated conversation with his host and hostess (which no one could overhear) and calling forth frequent bursts of laughter.

That was on Saturday, January 9, 1937. Though no one in the room heard him say it, Mr. Lewis remarked to Mr. Taylor that he would like a meeting

with him sometime in the near future. And Mr. Taylor at once suggested the
next day. The next day was Sunday, a day on which Mr. Lewis never talks
business; but this matter was apparently so important that he acquiesced, and
after some little palaver it was decided that Mr. Taylor's suite in the Mayflower
would make the least conspicuous rendezvous. . . .

The Chairman was confronted with a problem in metamorphosis. The metamorphosis, to be sure, was never at any time so violent as some people like to
suppose. To begin with, when the traditional labor policy of the Corporation
is boiled down to its essentials it is seen to consist in the theory of little more
than an insistence upon the open shop. Here and there the Corporation has had
dealings with unions. For many years it has been constrained to recognize the
United Mine Workers in the state of Illinois—a situation which has not worked
badly. And other contracts have been made with the U.M.W.A. in recent times,
notably those concerning the captive mines. But the trouble with the Corporation's labor policy was that, in practice, it *overdefended* the open shop, resorting to the most violent methods of labor warfare, including the late Coal and
Iron Police, state troops, local cops, and spies.[1] In this way it earned its reputation of being, not the champion of the open shop, but the enemy of all
organized labor. The lurid atmosphere thus created was also breathed by the
independents, some of which were even more aggressive than big steel. And the
result was incipient war. On June 29 last, when the industry (including the
Corporation) issued the proclamation reproduced on p. 35 through the American Iron and Steel Institute, the war was actually declared. For that proclamation was directed squarely at John L. Lewis, against whom it sought to set up
the company-union system.

Now Mr. Taylor, as we have seen, sailed for Europe on June 27, two days
before this manifesto appeared. Just before he sailed he had gone on record
against it—not strongly enough to stop it, certainly, but nevertheless on record
to some of his associates. And he did strenuously oppose the Institute's subsequent move, by which it published the manifesto as an advertisement in leading
newspapers at a cost of some $150,000. Which leads to some interesting points.
Mr. Taylor is a different sort of man from Judge Gary or anyone else who has
ever had an important position in steel. He is not a steel man and hence is not
particularly fascinated with the traditions of the steel country. And after his
own deliberate fashion, he is a liberal. Mr. Taylor's liberalism is not of any
standard variety. The Chairman is perhaps the closest thing in the U.S. to a
British Conservative—a man who, having measured the strength of a progressive adversary, has the foresight to anticipate him. The U.S. steel industry as
a whole, on the other hand, is characterized by conservatives of another stripe.
Most of them would rather be damned than give in to the Left. Mr. Taylor
played along with them for years, and then, in the course of fifty days, simply
decided not to.

Two facts support the contention that Mr. Taylor is a U.S. model of a British
Conservative. The first takes us back to the time when he bumped into

[1] Mr. Taylor sent out an order liquidating U.S. Steel's spy system two years ago,
but ambitious underlings have clung to the practice nevertheless.

TO THE PUBLIC
AND THE EMPLOYEES
in the
STEEL INDUSTRY

A campaign to unionize the employees of the Steel Industry has been announced.

In order that the employees and the public may know the position of the Steel Industry in the face of the threatened drive, the Industry makes this statement through the American Iron and Steel Institute.

Persons and organizations not connected with the Industry have taken charge of the campaign.

There are many disturbing indications that the promoters of the campaign will employ coercion and intimidation of the employees in the Industry and foment strikes.

The objective of the campaign is the "closed shop," which prohibits the employment of any one not a union member. The Steel Industry will oppose any attempt to compel its employees to join a union or to pay tribute for the right to work.

No employee in the steel industry has to join any organization to get or hold a job. Employment in the Industry does not depend upon membership or nonmembership in any organization. Advancement depends on individual merit and effort. These are fundamental American principles to which the Industry will steadfastly adhere.

The Steel Industry believes in the principles of collective bargaining, and it is in effect throughout the Industry.

The overwhelming majority of the employees in the Steel Industry recently participated in annual elections under their own representation plans and elected their representatives for collective bargaining. The elections were conducted by the employees themselves by secret ballot. One of the purposes of the announced campaign is to overthrow those plans and the representatives so elected.

The Steel Industry is recovering from six years of depression and huge losses, and the employees are now beginning to receive the benefits of increased operations. Any interruption of the forward movement will seriously injure the employees and their families and all businesses dependent upon the Industry, and will endanger the welfare of the country.

The announced drive, with its accompanying agitation for industrial strife, threatens such interruption.

The Steel Industry will use its resources to the best of its ability to protect its employees and their families from intimidation, coercion and violence and to aid them in maintaining collective bargaining free from interference from any source.

AMERICAN IRON AND STEEL INSTITUTE

Mr. Lewis in the coal strike of 1933. Of the 16,000 men employed in the Corporation's captive mines Mr. Lewis then controlled only about 4,000, but in spite of this fact he was holding out for a closed shop and exclusive bargaining rights for U.M.W.A. Mr. Taylor's opposition to this idea was insuperable and adamant—but not negative. On the subject of whether or not labor should be given the power to bargain, the Chairman was of an open mind, and the net result of the conversations was a compromise, prototype of the formula we have already set forth. By that compromise Mr. Lewis's wage and hour demands were granted. But the U.M.W.A. was recognized as a bargaining agent *for its own members only* and the open shop preserved.

That is one supporting fact; the second was more spectacular. Some time after Mr. Taylor returned from Europe in the late fall, when the storm was gathering over Alfred P. Sloan Jr. in the automobile country, a movement got under way among a number of the big industrialists for the formation of a "united front." Chief instigators of this idea were certain of the steel independents and General Motors, though (as Mr. Lewis has publicly stated) glass and "to a lesser extent coal" were on the fringes of it. Mr. Taylor went so far as to attend a meeting of the united front at which he was told that the time had come for a showdown against labor and that the allied industries must be prepared to dump their capital into a do-or-die fight. At which point Mr. Taylor arose and said that he would have nothing to do with the idea. He even went so far as to say that any such concerted action would be interpreted only as a capitalistic conspiracy to gang up on labor. So strong was his attitude that the united front fell apart.

Such, then, was the Chairman's faith in the Myron Taylor formula for industrial peace, which he had worked out that summer. And having come so far one might have expected him to plunge on. Characteristically, however, he did nothing of the kind. On one occasion, when discussing labor with business associates, he went so far as to wonder out loud whether it would be advisable to talk with Mr. Lewis; and one of the men present said, "Why of course you should. You did it in 1933 and you ought to try again." But even after this prodding Mr. Taylor hung back, not from indecision (for he is not the indecisive sort) but because, being instinctively a diplomat, he felt that the strategical moment had not yet arrived.

The moment

Thus the accidental meeting in the Mayflower, like all historical accidents, had been amply prepared, and as Mr. Taylor and Mr. Lewis stood chatting before the excited guests they knew of things more exciting than any of the guests could suspect. The next day we find Mr. Lewis in a Mayflower elevator on his way up to Mr. Taylor's suite. And a few minutes later the historic conferences had begun.

Here we may indulge in some speculation of a fairly foolproof variety. Neither Mr. Lewis nor Mr. Taylor will reveal what was discussed at that first meeting, but it seems clear that the sit-down strike at General Motors must have had some attention, and that Mr. Taylor must have expounded the principles of his formula—collective bargaining combined with the open shop. In this event he would have pointed out that if Mr. Lewis wanted to settle with General Motors, the closed shop and the checkoff would have to be thrown out of the window. Mr. Lewis has an intuitive and an agile mind. Whatever Mr. Taylor may have said or left unsaid, it seems certain that labor's chieftain left the conference with no illusions on most points. At any rate, his settlement with General Motors followed the formula closely.

Mr. Lewis and Mr. Taylor met again. And again. But such was the big laborite's skill in lumbering in and out of the crowded Mayflower that no one had the least suspicion of what he was up to, a few of the more observant Washington correspondents noting merely that he disappeared on several occasions without leaving any trace of himself. On January 14 Mr. Taylor swung out to Pittsburgh to plead for industrial peace at the opening of the new $10,000,000 plate mill at Homestead. But by the seventeenth he was back in Washington again. Here he found Mr. Lewis in one of his wildcat fighting moods, roaring at Alfred Sloan and calling upon the President to pay up for the support that labor had given him in the elections. The atmosphere of Mr. Taylor's suite after one of those hell-raising days, with the Chairman sitting thoughtfully in an armchair and Mr. Lewis trudging the floor, is better imagined than written. One must in any case admire the open-mindedness of the steel master no less than the huge courage of the laborite, who had the President of the U.S. and the automobile and steel industries on his hands at one and the same time. On the twenty-eighth, when Mr. Taylor left Washington, the friendly conspiracy was postponed. And on February 2 Mr. Lewis moved in person on Detroit.

The critical days

What Mr. Lewis accomplished in Detroit has a direct bearing on our tale, but in order to simplify it we must transfer ourselves first to New York. There, on February 4, the coal operators met with Philip Murray, Mr. Lewis's smart Scotch lieutenant, to negotiate new contracts with the United Mine Workers. Embroiled with Mr. Sloan in Detroit and then laid up for a spell with flu, Mr. Lewis was unable to attend these meetings until February 17, when he settled himself into the St. Regis Hotel and went to work for his own U.M.W.A. But he did not spend all of his time at the coal conferences. Muffling his unforgettable physiognomy in his coat collar as best he could, he often slipped away and out of sight. And no one knows where. But it is a safe bet that if some curious idler had been standing in East Seventieth Street hard by Myron C. Taylor's triple house he would have seen a cab draw up night after night and a big man step out with his hat cocked stubbornly forward over his forehead.

The fact that Mr. Lewis came secretly and frequently to the house of steel is one of the reasons why the story of these negotiations has never been told. It was, to say the least, an embarrassing spot in which to argue the proletarian cause. But that aspect of the situation is only superficial. Mr. Taylor and Mr. Lewis had now come a long way toward understanding each other, and it did not much matter in whose house they conferred—the truth could be spoken just the same. . . .

The lucky thing was that Mr. Taylor, for all his formality, is a sociable sort of man who likes a foursome in the afternoon and a long, sparkling dinner table in the evening; and Mr. Lewis, while he has generally held aloof from the industrial tycoons, is a conversationalist of power and versatility who delights in nothing better than to exercise his wit among folk who have thought of labor leaders in terms of William Green. It was this interplay of conversation that led them on. Yet it is not to be supposed either that they spent their stolen evenings in defining the amenities. Now and then one of them would, so to speak, pull out the diapason, and the great, solid theme of steel would be heard, and rise up to engulf them both for an hour or so.

And it was during these tonic moments that Mr. Taylor, diplomatist extraordinary, executed his plot. It was a simple plot and certainly not reprehensible, but plot it was nevertheless. It consisted in erecting before Mr. Lewis, in vivid word pictures, the great, forbidding specter of U.S. Steel's Board of Directors. As a matter of fact Mr. Taylor had been consulting his Board ever since his return from Europe in September and had turned the heat on all the way while Mr. Lewis was in Detroit. And although he had met with considerable resistance to his new labor philosophy from half a dozen of the Directors, he had met with encouragement from as many others. Nevertheless Mr. Taylor did not dwell upon the encouragement. To Mr. Lewis rather he relayed the vigorous objections of men who had hundreds of thousands of employees on their aggregate payroll, and who reasoned that if C.I.O. were allowed to get a foothold in steel it would eventually invade every industry in the land. This opposition, never in reality an insuperable threat to his statesmanlike plan, became in Mr. Taylor's skillful hands a jack by which to lift labor into a trading mood. With the result that in the end Mr. Lewis traded out the closed shop just as Mr. Taylor had advised him to do (and as he did do) in the automobile strike.

It is probable, however, that Mr. Taylor had his Board already in hand by the time Mr. Lewis arrived at the St. Regis to attend the coal meetings. The arguments he used to convince them would lead us astray into complexities, but they may be summarized briefly as follows:

1. The steel industry was participating in the domestic prosperity and might even be on the verge of a boom. To become tied up in a labor war would be to forfeit net profits the like of which had not been seen since before the depression.

2. Besides the domestic boom, Britain was about to call for bids on steel for her new $7,000,000,000 armament program.

3. The Walsh-Healey Act had tied the industry up in knots that could be untied only by raising wages and shortening hours; but if these steps were taken ex C.I.O., Scotch Mr. Murray would claim them as victories for C.I.O. anyway.

4. One of the big jobs that Mr. Taylor had set himself when he took over the chairmanship was the reorganization of steel production. Without entering the intricacies of this subject, it is clear that a reorganization of production implied a considerable simplification in the labor structure. The Carnegie-Illinois Steel Co. (to cite one example only) had built up a fantastic system of

wage scales resulting in no less than 11,000 different rates of pay applicable to 100,000 employees in twenty-eight mills. A wage structure as complicated as that is an almost insuperable obstacle to labor organizers, since it facilitates favoritism and job politics. But the system had backfired upon its inventors because it made a scientific analysis of production all but impossible. It was evident to anyone who thought about the situation objectively that a reliable contract with a vertical, industrial union such as that being organized by the S.W.O.C. would constitute a necessary first step toward a new and simplified industrial technique.

5. The C.I.O. drive in the steel country was probably the most intelligently directed labor drive ever organized in the U.S., complete with a fast-footed legal staff, high political connections, and a counter espionage system that was feeding the La Follette Committee with information just as distasteful to the gentlemen on the Board of U.S. Steel as it was to their Chairman. And here Mr. Lewis's exploit at Detroit weighed heavily upon the minds entrusted with the destiny of big steel. Whether General Motors had had a right to eject the sitdowners from its plants did not seem to the gentlemen to be the question, because very obviously they could not have been ejected without bloodshed. But if this sort of thing could tie up the automobile industry, which had been hastily organized, what would prevent it from tying up steel, where the C.I.O. was firmly and forethoughtedly entrenched?

Moreover, it had begun to look very doubtful whether the steel operators could win a strike, at any rate in Pennsylvania. Time was when they could have called upon the trusty Coal and Iron Police, but that faithful little band of desperadoes had been outlawed some years previously by Governor Pinchot. And time was when they could have counted on Harrisburg for the state troops, but as of February, 1937, it looked as if the resources of Harrisburg would be thrown chiefly to the other side. The rise of Governor Murphy of Michigan into the national limelight had indeed been a disturbing phenomenon to Pennsylvania's Governor Earle, who had presidential ambitions and would like nothing better than a chance to eclipse Governor Murphy in the headlines by refusing the economic royalists the use of the state militia. Obviously any resistance from the operators would simply make good political fodder for Mr. Earle. Which was one expedient reason for not starting trouble.[2]

Obviously all these points could be summed up in the simple statement that the Corporation had an enormous dollars-and-cents stake in heading off an industrial war. But before the august Directors achieved unanimity on the matter, another war broke out on a different front.

The independents

Go back momentarily to June 29, 1936, when the Iron and Steel Institute issued its manifesto to labor. That document defined the attitude of the independents toward John L. Lewis and all other outsiders. But while the inde-

---

[2] At the conclusion of the agreement Governor Earle wired warm congratulations to C.I.O. and Carnegie-Illinois.

pendents were holding this fixed position, Mr. Taylor had written his formula and taken steps to put it into action; and sooner or later a clash was inevitable. About the second week in February three of the independents, through the watchfulness with which all good industrialists compliment each other, got wind of the fact that Mr. Taylor and Mr. Lewis were holding conversations, and they went to see the Chairman. But before they got around to the subject, Mr. Taylor himself broached it. Inviting them to lunch with him in his office, he said that he was holding conversations with Mr. Lewis and he showed them the formula with which he was negotiating.

There ensued a heated debate, from which there emerged the fact that the independents wanted to meet the situation by raising wages. Mr. Taylor, however, did not want to raise wages. And for this he had two reasons. First, he believed that if Mr. Lewis were granted collective bargaining along the lines of the formula, the C.I.O. would not insist on a wage increase. Second, he said that he did not think that the wage increase was the point at issue out in the field. To the independents' insistence that it was, he replied that he was so differently informed that he wanted to check back with his own people. And with this the meeting was adjourned until a week later.

The next meeting came on Friday, February 26, and it broke the steel industry wide open. Mr. Taylor said that he had talked with his executives, who concurred with him that the wage issue was not the leading issue among the men. The independents, however, adhering to the policy by which the steel industry (but especially, be it noted, the Corporation) had lost ground to labor all summer, insisted that labor could best be handled by increasing wages, at the same time bolstering the company unions. Parenthetically it should be pointed out here that the company-union idea had had a boomerang action in many mills, serving to educate the workers in organization practices; and in certain cases the C.I.O. had been able to swing these organizations into the ranks *in toto*. Whether because Mr. Taylor had this fact in mind, or because he was only part way through his negotiations with Mr. Lewis and believed that wages could be traded out, he refused to countenance an increase at that time, and he went so far as to say that he did not think he could sell the idea to his Board. So this meeting adjourned also, with the understanding that Mr. Taylor would consult the Board on Monday and reconfer on Tuesday.

Thereafter the pace became breathless. The Chairman had a long conversation with Mr. Lewis Friday night at which two other men were present who had been in and out of the situation all along. These were Thomas Moses, President of the H. C. Frick Coke Co., who handled details for Mr. Taylor, and Philip Murray, Mr. Lewis's smart, aggressive lieutenant, who had been studying the steel situation since he was put in charge of the S.W.O.C. drive last spring. The next day (Saturday, February 27) Mr. Benjamin Fairless, President of the Carnegie-Illinois Steel Co., returning from a week's tour of his plants during which he had made a great number of speeches assuring the company unions that the management stood behind them, found a telegram on his desk. It was a brisk message requesting him to come to New York for an urgent conference on Sunday. Mr. Fairless went. Arriving in New York he stepped unawares into the situation that we have now traced from its origins. And having assimilated it as well as he could, returned to Pittsburgh.

On Sunday night Mr. Taylor had a final meeting with Mr. Lewis. On Monday morning he met with his Board. And then things began to happen out in the steel country. About two o'clock independent spies arrived breathessly in the offices of their executives to report that Mr. Benjamin Fairless and Mr. Philip Murray were about to sit down at a conference table at Carnegie-Illinois. Most of the executives did not credit the news, but at three o'clock Mr. William A. Irvin, President of U.S. Steel, called them all up in person and said that the C.I.O. and the Corporation were going to sit down that afternoon. Bending forward incredulously in his chair, one of the independents shouted, "I can't believe you. What time this afternoon?" Mr. Irvin said three o'clock. At this the steel master banged his fist on the desk. "It's three o'clock now!" he roared. And Mr. Irvin said, "So it is."

Thereafter the independents clutched their phones and began to crisscross the country with long-distance calls. The first news that the men in Mr. Fairless's office were S.W.O.C. representatives went on the wire at three twenty-six; and at three thirty-five Mr. Fairless handed out a statement verifying this fact. All during the conference the independents continued to check with each other. And they did so to such good effect that within an hour and forty-five minutes after the meeting ended no less than five of them had announced a new minimum wage, the first flash coming from Ernest Weir's National Steel Co. at 4:49 p.m.

Viewed in the calm light of history, this is the kind of affair in which it is impossible for the outsider to take sides. Mr. Taylor, it is now evident, was in an extremely delicate position. Though he had won Mr. Lewis's confidence and had obtained the backing of his Board, there was obviously no hope of swinging the independents over to his way of thinking; and in order to protect Mr. Lewis as well as himself, about the only thing to do was to beat them to the draw. If he had not done so his whole edifice might have collapsed, in which event this story would not have been written and the industrial world would not have been treated to the spectacle of the U.S. Steel Corp. and the C.I.O. shaking hands. Many men do not believe that they should have shaken hands. Many, many more believe that the handshake began a new era in industrial labor relations. At which point we can perhaps do no better than to quote the generous Mr. Lewis. He said: this agreement "has been made possible by the farseeing vision and industrial statesmanship of Myron C. Taylor. From time to time over a period of several months in New York and Washington, Mr. Taylor and I have engaged in conversations and negotiations. We were each conscious of the great weight of responsibility and the far-reaching consequences attached to our decisions. Labor, industry, and the nation will be the beneficiaries."

In the form in which our story has been constructed, Mr. Taylor has been cast in the heroic role. But that is largely because Mr. Taylor's motives, being less obvious than those of Mr. Lewis, have been followed in closer detail. According to the laws of drama Mr. Lewis is the real hero because Mr. Lewis is in the midst of a great, unfinished struggle in which this episode represents only one advance. Both Mr. Taylor and Mr. Lewis tasted victory; but for Mr. Lewis that victory must sooner or later resolve itself again into strife, whereas for Mr. Taylor it is a monument, fixed and immovable. Mr. Taylor took the chair of the U.S. Steel Corp. with the expressed intention of resigning in the not too distant future, and so far as his career is concerned, he could tender that resignation tomorrow and the world would acclaim him a successful man. He is free at any time to follow his bent toward diplomacy, and the gossip that he will be the next Ambassador to the Court of St. James's is worth paying some attention to, if only for that reason. No such fateful reward awaits Mr. Lewis, and one might add that none such is desired. The man who brought big steel to terms will probably die with his boots on.

A PAGEANT OF PROGRESS

A union official once said of his fellow unionists, with rare objectivity, "They glory in their past wars like American Legionnaires." Like American citizens recalling the events of their country's greatness or veterans remembering their campaigns, old-time union members frequently dust off reminders of the grim struggle for existence in the union's formative days, the historic strikes—won or lost—to compel some recalcitrant employer to recognize the union or concede some principle. This lore is especially important to an organization which considers itself part of a movement, which expresses its objectives not only in terms of day-to-day bread-and-butter gains but of ideals and principles. There is a strong emotional undertow to unionism, without an understanding of which it is impossible to comprehend the allegiance it arouses in the hearts of its most ardent leaders and its most loyal followers. In some respects it is more akin to a religious than an economic movement. The following reading should convey something of that impression.

From *Ammunition*, published by the United Automobile Workers, January, 1956, pp. 21–26

What was CIO's meaning? What were its accomplishments? How did it affect history? These were the themes of a pageant presented during CIO's final convention just before it and the AFL joined forces in an historic merger. Memories rushed back as the audience in the darkened hall watched the performers led by narrator Melvyn Douglas and labor songster Joe Glazer recall noted events in CIO history, bring to life once more its historic words. Excerpts from the pageant script are reprinted here.

MUSIC: "I'm gonna call the roll of unions in the CIO
I've got 'em right here—on my old banjo
I'm gonna call the big ones, gonna call the small—

I'll call in the in-between ones—let's call 'em all
Let's call the roll . . . of the CIO.
"There's Uniteds—Amalgamateds—and Internationals
They've organized the workers in the shops and mills
In the mines, on the busses and the ships on the seas
In the offices, the stores and in the factories . . .
Let's call the roll . . . of the CIO.
"Every group has played a part in the CIO
Every Union's left its mark in the CIO
Every member's helped to build the CIO . . .
"Yes! Let's call the roll—of brotherhood
Let's call the roll—of dignity
Let's call the roll—of solidarity
Let's call the roll—of the CIO."

NARRATOR: There are other names, too. Names of places—big cities and tiny one-factory towns; names of leaders, some known to all, many never identified; names of friends; names of allies. A rollcall only history itself can put together . . . the rollcall of CIO . . .

MUSIC: "CIO . . . CIO
And we'll never stop till we are on top
For we are the CIO . . ."

NARRATOR: The story of CIO is the story of people—millions of them—working and crying and struggling and rejoicing together. It is the story of practical men who dared to dream, of dreamers who dared to be practical. It is the story of Matthew proclaiming again: "Come unto me, all ye that labor and are heavy laden, and I will give you rest." It is Isaiah declaring again: "Learn to do well; seek judgment; relieve the oppressed; judge the fatherless; plead for the widow. Come now and let us reason together."

MUSIC: "We will overcome, we will overcome
We will overcome some day
Oh, oh, down in my heart, I do believe,
We will overcome some day."

NARRATOR: How tell the story of the CIO? Perhaps some day your grandchildren will be reciting in school . . .

SCHOOL BOY: The CIO was a labor organization during the period 1935 to 1955. It had three presidents: John L. Lewis, Philip Murray and Walter P. Reuther.

NARRATOR: Is that the story of CIO? In a way—for it does relate some of the facts. But in a real sense CIO was born long before that official birthdate of November 9, 1935. You might say the beginnings go back to the Philadelphia shoemakers sent to jail in 1806, back to the Pullman strikers standing up to the bayonets of the U.S. Army in 1894, back to the Steelworkers strike in 1919, back to the many years of hopes and dreams and unheeded cries of millions of workers for organization.

And is there an ending to the CIO? Of course not. For it is more than an organization—a name—a set of initials.

There can be no end to the unions built and strengthened under the banner of the CIO, to the pensions being paid, to the ideals instilled, to the friendships formed . . .

MUSIC: ". . . Since I been introduced to the CIO, I ain't, no I ain't, no stranger now . . ."

NARRATOR: No, there is no real beginning and no end. But these 20 years are a chapter—a particular chapter with particular accomplishments. It fell to us in our generation to meet desperate needs with daring answers, to be the vehicle for organizing Americans to meet those needs.

It has been said that we can never know how far we have gone unless we know from where we came. Philip Murray reminded us often from where we came.

VOICE: "I went into towns where children were eating out of garbage pails. People were living in hovels. No pictures on the walls, no carpets on the floors, no music in the homes. The working population was suffering, and in too many instances, was starving. Disease, sickness and poverty were rampant, and death stalked in the wake of every worker's family because he could not purchase medicine."

NARRATOR: ". . . pictures on the walls . . . music in the homes." What does this have to do with CIO? Let's listen again to Phil Murray.

VOICE: "What is a union for? To feel the pulse beats of the people, to live close to the people, to understand the people's problems, and then to use constructive, intelligent strength of the organization to promote the well-being of families, and by doing so, to promote the well-being of nations."

NARRATOR: ". . . to promote the well-being of families . . . the well-being of nations." How far have we come in the realization of these goals? How does one measure our progress? There are statistics, of course . . .

VOICE: "From the Bureau of Labor Statistics: Average hourly earnings, all manufacturing employees in 1935, 55 cents. 1955, $1.89. Percentage increase—261%."

NARRATOR: "Percentage increase—261%." Not too bad for 20 years. But these are cold statistics. What does it mean to one man? Let's hear from Frank Tuttle, the first man to retire in his plant on CIO-negotiated pension. He felt pretty good, and he wanted to tell everybody about it. Listen to what he said, and remember this was 1950 . . .

VOICE: "Today I punched my last clock card at the plant. I am now balancing my account.

"In 1933, my pay was down to 60 cents an hour. Then came the union. By 1950 my wages were $1.83 an hour. Throw in the fringes—like holidays and vacations—and it comes to an even $2.00. Sixty cents before the union, two dollars now.

"Altogether, I figure the union got me about $24,000 extra in wages, and my pension and my insurance is worth an additional $16,000. That makes a total of $40,000 won for me by the union.

"I have paid $225 in dues and I've lost about $1,200 walking a picket line. For every dollar of dues and lost time, I have gotten back $28."

NARRATOR: 28 for 1. And the same kind of arithmetic can be done by telephone workers, and clothing workers, merchant seamen or oil or rubber or any and every other group of organized workers.

But that's not all Frank Tuttle had to say the day he retired. Let's listen . . .

VOICE: "28 for 1. That much is simple arithmetic. But who can calculate the extra years of usefulness to thousands of us because the union didn't let the company say we were too old to work when we reached 40 or 50?

"How much is it worth to know that when we were laid off, we would be called back in our exact turn?

"Above all, what allowance for the fact that we have been building a better world to work in which we can leave as an inheritance to our children and grandchildren?

"Even Albert Einstein can't give you an equation that will measure these things."

NARRATOR: No. There is no equation which can measure self-respect or industrial democracy. And who could measure, with statistics, the sense of human dignity that CIO brought to America—the millions once considered faceless card numbers who are today treated as human beings and think of themselves as human beings?

Oh, you can measure the financial value—but not the spiritual value—of protection against sickness and old age, of medical centers, of cooperative housing. You can calculate the cost of guaranteed annual wages—but not its value.

How far have we come? Oh, we've been coming—and we haven't stopped. New tomorrows, new horizons, new goals. And sometimes we even dream . . .

MUSIC: "I dreamed that I had died and gone to my reward,
A job in heaven's textile plant on a golden boulevard.
The mill was made of marble, the machines were made out of gold,
And nobody ever got tired and nobody ever grew old."

NARRATOR: And sometimes dreams come true . . . but not easily.

VOICE: "They picked me up about eight different times and threw me down on my back on the concrete. While I was on the ground, they kicked me in the face, head and other parts of my body. . . . After they kicked me down all the stairs they started to hit me at the bottom of the stairs, hit me and slugged, driving me before them, but never letting me get away."

NARRATOR: Lest we forget. Dreams don't come easy. The words you just heard were those of an auto worker named Walter Reuther testifying about how he had been attacked by thugs in May, 1937, for the crime of distributing leaflets at the Ford plant. But many others never lived to tell their story.

VOICE: "Coroner's Report: Frank J. Walsh, Coroner, Cook County, Illinois. Name: Otis Jones. Sex: Male. Nationality: American. Date of Death: June 8, 1937. History of Cause of Death: Injured in riot at Republic Steel Mill, May 30, 1937. Died in Burnside Hospital. Diagnosis: Bullet Wound in Back."

MUSIC: The Oath. (Continues through Reading.)

NARRATOR: What was Otis Jones' "crime" that he was shot in the back? On Memorial Day in 1937, there was a peaceful parade of strikers at the South Chicago plant of the Republic Steel Company. There were 150 policemen, too.

And fortunately, so that all the world could soon know the truth, there were also newsreel photographers present. A columnist for the St. Louis *Post Dispatch* examined the films over and over again and then he wrote of the Memorial Day Massacre . . .

VOICE: "A vivid close-up shows the head of the parade being halted by a group of 150 policemen . . .

"Suddenly, without apparent warning, there was a terrific roar of pistol shots . . .

"The ground is strewn with dead and wounded. In several instances from two to four policemen are seen beating one man . . .

"Thirty persons, including one woman and three minors, received gun shot wounds.

"Ten men died, seven shot in the back and three in the side; none was hit in the front."

NARRATOR: That was 1937. Others died before them, and others since, in the exercise of their democratic rights.

And many others were prepared to make the same sacrifice. In February of 1937, for example, sitdown strikers in Fisher Body Plant Four at Flint were threatened with ejection as a result of an injunction which had just been issued. Strikers wired the Governor of Michigan . . .

VOICE: "We, the workers in the plant, are completely unarmed, and to send in the military, armed thugs, and armed deputies, will mean bloody massacre. We fully expect that if a violent effort is made to oust us, many of us will be killed. We take this means of making it known to our wives, our children, to the people of Michigan and of the country. We have decided to stay in."

MUSIC: "We shall not be, we shall not be moved.
We shall not be, we shall not be moved.
Just like a tree, that's planted by the water
We shall not be moved."

NARRATOR: Yes, these were the raw materials out of which CIO was built. Was it all worth while? Perhaps the answer is to be found in an essay written by a 16-year-old high school boy in Bemis, Tennessee. He had a kind of special reason for knowing.

VOICE: "Organized labor is not just a union you join. It is an organization which you must mingle in, contribute time and valuable thinking to.

"It is an organization that has not sprung up over night; it has taken years of painful, hard fighting to get it. Some lived so that they could work and contribute their time in organizing many plants, factories, and mills.

"No matter what kind of union, it cannot run itself. It must be taken care of.

"Make preparations for your children and theirs. Build your union as you would build your home. For without it, you're without a real home."

NARRATOR: "Build your union as you would build your home," wrote 16-year-old David Simmons, the son of Lowell Simmons. Lowell Simmons was a local leader of the CIO Textile Workers. On Christmas Eve, 1951, during a strike at Bemis, Tennessee, he was shot to death by a strikebreaker.

MUSIC: "I dreamed I saw Joe Hill last night.

Alive as you and me.
Says I but Joe you're ten years dead.
I never died says he—
I never died says he.
The copper bosses killed you Joe.
They shot you Joe says I.
Takes more than guns to kill a man
Says Joe I didn't die—
Says Joe I didn't die."

NARRATOR: Let the record show that as we grew and became stronger and developed maturity, there was too a growing maturity in the ranks of management. Sure, it wasn't an easy road—there have been many bumps on the way—but today . . . well, let us listen to David J. McDonald reporting to the Steelworkers.

VOICE: "At first our struggle was to gain recognition—and we lost in those early days. With patience, feeling and believing in justice and right and the full knowledge that our course was sound, we later did gain recognition. After this recognition came growth and strength, and now—we have heard the top leaders of the American steel industry say, 'We not only recognize the United Steelworkers of America; we accept the United Steelworkers of America.'"

NARRATOR: And let the record also show that we haven't been alone. We've had our enemies, yes. But we've had our friends, too. Wherever men of good will and democratic conviction were to be found, there you found friends of organized labor. All we asked was the right to organize. Franklin Delano Roosevelt agreed. So did the Congress which passed the Wagner Act. And so did the Supreme Court in 1937, when it declared . . .

VOICE: "We say that labor organizations come out of the necessities of the situation; that a single employee is helpless in dealing with an employer . . . that the union is essential to give laborers an opportunity to deal on a basis of equality with their employers . . ." The Wagner Labor Relations Act is constitutional.

NARRATOR: And men of religion were to be found speaking out fearlessly for labor. Leaders of every faith identified the aims of organized labor with the basic foundations of religion itself. A priest once told a CIO convention: "I am glad to come here because I belong here. To the eyes of other men, the Saviour appeared as a tradesman, a worker . . ." A rabbi declared: "For me the labor movement is a spiritual movement in the same sense that the church is—an organization to lift one up above materialistic needs, and to give one a vision of what can be . . ." And a minister said: "I am convinced that the organization of labor is essential to the well-being of the working people. It is based upon a sense of the inestimable value of the individual man."

MUSIC: "We will build a new world . . ."

NARRATOR: Sidney Hillman once declared: "There is no welfare without the social welfare." CIO has always recognized that its members could not be fully served at the collective bargaining table alone. Economic progress, peace, democracy in all its forms—these objectives of society were the objectives of organized labor. CIO has said that "what is good for America is good for the CIO." Shortly before he died, Hillman stated, with simple eloquence . . .

VOICE: "We want a better America, an America that will give its citizens, first of all, a higher and higher standard of living so that no child will cry for food in the midst of plenty. We want to have an America where the inventions of science will be at the disposal of every American family, not merely for the few who can afford them. An America that will have no sense of insecurity and which will make it possible for all groups, regardless of race, creed, or color to live in friendship, to be real neighbors; an America that will carry its great mission of helping other countries to help themselves."

NARRATOR: On many fronts, CIO has been working and fighting to create this kind of America, this kind of world. It has provided the training grounds for citizenship. Thousands of men and women have served . . . wherever people are working together to further the social good.

In the field of civil rights, for example. In 1947, James B. Carey spoke for millions of CIO members and their families when, as a member of President Truman's Committee on Cvil Rights, he joined in the declaration that:

VOICE: "We abhor the totalitarian arrogance which makes one man say he will respect another man as his equal only if he has 'my race, my religion, my political views, my social position.' In our land, men are equal, but they are free to be different. From these differences among our people has come the great human and national strength of America."

NARRATOR: Yes, it has been well said that the letters CIO really stand for Citizenship in Operation . . .

CIO's political and legislative activities have been directed at labor objectives, of course. Against Taft-Hartley—for improved unemployment insurance, for example. But CIO has never been found wanting in campaigns for the public good.

For the elimination of segregation in our public schools; for a liberal immigration policy; for the safeguarding of our civil liberties; for aid to farmers; for fair tax laws; for adequate housing and social security and health measures.

For CIO believes that there is no welfare without the social welfare.

MUSIC: "If each little kid could have fresh milk each day.
If each working man had enough time to play.
If each homeless soul had a good place to stay.
It could be a wonderful world.
If we could consider each other
A neighbor, a friend or a brother
It could be a wonderful world."

NARRATOR: ". . . if we could consider each other a neighbor, a friend, or a brother . . ."

CIO recognizes no national boundary lines to brotherhood. It has united with free workers, through the ICFTU, to create a world of peace and justice . . . a good world.

CIO has been privileged to play its part in the creation of such a world.

. . . We have come a long way here in America these 20 years. But so much remains to be done.

Count the hungry faces then, and count the strong ones now. But remember ones still unfed. . . .

Count the ragged children then . . . and rosy-cheeked ones now . . . but remember the millions still in slums. . . .

Count the victims of the wars we've seen in our short life . . . and count the blessings for each day of peace . . . but remember the fears and doubts still haunting us. . . .

Yes, count the millions then yearning for union strength, and count the union members now. But remember the millions still unreached, millions still yearning, still daring to hope. . . .

There is indeed much for American labor to do. And it will take more unity and more strength than ever. Remember well the words of Allan Haywood who until his very last breath kept driving us to build our union strong. . . .

VOICE: "The fact is that the CIO was born in an atmosphere of hunger and poverty—yes, and desperation. We organized, and we went on strike. We challenged the great corporations and we resisted the nightsticks and the tear gas of our police. Today trade unions of America have fought their way to acceptance by the corporations and the government. But keep this in mind: no government, no administration, no group of public officials, no matter how friendly, can hold our gains for us. It is only our unions supported by the solid determination of our members, which can insure our future."

NARRATOR: It is 20 years now since the letters CIO first made an indelible mark upon American history. And those who have been privileged to be associated with this stirring chapter are not content merely to look back upon that chapter with pride; they again turn their eyes to the future, a future of new opportunities, new goals, new dreams.

VOICE: "This is the beginning of what can be the most glorious chapter in the history of the American labor movement. . . . Let us join hands with the men and women of good will in the AFL and together face the future with the will, the courage, and dedication that we have demonstrated in the past. . . . Together we can be among the important architects in the building of that better tomorrow, that better world, and we can fashion it in the image of freedom and justice and decency and human brotherhood."

NARRATOR: Those were the words of hope and confidence of the President of the CIO—the words of Walter P. Reuther when the historic merger agreement was adopted earlier this year. Hope and confidence that flow from strength, from unity, from solidarity. . . .

VOICE: "When the Union's inspiration through the worker's blood shall run,
There can be no power greater anywhere beneath the sun;
Yet what force on earth is weaker than the feeble strength of one,
But the Union makes us strong."

NARRATOR: Some have sung just the last words—words of hope, words of strength, words of brotherhood—

"Solidarity forever. Solidarity forever. Solidarity forever.
For the Union makes us strong."
(Audience joins in singing. The curtain falls.)

EVOLUTION OF LABOR RELATIONS IN U.S. STEEL

By John A. Stephens, Vice President, Industrial Relations, U.S. Steel, 1955, pp. 8–9

We have made substantial progress since the early years of our union relationship. Those early years were difficult. I don't mean that the present are not difficult, too, but we do have improved relationships. We then learned, and continue now to learn, that man has an almost infinite capacity for disagreement and that decency, good will, and understanding cannot be induced by law or discipline alone. The relationship some years ago was, of course, new on both sides. Adjusting to it required time, patience, tolerance, integrity of character. . . .

During these years many serious men on both sides were slowly, painfully at times, learning to adjust, to work together. We were developing new skills in human relationships, social imagination—the ability to put one's self in another's place and see his point of view. And there was slowly emerging a spirit of tolerance. I do not mean by this an easygoing broadmindedness which has no fixed standards of right or wrong, but rather respect for the beliefs, practices, and behavior of others without necessarily sharing or accepting them.

FOR DISCUSSION AND ANALYSIS

1. American legal philosophy prior to the 1930s made individual rights superior to group rights. An individual labor contract took precedence over a collective agreement. The right of a worker to refrain from joining a union was greater than the right of a union to require his membership in an organization as a condition of employment. As one court said in a case arising in 1870:

Freedom is the policy of this country. But freedom does not imply a right in one person, either alone or in combination with others, to disturb or annoy another, either directly or indirectly, in his lawful business or occupation, or to threaten him with an annoyance or injury, for the sake of compelling him to buy his peace; or . . . "with intent to extort money or any pecuniary advantage whatever, or to compel him to do any act against his will."

Or, as the Supreme Court remarked in another but apposite context: "To sustain the individual freedom of action contemplated by the Constitution, is not to strike down the common good but to exalt it; for surely, the good of society as a whole cannot be better served than by the preservation against arbitrary restraint of the liberties of its constituent members."

Beginning with the 1930s, however, this legal attitude has been reversed. Individual rights in the employment relationship, at least in the important particulars, must be subordinated to group interests. Here again the words of the Supreme Court reflect this attitude:

But it is argued that some employees may lose by the collective agreement, that an individual workman may sometimes have, or be capable of getting, better terms than those obtainable by the group and that his freedom of contract must be respected on that account. . . . We find the mere possibility that such agreements might be made no ground for holding generally that individual contracts may survive or surmount collective ones. The practice and philosophy of collective bargaining looks with suspicion on such individual advantages. . . . The workman is free, if he values his own bargaining position more than that of the group, to vote against representation; but the majority rules, and if it collectivizes the employment bargain, individual advantages or favors will generally in practice go in as a contribution to the collective result.

How do you account for this apparent 180-degree shift in the legal view of the relative rights of individual and group?

2. Chief Justice Beasley, in *State v. Donaldson* (excerpted above) asserted that a right of workers to organize and strike in support of their demands would constitute a right to control the business of another. (*a*) Do you agree with this assertion? (*b*) To whatever extent you may concur, what, if any, justification may warrant granting such a "right"? (*c*) Would you impose any limitations on the right of workers "to control the business of another" by organization and the power of the strike?

3. The great contribution which Samuel Gompers is said to have made to the labor movement was to base the AFL, of which he was the first president, on principles of business unionism. This was in contrast to the utopian objectives of earlier labor organizations, which had sought radical social changes to better the lot of workers. The AFL has always accepted the prevailing economic system and sought simply to get out of it a bigger share for its members. Thus, when Gompers was once asked in a congressional committee what labor's objectives were, he responded, "More, more, more." This outlook has been termed "bread-and-butter unionism," or "pork-chops unionism," or "business unionism." American unions are generally said to be of this nature.

This would appear to be essentially a materialistic philosophy—the only objective, the only purpose, the only goal is more money and more goods. Yet the labor movement is also usually considered to be idealistic and reformist, in contrast to the conservatism of business interests. One of the most influential of current labor leaders once remarked: "Workers want something more than the assurance of a full belly. . . . I wouldn't be here if I didn't think there was more to unionism than just bread and butter."

Can these two apparently contradictory views of the philosophy of organized labor be reconciled?

4. The background of union-management relations in the United States has been one of violence to a degree not known in other Western countries. There have been shooting, dynamiting, and other manifestations of industrial warfare recurring from the time when unions first began to create organizations of any strength (about 1850) down to 1940, with occasional outbreaks even now.

(*a*) How can you explain this record of labor violence, peculiar to the United States among Western countries? (*b*) In the light of this background, how can you explain the widespread acceptance by American business of collective bargaining—however reluctant by management, or suspected by unionists—within a decade after passage of the Wagner Act?

5. On April 26, 1956, Crawford H. Greenewalt, president of E. I. du Pont de Nemours & Co. delivered an address before the Bureau of Advertising of the American Newspaper Publishers Association. His remarks were not addressed to personnel matters but, rather, to the place of business in the American scene. But one paragraph from that address is relevant to the subject matter of this chapter.

Much has been said in recent years of the "new type of business man," as if, by some process of sexless eugenics, the bull terriers and bloodhounds of the business past had been crossbred to produce a race of intelligent and kindly poodles. I have never been able to accept this concept. It seems to me that men will always reflect the society in which they live, will respond to its pressures, its ideals and its customs. As society as a whole develops and grows both spiritually and materially, the individuals comprising it will, on the average, grow and develop with it.

In what ways might it be said that management's personnel outlook of the present, changed as it is from the past, is a reflection of changed conceptions by society at large of the place of the worker in industry? What circumstances were responsible for the changes in society's views of the rights of workers?

6. Outline the basic differences between "employee representation" and "collective bargaining," doing such additional investigation as may be necessary. Employee-representation plans are now outlawed in interstate commerce by the Taft-Hartley Act, and were outlawed by the Wagner Act before it. What grounds do you see for making these plans illegal?

3: The Unions

Beneath the catch-all term "the Labor movement" is a complex of organizational structures. The documents and readings of this chapter are designed to give some impression of the nature of the institutions which compose the labor movement. These operate in three primary spheres: (1) the over-all national federation, the AFL–CIO, formed in 1955 out of a merger of the two previously independent federations, with which almost 200 national unions are affiliated; (2) the national unions themselves, such as the Automobile Workers, the Mine Workers, the Machinists, the Brotherhood of Locomotive Engineers, most but not all of which belong to the AFL–CIO; (3) the local chapters of the national unions, almost 80,000 in number. Each of these three types has its own function and its own form of government.

In the first selection, the Bureau of Labor Statistics analyzes statistically the American labor movement. This is a modified portion of its 1955 Directory of National and International Unions, *the most complete and authoritative source of such information now available.*

STRUCTURE AND MEMBERSHIP OF THE LABOR MOVEMENT

By William Paschell, Bureau of Labor Statistics, in Monthly Labor Review, vol. 78, 1955, pp. 1231–1239

Membership of national and international unions with headquarters in the United States was approximately 18 million at the beginning of 1955. The distribution of membership, by affiliation, based primarily on union reports and, in part, on Bureau estimates, was as follows: American Federation of Labor, 10.9 million; Congress of Industrial Organizations, 5.2 million; and not affiliated with either federation, 1.8 million. The 18 million total represents an increase of at least 1 million over the last published Bureau estimate of 16½ to 17 million for 1951. However, membership in 1954 was virtually unchanged compared with 1953 data which were also obtained in the current survey.

The 199 [1] national and international unions [2] known to the Bureau in 1954

[1] Because of union mergers which occurred through the fall of 1955, the number of national and international unions listed in the current Directory was reduced to 195.

[2] Henceforth, international is used generally to designate national and international unions alike. The latter claim jurisdiction and organize members beyond continental boundaries of the United States.

included unions which had slightly more than 1 million members located outside the continental United States, mainly in Canada. With this million-member segment excluded, total union membership in the United States was approximately a fourth of the Nation's labor force and a third of all nonagricultural wage and salaried workers. Almost 3 million women are union members, comprising approximately 1 of every 7 in the Nation's female labor force.

In size, the national and international unions ranged from fewer than 100 members to more than 1 million. One hundred twenty-four unions had fewer than 50,000 members and accounted for a combined membership of slightly more than 1½ million. In contrast, 6 unions, each with more than 500,000 members, represented an aggregate of nearly 6 million members or one-third of all union members.

Nearly 77,000 local unions were affiliated with the international unions. More than half were affiliated with 19 unions, each with 1,000 or more locals. Some small, highly centralized unions had no local affiliates. Both local and international unions, in varying degrees, shared the responsibility for the negotiation and administration of at least 125,000 collective bargaining agreements.

These figures are from the fourth survey conducted by the Bureau in recent years on union membership, the identity of all national and international unions, union officers, headquarters, the frequency of conventions, publications, the number of locals, and related matters. All affiliates of the AFL and CIO were surveyed. Unions not affiliated with either of these federations were included if they indicated that they were "interstate" in scope, i.e., had negotiated collective bargaining agreements with different employers in more than one State.[3] Information was obtained by means of a mail questionnaire sent to all unions which might be national or international in scope, as defined; it was supplemented in a number of instances through other sources, including union periodicals, convention proceedings, and the collective bargaining agreements on file in the Bureau.

It is important to emphasize at this point that the membership figures used in this study are based upon reports voluntarily submitted by the various unions, without a field check on the accuracy or consistency of these reports,

[3] The criteria concerning the geographical scope of collective bargaining agreements were waived for unions which organize government workers and, therefore, generally do not negotiate agreements. A few independent unions did not reply to the Bureau's questionnaire and were excluded because it could not be determined whether they met the "interstate" definition. In addition, some unaffiliated unions which may have been interstate in scope were not included because adequate identification was not available.

The criteria for listing as an unaffiliated union in the 1955 Directory differed from those used in the 1953 edition. In that Directory, "independent or unaffiliated unions were included where information existed that the union had at least 2 locals and was a party to collective bargaining agreements with more than 1 employer. In the absence of local branches, exceptions were made if the union had negotiated at least 10 collective bargaining agreements with different employers." (See Directory of Labor Unions in the United States, 1953, BLS Bull. 1127, p. 1, footnote 2.)

and upon Bureau estimates or other information where no membership count was submitted.

STRUCTURE OF THE LABOR MOVEMENT

It was just 20 years ago that the controversy over the organization of the mass-production industries flared at the convention of the American Federation of Labor, and the Committee for Industrial Organization was formed. In 1938, the new organization held its first constitutional convention as the Congress of Industrial Organizations. Since then, as a result of a variety of factors, the American labor movement has more than doubled in size, a growth accompanied by awareness of increased responsibilities at home and abroad. The importance of a free labor movement, at present covering 1 of every 4 in the Nation's total labor force, can be gaged by the breadth and impact of its activities. Probably best known are those which center upon union-management collective bargaining negotiations involving wages and working conditions. Collateral activities, including the use of educational media and the techniques of political action which seek to enlist public and government support for labor's goals, are found on community to national levels. Moreover, recognition that a mutuality of interests exists among democratically rooted labor organizations the world over has led to increased cooperation with free trade union movements abroad. These and other activities were carried out within the framework of union organizations discussed below.

AFL and CIO. The AFL, with 108 internationals [4] and 50,000 local affiliates, is the oldest and largest federation. In the CIO, there are 30 internationals with 10,000 locals. In addition, both federations have directly affiliated unions which are not part of any international; there were 900 federal labor unions (FLU) in the AFL as of June 30, 1954, and approximately 100 local industrial unions (LIU) in the CIO at the end of 1954.[5] A number of FLU's with common industry ties are affiliated with 1 of 3 organizing councils in the AFL. These represent a stage prior to the attainment of full-fledged international union status. The CIO has, on a comparable level, two organizing committees.

An integral part of AFL structure are its 5 departments,[6] 4 of which are composed of unions with mutual trades interest; the other, concerned with the union label, promotes the interests of all AFL unions with labels or emblems. Research and education departments and special committees in both the AFL and CIO compile data, disseminate information, and recommend action on affairs which directly affect the member's welfare as worker or citizen, includ-

---

[4] Two international unions were not included in this total. The Diamond Workers' Protective Union of America (AFL) effected a merger with the International Jewelry Workers' Union (AFL) in November 1954, and the National Association of Postal Supervisors withdrew from the AFL in February 1955.

[5] In 1954, a special effort to transfer local industrial unions to international unions of proper jurisdiction more than halved the number of LIU's.

[6] The Building and Construction Trades, Metal Trades, Railway Employes', Maritime Trades, and Union Label and Service Trades Departments.

ing collective bargaining, social security, housing, atomic energy, public power, and safety measures. The AFL's political arm, Labor's League for Political Education, and the CIO's Political Action Committee stimulate political support for labor's objectives.

Each federation holds annual conventions where summary reports are delivered, major policy is decided, and elections are held for key offices. Between conventions, federation affairs are directed in the AFL by the president, secretary-treasurer, and 15 vice presidents who together constitute the Executive Council; and in the CIO by an Executive Board consisting of the president, executive vice president, secretary-treasurer, 8 vice presidents, and 1 member from each CIO international union and organizing committee. All of these officers are elective positions.

To cope with problems at State and local levels, AFL and CIO bodies are maintained on a geographic basis. Early in 1955, the AFL had 48 State federations of labor; 2 territorial bodies covering Alaska and Puerto Rico; and 829 city central labor unions. The CIO had 44 State industrial union councils, including the District of Columbia; 1 territorial organization for Puerto Rico; and 296 city and county councils.

It would appear that the immediate impact of the AFL-CIO merger, from a structural viewpoint, would be inconsequential, at the outset, on the number and identity of subordinate bodies. The proposed constitution provides for the retention of the same organizing jurisdictions held by international unions through prior affiliation with either the AFL or CIO. A reliance upon voluntary action to solve interunion problems is stated in article III, section 10:

> Affiliates of the federation shall be encouraged to eliminate conflicts and duplications in organization and jurisdictions through the process of agreement, merger, or other means, by voluntary agreement in consultation with the appropriate officials of the federation.

State, territorial, and local bodies are to merge within 2 years, according to present merger plans.

In recognition of the principle stated in the proposed constitution "that both craft and industrial unions are appropriate, equal and necessary as methods of union organization," a new department for industrial union affiliates would be added to those presently in the AFL.

Conventions would be held every 2 years instead of annually and 3 executive bodies would guide the federation between conventions: (1) the Executive Council, a government body, composed of president, secretary-treasurer, and 27 vice presidents, would meet at least 3 times a year; (2) the Executive Committee, an advisory body, composed of president, secretary-treasurer, and 6 vice presidents, would meet every other month; and (3) a General Board, composed of Executive Council members and a principal officer of each national or international union, would decide policy questions referred by the Executive Council or Committee, meeting at least once annually.

RLEA. The Railway Labor Executives' Association is composed of the chief

The Unions   57

executive officers of 19 labor organizations; 16 are AFL affiliates; 1, CIO; and 2, independent. Twelve of the organizations have virtually all their membership in the railroad industry; the remaining seven are principally in other industries. Except for operating employees organized by three unions which are not members,[7] the RLEA's affiliates represent most of the organized railway workers in the United States. RLEA is not a federation of unions; rather, it functions as a policymaking body on legislative and other matters of interest to railroad workers.

Other Federations. There are 3 organizations which function as federations or have some of the characteristics of a federation such as the issuance of charters to, or the maintenance of a formal affiliation among, autonomous labor organizations in more than 1 industry. These are the Confederated Unions of America, the Engineers and Scientists of America, and the National Independent Union Council. Unions affiliated with these organizations which had negotiated agreements covering different employers in more than one State are included among the unaffiliated or independent unions discussed below.

Unaffiliated or Independent Unions. A total of 57 international unions commonly known as unaffiliated or independent unions, that is, not affiliated with the AFL or CIO, were known to the Bureau in late 1955. Their combined membership for 1954 was estimated at 1.8 million.[8] This group includes such long-established and well-known organizations as the four "operating" railroad brotherhoods and the United Mine Workers of America. All unaffiliated unions listed, other than those organizing government employees, reported agreements covering different employers in more than one State.

Of the 11 unions expelled from the CIO during 1949–50 on charges of Communist domination, only 4 remain as unions today.[9] Their combined membership is approximately a third of the 850,000 to 900,000 estimated for the 11 unions when the expulsions occurred.[10] The membership decline for the group is traceable to several factors, including (1) inroads by rival affiliated unions such as the CIO Electrical Workers and the CIO Auto Workers; (2) the collapse of some leftwing unions and absorption of their membership by affiliated

[7] The Brotherhood of Locomotive Engineers, the Order of Railway Conductors and Brakemen, and the Brotherhood of Railroad Trainmen. The latter two unions are scheduled to affiliate with RLEA on January 1, 1956.

[8] The estimate of 1.8 million members represents a decrease from the previous Bureau estimate of 2½ million for 1951. Among the factors accounting for this decline were: (1) membership losses in a few large unions, (2) mergers bringing unaffiliated unions into the AFL or CIO, (3) revised Bureau procedures for listing unaffiliated national unions which resulted in a reduction in the number listed, and (4) the exclusion of "other federations" from the membership count and the inclusion only of those affiliates which were "interstate" in scope.

[9] The United Electrical, Radio and Machine Workers of America; the International Union of Mine, Mill and Smelter Workers; the International Longshoremen's and Warehousemen's Union; and the American Communications Association.

[10] See Twelfth Convention of the CIO, Monthly Labor Review, January 1951, footnote 4 (p. 12).

unions; (3) the entrance of some into affiliated ranks through merger action; and (4) opposition to Communist-dominated organizations both by labor leaders and American workers.

TOTAL MEMBERSHIP

Reports from 177 national and international unions, supplemented by Bureau estimates for 22 unions which did not report membership, yielded a total count of 17,757,000 members for 1954 (table 1). It was estimated that the addition of membership of AFL federal labor unions (184,000) and CIO local industrial unions (15,000) would bring the total to approximately 18 million.[11] By affiliation, membership was distributed as follows: AFL, 10.9 million; CIO, 5.2 million; unaffiliated, 1.8 million. Slightly over 1 million members were located outside the continental United States.[12]

The 18 million membership figure does not reflect the total number of persons attached to the labor movement in the United States. At least 355,000 "members" were excluded by certain unions from membership reports, i.e., unemployed, those involved in work stoppages, those in the Armed Forces, apprentices, and retired workers, who were typically exonerated in whole or in part from the dues-paying requirements. Moreover, membership of unaffiliated or independent unions which are not interstate in scope is not included. At least 500,000 workers, according to available collective bargaining agreements, may be in this category.[13]

Membership Outside the Continental United States. Of the 199 national and international unions, 132 [14] claimed jurisdiction and had organized workers in areas outside the continental United States (table 1). Of these unions, 73 had members in Canada only; 45 in Canada and other areas; and 14 in areas exclusive of Canada.

- Total membership in all areas outside of the United States amounted to 1,039,000 in 1954. The largest concentration was in Canada, where 118 unions had 933,000 members. Elsewhere, the combined total reported was approximately 105,000, with virtually all members in territories and possessions of the United States: Puerto Rico had 53,000; Hawaii, 33,000; Alaska, 16,000; and the Canal Zone, 2,000. One union accounted for most of the members in Puerto Rico, and another for most members in Hawaii; in Alaska and the Canal Zone,

[11] Previous Bureau estimates of total membership included the FLU's and LIU's; hence the figure of approximately 18 million should be used for time comparisons.

[12] Many international unions traditionally include in their membership count members who work and live outside of the continental borders of the United States. To obtain detailed information, the Bureau for the first time asked each union to specify the number of dues-paying members outside United States continental borders who were included as of the end of 1954 or "any other appropriate current period."

[13] The Bureau's file of collective bargaining agreements contains agreements negotiated by over 300 unions of this type, covering approximately a half-million workers. Coverage of collective bargaining agreements in these cases probably exceeds the number of union members.

[14] One additional union reported members outside of the United States but excluded these from its membership total.

Table 1. Membership Reported by National and International Unions, by Geographic Area and Affiliation, 1954

Geographic area	All unions — Number	All unions — Members (in thousands) Number	All unions — Members Percent	AFL Number of unions	AFL Members (in thousands)	CIO Number of unions	CIO Members (in thousands)	Unaffiliated Number of unions	Unaffiliated Members (in thousands)
Total membership reported [1]	199	[1] 17,757	100.0	109	[1] 10,746	32	[1] 5,185	58	[1] 1,826
In continental United States	199	16,718	94.1	109	10,234	32	4,827	58	1,657
Outside continental United States [2]	132	1,039	5.9	91	512	19	358	22	169
Canada	118	933	5.3	84	487	18	307	16	139
Hawaii	32	33	.2	27	8	2	(3)	3	25
Puerto Rico	14	53	.3	9	1	1	50	4	3
Alaska	43	16	.1	33	14	1	(3)	9	3
Canal Zone	20	2	(4)	16	2	1	(3)	3	(3)
Other	5	1	(4)	3	(3)	..	....	2	1

[1] National and international unions were asked to report their *average dues-paying membership* for 1954. 177 national and international unions reported a combined total of 16,385,231 members, and the Bureau estimated on the basis of other information that membership of the 22 unions which did not report was 1,371,300. Members of federal labor unions directly affiliated with the AFL and members of CIO organizing committees or local industrial unions directly affiliated with the CIO are not accounted for in these estimates. Also excluded are members of unaffiliated unions not national in scope, as defined in this article.

[2] Membership figures outside the continental United States were compiled primarily from union reports to the Bureau. For unions which did not report Canadian membership, data were secured from Labor Organization in Canada, 1954 edition (Department of Labor, Economics and Research Branch, Ottawa, Canada). The number of unions does not add because many had members in more than one area.

[3] Fewer than 500 members.

[4] Less than 0.05 percent.

no one union was predominant. An additional thousand members of five unions
were located in widely scattered areas throughout the world.

Membership Changes. Following a steady decline in total union membership
at the beginning of the depressed 1930's, membership grew at an unprecedented rate until the mid-1940's. (See chart 1.) From 1935 to 1940, membership more than doubled, from approximately 3½ million to more than 8½
million. It continued sharply upwards to nearly 14½ million by 1945. Since
then, growth has been relatively moderate.

Chart 1. Membership of National and International
Unions, 1930–54 [1] (Exclusive of Canadian Members [2])

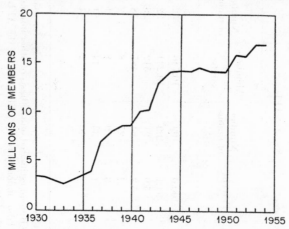

UNITED STATES DEPARTMENT OF LABOR
BUREAU OF LABOR STATISTICS

[1] For the years 1948–52, midpoints of membership
estimates, which were expressed as ranges, were used.

[2] Reflects a relatively small number of trade union
members in areas outside the continental United States
other than Canada. In 1954, approximately 105,000 members were in this category; such membership, however,
was not excluded, as in the case of Canadian membership, because data were not available for prior years.

The relationship between various labor force data and union membership
figures presents perspective on the rate of growth, since the labor force represents the universe from which union members are drawn. For this comparison, two labor force series were selected: (a) total labor force, which includes
both employed and unemployed workers in all industries, self-employed persons, members of the Armed Forces, etc.; and (b) employment in nonagricultural establishments, which excludes the Armed Forces, the unemployed, agricultural workers, proprietors, self-employed persons, unpaid family workers,
and domestic servants—groups which have not been particularly susceptible

to organization. To derive ratios of union membership to these labor force data in the United States, membership in Canada was eliminated.[15]

From 1930 to 1945, union membership as a percentage of the labor force grew from 7 percent to 22 percent (chart 2). By 1954, it had increased further

Chart 2. Membership [1] as a Percentage of Total Labor Force and of Employees in Nonagricultural Establishments

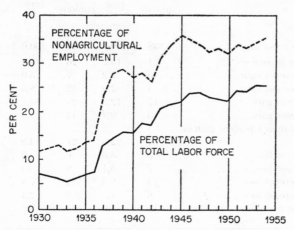

UNITED STATES DEPARTMENT OF LABOR
BUREAU OF LABOR STATISTICS

[1] Excludes Canadian membership. See chart 1, footnote 2.

to about 25 percent of the total labor force or 1 out of every 4 workers. In terms of nonagricultural employment—where most union members are found —these ratios were somewhat higher, moving from 12 percent in 1930 to almost 36 percent in 1945, at the close of World War II. Since that time, the rate of expansion in union membership has matched but not exceeded that in nonagricultural industries. Thus, a ratio of about 1 union member out of every 3 nonagricultural workers has typically prevailed during the past decade.

Year-to-year comparisons of total union membership tend to obscure the constant flux in membership among individual unions. For instance, while total membership rose approximately 0.5 percent between 1953 and 1954, membership in more than one-fifth of the unions which reported data for both years fluctuated by 10 percent or more (table 2). Between 1951 and 1954, approximately half of the reporting unions experienced a rise or fall in membership

[15] The total membership figure used for these comparisons included the approximately 200,000 members of the FLU's and LIU's with the membership of national and international unions. This procedure conforms to the previous practice of the Bureau in the construction of its historical series.

Table 2. Distribution of National and International Unions, by Percentage Change in Membership Reported, 1951–54

	1951–53		1951–54		1953–54	
Percentage change in membership	Number of unions	Percent	Number of unions	Percent	Number of unions	Percent
Total unions reporting [1]	138	100.0	141	100.0	167	100.0
20 percent or more gain	21	15.2	26	18.4	11	6.6
15 to 19.9 percent gain	10	7.2	7	5.0	1	.6
10 to 14.9 percent gain	4	2.9	12	8.5	13	7.8
5 to 9.9 percent gain	17	12.3	20	14.2	14	8.4
1 to 4.9 percent gain	13	9.4	14	9.9	36	21.6
None or less than 1 percent gain or loss	31	22.5	21	14.9	56	33.5
1 to 4.9 percent loss	5	3.6	6	4.3	16	9.6
5 to 9.9 percent loss	7	5.1	9	6.4	7	4.2
10 to 14.9 percent loss	13	9.4	11	7.8	9	5.4
15 to 19.9 percent loss	6	4.3	3	2.1	...	...
20 percent or more loss	11	8.0	12	8.5	4	2.4

[1] Only membership figures as reported by unions to the Bureau were used as a basis for the comparative data shown. The 1953 and 1954 membership figures were obtained from the questionnaire which was used to compile the current Directory. The 1951 membership reports appeared in the Directory of Labor Unions in the United States, 1953, BLS Bull. 1127.

of 10 percent or more; only 3 out of 10 union reports indicated a net gain or loss of membership of less than 5 percent.

It is difficult to isolate all the factors responsible for these changes and to evaluate their significance. Some of these, such as interunion rivalry resulting in gains for one union at the expense of another and union mergers involving wholesale transfers of membership, bring no net gains in membership for the labor movement as a whole. Other factors, such as declining or expanding employment in industries where unionism is well established, bring losses or gains which may have a real impact on total union membership. The effects of union-shop arrangements, which require membership as a condition of employment, although operative for many years in some industries, have undoubtedly been a significant factor in the increases recorded in union membership during recent years.[16]

Size of Unions. The heavy concentration of membership in a few unions remains a characteristic of the labor movement. Thirteen of the 199 unions

[16] See Union-Security Provisions in Agreements, 1954, Monthly Labor Review, June 1955 (p. 649).

had nearly half of the total membership. Six unions, with more than 500,000 members each, had a combined membership of 5.9 million, or a third of the total (table 3). Sheer size, however, is not necessarily the key index to union

Table 3. Distribution of National and International Unions, by Number of Members Reported and Affiliation, 1954

Number of members reported [1]	All unions				Unions by affiliation		
	Unions		Members		AFL	CIO	Un-affili-ated
	Num-ber	Per-cent	Num-ber (in thou-sands)	Per-cent			
All unions [1]	199	100.0	17,757	100.0	109	32	58
Under 1,000 members	16	8.0	8	([2])	8	..	8
1,000 and under 5,000 members	34	17.1	82	0.5	12	2	20
5,000 and under 10,000 members	23	11.6	170	1.0	8	4	11
10,000 and under 25.000 members	27	13.6	452	2.5	21	2	4
25,000 and under 50,000 members	24	12.1	852	4.8	15	5	4
50,000 and under 100,000 members	34	17.1	2,431	13.7	19	9	6
100,000 and under 200,000 members	17	8.5	2,336	13.2	10	4	3
200,000 and under 300,000 members	11	5.5	2,655	14.9	9	1	1
300,000 and under 400,000 members	3	1.5	1,047	5.9	...	3	..
400,000 and under 500,000 members	4	2.0	1,762	9.9	3	..	1
500,000 and under 1,000,000 members	3	1.5	2,298	12.9	3	..	..
1,000,000 members and over	3	1.5	3,664	20.6	1	2	..

[1] See footnote 1, table 1.
[2] Less than 0.05 percent.

strength. The larger international unions can, of course, muster greater support, financial and otherwise, to help their affiliated locals. However, smaller unions organizing in industries with a small labor force, or those strategically situated because of the nature of the work done by members, have an inherent strength not readily apparent from membership figures.

Women Members. Almost 3 million, or 1 of every 6, members of international unions in 1954 were women. This is based on reports from 135 unions and estimates made from available information for most of the 64 unions which did not report (table 4). The total of women unionists represented

Table 4. Distribution of National and International Unions, by Proportion of Women Members, 1954

Percent of women members	All unions			
	Unions		Women members reported	
	Number	Percent	Number (in thousands)	Percent
Total unions reporting [1]	135	100.0	2,098	100.0
No women members	40	29.6	....	....
Under 10 percent	44	32.6	85	4.1
10 and under 20 percent	11	8.1	168	8.0
20 and under 30 percent	11	8.1	134	6.4
30 and under 40 percent	6	4.4	275	13.1
40 and under 50 percent	5	3.7	173	8.2
50 and under 60 percent	2	1.5	133	6.3
60 and under 70 percent	9	6.7	366	17.4
70 and under 80 percent	4	3.0	690	32.9
80 and under 90 percent	3	2.2	74	3.5

[1] 64 unions which did not report the number of women members are not included. It was estimated that 51 of these had approximately 851,000 women members and 9 unions had no women members. For the remaining 4 unions, appropriate information was not available. Union reports supplemented by Bureau estimates yield a total of approximately 2,950,000 women members of national and international unions. In terms of affiliation, it is estimated that these members were distributed as follows: AFL, 57 percent; CIO, 36 percent; not affiliated, 7 percent. Women members of AFL federal labor unions and CIO local industrial unions and organizing committees are not included in these estimates.

approximately 1 of every 7 in the Nation's female labor force. A similar proportion was found to be organized in the Bureau's last survey.

Based on both reported and estimated data, a combined total of slightly over 1.3 million women were in 22 unions, and in each, women accounted for at least half of the total membership. Nearly as large a group was in 18 large unions where the ratio of women was much less than half of all members, but numbered 25,000 or more in each union. Accordingly, 40 unions accounted for more than 2½ million women, or 5 of every 6 women members. However, in 61 unions, women represented less than 10 percent of the membership. In addition, 49 unions had no women members.

Among unions with large numbers of women members are those having their principal jurisdiction in the needle trades, service industries, electrical goods manufacturing, communications work, and textile mills. The number of women members who worked at office occupations could not be determined from the reports compiled in this survey. Some large industrial and semi-industrial unions reported a relatively large number of women, but they comprised only a small fraction of their total membership.[17]

UNION FUNCTIONS AND ADMINISTRATION

The rules for union government and basic provisions for services needed to carry on union affairs are found in union constitutions.[18] Formal constitutional provisions vary among unions as to the allocation of responsibilities between the international and its local unions. Regardless of how this is resolved, basically both union levels mutually seek to achieve the same goals through the improvement of collective bargaining agreements and the economic and social status of their membership.

Number of Locals. The distribution of unions by number of locals had characteristics similar to the distribution by membership, i. e., a few unions with a large number of locals accounted for the majority of locals (table 5). Of the estimated 77,000 local unions affiliated with the 199 international unions surveyed,[19] 19 unions had approximately 40,000 local unions, or more than half of all locals; 80 unions, each with less than 100 locals, had slightly more than 3,000 local unions, or only 4 percent of the total.

Twelve AFL international unions had half of the AFL total of approximately 50,000 locals; 2 CIO unions had nearly 40 percent of the more than 10,000 in the CIO; and 5 unaffiliated unions had almost 70 percent of the more than 15,000 chartered by unaffiliated international unions.

International unions which had large membership generally had a large number of locals. However, the largest number of locals (13,000) was found

[17] A recent BLS study revealed that two-thirds of the contracts covering office workers in establishments in 17 major labor markets were with unions which also represented plant workers in the same establishment. See Monthly Labor Review, January 1955 (p. 68).

[18] Recent Bureau studies based on union constitutions are: Financing of Union Activities, Monthly Labor Review, October 1952 (p. 373); Strike-Control Provisions in Union Constitutions, Monthly Labor Review, May 1954 (p. 497); and Anti-Communist Provisions in Union Constitutions, Monthly Labor Review, October 1954 (p. 1097).

[19] As international unions were asked to report the total number of locals, this figure includes locals outside the continental United States.

Table 5. Distribution of National and International Unions, by Number of Locals and Affiliation, 1954

Number of locals	All unions — Unions Number	Percent	All unions — Locals Number	Percent	Union affiliation — AFL Number of unions	AFL Number of locals	CIO Number of unions	CIO Number of locals	Unaffiliated Number of unions	Unaffiliated Number of locals
All unions ¹	189	100.0	76,927	100.0	106	50,560	32	10,672	51	15,695
Under 10 locals	20	10.6	94	0.1	5	32	2	7	13	55
10 and under 25 locals	13	6.9	220	.3	5	78	...	...	8	142
25 and under 50 locals	20	10.6	722	.9	8	291	5	181	7	250
50 and under 100 locals	27	14.3	1,993	2.6	16	1,187	4	339	7	467
100 and under 200 locals	26	13.8	3,334	4.3	15	1,904	6	786	5	644
200 and under 300 locals	16	8.5	3,775	4.9	10	2,295	4	1,014	2	466
300 and under 400 locals	17	9.0	5,755	7.5	11	3,649	5	1,786	1	320
400 and under 500 locals	6	3.2	2,512	3.3	6	2,512	...	...	...	...
500 and under 600 locals	6	3.2	3,259	4.2	5	2,684	1	575	...	...
600 and under 700 locals	5	2.6	3,200	4.2	3	1,964	1	636	1	600
700 and under 800 locals	5	2.6	3,797	4.9	3	2,299	2	1,498	...	...
800 and under 900 locals	3	1.6	2,500	3.2	3	2,500	...	...	...	...
900 and under 1,000 locals	6	3.2	5,653	7.3	4	3,745	...	...	2	1,908
1,000 and under 1,500 locals	9	4.8	10,931	14.2	6	7,364	1	1,250	2	2,317
1,500 and under 2,000 locals	4	2.1	7,142	9.3	3	5,642	...	...	1	1,500
2,000 locals and over	6	3.2	22,040	28.7	3	12,414	1	2,600	2	7,026

¹ 21 unions did not report the number of local unions. For 11 unions, sufficient information was available on which to base estimates. For 10 small unions, appropriate information was not available.

The Unions 67

in 3 moderate-size unions of Government postal employees with a combined membership of only 250,000.

Collective Bargaining Agreements. The major efforts of unions are devoted to the negotiation of collective bargaining agreements—the embodiment of trade union aims for improved wages and working conditions. It is estimated that upwards of 125,000 labor-management contracts exist. This is based on returns from 133 unions, which reported nearly 70,000 agreements with employers, and an overall estimate prepared for 66 unions which did not reply.[20]

On the basis of union reports only, 57 unions had less than 100 agreements each; 36 had more than 100 and less than 500; 12 had from 500 to 1,000; 19 unions had 1,000 or more; and 9 unions, primarily organizations of government workers, reported no agreements. The 19 unions which each reported more than 1,000 contracts accounted for more than 50,000 agreements in all.

Union Conventions. The highest policymaking body in the international union is the union convention. In many unions, the convention also functions to decide appeals from actions taken at all union levels. Local union members customarily elect a number of delegates from their ranks, usually in some fixed proportion to total local membership. Conventions were held at intervals of 2 years or less by 114 unions; 2 years was the most common interval (71 unions). (See table 6.)

Table 6. Intervals at which National and International Unions Hold Conventions, 1954

Interval between conventions	All unions		Unions, by affiliation		
	Number	Percent	AFL	CIO	Unaffiliated
All unions..................	199	100.0	109	32	58
3 months...................	1	0.5	...	..	1
6 months...................	2	1.0	...	..	2
1 year.....................	39	19.6	16	6	17
18 months..................	1	.5	...	1	..
2 years....................	71	35.7	37	20	14
3 years....................	19	9.5	15	2	2
4 years....................	29	14.6	22	1	6
5 years....................	13	6.5	12	..	1
Referendum [1].............	5	2.5	4	..	1
No convention.............	12	6.0	3	1	8
Information not available ...	7	3.5	.	1	6

[1] Referendum determines whether and when a convention should be held.

[20] The Bureau requested that unions exclude from their count various supplements, e.g., pension, health, or welfare agreements, that might be provided in separate documents.

Union Professional Staff. Unions have increasingly made use of analyses prepared by statisticians, economists, and lawyers to support arguments advanced in contract negotiation, in public discussions, and in connection with legislative issues. Expert assistance is also frequently needed in drafting collective bargaining agreements, which have expanded considerably in scope and complexity over the years. After the agreement is signed, union representatives at the shop level may need assistance in the interpretation, application, and enforcement of the formal provisions. In recognition of the need for specialized staff, international unions have assigned personnel to research and education functions, on a full- or part-time basis. A more recent development is the employment of research and education directors by State federations of labor (AFL) and State industrial union councils (CIO).

Of the 199 international unions surveyed, 96 reported research directors and 81, education directors; in the 95 AFL and CIO State organizations, 22 reported research directors and 29, education directors.[21]

In recent years, the rapid growth of collectively bargained health, insurance, and pension programs has enlarged and complicated union responsibilities for protection of the well-being and security of workers represented. To meet complex problems involving policy, financial practices, benefit levels, worker eligibility, and similar matters, unions have assigned specialized personnel in this field. Ninety-two of the 199 international unions reported personnel who held a position related to various social insurance programs.[22] Of these, 60 unions reported that the individuals also had duties as president, secretary-treasurer, research director, or education director. In 32 unions, other individuals were designated.

Union Publications. Union publications serve as a means of communication between international unions and their members in affiliated local unions. They keep members informed of international union affairs, as well as matters of general interest in the labor movement. In format, they vary from mimeographed single sheets to attractively printed newspapers and magazines.

Of the 199 international unions surveyed, 166 issued publications. Nine unions reported 2 publications, bringing the total issued to 175. Most publications (122) appeared monthly; 15, biweekly or semimonthly; 14, bimonthly; 13, quarterly; 7, weekly; and the period of publication was not specified for 4.

Of the 95 AFL or CIO State and territorial bodies, 49 issued publications; 3 of these issued 2 publications each, making a total of 52. Twenty-three were published monthly; 13, weekly; 2, biweekly or semimonthly; 1, bimonthly; 1, quarterly; 9, annually; and for 3, no time interval was specified.

[21] These reports cover positions which are formally established and probably understate the extent to which unions use research and education techniques. Some unions assign personnel as needed from other regular staff, and others contract with private consultants to handle problems as they develop.

[22] This count does not include personnel assigned in government unions because the social insurance benefits received by government workers are not collectively bargained.

Union Headquarters Locations. In 1954, headquarters of 144 of the 199 international unions were located in 10 cities (table 7). The greatest concentration was found in Washington, D.C., where 46 unions representing nearly 6½ million members maintained central headquarters. Headquarters of the two

Table 7. Cities with Five or More International Union Headquarters, 1954 [1]

City	All unions		Union affiliation					
			AFL		CIO		Unaffiliated	
	Number	Members (in thousands)	Number of unions	Members (in thousands)	Number of unions	Members (in thousands)	Number of unions	Members (in thousands)
Total...........	144	14,164	84	9,114	25	3,506	35	1,544
Washington, D. C.	46	6,478	30	4,802	8	973	8	703
New York, N. Y..	32	2,043	13	691	11	1,070	8	282
Detroit, Mich.....	6	1,699	2	409	2	1,264	2	26
Indianapolis, Ind..	5	1,061	5	1,061	...	...	...	...
Chicago, Ill.......	23	1,042	15	875	3	137	5	29
Cincinnati, Ohio..	5	853	4	791	1	62	...	...
Cleveland, Ohio...	7	477	3	100	...	...	4	377
St. Louis, Mo.....	7	256	7	256	...	...	...	...
Philadelphia, Pa..	8	244	5	128	...	...	3	117
Milwaukee, Wis...	5	11	...	...	...	...	5	11

[1] Not included are offices established by unions for special functions, e. g., legislative activity or research.

major federations are also located there. Other locations where there were at least five international unions and the combined membership exceeded a million were New York, N. Y.; Detroit, Mich.; Indianapolis, Ind.; and Chicago, Ill.

UNION CONSTITUTIONS

Constitution of the American Federation of Labor and Congress of Industrial Organizations, 1955

PREAMBLE

The establishment of this Federation through the merger of the American Federation of Labor and the Congress of Industrial Organizations is an expression of the hopes and aspirations of the working people of America.

We seek the fulfillment of these hopes and aspirations through democratic processes within the framework of our constitutional government and consistent with our institutions and traditions.

At the collective bargaining table, in the community, in the exercise of the rights and responsibilities of citizenship, we shall responsibly serve the interests of all the American people.

We pledge ourselves to the more effective organization of working men and women; to the securing to them of full recognition and enjoyment of the rights to which they are justly entitled; to the achievement of ever higher standards of living and working conditions; to the attainment of security for all the people; to the enjoyment of the leisure which their skills make possible; and to the strengthening and extension of our way of life and the fundamental freedoms which are the basis of our democratic society.

We shall combat resolutely the forces which seek to undermine the democratic institutions of our nation and to enslave the human soul. We shall strive always to win full respect for the dignity of the human individual whom our unions serve.

With Divine guidance, grateful for the fine traditions of our past, confident of meeting the challenge of the future, we proclaim this constitution.

ARTICLE I

NAME

This Federation shall be known as the American Federation of Labor and Congress of Industrial Organizations. It is established pursuant to and as a result of a merger agreement between the American Federation of Labor and the Congress of Industrial Organizations. It shall consist of such affiliates as shall conform to its constitution and the rules and regulations adopted thereunder.

ARTICLE II

OBJECTS AND PRINCIPLES

The objects and principles of this Federation are:

1. To aid workers in securing improved wages, hours and working conditions with due regard for the autonomy, integrity and jurisdiction of affiliated unions.

2. To aid and assist affiliated unions in extending the benefits of mutual assistance and collective bargaining to workers and to promote the organization of the unorganized into unions of their own choosing for their mutual aid, protection and advancement, giving recognition to the principle that both craft and industrial unions are appropriate, equal and necessary as methods of union organization.

3. To affiliate national and international unions with this Federation and to establish such unions; to form organizing committees and directly affiliated local unions and to secure their affiliation to appropriate national and international unions affiliated with or chartered by the Federation; to establish, assist and promote state and local central bodies composed of local unions of all affiliated organizations and directly affiliated local unions; to establish and assist trade departments composed of affiliated national and international unions and organizing committees.

4. To encourage all workers without regard to race, creed, color, national origin or ancestry to share equally in the full benefits of union organization.

5. To secure legislation which will safeguard and promote the principle of

free collective bargaining, the rights of workers, farmers and consumers, and the security and welfare of all the people and to oppose legislation inimical to these objectives.

6. To protect and strengthen our democratic institutions, to secure full recognition and enjoyment of the rights and liberties to which we are justly entitled, and to preserve and perpetuate the cherished traditions of our democracy.

7. To give constructive aid in promoting the cause of peace and freedom in the world and to aid, assist and cooperate with free and democratic labor movements throughout the world.

8. To preserve and maintain the integrity of each affiliated union in the organization to the end that each affiliate shall respect the established bargaining relationships of every other affiliate and that each affiliate shall refrain from raiding the established bargaining relationship of any other affiliate and, at the same time, to encourage the elimination of conflicting and duplicating organizations and jurisdictions through the process of voluntary agreement or voluntary merger in consultation with the appropriate officials of the Federation, to preserve, subject to the foregoing, the organizing jurisdiction of each affiliate.

9. To aid and encourage the sale and use of union made goods and union services through the use of the union label and other symbols; to promote the labor press and other means of furthering the education of the labor movement.

10. To protect the labor movement from any and all corrupt influences and from the undermining efforts of communist agencies and all others who are opposed to the basic principles of our democracy and free and democratic unionism.

11. To safeguard the democratic character of the labor movement and to protect the autonomy of each affiliated national and international union.

12. While preserving the independence of the labor movement from political control, to encourage workers to register and vote, to exercise their full rights and responsibilities of citizenship, and to perform their rightful part in the political life of the local, state and national communities.

ARTICLE III

AFFILIATES

Section 1. The Federation shall be composed of (1) affiliated national and international unions and organizing committees, (2) directly affiliated local unions (such as Local Trade Unions, Federal Labor Unions, and Local Industrial Unions) and national councils thereof, (3) state and local central bodies (such as State and Territorial Federations, City Central Labor Unions and Industrial Union Councils), and (4) trade and industrial departments.

Sec. 2. Each national and international union and each federal labor union affiliated with the American Federation of Labor at the time of the adoption of this constitution by reason of a charter or certificate of affiliation granted by that federation and each national and international union, organizing committee and local industrial union affiliated with the Congress of Industrial Organizations at the time of the adoption of this constitution by reason of a charter or certificate of affiliation granted by that federation shall retain its charter or certificate, which shall become and be a charter or certificate of this Federation and, by virtue of the same and as a result of the merger between the American Federation of Labor and the Congress of Industrial Organizations, shall be an affiliate of this Federation and subject to its rules and regulations.

Sec. 3. Each such affiliate shall retain and enjoy the same organizing jurisdiction in this Federation which it had and enjoyed by reason of its prior affiliation with either the American Federation of Labor or the Congress of Industrial Organizations. In cases of conflicting and duplicating jurisdictions involving such affiliates the President and the Executive Council of this Federation shall seek to eliminate such conflicts and duplications through the process of voluntary agreement or voluntary merger between the affiliates involved.

Sec. 4. The integrity of each such affiliate of this Federation shall be maintained and preserved. Each such affiliate shall respect the established collective bargaining relationship of every other affiliate and no affiliate shall raid the established collective bargaining relationship of any other affiliate. When a complaint has been filed with the President by an affiliate alleging a violation of this section by another affiliate, that has not been settled under the provisions of the No-Raiding Agreement referred to in Article XVIII, the President shall endeavor, by consultation with the appropriate officers of both affiliates, to settle the matter by voluntary agreement between such affiliates. In the event no such voluntary agreement is reached within a reasonable time the President shall report to the Executive Council with such recommendations as he may deem appropriate. Upon such report being submitted, the Executive Council shall consider the same, shall hear the appropriate officers of the affiliates involved, and shall make such decision as it believes to be necessary and proper to carry out the provisions of this section. In the event an affiliate shall fail to comply with such decision, the Executive Council shall submit the matter to the convention for such action as the convention may deem appropriate under the provisions of this constitution.

Sec. 5. State and Territorial Federations of Labor and Local Central Bodies affiliated with the American Federation of Labor at the time of the adoption of this Constitution, and State and Local Industrial Union Councils affiliated with the Congress of Industrial Organizations at the time of the adoption of this constitution, shall become and be affiliates of this Federation and shall, as such, continue to exist as state, territorial and local central bodies, each representing the respective federal labor unions or local industrial unions now affiliated to such central body and such local unions now affiliated to such central body as are affiliated with a national or international union or organizing committee affiliated with this Federation. Provided, however: That a merger of these state, territorial and local central bodies, heretofore affiliated with the American Federation of Labor or the Congress of Industrial Organizations, shall be effected within two years after the adoption of this constitution, through the process of negotiation and agreement under the guidance of the President of this Federation and its Executive Council.

Sec. 6. Existing departments of the American Federation of Labor at the time of the adoption of this constitution shall continue as trade departments of this Federation with the rights of and subject to the rules governing trade and industrial departments provided in Article XII.

Sec. 7. The Executive Council shall have power to issue charters or certificates of affiliation to organizations desiring to affiliate with this Federation. This power may be delegated to the President. Subject to the provisions of Sections 2 and 3 of this Article, charters or certificates of affiliation shall not be issued to national or international unions, organizing committees, or directly affiliated local unions in conflict with the jurisdiction of affiliated national or international unions, except with the written consent of such unions, and shall be based upon a strict recognition that both craft and industrial unions are equal and necessary as methods of trade union organization, and that each affiliated national and international union is entitled to have its autonomy, integrity and jurisdiction protected and preserved.

Sec. 8. Except as otherwise provided in this constitution no national or international union chartered by or affiliated with this Federation may be suspended from membershp in the Federation except by a majority roll-call vote at the convention. No such national or international union shall have its charter or certificate of affiliation with the Federation revoked except by a two-thirds majority roll-call vote at the convention.

Sec. 9. No organization officered, controlled or dominated by communists, fascists, or other totalitarians, or whose policies and activities are consistently directed toward the achievement of the program or purposes of the Communist Party, any fascist organization, or other totalitarian movement, shall be permitted as an affiliate of this Federation or any of its state or local central bodies.

Sec. 10. Affiliates of the Federation shall be encouraged to eliminate conflicts and duplications in organization and jurisdictions through the process of voluntary agreement or voluntary merger in consultation with the appropriate officials of the Federation.

ARTICLE IV

CONVENTION

Section 1. The convention shall be the supreme governing body of the Federation and, except as otherwise provided in this Constitution, its decisions shall be by a majority vote.

Sec. 2. The regular conventions of the Federation shall be held every two years, beginning in 1955, at a time during the last four months of the year. The time and the place for holding the regular conventions shall be designated by the Executive Council which shall give at least 90 days' notice of the time and place designated.

Sec. 3. (a) Special conventions may be called by direction of a regular convention, by order of the Executive Council, or on request of national and international unions representing a majority of the total membership of the Federation, as evidenced by the records of the Secretary-Treasurer to the last convention.

(b) In the event a special convention has been called all affiliated organizations shall be given at least 30 days' notice, together with a statement of the particular subject or subjects to be considered at such convention.

(c) Representation to special conventions shall be on the same basis and subject to like qualifications and procedure governing regular conventions.

(d) A special convention shall be clothed with like authority and power conferred upon regular conventions, its decisions shall be equally binding and it shall be governed by the same procedure applicable to regular conventions; however, such special conventions shall be limited solely to the subject or subjects specifically and definitely indicated in the call for such special convention.

Sec. 4. Each national or international union and organizing committee shall be entitled to the number of delegates indicated in the following scale:

Less than   4,000 members.........1 delegate
Over   4,000   "   ....2 delegates
  "   8,000   " 3   "
  "   12,000   " 4   "
  "   25,000   " 5   "
  "   50,000   " 6   "
  "   75,000   " 7   "
  "   125,000   " 8   "
  "   175,000   " 9   "
plus one additional delegate for each 75,000 members over 175,000.

Each directly affiliated local union and each national trade and industrial department shall be entitled to one delegate. Each industrial union council and each state or local central body shall be entitled to one delegate. Directly affiliated local unions, with the approval of the President, may combine with other such unions within a reasonable distance to elect a single delegate to represent such unions.

Sec. 5. Delegates to a regular convention of the Federation shall be elected or otherwise designated by the affiliate at least 30 days prior to the convention, except in cases in which the convention of the affiliate meets within this 30-day period. The names of the delegates shall be forwarded to the Secretary-Treasurer of the Federation immediately after their selection.

Sec. 6. No organization that has seceded or has been suspended or expelled by this Federation, the American Federation of Labor, or the Congress of Industrial Organizations, or by any national or international union or organizing committee affiliated with this Federation shall, while under such penalty, be allowed representation or recognition in the Federation, or in any subordinate body thereof, or in any national or international union or organizing committee affiliated with this Federation, under the penalty of the suspension of the body violating this section. No affiliate which, at the opening date of the convention, is in arrears to the Federation for per capita tax or assessments for two months or more, shall be entitled to recognition or representation in the convention.

Sec. 7. No organization shall be entitled to representation unless such organization has applied for and obtained a certificate of affiliation at least one month prior to the convention, and no person shall be recognized as a delegate who is not a member in good standing of the organization he is selected to represent.

Sec. 8. The number of members of each national and international union, organizing committee and directly affiliated local unions for the purpose of selecting delegates and for roll-call votes at the convention shall be the average monthly number on which per capita tax is paid for the 24-month period prior to and including the second month preceding the month of the opening date of the convention. Where affiliation has occurred during this 24-month period, the average shall be computed from the month of affiliation, and the number of members shall be deemed to be one twenty-fourth of such average for each month for which per capita tax has been paid. The Secretary-Treasurer shall prepare for the use of the convention and submit to it a printed list showing the number of votes and the number of delegates to which each affiliate is entitled.

Sec. 9. The President shall appoint, in consultation with the Executive Council, prior to the opening date of the convention and subject to the approval of the convention, such committees as are necessary to conduct the affairs of the convention. Such committees may meet before the opening date of the convention and shall proceed to consider all resolutions, appeals, reports, and constitutional amendments submitted to the convention, and shall report thereon to the convention.

Sec. 10. (a) All resolutions, petitions, memorials and appeals to be considered by any convention of the Federation must be received by the Secretary-Treasurer at headquarters in Washington, D. C., 30 days immediately preceding the opening of the convention; except in instances where such matters have been acted upon and approved at a regular convention of a national or international union, or state central body, or national trade and industrial department held during this 30-day period in which event such proposals shall be received up to the opening date of the convention.

(b) All resolutions, petitions, memorials and appeals received or submitted after the time stipulated above or during the convention shall be referred to the Executive Council, and the Executive Council shall refer all such proposal or proposals to the convention with the understanding that consideration of such proposal or proposals is dependent upon the unanimous consent of the convention.

(c) Any or all proposals emanating from directly affiliated local unions shall be referred to the Executive Council for consideration and disposition. The Executive Council shall in turn advise the convention of the disposition made of such proposal or proposals.

(d) Proposals emanating from state central bodies to receive consideration of a convention must first have received the approval of the previous convention of the state central body involved. In the case of local central bodies any proposal or proposals to be considered must have first received the approval of such central labor body at a regularly constituted meeting of such organization.

(e) Each resolution, memorial, petition, or appeal properly received for consideration by the convention, as soon as practical after receipt thereof, shall be classified by the President as to nature, contents and subject matter and referred by him to an appropriate committee, which committee shall make a report thereon to the convention prior to consideration of any such matter by the convention. He shall cause to be distributed copies of such resolutions, petitions, memorials or appeals to the delegates of the convention at the opening session thereof or as soon thereafter as practical, but before any such matters are considered by the convention.

Sec. 11. Not less than 60 days prior to the opening of each regular convention, the Secretary-Treasurer shall furnish each affiliate with credential blanks in duplicate, which must be attested as required on the blanks. The duplicates shall be retained by the delegate, and the original sent to the Secretary-Treasurer. Subject to the provisions of Section 5 of this Article, no credentials shall be accepted later than 20 days prior to the opening date of the convention.

Sec. 12. Prior to the opening date of the convention, the Executive Council shall meet and constitute itself or a subcommittee as the Credentials Committee for the convention. Appeals from its decisions may be made to the floor of the convention. The convention shall not be constituted for business until after the Credentials Committee shall have examined and reported on credentials of all delegates present at the scheduled time on the opening date of the convention.

Sec. 13. All members of the Executive Council who are not elected as delegates shall be ex-officio delegates to the convention with all the rights and privileges of elected delegates, but without vote.

Sec. 14. Fraternal delegates attending conventions of the Federation shall be entitled to all the rights of delegates but shall not be entitled to vote.

Sec. 15. At the opening of the convention the President shall take the chair and call the convention to order, and preside during its sessions.

Sec. 16. One-fourth of the delegates seated at any convention shall constitute a quorum for the transaction of business.

Sec. 17. Questions may be decided by division or a show of hands, but a call of the roll may be demanded by 30 percent of the delegates present. Upon such roll-call each delegate representing affiliated national or international unions, organizing committees and directly affiliated local unions shall be entitled to cast one vote for every member whom he represents. Each state and local central body and national trade and industrial department shall be entitled to one vote.

Sec. 18. The rules and order of business governing the preceding convention shall be enforced from the opening of any convention of the Federation until new rules have been adopted by action of the convention.

Sec. 19. Unless otherwise specified, any action taken by the convention shall take effect immediately upon adoption.

ARTICLE V

OFFICERS

Section 1. The officers shall consist of a President and a Secretary-Treasurer, who shall be the Executive Officers, and 27 Vice Presidents.

Sec. 2. Each officer shall be a member of an affiliated organization.

Sec. 3. The officers shall be elected by the convention by majority vote. Such election shall take place on the last day of the convention, unless otherwise determined by the convention. In the event that more than two candidates are nominated for any office and no one candidate receives a majority of the votes cast, all except the two candidates receiving the highest votes shall be eliminated from the list of candidates and a second vote taken.

Sec. 4. Each officer elected at the convention shall take office immediately upon his election and shall serve until his successor is elected at the next regular convention.

Sec. 5. In the event of a vacancy in the office of either the President or the Secretary-Treasurer by reason of death, resignation or otherwise, the remaining executive officers shall perform the duties of the vacant office until a successor is elected. It shall be the duty of such executive officer to issue, within ten days of the date of the vacancy, a call for a meeting of the Executive Council of this Federation, upon ten days' notice, for the purpose of electing an executive officer to fill said vacancy for the unexpired term.

Sec. 6. In the event of a vacancy in the office of Vice President by reason of death, resignation or otherwise, the Executive Council shall have the power to fill the vacancy by majority vote of all its members for the period of the unexpired term.

Sec. 7. The national headquarters of the Federation shall be maintained by the Executive Officers at Washington, D. C.

Sec. 8. The Executive Officers shall, by virtue of their office, hold title to the real estate of the Federation as trustees for the Federation.

Sec. 9. The President and Secretary-Treasurer of the Federation or either of them may retire after reaching age 65 years, and after having served 20 years. Time served as an officer of any organization affiliated with the Federation, or with the American Federation of Labor or the Congress of Industrial Organizations, shall be included in determining length of service hereunder. In the event of retirement such officers shall have the title of President Emeritus, or Secretary-Treasurer Emeritus and shall render service to the Federation in an advisory and consultative status. They shall be compensated for such service by the Federation for life in an amount, payable weekly, equal to 75 percent of the annual salary paid to the corresponding Executive Officer of this Federation.

Sec. 10. No individual shall be eligible to serve either as an Executive Officer or as a member of the Executive Council who is a member of the Communist Party, any fascist organization, or other totalitarian movement, or who consistently pursues policies and activities directed toward the achievement of the program or the purposes of the Communist Party, any fascist organization or other totalitarian movement.

ARTICLE VI

DUTIES OF THE PRESIDENT

Section 1. The President shall function as the chief executive officer of the Federation. He shall exercise supervision of the affairs of the Federation, sign all official documents and preside at regular and special conventions, and at meetings of the Executive Council, Executive Committee and General Board. He shall call meetings of the Executive Council at least three times each year and a meeting of the General Board at least once each year.

Sec. 2. The President shall have authority to interpret the constitution between meetings of the Executive Council and his interpretation shall be conclusive and in full force and effect unless reversed or changed by the Executive Council or a convention.

Sec. 3. The President shall receive for his services a salary of $35,000 per annum payable weekly.

Sec. 4. The appointment and compensation, direction, suspension and removal of organizers, representatives, agents and employees of the Federation shall be under the direction of the President.

Sec. 5. The President shall make a report of the administration of his office and of the affairs of the Federation to the convention through the report of the Executive Council.

ARTICLE VII

DUTIES OF THE SECRETARY-TREASURER

Section 1. The Secretary-Treasurer shall be the chief financial officer of the Federation and shall receive and collect all moneys due the Federation which moneys shall be paid out only on the approval of the President.

Sec. 2. The Secretary-Treasurer shall be in charge of and preserve all moneys, properties, securities and other evidences of investment, books, documents, files and effects of the Federation which shall at all times be subject to the inspection of the President and Executive Council.

Sec. 3. The Secretary-Treasurer shall issue the call for and act as secretary at conventions, and shall cause the proceedings of all conventions and all sessions of the Executive Council and General Board to be recorded.

Sec. 4. It shall be the duty of each national and international union, organizing committee, each trade and industrial department, state and local central bodies and each directly affiliated local union, to furnish the Secretary-Treasurer a copy of all official reports issued by such affiliated organizations together with a statement of their membership in good standing and to furnish such additional statistical data in their possession relating to the membership of such organizations as may be called for by the Secretary-Treasurer of this Federation.

Sec. 5. The Secretary-Treasurer shall give a bond for the faithful performance of his duties in such amount as may be determined by the Executive Council and shall report to the biennial convention of the Federation through the report of the Executive Council, and for his services he shall receive $33,000 per annum, payable weekly.

Sec. 6. The Secretary-Treasurer shall print quarterly, as a separate document, a financial statement of the Federation and forward a copy thereof to all affiliated national and international unions, organizing committees, directly affiliated local unions and state and local central bodies.

Sec. 7. The Secretary-Treasurer shall be required, from time to time, but no less than semiannually, to provide for an audit of all books, accounts, records and financial transactions of the Federation by an independent public accountant. Such audits shall be furnished to the Executive Council and a biennial audit shall be furnished to the Convention.

Sec. 8. The Secretary-Treasurer shall, under the direction and instructions of the Executive Council, invest the surplus funds of the Federation in sound securities or deposit the same in a bank or banks.

ARTICLE VIII

EXECUTIVE COUNCIL

Section 1. The Executive Council shall consist of the President, the Vice Presidents and the Secretary-Treasurer.

Sec. 2. The Executive Council shall be the governing body of this Federation between conventions. It is authorized and empowered to take such action and render such decisions as may be necessary to carry out fully and adequately the decisions and instructions of the conventions and to enforce the provisions contained in this constitution. Between conventions it shall have the power to direct the affairs of the Federation and to take such actions and render such decisions as are necessary and appropriate to safeguard and promote the best interests of the Federation and its affiliated unions, including the organization of unorganized industries by means most appropriate for that purpose.

Sec. 3. The Executive Council shall meet upon the call of the President at least three times within each year at a time and place designated by the President.

Sec. 4. It shall be the duty of the Executive Council to watch legislative measures directly affecting the interests of working people, and to initiate, wherever necessary, such legislative action as the convention may direct.

Sec. 5. The Executive Council shall prepare and present to the convention in printed form a statement of all matters of interest to the convention and of the activities of the Federation between conventions.

Sec. 6. The Executive Council shall have power to make rules to govern matters consistent with this constitution and shall report accordingly to the Federation.

Sec. 7. It is a basic principle of this Federation that it must be and remain free from any and all corrupt influences and from the undermining efforts of communist, fascist or other totalitarian agencies who are opposed to the basic principles of our democracy and of free and democratic trade unionism. The Executive Council, when requested to do so by the President or by any other member of the Executive Council, shall have the power to conduct an investigation, directly or through an appropriate standing or special committee appointed by the President, of any situation in which there is reason to believe that any affiliate is dominated, controlled or substantially influenced in the conduct of its affairs by any corrupt influence, or that the policies or activities of any affiliate are consistently directed toward the advocacy, support, advancement or achievement of the program or of the purposes of the Communist Party, any fascist organization or other totalitarian movement. Upon the completion of such an investigation, including a hearing if requested, the Executive Council shall have the authority to make recommendations or give directions to the affiliate involved and shall have the further authority, upon a two-thirds vote, to suspend any affiliate found guilty of a violation of this section. Any action of the Executive Council under this section may be appealed to the convention, provided, however, that such action shall be effective when taken and shall remain in full force and effect pending any appeal.

Sec. 8. Subject to the provisions of Article III, Section 7, the Executive Council shall use every possible means to assist affiliated unions in the organization of the unorganized and to organize new national and international unions, organizing committees, and directly affiliated local unions.

Until such time as it is feasible to form a new national or international union composed of directly affiliated local unions or to affiliate such unions with an existing affiliated national or international union within whose jurisdiction they might properly come, the Executive Council may group such directly affiliated local unions, in a particular craft or industry, into national councils or organizing committees which shall be under the direct supervision and control of the Executive Council and the President.

Sec. 9. In carrying out the provisions of this Article the Executive Council shall recognize that both craft and industrial unions are appropriate, equal and necessary as methods of trade union organization and that all workers whatever their race, color, creed or national origin are entitled to share in the full benefits of trade union organization.

Sec. 10. A majority of the members of the Executive Council shall constitute a quorum for the transaction of the business of the Council.

Sec. 11. The Executive Council shall have the power to file charges and conduct hearings on such charges against any Executive Officer of the Federation or other member of the Executive Council on the ground that such person is guilty of malfeasance or maladministration, and to make a report to the convention recommending appropriate action. The Executive Council must serve such officer with a copy of the written charges a reasonable time before the hearing.

Sec. 12. The Executive Council shall have the further power to refuse to seat or to remove from office any member of the Executive Council, or to remove from office any officer, who is found by the Council, by a two-thirds vote after notice and hearing, to be ineligible to serve under the provisions of Article V, Section 10. Any action of the Executive Council under this section may be appealed to the convention, provided, however, that such action shall be effective when taken and shall remain in full force and effect pending any appeal.

Sec. 13. In any case in which an affiliate has been suspended from membership in the Federation by the convention, or by a two-thirds vote of the Executive Council in the cases set forth in Section 7 of this Article, and in which it is shown that the cause for such suspension no longer exists, the

Executive Council shall have the power, upon a two-thirds vote, to terminate such suspension.

Sec. 14. No affiliated national or international union or organizing committee shall be permitted to change its title or name without first having obtained the consent and approval of the Executive Council or the convention.

Sec. 15. The Executive Council shall be authorized to reimburse members of the Council for necessary expenses in performing their duties for the Federation.

ARTICLE IX

EXECUTIVE COMMITTEE

There shall be an Executive Committee which shall consist of the President and the Secretary-Treasurer and six Vice Presidents to be selected by the Executive Council. The Executive Committee shall meet every two months and shall advise and consult with the President and Secretary-Treasurer on policy matters.

ARTICLE X

GENERAL BOARD

Section 1. The General Board of the Federation shall consist of all of the members of the Executive Council of the Federation and the president or other principal officer of each of the affiliated national or international unions and each trade and industrial department.

Sec. 2. The General Board shall meet upon the call of the President of the Federation, but such meeting shall be called at least once each year.

Sec. 3. The General Board shall decide all policy questions referred to it by the Executive Officers or by the Executive Council.

Sec. 4. Questions coming before the General Board shall be decided in accordance with the applicable provisions of Section 17 of Article IV of this Constitution with the president or other principal officer of each affiliated national or international union casting the vote of such union and with the president or other principal officer of each department casting the one vote of such department. The number of members of each national or international union on a roll-call vote of the General Board shall be deemed to be the number of members represented at the last preceding convention except in the case where affiliation has occurred subsequent to such convention or within a 24-month period prior to and including the second month preceding such convention. In such cases the number of members of such affiliate shall be deemed to be one twenty-fourth of the average membership for which per capita tax was paid for each month, prior to the meeting of the General Board, for which such tax was paid.

ARTICLE XI

DEPARTMENT OF ORGANIZATION

Section 1. The organizing work of this Federation as set forth in Article VIII, Section 8, shall be conducted by the Department of Organization under the general supervision of the President. The Department of Organization shall be provided the staff and resources necessary to conduct such activities.

Sec. 2. The Department of Organization shall be headed by a Director of Organization who shall be appointed by the President after consultation with the Executive Committee, subject to the approval of the Executive Council.

ARTICLE XII

TRADE AND INDUSTRIAL DEPARTMENTS

Section 1. The Trade and Industrial Departments shall be subordinate to the Federation and shall consist of the following: Building and Construction Trades Department; Metal Trades Department; Union Label and Service Trades Department; Maritime Trades Department; Railway Employees Department; and a department of industrial organizations to be known as Industrial Union Department, and such other departments as may be established by the Executive Council or the convention. Each department is to manage and finance its own affairs and may establish local councils or railway system federations of departments. Affiliation to the departments in the Federation shall be open to all appropriate affiliated national and international unions and organizing committees.

Sec. 2. To be entitled to representation in any department, international unions and organizing committees eligible to join it must first be and remain in affiliation to the Federation.

Sec. 3. To be entitled to representation in local councils or railway system federations of Departments, local unions are required to be part of affiliated national and international unions and organizing committees affiliated to departments or to be directly affiliated to the Federation.

Sec. 4. The fundamental laws and procedure of each department are to conform to and be administered in the same manner as the laws and procedure governing the Federation. No department, local council or railway system federation of the same shall enact laws, rules or regulations in conflict with the laws and procedure of the Federation, and in the event of change of laws, rules, regulations and procedures of the latter, departments, local councils and railway system federations are to change their laws, rules, and regulations to conform thereto.

Sec. 5. Each department is to be considered an official method of the Federation for transacting the portion of its business indicated by the name of the department, in consequence of which affiliated and eligible organizations should be part of their respective departments and should comply with the actions and decisions of such departments, subject to appeal therefrom to the Executive Council and the conventions of the Federation. An organization affiliated with one or more departments shall pay per capita tax to each such department upon the number of members whose occupation comes under such department.

Sec. 6. The officers of the various departments shall submit a quarterly report to the Executive Council of the Federation of the work done by their department and its general conditions.

Sec. 7. At all regular meetings of the Executive Council of the Federation, there shall be present, during some period of the Council meeting, the executive officer or officers of each department, to take up with the Council matters that may be of mutual interest.

Sec. 8. Departments of the Federation shall have their headquarters in Washington, D. C., and in the headquarters of the Federation unless permitted to locate elsewhere.

ARTICLE XIII

COMMITTEES AND STAFF DEPARTMENTS

Section 1. The President of the Federation shall appoint the following standing committees and such other committees as may from time to time be necessary. The President with the approval of the Executive Council may combine standing committees. The committees, under the direction of the President, and subject to the authority of the Executive Council and the Convention, shall carry out their functions as described herein:

(a) The Committee on Legislation shall undertake to carry out the policies and programs of the Federation in the Congress and in the legislatures of state and local governments;

(b) The Committee on Civil Rights shall be vested with the duty and responsibility to assist the Executive Council to bring about at the earliest possible date the effective implementation of the principle stated in this constitution of non-discrimination in accordance with the provisions of this constitution;

(c) The Committee on Political Education shall be vested with the duty and responsibility to assist the Executive Council in meeting the need for sound political education and in bringing about the effective implementation of the objectives stated in this constitution of encouraging workers to register and vote, to exercise their full rights and responsibilities of citizenship and to perform their rightful part in the political life of the city, state, and national communities;

(d) The Committee on Ethical Practices shall be vested with the duty and responsibility to assist the Executive Council in carrying out the constitutional determination of the Federation to keep the Federation free from any taint of corruption or communism, in accordance with the provisions of this constitution;

(e) The Committee on International Affairs shall be concerned with international developments facing our nation and the Federation's relationships with the international trade union movement;

(f) The Committee on Education shall promote the widest possible understanding among union members of the aims of the Federation, shall assist affiliated unions in developing their own educational programs and shall implement the Federation's interest in providing the nation with the highest standard of education at all levels;

(g) The Committee on Social Security shall have the responsibility of providing guidance and information in the fields of social insurance and welfare;

(h) The Committee on Economic Policy shall undertake to recommend programs and policies toward the end of promoting prosperity, full employment and full utilization of our resources;

(i) The Committee on Community Services shall stimulate the active participation by members and affiliated unions in the affairs of their communities and the development of sound relationships with social agencies in such communities;

(j) The Committee on Housing shall advise on all matters relating to housing programs and policies;

(k) The Committee on Research shall have the responsibility of reviewing and appraising the research activities of the Federation to the end that adequate research facilities are available to the Federation;

(l) The Committee on Public Relations shall review and appraise the needs of the Federation in keeping the general public informed of the goals and policies of the Federation, the extent to which these needs are being met and shall make recommendations in this field;

(m) The Committee on Safety and Occupational Health shall be vested with the responsibility of recommending and promoting ways in which the work places of our nation can be made safe and healthful;

(n) The Committee on Veterans Affairs shall keep all affiliates informed of the rights and benefits available to veterans under federal and state laws and shall propose measures to protect such rights and benefits;

(o) All other committees shall have the function vested in them by the President, the Executive Council, or the convention, consistent with this constitution.

Sec. 2. Staff departments shall be established where appropriate under the direction of the President to function in the fields of activity described above and in such other fields as may be determined by the President, the Executive Council or the convention.

Sec. 3. The Committees and staff departments shall have adequate staff which shall be under the general direction of the President of the Federation.

ARTICLE XIV

STATE AND LOCAL CENTRAL BODIES

Section 1. Central bodies subordinate to the Federation may be established upon a city, state or other regional basis as may be deemed advisable by the Executive Council and shall be composed exclusively of locals of national and international unions and organizing committees affiliated with the Federation, directly affiliated local unions, local central bodies within the geographical limits of state and regional bodies, and such other subordinate bodies as the Executive Council may determine are eligible for affiliation.

Sec. 2. It shall be the duty of all national and international unions and organizing committees affiliated with the Federation to instruct their local unions to join affiliated central labor bodies in their vicinity where such exist.

Similar instructions shall be given by the Federation to all local unions affiliated directly to it.

Sec. 3. The Executive Council of the Federation shall issue rules governing the conduct, activities, affairs, finances and property of central labor bodies and providing procedures for the discipline, including suspension and expulsion, of such bodies or their officers. Such rules shall define the powers of the President, or his designee, with respect to disciplinary action against central labor bodies, or their officers. They shall provide for notice and hearing in all cases in which such action is taken, but shall permit emergency action (including the authority to suspend officers and establish a trusteeship over such central bodies and their property) prior to hearing where in the opinion of the President the interests of the Federation so require. The rules shall further provide for appeals to the Executive Council and to the convention, but shall provide that decisions appealed from shall remain in full force and effect pending any appeal.

Sec. 4. Upon the dissolution, suspension or revocation of the charter of any state or local central body, all funds and property of any character shall revert to the Federation to be held in trust until such time that the suspended or defunct organization may be reorganized and be able to confine its activities and actions to conform with the constitution and laws of this Federation. It shall be the duty of the officers of a state or local central body which has been dissolved or whose charter has been suspended or revoked, or which has been placed under trusteeship under Section 3 of this Section, to deliver all funds and property to the President of the Federation or his designated representative. In the event of a failure or refusal to so deliver such funds and property, all expenses incurred by the Federation in recovering such funds and property shall be a lawful charge upon the funds and property involved and, on recovery thereof, the Federation shall reimburse itself from the funds and property recovered.

Sec. 5. Merger of existing state and local central bodies of the American Federation of Labor and the Congress of Industrial Organizations shall be accomplished as provided in Article III, Section 5. Pending such merger state and local central bodies of both the American Federation of Labor and the Congress of Industrial Organizations shall be permitted to continue to exist as state and local central bodies representing the respective local unions or organizations now affiliated to such central bodies.

ARTICLE XV

LOCAL UNIONS DIRECTLY AFFILIATED TO THE FEDERATION, ORGANIZING
COMMITTEES AND NATIONAL COUNCILS

Section 1. Subject to the provisions of Article III, Section 7, the Federation is authorized to issue charters and certificates of affiliation to organizing committees and directly affiliated local unions.

Sec. 2. The Executive Council of the Federation shall issue rules governing the conduct, activities, affairs, finances and property of organizing committees, national councils, and directly affiliated local unions, and governing the suspension, expulsion and termination of such organizations. Such rules shall define the powers of the President, or his designee, with respect to disciplinary action against such organizations, or their officers. They shall provide for notice and hearing in all cases in which such action is taken with respect to directly affiliated local unions, but shall permit emergency action (including the authority to suspend officers and establish a trusteeship over such local unions and their property) prior to hearing where in the opinion of the President the interests of the Federation so require. The rules shall further provide for appeals to the Executive Council and to the convention, but shall provide that decisions appealed from shall remain in full force and effect pending any appeal.

Upon the dissolution, suspension or revocation of the charter of any such organizations, all funds and property of any character shall revert to the Federation, which shall to the extent appropriate hold such funds and property in trust until such time that the suspended or defunct organization may be reorganized and be able to confine its activities and actions to conform with the constitution and laws of this Federation. It shall be the duty of the officers of any such organization which has been dissolved or whose charter has been suspended or revoked to deliver all funds and property to the President of the Federation or his designated representative. In the event of a failure or refusal to so deliver such funds and property, all expenses incurred by the Federation in recovering such funds and property shall be a lawful charge upon the funds and property involved and, on recovery thereof, the Federation shall reimburse itself from the funds and property recovered.

Sec. 3. It shall be the duty of the Executive Council to combine directly affiliated local unions in related fields into national or international unions, organizing committees or national councils when such action appears to be appropriate. Any local union directly affiliated to the Federation or a group of such local unions may request the Executive Council to authorize such combination.

When directly affiliated local unions are grouped into an organizing committee they shall become locals of the organizing committee. The organizing committee shall have the same status as a national or international union under this constitution except that it shall be under the direct supervision and control of this Federation, as provided herein.

When directly affiliated local unions are grouped into a national council they shall remain local unions directly affiliated with this Federation.

Sec. 4. The per capita payment to the Federation by local unions directly affiliated to it shall be determined by the Executive Council but shall not be less than eighty cents per month.

Sec. 5. Local Trade and Federal Labor Unions and Local Industrial Unions which are affiliated with this Federation pursuant to Article III, Section 2, of this constitution shall be for all purposes local unions directly affiliated to the Federation under this and all other sections of the constitution.

Sec. 6. The Defense Fund for Local Trade and Federal Labor Unions of the American Federation of Labor, created under its constitution, shall be continued as a defense fund for local unions directly affiliated with this Federation, subject to the rules provided for in Section 2 of this Article and subject to such provisions concerning contributions by and the eligibility of Local Industrial Unions formerly affiliated with the Congress of Industrial Organizations as may be determined by the Executive Council.

ARTICLE XVI

PER CAPITA TAX AND ASSESSMENTS

Section 1. A per capita tax shall be paid upon the full paid up membership of each affiliated national or international union, organizing committee and directly affiliated local union.

Sec. 2. Each national or international union and organizing committee shall pay on or before the fifteenth day of each month, for the preceding month, a per capita tax of 4 cents per member per month.

Sec. 3. Each directly affiliated local union shall pay on or before the fifteenth day of each month, for the preceding month, a per capita tax of not less than 80 cents per member per month, as provided for in the rules governing the organization and activities of such directly affiliated local unions. Each directly affiliated local union shall also pay to the Federation a portion, to be fixed by the Executive Council, of the initiation fee received by such union from its members, but such payment to the Federation shall in no case be less than $1.00 per member.

Sec. 4. Revenue may also be derived from assessments when and as ordered by a majority vote of a convention. The Executive Council may also declare an assessment of not to exceed 4 cents per member per month on all affiliated unions for a period not to exceed six months in any one year when the interests of the Federation require and when funds available from per capita tax are insufficient to meet the needs of the Federation.

Sec. 5. Any affiliated organization which does not pay its per capita tax on or before the fifteenth of each month, and assessment or assessments when due and payable, shall be notified of that fact by the Secretary-Treasurer of the Federation. Any affiliated organization three months in arrears in payment of per capita tax or assessments automatically becomes suspended from membership in the Federation and can be reinstated only after such arrearages are paid in full.

Sec. 6. Each affiliate, upon the issuance of a certificate of affiliation, shall pay to the Federation the sum of $15.00.

Sec. 7. Each state and local central body affiliated with the Federation shall pay to the Federation an annual fee of $20.00.

Sec. 8. The Executive Council may exonerate any national or international union, organizing committee and directly affiliated local union from the payment of per capita tax or assessments due to the Federation for any month upon a proper showing that, in the opinion of the Executive Council, good cause therefor exists. Exonerated members shall be regarded, for the purposes of this constitution, as paid up members for the period of exoneration.

ARTICLE XVII

AMENDMENTS

This constitution can be amended or altered only by the convention, by a two-thirds vote of those present and voting, either by a show of hands, or, if a roll-call is properly demanded as provided in this constitution, by such roll-call.

ARTICLE XVIII

EXISTING AGREEMENTS

Section 1. The agreement for the merger of the American Federation of Labor and the Congress of Industrial Organizations, as approved by the Executive Council of the American Federation of Labor and the Executive Board of the Congress of Industrial Organizations and the conventions of both federations is incorporated herein and made a part of this constitution.

Sec. 2. The AFL-CIO No-Raiding Agreement shall be preserved and, with the consent of the signatories, shall be extended for a period of two years from its present expiration date and amended to make it effective as between all unions signatory to it irrespective of their former affiliation. The CIO Organizational Disputes Agreement shall be maintained in force for its term as between the unions which have adhered to it. The AFL Internal Disputes Plan shall be maintained in force for its term with respect to the unions which have adhered to it. A Joint Committee shall be established by the Executive Council to formulate the means for incorporating these three agreements into a combined no-raiding and organizational and jurisdictional disputes agreement which can be effective as between all of the unions becoming signatory to it irrespective of their former affiliation and for the purpose of extending, by voluntary agreement, such provisions to all affiliates of this Federation.

ARTICLE XIX

INITIAL CONVENTION

Section 1. The provisions of this constitution shall govern the initial convention of the Federation except as otherwise provided in this Article.

Sec. 2. The initial convention shall be called, and the time and place determined, by the Joint AFL-CIO Unity Committee, subject to the approval of the Executive Council of the American Federation of Labor and the Executive Board of the Congress of Industrial Organizations, and the conventions of the two federations.

Sec. 3. The Joint AFL-CIO Unity Committee shall act as the credentials committee for the initial convention and shall be empowered to accredit as delegates to such convention all of the delegates who have been duly accredited to the conventions of the American Federation of Labor and the Congress of Industrial Organizations which approved this constitution. Where the total number of such delegates of any affiliated organization is less than the number of delegates to which such organization is entitled under Article IV, Section

4, the Joint AFL-CIO Unity Committee shall be empowered to accredit additional delegates from such organization up to such number.

Sec. 4. Delegations representing national and international unions, organizing committees and directly affiliated local unions shall each be entitled to a total number of votes based upon the membership represented by such delegation at the conventions of the American Federation of Labor and the Congress of Industrial Organizations approving this constitution. State and local central bodies and national departments shall each be represented by one delegate and shall each be entitled to one vote.

Sec. 5. The Joint AFL-CIO Unity Committee shall report to the convention, designate temporary officers for the convention, appoint all convention committees, and take such other action with respect to the conduct of the convention as may become necessary by virtue of the fact that it is an initial convention.

ARTICLE XX

EFFECTIVE DATE

This constitution and the Merger Agreement between the American Federation of Labor and the Congress of Industrial Organizations shall become effective upon approval by the separate conventions of the American Federation of Labor and the Congress of Industrial Organizations and shall govern the affairs of the Federation beginning with the first convention of the Federation.

AGREEMENT FOR THE MERGER OF THE AMERICAN FEDERATION OF LABOR AND THE CONGRESS OF INDUSTRIAL ORGANIZATIONS

Signed February 9, 1955

1. AGREEMENT TO MERGE

The American Federation of Labor and the Congress of Industrial Organizations agree to create a single trade union center in America, through the process of merger which will preserve the integrity of each affiliated national and international union. They further agree upon the following principles and procedures to accomplish this end.

2. PRINCIPLES OF MERGER

(a) It is recognized, as a fundamental basis for the merger of the AFL and CIO, that each national and international union, federal labor union, local industrial union and organizing committee (hereafter referred to as affiliated union) holding a charter or certificate of affiliation granted by either federation shall retain its charter or certificate and become, by virtue of the merger, an affiliate of the merged federation.

(b) It is further recognized and agreed that the integrity of each affiliated union in the merged federation shall be maintained and preserved. In order to effectuate this principle, the Constitution of the merged federation shall contain a constitutional declaration for respect by each affiliate of the established bargaining relationship of every other affiliate and against raiding by any affiliate of the established collective bargaining relationship of any other affiliate. The merged federation shall provide appropriate machinery to implement this constitutional declaration.

(c) The parties further agree that, subject to the foregoing, each affiliated union shall have the same organizing jurisdiction in the merged federation as it had in its respective prior organization.

(d) The parties recognize that the above provisions may result in conflicting and duplicating organizations and jurisdictions. Where such is the case, affiliates of the merged federation will be encouraged to eliminate conflicts and duplications through the process of agreement, merger, or other means, by voluntary agreement in consultation with the appropriate officials of the merged federation.

(e) The merged federation shall be based upon a constitutional recognition that both craft and industrial unions are appropriate, equal and necessary as methods of trade union organization.

(f) The merged federation shall constitutionally recognize the right of all workers, without regard to race, creed, color or national origin to share in the full benefits of trade union organization in the merged federation. The merged federation shall establish appropriate internal machinery to bring about, at the earliest possible date, the effective implementation of this principle of non-discrimination.

(g) The merged federation shall constitutionally affirm its determination to protect the American trade union movement from any and all corrupt influence and from the undermining efforts of communist agencies and all others who are opposed to the basic principles of our democracy and of free and democratic trade unionism.

The merged federation shall establish appropriate internal machinery with authority effectively to implement this constitutional determination to keep the merged federation free from any taint of corruption or communism.

3. GOVERNMENT AND STRUCTURE OF THE MERGED FEDERATION

(a) There shall be established within the merged federation a Department to be known as the Council of Industrial Organizations. Such Department shall have the status of, and, in general, be comparable to, the existing Departments of the American Federation of Labor, which Departments shall be continued within the merged federation. This Department shall be open to all industrial unions within the merged federation. All other Departments in the merged federation shall be open to all appropriate unions.

(b) The executive officers of the merged federation shall be a President and a Secretary-Treasurer, who shall be elected at the regular conventions of the merged federation. Initially, the President and Secretary-Treasurer shall be elected from the unions now affiliated with the American Federation of Labor.

(c) The Department of Organization of the merged federation shall be headed by a Director of Organization who shall be appointed by the President, after consultation with the Executive Committee, subject to the approval of the Executive Council.

Initially, the Director of Organization shall be selected from a union now affiliated with the Congress of Industrial Organizations. The Department of Organization shall be provided the staff and resources necessary to conduct organizational activities in cooperation with the various affiliated unions, in the common effort to organize the unorganized into collective bargaining units which experience has shown to be the most effective and appropriate for the protection of such workers.

(d) The Convention of the merged federation shall be its supreme governing body. The convention shall meet regularly every two years. The delegates of affiliated unions to such convention shall vote the per capita membership of the unions which they represent. State and local central bodies shall be entitled to one vote each at conventions.

(e) In addition to the officers set forth in paragraph (b), there shall be twenty-seven Vice Presidents, to be elected at the regular conventions of the merged federation. The Vice Presidents shall, with the executive officers, constitute the Executive Council. The Executive Council shall meet not less than three times each year. It shall be authorized and empowered to take such action and render such decisions as will be necessary to carry out fully and adequately the decisions and instructions of the conventions and between conventions shall have the power to direct the affairs of the federation and to take such actions and render such decisions as are necessary and appropriate to safeguard and promote the best interests of the federation and its affiliated unions, including the organization of unorganized industries by means most appropriate for that purpose. At the first convention of the merged federation, seventeen of the Vice Presidents shall be elected from unions now affiliated with the American Federation of Labor and ten shall be elected from unions now affiliated with the Congress of Industrial Organizations.

(f) There shall be an Executive Committee which shall consist of the Executive Officers and six of the Vice Presidents to be selected by the Executive Council. The Executive Committee shall meet bi-monthly and shall advise and consult with the executive officers on policy matters. Initially, three of the Vice Presidents constituting the Executive Committee shall be selected from unions now affiliated with the AFL and three of the Vice Presidents shall be selected from unions now affiliated with the CIO.

(g) There shall be a body known as the General Board which shall consist of the members of the Executive Council and the President or other principal officer of each of the national or international unions affiliated with the merged federation. The General Board shall meet at least once each year and shall decide all policy questions referred to it by the executive officers, and the Executive Council. The rules of the convention as to voting shall govern the General Board.

(h) The constitution of the merged federation shall provide for standing committees of the federation in appropriate fields of action. These committees shall have appropriate staffs and due recognition shall be given to unions now affiliated with the AFL and the CIO in determining the chairmanships of, and in staffing, such committees.

(i) The constitution shall provide for state and local central bodies of the merged federation. In addition, the constitution shall permit the Council of Industrial Organizations to maintain subordinate councils, as now provided for departments of the American Federation of Labor. Existing state and local bodies of the AFL and CIO shall be merged as provided for in paragraph 6(g) of this Agreement.

4. FINANCES

(a) The merged federation shall succeed to all the assets of the American Federation of Labor and shall assume all of its liabilities and contractual obligations. The merged federation shall succeed to that part of the net assets of the Congress of Industrial Organizations which bears the same relationship to the membership of the Congress of Industrial Organizations (as measured by per capita tax paid as of the date of the 1954 Congress of Industrial Organizations Convention) as the net assets of the American Federation of Labor as of the date of merger bear to the membership of the American Federation of Labor (similarly measured as of the date of the 1954 American Federation of Labor Convention). The Council of Industrial Organizations to be established within the merged federation shall succeed to the balance of the assets of the Congress of Industrial Organizations, after all of its liabilities, both accrued and potential, have been provided for. The term assets shall include real estate held in trust for the respective federations.

(b) The per capita tax payable to the merged federation by national, international unions and organizing committees shall be 4 cents per member per month. The per capita tax of federal labor unions and local industrial unions shall be not less than 80 cents per member per month. The Council of Industrial Organizations, acting as a department of the merged federation, shall establish its own per capita tax, as shall all other departments of the merged federation.

5. EXISTING AGREEMENTS

The AFL-CIO No-Raiding Agreement shall be preserved and, with the consent of the signatories, shall be extended for a period of two years from its present expiration date and amended to make it effective as between all unions signatory to it irrespective of their former affiliation.

The CIO Organizational Disputes Agreement shall be maintained in force as between the unions which have adhered to it. The AFL Internal Disputes Plan shall be maintained in force with respect to the unions which have adhered to it. A Joint Committee shall be established to formulate the means for incorporating these three agreements into a combined no-raiding and organizational and jurisdictional disputes agreement which can be effective as between all of the unions becoming signatory to it irrespective of their former affiliation and for the purpose of extending, by voluntary agreement, such provisions to all affiliates of the merged federation.

6. METHODS OF MERGER

The merger shall be effected by the following procedure:

(*a*) This agreement shall be submitted for approval to the Executive Council of the American Federation of Labor and the Executive Board of the Congress of Industrial Organizations.

(*b*) Upon approval by them, a proposed constitution for the merged federation, reflecting the provisions of the merger agreement and containing such other necessary and appropriate provisions as may be agreed to, shall be drafted by the Joint AFL-CIO Unity Committee. The proposed constitution of the merged federation shall, consistent with the merger agreement, preserve the essential features of the present AFL and CIO constitutions and the basic rights and obligations of the affiliates of both federations.

(*c*) The proposed Constitution shall be submitted for approval to the Executive Council of the American Federation of Labor and the Executive Board of the Congress of Industrial Organizations.

(*d*) Upon approval by them, this Agreement and the proposed Constitution, and such other agreements as are necessary to accomplish the merger shall be submitted to separate conventions of the American Federation of Labor and the Congress of Industrial Organizations.

(*e*) Upon approval by the separate conventions of the two federations of the Merger Agreement and the proposed Constitution of the merged federation, a joint convention shall be held. Such joint convention shall constitute the first regular biennial convention of the merged federation.

(*f*) Initially, the headquarters and field staff of the AFL and the CIO shall be retained as the staff of the merged federation. A special committee shall be established of the present executive officers of the AFL and the CIO which shall, in conjunction with the executive officers of the merged federation, make just, fair and equitable provision for the integration of the staffs of the AFL and the CIO into a single staff for the merged federation.

(*g*) Merger of existing state and local central bodies of the AFL and CIO shall be accomplished within two years after the date of the merger of the two national federations by the process of negotiation and agreement under the guidance of the officers of the merged federation. Pending the conclusion of such agreements state and local central bodies of both the AFL and CIO shall be permitted to continue to exist as state and local central bodies representing the respective local unions now affiliated to such central bodies.

There is no national union which can in any sense be considered "representative." The constitution below is, however, one example of the organizational structure of an important national union.

Constitution of the International Union, United Automobile, Aircraft
and Agricultural Implement Workers of America, 1955

TABLE OF CONTENTS

PREAMBLE

We hold these truths to be self-evident, expressive of the ideals and hopes of the workers who come under the jurisdiction of this International Union, UNITED AUTOMOBILE, AIRCRAFT AND AGRICULTURAL IMPLEMENT WORKERS OF AMERICA (UAW-CIO); that all men are created equal, that they are endowed by their Creator with certain inalienable Rights, that among these are Life, Liberty and the Pursuit of Happiness. That to secure these Rights, Governments are instituted among men, deriving their just powers from the consent of the governed. Within the orderly processes of such Government lies the hope of the worker.

We hold that the exigencies of the times, the complete subdivision of Labor in the development and operation of the industrial mass production system imposes conditions under which the worker is gradually but surely absorbed and controlled by the machine.

We hold these conditions to be utterly at variance with the spirit of justice and the needs of mankind. We believe the right of the workers to organize for mutual protection is the culminating growth of a great industry, which is evidence not only of its increased power but also of an economic and social change in our civilization.

We believe that organized labor and organized management possess the ability and owe the duty to society of maintaining, through co-operative effort, a mutually satisfactory and beneficial employer-employee relationship based upon understanding through the medium of conference.

The worker does not seek to usurp management's functions or ask for a place on the Board of Directors of concerns where organized. The worker through his Union merely asks for his rights. Management invests thousands of dollars in the business. The worker's investment in the business is his sinew, his blood and his life. The organized worker seeks a place at the conference table, together with the management, when decisions are made which affect the amount of food he, his wife and family shall consume; the extent of education his children may have; the kind and amount of clothing they may wear; and their very existence. He asks that hours of labor be progressively reduced in proportion as modern machinery increases his productivity. He asks that the savings due to the inauguration of machinery and changes in technical methods shall be equitably divided between management and the worker. The organized worker asks that those who may be discharged be paid adequate dismissal wages to enable him to start afresh in another field; that society undertake to train him in new skills and that it make provisions through ameliorative social laws for the innocent and residual sufferers from the inevitable industrial shifts which constitute progress.

ARTICLE 1

NAME

The Organization shall be known as the "International Union, UNITED AUTOMOBILE, AIRCRAFT AND AGRICULTURAL IMPLEMENT WORKERS OF AMERICA (UAW-CIO)," hereinafter referred to as the International Union.

ARTICLE 2

OBJECTS

Section 1. To improve working conditions, create a uniform system of shorter hours and higher wages; to maintain and protect the interests of workers under the jurisdiction of this International Union.

Section 2. To unite in one organization, regardless of religion, race, creed, color, political affiliation or nationality, all employees under the jurisdiction of the International Union.

Section 3. To improve the sanitary and working conditions of employment within the factory, and in the accomplishment of these necessary reforms we pledge ourselves to utilize the conference room and joint agreements; or if these fail to establish justice for the workers under the jurisdiction of this International Union to advocate and support strike action.

Section 4. To educate our membership in the history of the Labor Movement and to develop and maintain an intelligent and dignified membership; to vote and work for the election of candidates and the passage of improved legislation in the interest of all labor. To enforce existing laws; to work for the repeal of those which are unjust to Labor; to work for legislation on a national scale, having as its object the establishment of real social and unemployment insurance, the expense of which to be borne by the employer and the Government.

Section 5. To work as an autonomous International Union affiliated with the Congress of Industrial Organizations together with other International Unions, for the solidification of the entire Labor Movement.

ARTICLE 3

CONSTITUTION

This Constitution as amended at the Cleveland Convention convened on March 27, 1955, and as may hereafter be amended, shall be the supreme law of the International Union, UNITED AUTOMOBILE, AIRCRAFT AND AGRICULTURAL IMPLEMENT WORKERS OF AMERICA (UAW-CIO), and can be amended only by a majority vote of the delegates at succeeding Conventions.

ARTICLE 4

INTERNATIONAL UNION HEADQUARTERS

The headquarters of the International Union shall be located in the City of Detroit, State of Michigan.

ARTICLE 5

JURISDICTION

The International Union, UNITED AUTOMOBILE, AIRCRAFT AND AGRICULTURAL IMPLEMENT WORKERS OF AMERICA (UAW-CIO), shall take in and hold jurisdiction over all employees of plants and shops engaged in the manufacture of parts (including tools, dies, etc.), and the assembly of these parts into farm, automobile, automotive propelled products, aircraft and agricultural implements, including employees engaged in office work, sales, distribution and maintenance thereof and such other branches of industry as the International Executive Board shall decide in accordance with the Jurisdiction Committee of the Congress of Industrial Organizations. The jurisdiction of this International Union shall be full and final.

ARTICLE 6

MEMBERSHIP

Section 1. The International Union shall be composed of workers eligible for membership in the International Union, UNITED AUTOMOBILE, AIRCRAFT AND AGRICULTURAL IMPLEMENT WORKERS OF AMERICA (UAW-CIO).

Section 2. Any person eligible to become a member of the International Union who is not affiliated with any organization whose principles and philosophy are contrary to those of this International Union as outlined in the Preamble of this Constitution, may apply for membership to the Local Union having jurisdiction over the plant in which he is employed. The applicant must, at the time of application, be an actual worker in and around the plant. All applicants for membership in any Local Union of the International Union shall fill out an official application provided by the International Union, answering all questions contained in such application, and sign a promise to abide by all laws, rules and regulations and the Constitution of the International Union. All applications thus received shall be referred to the Local Union for consideration, and shall be acted upon as soon as possible, but not later than sixty (60) days from the date the application is received by the Financial Secretary of the Local Union.

Section 3. Upon acceptance of the application, membership shall date from the first day of the month for which dues are paid.

Section 4. Applications for membership rejected by the Local Union shall not be reconsidered until thirty (30) days have elapsed.

Section 5. Unless waived by the Local Union, or unit of an Amalgamated Local, any candidate failing to present himself for initiation within four (4) weeks after notification of his being accepted to membership, without good and sufficient reason being given, shall forfeit all money paid by him.

Section 6. The original application signed by each member shall be retained by the Local Union for its record and official receipt shall be given to each new member for all monies paid. All receipts shall be made out in duplicate, the original to be given to the member, the duplicate to be retained by the Local Union and made available to the International Union upon request. These duplicate receipts may be destroyed after a Local Union audit upon written approval of the International Secretary-Treasurer.

Section 7. No new member will be recorded at the International office nor will initiation fee or per capita tax be accepted for new members until a monthly report is received from the Financial Secretary of the Local Union.

Section 8. Any Local Union or International Union Trial Committee expelling any member for cause shall notify the International Secretary-Treasurer and the latter shall notify all Local Unions of this fact forthwith. A person who has been suspended or expelled by any Local Union or International Union Trial Committee shall not be eligible for membership in any other Local Union until all claims or charges against such person have been satisfactorily settled with the Local Union or International Union Trial Committee suspending or expelling and written notice to this effect furnished the Local Union to which such person seeks admission.

Section 9. No member shall be allowed to hold membership in more than one Local Union of the International Union at the same time, except by permission of the International Executive Board. No member of the Union who is fully employed in one plant under the jurisdiction of the UAW, shall accept work in any other plant under the jurisdiction of the UAW. Any member violating this section may be subjected to charges of conduct unbecoming a union member.

The above shall not apply in the case of members of a Local Union or unit of an Amalgamated Local Union who are conducting an authorized strike and have received written approval from the Local Union officers to obtain employment elsewhere.

Section 10. No application shall be accepted from the one designated as the head of a department, directing company policy or having the authority to hire and discharge workers. Members of the Union who are promoted to such positions shall be issued a withdrawal card immediately by the Local Union, in conformity with Article 17 of this Constitution. Members promoted to minor positions where they work with their fellow workers and do not have the power of discipline by hiring or discharging employees may retain their membership in the Local Union at the discretion of the Local Union.

Section 11. The names of all applicants for admission about whose applications there is the least doubt may be published in the "official publication." No applicants whose names have been published shall be received into membership until thirty (30) days after the date of such publication.

Section 12. Any member in good standing who shall have become totally incapacitated by accident or illness may, at the discretion of his Local Union, be granted a gratuitous membership, continuing during incapacity. Appropriate cards denoting such membership shall be prepared by the International Union and furnished to Local Unions upon request, and at cost.

Section 13. All members of the Local Union are also members of this International Union and subject to the orders, rulings and decisions of this International Union and the properly constituted authorities of the same.

Section 14. The International Union and the Local Union to which the member belongs shall be his exclusive representative for the purpose of collective bargaining in respect to rates of pay, wages, hours of employment or other conditions of employment, and for the negotiation and execution of contracts with employers covering all such matters, including contracts requiring his membership or the continuance of his membership in the Union as a condition of his employment or continued employment, and contracts requiring the employer to deduct, collect, or assist in collecting from his wages any dues, initiation fees, reinstatement fees or fines, payable to the International Union or his Local Union.

Section 15. The International Union and the Local Union to which the member belongs, and each of them, are by him irrevocably designated, authorized and empowered exclusively to appear and act for him and in his behalf before any board, court, committee or other tribunal in any matter affecting his status as an employee or as a member of his Local Union or the International Union, and exclusively to act as his agent to represent and bind him in the presentation, prosecution, adjustment and settlement of all grievances, complaints or disputes of any kind or character arising out of the employer-employee relationship, as fully and to all intents and purposes as he might or could do if personally present.

Section 16. A member may resign or terminate his membership only if he is in good standing, is not in arrears or delinquent in the payment of any dues or other financial obligation to the International Union or to his Local Union and there are no charges filed and pending against him. Such resignation or termination shall be effective only if by written communication, signed by the member, and sent by registered mail, return receipt requested, to the Financial Secretary of the Local Union within the ten (10) day period prior to the end of the fiscal year of the Local Union as fixed by this Constitution, whereupon it shall become effective sixty (60) days after the end of such fiscal year; provided, that if the employer of such member has been authorized either by such member individually or by the Collective Bargaining Agreement between the employer and the Union to check off the membership dues of such member, then such resignation shall become effective upon the effective termination of such authorization, or upon the expiration of such sixty (60) day period, whichever is later.

Section 17. A member who resigns or terminates his membership shall have no right or interest in any property of the Local Union or of the International Union, including any dues or other financial obligations paid by him in advance of the effective date of such resignation or termination.

Section 18. Any member in good standing who is retired under the terms of a retirement or old-age pension plan shall be entitled to a "retired membership status" which shall entitle him to all of the privileges of membership except that he shall not be required to pay membership dues during the period of such retirement. Appropriate cards denoting such membership status shall be prepared by the International Union and furnished to Local Unions upon request and at cost. The regular withdrawal-transfer provisions of this Constitution shall be applicable if such retired member returns to active employment.

ARTICLE 7

POWERS OF ADMINISTRATION

The International Union shall be governed by its membership in the following manner:

(a) The highest tribunal shall be the International Convention composed of delegates democratically elected by the membership of Local Unions.

(b) Between conventions the highest authority shall be the International Executive Board, which shall meet at least once every three (3) months.

(c) Between meetings of the International Executive Board the administrative authority of the International Union shall be vested in the International President. The International President shall be responsible to the International Executive Board for the administration of the Union between International Executive Board meetings, according to the Constitution, the actions of the International Convention and the decisions of the International Executive Board. On all matters of major importance he shall consult the other International Executive Officers. He shall report his actions to the International Executive Board for its approval or rejection.

(*d*) In case of the absence or incapacity of the International President his powers and duties shall be assumed by the International Secretary-Treasurer.

ARTICLE 8

CONVENTIONS

Section 1. The International Union shall hold Constitutional Conventions bi-ennially in the month of May, provided that the date of holding such Convention may be advanced or delayed one (1) month upon a resolution to that effect adopted by the International Executive Board.

Section 2. The business of the International Convention shall proceed in the following order unless otherwise ordered by the Convention:

(1) Call to order.
(2) Report on Credentials.
(3) Reading of Convention Rules.
(4) Appointing Committees.
(5) Communications and Bills.
(6) Resolutions, etc.
(7) Reports of Committees.
(8) Report of Officers and International Executive Board.
(9) Nomination and Election of Officers and International Trustee.
(10) Unfinished Business.
(11) New Business.
(12) Adjournment.

Section 3. Twenty-five per cent (25%) of all of the delegates seated at any International Convention shall constitute a quorum. No business shall come before or be considered by the Convention at any session unless a quorum is present. In the event the Chairman of the Convention is unable to obtain a quorum on the last day of the Convention, all unfinished business of the Convention shall be referred to the International Executive Board.

Section 4. Special Conventions of the International Union shall be called by the International President, (1) when so instructed by a two-thirds vote of the International Executive Board or in the event of the failure of the International President to do so, by such other Board Members as the Board may designate. (2) By a referendum vote of the membership initiated upon the written request of at least fifteen (15) Local Unions from five (5) different states or provinces, having an aggregate membership of not less than twenty per cent (20%) of the total membership as reported to the last preceding Convention. The Local Unions demanding a Special Convention must state the reason or reasons why such Convention is desired, the place and date for the Convention and the dates for mailing out and returning the ballots. It shall be the duty of the International President, or the person designated by the International Executive Board to send out the call, to state such reason or reasons and the place and dates involved in transmitting the proposal to Local Unions for a referendum vote. The reasons for and against such Convention shall be published and forwarded to all Local Unions. Such Convention shall not have authority to consider any matter other than that which is specifically stated in the Call to the Convention. It shall be mandatory that all Local Unions hold a secret vote on the question of calling a Special Convention. All Local Unions shall vote their decision on the question involved, through Local Union procedure, by secret ballot. Local Union election boards shall tabulate the ballots and send the Local Union's vote to the International Secretary-Treasurer, who, within thirty (30) days after the setting of a deadline of a return date, shall publish the "yes" and "no" vote of each Local Union in the "official publication." If a majority of all the members voting in all Local Unions is in favor of a Special Convention, a Special Convention shall be mandatory. The Local Unions shall elect whatever qualified delegate or delegates they desire to attend the Special Convention. Local Union representation in the Special Convention shall be on the same per capita basis as governs regular Conventions.

Notwithstanding the above, should a Special Convention be called for the purpose of discussing International Union finances and/or collective bargaining programs within a six (6) month period following the 15th Constitutional Convention, the delegates elected to the 15th Constitutional Convention shall serve as delegates to such Special Convention.

Section 5. Each Local Union shall have one (1) delegate for two hundred (200) members or less and one (1) additional delegate for the next three hundred (300) members or major fraction thereof, and one (1) additional delegate for each additional eight hundred (800) members or major fraction thereof except Amalgamated Local Unions which elect as many delegates as they have manufacturing units who average two hundred (200) dues-paying members or more, and that those manufacturing units who have two hundred (200) members or more may elect their own delegates to the Convention and those with less than two hundred (200) shall be grouped together and vote as a miscellaneous group. In the event the miscellaneous group within an Amalgamated Local Union has less than two hundred (200), the International Secretary-Treasurer shall allocate such membership to some other unit of the Local Union in such a manner as will result in the maximum number of delegates.

Section 6. Each manufacturing unit of an Amalgamated Local Union shall be allotted its share of the number of delegates in proportion to the amount of per capita tax paid by the manufacturing unit through the Amalgamated Local Union. Any fractions remaining from the manufacturing units following such allocations shall be allotted to the Local Union's Joint Council, where such body exists. Delegates representing the total of all fractions shall be elected on the basis of one (1) for each eight hundred (800) or major fraction thereof. Any member of the Local Union who has qualified may be nominated and elected by the Joint Council, provided he has not accepted nomination in his manufacturing unit. In order to be eligible for nomination as a delegate representing a manufacturing unit of an Amalgamated Local Union, a member must be a member of such manufacturing unit.

Section 7. Each Local Union shall have one (1) vote for the first one hundred (100) members or less and one (1) additional vote for each additional one hundred (100) members or major fraction thereof, but no delegate shall have more than eight (8) votes. The votes shall be equally apportioned among the elected delegates of each Local Union, except that an Amalgamated Local Union may apportion its votes in such manner as the Local Union decides with no delegate having more than eight (8) votes. The total number of votes of the units of an Amalgamated Local Union shall not exceed the total votes which the Local Union is entitled to under Section 9 of Article 8 of this Constitution.

Section 8. Local Unions may elect alternate delegates if they so desire. The number of alternates may be less but not more than the number of regular delegates. Local Unions shall determine the manner and order in which an alternate will replace a regular delegate and shall so advise the Credentials Committee. Regular delegates may be replaced only if recalled by their Local Union in the manner they were elected or if unable to serve.

Section 9. The number of members in each Local Union, for the purpose of this Article, shall be determined by the average number of monthly per capita taxes paid by the Local Union to the International Union for the period from and including the third month preceding that in which the last bi-ennial Convention was held to not less than three (3) months nor more than four (4) months prior to the next Convention for which representation is to be determined. Per capita from Local Unions shall be accepted in the regular manner.

Local Unions or units of Amalgamated Local Unions which have engaged in authorized strikes or in lockouts shall have their representation to the International Convention determined by having subtracted from the base period the months of such authorized strikes or lockouts in which the membership of the Local Union or unit of an Amalgamated Local Union did not work in the plant forty (40) or more hours.

Section 10. Not less than sixty (60) days previous to the convening of the regular or special Convention, the International Secretary-Treasurer shall issue the Call to the Convention and shall furnish all Local Unions with credentials and alternate credential forms in contrasting colors, in duplicate, which must be attested as required on the forms. The original of each credential and alternate credential shall be retained by the delegate or alternate delegate and the duplicate copies shall be forwarded to the International Secretary-Treasurer. No credentials shall be accepted later than fifteen (15) days prior to the date for the convening of the Convention.

Section 11. No member is eligible to serve as a delegate from his Local Union unless he has been in continuous good standing in this International Union for twelve (12) months immediately preceding the first day of the month in which the Convention is held and shall also have been a member of the Local Union electing him for three (3) months immediately preceding the first day of the month in which the Convention is held. For the purpose of this section of the Constitution, members must pay their dues or secure out of work receipts in accordance with the provisions of this Constitution.

Section 12. Local Unions, in order to be entitled to representation at the Convention shall have been affiliated with the International Union for at least three (3) months prior to the holding of the Convention. New Local Unions shall have paid at least two (2) months' full per capita tax prior to the month in which the Convention is to be held. If such newly chartered Local Union

has been in existence since the last preceding Convention, it shall be entitled
to its full quota of delegates based upon the average number of months per
capita tax paid to the International Union during the period of time since the
last preceding Convention. With respect to newly chartered Local Unions who
received their charter subsequent to the last Convention, representation shall
likewise be based upon the per capita tax paid to the International Union,
averaged over the period of time from the last preceding Convention. In the
case of an Amalgamated Local Union where a shop has been organized for
over a year and secures a separate charter, it shall not be considered a new
Local Union. Members representing Local Unions or shop organizations within
Amalgamated Local Unions, which have not been in existence for twelve (12)
months prior to the Convention, shall be exempt from the provisions of Section 11 of this Article, provided they become members of their Local Union
or shop organization not later than thirty (30) days after the issuance of or
acceptance under the charter thereof.

Section 13. International Officers and International Representatives of the
International Union shall have a voice but no vote in the Convention of the
International Union unless they are duly accredited delegates from Local
Unions. Any member who is eligible may be elected to office whether or not
he is a delegate to the International Convention.

Section 14. Copies of all resolutions, grievances and constitutional amendments to be considered by the Convention must be sent to the International
Secretary-Treasurer not later than (3) weeks prior to the date set for the Convention. These will then be sorted and distributed by the International
Secretary-Treasurer among the chairmen of the various and proper committees.

Section 15. The International Executive Board shall select from the credentials of the delegates presented, a Constitution Committee, which shall
assemble at least two (2) weeks prior to the meeting of the Convention at the
place designated. It shall be the duty of said committee to take up all recommendations concerning changes or additions to the Constitution submitted by
the International Officers, International Executive Board and Local Unions to
act thereon. This Committee shall have authority to originate amendments to
the Constitution.

Section 16. The International Executive Board shall select from the credentials of delegates a Credentials Committee, which shall assemble at least ten
(10) days prior to the meeting of the Convention. The Committee shall examine
all credentials received at the International Office and investigate the standing
of the delegates and the Local Unions they represent; they shall receive the
original credentials of the delegates elected to attend the Convention, and be
in a position to report at the opening of the Convention.

Section 17. The International Executive Board shall select from the credentials of delegates to each International Convention a Resolutions Committee
of not less than seven (7) members, which shall assemble at least ten (10) days
prior to the convening of the Convention. It shall be the duty of said Committee to consider such resolutions as may be properly referred to it under this

Constitution. This Committee shall have authority to originate resolutions to be presented at the Convention.

Section 18. The International Executive Board shall select from the credentials of delegates to each International Convention, the several other committees necessary to successfully promote and execute the efficient operation of the Convention. Such committees shall convene not later than two (2) days prior to the opening of the Convention.

Section 19. All Convention Committees shall have an odd number of, and not more than eleven (11) members.

Section 20. Following the issuance of the Convention Call by the International Secretary-Treasurer, each Local Union shall issue a call for the nomination of its delegates to the Convention. In the absence of a democratically elected standing election committee (Article 36, Section 10), an election committee shall be elected by the Local Union at a regular or a specially called meeting for that purpose not later than the day on which nominations of delegates are made. A list of nominees shall be available to the membership. Candidates shall not serve on the election committee or as challengers or observers.

Section 21. The membership shall be duly notified at least seven (7) days in advance of the time and place of nominations and of the election of the election committee. The election committee shall handle all the details, insofar as they relate to the procedure of the election, and adopt such safeguards as are necessary to insure a fair election. After the deadline on accepting nominations has expired, no election of so-called "sticker" or "write-in" candidates shall be considered legal. Polling places must be open a sufficient number of hours on one (1) or more days to allow all members of the Local Union an opportunity to cast their ballots.

Section 22. At least seven (7) days shall elapse between the time of nomination of delegates and the date the election shall take place. All members shall be duly notified, at least seven (7) days in advance, of the time and place of said election and the hours the polls will be open.

Section 23. Delegates to the International Convention shall be elected by secret ballot of the Local Union of which they are members and in no case shall be appointed. Whenever there are unopposed candidates for delegate to the International Convention such candidates shall be considered elected without the necessity of an election.

ARTICLE 9

POLITICAL REQUIREMENTS OF UNION OFFICIALS

International Officers, International Board Members, International Representatives and Local Union Officers shall, from the date of taking office, be required to register and vote in elections for civil officers in the area in which their homes are located, provided they are eligible under the laws of the area and that it is a physical possibility for them to do so. Violation of this section shall subject the person charged to discipline, in pursuance of the procedure provided for in this Constitution.

ARTICLE 10

OFFICERS AND ELECTIONS

Section 1. The elective officers of the International Union shall be one (1) International President, one (1) International Secretary-Treasurer, four (4) International Vice-Presidents, whose duties shall be to assist the International President, and such International Executive Board Members as the Convention may determine.

Section 2. The International Executive Board Members shall be nominated and elected in the regions now established by the International Executive Board within the geographical districts as determined by the International Constitution. Only the delegates from the Local Unions in such regions shall nominate and vote for their International Board Member. Any member in continuous good standing for one (1) year, and who has worked at least ninety (90) working days in a plant or plants located within the region, whose Local Union is located within the region can be nominated and elected. It shall require a two-thirds (⅔) vote of the International Executive Board to change the composition of any region within a geographical district.

Section 3. The term of office of all elective officers shall be for the period up to the next Convention and the term of office shall begin immediately upon installation. The term of office of the Trustees shall be as provided for in Article 50.

Section 4. Nomination and election of all elective officers and Trustees shall take place in the regular order of business of the Convention and election shall be determined by a majority vote of the delegates voting. Candidates shall be elected to various offices by one (1) roll-call vote. In the election of the Vice-Presidents each delegate may vote for four (4) candidates. If there are eight (8) or more than eight (8) nominees for the four (4) offices and less than four (4) candidates receive a majority vote, the candidate receiving the lowest number of votes shall be eliminated in the run-off election, and in each successive run-off election the candidate receiving the lowest number of votes shall be eliminated, unless such elimination would result in reducing the number of candidates in nomination to a figure equal to the remaining vacancy or vacancies.

Section 5. All elections of International Officers and International Executive Board Members shall be by roll-call vote.

Section 6. No member shall be nominated or elected as an elective officer of the International Union unless he has been in continuous good standing for a period of one (1) year.

Section 7. No member of any Local Union, located in the United States of America, or Canada, shall be eligible to hold any elective or appointive position in this International Union or any Local Union in this International Union, if he is a member of any organization which is declared illegal by the government of the United States of America, or Canada, through Constitutional procedure.

Section 8. No member of any Local Union shall be eligible to hold any elective or appointive position in this International Union or any Local Union in this International Union if he is a member of or subservient to any political organization, such as the Communist, Fascist or Nazi Organization which owes its allegiance to any government other than the United States or Canada, directly or indirectly.

Section 9. No member of any Local Union shall be eligible to hold any elective or appointive position in the International Union, or any Local Union, if he is affirmatively engaged in the promotion, implementation, furtherance, or support of organized in-plant rackets, such as numbers, bookmaking, etc.

Section 10. The acceptance of an elective or appointive office or position or of nomination to an elective office or position by any member who is ineligible under Sections 7, 8, or 9 of this Article is an offense against the Union punishable by a penalty up to and including expulsion.

Section 11. When a charge is preferred that a member is violating Section 10 of this Article, it shall be made and the accused member shall be tried according to the appropriate provisions of Articles 29 and 48. Resignation from an elective office or appointive position, or withdrawal of candidacy by any member charged with violation of Section 10 shall not require the dismissal of such charges.

Section 12. Upon conviction of a member by a Trial Committee of a Local Union or by an International Union Trial Committee of violation of Section 10 of this Article, any elective or appointive office or position then held by such member shall be automatically vacated regardless of any other penalty imposed.

Section 13. No member removed from office or position by reason of a conviction of any offense enumerated in Section 17 of Article 48 by a Local Union Trial Committee, shall be restored to office or position by reason of a reversal of such conviction by the body which elected the Trial Committee, until after the lapse of sixty (60) days following such reversal, without a review having been ordered by the International Executive Board.

Section 14. Whenever any member removed from elective office or position by reason of having been convicted of an offense shall have taken an appeal under Article 30, and whenever a review of any such conviction shall have been ordered by the International Executive Board under Section 18 of Article 48, the vacancy in office or position may be filled according to the applicable provisions of Section 11 of Article 36 or Section 18 of this Article, but any successor in such office or position shall hold the office or position subject to the right of restoration of the removed officer upon reversal of his conviction subject to Section 13 of this Article.

Section 15. No member shall be entitled as a matter of right to restoration to any appointive position by reason of acquittal or reversal of a conviction.

Section 16. Incoming elective officers of the International Union shall be obligated and installed immediately after being elected. The obligation shall be the same as that provided for Local Union officers.

Section 17. In the event of the death, removal or resignation of the International President, International Secretary-Treasurer and/or International Vice-President, he shall be replaced by a member of the International Executive

Board. It shall require a majority vote of all members of the International Executive Board to elect a successor.

Section 18. In the event of the death, removal or promotion of a member of the International Executive Board, the International Executive Board shall, within thirty (30) days, call a special convention for the region which the International Executive Board member represented. Such vacancy shall be filled by a member elected by the delegates from the Local Unions in the region. Representation shall be in accordance with Article 8 of this Constitution. In the event of such death or removal from office within sixty (60) days of a convention no election shall take place and the office shall remain vacant.

Section 19. The International Executive Board shall consist of the International Executive Board Members elected from the regions together with the International President, International Secretary-Treasurer and the International Vice-Presidents.

Section 20. Voting strength of International Executive Board Members:

(a) Questions coming before the International Executive Board may be decided by unit vote of its members, but any member may demand a roll-call vote on any question.

(b) Each member of the International Executive Board shall have one (1) vote for each one thousand (1,000) members or major fraction thereof represented by him in his region.

(c) In regions where there are more than one (1) member of the International Executive Board the votes of the entire region shall be equally divided among each of the respective Board Members from that region.

(d) Voting strength of each region shall be computed on the basis of average monthly per capita tax payments from each respective region through the period of twelve (12) months commencing thirteen (13) months preceding each quarterly meeting of the International Executive Board. The voting strength of Executive Board members at special Executive Board meetings shall be on the same basis as at the preceding regular Executive Board Meeting.

(e) The International President, International Secretary-Treasurer and the International Vice-Presidents shall each carry the same number of votes, which shall be equal to the largest number of votes carried by any individual member of the Executive Board.

(f) Members of the International Executive Board may cast their votes by proxy.

Section 21. The following shall be the geographical districts and the number of International Executive Board Members for each district of the International Union:

1. Michigan 7
2. Ohio, West Virginia, and those parts of Pennsylvania west of and including the counties of McKean, Cameron, Clearfield, Cambria and Somerset 3
3. Indiana, Kentucky 1

4. Illinois, Iowa and Nebraska 1

5. Missouri, Arkansas, Louisiana, Kansas, Oklahoma, Texas, Colorado and New Mexico 1

6. Washington, Oregon, California, Idaho, Nevada, Utah and Arizona.. 1

7. Dominion of Canada 1

8. Tennessee, Virginia, North Carolina, South Carolina, Mississippi, Alabama, Georgia, Florida and the District of Columbia, Maryland, Delaware and the following counties of Pennsylvania, Franklin, Cumberland, Adams and York 1

9. New York, New Jersey, Rhode Island, Connecticut, Massachusetts, Vermont, New Hampshire, Maine and those parts of Pennsylvania east of and including the counties of Potter, Clinton, Center, Blair and Bedford, but excluding the counties of Franklin, Cumberland, Adams and York......... 2

10. Wisconsin, Minnesota, North Dakota, South Dakota, Wyoming and Montana 1

ARTICLE 11

SALARIES

Section 1. The salaries of the International President, International Secretary-Treasurer, International Vice-Presidents and International Executive Board Members in full for services rendered by each of said officers during his term of office shall be the following sums:

International President, $18,000.00 per annum.

International Secretary-Treasurer, $14,000.00 per annum.

International Vice-Presidents, $12,500.00 per annum.

International Executive Board Members, $10,000.00 per annum.

Salaries shall be payable in bi-weekly installments.

Section 2. The International President, International Secretary-Treasurer, International Vice-Presidents and International Executive Board Members shall devote their full time to their duties and shall not serve as an officer of a Local Union, District Council or any other Subordinate Body, beyond ninety (90) days after being elected as an International Officer.

Section 3. An International Executive Board Member shall serve under the general direction of the International President, subject to the decisions of the International Executive Board.

Section 4. The International President, International Secretary-Treasurer, International Vice-Presidents, International Executive Board Members and International Representatives, when traveling on union business or when away from their duly designated home offices, shall be allowed first class transportation fare by the shortest route to and from their destination, plus personal hotel and incidental expenses up to twenty dollars ($20.00) per day. In addition to the above, when these officers are required to incur organizational expenses for the good of this International Union, such organizational expenses shall be presented in itemized form for payment, it being understood that payment of all such items is under control of the International Executive Board.

The expense accounts of International Executive Board Members and International Representatives shall be strictly itemized and checked and these accounts be made available to any interested Local Union.

Section 5. The compensation of any member of the International Union, performing service under direction of the International Executive Board shall be an amount for time lost equal to his earning capacity, except that this remuneration shall be not less than fifteen dollars ($15.00) per day, or in case of International Representatives their weekly salary.

Section 6. International Representatives shall be paid not less than ninety-five dollars ($95.00) nor more than one hundred and fifteen dollars ($115.00) per week. The hiring rate for International Representatives shall be not less than ninety-five dollars ($95.00) per week and thereafter such rate shall be increased five dollars ($5.00) per month until the maximum of one hundred and fifteen dollars ($115.00) per week is reached. Minor department heads shall be paid not less than one hundred and fifteen dollars ($115.00) nor more than one hundred and twenty-five dollars ($125.00), and major department heads shall be paid not less than one hundred and thirty dollars ($130.00) nor more than one hundred and forty dollars ($140.00).

The International Executive Board shall determine the remuneration for professional specialists and key personnel.

Section 7. When any member is required by the International Union to perform service away from his home, he shall be allowed in addition to the amounts set forth above, first class transportation fare by the shortest route to and from his destination and actual hotel and incidental expenses not to exceed twenty dollars ($20.00) per day, provided that an itemized bill shall in all cases be rendered to the International Secretary-Treasurer.

Section 8. The International President, International Secretary-Treasurer, International Vice-Presidents and International Executive Board Members shall, on their first election, be entitled to traveling expense for themselves and families and the moving of household goods from their home to their assigned location and also on return at the close of their official terms.

Section 9. International Officers, International Executive Board Members, International Representatives and permanent employees shall be allowed a yearly vacation as follows:

(a) Service of six (6) months but less than one (1) year—one (1) week's vacation with pay.

(b) Services of one (1) year but less than five (5) years—two (2) weeks' vacation with pay.

(c) Services of five (5) years or more—three (3) weeks' vacation with pay.

Such vacation shall be mandatory and shall not interrupt the ordinary working of their office. Vacation arrangements for employees covered by contracts between the UAW-CIO and other unions shall be subject to negotiations between the unions involved.

Section 10. No person in the International Union who holds a paid full-time job in the Union shall hold any other paid position in the Union at the same time.

ARTICLE 12

DUTIES OF THE INTERNATIONAL EXECUTIVE BOARD

Section 1. The International Executive Board shall execute the instructions of the International Convention and shall be the highest authority of the International Union between Conventions, subject to the provisions of this Constitution, and shall have the power to authorize strikes, issue charters and punish all subordinate bodies for violation of this Constitution.

Section 2. The International Executive Board shall have power to revoke charters and to reorganize subordinate bodies in one of the two following manners:

(a) In case of disputes or conditions within a subordinate body that might threaten its existence the International Executive Board, by majority vote, may reorganize the subordinate body by ordering a Special Election to be held within thirty (30) days after the members in good standing are notified by mail. Under no circumstances shall more than one (1) such Special Election be held within a year's period in any one (1) subordinate body. Under this provision the elected officers of the subordinate body shall continue to hold office until the election and may run for re-election. The International Executive Board may have two (2) representatives to work with the elected Local Union Election Committee.

(b) For violation of this Constitution or of the laws of this International Union, or in case of disputes within any subordinate body affecting the welfare of its membership or its existence, the International Executive Board may, by two-thirds (⅔) vote of the entire Executive Board, after a hearing, revoke the charter or suspend any officer or officers from office and take over supervision of the subordinate body until its affairs have been properly adjusted. In any case of suspension of officers, an election of new officers shall take place within sixty (60) days from date of order, whereupon the subordinate body shall be returned its autonomy under this Constitution.

Section 3. The International President, International Secretary-Treasurer and the International Vice-Presidents shall be members of the International Executive Board with voice and vote.

Section 4. In case of vacancy, the Board shall cause such vacancy to be filled until the next Convention, in accordance with Article 10.

Section 5. It shall repeal any By-Laws of any subordinate body, which do not conform to this Constitution.

Section 6. It shall furnish all charters and initial supplies necessary to operate the subordinate bodies of the International Union.

Section 7. It shall decide all questions involving the interpretation of this Constitution between Conventions.

Section 8. It shall pass upon all claims, grievances and appeals from the decisions of subordinate bodies of the International Union, in the manner provided by this Constitution.

Section 9. It shall transmit a report of the activities of the International Union and a summary and explanation of the actions of the International

Executive Board relating to International finances to each Local Union of this International Union.

Section 10. If any elective officer is found guilty and removed from office through trial procedure, the vacancy shall be filled in accordance with this Constitution.

Section 11. Upon written request of three (3) members of the International Executive Board, the International Secretary-Treasurer, within forty-eight (48) hours of receipt of such a request, shall poll the International Executive Board on the question of a Special Board meeting. Upon a majority vote for such a meeting, the President shall convene the Board within five (5) days. In case the International President fails to convene the Board within the time allotted, the International Secretary-Treasurer or a Board Member previously designated by the Board shall convene the Board.

Section 12. Two-thirds (⅔) of the number of members comprising the International Executive Board elected at the preceding Convention shall constitute a quorum.

Section 13. Only a majority of the International Executive Board can adjourn a Board meeting.

Section 14. The International Executive Board shall set up such departments as provided for in this Constitution. It may, if voted by a two-thirds (⅔) vote, create additional departments for promoting the business of this International Union or the welfare of its membership. It may hire professional specialists not members of the International Union for such departments if they are not available within the membership.

Section 15. If and when a strike has been approved by the International Executive Board, it shall be the duty of the International Executive Board to render all financial assistance to the members on strike consistent with the resources and responsibilities of the International Union.

Section 16. Financial Officers (including Presidents) of the Local Unions of this International Union shall be bonded by such methods and agencies as the International Executive Board may determine. It shall be mandatory that such Financial Officers be bonded in an amount which shall cover at least seventy-five per cent (75%) of the funds available to them, and in no case for less than one thousand dollars ($1,000.00).

Section 17. The International Executive Board shall have power to adjust disputes between employers and employees and to make contracts with employers in accordance with this Constitution.

Section 18. The International Executive Board may rescind, reverse or repeal any action of any of the International Officers or Representatives.

Section 19. Verbatim minutes shall be taken at all meetings of the International Executive Board. Such minutes shall be transcribed immediately and copies thereof shall be distributed to all elected officers of the International Union as soon as completed. Such copies shall be made available to any interested member in good standing for inspection at the offices of the International Secretary-Treasurer and of each International Executive Board member. In addition, the Secretary-Treasurer shall prepare a summary of official International Executive Board action after each International Executive Board meeting, which shall be sent to each Local Union.

ARTICLE 13

DUTIES OF INTERNATIONAL OFFICERS

International President

Section 1. The International President shall preside at all sessions of the International Convention and all sessions of the International Executive Board. He shall perform such other duties as are necessary to protect and advance the interests of the International Union, and shall report his activities to all Local Unions and the general membership through the official publication. He shall report his activities to the quarterly meeting of the International Executive Board for approval or rejection and to the International Convention.

Section 2. Between sessions of the International Executive Board, he shall execute the instructions of the International Executive Board and have full authority to direct the working of this organization within the provisions of this Constitution and shall report his acts to the regular quarterly meeting of the International Executive Board.

Section 3. As set forth in this Constitution or voted by the International Executive Board, he shall assign any elected officer to represent or direct the workings of this International Union.

Section 4. The International President shall have power to withdraw any field assignment made to any elected officer when he becomes convinced that the officer has been derelict in his duty or been guilty of a dishonest act. Such withdrawal of assignment shall not act to suspend the vote or pay of such an officer, which power lies only in the International Executive Board as provided in this Constitution. Any officer whose assignment is withdrawn may follow the procedure outlined in Article 12, Section 11, to convene the International Executive Board. If the International Executive Board reaffirms the original assignment then the President shall not again suspend this assignment.

Section 5. He shall appoint such Representatives as he may deem necessary from time to time, such appointments to be pending the approval of the International Executive Board. He may remove from the payroll any Representative derelict in the performance of any duty, guilty of any dishonest act, or to conserve the finances of this International Union, pending the approval of the International Executive Board at its next session.

Section 6. After submitting his recommendations to the International Executive Board, he shall hire such legal, technical or professional help as is necessary to efficiently operate such departments of this International Union, except in the department of the International Secretary-Treasurer.

Section 7. He shall fill by appointment all vacancies occurring in the International Office Staff, except in the department of the International Secretary-Treasurer as otherwise provided for in this Constitution.

Section 8. He shall decide disputes or questions in controversy, except such cases as follow the procedure and conditions as outlined in this Constitution, all his decisions being subject to appeal, first to the International Executive Board, and then to the Convention. Notice in writing of appeal of any decision of the International President must be filed with the International Secretary-Treasurer and the International President within thirty (30) days from date of decision.

Section 9. He shall have authority to call special meetings of Councils or Local Unions whenever he deems such meetings necessary to protect the interests of its membership, after proper notification or consultation with officers of subordinate bodies involved. He shall have the authority to delegate such duties to any International Officer or Representative he may name, provided such delegation of authority is written, signed by him and bears the seal of the International Union.

Section 10. He shall be a delegate to all Conventions of the Congress of Industrial Organizations.

Section 11. He shall convene regular and special sessions of the International Executive Board whenever necessary.

Section 12. He shall be empowered to grant district or territorial dispensations relating to initiation fees and payment of per capita tax to the International Union with the approval of the International Executive Board, when in his judgment such dispensations will add to the growth of or conserve the interests of this International Union.

Section 13. He shall devote all his time to the affairs of this International Union, executing the instructions of the International Executive Board and exercising general supervision over all departments of this International Union.

Section 14. During his term of office he shall establish his residence in the metropolitan area of the city where the headquarters of this International Union is established.

International Secretary-Treasurer

Section 15. The International Secretary-Treasurer shall attend all sessions of the International Convention, and of the International Executive Board. He shall cause to be recorded the proceedings of the International Convention and meetings of the International Executive Board. He shall have charge of and preserve all books, documents and effects of the International Office except such records as properly belong to the office of the International President. He shall issue receipts for all monies paid to the International Union; pay all bills and current expenses, unless otherwise ordered by the International Executive Board. All expenditures shall be paid by checks countersigned by the International President when the latter is satisfied of their correctness. The International Secretary-Treasurer shall keep copies of all important correspondence sent out and received by his office. He shall submit expenses of each officer and employee, together with a detailed statement of receipts and disbursements of all money belonging to the International Union, to the International Executive Board and to the International Trustees.

Section 16. The International Secretary-Treasurer shall be the custodian of the funds of this International Union, and at the direction of the International

Executive Board shall deposit all funds of the International Union in some responsible bank or banks. He shall invest all funds in excess of two hundred fifty thousand dollars ($250,000) with banks giving interest-bearing "Certificates of Deposit"; invest such excess in bonds of the United States Government; or he may, with the approval of the International Executive Board, invest not more than forty per cent (40%) of such excess funds in securities which are considered legal investments for life insurance companies incorporated under the laws of the State of New York.

Section 17. The seal of the International Union shall bear the following words: "International Union, United Automobile, Aircraft and Agricultural Implement Workers of America (UAW-CIO), chartered August 26, 1935, affiliated with CIO." The seal of this International Union shall bear the design representing the Automobile, Aircraft and Agricultural Implement divisions of this International Union. The International Executive Board shall be authorized to adopt a seal appropriate with the above provisions. The seal of the International Union shall be held by the International Secretary-Treasurer in trust, for the use of the membership in their organization affairs; and he shall prosecute any and all proceedings proper to prevent the wrongful use of or imitation of the seal or of the name "International Union, United Automobile, Aircraft and Agricultural Implement Workers of America." He shall also take such measures as may be necessary to register or copyright the seal, and the International name, the label, insignia and any other property of the International Union that he may consider necessary to copyright or register.

Section 18. The International Secretary-Treasurer shall give a bond, amount of which shall be determined by the International Executive Board and paid for by the International Union, to insure faithful discharge of his duties. The International President shall act as trustee of and hold the bond. The International Secretary-Treasurer shall not have more than two hundred fifty thousand dollars ($250,000) subject to his order at any time.

Section 19. The International Secretary-Treasurer shall perform such other duties as are herein provided for in this Constitution or may be assigned to him by the International Executive Board.

Section 20. When a Local Union has failed to report and pay the per capita tax as provided for herein, the International Secretary-Treasurer shall notify the Local Union President and Board of Trustees of that fact.

Section 21. The International Secretary-Treasurer shall keep a complete record of the membership of the International Union.

Section 22. The International Secretary-Treasurer shall, with the consent of the International Executive Board, employ such assistants as may be necessary to conduct the affairs of his office.

Section 23. The International Secretary-Treasurer shall issue a standard "Work Permit" card which shall be furnished to Local Unions at cost. Such work permit shall be cancelled or renewed thirty (30) days following the date contained thereon. The charge for each work permit or renewal by the Local Union shall be not less than the amount of the monthly dues set by the Local Union, and one-half of which shall be paid to the International Union. It shall be left to the discretion of the Local Union to determine the duration of the period for which work permits are issued. In no case, however, shall work permits be issued to any worker for a period of more than three consecutive months.

Section 24. The International Secretary-Treasurer shall be a delegate to all Conventions of the Congress of Industrial Organizations.

Section 25. The International Secretary-Treasurer shall assume the powers and duties of the International President in case of the latter's absence or incapacity.

International Executive Board Members

Section 26. An International Executive Board Member shall have direct supervision over all organizational activities within the region from which he is elected. In case a geographical district has more than one regional board member, his activity shall be confined within a definite area within his region, which area shall be clearly defined by the International Executive Board.

Section 27. His field of activity shall be limited to shops within his region unless directed to other activities at the direction of the International Executive Board or the International President.

Section 28. He shall examine all contracts negotiated within his region before they are signed and submit them to the International Executive Board with his recommendation, negotiate disputes with the bargaining committees wherever possible, act to obtain favorable legislation for labor and work for the general welfare of the membership.

Section 29. Where district councils are established within his region, he shall attend their meetings when possible and work in cooperation with such councils. He shall submit quarterly reports of organizational activity within his region to the International President and also to the International Executive Board fifteen (15) days prior to the convening of the quarterly meeting of the International Executive Board, for its approval.

ARTICLE 14

INTERNATIONAL REPRESENTATIVES

Section 1. International Representatives' commissions must be approved and signed by the International President and shall be countersigned by the International Secretary-Treasurer and be subject to the approval of the International Executive Board.

Section 2. International Representatives shall work under the jurisdiction of the International President subject to the approval of the International Executive Board and under the direct supervision of the International Executive Board member of the region to which he is assigned, unless otherwise commissioned.

Section 3. No person can be appointed an International Representative unless he is a member in continuous good standing of the International Union for a period of one (1) year.

Section 4. Appointed International Representatives may be removed by the International President subject to the approval of the International Executive Board.

Section 5. An International Representative shall not, while holding such position, be eligible as a candidate for, or hold, any elective office or position in a Local Union, but an officer of a Local Union may be appointed to act as an International Representative on a part-time basis for parts of the day, or for full days not to exceed ninety (90) in any calendar year. An International Representative shall be eligible as a candidate for an elective office in the International Union or in the Congress of Industrial Organizations or a subordinate body of the Congress of Industrial Organizations or for delegate to the International Convention or to Conventions of the Congress of Industrial Organizations.

ARTICLE 15

FISCAL YEAR

The Fiscal Year of the International Union shall begin the first day of January of each year and end on the 31st day of December of the same year.

ARTICLE 16

INITIATION FEES AND DUES

Section 1. The initiation fee, no part of which shall be considered as a Local Union fine, shall be not less than five dollars ($5.00) nor more than fifteen dollars ($15.00) for membership in a Local Union of the International Union except that men and women returning from service in the Armed Forces of the United Nations shall be exempt from payment of an initiation fee upon presentation of military discharge papers to the Local Union Financial Secretary within one (1) year of the date of their discharge. One dollar ($1.00) of each initiation fee shall be forwarded to the International Secretary-Treasurer.

Section 2. All dues are payable on or before the first day of the month to the Financial Secretary of the Local Union. Monthly membership dues shall be two dollars and fifty cents ($2.50), or three dollars and fifty cents ($3.50), or seven dollars and fifty cents ($7.50), as specifically provided for in this Article. Nothing in this Article shall prevent any Local Union or unit of an Amalgamated Local Union from establishing, in accordance with the provisions of Article 45, dues in a greater amount than provided for in this Article. All dues established by this Article shall be uniformly required of all its members by each Local Union or unit of an Amalgamated Local Union except as exoneration may be granted pursuant to Section 14 of this Article or Section 12 of Article 13.

Section 3. Membership shall date from the first day of the month in which the application is received or the first day of the month in which dues are paid, whichever is the earlier, provided that if the application or first dues payment is received after the 25th day of the month, membership and the first dues payment shall date from the first day of the succeeding month.

Section 4. The Local Union shall set aside five cents (.05) of each month's dues payment as a Special Citizenship Fund to be used for the purpose of strengthening democracy by encouraging members, and citizens generally, to register and vote in community, state, and national elections and to carry on organizational and educational programs directed toward the achievement of an ever higher understanding of citizenship responsibility and the need for active participation in the affairs of a free and democratic society. Local Unions are obligated to carry out such programs in conjunction with city, county, and state CIO Councils. Three cents (.03) of each month's dues payment must be laid aside by the Local Union as a special fund to be used only for educational or recreational purposes as outlined in Article 26 of this Constitution.

Section 5. Any member becoming in arrears in dues within the time required by a Local Union (while working in a plant under the jurisdiction of such Local Union), which in no case shall be more than two (2) calendar months, unless officially exonerated from the payment of same by the Local Union (Local Unions cannot exonerate the International's share and are responsible for collection of same), shall automatically be suspended from membership and can be reinstated only by paying the reinstatement fee established by his Local Union.

Section 6. The reinstatement fee established by a Local Union shall be not less than the regular initiation fee charged by the Local Union, plus the dues for each month of delinquency in dues up to either the date of his automatic suspension or the date of his reinstatement, as the Local Union in its discretion may determine, plus the current month's dues. Such reinstatement fee shall be uniformly applied to all delinquent members of the Local Union. Individuals suspended as a result of their failure to pay dues while employed in a shop under the jurisdiction of another Local Union shall be dealt with in conformity with Article 17, Section 3.

Section 7. Local Unions may notify members of their delinquency. However, failure of the Local Union to notify the member of delinquency shall not exonerate such member from automatic suspension except as provided in Section 22 of this Article.

Section 8. (a) In months when the dues provided for in this Article shall be two dollars and fifty cents ($2.50), the member's monthly per capita tax shall be one dollar and twenty-five cents ($1.25); in months when such dues shall be three dollars and fifty cents ($3.50), said per capita shall be two dollars and twenty-five cents ($2.25); in months when such dues shall be seven dollars and fifty cents ($7.50), said per capita shall be six dollars and twenty-five cents ($6.25). The member's monthly per capita tax shall be forwarded to the International Secretary-Treasurer.

(b) One dollar ($1.00) of each reinstatement fee shall be forwarded to the International Secretary-Treasurer.

(c) If the Local Union does not charge back dues for the period following the date of automatic suspension to the date of reinstatement, but imposes a fine based upon the length of such period, the Local Union must forward to the International Union one-half of the fine so collected.

Section 9. When a member has been suspended for non-payment of dues and the Financial Secretary or other officers of the Local Union accept such payment thereafter, acceptance of his dues shall not operate to exonerate or reinstate the member, or to waive the provisions of the Constitution relative to forfeiture and reinstatement of members.

Section 10. The provision of Section 5 shall not apply to a member who has entered the military service of the United States of America or the Dominion of Canada, who shall be entitled to an honorable military service membership and whose membership in continuous good standing in the Local Union shall not be broken by such service, provided he reports to his Local Union at the time of entering such service or thereafter furnishes the necessary proof of military service. He shall become subject to the provisions of this section at the end of such military service.

Section 11. The International Union shall set aside from each member's monthly per capita tax all amounts in excess of one dollar ($1.00), and the funds resulting shall be a special fund to be known as the International Union Strike Fund to be drawn upon exclusively for the purpose of aiding Local Unions engaged in authorized strikes and in cases of lockouts, and for that purpose only, and then only upon a two-thirds (⅔) vote of the International Executive Board. From the remaining one dollar ($1.00) of each member's per capita tax, the International Union shall set aside:

1. Five cents (.05) which shall be expended only for publication of the "United Automobile Worker," the official publication of the International Union or of any successor official publication.

2. One cent (.01) to the Fair Practices and Anti-Discrimination Fund to be expended only for the support and promotion of the programs and activities of the International Union in support of fair employment practices and in opposition to all discriminatory practices in employment.

3. Three cents (.03) as the International Union Education Fund to be expended only for the programs and activities of the International Union Education Department.

4. One cent (.01) as the International Union Recreation Fund which fund shall be apportioned to each region on a per capita basis.

5. Five cents (.05) as the Special Citizenship Fund to be used for the purpose of strengthening democracy by encouraging members and citizens generally to register and vote in community, state and national elections and to carry on organizational and educational programs directed toward the achievement of an ever higher understanding of citizenship responsibility and the need for active participation in the affairs of a free and democratic society.

Section 12. Monthly dues shall be two dollars and fifty cents ($2.50) per month through April, 1955. Beginning with the month of May, 1955, the monthly dues shall be seven dollars and fifty cents ($7.50) and shall continue at that rate until the International Officers shall certify that there is twenty-five million dollars ($25,000,000.00) in the International Union Strike Fund.

Following such certification, dues shall be two dollars and fifty cents ($2.50) per month beginning with the following month and shall continue at such rate until the International Officers shall certify that there is less than twenty million dollars ($20,000,000.00) in the Strike Fund. Upon such certification, the monthly dues shall be three dollars and fifty cents ($3.50) beginning with the following month. Thereafter dues shall from time to time be decreased to two dollars and fifty cents ($2.50) or increased to three dollars and fifty cents ($3.50); a decrease becoming effective in the month following the month in which the Strike Fund shall have increased to the sum of twenty-five million dollars ($25,000,000.00), and an increase becoming effective in the month following the month in which the Strike Fund shall have declined to twenty million dollars ($20,000,000.00) or less.

Section 13. At least once each month, the International Secretary-Treasurer shall advise all Local Unions of the exact Strike Fund balance.

Section 14. Where Local Unions deem it necessary they may exonerate certain members from the payment of dues to the Local Union. However, such members, with the exception of those holding gratuitous life membership, shall be considered as dues-paying members and per capita tax shall be paid on such members.

Section 15. All per capita taxes, and all other monies collected for the International Union shall be transmitted to the International Secretary-Treasurer by the twentieth of each month following collection. All such per capita taxes and other monies are strictly the property of the International Union and in no case shall any part thereof be used by Local Unions, except upon permission of the International Executive Board.

Section 16. The International Secretary-Treasurer will issue the official receipt of the office of Secretary-Treasurer for all monies collected.

Section 17. Any member who has not worked forty (40) hours or received remuneration in lieu of work equivalent to forty (40) hours' pay within any calendar month shall be entitled to exemption of payment of regular monthly dues in the following manner:

Said member shall report his unemployment in person, or otherwise, to the Financial Secretary of the Local Union within one (1) month of the date he became unemployed. The Financial Secretary shall issue to such member an official memorandum indicating the date upon which the member became unemployed, provided, that no such memorandum shall be issued to the member unless he shall have paid all dues owing by him up to and including the current month. Such member shall be entitled to "out-of-work" receipts bearing the words "Out of Work" or the letters "O/W" upon application made by him within one (1) month after his re-employment or at any time during his period of unemployment, provided that he is eligible to receive the same under the provisions of this Section. Such member shall be exempt from dues payment for the period of his unemployment, provided that he shall have reported his re-employment in person, or otherwise, to the Financial Secretary of the Local Union within one (1) month from the date he became re-employed and provided that he had not worked on any compensable job forty (40) or more hours in any calendar month of unemployment. In those Local Unions covered by check-off provisions, where management notifies the Local Union of members who are on leave of absence, quit, laid off or rehired, the local Financial Secretary shall note such changes on the financial records of the Local Union and it will not be necessary to issue an "out-of-work" receipt.

Section 18. Any member becoming out of work because of illness or injury shall be exempt from the above section. Such members shall be automatically exonerated from the payment of dues and shall be issued out-of-work credits provided good and sufficient proof is submitted to substantiate illness or injury.

Section 19. Any member who has paid his dues by check-off for any month for which the member is exempted from payment of dues under Sections 15 or 16 of this Article shall be entitled to a refund of such dues if he claims the same in person or in writing from the Financial Secretary of the Local Union within two (2) months following the month for which the refund is due. Any member who has paid his dues in advance other than by check-off, for any month for which the member is exempted from payment of dues under Section 15 or 16 of this Article shall when he returns to work, be given credit on future dues for any such month.

Section 20. The Local Union shall use a receipt book or receipting register and form of official receipt furnished by the International Union. All receipts shall be made out in duplicate, the original to be given to the member, the duplicate to be retained by the Local Union and made available to the International Union upon request. The International Secretary-Treasurer may order the destruction of the duplicate receipts when they are no longer necessary.

Section 21. Local Unions covered by check-off agreements or having a check-off arrangement will be exempt from the provisions of the preceding section, providing the company clearly shows on the check stub or pay envelope of each Union employee the amount of the deduction and the reason therefor.

Section 22. A Local Union failing to pay full per capita tax due the International Union within a two (2) months' period, shall stand automatically suspended until the Local Union has been reinstated through payment of deficiency incurred, unless exonerated from payment of same as provided for in this Constitution.

Section 23. A Local Union failing to pay all of its financial obligations due the International Union shall not be entitled to a voice or vote in the International Convention.

Section 24. The failure of a Company to check off and pay to a Local Union the dues of a member as required by a contract will not make the member delinquent if the member has signed a Dues Check-Off Authorization Card. Where a member has signed a Dues Check-Off Authorization Card authorizing the deduction of dues for a given month, the member shall be considered as having paid his dues for that month even though the Company fails to deduct same. Upon the failure of the Company to deduct dues, the Financial Secretary of the Local Union must notify the member to pay his dues. The member shall have sixty (60) days in which to pay his dues after being notified. Failure on the part of the Financial Secretary to so notify a member of his pending delinquency will not affect the member's standing and he shall be considered in good standing in the Local Union.

ARTICLE 17

HONORABLE WITHDRAWAL TRANSFER CARDS

Section 1. All honorable withdrawal transfer cards shall be supplied by the International Secretary-Treasurer; they shall be available to the Local Union in duplicate form in pads and shall be sold at cost.

Section 2. Any member laid off from his plant but regularly employed on jobs outside the jurisdiction of the International Union shall take an honorable withdrawal transfer card, or in order to maintain himself in good standing in his Local Union, shall pay dues in accordance with Article 16 and Article 45.

Any member who has voluntarily separated himself from the jurisdiction of the UAW-CIO shall be issued a withdrawal card immediately by his Local Union. The above shall not apply to those members who are employed by or officially represent the UAW-CIO, National CIO, CIO State, County or City Councils.

Section 3. Any member in good standing at the time of leaving the jurisdiction of his Local Union shall establish his membership in the new Local Union by either of the following:

(a) By obtaining an honorable withdrawal transfer card and depositing same immediately in the new Local Union, but in no case later than the two (2) calendar months in which forty (40) hours are worked.

(b) By payment of an initiation fee and dues to the new Local Union, in which case such member's good standing will start as of the date of such payment.

This shall not apply to members holding a Local Union constitutional office who involuntarily left the jurisdiction of their Local Union. However, while holding such office such member shall not be eligible to hold any constitutional office in, or be a delegate to the International Convention from any Local Union other than the one which he involuntarily left.

Section 4. A member shall be entitled to an honorable withdrawal transfer card provided he shall have his dues paid up to and including the current month, or out-of-work receipts, and there are no charges or debts owed to the Local Union.

Section 5. A member who is transferred to another Local Union and who has paid his dues in advance shall not be required to pay duplicate dues. The Local Union to which the advance dues payments have been made shall forward them to the Local Union to which the member is transferred or refund them to the member.

Section 6. All honorable withdrawal transfer cards issued shall bear the seal of the subordinate body from which issued.

Section 7. A subordinate body may charge a maximum of twenty-five cents (.25) for each honorable withdrawal transfer card issued. No charges shall be made for honorable withdrawal transfer cards received.

Section 8. When a holder of an honorable withdrawal transfer card loses the same he can only receive a duplicate thereof by applying to the Local Union Financial Secretary who issued the same. The Financial Secretary of the Local Union, after sufficient time has elapsed for an investigation to be made, will issue a duplicate honorable withdrawal transfer card upon receipt of the payment of one dollar ($1.00) from the applicant.

Section 9. The International Executive Board shall be empowered to draw up or draft a type of honorable withdrawal transfer card suitable to the requirements of the organization.

Section 10. Honorable withdrawal transfer cards may be terminated by the Local Union issuing them or by International Officers for good and sufficient reasons.

Section 11. A person who has deposited his honorable withdrawal card and thus resumed membership in the Union shall thereupon be subject to charges and trial for acts of conduct detrimental to the interests of the Union or its members, committed while he was out of the Union on honorable withdrawal transfer card. The provisions of Article 48 shall be applicable in such cases.

Section 12. Members transferred from another CIO union to the International Union upon showing evidence of good standing membership in such other CIO union, by depositing said evidence immediately upon coming within the jurisdiction of the UAW Local Union, but in no case later than the end of the first two (2) calendar months in which forty (40) hours are worked, shall be admitted into the International Union, United Automobile, Aircraft and Agricultural Implement Workers of America (UAW-CIO), without payment of an initiation fee or any other type of entry fee. Within Canada the above shall also apply to members of Unions affiliated with the Canadian Congress of Labour.

Section 13. Any Local Union Officer, Shop Committee Member or Shop Steward offered a personnel or labor relations position with management shall secure permission from his Local Union before accepting such position in order to be entitled to an honorable withdrawal transfer card. Members violating this section shall be subject to expulsion from the Union.

Section 14. Any International Officer, Regional Director, International Representative or any other full-time employee of the International Union offered a personnel or labor relations position with management shall secure permission from the International Executive Board before accepting such position in order to be entitled to an honorable withdrawal transfer card. Members violating this section shall be subject to expulsion from the Union.

ARTICLE 18

UNEMPLOYMENT AND WELFARE

Section 1. The various regions where unemployment is a major problem shall make provisions for handling the welfare and unemployment grievances of members laid off from the shops either on a local, district or regional basis.

Section 2. The International Executive Board, upon recommendation of the Regional Board member, may appropriate funds to assist Local Unions or districts where their finances are insufficient to defray necessary expenses of Local

Unions or their district, provided the itemized expenses involved shall be submitted to the International Executive Board.

ARTICLE 19

CONTRACTS AND NEGOTIATIONS

Section 1. It shall be the established policy of the International Union to recognize the spirit, the intent and the terms of all contractual relations developed and existing between Local Unions and employers, concluded out of conferences between the Local Unions and the employers, as binding upon them. Each Local Union shall be required to carry out the provisions of its contracts. No officer, member, representative or agent of the International Union or of any Local Union or of any subordinate body of the International Union shall have the power or authority to counsel, cause, initiate, participate in or ratify any action which constitutes a breach of any contract entered into by a Local Union or by the International Union or a subordinate body thereof. Whenever a Local Union or a manufacturing unit of an Amalgamated Local Union becomes a party to an agreement on wages, hours or working conditions, it shall cause such agreement to be reduced to writing and properly signed by the authorized representatives of all the parties to the agreement.

Section 2. When a grievance exists between a Local Union and management and negotiations are in progress, and an International Union officer or representative is participating by request of the Local Union involved, a committee selected by the Local Union shall participate in all conferences and negotiations. Copies of all contracts shall be filed with the International Secretary-Treasurer.

Section 3. No Local Union Officer, International Officer or International Representative shall have the authority to negotiate the terms of a contract or any supplement thereof with any employer without first obtaining the approval of the Local Union. After negotiations have been concluded with the employer, the proposed contract or supplement shall be submitted to the vote of the Local Union membership or Manufacturing Unit membership in the case of an Amalgamated Local Union at a meeting called especially for such purpose; should the proposed contract or supplement be approved by the majority vote of the Local Union or unit members present at the meeting, it shall be referred to the Regional Director for his recommendation to the International Executive Board for its approval or rejection. In case the regional Board Member recommends approval, the contract becomes operative until the final action is taken by the International Executive Board.

Before contract or supplement demands affecting skilled workers are submitted to the employer, they shall be submitted to the Skilled Trades Department in order to effectuate an industry-wide standardization of agreements on wages, hours, apprenticeship programs, journeyman standards and working conditions.

Section 4. National agreements and supplements thereof shall be ratified by the Local Unions involved.

Section 5. The general meeting of the Local Union members of a manufacturing establishment under the jurisdiction of an Amalgamated Local Union shall be the highest authority for handling problems within the manufacturing establishment, in conformity with the By-Laws of the Local Union and this International Constitution.

Section 6. The International Executive Board shall protect all Local Unions who have succeeded in establishing higher wages and favorable conditions and have superior agreements, so that no infringement by Local Unions with inferior agreements in plants doing similar work may be committed against the Local Union with advanced agreements.

Section 7. Each Local Union or unit of an Amalgamated Local Union shall be required to maintain a complete and up-to-date schedule of job classifications and wage rates; a copy of which must be attached to each contract submitted to the International Union.

ARTICLE 20

NATIONAL AND CORPORATION BARGAINING COUNCILS

Section 1. In cases where there are a number of Local Unions involved in negotiations and bargaining with a major Corporation or an association of Corporations, the International Executive Board shall set up an Intra-Corporation Council. Such Local Unions so involved shall be members and shall participate through duly-elected delegates. When the large Corporation or National Association has widely scattered branches, the Intra-Corporation Council shall set up Sub-Corporation Councils.

Section 2. The International Executive Board shall determine the district in which Sub-Corporation Councils shall be established. The Intra-Corporation Council shall be composed of delegates from the Sub-Corporation Council.

Section 3. Directors to work with such Councils shall be appointed by the President subject to the approval of the International Executive Board.

Section 4. Voting at National Intra-Corporation Council meetings shall be based on per capita tax paid to the International Union by the various Local Unions participating.

Section 5. The purpose of the Intra-Corporation Council shall be to coordinate the demands of the separate members and to formulate policies in dealing with their common employer. The Intra-Corporation Council shall be convened not later than thirty (30) days prior to the opening of negotiations for a new National Corporation agreement to formulate new contract demands. The Council shall deal only with matters pertaining to problems arising in their immediate corporations. It shall be understood that such Intra-Corporation Council is not a legislative body of the International Union and shall not deal with policies of the International Union other than those concerning their own immediate corporation problems.

ARTICLE 21

NATIONAL AND REGIONAL WAGE-HOUR CONFERENCES

Section 1. Upon the written request of a representative number of Local Unions to the Competitive Shop Department and upon the approval of the

International Executive Board, National and Regional Wage-Hour Conferences may be called for the purpose of facilitating a discussion of problems related to wages, hours, production standards and other conditions of work within a competitive or allied group; and to assist in the establishment of uniform contractual provisions within the industry.

Section 2. Activities of both National and Regional Wage-Hour Conferences shall be coordinated through the offices of the Competitive Shop Department in cooperation with the Research Department of the International Union.

ARTICLE 22

NATIONAL AND REGIONAL WAGE-HOUR COUNCILS

National Wage-Hour Councils

National Wage-Hour Councils shall be established by the International Executive Board only in those cases where National Wage-Hour Conferences would prove inadequate in meeting the problem of organizing the unorganized competitive shops and coordinating the work of establishing uniform standards within a competitive group. In the event such Wage-Hour Councils are established, they shall be governed by the following provisions:

Section 1. The National Wage-Hour Councils shall consist of duly elected representatives from the Regional Wage-Hour Councils and plants where there are no Regional Wage-Hour Councils of a single industry.

Section 2. It shall be the duty of the National Wage-Hour Council to assist and cooperate with the Competitive Shop Department and the International President in the organization of unorganized plants.

Section 3. It shall be the duty of the National Wage-Hour Council to work in conjunction with the Competitive Shop Department and in cooperation with the Research Department of the International Union to standardize wages, hours and general working conditions of the organized plants in their industry, and to strive to get a single agreement covering their industry nationally.

Section 4. In case competitive plants in a given industry start negotiations on a national agreement, they shall make use of the National Bargaining Council provisions.

Regional Wage-Hour Councils

Regional Wage-Hour Councils shall be established by the International Executive Board only in those cases where wage-hour conferences would prove inadequate in meeting the problems of organizing the unorganized competitive shops, and coordinating the work of establishing uniform standards within a competitive group. In the event such Wage-Hour Councils are established, they shall be governed by the following provisions:

Section 5. A Regional Wage-Hour Council shall consist of duly elected representatives from plants or departments in plants doing similar work who can conveniently get together.

Section 6. It shall be the duty of the Regional Wage-Hour Council to gather and send to the Research Department of the International Union and the

atinr
ookinggion.

Section 7. It shall be the duty of the Regional Wage-Hour Council to assist in the organization of unorganized plants of their industry under the direction of the Regional Director.

Section 8. It shall be the duty of the Regional Wage-Hour Council to work toward standardization of improved wages, hours and general working conditions of the organized plants of their industry in their region, and to strive to get a single agreement covering their industry in their region.

Section 9. It shall be the duty of the Regional Wage-Hour Council to send regular reports to the National Wage-Hour Council in their industry and to the Competitive Shop Department of the International Union.

Section 10. It shall be the duty of the Regional Wage-Hour Council to send delegates to, and assist in the formation of, a National Wage-Hour Council for their industry.

Section 11. It shall be understood that such Wage-Hour Councils are not legislative bodies of the International Union and shall not deal with policies of the International Union other than those concerning competitive plant problems.

ARTICLE 23

COMPETITIVE SHOP DEPARTMENT

Section 1. The International Executive Board shall create a Competitive Shop Department for the International Union.

Section 2. The International President shall appoint a director for the Competitive Shop Department, subject to the approval of the International Executive Board, who is best qualified by experience and who now is and has been a member of the Union for at least two (2) years. The International Executive Board may remove the director of the Competitive Shop Department.

Section 3. It shall be the duty of the Competitive Shop Department to aid in organizing and calling National and Regional Wage-Hour Conferences. National and Regional Wage-Hour Conferences may be called by the Director of the Competitive Shop Department after consultation with the Regional Director concerned, subject to the approval of the International Executive Board.

Section 4. It shall be the duty of the Competitive Shop Department to direct the organization of unorganized competitive shops by making recommendations for assignment of organizers to the Regional Directors, the International President and the International Executive Board.

Section 5. Organizers working on such assignment shall make reports on the progress of organization to the Competitive Shop Department as well as to their Regional Directors.

Section 6. It shall be the duty of the Competitive Shop Department to check all agreements referred to it by the International Executive Board, and to make recommendations to the various Local Unions for the standardization of wage-hour provisions throughout given competitive industries.

ARTICLE 24

RESEARCH DEPARTMENT

Section 1. The International Executive Board shall create a Research Department for the International Union.

Section 2. The President of the International Union shall appoint a director for the Research Department who shall be selected from the International Union, if possible, and who is competent and qualified by previous experience and training to do such work; but such appointment shall not be considered final until it is approved by the International Executive Board at their next meeting. It shall be mandatory that the International Research Department shall be kept informed of changes in rates, working standards and so forth by all Local Unions.

Section 3. It shall gather and keep on file information on wages, hours and other conditions of employment and any general information about the automotive, aircraft and agricultural implement industries.

Section 4. It shall gather and keep on file any other information which the International Executive Board, Regional Directors, Local Unions, Wage-Hour Councils or any other subdivision of the International Union may require from time to time.

Section 5. It shall send to all International Executive Board Members, International Representatives, Local Unions and Wage-Hour Councils a periodic bulletin on problems of general interest to the members of the Union.

Section 6. It shall submit to the International Executive Board meetings, a regular report on general conditions in the automotive, aircraft and agricultural implement industries which are of importance to the International Union.

Section 7. It shall submit a complete and thorough report to the conventions of the International Union on the automotive, aircraft and agricultural implement industries and the International Union.

Section 8. It shall supply Wage-Hour Councils with financial reports of parts plants in their industry and such other material as they may request.

ARTICLE 25

FAIR PRACTICES AND ANTI-DISCRIMINATION DEPARTMENT

Section 1. There is hereby created a department to be known as the Fair Practices and Anti-Discrimination Department of the International Union.

Section 2. The International President shall appoint a committee composed of International Executive Board members to handle the functions of this department. He shall also appoint a director who shall be a member of the Union and approved by the International Executive Board. He shall also appoint a staff which shall be qualified by previous experience and training in the field of inter-racial, inter-faith and inter-cultural relations.

Section 3. One cent (.01) per month per dues-paying member of the per capita forwarded to the International Union by Local Unions shall be used as the Fair Practices and Anti-Discrimination Fund of the International Union as provided in this Constitution.

Section 4. The department shall be charged with the duty of implementing the policies of the International Union dealing with discrimination, as these policies are set forth in the International Constitution and as they may be evidenced by action of the International Executive Board and of International Conventions, and to give all possible assistance and guidance to Local Unions in the furtherance of their duties as set forth in this article, and to carry out such further duties as may be assigned to it from time to time by the International President or the International Executive Board.

Section 5. It shall be mandatory that each Local Union set up a Fair Practices and Anti-Discrimination Committee. The specific duties of this Committee shall be to promote fair employment practices and endeavor to eliminate discrimination affecting the welfare of the individual members of the Local Union, the International Union, the labor movement and the nation.

ARTICLE 26

EDUCATIONAL DEPARTMENT

Section 1. Education shall be a mandatory part of the business of the International Union and of each Local Union, particularly education in labor history, labor problems, the objectives of the International Union and the problems of the International Union, its members and their families.

Section 2. The International President shall appoint an Educational Director over the Educational Department, and such appointment shall be subject to approval of the International Executive Board.

Section 3. Four cents (.04) per month per dues-paying member of the per capita forwarded to the International Union by Local Unions shall be used as the Educational and Recreational Fund of the International Union, as provided in this Constitution.

Section 4. Three cents (.03) of such per capita tax shall be used for educational purposes and one cent (.01) shall be used for recreational purposes.

Section 5. It shall be mandatory that each Local Union set up an Education Committee. The duties of this committee shall be to promote all branches of education affecting the welfare of the individual members, the Local Union, the International Union, and the labor movement. It shall be the duty of the Regional Director to see that this provision of the Constitution is carried out.

Section 6. There shall be established educational areas throughout the International Union to which educational representatives shall be assigned. These educational representatives shall be appointed by the President to work under the direction of the International Education Director, and such appointments shall be approved by the Regional Director(s) in whose area(s) they shall serve.

Section 7. Each Local Union must set aside a separate fund of three cents (.03) per month per dues-paying member to finance the Educational and Recreational Activities of the Local Union. The pro-rating of this fund shall be in such manner as the Local Union may determine.

UNION LABEL

Section 1. The International Union shall have a union label and stamp.

Section 2. It shall be the duty of the International Secretary-Treasurer to copyright and protect said union label and stamp.

Section 3. It shall be the policy of the International Union and subordinate bodies to insist that all parts, stampings, tools, dies, machinery, fixtures, accessories and supplies used in the manufacture of articles under the jurisdiction of this International Union, bear the union label or union stamp of the International Union, or any other bona fide labor union.

Section 4. It shall be the duty of all representatives, business agents and union officials to insist that the above provisions be written into all contracts between employers and the International Union subject to approval of the International Executive Board.

Section 5. No manufacturer of products produced by workers under the jurisdiction of this International Union shall be permitted to use the union label or union stamp unless the plant is holding a contract approved by the International Executive Board, with the International Union.

Section 6. It shall be the duty of the Local Union Label Committee to see that the International Union label shall be molded, stamped or affixed to all parts manufactured, assembled or finished products where provided for.

Section 7. The above provisions shall in no case be used as a basis for the violation of existing agreements.

Section 8. All Local Unions shall have an appointed or elected Union Label Committee that must function.

Section 9. At all conventions of the International Union, a necessary qualification of delegates shall be the possession and wearing of at least three (3) union-made garments.

Section 10. The International Executive Board shall set up a Union Label Committee from members of the International Union to coordinate the activities of Local Union Label Committees throughout the International Union. It shall be the duty of this committee to work in conjunction with the Educational Department of the International Union and the Congress of Industrial Organizations' Union Label Committee.

ARTICLE 28

OFFICIAL PUBLICATION

Section 1. There shall be published at least once a month by the International Union a publication designed to educate the membership and to acquaint the membership with the activities of this International Union. The title of said publication shall be "United Automobile Worker," or its successor designation, Official Publication of the International Union.

Section 2. The "United Automobile Worker" shall be under the supervision of the International Executive Board who shall select a Publication Committee consisting of the International President and two other members of the International Executive Board. The Publication Committee shall be directly responsible to the International Executive Board in carrying out the task of publishing the "United Automobile Worker." The Editors of the "United Automobile Worker" shall be appointed by the International President, subject to the approval of the International Executive Board.

Section 3. The International Secretary-Treasurer shall allocate out of each per capita tax, five cents (.05) for a special fund for the "United Automobile Worker."

Section 4. The subscription rate of the "United Automobile Worker" shall be sixty cents (.60) per annum, payable as provided in this Constitution.

Section 5. This publication is to be sent through the United States mail to each member in good standing.

Section 6. To non-members the rate shall be one dollar ($1.00) per annum with postage additional for foreign subscribers.

Section 7. Price of single copies shall be five cents (.05).

Section 8. Local publications shall conform with the policies of the International Union.

ARTICLE 29

CHARGES AND TRIALS OF INTERNATIONAL OFFICERS

Section 1. Charges against International Officers or International Executive Board Members may be filed in either of these manners:

(a) Upon written affidavit signed by five (5) or more Board Members and filed with the International Secretary-Treasurer.

(b) Upon written affidavit signed by a Local Union member and endorsed by his own Local Union and by at least ten (10) additional Local Unions in the International Union, or in the case of charges against an International Executive Board Member, upon written affidavit signed by the Local Union member and endorsed by his own Local Union and a majority of the Local Unions within the region from which the International Executive Board Member is elected.

Section 2. In case the charges to be filed are against the International Secretary-Treasurer they shall be filed with the International President who shall in that case alone perform the duties with reference to the trial procedure.

Section 3. Upon receipt of the charges the International Secretary-Treasurer shall immediately send a copy of the charges by receipted registered mail to the accused and copies to all International Executive Board Members, notifying the accused that he has fifteen (15) days to prepare a defense and notifying the International Executive Board Members of a Special International Executive Board Meeting to be called ten (10) days following filing of the charges.

Section 4. Pending the trial, the International Officer or International Executive Board Member accused shall continue to function in his elected capacity unless a Special International Executive Board Meeting is convened and votes by a two-thirds (⅔) vote for his suspension as otherwise provided in this Constitution.

Section 5. The first order of business at the Special International Executive Board Meeting shall be the setting up of an International Union Trial Committee. This Committee shall be chosen from among present members in good standing who were seated delegates at the last preceding International Union Convention, but excluding any such who, at the time of selection of the Trial Committee panel, are officers or employees of the International Union or are members of the International Executive Board. The name of each member qualified as aforesaid for service on the Trial Committee shall be written on a slip of paper on which shall also appear the number and location of the Local Union from which he was a delegate, the said slips being all of uniform size and appearance. The said slips of paper shall be deposited in a box by the Secretary-Treasurer in the presence of the International Executive Board and the box shall be sealed and thoroughly shaken. The International Secretary-Treasurer shall then open the container and the member of the International Executive Board selected for that purpose and blindfolded shall draw the names of fifty (50) delegates, one by one. After these names are drawn they shall be read by the International Secretary-Treasurer in the presence of the International Executive Board and each name in succession shall be set opposite a number from one (1) to fifty (50).

Section 6. During the drawing of the names, the accused or his personal representative shall have the right to be present, as may the accuser or a representative of the accuser.

Section 7. Immediately following the drawing of the panel, the Trial Committee shall be chosen. The accused and the accuser shall each have the right to strike ten (10) names from the panel. Either may waive the right in whole or in part, striking in such case, less than ten (10) names but the right of either party to strike ten (10) names shall not be affected by any such waiver by the other. The parties shall proceed alternately in striking names from the panel, beginning with the accused.

Section 8. After these challenges have been made the first twelve (12) persons whose names remain on the list shall be notified to report to the International Office within five (5) days to proceed with the trial. Local Unions shall also be notified when any of their members' names are drawn for service on the International Trial Committee.

Section 9. Such an order shall be mandatory upon any member of the Union receiving this notice. Should he fail to appear, unless his absence is excused by a signed affidavit of illness or Local Union emergency, attested to by the Executive Board of his Local Union, such a member may be subject to charges in his Local Union, and to expulsion.

Section 10. Upon his appearance at the International Office, each member of the Trial Committee thus notified shall produce affidavit attesting his membership in good standing in his Local Union, signed by the Financial Secretary of his Local Union.

Section 11. In case one (1) or more members of the Trial Committee thus notified shall fail to appear for the above reasons or fail to produce such certificate of membership in good standing, the next member of the panel, numbering down from one (1) to fifty (50) shall be notified to report.

Section 12. The International Trial Committee shall go into session immediately upon arrival of the full panel and shall hear the charges brought by the accuser and all the witnesses named for substantiation, and shall hear the defense of the accused and all his witnesses for substantiation. The Trial Committee shall decide its own rules of procedure relating to the conduct of the trial and may elect its own Chairman and Secretary, providing that verbatim minutes of all evidence shall be reported by a court stenographer. The accused and the accuser shall have a right to be represented by counsel.

Section 13. The Trial Committee, upon completion of the hearing on the evidence and arguments, shall go into closed session to determine the verdict and penalty. A two-thirds (⅔) vote shall be required to find the accused guilty. In case the accused is found guilty, the Trial Committee may, by a majority vote, reprimand the accused or it may, by a two-thirds (⅔) vote, assess a fine not to exceed five hundred dollars ($500.00), with automatic suspension, removal from office or expulsion in the event of the failure of the accused to pay the fine within a specified time; or it may, by a two-thirds (⅔) vote, suspend or remove the accused from office, or suspend or expel him from membership in the International Union.

Section 14. In case a Trial Committee finds the accused innocent they may determine the honest or malicious intent of the accuser. If they find the accuser guilty of obvious malice in filing the charges they may assess a penalty against him in accordance with Section 13 of this Article.

Section 15. Charges against an International Officer or International Executive Board Member, concerning his own Local Union, shall not be filed according to Local Union trial procedure, but in accordance with the above provisions.

ARTICLE 30

APPEALS

Section 1. All subordinate bodies of the International Union and members thereof shall be entitled to the right of appeal.

Section 2. If a subordinate body, or member thereof, wishes to appeal from any action, decision or penalty, he shall appeal to the International Executive Board, and if it is desired to appeal the decision of the International Executive Board, an appeal may be taken therefrom to the next International Convention. The decision of the Convention shall be final. In all cases, however, the decision of the lower tribunal must be complied with before the right to appeal can be accepted by the next tribunal in authority, and shall remain in effect until reversed or modified.

Section 3. Any member wishing to appeal from the action, decision or penalty of his subordinate body shall do so in writing within thirty (30) days after the aforesaid action, decision or penalty, and he must notify said subordinate body of his intention in writing. It shall then be the duty of the subordinate body to forward to the International Secretary-Treasurer a complete statement of the matters in issue, including copies of all charges, records, minutes, transcripts of testimony, and all other material relating to the appeal.

Section 4. Any subordinate body or member thereof wishing to appeal from any action, decision or penalty of the International Executive Board to the Convention of the International Union, must serve notice of appeal upon, and file a written statement of his grievance with the International Secretary-Treasurer within sixty (60) days after such decision is rendered, provided, however, that in any case the appeal must be made, in conformity with this procedure, to the Convention next following the date of the action of the International Executive Board; and provided further, that where the action of the International Executive Board is taken less than sixty (60) days before the date of the Convention, the International Executive Board must give the parties immediate notice of the action taken on the appeal made to it.

Section 5. The International President may extend the time for filing any appeal if in his opinion justice will be served thereby.

Section 6. In no case shall a member or subordinate body appeal to a Civil Court for redress until he or it has exhausted his or its rights of appeal under the laws of this International Union. Any violation of this section shall be cause for summary suspension or expulsion, or for revocation of Charter, by a two-thirds vote of the International Executive Board.

ARTICLE 31

DISTRICT COUNCILS

Section 1. When a majority of Local Unions of this International Union representing a majority of the membership within their geographical district, request the establishment of a District Council, such Local Union representatives shall be assembled by the Regional Directors of that area for the formation of such a Council.

Section 2. When such a District Council is established, it shall be mandatory for all Local Unions of this International Union to affiliate with the Council of their geographical district and obtain a charter from the International Union.

Section 3. The purpose of the District Council shall be to recommend to the Regional Director and the International Union, constructive measures for the welfare of Local Unions and their members. It shall discuss comparative wages, rates, agreements, methods of approach, organizational problems, National, State and Provincial legislative programs and such other problems as may be of general interest to the Local Union membership.

Section 4. The District Council shall be composed of delegates elected from the Local Unions at the formation of the Council and each year thereafter on the basis of Convention procedure. To avoid unnecessary expense in District Councils, Local Unions may empower as many delegates as they desire to carry and vote the entire vote of the Local Union.

Section 5. Activities of the District Councils shall be financed by the payment of a per capita tax of not more than one cent (.01) per member per month by each Local Union affiliated with the District Council.

Section 6. The per capita tax may be used to assist in organizational work, prepare educational literature, lobby for legislative programs and programs of benefit to its affiliated Local Unions.

Section 7. When a subordinate body has failed to report and pay the per capita tax to the District Council, the District Council Secretary-Treasurer shall report this fact to the International Secretary-Treasurer; the International Secretary-Treasurer shall notify the Subordinate Body President and Board of Trustees. Such subordinate body shall stand suspended until such deficiency is made good.

Section 8. The District Council shall draft its By-Laws in conformity with this Constitution and subject to the approval of the International Executive Board.

Section 9. To dissolve a District Council the Regional Director(s), on the request of three (3) Local Unions within the geographical district, shall call a special meeting of the Council to be held within thirty (30) days of such request, with proper notice of the purpose of the meeting, to vote upon the dissolution of the Council. At this meeting the District Council may be dissolved by a vote of a majority of the Local Unions representing a majority of the membership within the geographical district.

ARTICLE 32

AMALGAMATED LOCAL UNIONS

Section 1. Any two (2) or more manufacturing units who are not a part of an Amalgamated Local Union may petition the International Executive Board for the formation of an Amalgamated Local Union. Such petitions must be approved by the membership of the manufacturing units desiring an Amalgamated Local Union in a specially called membership meeting for that purpose. Upon receipt of such petitions the International Executive Board shall investigate the feasibility of an Amalgamated Local Union and if their decision is that an Amalgamated Local Union be set up, the Regional Director shall without delay set up an Amalgamated Local Union comprising the manufacturing units as determined by the International Executive Board.

Section 2. Any two (2) or more manufacturing units of an Amalgamated Local Union may petition the International Executive Board to set up a Joint Council in their Local Union. The International Executive Board shall without undue delay investigate the practicality of a Joint Council for that Local Union and if they determine that a Joint Council shall be set up, the Local Union shall without delay set up a Joint Council based on the principles in Section 3 of this Article.

Section 3. The membership of the Local Union shall be guaranteed:

(a) Proportional representation from each manufacturing unit, based on the dues dollar each manufacturing unit pays to the Local Union. In no case shall any manufacturing unit be entitled to less than two (2) representatives to the Joint Council.

(*b*) The right to appeal from any decision of the Joint Council by referendum vote of the membership.

(*c*) That each manufacturing unit will have unit autonomy on matters pertaining strictly to that unit.

(*d*) That a percentage of every dues dollar which a manufacturing unit pays to the Local Union may be set aside as a fund for the use of that manufacturing unit for whatever purpose they so desire.

Section 4. Additional organized manufacturing units may be added to Amalgamated Local Unions only upon approval of the International Executive Board and subject to the majority vote of the membership of the unit and the Joint Council or membership of the Amalgamated Local Union. Unorganized manufacturing units may be added to an Amalgamated Local Union upon the approval of the Regional Director.

ARTICLE 33

LOCAL UNION CHARTERS

Section 1. A Local Union may be formed by fifteen (15) or more persons working within the jurisdiction of the International Union by applying to the International Secretary-Treasurer for a charter.

Section 2. The International Secretary-Treasurer shall furnish the applicants for a charter with an application blank, and when the same has been properly filled out and returned with fifteen dollars ($15.00) charter fee, upon approval of the International Executive Board, a charter shall be granted and a seal and initial supplies furnished.

Section 3. The charter fee for subordinate bodies shall be fifteen dollars ($15.00), which shall entitle the Local Union to a charter, one (1) membership receipt book, one (1) International bookkeeping set, one (1) Recording Secretary's minute book, fifteen (15) Constitutions, one (1) roll call book and one (1) gavel.

Section 4. The charter and supplies shall remain the property of the International Union, to be used by the Local Union only as long as said Local Union and its members comply with the laws of the International Union.

Section 5. The charters to be issued to subordinate bodies shall be in the following form:

CHARTER

To All Whom These Presents Shall Come:

Know Ye, that the International Union, UNITED AUTOMOBILE, AIRCRAFT AND AGRICULTURAL IMPLEMENT WORKERS OF AMERICA (UAW-CIO), affiliated with the Congress of Industrial Organizations, established for the purpose of effecting through organization of the Automotive Industry, and composed of Local Unions and Members in different sections of the country, doth, upon proper application and under conditions herein provided hereby grant unto

....

....

....

and to their successors, this Charter for the establishment and future maintenance of a Local Union at ....

....

to be known as Local Union No. ....

of ....

Now, the conditions of this Charter are such: That said Union forever and
under any and all circumstances shall be subordinate to and comply with all
the requirements of the Constitution, By-Laws and General Laws or other laws
of the International Union, UNITED AUTOMOBILE, AIRCRAFT AND AGRICULTURAL
IMPLEMENT WORKERS OF AMERICA (UAW-CIO), as they may from time to time
be altered or amended; That said Union shall for all time be guided and controlled by all acts and decisions of the International Union, UNITED AUTO-
MOBILE, AIRCRAFT AND AGRICULTURAL IMPLEMENT WORKERS OF AMERICA
(UAW-CIO), as they may from time to time be enacted; That should the
Local Union above chartered take advantage of any powers, privileges or rights
conferred under the laws as they may exist at any time, said action shall not
prevent the International Union, UNITED AUTOMOBILE, AIRCRAFT AND AGRI-
CULTURAL IMPLEMENT WORKERS OF AMERICA (UAW-CIO) from recalling,
amending, changing or abolishing any such powers, privileges or rights.

So long as the said Union adheres to these conditions, this Charter to remain
in full force; but upon infraction thereof, the International Union, UNITED
AUTOMOBILE, AIRCRAFT AND AGRICULTURAL IMPLEMENT WORKERS OF AMERICA
(UAW-CIO) may revoke this Charter, thereby annulling all privileges secured
hereunder.

In Witness Whereof, We have hereunto set our hands and affixed the Seal of
the International Union, UNITED AUTOMOBILE, AIRCRAFT AND AGRICULTURAL
IMPLEMENT WORKERS OF AMERICA (UAW-CIO) this .... day of
...................., 19 .....

INTERNATIONAL EXECUTIVE BOARD

....
International President.

....
International Secretary-Treasurer.

Section 6. No Local Union, Women's Auxiliary, or subordinate body shall
disband as long as fifteen (15) members or two (2) Local Unions desire to
retain the charter, and then only upon the approval of the International Executive Board. In localities where there are two (2) or more Local Unions and
where the membership of any Local Union drops below fifteen (15) members
in good standing, such Local Union may be merged with another Local Union
in that locality, at the discretion of the International Executive Board.

Section 7. The above section shall not apply to the issuance of charters
covering plants under the jurisdiction of a previously chartered Amalgamated
Local Union.

Section 8. If a Local Union disbands, or if a Local Union goes out of
existence by reason of cessation of production at the plant over which it has

jurisdiction, all of the funds, property and assets of the Local Union shall forthwith revert to and become the property and assets of the International Union. If, within one (1) year thereafter, a new charter is issued to a Local Union with the same or similar jurisdiction, the International Executive Board shall, in order to aid such newly chartered Local Union in the commencement of its operations, make an appropriation to it in an amount not to exceed the value of such funds, property and assets.

Section 9. If, as the result of a drastic reduction in the membership of a Local Union because of lay-offs or other reasons, the funds, property and assets of such Local Union become grossly disproportionate to the number of members remaining, the International Executive Board may, by seven-eighths vote, after a hearing, and for such period of time as it may deem necessary, take possession of and assume control over the expenditure and use of such funds, property and assets, for the purpose of insuring their application in furtherance of the objectives of the Local Union and the International Union, and their conservation in the interest of the membership of the Local Union, as then existing and as subsequently augmented.

Section 10. In case the membership of a unit covered by the jurisdiction of an Amalgamated Local Union desires to withdraw from the Local Union, such desire may be raised in any regularly called meeting. If approved by a majority vote of such meeting a date shall be set for a special meeting to discuss and decide whether a vote shall be taken on such proposed withdrawal. The membership of such unit shall be given at least seven (7) days' notice of the time, place and purpose of such special meeting. If at this meeting a two-thirds majority of the members present vote in favor of holding an election to decide the issue, the membership of such unit shall be given at least seven (7) days' notice of the time, place, and purpose of such election. Voting in such election shall be by secret ballot in booths conveniently located to allow all members an opportunity to vote.

All ballots shall have printed thereon the following words, "Are you in favor of applying for a separate UAW-CIO charter for .... Unit of Local ....? Yes ___ No ___."

In the event that the members present at the special meeting provided for in this Section decide against holding an election or in the event that the vote in such election does not obtain the required majority, the question shall not be acted or voted on again for a period of two (2) years.

Section 11. In the event an Amalgamated Local Union desires to discontinue the affiliation of a unit of the local Union, such desire may be raised in any regularly called meeting of the Local Union membership, or the Joint Council where such body exists. If approved by a majority vote of such meeting a date shall be set for a special meeting to discuss and decide whether a vote shall be taken on the proposed discontinuation of affiliation. The membership, or Joint Council delegates where such body exists, shall be given at least seven (7) days' notice of the time, place, and purpose of such special meeting. If at this meeting a two-thirds (⅔) majority of the members (or Joint Council delegates) present vote in favor of holding an election to decide the issue, the Local

Union membership shall be given at least seven (7) days' notice of the time, place, and purpose of such election. Voting in such election shall be by secret ballot in booths conveniently located to allow all members an opportunity to vote.

All ballots shall have printed thereon the following words only: "Are you in favor of discontinuing the affiliation of the .... Unit of Local ....? Yes — No —."

In the event that the members (or Joint Council delegates, where such body exists) present at the special meeting provided for in this Section decide against holding an election or in the event that the vote of the Local Union membership voting in such election does not obtain the required majority, the question shall not be acted or voted on again for a period of two (2) years.

Section 12. In case a two-thirds (⅔) majority of the unit membership voting vote in favor of applying for a separate UAW-CIO charter as provided for in Section 10 or two-thirds (⅔) of an Amalgamated Local Union membership voting vote in favor of discontinuing the affiliation of a unit as provided in Section 11, the International Executive Board may issue a separate charter.

Section 13. All funds and other assets of an Amalgamated Local Union shall be and remain the property of the membership of that Local Union, and any unit withdrawing from an Amalgamated Local Union and obtaining a separate charter shall only be entitled to the balance of such funds or property as may have been allocated to it by the Local Union up to the time of separation where such unit funds are established.

ARTICLE 34

DUTIES AND POWERS OF SUBORDINATE BODIES

Section 1. It shall be mandatory for all Local Unions of the International Union to affiliate with State or Provincial Industrial Union Councils.

Section 2. It shall be mandatory for all Local Unions to affiliate with CIO City or County bodies and Councils of the Canadian Congress of Labour wherever such bodies are established, unless this requirement is otherwise waived by the Executive Board of the International Union.

Section 3. All subordinate bodies shall submit any and all laws governing said subordinate bodies to the International Executive Board for ratification of same.

Section 4. Each Local Union, other than an Amalgamated Local Union shall hold a regular general membership meeting at least once a month.

An Amalgamated Local Union that has a Joint Council, established in accordance with Article 32, Section 2, shall have meetings of such Joint Council at least once a month, and shall hold a general membership meeting at least once a year. Amalgamated Local Unions without a Joint Council shall hold a regular general membership meeting at least once every three (3) months.

Plant units of all Amalgamated Local Unions shall hold membership meetings at least once a month.

Section 5. Local Unions may levy fines for non-attendance at membership meetings and for other reasons, provided that such fines do not exceed one dollar ($1.00), and further provided that the provisions for such fines (1) are properly adopted by the Local Union, (2) are approved by the International Executive Board, and (3) are administered on a reasonable and non-excessive basis. In cases where the facts involving the application of such fines are not in dispute, the Local Union is empowered to provide for the forfeiture of the membership of the delinquent member for non-payment thereof without the necessity of proceeding by the filing of charges and the conduct of a trial.

Section 6. Local Unions shall make reasonable provisions in their by-laws, or in case Local Unions have no by-laws, rules governing the attendance at meetings by members holding any Local Union elective position. The Local Union shall establish penalties that may include automatic removal from such office or position upon their failure to attend a stipulated number of meetings as required by their by-laws or rules. Local Union by-laws so amended or rules established where Local Union by-laws do not exist must be submitted to and approved by the International Executive Board before becoming effective.

Section 7. Each subordinate body shall strive to attain the objectives set forth in this Constitution; to maintain free relations with other organizations; to do all in its power to strengthen and promote the labor movement; to cooperate with Regional Board Members, the International Representatives and help promote organizational activities.

Section 8. No Local Union or other subordinate body, and no officer, agent, representative or member thereof shall have the power or authority to represent, act for, commit or bind the International Union in any matter except upon express authority having been granted therefor in writing by the International Executive Board or the International President.

ARTICLE 35

LOCAL UNION SEAL AND BUTTONS

Section 1. The International Union shall provide each Local Union with the official seal which shall be held in the custody of such Local Union officer or officers as each Local Union may decide and shall be used only on documents or communications for which its use has been specifically authorized by the Local Union.

Section 2. Any member who shall counterfeit, imitate or falsify the International Union dues receipts, insignia, seal, label or buttons, or knowingly use such imitations or counterfeits, shall be fined or expelled from this Union, as the circumstances may warrant after trial has been accorded the accused.

Section 3. The International Union shall provide uniform monthly dues buttons, at not more than cost, of a different color for each month. It shall be mandatory for Local Unions using dues buttons to use only those buttons provided by the International Union, which shall be supplied by the International Secretary-Treasurer to the Financial Secretaries of the Local Unions upon request. Local Unions covered by Union Shop or check-off agreements may, upon approval of the International Executive Board, use an annual membership button, membership card or other suitable identification of membership in lieu of monthly dues buttons.

ARTICLE 36

LOCAL UNION OFFICERS

Section 1. Each Local Union shall have the following Executive Officers: President, Vice-President or Vice-Presidents, Recording Secretary, Financial Secretary, Treasurer, three (3) Trustees, Sergeant-at-Arms and Guide.

Section 2. The election of Local Officers shall take place by secret ballot during May and June and installation shall take place at the next regular meeting following the election, except as otherwise authorized by the International Executive Board. After the deadline on accepting nominations has expired, no election of so-called "sticker" or "write-in" candidates shall be considered legal. Election of all Local Union Officers shall require a majority of the votes cast for the office. The membership shall be duly notified at least seven (7) days in advance of the time and place of nominations and of elections, and at least seven (7) days shall elapse between the time of nominations and the date the election shall take place.

Section 3. These officers shall serve for the period of one (1) year with the exception of the Trustees, who shall serve for three (3) years each. In the original election of Trustees, one shall be elected for one (1) year, one for two (2) years, and one for three (3) years, and at each subsequent election as the vacancies appear each Trustee shall be elected for a three (3) year term.

Notwithstanding the provisions of this section, however, a Local Union may elect its Local Union or unit officers for a two (2) year term by enacting appropriate membership action to that effect. Under these conditions the following provisions would apply:

These officers shall serve for a period of two (2) years with the exception of Trustees who shall serve for four (4) years each. In the original election of Trustees in new Local Unions two (2) Trustees shall be elected for a four (4) year term of office and one (1) for a two (2) year term and at each subsequent election the Trustee or Trustees as their terms expire shall be elected for four (4) year terms of office.

Section 4. No member shall be eligible for election as an Executive Officer of the Local Union until he has been a member in continuous good standing in the Local Union for one (1) year immediately prior to the nomination, except in the case of a newly organized Local Union.

Section 5. Eligibility for election to other Local Union offices, committees, etc., shall be determined by the Local Union.

Section 6. The Executive Board of each Local Union shall consist of all the elected Local Union officers and such members at large as the Local Union may deem necessary.

Section 7. The Executive Board shall be empowered to represent the Local Union between meetings of the Local Union when urgent business requires prompt and decisive action. In no case, however, shall the Executive Board transact any business that may affect the vital interests of the Local Union until the approval of the membership is secured, or of the shop organization in the case of an Amalgamated Local Union.

Section 8. Any member of the Executive Board who is not directly elected to the Board, but who holds such office by virtue of his holding some other office or position in the Local Union or shop organization shall, upon ceasing to hold the latter office or position, automatically cease to hold the office of Executive Board Member.

Section 9. At the discretion of the Local Union the offices of Financial Secretary and Treasurer may be combined.

Section 10. The following rules shall be mandatory in all Local Union elections:

(a) Every member in good standing shall be entitled to vote at all Local Union elections.

(b) All elections shall be held under the supervision of a democratically elected Election Committee.

(c) No candidate in any election shall be a member of the Election Committee having supervision over such election.

(d) Any eligible candidate in any election shall have the right to submit his commonly known name to the Election Committee in writing as he desires it to appear on the ballot; and it shall so appear.

(e) Each candidate shall have the right to have one (1) challenger present when the votes are cast and when they are tabulated, provided that such challenger shall be a member of the Local Union.

Section 11. All vacancies in Local Union offices, except the office of President, shall be promptly filled by election, provided that the Local Union may provide other means for filling such vacancies for the temporary period pending the holding of the election. In case of a vacancy in the office of President, the Vice-President shall fill the vacancy for the unexpired term, provided that where there are two (2) or more Vice-Presidents, the Local Union shall establish fair and reasonable procedure for determining which of the Vice-Presidents shall fill the vacancy.

Section 12. Local Unions may elect a Business Agent if they so desire, provided he has been a member of the International Union in continuous good standing for a period of one (1) year.

Section 13. If a member holding Executive Office, the term of which is not expiring, desires to become a candidate for another Executive Office, such member is obligated to notify the Local Union of his resignation from his present office sufficiently in advance of the nominating meeting to permit the nomination and election of candidates for both offices during the same election. Such resignation would become effective at the time of installation.

Section 14. Whenever there are unopposed candidates for Local Union Executive Office, such candidates shall be considered elected without the necessity of an election. Where run-off elections are necessary because a candidate for Local Union Executive Office fails to receive a majority vote, the run-off shall be confined to the two (2) candidates receiving the highest number of votes for the office involved.

ARTICLE 37

INSTALLATION CEREMONY

The installation ceremony may be performed by the retiring President, Acting President or any regular commissioned International Representative.

The Installing Officer says:

"Give attention while I read to you the obligation:

"Do you hereby pledge on your honor to perform the duties of your respective offices as required by the Constitution of this Union; to bear true and faithful allegiance to the International Union, UNITED AUTOMOBILE, AIRCRAFT AND AGRICULTURAL IMPLEMENT WORKERS OF AMERICA (UAW-CIO); to deliver all books, papers and other property of the Union that may be in your possession at the end of your term to your successor in office, and at all times conduct yourself as becomes a member of this Union?"

Officers respond, "I do."

The Installing Officer then says:

"Your duties are defined in the laws of the International Union, UNITED AUTOMOBILE, AIRCRAFT AND AGRICULTURAL IMPLEMENT WORKERS OF AMERICA (UAW-CIO) and in your obligation; should any emergency arise not provided for in these, you are expected to act according to the dictates of common sense, guided by an earnest desire to advance the best interest of the International Union and this Local Union. I trust you will all faithfully perform your duties, so that you may gain not only the esteem of your brothers, but what is of even more importance, the approval of your conscience.

"You will now assume your respective stations."

ARTICLE 38

DUTIES OF LOCAL UNION OFFICERS

President

Section 1. It shall be the duty of the President to preside at all meetings of the Local Union, sign all orders on the Treasury authorized by the Local Union, countersign all checks issued by the Financial Secretary against accounts of the Local Union when ordered by the Union, enforce the provisions of the Constitution and appoint committees not otherwise provided for. He shall be a member ex-officio of all committees.

Vice-President

Section 2. The Vice-President or Vice-Presidents shall assist the President in the discharge of his duties, and shall attend all sessions of the Local Union. In case of the absence or incapacity of the President, his duties shall be performed by the Vice-President, provided that where there are two (2) or more Vice-Presidents, the Local Union shall determine which of them shall perform such duties.

Recording Secretary

Section 3. It shall be the duty of the Recording Secretary to keep a correct record of the proceedings of the Local Union, sign all orders on the treasury authorized by the Local Union, read all documents and conduct the general correspondence received by the Local Union which does not pertain directly to the duties of the other officers of the Local Union, and keep same on file for future reference. He shall bring to the attention of the membership of the Local Union any correspondence upon which the membership must take action. He shall comply with the provisions of Article 49, Section 2. He shall furnish to the Research Department of the UAW-CIO and to his Regional Director, every six (6) months (in January and July): (1) Three (3) copies of the existing contract(s); (2) A complete revised list of all classifications and rates for the plant or plants covered by the contract(s); (3) Any additional information gained through negotiations with the respective plant management that may be useful to other Local Unions in their collective bargaining.

Financial Secretary

Section 4. It shall be the duty of the Financial Secretary to receive all dues, initiation fees, readmission fees, fines and all other income of the Local Union for any fund from any source and to give official receipts for same, as provided in this Constitution. Financial Secretaries of Local Unions having a check-off arrangement shall issue one (1) receipt for the check received from the company, and otherwise use the procedure outlined above for any other income. No receipt shall be issued to individual members unless the company does not show on the check stub or pay envelope the amount of the deduction and the reason therefor.

Section 5. He shall write all checks drawn on the Local Union funds and report in writing every month at a regular meeting of the Local Union giving the amount of monies received and paid out during the previous calendar month, divided as between the various income and expenditure classifications, and the remaining balances in the fund accounts of the Local Union.

Section 6. He shall deposit all collections either with the Treasurer, taking a receipt therefor, or in such banks as Local Union Trustees may direct, with advice to the Treasurer as to the amount so deposited.

Section 7. He shall, by the 20th of each month, send a report to the International Secretary-Treasurer on blanks furnished by the International Union, together with the correct amount of money due the International Union for the preceding month which begins on the first and ends with the last day of the month. He shall receive applications for membership and notify the candidates of their election or rejection. He shall assist the International Union in seeing that all members receive the official publication regularly when eligible, provide each member with an official receipt for all monies paid and provide each member with a copy of the Constitution and By-Laws. Union membership cards and/or dues buttons may be issued at the option of the Local Union.

Section 8. He shall furnish the International Secretary-Treasurer with the names and addresses of all the officers of the Local Union. He shall keep a record of all members initiated, suspended, expelled or deceased, transfers in and out and reinstatements, during his term of office and notify the International Secretary-Treasurer of same, and perform such other duties as the By-Laws prescribe or the Local Union may direct. There shall be maintained by the Financial Secretary a complete record of all active members of the Local Union. This record shall have the date of initiation, the date and cause of suspension or expulsion, the date of reinstatement, together with the date of death, home address and such other matters as may be deemed necessary to keep a record of the continuous membership of a member of the Local Union.

Section 9. He shall keep an inventory of all records and property of the Local Union, the same to contain, when possible, date of purchase and amount paid for each article. He shall notify all members in arrears of the amount of their indebtedness and turn over his books to the Trustees for audit and approval when called to do so. He shall, on the demand of the International Secretary-Treasurer, produce his books for examination and audit, and shall comply with the provisions of this Constitution.

Section 10. Should it be proven that any Local Union Financial Secretary has wilfully and intentionally failed to report monthly the full membership of his Local Union to the International Secretary-Treasurer or should it be proven than any Local Union President, Treasurer and/or Financial Secretary wilfully and intentionally refuses to sign a check to send in the full amount of per capita tax on the same number of members who have paid dues to the Local Union, the Local Union may be suspended from all privileges and benefits until the deficiency is made good and the officer or officers responsible for such failure shall not be allowed to again hold office in the organization for a period of two (2) years.

Treasurer

Section 11. The Treasurer shall give a receipt for all monies received from the Financial Secretary. The monies received must be deposited in such bank as the Local Union Trustees may direct for the several funds provided for in this Constitution and such other funds as the Local Union may set up in the name and number of the Local Union. He shall sign all checks, which must be countersigned by the President. He shall report in writing every month at a regular meeting of the Local Union the total receipts and total expenditures for the Local Union for the previous calendar month and the amount of money still on deposit. He shall deliver to his successor all monies and other property of the Local Union. He shall, on demand of the International Union or Trustees of the Local Union, produce his books for examination and audit.

Trustees

Section 12. The Trustees shall have general supervision over all funds and property of the Local Union. They shall audit or cause to be audited by a Certified Public Accountant selected by the Local Union Executive Board, the records of the Financial Officers of the Local Union quarterly as provided herein, using duplicate forms provided by the International Union, a copy of which shall be forwarded to the International Secretary-Treasurer immediately thereafter. It shall also be their duty to see that the Financial Officers of the Local Union are bonded in conformity with the laws of the International Union. The Trustees shall see that all funds shall be deposited in a bank subject to an order signed by the President and Treasurer and/or Financial Secretary. In Local Unions where safety deposit boxes are used the Trustees shall see that the signatures of the President, Treasurer and one (1) of the Trustees are required before admittance to the safety deposit box is permitted. In the event the books are not received for audit within fifteen (15) days after the end of each quarter the Chairman of the Trustees shall make a report to the next meeting of the Local Union for action.

Sergeant-at-Arms

Section 13. It shall be the duty of the Sergeant-at-Arms to introduce all new members and visitors and assist the President in preserving order when called upon to do so. He shall also take charge of all property of the Local Union not otherwise provided for, and perform such other duties as may be assigned to him from time to time.

Guide

Section 14. It shall be the duty of the Guide to maintain order, inspect the membership receipts, satisfy himself that all present are entitled to remain in the meeting of the Local Union and perform such other duties as are usual to the office.

Section 15. All Local Union officers, committees, stewards and other members handling funds or other property of the Local Union shall, at the completion of their duties, turn over all papers, documents, funds, and/or other Local Union property to the properly constituted Local Union officers.

ARTICLE 39

DUTIES OF LOCAL UNION MEMBERS

Section 1. It shall be the duty of each member to conscientiously seek to understand and exemplify by practice the intent and purpose of his obligation as a member of this International Union.

Section 2. It shall be the duty of each member to render aid and assistance to brother or sister members in cases of illness, death or distress, and in every way acquit himself as a loyal and devoted member of the International Union.

Section 3. It shall be the duty of each member to participate in all Local, State, Provincial and Federal elections through registration and balloting.

ARTICLE 40

OPENING AND CLOSING CEREMONIES

"I now declare this meeting of Local Union No. ...... of the International Union, UNITED AUTOMOBILE, AIRCRAFT AND AGRICULTURAL IMPLEMENT

WORKERS OF AMERICA (UAW-CIO) open for the transaction of such business as may properly come before it."

The following order of business is suggested, but it may be altered to suit the requirements of each Local Union:

1. Roll call of officers.
2. Reading of the minutes of the previous meeting.
3. Applications for membership.
4. Voting on applications.
5. Initiation of Candidates.
6. Report of Financial Secretary and/or Treasurer.
7. Reports of officers, committees and delegates.
8. Communications and bills.
9. Unfinished business.
10. Good and welfare.
11. Does any one know of a member out of work or in distress?
12. New business.
13. Closing.

(All questions of parliamentary nature shall be decided by Roberts Rules of Order.)

ARTICLE 41

INITIATION CEREMONY

The President shall say to the Guide:

"You will now place the candidate before me for the obligation." The Guide advances with the candidate and places him in front of the President's station. All newly elected members before being admitted to full membership shall subscribe to the following obligation:

"I .... pledge my honor to faithfully observe the Constitution and laws of this Union and the Constitution of the United States (or the Dominion of Canada, as the case may be); to comply with all the rules and regulations for the government thereof; not to divulge or make known any private proceedings of this Union; to faithfully perform all the duties assigned to me to the best of my ability and skill; to so conduct myself at all times as not to bring reproach upon my Union, and at all times to bear true and faithful allegiance to the International Union, UNITED AUTOMOBILE, AIRCRAFT AND AGRICULTURAL IMPLEMENT WORKERS OF AMERICA (UAW-CIO)."

ARTICLE 42

LOCAL UNION COMMITTEES

Section 1. The Local Union shall have the following standing committees: Constitution and By-Laws, Union Label, Education, Recreation, Community Services, Fair Practices and Anti-Discrimination, Legislative and Political Action, and such other committees as they deem necessary. All committees should be appointed or elected, subject to the direction of the Local Union or shop organization in the case of an Amalgamated Local Union.

ARTICLE 43

SHOP STEWARDS AND SHOP COMMITTEEMEN

Section 1. The Bargaining Committee may, but does not necessarily have to consist of the members of the Executive Board of the Local Union.

Section 2. All Shop Stewards and/or Committeemen shall be democratically elected and shall be required to take the oath of office as provided in Article 37. They may be recalled for good and sufficient cause by a two-thirds (⅔) vote of the members, whom they represent, present and voting at a special meeting called for that purpose, provided due notification of such meeting is given.

Section 3. All Local Union by-laws shall contain specific provisions on the Shop Steward system as applicable to their shop or plant, the general structure of which is outlined in an issue of the Educational Department of this International Union, dealing with Shop Stewards.

ARTICLE 44

LOCAL UNION FINANCES

Section 1. The funds of each Local Union shall be used to defray all necessary expenses which must be approved by the Local Union in regular meeting.

Section 2. All appeals by Local Unions to other Local Unions for funds must be approved by the respective Regional Director before they shall be recognized. Such appeals must be promptly approved or disapproved.

ARTICLE 45

LOCAL UNION DUES

Section 1. A Local Union or unit of an Amalgamated Local Union may establish membership dues in an amount exceeding the minimum prescribed by Article 16, Section 2. Such action by a Local Union or unit of an Amalgamated Local Union shall require ratification by a two-thirds (⅔) vote of the votes cast at a Local Union or unit meeting, due notice of which has been given to the membership at least seven (7) days prior to the date of said meeting and shall be subject to the approval of the Regional Director whose approval must be obtained before such dues are levied.

Section 2. A Local Union or unit of an Amalgamated Local Union is empowered to provide for the forfeiture of the membership of a delinquent member for the non-payment of dues without the necessity for proceeding by the filing of charges and the conducting of a trial.

ARTICLE 46

LOCAL UNION AUDITS

Section 1. The fiscal year of the Local Union shall be from January 1st through December 31st.

Section 2. It shall be the duty of the Trustees of each Local Union, as provided for in Article 38, Section 12, to audit or cause to be audited by a Certified Public Accountant the books and financial affairs of their Local Union quarterly on the forms supplied by the International Union, and this quarterly report shall be made to the Local Union and a copy forwarded to the International Secretary-Treasurer of the International Union and to the Local Union's Regional Director.

Section 3. Should inaccuracies or discrepancies appear to exist in a Local Union, the International Secretary-Treasurer, upon the approval of the International President or the International Executive Board, shall have the authority to designate a representative to take charge of and audit all financial books, records and accounts of said Local Union and/or may employ a Certified Public Accountant to audit same.

Section 4. The report and findings of the representative or the Certified Public Accountant shall be filed with the President of the Local Union and the International Secretary-Treasurer of the International Union.

Section 5. Should an audit by a Local Union or the International Union reveal a misappropriation of funds, the International President or the International Executive Board may summarily suspend from Local Union office or other Local Union position any member who appears to be responsible for such misappropriations, pending further investigation or action by the International Executive Board. If in the judgment of the Board the facts warrant, the Board shall conduct a hearing to determine the guilt or innocence of the member or members involved. It shall require a two-thirds (⅔) vote of the Board to find a member guilty. A member found guilty by the Board shall be removed from any office or position he may hold in the Local Union, and he shall not thereafter be eligible to hold any office or position in any Local Union or in the International Union or to represent the Local Union or the International in any capacity until and unless he shall make full restitution, and then only by action of the International Executive Board by a two-thirds (⅔) vote. The procedure provided in this section shall be in addition to, and not exclusive of, any other action which may be taken against such Local Union officers or members by or in the Local Union or by the International Union. Under no circumstances shall a misappropriation of funds be written off the books of a Local Union or a final settlement of same be made without the approval of the International Secretary-Treasurer.

ARTICLE 47

FRAUD IN LOCAL UNION ELECTIONS

Section 1. Any member convicted of misrepresenting returns, altering, mutilating, or destroying deposited ballots, voting fraudulently or of intimidating others by threats or otherwise interfering with a member in the exercise of his right to cast his ballot in Local Union elections and strike balloting, shall be punished in accordance with the Trial Procedure outlined in this Constitution. In no case shall the penalty be less than a fine of ten dollars ($10.00), and the member so convicted shall be disqualified for either elective or appointive office within the jurisdiction of the International Union for a period of not less than two (2) years or more than five (5) years.

Section 2. All ballots may be destroyed ninety (90) days after the close of the election and a notarized statement by the Election Committee shall be made with regard to the election results and the disposition of the ballots.

ARTICLE 48

TRIALS OF MEMBERS

Section 1. A charge by a member or members in good standing that a member or members have violated this Constitution or engaged in conduct unbecoming a member of the Union must be specifically set forth in writing and signed by the member or members making the charges. Two (2) or more members may be jointly charged with having participated in the same act or acts charged as an offense or with having acted jointly in the commission of such an offense and may be jointly tried.

Section 2. Charges must be submitted to the Recording Secretary of the Local Union or of the Shop Organization, as the case may be, within sixty (60) days of the time the complainant becomes aware of the alleged offense, provided, that if the charges are against the Recording Secretary, they shall be submitted to the President of the Local Union or the chief Executive Officer of the Shop Organization, as the case may be, and provided further, that charges preferred against one for acts or conduct detrimental to the interest of the Union or its members, committed while he was out of the Union on withdrawal card, shall be submitted within sixty (60) days from the time of the deposit of his withdrawal card.

Section 3. Upon charges being submitted, it is mandatory that a trial be held, unless the charges are withdrawn by the accuser.

Section 4. A member against whom charges have been filed shall be notified of such charges by receipted registered mail within seven (7) days after the charges have been submitted to the Local Union or, in the case of an Amalgamated Local Union, to the Shop Organization of which he is a member.

Section 5. A member preferring charges, and a member against whom charges are preferred shall be permitted representation by counsel of his own choice; such counsel, however, shall be required to abide by the Trial Procedure as established by the Trial Committee and as outlined in this Constitution.

Section 6. A member against whom charges have been filed may be suspended from office or membership in his Local Union or Shop Organization, as the case may be, pending trial, by a two-thirds (⅔) vote at such Local Union or Shop Organization meeting. In the case of a plant in which Union membership is a condition of employment, suspension from membership shall not require removal from the job, provided, that in cases of extreme emergency, removal from the job may be required by a two-thirds (⅔) vote of the body voting suspension.

Section 7. The accused member shall be tried by a Trial Committee consisting of at least seven (7) members, and such additional members as may be chosen to act as alternates, who shall be elected by the Local Union, or, in the case of an Amalgamated Local Union, by the Shop Organization, at the next membership meeting, which shall be not later than forty-five (45) days from the time the charges were submitted. A Trial Committee shall be separately elected for the trial of each case.

Section 8. Within seven (7) days after the Trial Committee has been elected, the accused member shall be notified of the time and place of the trial, which shall be held not less than fifteen (15) days nor more than thirty (30) days from the date of his receipt of such notification. The Trial Committee shall submit its findings to the Local Union not later than sixty (60) days from the time such committee was elected unless extended by the International Executive Board.

Section 9. Any Officer, Executive Board member or Joint Council delegate, where such council exists, if charged with a violation of the Amalgamated Local Union By-Laws or International Constitution or if charged with being derelict in performing his duties as a Local Union officer or failure to carry out the union obligation which he accepted, shall be tried by a Trial Committee elected either by the delegate body of such Amalgamated Local Union, where such delegate body exists, or by a Trial Committee established by the general membership meeting of such Amalgamated Local Union where no delegate body exists.

Section 10. The Trial Committee, upon completion of the hearing on the evidence and arguments, shall go into closed session to determine the verdict and penalty. A two-thirds (⅔) vote shall be required to find the accused guilty. In case the accused is found guilty, the Trial Committee may, by a majority vote, reprimand the accused; or it may, by a two-thirds (⅔) vote, assess a fine not to exceed one hundred dollars ($100) with automatic suspension, removal from office or expulsion in the event of the failure of the accused to pay the fine within a specified time; or it may, by a two-thirds (⅔) vote, suspend or remove the accused from office or suspend or expel him from membership in the International Union.

Section 11. The Trial Committee shall thereupon report its verdict and judgment to the body which elected them, at the membership meeting next following the determination of the verdict and judgment of the Trial Committee, and in case of a verdict of guilty, such verdict and judgment shall become effective only upon approval by a two-thirds (⅔) vote at the Local Union meeting, or the unit meeting, as the case may be. In case of a verdict of guilty the Local Union meeting or the unit meeting may, by a two-thirds (⅔) vote, modify the verdict or order a new trial. The vote shall first be upon the verdict of guilty. If such verdict is not approved by a two-thirds (⅔) vote, the accused shall stand acquitted. If the verdict of guilty is approved by a two-thirds (⅔) vote, the vote shall then be upon the penalty recommended by the Trial Committee. The vote upon any proposed modification of the penalty shall be either (a) By voting down the penalty recommended by the Trial Committee (by an adverse vote in excess of one third (⅓)) and then voting upon the proposed modification, or (b) By voting upon the proposed modification as an amendment to the committee's recommendation. In the case of a plant in which Union membership is a condition of employment, suspension from membership shall not require removal from the job, provided, that in cases of extreme emergency, removal from the job may be required by a two-thirds (⅔) vote of the body voting suspension. However, in the case of a plant in which Union membership is a condition of employment, expulsion from membership shall require removal from the job.

Section 12. A member found guilty by his Shop Organization may appeal in writing to the next meeting of his Amalgamated Local Union, his appeal to be considered by the Amalgamated Local Union's delegate body, where such exists, or the general membership meeting, where no delegate body exists. The Amalgamated Local Union shall review the appeal, with the aid of an investigating committee or otherwise, and shall determine the appeal but shall not select its own Trial Committee to retry the case. An appeal from the decision of the Amalgamated Local Union shall be carried to the International Executive Board.

Section 13. In the event that the penalty is suspension, the suspended member shall be required to pay all dues during the period of suspension. Suspended members shall not be entitled to "Out-of-Work" receipts.

Section 14. In case the Trial Committee finds the accused obviously innocent they may determine the honest or malicious intent of the accuser. If they find the accuser guilty of obvious malice in filing the charges, they may assess a penalty against him in accordance with Section 10 of this Article, provided, however, that such a penalty shall be limited to the following: A fine not to exceed one hundred dollars ($100.00), with automatic suspension in the event of failure of the accused to pay the fine within a specified time; or suspension from membership for a period not to exceed three (3) months. Such verdict and penalty in relation to the accuser shall become effective only upon approval by a two-thirds (⅔) vote at the Local Union meeting or the Shop Organization meeting, as the case may be. The Local Union meeting or the Shop Organization meeting may, by a two-thirds (⅔) vote, modify the verdict or order a new trial of the accuser. The vote shall be taken in the same manner as provided in Section 11 of this Article. In the case of a plant in which Union membership is a condition of employment, suspension from membership shall not require removal from the job, provided, that in cases of extreme emergency, removal from the job may be required by a two-thirds (⅔) vote of the body voting suspension.

Section 15. Any higher body to which an appeal from the decision of the Trial Committee is made shall have the authority not only to accept or reject the verdict, but may modify such a verdict or order a new trial.

Section 16. Where a member against whom charges have been filed has been duly suspended in compliance with the provisions of Section 6 of this Article and has been found guilty by the Trial Committee, he shall have the right to attend the meeting of the Shop Organization or of the Local Union, as the case may be, in which any verdict and judgment is presented for approval, and shall be afforded full opportunity to present to the meeting his position on all matters bearing upon his trial, verdict and judgment.

Section 17. In any case in which a member shall have been tried upon charges alleging one or more of the following offenses:

(a) Illegally seeking or holding office or position in violation of Section 10 of Article 10.

(b) Misappropriation or embezzlement of Union funds.

(c) Fraud in a Local Union election as defined in Section 1 of Article 47.

(d) Any other offense concerning which the International Executive Board has the present authority to act under the emergency provisions of Article 48, Section 21

an acquittal by the Trial Committee or by the Local Union may be reviewed only by the International Executive Board. Such appeal must be taken within thirty (30) days by any member of the Local Union or the Regional Director.

In case of a conviction, the penalty may be reviewed by the International Executive Board upon an appeal taken within thirty (30) days by any member of the Local Union or the Regional Director on the ground that the penalty imposed is grossly disproportionate to the gravity of the offense.

Section 18. Upon appeal from an acquittal, the International Executive Board shall review the record of the trial and subsequent proceedings in the Local Union and shall be empowered, if it finds that the verdict was against the great weight of the evidence, to set it aside and to order a new trial by an International Union Trial Committee in accordance with Sections 23 and 24 of this Article.

Upon appeal from a penalty, the International Executive Board may refer the penalty to an International Union Trial Committee selected in accordance with Sections 23 and 24 of this Article. The International Union Trial Committee may in any such case prescribe any penalty provided by this Constitution but without reviewing the verdict of guilt.

Section 19. Any member expelled or suspended from membership for more than two (2) years may be reinstated to full membership or to membership without right to hold office or appointive position at any time after two (2) years following the final action which effected his expulsion or suspension. Such reinstatement may be ordered by a majority vote.

(a) By the Local Union if its order of expulsion or suspension was not reviewed by the International Executive Board on appeal by the convicted member or under Section 17 of this Article, or

(b) By the International Executive Board if the expulsion or suspension resulted from its review of Local Union action, either on appeal or on review under Section 17 of this Article or from the decision of an International Union Trial Committee from which no appeal was taken to a Convention, or

(c) By a Convention of the International Union if the expulsion or suspension was by vote of a previous Convention upon an appeal.

Any such expelled or suspended member seeking reinstatement shall file a petition with the body having authority under this section to act thereon. If the petition is to a Convention, it shall be filed with the International Secretary-Treasurer at least ninety (90) days before the Convention convenes.

Section 20. A reinstatement by a Local Union pursuant to Section 19 of this Article shall be subject to approval by the International Executive Board before the reinstatement can become effective. The denial by a Local Union or by the

International Executive Board of a petition for reinstatement shall be appealable in the manner provided by Article 30.

Section 21. In cases of extreme emergency and when it appears to the International Executive Board that irreparable injury may result to the International Union or to a subordinate body from offenses punishable under this Constitution recently committed or being committed by any member or members unless the Board shall intervene, and, without regard to the existence of a present emergency, in any case in which it shall appear to the Board that two (2) or more members have engaged at any time since the original adoption of this section at the Twelfth Constitutional Convention in a conspiracy to commit an offense against the Union, the Board may, if two-thirds (⅔) of its members concur, prefer charges against such member or members for the violation of this Constitution or for conduct unbecoming a member of the Union, which charges shall be specifically set forth in writing and signed by the Secretary-Treasurer of the International Union. At the same session at which any such charges are voted the Board shall select one (1) of its members who shall serve as the representative for the Board in the trial of the charges.

Section 22. If it shall be charged by the International Executive Board that two (2) or more members have participated in the same act or acts charged as an offense or having acted jointly in the commission of an offense, or have engaged in a conspiracy to commit an offense punishable under this Constitution any such members may be jointly tried.

Section 23. Charges preferred against a member or members by the International Executive Board shall be tried by an International Union Trial Committee chosen in the manner provided for the selection of such a committee in Article 29, Sections 5 through 12, inclusive, except that the accused and the representative for the International Executive Board shall each be entitled to strike only five (5) names from the panel. In cases where two (2) or more members are charged jointly the panel drawn by the Secretary-Treasurer shall consist of a number of names equal to fifty (50), plus ten (10) times the number by which the number of accused exceeds one (1), so that if there are two (2) accused, sixty (60) names shall be drawn, if three (3) are accused seventy (70) names shall be drawn, and so on. Each of the accused shall be entitled to strike five (5) names and the representative for the International Executive Board shall be entitled to strike a number equal to five (5) times the number of accused. The accused shall proceed in striking names from the panel in the alphabetical order of their names and in the manner provided in Article 29, Section 7.

Section 24. Upon completion of the trial, the International Union Trial Committee shall go into closed session to determine the verdict and penalty. A two-thirds (⅔) vote shall be required to find the accused guilty. In the event the accused is found guilty the International Union Trial Committee may impose the penalties provided by Section 10 of this Article. In the event the International Union Trial Committee finds the accused guilty, the accused may appeal the decision to the next International Convention in the same way as provided in Article 30 for an appeal from the decision of the International

Executive Board. In the event the International Union Trial Committee finds the accused not guilty, the decision shall be final.

ARTICLE 49

STRIKES

Section 1. Whenever any difficulty arises within the jurisdiction of any Local Union within the shop involved, between its members and any employer or employers, growing out of reduction in wages, lengthening of hours of labor, or other grievances incident to the conditions of employment, or whenever any local Union desires to secure for its members an increase in wages, a shorter work day or other changes in the conditions of employment, the Local Union involved shall call a meeting of all members to decide whether the proposed changes shall be accepted or rejected. The majority vote of those present and voting on the question shall decide. If, as a result of this decision, a strike vote is decided upon, the Local Union Executive Board shall notify all members, and it shall require a two-thirds (⅔) vote by secret ballot of those voting to declare a strike. Only members in good standing shall be entitled to vote on the question of declaring a strike.

Section 2. If the Local Union involved is unable to reach an agreement with the employer without strike action, the Recording Secretary of the Local Union shall prepare a full statement of the matters in controversy and forward the same to the Regional Director and International President. The Regional Director or his assigned representative in conjunction with the Local Union Committee shall attempt to effect a settlement. Upon failure to effect a settlement he shall send the International President his recommendation of approval or disapproval of a strike. Upon receipt of the statement of matters in controversy from the Regional Director, the International President shall prepare and forward a copy thereof to each member of the International Executive Board together with a request for their vote upon the question of approving a strike of those involved to enforce their decision in relation thereto. Upon receipt of the vote of the members of the International Executive Board, the International President shall forthwith notify in writing the Regional Director and the Local Union of the decision of the International Executive Board.

Section 3. In case of an emergency where delay would seriously jeopardize the welfare of those involved, the International President, after consultation with the other International Officers, may approve a strike pending the submission to, and securing the approval of, the International Executive Board, providing such authorization shall be in writing.

Section 4. Neither the International Union nor any Local Union, nor any subordinate body of the International Union, nor any officer, member, representative or agent of the International Union, Local Union or subordinate body shall have the power or authority to instigate, call, lead or engage in any strike or work stoppage, or to induce or encourage employees of any employer to engage in a strike or a concerted refusal in the course of their employment to use, manufacture, process, transport or otherwise handle or work on any goods, articles, materials, or commodities, or to perform any services, except as authorized by the International Executive Board or the International President in conformity with the provisions of this Constitution. Such power and authority resides exclusively in the International Executive Board and the International President, and may be exercised only by collective action of the International Executive Board as provided in Section 2 of this Article or by emergency action of the International President as provided in Section 3 of this Article.

Section 5. Before a strike shall be called off, a special meeting of the Local Union shall be called for that purpose, and it shall require a majority vote by secret ballot of all members present to decide the question either way. Wherever the International Executive Board decides that it is unwise to longer continue an existing strike, it will order all members of Local Unions who have ceased work in connection therewith to resume work and thereupon and thereafter all assistance from the International Union shall cease.

Section 6. Any Local Union engaging in a strike which is called in violation of this Constitution and without authorization of the International President and/or the International Executive Board shall have no claim for financial or organizational assistance from the International Union or any affiliated Local Union.

Section 7. The International President, with the approval of the International Executive Board, shall be empowered to revoke the charter of any Local Union engaging in such unauthorized strike action, thereby annulling all privileges, powers and rights of such Local Union under this Constitution.

Section 8. In cases of great emergency, when the existence of the International Union is involved, together with the economic and social standing of our membership, the International President and the International Executive Board shall have authority to declare a general strike within the industry by a two-thirds (⅔) vote of the International Executive Board whenever in their good judgment it shall be deemed proper for the purpose of preserving and perpetuating the rights and living standards of the general membership of our International Union, provided, under no circumstances shall it call such a strike until approved by a referendum vote of the membership.

Section 9. In case of a general strike, it shall require a majority vote of the International Executive Board before the strike is officially called off.

ARTICLE 50

BOARD OF INTERNATIONAL TRUSTEES

Section 1. A three (3) member International Board of Trustees shall be created, charged with the duty of safeguarding all funds and property of the International Union by causing the books and accounts of the International Secretary-Treasurer to be audited quarterly. The Board of Trustees shall designate a certified public accountant to make such audits, and shall incorporate same in their report to the International Officers, Board Members, and all affiliated Local Unions as soon as completed. The Board of Trustees shall report its activities to the quarterly meetings of the International Executive Board and to the International Convention. It shall make recommendations to the Board and to the Convention for improving the handling of the finances of the International Union and for safeguarding its funds and property.

Section 2. Members of the Board of Trustees shall devote the time necessary to the performance of their duties, not to exceed a maximum of thirty (30) days in any quarter. Members of the Board of Trustees shall be compensated on the basis of maximum International Representative's salary, and expenses.

Section 3. Nominations and elections of Trustees shall take place in the regular order of business of the International Convention. Candidates shall be nominated and elected in one election. The candidates shall be nominated for a three (3) term trusteeship, for a two (2) term trusteeship, and for a one (1) term trusteeship. The candidate receiving the highest number of votes for each of these three (3) positions, respectively, shall be declared elected. At each Constitutional Convention, a Trustee shall be elected for a three (3) term period.

Section 4. In the event of the death, removal or resignation of a Trustee, the following procedure shall be utilized to fill the vacancy for the unexpired term until the next subsequent Convention only. The names of all regular delegates attending the preceding International Union Convention shall be copied from the official Convention roll call. The names of all delegates shall be written on uniform sized slips of paper and deposited in a box by the Secretary-Treasurer, in the presence of the International Executive Board, and the box shall be sealed and thoroughly shaken. The International Secretary-Treasurer shall then open the container and the member of the International Executive Board selected for that purpose, and blindfolded, shall draw the names of fifteen (15) delegates, one by one. After these names are drawn they shall be read by the International Secretary-Treasurer in the presence of the International Executive Board, and each name in succession shall be set opposite a number from one (1) to fifteen (15). The vacancy shall be filled by the first individual in numerical order on the list who accepts and who is eligible.

Section 5. A member of the Board of Trustees shall not, while holding such position, be employed by the International Union as an International Representative or in any other capacity whatsoever. Such member shall become eligible as a candidate for office in, or as an employe of, the International Union only subsequent to an International Convention which follows his resignation from the Board of Trustees.

ARTICLE 51

WOMEN'S AUXILIARIES

Section 1. Where there is a strong desire on the part of the wives, mothers, sisters and daughters of the members of any Local Union of the International Union to elevate the conditions, maintain and protect the interests of the UAW-CIO, a charter for a Women's Auxiliary shall be granted when application is made upon a blank furnished by the International Secretary-Treasurer of this International Union.

Section 2. The charter fee shall be ten dollars ($10.00) for charter and initial supplies.

Section 3. Dues to maintain such Auxiliary shall not be more than fifty cents (.50) per month. No per capita tax shall be charged by this International Union from dues so collected.

Section 4. The Auxiliary shall establish such laws as do not conflict with the By-Laws of their Local Union and this Constitution and shall submit same to the International Executive Board for ratification.

Section 5. So long as the Auxiliary adheres to the provisions of this Constitution and the Local Union By-Laws and does not adopt a policy contrary to that of the International or Local Union and adheres to the conditions of its charter, it shall remain in full force, but upon infraction thereof or upon request of the Local Union, the International Executive Board may revoke the charter, thereby annulling all privileges secured thereunder.

Section 6. Women's Auxiliaries shall be coordinated through an International Women's Auxiliaries Department.

Section 7. The President of the International Union shall appoint the director to direct, coordinate and supervise the activities of the Women's Auxiliaries.

Section 8. The Director of the Women's Auxiliaries may call regional conferences of the Auxiliaries.

Section 9. It is the duty of the Women's Auxiliaries to educate the wives, mothers, sisters and daughters of the workers to the principles and ideals of trade unionism; to adhere to the principles and policies of their Local Union and the International Union; to assist their local Unions in time of need and during labor disputes; to assist Local Unions in social affairs when called upon by their respective Local Union; to provide educational and cultural activities for the children of the workers. It shall be the duty of the Local Unions to assist in the formation of Local Women's Auxiliaries; the Regional Director shall assist the Director of Women's Auxiliaries in their respective regions. The Women's Auxiliaries shall not campaign for or against candidates seeking office in Local Unions. The Women's Auxiliaries shall not interfere with affairs of the Local Union unless officially called upon by their Local Union. Each respective Local Union shall select a Committee of not more than three (3) to assist the National and Regional Directors in supervising and formulating policies for their respective Auxiliaries.

Section 10. No one shall be eligible for membership in the Women's Auxiliaries who holds membership in any Local Union under the jurisdiction of the UAW-CIO.

SUBJECT INDEX

SUBJECT INDEX—(Continued)

As the Automobile Workers' constitution suggests, and as is true for every national union, the convention is the supreme authority. Below is a report of the convention activities of one important union.

THE 1956 CONVENTION OF THE MACHINISTS UNION

By Donald M. Irwin, Department of Labor, in Monthly Labor Review, vol. 79, (1956), pp. 1292–1294

The strength and goals of a growing democratic trade union were clearly demonstrated at the largest quadrennial grand lodge convention of the International Association of Machinists (IAM), held in San Francisco, September 4–13, 1956. There was no dominant issue or event facing the delegates. Intra-union problems, national and international affairs, and political action all received the attention of the 1,500 delegates who represented the union's 900,-000 members of more than 2,000 lodges in the United States, its Territories, and

Canada. Bargaining goals, set forth in a number of resolutions, included higher wages and improved health and welfare benefits.

INTERNAL UNION AFFAIRS

Growth Since 1952. Since the last IAM convention in 1952,[1] the net membership gain had been about 130,000, according to the officers' report submitted to the convention. Total membership had declined especially from March 1954 until April 1955, when the trend was reversed. Furthermore, membership turnover was high, as in other international unions. From January 1950 through March 1956, almost 1 million persons had become members and then left the organization. The aircraft and airframe lodges had the greatest increase in membership since 1950 while the automotive lodges had the largest decrease.

Increased emphasis on organizing was possible, President A. J. Hayes stated in his opening remarks to the convention, because of "the greatest development in the American labor movement in the past 4 years"—the merger of the American Federation of Labor and Congress of Industrial Organizations (AFL-CIO) which was followed by the merger of the Trades and Labor Congress of Canada and the Canadian Congress of Labor. George Meany and Claude Jodoin, presidents of the respective merged federations, addressed the convention.

Progress in the field of cooperation with other labor unions also contributed to the growth of the IAM, according to President Hayes, who reported that no-raiding agreements had settled many jurisdictional problems. In 1952, the IAM had one such pact with the United Automobile Workers (UAW). Since then, similar agreements have been signed with the following unions: Rubber Workers; Carpenters; Plumbers and Pipefitters; Iron Workers; Printing Pressmen; Teamsters; Boilermakers; and Electricians (International Brotherhood of Electrical Workers). Convention resolutions approved the progress made in this field. In addition, the delegates approved a resolution calling for a joint organizing drive with unions in the petroleum and chemical industries.

The net worth of the organization—approximately $15 million—was about one-third higher than in 1952. The officers' report to the delegates, however, noted that "the assets of an organization of the type and magnitude of the IAM should be much greater in order to more effectively carry on its diversified activities."

Constitutional Amendments. Over 250 amendments to the union's constitution had been submitted by IAM lodges for consideration by the committee on rules. Hearings on the amendments had been held by the committee for almost 2 weeks prior to the opening of the convention. The committee then presented its recommendations to the convention in the form of substitute resolutions or resolutions approving or opposing the amendments submitted by the lodges. Constitutional amendments proposed at the convention, such as those that follow, are subject not only to approval by the convention but also to a membership referendum.

[1] For a summary of the 1952 convention, see Monthly Labor Review, December 1952 (p. 639).

The delegates approved a resolution calling for cessation of publication of the Machinists' Monthly Journal. However, the union's weekly publication, The Machinist, would be increased in size to provide more complete coverage of matters of interest to the membership. President Hayes indicated that funds presently being used for publication of the Journal may be spent to aid organization of Canadian workers.

Substantial salary increases were recommended for grand lodge officers and representatives, including a raise in the annual salary of the international president from $18,000 to $25,000. Minimum monthly dues of $4 instead of $2 a month per capita were proposed for all members. (A resolution adopted by the 1952 convention favoring an increase in the dues from $2 to $3 a month was defeated in a referendum vote.) If higher dues are approved by the membership, 50 cents of the amount will be sent each month to the international for a "strike prevention fund" in order to build more adequate cash reserves and to pay increased strike benefits when necessary. Additional resolutions concerning changes in the IAM pension plan for its paid officials were adopted by the delegates.

Committee Reports. Reports covering such matters as appeals and grievances from executive board decisions, apprentice training, health and welfare plans, officers' report, publications, ritual, shorter workweek, and workers' education were presented by the appropriate committees.

Also, twelve industry committees reported to the convention on developments, goals, and problems in their respective fields. The committees, which had been established to report on industries with concentrations of IAM membership, were: aircraft and airframe (including guided missiles); air transport; atomic energy; automobile; construction and erection; government employees; machine tool and die and machine tools; marine; petroleum and chemical; printing machinery; railroad; and paper, pulp, and sulphite. The highlights of the reports by 3 of the industry committees are briefly summarized below; they are intended to illustrate the work done by the 12 committees.

The aircraft committee approved that section of the officers' report concerning their industry. It was emphasized that the industry is now the largest employer of workers in manufacturing in the United States, but that plant dispersal and abnormal plant expansion have made the bargaining position of unions there more difficult. The committee approved the policy of company-wide bargaining in the industry for the present, but set as a future goal, industry-wide bargaining. In both these areas, it recommended joint negotiations with the UAW where possible.

The railroad committee considered over 75 resolutions submitted by the lodges in that industry. The delegates approved proposals to be made in future contract negotiations for an increased differential for leadmen, shift premium pay, a shorter workweek, premium rates for Saturday and Sunday work, improved vacations, jury duty pay, restrictions on contracting-out work historically performed by machinists, and improved pension, health, and insurance plans.

The Government employees' committee noted with approval the substantial improvements made since 1952 in Federal legislation affecting Government employees. It presented resolutions to the convention urging legislation providing for triple-time pay for holiday work, furnishing of workers' tools by the Government, revision of the Hatch Act to permit Federal workers to joint political clubs, and curtailment of time studies in governmental establishments.

NATIONAL AND INTERNATIONAL AFFAIRS

Following the convention's discussion of various resolutions concerning the school integration decision of the United States Supreme Court, the delegates adopted a resolution committing the IAM "to raise the economic, social, and cultural standards" of all of its members regardless of the "area in which they live, or regardless of race, creed, color, or religion" by applying trade union principles.

The issue of automation was stressed by Secretary of Labor James P. Mitchell and by Canadian Minister of Labor Milton F. Gregg in their speeches to the convention. The IAM's position in this matter was stated in the officers' report; namely, that automation will increase the need for machinists and that automation is necessary for increased productivity. The report also stated that guaranties must be obtained to assure that the displacement of workers through automation does not cause unemployment and that increased facilities must be made available to train workers affected by automation for newly created jobs as well as other jobs to which they may be transferred.

A resolution approving supplemental unemployment benefit plans was adopted by the delegates although they considered that such plans were no substitute for needed improvements in existing public unemployment compensation programs and that such plans may be feasible in certain industries only. Other resolutions adopted by the convention were those favoring equal pay for equal work, a 30-hour workweek, and statehood for Hawaii, Alaska, and Puerto Rico. Resolutions encouraging the work of CARE, the Red Cross, and International Guiding Eyes, Inc., were also approved.

A number of guests addressed the delegates on a variety of issues concerning national and international affairs. In addition to those already mentioned, the speakers included: Omer Becu, general secretary of the International Confederation of Free Trade Unions and president of the International Transport Workers Federation; Israel I. Blumenfeld, West Coast director, American Trade Union Council for Labor, and representative of Histadrut (General Federation of Labor in Israel); Leon Keyserling, consulting economist and attorney; John I. Snyder, president, U.S. Industries, Inc.; James G. Patton, president, National Farmers Union; and Mrs. Elda Luebbert, president of the Ladies Auxiliary of the IAM.

POLITICAL ACTION

Political Action was stressed by many speakers and was emphasized in several resolutions adopted by the delegates. Adlai E. Stevenson and Estes Kefauver, the Democratic nominees for president and vice president, who addressed the delegates, received the convention's endorsement. Senator Wayne Morse, of Oregon, also spoke and was endorsed. Delegates also registered their support of the Machinists' Non-Partisan Political League, a voluntary organization of IAM members.

The center of power in American unions is in the national office. The national (usually called international, because of affiliates in Canada) unions wield more authority than the top federation, the AFL–CIO, on the one hand, or the local unions, on the other hand. But the vitality and life of the labor movement lie in the local unions. The public reads headlines about the national officers, but the things that matter most to the worker are taken care of by his local. We try next to get some impression of these organizations.

THE TWENTIETH ANNIVERSARY OF RITTMAN LOCAL 150

By Rudy Samic, President, from The Pulp, Sulphite and Paper Mill Workers' Journal, November–December, 1953

Rittman Local No. 150 will celebrate its twentieth anniversary this year. As President of the Local No. 150 this memorable year, I believe it will interest those who were members of this Local in its early years (in which they played such important parts) and also those who have joined in recent years to read an account of the history of the struggles and the heartaches and the internal strife which this Local has experienced. All of us can feel proud of our achievements. Not only do we consider that Rittman Local No. 150 is one of the best locals of our International Union, but we believe we have contributed, in no small measure, to making the Ohio Boxboard Company one of the best companies in this particular industry, and to making Rittman, Ohio a good town in which to live. This anniversary being an occasion of such importance, to so many, we are most desirous of having everyone acquainted with our record.

Twenty years ago (1933), Congress passed the National Recovery Act, which was signed by the late President Franklin D. Roosevelt. The Ohio Boxboard Company was one of the first big companies in Ohio to comply with the act. The eight hour day and the forty hour week was put into effect promptly. This shortening of the work week, even though a wage increase was granted, resulted in less take-home pay for the workers. This of course did not meet with the approval of the workers or the businessmen of Rittman.

In June, 1933, three members of the newly organized Akron (Ohio), Local 145 of our International Union decided to investigate the possibilities of organizing the workers at the Ohio Boxboard Company in Rittman. These men not only talked about it, but also acted. They traveled to Rittman and passed out the *Summit County Labor News* at the gates of the plant. This paper explained in detail the workers' newly acquired rights granted by Congress, to organize without fear of any discrimination by the company because of union affiliation and advertised a meeting to be held in Akron, Ohio (on the following Sunday), for the Ohio Boxboard workers.

Seventeen workers attended this meeting. Fourteen joined the Union, among whom was Paul Briggle, who took a number of application cards with him to Rittman. For the next ten days this man travelled to Akron every night, with signed application cards and initiation fees.

At this time the American Federation of Labor established an office in Akron, Ohio, with Coleman Claherty of Cleveland, Ohio, as Regional Director, primarily to assist the rubber workers in their efforts to organize and also to assist in the organization of workers in other industries in that area. Because of the intense interest and activity on the part of the Ohio Boxboard workers in their desire to be organized, they did not have too much difficulty in persuading the A.F. of L. to hold a mass meeting in Rittman for these workers. This meeting was held in the school hall. The success of this meeting can best be gauged by the fact that about 500 workers joined the Union that night.

An application was made to the International Brotherhood of Pulp, Sulphite and Paper Mill Workers for a charter, which was duly presented to the Local on August 8, 1933, at its first official meeting. At this meeting an election of officers was also held and the following elected: President, A. F. Fergison; Vice-President, Ernest Wald; Financial Secretary-Treasurer, Paul Briggle; and Ivan King as Corresponding Secretary (King resigned at the following meeting and Jay Kinch was elected).

To the late Jacob Stephan, that fighting little Organizer and Representative of our International Union, must go much of the credit for many of our accomplishments, because of his wise advice and counsel to our Local in the early years of our organization. He also assisted us in negotiating our first labor agreement with the Ohio Boxboard Company. Although by today's standards, this agreement would not be regarded as a great accomplishment, nevertheless, it was a great victory for Local 150. In addition to an increase in wages of 4c an hour, other gains were made at this time, while workers in other industries, in particular the rubber workers in Akron, were having difficulty to gain even recognition.

In 1934, Brother Hoey Taylor was elected President of Local 150. Again International Representative Stephan assisted us in negotiating another labor agreement with the company. Even though we obtained a general wage increase and other improvements, we were unable to get a "Union Shop" agreement, something so very dear to the heart of every true union-minded worker.

In 1935 Brother Ernest Wald was elected president; and that year the late Vice-President Maurice LaBelle of the International Union, assisted our Local in negotiating a new labor agreement. Being aware that very few members were attending union meetings or were paying union dues, the Ohio Boxboard Company was not very friendly during these negotiations. Several meetings were held before the company would agree to renew the labor agreement. The membership voted to accept the renewal of the labor agreement, which vote almost caused the breaking up of the local union. Subsequently, on December 1, 1935, the Company notified the local union officers that the Company was terminating the labor agreement as of January 1, 1936.

Notwithstanding the fact that International President Burke was shocked to learn of this action of the company, he was not too disheartened because he was confident that there were enough union-minded workers at the Ohio Boxboard Company who wanted to continue being members of the union. He did not ask for the return of the charter, but, instead, assigned Representative E. A. Mangan to reorganize and revitalize Rittman Local 150.

A careful investigation of the Local's condition by Representative Mangan disclosed that there were only fourteen members in good standing, that the Local had a bank balance of $5.89, but was in debt to the International Union for $60.00, and had not paid hall rent for some time, which represented another debt of $72.00. There was also much evidence of irregularities and also much dissatisfaction with the officers of the Local. No doubt most men would have sized up the situation as a hopeless case and would have picked up the charter and sent it back to the International Office, but Representative Mangan is not the type to admit defeat so easily. Instead, he set to work to resolve the financial difficulties of the Local and to re-organize it.

The payment of the overdue hall rent was extended for one month on condition that "Doc" Twineam, who owned property in Rittman, would guarantee payment. Alec Dostal also played a very important part in the reorganization, for it was at his shoe repair shop that Local meetings were held until the Local again had its own meeting hall.

The first week in January hand bills were passed out at the gate of the Ohio Boxboard Company, advising the workers of a union meeting. Thirty-seven workers responded. All paid their dues. Joseph Gaborski was elected President of the Local; other officers and committees were elected. The Local became very active, which was reflected in membership, which had grown to 200 paid-up members in about two months' time.

About this time a letter was sent to the Ohio Boxboard Company stating that we wished to meet with the officials of the company for the purpose of representing the workers. The company agreed to meet us; and the first conference was held in April, at which time we presented our demands. The company wanted time to study our proposals. After several meetings, the company agreed to give us their counter-proposal by June 8, 1936. The company's attorney notified us on that date that the company did not have a counter-proposal. We informed the company that we were having a meeting that night and that the workers were expecting some kind of an offer from the company, and as they had been very patient these several months, the attitude of the company would not be favorably received, and might have serious consequences. At that point the company's attorney remarked: "Hell! If the workers want to strike, let them strike."

During the course of the meeting that night, the outcome of the conference with the company that day was related and, as a result, a strike vote by secret ballot was taken, with only four dissenting votes. By 11:30 that night the entire plant was shut down, except the boiler room, which the Local members had agreed to operate for the purpose of plant protection.

The strike was a bitter one, as a group of business men, as well as the company, did everything possible to break the strike; but, to the undying credit of the workers, it must be said that they were firm in their conviction, and were determined to prove once and for all that there was a union in Rittman, to stay, regardless of what the sacrifice may be.

In the meantime, former Vice-President H. W. Sullivan of our International Union, with Mr. Hyland, Conciliator from Columbus, Ohio, came to Rittman and were successful in having negotiations resumed, with the result that an agreement was eventually reached, which was ratified by the Local membership. Even though many, many years have passed since the strike of '36, it is not unusual to hear remarks concerning the strike on the streets of Rittman to this very day.

During the years that followed since then, we were assisted in negotiations and other matters by Vice-President S. A. Stephens, Rasmus Anderson and Lambert Louy. During the early '40s, through the trying war years of labor shortage, Representative Mangan, upon our request, was again servicing Local 150. Though Rittman Local 150 does not expect anything in the way of appreciation, nevertheless, the citizens of Rittman owe a debt of gratitude to the Local Union for the manner in which this matter was handled.

During the years of 1943, 1944, 1945 and 1946 our Local had International representation in the persons of Henry Segal, Keith Wentz, and Ray Derhammer; and each year both monetary and working conditions were improved.

Because of the Taft-Hartley Act, a company cannot agree to give its workers a union-shop agreement without an election conducted by the National Labor Relations Board,* it being the contention of the sponsors of the bill that workers do not want a "union shop." Sorry to say that many, many people on the side of management had the same erroneous opinion. To comply with the act, much work was required on the part of the Local Union and again Representative Mangan came to our assistance and spent several weeks to get everything in readiness for an election, as required by law. Representative Carter Share was able to spend some time on this work for Local 150 also. The election showed that some 400 workers who were not even members of the Local Union then voted in favor of a "union-shop." Despite this overwhelming evidence in favor of a "union-shop," the management of the Ohio Boxboard to this day has denied Local 150 a "union-shop."

The year of 1949 was a year of internal strife. There were those workers at the Ohio Boxboard Company that had been carried away by headlines made in the daily press by the CIO, without stopping to make a true analysis of the facts. I am sure that had these workers followed the advice of Mr. P. F. Drucker, one of the foremost consultants on management problems in the United States, who had this to say: "The CIO makes the headlines; the AFL makes the gains," I am sure there would have been no problem. Although this Local is grateful to Representatives E. A. Mangan, William Lauman, and A. H. Patin for their untiring efforts to keep the Local intact, much of the credit for this belongs to Boyd Artrip, the President of Local 150 at that time, who could not be persuaded to leave our Local, regardless of the pressure exerted upon him, nor could he be bribed with any amount of money. He had taken an

* Editor's note: This provision was repealed in 1951.

obligation when he accepted the office as President and he intended to fulfill this obligation, come what may. Prior to the election to determine the bargaining agent for the workers, International President John P. Burke and other Representatives came to Rittman to address the workers at a mass meeting held at the school hall. When the election was held and the votes tabulated, the results showed that the CIO was defeated by a margin of about 2 to 1.

While I have mentioned only the highlights in the history of Rittman Local 150, and the Presidents that were in office during those periods, nevertheless, any and all of the members that were ever elected to office and those who contributed in any way to the success of Local 150, would make a list extremely long. I shall therefore, confine myself only to the past Presidents who have not been mentioned. My immediate predecessor was Lewis Lutz. He was preceded by Herbert Willems. Others were John Conrad, Joe Garborsky, Charley Kline, Andrew Graham and Thomas Clinkenbeard.

Though we have made continued progress in increased earnings and better working conditions and today are enjoying those things that were just wishful thinking twenty years ago, such as paid vacations, paid insurance, pensions, premium pay for overtime, seniority, etc., nevertheless, we must continually strive to improve our labor agreement. I am sure that if the local officers, committees, and members will cooperate with each other and with our International Union through our International Representatives, we will prove worthy of the task before us, and when the time comes for us to pass on to others the responsibility that is now ours, may it be said of us that we have been ever faithful to the trust that was given us, and that because of our contribution (though it may be small) the Ohio Boxboard Company is a better Company to work for and Rittman is a better place to live in.

FOR DISCUSSION AND ANALYSIS

1. Draw organization charts of (*a*) the AFL–CIO and (*b*) the UAW. Which has the most centralized organization?

2. Contrast the authority of the presidents of the AFL–CIO and of the UAW. How do you explain the difference?

3. Contrast the powers of the UAW president and executive board.

4. Itemize the powers which the UAW national office exercises over the local union. What justification for each of these powers can you see?

5. Some people believe that unions are undemocratic organizations. Do you find any provisions in the constitution of either AFL–CIO or UAW which support that criticism? In what ways does the formal constitutional government of an organization fail to reveal how democratic or undemocratic that organization may be?

6. What changes in the constitution of the Automobile Workers would you advocate in order to make it a more democratic organization—however democratic it may be now? Would the changes which you recommend have the effect of reducing its strength?

4: Union Leadership

There are two ways we could go about trying to acquire some compre-hension of the kind of men who run the unions. One would be statistical—the age, parental background, educational attainments, social status, political affiliation, and so on, of this group. Professor C. Wright Mills of Columbia University has used this approach in his book New Men of Power. There is another more restricted way, which we shall adopt here, of relying on the more detailed biographical sketches of some of these men. Below is a snapshot in action of the president of one national union, followed by another of the president of the Teamsters' St. Louis Joint Council 13. Two men do not make a sample, and these can hardly be viewed as "typical" union leaders, but they do help give some insight into the men of labor.

A DAY IN THE LIFE OF A LABOR LEADER

From Business Week, August 18, 1951, pp. 42–50, by special permission

6:00   It isn't quite 6 a.m. in the Rogers Park section of Chicago. [A] man has just asked the operator to connect him with a West Coast representa-tive of the Building Service Employees Int'l. Union. The man in Chi-cago is William L. McFetridge, president of the BSEIU. He's had a restless night worrying about a strike he had authorized a West Coast local union to call.

In a moment, McFetridge will be talking to his Coast officer—pulled away from a heated 12-hour bargaining session that seems fated to end in a walkout. McFetridge is going to tell him he has thought it over: A strike now looks like bad strategy; the local should agree to arbitrate. The West Coast local will do what McFetridge suggests. McFetridge's policies prevail in the BSEIU. They have built the union into a strong, respected, and well-run organization—a far cry from what it was under his predecessor, the notorious George Scalise.

To achieve that feat, and to rise as he has in the labor movement, McFetridge has used a combination of talent, shrewdness, and energy. Without being so well-known as some of his compeers, McFetridge is in some ways the model U.S. labor leader. For the log of an average day in the union executive's work life, [we continue].

7:45   McFetridge leaves his seven-room corner house. He has read two news-
       papers. [He has] homework under his arm.
8:00   He unparks his Cadillac and drives to work. It's usually his only half-
       hour of the day free from business details.
8:20   He reaches his office, just west of the Loop. The seven-story Building
       Service Center is owned by BSEIU.
8:30   Mail, memos, phone calls. Most deal with new contracts, union rival-
       ries, staff problems, employer relations.
10:30 Staff conferences begin. [On this day], one is with Martin Dwyer, of
       Local 66, on pay rates for elevator starters.
11:30 Meetings. [Today it is] a group of BSEIU agents. The agenda: em-
       ployer relations, rank-and-file sentiment, reports.
1:00   Lunch—always business. This time it's with Frank C. Wells, president
       of Chicago Real Estate Board, over effect of rent control on real estate
       income.
2:30   McFetridge budgets two afternoons a week for civic activity. [Today]
       he sits as a member of the Chicago Parks Commission. His associates,
       business and professional men, value his judgment.
4:00   At his office in the Park District's headquarters, he goes over all build-
       ing plans. He has been a member since 1943, is now chairman of the
       commission.
5:15   Back to his own office. If he hasn't got his second wind by this time,
       he'll have stopped for a single Martini.
5:30   And on until 7:30—or it may be 9, 10, or midnight—in his ceaseless
       battle to clear his desk before leaving.
8:30   Tonight it's a dinner on the far West Side, given by one of his locals
       to city bowling champions. He'll make a speech. . . . With luck, he'll
       be home by 1 a.m.

An opinion polling organization once asked loyal union members what they
thought employers did. Some of the answers were pretty sensible, but many
of them would hit the average businessman like a sharp jab in the solar plexus.
Reappearing frequently were such responses as: entertains customers at fancy
night clubs; clips coupons; goes to Florida; sits in his club and damns the
New Deal.

Shocking as these opinions are, they nevertheless bear some resemblance to
those held by some businessmen about labor leaders. The average union head
has some reason to believe that he is regarded in management circles as a
high-living, Florida-commuting, orating, trouble-maker.

In actual fact, job descriptions of the work of responsible union executives
and business executives would have a great deal in common. And even where
they would appear most divergent, there are subsurface similarities.

For example: The time spent by the labor man making speeches and talking
to the press is aimed at the same general object as the businessman's time for
advertising and public relations problems.

The labor man's parleys with fellow laborites are of the same stuff as the
management man's activities in his trade association.

And in one area now, it's almost impossible to tell whether it's a union or a business executive doing the complaining about the increasing amount of time required. That's in dealing with lawyers. How to operate under government regulations raises questions that have appreciably lengthened the workday of both. Opposed as may be their goals, philosophy, and interests, their executive responsibilities make them cousins, if not brothers, under the skin.

WOMB TO TOMB

Although labor executive William L. McFetridge gets pictured and quoted in the newspapers less than some other union leaders who preside over large organizations, his job is pretty much the same as those who are basking in the limelight.

He runs the union of 200,000 men and women who operate the elevators, do the building and grounds maintenance, wash the windows, dispose of the garbage, and perform other services in urban life.

His Building Service Employees International Union, like so many other labor organizations, is not accurately named. It includes men and women workers having nothing at all to do with building service.

It is, among other things, the world's only womb-to-tomb union. In the bizarre jurisdictional patchquilt that is the AFL, McFetridge has managed to get BSEIU membership cards into the soft hands of nurses' aides who prepare expectant mothers for their trip to the delivery room, and into the calloused palms of men who dig graves in some of the largest cemeteries in the United States.

BSEIU has contracts with Harvard College and California Tech; with burlesque theaters and Trinity Church; with Rockefeller (for Radio City), and more John Does and Richard Roes than possibly any other labor organization. The Does and Roes are the small landlords who sometimes employ only one man, a janitor.

But McFetridge wants that one employee to be in BSEIU and has made law by getting the courts to decide one employee is "an appropriate bargaining unit" for purposes of a labor board election.

RISE OF A LEADER

McFetridge will be 58 years old his next birthday. Up to a point his biography might be that of any one of scores of well-known businessmen. He was born in a Chicago factory neighborhood and was in the sixth grade at public school when the family moved to McFarland, Wis. His father, a teamsters union member, owned and operated a small ice delivery service.

McFetridge quit school and small-town life when he was 13; he got a $20-a-month office boy job at the Milwaukee Road in Chicago. Seventeen years later, he had worked himself up to traveling claims agent. Then he thought he saw a better opportunity with American Express. It wasn't there, and he went back to the Milwaukee Road, staying until 1923.

During these years, McFetridge felt squeezed between his ambitions and his limited education. To make up what he lacked, he went to night school "for more years than I want to remember," he says. Through high school, prelaw, and law school he dogged it three hours a night, night after night, year after year. It has given him one unusual attribute: No matter how tired he is, he can't nap after dinner. "I used to hold my breath to keep awake," he says, recalling the tedium of the grubby classrooms. "Now I couldn't fall asleep in a chair if I was drugged." It's an invaluable asset for a man who has to spend a great many of his evenings on a dais, listening to speech follow speech after a very hearty serving of roast chicken.

At the age of 30, McFetridge saw his star. He accepted a job offer from his uncle, William Quesse, who was then president of the Chicago Flat Janitors Union—Local 1 of BSEIU. The newcomer to the labor movement was employed as confidential secretary, general aide, investigator, and trouble-shooter; it was work for which his experience as claims agent was not badly suited.

On his own, the union tyro organized Chicago school maintenance workers. He became head of their new local, which affiliated with BSEIU. After that, his rise was sure, if not too rapid. By 1940 he was a national vice-president of BSEIU, an officer in both the Illinois and Chicago Federations of Labor, a well-known and important union figure in the Midwest. Having reached a secure position in the second magnitude, like so many corporation vice-presidents, it looked as though he had gone just about as far as he could go.

THE TURNING POINT

But then the lightning struck. When the storm was over, George Scalise, president of BSEIU was on his way to jail for extortion; the union had declined to fewer than 70,000 discouraged, embittered members; at least $1.5-million was missing from the union treasury; and McFetridge himself had gone through—and survived unsullied—marathon grand jury sessions where everything including his remote cousins' bank accounts were subpoenaed, audited, and examined.

The careful, almost-reluctant conclusion of the courts and prosecutors was that McFetridge was an honest man in a nest of thieves. It was that conclusion and his experience that made him the logical man for the job of putting the union back together after Scalise and the Capone mob had left it a shambles. Along with a few seasoned men—like David Sullivan in New York, Charles Hardy in San Francisco, and William Cooper in Milwaukee—who had been uncorrupted by the gangsters, he started the rehabilitation and rebuilding.

Under his presidency, BSEIU has become powerful, wealthy, and respected. It has achieved a record of peaceful bargaining, contract observance, and wage progress that not many other unions can equal. And rising with the union, McFetridge has now moved well into the first magnitude of labor leaders.

Today he is a member of AFL's top executive council, along with such other large men as Hutcheson of the carpenters, Tobin of the teamsters, Dubinsky of the garment workers. He is the newest member of that select group, having been elected to it only last year. But already some of the people whose ideas count are saying he might be the man to succeed Bill Green when the time comes for the federation to get a new president.

LOW-PRESSURE APPROACH

Meanwhile, McFetridge preserves a rare nonconformism for a labor leader. He doesn't mind being called a Republican and was unperturbed by the barbs tossed in his direction when he came out for Dewey in the Presidential election of 1948.

His union salary is $32,000 a year—cut back to $22,000 during the war at his request. His nonunion life centers on his wife and two now-grown daughters; on a summer home near Antioch, Ill.; on a lake where he can fish and swim; and now—like many another Chicagoan—on the ups and downs of the White Sox in the American League pennant race.

In negotiations with employers, McFetridge operates at a low pressure, is addicted to brief speaking, and is almost subdued in manner. He has a habit of looking at you, intent and unsmiling, while his fingers make and unmake a church steeple in moments of greatest concentration.

McFetridge will sometimes bowl an employer over with an observation or insight that could only come from a businessman. To the question, where did he get it, the answer is simple: He's a director of the Bank of Rogers Park and participates in the conservative management of its more than $11-million assets.

MEET HAROLD J. GIBBONS

From the St. Louis Globe-Democrat, by Con Kelliher, staff writer, August 26, 1956

POWERFUL BOSS OF ST. LOUIS TEAMSTERS
IS ONE OF CITY'S MOST CONTROVERSIAL FIGURES

The oft-quoted verse by the late Grantland Rice points out:
"When the Great Scorer comes to mark against your name, He'll not write 'won' or 'lost,' but how you played the game."

The tally sheet of Harold Joseph Gibbons, 46, the Teamsters Union version of an egghead, can be stamped V for victory right now.

But while there's no doubt about who'll bag all the marbles, supernatural powers probably would be required to determine precisely how Gibbons is playing the game.

He is an intent, hungry-looking and restless man. He can flit from picket line to pokey, if need be, and then to the lecterns of a number of universities—or across the seas on government or labor goodwill missions.

Looming as perhaps the city's most powerful political force, Gibbons denies being a Democrat and yet was a delegate to the Democratic national convention. He returned home from Chicago instead of going on a scheduled tour of Israel. Illness in his family, not the wildcat taxi strike, caused the change in his plans.

Gibbons obviously is a man of many sides, and few foes or spectators see him through the same mirror. Their reports, seldom impartial, add to the fog of rumor, propaganda, hero worship and downright hatred that surrounds one of St. Louis' most controversial citizens.

MEET MR. GIBBONS

So while Gibbons speeds indomitably toward personal goals known only to himself, the testimony of others as to what he's about and how he'll get there, must be weighed.

But first, a brief introduction of Exhibit A:

Gibbons was one of 23 children in a Pennsylvania coal miner's family. His father died when he was 14 and the family moved to Chicago. Gibbons learned the cook's trade and scrounged for an education in night classes. He attended a summer labor school at the University of Wisconsin, and thereby discovered his niche in life.

He had qualified himself as a WPA teacher of skills for young workers, and this led to membership and a leader's role in the American Federation of Teachers.

Soon he was in the midst of the Chicago labor organizing campaign, and he became a leader in the 1937 Chicago taxicab strikes. When the CIO was formed, he became an organizer for several of its new unions. Eventually he arrived in St. Louis in a patched blue serge suit, and began organizing warehousemen.

Local 688, of which he is secretary-treasurer, is a sort of monument to Gibbons' conception of a labor organization. He shaped it, led it out of a CIO international union in a factional fight, and found a shelter for it in the Teamsters Union.

The Teamsters, somewhat dazed to find a man with Gibbons' energies and new-fangled ideas in their midst, quickly decided they could use his talents over a wide field. He is now president of the Teamsters Joint Council 13, heading the 40,000 men who keep the truck wheels rolling in this region.*

SOCIAL SERVICE

Local 688, comprised of 10,000 warehousemen, operates like a small-scale international union. Through its Labor Health Institute (paid for by the employers), it provides medical care for members, and virtually cradle-to-the-grave medical care for members' families. This and other social action programs cause university professors, unionists and other delegations to visit Local 688 to observe first-hand its operations.

The first witness is another big St. Louis labor leader who has long kept a wary eye on Exhibit A:

A lot of other union officers go along with Gibbons because they're afraid to do otherwise. There's a lot of things to be said about Gibbons, but nobody's going to say them. But any one is mistaken to say he doesn't know how to develop a program and make it work. Gibbons has abilities, and is articulate in expressing those abilities.

* Editor's note: Since this writing Gibbons has also become vice-president of the international union.

An employer, who remembers the days when sugaring a business agent would sweeten negotiations: "Gibbons personally doesn't care about money, or what money will buy. You can't buy off the —–––."

OBEYS CONTRACTS

Almost all management men will candidly admit their side of the table cannot match the skill and polish of Gibbons' negotiating crews. The union negotiators are always backed by voluminous data compiled by Gibbons' statisticians, economists and researchers. "They pinpoint how the company makes its dollar, and just how it is spent," said one observer.

A builder declared: "You better know your business, or they'll take your coat as well as your pants in negotiations. But I'll say one thing for Gibbons: when you sign a contract, his union always lives up to it."

A management lawyer answers: "There's no reason for Gibbons not to observe a contract. They're written on his terms of heads-I-win, tails-you-lose. He deserves no credit for adhering to such agreements."

A boss says: "In this age when everybody is chasing a dollar, it makes you suspicious when you come across somebody like Gibbons, who doesn't have the same interest. If the guy isn't interested in money, what does he want?"

The answer may be supplied by an observer who finds diversion in his own continuing study of what makes Gibbons gallop.

"The man is interested in people—sincerely interested in them and their welfare," he declares, chuckling: "And what Gibbons thinks is good for people is good for them—period! They can't argue with him.

"Unfortunately, this interest does not conflict with the second great motivation in Gibbons' life—his desire for power!"

In rebuttal, a mortgage banker says: "Anyone interested in people usually shows a sense of humor. How often have you seen Gibbons laugh and mean it?"

AFRAID OF HIM

Derisive hoots also come from labor sources. Many other union leaders say Gibbons undoubtedly is interested in the welfare of "his own people"—the teamster members he serves so well—but they doubt if his interest flows benignly to other labor groups.

What serves the interests of the teamsters, not what is best for the labor movement as a whole, they charge, would cause Gibbons to ride roughshod over other unions.

These modifications on his original analysis are cheerfully accepted by the man who secretly keeps Gibbons under a microscope. He himself often wonders if Gibbons likes business and businessmen. He sometimes suspects that deeply rooted in the labor leader's subconscious and unknown to Gibbons himself, is a dislike for business that stems from Gibbons' earlier preoccupation with Socialism.

"I can also tell you Gibbons' weakness," says this observer. "It is his failure to realize when it's time to quit pushing management. He wants power and recognition, a sense of accomplishment. But a lot of us puzzle over how wisely he will use his power.

"We're not afraid of George Meany, president of the AFL-CIO. Meany has great power, but he also has a sense of judgment, an ethical sense of responsibility to restrain him. Hoffa (James R. Hoffa, an international vice president of the union) also has a sense of responsibility. He figures just how far he can go and stops there." *

A business observer agrees that Gibbons primarily seeks recognition.

"You usually find his kind on our side of the fence," he says. "I can show you several St. Louis executives just like him. Although income tax schedules make it impossible for a man to amass a personal fortune these days, these fellows keep fighting their way to the top—just for recognition.

"They cannot be stopped, they cannot stop themselves; it's an inner compulsion that keeps them driving to get to the top of the heap."

BLAMES BUSINESS

Gibbons, who can easily slip into the ungrammatical vernacular of the docks when addressing followers there, often talks like a business executive when examining his own problems in his office in Local 688, at 1127 Pine st.

He recently was reminded of the frequent charge that teamsters' contract demands often threaten to drive small businesses to the wall.

No industrial leader defending his organization in anti-monopoly hearings could answer more coolly or incisively than Gibbons when he said:

If any ever go to the wall, it will be because they were bound to fail anyway, even if we had not been in the picture. The fact is, some businesses cannot hope to operate successfully because they are undercapitalized; or, because their management simply isn't qualified to be management.

On the other hand, Local 688 can say this: "Not a single businessman has ever come in here with a valid complaint or problem who hasn't been given a break."

There are many thoughtful men who are gravely disturbed by the potential chain reaction that could blast loose if someone happened to rudely joggle the present mixture of Gibbons power and Gibbons personality.

FACES CHARGES

But they see little wisdom in the type of charges hurled by some of his non-admirers. For example, in 1954, an apparently highly financed publication of murky origin raked Gibbons in every issue. Among other things, it charged he was a Red.

The charge was made shortly after the American Legion in the District of Columbia had awarded Gibbons a citation—"for outstanding service in combating Communism."

Victor Riesel, the labor columnist and friend of Gibbons, wrote a column protesting the baseless charge. Riesel, whose articles appear in The Globe-

* Editor's note: Hoffa was elected Teamsters' president in 1957.

Democrat, and who is an arch foe of Communists and racketeers, recently was
blinded when a hoodlum threw acid in his face.

The publication that accused Gibbons was making its appearance at a time
when the union suspected a "get-Gibbons" drive was reaching its peak. A federal grand jury joined in the chase. It returned a shallow indictment based on
a bookkeeping technicality that allegedly violated the Taft-Hartley law. The
indictment was twice dismissed by the courts.

Gibbons also spent 43 hours in jail for contempt when he at first refused to
turn over union records to the grand jury. He said he was fighting the sub-
poena as a matter of principle, alleging the grand jury suspected no wrongdoing, but was just on "a fishing expedition."

The grand jury in an interim report rapped Gibbons' union for allegedly
driving industries from St. Louis through excessive contract demands. Gibbons
produced letters and statements from departed firms, speaking of their pleasant
relations with him and Local 688.

DRIVEN OUT?

The outgoing firms did not move to Georgia or Mississippi or other low-labor-
cost areas, but for the most part to regions where pay scales are higher, union
researchers point out.

"Basic changes taking place today in methods of wholesale and retail distribution, not unreasonable union demands, have been responsible for concerns
leaving," Gibbons says.

His research people expand on the statement. For example, rumor has it
that the J. C. Penney warehousing operation was "driven out of town by Gibbons." The facts seem to be that Penney was quitting warehouse operations
entirely, and had closed other installations before the St. Louis building was
affected.

Local 688 analysts warn that St. Louis, a recognized distribution center, has
a new basic problem the whole community should be considering. Modern
warehouse operations call for buildings not more than two stories tall, but covering lots of space, with conveyor belts and other efficient cost-cutting
equipment.

According to the researchers, other cities are more fortunate in finding adequate space on which to build the new type of warehouses. They say some
firms in St. Louis are therefore hard put to match the efficient type of operations going on in new warehouses in other cities.

CAN STOP WHEELS

In one respect, Gibbons should appreciate the grand jury's interest. Probably
no St. Louisan or institution ever underwent such a probing scrutiny as he
did. FBI agents, internal revenue men, special investigators—the government's
best—peered into every cranny of Gibbons' past and present, and tried to divine
his future.

Their failure to come up with anything, up to this time, at least, leaves him in the happy position to feel that his professional life bears the government's stamp for clean living.

If Gibbons has many admirable qualities, what is it that causes others to fear him?

Primarily, it's the thought of what he could do with his power. He could stop every vital wheel in this area—at least once—if he so chose. Such drastic action undoubtedly would lead to his downfall as a dominant labor leader.

"But Gibbons wouldn't do a thing like that!" protest his devoted colleagues. "If the stakes were big enough, who says he wouldn't?" growl the skeptical.

Labor and business got a sample of what could happen in 1953, when 500 construction drivers went on an 85-day strike against mixed-concrete firms to win their demands. The impasse made about 27,000 other workers jobless, with an estimated wage loss of $25,000,000.

The bitterness generated by the strike clouded the fact it was the first prolonged teamster walkout in 20 years.

Hoffa finally came in to negotiate. When the agreement was reached, at almost the terms originally asked by the union, the employers didn't want to let Gibbons sign the contract for the union.

SOME HATE HIM

Gibbons recalls that, as he and Hoffa left one session, Hoffa said: "Gibbons, there are some men in Detroit who dislike me—but those fellows back there actually hate you!"

Gibbons, who doesn't laugh much with strangers, chuckles when he relates this story, because: "That's the only time I have ever seen Hoffa impressed by anything."

Politicians fear Gibbons because he is on his way to becoming the most powerful among them. As to his political potential, one shrewd observer says: "Give me Gibbons and Local 688, and you can have the rest of the Democratic organization—Jack Dwyer, Tony Sestric, the whole lot. Gibbons is the man to watch."

Gibbons, a personal friend of Averell Harriman, says business has forced labor into the political arena.

"They used to beat us by bringing in the strike-breakers," he says. "Now they do it by passing laws hostile to unions. Ninety per cent of our troubles come from laws designed to put clamps on labor. So we're going to have to make our voices heard in legislative halls, as a matter of self-protection."

POLITICAL ACTION

Gibbons has begun one of the most effective local union political-action programs in the nation. Local 688 has "community stewards" throughout the city, to take up the citizens' grievances about slow removal of fallen trees or garbage, the need for playgrounds, location of bus stops and the like.

Most of the chores are of the type ward committeemen ordinarily handle. The difference, is, Local 688 is more alert than most committeemen. Increasingly more people look to the local to get things done in the neighborhood. When elections roll around, these same people might follow the union's recommendations on candidates.

Politicians are apt to brood about the union's community center at Bischoff avenue and Marconi street, in the "hill" area. The center is just a pilot plant. As soon as operational kinks are ironed out, Gibbons hopes to set up more such centers.

Citizens can go to the present community center to get notary public service, assistance in making out all tax returns, to pay utility bills, and to buy auto licenses and stickers, hunting and fishing licenses. There is a juke box, ping pong tables and other recreational facilities, and a "teen town" also has operated there.

Gibbons says it will be five years before the community action program hits full stride. But then he hopes the union will be devoting half its income, or $250,000 a year, to the program. Only $40,000 goes into it now.

The community program has scored one big victory. The union was successful in getting the courts to order St. Louis to enforce its rat-control in slums as well as in other parts of the city.

Some city officials earlier had taken the position that rat control was a waste in some areas where buildings might be torn down for slum clearance. Local 688 contended that as long as people were living in the old buildings, the fight against rats had to continue.

NATIONAL FIGURE

Just what tack the union will take in the upcoming political campaign remains to be seen. Gibbons undoubtedly will want to improve on the 1952 showing, when the teamsters' backing of Republican Howard Elliott for Governor didn't keep Phil M. Donnelly from winning.

Still another reason why Gibbons is feared by both business and labor is his steady climb as a national teamster union power. He has one paying job, that of secretary-treasurer of Local 688, at $15,000 a year.

He stands for re-election once every three years, and the secret ballot vote of the membership returns him to office by a five-to-one margin over opponents. The union is operated democratically and Gibbons is returned to office simply because he does a good job for its members.

He also is secretary of the Central States Conference of Teamsters, and Hoffa is conference president. They are long-range planners and shrewd field marshals who want uniform pay scales throughout their 13-state region, and the nation.

Formerly, most Teamster officials had operated in little baronies of their own, without any regional co-ordination of aims. They also are mainly "meat and potato" unionists, seeking only better pay scales and ignoring frills like Gibbons' Labor Health Institute, and community action programs.

One article has quoted a veteran labor leader as saying most teamster organizers are "old ducks with bellies hanging over their belts." This is not true of the sharp-thinking Hoffa, Gibbons and company.

Gibbons also is the director of the international union's warehousing division, and has a second office and staff in Washington.

HAS LAST WORD

He has an explanation as to why he is not popular with many labor leaders here: "Nobody loves a rich uncle."

"Our position is unique, in that we probably are the only union which touches on the basic operations of all others," he says. "Whenever another union considers a strike, the first question is, will the teamsters honor the picket lines. So they approach us for the answer."

If the teamsters don't cross the picket line, the striking union is almost virtually assured of a victory. But Gibbons realizes it must be galling to other union officials to have to come to his office to ask help. If he were in their shoes, he wouldn't like it himself.

Gibbons denies that his union seeks the work belonging to other crafts, or raids members of other unions. He cites instances, all of which seem minor, in which Teamsters have lost workers, like cafeteria employes, to some other union.

But obviously Teamsters have an economic lever, not available to other unions, to use in reclaiming what they consider their own, if they really want it. All they have to do is stop trucks rolling into the plant where the dispute lies.

Already the largest union in the world with about 1,500,000 members, the Teamsters are expanding rapidly and probably will not be stopped by either business or other unions which see the growth as ominous.

Gibbons probably will continue to advance in stature as the Teamsters grow.

"While Gibbons has not learned when to quit pushing," says his secret watcher, "he nevertheless is intelligent, energetic, tireless, and is a terrific driving force. It's impossible to keep down a man of his kind."

But whether Gibbons will be wearing the mantle of labor statesmanship that he covets when he reaches the top is still the unanswered question.

THE MANAGERS OF LABOR

One perceptive observer of the Labor scene, Dr. Marshal Scott, wrote the following in January, 1954.

The CIO national convention . . . now two months past . . . was the fifteenth constitutional convention of the CIO. The change in 15 years is almost unbelievable. Fifteen years ago the CIO was a genuine revolutionary upsurge among mass production workers. Men were sacrificially fighting and dying for freedom and justice. In the 1953 convention theme and goals (and speeches) there was not one revolutionary appeal—only a modest urge for refinements in our present social and political system.

The delegates were all comfortably dressed and fed middle-class executives. They are younger, smoke fewer cigars, and look more like big industry management than the AFL delegates. In fact, for the first time I realized that if it had

not been for the great depression of the 1930's most of these young men would
have become management. These are the alert, intelligent, aggressive younger
men who normally advance into management. The depression thwarted them
and they turned to the labor movement with zeal to right a wrong. . . . Now
these men are the executives in the labor bureaucracy.

*Professor Lloyd H. Fisher in "The Price of Union Responsibility," a paper
presented to the National Conference of Social Work at its Seventy-fourth
Annual Meeting, 1947*

In a complex society such as our own the distance between membership and
leadership grows daily wider. The separation between ownership and management which occurred long ago in the joint stock corporations has its analogies
in the labor union. The separation is not yet so great, but it continues to grow.
The union executive can often speak with the same authority that lends so
much weight to the statements of a corporation president. . . .

The labor leader lives partly in the world of management and partly in the
world of the worker. He has frequently to choose between the role of militant
rank-and-file leader and that of business envoy to management, between the
conduct of a military campaign and the negotiation of a commercial treaty.

LOCAL UNION POLITICS

*Wherever there are organizations which offer exceptional individuals a
chance to distinguish themselves from the crowd by exercising leadership
functions, there must be politics. People vie for office, seek to organize
followings, attempt to win the approval of the electorate. Unions inescap-
ably have their politics, and union politics sometimes "takes it out" on
management.*

*Excerpt from a personal letter written by an active member of a mailers union
local in the Middle West*

Last February I was removed from the presidency in one of the most beautiful smear campaigns I have ever seen. Up to then, there had been very little
action of a political nature in our local. I didn't think the boys wanted politics,
but, before I was aware of what was going on, there I was really ostracized.
There had been free beer and card parties for an ever widening secret group.
For more than a month before the elections, about half of the membership
would not even talk to me. I tried to find out what was wrong, but could get no
answers. I was defeated by a goodly figure by John Adams, the boss's brother.

Boy, I saw the company behind the whole thing. I couldn't picture "my boys"
doing that to me without some outside interference. I tried to give them everything and do the job right. Most of the boys were fairly intelligent, I thought.
I really got tough after the election and got down and played marbles the way
the opposition did. It wasn't long before I heard of some of the gossip spread by
the "boys." I robbed the treasury, and everything (but) hang my mother-in-law.
I was a communist, an office man.

As time marches on, I think the real analysis is that the whole thing was a reaction to the strenuous time spent in organizing. Extreme clannishness was the key to our success over office interference. Also, during our first year, we had continual action, while during the last year there was little activity. We had a two year contract and the boys craved action after the end of the first year. The contract was signed for two years, so there was only one outlet for the stored up energy. I was it.

Since Adams took over, he has stuck his neck out on every occasion. (Bragging) I had to straighten everything out.

Gradually the boys are regaining confidence in me, I hope. At any rate, when our Secretary-Treasurer was drafted, I sneaked into that office. That was a close election, but, it was encouraging to this poor old man.

Our scale is coming up shortly, and the boys are looking to me to fill their pockets "now, if ever." If the boys liked their little politics, I think I can give them a fairly good show.

A reply to a question addressed to William Gomberg, then Director, Management Engineering Department, International Ladies' Garment Workers Union, in a forum of the America Management Association, reprinted from The Union's Role in Production Management, American Management Association Production Series No. 189, 1950, pp. 23–24

QUESTION: Can absolute work standards be maintained by a union suffering from internal politics?

MR. GOMBERG: To the same extent to which they can be maintained by a management suffering from internal politics. That's what I call a loaded question. The assumption is that unions are more political than they are, because union bureaucracy is relatively public. Businesses are also political, but there the bureaucracy is private.

Politics enter into a union when various people vie for the confidence of the membership. And so a scramble ensues. Politics enter into a company when the various executive heads vie for the favor of the guy whose decision is final. Union politics take place in a democratic frame of reference—business politics in an authoritarian frame of reference. And with all those limitations, both management and labor have maintained production standards.

Here is the way the problem solves itself. Sooner or later, the fellow who tries to be a demagogue by continually pressing the company for an unreasonable production standard begins to get on the nerves of the membership, because they want to work—provided that they get a decent break from management—not to be kept in a state of perpetual turmoil. In the normal course of events, a local union election is held, and the fellow who has nothing more than a neurosis to recommend him to the membership is thrown out.

Why are wildcat strikes no longer a problem? Remember when everybody was so worried about wildcats? The reason wildcats are no longer a problem is that the fellows who would militantly march the boys out on the picket line, would then have to march them back a few days later without any improvement in working conditions. The boys got sick and tired of having these fellows

march them in and out, so they threw them out of office and that was the end
of that. These situations stabilize themselves. That is how production standards
get stabilized in a union.

Now, when union politics arise as a result of management's playing politics
—whether by trying to get rid of the union or by favoring the particular faction
with which it thinks it can make a deal—then management becomes a party
to the mess and things never get settled. But given an ordinary relationship,
where management has made up its mind that it ought to live with the union,
and the union is still wild—its heritage, doubtless, of the days when the very
existence of unions was challenged—certain stabilizing groups begin to assert
themselves in the union.

I cannot promise you that if on Monday you make up your mind to a sound
relationship with the union, on Tuesday you are going to have perfect peace
and complete acceptance of reasonable standards. But I can tell you this: Over
the course of two years or so, given a good relationship with management, the
political situation within the union will gradually stabilize. The union man who
is willing to take a stand and make it possible for these fellows to keep working
and make their wages will win and the result will be that you need fear no
politics in the union as far as you are concerned.

What you mean by politics, of course, is the ugly sort of politics, for the
very relationship of management and workers is politics. After all, what is
politics? It is the way men contest for authority, whether on the board of
directors or on the executive board of the union.

NATIONAL UNION POLITICS

*Occasionally union members who feel they have been denied their
democratic rights within the union have taken their complaints to courts
of law. The decision and opinion below arose from an internal dispute
within the National Brotherhood of Operative Potters concerning the
rights of members to electioneer on behalf of opposition candidates.*

*Crossen v. Duffy, Court of Appeals of Ohio, Seventh District, No. 689, June 11,
1951*

J. THOMPSON

The first case to reach this court was that of Finlay et al vs Duffy et al, 57
O.L.A. 442, decided by this Court on May 19, 1950. In the Finlay case, the
plaintiffs were certain members of the National Brotherhood of Operative
Potters and the defendants were national officers of that Union. The membership of the Union comprises operative potters belonging to separate local
unions scattered throughout the United States and Canada. These local
unions, some 114 in number, with a local membership of more than 28,000
members, are affiliated with and under the jurisdiction of the National Brotherhood of Operative Potters. In the Finlay case, the plaintiff members had
sought an injunction against certain salary increases of the national officers,

claiming that the increases were unauthorized and in violation of the Constitution of the National Union and of its subordinate locals.

The increased salary for the national officers had been voted by the Executive Board in early 1947. In May, 1947, a spirited campaign developed within the Union on the part of individual members (Finlay, Whippler et al) campaigning as a slate opposed to the then officers of the National Brotherhood. These members failed of nomination and the officers who for many years had guided the National Brotherhood policies were re-elected at the Annual Convention in June, 1947. In that National Convention a resolution was introduced and passed by the delegates amending the Constitution. The language of the resolution was as follows:

Report of Law Committee—recommendation

Whereas, the Law Committee has been instructed to offer a solution for unethical tactics and conduct in the past election; and

Whereas, The dignity of our organization has been lowered; therefore be it

Resolved, That any member contesting for national office shall conduct himself in a proper manner; and be it further

Resolved, That any member accused of making false accusations, misrepresentations, untruths or using degrading literature shall be called before the convention following said election, by a majority vote thereof.

The succeeding convention could try accused member or members or elect a body of five members to try said accused, or set up a special court with power to impose a reprimand, fine, suspension or expulsion.

Committee recommends adoption.

Motion by John Thorne that we concur in the report of the committee. Motion carried unanimously.

In March, 1949, in accordance with the Constitution of the National Brotherhood, the customary primary elections were held to select the national officers for the ensuing year and in May, 1949, run-off elections were held between the two highest candidates for each office at the primaries. In this May, 1949, election there was a slate known as the "Finlay Slate" opposing the then National Officers which we may refer to as the "Duffy Slate." The Finlay slate was unsuccessful.

In the contest in May, 1949, certain of the supporters of the Finlay slate had circulated a sheet referred to as the "Green Sheet" which is plaintiffs' Exhibit 7 in this case. The election campaign at the local union levels was decidedly spirited but the Duffy slate was successful. Subsequent to the 1949 Annual Convention and prior to the Annual National Convention to be held in June, 1950, certain of the candidates for office at the May, 1949 primaries and certain of their supporters who had backed them, and who had circulated what is referred to as the "Green Sheet" received notices to appear for trial at the National Convention to be held in June, 1950. We shall return to a more specific statement of the facts concerning the action taken at the June, 1950 Convention, but at this point we may summarize the events by saying that the

National Convention of 1950 tried and punished certain of the candidates for office at the May, 1949, primary and, also, tried and punished certain of their supporters who admitted that they had either signed or circulated the "Green Sheet" or handbill referred to as Plaintiffs' Exhibit 7.

In August, 1950, Finlay and Whippler and various other candidates for national office at the May, 1949, primary, who had been punished by the National Convention in June, 1950, filed suit in the Common Pleas Court of Columbiana County (#37226) asking that Court to set aside their fines and suspensions. At the same time, a separate suit was filed in the same Court (#37227) by five members of the Union, the plaintiffs appellees in this action, none of whom were candidates for office at the May, 1949 primary, but all of whom had been punished at the June, 1950 National Convention because of their circulation of the handbill referred to as Plaintiffs' Exhibit 7, which had been used in support of the unsuccessful candidates.

We are, in this decision, in no way concerned with the court suit by the candidates for office and the sole question in this action is the question of the legality of the punishment imposed by the 1950 Convention against the five members of the union who merely circulated handbills in behalf of the unsuccessful slate at the May, 1949 primary.

In order to determine the nature of the action by these five individuals and in order to consider the punishment meted out to them and the relief which they are now requesting in court, a further examination of the facts in this case is required.

We have previously referred to and quoted the resolution adopted at the National Convention in June, 1947. That resolution in modified form, which modification was made by the national Secretary without the authority of a convention of the Brotherhood or a referendum of the members, became embodied in the Constitution of the National Union as revised October, 1947, and is therein set forth as Section 37. . . .

Section 37 of the Constitution provides that *any members* contesting for National office shall conduct themselves in a proper manner, and declares that "false accusations or misrepresentations, untruths or use of degrading literature" shall be brought to the attention of the delegates in the next Convention and then states that any candidate convicted by a majority vote of delegates may be reprimanded, fined, suspended or expelled after due and proper hearing.

Section 37 declares that if the offending member candidate is not a delegate, the Convention shall, by majority vote, elect a body of five members as a special court to hear the case.

In addition to Section 37 of the Constitution, it must be noted also that at the 1948 National Convention the following resolution was enacted:

Recommendation of Law Committee

The Executive Board shall be empowered to summon any member or members before our National Convention for examination of any act or conduct in violation of their obligation, or anything in any manner detrimental to the N.B. of O.P. and its members.

The delegates in the Convention shall have authority to impose suitable and proper penalty in any case where guilt is established.

Failure to present themselves shall not prevent the delegates from disposing of the case in accordance with letter and spirit of this law.

If proven not guilty, the member or members shall be entitled to transportation and hotel expenses to be paid by the national organization.

This law to become effective immediately. Committee recommends adoption.

Motion by T. J. Desmond that we concur in the report of the committee. Motion carried unanimously.

Plaintiffs in this case are Crossen, Gilbert, Cranston, Hammond and Snyder. Of these five plantiffs, the handbill (Plaintiffs' Exhibit 7) bears the names of three, namely, Gilbert, Cranston and Snyder, as members of a committee of six urging a change in national officers and setting forth as worthy of election the names of eight individuals which we refer to in this opinion as the Finlay slate. None of the plaintiffs in this case was a candidate on that slate, the offense charged against the plaintiffs in this case and for which they were tried, being that they either published or circulated improper campaign literature.

Prior to the June, 1949, Convention, each of the plaintiffs in this case had received a letter dated June 20, 1949. Gilbert, Cranston and Snyder received similar letters containing the following notice:

Dear Sir and Brother:

You are hereby summoned to appear in the National Convention, June 27, 9:30 a.m. Atlantic City Auditorium, Atlantic City, N.J. to defend yourself for the act of publishing malicious misrepresentations regarding present national officials in the last election.

You are being charged with violating the law adopted in the 1947 Convention, prohibiting malicious political activity within the organization.

You are to assume all expense in connection with your getting to Atlantic City. If proven guilty you will not be reimbursed for any expense whatsoever. If adjudged not guilty the N.B.O.P. will pay expenses. We remain,

Fraternally,
James M. Duffy, President
Chas. F. Jordan, Secretary-Treasurer

The letters to Crossen and Hammond also summoned them to appear at the National Convention on June 27, 1949 at Atlantic City, but these two individuals not having signed the handbill, they were summoned to appear to explain their conduct in distributing handbills to local union memberships during the recent election. . . .

It becomes important now to examine the handbill, the publication or circulation of which gave rise to the charges in this case. We reproduce the handbill as follows:

"Election N.B.O.P. Officers First Meeting in May

VOTE

We believe the present administration should be changed

—because of its—

1. Reluctance to Accept Laws and Courts of U.S.A.
2. Illegal Salary Increases.
3. Arbitrary Disregard of Wishes and Opinions of Locals and Members.
4. Unfair Election Tactics.
5. Use of Potters Herald for Personal Propaganda Agency and to Impugn Motives and Attack Members.
6. Inefficiency in Office.
7. Denial of Help to W. Va. Federation of Labor in Efforts to Increase Silicosis Benefits.
8. Duffy's Open Shop Attitude.

RESTORE DEMOCRACY IN N.B.O.P.

The following are Honest and Capable—ELECT

PRESIDENT—*Larry Finlay*

SEC. TREAS.—*P. K. Calhoun*

FIRST VICE—*E. Curry*

SECOND VICE—*Harold West*

THIRD VICE—*E. C. Armstrong*

FIFTH VICE—*Verne Phillips*

SEVENTH VICE—*Charles Boso*

EIGHTH VICE—*George Brunt*

Committee:

Norman Whippler—No. 124
E. Cranston—No. 9
Frank Applegate—No. 59
Paul Gilbert—No. 33
H. Snyder—No. 133
O. L. Sullivan—No. 201"

Plaintiffs' Exhibit 7

It should be added that in addition to the five plaintiffs in this case who were summoned to appear at the Convention, one other individual not a party to this suit, O. L. Sullivan, had his name on the handbill as a member of the Committee in behalf of the Finlay slate. The latter did not come to the Convention, but he wrote a letter stating his signature had appeared on the handbill without his authorization and he was exonerated by the National Convention.

At the National Convention which commenced on June 27, 1949, the

Convention had a number of matters to dispose of and on July 5th, the Convention took up the matter of the alleged misconduct of Crossen, Gilbert, Cranston, Hammond and Snyder pursuant to the summons received by each. The proceedings of this Convention (Plaintiffs' Exhibit 2) thus summarized the action which then occurred as follows:

> The case of the next accused by the Executive Board for distributing malicious handbills in violation of the Constitution was taken up.

> Frank Applegate, Local Union No. 59, rose and stated that he wanted to go on record that he did not have anything to do with having his name on any handbills, but that he did distribute them because he believed they were true statements.

> The prosecution stated their charge and rests their case on the presentation of the green document. . . .

> The photostatic copy of a letter sent Brother O. L. Sullivan, Local Union No. 201 from Norman Whippler, Local No. 124, was read for the record. Motion by Delegate Morgan, Local Union No. 89 that Brother Sullivan be exonerated in the misuse of his signature on the green sheet. Motion carried 108 to 24.

> Delegate Applegate, Local Union No. 59 pleads not guilty. I knew nothing of the use of my name until I saw it on the green sheet. Motion by Delegate Williams, Local Union No. 4, seconded by Delegate Blake of Local Union No. 172 we exonerate Brother Applegate, Local Union No. 59 of the use of his name on the green sheet. Motion carried 134 yes 3 no.

The proceedings of the Convention further show that by resolution subsequently adopted, after hearing, a fine of $50.00 was assessed against Gilbert, Cranston, and Snyder for putting their names to the green sheet, subject to appeal to the Executive Board. As to the charge of distributing literature on the part of Crossen and Hammond, the fine was originally fixed at $50.00 but the fine as to Crossen was at a later point in the Convention suspended and he was placed on four years probation.

This modification as to Crossen was apparently the result of a statement attributed to Crossen at the Convention and carried in the printed proceedings in which he declared, "I am willing to rub off the war paint and co-operate 100%."

Thereafter, letters were written to each of the five individuals found guilty by the Convention, advising them of the $50.00 fine. As to Crossen, it was declared that his fine was suspended and he was placed on probation for four years. As to the other four individuals, letters informed them of the fine in the amount of $50.00 each and stated that the fine would be suspended if the individuals appeared before the National Executive Board and gave satisfactory explanation of their recent conduct and assurance of good conduct in the future. The letter closed as follows:

> You must however, satisfy the Executive Board in your explanation before the fine is suspended. The fine must be paid to the National Secretary.

Under date of September 2, 1949, Gilbert, Cranston, Snyder, Crossen, and

Hammond filed their petition in the Common Pleas Court of Columbiana County naming as defendants, the National President and the National Secretary of the Union in their individual capacities and as officers of the Union. Plaintiffs alleged that they were members in good standing of the Union, having paid all dues and assessments required by law and regulations of the Union. They recited the fact that in May, 1949, an election for national officers was held by the National Union in which the defendants were candidates for election to the office of National President and National Secretary. Plaintiffs further alleged that the said defendants were opposed by another slate of candidates headed by one L. A. Finlay, and that plaintiffs had campaigned to advance the cause of the slate headed by Finlay. Plaintiffs further alleged that they distributed literature in behalf of the Finlay slate, that their slate lost in the election and that the defendants Duffy and Jordan were re-elected to the office of National President and National Secretary. The petition then recited that plaintiffs were thereafter ordered by defendants to appear at the National Convention of the Brotherhood to be held on June 25, 1949 at Atlantic City, New Jersey and to stand trial. Plaintiffs further recited that at said Convention, and regardless of whether plaintiffs were present or not at the Convention, charges were brought against them for having campaigned against the slate headed by the defendants. Plaintiffs alleged that at no time did they submit to the trial, but that nevertheless each of the plaintiffs, with the exception of Crossen, was assessed a fine of $50.00 and that plaintiff, Crossen, was placed on four years' probation. Plaintiffs further alleged that under the rules and regulations of the National Union, the payment of the fine was required to be made, the same as dues, and that if not paid, plaintiffs would be suspended from their local unions and from the National Union thus preventing them from being bona fide members of the Union and endangering their ability to pursue their trade. Plaintiffs further alleged that because of the fines assessed against them, the good standing of plaintiffs was thereby taken from them, making them ineligible under union rules to run for any office or to hold any office in the National Brotherhood or in the local unions for a period of five years. Plaintiffs further alleged that any literature distributed by them was merely to enhance the cause of the Finlay slate, which they were advocating, and they denied that they had distributed any literature of a degrading, malicious or vicious nature such as to cast disrespect upon the National Union. Plaintiffs further alleged that the defendants had presented charges and acted as prosecutor before the Convention in June, 1949, to punish plaintiffs for campaigning against them and to prevent any further activities of plaintiffs, by placing plaintiffs in a position where they would not be in good standing in their unions. Plaintiffs further alleged in their petition that the various offices for which they could run, including that of delegate to wage conferences, were valuable property rights, that their good standing in the Union was a valuable property right and that plaintiffs lacked adequate remedy at law. Plaintiffs, therefore, prayed the Court to restrain the defendants from enforcement of the penalties meted out to the plaintiffs at the Convention of 1949 and for such other and further relief as might be just and proper.

The defendants in their answer admitted that at the Annual Convention of the Union in 1949, the plaintiffs were summoned to appear on charges brought against them for conducting a campaign for National Officers of the Brotherhood in a manner contrary to the Constitution and for the act of distributing handbills to union members or for publishing malicious representations regarding the National Officers. The defendants in their answer further averred that the charges against plaintiffs, the trial by the Convention and the findings were in accordance with the provisions of the Constitution, rules, regulations, custom and usage of the National Brotherhood of Operative Potters. The answer set forth the allegation that the action of the Convention was in accordance with, and pursuant to, the Constitution and expressly quoted the resolution of July 7, 1948, as authority for the action taken. Defendants asserted that the plaintiffs were found guilty of conducting or causing to be conducted a campaign for national officers in a manner in direct violation of the Constitution of the Union.

In their reply, the plaintiffs denied that they had published or distributed handbills containing malicious representations regarding the national officers and denied the other allegations of the answer.

On the hearing of this case for the Common Pleas Court, the testimony of the various witnesses called by plaintiffs and defendants consisted primarily of the narration of the events surrounding the trial of plaintiffs in the National Convention in 1949. The trial court was advised of the evidence proffered against the plaintiffs at that time and numerous exhibits were introduced, consisting of the Constitution and By-Laws of the Union, the charges against the plaintiff contained in the letters summoning them to the trial before the Convention, various issues of The Potters Herald, the Union newspaper published under authority of the national officers and the campaign literature distributed by the opposition slate including two copies of the Potters News and the so-called "green sheet" (Plaintiffs' Exhibit 7) which we have herein above reproduced.

The testimony of the defendant, Jordan, the National Secretary-Treasurer made it clear that the only evidence presented at the Convention against plaintiffs Gilbert, Snyder and Cranston was that their names were signed to the "green sheet" (Plaintiffs' Exhibit 7) and that they had ordered the distribution of it. Jordan further stated that none of these three men was present in person at the Convention.

As to the plaintiffs Crossen and Hammond, neither signed plaintiffs' Exhibit 7, and Hammond was not present at the Convention but there was testimony that both had helped to circulate plaintiffs' Exhibit 7, and possibly also, plaintiffs' Exhibits 10 and 11.

It is apparent from the proceedings of the Convention and the testimony of defendants Duffy and Jordan that plaintiffs' Exhibit 7 was the particular literature to which objection was taken and which furnished the basis for the charges against plaintiffs and trial by the Convention.

The trial court, after analyzing the eight charges contained in plaintiffs' Exhibit 7, came to the conclusion that to punish plaintiffs for publishing and distributing the handbill in question, as the Convention attempted to do, interfered with the plaintiffs' freedom of speech and freedom of the press.

In its journal entry, the trial court declared as follows:

The Court finds that a labor union does have a right to protect itself and its members from slander or libel; the Court further finds that a labor union does not have the right to abridge the freedom of speech or the press of its members; that the literature sponsored or passed out by the plaintiffs George Crossen, Paul Gilbert and Edward Cranston, Raymond Hammond and Harry Snyder, did not amount to slander nor libel and that any punishment that the defendants will mete out to the plaintiffs for sponsoring and passing out the literature introduced in this case would be an abridgement of the freedom of speech and press.

The Court found that none of the plaintiffs, with the exception of Crossen, consented to be tried by the 1949 Convention and that Crossen consented to accept probation at the hands of the Convention.

As to plaintiffs Gilbert, Cranston, Hammond and Snyder, the trial court held that the action of the 1949 Convention in trying these men, and imposing penalties upon them, was void and of no effect and the court therefore enjoined the defendants, Duffy and Jordan, individually and as President and secretary of the National Brotherhood and also, the National Brotherhood from collecting or attempting to collect the fines imposed upon plaintiffs. The injunction was denied only as to plaintiff, Crossen. The court found that under the Constitution of the Union, failure to pay a fine would subject the members involved to suspension from membership and consequent loss of property rights.

As a result of the appeal on law and fact to this Court by the defendants Duffy and Jordan from the trial court's judgment, this Court has studied carefully the evidence in this case, including the analysis by the trial court of the eight charges published or distributed by plaintiffs in the handbill referred to as plaintiffs' Exhibit 7. We do not find that any of these charges falls within the classification of libel. It seems to us rather that the charges complained of fall within the scope of free, if not fair, criticism and the free speech guaranteed by the United States Constitution and the Constitution of Ohio. It is admitted that plaintiffs' Exhibit 7 was circulated as part of an election contest in behalf of one of two slates of national officers being presented for election, and to be voted on by the constituent local unions. The slate advocated in plaintiffs' Exhibit 7 failed of election. Each slate was warmly espoused by adherents and, in turn, strongly attacked by its opponents. Defendants, as national officers seeking re-election, had available channels of publicity not open to the slate advocated by plaintiffs, since the defendant President was editor of the official newspaper of the Brotherhood sent to all members, and the columns of that paper understandably advocated the defendants' slate and vigorously criticized the opposition, terming these individuals "smear artists," and otherwise belittling them.

In reaching our decision, we recognize that the National Brotherhood of Operative Potters is a strong union, a democratic union. Its record for successful leadership in the industrial field has been outstanding. A strong organization pre-supposes strong leadership. Such leadership calls forth strong adherents and often strong critics and lively contests, not to be found, because not tolerated, in a totalitarian climate. In our political democracy and in our economic achievements a measure of our strength in this country has been our ability to permit, and benefit by, criticism and the competition which nurtures that strength.

The important and apparently original legal question squarely presented in this case is whether a rule adopted by a mutual benefit association of the character of a labor union may infringe upon and take away fundamental liberties otherwise granted by the Constitution of the United States and the Ohio Constitution. It is quite true that by joining a mutual benefit association an individual consents to be bound as a member by rules and regulations not affecting non-members. How far may a mutual benefit association go in restricting the freedom of members? In this case, the Association involved is an Ohio corporation and it is subject to the Constitution of Ohio and the Constitution and laws of the United States. The Constitution of the United States (Amendment I) declares that Congress shall make no law "abridging the freedom of speech, or of the press." The Constitution of Ohio (Article I, Sec. II) declares as follows:

> Every citizen may freely speak, write, and publish his sentiments on all subjects, being responsible for the abuse of the right; and no law shall be passed to restrain or abridge the liberty of speech, or of the press.

Having in mind the foregoing safeguards, we may consider the provisions of the regulation or by-law, if any, which the plaintiffs in this case may be said to have violated. Examination of Section 37 of the Constitution of the Union as revised in October, 1947, shows that despite the language of the summons to the Convention, plaintiffs could not have been properly tried for violation of Section 37 because it applies only to candidates. Plaintiffs were likewise not properly able to be tried under the resolution of June, 1947, because, under the procedure there outlined, any member accused of making false accusations, misrepresentations, untruths, or using degrading literature, could be called before the Convention following the election, but could be tried only by the *succeeding* Convention, or by a body of five members or by a special court selected at such succeeding Convention.

We find that despite the letter calling plaintiffs to appear before the June, 1949, Convention to defend themselves for "the act of publishing malicious representations regarding present national officers in the last election," as in the case of Cranston, Gilbert and Snyder, or to explain their conduct, "in distributing handbills to local union memberships during the recent election for National Officials," as in the case of Crossen and Hammond, the plaintiffs were actually tried or able to be tried by the June, 1949, Convention only for violation of the resolution adopted at the July, 1948, Convention covering "conduct in violation of their obligation or anything in any manner determental to the N.B.O.P. and its members." We are loathe to say, in view of the provisions of the Constitution of the United States and the state of Ohio, guaranteeing free speech, that we should construe this indefinite language as intending to deprive members of the union of the right of free and fair criticism, otherwise theirs, although the 1949 Convention appears thus to have construed it and to have punished plaintiffs on that basis. Examination of the facts before us impels us to hold that a member of a mutual benefit association continues to be a citizen of the United States, and the free speech guaranteed by the United States Constitution permits him freedom in criticizing his union officials, as well as his public officials generally, subject always to the limitations imposed by the laws of slander and libel. 64 Harvard Law Review 1071. In so declaring, we recognize that it is not generally the function of courts to control the policies or the internal affairs of labor unions, but the courts may and should protect the democratic processes within unions by which union policies and their leaders are determined. Upon this point, see the illuminating article entitled "Legal Limitations On Union Discipline" by Clyde W. Summers, 64 Harvard Law Review 1049, at page 1073 and also, the article by Joseph Kovner entitled "The Legal Protection of Civil Liberties Within Unions," Wisconsin Law Review (1948), at page 18.

Particularly important seems to us the realization that labor unions constitute a special type of mutual benefit association, standing in special relation to their members and to the state. Membership has become a frequent condition of employment, even as the right of every man to work has become increasingly recognized as one of the most valued rights of a free society. Viewing the important role of labor unions in this era, a court may well determine in a particular case that protection of their democratic processes is essential to the maintenance of our democratic government.

The right of free criticism of union officials was recognized in the recent case of Ames vs Dubinsky, 70 N.Y.S. (2nd) 706. The eleventh paragraph of the syllabus announces the following proposition—

Where a person offers himself as a candidate for office in a union or for re-election, his character for honesty and integrity and his qualifications and fitness for the office are presented as suggestions for fair comment by contrast, comparison or analysis.

See also, Polin vs Kaplan, 257 N.Y.S. 277.

In Gleeson vs Conrad, 81 N.Y.S. (2nd) 368, it was held that courts will examine into the internal problems of unions and other associations when the rules of the organization have not been substantially complied with and a member has been damaged by such non-compliance or where the rules are themselves unreasonable or contrary to law or public policy.

We hold that the action of the 1949 Convention in fining plaintiffs because of publication or distribution of the handbills constituted an infringement of the right of free speech on the part of plaintiffs, calling for exercise, under the peculiar circumstances of the case, of the equity powers of this Court to protect the plaintiffs in their property rights and in their calling. In so declaring, we consider that we are in no wise departing from previous decisions of this Court including Pfoh vs Whitney, 43 Abs. 417, decided by this Court on June 25,

1945, and Finlay vs Duffy, 57 Abs. 442, this Court's decision of May 19, 1950. It is our belief that our present ruling is a logical development of these two cases.

It is to be noted that in the Pfoh case there was no claim asserted by plaintiff that the section of the Constitution of the Union, on the basis of which plaintiff was expelled, was violative of the laws of the land or that it was not a valid part of the Union's Constitution.

In the Finlay case, the opinion declared that courts will not assume to act in place of those authorized to interpret the Constitution and by-laws of voluntary associations unless those upon whom the duty is placed, act in an arbitrary and unreasonable manner. The precise question in that case involved the regularity of adoption of a resolution determining the compensation of the national officers and Judge Skeel, in rendering the opinion of the court, expressly pointed out that this matter in no way affected a property right of any of the members. In the opinion, Judge Skeel stated: "The right to seek the power of injunctive relief in a court of equity cannot be invoked unless and until it is made to appear that a property right has been invaded for which there is no other adequate remedy afforded."

In the present case, we find that a property right on the part of plaintiffs is clearly involved, since failure within thirty days to pay the fines levied would subject plaintiffs under Section 181 of the Union's Constitution to suspension from the Union. Furthermore, by Section 255 failure to pay a fine expressly deprives any member of all privileges of local membership thus entailing loss of benefits, loss of right to seek office within the Union and possible loss of work opportunities.

Numerous cases hold that where the expulsion or suspension of a member of the Union affects the individual's property rights, a court of equity will award relief to a member wrongfully expelled or suspended from the Union by decreeing his re-instatement, at least where a resort to the internal remedies within the Union would be futile, illusory or useless, or would not accord to the members in question substantial or practical justice. See the note in 168 A.L.R. 1462 entitled "Exhaustion Of Remedies Within Labor Union As Condition Of Resort To Civil Courts By Expelled Or Suspended Member" and particularly the cases cited at page 1479.

In the court below, the trial judge in his opinion pointed out that the matter of exhaustion of remedies within the Union is not a required prerequisite to court action unless the tribunal is impartial, and in this case it was the Executive Board which brought the charges against plaintiffs and further appeal to that Board would presumably be unavailing. Particularly, was any such gesture to be deemed futile where the objectionable actions of plaintiffs constituted support of an opposition slate and where, in the companion case being decided by this Court today and involving attempted punishment of candidates on the rival slate, the action of the Executive Board had given evidence of intention of silencing further opposition.

Finding that plaintiffs exhausted their remedies within the Union, to the extent feasible, and finding that plaintiffs' property rights were involved, we therefore conclude that the injunction prayed for should issue against the defendants in favor of the five plaintiffs in this case.

Injunction granted.

SKEEL, P. J.; HURD, J. CONCUR.

UNION DEMOCRACY

Hearings before a special subcommittee of the House Committee on Education and Labor, 81st Cong., 1st and 2d Sess., 1950, pp. 468–473

In 1949 the House of Representatives Committee on Education and Labor appointed a special subcommittee to inquire into the existence or nonexistence of undemocratic processes in labor unions. In the course of those hearings the following interchange took place between Representative Andrew Jacobs of Indiana and James M. Duffy, president of the National Brotherhood of Operative Potters, who was involved in the above proceedings (which at that time were still on appeal).

MR. JACOBS: Mr. Duffy, I would like to ask you a few questions. This committee, of course, was not constituted for the purpose of deciding an election issue in your union. That is the function of the membership. Nor are we to sit in judgment upon the wisdom of the membership in electing or rejecting any slate of candidates.

You refer to this group as a "disturbing element," and I suppose they were a disturbing element. Personally, I have always considered the Republican Party in my district a disturbing element. [Laughter.]

I suppose that Mr. Werdel and Mr. Morton consider the Democratic Party a disturbing element in their districts. Down where Mr. Sims comes from, I suppose there is a Democratic faction that disturbs some of the people down there once in a while.

The thing that I see in your case here is this: That here is some literature that was gotten out. And, as I view the evidence that you have given here and the evidence that the other witnesses have given, it seems to be pretty well conceded that some of these men were actually tried and penalized for circulating literature in an election. It may have been a dirty campaign. I mean I have been in dirty campaigns myself. Of course, I never participated in any dirt now; you understand that.

MR. DUFFY: We are not used to them. It is new to us. Maybe that is why we dislike it.

MR. JACOBS: But doesn't it sort of seem to you that it is just a kind of part of a political campaign for people to print their ideas and their views and what they think about the other fellow, et cetera, and circulate it? That that is just a sort of part of the American system of election, and that we just more or less take it in our stride? Don't you think that is a pretty good American custom?

MR. DUFFY: What is evidenced in those handbills in all my experience in the trade-union movement I never knew any such thing to happen. What about my family?

MR. JACOBS: Well, I know they said some—

MR. DUFFY: Why should we be subjected to such accusations and so forth without some chance to defend ourselves and get some redress from those things?

MR. JACOBS: Well, I think that is right. I think that it is a rugged game. I have been in it. I have been in politics. And it is a rugged game. I remember, notwithstanding the fact that I am a teetotaler and don't drink anything, that the rumor got around in one neighborhood in Indianapolis that I was paralyzed drunk.

MR. DUFFY: I have had the same experience.

MR. JACOBS: Well, I think I asked for it when I went in politics.

MR. DUFFY: I had the same experience, and I am the same kind of "gink" as you. I don't drink and smoke.

MR. MORTON: Somebody spread the rumor in Kentucky I was a prohibitionist. [Laughter.] That is harder on me than what they spread on you.

MR. JACOBS: Well, it seems to me—of course, we can hardly discredit all of the statements that are made. There was some controversy over salaries; and, personally, I am not questioning the justice of your salary, but the court did decide with these men. I mean we can't get away from that. And, certainly, we are not questioning whether the court was honest or not. They may have been right or wrong, but they had a right to bring out these facts, circulate the literature. You had the right to print literature and answer it.

What I am driving at is this: I would like to ask this question. Do you think that unions should operate democratically?

MR. DUFFY: We do. We do.

MR. JACOBS: You believe they should?

MR. DUFFY: I have never known any base of operation but democratically.

MR. JACOBS: That means that the membership shall vote upon who shall be the officers. Is that not right?

MR. DUFFY: No one has ever questioned that.

MR. JACOBS: Don't you think that the membership naturally must have some information about how to vote—like we get in the campaigns? Sometimes you get publicity in the newspapers. Sometimes you like it, and sometimes you do not. I have had it both ways.

MR. DUFFY: Are you assuming, may I ask, Mr. Chairman, that if there are two men contesting for public office, equally worthy and clean in every respect, that if one of those individuals by making nasty charges and calling dirty, nasty names and definite insinuations of dishonesty, can you by any moral standard that you know of condone and regard that as decent and fair?

MR. JACOBS: I am not talking so much, Mr. Duffy, about whether it is decent or not as I am the fact that no one has even been able to find the line where censorship is to be drawn. I mean in order to have a free press, in order to have free speech, in order to have free elections, we have to endure a good many things that are very distasteful and quite often very unfair. Otherwise, we do not know where to draw the line in order to make a fair rule.

I mean someone may publish something about me or you when we are seeking office, and the inference may be very bad. And yet, if you draw the line there, the censor of that must always try the case and see whether or not it is justified. And I thought that it was pretty well determined in the American way of life that we have no censorship. Of course, you can always sue for libel if it is utterly false.

But, I have read these dodgers here. I would say they are a little "salty" in places, but it seems that at least there is some basis for what they said in the court's decision. And as to whether or not you could rebut them would be a question for you to print counteracting literature.

MR. DUFFY: We don't indulge in that kind of stuff, and we never are, so far as I am concerned. The statement that we disregard, show disrespect for decisions in courts—is that serious or not? Now, maybe, Mr. Chairman, I have had the wrong kind of "fetching up," as they say, to be in this kind of lousy campaign business.

I am not interested, or I am not going to be a party to it. I am not going to participate in it. And I am going to do everything in my power to prevent it.

Mr. Finlay is notoriously known around our neighborhood for having made the statement in barber shops—and God knows that's the place to be heard, in the barber shop—he has said on many occasions—speaking of intolerance—any laboring man who did not vote the Democratic ticket was crazy or a fool, or words to that effect.

MR. JACOBS: Well, I would say on that I don't know but what I would agree with him, but I certainly would not punish him if he didn't. I mean I would not punish him. I think he would be free.

MR. DUFFY: And how can you sit there and so facetiously and so humorously make a joke of a statement made by an individual that anyone that didn't vote a certain political way was a fool? How can you do that?

MR. JACOBS: I think that what I say is that he should not be penalized for being wrong if he wanted to be.

MR. DUFFY: He was not penalized, Mr. Chairman. But it just shows the state of mind and the inclination of the individual.

MR. JACOBS: In other words, I agree with your construction of that statement —that the man has a right to vote as he pleases. I think he has a right to argue whichever side he pleases, either verbally or in writing.

Now, let's get to the court case.

MR. DUFFY: If you give me one word—

MR. JACOBS: Sure; go ahead.

MR. DUFFY: There is nothing I would like better than everyone or anyone or all of you gentlemen to come to our convention. If I have been derelict or if I have been loose in anything in convention, it has been in my determination, as I always stated to the delegates, that no one is going to be deprived of getting up on this floor and speaking his piece. I have specifically said on many occasions that, if I must do violence to something in order to give every delegate, every individual an opportunity to speak his piece wholeheartedly and completely, I am going to do violence to parliamentary procedure and see they get on their feet and speak their piece.

Mr. Chairman, I take these things seriously, and I don't think anything in connection with a man's citizenship and his rights and privileges is anything to be making a joke over. Not one iota. I can't see that.

MR. JACOBS: Well, let's approach it in this way: I am inclined to be convinced, from what you have said here, that you have been forthright; you have been very frank. There is not any question but what these men were penalized for circulating this literature. I do not think that it is a question here of whether you are honest, but rather a question of whether you have mistaken the rights of citizenship of these men to circulate the literature.

I think you have been perfectly honest and frank about it. Well, after all, I asked you the question; you answered it. You seem to think that the union should have the right to penalize these men for circulating the literature.

MR. DUFFY: Because the constitution forbade such literature.

MR. JACOBS: I am inclined to be of the opinion that the constitution of an organization cannot forbid a member from exercising their natural rights, or, if it can, that it should be forbidden from so providing.

In other words, I have a feeling that, if your union is going to operate democratically, then the members must have a right to print and disseminate literature as they see fit—answering, of course, for libel.

MR. DUFFY: They do.

MR. JACOBS: Now, take the court case, for example. Some of them were suspended from or disfranchised, we will say, for a period of 10 years because they brought an action in court. But the court agreed with them. The court must have thought that under the law of the land they were not required to exhaust such remedies as may have been left to them. There must have been some reason, and there are many reasons, why a member of a union is not required to exhaust his remedies. Sometimes the remedies are considered inadequate.

On that I am passing no judgment. The court passed judgment on that. But doesn't it seem a good deal out of line that the union should penalize members for seeking remedy in court when the court agreed with him he was entitled to that remedy?

MR. DUFFY: In answer to that, may I state, Mr. Chairman, that I will just make use of a phrase or statement of lawyers and judges: "Coming into court with clean hands."

Now, let's assume that I have done my job conscientiously and wholeheartedly and earnestly. We have got as good increases in wages as any organization in this United States of America. We have maintained industrial peace, which means taking care of public welfare. Let's assume that I have done those things with the aid of my fellow officers. Then along comes an election. Here are men that couldn't be elected on their own ability, and so forth. Then they resort to that kind of business.

Now, listen, Chairman—Mr. Chairman—you know just as well as I do the peculiar workings of the human mind and in an eleventh-hour release what they can do by some insinuation and that sort of thing. And such things sometimes result in the more competent and better man being defeated and the lesser getting the job.

Now, surely—

MR. JACOBS: Let me ask you a question.

MR. DUFFY: Surely you are not going to give me an argument and say that is democratic procedure.

MR. JACOBS: Well, I don't believe you and I have the same comprehension of what democratic procedure is. I think you are honest. I give you credit for that. I believe that you believe that you are the best of two men in the race. And I believe that you believe that the things that were said about you in these circulars were not warranted.

MR. DUFFY: I know they were untrue.

MR. JACOBS: I think that you are honest in your views. But, on the other hand, I do not know just where you are going to draw the line on censorship. If you are going to have a censorship, you can draw the line at the wrong place as well as you can at the right place, and I do not believe that the one concerning whom the articles are being written least of all should be a censor. I mean those are my views.

But, after all, we cannot decide it here anyway, Mr. Duffy. The purpose of the hearing is not to determine whether you were right or they were right. The purpose of the hearing is to determine whether or not they were prevented from exercising democratic rights. And I do not believe you and I probably see it in the same light, so I think I have no further questions.

MR. DUFFY: Just a little comment. I disagree with you that you and I have any different comprehension as to democratic rights, and so forth. But have we not proceeded democratically? We depend on the majority.

MR. JACOBS: But curtailment of the right of free speech, free press, et cetera, those are things in our way of life that a majority cannot take away from a minority. We may be different in that.

MR. DUFFY: I agree with you in what you have said, Mr. Chairman, but surely you do not believe in compromising with falsehood and that sort of thing, and that can be involved.

MR. JACOBS: Well, my view of it is that with a good record such as you have described you should be able to meet it, and apparently you did, and that seems to me that that is the complete answer to your problem.

EXTERNAL REVIEW OF UNION INTERNAL ACTIONS

The charge has often been made that union members who are disciplined by their own unions often face an inadequate appeals procedure. To go through the several prescribed steps—including a final appeal to the convention, which may meet only every two or four years, is time consuming and expensive. The men who sit as judges on such appeals may be the same men who imposed the original penalty, or they may be factional friends of those who imposed the penalty. To meet these valid

criticisms the Upholsterers' Union established an impartial "review board"
to which a disciplined union member might appeal for a rehearing. In
1957 the United Automobile Workers became the first major union to
adopt a similar procedure. The recommendation of the union president,
below, was adopted at the Atlantic City convention.

The UAW is both democratic and clean and we intend to keep it that way. For some time, however, we have been giving consideration to providing a new step in the Union's internal trial machinery and of reviewing the trial procedure at the local level in an effort to insure the fullest possible protection of the democratic rights of each individual member.

The International Executive Board will make recommendations in this respect for consideration of the coming Convention.

1. We are recommending that the local union trial machinery be improved to provide among other things for the selection of the members of the Local Union Trial Committee by lottery at a membership meeting, rather than by election as presently provided.

It is felt that selection of the members of the Local Union Trial Committee by lottery will be more democratic and therefore will not be subject to the pressures of electioneering, which has occurred in certain cases where the Trial Committees were elected.

2. We are recommending that a member of our Union, having an appeal from the decision of the local union and then from the decision of the International Executive Board, have an alternate route.

At the present time a member having an appeal from the decision of the International Executive Board may appeal to the International Convention. We propose that we retain this provision intact but add an alternate step by creating by constitutional amendment a Public Review Board, composed of approximately seven outstanding public citizens whose integrity and general acceptance are beyond question.

We are recommending that this Public Review Board be given the constitutional authority and the needed staff and office personnel to conduct investigations, hold hearings, and to make decisions on cases appealed to it by any member of the UAW.

The Public Review Board would have the constitutional authority to uphold, modify, or reverse the decision of the International Executive Board on any appeal, and the decision of the Public Review Board would be final and binding upon both the International Union and the member.

The membership of the Public Review Board would be submitted for approval at each future convention of the UAW.

The UAW is not perfect, but I think it can be said in all good conscience that we have tried to the best of our ability to make decisions, with respect to appeals within the trial procedure of our Union, on the basis of fairness and honesty. The leadership of the UAW, while we have had no complaints on the conduct of the appeals procedure, does feel, however, that more and more the leadership of the labor movement must be prepared to have their stewardship and conduct of the affairs of the Union under their leadership subject to public review. The leadership of the UAW is prepared to have its stewardship reviewed, and we are proposing the creation of a Public Review Board for this purpose and to further strengthen and refine the internal machinery of our Union to insure that the justice which comes from the Union's internal appeal procedures, meets the standards of fairness and honesty consistent with public standards in a free society.

The leadership of the UAW will propose further to the coming Convention that the authority of the Public Review Board be broadened to include the additional responsibility of acting as a public watchdog in our Union to strengthen our efforts in our determination to continue to conduct the affairs of the Union in accordance with the high ethical and moral standards for which the UAW has stood.

We propose specifically that the Public Review Board be given the constitutional authority to conduct investigations and hold hearings and make findings on any matter which is a violation of, or in conflict with the ethical codes adopted by the AFL-CIO or any additional codes which may be adopted by the UAW as they relate to the conduct and activities of any officer or staff member of the International Union, local unions or any subordinate body of the UAW.

The Public Review Board would be required to issue periodic reports to the membership of the UAW and to the public on its findings both as they relate to the internal trial procedure of the Union and the broad question of ethical and moral practices.

The leadership of the UAW makes the above proposal because it is prepared to have the Public Review Board, composed of outstanding public citizens, review the conduct of UAW affairs and report its findings to the UAW membership and to the public at large. In a free society the voluntary acceptance and discharge of moral and social responsibility is the only effective alternative to government intervention and government compulsion. We believe that to the extent that the free labor movement develops and implements proper internal machinery to provide effective safeguards of the democratic rights of each individual member and provides further for an appropriate public review of the Union's affairs as they relate to high standards of ethical and moral conduct, to that extent free labor will preserve its voluntary character and will minimize the necessity for government interference and the justification for government compulsion. We shall urge affirmative action on these proposals at the Convention for we believe the UAW can make a valuable contribution in this area by pointing the way for other labor groups to follow.

INDIVIDUAL FREEDOM IN LABOR UNIONS

Remarks by Walter Gellhorn, Professor of Law, Columbia University, on receiving the Hillman Award, New York City, 1957

A lot of well-meaning people—as well as a few who are not so well-meaning —think that individual freedom is a luxury the country cannot afford today.

At least, they think that freedom for individuals whose views they happen not to share is something we can and should readily surrender. Many of these let's-give-it-up folk are active flag wavers, and are sincerely convinced that they are preserving the American way of life. The fact of the matter is that, despite their patriotic intent, they are subverters of the national interest they seek to uphold.

Individual freedom is not a luxury at all. Its justification is not that this or that individual is made happier by being unchained—though certainly that is a rather good justification in itself. The real point about maintaining differences by permitting freedom of expression is that a free and diverse society is, in the long run, likely to be healthier than a society which levels out dissent by running a steam roller over dissenters.

When speech is allowed to be free, we can be certain that a very considerable amount of rot is going to be spoken. Sometimes dissent is silly. Sometimes, even, it is purposefully intended to stir up troubles and to cause confusion and to intensify divisions. Sometimes it creates uncertainties that delay necessary governmental decisions, or that hamper their effective administration. But—as against all of these demerits which might make us feel how lovely it would be if everyone thought alike, or at least were not allowed to think out loud—untrammeled expression does have one great and moving merit. It allows people to vent dissatisfaction before they build up into disasters. Every time some "crackpot" or "radical" or "intellectual" or "union agitator" gets up on his hind legs to complain about things as they are, the rest of us have a chance to take a fresh look at the problem and to consider whether the complaint has merit.

Now the mere fact that a new point of view has been expressed does not, of course, mean that we have to accept it. Most of the time we reject the new and cling to the old. But often enough to make the whole thing worthwhile, we do find that there is something to be said on the side of the complaint— very probably not as much as the complainants said, but nevertheless something—and we set about to correct the defects. That is why, in the United States, we manage constantly to alter and improve the shape of our country, without having to shatter it and start over again. We live like prudent house-holders. If someone tells us that there is an inch of water in the basement, we do not cut out the tongue of this bearer of bad tidings, but we go take a look at the basement and try to find out how the water got there. Possibly there is an easily repaired leak in a pipe; perhaps there is a more serious problem in the foundation. Whatever caused the trouble, we have a chance to deal with it before it becomes a major crisis. And precisely the same is true in political affairs. We do not attempt to sit on the lid of discontent until pressures accumulate into an explosion, as has happened in repressive countries like Hungary and Poland. Instead, we have traditionally—and most wisely—encouraged freedom of expression by faultfinders as well as by upholders-of-things-as-they-are. America became great in the process, for its people were not afraid to be dissatisfied and they never accepted the deadening belief that the country had gone just about as far as it could go.

Oddly enough, the labor movement—which has, I believe, experienced many direct proofs of what has just been said about the virtues of political freedom —has not always been equally perceptive about the need for safeguarding free expression by its own members. Part of the present mess in which it finds itself stems from that fact.

Many people nowadays are being revolted by revelations that high union leaders have been corrupt. Why, it is sometimes asked, don't the members throw those bums out? And why did the members need the prodding of Senator McClellan of Arkansas to start being worried about the stench beneath the floorboards? I suggest that one powerful explanation is to be found in restraints upon the members' freedom to criticize. Too many unions have made it too perilous for their members to be effective complainers. And when complaining has been deterred, troubles have accumulated. Now they are piled so high that the whole labor movement—the thoroughly innocent parts along with the guilty—may find itself wide open to attack.   .

As in society at large, the chief problem, I suppose, has to do with failure of people to exercise the citizenship rights they do undoubtedly possess. It takes a supine citizenry to create a climate in which corrupt machine politics flourish. And the same thing is true in labor organizations. By and large people are content to leave the worrying and the work to someone else. Nobody has to put pressure on them to stop being active. The more difficult task is to get them to be active enough to get up off their big fat hassocks long enough to listen to someone else tell them the facts of life.

Occasionally, however, someone with imagination and zeal—or just pure cussedness—does want to ring the alarm bells. Then the question arises whether he will be allowed to ring away, to his heart's content, or whether he is going to be shut up before anyone is waked up.

Freedom of expression by viewers-with-alarm in unions has sometimes been limited by the use of unadorned thuggery. The heavy fist, occasionally decorated with brass knuckles, is a pretty effective instrument for closing mouths. I have no easy prescription for ending hoodlumism. Fortunately it is not commonplace in unions. It presents there as it does elsewhere in society a serious challenge to law enforcement. Violence on the waterfront or on the highway must be stamped out by vigilant police work and prosecution. It is a major problem. But physical gangsterism is by no means the heart of the problem that besets labor unionism. The core of the matter lies, rather, in the lack of protection accorded a member who faces penalties in the form of union disciplinary proceedings or other reprisals because he has tried to set aright things that he thought were wrong. We are fond of saying that a man should have the courage of his own convictions. But I have always thought that, in a democracy, a man should feel free to have convictions even though he might not in fact be very courageous. Some labor organizations seemingly proceed on the theory that a dissenter must be an absolute hero. At any rate, they make it so dangerous for a man to have convictions at all that a person must be very brave indeed before he dares to speak out of turn.

Interestingly enough, the big scandals do not pop up in unions which, like the Amalgamated Clothing Workers, believe that what is a good enough policy for the United States of America is good enough for them. The scandals pop up in unions with a more dictatorial outlook on life: unions which discourage protest and questioning, unions which have made plain their belief that freedom of speech is not a good to be nourished, but an evil to be suppressed.

Suppression has been achieved for the most part not by violence but by economic pressure. The dissident member does not get job opportunities. Or, by formal proceedings, he is fined or, even, thrown out of the union entirely, with all the losses that expulsion may entail. In a single year one powerful union reportedly disciplined over 4,000 members, levying fines on them that totaled nearly $300,000 and imposing suspensions that added up to the neat figure of 150,000 years. One unpopular fellow was told that he would not be expelled from the union—that would be too harsh a penalty for his having been bold enough to buck the boss. Instead, he was given a lighter sentence: suspension from the union for 99 years.

Now of course not all of these cases represented an abuse of power. A union certainly has a right to preserve itself by expelling or penalizing members whose misbehavior might destroy it. Offenses against the union as a whole may range all the way from embezzlement of funds to the leading of wildcat strikes, from company espionage to Communist intrigue; and, given fair procedures, a labor organization like any other group has an entirely defensible power to protect itself against those who are sawing away at its gizzard.

The trouble comes when offenses are too broadly defined. Most unions provide that a man may be disciplined for "conduct unbecoming a union member" or for "conduct detrimental to the best interests of the union" or for "slandering an officer" or for "undermining the constitution." Needless to say, clauses like these can be worked overtime by those who want to frighten dissenters. Uncertainty about the way they may be applied means that in some unions a critical member must think twice before he undertakes to challenge those who are in the seats of power.

Bear in mind how these things work in shady or hardshelled unions. A trial is had before a committee; the local membership, sometimes already frightened and finding it much more comfortable to hunt with the hounds rather than run with the hares, confirms the result; and then there is a grand round of appeals that seem adequate in form but may be a sham of purest ray serene. Suppose that an appeal lies to a district board that is packed tight with the henchmen of the ruling clique, and from that board to the national executive council that is the clique itself, and thence to the president himself—the man for whom our local hero has been gunning. Finally, as a supreme expression of the democratic faith, our little defendant—if he has not long since sunk into a bitter grave—is given a chance to appeal to the national convention. All he has to do is travel from where he lives and works—say, Minneapolis—to Miami Beach and there, amidst the splendors of the newest hotel, try to persuade the well-packed delegates that all is not as it should be in the union. Sometimes, of course, he may have to wait a while for the convention to meet; not very many years ago, to cite an extreme example, the Hod Carriers managed to get around to holding their first convention after a lapse of a mere thirty years.

I do not for a moment suggest that all unions do constantly use their disciplinary procedures to harass rather than to protect their members. But the danger of abuse is certainly there—and it has occurred often enough to give concern.

Precisely at this point a great deal can be accomplished—and easily accomplished—to polish up the labor movement by preserving the freedom of individuals. The Upholsterers and the Auto Workers have made a beginning in the right direction by setting up a final appeals board of distinguished private citizens, to decide whether a member has been unjustly disciplined by the union. This is good, but not good enough. A distant body of luminaries— bishops, and university presidents, and the like—may be comforting as a symbol; but it remains a distant body. By the time a disappointed suitor reaches that august tribunal, if he ever does, too much damage will already have been done. Not very many wage earners will be emboldened to speak out against abuses by the existence of a central board—no matter how distinguished by piety, learning, and disinterest—that is just about as hard to reach as the pot of gold at the end of the rainbow. I join in the round of applause that has greeted unions that have made a beginning. But let us not delude ourselves into thinking that this is much more than a gesture of good will.

A better answer, in my opinion, would be for the whole union movement— by joint rather than single action—to set up a decentralized grievance machinery to which any individual member may have recourse if he thinks his organization has abused him. From coast to coast, from Canada to Mexico, this country has developed an able, richly experienced corps of impartial labor umpires. By agreement with unions, employers have bound themselves to allow these third parties—these outsiders, if you will—to pass upon their disciplinary actions against employees. Every watcher of the nation's industry in the past two decades has seen how workers have grown in pride and stature as they have grown in confidence that whimsical discharges can be challenged. They have not become insubordinate; but they have become more manly as they have become less defenseless. Men and women have stood up for their rights in the shop because they know that their rights are not mere words, but are realities that cannot be snatched away by a vindictive reprisal. Something of the same sort can be and should be done by the labor movement for itself. A cheap, accessible, and trustworthy tribunal ought to be provided for all members of all unions. What can the labor movement lose if it permits a qualified and dispassionate inquiry to be made into the validity of a penalty imposed on a member? How much it can gain in public respect and, indeed, in the loyal support of its own members if an end can be put to the suspicion that inequitable and coercive decisions are sometimes made by kangaroo courts!

Unions have become the economic government of vast numbers of American men and women. Many of the conditions of their lives—their wages, their job tenure, their hopes for the future—are controlled by the decisions of those who speak for them through their labor organizations. By exercising the normal rights of citizenship they must have opportunity to control their economic government just as they have opportunity to control their political government. The "economic ballot" needs more protection than it has up until now been given. In my estimation, the labor movement had better hurry to provide the needed protection itself, before the problem is snatched from its hands by ill advised or perhaps even hostile forces. The problem is not insoluble. More than anything else, it needs to be attacked with real conviction that the preservation of individual rights is a mighty important thing to achieve in this century of big organizations and little people. As to that, the words of my favorite author bear repeating: "Today is a perfectly good day for reminding ourselves that the blessings of liberty have been hard won in the past and should not be softly lost in the present through slothfulness, inattention, or doubt."

RACKETEERING

A perennial problem within the labor movement has been racketeering. This has taken several forms: the shake-down of employers under threat that strikes would be called against them or—when unorganized—that they would be organized and forced to pay exorbitant wage increases; violence to wrest control of a union away from another group, without respect to membership interests, for the exploitation either of union members or of employers with whom the union deals or both; kickbacks from members for special favors, such as priority in employment, or sale of membership in the union without the applicant's having to pass standard apprenticeship tests.

No one knows how much labor racketeering goes on in the United States. It seems probable, however, that it represents a rather small fraction of total union activity. The more serious consideration, however, is that such racketeering as does exist may be concentrated—in certain unions, or certain industries, or certain areas—so that its impact in particular spheres may be very considerable. It is a matter of fact that the unions most frequently mentioned as harboring such elements are the powerful Teamsters and the building trades unions.

As can readily be appreciated, such activities within the labor movement are a source of concern to legitimate union leaders, since it colors the popular impression of unions in general and damages their acceptability in a society which has only lately come to accept them. The exposures in 1957 before the Senate Select Committee on Improper Practices in the Labor and Management Field, although largely confined to a few unions, constituted a sharp blow to the labor movement as a whole. Nevertheless, until recently the unions have done relatively little to clean their own house. The AFL ultimatum to the International Longshoremen's Associa-

*tion makes clear that in part this relative inaction has been due to
the jealous regard for the autonomy of the constituent international
unions.*

**From Report on Certain Aspects of Labor Union Responsibility and Control,
by the Subcommittee on Labor Unions of the Committee on Legislation, City
Club of New York, 1937, pp. 7–9, 12–13**

Racketeering exposed in connection with labor unions is in no sense peculiar
to labor unions; it is part of a criminal pattern that has manifested itself in such
diversified fields as prostitution, lottery and policy games, bail bonding, and in
liquor traffic, both now and prior to repeal of the Eighteenth Amendment, as
well as in legitimate forms of business activity. In each case the purpose is the
unlawful extortion of tribute for the personal gain of a few individuals; in each
case these individuals are found to be criminals who may be cloaked in the
trappings of respectability but whose illegal activities are not confined to the
labor racket.

One feature which is sometimes considered peculiar to labor racketeering is
that the means employed may include practices not intrinsically illegal, namely,
the threat of union sanctions such as strikes and picketing. But the threat of
lawful action is made in connection with other types of extortion. For example,
the blackmailer menaces his victim with the threat of making public what may
be a completely true statement of facts, or of reporting to law enforcement
officers the commission by his victim of a crime. And a similar technique is
found in unfair trade practice such as tying contracts or block-booking in the
motion picture industry, through which a purchaser, in order to obtain a
desired article, is compelled at the same time to purchase an undesired article.
In each case the means, intrinsically lawful, become unlawful only because of
the element of extortion.

That the means employed by the labor racketeer may not be unlawful makes
it all the more important that the problem be approached with circumspection
and with appreciation of the fact that labor racketeering is but a symptom of a
far larger problem. Otherwise, proper efforts tending to bring into disrepute
the lawful means employed by labor racketeers for unlawful ends may also
tend to discredit legitimate labor activity for legitimate ends. . . .

"Labor racketeering" consists in essence of the use of a labor union by
racketeers to exact payments to the racketeers from the employer, from members of the union, or from both. The racketeer may himself be a union official
or he may operate from without the union either through his agents or through
the exercise of coercion upon intimidated union officers. The labor racketeer is
often enabled to maintain his dominant position through cooperation, passive
or even active, on the part of the employer, whose inertia to the existence of
a racket may be partially explained by the fact that the cost of the racket is
usually passed on to the consumer, or to another branch of the industry, rather
than borne by the employer himself. A further explanation may be found in the
fact that the employer may actually profit by the racket. Thus, the employer
may find it profitable to make periodic payments to a union officer in order to

avoid compliance with a union rule, such as payment for overtime, or a requirement that members of the union shall not work with, or on the products of, non-union labor. Or the employer may believe that the improvement of working conditions which may follow upon effective collective bargaining will cost him more than the labor racket.

Again, the employer may take advantage of the racket to drive a competitor out of business or to maintain prices in connection with certain types of so-called trade associations. This type of trade association, in conjunction with which labor racketeering flourishes most effectively, is usually organized and maintained in a large city and in a demoralized industry in which legitimate employer-organization is not possible or its advantages not appreciated. The initial purpose of the association, which in its more refined forms may escape the sanctions of the anti-trust laws, is to obtain higher prices or to stabilize competitive conditions. Ultimately, the visible gains to the members of the association may be so costly or the temptation to attract business by price-cutting so strong that coercion becomes necessary to compel members to remain in the association or to compel competitors to join it. An effective instrument for such coercion is found in the labor racketeer, who directs threats of labor trouble against those who might otherwise be unwilling to join or maintain membership in the trade association itself but also in other branches of the trade or industry in which the association functions.

Variations in the labor racket occur under varying conditions but the fundamental technique remains the same; upon analysis most labor rackets are found to be surprisingly similar.

The labor racketeer sometimes obtains such power that he is able to create an unnecessary type of work from which he obtains income. For example, an indictment against racketeers in a local of the teamsters' union charges that these racketeers through their control of trucking forced upon the dairy industry a duplication in terminal operations, resulting in a $300,000 annual increase in handling costs.

Through his dominance of the industry, the racketeer may even set up an independent business servicing the industry, patronage of which is required of employers wishing to avoid labor trouble. An outstanding example is a case in New Jersey in which a racketeer compelled contractors to patronize his construction-bonding business. Another instance is that of a racketeer in control of a motion picture operators' union who forced theatre-owners to purchase supplies from him.

While the membership of a union dominated by a racketeer may on the whole be better off by reason of improved conditions than in the absence of any union, the membership also suffers from labor racketeering. Exploitation of union members by the racketeer takes the form of the "sell out," most commonly in the form of agreements unduly favorable to the employer, the "kickback," through requiring union members to return part of their wages to the employer or to union officers, the exaction of excessive dues, discrimination in union privileges or in the distribution of work, waiver of union rules or contract provisions, payment of excessive salaries to union officials or diversion or embezzlement of union funds. The racketeer-controlled union may also be used as a device to combat legitimate union activity.

While the employer may in the first instance pay the cost of a racket, that cost, like the cost of any other anti-social activity, is ultimately borne by the public in the form of increased prices and industrial strife. Some employers, such as small retailers, may suffer through being unable to pass on the racket cost, but, as we have pointed out, employers may obtain benefits from the labor racket through the maintenance of the price level and the elimination of effective collective bargaining. It is an interesting commentary upon the relationship that sometimes exists between the employer and the labor racketeer that the head of an employers' association in a notoriously racket-ridden industry is reported to have asked that one of the principal convicted defendants be paroled in his custody pending an appeal. And in the recent trial of restaurant racketeers, it was brought out that substantial contributions to their defense fund were made by restaurant owners. It is true that employer groups protest the labor racket, but such protests are chiefly in the form of proposals for curbing all unions, whether corrupt or not, and, moreover, often come from groups not affected by racketeering. . . .

CONCLUSIONS

To treat the problem of "labor racketeering" as a problem peculiar to labor is fundamentally to misconceive the nature of the crime. Racketeering, according to a definition approved by Thomas E. Dewey, is "the systematic extortion of money or property by the use of force or fear from the various members of a legitimate or illegitimate industry." This definition applies with equal force to all forms of racketeering, including racketeering exposed in connection with labor unions.

Nor is racketeering in any proper sense typical of the labor movement. On the contrary, it is merely an invasion of that movement by a relatively negligible element. It is only in a few large cities that one hears of racketeers.

Moreover, racketeering by and large has been and is being eradicated. The number of prosecutions and convictions are impressive. Indeed, there appears to be a tendency to exaggerate the problem in order to lend weight to proposals for union regulation.

This is not to say that no problem exists. But that problem is not one of remedies, which are ample; it is one of enforcement. To meet the problem, the Subcommittee makes the following proposals:

First. The Subcommittee believes that *measures should be taken to overcome the inertia of persons who, knowing of the existence of a crime fail to take any action to assist in its exposure and prosecution.* . . .

Second. Prior to public announcement of the organization of the Citizens Committee on the Control of Crime in New York, Inc., the Subcommittee had given consideration to the establishment of a racket bureau to operate in connection with the Police Department as a permanent organization to which complaints could be made and which could initiate, assist in and ensure impartial investigation. Mr. Dewey has recently endorsed the work of the Citizens Committee and has expressed the opinion that with it may lie the remedy. The Subcommittee believes that *a bureau such as the Citizens Committee could prove most effective* provided that it is not associated with any political organization, but that in any event the bureau should be established on a permanent basis with police powers.

Third. Experience has shown that *eradication of racketeering from a union can come only from an aroused and determined membership.* Sporadic prosecution is of little avail; one or two dishonest leaders are removed and others come to take their place for the conditions which enabled racketeering to flourish are not thus removed. The building trades and the poultry rackets are notable examples. On the other hand, when the membership does take action, as in the musicians' union and the painters' union, the evil is removed apparently not to return.

The Subcommittee believes that the elimination of racketeering within a union must be primarily the concern of the membership, which is most directly affected by the racket. The problem is fundamentally one of promoting democratic control. . . .

Address delivered before the Southwestern Legal Foundation and Southern Methodist University School of Law, Dallas, Texas, April 22, 1955, by Herbert Brownell, Jr., Attorney General of the United States, pp. 2–6

THE DEPARTMENT OF JUSTICE MOVES ON LABOR RACKETEERS

During the past two years the Department of Justice has engaged in a most strenuous effort to enforce the federal criminal laws against parasitic racketeers who in many parts of the country have infested and poisoned the relations between business management and labor. . . .

There are three laws which constitute the principal weapons in the armory of the Department of Justice in combatting this kind of racketeering. Two of them apply directly; the third indirectly. The first of these is the federal Anti-Racketeering Statute, originally enacted in 1934, and often referred to as the Hobbs Act. The second is section 186 of the Labor-Management Relations Act, passed by Congress in 1947 and usually called the Taft-Hartley Act. The third, which applies indirectly, is the federal Income Tax law.

Two different types of cases are encountered so frequently as to be typical of violations of these laws. First, there is the case, covered by the Hobbs Act, where some racketeer who is in control of a labor union as an official demands a pay-off from an employer, usually in the form of cash, for his own personal enrichment under threat of damaging the employer if the pay-off is not made with strikes, slowdowns, or violent injury to his property, person or family. Such a case amounts to extortion.

The second situation, covered by section 186 of the Taft-Hartley Act, is where a crooked employer induces a union official to betray and sell out the interests of his union members in return for cash or other bribe for his personal benefit.

Both situations involve the payment of money in secret and usually when that occurs the receipt of the money is not declared for income tax purposes.

That is why investigation of such cases not infrequently results in a prosecution for income tax evasion. . . .

In the little more than two years since [January 1953] there have been approximately 56 Anti-Racketeering indictments charging 126 defendants. In two other trials the jury failed to agree and the cases will have to be retried. Three indictments have been dismissed. The remaining 33 cases are on active calendar and will be tried in due course. During this same two year period there have been 14 indictments charging 23 defendants with violating section 186 of the Taft-Hartley Law. Four of them have been tried resulting in seven convictions, one has been dismissed and the remaining nine are awaiting trial.

Since January 1953, at the request of the Department, the FBI has undertaken about 1,400 investigations of possible violations of these two laws and is continuing to open new cases at the rate of approximately 50 per month. These cases have originated in such far-flung cities as St. Louis and Kansas City, Missouri; East St. Louis, Springfield and Chicago, Illinois; Detroit; St. Paul; Cleveland; New Orleans; Boston; Pittsburgh; Los Angeles; Seattle; Las Vegas; New York City; Jersey City; Providence; Louisville and Washington, D. C.

The expulsion of the International Longshoremen's Association from the AFL was preceded by the following ultimatum, issued February 3, 1953, by the executive council—the first such ultimatum issued in the Federation's history.

AFL ultimatum to ILA

To the officers and members of the International Longshoremen's Association:

The executive council of the American Federation of Labor, at its present session, has given thorough consideration to the disclosures developed by the New York State Crime Commission affecting international and local union officers of the International Longshoremen's Association.

We have followed this investigation with interest and the reported widespread alleged crime, dishonesty, racketeering and other highly irregular and objectionable practices in which it is reported that officers of your international and local unions have been and are involved.

One of the most serious features of the New York City situation as pertains to your international union and its local unions, as outlined by recent testimony before the Crime Commission, is the clear and definite indication that these workers of the Port of New York are being exploited in every possible way and that they are not receiving the protection which they have every right to expect as trade unionists and members of your organization.

We have concluded that these disclosures are of such a serious nature as to call for immediate action by us. We wish to make clear the position of the A.F.L. on crime and racketeering within your international and its local unions.

Your relationship with the A.F.L. demands that the democratic ideals, clean and wholesome free trade unionism must be immediately restored within your organization and all semblance of crime, dishonesty and racketeering be forthwith eliminated.

Reported practices of international and local union officers accepting gifts and bribes from employers and the appointment of representatives with criminal records is denounced and those persons guilty of these practices must be forthwith removed from office and eliminated from your organization.

The so-called shape-up, which encourages the kick-backs and other objectionable practices, must be supplanted by a system of regular employment and legitimate hiring methods, and we request that you immediately take vigorous and effective action to institute this reform.

Union representatives with criminal records cannot be tolerated in any official capacity and they must be immediately removed from all positions of authority within your organization.

Recognized democratic procedures of the A.F.L. must be put into operation in your local unions so that members who work on the waterfronts will be able to select true and capable trade union leaders who will serve the best interests of the A.F.L. and be free from the taint of crime and racketeering.

We deplore the reign of lawlessness and crime which has been disclosed on the New York City waterfront and we call upon those officials charged with the responsibility of law enforcement to bring to justice all those persons who may be guilty of any illegal acts.

The A.F.L. is not clothed with authority, nor is it our responsibility to do this job. We do feel, however, that your international union must forthwith take the necessary action to remove any and all of those representatives who may be participants in these unlawful activities.

The A.F.L. is, as you know, a voluntary association of free and autonomous national and international unions. The founders of the A.F.L. deliberately set up an organizational structure which would preclude the domination of our organization by any one man or group of men operating from the top.

The founders of the A.F.L. saw to it that there was no police power given to the central organization which it could use to interfere with the internal affairs of national or international unions affiliated to the A.F.L.

The executive council has no intention of changing the traditional position of the A.F.L. in regard to the freedom and autonomy of its affiliated units. We feel that the greatest factor in the strength and vigor of the A.F.L. over the years has been its adherence to the principles of freedom and voluntarism.

However, no one should make the mistake of concluding that the A.F.L. will sit by and allow abuse of autonomy on the part of any of its affiliates to bring injury to the entire movement.

The exercise of autonomy by affiliated units in an organization such as ours presupposes the maintenance of minimum standards of trade union decency. No affiliate of the A.F.L. has any right to expect to remain an affiliate "on the grounds of organizational autonomy" if its conduct, as such, is to bring the entire movement into disrepute.

Likewise, the cloak of organizational autonomy cannot be used to shield those who have forgotten that the prime purpose of a trade union is to protect and advance the welfare and interests of the individual members of that trade union.

The failure of your organization and its officers to protect your membership from exploitation and oppression by employers as well as by thugs cannot be justified or defended on the ground of autonomy.

A.F.L. affiliates have autonomy in the conduct of their affairs but it must be conceded by all that there is an unwritten law that this freedom of action must be used to advance the interests of labor and not to exploit the workers. The executive council of the A.F.L. concludes that the I.L.A. must immediately, as a condition of continuing affiliation with the A.F.L., take such actions necessary to place the I.L.A. and its local unions above suspicion and completely free of all racketeering, crime, corruption and other irregular activities disclosed by the recent investigation of crime on the New York City waterfront, to the end that the I.L.A. will serve the legitimate social and economic needs of its members in keeping with true trade union principles traditionally established by the A.F.L.

The executive council will expect a report from you advising that the above recommendations have been and will be complied with on or before April 30, 1953.

The following code was proposed by the Ethical Practices Committee and adopted by the Executive Council of the AFL-CIO in 1957.

AFL Ethical Practices Code III: Racketeers, Crooks, Communists, and Fascists

This is the third in a series of recommended codes which the committee on ethical practices has developed in accordance with the direction of the Executive Council that it should "develop a set of principles and guides for adoption by the A.F.L.-C.I.O. in order to implement the constitutional determination that the A.F.L.-C.I.O. shall be and remain free from all corrupt influences." *

Article VIII, Section 7 of the constitution of the A.F.L.-C.I.O. establishes that "it is a basic principle of this federation that it must be and remain free from any and all corrupt influences and from the undermining efforts of Communist, Fascist or other totalitarian agencies who are opposed to the basic principles of our democracy and of free and democratic trade unionism." Under this constitutional provision there is no room within the federation or any of its affiliated unions for any person in a position of leadership or responsibility who is a crook, a racketeer, a Communist or a Fascist. And it is the obligation of every union affiliated with the A.F.L.-C.I.O. to take appropriate steps to insure that this principle is complied with.

To be sure, neither the A.F.L.-C.I.O. nor its affiliated unions are law-enforcing agencies. It is not within the purview or authority of a trade union to convict its members of a violation of statutory law. But it is the duty and

---

* Editor's note: The first code stigmatized the issuance of charters covering "paper locals" (having no actual membership) which are used "to enter into conspiracies with corrupt employers to prevent, for a price, the genuine organization of workers into legitimate unions." The second code set out certain principles designed to avoid the dishonest administration of health and welfare funds. A fourth code dealt with "conflicts of interest in the investment and business interests of union officials."

responsibility of each national and international union affiliated with the federation to see to it that it is free of all corrupt, Communist or Fascist influences. Consequently, a trade union need not wait upon a criminal conviction to bar from office corrupt, Communist or Fascist influences. The responsibility of each union to see to it that it is free of such influences is not a responsibility placed upon our unions by law. It is a responsibility which rests upon our unions by the A.F.L.-C.I.O. constitution and by the moral principles that govern the trade union movement. Eternal vigilance in this area is the price of an honest democratic trade union movement.

It is not possible, nor is it desirable, to set down rigid rules to determine whether a particular individual, in a position of responsibility or leadership in the trade-union movement is a crook, a racketeer, a Communist or a Fascist. Obviously, if a person has been convicted of a crime involving moral turpitude offensive to trade-union morality, he should be barred from office or responsible position in the labor movement. Obviously also, a person commonly known to be a crook or racketeer, should not enjoy immunity to prey upon the trade-union movement because he has somehow managed to escape a conviction. In the same manner, the fact that a person has refrained from formally becoming a member of the Communist party or a Fascist organization should not permit him to hold or retain a position of responsibility or leadership in the trade-union movement if, regardless of formal membership, he consistently supports or actively participates in the activities of the Communist party or any Fascist or totalitarian organization.

In this area, as in all others, determinations must be made as a matter of common sense and with due regard to the rights of the labor unions and the individuals involved.

On the basis of these considerations, the Ethical Practices Committee, under the authority vested in it by the constitution of the A.F.L.-C.I.O., pursuant to the mandate of the first constitutional convention of the A.F.L.-C.I.O., recommends that the executive council of the A.F.L.-C.I.O. adopt the following policies to safeguard the good name of the A.F.L.-C.I.O. and its affiliated unions:

[1]

The A.F.L.-C.I.O. and each of its affiliated unions should undertake the obligation, through appropriate constitutional or administrative measures and orderly procedures, to insure that no persons who constitute corrupt influences or practices or who represent or support Communist, Fascist or totalitarian agencies should hold office of any kind in such trade unions or organizations.

[2]

No person should hold or retain office or appointed position in the A.F.L.-C.I.O. or any of its affiliated national or international unions or subordinate bodies thereof who has been convicted of any crime involving moral turpitude offensive to trade union morality.

[3]

No person should hold or retain office or appointed position in the A.F.L.-C.I.O. or any of its affiliated national or international unions or subordinate bodies thereof who is commonly known to be a crook or racketeer preying on the labor movement and its good name for corrupt purposes, whether or not previously convicted for such nefarious activities.

[4]

No person should hold or retain office or appointed position in the A.F.L.-C.I.O. or any of its affiliated national or international unions or subordinate bodies thereof who is a member, consistent supporter or who actively participates in the activities of the Communist party or of any Fascist or other totalitarian organization which opposes the democratic principles to which our country and the American trade union movement are dedicated.

From The Truth about the Taft-Hartley Law and Its Consequences to the Labor Movement, published by the International Association of Machinists, 1948, pp. 30, 32

How about graft and corruption elsewhere than in the labor movement and on levels which are above the status of economic security? There is graft and corruption in the business community which has become so commonplace that it is hardly noticed as news until it amounts to a major scandal. Similar misdeeds occur constantly and are as taken for granted in the industrial-manufacturing world. . . .

Corruption is not a stranger either in city or state governments and it is not unknown in the federal Congress although all these institutions are run by those who singularly occupy positions of public confidence. . . .

When the amount of malpractice in organized labor is compared without prejudice and from any angle to serious misconduct and irresponsibility elsewhere in our society, then the record of trade unions in this regard is surprisingly clean.

The following editorial appeared shortly after Dave Beck, president of the International Brotherhood of Teamsters, had declined to answer any questions concerning his personal finances and their relation to union funds posed by the Senate Select Committee on Improper Practices in the Labor and Management Field, pleading the Fifth Amendment to the Federal Constitution as excusing him from testifying on the ground that he might incriminate himself.

From the AFL-CIO News, March 30, 1957

UNPLEASANT STUFF

The transcript of the hearings of the McClellan Committee does not make pleasant reading.

Union Leadership

	225

The record strongly suggests the absence of a real sense of trade union responsibility or morality on the part of several leaders of the Teamsters Union.

From the testimony; from the repeated use of the Fifth Amendment against self-incrimination; from the documents and evidence introduced by the committee staff—from all of this, there emerges a strong indication that ethical, responsible practices were too often flouted.

The McClellan Committee, needless to say, is not a court of law. On the other hand, it is not, on the record of the first few weeks, a witch-hunting group nor a group of irresponsibles. To date, it has performed a public service in bringing to light facts and figures which only a governmental agency could uncover.

Repeatedly the committee members and their counsel have pointed out that the practices which they have uncovered are not typical of the labor movement, and indeed that they run counter to the ethical standards developed by the AFL-CIO and the vast majority of its affiliated unions.

In other words: what has been harmful to labor during the first few weeks of the hearing has been not the committee but the practices and attitudes it has brought to light.

Perhaps, as the next few months unfold, anti-labor forces will use these disclosures in an effort to hamstring the entire labor movement. Fair legislation will win support. But anti-labor legislation will be resisted by the great majority of the labor movement—the multitude of honest, devoted members and leaders who have worked and sacrificed to build their unions and to make them honest, effective instruments for the public welfare.

The morality of the American labor movement has always been high—higher than those of profit-making corporations and the business community in general.

As AFL-CIO Sec.-Treas. Schnitzler has said: "I don't give a damn what a corporation does—that doesn't justify a union representative taking a 3-cent stamp."

That attitude—and only that attitude—can maintain the wonderful record of integrity of the overwhelming majority in our trade union movement.

THE PUBLIC IMAGE OF UNIONS

There are two conceptions of unionism which find a considerable public acceptance. One is of the union as an instrument through which a worker achieves some measure of independence and dignity in industry, the only means by which he can ensure that the employer's authority is not exercised autocratically or paternalistically, in the words of Professor J. M. Clark of Columbia University, the worker's "alternative to serfdom." The other image is of the union as a bureaucracy manned by labor bosses living in plush comfort off the dues which their members are forced to pay, as an organization over which members have relatively little control and which becomes, along with the employer, simply another instrument of control over workers.

Some members of the public adopt one or the other of these views and adhere steadfastly to it out of a prejudice or bias the roots of which they might themselves have difficulty in understanding. Other members of the public may accept both of these images as at least partially true, superimposing one on the other in a kind of Picasso-like conception. Still others, with greater ambivalence, may move back and forth between these views depending on the circumstances of the moment, depending on whether a congressional committee is one day exposing the cynical selfishness of some labor baron or whether the public press, another day, carries an account of how some railroad company has moved its headquarters offices, secretly and without notice to its employees, to a city 500 miles removed.

This chapter, which has focused on problems internal to unions, may have encouraged some acceptance of Image 2 in the mind of the reader, the conception of unions as autocratically controlled bureaucracies. If so, it would be to the reader's benefit to turn the pages of Chapter 2 again to see that Image 1, of unions as the voice of employee interests, likewise has its claim to validity.

As unions continue to struggle for greater social acceptance, which means, among other things, adding to their memberships, their appeal to workers not organized depends on which of these two images is the more credible. The next two selections point up how these two conceptions contend with each other.

From The Nation, December 10, 1955, pp. 497–500

ORGANIZING THE UNORGANIZED

When John W. Livingston, director of organizing for the merging A.F. of L.-C.I.O. surveys his job he will be looking beyond heavy industry, public utilities, and transportation. These, already fairly well organized, compose the bulk of the 16,000,000 members to whom President George Meany will be pointing with pride. Livingston, the husky auto worker from the Ozarks, will be concerned rather with the 45,000,000 wage-earners outside the union fold. They include most women workers, most white-collar employees, and most of the men and women, white and Negro, employed in the South. If, within the next ten years he would double the membership of the A.F. of L.-C.I.O. his name would go down in labor history alongside that of John L. Lewis.

The car you now drive, the house you live in, the meat and bread you eat—these are all pretty likely to be union-made. Likewise the electrical gadgets you live by, your means of getting hither and yon, the structures you work in, the things you read are produced, chances are, by hands that hold a union card. It's not nearly so likely that the clothes you wear (unless you insist on the union label) will be union-made. Most of the food you eat, most of the personal services you receive, the host of small and inexpensive things—these are, by and large, without benefit of union protection to their makers, processors, and handlers.

The statistics which face Livingston in his organizing drive do not give the whole picture. For instance, Chicago. This cradle of American labor is less unionized, factory-wise, than Richmond, Virginia, or Birmingham, Alabama. Enormous segments of heavy industry, particularly in oil and chemicals, remain untouched by orthodox unionism. In certain industries where both A.L. of L. and C.I.O. have competing unions, as in meat packing, textiles, and chemicals, internecine strife has taken a heavy toll. But the key to Chicago's poor showing is the small factory. In this metropolitan area there are not fewer than 14,000 factories employing one million workers, and most of them have fewer than a thousand employees. Here unionism runs into cost factors and the law of diminishing returns. A union administrator will tell you that it costs only about twice as much to furnish union services in a plant with 1,000 members as in one with a hundred. The temptation here is to organize not the workers but the employers into associations to be more easily policed by association-wide contracts. Small factories are a major union problem almost everywhere; in the aggregate they may well account for 10,000,000 unorganized workers.

Another roadblock to unionism is the white-collar employee. The factory workers tend to be output minded and to tie this in with severely regimented wage scales, seniority and working rules. The office workers in the big industrial plants look with no little envy on the status production workers have attained; whether unions can modify their rigid notions to fit the white collar, while the white collar abandons some of his notions of superiority, will determine union success in this most promising of all the big unconquered sectors.

Women are a problem, too. Or rather, union men are the problem in their attitude toward organizing women. The traditional male idea has been that the husband, as family breadwinner, should earn enough to support his family. Unions helped mightily to get the children out of the factories, and some of them thought woman's place, too, was in the home. However desirable this old American dream may have been, the facts of life negate it. Women constitute one-third of the labor force; one-third of women over fourteen are at work. The new A.F. of L.-C.I.O. director of organization may know better than to try to stretch women on unionism's procrustean bed. Since he'll likely be too male-conscious to see the problem (not a single woman has ever been elected to the executive board of either labor federation), perhaps there should be a woman codirector of organization. That might rectify the present situation where men are averaging $3,469 in yearly earnings against $1,252 for women, who are actually 13 percent worse off, wage-wise, than they were thirteen years ago. The catch phrase, so dear to both Republican and Democratic vote-catchers, that labor never had it so good, certainly doesn't apply to women.

Whatever his other problems, Director Livingston is not going to be bothered much by the size of his organizing budget. The new federation starts with a built-in annual deficit of between three and four million dollars. This stems from the facts of merger. Governed by sacrosanct rules of tenure and seniority, the merged federation will enjoy no economies but rather a two-headed bureaucracy in which every officeholder is assured of his job. The lack of money doesn't mean too much. There were hardly pennies available back in the 1930's when steel, auto, electrical, and machine workers organized themselves. Sending scads of paid organizers into virgin territory usually doesn't pay off. The paid organizers are apt to limit their efforts to getting signatures on application cards; that indeed is the criterion of success in many a union headquarters. It is assumed that there is some magic in the word "union" and that this *deus ex machina* will do the job somehow by remote control. Wherever workers have been genuinely organized into unions, they have accepted the union as a vehicle which they must pull to success by their own efforts. It is true that there are many unions organized by bureaucratic methods, but they can better be described as workingmen's business organizations which come to life once a year when the contract expires. Unionism as a way of life, which is the biggest asset Director Livingston has in doubling the A.F. of L.-C.I.O. membership in the next decade, is a lot bigger than most union officials care to admit; in fact there is a certain tendency to lean over backwards and insist that the immediate pork chop is the sole goal of labor. A certain type of university intellectual who dabbles in labor matters fiercely loves this concept of business unionism, perhaps because it is supposed to be anti-Marxist, but few average citizens love it. It is a bit too materialistic to enlist widespread admiration among those not directly involved.

Business unionism will offer certain obstacles to Director Livingston's program. As these unions achieve a certain limited success, and their officials acquire financial and social status in rather sumptuous headquarters, bureaucratism becomes a factor. So long as the dues continue to roll in, these cumbersome machines tend to rely on their own momentum to survive. While every union covets more per capita, the imagination and drive needed for organizing become dulled and the machines become involved in contemplating their own internal problems. Unable to cope with the challenge within their own industries, they look only with vague interest toward ambitious programs for organizing women, white collars, or the South. The typical union official today is an administrator, not an organizer. The situation was highlighted when the United Auto Workers offered to toss $1,250,000 into a general organizing kitty if other unions would also chip in. The idea lies vegetating in the fields and it will be interesting to see how much luck Director Livingston has in resurrecting it.

An exception must be noted. The Teamsters, an extremely self-centered and businesslike union, has garnered a rich harvest of small factories, warehouses, and processing plants. Almost any unorganized plant that a truck may enter to deliver or take away goods is subject to Teamsters' interest; so widespread has become its jurisdiction that it parallels in structure and scope the great British Transport and General Workers Union. While the Teamsters organize on a strictly self-centered basis which may afford little help to A.F. of L.-C.I.O.'s general campaigns, the success they have attained in aggressive organizing shows the possibilities lying around unrealized.

Another encouraging factor with which Director Livingston is well acquainted is the proletarianizing of the supervisory and technical staffs in heavy industry. In oil refineries, for example, there is now one supervisor for every five or six hourly workers. These, along with the technicians and professionals in the factory, are tending to become "the masses" and inclined to like the kind of protection that unionism affords.

This generation has seen two upsurges of organization, the first growing out of the desperation of the Great Depression, the second out of World War II. In the first, workers organized themselves. In the second, the unions did the job through labor-board ballots with a powerful assist from the government which needed to have war workers mobilized for more effective direction.

The current era differs from both. It can hardly be said that the unorganized show desperation today, particularly in the North. Many of them bask in the shade of the union umbrella without having to pay dues. Perhaps as many workers enjoy the wage benefits of unionism outside the unions as inside—they are the free riders. Then there are the millions of capitalism's captives, the indentured servants of instalment purchases. They feel they can't afford to risk strikes for the union because the sheriff might haul away the cherished TV, the beloved new car, or the housewife's proud badge of freedom, her machines for washing and cleaning. Not in their ranks of course are the appalling numbers even in the North who earn less than $1 an hour, but still are an influential minority among the unorganized.

Employers too have their umbrella, the Cadillac Cabinet in Washington, basically hostile to unionism. Lothair Teetor, former Assistant Secretary of Commerce whose Perfect Circle firm in Indiana believes in shooting it out with the United Auto Workers, hastily abandoned his Washington post not, perhaps, because his hostility to the union was repudiated but because this display of pre-Rooseveltian anti-unionism was embarrassing. The Secretary of the Interior, whose struck Oregon firm depends more on starvation than bullets to beat down the union, rides more easily in the Cabinet. Under Eisenhower, the National Labor Relations Board has become a coolly hostile force from which unions can expect no favors. Insofar as possible, they bypass the very board which was set up originally to protect the right to organize. If a minor depression should set in, the unions, under the present Administration, might well find themselves entrenched in a war of self-preservation rather than in seeking more millions to organize.

Director Livingston then must face the intrinsic differences of this period, which contrasts with the 1930's and with the war years. There is an undeniable passivity among many unorganized workers and a growing intransigence among hard-boiled employers. These are high hurdles.

Any serious proposal to add millions to the labor movement must take into account the South, where industry is burgeoning, wages are low, and security generally non-existent. The emancipation of Southern labor is the key not only to the creation of a truly national labor movement, but to the refreshment of American political life. A South brought up to national wage standards, liberated from industrial-plantation feudalists, and freed from bondage to the race issue would give a new turn to the national life. This long overdue emancipation can be labor's greatest gift both to the South and to the country at large. It will be achieved when Southern workers find the union key. They are ready, they are good joiners, and when they have pledged their work they are loyal to it (a mighty asset on the picket line). Here especially the spiritual values that labor can express find a ready response. Southern workers are tired of being second-class industrial citizens, of being told that sunshine is a good substitute for adequate pay and the self-respect that unions bring. Nor will the chains of instalment-buying bind them; they have little to lose and much to win in a fight.

The textile baronies along the Atlantic Piedmont differ as sharply from the industrialized Birmingham region as does oil-rich Texas and the Southwest from either. There is no unified "South." Alongside the peonized sugar workers of Louisiana are unionized oil workers on the Gulf Coast who have wiped out the North-South wage differential. The Birmingham steel workers have just erased the wage differential; the meat packers are narrowing the margin. Along the bayous and in the piney woods giant new plants are mushrooming, most of them built by Northern corporations accustomed to dealing with unions up North. Any Southern organizer will tell you that a new plant is twice as easy (or half as difficult) to line up as an older one.

Nevertheless repeated "Southern drives" have petered out. A good bit of the blame must be placed at labor's door because of its hesitant attitude toward Negroes. A firm stand has been diluted out of concern for the prejudice of the white worker; as a result neither white nor Negro is organized.

There is no disguising the stubbornness of racial prejudice; on the other hand it has been magnified out of all perspective by the racist press and agitators. It is becoming increasingly clear to Southern workers that discrimination is holding back both races. All the way from Richmond to Corpus Christi union leaders can give concrete examples of success in fighting discrimination. The Negro, as an ally, can decide the issue of unionism in the South; if he is left uninterested, he can defeat unionism by his mere passivity. When the A.F. of L.-C.I.O. brings its fight for economic and political equality out of the clouds of convention oratory and pious resolutions into a genuine fighting program, the next drive in the South will need neither millions of dollars nor thousands of paid organizers. To paraphrase Marx, the emancipation of the Southern workers will be achieved by the Southern workers themselves, once Negroes are assured a position in the labor movement fully equal to their white brothers.

The main reason organized labor has made little progress in recent years can be found in "public opinion." Director Livingston will find this public opinion the all-important factor in his organizing plans. Not the public opinion so readily manufactured by the mass media controlled by the business elements, but rather that of the grapevine, of word-of-mouth that spreads among unorganized workers as they eye unionism as it is. In this, the spiritual factors far outweigh the material, odd as that may seem. The name of John L. Lewis was magic to millions in the 1930's because at last one of their own stood up, fought back, and won against the titans of his time. That exhilaration of spirit was worth more than millions in the treasury. The image of Organized Labor as the protector of the poor, the apostle of public education, the champion of better health, and welfare, the watchdog against private plunder of the national resources, the advocate of world brotherhood, is the most valuable asset the A.F. of L.-C.I.O. director of organization can possibly have. That is why the business press has been so keen to show up sporadic pilfering of union welfare funds and to front-page the mansions of a few labor leaders. If the labor movement can be reduced in public estimation to a selfish materialistic concept in which a favored class advances its own pay (and prices to the public, as the press insists) and collaborates with municipal corruptionists for special privilege, the vast majority of men and women still outside the House of Labor will remain there. If labor's political action, in practice, seems aimed at seeking favors, in advancing the interests of political shysters, in urging expanded military expenditures so that unionized war workers in plane factories and other munitions plants may be sheltered, there will be little spark of response from the unorganized. Even if their aspirations are unverbalized, they seek security, dignity, peace.

In truth there have always been the two drives within the labor movement, the one animated by the highest concern for humanity, the other rather desperately seeking to find safety for some behind barriers. Across the country from coast to coast there are thousands dedicated to the proposition that unions are the engines of democracy in an industrial society; their voices are going to be heard increasingly as the bankruptcy in imagination and drive of the business unionists continues to breed sterility. It is to them that Director Livingston will need to be looking for the organizers, largely unpaid, of the millions who should be in the unified House of Labor.

By David S. Burgess, reprinted by permission of The Christian Century from the issue of May 13, 1953

IN DEFENSE OF LABOR

Recently it has become fashionable in Protestant liberal circles to criticize the labor movement. Chief among its current critics is Kermit Eby, former educational director of the national C.I.O. and now professor at the University of Chicago. Only four months ago Charles Clayton Morrison, former editor of The Christian Century, joined the ranks of the critics. (See the Century for January 21.) Fortunately, both are friends and sympathetic in their approach. Yet, in their anxiety to set forth their new insights, they have presented to the relatively uninformed layman a distorted picture of the total labor movement. They have used such emotionally colored phrases as "entrenched bureaucracy" and "autocratic leadership" with careless liberality. And they have failed to list the positive contributions which today's labor movement is making to the life of America.

Dr. Morrison has awakened to the undeniable truth that the labor movement is not without sin and that many well meaning churchmen have displayed a woeful ignorance of this fact. Then, like the husband who has come to discover that his wife has many human failings, he proceeds to describe the democracy of the labor movement as "akin to the democracy of fascism and sovietism," and concludes by calling upon all good churchmen "to condemn as morally and socially vicious the alleged right to strike."

Loss of early enthusiasm

Having first-hand knowledge of the A.F.L. and C.I.O., Prof. Eby is less severe in his description of the slow but almost inevitable institutionalizing of the labor movement. He pines for the exciting days of the thirties when he was among the "shock troops," when idealism, courage and sacrifice were the ingredients of the new unions. But today, he claims, the fire of enthusiasm is almost out. "The revolution has been stabilized." Well-paid "pork-choppers" of this newly "entrenched bureaucracy" rule the unions. The rank and file, with decreasing interest and participation, are supposed to "applaud uncontested slates and agreed resolutions." All in all, the American labor movement has become complacent and inclined to middle aged mediocrity.

Despite the truth in these insights, the two critics err in their implied assumption that the whole labor movement suffers from middle age or bureaucracy or a combination of both. The fact is that local unions, international unions and the various labor movements of our nation differ radically in this regard. Around Chicago and other northern industrial centers, as Dr. Morrison claims, the labor movement may be settling back, since "many if not most of the injustices [which created the labor movement] have been corrected or are on their way to correction." But this is not the case in most of America, and especially in the south. Here union organizers are still slugged. The right of collective bargaining is flouted by employers. In such a hostile atmosphere, the average member regards the union as a "way of life," for he knows that the struggle must be continued.

Standing outside the circle of the 16 million union members of America are more than 40 million unorganized workers—agricultural laborers, retail clerks, white-collar employees, domestic and service workers. In time many of them will be seeking admittance to the labor movement, for despite Dr. Morrison's assertions a wealth of injustices still exist among working people and must be righted.

Problem of institutionalism

In fairness, however, we must admit that the critics' basic analysis of the older and better established unions often rings true. The more enlightened leaders of American labor are acutely aware of this growing problem of institutionalism. Like any other human organization built on sacrifice and blood, the labor movement undergoes a change when its charter members pass on and leave in their place the leaders of the second generation. Many of these new officials rose in the movement *after* the battle for recognition had been won. They are now called upon to direct and inspire many union members who have never experienced a strike and who tend to take for granted the hard-won benefits of their own unions.

Aware of this problem of the second generation are President Walter Reuther and other new chieftains of the C.I.O. In Reuther's own union, the United Auto Workers, an active program of education has been launched to train the 60 per cent or more of the members who were too young to have participated in the early struggles of their movement. The same type of program has been started in the A.F.L. International Ladies Garment Workers Union. Good wages, war prosperity, TV seductions, and the constant antiunion barrage of the "one-party" press tend to make some workers soft, content, uninformed about their own movement, and therefore easy prey to every passing wind of hostile gossip.

Ethics of labor power

The second basic criticism by these two friendly critics centers on the puzzling question of power—the ethics of "entrenched bureaucracy," as Prof. Eby terms it, and the "prodigious concentration of power wielded by a few men," in Dr. Morrison's phraseology. In all candor it must be granted that labor has often fallen victim to the vices of power. A few leaders have developed an inordinate lust for power and recognition. In an atmosphere of internal competition within a union, loyalty to a faction or a superior has often taken precedence over loyalty to the union or to the public welfare. As a result, favors, political jobbery and purges of the opposition have often been a part of trade union history.

But again the critics have failed to tell the whole truth. The simple fact is that, despite certain aberrations of the democratic process, most labor unions were founded and still operate on a democratic foundation. Unlike the officials of corporations, union presidents, executive board members and regional directors are elected by the membership in a referendum or at a convention, and in the end they are held accountable to all the union members.

At the same time, members have learned that their elected leaders must be vested with strong powers if the international union or the labor movement as a whole is to be effective and able to survive the onslaughts of hostile industrialists. Labor knows that in the mass industries of America, wage, hour and fringe decisions are not made by a single employer, but by a combination of employers working in close, day-to-day collaboration. This elemental fact of our semimonopolistic system of capitalism is the reason why the structure of an effective international union tends to parallel the structure of the industry it attempts to organize. Hence regional and industry-wide bargaining is absolutely essential to the preservation of industrial democracy, and elected union officials have to be vested with power. Without this concentration of power in the hands of the elected union leadership, collective bargaining in the great industries of America would be a mockery and giant corporations would rule undisputed.

Labor and government intervention

The necessary power of labor's top leaders, however, has created certain problems for the public at large. The coal strikes of the 1940s are the most dramatic example of this phenomenon. These stoppages disrupted the national economy and in the end caused the federal government to intervene. In time, miners' wages were raised, though John L. Lewis' union was forced to pay a heavy fine during the last settlement.

Dr. Morrison argues that such strikes are morally wrong and contrary to the public interest. He sharply criticizes labor leaders for allegedly precipitating such strikes with full knowledge that the federal government would intervene and come to the rescue of the union. Leaving out of account the morals of coal operators, the criticism may have had a limited validity one, five or ten years ago, but it has little meaning today. The Republicans rule Washington and most of organized labor no longer regards the federal labor agencies as sympathetic or even impartial. In the years immediately ahead, public members of tripartite investigating boards are much more likely to wind up on the employer's side of the bargaining table.

Moreover, Dr. Morrison's statement about labor's depending on government intervention during the days of a "favorable" administration in Washington can be disputed by two outstanding examples. Back in 1946, the U.A.W.-C.I.O. workers at General Motors offered to settle their strike without a desired wage increase if the corporation would open its books and prove that the requested wage increase would lessen profits or justify any price increase for the product. The corporation kept the books closed. In 1952 the United Steelworkers-C.I.O., after months of bargaining and government investigation, refused to be a party to a deal giving the workers the desired pay raise at the price of an unjustifiable increase in steel prices. The corporation refused to accept a reasonable settlement. In both instances, powerful labor leaders showed that their sense of responsibility to the public interest could outweigh their desire for tangible improvements for the members of their unions.

How powerful are the unions?

Dr. Morrison, I fear, overrates the *real* power of organized labor. He states rather categorically that "virtually the whole labor community has been organized until labor now represents the most powerful bloc in our economy." Labor is so strong that it supposedly controls a place on President Eisenhower's millionaire cabinet, even though it is "opportunistic and short-ranged" in its program and is seeking "to gain a whip hand over industry."

Without attempting to refute all Dr. Morrison's opinions, I submit that a comparison of the financial resources of labor and capital in two basic industries will create a reasonable doubt in the reader's mind about their justification. In 1950 the United Steelworkers-C.I.O., which has about 90 per cent of the industry organized, had total assets of $9,000,000; in the same year the Bethlehem Steel Corporation could boast assets of $1,155,000,000, and U. S. Steel had $2,556,000,000. The United Auto Workers-C.I.O. had only $4,000,000 in assets, but General Motors Corporation had $2,824,000,000. These corporations had by far the more effective propaganda facilities. Their executives were recognized as civic leaders. The unions, in contrast, were financially weak and limited in their ability to reach and to influence the general public. Their officials were seldom given sympathetic treatment in the press or over the radio. Now that General Motors Corporation has three former officials in the President's cabinet and Big Business rides firmly in the Washington saddle, the comparative strength of the contending groups within industry is even more disproportionate. Therefore, we need a stronger rather than a weaker labor movement if industrial democracy is to remain a reality.

Amid all their criticisms, Prof. Eby and Dr. Morrison do not mention the positive contributions of the labor movement to our nation's life. During the early organizing days of "shock troops" and "brickbats," organized labor could not make its contribution to welfare in the broader sense of the word. Fighting against low wages and long hours, working men and women were so engrossed in the rudimentary struggle to get a union that they had no time to give to the larger questions of public welfare—the community chest, the March of Dimes, civic improvements, rights for teachers, election of decent public officials. Life was too full of blacklists, company "goons" and "kept" sheriffs. First things had to come first if the labor movement was to live at all.

Labor's positive contributions

But today this narrow emphasis on the basic problems of recognition and economic subsistence no longer characterizes the operating philosophy of the C.I.O. and the A.F.L. In labor's ranks the broader public interest now supersedes the so-called labor interest. Even where the labor movement is numerically weak, unions have shown a remarkable concern for the welfare of *all* working people. In the recent session of the Georgia general assembly, for example, the C.I.O. and A.F.L. had a simple, two-point program: to increase unemployment benefits and to overhaul completely the state's antiquated workmen's compensation law. Few A.F.L. or C.I.O. members are now unemployed. Fewer still draw workmen's compensation payments, because labor-management cooperation in developing safety programs in unionized plants has kept the accident rate to a minimum. Yet here in the Georgia legislature were the A.F.L. and C.I.O. organizations, representing only 15 per cent of the workers, lobbying for two measures that would benefit *all* Georgia workers. Again and again, this story of labor's fundamental altruism has been repeated in other legislatures.

But the most striking proof of labor's concern for the general welfare is exhibited daily in Washington. Because union members pay dues and can therefore employ full-time representatives, the labor lobby in the capitol has become in effect the lobby for the great mass of unrepresented consumers—housewives, small farmers, unorganized workers and millions of voiceless Americans. The truth of this claim is borne out by an examination of labor's legislative program. It calls for extension of social security benefits, decent public housing, channeling of tidelands oil billions into the needy schools of America, national health insurance for all people, civil rights for all minorities, freedom of conscience and thought for every American. This program is broad and inclusive because organized labor has learned that it cannot grow or prosper if it confines its efforts to improving the lot of its own members. To grow it must try to represent all working people.

"The Protestant ethic"

As professing Protestants, we cannot be satisfied by listing labor's past accomplishments or by proclaiming our faith in its future destiny. Our main and oft-neglected task is a present one—applying the insights of the gospel to the everyday problems of an institutionalized labor movement. Neither of our critics has discussed this fundamental problem. They have failed to mention the Protestant principle of "rebirth"—the "Protestant ethic," as Paul Tillich so aptly terms it. For the individual it takes the form of self-examination, of forgiveness from God, of being "born again." For the institution which suffers from selfishness or dullness of vision, this transformation can come about, this rebirth can occur, if the leaders and members examine their own motivations and the mores of their own organization. Then, with the help of God, they may be fit to put their own house in order.

But such a message of salvation can seldom reach the labor movement when the critics sound their denunciations from the balcony. It can be transmitted best by those in the labor movement or by friends outside the ranks whose depth of comprehension regarding corporate sin is balanced by their breadth of compassion for the alleged sinners. By those few Protestants who by choice or circumstance are still in the labor movement, this message of salvation is seldom heard. We are criticized without sympathy and reviled without understanding. But we keep praying for a church that can speak the truth unafraid, freeing men from their sins and transforming even the most worldly institution.

FOR DISCUSSION AND ANALYSIS

1. Are there reasons why we should be more concerned about the democratic character of labor unions than of other kinds of organizations? Do you think it is any less important for corporations to be democratic, for example?

2. Describe the steps by which (a) a member of the United Automobile Workers and (b) a local union may appeal disciplinary action believed to be unfair, referring to the UAW constitution in Chapter 3. Comment on the adequacy and fairness of these procedures.

3. "Resolved: Labor unions are the most democratic organizations in our society." Outline the arguments on the affirmative and negative sides of this proposition.

4. Professor Clark Kerr once remarked it was a rather sad commentary on industrial relations that the situations which most conduce to local union democracy are also the situations which make a peaceful and cooperative relationship between union and management difficult to maintain. Why should this be so?

5. If the AFL-CIO executive council believed that one of its constituent unions was dominated by racketeers or communists, what action could it take against that union to remedy the situation? Refer to the provisions of

the constitution (Chapter 3) to support your conclusion. Does the Ethical Code against labor racketeers adopted in 1957 strengthen the constitutional powers to deal with such a situation?

6. Do you feel more favorably disposed towards business firms than towards labor unions? Do you think that unions are too powerful and should be "cut down to size" by governmental action or legislation? Do you think that unions benefit their officials at the expense of their members?

If you answer all the foregoing in the negative, you then hold Public Image No. 1 of the unions, that they are necessary instruments for the achievement of worker rights in our society. If you answer all the foregoing in the affirmative, the chances are that you hold Public Image No. 2, that they are bureaucratic organizations fastened on the worker, who has been hoodwinked or cajoled into believing that they are good for him or who has been coerced to join, against his will. If your answers are split, you probably hold both these views in varying proportions or waver between them.

Whatever your answers and the image which you hold, try to analyze the reasons why you have this conception of the unions, being as honest with yourself as possible, distinguishing ratiocination from rationalization.

5: Management Outlook and Practice

Management's attitudes towards its employees and towards unions flow from its structure of aspirations, including the values which it would like to see incorporated in the society around it. Its philosophy of efficiency may lead it to oppose employee and union practices which are rational only in terms of a philosophy of security. Its predisposition towards individual effort and responsibility may militate against its acceptance of collective action by its employees. Its traditional belief in the necessity of management's possessing final authority may lead it to question the place of representative institutions in business. The readings which follow illustrate and suggest the values and aspirations which characterize management, from which flow its personnel practices. The same beliefs do not, of course, always result in the same practices; the latter are also some indication of the degree of sophistication of their source and their object.

INDUSTRIAL POLICIES AND THE DRIVE FOR IMPROVED METHODS

From Industrial Engineering, report of a visit to the United States in 1953 of a British specialist team in industrial engineering, British Productivity Council, 1954, pp. 11–12

We were convinced that the drive for improved methods in the individual firm comes from top management, is felt through middle management and finds strong expression on the shop floor. Functional specialists such as industrial engineers (under this or other names), controllers, cost-accountants and personnel officers make effective contributions towards this drive. Line management, including foremen, plays its part, whether or not functional specialists form part of the organisation and irrespective of whether their influence is strong. The drive is not transmitted in any one way, by any one type of organisation or by any one technique; the variety of organisation and techniques is remarkable.

But what, then, makes senior management itself method-conscious? We find the answer in the competitive atmosphere of American industry already noted. Method-consciousness has resulted from the keen attention to production costs which in itself is one of the major features of the American competitive econ-

238

omy. *The top executive knows that continual improvement of his methods will reduce his costs and keep him in the race:* he cannot afford to stand still since his competitors are advancing all the time. Therefore he keeps his managers, foremen and workers aware that they personally are as vitally concerned in this as the firm itself. If they lead in the race all will benefit by higher earnings, security of employment and greater chances for promotion as the company grows; higher earnings mean a higher standard of living; greater chances of promotion mean not only higher earnings but elevated status in society. If they fall behind, they all lose together; short time, reduced earnings, lowering of living standards, or even unemployment may result. We believe this line of reasoning is understood and accepted by most if not all in American industrial life, certainly by trade union leaders. Naturally the workers insist on certain safeguards. They sometimes enforce rigid rules governing the introduction of labour-saving machinery and the treatment of workers made redundant by technological improvement. They aim, through their unions, at getting as big a share of the cake as they can, but realise that they must accept new methods so that the cake can become bigger. . . .

How is it that the right men get to the top? We believe that the answer is two-fold: competition again, and good selection. The reward for men in top positions is high; salaries of senior executives are much more generous than is usual in this country, and personal taxation is less punitive. Reward is nearly always related to the results achieved; and, as elsewhere, the sky is often the limit. There is more ruthlessness than there is in this country with those who fail; they have to quit or are given other, subordinate positions. Youth is no bar to advancement. The mobility of labour applies equally to executives. They move far more frequently than is usual here and in this way they gain broader experience. Indeed, moves are encouraged; some large firms have within their own organisations a formal system of job-rotation for all their executives.

A good executive was defined to us as one who is "dissatisfied with the present method of doing anything," who is "constantly learning new tricks," and is "ready to listen to advice, both from inside and outside his organisation." Being prepared to take outside advice is a characteristic that struck us as particularly notable. It expresses itself not only in the widespread use of professional consultants and other outside advisers, but also in the readiness of executives to participate in the meetings and conventions of management and professional societies, to attend courses and lectures and to visit one another's factories. This last point is the one which impressed us most of all.

STRENGTHENING JOBS IN AN EXPANDING ECONOMY

Excerpt from an Address by Charles R. Sligh, Jr., President, Sligh Furniture Companies, Grand Rapids, Michigan, and Chairman of the Board, National Association of Manufacturers

I wish that I had some dramatic way of driving home the message that anything which shackles, restricts or smothers free movement—anything that shods progress with lead—is false to the American principle.

Let me try to paint the picture in a few broad strokes.

Until a few hundred years ago the history of the world was a drab recital of misery. Our forefathers tore themselves loose from that sterile soil, came to America and founded a nation based on freedom of worship, freedom of speech and freedom of enterprise. Our forefathers lived daringly. They staked their all for a better America. They had the courage to overcome fear, the resourcefulness to overcome want.

Over and over again our free economy has proved itself equal to the task of creating job opportunity. According to a recent survey by the Council for Technological Advancement, "The basic economic strength of the United States stems from added opportunities of employment provided by proper utilization of machinery. Since 1939 jobs in manufacturing have increased 70 per cent while population has gone up 22 per cent."

Each new factory rises as a symbol of new productive might. It contributes to the growing strength and security of America. Each new enterprise sows the regenerating seeds of new jobs. A vital part of our overall freedom is industrial freedom which consists of—

First. The element of *change*, the principle that all things are in a constant state of flux and flow. From this change often comes economic growth and personal advance.

Second. Invention and innovation. As new devices are invented, new materials developed, new methods worked out, and as productivity advances, the resulting expansion in our economy means not only more jobs but a higher standard of living for everybody.

Third. From year to year—even from month to month—the foundation of industry feels economic ground swells. No growth is possible without recognition of the need for *flexibility* and the ability of employers, workers and the government to "ride with the punches."

Fourth. Accompanying these earth tremors are *movements of population.* People move from job to job within a city and from one city to another. Always the incentive is to increase the scale of living and allow higher income, more satisfying jobs, better homes and living arrangements.

Fifth. Over and above all of these is the *incentive* for the individual *to risk* his savings, in the hope of reward. Very often an employee who has a good, steady job with security, surrenders it willingly for one in a more dynamic organization that has promise of future growth.

To restate the problem *we must have new jobs*, a million of them a year—and at the same time *we must strengthen jobs* in our expanding economy.

Such surging economic growth can be realized only by the *preservation of four conditions.*

. . . We must preserve our *Freedom* with a capital "F," for that freedom includes the industrial freedoms to act, to work and to choose as the master, not the servant, of the government.

. . . We must preserve *free competitive markets* with a government that acts on the principle that government governs *best*—which governs *least*.

. . . We must preserve *a climate of government favorable to individual op-*

portunity and dynamic expansion, which recognizes a fair tax structure, sound money, aggressive marketing, good labor-management relations, conservation of resources and the importance of profits.

. . . We must preserve *faith in industry,* its motivation and its ability to seed job-growth in the national interest.

Both the guaranteed annual wage and company policies which completely ignore human needs fall far short of these four requirements.

On the national level we must have the kind of governmental policies which encourage incentive for investment and business expansion.

On the community level we must have a better understanding of the elements of job-making—the role of capital investment, competition, research and management skills, and a recognition that the role of government must be limited.

On the company level we must have all-out efforts by management to provide the highest possible level of *steady work and steady pay* through more effective handling of factors lying within company control.

It would be poor business for management to guarantee work or wages. Free government can't guarantee employment without freezing over the economy with an icecap of socialism. And the unions aren't going to guarantee *anything.* That sums up the situation.

We have come full circle—back to management. Security rests right where it has always rested—on the businessmen who take the risks.

There's no road for us but the hard, level highway we have always trod. The primrose path may be inviting. But it doesn't lead to security, to prosperity, or to any form of economic fulfillment. It runs downhill into ruin— national and individual. The risk—the responsibility—the worry—all of these we must accept.

We must find the ways of stabilizing production and work.

We must do everything humanly possible to eliminate such things as seasonal lay-offs. We must level out the peaks and valleys on the sales charts.

In short, we must *strengthen jobs*—in an expanding economy—because that's the only way we can have a stronger people—a stronger nation—and a stronger industrial freedom.

THE DOLLARS AND CENTS OF INDUSTRIAL RELATIONS

By Samuel L. H. Burk, Director, Industrial Relations Division, National Association of Manufacturers, before the Roundtable in Labor Relations, Graduate School of Business, Columbia University, February 26, 1957

The title assigned to my formal remarks this afternoon, and which also describes the subject matter of our discussions to follow, is—I am afraid—just a little too restrictive for what I understand to be our purposes. My invitation to address you at least implied, if not emphasized, that the pure cost aspects of industrial relations are the determing factors in management decisions in the broad field of personnel administration; or, if they are not, they should be.

In the field of industrial relations—in fact, in all phases of management—it is well-nigh impossible to isolate consideration of costs from a great number of other imponderable factors which enter into the making of management decisions. In fact, even to hint that a manager is nothing but a kind of super electronic computer would be dangerously misleading—in one sense defamatory and in another sense unfortunate. In spite of many opinions to the contrary, which are sometimes deliberately fostered by anti-management groups and at other times innocently caused by actions of managers, there can be no doubt that members of management are human beings. As human beings, they are subjected to the same powerful influences which contribute to all human behavior. An examination of some of these influences and some consideration of the behavior of individual human beings in managerial positions are appropriate before getting down to the bedrock subject matter.

Let us first take a brief look at the nature of organizations. Professor Harold Thuesen in his book "Engineering Economy" has stated "Organizations are the means for overcoming the limitations of people through cooperative effort." While in my opinion this definition alone is worth the price of the book, the thing that Professor Thuesen failed to bring out in the statement was that, no matter how cooperative individuals may be or want to be, their effectiveness in organizations will vary in direct proportion to the quality of coordination which is provided by assigning to certain individuals authority to direct and command the activities of cooperating individuals. Coordination is, together with the employment of people of widely varying make-up, the essence of organizational effectiveness. Thus, the quality of the management is the chief determinant of coordinative success.

We could continue a philosophic discussion of the administrative activities of the manager and what it takes to achieve the optimum of coordination with some profit but with little progress toward any conclusions concerning our immediate subject. We must move toward some definition of why these managers tend to make certain kinds of decisions and take some kinds of actions in carrying out their function of coordinating and directing the work of others. We have pointed out that managers are human beings. Like other human beings they are largely emotional, but we like to think that rational reasoning processes are more a part of the manager's individual make-up than they are of people who do not succeed in administrative and executive assignments. Moreover, because of the responsibility which is a concomitant of that managerial authority which is inherent in any organization, we must assume that a large part of the managerial function is discharged in accordance with some individual general code of principles which in total constitutes a manager's personal philosophy. In the case of any one manager, this may differ from or follow closely the over-all administrative philosophy of any business organization.

We see, then, that managerial decisions and actions are a combination of principles, emotions and reasoning. This is perhaps oversimplification. Certainly we cannot overlook the national, social and economic atmosphere in which managers operate or have operated.

Management decisions and actions with respect to employee or industrial relations are therefore a complex of the principles, emotions and reasoning powers of the most influential members of any single management group. To imply that a wholly rational approach based only upon an extremely intelligent balancing of the cost factors is the sole manner in which managers make their decisions would be foolish. Similarly to imply that there are some general mathematical formulas adopted by all managers in arriving at their decisions, or that there is some formula which can be given to a management on the basis of which decisions can be made would be just as foolish as was the expectation that people's habits with respect to alcoholic beverage consumption could be regulated legislatively.

Let us take some sample questions in order to develop our points further. The question has been asked "How can a management determine whether to settle on the union's terms or take a strike?" What actually happens when a management is faced with this issue? The cost of shutting down the plant is usually fairly well known or can be approximated with a reasonable degree of accuracy. Added to possible strike costs must be estimates of the dollars and cents impact on relations with the company's customers and suppliers. Most managements will also consider the effect of wage and salary losses on its em- ployees and the estimated resulting cost effect of lowered production caused by reduced morale when the strike is finally settled. There will, of course, be other matters taken into consideration—such as stockholder or owner reaction to measurable as well as imponderable losses and the effect of such reaction on the tenure or progress of the members of the top management group.

From just these few sample considerations it will be evident that we progress very swiftly from hard monetary facts to matters which are pure conjecture, coupled with the dictates of experience in similar past situations. When a company is closely held or family owned, and the members of the management group are largely members of the family most directly interested financially, the decision may well be appreciably different than in the more widely held corporations. Again at the risk of oversimplification, we can define this differ- ence as the difference between ownership management and professional management.

However, experience does not enable us to point to typical decision situa- tions which differentiate between ownership management and professional management—again because managers of each of these general types differ widely as individuals. Generally speaking, we find that the owner-manager will tend to be somewhat more emotional than the professional manager in a potential strike situation. To the owner-manager the threat is a distinctly personal one. To the professional manager, while the threat is directed at his managerial ability, it is largely directed toward the security and profitability of money that belongs to someone else.

From the point of view of principles, there is little distinction that can be made between the owner-manager and the professional manager. We have individuals in both groups who place great weight on their philosophies with respect to the people that make up their organization. We have others who have not troubled to establish in their own minds any fundamental body of principles in these respects. But, generally speaking, professional management seems to be less governed by personal principles of individual managers than is ownership management. This is not to say that big business is "unprincipled." It merely means that the professional manager *as an individual* is more likely to subordinate both his personal principles and his personal emotions to the needs of the corporate enterprise than is the owner-manager. This, of course, is because the owner-manager has more freedom to do as he will with his own property. On the other hand, many very successful large companies, widely owned by the general public, have established organizational philosophies based on what they believe to be sound principles of human relations. Many of these companies have adhered to these principles regardless of the estimated effect upon immediate profit. It would appear that, where the principles have been sound over the long run, adherence to such principles in spite of current expedience has carried the company successfully through the crisis. On the other hand, however, where the principles have been unsound, adherence to such principles has inevitably led to deterioration of the organization in one way or another.

Therefore, at the outset management is faced with the decision as to the soundness of its principles. The soundness of such principles must be evaluated in the light of the changing economic and social atmosphere in which the organization operates. This in itself is no small assignment. Part of the management job, therefore, is to examine the fundamental principles on which it operates. In order to do so, it must do more than philosophize about the principles but must compare its principles with the principles of other well-known and successful corporations. Let us look at an actual company which we shall call Company U. For many years the company had stood firmly against compulsory unionism. Prior to contract negotiation time, it made a complete survey of its suppliers and customers and came to the conclusion that, despite its conviction that its previous principles were morally and ethically right, it could not afford to take a strike solely on the basis of that issue because it could not get support for such a stand from its shareholders, its consumers or its suppliers. It is apparent that, although extremes of emotions were involved in arriving at this decision and although no individual member of the management was willing to change his individual conviction as to principle, some imponderable dollars and cents value was placed on stockholder, customer and supplier reaction. The dues shop clause was inserted in the contract without any argument after years of bitter holding out for the right to work. Certainly no absolute dollars and cents value could be attributed to this concession. There was no way for the management to put a dollar value on how much business would be lost or how much good or ill will would be accumulated and what the actual gain or loss to the company would be as a result of such accumulation.

On the other hand, take the case of Company S. Company S is largely a family-owner managed corporation. This company is still in the throes of a long strike. They have steadfastly held to what they consider to be a fundamental principle, namely the right to work. One would suppose that a great deal of emotion has entered into this stand. The company has lost some business to its several competitors largely because a few potential customers are uncertain of Company S's ability to meet its sales obligations. Again, however, the company has been unable to put a dollars and cents value on the amount of business lost that can be attributed solely to their having taken a strike over this one issue.

All of the above adds up to a conclusion in answer to our first question that there has been no successfully demonstrable way for a company to determine, on a purely financial basis, as to whether to settle on the union's terms or take a strike.

Let us examine another question. How far can management afford to make concessions for the sake of what it hopes will be improved morale or because of fear that failure to make concessions will adversely affect productivity in the shop? This question starts from a doubtful assumption in the first place. We have no general assurance that making concessions to union demands affects morale favorably or adversely. We have no *statistically demonstrable* broad assurance that even employee morale affects individual productivity one way or another, although isolated studies have indicated such a possibility. On the other hand, American industry has *assumed* that increased morale has a favorable effect on individual productivity, and research experiments such as those conducted by Rexford Hersey at the Pennsylvania Railroad and by the instigators of the well-known Western Electric Hawthorne experiments would indicate that there is a definite relation between productivity and certain aspects of morale but that the relationship will vary widely depending upon the individuals affected. However, for our purposes I am willing to assume with the great majority of American businessmen that good morale is good business, and that good business starts with improved individual productivity. It is not so easy for me to agree that making concessions to union demands affects morale one way or the other. One would first have to determine how basic, prevalent and wide-spread the desire for consummation of the demands may be among the workers affected as against the possibility that at least some of the demands may have been cooked up by union leaders at a national or international level for pur-poses not directly related to satisfaction of the needs of their members. All practical contract negotiators know that the union demands do not always represent either rank and file wishes or union expectation that the demands will be met. Management decision with respect to conceding to union demands is based more on its judgment as to what the union will settle for and how basic the demand itself may be to the rank and file. The increasingly prevalent prac-tice of "organizing from the top" even indicates that employees are having less to say about organizing, let alone negotiating. The use of a man's dues money to support a political party or candidate not of his choice is not going to add to his morale, particularly if he has to pay dues to get or hold a job.

Moreover, a large number of union demands are not direct cost items. Cer-tainly wages, the so-called "fringe benefits" and certain other matters are. If we confine our reply to the "direct" cost factors, we can see, of course, that management must take into account the manner in which an increase in basic hourly wage or the cost of a new pension program will affect its products' cost and, through cost, affect its sales price, and study the effect of an appropriate increase in price, if any, on its sales volume. In these days of high break even points, maintenance of close to 100% capacity is essential to the continuity of the business. This is one area, then, in which management is very dollar conscious. It is perhaps the single point at which, in deciding whether to take a strike, a management looks at the hard, cold dollars and cents. It is the one decision made on what the hard-boiled operating executive calls a practical basis. This is not to say, however, that the decision is always a rational one. Again, principles and emotions enter into the decision. The company may have principles against increasing the price to meet the increased cost. It may have principles with respect to the proportions of profit to be distributed among employees as against stockholders. Certainly the management has varying kinds of emotions about what constitutes adequate wage and benefit levels. So again we arrive at the conclusion that, although direct cost wage and benefit increases are measurable with a high degree of accuracy, we cannot conclude that the decision to take a strike or not to take a strike is based solely on cost considerations.

While we are on the subject of union relations as against the subject of employee relations, it might be well to examine two additional related questions which have been suggested. The first is: What are the principal costs in the union-management relationship which management regards as unwarranted, and is there any way by which these may be reduced? The second is: How does dealing with the union affect management's effort to reduce the labor-cost element of total costs? These two suggested questions can obviously be answered best as one question, starting with the emphasis on the implications of the second.

It should be obvious to begin with that union negotiations involve a very direct series of costs. The series starts with the time of the managers who must necessarily be involved in such negotiations—time which, in the minds of many managers at least, could be more profitably spent on other phases of their jobs. If the time of operating executives is not to be used, then, of course, there arises the cost of paying a specialist in the field of labor negotiations, whether he be a member of the corporate family or an outside consultant engaged on an ad hoc basis. The next element of cost is the cost of the time of the employees themselves expended in taking part in negotiations. In some cases the union may bear all or part of the cost of this time; in other cases, companies contribute negotiation time of workers who are on the negotiation committees. These more or less incidental costs are, however, unimportant. The main point is that, when a management is required to deal with a union, certain limitations are placed on the freedom of management to manage. At this point we raise no question as to the desirability or undesirability of collective bargaining. We merely point out that in a situation in which management is free to do as it pleases in the employee relations field, subject only perhaps to the dictates of good conscience, it makes decisions and takes actions aimed at keeping costs low. Many such decisions and actions are definitely limited by the union agreement. Perhaps the drive on the part of employees and their unions to remove from the unilateral rights of management certain aspects of the employment situation can be justified both from the ethical as well as the economic point of view. Examining the economics of the situation, it can be said that many of the limitations on management which have been created by collective bargaining agreements are things which most good managements would attempt to do anyway. In other words, so-called sound human relations have been reduced to a written formula in the labor agreement, in some cases. In other cases, however, union agreements have so impinged upon the freedom of management to manage that there can be serious question as to the propriety of this kind of contract clause.

This leads us into the other suggested question in connection with the principal costs which management considers unwarranted in the union-management relationship. In the first place, management is usually saddled with the cost of collecting union dues through checkoff agreements. Certain records are required by the contract to be kept and given to the union which would not ordinarily be maintained for management use. From this very simple and elementary type of added cost we move into the more complex situation of seniority clauses, contracting out work, introduction of new methods and machinery, enforcement of discipline and other much more cost raising aspects of the union agreement. The more complex the contractual provisions in these respects, the more difficult it is to assign a direct cost to them. For example, how can you put a definite dollar value or cost to the company on a strict seniority clause as applied to promotions or lay-offs or recall? Even assuming that some reasonably accurate estimate of the cost of such possible application might be made, is there any offset against the cost resulting from having better satisfied employees on the job? It is possible that we might accumulate the possible cost of past actions in which unqualified employees have been assigned to a certain job because of seniority provisions, but it is extremely difficult either to project these data accurately into the future or to judge what promotions, for example, might have been given to the senior employee in any case if the seniority provisions had not existed. Similarly, we could with all justice ask what losses in production might have taken place because employees were dissatisfied with the manner in which foremen or supervisors assigned promotions under a system that was not regulated by some seniority agreement.

We could explore in much more detail the various sources of added cost which result from collective bargaining process and perhaps enumerate many other such sources. This, however, is not a dissertation on maintaining management's ability to manage and we need only point out that, when management in any way cedes to employees or their representatives those phases of management authority which are essential to coordination, management incurs the probability of increased labor costs. In all fairness, however, it must be admitted that there would appear to be some justification for the argument of some people that these additional costs are counterbalanced by increased productivity resulting from the belief or feeling of employees that they have something to say about the conditions of work which directly affect them.

Examination of the potential labor-cost effects of the collective bargaining aspects of personnel administration leads us into the much more rarefied atmosphere of the potential cost of the other aspects of personnel administration. Two questions also quite closely related suggest themselves at this point: namely, (1) How far can management go in undertaking a "human relations" program in the hope of unleashing worker motivations that will compensate for any costs which such a program may entail? (2) How can one measure the return against the cost in the operation of a personnel program? We could greatly shorten this whole discussion if we were to say in answer to the first question that there is no measurable or objective way that we can define a limit to how far management can go, and second, one cannot measure the return against the cost in the operation of the personnel program. In the first place, any so-called personnel program is merely the development and maintenance of the tools used by management in directing the work of other members of what should be a well-coordinated, cooperative production team. American industry seems to be satisfied in general that sound personnel administration pays off. On the other hand, I know of no more frustrated group of people in American management than the personnel men themselves. They are frustrated because they are continually being charged with being just another expensive overhead department and don't seem to be able to do anything about justifying their own maintenance and upkeep from a dollars and cents viewpoint. They are frustrated because the tools that they develop and maintain must primarily be used by others. Therefore, any credit that may accrue to the specialized personnel staff unit is almost entirely indirect. If the tools are not used or not used well, then the money spent in their development and maintenance has been wasted. If the tools are used adequately, then the credit for their use goes to the line people who use them. All of this is quite proper but it is fairly common practice to find that, when things are not going so well on a company-wide basis, one of the first—if not the very first—organization units that is made the target of retrenchment activities is the personnel unit. We believe this to be so because, of all of the facilitative (commonly called "staff") activities, the personnel department can tie itself least closely to demonstrable dollar results. Industrial engineering has its methods and incentive savings. Even the accounting department can point to savings which have been made by the line as a result of control data which have called the opportunity for such savings at least to the attention of the line. The law department can point to cases won and money saved thereby. The treasurer's department can point to money secured for the operation of the business, savings made in corporate financing, etc.

All of this leads us into what some of you may regard as a digression, but it is necessary that we should set some criteria, as subjective as they may be and as far removed from dollar values as they will be, in order to determine how far management can go in its human relations programs and to what extent one can measure the return from such programs against the cost.

I have enumerated for other purposes some twenty-five essential requirements of a personnel program which, if adequately fulfilled in total, make for the achievement of the optimum in sound personnel administration. The first two of these requirements are the essential and irreplaceable elements.

1. The first essential element requires that there be in writing and widely disseminated, inside and outside of the company, a statement of the fundamental philosophy of the enterprise with respect to the people who are the organization. A philosophy is defined in the unabridged dictionary as follows: "an integrated and consistent personal attitude toward life or reality, or toward certain phases of it, especially if this attitude is expressed in beliefs or principles of conduct." For our purposes, this might be paraphrased as follows: "A philosophy of personnel administration is an integrated and consistent corporate attitude toward the people who go to make up a business organization, especially if this attitude is expressed in firm beliefs and principles of conduct governing employer-employee relationships." I realize that not many firms have such a statement of fundamental philosophy, but I submit that without it there can be no fully effective and consistent management drive toward achievement of sound personnel administration.

2. The second element is just as essential and irreplaceable as the first. It requires that the chief executive truly believe in and, by precept and example, support and insist upon the application of this philosophy at all levels of the organization. This means that the chief executive must be the leader of those who report directly to him and that his leadership be evidenced by his own actions. It also means that he be continually alert to the probability that the philosophy will not be applied all the way down the line unless he delegates to someone the responsibility and authority for getting the facts necessary for reporting on consistent and continuing application at all organization levels.

(We should not depreciate by brevity the significance and importance of the other twenty-three elements, but we do have time limits which require that we merely list these elements in order to get on to an answer to the question posed by the title of this speech.)

3. There should be a *plan* for dividing into functions and positions the overall job of the enterprise.

4. The duties and responsibilities of each of these positions should be defined in writing, and the definitions should be kept up-to-date as changing circumstances require changes in the organization structure.

5. The inter-relationships of the positions so defined should be set forth in such a way that they can be understood and practically worked out among incumbents of the positions at all levels of the organization.

6. The human requirements for success in the various positions should be determined.

7. Recruitment and selection of people to fill the positions so defined should be carried on in such a way as to result in the hiring of the people most highly qualified to meet the job requirements.

8. When we have found the best qualified people we must gain their cogent acceptance of the defined positions and the terms of employment involved.

9. Every individual in the organization must understand and accept both the scope of his responsibilities and the criteria which will be used by his superiors in appraising the quality of his performance.

10. Every employee must be familiar with the corporate policies within the limits of which he must discharge his duties and responsibilities.

11. Every member of the productive team must be given the necessary mechanical and material as well as the developmental aids required for improvement of his performance.

12. The individual employee should have his performance appraised periodically and he should be informed of the specific and detailed results of such appraisals.

13. There should be adequate provision for reward for satisfactory or better performance and encouragement toward improvement.

14. Definite provisions must be made for transfers and retraining when these actions may be necessary to make the fullest use of an individual's capacity.

15. Perhaps unfortunately, it is also extremely necessary to make sure that there is provision for prompt replacement of the incompetent.

16. Each individual must be equitably compensated for his efforts, with the understanding that equity involves maintenance of favorable internal and external comparisons in job rates as well as provision for financial recognition of differences in individual performance.

17. Full provision must be made for maintaining a safe and healthful working environment and for encouraging and aiding employees in maintaining an optimum level of both mental and physical health.

18. The employee must be aided in protecting himself against the economic insecurities arising from the risks of modern industrial life.

19. Every individual must be adequately protected against the possible results of arbitrary, dictatorial, capricious, or even whimsical actions of his superiors.

20. Provisions must be made for encouraging and aiding employees in getting social satisfactions from the associations arising out of their employment.

21. Every man's assignment must afford opportunity for the development and eventual utilization of his maximum capacities.

22. Every possible opportunity must be grasped for appropriately and adequately recognizing individual accomplishment and growth by non-financial as well as financial means.

23. All members of the organization must be afforded sufficient opportunity to be informed of or to inform themselves concerning the formation of the organization's plans and decisions which affect their jobs and their welfare. In this connection it is well to recognize that participation is the outstanding road to understanding and acceptance of such plans and decisions. It is also essential that there be sufficient opportunity for the individual to get his thoughts to his superiors, particularly when there is some real or imagined grievance in the mind of any employee at any level.

24. When employees are represented by a union, there must be established a feeling of mutual respect and confidence between union officers and members of the management group as a firm basis for meeting the best interests of all

parties to this relationship, while, at the same time, there must be no weakening or surrender of management's authority to manage or consideration of the basic rights and needs of the individual.

25. The entire process represented by the preceding list of requirements must be under constant examination by all members of the management group so that it is at all times dynamic and kept in phase with changing economic and social conditions.

We should restate for purposes of emphasis that the responsibility for the maintenance of such a program begins with and lies with top management. Naturally, other executives in the line of command must participate at their appropriate levels in the determination of policies and assure maintenance of appropriate relationships among their management subordinates.

If we examine these criteria, it is evident that they could be all summed up into the statement that personnel administration aims at the conservation of the human resources of a business enterprise. This conservation is not undertaken because managements in general believe that conservation of human resources is the nice thing to do. They do it because long years of experience in the profitable operation of a business enterprise have indicated that waste of human resources is unprofitable. To put it another way, very nearly every experienced manager is agreed that the employee who finds that he can satisfy his economic, social and spiritual needs through his work is the more productive employee.

Defining the over-all objective of personnel administration as conservation of human resources brings us closer to an answer to our problem. If we label what happens in the absence of sound personnel administration as *waste* of human resources we may start toward some top level acceptance of the function.

Undoubtedly we do need some way to hang a price tag on good personnel administration. Undoubtedly people in personnel administration, as well as in top management, have spent too much time reviewing the elements which make dollars and cents value determination "impossible" as against spending the same amount of time on "accentuating the positive." Many companies do estimate how much it costs to replace a production or maintenance worker. Some very few have gone even further to hang a similar price tag on the replaced management man. It seems to me that such studies point in the right direction because they put the emphasis on saving as against wasting. Of course, the chief need is to go much further. What is the total per hour cost of *keeping* a man on the payroll? What should we reasonably expect in the way of production for the expenditure? What are our current variances from a standard unit cost so established? Plus variances are wastes of human resources; minus variances are savings.

If we assume that by long term use of such data we can validate our standards satisfactorily (and this would probably be on a group rather than individual basis) we would then get into real "blue sky" research. I submit that if we took each of our twenty-five points and, through clinically controlled experiments, determined the cost effects of both meeting or not meeting the optimum of each point we should ultimately arrive at at least some reasonable value for each alleged requirement of good personnel administration. Then and only then would we be able to tell "how far a management can economically go" in setting up a personnel program.

It is obvious that such a research job would in itself be tremendously expensive—perhaps well beyond the reach of any one company. But each step taken toward the goal would move certain aspects of human relations management from the emotional to the rational side of determining values. It is certainly one field in which the new science of "operations research," aided and abetted by the new computers, could be put to profitable use.

Human resources will, according to our best thinkers, be in shorter and shorter supply over the next decade or two at least. Business and industry has a tremendous responsibility for conserving these resources. We cannot discharge this responsibility unless we know where the greatest wastes occur and start to eliminate them. We can't find these opportunity spots by the emotional approach or even by past experience based on quite different situations. It seems incredible that a country that is famed for its achievements in "scientific management" should find itself balked at this kind of a problem.

ONE COMPANY'S PERSONNEL POLICY

Few company programs in personnel and industrial relations have captured so much attention as has that of General Electric in the years following World War II. Popularly dubbed "Boulwareism," after Lemuel R. Boulware, formerly G. E. Vice President of Public and Employee Relations, it has been imitated by some managements, regarded dubiously by others, and criticized vigorously by unions. Below, General Electric explains the genesis and content of this program.

General Electric Employee Relations News Letter, December 31, 1954

YEAR-END REVIEW: WHERE WE WERE, WHERE WE ARE, WHERE WE ARE TRYING
TO GO IN EMPLOYEE, PLANT COMMUNITY, AND UNION RELATIONS

1. WHERE WE WERE

In May 1947 General Electric came reluctantly to a very important conclusion.

It had been evident for some time that, however successful we might be in other fields, we enjoyed only limited success in employee and plant community relations.

But the new and distressing conclusion was that, if we continued to follow past practices, we were likely *never* to accomplish in proper degree the good relationships which were so important to our employees and neighbors themselves as well as to our customers, vendors, shareowners, and the rest of the public.

That our course was then failing was surprising. By any available standards, our thinking had been quite advanced. We had made large expenditures on what we had thought was right and had hoped would result in job and community satisfaction.

A pioneer

Our primary product is progress. To pioneer has been our traditional determination. This has applied not only to providing the best values on the best products and services. It has applied also to making and keeping jobs right up to what's good in every proper material and human respect. Likewise, it has applied not only to our bringing important money into the communities but also to our determined efforts to be generally useful as a good citizen there.

For instance, at the time of this 1947 decision, we looked back not only on having paid wages that were right up to the top of what was feasible and proper by all the standards, but also to our having voluntarily pioneered our employee suggestion systems in 1906, our safety and health programs in 1907, pensions in 1912, savings plans in 1917, insurance in 1920, relief and loan plans in the 1930's and our ambitious experiments in work and pay guarantees—including the guaranteed annual wage—in the 1930's, and our profit sharing plans in the 1930's and 1940's.

Not only had we provided good and remarkably steady jobs, but the number of them had more than doubled in just a single decade. This doubling of jobs had been accomplished in a continuing "sellers' market" on employee services. Anyone dissatisfied with his job could get another one most anywhere he wanted it. Yet we not only kept our old employees but more than doubled their number.

A typically-held view was: "General Electric ranks high among corporations in its treatment of workers." [1]

We had had national and independent unions at various of our plants from time to time. We had always dealt with them in accordance with our employees' wishes. When the new wave of unionization came along in the 1930's and the U.E.-C.I.O. had been certified to us in a number of our plants as our employees' choice, we voluntarily entered into one of the first—if not the first—multi-plant contracts. We continued to deal with this union in good faith, as our employees apparently wished and as the United States Government kept ordering us in no uncertain terms to do—even after the suspicion had become widespread that this union was Communist dominated.

What was apparently not realized by the employee and community beneficiaries in 1947 was that our pay and benefits had increasingly made our jobs so attractive that many of the communities were already having difficulty both in persuading other employers to expand there and in persuading new ones to move in beside us. For instance, a July 24, 1954 Berkshire Evening Eagle editorial points out that General Electric is "the employer of nearly 75% of Pittsfield's wage earners" and that "trying to lure new business here . . . won't be easy."

[1] "How Collective Bargaining Works," Twentieth Century Fund, 1942.

Starting from scratch 70 years before, we had persevered until we were bringing into our communities in 1947 an overall amount of business activity that has been estimated to be the major support of 40,000 retail establishments; to maintain 1200 schools with 21,600 teachers; to supply opportunities for 28,800 professional men outside General Electric; to supply livelihoods to over 1,000,000 people outside our employees and their families; to support the selling and servicing of 540,000 automobiles a year; to mean $240 million revenue for the railroad traffic in and out of the communities; to create a taxable valuation of $3 billion; to give markets for $420 million of farm products, and create an annual expenditure in trade in our communities of $1,800 million.

What this meant to newspapers, churches and endless individual enterprises, groups, and institutions can be well imagined.

Over and beyond all this, our strenuous efforts to wed science with human needs and desires resulted in our taking still more drudgery out of work in homes and factories—including our own plants—as well as helping otherwise to raise the level of living by the additional products and services we were aiding more people all the time to be able to buy.

Our activity also benefited many small businesses. This resulted from our willingness to take on large assignments and then break them up into smaller assignments which could be carried out by smaller suppliers who would not be in a position to get the orders direct.

Furthermore, the benefits of the technology which we were developing were not only being spread across our growing industry, but also being diffused throughout the whole of industry here and abroad for the good of all.

And our Presidents and Board Chairmen—along with countless more of the managerial, professional and other members of the General Electric family— had always been freely available and had served with distinction in our country's emergencies in peace and war over a long period here and abroad.

But was all this understood? Had it resulted in employees and neighbors approving our accomplishments or even having a favorable attitude toward our efforts in their behalf? Had it resulted in job satisfaction or community satisfaction?

Generally, it had not. In fact, the harder we tried and the more we got done, the more misunderstanding and disapproval we seemed to experience.

The search

So, our General Electric management set out with a firm resolve, first, to begin to do *whatever was necessary* to achieve ultimately the same success in *job marketing* that we had accomplished in *product marketing*. In other words, we wanted *good* job customers and *satisfied* job customers.

In the selling of products, we learned long ago that we needed reliable market research to determine what the customer wanted, why he wanted it, when he wanted it, and how much he was willing to pay for it. We also learned that in order to accomplish a satisfactory product marketing program, it was necessary to have sound *product planning, market development*, and *merchandising*, including advertising, sales promotion, sales training, and the like.

What we were examining was the question of whether or not we could use these same *methods* and *human considerations* in genuinely *pleasing people with jobs* in practically the same way we had used them so successfully for so long in *pleasing people* with *products*.

Could we use these considerations and methods in periodically designing, accurately presenting, and delivering "new-model" *jobs* which would *deserve* to achieve—and would then *succeed* in achieving—the maximum job satisfaction available within the framework of what's feasible and fair—and recognized as such?

Could we pass on to our employees—our "job customers"—the benefits of what we had learned in many years of pleasing *product* customers through the application of humility, ingenuity and diligence to market research, to product planning, to organization and training, to personal man-to-man information transfer, to the use of mass communication to supplement the man-to-man process, and finally, to servicing the inevitable customer complaints? We decided to try.

So we went out to ask our employees what they wanted in their jobs, and in what ways they felt their present jobs fell short of that. We tried to diagnose what they liked and disliked about their jobs; what they understood, misunderstood, or just didn't know about their jobs. We inquired into what they did and did not understand about the economic, social and political influences which surround their jobs with opportunities, obligations and limitations.

We looked for the motives and beliefs which determined whether or not they came to work promptly, regularly, and in an agreeable mood; the things that determined whether or not they gave their full interest, skill, care, and effort while working; and the events and impressions that determined whether or not they went home reasonably satisfied with their accomplishments and associations at the end of the day.

The nine-point job

This search for the facts resulted in the clear indication that General Electric employees wanted a packaged job that contained nine distinct ingredients. They wanted:
1. Good pay and other material benefits
2. Good working conditions
3. Good bosses
4. A fair chance to get ahead
5. Steady work
6. Respectful treatment
7. Full information
8. Important and significant work
9. Rewarding association on the job.

There was obviously nothing here but what we had *intended* to provide all along. We would simply redouble our efforts to supply such a job package and have it more intimately in step with the expressed wishes of employees. Our employees, in turn, had indicated that they were perfectly willing to pay the proper price for such a job package in interest, skill, care and effort—provided they could be confident they knew what the proper price was and that the deal was fair all around.

Balanced best interests

Our efforts to this end had, of necessity, to be geared to the Company's overall objective. That objective is to do our utmost, in every word and deed, to operate in the *balanced* best interests of all the contributors to and corresponding claimants on our output of goods and services.

These contributor-claimants are, of course, not only our employees but also— and just as importantly—our customers, owners, vendors, and neighbors or public along with the government.

Each contributor-claimant must be dealt with realistically and fairly. Each must do his part and get his proper return for what he does. Each must *know* he is being thus fairly treated.

If any one or more of them is not—or *thinks* he is not—being dealt with fairly in either the financial or non-financial areas, he will not do his part, and he and all the others suffer.

If there is any attempt to favor any *one* at the expense of one or more of the others, the attempt is bound to backfire shortly with damage to the interests of the one so favored as well as to the rest of the contributor-claimants.

Thus, the overall *material results* of employee and other contributions have to go on the market, and be rewarded financially with fair shares of what the free customer regards as the material and emotional *money value* of what we do for him.

Two more requirements

But our market research into employee and public activities had revealed that there were two more things to be done:

1. *Deserving and Getting Confidence.* The bitter 1946 strike called by U.E.-C.I.O. had indicated clearly that not only a majority of our employees, but also of the press, merchants, clergy, teachers, politicians and seemingly the community citizens in general, misunderstood both our performance and our intentions. A long, tough job lay ahead in overcoming this. Regardless of how good and attractive our jobs were already in the financial and other basic aspects, we had many problems. We had to develop a more adequate understanding of our past good performance in order to get the recognition and credit we already deserved. We had to review our current performance to see how we could *improve* it. We had to deserve and gain the understanding and approval of our employees and community neighbors.

We initiated the nine-point job program explained above, and immediately began trying to make it become a reality for all concerned. Our research indicated that many foremen, as well as many others throughout management, just couldn't *believe* at first that the nine-point job was going to be given them by *their* bosses. Some regarded it as just another case where we were not going to be *practicing* with our own management people what we were *preaching* for employees further down the line. So we redoubled our efforts at the top.

Meanwhile we expended every effort to earn and get general employee approval of our good *intentions* and steadily improving *performance* in making General Electric jobs the best available in both material and human ways. This effort included constant emphasis on the need for all operating managers to give full, earnest, personal attention to problems in the area of employee and plant community relations, as well as to their problems in the traditional areas of marketing, engineering, manufacturing, and finance.

2. *Lessening Unwarranted Trust.* The second problem we faced was the regrettable and *distasteful*, but *vitally necessary* task of doing our part to correct any unwarranted confidence in any unsound proposals by union officials.

Skillful propaganda by certain union officials and other of our critics had filled the communication void created by the traditional reluctance of ourselves and other businessmen to speak up about our good intentions and performance.

This had prevented too many people from recognizing the growing gap between the thoroughly good theory and potentiality of unions and the too-frequently bad ideas, practices and proposals of certain individual union officials.

Regardless of how untrue it was, every improvement in employee welfare was getting to be regarded as something which we had greedily and viciously resisted, and which had had to be *forced* out of us *unwillingly*.

And certain of these union officials were too often regarded as friends of the worker and public even when sponsoring ideas and action quite contrary to the best interests of employees and public.

There was obviously wide and dangerous misinformation to combat in the balanced best interests of all.

Who had been at fault in letting this misinformation go unchallenged and grow to such proportions? The main fault was clearly ours. It seemed incredible that our intelligent employees would look right at our superior jobs and see them as bad instead of good. But even intelligent people have to have access to the facts, so we reluctantly entered upon what positive informing—and what debunking and disillusioning—was necessary to have the true facts stand out more clearly in the future.

The program

We resolved that our revised or broadened course of action would have our jobs measure up in every fair and feasible way not only to the material needs and desires of our employees but also to all worthy hopes and aspirations of themselves, their families and neighbors in all the human or spiritual areas over and beyond the purely financial.

We were not only going to *do right voluntarily*—we were going to have it *known* that we were.

At the same time, we realized this was no one-way street. We could not do the job alone. To supply good jobs, we would have to have the enlightened cooperation of well-informed and diligent employees and neighbors in helping us get and keep the business that brought the money and progress into the pay envelopes and the community.

As a result, we resolved to help our employees achieve the kind of jobs they said they wanted by exhausting the possibilities in these four principal areas of thought and effort:

1. *Good Pay for Good Work.* We in management wanted to do right and also knew we certainly must do right—competently and voluntarily—about pay, benefits, physical working conditions and other material aspects of jobs.

And we had to be sure our employees and neighbors *realized* we were doing our best to do right voluntarily in the balanced best interest of employees as well as all others concerned and that we did not have to be dragged *unwillingly* to do what we had learned we should from whatever sources.

We were just as anxious as anyone could be to see that each claimant got his fair share in accordance with the market value of his contribution from his own resources. In fact, we believed then as now that the good of *all*, and therefore even the jobs of *employees* themselves, depends on *each* contributor and claimant getting neither more nor less than his fair share.

But we had been drifting along with the developing fashion of the times. We had been falling into the habit of making our bargaining offers on the low side, with the full expectation that we would be "traded up" step by step to the final settlement—often to the accompaniment of much union bally-hoo while we remained silent.

For instance, if everything pointed to a 5¢ increase being about right, there was a great tendency among employers in those days to offer nothing at first. Then, under later strike-threat pressure, about half would be offered. Then, after all the union representatives had been called in from the plants and the resulting vote for a strike had been well aired in the press—management would "capitulate" by upping the offer to the full 5¢ per hour.

This was, of course, exactly what the union officials required for a conspicuous "triumph over greedy and vicious management." It could not have been carried off any more effectively if the whole thing had been rehearsed beforehand.

While all this may have been amusing amateur theatricals to the bystander who thought he was not concerned, any tendency on our part to go along further with the fashion would have seriously misled our employees and neighbors. We could not be silent about our good intentions and good deeds— nor about false charges against us. Once we began to realize the extent of the false impression the currently fashionable behavior would create, simple honesty compelled us to avoid henceforth acting out any part that might help certain union officials *look* useful in ways they were not. Otherwise, we would have been helping them fool our employees about themselves *and about us.*

We felt then and now that a union representing our employees should have every bit of credit for every good thing it does. But we believe it should certainly have a sounder and nobler function to perform than fooling its members about a particular task that is made to appear difficult but may be easy or even non-existent.

In addition, we had begun to realize we were employing here with our job customers something other than that high "single-standard" of research, preparation, value, full information and courageous public forthrightness which had been so rewarding in our relations with our product customers.

We had also begun to see that the old course was dangerous for all concerned from a *financial* as well as a relations standpoint. If, because of some difference in bargaining skills or other factors, the settlement mentioned above had been 3¢ instead of the 5¢ management privately recognized as right, it would have been unfair not only for employees *but for all concerned.* If it had been 7¢ it would still have been bad for all concerned in the end—*including the employees who got the 7¢.*

To serve the interests of employees and all others, there was nothing to do but try to arrive at what was right for all. No one should even consider *trying* to get the better of the other in such an important matter of honor affecting close associates. And we certainly were not going to go to the bargaining table and let it wrongly *appear* that we were there trying to settle for anything we could get away with. Fortunately, there was already a whole lot less actual difference between the parties than the initial demands and offers would indicate. Nevertheless, there was lots to do.

We resolved we would henceforth carry on much more intensive and continuing research in all matters affecting our employees—including those about which we bargained with our unions.

We resolved to prepare for coming negotiations by the steady accumulation of all facts available on matters likely to be discussed.

We would then add to, discard or revise these facts on the basis of any additional or different facts we learned from union or other sources *during* negotiations as well as before.

Then at the appropriate time, and when seemingly all the available significant facts were in and had been fully discussed, we would offer what the facts from all sources seemed to indicate was fully up to all that was right in the balanced best interest of all. This was to be the full truth as we saw it—with nothing held back for future jockeying.

We would stand ready and willing to alter what we had offered immediately upon our getting new or old additional facts—from union or any other source—which would indicate changes that were in the interest of all.

Incidentally, we reached agreement in a day or two without any change in one of our early national offers several years ago. But that was the first and only time, and we recall now no subsequent negotiation where such an initial offer has not been revised in some major or minor ways.

Upon questioning, we have freely admitted we do not regard the threat or the actuality of a strike as being the kind of fact that ought to change what we honestly think is right. But that opinion on our part obviously changes in no way the full right and opportunity of any union to employ the strike weapon.

We decided at the same time that we should and would publicize our offers when made. We would keep our employees and neighbors advised of the course of negotiations—including any changes in our offers in response to union representations or by reason of any other developments.

While we were spending most of our thought and action on what *we* were going to do to try to live up to doing *our* part, we had clearly in mind this was still not going to work as a one-way matter and that our individual employee had to do *his* part. We had to try to help him understand—and we hoped other economic and moral teachers would help—that he must, in his own interests, do right voluntarily about applying honestly his skill, care, and effort to giving value received through doing a full day's work by reasonable modern standards.

Here was a vast job of study and communication to enable us all to try together to develop a commonly accepted set of facts and opinions. This was needed to aid management and employees in *being* right as well as in *knowing* how and why they each were sound and right in their conclusions and actions in these material matters involving their association with each other.

But to be able to get together in any sort of agreement as to the facts in just this financial or material area alone—as well as being able to go on to substantial accomplishments in the all important non-material or human areas of job satisfaction—both management and employees had to apply themselves conscientiously to these other three remaining areas described below.

2. *Good Human Interest—Both Ways.* We wanted to do right voluntarily and sincerely in the area of human association. We wanted to be sure—no matter what might be any failings of the moment—that our *intentions* were good, our performance was improving, and our efforts were being recognized for what they were.

Our employee did not live by bread alone.

He wanted—and we wanted to give him—a boss who was on his side, who put the human consideration first, who respected and protected employee dignity, who engaged in genuine and forthright two-way, man-to-man communication on the things that counted to the employee's way of thinking.

He wanted—and we wanted to give him—a boss who provided him a sense of importance, significance, and genuine participation, and who had a real head and heart interest in the employee both as a person and as a welcome and appreciated associate in the rewarding activity they were carrying on together.

We knew the fellow we formerly called "boss" had to become recognized as a teacher and leader. The supervisor now had to depend entirely—as he should —on getting things done right by getting employees to *know* what was the right way and to *want* to do them that way.

We realized that any group of trainees in foremanship, in office management, or in engineering management, who would not be almost as acceptable for training as *sales-engineers for the product* of that plant, did not belong in the supervisory training group as future suppliers of genuine *job satisfaction*.

Our *employee*, in turn, would need to be especially firm in his determination *to do right himself*—and to *want* to do so—in this human relationship. As a simple matter of economics and morals, *he* would obviously have to do *his* part to make it a rewarding two-way street.

But we realized such two-way human relations could not be accomplished by any superficial or spurious back-slapping or baby kissing, or by any sheer force of personality. It had to be based on a sound, deep, and deserved impression that *both* parties *intended* to do right and were not just trying to "get away" with what *looked* like it was right. It had to be based on both parties doing their best to *be* right through following the proper ideas and measures to find out *what* was right.

This search by both for the facts would almost surely result in a rather common set of ideas or values or measures about what's right in the material and non-material areas of motivation and association. And then the actions of both, and even the silences of both, would have to speak as loudly and as favorably as any words in proving they were able and committed to do right.

Here again was a vast job of two-way communication—man-to-man communication, mass communication, formal and informal surveys, and other such aids—to get the facts, to resolve misunderstandings, to pursue programs, and otherwise to implement and measure the progress we all were seeking in the human and moral and emotional forces and satisfactions.

3. *Good Understanding of Jobs and of the Economic Relationships among Interdependent Specialists.* To accomplish anything like what has already been indicated as our goals, we believed it was imperative that we in top management ourselves learn to understand—and then teach—where jobs come from, how free people act in a free market, how we all work for each other as interdependent specialists, and how in general our business and economic system operates.

We felt we had to learn and teach the facts about money; about taxes; about private enterprise as differentiated from collectivist systems; about the value of incentives, savings, technology, risk, competition, profit and loss and other rewards varying with performance; about war booms and readjustments.

We felt we must show employees and public what money comes into the business and how much of it goes to outside suppliers, to taxes, to employees, to reinvestment in growth and strength, and to shareowners in dividends.

Some union officials were loudly and scornfully claiming they knew more about our businesses and our economic system than management did. And too many people believed them—with what justice we will leave to you.

But, in any event, the most startling change seemingly needed to be made by us businessmen in our personal equipment—and of use not only in employee relations but in other fields—was in our understanding of economics and in our ability to make ourselves understood and convincing in this area.

We felt this acquisition would give us the courage—of which we had too little in the past—to speak up boldly and confidently with the truth to employees and neighbors—no matter how unpalatable it might be at first to those in whose interests we were working and whom we wanted to respect and like us in the end—and no matter who had to be contradicted among those of good or evil power.

Happily, there was already ample encouragement to the hope that our employees and other fellow citizens wanted to depend on, and be on the side of, the stout and honest leader who told the truth as he saw it.

They were already getting properly suspicious of the executive who—despite his known convictions—always said what he thought his listeners wanted to hear, and who showed outward approval for people and ideas he was known to condemn rather violently in the privacy and safety of his panelled office.

Business executives are supposed to be leaders, and never in history has there been an instance of people having confidence in a *frightened* leader.

We hoped to find the individual employee increasingly desirous of learning the economics, morals and politics of his particular role as a contributor, claimant and citizen—as compared with the roles of his interdependent fellow producers, claimants and citizens in and out of our business.

We were sure that our employee could not possibly know whether we as his employer were being fair with him—and not exploiting him—unless he appreciated that there were two kinds of work done in a business—one kind by minds and muscles, and the other by people's savings—and that *both* kinds of work had to be paid for at the market price or they would not get done and there would soon be no jobs.

Obviously this two-way economic education process of both management and employees was to be a two-way *communication* job of the first order.

4. Good Outside Understanding and Relationships. We had come to suspect that good pay for good work, good human relationships and good economic, moral and political teachings *inside* our business would not likely *of themselves* produce harmonious over-all employee-employer relationships.

The outside influences were too many and too strong.

We were afraid it was going to prove practically impossible to have good employee relations by dealing with our employees alone and without going out among our neighbors to get good community understanding and approval of us and our activities.

We suspected we would have to take every available means to deserve and get a firm belief by the community that we were trying to be a good employer, a good purchaser of local goods and services, a good taxpayer with no bargains asked, a good contributor to charities and not a drain on them, and a good business and personal citizen and neighbor.

But, we also understood already, of course, that no one employer and his employees could alone make a given community an understanding and properly rewarding place in which to operate, work and live. It was the job of *all* businessmen, *all* leaders and *all* citizens there—including *all* employees.

We knew that we and other businessmen would have to work hard at developing and promoting proper standards of good employee compensation, understanding, and relationships in our various individual local businesses—and then try to have the public know and approve what was being done generally by local business for the overall economic and social good of the community.

Then we felt all businessmen would need to join with all other leading or interested citizens in promoting economic education, moral re-awakening and political sophistication among all the local public and among all others elsewhere who have been the sources of the unfavorable influences that came into the community.

We suspected we would find need to learn and help teach all concerned the impact of local, state, national and union politics on the day to day operations of our individual jobs and our individual businesses locally.

We felt we would certainly need to become skilled at recognizing particular types of demagogues and merciless in boldly exposing them to our employees and neighbors when job-related interests were at stake.

We felt we otherwise were going to have to try to do whatever was our proper part to help employees and public be adequately informed as to what was right or wrong politically from the standpoint of *their own best interests*.

Through our constant vigilance to be sure that our actions were genuinely in the balanced best interests of all concerned, we had hoped to *deserve* having politicians consider it "good politics" to be *for* what business is for.

We realized our employee, in turn, had to be aided by us in management to understand why he had a particular selfish duty to his job and himself, both as an employee and as a citizen, to try to help in correcting any misinformation anybody spread about his employer. He had then to go beyond to help promote sound understanding of his employer's business, of business in general, and of the whole economic system of incentives and competition within which business operated to provide jobs and our unbelievably high level of living.

Here again was a real job for communication, and maybe the one most of us would be reluctant to embrace, for it was in a highly controversial area to which businessmen were unaccustomed. But the need here was vital to the survival of free business and free persons, and we resolved to *try* to do our part.

Early obstacles

The most immediate, serious and surprising obstacle—and yet the most logical one—showed up widely among us in management soon after the redoubling of our efforts in 1947.

As already indicated, some managers at each successive level, including many foremen, found it simply too much to believe that they were really going to get from their immediate bosses the 9-point job they were being urged to try to work out for those under their supervision.

This incredulity did not begin to disappear until the distortions from wartime salary freezes began to be smoothed out, and even then until the President began to hold the now regular individual two-way sessions with Vice Presidents on *their* jobs—with always the firm plea to the latter to go then and do likewise with *their* associates next in line.

Even then the overload from shortages, substitutions and stop-and-start change-overs between military and civilian production kept managers in general simply handcuffed with mechanical problems that prevented the new and broader and deeper attention everybody wanted to give to the human considerations and to a more understanding and rewarding association together.

And then there was the old problem of habit as to both the organization of the manager's time and the manner in which he dealt with his employees. Many managers wanted to "be themselves," believed *their* employees understood thoroughly their intentions and accomplishments in the employees' behalf, and naturally felt a little diffident about any sudden, obvious change in the degree of time and interest spent in exploring further the possibilities in old and new areas of rewarding job-satisfaction activity.

When it came to our non-supervisory employees, however, the situation proved surprising and encouraging in many important respects. This was all the more so because our employees had not yet, of course, been anything like persuaded that they were all going to get, any time soon, all the good results which we were now obviously aware they wanted and which we claimed we wanted to supply to the degree possible and feasible.

Our employees very early seemed quite unreserved in their open approval of our willingness to discuss a great many subjects we had never discussed before. They seemed encouraged by our even professing to take an interest in a lot of things they had not been too sure we realized were important to them.

They seemed obviously ready to believe a calm statement of fact over the Company's or an officer's signature. They appeared open-minded on any calm and thoughtful statement from us on any controversial subject of mutual interest.

The initial surprise and gratification from this was in no way lessened, when we learned that a great many of our employees and neighbors understood that— whether or not we *wanted* to tell the truth (and we certainly did)—we *had* to tell the truth and *had* to be very circumspect as to the soundness and fairness of our opinions in controversial matters.

The reasons for this were reported to be their conviction, happily correct, that all material of this kind, before publication, had to be checked by accountants, lawyers and other top management representatives, since any big employer and his reputation and bank account were a "sitting duck" for certain enemies or critics in government, union or other sources who would be delighted to pounce on and magnify the very first small slip.

Over and above all this, we discovered what we should have known all along—which is that our employees had a very natural and quite unsatisfied desire and *need* for prompt and adequate information that might affect their interests, their worries or their hopes about their jobs or their personal plans in either material or other ways. Incidentally, it was very evident that this sort of information would help our employees *help us* in all sorts of areas of mutual interest.

Meanwhile, it was also evident that some of even this early information was already resulting in some disillusionment about some of the claims and actions of certain of their union officials. This is normally a very unpopular process. Nevertheless, in this case, here and there were instances of people taking a somewhat altered view of the situation—with the result that we were not regarded with quite the same unfavorable misunderstanding as before. And it was beginning to be recognized and understood that there was a wide and important difference between the good theory and potentiality of unions as distinguished from some of the individual ideas, motives and practices of certain union officials.

In any event, we were on the way with our program to make whatever initial investment was necessary in trying to employ belatedly in employee and community affairs that same *single standard* of gumption, honor, diligence and courageous forthrightness which had been so rewarding in the product field.

Incidentally, we were sometimes little short of startled at the ready response of good people to even a beginning realization of the good aims and efforts—and results—of our management in their behalf.

This was no unorthodox program. There was nothing new or experimental—as everything we were starting to do had been blessed by years of practical experience in the product area where we had been successful in doing what people said they wanted us to do for them and in having those people understand and thus favorably regard what we were getting done for them as well as what more we were *trying* to do.

There was no guarantee we would succeed along this path, of course. But it was the only path we felt we could be the least justified in *trying*.

2. WHERE WE ARE

In pausing now to take stock of where we are, it's hard to realize that seven and a half years have slipped away since we undertook to go ahead with finding out how much more or different we and others had to do to exhaust the possibilities of providing the job-understanding and job-satisfaction our employees were seeking.

There were many material or mechanical difficulties to overcome. The plants were still unraveling the disarray in product lines and machinery caused by World War II when the fresh distortions of Korea mixed up the equipment, material distribution, market problems and employment difficulties all over again. After fifteen years of these unnatural and unpredictable influences—and with the easing of material shortages and controls—we are now trying again to accomplish some rearrangements required for a more normal or at least steadier relationship between military and civilian production. But the rapid shifts in the very nature of military and civilian goods, as well as in the ratio of the one to the other, promise to continue to complicate our problem.

One of our acute management, employee, and community problems arises from the supply of technical personnel and varied equipment which makes us so readily available for designing and producing defense products. The periodic bulges in military demand force us to do two things of particular moment in this respect. First, we have to let large portions of our civilian business get away to others. Second, we have to draw the needed extra employees from other employers and usually from a great distance. When general employment later shrinks through drop-off in military or other demand, these extra employees, including even those from a distance, do not want to go back to their old jobs or old locations. We thus frequently find ourselves with employees driving 50 or 60 miles to work for us, while local citizens of little or no service with us are unemployed.

We also hear of frequent instances of local employees, with some or no service with us, being hesitant to take other work locally because of a desire to wait for the higher pay, benefits and other attractions of jobs with us. As pointed out earlier, local newspapers are beginning to point out the difficulty of getting other old employers to expand in communities where we operate or to get new employers to move in—because of the cost of competing with the overall attractions of our jobs.

But, whatever the difficulties, we have to keep looking ahead and struggling to stay ready to take on the emergency engineering and production our government wants us to do—while continuing to stay fit and equipped to take as big a portion as possible of whatever civilian business we can merit by the attractions of the products and prices we can offer. In a country as wonderful as this, we feel anybody's obligations are just as great as their opportunities to serve, and we are glad our facilities and people make us so conspicuously available to meet emergency as well as other needs or desires. So, in war and peace we keep expanding and improving in order to try to continue able to take on as big a portion of emergency work as is required of us and, at the same time, to stay competitive and get as much as possible of the civilian demand which seems destined to grow by about an average 10% a year regardless of how fitful is that progress.

In addition to these material or mechanical obstacles, there have of course been the usual human barriers to fast progress. We are dealing with illusions, prejudices, habits of mind, and the memory of former actual or suspected indifference or neglect on our part. It takes time for misinformation to disappear, as well as for emotions to die down, even when the required facts are presented with the utmost accuracy and thoroughness and with the simplest and most temperate clarity. And we naturally were by no means so much at home in discussing these matters as we had become in the more well-developed and familiar areas of communication. Nevertheless, the developments have been very encouraging despite our understandable tendency to criticize ourselves for not making that faster progress in these directions which we are sure will be for the good of all.

Managers and employees

Our managers in every area of responsibility, including foremen, have certainly devoted themselves to trying to put more *in* jobs so our employees could get more *out* of their jobs.

Our managers have constantly before them the example of what we find is necessary to succeed in the product field.

In trying to learn how best to apply these same principles of pleasing people in the job field, most every one of us in management has come unmistakably to realize the degree to which we have been ignorant as to the various additional things our employees feel are important.

We have accordingly put major emphasis on trying to encourage and help our employees to tell us what are all the things that are important to them from *their* standpoint. Through two-way, man-to-man communication our managers have been trying to meet the need and desire of employees to be influential in getting things satisfactorily settled in the areas that count to their individual way of thinking.

We believe that our employees are finding this helpful and that they are encouraged to expect it to be still more so in the future. Certainly our managers, in turn, are getting rewarding new help in their daily problems affecting all.

The great majority of our employees seem ready to listen thoughtfully to anything important we have to say on any matter of mutual interest, no matter how controversial, and no matter whether the things we say agree with what our employees have heard from others.

They also show a growing and obviously healthy tendency to demand all the facts on both sides of any controversial matter, and then make up their own minds as to who is right or wrong in the particular instance, or what is the sensible course for them to take in their own interests. With so many special pleadings coming in from so many sources in our lives of growing complexity, it is both understandable and laudable that one of the main objectives of our employees seems to be to learn better whom to trust, and how to get facts that will keep them from being fooled.

We think we see rewarding evidence already that our employees are beginning to believe we are really trying to supply the kind of information they want. And we are still trying—by explaining our needs, telling our plans, describing our problems, reporting our decisions and the reasons for them, and analyzing any disagreement in areas where we believe our employees are concerned or interested.

We sense that our employees are gaining for themselves a good grounding in where jobs come from and how jobs can be made and kept better. They seem wisely eager to learn anything available on how we all work for each other and on the rapidly mounting complications of our free markets and free way of life.

Our employees have seemed particularly eager to learn more of how our business system in general operates and what the plans and problems are in our own local plants and offices. We feel our average employee is rapidly approaching as good an understanding of our business, and maybe of business in general, as is possessed by our average customer, shareowner, or supplier.

We believe our individual employee has already gained a quite new appreciation of his own importance and corresponding duties and services to others, as well as an appreciation of the importance to himself of the presence, duties and services of all the other individual contributors and claimants.

We think the average employee is beginning to see that management is not lined up against him or his union, but is just as interested as he or his union can possibly be in seeing the employee gets right up to the top of all that's fair. The manager must—and does—try to provide customers, suppliers, shareowners, employees and public with what is no less (and no more) than the fair share of each. That is the only way the manager can be successful today. It is the only way any honest man would try to discharge his obligations.

Quite beyond these purely material or financial considerations, we think we see some encouraging signs that employees are beginning to appreciate we are *on their side* in lots of other areas of their interest. An important and distressing consequence of our prior inadequate efforts at contact on matters of importance to employees was that employees did not believe we were on their side.

They recognized we were able, honorable, diligent and effective in the areas of our *real* interest. But too many of them had been wrongly persuaded that they were not a real interest of ours and that we were using our ability and energy to exploit them for ourselves or others elsewhere.

A broader understanding of what management's responsibilities, problems and accomplishments are in the financial or material field, and a more intimate knowledge of what management's personal intentions and efforts are in the non-financial or human areas of employee interest, appear to have started the clearing up of a lot of misinformation of the past.

A new realization seems to be dawning as to how much management strives to provide jobs that don't just have to be endured for the necessary financial returns but jobs which make it unnecessary to leave work to find dignity and pleasant human association in areas of lively interest, enthusiastic participation, recognized significance and warmly rewarding accomplishment.

What each manager has in one way or another been trying to do is to complete the shift from any tendency toward the old time "boss" type of managing and arrive at the modern type of association and leadership—or salesmanship—or managerial skill—or whatever we may wish to call that combination of competent teaching and firm direction and patience, fairness and genuine, warm, friendly interest of one upstanding American in another. Those are regarded as the things most likely to make the employee *want* to do what the supervisor wants done because the employee would have the facts to *know* the supervisor is urging what's right for all concerned.

The foregoing are some overall impressions from here as to beginnings of progress over the company-wide area. They will vary in degree with each location, and even for any group of a single supervisor and his employees. You will have to be the judge as to how any or all of this applies to your location in general and to your own employees in particular.

Managers and neighbors

Our community neighbors have appeared genuinely interested in taking a new look as to the value of the economic and social function we perform in the direction of needs and desires of the community in general.

Their already great interest has reportedly been even further heightened at most locations during the year since the cut-backs from the peak of the Korean military and civilian demand. The reason for this seems to be that the bulk of our operations is in the industrial northeast which was most seriously affected by the unnatural World War II and Korean build-up and which has, in many instances, been distressed by even the relatively small recent readjustment from the artificial levels developed over the past fifteen years.

The sellers' market generally prevailing during those fifteen years—plus the added preoccupation with a huge volume of military production—masked the competition that was growing up in foreign countries and in the newer areas of population growth in this country away from the older industrial communities. Also masked had been the growing cost differentials in favor of this new competition from abroad and from these newer areas here at home.

These cost disadvantages arose in some cases from size and age. There has also been some failure in the past to move on problems soon enough, such as where there was too much dependence on one or two employers. In other cases, the unfavorable cost factors had grown up in one or more of such items as local taxes, local housing and transportation costs, local welfare practices, wage rates, degree of interest or effort by employees, attitude toward technological progress, spread-the-work practices, political considerations in such matters as law enforcement, and whether there was an encouraging or discouraging "climate" of understanding and opinion about the services and just deserts of one employer in particular or of business in general.

Some of our communities, which felt they had or might have such a competitive problem, were immediately anxious to determine what would be necessary to overcome their cost handicaps in order to get old employers to expand and new ones to come in.

We are naturally very much interested in such communities. We want them to succeed in becoming competitive again and in being able to rebuild employment by keeping old employers and attracting new ones. This is because of our desire, from a human standpoint, for the citizens not to be so wholly dependent on us for jobs and local prosperity. This is also because of our equally understandable desire to keep taxes and other local costs reasonable for the company and for everybody else through having many of these costs spread over a broader base.

Our own employment has held up remarkably well in these locations despite our problem with military and civilian sales and plans. We are trying our best to rebuild our volume of business and employment to the full level we can reasonably expect to sustain. We and others appreciate, however, that it is not in the interest of our employees and communities, as well as of the others concerned, to overload and complicate the problem by having too much dependence on any one employer.

But even in those few latter locations, we are cooperating in trying to get the sales to put our own employment up to where it ought to be and in trying to help find and attract new employers. It has been a blessing that the correction—after the sharp Korean cutback and 15 years of other distortions—has not been still more serious. Any cutback is a distressing matter, and we are hopeful we can—with the help of all concerned—bring in work and resulting local business right up to what we should do in the interest of all.

At two or three of these locations—where we are the largest and even now the steadiest employer in town—certain shortsighted critics have sought to make political capital of our necessary but still relatively few layoffs. They have ignored other employers who are practically shut-down or who have moved away. They have advertised the situation in such a way as to seek the incorrect and damaging impression across the country that the particular locations are destitute and also cursed with labor trouble.

Such defamation of a community is obviously an unwise way to try to attract new employers or get old ones to expand—or to get business for any employers continuing to do their best there.

The accompanying unwarranted local and nationwide public attack on us is also a questionable course of encouragement and other aid to our trying to take up the local slack. These union critics and distant agents have attempted to injure our reputation through irresponsible charges and misrepresentation of facts. If our customers had believed even a part of these charges there would undoubtedly be much less business coming into our plants—and consequently smaller pay rolls and fewer other local benefits.

However, we are obeying the Biblical injunction to "turn the other cheek." We are going ahead to do what's right and contribute as best we can to the long-term best interests of these communities. Anyhow, we judge both the local and distant public is not anything like as gullible as these few agents seem to continue to suspect.

One of these agents stood on the platform as an officer at a national convention recently and made a newly startling but entirely unfounded charge of the front-page type against us. Forty reporters reputedly sat at the table for the public press and, so far as we have yet been able to learn, not a one of them trusted the charge to the point where he chose to report it to his newspaper or magazine.

Meanwhile, our managers and, happily, a great number of our employees have been impressing on our community neighbors that—while of course suffering the usual human failings—we are really *trying* to be a good employer in the best sense of the word, that we are *trying* to spread the maximum amount of money in town by purchasing all possible goods and services locally, that we pay our full share of the taxes with no bargains asked, that we are a good contributor to charities and not a drain on them, and that we are trying in all other appropriate ways to be a good corporate neighbor and citizen.

We are encouraged to believe that the merchants, press, educators, clergy, public servants and other economically, socially and spiritually conscious leaders are slowly gaining a more adequate impression of what we are trying to do, what we are getting done, and how we want to direct our further efforts to measuring up in every feasible way to what fits in with the needs and aspirations of the community.

Incidentally, ever since business first fell from grace sixty years ago because of abuse of power, it has continued to be considered by many public servants to be "bad politics" to be for what business is for—no matter how right business may be. As indicated earlier, we have been trying to *deserve* to have public servants find it "good politics" to do their best to do right by us—through their finding that we are doing our best to do right by all concerned. This fact seems to be getting more and more widely understood all the time.

We have encouraging evidence that public servants—and the public itself when courageously given the facts—do not want law-breakers to go unbridled at any time. Especially is this so when the object of those law-breakers' illegal attacks is the property of loyal employees of a law-abiding, productive, local employer who needs to be protected and encouraged in what he is trying to do in the community's interest.

This is in keeping with the findings of many other researchers who observe that developments here and abroad in recent years have given individual citizens a new determination *not* to have their "destinies planned and controlled by a small group of men whether they be politicians, employers, or union leaders." [2]

The foregoing again are overall impressions from here as to initial progress in the company-wide area. There will naturally be variations at each location, and you will have to be the judge as to what the current situation is at your location in general and with your own neighbors and other local associates in particular.

Managers and union officials

UE's difficulties over the Communist issue provided the opportunity for IUE-CIO to take over most of the former's locals and local officials. UE still bargains for about 20,000 employees, and IUE-CIO now represents about 80,000. We negotiate on a national basis with these two.

Our local managers negotiate separate local contracts with local employee representatives of around 90 bargaining units, even though most of these units are affiliated with one or another of various CIO and A.F. of L. national unions.

Occasionally, a national headquarters will succeed in promoting a strike or in forcing delay in putting into effect an agreement the local employees have voted to approve. Last year the members of some locals of one national union had for many weeks to lose an increase they had voted to approve. This was due to a national union president reportedly ordering the local business agents to refuse approval of the local employees' wishes. This apparently was an effort to bolster up the momentarily fading personal prestige of another national union president who had worked himself into another of the impossible situations which are such an annual embarrassment to his more sober and responsible associates and often such a loss to the employees he represents.

But, in the main, these autonomous local negotiations are conducted under the eye of the local members who are getting more and more determined and effective in their demand that their union or local representative in each case be their servant and not their master and be vigilant and skilled in what the local employees regard as necessary or desirable.

Including the usual temporary local misunderstandings, which are normally rather promptly adjusted to most everybody's reasonable wishes, our relations with most all the local officials of these more than 90 union groups are on a constructive and agreeable basis of confidence and fairness.

The principal exception is when some one or more of them get involved in printing or backing some inapplicable idea that has been sent down as a

[2] "Basis for Industrial Relations" by Waldo E. Fisher.

"must" from the national union headquarters. But, in general, we live in peace and harmony—despite occasional and thoroughly helpful arguments—and the local union officials and members seem just as approving and proud of this constructive relationship as we are.

In fact, we are deeply impressed and greatly encouraged by the increasing number of employees and local union representatives who seem to realize we are really trying to seek the truth and then gain acceptance of it by others in support of sound understanding and relations. They are less and less tolerant of the old familiar fallacies and the old dog-eared misrepresentations calculated to rouse the emotions and obscure the facts.

They don't want something for nothing—or more than their fair share. They want to do right. They want to know what's sound economically in the fair and balanced best current and future interests of all the contributors and claimants. They would now be properly suspicious of spurious back-slapping or baby-kissing or any acting like we agree when we believe the facts to be different. They want us to have the honesty and courage to tell them what we believe we have found is right in controversial matters—even when we suspect it is going to be a little or a lot different from what they have been thinking. But there's nothing new about any of that. As already indicated, nobody follows or even pays any attention to a leader who is scared to tell the truth.

But all the employee wants from his job and his life cannot be secured by the economic route alone. Employers, employees, and union officials overlooked this fact for a long time. They failed to take the full measurements as to what job-satisfaction and human significance involved. Too many top union officials are still making this mistake and are trying to keep employees, employers and public convinced that there is a material route even to spiritual satisfactions.

For our part, we have certainly been trying to learn this lesson ourselves. We have been doing everything indicated as appropriate from a material standpoint. We have then been going beyond and trying to help provide a *human* association that will be rewarding in the additional spiritual ways our employees and our managers seek. We believe our employees sense that we are trying to do our part, despite the inevitable mistakes we often make.

We are happy to observe so many local union leaders moving up to help obtain these true extra objectives their members seek. We are confident this influence will proceed on upward until those top union officials, who have not yet embraced the change, will be seeking to help spread true understanding and to eliminate rather than create groundless emotional dissatisfaction.

Good employers want any unions chosen by employees to be *good* in just the same way good union *members* do. *Good* union officials want to *aid* both job satisfaction from the economic standpoint, when it is warranted, and emotional or spiritual satisfaction when it is warranted.

The exceptions to this in our experience are even now coming to be confined in the relatively narrow area of a few union officials who cling to an outmoded and wrong concept as to our intentions and activities and, we believe, to an equally outmoded and wrong concept as to what our employees really want a union to do as their representative.

An occasional top union official will keep himself particularly upset about us because we don't think we can honorably and otherwise sensibly go along with the way he demands we conduct ourselves for his benefit as contrasted to what we honestly believe is not only the high-grade way to act but also what is to the direct and balanced benefit of our employees, neighbors, and all others concerned.

For instance, one gets upset because we do not keep silent in the face of the steady stream of false public charges such as our being "greedy", "vicious", "agnostic", "anarchist", "rough, tough and nasty", etc. Now, being human beings, we of General Electric management have undoubtedly about the usual human frailties. We are not infallible. As already indicated, we know we make mistakes. We do not—every one of us in every case—manage to follow Company policies exactly. We have not even always been successful—despite our best conscientious efforts and the repeated directives of top Company officers—to see that in every case and at all times the many representatives of the Company act strictly in accord with the applicable details of many complex laws and with the constantly developing interpretations which courts put upon them.

But we are certainly *trying* to learn how to do right and *then* do it. Meanwhile, we don't think there should be any silence on our part that might be taken to admit these false charges. We think we should speak up with what we claim is the truth—and then let all concerned decide who and what to believe.

Another thing that upsets one particular union official is that he feels we don't "bargain" the way we should to fit in with his particular skills and personal desires. He wants us to discuss with him his and our ideas on any important subject before we exchange ideas with any of the representatives of the other 90-odd groups or even before we exchange ideas with him in the presence of his own bargaining committee from our plants.

He wants us to make him a better offer than we do any others—or make him an offer ahead of any applicable offer that might be made to any other union whose contract may have actually or nearly the same termination date. He seems to want to divert to himself any credit any other officials might be given by their members. Many of these others, incidentally, are officials in a union group of which he is an officer.

He wants us to make an offer and then, almost immediately, raise it for no good reason except to prove we are "bargaining."

He wants us to be very sure to conduct ourselves—by silence or by our public protestations—so that any final settlement appears to be one to which we are not at all agreeable but one into which we have been driven unwillingly by brute force.

We think all this is out of keeping with the change from bargaining as a "class struggle" to bargaining as a joint search for what is accurately and honestly in the fair and balanced best interests of all concerned.

To be sure, some may yet for a while associate bargaining with horse trading, or with downright deceit, or with the fleabitten Eastern bazaar type of cunning and dishonest but rather pointless haggling.

But the objective of competent and honorable "collective bargaining" is for employees to get for their individual contribution no less and no more than what is fairly coming to them in keeping with what is in the balanced best interests of all.

Thus, our bargaining has as its objective the most mature approach possible by management and union representatives: to arrive at the facts and then take the action which will be in the balanced best interest of all. We don't want any more or any less than what's right for anybody. We are seeking the facts and sound conclusions. We don't care where the facts come from, or when. We are not concerned with credit or face-saving. We just want to do right.

We have to be fair with all the union officials involved. In the first place, any favor to one over the other would be unfair to the other officials—no matter how big or small is the bargaining group involved. And, also, any variation that resulted in our treating one group of employees unfairly for what they do at their jobs, as compared with any or all the other groups of employees, would certainly be a very unfair or incompetent or unfortunate kind of bargaining.

When it comes to making offers, the only way we know to do this ably and honorably is

. . . to study all the evidence all year long as to employee compensation and benefits,

. . . to study all the applicable union statements made meanwhile,

. . . to listen to the union demands made in negotiation,

. . . to consider carefully these demands along with all other old and new information available or that may become available,

. . . to make offerings at the proper time and voluntarily include absolutely everything our research from all sources, including unions, has indicated should be included to measure up to what's fully right by every reasonable standard,

. . . to discuss fully with the unions, and

. . . to make promptly any modifications in our offers that are indicated as right by any new light on the subject from any source.

Incidentally, we are always freshly amazed when a top union official now and then will claim—despite his direct experiences with us—that this is a "take it or leave it" program and that our efforts at "doing right voluntarily" represent some sort of challenge to the whole usefulness and survival of unions. For nothing could be farther from the facts.

In the first place, this is no "take it or leave it" program as the experience of every union official with it must make him admit to himself. Every one of our offers has stated we would be glad to change on learning of any valid reason why we should—and that was the truth, as proved in practice. One of the early offers was accepted within a day or two for the surprisingly and completely acceptable offer it was. But as already indicated, in every other case we can now recall, we have made any number of modifications in our original offer—some substantial, some minor.

What one particular group of top officials is really complaining about is that we voluntarily come so close to what's obviously right that they can't make it appear that we have been dragged unwillingly to make substantial changes through pure force. Apparently they want us to adopt the outmoded "cooperating" method of making a very low offer we would know is not right and then be publicly bludgeoned up to what's right.

In the first place, we have wanted to tell the full truth in the beginning as to what our studies indicated was right. We have refused to try to fool our employees into thinking we were trying to get away with less than we thought was fairly coming to them. In the second place, where old or new facts show we ought to improve a previous offer, we are always happy to do so at once and in no sense have to be beaten into doing so.

Furthermore, we try to tell such top officials that we believe—and we think our employees believe—that they should concentrate on seeing that we do right for those they represent no matter whose ideas or what combination of them are used in the end. We believe there is no demand on them from the employees to stage a great emotional or political victory to get more than what is right or more than is willingly available if that's right. We believe—and we think our employees believe—that any good union official of theirs has a better and nobler function to perform than trying to persuade or force us to help fool our employees about something we are perfecting willing to do and should be fired if we weren't willing to do.

Still, one final major irritation to one of the top union officials is in connection with his annual and interim strike promotions here. For industry as a whole, about 95% of strikes are reported to be settled the first week by the employer giving in completely. This critic is reported to complain that in our case, in contrast, "when the plants are down, the company does nothing but emit propaganda."

Now we feel deeply that a strike is a tragic thing, and we are greatly distressed for all concerned whenever a few or many of our employees are persuaded or forced to respond to a strike call by a union official.

We do our level best to see that no employee ever has a valid reason to strike—and we mean "valid reason" from *his* standpoint on the basis of all the facts.

Yet we would defend to the last our employee's right to strike voluntarily of his own choice—regardless of how we may have failed to convince him of what we believe to be the facts.

But likewise, if the strike instrument is available to the one for what he feels is a just cause, the other should also be permitted to stand the strike in order to keep from being forced to do what he believes to be wrong for the balanced best interest of all those for whom he is responsible.

The real complaint is that the strikes called here by the official in question have been unrewarding. But that has been because, when all the initial charges and emotions have had a chance to clear up, our employees and their families and neighbors have realized the issues had been misrepresented or misunderstood and the strikes were not the kind of activity they thought proper in their own interest as well as in the interests of others affected.

To try to clear up the misinformation at such times we take as a matter of honorable duty.

But, despite these few problems at the top, we are encouraged to believe that more and more union officials at various levels are coming to believe in our good intentions toward better management from the employees' standpoint, better union practices from the employee and good union leader's standpoint, and better union management relations on the same sound and forthright and non-artful basis on which mutually able and trustworthy people deal in the other important areas affecting us all.

And this is especially good, because we believe in the good theory and potentiality of unions when addressing themselves to worthy services which fully informed employees really want to pay for having outside agents do for them. This is not to say we do not have many disagreements with some top union officials—especially where they misrepresent the facts in organizing or bargaining matters. It is also not to say many of our employees themselves do not disagree with these top officials.

Our employees at some locations have not been persuaded to have any union at all, and many more of our employees elsewhere have felt that they individually had no need for the services of an outside paid agent. We, of course, believe our employees should be just as free to decide not to have or join a union as they are free to carry out a decision to be unionized. But— whether our employees have unions or not at a given location—we continue our efforts there as elsewhere to do right voluntarily in the balanced best interests of all.

Meanwhile, we are particularly impressed with the new generation of union leaders now coming up through the local ranks where we do have unions. They are intimately conversant with what we are trying to do to lay a foundation for peaceful fair-dealing and rewarding association with employees and with employee representatives who are businesslike.

They know that our employees are getting better and better informed all the time on general economic and political matters as well as on our own good intentions and improving practices.

They give every evidence of welcoming the higher grade pursuit thus opening to them as the dignified and responsible representative who can look forward to dealing in unemotional and accurate facts as opposed to any necessity or fashion of conducting themselves in the old rabble-rousing manner amid the old false charges that we in management are greedy and brutal and have to be bludgeoned into doing any least thing that is good.

They already seem to be not only bored with, but at times embarrassed at, having to be a party to misrepresentations obviously calculated to mislead the very people within their communities whom they are supposed to serve and with whom they must live on a day to day basis.

From men of this type we hope will soon emerge the kind of top union leadership which will match the growing knowledge, sophistication and maturity of their membership and will live up to their great opportunity for good as opposed to following the less constructive paths of some of their predecessors.

Our entire program of mutual study and public discussion of the facts—and of honest, forthright, non-artful bargaining—is intended to encourage the development and aid the influence of such honest, direct and responsible union leaders. In contrast, our program is bound to be somewhat discouraging to any who want to go back to the old double-standard or "fleabitten Eastern bazaar" type of bargaining.

We think this is the right basis on which to come together to settle a matter of mutual interest—since it is *not* to any one's real advantage to seek or get a temporary advantage to the unfair disadvantage of the other contributors and claimants.

We confidently expect that most of the old remaining fallacies and emotions about bargaining will soon fall of their own weight. We just as confidently anticipate that this kind of an economic and human process can only survive by "going high-grade" in the same way the older relationships in economic and human affairs had to do to survive.

It may seem naive to admit it, but we see no reason why collective bargaining cannot be conducted with both parties accepting and applying practically the same facts and standards toward a common end, and seeking at the same time to be sure emotion and misinformation do not obstruct a settlement that is fair and just for all concerned.

In such a situation, there is every reason why both parties will eventually come to the bargaining table with a fairly common set of facts about a common objective—with both sides later frankly stating publicly that they found themselves initially in such admittedly substantial agreement that they only had to work out the remaining small differences in an atmosphere of confidence and good will.

In any event, we believe that the entire concept of unions is too big to be forever perverted by the pettiness of any few union officials. We believe the concepts of fairness of the union members themselves are too sound to do other than encourage every possible trend toward the same kind of honorable, forthright and honest dealing as is employed in all other responsible and rewarding walks of life.

What the particular progress has been in these respects thus far with the union officials and employees within the area of your contacts, you will of course have to be the judge. But again, we are encouraged—despite this whole vast area being one of slow change and thus slow progress. We are *trying*. We believe others are beginning to understand and approve our trying. We think we should keep right on diligently seeking the best possible common basis of thought and action with our employees and neighbors and, of course, with their agents and spokesmen in unions, politics, education, clergy, and elsewhere among all leaders and citizens.

This is a *job-improvement* program. We want to be able to put more *in* so our employees can get more *out*. We want the interest and help of all who have such aims.

3. WHERE WE ARE TRYING TO GO

Where we are trying to go in the future is where we have been trying to go for seven and a half years. It is where we are trying to go now day by day. As we said in last year's summary, we are in pursuit of these twin objectives:

1. Our *learning* to do—and *doing*—what we should for our employees.
2. Their *wanting* to do what they can and should in fair return.

For our part, we are sure that our managers, as never before, will be trying to do what's right about pay, benefits, working conditions, information, participation, and the development of ever more rewarding human associations. This is our philosophy and practice of *doing right voluntarily*.

For their part, we are certain our employees will just as surely strive to do what's right for all concerned through applying interest, skill, care, and effort —as they come more and more to know the facts of our intentions and practices, and as they come more and more to see the evidence of the warmth of our human interest.

And for all the other leaders and citizens so intimately concerned—our employees' families and union representatives, our local suppliers, our public officials and civic workers, our educational and religious leaders, and all our other neighbors—we will be seeking to achieve a still more mutually rewarding association.

EMPLOYEE AND PLANT COMMUNITY RELATIONS
SERVICES DIVISION
NEW YORK

A VOTE OF CONFIDENCE

From the president's letter of a company house organ, April, 1952

The compensations for managing a private business have been diminishing consistently over recent years. On the monetary side, because of the increase in other business expenses, inflation, and higher and higher taxes, the executive is constantly losing ground. In the matter of personal satisfaction, the multiplicity of problems induced by a socialistically inclined government have seriously cut into that intangible compensation, the thrill of success and of knowing that one merits commendation.

However, once in a while, there occurs an incident which does give one a very satisfying mental lift. One such incident happened recently in our organization.

Those of you who have been familiar with the Gear Works for any length of time know that our consistent policy has been to be equally considerate of *all* employees, regardless of affiliations, creeds or nationalities. It has always been our policy to recognize every man as an individual and to accord him the dignity which is called for by Christian principles and by the principles which guided the founders of our country. We have maintained that it is not necessary for people at the Gear Works to employ outsiders to obtain for them what is justly theirs. I regret that at times we have felt somewhat discouraged when our policies seemed to be misinterpreted, or at least were not fully understood. Now, however, we have received a vote of confidence which made us both happy and proud.

It came about like this. Some years ago, the National Labor Relations Board ruled that the Lynwood Plant must recognize an international union for bargaining purposes with certain of our plant employees. That obligation has been carefully discharged since that time. More recently, for reasons which may or may not have been well advised, the union approached your Management regarding extension of its jurisdiction. Ultimately, the matter of extension came up for a vote under the supervision of the National Labor Relations Board.

The result was the gratifying experience to which I referred. The vote of confidence is very much appreciated. Personally, I wish to express my appreciation and commendation to all those in the departments concerned. It is a matter of official record that the vote was 20 to 1 against affiliation.

You may be assured that the policies of your Management in this regard will not be changed. We will try to work with unions when the majority in a bargaining unit designate that it is their desire that we do so. On the other hand, we hope that we do nothing to make it necessary. And we hope we will never be prevented from treating all our people alike, and as dignified individuals, regardless of their associations.

ELECTIONEERING IN ONE COMPANY

About one week prior to a scheduled NLRB election to determine whether the employees of an Arkansas firm manufacturing men's shirts, underwear, and pajamas wished to be represented by the Amalgamated Clothing Workers (ACW-CIO), leaflets of undisclosed origin, containing eighteen questions and answers agitating against the union, were found scattered about the plant. Employees testified without contradiction that the leaflets were on the machines when they arrived in the morning. This occurred during World War II, but opposition to unionization continues in many Southern communities and employs many devices, including pamphleteering such as this.

FACTS YOU SHOULD KNOW ABOUT THE AMALGAMATED
CLOTHING WORKERS OF AMERICA, C.I.O.

1. Who is at the head of the Amalgamated Clothing Workers of America, C.I.O. Union?
    a. Sidney Hillman.
2. Who is at the head of the Political Action Committee of the C.I.O.?
    a. Sidney Hillman.

3. Who is Sidney Hillman?
   a. A foreign born Jew, educated in Russia.
4. What is his political background?
   a. Communist.
5. What is his salary?
   a. $15,000.00 a year as head of the Amalgamated Clothing Workers of America only. He pays $125.00 per month for his apartment.
6. Who pays his salary?
   a. Low paid workers who sign union cards.
7. Who forced racial equality plank into the Democratic National platform, against the wishes of all Southern delegates?
   a. The C.I.O., headed by Sidney Hillman.
8. Does the C.I.O. and Sidney Hillman believe that negro women and men should work side by side with white workers in Southern factories?
   a. Absolutely, they have said so.
9. Has the C.I.O. recently caused stoppage of war production in order to force white workers to work with negroes as equals?
   a. Yes—in Philadelphia week before last the C.I.O. Transportation Union insisted that eight negro workers be promoted to places formerly held by white workers. The entire transportation system [more than 3000 street car, busses and subway cars] ceased to operate for 5 days in protest. As a result war production dropped to almost nothing.
10. What has been the main cause of racial trouble recently throughout the United States?
    a. The C.I.O., headed by Sidney Hillman.
11. Who said the following: "I would rather see Americans die in battle for want of equipment than to see my union lose any rights"?
    a. Thomas De Lorenzo, United Automobile Workers local president at Brewster Aircraft plant.—Another union.
12. What would your soldier husband, sweetheart or friend think of your joining the union?
    a. You know what our fighting men think of the C.I.O.
13. Do you have to vote "Yes" at the coming election because you have signed a union card?
    a. No—The ballot is secret. No one will know how you voted. You can vote no.
14. If the union receives a majority will it be possible for those who have signed a union card to withdraw from the union?
    a. Yes. You have a 15 day escape period.
15. If the union requests and is granted a maintenance of membership clause, what will be the status of the union and the non-union employees?
    a. Union members will have to pay their dues for one year or the Company will be compelled by law to discharge them. But non-union members will receive all rights and privileges that union members will and pay nothing to the union.

16. Can the union fulfill its promises of quick benefits if the union gains a majority?

    a. No—A nearby factory has been operating as a union factory now for one year and the union has not been able to fulfill one single promise which it has made.

17. Should I as a free born American citizen, vote "yes" or "no" in the coming election?

    a. Every statement made above is absolutely true. After reading them carefully use your own judgment and let your conscious [*sic*] be your guide.

18. Who are my real friends—The foreign organizers bossed by the foreigner, Sidney Hillman, or the American men of Blytheville and my employers?

    a. You know who your real friends are.

FOR DISCUSSION AND ANALYSIS

1. One industrial relations manager (C. Wilson Hudson, Division Manager of Personnel, Radio Tube Division, Sylvania Electric Products) has said that "the essential skills of the personnel man emerge as those of working with the people in their organization and assisting them to analyze and think through their problems."

One union leader (Solomon Barkin, Research Director, Textile Workers of America) has given this view of company personnel policy:

> Traditionally, a personnel program is simply one of management's tools for the control and direction of the enterprise. Like the others, it seeks greater efficiency and higher profits. Personal values do affect the application of this guide, but the ultimate ends are the same. As a result, plant efficiency is the basic unit for testing conduct. The personnel program pursues these ends by seeking to induce the worker to accept or adapt himself fully to management's code of values and management's goals.

Identify the differences between these two conceptions. What merit do you find in the position of each?

2. Mr. Burk in his paper reproduced above has said that "managerial decisions and actions are a combination of principles, emotions and reasoning." Construct a hypothetical industrial relations or personnel situation the circumstances of which illustrate this proposition, identifying the elements of principle, emotion, and reason.

3. One sage observer of the American industrial scene has said:

> Prerequisite to all else in human relations, then, the manager must learn to know himself, to understand his own emotional reactions to unpalatable developments, to accept his fears and angers as entirely natural responses to those situations, so that he can control them as influences upon his action. But when he has achieved such insights into his own behavior, he must next recognize

that his employees' responses to these same stressful situations, even when they
generate conflict, are equally normal. Seldom indeed does the plant manager
proceed from such a premise. He does not, accordingly, accept the emotions
animating his turbulent, restive workers objectively, as integral components of
daily reality that must be handled dispassionately. Instead, with conclusive
"logic" he establishes the unreasonable character of the demands made by his
workers. He looks for formulas to handle the specific exasperations of specific
strikes and walkouts and slowdowns. He traces the "irresponsibility" of union
leadership and the incitements of "agitators" in the shops. . . .

The quest for ever higher wages is part of the ambition to get on, to improve
living standards, to give one's children better opportunities than his father
enjoyed—all of which is sanctioned by the basic American creed. But time and
again when concrete demands for wage increases, job assignments, or some
other improvement must be denied, the manager seems impelled to pass judgment upon the claimants as well as the claims.[1]

Is the understanding of and objective attitude towards one's own behavior and motivations, as well as of the behavior and motivations of
others, which Professor Selekman says is necessary if managers are to be
effective, something which can be taught? What is there, if anything, in
the curriculum of the college which you are now attending or previously
attended which helps to provide that understanding? What fields of study
do you consider most important to the achievement of this kind of understanding? How can such attitudes best be cultivated?

4. American business has frequently been criticized as autocratic, based
on lines of an almost military-like authority, in which subordinates are not
free to dissent effectively, in which they must conform to orders as given
to them, in which power is concentrated at the top of a hierarchical pyra-
mid. To what extent is *some* authoritarian structure made necessary and
inescapable by the peculiar requirements of business enterprise? Is there
any way in which people in a business enterprise may be allowed greater
independence on the job and greater freedom of decision concerning the
conduct of their duties?

5. There are two basic views of the union-management relationship
which a management might adopt. The viewpoint adopted colors all its
approaches to the union and influences its collective bargaining policies.
(*a*) It may view the union leadership as an opposition force obstructing
management's contact with the workers and seeking to substitute its own
authority over the workers. This view pictures the union as a kind of
intruder or gangster force "muscling in" on management's territory. (*b*) It
may view the union leadership as an influence over its workers (whether
that influence was acquired through the ready grant of power by the mem-

[1] From Benjamin M. Selekman, *Labor Relations and Human Relations*, New York:
McGraw-Hill Book Company, Inc., 1947, pp. 152–154.

bership itself or through the pressures and "false promises" of union organizers) to be recognized and used as possible to further management's own aspirations. The second view still permits a belief that unions are undesirable.

Look back over this chapter to see which of these views seems to underlie each of the selections. Pay particular attention to the General Electric philosophy. Unions have frequently condemned the outlook and policy expressed there as basically antagonistic to the unions and as designed to keep unions "at arm's length." Analyze the policy statement and construct a rebuttal or defense of this union criticism.

6. Managements have frequently objected to the unions on the ground that they divide an employee's loyalty, that they play up the antagonisms between worker and management (whether real or imaginary), that they seek to have ascribed to them the credit for any improvement in working conditions (as though won against the stubborn resistance of management). What do these criticisms reveal of management's philosophy of worker-management relations? Assuming they are valid, what do they reveal of unionists' attitudes towards worker-management relations? Do you believe that a vote against the union is a vote of confidence in management, and vice versa?

6: Political Activity

Unions and managements bargain not only across the table, over the terms of a collective agreement, but across the ballot box, over the terms of legislation. Both groups are concerned with the basic labor legislation, to be sure, but both are also concerned with many other types of laws which Congress and the states may consider—laws dealing with taxation, housing, education, social security, minimum wage, and so on.

As each group seeks to influence the terms of such legislation by putting into office friendly legislators and administrators and by keeping the pressure on such legislators and administrators once elected, they inevitably find themselves engaged in highly organized political activity. In recent years public attention has been more fastened on union political action, but businesses have been no less active in their own way.

RESTRICTION ON POLITICAL CONTRIBUTIONS

From the Labor-Management Relations Act of 1947, Sec. 304

It is unlawful for any national bank, or any corporation organized by authority of any law of Congress, to make a contribution or expenditure in connection with any election to any political office, or in connection with any primary election or political convention or caucus held to select candidates for any political office, or for any corporation whatever, or any labor organization to make a contribution or expenditure in connection with any election at which Presidential and Vice Presidential electors or a Senator or Representative in, or a Delegate or Resident Commissioner to Congress are to be voted for, or in connection with any primary election or political convention or caucus held to select candidates for any of the foregoing offices, or for any candidate, political committee, or other person to accept or receive any contribution prohibited by this section. Every corporation or labor organization which makes any contribution or expenditure in violation of this section shall be fined not more than $5,000; and every officer or director of any corporation, or officer of any labor organization, who consents to any contribution or expenditure by the corporation or labor organization, as the case may be, in violation of this section shall be fined not more than $1,000 or imprisoned for not more than one year, or both. For the purposes of this section "labor organization" means any organization of any kind, or any agency or employee representation committee or plan,

284

in which employees participate and which exists for the purpose, in whole or in part, of dealing with employers concerning grievances, labor disputes, wages, rates of pay, hours of employment, or conditions of work.

AFL-CIO COMMITTEE ON POLITICAL EDUCATION

From the Guild Reporter, published by the American Newspaper Guild, February 10, 1956

COPE INTRODUCES ITSELF

Webster defines the intransitive verb "cope" as: (1) to strike; fight; (2) to enter into or maintain a hostile contest; (3) to meet or have to do (with).

Which all makes very appropriate the adoption of the initials to describe the combined political program of the newly-merged AFL-CIO. It's our old friend, CIO-PAC, actually, but let's have COPE speak for itself. Here's the text of a leaflet available for general distribution from the COPE office at 1625 Eye Street, N.W., Washington 6, D. C.

What is COPE?

The letters COPE stand for Committee on Political Education, the committee of the American Federation of Labor-Congress of Industrial Organizations to advance and promote the general welfare of America by political education and political activity.

As stated in the AFL-CIO Constitution, COPE has the task "of encouraging workers to register and vote, to exercise their full rights and responsibilities of citizenship and to perform their rightful part in the political life of the city, state, and national communities."

COPE is made up of local and state committees of AFL-CIO members, and a national committee consisting of the AFL-CIO Executive Council, George Meany, chairman.

Why is the AFL-CIO in politics?

The AFL-CIO fights to secure a better standard of living for American working men and women and their children. Its unions fight for better wages and working conditions.

But the gains won at the bargaining table can be whittled down or wiped out by decisions of Congress, a state legislature, or a city council. That is where the small but powerful core of reactionary business groups is attempting to kill labor's efforts to achieve greater welfare and security.

To protect and enlarge our gains on the economic front, we must also fight on the political front. In the complicated world of today the two cannot be separated.

COPE is the means through which AFL-CIO members exert their collective strength to obtain good government—good officials acting under good laws. It seeks to inform union members and their neighbors about the issues and the candidates for public office and to organize them so they can act upon this information.

How does COPE work?

COPE reports the facts about issues and candidates. It closely follows the voting records of our elected officials. It helps to educate AFL-CIO members so that they will vote and vote intelligently.

COPE workers carry on registration drives and try to get out the vote on election day so that the result will be a decision of the true majority of the people.

What is the COPE program?

The AFL-CIO stands for world peace founded on justice, freedom and security. To secure such a peace, America must be strong and prosperous. Our country must be free from economic and social injustice, and racial or any other type of discrimination. The AFL-CIO stands for full employment based on an economy in which our increasing productivity is matched by increasing consumer purchasing power.

It stands for the re-establishment of sound and fair labor relations, for better education, housing, social security, unemployment insurance and workmen's compensation.

It stands for an equal distribution of the tax burden, the protection of our natural resources, adequate health services, fair treatment of immigrants, and the extension of civil rights and civil liberties to *all* our citizens.

Who determines COPE policies?

The policies of COPE are determined by the national committee of COPE in the light of actions of the AFL-CIO convention.

Is COPE a political party?

COPE is not a political party. The resolution on political action passed unanimously by the first AFL-CIO Constitutional Convention states: "We reaffirm organized labor's traditional policy of avoiding entangling alliances with any other group and of supporting worthy candidates regardless of party affiliation." The Convention also called for voting records to be placed in the home of every AFL-CIO member.

Does COPE work alone?

COPE cooperates as broadly as possible with other groups who have the same ideals and aims as our organization. It will work with all citizens of good will who have the same ideals.

How does COPE get its money?

COPE funds come from the voluntary contributions of AFL-CIO members.

Where does the money go?

Of every dollar contributed to COPE, half is used by local and state Committees on Political Education, the other half is used by national COPE to aid worthy candidates for national offices.

Testimony of Jack Kroll and James L. McDevitt, Codirectors, AFL-CIO Committee on Political Education, in 1956 Presidential and Senatorial Campaign Contributions and Practices, hearings before a subcommittee of the Senate Committee on Rules and Administration, 84th Cong., 2d Sess., part 1, pp. 48–63

. . . the Committee on Political Education was formed on December 5, 1955, by action of the first convention of the American Federation of Labor and Congress of Industrial Organizations.

That convention also adopted a resolution, which we submit here for the record, outlining our tasks and our goals.

The committee chairman is George Meany. Its secretary-treasurer is William Schnitzler. It consists of the 27 vice presidents of the AFL-CIO plus 27 other officials of affiliated unions. The day-to-day operations of the committee are carried on by the codirectors, James L. McDevitt and Jack Kroll, and their staff. The staff consists of 41 persons at the headquarters in Washington plus 13 people who devote their time and attention to the field activities of our organization.

The work of our committee falls into three general categories.

We have it as our first responsibility, as we have indicated, the education of our own membership on the issues which we conceive to be of prime concern. We believe they should be as fully informed regarding these questions, and the stands of those they elect to positions of responsibility and trust in government, as possible.

We therefore publish a wide variety of literature which ranges from methods of political organization to discussion of such subjects as the Taft-Hartley Act, social security, and welfare legislation.

We have undertaken this year to provide each member of our organization with a voting record of his Senators and his Representative dealing with about 20 labor, general welfare, domestic policy, and foreign aid issues over the years so that the member can form his own judgment as to the character of his representation.

The AFL-CIO has appeared before the platform committees of both major parties and presented its views on the major public questions.

We have held meetings in various parts of the country at which men and women have gathered to talk about the problems which confront them and the country. Our field representatives are meeting constantly with local union organizations assisting them in discussing issues and in formulating programs. Our State conventions and other large bodies have gone out of their way to invite candidates from both parties to address them and give them the benefit of their views.

And we would like to emphasize that the program and policies we are concerned with are not narrow, partisan, group-interest issues. They are issues which affect every American, whether or not he or she is a member of our organization and whether or not he or she is engaged in industry, agriculture, or a profession.

We do not believe that we control any votes. We would not want that power were it within our grasp because such power in the hands of any individual can only run counter to the interests of democratic government. Nor are we so arrogant or naive as to believe that any American citizen would surrender his conscience and his judgment to anyone.

We have faith in the good sense and judgment of the American people and we are willing, at all times, to abide by the will of the majority however distasteful that decision, at any given moment, may be to us.

What is important, however, is that as many citizens as possible participate in our elections and this is the area in which the second category of our activities falls.

We are currently engaged in a registration campaign that will raise the level of political participation to what we hope will be its highest peak. We want to be content, after election day, that no member of our organization failed to understand the privileges available to him through any fault of ours.

We have designated appropriate weeks in the various States "R Week" during which time we will seek to utilize all the channels of communication open to us to inform our members of where they can register, when they can register, and what the registration procedures are.

We are proud that we have succeeded as well as we have in making the Nation registration-conscious. It is a campaign we have been conducting for the last three national elections and throughout all the intervening State and local elections.

Today there are many organizations engaged in this activity. We are proud of the contribution we have made in being among the first to call attention to this problem.

In this connection you will note that among the resolutions adopted by the convention of the AFL-CIO is one which calls for a uniform registration system throughout the States which will eliminate the many unnecessary and cumbersome rules and regulations which now prevail in many places.

The third category of our activities deals with the support of candidates for public office. As we have indicated the first deals with information respecting the issues while the second concerns itself with voter participation.

We should like to make it clear that our organization, the Committee on Political Education, does not and will not recommend candidates for senatorial, congressional, State, or local offices. That is not our job. It is the job of the local and State organizations and the local voters, and they would and properly do resent any attempt to have an outside judgment imposed upon them.

We do not, therefore, as we have many times stated, have any purge list either public or secret and all attempts to concoct one are the mere products of a political campaign.

That does not mean that we do not consult with our local and State organizations or that we do not make available to them such facts and materials as we may have in our possession which would assist them in forming their own opinions. On the contrary, we believe one of our important functions is to keep them as fully informed as possible.

The recommendations with regard to candidates for the President and Vice President are the province of the general board of the AFL-CIO which will be meeting in Chicago on September 12 for the purpose of considering such action.

There is one additional phase of our activity that may be of some interest.

We have made, and we will make, modest contributions to candidates for public office who have been commended to us by the local and State organizations.

We have filed a statement of such contributions, as well as the other details of our finances as the law requires, with the proper authorities.

It will be apparent to you as you examine this statement that our treasury and financial resources hardly merit the attention which has been paid them by certain opponents of labor. Our total expenses this year were just about matched by the political contributions of just four families in the 1954 congressional elections. We assume these families will not be less interested this year.

We do not believe that the power of money can or should win elections. We believe that it is the power of ideas which can and does win elections. It is ideas, not money, which generate the kind of enthusiasm and willingness to participate that you gentlemen know is the essential ingredient of successful elections. It is a program, a record of promises made and kept, a devotion to public service and public service alone that moves people to the kind of activity which results in election victories.

If we have been successful in our program it has not been because of our financial resources. It has been because of the kind of activity we engage in. We believe it has been wholesome and beneficial and it has won adherents on that account and on that account alone. . . .

SENATOR GORE: The committee would like to know the exact amount of funds which the organization you represent, AFL-CIO Committee on Political Education had on hand as of September 1. . . .

MR. MCDEVITT: $215,360.60. In the educational fund we have $117,754.41.

SENATOR GORE: How do you differentiate between the educational fund and the campaign fund or the funds of the Committee on Political Education?

MR. MCDEVITT: The explanation for those two funds, Mr. Chairman, are that the political fund is raised through voluntary contributions for political purposes only.

The educational funds are for educational activities only and do not become a part of any expenditures in behalf or in opposition to any candidate.

SENATOR GORE: Now, I failed to make note of the educational fund of $100,000-some, you said?

MR. MCDEVITT: That's right. To be exact again, Mr. Chairman, $117,754.41.

SENATOR GORE: Do I correctly understand you to testify that at no time do you plan to use for purposes of a political contribution any funds derived from your ordinary membership dues?

MR. MCDEVITT: That's right.

MR. KROLL: That is quite correct.

SENATOR GORE: Are these funds maintained separately in a bank account or are they commingled?

MR. MCDEVITT: They are maintained as separate accounts, Mr. Chairman.

SENATOR GORE: What is your budget for the political year 1956?

MR. MCDEVITT: Are you referring to a budget involving the political fund?

SENATOR GORE: I would like that, please, sir.

MR. MCDEVITT: There is no budget for the political funds, Mr. Chairman.

SENATOR GORE: There is no budget for the political fund?

MR. MCDEVITT: No. That is a voluntary fund. That is what we call the voluntary dollar, and we are necessarily guided in our expenditures by the amount of dollars we receive, and therefore there isn't any way in establishing a budget for that approach. . . .

SENATOR GORE: Well, if you do not have a specific budget, is it reasonable to presume that you do have some plans, some estimates of the amount of funds that you will have for political activity?

MR. KROLL: May I answer that, Jim. We cannot do it because we never know from day to day how many voluntary or political dollars we will be getting in. And we do it this way. If we think a candidate merits our support because of the action of the State or local code, then we give them a partial payment and if the rest of the money comes in we send them the balance that is recommended by the State. Do you follow me?

SENATOR GORE: Yes; I follow you.

MR. KROLL: Do I make myself clear? We make no commitments until we have the money. We can't spend the money until it comes in, and we have no way of knowing how much money comes in.

SENATOR GORE: You have no estimate of the amount of funds you may raise? How much did you raise by this method in 1952?

MR. KROLL: Well, 1952 we were not merged. I think between the 2 organizations we made about $700,000. I think that was about what it was.

SENATOR GORE: The two organizations?

MR. KROLL: Combined.

MR. MCDEVITT: Ours averaged out at less than 3 cents per member for all of the membership of the American Federation of Labor in the year of 1952.

SENATOR GORE: Do you think you will do as well in 1956?

MR. KROLL: We certainly hope so.

SENATOR GORE: Do you expect to do so?

MR. KROLL: We are trying to do better.

SENATOR GORE: What is your goal?

MR. KROLL: Our goal, as Mr. McDevitt has said, our goal is every member 25 cents.

SENATOR GORE: Do you think you will reach as much as $1 million?

MR. KROLL: I doubt it.

MR. MCDEVITT: I doubt it. . . .

MR. KROLL: Mr. Chairman, if I may add this up, as a trade-union movement it is traditional with us that when we are solicited for help by any organization in any State in the Union that are in difficulties, the trade-union membership is more than anxious to help, and that is traditional. We carry that into the political field when an organization in a given State needs help to elect, financial help to elect a good candidate or defeat a bad candidate, the organizations are more than willing to help. As I said, it is traditional.

SENATOR GORE: Are you not willing to leave, Mr. Kroll, to the judgment of the people of a given State or a given congressional district the exercise of their judgment as to who is a bad or who is a good candidate?

MR. KROLL: Oh, sure, sure, we are. But Mr. Chairman, these Senators or Congressmen who come here vote for good or bad legislation affecting the trade-union movement, not of just the one State. They legislate for the entire 48 States, and a bad Congressman from 1 State can affect the membership in New York State just as effectively as if he comes from New York State alone.

These Senators don't legislate for one State alone. They legislate for the Nation as a whole.

SENATOR GORE: Well, would not that be equally true with respect to a corporate interest?

MR. KROLL: I don't know if corporate interests wait for solicitation from the members in their State. We wait until that State asks us for help.

SENATOR GORE: Is that the only distinction you draw?

MR. KROLL: At the moment. . . .

SENATOR CURTIS: The point is your whole educational expenditure is for political purposes now; isn't it?

MR. KROLL: That is not true.

MR. MCDEVITT: Definitely not true.

SENATOR CURTIS: What is it for?

MR. MCDEVITT: Educational purposes. Everything that the word implies, educational.

SENATOR CURTIS: Don't the political parties carry on that?

MR. MCDEVITT: What's this?

SENATOR CURTIS: The Republican Party carries on a tremendous educational program. They tell people about the President, they tell the people about what it has accomplished. That is education.

MR. MCDEVITT: Is it?

SENATOR CURTIS: I think it is.

MR. MCDEVITT: I'm inclined to think, Senator, I think that is designed by the Republican National Committee in its behalf.

MR. KROLL: Senator, we talk about no candidate. We talk about issues as those issues affect our people. We talk about no candidate at all. When we talk about a candidate, we use voluntary money. Now, let's understand that clearly. We talk about issues, no President. . . .

SENATOR MANSFIELD: Now, just to reiterate one particular point again, because the question has been raised in this committee and elsewhere, the contributions made to COPE are all on a voluntary basis and there is no coercion used.

MR. MCDEVITT: As far as for political purposes, that is either in behalf of or in opposition to a candidate, that's right.

Now, we accept contributions to our educational fund, but that is not used at any time under any circumstances in connection with anyone's campaign.

SENATOR MANSFIELD: Is the purpose of the educational fund indirectly connected with campaigns to the extent that records of Members of Congress, analysis of bills and things of that sort are put down on paper and distributed?

MR. MCDEVITT: We pay out of the educational fund the cost of distributing that voting record. That is for information, and there is nothing in the voting record, Senator, if you will wait just a second, there is nothing in the voting record—this is the set here that was put out for 48 States, there is nothing in that record that suggests that you vote for Jones or Smith or not vote for Jones or Smith. We make no recommendations. We simply take the bills that we had an interest in, where the AFL-CIO took a position, and we announce to the State, to our membership, just how the Congressman and the Senators voted on that particular measure or that series of measures.

MR. KROLL: I'd like to add to that. We also use the educational money for urging registration, urging the memberships to register.

MR. MCDEVITT: And also on forum discussions in classes and instructing them on legislation and how to operate their unions insofar as our interests are concerned.

SENATOR MANSFIELD: The educational fund is used strictly for educational and public-service functions.

MR. KROLL: Right.

MR. MCDEVITT: Exactly.

POLITICAL SCOREKEEPING BY THE UNIONS

Below is an example of how the unions select issues which are of particular importance to them, and "educate" their memberships on the voting records of senators and congressmen on those issues.

From the *IUE News* of September 10, 1956

HOW SENATORS VOTED, 1947–1956

THE ISSUES

Labor

1 *Taft-Hartley (HR 3020)*—June 23, 1947 Veto overridden 68–25. *Nay–R.*

Vote to override President Truman's veto of act destroying protection of Norris-LaGuardia and Wagner Acts; subjecting unions to injunctions and suits for damages; outlawing closed shop, secondary boycott and union hiring halls.

2 *Lucas Anti-Injunction Amendment (S 249)*—June 28, 1949 Defeated 44–46. *Yea–R.*

Amendment to Taft-Hartley by Senator Lucas (D. Ill.) would have abolished injunctions in so-called national emergency strikes.

3 *Byrd Injunction Amendment (S 2594)*—June 10, 1952 Passed 49–30. *Nay–R.*

Asked President Truman to use Taft-Hartley injunction against striking Steelworkers. (He refused.)

4 Bacon-Davis Amendment (HR 10660)—May 29, 1956 Passed 42–37. *Yea–R.*

Amendment to give the Secretary of Labor, rather than local agencies, the right to fix minimum wage rates on interstate highway construction.

5 Minimum Wage (S 653)—Aug. 31, 1949 Defeated 26–51. *Nay–R.*

Amendment by Sen. Ellender (D. La.) to hold hourly minimum wage at 65c instead of raising it to 75c and to permit it to drop even lower in times of business recession.

6 Civil Service (HR 4974)—June 3, 1953 Defeated 35–36. *Nay–R.*

Motion to permit vote on amendment by Sen. Carlson (R. Kans.) creating patronage plums and letting government agencies fire career employees arbitrarily, without regard to veterans' preference.

7 Postal Pay (S 1)—May 24, 1955 Defeated 54–39. *Yea–R.*

Vote to override President Eisenhower's veto of bill increasing postal workers' pay 8.59%.

General welfare

8 Unemployment Compensation (HR 5173)—July 13, 1954 Defeated 30–56. *Yea–R.*

Amendment by Sen. Kennedy (D. Mass.) would have raised weekly benefits and provided 26 weeks of coverage in all states. The Eisenhower administration argued these improvements should be left to the states and opposed the bill.

9 Offshore Oil (HR 5134)—July 30, 1953 Passed 45–43. *Nay–R.*

Vote to overrule Supreme Court and give offshore oil, gas and mineral resources valued at $50 billion to $300 billion to coastal states. An amendment by Sen. Hill (D. Ala.), stricken from this bill, would have applied revenues from offshore leases to aid education in all states.

10 Public Housing (S 866)—April 21, 1948 Defeated 35–49. *Nay–R.*

An amendment to strike provisions for public housing from the Taft-Ellender-Wagner Housing Bill.

11 Public Housing (S 3855)—May 24, 1956 Defeated 38–41. *Nay–R.*

Capehart (R. Ind.) amendment to the Housing Act to cut the number of new low rent public housing unit starts authorized from 135,000 each year to 35,000 each year.

12 Social Security (HR 7225)—July 17, 1956 Passed 47–45. *Yea–R.*

Vote on a provision to expand the social security program to include pensions at age 50 for persons totally disabled. The Eisenhower administration opposed the measure.

Domestic policy

13 War Profits Tax (HR 4473)—Sept. 26, 1951 Defeated 33–54. *Yea–R.*

An amendment by Sen. Lehman (D. N.Y.) to set Jan. 1, 1951, as starting date on new taxes on corporation profits, instead of April 1, 1951. This amendment's defeat permitted corporations, with record profits, to escape payment of $500 million in taxes.

The Vote

	1	2	3	4	5	6	7	8	9	10	11	12	13	14	15	16	17	18	19	20
California																				
William F. Knowland†..	W	W	W	W	R	W	W	W	W	R	W	W	W	W	W	W	R	W	W	W
Thomas H. Kuchel†.....	*	*	*	R	*	W	R	W	W	*	W	R	*	W	W	W	*	W	W	*
Connecticut																				
Prescott Bush†.........	*	*	*	R	*	|	W	W	W	*	R	W	*	W	R	W	*	W	W	*
William A. Purtell†.....	*	*	*	R	*	|	W	W	W	*	R	R	*	W	R	W	*	|	W	*
Illinois																				
Paul H. Douglas‡.......	*	R	R	R	R	R	R	R	R	*	R	R	R	R	R	R	R	R	R	R
Everett M. Dirksen†.....	*	*	W	W	*	|	W	|	W	*	W	W	W	W	W	W	*	W	W	*
Indiana																				
Homer E. Capehart†.....	W	W	W	R	R	W	R	W	W	W	W	W	R	W	W	W	R	W	R	W
William E. Jenner†......	W	W	W	W	|	W	W	W	W	W	W	W	W	W	R	W	R	|	W	W
Kentucky																				
Earle C. Clements‡......	*	*	R	R	*	R	R	W	R	*	R	R	R	R	R	R	*	R	R	*
Vacancy................																				
Massachusetts																				
Leverett Saltonstall†.....	W	W	W	W	R	|	W	W	W	R	W	W	W	W	W	W	R	W	R	W
John F. Kennedy‡.......	*	*	*	R	*	R	R	R	R	*	R	R	*	*	R	R	*	|	W	*
Michigan																				
Charles E. Potter†......	*	*	*	R	*	W	W	|	W	*	W	R	*	W	R	W	*	W	W	*
Patrick V. McNamara‡..	*	*	*	R	*	*	R	*	*	*	R	R	*	*	R	*	*	R	R	*

294

	Minnesota		Missouri		New Hampshire		New Jersey		New York		Ohio		Pennsylvania	
	Thye†	Humphrey‡	Hennings‡	Symington‡	Bridges†	Cotton†	Smith†	Case†	Ives†	Lehman‡	Bricker†	Bender†	Martin†	Duff†

Minnesota
- Edward J. Thye†
- Hubert H. Humphrey‡

Missouri
- Thomas C. Hennings‡
- Stuart Symington‡

New Hampshire
- Styles Bridges†
- Norris Cotton†

New Jersey
- H. Alexander Smith†
- Clifford P. Case†

New York
- Irving M. Ives†
- Herbert H. Lehman‡

Ohio
- John W. Bricker†
- George H. Bender†

Pennsylvania
- Edward Martin†
- James H. Duff†

R Voted right or paired right
W Voted wrong or paired wrong
— Absent or general pair
* Before taking office
† Names of Republicans
‡ Names of Democrats

14 $700 Income Tax Exemption (HR 8300)—June 30, 1954 Defeated 46–49.
  Yea–R.
  An amendment by Sen. George (D. Ga.) to increase the $600 tax exemption
by $100 for all taxpayers and dependents and to eliminate loopholes.
15 Natural Gas (HR 6645)—Feb. 6, 1956 Passed 53–38. *Nay–R.*
  Passage of bill to permit producers of natural gas to increase prices without
government approval.
16 Dixon-Yates Giveaway (S 3690)—July 21, 1954 Defeated 36–55. *Yea–R.*
  An amendment to forbid President Eisenhower to carry through a plan to
weaken TVA and give the Dixon-Yates power combine a contract to make $40
million profit on a $5.5 million investment.
17 Segregation in Armed Forces (HR 6826)—June 22, 1950 Defeated 27–45.
  Nay–R.
  An amendment by Sen. Russell (D. Ga.) to permit racial segregation in the
Armed Forces.
18 Honesty in Government (S 2391)—Aug. 1, 1955 Passed 36–34. *Nay–R.*
  A motion by Sen. Capehart (R. Ind.) to excuse businessmen holding nonpaying jobs in government from filing personal financial statements. Such statements were recommended to prevent the use of a government position for
private gain by an individual or firm.
19 Farm Price Supports (HR 12)—April 11, 1956 Passed 50–35. *Yea–R.*
  Passage of bill, later vetoed by President Eisenhower, to support basic crops
at 90% of parity and to assist farmers with soil bank provisions.

Foreign aid

20 Point Four (S 3304)—May 5, 1950 Passed 37–36. *Yea–R.*
  Motion by Sen. Connally (D. Tex.) to add the Point Four Program to the
Foreign Economic Cooperation Act. This was a necessary step to prevent Communist expansion by relieving distress and raising the standard of living in
backward areas of the world.

1956 GENERAL ELECTION SUMMARY OF INFORMATION ON DIRECT EXPENDITURES BY CAMPAIGN COMMITTEES

*From 1956 General Election Campaigns, Report of the Subcommittee on
Privileges and Elections, Senate Committee on Rules and Administration, 85th
Cong., 1st Sess., 1957, p. 38*

EXHIBIT 1

  Summarized in the table below is the information about direct campaign
expenditures in 1956 that has been available to the subcommittee. The information has come from reports filed with the subcommittee and with the Clerk of
the United States House of Representatives.
  "Direct expenditures" include only funds spent by a campaign committee
itself. Because direct expenditures do not include funds transferred to other
organizations or to individuals, there are no duplications in the amounts
reported. . . .

	Republican	Democratic	Labor	Miscellaneous	Total
Jan. 1 to Dec. 31, congressional [1]	2,271,135	41,291	......	......	2,312,426
Jan. 1 to Aug. 31, other national [2]	2,013,219	813,385	133,385	319,811	3,279,800
Sept. 1 to Nov. 30, other national [3]	3,381,977	3,250,985	407,350	260,060	7,300,372
Subtotal	7,666,331	4,105,661	540,735	579,871	12,892,598
State	6,983,727	3,135,292	161,556	791	10,281,366
Local	3,854,779	2,415,190	238,980	615	6,509,564
Senatorial [4]	1,014,753	1,272,016	......	......	2,286,769
Special cases [5]	1,165,797[6]	49,631	......	......	1,215,428
Grand total	20,685,387	10,977,790	941,271	581,277	33,185,725

[1] This is information for the Republican and Democratic congressional campaign committees, derived from reports filed with the Clerk of the U.S. House of Representatives.

[2] This information is derived from reports filed with the Clerk of the U.S. House of Representatives.

[3] Information for this period was derived from reports filed with the subcommittee.

[4] This is information for committees supporting senatorial candidates and does not include information reported by candidates themselves.

[5] Reports were received from 4 committees as this exhibit was going to the printer. Another committee provided partial information. For none of these cases is a detailed breakdown included in subsequent exhibits.

[6] This figure may include some transfers of funds.

EXHIBIT 1A

1956 GENERAL ELECTION SUMMARY OF INFORMATION ON RECEIPTS BY CAMPAIGN COMMITTEES

Summarized in the table below is the information about total campaign receipts in 1956 that has been available to the subcommittee. . . .

	Republican	Democratic	Labor	Miscellaneous	Total
Jan. 1 to Dec. 31, congressional [1]	2,870,987	250,315	....	......	3,121,302
Jan. 1 to Aug. 31, other national [2]	3,162,932	976,202	957,225	383,584	5,479,943
Sept. 1 to Nov. 30, other national [3]	3,121,553	3,564,179	955,765	291,787	7,933,284
Subtotal	9,155,472	4,790,696	1,912,990	675,371	16,534,529
State	14,905,881	4,046,830	388,553	527	19,341,791
Local	6,449,056	2,593,910	276,638	1,242	9,320,846
Senatorial [4]	1,033,484	1,326,315	....	......	2,359,799
Special case [5]	886,694	133,390	....	......	1,020,084
Grand total	32,430,587	12,891,141	2,578,181	677,140	48,577,049

[1] This is information for the Republican and Democratic Congressional Campaign Committees, derived from reports filed with the Clerk of the U.S. House of Representatives.

[2] This information is derived from reports filed with the Clerk of the U.S. House of Representatives.

[3] Information for this period was derived from reports filed with the subcommittee.

[4] This is information for committees supporting senatorial candidates and does not include information reported by candidates themselves.

[5] Reports were received for 4 committees as this exhibit was going to the printer. Another committee provided partial information. For none of these cases is a detailed breakdown included in subsequent exhibits.

The receipts include transfers of funds from other campaign committees, as well as receipts from individual contributions and other sources. The same money may be transferred several times, showing up in each transaction as a receipt by one organization and as a disbursement by the other. Consequently, when the total receipts of a number of campaign committees are added together, some of the same money is counted more than once. The total receipts reported in this table are therefore not an accurate reflection of the financial resources of the parties and other groups. The best index is the summary of direct expenditures reported in exhibit 1. . . .

REACHING THE VOTER

Below is a detailed account of the part played by one large local union in a state election. Teamsters Local 688, under the leadership of Harold Gibbons, whose biographical statement appeared in Chapter 4, is located in St. Louis, Mo.

Report to the 14th Annual City-wide Shop Conference, Teamsters Local 688, January 27, 1957

THE 1956 PENTLAND CAMPAIGN

In 1956, running for his third term in the Missouri Senate, Robert Pentland was faced with the stiffest contest of his political career.

1. His area had been redistricted. The heavily-Democratic 10th Ward was taken from his district, and the predominantly Republican 13th Ward was substituted.

The 10th Ward had provided the winning margin in both 1948 and 1952:

Year	10th ward margin	Total winning margin
1948.	1,377	1,306
1952.	2,133	1,541

Loss of the 10th Ward, on the face of it, therefore, made 1956 a losing battle.

2. Pentland's opponent was a popular and respected ex-Senator, Milton Napier, whose home ward was Pentland's newest—the 13th.

3. Faced with the national popularity of President Eisenhower, and a strong-running and popular Republican candidate for Governor, the outcome in this predominantly Republican Senatorial district was distinctly in doubt.

Faced with this challenge, more than 350 rank-and-file members of Pentland's union—Teamsters Local 688—turned out to work in his campaign.

When the votes were counted, Pentland's victory margin was the largest ever. Not counting absentee ballots, he had carried the district by 1,927 votes. He had not only won the Democratic 11th Ward, but had carried the Republican 23rd Ward (which he lost by 1,000 votes in 1952), and the 13th Ward as well. He had lost the Republican 12th Ward by only 278 votes, compared with 1,239 in 1952.

(Absentee ballots reduced his margin by 245 votes, but gave him an overall majority of 1,682—still his largest victory margin. They also carried the 23rd Ward into the Republican column by 66 votes, and raised the 12th Ward margin to 358). . . .

The campaign

The approach used in the 1956 Pentland campaign represented a departure from usual practices. Political organizations ordinarily "play from strength"— that is, they concentrate on bringing out the votes in their best precincts.

In the Pentland campaign, it was felt that it was necessary to reach Republican and Independent voters, rather than Democratic voters, in order to overcome the deficit he faced on paper.

Accordingly, two principal means of approach were decided upon:

1. Of the 127 precincts in the district, Pentland had lost 72 of these, either in 1948 or 1952, or had won by a very narrow margin. It was decided to cover every home in each of these 72 precincts on a door-to-door basis.

2. In an effort to reach every home in the district with something other than a routine mailing, it was decided to publish a four-page, tabloid newspaper, called the "Pentland Record." This paper detailed the candidate's record, platform, qualifications, endorsements, etc. Two issues of this paper were mailed to each of the 42,000 homes in the area.

Numerous other campaign devices were also used—a card party, a parade, a Citizens' Committee, balloon distribution in the schools, etc.

While concentrating largely on the Republican and borderline precincts in the 12th and 23rd Wards in the pre-election campaigning, Pentland and his co-workers on election day worked closely with the regular Democratic ward organizations, with the majority of the Pentland workers engaged in the 11th and 13th Wards.

The overall strategy seems to have paid dividends, resulting as it did in his largest victory.

Evaluation

As with any statistics, a number of interpretations could be given to the results in the First Senatorial District.

The picture is complicated by the fact that in 1952, in the Eisenhower landslide, most Democratic candidates dropped considerably in the percentage of votes they received. Pentland, due to a strong campaign in that year, held his own or improved.

In 1956, due to the intensive door-to-door campaign and the "Pentland Record," Pentland's percentage of votes increased substantially in the 12th and 23rd Wards, where the bulk of the effort was made. By contrast, the Governorship race showed a continued decline, and the Presidential race remained virtually the same.

In such other races as U. S. Congress and Missouri Secretary of State, their percentage increased substantially over 1952, but still did not reach their level of 1948.

Pentland not only had to reach his level of 1948 or 1952 to win. He had to increase it substantially in the 12th and 23rd Wards. This he did, and without a concentrated campaign, it could never have been done.

Here is the Pentland picture, by percentage (omitting the 13th Ward, for which there were no comparisons):

Percentage of Votes

Ward	1948	1952	1956
11th....................	56.2%	57.2%	57.9%
12th....................	46.3%	46.7%	49.2%
23rd....................	47.8%	47.8%	50.0%

It is significant, in this table, that the minimum door-to-door effort was made in the 11th Ward, the maximum in the 12th and 23rd Wards.

Also of interest is the composite picture for the 11th, 12th, and 23rd Wards, comparing Pentland with the Democratic candidate for President (Truman and Stevenson), and for Governor (Forrest Smith, Phil M. Donnelly, James T. Blair, Jr., all victorious statewide):

Percentage of Votes, 11th Ward

Democratic candidate	1948	1952	1956
President................	62.3%	56.1%	54.9%
Governor................	60.2%	61.8%	54.3%
Robert Pentland..........	56.2%	57.2%	57.9%

Percentage of Votes, 12th Ward

Democratic candidate	1948	1952	1956
President	50.9%	45.1%	45.1%
Governor................	49.9%	45.5%	43.5%
Robert Pentland.	46.3%	46.7%	49.2%

Percentage of Votes, 23rd Ward

Democratic candidate	1948	1952	1956
President...............	50.0%	46.0%	46.4%
Governor...............	47.4%	48.6%	44.5%
Robert Pentland.........	47.8%	47.8%	50.0%

Doubtless, many factors enter into an election campaign. But it seems evident that 135 volunteer workers engaged in door-to-door campaigning in 72 doubtful precincts, plus the "Pentland Record," were able to increase the percentage of votes for Pentland substantially and thus achieve a victory which at first seemed beyond grasp.

The candidate

Effective as the work of the campaign proved to be, it must be emphasized that Local 688 was backing a candidate whose record and abilities gave the union something to boast about.

Robert Pentland was a rank-and-file shop steward at J. C. Penney Co. warehouse in St. Louis when he was first elected in 1948. The first victory was a surprise to political veterans. Even at that time, his district was considered safely in the Republican column.

Following his 1948 victory, two heavily Republican precincts in the 13th Ward were added to his district. Again in 1952, Pentland won.

In 1956, it appeared that an even stronger effort was being made to unseat Pentland, when the 10th Ward was taken away from him and the 13th Ward was substituted.

This redistricting, combined with Pentland's noteworthy legislative record in such areas as unemployment compensation, workmen's compensation, labor legislation, and other matters of concern to working people, provided strong incentive to rank-and-file union members to work for his re-election.

In addition, such things as Pentland's tireless efforts in behalf of honest elections (voting machine bills, modernization of voting procedures), his support of good social welfare legislation, his perfect attendance record, and numerous testimony about his conscientious and able performance in the State Legislature, were matters upon which he could capitalize in reaching the voters of his district, the majority of whom have no particular affinity for organized labor.

Recruiting workers

To pursue the type of campaign envisioned, a large number of volunteer workers would be required. Beginning with the union's 500-member Stewards Council in July, and later in the union's regular shop meetings, members of the campaign committee began to emphasize the importance of the Pentland campaign to Local 688 and its members.

Most important, of course, was Pentland's record in behalf of legislation affecting working men and women, and social welfare laws which involved the whole community.

Continual redistricting made it appear that some interests were concerned about Pentland's consistent success. If they could beat Pentland, it was reasoned, they would be encouraged to seek victories over other progressive candidates.

Another important consideration was the fact that Local 688, itself, was a target. Known, respected, and in certain quarters feared as a militant and progressive union, Local 688's defeat in the political arena, after considerable success, would gladden the hearts of some people.

Even more, with the effort to restrict labor's freedom and growth having moved from the bargaining table and picket line, and into the legislative halls, many people hoped that a defeat for labor in this key contest would signal a mounting campaign against labor's proportionate representation in law-making assemblies.

Among a membership which has been schooled through the years in its stake in political and community affairs, this appeal was realistic. Shop stewards took special volunteer cards and endeavored to enroll their fellow employees as campaign workers.

The fact that Pentland himself was a former rank-and-filer and a close personal friend of many of the members, added to the appeal.

All volunteer work during the campaign was unpaid, except for election day, when workers were paid the equivalent of the wages they lost by taking off work.

Yet a grand total of 324 rank-and-file workers took part in various phases of the campaign, including the 135 who worked door-to-door.

Some of the larger Local 688 shops produced numerous volunteers. At Crown Cork, chief steward Dorothy DeBlaze was successful in recruiting 51 volunteers. At Cupples-Hesse, steward Norma Ellerbrock produced 36 workers. Brown Shoe, long a stalwart of union activity and interest, had 31. But the rank-and-file volunteers also came from far and wide, from small shops as well as large, and represented a wide cross-section of the union.

The door-to-door campaign

To cover 72 precincts door-to-door, especially when each worker was to take only one-half precinct, would require many workers. Ultimately, 135 people were working at this project, with some taking several assignments, and union staff members completing the remainder.

The purpose of the campaign was to swing normally Republican and Independent votes into Pentland's column, on the basis of his record. Door-to-door workers were cautioned, therefore, not to engage in political controversy or to inquire about political affiliations.

A special brochure was prepared, which proclaimed: "South St. Louis Has the Best—Let's Keep Him." This folder outlined Pentland's voting record, quoted from laudatory newspaper editorials, and set forth his platform for the coming session.

Workers were instructed to do simply the following: to greet the resident, state his interest in Pentland's re-election, present the folder and ask that it be read, and encourage a vote for Pentland.

Kits were prepared in advance for each half-precinct, containing: a half-precinct list, instruction sheet, supply of folders, and special cards which offered election day information, services such as baby-sitting and transportation, and an invitation to call upon the candidate for help.

On the basis of those volunteers who had indicated a willingness to work door-to-door, assignments were made in advance and were ready for the first general volunteers' meeting on October 8. More than 100 workers turned out for this meeting and accepted kits. For those who would work but could not be at the meeting, kits were delivered to their shops.

A number of follow-up procedures were established. Meetings in each of the four Pentland ward headquarters were set up for the following week. The turnout for those meetings was very small. In retrospect, they were needless meetings, taking out a valuable night that could otherwise be used for canvassing.

An effective technique, however, was the appointment of a telephone committee composed of volunteers from the truck line offices. They divided the list of volunteers and followed up by telephone. This seemed to be helpful in encouraging workers to complete their assignments.

On Oct. 29, the Political Education Committee of Local 688 (P.E.C.), most of whose members were active in the door-to-door campaign, was called together and asked to help in completing the precinct assignments. Several additional kits were distributed in this way.

In the final week of the campaign, union staff members took on the responsibility of completing the list of 72 precincts.

The "Pentland Record"

The second principal approach used in the campaign was publication of a special, four-page tabloid newspaper called the "Pentland Record," co-edited by Carl Leathwood and Jake McCarthy.

Dealing with issues, qualifications, and platform, and sprinkled liberally with photographs, the "Record" was felt to be a particularly effective medium, certainly more than a normal political mailing would have been.

Two issues of the paper were mailed—to a total of 42,472 homes each, or every home in the district.

The economy of such a campaign device was interesting. Not only was a saving made in postage, compared with an ordinary first-class mailing. Printing of the "Pentland Record" actually represented less an expenditure than an effective advertisement in the daily press would have cost.

Members of the P.E.C. Committee and other volunteers took care of the large task of addressing an original and carbon copy of the names and addresses of all registered voters in the district, a project which began in August.

The results

The fact that Republican or borderline precincts had been selected for intensive work, and that so-called "safe" precincts were not covered, resulted in some interesting figures.

Not only was there a substantial swing to Pentland in the apparently Republican precincts. In the 12th Ward, for example, there was a heavy swing *away* from Pentland, and other Democratic candidates, in those precincts which were *not* worked.

Another interesting occurrence developed. Apart from ticket-leading races such as President and Governor, where there were declines, a number of other Democratic candidates also experienced similar upswings.

One conclusion is obvious: there is a shifting pattern of voting habits in the district, particularly in the 12th and 23rd Wards.

How much of this was due to Pentland's campaigning, and how much was due to other factors, is hard to determine.

But it was certainly true that the results of the Pentland campaign were gratifying. And, remembering the pessimistic picture in the First Senatorial District before the campaign got under way, it would be difficult to say that the Pentland victory was due to anything but hard and effective work.

Certainly, there were other factors. The tremendous popularity of U. S. Senator Thomas C. Hennings, Jr., who led the Democratic ticket, no doubt helped. But the continued decline of Democratic vote percentages in the races for President and Governor indicated a heavy pattern of "ticket-splitting," and Pentland, with a popular opponent, probably could not have won in a traditionally Republican district without a concentrated effort. . . .

The citizens committee

In addition to the "Pentland Record," a principal mailing piece used was the "Citizens-for-Pentland" committee letter, which also went to the more than 42,000 homes in the district.

With Circuit Attorney Edward L. Dowd as chairman, the letterhead also included the names of other prominent South Side Democrats.

This letter, mailed in a plain envelope to minimize its chances of being ignored as "another campaign piece," was sent the last week of the campaign as a final reminder.

Other unions

A number of other labor unions also gave generous cooperation to the campaign. The following unions, through their officers, sent letters to each of their members in Pentland's district, calling attention to his labor record:

International Brotherhood of Electrical Workers, Local No. 1, Paul Nolte; Amalgamated Meat Cutters and Butcher Workmen, Local No. 88, Nick Blassie; United Hat, Cap, and Millinery Workers, Isadore Drucker; and Street Car and Bus Operators, Local No. 788, John Rowland. The Meat Cutters also invited Pentland to address their regular monthly meeting just prior to the election.

The great majority of local unions in Teamsters Joint Council No. 13 also provided lists of their members residing in that area. One mailing went to these Teamster members, inviting them to the kick-off meeting on Oct. 1; the second was a last-minute reminder just prior to the election.

Mailing

In a comprehensive campaign such as this, the task of addressing envelopes and labels is monumental. Large numbers of volunteers undertook this job, which was one of the most important of the campaign. A special meeting was also called, late in October, to stuff the Citizens Committee mailing. Some 60 volunteers attended.

Pentland parade

On Saturday, Nov. 3, the campaign committee organized a colorful parade through Pentland's district. With a special motorcycle escort of young ladies who belong to the St. Louis Cyclettes, about 15 highly-decorated automobiles attracted a good deal of attention along the parade route. The Cyclettes' president, Lois Schroeder, is employed by the union's Labor Health Institute.

Card party

On Sunday, Nov. 4, the campaign was brought to a peak with a free card party at Kolping House. This was advertised throughout the district in the final issue of the "Pentland Record."

Some 400 persons attended this afternoon event, which was supervised by a group of union volunteers from Rice-Stix, with Martha Fannen as chairman.

A number of employers generously donated prizes for the free event. Some 300 attendance prizes were given away, and the card party was considered to be another effective device in the campaign. . . .

Balloon distribution

In the last two weeks before election, some 20,000 Pentland balloons were distributed to children of the public and parochial schools of the district.

While it is difficult to assess the value of this project, particularly compared with the man-hours required to distribute them, an excellent suggestion was made that would bear consideration in future campaigns.

This was the suggestion that the balloons might more effectively be used if they were distributed as favors by those campaigning door-to-door.

Kickoff meeting

The Pentland kickoff meeting, held Oct. 1 at Alhambra Grotto, was attended by Local 688 members living in the district, in lieu of their regular union "community meetings" held during October.

U. S. Senators Stuart Symington and Thomas C. Hennings, Jr., and the successful candidate for Governor, James T. Blair, Jr., headlined the speaking program.

The event gained useful newspaper publicity, and the laudatory comments of the speakers were successfully used in the final issue of the "Pentland Record."

Other projects

On Saturday, Oct. 13, a group of volunteers, chiefly from the union staff, put up Pentland placards on telephone poles along the main streets of his district.

Those placards, along with some 2,000 bumper strips, were also distributed to members living in that area, via their regular shop meetings during September.

Pentland match-books were distributed in stores and taverns in the area by A-1 Cigarette and American Cigarette vending companies, whose employees are members of Local 688.

Publicity

During the campaign, the committee was successful in gaining publicity in the daily press. Coverage was given to the kickoff meeting. In addition, the press gave good coverage to such Pentland campaign proposals as: annual sessions for the State Legislature, abolition of the household "nuisance" tax, and the establishment of a Missouri State Youth Authority.

While not giving a strong editorial endorsement, the Post-Dispatch commended Pentland's record in the closing days of the campaign, and this was helpful in his district, which is comprised of so-called "newspaper wards."

In addition, Pentland appeared on a League of Women Voters TV panel on Channel 9, and on the Teamsters' TV panel, "Labor Views the News," on Channel 36, discussing his proposal for a Youth Authority.

Election day

Whereas the bulk of pre-election campaigning had been done in 72 Republican and borderline precincts, it was deemed important to do the bulk of election-day work in the Democratic precincts.

Accordingly, although most of the pre-election efforts had been in the 12th and 23rd Wards, on election day the emphasis shifted to the 11th and 13th Wards.

Working closely with the ward organizations, the Pentland committee assigned its volunteer workers as follows: 33 in the 11th Ward; 36 in the 13th; 15 in the 12th; and 14 in the 23rd.

Pentland workers wore the candidate's lapel ribbons, and handed out "last minute reminder" Pentland cards, in addition to the regular ward literature.

On election day, staff members manned the ward headquarters in the hope of providing baby-sitting services and transportation, as promised on cards handed out door-to-door.

Election day was a day of excellent weather, however, and there were few calls for transportation. Nor were there more than one or two calls for baby-sitters. The offer of such services, however, had been another gesture of good will during the campaign. . . .

UNION POLITICAL DOMINATION—REALITY OR NIGHTMARE?

Management's reaction to union political activity has usually been sharp. Two examples are provided by the remarks of Mr. Parker and Mr. Sligh, below.

An address by Cola G. Parker, President, National Association of Manufacturers, and Director, Kimberly-Clark Corporation, before the Economic Club of Detroit, October 15, 1956

A TIME FOR PLAIN SPEAKING

This could be a decisive year in the history of America.

It is the year in which organized labor leadership has proclaimed an all-out effort to elect a Congress, and if possible an Administration, which will do the bidding of the handful of men who have the effrontery to claim the American working man as their chattel and possession—who have the gall to say that they, and they alone, speak for American working people. Even many of their own members are unwilling captives, and their total enrollment represents only about one-quarter of the nation's work force.

What I'm telling you is not news. There has been no effort to conceal this power-grab from the nation. Heady with the power they already possess by virtue of holding millions of American working people within the iron grasp of compulsory unionism, the leaders of organized labor boldly announce their intention of seizing political control of the country.

As I say, this is not news to this audience. Nor is it news to anyone who reads the papers. But what appalls me is the stark indifference—an indifference which is alarming—which prevails all over the country. As I read the situation, the people are relying on business and professional men to meet and turn back this challenge to their political traditions. But, I speak for businessmen. And so my remarks will be confined to them.

The businessmen of America sit like rabbits hypnotized by a snake, seemingly helpless to organize a program to defend the American political and economic system, which is essential to the welfare of the American people and to their own welfare. Worse still, they seem too indifferent, or lethargic, or paralyzed by a feeling of hopelessness to seize upon and use the weapons of defense which are available to them.

I should tell you at the outset that NAM does not deny the right of employees to form or join unions and to bargain collectively. We are not out to "bust" unions. But we are opposed to monopoly power in the hands of either business or unions. We are against illegal and unethical practices in the operation of unions. And we are against the use of union funds and union organizations for partisan political purposes. . . .

The intentions, and the program of action, of organized labor in this political campaign are amply documented. Like Hitler when he wrote "Mein Kampf," and like Karl Marx when he wrote "Das Kapital" and the "Communist Manifesto," the leaders of the AFL-CIO have proclaimed in writing and in public statements exactly what they intend to do.

George Meany said last November: "The scene of the battle is no longer the company plant or the picket line. It has moved into legislative halls of Congress and the state legislatures."

The use of the term "battle" is revealing as to the mental attitude and processes of organized labor's leadership.

The union objective, according to their spokesmen, is to elect their own definition of liberal representatives at all levels of government and, if possible, a President and state governors, mayors and other local officials, who will be pliable to the demands of Mr. Meany and his associates.

Now, how are they going about it? What are they actually doing in this campaign, today, to gain their objectives?

They are pouring money and manpower in the election drive at a rate which makes previous efforts seem strictly bush league.

They are diverting to political activity the services of more than 60,000 full-time paid union officers—men and women who are well versed in and capable of applying to electioneering the same tactics of misrepresentation and intimidation which have been used so frequently in industrial disputes.

They have organized election workers from their ranks in as many of the nation's 140,000 voting precincts as possible.

They have turned more than 1,000 union newspapers, with circulation in the millions, into outright propaganda sheets for favored candidates.

They have stepped up the political voltage and the slant of their two regular nationwide network broadcasts as well as union-controlled sectional radio and TV programs.

They are buying time on radio and television for their candidates to appear before the public.

As they did with one of the great political parties here in Michigan, they are taking over political organizations where they are weak at state as well as local levels.

They are infiltrating community organizations of all kinds, from Parent-Teacher Associations, to school boards and social service agencies.

They are wooing the votes of everyone—farmers, white collar people and non-union as well as union members—with the pocketbook approach, promising lower taxes, higher wages, greater social security, less work hours, and larger unemployment and workmen's compensation payments.

They are preparing and distributing every conceivable type of campaign aid for the candidates who have their endorsement.

And, perhaps most effective of all, they are enlisting some 2,000,000 campaign workers with the proclaimed objective of calling at every home in the land they can reach. . . .

But, this is only the beginning. The union political organization will grow and be perfected. And the union leaders will try and keep trying, until they win. In 1958, they will be more effective than in 1956, and in 1960 they will know better what to do and how to do it than in 1958. Unless halted, organized labor eventually will dominate the American political scene. Our history will become the history of Socialist England all over again. . . .

Laws are made by politicians, and politicians want to be elected and re-elected. We cannot rely on the politicians of either party to take forthright action against the political machine the unions already have built up, and which they are putting through its paces in this election. As time goes on and the machine grows stronger, the chances of their doing so will become less and less.

The only effective action is to create a countervailing force—an organization which gets down to the people in every state, and every county, and every precinct—an organization which can carry the truth to the people in their homes. . . .

The preservation of what we call the American way of life transcends the personal or corporate interest of every one of us. No sacrifice is too great, no task too onerous, no foe too fearsome—Walter Reuther or Dave McDonald or anyone else—in this struggle to keep America a nation of all the people.

It is a time for plain speaking, and—as one American—I have tried to speak plainly.

On October 17, 1956, the AFL-CIO News Service released a story carrying a reply to Mr. Parker by George Meany, AFL-CIO president. It included the following paragraphs.

When Parker "wakes up from his nightmare," Meany retorted, he will find "that the former head of General Motors runs the Defense Dept. and that other big business leaders occupy virtually every key post in our national government."

If Parker "thinks labor would like to change this situation, he is right," Meany said. "But our political activities are being conducted by democratic and legal methods" and "every citizen has the right to vote and speak his mind on politics."

Excerpt from an address on the AFL-CIO merger by Charles R. Sligh, Jr., Chairman of the Board, National Association of Manufacturers, and President, Sligh Furniture Companies, Grand Rapids, Mich., at the 60th Congress of American Industry, December 9, 1955

WHAT INDUSTRY EXPECTS FROM ORGANIZED LABOR

Will the new organization become in effect a labor monopoly? Union leaders point out that their organization still represents only about one-fourth of the total labor force and hence cannot be accused of being a labor monopoly. This it seems to me is begging the question. A monopoly exists wherever the entire labor supply of an industry is under the control of one union—and the new federation has announced its intention of organizing industry to the greatest possible extent. When the unions which control the labor supply of a number of major industries are gathered together in a body like the new federation—where they can be made to wheel and turn in response to the voice of the high command—the entire economy of the country is threatened with monopoly control.

Will this new organization become in effect a "ghost government"? Will a handful of men, not elected, not authorized by the American people pull strings behind the scenes to direct the destinies of the nation? It is the potentials of this situation which worry industry—and many other thoughtful citizens as well.

Organized labor and industry will be able to work together in far greater harmony if the leaders of labor will be guided more by economic reality and abandon efforts to achieve by political means what cannot be justified economically at the bargaining table.

UNION FINANCES AND POLITICAL POWER

One criticism of union political activity (their use of common funds for purposes to which individual union members might object) is suggested in the following.

Testimony of Robert R. Nathan, Chairman, Executive Committee, Americans for Democratic Action, in 1956 Presidential and Senatorial Campaign Contributions and Practices, hearings before the Subcommittee on Privileges and Elections, Senate Committee on Rules and Administration, 84th Cong., 2d Sess., 1956, pp. 293–295

SENATOR CURTIS: Now, this—what labor union was it that gave you a thousand dollars?

MR. NATHAN: United Automobile Workers, sir.

SENATOR CURTIS: Did they give you that before or after you declared for Stevenson-Kefauver?

MR. NATHAN: That is given on a monthly basis, sir, throughout the year.

SENATOR CURTIS: They give you that much every month?

MR. NATHAN: Yes, sir; we get $1,000 a month from UAW. . . .

SENATOR CURTIS: Now, this $1,000 that comes from the UAW, that comes from the dues?

MR. NATHAN: That comes from the regular treasury of the union.

SENATOR CURTIS: Yes; and that is money that is collected under the union shop and other compulsory membership of individuals.

MR. NATHAN: Yes, sir.

SENATOR CURTIS: In other words, you got money paid in by people that had to pay it to hold their jobs, and they may not believe that any of the things you stand for are good for America; is that right?

MR. NATHAN: Well, their leadership, however, feel our support of minimum wages, our support of broadening the coverages of social security, our support of international economic-aid programs, and so forth, is consistent with the well-being of the union membership.

SENATOR CURTIS: I know, but a lot of these union members are for the reelection of Mr. Eisenhower.

MR. NATHAN: That is correct.

SENATOR CURTIS: And money was extracted from them in order to hold their job and turned over to a group that consistently, without exception, has supported the Democratic candidates for President and, according to your statement, about 90 percent of the time Democratic candidates for the House and Senate.

I can understand how a political party anxious to get into power would grab such money, but I cannot understand how anybody who claims himself to be a liberal would have anything to do with such involuntary, compulsory collection of money.

MR. NATHAN: Well, we use that money to—for instance, we tried to do a job, if I may use those words, on Republicans as well as Democrats on issues. We came down and testified before committees here on all these legislative measures.

SENATOR CURTIS: This may come, this money, from people who disagree with your every issue. And even if they are in the minority, regardless of what percent it is, it is still involuntary money extracted from people to hold a job. How it can be defended under our American system is just beyond me.

MR. NATHAN: Well, I would like to say this, Senator Curtis: The democratic process has never been a perfect one. I have many friends in business, and big business, too, who disagree violently with the NAM, but for business purposes they pay their NAM dues, and they come down here and they hear testimony which is truly revolting to these individual businessmen, but they pay their dues.

SENATOR CURTIS: They don't have to pay their dues.

MR. NATHAN: Well, they don't have to, but it isn't very easy sometimes, in some organizations, to go along sideways with them.

SENATOR CURTIS: But there is no contract supported by law that if they failed to support their NAM dues, pay their dues, in 30 or 60 days, they are out.

MR. NATHAN: No. That is right. It is not, true, a contract, but it is certainly true in the business practice, and one can say it is quite an important pressure on them.

The same thing is true in the professions. A doctor doesn't have to belong to the AMA, but in many, many communities he has great difficulty in the hospitals and in various professional activities if he doesn't. And yet you get testimony by AMA which is so, what I would call reactionary, personally, that many doctors just can't take it. They just disagree violently, but they continue to pay their dues.

This is part of the imperfections of the democratic processes.

SENATOR CURTIS: I do not think it is imperfection. I think it is taking away money from people. It is dishonest.

MR. NATHAN: We would never have organizations, in my judgment, Senator Curtis, if the sort of majority kind of operation didn't prevail.

I know there are injustices that develop where a person's resources or talents or efforts are sometimes used to an end to which he does not subscribe, but at least if the majority provision is taken care of, then I think we are trying to do the best we can.

And, after all, these unions do have annual elections, and if Walter Reuther is following political issue stands that most of his membership are against, I think in time—it may not be overnight—I think there would be a change.

SENATOR CURTIS: I think the whole discussion, including the issues raised in these court cases, disregarded the rights of individuals. It is not a question of free speech of a union. It is what they do with somebody else's money that they took away from them in order for them to get a job.

MR. NATHAN: What would I do, Senator Curtis, if I held stock in General Motors, and I objected to General Motors' membership in the NAM? I couldn't do anything about it. And I would object violently, and I do have securities in some companies, and I find it quite antagonistic to my judgment as to what is in the best interests of America for them to belong to the NAM.

I would much prefer to see them belong to a Committee for Economic Development or an industry organization that is more in line with constructive, forward-looking principles. But the majority decides that, and there is nothing I can do about it.

SENATOR CURTIS: Well—

MR. NATHAN: I can sell the stock.

SENATOR CURTIS: You can sell your stock and make a choice from a wide selection. There will be a lot of sales.

MR. NATHAN: It would be very difficult, however—

SENATOR CURTIS: I would be glad to assist you in making the change.

MR. NATHAN: Yes.

SENATOR GORE: You could even make a political contribution.

MR. NATHAN: Yes.

SENATOR CURTIS: But the individual workman, living in a locality, possessing certain skills, where there are only a few places to work at, maybe only one, he is made a political prisoner in this process.

I am shocked that an organization proclaiming liberalism would endorse it or defend it or share in the proceeds.

MR. NATHAN: Well, we certainly wouldn't take any funds from any union where the convention, for instance, let us say, had adopted policies which we could find utterly inconsistent with ours.

FINANCING POLITICAL ACTIVITY

Among the unions which have been politically most active has been the United Automobile Workers. In the selection which follows, Walter Reuther outlines his views on the kind of limitation on political activity which is desirable.

Testimony of Walter Reuther, President, United Automobile Workers, in 1956 Presidential and Senatorial Campaign Contributions and Practices, hearings before the Subcommittee on Privileges and Elections, Senate Committee on Rules and Administration, 84th Cong., 2d Sess., 1956, pp. 334–335, 378–381

. . . Our basic problem is that more and more, with the cost of campaigns pyramiding to astronomical heights in terms of television costs, and so forth, more and more reliance is being placed upon big contributions from a small group of wealthy families.

That is the danger; not the degree of public participation in debate. And that is why we believe, Mr. Chairman, that the problem must be solved, not by limiting free discussion, but by limiting the size of contributions.

And I would like to conclude by renewing a recommendation that we made some time back. We propose, and it is incorporated in our statement, that there ought to be a $5 limitation per voter; that grandchildren at the age of 3 should not be able to make contributions of $5000, because they have analyzed the issues and looked into the candidate's merits.

We believe that you ought to have to be a voter, and you ought to be limited to a $5 contribution for the person whom you want to support for the Presidential position. You can give it direct to his committee, or to the National Campaign Committee, but you can only spend $5 to help elect somebody for President.

Five dollars additional to elect a Senator; you can give it to any Senator. You can split it $2.50 to this fellow and $2.50 to another, but you can only spend $5.

Five dollars for Congressman, and $5 contribution to a committee or a political party—$20 in a Presidential election year, $15 in a congressional year, $5 in a nonelection year.

Then there will be no problem of corruption, because you can't corrupt a person seeking office for $5. The price has got to be much higher than that.

And when you give $5, when you give $5, you don't have to worry about the impact of that money upon the legislative processes or the structure of American democracy.

When we talk about a limitation of $5,000, the $5,000 thing, Professor Heard, I think it was, was here the other day, and he said that the officials of 24 big corporations gave, in 1952, $1,064,934.

That is the problem, not free political debate. If the General Motors Corp. wants to talk about atomic energy—that it ought to be given to the private utilities, let them talk about it, let them express their point of view, and let them try to influence the ultimate judgment of the American people.

There is nothing wrong with that. That isn't the danger. The danger is when this money is under the table, when this money is used to influence, when Texas oil millionaire money flows into Arizona, flows into other States all over this country.

That is the danger.

And if we had a $5 limit on individual contributions in any contest, then you would not have to worry about jeopardizing the basic integrity of the system that we are trying to make secure. . . .

SENATOR GORE: Well, when you make a large financial contribution to the campaign of a given candidate for governor or Congress or for the Senate in a State other than that in which you have citizenship, is not that an attempt to interfere with the untrammeled right of the people of that State or district to exercise their own right of selection of their own officers and representatives without undue interference from without?

MR. REUTHER: Well, if the membership in the State of Illinois endorses Senator Paul Douglas, as they did in the last election, we have a large membership there—I think we are, perhaps, the largest trade-union group in the State of Illinois—now, if the membership there makes the decision and then says to us, "Now, we have sent you so much money and COPE so much money, we would like to get some of that back now to help on this." I don't think that is wrong.

Or, supposing we send them a few more dollars than they send us? If in that situation there is big money in there from industry and the fellow who is running has a hard row, it seems to me that the decision that really this turns on is who made the first decision, was it hand-picked from the top down or did the people at the local level make the decision.

In our case the people at the local level make the decision. We do not make that decision.

I have not participated in a single meeting in which they selected a senatorial candidate or congressional candidate. I have participated in the question of the decision of the Presidency and the Vice Presidency.

SENATOR GORE: You understand I raise no question whatever about the right of the members of your organization who are citizens of a State to fully exercise and vigorously exercise their right of citizenship. The more vigorous they are, the better.

I really cannot see anything basically wrong with that proportion of the political fund which the membership of that State has contributed being used in that State.

I cannot go with you that last step, however, when you attempt to justify one wrong by another. The two do not make a right.

I certainly would concur that there is some equity involved when large funds are being expended from one particular economic source to encourage the offsetting thereof by funds from another source.

However, I still cannot arrive at a right being made by the two wrongs.

It seems to me that we must preserve, if we are to have truly representative government, as inviolate as it reasonably can be preserved, the right of people within a given jurisdiction to elect their own officers and representatives——

MR. REUTHER: Senator Gore——

SENATOR GORE (continuing): Without undue influence from without.

MR. REUTHER (continuing): I am in complete sympathy with the point of view which I know you share because I heard you discuss this very ably the last time I appeared before the committee on the gas bill, but I think you have got this kind of problem, which disturbs me greatly, as I know it does many other people who are concerned about the future of American democracy.

Here we have an imbalance in the political situation where four families contributed more in 1952 than the one and a half million members in my union. That is with all the hard work we put in, still four powerful families contributed more money.

Where did that money go? It didn't go in the congressional district where they lived.

The Du Ponts live in Delaware, at least part of the year; but that went all over America.

If you will look at the big oil interests, just check and see what is happening in the campaign of Senator Wayne Morse out in Oregon, and you will find out how much money is going there from the oil industry and its powerful financial groups, so you have got this imbalance.

And I say, Senator Gore, you cannot correct that excepting by limiting the size of the contributions. You get it down to $5 so that the Rockefeller family can give $5 per voter in a senatorial campaign, and you will not have to worry about how much of that crosses State lines because the volume will be so reduced in terms of the impact of wealthy families or any other group that it will not constitute a threat to the integrity of American democracy.

It is the volume of this thing that creates the problem, and I say that politics have got to be practical, too. You cannot save democracy in a vacuum of idealism. You have got to be motivated by idealism, but you have got to also be fighting the hard problem of practical politics. . . .

I mean, these are the facts of life; and I agree with you, your motivations are a thousand percent right, I am sympathetic with what you are talking about. But the way to correct it is to put a $5 limitation upon this so that the Du Ponts and the Rockefellers can send $5 to Arizona, but they can't send $5—I mean, they can send $5 but they can't send $5,000.

SENATOR GORE: It seems to me that it is a basic threat to popular government, when roughly 1 percent of the people finance 95 to 98 percent of our political campaigns—we need to reform our system. Were it not for the interlocking and complex relationships between the Federal Government and the States, I would very readily say to you and to the public that I would favor an absolute prohibition against any monetary contribution to any campaign for Federal office.

I am not sure that it can be put into effect. Of course, you know that former President Theodore Roosevelt favored something along this line.

MR. REUTHER: I would favor that, too.

SENATOR GORE: But this committee is engaged in the serious study of election reform, and we will have further hearings in January, and it may be that we will invite you back.

MR. REUTHER: I think the tax credit which we have proposed, Senator Gore, on the $5 contribution will create the kind of incentives where we can broaden, really, the great financial base upon which American politics must rest. Get more and more people to contribute smaller amounts, and the parties and the candidates will get adequate financial help, but they will get it from a lot of little people rather than a few big people.

I think that is the approach, the tax credit thing, would be a tremendous incentive.

Now, we would lose a few dollars in Federal revenue, but that would be a very small price to pay for the fact that American democracy would be stronger and healthier.

Political activity may involve more than bargains with candidates and efforts to get people to vote for the right man. In recent years the unions have been countering business charges that huge political machines have been formed out of the labor movement with the charge that business has its more subtle instruments for molding public sentiment in support of its programs. *Again it is the politically conscious UAW which authored the article.*

THE SECRET STRUGGLE TO CHANGE YOUR IDEAS

From Ammunition, published by the United Automobile Workers, September, 1955, pp. 6–10

"During the past two decades, top management slowly awoke to the fact that what employees thought, and how they subsequently voted, were vitally important factors—and that these factors had a direct and telling effect on the climate in which business had to operate," a recent article declared in the *Public Relations Journal*.

Increasingly, industry is trying to change the way its workers and members of their families have been thinking. It's pulling the strings and paying the bills for this super-expensive campaign, and not just because the way its workers vote can affect the "climate" in which corporations operate.

Equally, it's trying to coax workers into accepting management policies and decisions they normally would oppose through their unions, along with political policies which would bring the same reaction.

The task of manipulating such policies and decisions to make them more palatable to the public is being taken over now on a larger scale than ever before by so-called public relations men, a new injection in the top management structure.

Once upon a time, they were known as press agents. Their only function then was to get publicity for the company, its product and its officers.

Now, however, they're striving—with management help—to become one of the most powerful opinion-swaying groups in the country. Their big push toward that objective moved forward rapidly after the 1952 election which might be said to have been aided more by the gimmicks of Madison avenue advertising agencies than by Republican doorbell ringers.

How important their function is considered by top management was summarized by *Time* magazine which, in an article on industry's use of public relations, declared:

"Public relations is a long and continuous campaign, aimed at molding public opinion on a broad basis for the benefit of a corporation."

And you're the target!

You're the target, and management's ideas are being aimed at you in every possible way, shape and form all through the day. Daily newspapers, radio and television programs, reading racks, house organs, movie shorts—all these and other methods of reaching vast numbers of people are being used intensively in industry's unending efforts to get people to accept its ideas as their own.

These efforts, of course, take place behind the scenes. They couldn't be effective otherwise. Propaganda loses its value when it's recognized for what it is. Newspapers particularly are aware of this.

Almost all slant the labor, political and economic news they print to favor management and the political policies and candidates management supports. But the papers also attempt to give this respectability by tying it to a news source or event or occasionally by printing "the other side."

Newspapers particularly are susceptible to industry's propaganda campaigns. For the most part, industry pays their bills. The papers depend on industry-bought advertising for the bulk of their income. The majority, therefore, have listened willingly to the siren song of the corporation Loreleis.

Additionally, newspapers themselves are big business. They operate, as other companies do, to make a profit. They hire and fire, buy and sell, depreciate buildings and machinery, turn out products, meet payrolls—and don't stay in business very long if they lose money.

The radio and television industry is in somewhat the same position. It, too, depends on advertisers for its income. Instead of buying space on the printed page, the advertisers dealing with radio and TV stations buy time.

Often, however, they use that time to sell the corporation's ideas more than its products. Many huge corporations, which sell only to other companies and not to the public, now sponsor lengthy, expensive programs as well as those featuring news analyses or commentaries. It is not surprising that the corporation's economic, labor and political ideas turn up on these broadcasts in the form of "comments" or commercials.

They also turn up in pamphlets on factory reading racks and in company house organs. Management has been using both increasingly in the campaign to get its views across to workers and their families.

The house organs—a trade name for company magazines—are an obvious setup for industry propaganda. They're where readers would expect to find management's point of view. They're financed by the plant to tell its own story. It's expected that what a company magazine prints will be written to emphasize management's ideas.

This, however, is vastly different from the hypocritical appearance of "impartiality" that industry tries to tack on to its propaganda in other forms of reaching people.

Aside from newspapers and radio and television, reading racks are a strong example of this. About 4,000 corporations now are estimated to have reading racks in their plants. The *Wall Street Journal* has estimated that in-plant pickups of reading rack pamphlets total more than 30 million individual copies a year.

Many of these contain the names of apparently disinterested organizations as their publishers. Actually, they're put out by companies financed by industry or business organizations. These are paid to prepare the reading rack material to tell a particular story so it can be used in management's propaganda campaign. The Foundation for Economic Education, the Good Reading Rack Service, the Advertising Council, Inc., the American Economic Foundation, and the Committee for Constitutional Government are among the industry-financed propaganda groups preparing and supplying these pamphlets.

One purpose of this multi-million-dollar-a-year industry is to "lessen employee resistance to information considered to be a management story," the *Wall Street Journal* declared. General Motors Corp. alone spends a half-million dollars a year on its plant rack program, *Fortune* magazine has disclosed.

Additionally, company magazines now are published regularly by more than 8,000 corporations, the *Journal* reported earlier this year. Each issue of these magazines combines to total some 19 million copies, and about 80 million people read them, the newspaper added.

The companies mail them to their workers' homes or hand them out at plant gates; they're put on dealers' counters, given to salesmen to distribute, sent to customers.

"Managements around the country think enough of these publications to spend about $140 million annually on them," the *Journal* stated. And, it added, companies are "getting their money back many times over."

Increasingly, the public relations experts are taking over supervision of these company-financed publications and programs, and representing management in dealing with the others. In the past, they talked in terms of these operations as methods to boost morale and production and to "help the worker appreciate the company."

But now, their field is becoming broader by their own action. They not only want to stimulate but also to manipulate how workers think and react. They believe they're developing the tools to accomplish that.

And one way in which some public relations specialists themselves see their new role was stated by Kieber R. Miller, public relations director for the Hawaii Employers Council. He said:

"Through the adroit application of psychology and social physics, it should be possible for the public relations man to transform left-wing union leadership into an enthusiastic corps of Christians and ideological capitalists."

To the employers Miller represents, all union leadership is left-wing, and only those who conform to management's ideas and programs can be saved.

Industry's campaign to win the minds of its workers and their families has been under way for many years. From time to time, its methods change but its objective remains the same. As recently as the 1930s many bosses still tried to dictate how workers were to vote. And wage earners in many instances were fired just for expressing an idea with which the boss disagreed.

Although such tactics still take place in some shops, they generally have been replaced by more subtle and hidden efforts to sway workers' thinking. Policies which companies sponsor and advocate strongly are passed along to workers increasingly in the form of publications or messages from sources which appear to have no direct connection with management.

Striving to speed up the headway made through this approach, however, the public relations and advertising men have been plugging the development of improved methods for influencing people. One they've been working on involves adapting the gimmicks which persuade people to buy particular products so they can be used to coax them into "buying" particular ideas.

Still in its formative stage, the new technique is a combination of advertising and psychology. The advertising and public relations specialists call it "motivation research." It's based on what they find out in "depth interviews" which plumb your innermost feelings—or those of others like you.

The idea is when the researchers know why you go for certain products or ideas—when they know what factors cause you to react as you do—they'll know how to aim their advertising and messages to get the biggest response.

Miller, the Hawaii Employers Council public relations chief, indicated the extent to which public relations men believe this technique can be carried when he asked:

"In employing the variety of techniques available, what degree of intensity is proper in seeking to arouse desire, hatred, envy, cupidity, hope of immediate reward, or any of the great gamut of human emotions on which the public relations man must play?"

Until now, motivation research largely has been confined to selling. It's based on a theory of some psychologists that emotional factors more than technological factors determine why consumers buy certain products.

These research specialists say consumers are faced with a choice of many brands when they are ready to make a purchase. What brings them to buy or to not buy, to pick a specific brand over the others, is determined by such personal factors as hidden emotional judgments, beliefs, prejudices, desires, fears, even an individual need for security, they declare.

That's why tea manufacturers no longer advertise their product with slogans such as "Tired? Nervous? Try Tea." The motivation researchers had found people developed the impression tea was only for the weary and nervous.

Airlines were told many husbands were refusing to travel by plane, not on the chance the plane might crash but that, if it did, their wives would say, "The fool should have taken a train." Brewers now shy away from labeling beer a healthy food because the psychologists told them this brought ideas of fat and "beer bellies."

Some researchers now are hard at work trying to speed the development of these techniques so they can be used to sell company programs and ideas on a large scale as well as company products.

One such study recently recommended that management use two different programs to influence the attitudes of the people on its payrolls. Supervisors ought to be given both sides of an issue, according to this report, while rank-and-file workers should get only a one-sided propaganda campaign.

The recommendation was based on the researchers' theory that supervisors are better educated than workers. The fact that supervisors generally come from the ranks of workers seems not to have been considered in forming either the theory or the recommendation.

Nor was the tradition that all people have the right to know both sides of a question so they can make up their own minds about it.

Disregard for the basic rights of individuals and the attempts to manipulate them for selfish corporation purposes are two of the most serious current drawbacks of the public relations industry, neither of which ever have been exactly sure of their general public standing or acceptance.

Each field constantly is examining itself, but almost always confines its soul-searching to how it might achieve greater recognition from industry and the public. "Can We Measure Up?" is the title of a book recently authored by an official of the Public Relations Society of America. "Can a Public Relations Man's Job Be Defined and Respected?" was the subject of a panel discussion at the American Public Relations Association's recent convention.

But this self-examination is as much a behind-the-scenes affair as the public relations techniques themselves. Outwardly, public relations men urbanely insist their methods provide the answers to most problems which confront businessmen, politicians, economists and a host of others.

They consider themselves combination lawyers, writers, psychologists, social engineers, lobbyists, economists, scientists, politicians, experts on international relations and even more.

Industry's acceptance of the methods they have developed and adapted—which also has meant their increasing acceptance by politicians since the Republican administration took office—has helped bring on this largely-inflated appraisal. One leading member of the profession spoke of its activities in the 1952 national political campaign as "selling a product."

There are vital distinctions, however, between appraisal and result which members of the profession obviously disregard. A customer doesn't necessarily have to buy a product. If he does, he can return it or toss it away if it turns out to be unsatisfactory.

But when the "product" turns out to be a disappointing public official or a poor law or a miserable administration policy, he's stuck with being ruled by it quite a while.

Moreover, industry's acceptance of public relations functions as part of its top management setup has given the field a high degree of policy-molding importance. Management not only wants its workers and the public to know and understand its policies and ideas; it wants them to accept these.

Both in factories and communities where workers and citizens have widely-varied interests and loyalties, the public relations campaigns to shape the acceptance of corporation thinking could have only one result if it were not being met by opposing forces—and that would be to build conformity, to turn back progress, to weaken workers' job security, to stifle union gains and ultimately to patternize the thinking of individuals.

The struggle to get one's ideas and policies generally accepted is natural in democracy. Ideas are offered; they compete; when they come to be believed, they are acted on.

The apprehension and concern over industry's public relations programs for spreading acceptance of its ideas and policies doesn't involve this process as such.

Instead, it's aimed at the fact that issues are not put squarely before the people. Rather, efforts are made to "sell" them through the use of laboratory-developed hidden methods, guinea-pig-tested techniques, deliberately misleading impressions, and scientifically-prepared propaganda devices.

Motivation research is a startling example. Efforts to sway men's minds "through the adroit application of psychology and social physics," as Kieber Miller described an aim of industry's public relations program, can only give rise to general suspicion.

So, too, have the public relations programs designed by public relations men on corporation payrolls to "sell" acceptance of both federal and state laws which are aimed at weakening the bargaining and organizing activities of unions.

Similar criticism has been heard increasingly of industry's influence on newspapers. This, too, is a behind-the-scenes operation. But extensive research has shown most newspapers kowtow to business and industry, largely as a result of publishers' heavy dependence on advertising revenue.

How corporations can make their influence felt in this way was described baldly some years ago by Charles F. Kettering, then a General Motors vice-president. Speaking at a GM dinner for Associated Press managing editors, Kettering said:

"We always sort of felt we owed the newspapers something in the form of advertising for the other things they did. We really didn't advertise to sell cars at all. We had to advertise to keep the newspapers going."

To get heavy advertising revenue, too many newspapers have been willing to continue doing "the other things." According to industry reports, the three Detroit newspapers got a total of about five-and-a-half million dollars in display advertising from the auto industry during 1954. But the newspapers would be the first to deny any connection between that and their outright opposition to the Guaranteed Annual Wage.

How can people guard against these usually-secret efforts to influence their ideas?

Propaganda appeals can be recognized. They can be looked into. They can be analyzed.

You should decide whether the source is reliable or not.

You should know whether the appeal is emotional or factual.

You should see whether you're being told the whole truth or just part of it—or if you're not being told the truth at all.

When you look at the source, you know whether it can be trusted to tell you the truth or not.

You know if it's fought for you in the past or against you.

If its name doesn't give you any indication of this, see if what it says sounds as if it comes from a source you do know.

If the appeal is made to your emotions instead of your ability to think and analyze, ask yourself why. Are the emotional appeals put there because there aren't facts to support the appeal? Are they trying to play up to emotional drives, such as the desire of many people to feel important? If they are, will it benefit you or them?

Do they use words which can mean different things to different people? If your boss or a newspaper editorial talks about security, do they mean the kind of security that would benefit the many or the few? If the company or a reading rack pamphlet or an editorial or a Republican politician talks about reduced taxes, does that mean your own taxes have been reduced? Can a law which reduces taxes just send them down for industry but not for you? Can it give people with big incomes much more of a tax cut than you?

Are you being told the whole story by what you read or hear or see? Not in every detail, perhaps, but so you get a full picture of what's going on? Are you being given both sides or not? Is the appeal only a mixture of opinions and a few facts put together to get you thinking in a certain specific line?

Finally, what results are being sought by those trying to influence the way you think? Who'll benefit—you or they?

For that's the key to why the appeal was made to start with.

PROPERTY VS. LABOR?

In its final report on the 1956 General Election Campaigns, the Subcommittee on Privileges and Elections of the Senate Committee on Rules and Administration expressed concern at the apparent alignment of propertied and business groups with the Republican party, and of labor groups with the Democratic party. It implied that remedial action is necessary, but no recommendations as to the nature of such action were made.

The 1956 General Election Campaigns, 85th Cong., 1st Sess., p. 3

Examination of the facts developed by the subcommittee discloses, as is revealed by the exhibits included herewith, heavy campaign expenditures by persons affiliated with big business, and large vested interests, and by wealthy individuals, on the one hand, and organized labor, on the other, the contributions of the former being largely to Republican committees and candidates, and of the latter almost entirely to Democratic committees and candidates.

The subcommittee views this with deep concern, feeling that it is an unhealthy state of political affairs that may grow worse instead of better unless remedial action is taken by the Congress. As an example, the contributions in excess of $500 made by the officers and directors of 225 of our largest corporations totaled $1,816,597 to the candidates and committees of the Republican Party and $103,725 to candidates and committees of the Democratic Party. The contributions of $500 or more made by officials of labor organizations totaled $16,500 to the candidates and committees of the Democratic Party and $2,500 to the candidates and committees of the Republican Party. The expenditures of labor's political action committees, totaling $941,271, as has been shown, was spent almost entirely on behalf of candidates of the Democratic Party. On the other hand, 12 selected wealthy families contributed $1,040,526 to Republican candidates and committees and only $107,109 to Democratic candidates and committees.

FOR DISCUSSION AND ANALYSIS

1. Are union expenditures to ensure that all their members are registered for voting a "nonpolitical" expenditure, in your view, hence not subject to any of the legislative restrictions on political expenditures by unions? How about expenditures to publicize the voting records of candidates?

2. Is there anything wrong with the kind of political campaign that Teamsters Local 688 put on in connection with the Pentland campaign for reelection, described in the readings above? Are Mr. Parker's fears about the effect of union political activity only a "fear of democracy," as some of his union critics have argued?

3. In the 1953 Senate hearings on proposed revisions to the Taft-Hartley Act, President Meany of the AFL objected to the section prohibiting political expenditures by labor unions in any Federal primary or election. He made the following statement on behalf of the labor group:

> The prohibition against political expenditures by labor unions written into the Taft-Hartley law rests upon the false assumption that labor unions should be given identical treatment with corporations. It is a dangerous fallacy to lump unions and corporations together in this fashion.
>
> A corporation is an artificial creature of the law, a business operated for profit whose owners generally meet only by proxy and have very little to say about the spending of corporate income. The union is a nonprofit association of individuals meeting regularly whose limited financial funds represent contributions from members.
>
> Under these circumstances, it is hardly reasonable to equate the small political expenditures which unions can make only by the specific authorization of their members with the vast sums that corporations would have available for political expenditures if these were permitted.

Do you agree?

4. In the 1956 Senate hearings on political activity by unions and corporations, Senator Carl T. Curtis, Republican, Nebraska, expressed concern that unions had power to require dues payments of workers, under union shop agreements, and then might use such funds for political purposes to which at least some members might be antithetical. In his minority report he stated:

> Some labor unions have now become more powerful than any business in history. What was formerly a danger to a stockholder minority or to individual stockholders has now become even more dangerous to a union minority or to an individual union member. There is now the genuine

possibility of creating in this country a large group of second-class citizens who can be required, by the heads of their organization, to support a political cause or candidate as a condition of membership in the union. A shareholder may withdraw from an organization by selling his stock; a union member, in a union or closed shop, must remain in the union if he is to continue to make a living at his trade. The danger for the union member is now greater than for the shareholder 50 years ago.

With the creation, in 1956, of 1 union of more than 16 million members, it now becomes, for the first time, possible for 6 or 7 million political dissidents within a single union to be required by the majority to finance a political candidate or cause to which they, as citizens may be opposed.

Analyze this statement point by point, indicating the reasons for your concurrence with or dissent from each point made.

5. In a study of the voting behavior of unionized automobile workers in the city of Detroit, *When Labor Votes*, published in 1956 by University Books, the three authors (Arthur Kornhauser, Albert J. Mayer, and Harold L. Sheppard) raised a number of interesting issues. One in particular deserves attention. First, they accepted the proposition that there is a predominantly business-oriented presentation of the news, ideas, and interpretations in American society. Then they suggested that unions would probably move to counter this "one-sided influence" on public opinion (see the UAW article above, "The Secret Struggle to Change Your Ideas") and that both "sophisticated labor and business leadership will increasingly perceive their long-run power relationship as determined in great measure by public opinion (including workers' opinions) and its political expression." (In this connection, think back to the GE program on employee and community relations.)

But this probability that unions will move more and more into the arena of seeking to influence public opinion poses some real issues for the unions—and for public policy. As Kornhauser, Mayer, and Sheppard remark (p. 296):

> On the one hand, there is the question whether democratic doctrine can be reconciled to the employment of dissenting members' dues for political purposes that run contrary to the wishes of those individual members—in an organization to which the individuals must belong for other reasons. This question persists even though the use of funds may be approved by an overwhelming majority of the members. But on the other hand, we have the question whether it is not right and necessary for a democratic majority to be free to act. For example, it is generally agreed that unions can properly decide by majority vote whether to accept or reject an employer's bargaining offers, to strike or not to strike, and almost no one would now contend that the dissenters from such decisions should be entitled to refuse the use of their dues money to implement the

will of the majority. Where is a line to be drawn between such core
economic activities of the union and political types of action which a
majority may also approve as being in the interests of the organization
and its members?

This is the same kind of issue which Senator Curtis raised in his
colloquy with Robert Nathan, excerpted above. Although Senator Curtis
himself has concluded the matter in his own mind, others who have
reflected on this issue are uncertain as to how the above question should
be answered. Where would you draw the line?

6. Mr. Reuther has proposed that political contributions be limited to
$5 per voting person in any presidential or senatorial election.

Others who have agreed with him that present limitations on political
contributions are ineffective have gone to the other extreme, suggesting
that all limits be removed. Which of these two approaches do you prefer?
Can you suggest a preferable alternative?

7: Collective Bargaining

Collective bargaining is the process whereby management and union agree on the terms under which workers shall perform their duties. This includes a spelling out of management's obligations to its employees and to the union which represents them. Historically, it is this principle of agreed and enforceable managerial responsibilities which has given collective bargaining its chief significance. It marked a break with a work system under which management's obligations were only self-assumed or imposed by the competitive market.

With the growth of union power, however, collective bargaining has evolved into a system for obtaining joint agreement on reciprocal responsibilities. Not only the obligations of management, but also the obligations of workers and unions are agreed and enforceable. Agreement on these obligations is achieved through periodical renegotiation of the collective contract.

It is this phase to which attention is given in this chapter. Enforcement of the obligations agreed upon comes through the grievance procedure, to which the materials of the next chapter refer.

COLLECTIVE BARGAINING TODAY

Excerpts from an address by Paul L. Styles, member, National Labor Relations Board, before the 39th convention of the American Federation of Hosiery Workers, Philadelphia, May 7, 1951

Essentially, there are only four ways in which terms and conditions of employment can be determined: (1) They can be fixed by the employer; (2) They can be imposed by the union; (3) They can be ordered by government decree; and (4) They can be determined by collective bargaining. . . .

The fourth course—collective bargaining between the chosen representatives of management and labor—may not be the perfect system, but it is the best ever devised by free men conscious and jealous of their liberties.

It is just 25 years ago this month that Congress first adopted as a national policy the requirement that employers meet and bargain in good faith with the representatives of their employees as a group. At first, Congress adopted this policy only for the railway industry. Nine years later, Congress applied it to all industry affecting interstate commerce, except agriculture.

That does not mean that collective bargaining was born just 25 years ago. Not by any means. Historians trace the first collective bargaining in America back to 1636, only 16 years after the Pilgrims landed at Plymouth Rock and nearly a hundred and fifty years before the establishment of our national government. The men involved in this incident were a group of so-called "bound" workmen and fishermen. They met with an agent of their employer and tried to persuade him to pay them a year's wages which he was withholding. The men finally resorted to mass desertions, which the employer's agent described as "a mutiny." Five years later the same employer's agent was complaining that his workmen had engaged in a work stoppage one afternoon to protest inadequate food. Those probably were the first attempts by employees at collective bargaining in America. You will note that America's first recorded attempt at collective bargaining preceded its first recorded strike by five years. And it was not until 150 years later that the first trade union actually resembling the unions of today appeared. Even then, the first union came only after organizations of employers had pointed the way by demonstrating in a number of instances what collective action and organization could mean in the way of fixing wages.

I think it is important to note that sequence: Collective bargaining first, then strikes to back up bargaining, then labor unions. In short, history teaches that labor organizations appeared in response to the need of employees for continuing and effective representation. The appearance of organizations of employees devoted to bargaining on a collective basis at a time almost exactly coincident with the rise of the democracy is not just one of those odd accidents of history. Collective bargaining is merely another manifestation of the democratic idea. Collective bargaining is a big-sounding word, but, you know as well as I do that there is no mystery about it. It happens whenever a group of employees get together and choose a representative to bargain for them as a group—and their employer deals in good faith with the representative chosen by the majority of the employees. Properly conceived, it is simply the application of the principle of democracy to the relationship between employer and employee. It is just a matter of bringing democracy into the factory or workshop.

The importance of collective bargaining in a democratic society was well summarized by Congress in the National Labor Relations Act of 1935, better known as the Wagner Act. The Act said, in its statement of policy:

The inequality of bargaining power between employees who do not possess full freedom of association or actual libery of contract, and employers who are organized in the corporate or other forms of ownership association substantially burdens and affects the flow of commerce, and tends to aggravate recurrent business depressions, by depressing wage rates and the purchasing power of wage earners in industry and by preventing the stabilization of competitive wage rates and working conditions within and between industries.

Experience has proved that protection by law of the right of employees to organize and bargain collectively safeguards commerce from injury, impairment, or interruption, and promotes the flow of commerce by removing certain recognized sources of industrial strife and unrest, by encouraging practices fundamental to the friendly adjustment of industrial disputes arising out of difference as to wages, hours, or other working conditions, and by restoring equality of bargaining power between employers and employees.

That is still the national policy. In 1947, when Congress was revising the labor-management relations statute, the lawmakers found no reason to change a word of this seldom-read statement. Experience has proved beyond doubt the wisdom of it.

BATTLE OF THE FISHWIVES

Excerpt from a personal letter written by the assistant to the industrial relations director of a Middle Western manufacturing plant

Recently, we have been negotiating another general wage increase, and my naive soul has seen the two giants in the pit both grappling for *money!* For my part, any of the idealistic concepts of the motives of either party are again given a crack in the head. When the chips are down the boys shed the remnants of fine manners and fair speech and the talk is plain and the gestures simple. Reason is brushed aside—appealed to only as a defense, and the battle of the fishwives in the marketplace is no more intense.

Lest it sound like we are having a knock down drag-out fight out here—let me assure you that we are not—in fact, the meetings are rather orderly and pleasant under the circumstances, but when the union came in with their request for a 25¢ general increase based on the BLS C/L figures and the $3400 family budget and we very honestly and clearly showed them that they were unable to hold that argument—as it simply didn't stand up to the facts—they very undauntedly abandoned it and took off on the profit side of the picture. There in spite of frank, honest explanation by the top men of the company of increased costs of materials—with profuse examples, doubled replacement costs of plant and equipment, a good picture (from the company's point in the argument) of profit based on dollar volume of sales rather than on an outmoded and unrealistic capitalization figure—there in spite of these things and with an offer of more than their basis of argument would justify, they rejected all offers and demanded more.

Afterwards in talking to the Chief Shop Steward I pointed out to him that profits compared to capital structure was not taking into consideration present costs of replacements (which we are confronted with on a huge scale) and he admitted that such was the case—but replied—How could he even admit that when it would knock the props out from under their arguments. So even if you do present a sound logical argument, they can utterly ignore it—profess ignorance of your arguments and still threaten to tie you up with a strike unless you meet what they *feel* should be given them. At that point reason has left the bargaining and the muscles start to flex!

Neil, the materials in our product make up about 80% of its cost, and on the overall that cost has gone up 267% since 1939 based on our cost figures. One component of the unit alone accounts for 54% of its cost and that figure is 300% of 1939. Yet neither the price of our product, nor the profit on them has gone up that % per unit or anywhere near that. That would seem to be a reasonable fact to justify our position, wouldn't it—yet the boys on the other side of the table simply shrug their shoulders and pass it off with a—That's your problem attitude. It's not our problem alone—if the thing isn't handled skillfully it will be their problem when we are no longer in position to compete with lower cost companies. . . .

In wage negotiations some of the remarks made display their lack of appreciation of business practices and the VP of the union was amazed when he learned that our contract with one of our principal customers didn't allow for an increase in price when costs—including labor costs—went up!

There's an awful gulf between the two before you can even get on common ground with the ground floor union officers. This is the distinction I feel is existing between these boys in local offices and your international officers (many of whom are well educated, well trained boys). Then even if you do get on common ground, it's a question of expediency whether or not they will argue in good faith.

IN DEFENSE OF INSULTS

An editorial from Business Week, April 7, 1956, following a 150-day strike at Westinghouse by members of the International Union of Electrical Workers

James Carey, the union president who led the unconscionably long Westinghouse strike, has been severely criticized for the bad temper, rough language, and acrimonious attitude he introduced into the six months of negotiations. His uncontrolled behavior, which some believe actually protracted the strike, will not be defended here.

But abhorrence of Carey should not lead his critics to embrace an attractive fallacy. That would be the notion that collective bargaining is best conducted in an atmosphere of sweetness and light. Though reasonableness is always welcome in labor-management negotiations, affability can subvert the process and sow the seeds of trouble. If preserving the benign comity of friendliness is put above the unpleasant business of reaching precise understanding, the result may be so ambiguous and equivocal as to be the direct cause of even more bitter conflict.

Real collective bargaining is by its very nature a rough, tough undertaking. Its essence is the reluctant exchange of commitments; both parties want to yield less and get more. It is not qualitatively different from a business deal in which both negotiators have something less than 100% trust in one another. Nor is it much different from the practice of diplomacy in a mutually suspicious world. In all three forums, the calculated insult and simulated anger are familiar tactics.

In writing about Pres. Eisenhower's amiable sojourn in White Sulphur Springs with the President of Mexico and the Prime Minister of Canada, James Reston of the New York Times quoted Sir Harold Nicholson, expert on the practice of diplomacy, as follows:

"Diplomacy is the art of negotiating documents in a ratifiable and therefore dependable form. It is by no means the art of conversation. The affability inseparable from any conversation between [representatives] produces allusiveness, compromises and high intentions. Diplomacy, if it is ever to be effective, should be a disagreeable business. . . ."

That observation applies with equal cogency to collective bargaining.

COLLECTIVE BARGAINING: HOW TO MAKE IT MORE EFFECTIVE

Excerpt from a statement on national policy by the Research and Policy Committee of the Committee for Economic Development, February, 1947

VOLUNTARY PROCEDURES FOR EFFECTIVE COLLECTIVE BARGAINING

Orderly bargaining between management and union requires adequate "ground rules." While some of the rules must be established by government and should have legal status, many of the most important rules must stem from mutual agreement between management and union. Without this mutual agreement collective bargaining will not function effectively. Unless union and management bring sanity, moderation and tolerance to the bargaining table, agreement becomes difficult.

SUGGESTED VOLUNTARY PROCEDURAL STEPS FOR CONTRACT MAKING

In contract making there is a mutual responsibility for establishing procedures which will permit continuity of production. Among procedures which have been found of value, and are recommended, are the following:

(a) Pre-negotiation exploratory discussion should be held on problems which each side feels are vital and of mutual interest. Such discussions should take place before formal contract demands and proposals are formulated by either side.

(b) Negotiations over contract terms should start well in advance of contract termination, where a termination date exists, with provisions for contract extension if agreement has not been reached by that date.

(c) Proposed contract changes should be presented in writing in advance of formal negotiations so that both sides may have ample opportunity to study the proposals.

(d) Prior to, or at the start of, contract negotiation meetings, the parties should specify the rules of the meetings; time and length of meetings; procedure on such matters as press releases; a list of representatives of each side and their authority; what, if any, transcript or record should be made of meetings; and like matters. All these are important in ensuring smooth and ultimately successful meetings.

THE STEEL NEGOTIATIONS OF 1956

In June of 1956 the United Steelworkers of America, David J. McDonald, president, served demands on the steel industry in anticipation of the expiration on June 30 of the existing contract. The union's demands—twenty-two in all—centered chiefly on a "substantial" but unspecified wage increase; premium pay for Saturdays, Sundays, and holidays; improvements in such "fringe" benefits as holidays, vacations, insurance, shift differentials; a supplementary unemployment benefit plan, and a full union shop. The duration of the agreement was not specified; traditionally agreements in steel have been for two years with a one-year reopening.

The steel companies came back with a counterproposal of a five-year contract, without any possibility of reopening it during that period. Every year wages would rise by an amount ranging from 6 cents to 12 cents an hour, averaging a 7.3 cents-per-hour increase every year over the five-year period. A cost-of-living clause would be included, protecting the real value of these increases. An SUB program, a 10-cents-an-hour premium for Sunday work, and improvements in a number of fringe benefits were also offered.

The parties did not appear so far apart, so that a considerable optimism began to develop that an agreement might be reached without a strike. Strikes in steel during the postwar period had become a familiar part of the bargaining pattern.

With the stage so set, let us follow the developments.

From The New York Times, June 14, 1956

David J. McDonald, president of the United Steelworkers of America, made it clear that the offer would require further bargaining. But he expressed hope that a full accord would be reached by Sunday, thirteen days before the June 30 strike deadline. . . .

Steel stock prices on the New York Stock Exchange pushed upward in late trading yesterday as optimism about a peaceful outcome of the crucial union negotiations rose in Wall Street.

Company and union leaders have made Sunday their target date for a new contract. The day marks the twentieth anniversary of the union's founding. Mr. McDonald believes the most appropriate "birthday present" he could give his members would be a wage increase and the assurance that there would be no shutdown of the industry this year.

However, union officials cautioned against too hasty assumptions that the contract was "in the bag." Mr. McDonald declined to say whether he thought an agreement by this week-end was "probable" or merely "possible."

From an article by A. H. Raskin, in The New York Times, June 16

STEEL UNION BARS BIG 3 WAGE OFFER; COMPANIES FIRM
LABOR CHIEF CALLS PROPOSED 5-YEAR BENEFITS 'PICAYUNE'—NEGOTIATIONS RESUMED

Leaders of 650,000 union steel workers rejected yesterday a proposed five-year no-strike contract with fixed annual wage increases, a fifty-two-week unemployment pay plan and other employe gains.

The country's three biggest steel producers promptly announced that they would not cut the five-year term or increase the total wage and fringe benefits provided in their offer.

A bitter exchange of statements by union and company officials torpedoed hopes both had expressed Wednesday for a contract settlement by tomorrow. But the negotiators still had two weeks in which to head off a strike that would halt nine-tenths of national steel production.

The proposal by the industry's "Big Three"—United States Steel, Bethlehem and Republic—would have provided a package increase this year of 14 to 15 cents an hour. The companies estimated that the total rise in their labor costs over the five-year period would be more than 65 cents an hour. However, statisticians for the union, the United Steelworkers of America, put the figure at just over 45 cents.

David J. McDonald, president of the union, denounced the pay proposal as "picayune." He said the increase in actual take-home pay this year would be only 5 cents an hour. He called the entire package "too little, too late and too long."

"The titans of industry have labored and brought forth a louse," the tweedy, silver-haired union chief said.

"Do you mean mouse?" a reporter asked.

"I mean louse," Mr. McDonald replied.

Executives of the three companies said they felt their offer had gone "as far as we can go" in total benefits. They put special emphasis on the five-year term as a contribution to stabilized planning for the industry, the workers and the national economy.

The industry's past practice has been to sign two-year contracts with a wage reopening and the right to strike in the off-year. This has raised a strike possibility each year. The industry was shut down for periods of four to eight weeks in 1946, 1949 and 1952. Last year it had a twelve-hour strike.

The "Big Three" proposal was voted down unanimously at a meeting of the union's 170-member Wage Policy Committee in the Roosevelt Hotel. Four-man committees from the union and the companies then resumed negotiations. They will meet again this morning.

Both sides promised that they would make every effort to hammer out a "fair and constructive" settlement before the June 30 strike deadline. But the expressions of optimism that had marked their earlier meetings were conspicuously absent.

Union statement

The United Steelworkers of America rejects as entirely inadequate the wage and contract proposal made by the Big Three steel corporations. The industry offer is too little, too late and too long. The wage offer is too little. The fringes are inadequate and become effective too late to have any significance. And the whole contract, instead of being modernized, is to be extended, with its obsolescent features, for too long a period.

After a year of record profits and productivity, the industry has offered the Steelworkers a wage increase for this year of 6 cents an hour and a minor adjustment for skilled employes of two-tenths of a cent in their job increments. At the same time, the industry's offer would require the employes to contribute 1½ cents more for insurance. The industry's wage offer, therefore, would result in a take-home-pay increase to the average steelworker this year of about a nickel an hour—about 2 per cent. This 2 per cent increase would be the Steelworkers' reward for increasing their productivity by a record-breaking 11 per cent in the last year.

To get this trifling 2 per cent wage increase the Steelworkers would be required to mortgage an unpredictable future by agreeing now to settle their fate and that of their families for a similar wage settlement for each year of a five-year term.

The steel industry has attempted to dress up this unacceptable wage proposal by offering a supplemental unemployment benefit plan which is far less in actual benefits than those negotiated by the union in the can industry last year. Furthermore, the industry offer would result in no benefits whatsoever to a substantial part of the union's membership employed in such key steel states as Ohio and Indiana. The union has proposed a practical way to ensure full payment of benefits to unemployed steelworkers in such states. The companies, by spurning the union's proposals to this end, have made it clear that their supplemental unemployment benefit proposal is for propaganda.

To further disguise its picayune wage offer, the companies have proposed a few fringe benefits—effective at dates far in the future. Thus, an additional holiday is offered—but not until next year. An additional half week of vacation is offered for a minority of the employes—but not until two years from now. A one-cent increase in afternoon and night shift premiums is offered—but again, not for two years. Jury pay, the cost of which is so infinitesimal that it cannot be computed, is offered—but not for three years. Also three years away the Steelworkers are offered, instead of double time for Sunday work, now almost universal in American industry, one twenty-fifth time—and no premium whatsoever for Saturday work.

To cap it all, in 1987—thirty years from now—a retiring Steelworker is offered minimum pension benefits not quite equal to the pension benefits now being paid in the can industry.

The plain fact is that virtually all of the fringes offered are already, and more generously, incorporated in labor contracts throughout American industry and will be further improved by the time that they are to become effective in the steel industry under the offer that has been made.

The industry has also refused to modernize the labor agreement in other respects, such as union security, to bring it up to the practice prevailing throughout major segments of American industry where good labor-management relations prevail. Instead, the industry has proposed to turn the clock back in the handling of labor relations by substituting for a tried and tested program of achieving industrial peace an artificial system of unwarranted penalties.

The unfair and one-sided character of the industry's proposal is demonstrated by the absence of any protection for the employes against a rise in the cost of living during the five-year term, while the companies reserve for themselves the right to cancel the meager future benefits proposed in the event the Government finds it necessary at any time within the five-year term to impose controls on the economy.

Our members and the public will not be deluded by industry propaganda as to the "package value" of the offer. No mathematical juggling can obscure that the Steelworkers are being offered an increase in take-home pay this year of 5 cents an hour. It is this amount and not a fictitious package that is available to buy groceries. And, in each of five years, the situation would be the same.

It would be a major step backward for our national economy, as well as for each steelworker, to accept the industry's proposal. The future prosperity of our country depends upon a steadily increasing standard of living for all our citizens. Through their work and productivity they must be provided with the wherewithal to purchase the ever-mounting output of our mills and factories.

The industry's proposals do not meet this need.

We call upon the leaders of the steel industry to measure up to their responsibilities to the steelworkers and the nation. We stand ready to negotiate, through genuine collective bargaining, a fair and reasonable settlement based upon the union's constructive proposals.

Companies' statement

Informed that the United Steelworkers of America had rejected the steel companies' offer which would increase employment costs by more than 65 cents an hour over the next five years, representatives of United States Steel Corporation, Bethlehem Steel Company and Republic Steel Corporation today disclosed full details of the proposals they presented to the union earlier this week.

The offer made by each of the three companies to the U.S.W. included a wage increase in each of the next five years; a fifty-two-week supplemental unemployment benefit plan; a premium for Sunday work and increases in the present premiums for work on the second and third shifts; improved insurance and pension benefits; an additional paid holiday, and increased vacation pay.

After meeting with the union on Wednesday, the negotiators for the three companies recognized that the purchasing power of their employes might be reduced by an increase in the cost of living. The company negotiators therefore offered at today's meeting to include in the proposed agreements provisions to protect employes against a further rise in the cost of living.

The three companies' proposal would increase their labor costs by the end of the five-year period, by more than 65 cents per hour worked; and of this sum, 17⅔ cents an hour, per employe, would be effective this year.

The supplemental unemployment benefit plan offered by each of the three companies provides for the creation of a trust fund into which the company would pay 5 cents per employe-hour worked.

In the event of a lay-off, employes with a minimum service of three years would receive 65 per cent of their after-tax take-home pay, less whatever amounts they receive in state unemployment compensation benefits. Payments out of the trust fund would be a maximum of $25 a week while state benefits were being collected, and $47.50 after the state benefits expired. The maximums would be increased by $2 for each dependent up to four. Benefit amounts and weeks of payment would be reduced if the fund fell below specified levels and until it was restored to those levels.

Each of the three steel companies offered substantial increases in benefits under programs for life insurance, sickness and accident insurance, hospitalization and surgical benefits. Sickness and accident disability benefits would be increased to a range of $42 to $57 a week, as would benefits supplementing state workmen's compensation, in cases of sickness and disabling accidents. A life insurance schedule would provide maximum coverage of $6,000 per employe and life insurance amounts after retirement would be increased to a scale ranging from $1,300 to $1,550. Similarly increases in amounts paid through hospitalization insurance and allowances for surgical fees would be provided.

The companies' offer also provided improved pension benefits. Upon retirement at age 65 or afterward, a steelworker would receive a minimum monthly pension, for each year of continuous service up to a maximum of thirty years, of $2 per month for each year of service prior to Nov. 1, 1957, and $2.50 per month for each year of service after that date. This is in addition to Social Security benefits. Under existing contract provisions, employes with thirty years of service receive a minimum of $1.83 per month for each year of service, upon retirement. The new contract offered by the steel companies would also permit an employe to retire on pension at age 60, if he chose to do so instead of 65 as at present.

The negotiators for the three steel companies said that the original demands made by the United Steelworkers would, if accepted, increase their employment costs immediately by approximately 25%.

"Increases of that magnitude would unquestionably touch off another ruinous round of inflation and undermine the business of the companies," the negotiating companies declared.

"The companies believe that no increase in employment costs at this time would be in the nation's best interests, but adherence to such a position would mean a prolonged strike at the companies' plants and would work grave hardship on our whole economy, in which steel is the basic product," the companies continued.

"Even though steelworkers are already among the highest paid in all American industry, and have made more rapid economic progress in recent years than employes in almost all other major industries, the three companies felt that a proposal of a five-year, nonreopenable agreement with the union would afford the employes further material increases and benefits over the period of the agreement. At the same time, such a contract would give the employes, the customers of the companies and all others affected by their operations a substantial period in which they would be free of any threat of interrupted steel production due to labor difficulties," the company spokesman added.

A period of assured freedom from work stoppage is, they asserted, "sorely needed to enable the companies to plan for and carry out the extensive and costly expansion programs which they have scheduled. It is also needed to enable consumers of their products and all those dependent on the production of steel, to carry forward their business in an orderly fashion, free from the threat of a shutdown of steel operations each year."

The five-year contract, the negotiators said, would permit steel workers to plan for and carry out family programs and responsibilities "without fear of loss of employment due to strikes at annual contract reopenings that have prevailed in the steel industry for many years."

From Business Week, June 16, 1956

STEEL'S DECISIVE DEADLINE

Technology dictates that steel's work-or-shutdown decision come 48 hours before contracts end. So pressure is on for fast settlement to avoid last-minute trouble.

The steel contracts run until midnight, June 30. So it's widely assumed that expiration date sets the deadline for a work-or-shutdown decision. Actually, it doesn't. Whether there will be an interruption of steel production can't be decided in the last few hours of the present contracts' life. The decision must come well in advance, and the negotiators don't have all the time that the contract would appear to provide.

The reason for the earlier deadline is inherent in the technology of steel-making. Basic mills can't be shut down on short notice. So bargaining must take account of these practical, realistic deadlines:

If there's no contract agreement by midnight, June 28, the steel industry must begin then to curtail operations.

Once started, curtailment must be continued over a period of 48 hours, as various production cycles are completed.

If there's no agreement before 4 p.m. on June 30, it's possible that production will cease then in all USW-organized steel mills.

A decision to slow down—and ultimately stop—steel production won't be taken lightly. It's expensive to close a mill and start it up again. The lost tonnage is just a part of it. There are other hefty technical costs, and there are genuine dangers to workers and to equipment in shutting down and then restarting a mill.

From The New York Times, June 18

Negotiations between the United Steelworkers of America and the country's three biggest steel producers reached a deadlock yesterday, two weeks before the deadline for a national steel strike.

The union recessed joint contract talks with the "Big Three" companies— United States Steel, Bethlehem and Republic—after "getting nowhere" in efforts to iron out a dispute over the companies' proposals for a five-year no-strike agreement.

David J. McDonald, president of the union, said it would turn this week to individual negotiations with the industry's three leaders and eight other major steel companies. However, he acknowledged that it was "most unlikely" that any settlements could be reached until the union went back into joint session with the "Big Three."

The gloomy outlook for heading off a walkout of 650,000 steel workers at midnight June 30 was further reflected in an announcement by Mr. McDonald that the union's Wage Policy Committee would be sent home tonight.

Industry advertisement, New York Times, June 20
A RAISE EVERY YEAR FOR FIVE YEARS IS OFFERED
STEELWORKERS

Five year package will increase companies' employment costs 65 cents per hour worked—17⅔ cents in first year

The undersigned steel companies have offered the United Steelworkers of America the largest single pay package in the history of the industry.

The companies' offer covers wage increases and additional fringe benefits for workers over the next five years, amounting, by the end of that period, to a total increase of employment costs of 65 cents per hour worked. Of this sum, 17⅔ cents will be incurred in the first year.

Some important features of the companies' offer follow:

A raise every year for five years

The offer provides for an increase in hourly wage rates averaging 7.3 cents on July 1 of each year for five years; ranging from 6 cents an hour to 12 cents an hour in each year, and totaling from 30 cents to 60 cents by the end of five years.

Protection against increased living costs

The offer provides, additionally, compensation for cost of living increases that may occur during the life of the contract.

52-week unemployment pay

The offer provides for a 52-week Supplemental Unemployment Benefit plan for the protection of eligible employees and their families in case of layoff.

Premium pay for Sunday work

The offer provides a premium for Sunday work for the first time in the necessarily continuous-process steel plants of the companies. It also would increase premium pay for work on the afternoon and night shifts.

Improved insurance plan

The offer provides substantial increases in life, sickness, accident insurance, and in hospitalization benefits. Sickness and accident disability benefits would be increased from a flat $40 to a range of $42 to $57 a week. Life insurance would provide maximum basic coverage of $6,000 per employee. Hospitalization benefits would be improved and maximum allowances for surgical fees would be increased by 50 per cent. The cost of this program would continue to be shared equally by the companies and the employees.

Improved pension plan

The offer provides for higher minimum pension payments for employees retiring after October 31, 1957.

An additional paid holiday and liberalized vacations

The offer provides for a seventh paid holiday and makes provision for liberalized vacation pay.

Effective Dates for Proposed Improvements

1956

July 1—A direct wage increase averaging 7.3 cents an hour.
July 1—Advance all job class 1 employees to job class 2 with a consequent additional increase of 6 cents an hour for these employees.
July 1—Establish Supplemental Unemployment Benefit fund with company contributions of 5 cents an hour per employee per hour worked, to provide up to 52 weeks of layoff benefits for workers with 3 or more years of service.
November 1—Establish improved insurance program.

1957

July 1—A direct wage increase averaging 7.3 cents an hour.
July 1—Add a seventh paid holiday.
November 1—Increase minimum pensions for employees retiring on or after this date.

1958

January 1—Increase vacation pay of employees with 3 to 5 years of service to 1½ weeks and increase vacation pay of employees with 10 to 15 years of service to 2½ weeks.

July 1—A direct wage increase averaging 7.3 cents an hour.

July 1—Increase shift premiums to 7 cents for afternoon shift and 10 cents for night shift.

1959

July 1—A direct wage increase averaging 7.3 cents an hour.

July 1—Establish new premium for Sunday work equal to night shift premium.

July 1—Make up pay lost due to jury service.

1960

July 1—A direct wage increase averaging 7.3 cents an hour.

July 1—Increase shift premiums to 8 cents for afternoon shift and 12 cents for night shift.

July 1—Increase premium for Sunday work accordingly.

In addition, the proposal would provide compensation for cost of living increases which may occur during the life of the contract.

These proposals reflect our desire to assure steelworkers a continuous, progressive program toward ever-higher standards of living. . . . We believe these proposals are as fair to the workers as they could possibly be without being unfair to all other Americans, who also have a stake in the outcome of the negotiations.

These proposals were rejected by the United Steelworkers of America. We hope that in the national interest, and in the interest of the steelworkers themselves, the union will reconsider its decision.

United States Steel Corporation	**Inland Steel Company**
Bethlehem Steel Company	**Great Lakes Steel Corporation**
Republic Steel Corporation	**Wheeling Steel Corporation**
Jones & Laughlin Steel Corporation	**Pittsburgh Steel Company**
Youngstown Sheet and Tube Company	**Allegheny Ludlum Steel Corporation**

From an article by A. H. Raskin in The New York Times, June 24

STEEL INDUSTRY FACES STRIKE NOBODY WANTS

BASIC DIFFICULTY IS OVER INDUSTRY DEMAND FOR FIVE-YEAR CONTRACT

Starting a strike is always easier than stopping one. That is the somber realization that presses in on industry and union negotiators in steel as they trudge down "the last mile" toward next Saturday's strike deadline.

The prospect of a short tie-up holds no terrors for either side. Most of the 650,000 union members are entitled to two weeks' paid vacation, and being out of the mills in July's heat is a welcome thought. Even if the shutdown lasted a week or two longer than their vacation checks, few steel workers would be too upset.

The companies, now turning out steel at a record rate, have fewer orders to fill for the third quarter. They face a dip to 80 per cent of capacity in the next three months. A strike of two or three weeks' duration would restore demand to peak levels. It also would make it easier to put across a substantial increase in steel prices.

But there is no reason to believe that tidy limits could be set to a strike this year, even with the powerful deterrents that operate to curb any major test of economic strength in a Presidential campaign period. The strike of 55,000 Westinghouse Electric workers earlier this year lasted five months. Twelve thousand strikers at the Republic Aviation plants in Long Island were away from their jobs sixteen weeks.

Strike in 1952

The steel industry itself was idle for nearly eight weeks in 1952, when the pressures of the Korean war were added to those of a Presidential year.

The fact that a steel stoppage impends at all is a reflection of the juvenile state of collective bargaining after twenty years of industrial unionism in a vital sector of the national economy. On the surface, this would appear to be a year in which the steel producers and the union should have little difficulty in working out an agreement fair to both sides and consistent with the economic welfare of the country.

The industry is enjoying unparalleled prosperity and productivity. The profits of the eleven big steel companies that have formed a united front for bargaining purposes are running 40 per cent ahead of last year's high levels. Their net earnings in the first quarter came to $257,392,000, with United States Steel alone accounting for $104,160,000 of this total.

The smaller steel companies are doing even better on a relative basis. The profits of twelve second line companies are up 61 per cent over last year. This compares with an 11 per cent increase for industry generally.

Ahead in wages

The union members also "never had it so good." Their wages had been going up faster than those of workers in any other major industrial group in the three and one-half years since David J. McDonald became president of the steel union.

Their weekly wage topped $100 in April, the last month for which figures had been compiled by the Federal Bureau of Labor Statistics. Their hourly earnings of $2.47 were 21 cents above the average for automobile workers and 51 cents above the general factory level.

The union is under conservative leadership. Since 1953 Mr. McDonald, a champion of stable industrial relations, has made joint visits with company executives to 128 steel plants to build more friendly labor management relations. The union holds its quadrennial election of officers next February, and a bitter strike now would pitch the whole campaign on the "hate the boss" lines that marked the union's early struggles.

Politically a long shutdown in steel would jeopardize the national prosperity that plays so big a part in Republican hopes for election success. It also would force the White House to decide whether to obtain a no-strike injunction under the National Emergency provisions of the politically explosive Taft-Hartley Act.

Humphrey's influence

The Secretary of the Treasury, George M. Humphrey, former chairman of the Pittsburgh Consolidation Coal Corporation, has great influence with the steel companies, but there has been no indication that he or any other officer of the Eisenhower Administration plans to step into the situation.

On the union side Mr. McDonald will be a Pennsylvania delegate to the Democratic National Convention. However, he has always been on cordial personal terms with President Eisenhower and has privately expressed doubt that the President can be beaten. Labor officials outside of steel are far from sure that a steel strike would hurt the Republicans as much as it would the Democrats.

The make or break issue in the deadlocked negotiations is the industry's insistence on a five-year contract that would prohibit strikes until 1961. The companies are tired of what they call the "guaranteed annual argument." They want a long period of stability in which they can carry forward their expansion plans without fear of work stoppages or unanticipated rises in labor costs. . . .

Shorter term

The McDonald union has indicated that it would be receptive to a three-year term. This would mean a stabilization period three times as long as the industry and its workers have been accustomed to. It would give the union and the companies a chance to judge the value of an even longer pact the next time round.

The worst thing about the present situation is the union's feeling that its manhood has been challenged by the "take it or leave it" flavor of the industry's offer. Substantial as many of the provisions are, the companies' refusal to consider any compromise on the contract term or on the total value of the wage and fringe benefits contained in their original proposal has revived all the union's long dormant suspicions that the industry still is not reconciled to its existence. This is the kind of feeling that makes for long strikes.

From The New York Times, June 25

On Saturday night, David J. McDonald, the union president, charged in a national television address that the steel companies were guilty of a "flagrant" effort to provoke labor strife by presenting the five-year, no-strike contract to the workers as an ultimatum.

Mr. McDonald characterized the companies' offer as constituting a "nickel increase in net pay," and said that the workers were being asked to take a "long-term" gamble in return for an inadequate contract. . . .

The producers asserted that the $2,310,000,000 increase in wages and benefits which the contract represented was equal to half of the total employment costs of the steel industry last year.

They said that under their proposal, the 550,000 union workers would gain an average of $350 the first year of the contract and an average of $1,300 in the fifth year of the contract.

The company spokesman said that beyond their commitments to members of the United Steelworkers, they would have to give benefits to another 100,000 employes not covered by contracts with the steel union.

In addition to the contract increases, the companies said, the wages of the steelworkers would be increased to compensate for any increase in the cost of living as measured by the consumer price index of the Bureau of Labor Statistics.

From an article by A. H. Raskin in The New York Times, June 28

STEEL WALKOUT SEEMS CERTAIN; TRUCE BIDS FAIL

Industry bars union plan for strike delay after its proposal is rejected

RETROACTIVE PAY ISSUE

Mills start shutdown task—650,000 workers await Saturday deadline

Industry and union proposals for postponing a national steel strike broke down last night over the issue of retroactive pay.

The collapse of the truce efforts made virtually certain a walkout of 650,000 members of the United Steelworkers of America at midnight Saturday.

However, both sides are expected to make a final attempt today and tomorrow to hammer out a contract agreement. They will negotiate against a backdrop of cooling blast furnaces and open hearths.

The cumbersome process of shutting down the mills that turn out nine-tenths of the country's steel began at midnight. It will go into high gear today.

What seemed the last real chance to avert a crippling stoppage vanished at 9:45 P.M. when the twelve biggest steel producers rejected a union offer to delay strike action for fifteen days.

The companies' action was based on a union demand that any wage increases and other benefits eventually agreed upon become effective as of Sunday. The employers asserted that negotiations for a new contract should go forward "with equal pressure on both parties."

They said such a condition could not exist "when the union is guaranteed by retroactivity that, no matter how it may delay agreement, it has nothing to lose."

The industry has consistently contended that it would need higher steel prices to offset higher wages. No retroactive rise in prices could be imposed to pay for a retroactive wage increase.

A company suggestion that the present pact be extended indefinitely with no change in wages or working conditions was turned down by the union. The industry had coupled its suggestion with a demand that the union commit itself to give three days' advance warning before calling its members off the job.

David J. McDonald, president of the union, said it wanted a settlement, not a "premium on procrastination."

He asserted that continuing operations without retroactivity would mean that the union's members would be "working during the next contract year for last year's wages." The union head said this would not be "fair, equitable or customary."

The bitter exchange of statements developed after the twelve big companies had expressed willingness for the first time to recede from their insistence on a five-year no-strike contract.

However, their offer to substitute a four-year, four-month pact, with a proportionate cut in the wage increases and other benefits originally proposed, met with no union favor.

Each side blamed the other for the deadlock in negotiations, and each insisted that a change of attitude on the other's part would clear the way for a quick accord. No specific arrangement was made for a new meeting today.

The union's 170-member wage policy committee will meet here tomorrow to give the formal signal for a strike. Wildcat stoppages may begin in some areas before the midnight Saturday deadline.

White House intervention represented the chief remaining hope for staving off a shutdown. President Eisenhower could move for an eighty-day no-strike injunction under the national emergency provisions of the Taft-Hartley Act, but it was believed unlikely that any action along this line would be taken until a strike had been in progress several weeks.

However, some belief was held that high Federal officials might step in to try to revive the strike postponement efforts. A prolonged shutdown in steel would be the worst labor trouble in the three and one-half years of the Eisenhower Administration.

The steel industry was shut by a twelve-hour strike last year. However, leaders on both sides are convinced that a walkout this time will be far more extended. In 1952 the steel mills were shut for nearly eight weeks. Similarly long strikes paralyzed the mills in 1946 and 1949.

Hopes had been high Tuesday that the industry would put forward a three-year contract proposal at yesterday's bargaining sessions in the Roosevelt Hotel. However, a division was reported to have developed within the industry's high command on the tactical wisdom of making such an offer without specific assurance from the union that it would be acceptable.

One wing of the industry was said to have argued that any major shift in the companies' position would be interpreted as a sign of weakness that would send the union's demands "so high in the sky" that a settlement would be hopeless.

The section of the industry that supplies steel for the automobile industry was understood to be especially insistent on this view. With auto production at low ebb and the motor companies well stocked with steel, this section of the industry faced a sharp drop in orders in the third quarter, even if the mills stayed open.

COMPANIES' PROPOSAL

The undersigned companies have been negotiating with representatives of your union for over four weeks in an effort to agree on terms of new agreements to replace those expiring at midnight, June 30, 1956.

Two weeks ago proposals for new five-year agreements were made by certain of the undersigned and, later adopted by all, in an endeavor to reach a settlement and to satisfy the union's demands to the fullest extent consistent with the companies' responsibilities to their stockholders, customers and the general public. Two days later, however, you rejected those proposals and, among other comments, you then and subsequently characterized the suggested five-year term as too long. You have declared also that the companies' insistence on what they regard as a desirable period of stability constitutes an arbitrary "take-it-or-leave-it" attitude.

The companies, in their proposals, asserted that a period of stability free of strikes is sorely needed in steel. They declared that their proposals were carefully designed with a view to equity to employes, to the companies and to the public generally. They put forth in good faith proposals by which their employment costs would have been increased by 65 cents per employe hour worked, by the end of the five-year span. They have continued to advocate the acceptance of their proposals. Agreement, however, has not been reached and the companies are forced reluctantly to conclude that the prospect of reaching a settlement by midnight, June 30, is not good.

You have recently reasserted the historical policy of your union of "no contract, no work." If a strike is to begin at midnight, June 30, it will be necessary to start curtailing operations not later than 12 o'clock tonight in order to accomplish an orderly shutdown without risk of serious injury to employes and extensive damage to facilities and equipment.

The companies assert again that they desire to do whatever they can in good conscience to avoid a strike. Accordingly, the companies propose that you postpone any strike at this time, that the parties continue to negotiate beyond midnight of June 30 (should agreement not have been reached by that time) and that you agree to give the companies at least seventy-two hours' prior written notice, after the date of this letter, of any strike beginning at any time after June 30.

If the union shall accede to this proposal which is, the companies believe, in the interests of employes and the country as a whole, the companies in subsequent negotiations will be agreeable to reducing the five-year term of the proposed agreements to a shorter term running from the date of execution of the new agreements to Oct. 31, 1960, with, of course, a proportionate reduction of the benefits provided in their five-year proposals.

In the absence of an agreement by the union not to strike at any time after June 30 without hereafter giving the companies at least seventy-two hours' prior written notice, the companies will, for the reasons stated above, be forced to start curtailing operations at midnight tonight.

Please be good enough, in light of the time and the urgency of this matter, to advise us whether you are willing to make such an agreement by replying to this letter in writing to John A. Stephens, Room 820, Biltmore Hotel, New York, New York, not later than 5 P.M. today.

UNION COUNTER-OFFER

The United Steelworkers of America commenced negotiations with the leading companies in the steel industry on May 28–29 in Pittsburgh.

The representatives of the union have been meeting almost daily since then with the representatives of United States Steel Corporation, Bethlehem Steel Company and Republic Steel Corporation. Our contracts with the companies do not expire until midnight, June 30.

The time consumed in negotiations was ample to have concluded mutually satisfactory agreements, had the steel companies bargained with the union in good faith toward a reasonable and honorable settlement.

Unfortunately, a settlement has been road-blocked by the companies' adamant insistence upon their proposal for a fixed five-year agreement, with benefits each year less than the union had negotiated in past years.

The union in rejecting this proposal as too little, too late and too long, made it clear that, on its part, the union, without stipulating any prior conditions, was ready and willing to negotiate a reasonable settlement.

At the eleventh hour, the twelve leading companies in the industry now propose a contract for a four-year, four-month term with a proportionate reduction in the already rejected companies' first proposal. The companies condition their present offer with a proposal that the parties continue to negotiate beyond midnight, June 30, and that the contract be extended indefinitely subject to termination upon seventy-two hours' notice.

The companies' present offer meets none of the union's reasoned objections to their original proposal. An indefinite extension, subject to termination on seventy-two hours' notice, will create instability and intensify present tensions to the detriment of the industry, its employes and the public.

The present situation calls for a settlement—not continued procrastination. Regretfully, and due to no fault of the union, the deadline is upon us. The union is conscious of its responsibilities to the nation. It is prepared to meet these responsibilities four-square and not by indirection.

Accordingly, the union stands willing to extend the present labor agreements until midnight, 12:01 A.M., July 16—an extension of fifteen days—with the understanding, of course, that the benefits provided in the settlement which would otherwise be applicable on July 1, 1956, shall be retroactive to that date.

The union's negotiators, without stipulating any prior conditions, will continue to negotiate with the representatives of the companies with the sole end of arriving at a reasonable and honorable settlement.

COMPANIES' REJECTION

Our letter of today asked you to advise the companies whether you would strike June 30, midnight, in accordance with your union's traditional policy of "no contract, no work." It proposed postponement of the threatened strike and continuation of negotiations beyond midnight, June 30.

It also requested you to agree to give the companies at least seventy-two hours prior written notice of any strike beginning at any time after June 30, so as to avoid the necessity for curtailing operations beginning at midnight tonight in anticipation of a strike at the termination of our agreements on June 30.

We have received your reply. In it you propose as a condition an extension of our existing agreements to July 16, 1956, that benefits which may be resolved in our bargaining and which are applicable shall be retroactive to the June 30, midnight termination date of the present agreements.

The companies, while desirous of continuing the negotiations and postponement of the strike, cannot, nevertheless, accept the retroactivity condition which you attach to your willingness to extend. Continued negotiations should be conducted with equal pressure on both parties, a condition not present when the union is guaranteed by retroactivity that no matter how it may delay agreements it has nothing to lose.

We agree that the present situation most certainly calls for settlement rather than continued procrastination. Today we tried to meet one of your main objections to the companies' proposals by offering to reduce the term by two-thirds of a year. Our proposals were fair, reasonable and in the employe, company and national interest. Under them employes are assured of steady and orderly progress without loss due to strikes.

The companies must disclaim responsibility for failure to reach agreement. The union has blocked settlement; blocked settlement by insistence upon extravagant concessions far beyond fairness and reason.

Tonight we face a crisis in the steel industry—and the union, not the companies, is responsible. It is not too late, however, for the union to depart from its position. If it does, that crisis can at least be deferred—perhaps completely eliminated—should negotiations proceed as the companies have suggested, without the retroactivity condition proposed by you which would put a further premium on procrastination.

UNION'S COMMENT

You asked us for an extension. We agreed; you rejected. Of course we ask for retroactivity. Otherwise we would be working during the next contract year for last year's wages. This, you know, would not be fair, equitable or customary.

We want no premium on procrastination. There has been too much on your part. We stand ready to negotiate a settlement with you tomorrow and to remain in continuous session to complete all necessary documents. We have met this time schedule before. We can do it now. All that is necessary is for the industry to stop this nonsense of a four-year, four-months contract for reduced benefits.

Despite contrary newspaper reports, this is the only offer now before us.

We give you a plain option. Negotiate and conclude a settlement tomorrow —or, if you feel additional time is necessary extend for such part of fifteen days as may be required to conclude a settlement with customary retroactivity. Your rejection of both alternatives will make it crystal clear that the companies are intent upon forcing a shutdown in steel production. The nation will suffer from this, your stockholders will suffer from this and so will your employes.

There is no need for a crisis in steel—but the steel companies are forcing one on the nation.

From The New York Times, June 29

The Eisenhower Administration announced yesterday that it planned no action to head off a national steel shutdown at midnight tomorrow.

The Administration's position was made known in Washington by James P. Mitchell, Secretary of Labor. He spoke as a three-hour negotiating conference between industry and union leaders here "got nowhere" in efforts to prevent a stoppage by 650,000 workers in mills that turn out nine-tenths of the country's steel.

With the banking of blast furnaces already well advanced in most steel centers, the negotiators again will attempt to forge an agreement this morning. But yesterday's developments engendered no hope of success.

Indeed, the chief concern of each side now seemed to be to convince the public that a shutdown would be the other side's fault.

David J. McDonald, president of the United Steelworkers of America, asserted that the union considered the shutting down of the mills a "lockout" by the industry.

His assertion presaged an attempt by the union members to claim unemployment insurance benefits in states that bar benefits to strikers but give them to workers whose idleness is caused by their employers. Industry spokesmen made it plain that they would oppose such payments from state funds.

Admiral Ben Moreell, retired, chairman of the Jones & Laughlin Steel Corporation, went on a coast-to-coast television network of the Columbia Broadcasting System last night to deny that the industry had conspired to force a shutdown.

Moreell's address

At this moment steel furnaces all over the nation are being banked. This must be done to protect employes against the danger of accidents and to prevent severe damage to costly equipment if the strike, called by the Steelworkers Union, begins fifty hours from now.

Next Saturday, at midnight, steel production in America will virtually have ceased. This will affect every man, woman and child in the country. That is why I want to talk to you tonight—to explain the facts of this dispute, as I see them.

It has been charged that the steel companies have conspired to force this shutdown. That charge is not true. The steel companies of America exist to produce steel—not to lie idle.

In fact, the mere shutting down of our furnaces means an enormous loss to the companies. And even if a strike were to last only twelve hours—as it did last year—the companies would lose millions upon millions of dollars. So, it stands to reason that it isn't the companies who want this strike.

To prevent this strike, the companies have been bargaining almost continuously for the past month. Let us review these negotiations. But first, let us look at the present status of the steelworker.

He is now among the highest paid industrial workers in the nation. His wages alone average more than $5,200 a year. His average hourly earnings are already 52 cents above those of the average in all American manufacturing industries. They are substantially higher than those of the automobile and electrical industries.

During the past six years the steelworker's earnings increased by an average of more than 80 cents an hour. No other group of industrial workers has gained so rapidly during this period.

Since 1940 total employment costs per hour of the steel companies have risen each year at a compound rate of 7.5 per cent. At the same time our total costs, including wages, materials, services and all the things we buy, have gone up even more.

Actually, they have gone up at a compound annual rate of 8.2 per cent. From personal experience I can tell you that the only source of revenue which my company has is our customers. And to meet these rapidly rising costs—to pay our bills—we have had to increase prices.

But figures published by the United States Department of Labor show that prices of steel products during this period have gone up only at a rate a little less than 5.5 per cent a year, compounded. And this did not fully cover our increased costs. Had it done so, our profit rate would be the same today as it was in 1940. But it is not.

Not long ago the profits earned by the steel companies were published. This record shows that in 1940 these profits amounted to 8.1 cents on each dollar of sales. Last year they were only 7.8 cents—a decline of a little over 3 per cent.

That was the situation a month ago when the union leaders formally presented their original proposals. Without going into detail, I will merely say that they would have increased our employment costs immediately by about 25 per cent.

An abrupt increase of such large amount would have set an inflationary employment cost pattern for all of American industry, and so would have had no lasting benefits. In fact, it would have done great harm.

Certainly our total manufacturing costs would have risen in like degree, as they always have, following every wage increase, and certainly in my company our prices would have had to do the same.

Faced by these demands, the steel companies realized that they had two responsibilities which were in conflict. The first was their responsibility to the nation; to retard—as much as is within the power of any one industry—the inflationary spiral which has become almost chronic.

The second was to meet, as fully as practicable, the basic proposals of the union and thus avoid, if possible, a strike which would disrupt the entire national economy. So, in an effort to reconcile these two grave responsibilities, instead of thinking in terms of a single year, we offered to spread increases in wages and benefits over the next five years. But the total offer was the largest single package ever advanced by the companies in the history of the steel industry.

Instead of an inflationary employment cost rise in one short year—the benefits of which could quickly disappear—the companies' proposal would have dispersed the effects of these added costs in an orderly pattern over a five-year period.

The corresponding increases in total steel manufacturing costs would also have been distributed, and the economy would have been able to adjust itself gradually to the increased employment-cost levels.

Now let us look at the companies' offer. In the first year, it would have increased the companies' employment costs by an average of 17⅔ cents per hour worked. Further increases in wages and benefits, in each successive year, would have lifted this cost increase to 65 cents an hour in the fifth year. Here is where that 65 cents per hour would go:

¶ The figure at the top—36½ cents—is the total of the average direct increases in the wage rates that would be paid to steelworkers.

¶ Then the worker also would get other direct cash benefits amounting to an additional 16.8 cents per hour. These benefits would include increased vacation pay, increased holiday pay, a premium for Sunday work, increased premium pay on the afternoon and night shifts, and the increases in incentive and overtime payments that would result automatically from the rising wage rates throughout the five-year period.

Thus 53 cents an hour would go directly into the worker's pay envelope.

¶ The third figure—11.7 cents—is additional cash which would be paid out by the companies for the worker's benefit. Included here are increased insurance coverage, larger pensions, and bigger contributions for social security. Also included is the cost of a new kind of security for American steelworkers—Supplemental Unemployment Benefits, to help tide them over periods of layoff.

These Supplemental Unemployment Benefits, coupled with the sums which laid-off workers could collect through state unemployment insurance payments, would be designed to give the eligible steelworker 65 per cent of his take-home pay for a period up to fifty-two weeks if he is laid off or discharged for lack of work.

The total cost, as you see, adds up to 65 cents an hour.

Let's take a look at what these increased wages and benefits would mean to the steel worker:

¶ In the first year—beginning next Saturday at midnight—the average increases paid by the companies for the benefit of the steelworker would amount to $350. And this $350, of course, would continue throughout the remaining four years.

¶ In the second year, there would be an additional increase of $280 in these wages and benefits.

¶ In each of the third and fourth years would come a further increase worth $220.

¶ And in the final year, the increase would amount to $230.

The average total increase paid for the benefit of the steelworker each year is shown on the bottom line—starting with $350 in the first year and mounting to $1,300 a year in the fifth year. And at the end of the five-year period, the steelworker would have received in equivalent wages and benefits $4,200 more than he would receive under the present contract. This is for each worker, on the average. When applied to all workers covered by the contract, this would mean a total increase in employment costs to the companies of nearly $2,333,000,000.

The companies were willing to commit themselves to this added outlay because they have confidence in the future of America. We recognize the hazards involved in this long-range commitment if there should be a falling-off of business. But there is no way to protect the companies from such hazards. It is a risk we are willing to assume.

But when we presented this offer to the union, they quickly pointed out a major hazard to the steelworker—the hazard of inflation. A rapid rise in the cost of living, they said, could wipe out these gains entirely.

Conceding this point, the companies amended their proposal to include assurance that any increase in the cost of living, which might occur during the life of the contract, would be compensated by additional increases in wages.

With this added protection, the package offered to the steelworkers represents the largest increase in actual purchasing power they have ever attained in any consecutive five-year period of the union's history.

Would you like an inflation-proof wage increase every year for the next five years?

We believe that this offer is a fair one. We believe that five years of peace in the steel industry—with no strikes to drain away the workers' savings; no strikes to halt the companies' expansion and improvement programs; no strikes to threaten those industries, large and small, which depend on a steady supply of steel; and no strikes to interrupt the orderly march of progress throughout our economy—that this kind of industrial peace would be a boon to all of us and to our nation.

But the union promptly rejected this offer. While expressing willingness to bargain on other points, and making concessions which represented only small retreats from their original proposals, they refused to accept a five-year contract on any terms. And for many weary days a stalemate resulted, during which they have accused the companies of presenting a "take-it-or-leave-it" ultimatum.

Yesterday, in a final attempt to prevent a nation-wide strike, the companies proposed an extension of the strike deadline. And we further offered to shorten the contract by eight months with corresponding adjustments in the scale of wages and benefits provided in our original proposal.

This period was suggested because the present pension agreement, if extended by the customary three-year period, would expire on Oct. 31, 1960— fifty-two months from now. All phases of the contract would then be re-openable for negotiation at the same time.

The union leaders flatly rejected the companies' offer, but agreed to extend the strike deadline until midnight, July 15, provided that any benefits which were scheduled to begin with the new contract would be dated back to begin July 1.

The companies had to decline the union's counter-proposal, because every day that the plants continued to operate under such a retroactive agreement would leave the companies facing an additional unknown and potentially excessive cost. Thus, with every passing day, the pressure on the companies to accept the union demands would increase—while the union, on its part, would be under no pressure whatsoever to reach a speedy settlement of the issues.

We now have less than fifty hours in which to reconcile our wide differences. That is not an easy task.

Yet, between men of good will, agreement could be reached within that time. I believe that reasonable men can always settle honest differences. But, in saying this, I must repeat what I regard as the obligation of the steel companies to the American people: first, to retard, if possible, the inflationary spiral of rising costs; second, to meet the legitimate needs and aspirations of our workers, and third, to provide steel of qualities and quantities adequate to meet the nation's requirements.

Within the framework of these obligations I can assure you that the steel companies will do their utmost to reach an agreement that will be fair and in the best interests of every one of us.

McDonald's reply

Tonight Admiral Moreell made an address to the American people on behalf of the twelve leading steel companies.

In his address, Admiral Moreell pointed out that at this very moment steel furnaces all over the nation are being banked. He said that we now have less than fifty hours in which to reconcile the differences between the steel industry and the Steelworkers Union. Yet, he added, "Between men of goodwill, agreement could be reached within that time. I believe that reasonable men can always settle honest differences."

I agree with Admiral Moreell. Agreement can be reached in time to avert a shutdown in steel. Reasonable men can settle honest differences. I regard Admiral Moreell to be a reasonable man. I trust he so regards me.

I propose that the differences between the steel industry and the steel union be settled. To this end, I invite Admiral Moreell, chairman of Jones & Laughlin Steel Corporation; Roger Blough, chairman of United States Steel Corporation; Eugene Grace, chairman of Bethlehem Steel Company; Charles White, president, Republic Steel Corporation; Tom Millsop, president, National Steel Corporation, and the chief executive officers of the remaining twelve companies to meet with me and my fellow-officers tomorrow morning at the Roosevelt Hotel in New York City for the purpose of reconciling our differences and, as men of goodwill, reaching agreement.

From The New York Times, June 30

Steel negotiations failed again yesterday as mill shutdowns went forward in preparation for a full blackout of steel production at midnight tonight. . . .

However, there were reports that influential leaders in other industries were attempting to find a "face-saver" that would make possible a full-fledged peace or a truce to allow continued negotiations. No immediate signs of success attended these endeavors. . . .

David J. McDonald, the union's president, asserted that its rank-and-file members in the mill towns were "hot—really hot" against acceptance of the industry terms. However, company officials contended that there was no enthusiasm for a walkout and that the workers would go out reluctantly at the union's call.

Union statement

Today the steel companies across the nation are banking their furnaces. Instead of a settlement, we are confronted with an industry decision to shut down operations.

Negotiations between these companies and the union began in Pittsburgh on May 28 and 29. At that time the union presented proposals to bring its contracts with the companies up to date and to provide for the employes a reasonable share in the tremendous, record-breaking prosperity which the steel companies are enjoying and a reasonable reward for the large increase in the productivity of their employes!

Following the meetings in Pittsburgh, the officers of the international union met in New York in almost daily session with the representatives of the big three steel companies.

Finally, on June 13, two weeks after negotiations had begun, these representatives of the industry made their first proposal. The essential element in this proposal was that the union agree to a rigid, closed, five-year contract. In return, the companies offered wage increases far less than the union has negotiated in past years and far less than the employes are entitled to on the basis of the industry's record-breaking profits and the employes' record-breaking productivity.

They coupled this inadequate wage offer with a proposal to increase fringe benefits so little that, even by July 1, 1961, they would still be far below the level of benefits generally prevailing in American industry at this moment.

They proposed a supplemental unemployment benefit plan in name only. Their plan was so loaded with newly invented gimmicks that practically no benefits could be paid to our members.

The other fringes offered were not only inadequate and substandard, but were effective at dates far in the future.

The union's proposal for premium pay for Saturday and Sunday work—pay which workers in almost every industry in America now receive—was virtually denied. Instead, the companies offered, effective three years from now, to pay 10 cents an hour (1/25th time) as a premium for the Sunday work which is generally paid for at double time in America. They denied completely our request for premium pay for work on Saturdays and holidays.

The companies also offered an improved insurance program containing benefits actually costing $2.25 per employe per month. But they insisted that in order to receive this $2.25 improvement, the employes should increase their own contributions by $2.55 per month.

To cap their offer, the companies insisted that we renegotiate our pension agreement, which does not expire until next year, so as to extend it until 1961. In return, they offered a pension plan which would not expire until 1987—thirty years from now—provide minimum pension benefits equal to those now in effect under contracts negotiated last year by the union with the can industry.

The companies' total offer, based on their own figures, was worth no more than 28.5 cents per hour on the average for a five-year term. But the companies, more intent on advertising than on bargaining with their employees, advertised across the land that ultimately, in 1961, the offer would cost them 65 cents per hour—a wholly unjustified figure, prepared solely to mislead our membership and the public.

The International Wage Policy Committee, on Friday, June 15, unanimously rejected the inadequate proposals and the unreasonable demands of the companies, and instructed the union's officers immediately to resume negotiations with the representatives of the big three steel companies to see if a fair and reasonable settlement, based upon the union's constructive proposals, could be achieved. Such meetings took place. But the company representatives took an adamant position. They said flatly that they demanded, as a condition of settlement, that the union agree to accept their shockingly inadequate economic proposal for a five-year term. They said that their first proposal was a "take-it-or-leave-it" proposition.

Again the matter was brought before the International Wage Policy Committee on June 18. And again the committee unanimously rejected the companies' wage and contract proposal, and authorized our president, David J. McDonald, and the other international officers to take whatever action was appropriate under the circumstances.

Our officers were not content merely to reject the companies' proposals. They sought in every conceivable manner to find a method of negotiating a reasonable settlement. On June 19 and 20, each of the union's full negotiating committees met separately with the companies to see if a fair and honorable settlement could be negotiated. Each company took the same unyielding and adamant position. And each of the committees again expressed the union's desire to negotiate a reasonable settlement if the companies would eliminate the pre-conditions which they had established to road-block such a settlement.

When negotiations with the individual companies failed, the officers again resumed their meetings with the representatives of the big three companies. Again these representatives of the industry reiterated their take-it-or-leave-it position.

Finally, on June 27, a month after negotiations began and two weeks after the companies made their obviously unacceptable first proposal, the companies proposed that the contracts be extended indefinitely, subject to a seventy-two hour termination notice.

If the union agreed to this, they said that they would be agreeable to reducing the five-year term of their proposal by a total of eight months, with, they said, "of course, a proportionate reduction of benefits." Instead of moving toward a reasonable settlement with the union, for this four-year four-month agreement, they proposed to take away some of the benefits which they had already offered.

Again, the representatives of the union sought to avert a crisis. They proposed a fifteen-day extension of the contract, but with the understanding that the benefits provided in any agreed-upon settlement which, were it not for the extension, would have been applicable on July 1, 1956, should be made effective retroactively as of that date.

Again, the companies said "No." Instead, they proposed to take away even the inadequate increases which they had offered to make effective on July 1 by refusing the fair, equitable and customary provision for retroactivity. They proposed to profit by their own delay by asking steel workers to continue to work during the next contract year for last year's wages.

The union's negotiators, in a final effort to prevent a crisis, called for still further meetings with the companies. Again, in meetings just yesterday, the companies rejected any suggestions that they retreat from their adamant position that the Steelworkers Union either agree to their take-it-or-leave-it offer or continue to work at last year's wages.

Steel production is now coming to a halt. The companies have so willed it.

We, the International Wage Policy Committee, reaffirm the desire of the union to reach a fair and reasonable settlement with the companies.

We commend our president, David J. McDonald, for his untiring efforts to persuade the companies to join with us in the search for such a settlement. We assert again our offer to engage in genuine give-and-take collective bargaining, without pre-conditions or other artificial road-blocks to mutual agreement.

Our cause is just. Our union is strong and united. Our determination is firm. We shall succeed.

Companies' telegram

Your telegrams to executives of the undersigned companies inviting them to meet with you for the purpose of endeavoring to reach a settlement in the current contract negotiations with your union are hereby acknowledged.

For the past three weeks the negotiations with you have been conducted by the authorized representatives of three of the companies. Those representatives have been, and are now, in constant consultation with the officials of all of our companies and the position that they have taken in the negotiations fully reflects the views and policies of the undersigned companies and they have our full support. No useful purpose can possibly be served by changing the present negotiating procedures.

We are just as anxious as you are to reach an agreement in the interests of employes, customers, stockholders and the public. Negotiations with the representatives of the three companies should be continued.

From The New York Times, July 9

Lay-offs in industries dependent upon steel are expected to near 100,000 this week as the national steel strike extends its grip on the economy. Federal mediators plan to renew their contact with industry and union leaders by telephone today.

But there is little belief in either Washington or Pittsburgh that the second week of the walkout of 650,000 steel workers will bring any real headway toward a settlement.

With steel output down to 11 or 12 per cent of capacity, the walkout and the preliminary banking of blast furnaces already have cost 2,500,000 tons of steel. It is estimated that the shutdown will bring idleness this week to 50,000 coal miners, railroad workers, truck drivers and other workers in allied industries. An equal number were laid off last week.

From The New York Times, July 13

WASHINGTON, July 12—The Administration is not exercised at this point about the general economic effect of the steel strike.

Top economists in the Government said today that a three-week or four-week strike would cause no important damage to the economy. The general expectation is that the strike will run at least that long.

Sinclair Weeks, Secretary of Commerce, said that the "impact has been hardly noticeable" despite the twelve-day-old strike of 650,000 steel workers and the lay-off of others in transportation and related industries.

Industry advertisement, New York Times, July 13

WOULD YOU LIKE LABOR PEACE PLUS AN ANNUAL RAISE FOR FIVE YEARS?

That is what the steelworkers were offered by their companies—
plus protection against increased living costs

Steel mills throughout the country have been closed down by a strike called at midnight, June 30, by union leaders. Each week the striking steelworkers are losing more than $50,000,000 in wages. The country is losing about 2,000,000 tons weekly in steel production.

This strike was in the face of a package offer by steel companies which would give employees and their families a bigger increase in actual buying power the next five years than they have had over any consecutive five-year period. It included the following proposals:

1 Increases in hourly wage rates every year for five years, ranging from 6 cents to 12 cents, and averaging 7.3 cents for each of the years.

2 A cost-of-living adjustment to protect the wages of employees against the effect of rising prices.

3 A supplemental unemployment benefit plan for employees with three years or more of service to help tide them over periods of layoff up to 52 weeks.

4 Many other fringe benefits including improvements in insurance and pensions, holidays and vacations.

5 A contract providing progress, stability and labor peace for five years.

Those increases would cost the companies 17⅔ cents more per employee hour worked in the first year and by the fifth year the increases would reach a total cost of 65 cents per hour more than at present. Any cost of living adjustment would be in addition to these costs.

This amounts to a total cost increase of $2⅓ billions over the five-year period.

The steelworker is already among the highest paid industrial workers in the entire nation. His wages alone have recently averaged $100 a week, or $20 a week above the average in all manufacturing industries.

The companies were deeply hopeful that by making this offer early in the negotiations, a strike could be avoided.

But at the same time the companies are keenly conscious of their public obligation to retard—as much as is within the power of any one industry—a new inflationary spiral.

This could be accomplished by spreading increased wage costs in the industry over a long-term, no-strike contract.

Would not the best interest of steelworkers, the industry, and the country be served by acceptance of this offer?

United States Steel Corporation	Armco Steel Corporation
Bethlehem Steel Company	Great Lakes Steel Corporation
Republic Steel Corporation	Colorado Fuel & Iron Corporation
Jones & Laughlin Steel Corporation	Wheeling Steel Corporation
Youngstown Sheet & Tube Company	Pittsburgh Steel Company
Inland Steel Company	Allegheny Ludlum Steel Corporation

From Business Week, July 14

A STRIKE THAT FEELS LIKE A PICNIC

Like Sleeping Beauty, the steel industry lay in its second week of trance.

"Damndest strike I ever saw," said a grizzled city cop in Ambridge, Pa., after he had jawed for a while with the pickets and the plant protection men bunched around American Bridge Co.'s gates. "Those guys are making up a pool on which Pirate gets the most hits in the All-Star game."

Memories are short; most strikes nowadays start in a holiday spirit, camaraderie between the men on the line outside and the housekeeping crews inside are a characteristic of their early stages. The bitterness and rough stuff comes later. Even so, the big 1956 steel strike was strange.

Listless. The fruitless bargaining that preceded it was listless, almost lazy. Government mediators gave the conferences a wide berth. There were no lengthy sessions, no burning of the midnight oil. None of the negotiators missed a lunch, dinner, or was late for cocktails. Nor did they raise their voices. When bargaining dead-ended, the statements from the industry and union antagonists hardly satisfied the name-calling conventions.

Then, after the strike was on, union and industry negotiators returned from New York to their respective offices in Pittsburgh and just waited. Toward the end of the first week, Joseph Finnegan, head of the federal mediation service, turned up in town with two of his aides. They had separate conversations with union Pres. David McDonald and U.S. Steel Vice-Pres. John Stephens. When the federal men got back to Washington, they reported that they were just getting "background." For this week, more separate conversations in Washington and a joint meeting in Pittsburgh. Thus far, the government, like the parties themselves, was being very relaxed.

Biding Time. Not that the Administration was indifferent. Its appraisal of the situation—by Labor Secy. James P. Mitchell and Treas.-Secy. George M. Humphrey, as well as by its mediators—convinced the Administration that this week was too early for pressure. It bided its time, waiting for a sign that either party was willing to do a little bending. The industry's offer of an average 7.3¢ a year wage increase, fringe benefits, and a long-term contract still stood against the union's adamant rejection. And the belief was widespread that if steel raised its offer by a nickel and made concessions on the fringes it could settle for a three-year contract.

Meanwhile, the country gaped at what was probably the biggest strike ever patrolled by such a handful of pickets. There wasn't a melee anywhere. The only casualty reports were from Youngstown, where some Youngstown Sheet & Tube Co. pickets had removed their shirts and blistered badly under the hot July sun. There was plenty of parking space on the main street of Aliquippa the Saturday after payday. Gary was a ghost town, with an estimated 10,000 having taken off for the Michigan and Wisconsin woods. Hardware stores in all the mill cities did a rushing business. Their big items: Paints and window screening as strike-idle workers got jobs around the house.

Sub-Surface. But while the picket lines were peaceful, they were buzzing. Visits of BUSINESS WEEK reporters to picket lines in towns from Provo, Utah, to Sparrows Point, Md., found animated discussion everywhere, and revealed a simplified, but firm, picture of what the strike was all about in the strikers' minds.

First, the union seems to have succeeded in convincing its rank and file that the industry wanted the strike to cut down its customers' inventories. Again and again, BUSINESS WEEK found expert expressions among pickets on steel supply and demand. A Bethlehem Steel picket's views were typical. "Look, Mac," he declared, like a teacher lecturing a backward pupil, "it's smart business. The orders weren't coming in, see. Everybody in the plant knew that. So shut her down. Then what happens? Boy, are they pouring in now. I told the wife not to worry. There'll be plenty of overtime when we go back."

Second, the premium pay for Sunday work seems to be, for the pickets at least, the big dramatic issue. It's easy to understand, easy to get a sense of grievance about. A laid-off railroadman was kicking it around with some Jones & Laughlin pickets. "It just ain't right," the switchman was told, "a man should be able to go to church with his wife and family on Sunday."

"When did you go to church last?" the switchman asked the most vociferous of the pickets.

"What the hell has that got to do with it," came the response as the other pickets nodded and bristled, "it's the principle of the thing."

Third, the long-term contract issue gets an interpretation on the picket line that it did not have in the collective bargaining. At more than one plant gate, reporters found strong talk about "automation," variously pronounced and understood. "If we were tied up with a five-year contract," a Republic Steel striker stated solemnly, "everything would be automation before we could do anything about it." Significantly, it has been the auto union, not the Steelworkers, that has been sounding the alarms on automation, but some of it seems to have penetrated the mills.

Fourth, there's a lot of political talk on the lines. That's natural enough, given an election year and all the portable radios blaring about Pres. Eisenhower's decision to run again. And it's Democrat talk, of course. "They'll set this up so Ike can settle it, like they did with Korea," an Inland Steel picket says, and none of his colleagues resting in the shade of a shed in Indiana Harbor disagree. Elsewhere, politically minded pickets who double as steelworkers and party wardheelers remind their fellows that in previous strikes Roosevelt or Truman was "in there fighting" for labor.

Over-all, however, the attitudes of the strikers were low-keyed and unemotional.

From The New York Times, July 19

PITTSBURGH, July 18—Industry and union leaders received a blunt warning today that President Eisenhower expected them to end the crippling tie-up of the steel industry within a week.

The parties were told that the White House would take action that neither side would like if no progress toward settling the walkout of 650,000 steel workers came out of Government-sponsored negotiations here.

Reliable sources reported that the settle-or-else warning was brought from Washington by Joseph F. Finnegan, director of the Federal Mediation and Conciliation Service. He flew here direct from a White House meeting with the President and key members of the Cabinet.

Letter sent on July 22 to members of the Cabinet, members of Congress, and other Federal and state officials by President McDonald of the Steelworkers

Dear Sir:

Since midnight of June 30 the basic steel industry has been idle because of the decision of the companies to shut down operations when labor contracts with the United Steelworkers of America terminated.

Instead of engaging in good faith bargaining with the union prior to June 30 to work out new contracts which would meet the needs of the employes and provide them with an adequate share in the tremendous prosperity of the industry, the companies forced 650,000 of their employes and thousands in other industries into unemployment with consequent harm to the economy.

We of the United Steelworkers did not want this shutdown to happen. We did everything in our power to prevent it. We made reasonable proposals for an honorable settlement which would be fair to the employes, the stockholders and the public. However, we were confronted by a totally inadequate "take-it-or-leave-it" proposition from the industry.

We are not indulging in wild charges, but stating our sober conviction, when we say that the leaders of the steel industry forced the shutdown—for ulterior reasons which they must be better able to explain than anyone else. You will recall that the Steelworkers Union, just before contract talks with the industry spokesmen were broken off, made a forthright offer to extend our agreements for fifteen days with customary retroactivity to provide more time for negotiations. The industry showed its true purpose of forcing a shutdown when it flatly rejected this offer.

Thus we stand at the present impasse—with time ticking away, with a needless great loss in production, in wages, in purchasing power to keep the wheels of our economic machine turning.

I realize that you, as a public-spirited citizen, would like to know more of the facts on this situation than can be found in the newspapers. Ours is a responsible union. We believe that you—and the public in general—have a right to know the facts because all of us have a stake in the outcome. It is in recognition of your right to know that the United Steelworkers of America has prepared two well-documented studies of the facts and real issues involved in our present dispute with the steel industry. For it is only through a study of the clear facts that the issues can be reasonably appraised and intelligent negotiations carried on.

Unfortunately the spokesmen for the industry have not been willing to engage in genuine negotiations based on the irrefutable facts contained in these two studies. Rather, they have substituted press releases, press conferences and newspaper advertisements for genuine negotiations. Because their inadequate proposals, which they well knew the union could not accept, were handed down with a "take-it-or-leave-it" attitude which cannot be defended, they have obscured or misrepresented the facts.

So I commend, then, for your judgment, the facts in our two studies here summarized. In the one entitled "Steel and the National Economy 1956," there is a thorough analysis of the current state of the economy and the over-all effect of the steel industry on the national economy, with special emphasis on the question of inflation. In the other study entitled "Facts on Steel: Profits, Productivity, Prices and Wages 1956," there is a detailed examination of the financial position of the industry, with significant comparisons of the relationship of profits, productivity, prices and wages.

You recall that steel industry spokesmen have sought to justify their failure to offer a reasonable wage increase by invoking the word "inflation." They said that "no increase in employment costs at this time would be in the nation's best interests . . ." since it would set off "another ruinous round of inflation." Now, there are very few people indeed who want inflation, but we sharply disagree with the industry's contention that inflation is caused by wage increases—for to say this is tantamount to saying that it is impossible for the living standards of the working population to improve at all. Indeed, any inflationary tendencies that may exist in our economy stem not from wage and salary increases, which are vitally needed, but from pricing policies of industry generally and particularly the steel industry. Let us see what our studies have to say on this and related subjects.

Steel and the national economy

The volume which addresses itself to the problem of inflation and the present state of our economy contains the following facts and essential policies:

Concern is expressed by the union as to the need to safeguard and improve the health of our economy as a whole. Note is taken of the fact that there have been some serious "soft spots" in the fabric of the economy, which has been on a plateau for some nine months. Despite precarious inventory accumulations and higher consumer debt, the full employment levels of 1952 and 1953 have not been matched. Prosperity in the last decade has been sustained by wage and salary increases and labor's rising share of the total income. (Though in steel labor's total-income share has fallen in this decade.) But labor's share in the economy, as well as in steel, has fallen in the last year and consumer purchases are lagging. Unless corrected, this could spell trouble.

With confidence in the fundamental strength of our economic system, and with faith in its potential growth, we also in this study take into account the possibilities and challenges of the years ahead. A growing labor force and rising productivity make possible a doubling of our production and our standard of living within the next twenty years. These can be achieved only if there is an active market for the goods and services we can produce.

Consumers buy five of every six dollars worth of goods and services purchased privately. Since consumer purchasing power arises largely from wages and salaries, wages and salaries must increase if economic expansion is to be resumed and a market provided for this doubled production.

Our study refutes any alleged relation between wage increases and inflation and states: "Experience has proved that wage increases have not caused inflation, that wages can be increased without prices being raised, and that rising real wages give us stable prosperity and growth."

Wage increases, says our report, lagged behind price increases in the immediate postwar and Korean inflations and obviously could not have caused inflation. The pattern of inflation is rising prices, rising real profits and lagging real wages. In the stable period since mid-1951, on the other hand, wage rates in manufacturing have risen 23 per cent, living costs less than 4 per cent and industrial prices 4 per cent. Yet total profits before taxes reached record levels in 1955.

Rising real wages, stable prices and sustained high profits, made possible by constantly increasing productivity, are thus the keys to economic stability and perpetuation of prosperity for all segments of our economy. Our study points out:

"Productivity . . . has been increasing more than 3 per cent per year. In manufacturing industries, the annual rate has been exceeding 4 per cent. Automation will increase the pace. . . . Real hourly earnings in manufacturing fell behind the rise in productivity at the time of the Korean War and have not caught up yet. This disparity must be corrected through rising real wages."

With steel a conspicuous exception, the union's report says, rising volume of business in industry generally has tended to be associated with lower profit margins per unit of production in periods of stability. This policy has yielded prosperity and high total profits. The spurt of industrial prices ahead of wages and the sharp rise in profit margins in 1955, after four years of moderate decline, spell danger and must be reversed.

Our study reveals a disturbing irresponsibility in the pricing and profit margin policies of the steel industry. Our study states:

"The contrast between the pricing policies of the steel industry and of all manufacturing industries as a whole is rather startling. Steel prices have increased proportionately with wage rates since 1947 ignoring rapidly rising productivity in its pricing policies. For all manufacturing, industrial prices increased considerably less than half as much as wage rates from 1947 to 1955.

"The steel industry does not follow the principle of higher volume and lower margins. If there is any single industry that has followed inflationary pricing practices; that has shown a disregard for the economic welfare of the country, especially relative to its key role in the economy; that has truly practiced inflation; that has the least right to hide behind the cloak of favoring a sound dollar and to contend that wage increases are inflationary; it is the steel industry."

Before the union commenced negotiations with the industry, several steel company spokesmen had issued public statements calling for higher prices for their products. They based this mainly on the plea that price increases were required to finance expansion. Our study says of this:

"Contentions by leaders of the steel industry and other industries that prices must be increased so that there will be more profits with which to finance expansion are astounding. Raising prices to secure funds for new plant and equipment, in effect, forces the consumer to put up the money for new plants for the benefit of existing stockholders. The consumer gets nothing for his forced 'investment.' The opportunity for American citizens to participate in the growth of American industry is denied when expansion is financed entirely through exorbitant profits, rather than security flotations."

Facts on steel: profits, productivity, prices and wages

Now let me refer you to the second of our two economic studies, which deals with the financial position of the steel industry in relation to industry as a whole and in relation to profits, wages, prices and—of special significance—productivity in relation to all of these factors.

Our study emphasizes productivity as the key to the entire question of wages, prices, profits and the health of the over-all economy.

"It is now commonly accepted that, over long periods, wage gains and rising living standards must come largely from increased productivity, i. e., rising output per man-hour," states our report. "With this concept the union has no quarrel as long as one prior condition is met—namely, that the income shares as between management and investors on the one hand and labor on the other . . . are fair and equitable. There is no such equitable sharing in the steel industry today."

Here is what our analysis of the productivity record in steel reveals:

Taking note of the great, continuing rise in productivity for many years, we observe especially "the sharp acceleration in the productivity rate in the most recent years."

For example, productivity in the steel industry currently has been running at a rate 4.7 per cent higher than in 1955. And the rate in 1955 was a phenomenal 11.2 per cent above 1954. In short, steelworkers are producing more and more steel per year, . . . productivity in steel has run well in excess of the increase in the economy as a whole and in manufacturing industries.

Yet what does a comparision show us? Taking the years 1939-1956 (more than sixteen years), we find the "real" productivity increase in the steel industry to be 68.8 per cent. For the same period, the "real" straight time average hourly earnings of the steelworker rose only 47.1 per cent.

It is evident that increasing productivity is the key to providing higher wages, higher standards of living, broader and more stable prosperity—and all without the need to boost prices beyond reason and without harm to the rightful profits of the industry and its investors. For if the millions of workers in industry do not receive a fair share of these benefits of increased productivity, then our free enterprise economy cannot continue to function. And it is in this area that the leaders of the steel industry have, so far, been far too backward and short-sighted.

Our study of the industry contains interesting revelations as to steel profits. Far from being in dire straits, profit-wise, the steel corporations under examination have been showing a 1956 profit rate of 15.3 per cent higher than last year and—believe it or not—107.4 per cent higher than in 1954! These are profits before taxes, and it should be remembered that wage increases are offset from profits before, not after taxes. As to profits after taxes, you will find that these companies have been reaping—at the 1956 rate—net profits 13.1 per cent higher than in 1955 and 95.6 per cent higher than in 1954.

That is not all of the story, however, for any such gain in profits has to be compared to profits in other lines of manufacturing to make real sense out of the comparison. You will find in our study that such a comparison shows that the steel industry has done very well indeed.

Take a look at this, if you will, from the point of view of profits as a share of the "sales dollar," which is a favorite approach of many companies. What we discover is this:

While net profits as a share of the sales dollar in the steel industry went up from 6.2 cents in 1947 to 7.9 cents in 1956 the record shows that net profits for all manufacturing companies went down from 5.7 cents in 1947 to 4.3 cents in 1956.

And these figures, by the way, do not at all mean that companies in other manufacturing lines are in bad condition, profit-wise, or are ill-managed. Rather, it means simply that with increased productivity and higher volume of business these companies are taking less profit per dollar of sales. In contrast to this, the steel industry has been siphoning off more and more profit from each and every sales dollar—instead of passing on more of the benefits of increased productivity and high-level sales to their employes and their customers.

You will find, too, a striking contrast in the rising size of dividend payments by the steel companies, whose dividends more than tripled between 1947 and 1956 while the dividends from all corporations were not quite doubled.

This study discloses, as does our other study, that the pricing policies of the steel industry have shown little concern for the welfare of the public. Traditionally the industry has sought to justify price increases as being necessitated by wage increases, increased materials costs, alleged "too low" profit margins, and more recently, the "need" to finance expansion out of profits. We have already seen from our studies that profit margins certainly are not "too low" and that the concept of financing expansion out of profits is untenable and in contradiction to the traditional system of obtaining expansion capital through flotation of securities.

The facts in our study likewise contradict the industry's assertions that increased wages and materials costs have necessitated price increases. The industry has increased prices out of all proportion to increased costs. For each $1 increase in labor costs since 1945, exorbitant price increases have yielded $3.19 in additional revenues. The figures on materials costs are equally startling. Materials costs since 1947 have risen about 28 per cent, but steel prices in the same period have risen 78.2 per cent—an excess of price increases over cost increases of nearly 3 to 1.

A central and overriding fact relative to the current dispute which emerges from our study of the steel industry is the ability of the industry to absorb a truly substantial wage increase without a price increase. This is due to the relatively small portion of total costs represented by wage costs—about one-third only—and to the great profitability of the industry.

Within the framework of its 1956 operations, the steel industry could absorb for a full year a wage "cost" increase which would meet the needs of its employes, forego a price increase, and end up with net profits comparable to the huge profits of prior years. The return on net worth would still be nearly double the fair and reasonable rate of 6 per cent—and the return on sales would be well above the 4.3c for all manufacturing corporations in 1956.

The picture becomes even more overwhelming when we realize that the foregoing figures are based on an assumption of no increase in productivity. Clearly, even a modest productivity increase of 4 or 5 per cent will facilitate the industry's ability to absorb wage increases without increasing prices and still end up with enormous profits.

What does all of this prove? Certainly not that the industry should not make good profits nor that the stockholders should not receive good dividends. Rather, what it demonstrates is that the steel companies can well afford, beyond the shadow of a doubt, to meet the Steelworkers' proposal for a substantial wage increase and the other benefits we ask for our members and that they can do so without raising prices.

The Steelworkers Union presented reasonable, practical and justifiable proposals to the steel industry.

We asked for a substantial wage increase which is vitally needed to permit steelworkers to improve their living standards, to share in the industry's record prosperity and productivity which they have greatly helped to fashion, and to provide them with the increased purchasing power needed for a prosperous and expanding economy.

We asked for Sunday premium pay at double time and Saturday premium pay at time and one-half in line with the predominant practice in American industry.

We asked for improvements in "fringe" benefits such as holidays, vacations, shift differentials and insurance.

These provisions of our contracts have fallen far behind practices now prevalent in American industry as indicated by the following table taken from our report:

	American industry practices	Steel industry practices
Pay for Sunday work	Double time	Single time
Pay for Saturday work	Time and one-half	Single time
Paid holidays	7	6
Premium above holiday pay for work on holidays	One-half time or better	None
Vacations for:		
3 years of service	2 weeks	1 week
10 years of service	3 weeks	2 weeks
Over 15 years of service	3 or 4 weeks	3 weeks
Shift differentials:		
Evening	10¢	6¢
Night	15¢	9¢

We asked for a supplemental unemployment benefits plan to protect steel workers against the ravages of unemployment which occasionally occurs in this industry.

We asked for improvements in other contract provisions which need modernization.

Our study points out that the steel industry has refused to make a wage offer or an offer on the other contract items which even begins to meet the needs here noted. Customarily, the industry and the union have signed two-year contracts with provision for wage reopening after one year. Now the industry has demanded a closed-term, five-year contract, the provisions of which are decidedly substandard. The industry has flatly refused to make any wage or contract proposals for the customary two-year term.

The industry has advertised far and wide that the "take-it-or-leave-it package" which they have offered us, over the five-year term, would cost 65c an hour.

This industry figure, as our study proves, is propaganda rather than fact. Giving the companies the benefit of any doubt, the ultimate value of the industry's offer, when they all finally go into effect in 1961, would be 45.3 cents per hour. Moreover, the *average* benefit over the five-year term amounts only to 28.5 cents per hour since many of the offered benefits would not become effective for several years. This is much less than we have received on the average during the past ten years under one and two-year contracts.

The industry has alleged that any substantial meeting of the union's demands would:

1. represent a cost too great for the industry to bear,
2. force a large hike in steel prices,
3. be highly inflationary in steel and in the economy.

These allegations are, as our studies have shown, wholly unsupported by the facts. They are a deliberate attempt to mislead the public. It is plainly not true that increases in employment costs in steel would set off another round of inflation. Inflation is an increase in prices—and it is the companies' price policies which have an inflationary effect, not its wage policies. As has been shown above, the steel industry—unlike almost every other American industry—has refused to absorb wage increases in the past and has, instead, passed on to the consumer three times the cost of each wage increase. The steel industry—unlike almost every other American industry—has increased its profit on each dollar of sales, instead of lowering it, as volume increased. The steel industry—unlike almost every other American industry—has refused to recognize that wages should increase without a price increase when workers produce more steel for each hour they work.

In short, the steel industry can afford to meet the Union's proposals without increasing prices, and without setting off any inflationary effect whatsoever.

Not only can they afford it, but they have a responsibility to do so—in order that the benefits of increased productivity and profits shall be shared by their employes and thus keep purchasing power in balance with output to ensure a healthy economic situation.

For you will find in our study of the industry that the steel industry's share of the sales dollar in gross profit has risen from 10.9 cents in 1947 to a rate of 16.2 cents in 1956. But in shocking contrast to this, an analysis of the eleven companies on which proper information was available reveals that wages and salaries, as a share of the sales dollar, have been reduced from 40.5 cents in 1939 to 35.5 cents in 1955! In other words, as we state in our report, "the wage earner's portion of the sales dollar has grown smaller and smaller." The facts reveal, for example, that despite the hourly wage increases (plus pension and insurance improvements) in 1954 and 1955, the actual labor cost per ton of steel produced is less in 1956 than it was in 1954!

All this is, indeed, a far cry from the impression created by steel industry propaganda, with its complaints of rising "wage costs" and "too-small" profits. And, of course, the factual record of their pricing policies do not jibe with their piously expressed concern over "inflation." The facts, as our two studies prove, are that the industry's profit position has been steadily improving while its wage and salary costs have been substantially reduced.

Obviously, if such a trend as this were prevalent throughout all industry, there would spread such a gap between the output of mass production and the buying power of the consumers as to create a serious danger to the economy. There must be a balanced sharing of the benefits derived from increased productivity to keep the economy going forward.

The steel industry leaders should face the plain economic facts which are presented in our two studies and which I have outlined to you here.

Admiral Ben Moreell of Jones & Laughlin Steel Corporation, speaking in behalf of the steel industry over a nation-wide television network on June 28, said that agreement could be reached between men of good will. We in the Steelworkers concurred in that, and we still concur. Added to good will must, of course, be reason. And reason must operate within the framework of the economic facts.

The union has been willing throughout, and is willing now, to negotiate a fair and honorable settlement based on our proposals, which our studies prove are reasonable, practical and entirely justifiable. It is the plain duty of the industry, now that it has succeeded in forcing a steel shutdown, to begin—for the first time—the process of give-and-take negotiation which alone can end the present crisis.

Sincerely yours
DAVID J. MCDONALD

Memorandum prepared by a Wall Street stock brokerage firm, under date of July 24, 1956

RE: STEEL SETTLEMENT

BASIC ASSUMPTIONS

In order to gauge the impact of the expected wage settlement and subsequent price increase on the earnings of the steel industry a number of assumptions have to be made:

1. While at the time of this writing it is not known by what amounts wages and prices will be raised it appears reasonable to assume that employment costs will go up by 20¢ per hour and prices by $10 a ton on average. It may be

noted that as long as wage negotiations are in progress the industry tends to overstate the money value of a wage offer while the union is likely to understate it. Once a settlement is reached, however, both parties may be inclined to evaluate the "package" rather generously.

2. The number of man-hours that go into the production of a ton of finished steel varies from product to product, being much higher for specialty steels than for tonnage products, and fluctuates inversely with the operating rate of the individual company. Over the years the actual number of man-hours per ton of steel shipped has declined for five major steel producers. . . .

If it is assumed that 20 man-hours are needed to produce one ton of finished steel, a wage increase of 20¢ per hour raises the labor cost per ton by $4.00.

3. Higher steel wages necessarily result in higher materials cost for the steel industry as the wage rise spreads to other industries and forces up the price of raw materials for steel making, as for instance iron ore. The steel industry has traditionally taken the position that sooner or later its materials costs rise by an amount equivalent to the wage increase. A statistical comparison of employment costs and expenses for products and services shows, however, that it takes considerable time before raw materials costs catch up with the rise in wages. The following tabulation shows the relationship of the two cost factors for U.S. Steel between 1940 and 1955:

1955 in % of	Employment costs	Products and services bought
1940.	348%	378%
1950.	137	121
1952.	122	104

Furthermore, the position of the industry does not take into account that at least part of the direct and indirect cost increases following a wage rise is being offset by higher productivity. If it is assumed that the increase in materials costs will be about 50% of the wage increase, a 20¢ wage rise per hour would cause materials to go up by $2.00 per ton of finished steel produced.

ESTIMATED EFFECT ON EARNINGS

Based on these assumptions, a wage increase of 20¢ per hour and an average price rise of $10 per ton would, if in effect for a full year, increase per share earnings of the eight leading steel companies [shown on p. 368].

It may be noted that the expected earnings improvement ranges from 9% to 16% of previously estimated earnings with the highest relative benefits accruing to those companies which show the lowest profits per ton of steel produced.

		% of est. earnings before price increases
U. S. Steel	$0.90	12%
Bethlehem	2.20 [1]	12
Republic	0.85	13
Jones & Laughlin	1.30	16
National	1.03	13
Youngstown	2.19	15
Inland	1.17 [1]	12
Armco	0.62	9

[1] Assuming full conversion of convertible issues.

From an article by A. H. Raskin in The New York Times, July 24

NEW STEEL TALKS OPEN TOMORROW; PEACE HOPES RISE

Union accepts surprise call to parley here—attacks companies' price policies

A dizzying about-face by industry and union leaders resulted in a decision last night to resume negotiations to end the national steel strike.

The peace talks, which were abandoned in Pittsburgh Saturday, will be resumed in New York tomorrow. There was no official explanation from either side of the fresh attempt to settle the twenty-two-day-old walkout of 650,000 steel workers.

However, it was believed that the decision presaged a new settlement offer by the twelve major steel companies. Authoritative industry sources reported that the steel producers were prepared to give a three-year contract if union bargainers would bring down their wage and fringe demands. . . .

The renewal of peace talks came at the request of John A. Stephens, vice president of the United States Steel Corporation and chief negotiator for the industry. Mr. McDonald had been scheduled to leave Pittsburgh last night to address a series of strike rallies in major steel centers. But he canceled the tour after getting a telephone call from Mr. Stephens.

The conference arrangements were accompanied by a disclosure that company negotiators had expressed a willingness to grant a three-year agreement during the unsuccessful conferences with union leaders last week.

The companies made no official change in their pre-strike insistence on a fifty-two-month no-strike contract, with package increases of 14 to 15 cents an hour in the first year. However, responsible industry sources said they had let the union know it could have a three-year agreement if it would scale its economic demands down to the level embodied in the original management proposal.

No accord could be reached, these sources said, because the union had continued to insist that the wage offer was too low. The union was reported asking for total first-year gains of 28 cents an hour. However, most observers believe it would accept a three-year pact, with a 20-cent package in the first twelve months. Pre-strike wages averaged $2.47 an hour.

The negotiations will get under way against a background of controversy between the union and the industry over the extent to which steel wages and prices have contributed to inflation.

The twelve principal steel companies attacked David J. McDonald, president of the union, for his charge that the industry had been guilty of a "disturbing irresponsibility" in its price and profit policies.

The companies accused Mr. McDonald of making "many misrepresentations and distortions" in a letter he sent to members of Congress and high Administration officials Sunday.

Reply of representatives of the twelve negotiating steel companies to the McDonald letter of July 22

The letter sent to Congress by David J. McDonald, president of United Steelworkers of America, and released to the press, contains many misrepresentations and distortions about wages and profits in the steel industry, it was charged today in a statement issued in behalf of the twelve steel companies involved in the negotiations with the steel workers' union.

The companies pointed out that a basic statement just compiled from Government and other authoritative sources completely refutes the unfair allegations contained in the McDonald letter.

Salient facts in the companies' statement follow:

Steel's employment costs per hour have risen to a level now triple that of 1940. They have been advancing since 1940 at the rate of 7.6 per cent each year—meaning 7.6 per cent compounded annually.

Total costs in the steel industry, per hour worked, have advanced since 1940 at the rate of 8.2 per cent a year, compounded.

But figures published by the United States Department of Labor show that the prices of steel products during this period have gone up only at a rate of 5.4 per cent per year, compounded.

And this did not fully cover the companies' increased costs. Had it done so their profit rate would be the same today as it was in 1940. But it is not.

Published figures reporting earnings of steel companies show that their profits in 1940 amounted to 8.1 cents on each dollar of sales. Last year they were only 7.8 cents—a decline of a little over 3 per cent.

Earnings of employes in the steel industry since World War II show larger gains—both in terms of cents per hour, and in percentages—than those of other manufacturing workers.

The steel worker's average hourly earnings of $2.47 in April of 1956, were 51 cents above the average in all manufacturing, 39 cents above the average in the durable goods industries, 20 cents above the average in the automobile industry, 51 cents higher than the average in the electrical machinery industry.

Since 1948, the average steel worker's earnings have increased by an average of more than 80 cents an hour. No other comparable group of industrial workers has gained so rapidly during this period.

Increased wages mean very little to a worker if rising living costs consume the increase. Therefore, the true measure of improved living standards is only to be found in the greater buying power of the worker.

Since 1949, the average steel worker's hourly wages and benefits—after being adjusted for price changes—show an increase of 43 per cent. National productivity has meanwhile increased less than 22 per cent, according to extension of data reported by the Joint Committee on the Economic Report.

The increase in national productivity reflects the increase in the efficiency with which the economy produces goods and services, and is a measure, therefore, of the rate at which the general standard of living is rising. It results largely from the investment in labor-saving machinery and in new and more efficient facilities of all kinds that permit much higher output per man hour. The steel worker's standard of living has thus improved far more than that of most workers in other areas of the economy. The 43 per cent increase in his "real" wage and benefits is a fair measure of the actual rise in his standard of living.

The package proposed by the steel companies in June, 1956, would increase the hourly cost of wages and benefits by about 23 per cent over a five-year period—or an average increase of more than 4 per cent per year. Since this is considerably more than the average annual increase in productivity, it would further improve the steel worker's standard of living, in comparison with that of other workers.

While steel workers are among the highest paid workers in manufacturing industries, steel company profits on sales give the industry no such top rating. Steel's margin of profit on sales in 1955 ranked it tenth from the top, among the manufacturing industries reported by the First National City Bank of New York. In the hourly earnings of its employes, by contrast, it ranked side by side with petroleum refining, an industry with a much higher profit margin.

The industry's profit rate per dollar of sales was less in 1955 than in 1940. The decline between these two years was from 8.1 per cent to 7.8 per cent in 1955, according to calculations for steel companies by First National City Bank of New York.

This 7.8 per cent in 1955 was, of course, earned on a much larger volume of sales, which totaled $14,000,000,000 in 1955 against $3,500,000,000 in 1940. Hence 1955 profits looked much larger, in terms of dollars. But billions of dollars of new investment were necessary to produce the higher sales volume.

The investment of these companies in steel plant rose, for instance, from $3,300,000,000 to $7,200,000,000 between 1940 and 1955. Much of this rise took place in the brief 1950–1955 period, when the investment increased by 40 per cent. In 1955, it therefore took 40 per cent more dollars of profit than in 1950 to pay the same return on the increased investment.

Somewhat similarly, millions of dollars of so-called increased profit now have to be used by the steel industry for use in replacing old plant. The depreciation funds that should pay for this rebuilding are now wholly inadequate because of today's inflated costs.

The amount of so-called profit thus used for replacement might well be called "phantom" profit because—as a result of the inadequacy of depreciation reserves —what otherwise would be profit available for payments to owners and available in some measure for expansion, must be applied to the replacement of present facilities.

Since 1946, about 55 per cent of the total profit, after taxes, of the steel companies have been plowed back into the business for expansion and modernization, while 45 per cent of the profit was used for the payment of dividends.

Steel companies have devoted most of their profits to replacement of existing equipment, expansion of facilities, and increase in working capital. This source of capital having proved inadequate, the industry has found it necessary to borrow heavily. Steel's long-term debt has tripled since 1946.

Union advertisement in Cleveland Plain Dealer, July 24

STEEL INDUSTRY'S ULTIMATUM TO THE STEELWORKERS

Take the industry's 5 year contract! March backwards while the industry moves forward! Lock the doors to any changes or improvements despite the countless problems arising daily! Use the old, worn out contract to meet the new problems!

Take 80c for working all day on Sundays . . . away from church, rest and recreation with the family! But wait until 1959 for this 80c! Until then . . . absolutely nothing more for Sunday work! Other industries generally are today paying 25 times as much! Perish thoughts of any extra pay for Saturday work! Don't be like other workers! Be sub-standard!—Be second-class!

Take the kind of grievance procedure the industry wants! Let the industry alone decide crew sizes, incentive pay and pace! Forget the old timers and their needs for more adequate pensions! Wait until 1987 to get a 1956 style pension plan! The industry will dictate whether Steelworkers should have a vacation or work instead!

Take a nickel in net wage increases! Fix wages in advance for five years and freeze them there. Work harder so industry can expand without borrowing money . . . so industry can install new equipment for increased production, with profits solely for industry. Don't ask for a just share of industry's almost $4,000,000 net profits every 24 hours. Set aside any plans for improving the family life . . . a newer car, an addition to the house, education for the children! *Take it or leave it!*

IS THIS COLLECTIVE BARGAINING?

We Steelworkers don't like being handed ultimatums. We don't deserve such treatment from industry—the industry we help build. Our union did everything possible to reach a fair settlement before June 30. We even offered in good faith and in the interest of the Nation to extend our old contract for 15 days and continue working to get an agreement and avert a national steel shutdown. But the industry said "No."

We asked to talk with the top officials of our individual companies. Again, the industry said "No."

Our union has worked diligently to break all production records—to stabilize the industry. As a result profits are the highest in history, with enough for the managers, the stockholders and for a substantial wage increase for us.

Our union officers joined with industry officials in tours of mills across the nation . . . to promote better understanding between labor and management; to achieve industrial peace.

Was all this just wasted effort? Is this ultimatum our reward from the industry?

> UNITED STEELWORKERS OF AMERICA
> 1500 Commonwealth Building
> Pittsburgh 22, Pa.

Joint statement issued on July 24 by the conferees, who had resumed negotiations the previous day

The negotiators for the twelve companies and the negotiators for the union have met today and have exchanged ideas as to terms of settlement.

To expedite matters, subcommittees have been appointed to further explore various issues. These subcommittees will start to meet this afternoon.

The negotiators for the twelve companies and the union will meet again tomorrow morning at 10 A.M.

The parties have not yet reached agreement but believe that they are making progress.

The International Wage Policy Committee of the union has been called to stand by for a meeting on Thursday at 2 P.M. at the Roosevelt Hotel in New York City.

From The New York Times, July 25

Authoritative sources supplemented this announcement with a disclosure that the industry had made "substantial" changes in its pre-strike offer of a fifty-two-month no-strike contract, with fixed annual wage increases averaging 7.3 cents an hour, a full-year lay-off pay plan and other benefits.

The industry did not put its revised package in the form of an official offer, but made it clear that it was ready to do so whenever agreement was reached on all points. The new plan was understood to call for a three-year pact, with annual pay rises averaging 9 to 10 cents an hour and improvements in other features of the original proposal.

Differences in the computing methods used by the union and the industry made it difficult to arrive at a clear estimate of the total cost of the revised management package. Some sources said total benefits in the first year would come to 25 cents an hour. The full three-year figure was put at 50 cents an hour.

However, both of these figures were believed to include increases in Social Security taxes, overtime and vacation payments and other factors the union does not recognize as valid in calculating a wage offer. With these items eliminated, the reported package increase in the first year would be roughly 20 cents an hour. For the three years the figure would be 40 cents.

Reason for shift undisclosed

The first-year benefits in the offer made by the companies before the strike came to 17⅔ cents an hour, according to the industry's accounting system. The union estimated the benefits at 14 cents an hour. Pre-strike wages averaged $2.47 an hour.

The unanswered question in the abrupt shift from war to peace on the strike front was what happened between 4 P.M. last Saturday and noon Sunday to cause the industry to sweeten the settlement pot. Government-sponsored negotiations in Pittsburgh collapsed Saturday. Both sides expressed certainty that further meetings would be fruitless.

Twenty hours later the industry's chief bargaining representative, John A. Stephens of the United States Steel Corporation, called David J. McDonald, president of the union, and proposed that the talks get under way again in New York Monday. Announcement of the new conferences brought an immediate declaration from James P. Mitchell, Secretary of Labor, that he hoped for a quick agreement.

This led to renewed reports of intense White House pressure to hasten a reopening of mills that normally turn out 85 per cent of the country's steel. It was learned that Mr. Mitchell had attended a private meeting of steel executives in this city last Tuesday.

On the next day the Labor Secretary met with President Eisenhower and other key members of the Cabinet to discuss the strike. Joseph F. Finnegan, director of the Federal Mediation and Conciliation Service, flew from the meeting to Pittsburgh.

There he informed industry and union leaders that the President would act if the strike did not end this week. The White House denied that the President had meant to imply any "ultimatum". or fix a specific deadline for a settlement.

Union sources made no secret of their belief that the Administration had intervened again after the talks broke down Saturday, although both Mr. Mitchell and Mr. Finnegan denied that they had anything to do with the industry decision to request fresh talks.

There was unconfirmed speculation that George M. Humphrey, Secretary of the Treasury, had been in touch with heads of the principal steel companies over the week-end. Mr. Humphrey has been on intimate terms with many steel executives for thirty years. He is a former chairman of the Pittsburgh Consolidation Coal Company.

Price rise to follow

Company officials said a rise in steel prices would follow the wage settlement. They declined to forecast the amount of the increase. But most observers expected that the average rise would be $8 to $10 a ton. Pre-strike prices averaged $130 a ton.

If an end of the tie-up comes this week, the net loss to the companies or the strikers will not be great. Most of the workers were entitled to two or three weeks of paid vacations and many mills have informed the men that they can count their strike absence as vacation time.

Also, the reopening of the steel plants will be accompanied by a period of overtime work that will counteract some of the strike losses.

The industry had expected to run at 80 to 85 per cent of capacity in this quarter because of a slackening of orders.

From Business Week, July 28

Ending the strike when they did and producing the package of 36-month benefits for steelworkers that resulted was optimum collective bargaining by steel industry and steel union negotiators. Settling wages for three years instead of one is exactly three times more difficult.

This is the common ground the bargainers reached:

The 10¢ average hourly pay boost for the first year, followed by two more at annual intervals of about 7.3¢, will not upset the national wage equilibrium.

The supplementary unemployment benefit plan, to be financed by a company contribution of 5¢ per working hour carries the auto industry pattern along but breaks no radically new ground.

More liberal holiday, vacation, insurance, and pension provisions were predictable, as steel has always lagged somewhat behind other industries in these areas.

The thorniest substantive issue of all was the premium pay for Sunday.

Give and Take—The bargainers on both sides were at their skillful best in the trading over the two trickiest issues: premium pay, and length of contract. The companies could yield on one, the union on the other. Extra compensation for Sunday work in continuous-production plants represents a real concession for steel and will have an impact on other continuous-production industries. But in its original proposal to the union—a 10¢ per hour Sunday bonus—steel had made the concession on the principle. From there on, it was bargaining over the amount.

New Technique—The industry tried, with great success, a new bargaining technique this year. In the past, one principal negotiator for one steel company—usually John A. Stephens of U.S. Steel—did all the negotiating with the union. Then the agreement ultimately reached—either with or without a strike—set terms to which the entire industry subscribed, although only the one company did any bargaining.

This year, Stephens for The Corporation was flanked by Thomas Patton for Republic and John Morse for Bethlehem in all the negotiations with David McDonald and Arthur Goldberg for the United Steelworkers. Behind this three-man industry team was a 12-man panel made up of the presidents of the principal steel companies. For all practical purposes, steel was engaging in industrywide bargaining with industrywide participation.

Big Test—The experiment was made triply hazardous by two complicating factors. These negotiations were the first really big test of McDonald's leadership of the steel union—a post in which he had succeeded the late Philip Murray, one of labor's most seasoned and successful bargainers. The two previous negotiations in which McDonald had participated were, for many reasons, much simpler affairs, and he was still enjoying a "honeymoon" in the union's presidency.

Even thornier, however, was the problem of these being "wide open" negotiations. Every major contract written in steel since the '30s was written in large part by government boards. The National War Labor Board, the Wage Stabilization Board, special Washington-named fact-finding tribunals, and a Taft-Hartley board had been chief authors, if not White House amanuenses, of steel's new contracts. This time the parties took at face value the Eisenhower Administration's "hands-off" policy in labor disputes. They assumed, and correctly so, that there would be no "recommendations" from the government.

The Administration did, however, play a role—and an important one—in keeping the free and face-to-face bargaining on the track.

Before the Strike—During June, while pre-strike bargaining went on, Secy. of Labor James P. Mitchell met privately in Washington with top union and industry representatives. They kept him informed, and he in turn informed the White House, of all pre-strike developments.

Mitchell's advice was to keep government firmly out of the dispute. No one in the Administration questioned it, though it was opposed by some Republicans in the Senate.

Early Stage—Mitchell worked closely with Joseph Finnegan, director of the Federal Mediation & Conciliation Service, and with Treasury Secy. George M. Humphrey, who has close and intimate relations with steel industry leaders. He got almost hourly reports on the parties' state of mind and on developments during the strike.

When the strike began and negotiators left New York in a huff, Finnegan went to Pittsburgh to get them back into the same room and talking settlement terms.

When the first week of the strike ended, Finnegan reported that negotiations were still desultory. At that point Mitchell, through Humphrey, arranged a meeting in New York with the three top steel company presidents: Clifford F. Hood of U.S. Steel, Arthur B. Homer of Bethlehem, and Charles M. White of Republic. Nine other steel company top executives also came to New York to be available. Mitchell had McDonald and Goldberg come from Pittsburgh and stand by.

Bearing Down—Mitchell did no bargaining with the company presidents at this crucial meeting. He explained the Administration's policy, spelled out the economic effects of a continuing strike, and asked them to meet with McDonald directly and get the bargaining going in earnest.

They agreed to do this, and Mitchell called McDonald in, going over with him the same points he made to the industry. Later that night, McDonald and White arranged for the union president to meet the three company presidents. From this meeting came the resumption of negotiations in Pittsburgh.

Finnegan audited those conferences carefully but kept strictly out of negotiations, determined to have all the initiative for settlement come from the parties themselves.

Into the Weekend—No settlement formula emerged from those sessions. And early last weekend Finnegan left Pittsburgh to dramatize the gravity of the deadlock.

At the start of the weekend, the outlook was bleak. McDonald was all set to make a cross-country series of visits to local union mass meetings and picket lines. No one expected him to spread any sweetness or light. He would do the orthodox job of a labor leader dealing with a striking rank-and-file: heat them up. The possibility of settling the strike on moderate terms and getting those terms accepted by the union's membership would be considerably slimmer once McDonald put on his war paint and took to the road.

Turning Point—Mitchell again talked directly with steel company presidents. While outsiders believed last Sunday that a settlement was further away than ever, top industry executives were in fact formulating the terms on which a settlement was based. When John Stephens called McDonald later in the day, and McDonald was induced to give up his circuit-riding program, everything was set for the windup.

Within 24 hours, Mitchell could inform Pres. Eisenhower in Panama that his biggest domestic worry was over, that only details and drafting remained to be worked out before the 1956 steel strike became history.

From *The New York Times*, August 7

PITTSBURGH, Aug. 6—Steel prices were increased by an average of $8.50 a ton today by the United States Steel Corporation, the country's largest producer.

Other companies were expected to move quickly to raise their prices in the wake of the thirty-four-day steel strike.

From an editorial in *Business Week*, August 4, 1956, following the steel strike

A STEP FORWARD IN LABOR RELATIONS

Collective bargaining, that relatively recent invention of free economic systems, is at best a crude mechanism for determining wages and conditions of employment. It is, more accurately, a test of strength between the bargainers who hold apocalyptic threats of strike and lockout. The test is scored by how much is gained and how much conceded. Any employer, union leader, or detached economist is sure that he can set wages and conditions more scientifically and sensibly through cost accounting, opinion poll, and slide rule—or by his superior judgement. And perhaps he can.

But rough though collective bargaining is, and wasteful as its consequences may be, it is a small part of the cost we pay for maintaining economic freedom, the entire bill for which buys what is still the world's greatest value.

Collective agreements in the steel industry are very similar but not identical for all the major companies. Below is reproduced the collective agreement negotiated in one of the steel companies, Bethlehem, including such modifications as were hammered out in the negotiations described above. In addition to this principal agreement there are separate agreements, not here given, covering such matters as the pension and supplementary unemployment benefit programs.

**AGREEMENT BETWEEN THE BETHLEHEM STEEL CO.
AND THE UNITED STEELWORKERS, 1956**

INDEX

AGREEMENT dated August 3, 1956, between BETHLEHEM STEEL COMPANY, BETHLEHEM PACIFIC COAST STEEL CORPORATION, BETHLEHEM CORNWALL CORPORATION, BETHLEHEM LIMESTONE COMPANY, BETHLEHEM SUPPLY COMPANY, BUFFALO TANK CORPORATION, THE DUNDALK COMPANY and UNITED STEELWORKERS OF AMERICA.

The above-named parties hereby agree as hereinafter set forth, each of the above-named corporations agreeing severally for itself and not for the other of said corporations and only in respect of rates of pay, hours of work and other conditions of employment of the Employees (as hereinafter defined) who shall be employed at any Plant (as hereinafter defined) which shall at the time be operated by said corporation.

The provisions of this Agreement shall become effective August 3, 1956, except as otherwise specifically provided herein.

ARTICLE I—DEFINITIONS

Except as otherwise stated in this Agreement, wherever used herein the respective terms hereinafter in this Article mentioned shall have the respective meanings hereinafter set forth.

(a) The term "the Company" means Bethlehem Steel Company, Bethlehem Pacific Coast Steel Corporation, Bethlehem Cornwall Corporation, Bethlehem Limestone Company, Bethlehem Supply Company, Buffalo Tank Corporation, or the Dundalk Company, as the case may be.

(b) The term "the Union" means United Steelworkers of America, and wherever said term is used with reference to a particular Plant said term includes the Local or Locals of the Union at such Plant.

(c) The term "Plant" at any given time means one of the steel plants, fabricating works, mines, quarries or other operations of the Company listed in Appendix 1 to this Agreement, if at that time it shall be operated by the Company.

(d) The term "Unit" means the unit at a Plant as such unit is defined in Article II of this Agreement, and the term "Units" means two or more or all (as the case may be) of such units.

(e) The term "Employee" means an employee of the Company who is included in a Unit, and the term "Employees" means two or more or all (as the case may be) of such employees.

(f) The term "the Management" means the management of the Company at the particular plant.

(g) The term "Grievance Committee" means the grievance committee of the Union for the Plant.

(h) The term "term of this Agreement" means the period during which this Agreement shall be in effect as provided in Article XIX hereof.

ARTICLE II—APPLICATION OF AGREEMENT

Section 1. It is the intent and purpose of the parties hereto to set forth herein the agreement between them in respect of rates of pay, hours of work and other conditions of employment of the Employees in the respective Units as hereinafter defined at the respective Plants listed in Appendix 1 hereto.

Section 2. (a) The Unit at each of such Plants shall include all production and maintenance employees of the Company there and firemen at the Bethlehem, Lackawanna, Lebanon, Sparrows Point and Steelton Plants, and shall exclude all executives, office and salaried employees, foremen, assistant foremen, supervisors who do not work with tools, draftsmen, timekeepers at Plants other than the Sparrows Point and Lackawanna Plants, watchmen and guards, full time first aid and safety employees, and employees in the Die Sinking Division (DWM) at the Bethlehem Plant.

(b) Any difference which shall arise between the Company and the Union as to whether or not any individual employee is or is not included within the Unit at any Plant as hereinbefore defined shall be handled as a grievance in accordance with the procedure set forth in Article XI hereof.

Section 3. The term "local working conditions" as used in this Section means specific practices or customs which reflect detailed application of the subject matter within the scope of wages, hours of work, or other conditions of employment and includes local agreements, written or oral, on such matters. It is recognized that it is impracticable to set forth in this Agreement all of these working conditions, which are of a local nature only, or to state specifically in this Agreement which of these matters should be changed or eliminated. The provisions set forth below provide general principles and procedures which explain the status of these matters and furnish necessary guideposts for the parties hereto and the impartial umpire. The provisions of this Section are not intended to prevent the Management from continuing to make progress. Any arbitrations arising hereunder shall be handled on a case-by-case basis on principles of reasonableness and equity.

(*a*) It is recognized that an Employee does not have the right to have a local working condition established, in any given situation or plant where such condition has not existed, during the term of this Agreement or to have an existing local working condition changed or eliminated, except to the extent necessary to require the application of a specific provision of this Agreement.

(*b*) In no case shall local working conditions be effective to deprive any Employee of rights under this Agreement. Should any Employee believe that a local working condition is depriving him of the benefits of this Agreement, he shall have recourse to the grievance procedure and arbitration, if necessary, to require that the local working condition be changed or eliminated to provide the benefits established by this Agreement.

(*c*) Should there be any local working conditions in effect which provide benefits that are in excess of or in addition to the benefits established by this Agreement, they shall remain in effect for the term of this Agreement, except as they are changed or eliminated by mutual agreement or in accordance with paragraph (*d*) below.

(*d*) The Management shall have the right to change or eliminate any local working condition if, as the result of action taken by Management under Article XIII hereof, the basis for the existence of the local working condition is changed or eliminated, thereby making it unnecessary to continue such local working condition; provided, however, that when such a change or elimination is made by the Management any affected Employee shall have recourse to the grievance procedure and arbitration, if necessary, to have the Management justify its action.

(*e*) No local working condition shall hereafter be established or agreed to which changes or modifies any of the provisions of this Agreement. In the event such a local working condition is established or agreed to, it shall not be enforceable to the extent that it is inconsistent with or goes beyond the provisions of this Agreement, except as it is approved by an International officer of the Union and the Manager of Industrial Relations of the Company.

ARTICLE III—RECOGNITION AND UNION MEMBERSHIP

Section 1. Subject to the provisions of the National Labor Relations Act, the Company recognizes the Union as the exclusive representative of all the Employees for the purposes of collective bargaining in respect to rates of pay, wages, hours of employment or other conditions of employment.

Section 2. (*a*) Each Employee who, on the date of this Agreement, is a member of the Union in good standing and each Employee who becomes a member after that date shall, as a condition of employment, maintain his membership in the Union. Each Employee hired on or after July 1, 1956, shall, as a condition of employment, commencing on the 30th day following the beginning of such employment or the date of this Agreement, whichever is the later, acquire and maintain membership in the Union. The foregoing provisions shall be effective in accordance and consistent with applicable provisions of federal and state law.

(b) At the time of his employment the Company will suggest that each new Employee voluntarily execute an authorization for the checkoff of Union dues in the form agreed upon. A copy of such authorization card for the checkoff of Union dues shall be forwarded to the Financial Secretary of the Local Union along with the membership application of such Employee.

(c) For the purposes of this Section, an Employee shall not be deemed to have lost his membership in the Union in good standing until the International Secretary-Treasurer of the Union shall have determined that the membership of such Employee in the Union is not in good standing and shall have given the Company a notice in writing of that fact.

(d) Upon receipt by the Management's Representative at any Plant of a voluntary written assignment (in a form agreed to in writing by the Company and the Union) by an Employee at such Plant, the Company will deduct from the first pay of such Employee each month thereafter during the existence of such assignment his periodic Union dues for the preceding month and the Company shall also deduct any assessments against him which shall be general and uniform among Employees who shall at the time be members of the Union, and, if owing by him, an initiation fee, all as payable to the Union in accordance with its constitution and by-laws. The Company shall promptly remit any and all amounts so deducted to the International Secretary-Treasurer of the Union, who shall notify the Company in writing of the respective amounts of the dues, initiation fees and assessments which shall be so deducted.

Section 3. The Union shall indemnify the Company and hold it harmless against any and all suits, claims, demands and liabilities that shall arise out of or by reason of any action that shall be taken by the Company for the purpose of complying with the foregoing provisions of this Article or in reliance on any list, notice or assignment which shall have been furnished to the Company under any of such provisions.

ARTICLE IV—RATES OF PAY

Section 1. (a) Beginning as of each date specified in Appendix 2 hereto, the standard hourly wage rate for each job class shall be the rate specified for such job class under such date in Appendix 2.

(b) Beginning as of the date of each general increase in the standard hourly wage rates as specified in Appendix 2 hereto, the hourly earnings (not including overtime compensation, shift and Sunday premiums and any Cost of Living Adjustment, but including the Adjustment Factor provided for in Section 2 of the Supplemental Agreement dated May 25, 1956) of each Employee whose job shall be paid on an incentive basis (for each hour worked by him and for which he shall be paid incentive earnings) shall be increased by the percentage by which the standard hourly wage rate for his job resulting from such general increase exceeds the standard hourly wage rate which was in effect for such job on the day before such general increase. Except for Employees receiving an interim hourly rate under Article V, the provisions of this paragraph shall not apply to any job after the incentive base rate for such job shall be the standard hourly wage rate applicable to such job.

(c) Beginning as of the date of the combination of job classes 1 and 2, the increase in rate resulting from such combination shall be applied to reduce or eliminate any personal out-of-line differential of any Employee in job class 1 who has a "red circle" hourly wage rate or a "red circle" guaranteed occupational hourly rate. Beginning as of the date of each general increase in standard hourly wage rates specified in Appendix 2 hereto, the increase in the standard hourly wage rate for any job which is attributable to the increase in the increments between job classes shall be applied to reduce or eliminate any such personal "red circle" rate. Except as so reduced or eliminated, such "red circle" rate shall remain in effect for such Employee while he shall be employed on such job or any other job to which he shall be promoted or transferred at the direction of the Management.

Section 2. (a) If the Consumer Price Index of the Bureau of Labor Statistics, U.S. Department of Labor (1947–1949 = 100), hereafter referred to as the BLS Consumer Price Index, shall increase from the June 15, 1956, level of 116.2 to a level above 116.5, there shall be added to the straight time hourly earnings of each Employee a Cost of Living Adjustment in accordance with the following table and provisions:

BLS consumer price index	Cost of living adjustment
116.5 or less	None
116.6–117.0	1¢ per hour
117.1–117.4	2¢ per hour
117.5–117.9	3¢ per hour
118.0–118.3	4¢ per hour

and so forth, with a one cent change in the Adjustment for each 0.4 or 0.5 point change in the Index, whichever is appropriate, based on the sequence of changes set forth in the above table.

(b) Changes in any Cost of Living Adjustment shall be made, if appropriate, only commencing with the first pay period beginning on or after each January 1 and July 1, beginning January 1, 1957, and shall be based on the first published BLS Consumer Price Index as of the prior November 15 and May 15, respectively. The amount of the change in the Cost of Living Adjustment shall be the difference between the amount provided in the above table and any Cost of Living Adjustment already in effect pursuant to this Section 2.

(c) Notwithstanding any decrease in the BLS Consumer Price Index, there shall not be any decrease in any existing Cost of Living Adjustment in accordance with the above table, unless the amount of the decrease in the Cost of Living Adjustment under such table is at least 2 cents, at which time the full amount of the appropriate decrease shall be made.

(*d*) If the BLS Consumer Price Index for any November 15 or May 15 shall not be available by the following January 1 or July 1, as the case may be, any change in the Cost of Living Adjustment pursuant to such late reported Index shall be made effective as of the pay period beginning on or after January 1 or July 1 which would have been applicable had the Index not been published late.

(*e*) If the BLS Consumer Price Index in its present form and calculated on the same basis shall be revised therefrom or discontinued, the parties shall attempt to adjust this clause, or, if agreement is not reached, the parties shall request the Bureau of Labor Statistics to provide an appropriate conversion or adjustment, which shall be applicable as of the appropriate adjustment date and thereafter.

Section 3.   The standard hourly wage rate for each job class as set forth in Appendix 2 shall be the hourly rate of pay for each Employee on each job in such class for all work which shall not be incentive rated or covered by an incentive, and any other hourly wage rate or other payment, whether higher or lower, for such work is eliminated except as is otherwise specifically provided in this Article and Article V of this Agreement and in the Supplemental Agreement, dated May 25, 1956.

Section 4. Each Employee paid on an incentive basis shall be guaranteed and shall receive for each day that he shall work an amount (in addition to any premium for shift work or Sunday work and any Cost of Living Adjustment payable to him under this Agreement) which shall be the greater of

(*a*) the standard hourly wage rate for the job worked by him on that day multiplied by the number of hours worked by him in that job on that day, or

(*b*) the amount of his incentive earnings for that day; provided, however, that, if an Employee shall be paid on an incentive basis and it shall not be reasonably practicable to compute his incentive earnings on a daily basis, the foregoing guarantee shall be applied on the basis of the shortest reasonably practicable period of time for which such incentive earnings can be computed, and any and all other guarantees, whether stated in money or time or based on tonnage or any other factor, for such job are eliminated, except as is otherwise specifically provided in this Article and Article V of this Agreement and in the Supplemental Agreement, dated May 25, 1956.

Section 5. Neither the putting into effect of the standard hourly wage rates in accordance with the provisions of this Article, nor any change in job titles made in connection therewith, shall of itself alter or affect in any way any incentive rate (including any hourly base rate in so far as it is used in the computation of incentive pay). Neither the Union nor any Employee shall claim that any wage inequity exists and a grievance on behalf of an Employee based on an alleged wage inequity shall not be filed or processed, whether such Employee shall be paid on an hourly or on an incentive basis.

Section 6. If an Employee shall be assigned temporarily for the Company's convenience to a job other than his regular job when work is available to the Employee on his regular job, he shall receive the established rate of pay for the job performed or for his regular job, whichever is higher.

Section 7. Adequate provisions shall be made at each of the Plants whereby each Employee there shall be currently informed of his standard hourly wage rate and, in the case of an Employee who is paid on an incentive basis, of the method of computing his incentive earnings.

ARTICLE V—JOB CLASSIFICATIONS AND INCENTIVES

Section 1. (a) Each job classification now in effect or hereafter established shall remain in effect, except as changed in accordance with the provisions of this Section.

(b) Whenever a new job shall be established or, after the effective date of the last classification or reclassification of an existing job, the requirements of such job as to training, skill, responsibility, effort and surroundings shall have been altered to the extent of a whole numerical classification of 1.0 or more, the Management shall classify or reclassify such job, as the case may be, and the new classification shall be put into effect in accordance with the procedure set forth in this Section.

(1) The Management shall describe and classify such job in accordance with the Manual for Job Classification of Production and Maintenance Jobs (hereinafter referred to as the Manual) a copy of which is annexed to the agreement dated April 11, 1947, between the Company and the Union, and shall present such description and classification to a representative of the Union designated for the purpose and shall afford to such representative a reasonable opportunity to be heard with respect to such proposed new classification. If the Union shall not have designated such representative, the Company may present such description and classification to any officer or grievance committeeman of the Union as its representative for such purpose.

(2) If the Union, acting by such representative, shall agree to such proposed new classification, it shall be established for such job.

(3) If the Union, acting by such representative, shall not agree to such proposed new classification for such job, the Management may nevertheless put such new classification into effect and it shall continue in effect, unless it shall be changed in the manner provided in subparagraph (b) (4) of this Section.

(4) The Union may, at any time within 30 days after the date on which such new classification shall have been put into effect without the agreement of such representative, initiate a grievance regarding such new classification, in which event such grievance shall be handled in accordance with the procedure set forth in Article XI hereof. If such grievance shall not be so initiated before the expiration of said 30 days, the Union shall be deemed to have agreed that such new classification shall become established for such job. If such grievance shall be submitted to arbitration as provided in said Article XI, the impartial umpire shall, subject to the limitations hereinbefore set forth in this Section, decide such grievance in accordance with the Manual and his decision with regard thereto shall be effective as of the date when the new job was estab-

lished or the change or changes installed but in no event earlier than 30 days prior to the date on which the grievance shall have been presented in written form under Step No. 1 of the procedure set forth in said Article XI.

(c) If any Employee shall claim that after the effective date of the last classification or reclassification of an existing job the requirements of his job as to training, skill, responsibility, effort and surroundings shall have been altered to the extent of a whole numerical classification of 1.0 or more, he may initiate a grievance in respect of his job classification and such grievance shall be handled in accordance with the procedure set forth in Article XI hereof. If such grievance shall be submitted to arbitration as provided in said Article XI, the impartial umpire shall, subject to the limitations hereinbefore set forth in this Section, decide such grievance in accordance with the Manual and his decision with regard thereto shall be effective as of the date when the new job was established or the change or changes installed but in no event earlier than 30 days prior to the date on which the grievance shall have been presented in written form under Step No. 1 of the procedure set forth in said Article XI.

(d) The classification of any job may be changed by agreement in writing between the Management and the representative of the Union referred to in subparagraph (b) (1) of this Section.

(e) Whenever the Management shall record a change on a job description form or a job classification form, it shall give such representative written notice of such change.

(f) The Union and the Company shall each designate three representatives to a joint committee to review the Manual and job classifications with a view to achieving maximum understanding between the parties.

Section 2. (a) Each incentive now in effect or hereafter established shall remain in effect, except as changed in accordance with the provisions of this Section or of the Supplemental Agreement dated May 25, 1956, between the parties hereto.* The term "incentive" as used in this Section means any incentive plan and the incentive rates under such plan (including: tonnage rates; premium rates; piece rates of continuing application; and standards and guides used in the calculation of piece rates other than those of continuing application).

(b) The Management shall have the exclusive right to establish an incentive (1) for any new job (other than a new job which replaces a job to which an incentive had been applicable), (2) for work which shall not at the time be paid on an incentive basis, or (3) where the Management shall eliminate an incentive in accordance with the provisions of paragraph (g) of this Section. Any such new incentive shall be established in accordance with the procedure set forth in paragraph (d) of this Section, shall be based upon the applicable standard hourly wage rate and shall provide equitable compensation.

(c) The parties hereto recognize that it may become necessary or desirable from time to time that a then existing incentive be adjusted or replaced because of changes in equipment, changes in manufacturing processes or in materials processed or in methods or standards of manufacture or production, the development of new manufacturing processes or methods, or mechanical improvements

* Not reproduced here.

made by the Company in the interest of improved methods or products. Whenever any of such changes or such other events occurs and for that reason the Management shall deem it necessary or desirable to adjust an existing incentive (or, if appropriate in view of the changes, to replace an existing incentive plan) the Management shall establish a new incentive in accordance with the procedure set forth in paragraph (d) of this Section. Such new incentive shall be based upon the applicable standard hourly wage rate and shall, giving due effect to the change or other event by reason of which the new incentive shall have been established, be designed to provide compensation at least equal to the compensation that would have been provided under the incentive which it replaced and shall provide equitable compensation.

(d) Any new incentive shall be established in accordance with the following procedure:

(1) The Management shall develop the incentive and furnish to the steward of the Union for the applicable department such information and explanation with regard to the proposed incentive as shall reasonably be required to enable him to understand the new incentive. After notifying such steward of the date on which the incentive shall be made effective, the Management may put the incentive into effect.

(2) Any incentive may be installed on a trial or experimental basis, provided the Management and steward so agree, in which case such agreement shall include the duration of such trial or experimental period and any special guarantees which may be made applicable.

(3) The Union may, at any time after 30 days but not later than 60 days following the effective date of a new incentive, initiate a grievance regarding such incentive, in which event such grievance shall be handled in accordance with the procedure set forth in Article XI hereof. If a trial or experimental period has been agreed upon, the applicable time limit for initiating a grievance regarding such incentive shall apply as of the end of such trial or experimental period. If such grievance shall not be so initiated before the expiration of said 60 days, the Union shall be deemed to have agreed that such new incentive shall become established. If such grievance shall be submitted to arbitration as provided in said Article XI, the decision of the impartial umpire with regard thereto shall be effective as of the date when the Management shall have put such new incentive into effect.

(4) If the Management, in accordance with the provisions of this Section, shall cancel an existing incentive applicable to any work prior to the establishment of the new incentive which is to replace it, or if an Employee shall perform work which, except for one of the changes specified in paragraph (c) of this Section, would have continued to be paid for on an incentive basis, during the period preceding the establishment of the new incentive on such work each Employee who shall perform such work shall be paid, for all such work performed by him, at an interim hourly rate. Such interim hourly rate shall be equal to the average hourly earnings (not including overtime compensation or shift or Sunday premiums or any Cost of Living Adjustment) of all Employees who were assigned to the job on which the work was performed during the 3

months' period next preceding the cancellation or non-payment of such existing incentive or it shall be such other interim hourly rate as shall be agreed to by the Management and the Union steward for the applicable department. Such interim hourly rate shall be paid to such Employee only so long as he maintains the average performance on such job during such prior 3 months' period. If he voluntarily maintains a performance appreciably below such average performance of such prior 3 months' period, after notification to such Employee and such Union steward, the Management may suspend payment of such interim hourly rate.

(e) Subject to the provisions of Section 5 of Article XI of this Agreement, if any Employee shall claim that by reason of any change or other event specified in paragraph (c) of this Section which shall occur, his incentive has become unreasonable and unfair, he may initiate a grievance in respect thereof and such grievance shall be handled in accordance with the procedure set forth in Article XI hereof. If in the determination of such grievance such incentive shall be changed, the new incentive shall be established in accordance with the principles set forth in paragraph (c) of this Section.

(f) Any incentive may be revised or replaced by agreement in writing between the Management and the Union steward for the applicable department or other designated Union representative.

(g) If the average straight time hourly earnings of the Employees paid under a particular incentive plan, for the pay periods ended during the preceding calendar quarter, are lower than or equal to the standard hourly wage rates of such Employees, the Company may eliminate such plan provided the Management replaces such plan with a new or adjusted plan in accordance with the provisions of paragraph (b) of this Section.

(h) The Union and the Company shall each designate three representatives to a joint committee to review incentive problems with a view to achieving maximum understanding between the parties.

Section 3. If prior to the time when an existing incentive plan shall be replaced with a new incentive plan under the provisions of Section 5 of the Supplemental Agreement dated May 25, 1956 (a copy of which is attached hereto as Appendix 3) an existing incentive wage rate shall be adjusted because of the occurrence of any of the changes or events set forth in Section 2(c) of this Article, such adjustment shall be made in accordance with the procedure of Section 2 of this Article and the adjusted incentive shall be developed by the Management in accordance with the usual practice now in effect with it at the Plant and on the principle that the new incentive shall, giving due effect to the change or other events by reason of which the new incentive shall have been established, be in equitable relationship to the incentive which it replaced and provide equitable compensation.

ARTICLE VI—SHIFT AND SUNDAY PREMIUMS

Section 1. For the purposes of this Article:

(a) All shifts beginning between 6 a.m. and 9 a.m., inclusive, shall be considered day shifts.

(*b*) All shifts beginning between 2 p.m. and 5 p.m., inclusive, shall be considered middle shifts.

(*c*) All shifts beginning between 10 p.m. and 1 a.m., inclusive, shall be considered night shifts.

Section 2. (*a*) Each Employee scheduled to work on the middle shift shall be paid a middle shift premium of 6 cents per hour for all hours worked by him on that shift, and each Employee scheduled to work on the night shift shall be paid a night shift premium of 9 cents per hour for all hours worked by him on that shift.

(*b*) Effective July 1, 1958, the middle shift premium shall be increased to 8 cents per hour and the night shift premium shall be increased to 12 cents per hour.

Section 3. An Employee who begins work at a time not specified in Section 1 of this Article shall be paid the middle shift premium for all hours worked by him within the hours of the prevailing middle shift in his department and the night shift premium for all hours worked by him within the hours of the prevailing night shift in his department. If there is no such prevailing middle shift or prevailing night shift, such Employee shall be paid the middle shift premium for all hours worked by him between 3 p.m. and 11 p.m. and the night shift premium for all hours worked by him between 11 p.m. and 7 a.m.

Section 4. (*a*) For the purposes of this Article, except as hereinafter in this Section provided, all consecutive hours (exclusive of meal periods) worked by an Employee who begins work at a time specified in Section 1 hereof shall be deemed to be worked by him on the shift on which he begins work.

(*b*) If an Employee who is scheduled to work on the day shift works throughout such shift and continues to work for more than 4 hours into the middle shift, he shall be paid the middle shift premium for all hours worked by him after such 4 hours.

(*c*) If an Employee who is scheduled to work on the day shift works throughout that shift and, after leaving the Plant, is called back to work on the middle shift or the night shift, he shall be paid the middle shift premium for all hours worked by him on the middle shift and the night shift premium for all hours worked by him on the night shift.

Section 5. Shift premiums payable under the foregoing provisions of this Article shall be included as part of the Employee's regular rate of pay for the purpose of computing overtime under Article VII of this Agreement, but such premiums shall not be added to hourly base rates for the purpose of calculating incentive earnings.

Section 6. For all time worked on Sunday which is not paid for on an overtime basis, a premium based on the regular rate as defined in Section 5 of Article VII of this Agreement shall be paid, as follows:

> September 1, 1956, to June 30, 1957: 10%
> July 1, 1957, to June 30, 1958: 20%
> July 1, 1958, to June 30, 1959: 25%

For the purpose of this provision, Sunday shall be deemed to be the 24 hours beginning at 12:01 a.m. Sunday or the turn-changing time nearest thereto.

ARTICLE VII—HOURS OF WORK AND OVERTIME

Section 1. (a) In accordance with the practice prevailing at the respective Plants, the normal daily hours of work shall be 8 consecutive hours, excluding luncheon periods and rest periods where such periods are provided, and the normal weekly hours of work shall be 40 hours. The Management will make a diligent effort so to schedule Employees for work that at least 85% of the Employees at any Plant shall be scheduled for work on a normal work pattern of 5 consecutive workdays followed by 2 consecutive days off in each 7 consecutive days. If an Employee shall receive 4 consecutive days off in each 14 consecutive days pursuant to an agreement between the Management and the Grievance Committee, such Employee may be included in computing such 85%. Each Employee assigned to a working schedule agreed to by the Management and the Grievance Committee and which does not provide 2 consecutive days off in each 7 consecutive days or 4 consecutive days off in each 14 consecutive days may be included in computing such 85%. If an Employee shall be paid at the overtime rate hereinafter in this Article specified for all hours worked by him on any day, then, for the purpose of computing such 85%, that day shall be counted as a day off. The Management will also endeavor to give Employees notice of any changes in their weekly working schedules in time to enable them to make changes in their plans in order to meet such schedules.

(b) Schedules of the Employees' regular workdays shall be posted or otherwise made known to Employees in accordance with prevailing practices at the respective Plants, not later than Friday of the week preceding the calendar week in which they shall be effective; provided, however, that in the case of breakdowns or other conditions beyond the control of the Management or because of the requirements of the business the Management may change such schedules after Friday of the week preceding the calendar week in which they shall be effective.

(c) The foregoing provisions of this Section shall not be construed as guaranteeing to any Employee any number of hours of work per day or per week. The Management will from time to time furnish to the Grievance Committee such information as such Committee shall reasonably request with regard to the compliance by the Management with the provisions of this Section.

Section 2. The starting times of regular turns at the respective Plants shall be determined from time to time by the Management, and, in so far as practicable, notice of any change in any such starting time shall be posted on the bulletin boards in the departments affected thereby at least 48 hours before such change shall become effective.

Section 3. (a) Overtime compensation at the rate of one and one-half times the Employee's regular rate of pay (as hereinafter in Section 5 of this Article defined) shall be paid for all time worked by such Employee,

(1) in excess of 8 hours within a workday; provided, however, that the same hours shall not be included in more than one workday, or

(2) in excess of 40 hours within a payroll week, or

(3) on any workday within a payroll week after he shall have worked on 5 previous days in that week; provided, however, that for the purpose of this clause (3) an Employee shall be deemed to have worked on any of such 5 previous workdays on which he shall have been scheduled to work and on which he did not work because his schedule was changed after Friday of the preceding week, but this proviso shall not be applicable to changes in schedules in the case of breakdowns or other conditions beyond the control of the Management, or

(4) on any sixth or seventh workday of a 7-consecutive-day period during which the first 5 days were worked by the Employee whether or not all of such days fall within the same payroll week as defined in Section 5(b) of this Article, except when that day is worked pursuant to a schedule approved by the Grievance Committee; provided, however, that no overtime compensation under this provision will be due unless the Employee shall notify his foreman of a claim for overtime within a period of one week after such sixth or seventh day is worked; and provided further that on shift changes the 7-consecutive-day period of 168 hours may become 152 consecutive hours depending upon the change in the shift. For the purposes of this clause (4) all working schedules now normally used in any department of any Plant shall be deemed to have been approved by the Grievance Committee. Such approval may be withdrawn by the Grievance Committee by giving 60 days' prior written notice thereof to the Management.

(b) Overtime compensation shall be paid for all time worked by an Employee on a holiday as defined in Article VIII of this Agreement at the rate of

(1) until June 30, 1957, two times the Employee's regular rate of pay;

(2) from July 1, 1957, to June 30, 1958, two and one-tenth times the Employee's regular rate of pay; and

(3) after June 30, 1958, two and one-fourth times the Employee's regular rate of pay.

Section 4. (a) For the purpose of computing overtime compensation under this Article, if more than one of the provisions of this Agreement with regard to the payment of overtime compensation shall be applicable to any time worked by any Employee, he shall be paid for such time at the highest overtime rate specified in any of such applicable provisions but he shall not be entitled to additional overtime compensation for such time under any other of such provisions.

(b) Hours compensated for at overtime rates shall not be counted further for any purpose in determining overtime liability under the same or any other provisions; provided, however, that a holiday, whether worked or not, shall be counted for purposes of computing overtime liability under the provisions of clause (3) of Section 3(a) of this Article, and hours worked on a holiday shall be counted for purposes of computing overtime liability under the provisions of clause (1) of Section 3(a) of this Article. Except as provided in this paragraph (*b*), hours paid for but not worked shall not be counted in determining overtime liability.

Section 5. The following provisions shall apply in the computation of overtime compensation under this Agreement:

(*a*) The term "regular rate of pay" shall mean

(1) in the case of an Employee who shall be paid at a fixed rate of pay per hour, such rate of pay; or

(2) in the case of an Employee who shall be paid on an incentive basis, the amount of his average rate of earnings per hour on the position on which he shall work the particular overtime for the payroll week (or for the other period for which such earnings are regularly computed) during which such overtime shall be worked; provided, however, that if he works on a position for which it is the regular practice to compute such average rate of earnings for the position as such, such average rate shall continue to be computed on that basis for the purposes of this paragraph; and provided, further, that overtime compensation and shift and Sunday premiums shall not be included in computing such average rate of earnings per hour, but any shift premium to which such Employee shall be entitled under Article VI of this Agreement for the overtime hours worked shall be added to such average rate of earnings per hour in computing such regular rate of pay.

(*b*) A payroll week means a period of 7 successive days (of 24 hours each) beginning at 12:01 a.m. Sunday or at the turn-changing time nearest thereto; and a workday means the 24-hour period beginning with the time the Employee begins work, except that the workday of an Employee who reports late shall begin at the time it would have begun had he not reported late.

(*c*) In computing the number of workdays in which an Employee has worked for the purposes of this Section: (1) if a shift includes a part of each of 2 workdays, an Employee who works on that shift shall be deemed to have worked only on the first of such days; (2) if an Employee works beyond the end of his scheduled shift into the next succeeding workday, he shall not be deemed to have worked on such succeeding day, unless he shall work more than 4 hours on that day or shall have been called back to work on that day after leaving the Plant; (3) if an Employee begins work before the regular starting time of his shift and the time at which he so begins work falls within the workday preceding the workday on which such shift so starts and he has not previously worked on such preceding day, it shall not be counted as a day worked by him unless he shall have worked at least 4 hours on that day.

Section 6. If an Employee shall be required by the Management to report for work on any day and he shall report at the time and place at which he was required so to report, he shall be paid a minimum of 4 hours' pay at the standard hourly wage rate which would have been applicable had he worked such 4 hours in the position for which he was required so to report. When an Employee who starts to work is released from duty before he works a minimum of 4 hours, he shall be paid for the hours worked by him in accordance with the provisions of Article IV hereof and credited with an amount equal to the standard hourly wage rate which would have been applicable had he worked in the position for which he was scheduled or notified to report multiplied by the unutilized portion of the 4-hour minimum. Any pay under this Section shall include any applicable shift premium and Sunday premium (computed solely on the basis of the standard hourly wage rate). The provisions of this Section shall not apply to an Employee if

(a) at his own request or because of his own fault, he shall not be put to work or shall not complete 4 hours of such work after having been put to work, or

(b) he shall be assigned to another position of at least equal job class which he shall be qualified to fill and shall refuse to work at such other position or because of his own fault shall not complete 4 hours of such work after having been put to work at such position, or

(c) he shall not be put to work or shall not complete 4 hours of work after having been put to work by reason of any strike or other stoppage of work in connection with any labor dispute or any failure of utilities beyond the control of Management or Act of God.

ARTICLE VIII—HOLIDAYS

Section 1. Whenever used in this Agreement, the term "holiday" means one of the following days: January 1, Good Friday, Memorial Day, July 4, Labor Day, Thanksgiving Day and Christmas Day. If any of such holidays shall fall on a Sunday, the following Monday (and not such Sunday) shall be observed as such holiday.

Section 2. An eligible Employee who does not work on a holiday shall be paid 8 times the applicable hourly rate of the job to which he is regularly assigned, exclusive of shift, Sunday and overtime premiums (in the case of an Employee who is paid on an incentive basis, the Employee's average hourly earnings exclusive of shift, Sunday and overtime premiums for the pay period preceding the one in which the holiday is observed shall be used, except that if he does not perform any work in such pay period, the pay period in which the holiday is observed shall be used); provided, however, that if an eligible Employee is scheduled to work on any such holiday, but fails to report and perform his scheduled or assigned work, he shall become ineligible to be paid for the unworked holiday, unless he has failed to perform such work because of sickness or because of death in the immediate family (mother, father (including in-laws), children, brother, sister, husband, wife and grandparents) or because of similar good cause. As used in this Article, an eligible Employee is one who

(1) has worked 30 turns since his last hire;

(2) performs work or is on vacation in the pay period in which the holiday is observed (or where there are weekly pay periods, the pay period in which the holiday is observed or the next preceding pay period); and

(3) works as scheduled or assigned both on his last scheduled workday prior to and his first scheduled workday following the day on which the holiday is observed, unless he has failed so to work because of sickness or because of death in the immediate family or because of similar good cause.

Section 3. An eligible Employee who would otherwise be entitled to pay

for an unworked holiday and who shall be scheduled pursuant to the provisions
of Article IX to take a vacation during a period when a holiday occurs, shall
be paid for the unworked holiday in addition to his vacation pay. The provisions of clause (3) of Section 2 of this Article shall not apply to a day on which
an Employee is scheduled on vacation.

Section 4. An eligible part-time Employee shall receive pay for holidays in
accordance with the foregoing provisions of this Article, but the pay that he
shall receive for any such holiday shall be an amount equal to his applicable
hourly rate (as defined in Section 2) times the lesser of 8 or the average number
of hours worked by him per day in the preceding 2 pay periods.

Section 5. No Employee shall receive more than the compensation specified
in Section 3(b) of Article VII for hours worked on any holiday.

Section 6. A holiday shall be deemed to be the 24-hour period beginning
at 12:01 a.m. of the holiday or at the turn-changing time nearest thereto.

ARTICLE IX—VACATIONS

Section 1. Subject to the provisions of this Article, an Employee who has
completed the years of continuous service indicated in the following table in
any calendar year during the term of this Agreement shall receive during
such year a vacation corresponding to such years of continuous service and,
effective January 1, 1958, extra vacation pay, as shown in the following table:

Years of continuous service	Vacation	Extra vacation pay effective 1/1/58
1 or more...............	1 week	0
3 or more...............	1 week	½ week
5 or more...............	2 weeks	0
10 or more...............	2 weeks	½ week
15 or more...............	3 weeks	0
25 or more...............	3 weeks	½ week

Section 2. To be eligible for a vacation in any calendar year during the
term of this Agreement, the Employee must:

(a) have one year or more of continuous service; and

(b) not have been absent from work for 6 consecutive months or more in
the preceding calendar year; except that in the case of an Employee who completes one year of continuous service in the vacation calendar year, he shall
not have been absent from work for 6 consecutive months or more during the
12 months following the date of his original employment; provided, that an
Employee with more than one year of continuous service who, in any year, shall
be ineligible for a vacation by reason of the provisions of this paragraph as a
result of an absence on account of layoff or illness shall receive one week's
vacation with pay in such year if he shall not have been absent from work for

6 consecutive months or more in the 12 consecutive calendar months next preceding such vacation.

An Employee, even though otherwise eligible under this Article, forfeits the right to receive vacation benefits under this Article if his employment shall be terminated prior to January 1 of the vacation year.

Section 3. For the purposes of this Article the length of continuous service of an Employee with the Company shall be computed in accordance with the provisions of Section 3 of Article X of this Agreement.

Section 4. Vacations shall be scheduled between April 15 and December 31, except that an eligible Employee may request and be given his vacation at another time subject to the approval of the head of the department. While every effort will be made to meet the desires of Employees, Employees having longer service at the Plant being given preference as to choice, vacation schedules must conform to the requirements of operations and vacations must be taken as scheduled by the department heads. An Employee shall take his vacation in one continuous period, unless the head of the department in which he shall work shall, for some exceptional reason, approve of his breaking his vacation into two or more periods. Where an Employee's vacation is broken into two or more periods, the amount of his vacation pay for each of such periods and the amount of any payment to which he may be entitled in lieu of any portion of his vacation shall be based upon the rate of his vacation pay and the number of hours for which he shall be paid for the first of such periods; provided, however, that the vacation pay of any Employee for any part of his vacation taken after the effective date of a general wage increase under the provisions of this Agreement shall include such increase.

Section 5. The rate of vacation pay of an Employee shall be based on his average rate of earnings per hour for the last 2 non-holiday pay periods (or 4 pay periods where pay is computed weekly) for which the payrolls have been closed immediately preceding his vacation. The number of hours for which such Employee shall be paid for each vacation week shall be the average number of hours worked by him per week as computed for the pay periods so used, with a minimum allowance of 40 hours or the scheduled workweek of the Plant for the last week of the pay periods so used, whichever is larger, and a maximum of 48 hours or the scheduled workweek of the Plant for the last week of the pay periods so used, whichever is larger; provided, however, that the minimum allowance hereinbefore provided shall not be applicable to Employees who, for their own convenience, are regularly scheduled to work on a basis other than full time.

Section 6. The Union and the Company agree that their mutual objective is to afford maximum opportunity to the Employees to obtain their vacations and to attain maximum production. All Employees eligible for vacation shall be granted their vacation from work. However, the Company may, due to operating requirements and employment conditions, arrange, with the consent of an Employee, that such Employee receive vacation allowance in lieu of actual vacation. The vacation allowance paid to such an Employee shall be the same as it would have been had he taken his vacation beginning on the first Monday in November. The vacation allowance due such Employee shall be included in the first pay which shall be paid to him in December or as soon thereafter as shall be practicable.

ARTICLE X—SENIORITY

Section 1. In the promotion of Employees to non-supervisory positions and for the purpose of demotions, or layoffs in connection with the decreasing of the working force and of the recalling to work of men so laid off, the following factors shall be considered, and if factors (b) and (c) are relatively equal, length of continuous service shall govern:

(a) Length of continuous service in the applicable seniority unit determined as provided in Section 2 of this Article;

(b) Ability to perform the work; and

(c) Physical fitness.

In the filling of a temporary vacancy within a seniority unit, the Management shall, to the greatest degree that shall be consistent with efficiency of the operation and the safety of Employees, fill the vacancy with the Employee having the greatest continuous length of service in the seniority unit or on the particular turn in such unit in which the vacancy shall occur.

Section 2. (a) The units within which the seniority rules set forth in this Article shall apply shall be those which have been or shall from time to time be mutually agreed to in writing by the Management's Representative and the Union at the respective Plants and any such agreement hereafter entered into at any Plant shall be posted by the Union on the appropriate bulletin board of the Union at such Plant. In any case in which local agreement cannot be consummated as to the seniority unit in which a new job is to be placed, Management shall include such job in the most appropriate seniority unit or in a new seniority unit, if appropriate, subject to the grievance procedures of this Agreement.

(b) To the end of encouraging application of the principle that employment security should increase with continuous service, consistent with Section 1 of this Article, the appropriate representatives of Management and the Union at each Plant shall review the existing local seniority arrangements in connection with layoffs and re-hiring after layoffs. The representative duly designated by the International Union for this purpose and the representative designated by the Company shall be available to advise and consult with the Plant representatives of the parties. Any revised agreements on which the local Plant representatives of the parties can agree shall be placed in effect as soon as possible.

Section 3. (a) Subject to the provisions of Section 4 of this Article and the provisions of Article XV hereof, the length of continuous service of an Employee in the applicable unit determined as provided in Section 2 of this Article shall be computed from the date on which he first began work there, except that such length of service shall be broken and no prior period or periods of employment shall be counted

(1) if he shall voluntarily quit his employment;

(2) if he shall be discharged;

(3) if his employment shall be terminated by the Company, because he shall have been absent from work for 10 days or more without reasonable cause or because he shall have failed without such cause promptly to return to work after a leave of absence or when recalled to work after a layoff;

(4) if he shall be laid off and not recalled for work within 2 years; or

(5) if his length of service shall be broken in accordance with the provisions of Article XVIII or Section 5 of this Article.

(b) If an Employee shall be unable to work because of sickness or bodily injury and shall present to the Company satisfactory proof of the facts to that effect, then his length of continuous service shall not be broken but the excess of his period of absence over 6 months shall not be included as a part of his length of continuous service; provided, however, that an Employee who shall be injured while on duty shall accumulate credit for continuous service until the termination of the period for which workmen's compensation shall be payable to him.

(c) In computing the length of continuous service of an Employee at a Plant, if such Plant shall have been acquired by the Company, there shall be included the period of continuous service of such Employee at such Plant prior to its acquisition by the Company.

(d) An Employee who has attained a higher position than other Employees through the failure of such other Employees to accept promotions shall have a higher seniority standing than such other Employees for the purpose of the provisions set forth in Section 1 of this Article relating to promotions.

Section 4. A new Employee and one who shall be reemployed after a break in his continuous service shall not acquire any seniority until the expiration of the period of 6 months following his employment and shall not receive any credit for continuous service during such period. If he shall be continued in the employ of the Company after the expiration of such 6 months' period, the length of his continuous service shall be computed from the date of his employment or reemployment in accordance with the provisions of Section 3 of this Article. During the first 30 days of such 6 months' period, he may be laid off or discharged as the Management shall determine and his layoff or discharge shall not be made the basis of any claim or grievance against the Company.

Section 5. Subject to the provisions of Section 3 and Section 4 of this Article, the following provisions shall apply in respect of transfers of Employees within any Plant:

(a) If an Employee has been or shall be transferred out of any seniority unit at his own request, his length of service in the seniority unit from which he was or shall be transferred shall be deemed to have been broken 10 days after his transfer from such unit.

(b) If an Employee has been or shall be transferred from one seniority unit to another seniority unit other than at his own request, he shall retain and continue to accumulate length of service in the seniority unit from which he was or shall be transferred for a period of not longer than 6 months or for such other period as shall be agreed upon by the Management and the Grievance Committee.

(c) If an Employee has been or shall be promoted to a supervisory position, he shall retain and continue to accumulate length of service in the seniority unit from which he was or shall be so promoted.

(d) If an Employee (1) who was or shall be disabled while in military service and was or shall be reemployed in accordance with the provisions of Article XV of this Agreement or (2) who was or shall be disabled in the course of his employment with the Company, was or shall be transferred by agreement between the Management and the Grievance Committee from one seniority unit to another to accomplish his rehabilitation or to restore him, after a period of rehabilitation deemed reasonable by the Company's medical department, to the seniority unit from which he shall originally have been transferred, he may, by agreement between the Management and the Grievance Committee, carry with him his total accumulated length of service in any and all seniority units from which he shall be so transferred.

(e) The Management shall furnish to each Employee who shall be transferred from a seniority unit a copy of the Return Notice on which shall be indicated whether the transfer is at the request of the Employee or at the direction of the Management.

(f) For the purposes of this Section, an Employee who shall be laid off or demoted out of his seniority unit in connection with the decreasing of the working force in his seniority unit and who thereafter shall be employed by the Company outside such seniority unit shall not be deemed to have been transferred out of such seniority unit.

Section 6. (a) Each member of the Grievance Committee and each Employee who at the time shall be the President, Vice-President, Recording Secretary or Financial Secretary and Treasurer of the Local or Locals of the Union at any Plant shall, for their respective terms of office, have top seniority rights in their respective seniority units for the purposes of layoffs in connection with the decreasing of the working forces in such units; provided, however, that a Grievance Committeeman or an officer of a Local of the Union shall not be retained in the employ of the Company unless work which he can perform is available in his seniority unit.

(b) At each Plant the District Director of the Union shall designate in writing to the Management's Representative the names of the Grievance Committeemen (not exceeding 10 at any Plant) who shall have top seniority rights in accordance with the foregoing provisions of this Section.

(c) Any Employee having a length of continuous service with the Company of one year or more who shall be appointed or elected to an office in the Union at the Plant at which he shall be employed, may, upon the written request of the Union, be granted a leave of absence for a period of one year. By agreement of the Company and the Union, such leave of absence may be extended or renewed for a further period of one year or for such other period or periods as shall be agreed upon. Such Employee's length of service record shall be computed as though he were continuously employed by the Company during such leave of absence.

Section 7. If, as a result of a decrease in work other than decreases which may occur from day to day, the average scheduled hours of work of the Employees in a seniority unit shall be reduced for a period of 2 consecutive weeks to less than 32 hours per week and in the judgment of the Management that level of work will continue for an extended period of time, the head of the department affected will discuss with the Grievance Committeeman in such department the question whether a decrease of the working force shall be effected in accordance with the provisions of this Article or whether the available hours of work shall be distributed among the Employees in such unit so far as shall be practicable with due regard for the particular skills and abilities required to perform the work available there. If the head of the department and such Grievance Committeeman shall fail to agree, the working force in such unit shall be reduced to an extent which shall be sufficient to enable the Employees working there to average 32 hours of work per week.

Section 8. When a vacancy (other than a temporary vacancy) in any job in a seniority unit shall occur which is to be filled by promotion, the Management shall, so far as shall be practicable, post a notice of such vacancy in the department for a period of 30 days.

Section 9. The Management shall furnish to the Local Union concerned lists showing the continuous service of each Employee in each seniority unit agreed upon pursuant to Section 2 of this Article. Such lists shall be revised by the Management from time to time, as necessary, but at least every 6 months to keep them reasonably up to date. The seniority rights of individual Employees shall in no way be prejudiced by errors, inaccuracies or omissions in such lists.

ARTICLE XI—ADJUSTMENT OF GRIEVANCES

Section 1. (a) Should any differences arise between the Company and the Union as to the meaning and application of the provisions of this Agreement or as to any question relating to the wages, hours of work and other conditions of employment of any Employee, there shall not be any suspension of work on account of such differences, but an earnest effort shall be made to settle them promptly and in accordance with the provisions of this Agreement in the manner hereinafter set forth.

(b) The procedural steps for the settlement of grievances hereinafter in this Article set forth shall constitute a general standard which may be modified at any Plant by agreement between the Management and the Union, if, in the interest of prompt and orderly settlement of grievances, it shall be deemed advisable that such procedural steps be so modified.

Section 2. If an Employee shall believe that he has a justifiable request or complaint, he may discuss such request or complaint with his foreman, with or without a steward of the Union employed in his department being present, as he may elect, in an attempt to settle the matter. Any such request or complaint which shall not be satisfactorily disposed of within 2 days and which shall be presented in writing as hereinafter provided shall constitute a grievance and shall be handled under the procedure hereinafter in this Article set forth; provided, however, that a request for any change in any of the terms or provisions of this Agreement shall not be handled as a grievance under such procedure.

Step No. 1

Such a grievance shall be stated in writing on a form to be furnished by the Company, which shall be dated and shall be signed by the Employee involved and 4 copies of it shall be delivered to such foreman. Such foreman shall note in the appropriate place on such form his disposition of such grievance and shall sign and date the notation and return 2 copies of such form to such Employee or his steward and deliver or send one copy thereof to the superintendent of his department. Any grievance which shall not be so disposed of by the foreman within 3 days (excluding Saturdays, Sundays and holidays) after it shall have been so presented to him may be appealed to Step No. 2. Unless such grievance shall be appealed to such superintendent within 5 days after such disposition thereof by such foreman, such grievance shall be deemed to have been settled in accordance with such disposition and no appeal therefrom shall thereafter be taken.

Step No. 2

If such grievance shall be so appealed, it shall be discussed in an effort to settle it between a Union steward of such department and the superintendent thereof. The discussion shall be held and such superintendent shall dispose of such grievance within not more than 7 days after the date on which such grievance shall have been so appealed to such superintendent. If the superintendent shall fail to provide an opportunity for discussion of and shall fail to dispose of such grievance within 7 days, such grievance may be appealed to Step No. 3, unless an extension of time shall have been mutually agreed upon. The disposition of such grievance by such superintendent and the date thereof shall be noted on his copy and on the Employee's copy of the grievance form. If such grievance shall not be presented to the Management's Representative within 7 days after such disposition thereof by such superintendent, it shall be deemed to have been settled in accordance with such disposition and no appeal therefrom shall thereafter be taken.

Step No. 3

A grievance which shall not be settled by the procedure prescribed in the foregoing Step No. 2 shall be discussed promptly at a mutually satisfactory time between the Management's Representative and the Grievance Committee and a representative of the Union. At any meeting with the Grievance Committee the Management's Representative may be accompanied by such other representatives of the Management as he shall select.

There shall be one Grievance Committee at each Plant, which shall consist of such number of Employees as shall be mutually agreed upon between the

Management's Representative and the Union, but the number thereof shall not in any case be less than 3 nor more than 10.

At the meeting at which such discussion shall be held either the Management or the Union may produce persons who, being familiar with the facts involved, may aid in a satisfactory settlement of such grievance, but their presence at such meeting shall be limited to the time necessary for the presentation of testimony with regard to such grievance.

Unless otherwise agreed, such grievance shall be discussed at a Step No. 3 meeting which shall be held not later than 9 days after such grievance shall have been presented to the Management's Representative. If the Management's Representative shall fail to provide an opportunity for discussion of such grievance within such 9 days, such grievance may be appealed to Step No. 4, unless an extension of time shall have been mutually agreed upon.

If a grievance shall be presented to the Management's Representative which shall not have been taken up in accordance with the procedure prescribed under the foregoing Steps Nos. 1 and 2, respectively, it shall be referred back to the proper supervisory officials for handling in accordance with such procedure, unless it shall be of a general character which cannot be settled by such supervisory officials.

Minutes of each meeting under this Step No. 3 shall be prepared by the Management's Representative and shall be signed by the Chairman or Secretary of the Grievance Committee and the Management's Representative not later than 10 days after the date on which such meeting shall have been held. Such minutes shall be typewritten and shall conform substantially to the following outline:

(a) Date and place of meeting.

(b) Names and positions of those present.

(c) Identifying number and description of each grievance discussed.

(d) Brief statement of the Union's position with regard to each grievance.

(e) Brief statement of the Company's position with regard to each grievance.

(f) Action taken at such meeting with regard to each grievance.

(g) Statement as to whether or not the Union concurred in such action and of any exceptions taken by the Union thereto.

If an appeal from the action taken with regard to any grievance in accordance with the procedure under this Step No. 3 as shown in the minutes of the meeting at which such action shall have been taken shall not be made within 30 days after the date of such meeting or within 20 days after a draft of the minutes of such meeting shall first have been received by a representative of the Union, whichever of those periods shall last expire, such grievance shall be deemed to have been settled in accordance with such action and no appeal therefrom shall thereafter be taken.

Step No. 4

Any grievance which shall not be settled by the procedure prescribed in the foregoing Steps Nos. 1, 2 and 3 shall be discussed in an attempt to reach a mutually satisfactory settlement thereof between two representatives of the Union who shall be certified to the Company in writing as the representatives selected by the Union for the purpose and two representatives of the Company who shall be similarly certified by the Company to the Union. Notice of the intention of either party to take up a grievance under this Step No. 4 shall be given to the other party in writing within 30 days after the date of the meeting under Step No. 3 at which action with regard to such grievance shall have been taken or within 20 days after a draft of the minutes of such meeting shall first have been received by a representative of the Union, whichever of those periods shall last expire. Such notice shall state the identifying number and subject matter of such grievance and the objections made to the previous action taken with regard thereto.

Except as otherwise agreed by the Company and the Union, meetings which shall be required under this Step No. 4 shall be held at Bethlehem, Pa., and the number of such meetings and any other procedure which may aid in the effort to reach a satisfactory settlement of any grievance shall be agreed upon between the representatives of the Company and the representatives of the Union.

Minutes of each meeting for the discussion of grievances under this Step No. 4 substantially similar in form to those prescribed for meetings under Step No. 3 shall be prepared by the representatives of the Company and shall be signed by them and the representatives of the Union within 10 days after such meeting shall be held.

If an appeal from the action taken with regard to any grievance in accordance with the procedure under this Step No. 4 as shown in the minutes of the meeting at which such action shall have been taken shall not be made within 30 days after the date of such meeting or within 20 days after a draft of the minutes of such meeting shall first have been received by a representative of the Union, whichever of such periods shall last expire, such grievance shall be deemed to have been settled in accordance with such action and no appeal therefrom shall thereafter be taken.

Section 3. (a) The foregoing procedure, if followed in good faith by both parties, should be adequate to reach a fair and expeditious settlement of any grievance. In the event, however, that the procedure hereinbefore in Section 2 of this Article set forth shall have been followed in respect of any grievance and such grievance shall not thereby have been satisfactorily settled and if such grievance shall involve the meaning and application of the provisions of this Agreement, it may be appealed by notice in writing to the Company, within 30 days after the date of the meeting at which discussion of such grievance under Step No. 4 shall have been completed, or within 20 days after a draft of the minutes of such meeting shall first have been received by a representative of the Union, whichever of those periods shall last expire, to an impartial umpire to be appointed by mutual agreement of the parties hereto.

(b) Except as in this Agreement otherwise expressly provided, any grievance which shall involve any claim that any then existing wage rate should be changed shall not be submitted to arbitration under the provisions of this Section, unless the Company and the Union shall specifically agree in writing so to submit such grievance or unless such claim is that such wage rate was established or increased or decreased in contravention of the provisions of this Agreement.

(c) An umpire to whom any grievance shall be submitted in accordance with the provisions of this Section shall, in so far as shall be necessary to the determination of such grievance, have authority to interpret and apply the provisions of this Agreement, but he shall not have authority to alter in any way any of such provisions.

(d) The appointment of such umpire as hereinbefore provided and his decision on any matter which shall properly have been referred to him shall be final and binding upon the Company, the Union and all Employees concerned therein.

(e) The compensation of such umpire for his services hereunder and his expenses in connection therewith shall be shared equally by the Company and the Union.

(f) Except as in this Agreement otherwise expressly provided, an award of the impartial umpire in respect of any grievance which shall be so submitted to him shall not in any case be made retroactive to a date prior to the date on which such grievance shall have been first presented in written form under Step No. 1 of the procedure set forth in Section 2 of this Article. An award of the impartial umpire in respect of any grievance in respect to rates of pay (other than a grievance arising out of the provisions of Article V of this Agreement), overtime compensation, call-in pay, shift premiums, suspensions, seniority, holidays and vacations shall be made retroactive to the date of the occurrence or non-occurrence of the event upon which the grievance is based, but in no case prior to a date 30 days before such grievance shall have been first presented in written form in Step No. 1 of such procedure.

Section 4. (a) If any steward of the Union shall so request of his foreman, he shall be granted such time off without pay as he may reasonably require for the purpose of investigating the facts with regard to and of endeavoring to settle any grievance in Step No. 1 or Step No. 2 presented by any Employee in his department.

(b) If any member of the Grievance Committee shall so request of his foreman, he shall be granted such time off without pay as he may reasonably require for the purpose of investigating and of endeavoring to settle any grievance in Step No. 3 or Step No. 4 with which he shall be concerned and, by request to the Management's Representative, he shall be permitted to visit any department other than his own, when a visit there is necessary for such purposes.

(c) If a representative of the Union who shall have been certified to the Company in writing as the Union's representative for the purpose of handling grievances in Step No. 4 from a particular Plant shall so request of the Management's Representative, he shall be permitted to visit such Plant for the purpose of investigating any grievance which shall have been appealed therefrom to Step No. 4, subject to such regulations as shall be established by the Management's Representative.

Section 5. An alleged grievance shall not be presented or considered under the procedure for the adjustment of grievances hereinbefore in this Article prescribed, unless such alleged grievance shall be presented in writing to the Management within 30 days after the date on which the facts or events upon which such alleged grievance is based shall have existed or occurred; provided, however, that an alleged grievance in respect of a decision of the Management under Article XII of this Agreement shall not be presented or considered under such procedure, unless it shall be presented in writing to the Management's Representative within 10 days after the Employee involved shall have received written notice of such decision.

Section 6. Any alleged grievance which was presented in writing in Step No. 1 under a prior agreement between the Company and the Union and which is still pending and not finally disposed of at the date of this Agreement shall be handled in accordance with the provisions of this Article and shall be determined in accordance with the applicable provisions of such prior agreement which were in effect at the time when such alleged grievance arose.

ARTICLE XII—DISCHARGE OF EMPLOYEES

Section 1. Before discharging any Employee the Management shall give him written notice of its intention to discharge him. The Management may suspend such Employee pending a final determination of his case as hereinafter provided. If such Employee shall not within 5 days after receiving such notice file with the Management's Representative a request in writing for a hearing as hereinafter provided, the Management may at any time after the expiration of such 5 days discharge him and he shall not be entitled to assert any claim or grievance against the Company in respect of his discharge.

Section 2. (a) If such Employee shall, within 5 days after receiving such notice, file with such Management's Representative a request in writing for a hearing on the question as to whether or not he should be discharged, he shall within 5 days after the receipt of such notice by such Management's Representative be furnished with a written statement of the reasons why the Management shall intend to discharge him and of the time and place at which such hearing will be held, which time shall be not less than 5 days nor more than 10 days after the date on which such statement shall be so furnished to him.

(b) Such hearing shall be held before an official of the Company who shall be designated by it for the purpose, and at such hearing such Employee may be represented by one or more members of the Grievance Committee and shall be given a reasonable opportunity to present evidence on his behalf.

(c) Within 10 days after the conclusion of such hearing the Management shall notify such Employee in writing of its decision as to the action which it shall take in his case, which action may include the discharge of such Employee or such other action as it shall deem proper. If such Employee shall be aggrieved by such decision, he may within 10 days after receiving written notice of such decision present his grievance in respect thereof to the Management's Representative and such grievance shall be handled in accordance with the procedure set forth in Article XI of this Agreement beginning with Step No. 3. If he shall not so present such grievance within such 10 days, he shall not be entitled to assert any claim or grievance against the Company in respect of any such action.

(d) If such grievance shall be submitted to an impartial umpire as provided in Article XI of this Agreement and he shall determine that such Employee was discharged or suspended, as the case may be, without just cause, and that such Employee is entitled to compensation for time lost by him by reason thereof, such umpire shall award to such Employee back pay for the time which he shall have lost by reason of his suspension or discharge, as the case may be, at the rate of pay which would be applicable to such Employee for such time.

Section 3. The foregoing provisions of this Article shall not apply to a case in which an Employee shall be suspended or laid off for any reason (other than a suspension as hereinbefore provided pending a determination as to whether or not he shall be discharged), but any grievance relating to any such case shall be handled in accordance with the procedure set forth in Article XI of this Agreement.

Section 4. Any member of the Grievance Committee who shall have been designated by an Employee to represent him at any hearing which shall be held in accordance with the foregoing provisions of this Article shall, if such member shall so request to his foreman, be granted such time off without pay as he shall reasonably require in order to investigate the facts with regard to the subject matter of such hearing and to attend such hearing.

ARTICLE XIII—MANAGEMENT FUNCTIONS

The management of the Plants and the direction of the working forces and the operations at the Plants, including the hiring, promoting and retiring of Employees, the suspending, discharging or otherwise disciplining of Employees for just cause, the laying off and calling to work of Employees in connection with any reduction or increase in the working forces, the scheduling of work and the control and regulation of the use of all equipment and other property of the Company, are the exclusive functions of the Management; provided, however, that in the exercise of such functions the Management shall observe the provisions of this Agreement and shall not discriminate against any Employee or applicant for employment because of his membership in or lawful activity on behalf of the Union.

ARTICLE XIV—SAFETY AND HEALTH

Section 1. The Company will continue to make every reasonable effort to provide safe and healthful conditions of work for Employees at the Plants and to provide Employees with any necessary protective equipment in accordance with the practices prevailing at the respective Plants at the date of this Agreement. Goggles, gas masks, face shields, respirators, special-purpose gloves, fireproof, weatherproof or acid-proof protective clothing, when necessary and required, shall be provided to the Employees without cost, except that the Company may charge an Employee a reasonable amount for any loss or willful destruction of any of the foregoing by such Employee. In so far as reasonably practicable, considering the nature and requirements of the respective operations, suitable heating and ventilating systems shall be provided.

Section 2. (a) The Union will cooperate with the Company in encouraging Employees to observe the safety regulations which shall be prescribed by the Company and to work in a safe manner. To that end, a Safety Committee shall be established at each Plant to be composed of 3 representatives of the Company and 3 Employees at that Plant (unless otherwise agreed by the Management's Representative and the Union at such Plant), which shall assist, make recommendations to, and cooperate with, the head of the safety department at such Plant. The Employees on such Committee at each Plant shall be designated by the Union. The Employees who shall be nominated by the Union to be representatives on such Committee at any Plant shall be Employees who have knowledge of the practices at that Plant and who shall have worked there a minimum of one year.

(b) The Union and the Company shall each designate 3 representatives to a joint committee on safety which shall meet from time to time to review the operation of this Article with a view to achieving maximum understanding as to how the Company and the Union can most effectively cooperate in achieving the objective set forth in Section 1 of this Article.

Section 3. If an Employee shall believe that there exists an unsafe condition, changed from the normal hazards inherent in the operation, so that the Employee is in danger of injury, he shall notify his foreman of such danger and of the facts relating thereto. Thereafter, unless there shall be a dispute as to the existence of such unsafe condition, he shall have the right, subject to reasonable steps for protecting other Employees and the equipment from injury, to be relieved from duty on the job in respect of which he has complained and to return to such job when such unsafe condition shall be remedied. The Management may in its discretion assign such Employee to other available work at the Plant. If the existence of such alleged unsafe condition shall be disputed, the Chairman of the Grievance Committee and the Management's Representative or his designee shall immediately investigate such alleged unsafe condition and determine whether it exists. If they shall not agree and if the Chairman of the Grievance Committee is of the opinion that such alleged unsafe condition exists, the Employee shall have the right to present a grievance in writing to the Management's Representative or his designee and thereafter to be relieved from duty on the job as stated above. Such grievance shall be presented without delay directly to an impartial umpire under the provisions of Article XI of this Agreement, who shall determine whether such Employee was justified in leaving the job because of the existence of such an unsafe condition.

ARTICLE XV—MILITARY SERVICE AND JURY PAY

Section 1. (a) Employees, other than temporary Employees, who enter the armed forces of the United States or who have left or who subsequent to the date hereof leave their positions for the purpose of being inducted into, enlisting in, determining their physical fitness to enter or to perform training duty in said armed forces, shall be reinstated in accordance with the applicable federal statutes.

(b) A reasonable program of training shall be afforded to an Employee who shall not be qualified to perform the work on the job which he might have attained, if he had not been absent in such service.

(c) An Employee who is entitled to reemployment at any Plant under the provisions of this Section and who applies for such reemployment and who desires to pursue a course of study in accordance with the laws of the United States granting him such opportunity, shall be granted a leave of absence for such purpose. An Employee who desires such a leave of absence after returning to his employment with the Company shall have it granted only if he notifies the Company in writing, within one year after his reemployment, of his intention to pursue such a course of study. Such leave of absence shall not constitute a break in his length of continuous service and the period of such leave shall be included in his length of continuous service, if such Employee shall report promptly for reemployment after the completion or termination of such course of study and if he shall at least once each year notify the Management and the Union in writing of his intention to return to work at such Plant at the completion or termination of such course of study.

(d) An Employee who is entitled to reemployment in accordance with the provisions of this Section and who has been disabled in the course of such service in the armed forces shall, during the period of such disability, be assigned without regard to the provisions of Article X hereof relating to seniority to any vacancy which shall be suitable to his disability, provided that the disability of such Employee is of such nature that it shall be onerous or impossible for him to return to his own job or department and provided further that he shall have the minimum physical requirements for the work available.

Section 2. (a) If any Employee who would otherwise have been entitled in any year to a vacation with pay under the provisions of Article IX of this Agreement shall during such year enter the armed forces of the United States before he shall have taken such vacation or been paid an allowance in lieu of such vacation and if he shall furnish to the Company at least 14 days' prior written notice of his intention to enlist, he shall be paid an allowance in lieu of such vacation equal to the amount of vacation pay which he would have been entitled to receive for the period of such vacation.

(b) Any Employee who shall be reemployed under the provisions of Section 1 of this Article and whose length of continuous service with the Company determined as provided in Article IX of this Agreement shall qualify him for a vacation with pay in the year in which he shall so be reemployed shall receive such vacation with pay or a vacation allowance in lieu thereof irrespective of the date in such year on which he shall so be reemployed.

Section 3. An Employee who is called for jury service shall be excused from work for the days on which he serves and he shall receive, for each such day of jury service on which he otherwise would have worked, the difference between 8 times his average straight time hourly earnings (as computed for holiday allowance) and the payment he receives for jury service. The Employee will present proof of service and of the amount of pay received therefor.

ARTICLE XVI—UNION ACTIVITY

No Employee shall engage in any union activity on the property of the Company in any manner which shall interfere with production or engage in any union activity on Company time.

ARTICLE XVII—PROHIBITION OF STRIKES AND LOCKOUTS

During the term of this Agreement neither the Union nor any Employee shall (a) engage in or in any way encourage or sanction any strike or other action which shall interrupt or interfere with work or production at any of the Plants or (b) prevent or attempt to prevent the access of employees to any of the Plants. During the term of this Agreement the Company shall not engage in any lockout of Employees at any of the Plants. The Management may suspend and later discharge, in accordance with the provisions of Article XII of this Agreement, any Employee who shall violate any provision of this Article. Prior to discharging any such Employee for any such violation, the Management shall furnish the name, check number and address of such Employee to the Director of the District of the Union in which the Plant is located.

ARTICLE XVIII—SEVERANCE ALLOWANCE

Section 1. If the Company shall close permanently a Plant or discontinue permanently a department of a Plant or a substantial portion thereof, each Employee whose employment shall be terminated by the Company as a result thereof and who at the time shall have a length of continuous service with the Company of 3 years or more shall be entitled to a severance allowance all in accordance with the provisions hereinafter in this Article set forth.

Section 2. For the purposes of this Article, the length of continuous service of an Employee with the Company shall be computed in accordance with the provisions of Section 3 of Article X of this Agreement, except that, if an Employee shall be laid off for a period of over 6 months, the part of such period over 6 months shall not be included as part of his length of continuous service with the Company.

Section 3. The amount of severance allowance which an Employee shall receive in accordance with the provisions of this Article shall be 4 weeks' pay in the case of Employees having a length of continuous service of 3 years or more but less than 5 years, 6 weeks' pay in the case of Employees having a length of continuous service of 5 years or more but less than 7 years, 7 weeks' pay in the case of Employees having a length of continuous service of 7 years or more but less than 10 years and 8 weeks' pay in the case of Employees having a length of continuous service of 10 years or more. Each week of severance allowance shall be determined in accordance with the provisions for the calculation of vacation pay set forth in Section 5 of Article IX of this Agreement. The payment of a severance allowance to an Employee shall be made in a lump sum when his employment shall be terminated.

Section 4. If an Employee at any Plant who shall lose his job as a result of the permanent closing of such Plant or the permanent discontinuance of a department of such Plant or a substantial portion thereof shall be offered employment by the Company consistent with the provisions of Article X hereof in a job for which he is qualified at such Plant, in the same or a higher job class, he shall not be entitled to a severance allowance pursuant to the provisions of this Article. If he shall be offered employment by the Company in any other job, he shall have the option of either accepting such other employment or receiving the severance allowance herein provided. The length of continuous service of an Employee who shall be paid a severance allowance pursuant to the provisions of this Article shall be deemed to be broken as of the date of such payment.

Section 5. An Employee shall not be entitled to a severance allowance pursuant to the provisions of this Article, if he shall receive an amount equivalent to such allowance by reason of any other agreement, law or otherwise. If an Employee shall be entitled to any discharge, liquidation, severance or dismissal allowance or payment of similar kind (not including statutory unemployment compensation payments) by reason of any law of the United States or of any of the states, districts or territories subject to its jurisdiction, the total amount of any such payment shall be deducted from the severance allowance to which the Employee shall be entitled under this Article.

Section 6. Notwithstanding any other provision of this Agreement, an Employee who would otherwise have been terminated in accordance with the applicable provisions of this Agreement and under the circumstances specified in Section 1 of this Article may at such time elect to be placed upon layoff status for 30 days or to continue on layoff status for an additional 30 days if he had already been on layoff status. At the end of such 30-day period he may elect to continue on layoff status or be terminated and receive severance allowance if he is eligible for any such allowance under the provisions of this Article; provided, however, that the amount of any such severance allowance to which he would have been otherwise eligible at the commencement of such 30-day period shall be reduced by the amount of any Supplemental Unemployment Benefit payments received by him with respect to such 30-day period.

ARTICLE XIX—TERM OF AGREEMENT

Section 1. Except as otherwise expressly provided in this Agreement, this Agreement shall become effective on the date hereof and shall continue in effect to and including midnight of June 30, 1959.

Section 2. Either party may on or before May 1, 1959, give notice to the other party of the desire of the party giving such notice to negotiate with respect to the terms and conditions of a new agreement on wages, rates of pay, hours of work and other conditions of employment including insurance and pensions (the provisions of the Insurance Agreement and of the Pension Agreement, both of which are dated August 3, 1956, to the contrary notwithstanding); provided, however, that the terms and conditions of said new agreement with respect to insurance and pensions shall not be made effective before November 1, 1959. If the parties shall not agree with respect to insurance and pensions by midnight of June 30, 1959, either party may thereafter resort to strike or lockout, as the case may be, in support of its position in respect of such matter as well as any other matter in dispute (the provisions of the Insurance Agreement and the Pension Agreement, dated August 3, 1956, to the contrary notwithstanding).

Section 3. Any notice required or permitted to be given hereunder shall be deemed to have been given when it shall have been mailed by registered mail postage prepaid addressed to the party to which such notice is required or permitted to be given hereunder at the address of such party hereinafter set forth. Notices to the Company shall be addressed to the Company at Bethlehem, Pennsylvania, attention of the Manager of Industrial Relations. Notices to the Union shall be addressed to United Steelworkers of America, 1500 Commonwealth Building, Pittsburgh 22, Pennsylvania.

IN WITNESS WHEREOF, the parties hereto have caused this Agreement to be signed in their respective names by their respective representatives thereunto duly authorized.

> BETHLEHEM STEEL COMPANY,
> BETHLEHEM PACIFIC COAST STEEL CORPORATION,
> BETHLEHEM CORNWALL CORPORATION,
> BETHLEHEM LIMESTONE COMPANY,
> BETHLEHEM SUPPLY COMPANY,
> BUFFALO TANK CORPORATION,
> THE DUNDALK COMPANY,
>   by
>   J. M. Larkin, *Vice-President*
> UNITED STEELWORKERS OF AMERICA,
>   by
>   David J. McDonald, *President*
>   [and other union representatives]

APPENDIX 1—LIST OF PLANTS

[omitted]

Effective on the date of this Agreement, the job classes for apprentice jobs as contained in the Manual shall be increased by one job class.

APPENDIX 2

Job Class	Standard Hourly Wage Rate		
	Effective August 3, 1956	Effective July 1, 1957	Effective July 1, 1958
1 - 2	$1.82	$1.89	$1.96
3	1.883	1.955	2.027
4	1.946	2.02	2.094
5	2.009	2.085	2.161
6	2.072	2.15	2.228
7	2.135	2.215	2.295
8	2.198	2.28	2.362
9	2.261	2.345	2.429
10	2.324	2.41	2.496
11	2.387	2.475	2.563
12	2.45	2.54	2.63
13	2.513	2.605	2.697
14	2.576	2.67	2.764
15	2.639	2.735	2.831
16	2.702	2.80	2.898
17	2.765	2.865	2.965
18	2.828	2.93	3.032
19	2.891	2.995	3.099
20	2.954	3.06	3.166
21	3.017	3.125	3.233
22	3.08	3.19	3.30
23	3.143	3.255	3.367
24	3.206	3.32	3.434
25	3.269	3.385	3.501
26	3.332	3.45	3.568
27	3.395	3.515	3.635
28	3.458	3.58	3.702
29	3.521	3.645	3.769
30	3.584	3.71	3.836
31	3.647	3.775	3.903
32	3.71	3.84	3.97

APPENDIX 3

[Supplemental agreement on incentive rates omitted]

FOR DISCUSSION AND ANALYSIS

1. It has been said that the *philosophy* of collective bargaining has become widely accepted in our society because it has ethical connota-

tions according with our system of social values. Do you find in the *practice* of collective bargaining any behavior patterns which have attached to them ethical connotations *not* consonant with our system of social values? What explanations can you give for the presence of any such practices, if you find them? Again if you find such practices, what is the significance of the resulting conflict of philosophy and practice? How is it likely to be resolved?

2. One of the sessions of the 1952 annual meeting of the Industrial Relations Research Association was given over to a discussion of the value of statistics in collective bargaining. William J. Caples, Inland Steel vice president in charge of personnel and public relations, was among the most pessimistic of the participants. He commented:

> In my experience, the use of statistical indices are a waste of time in bargaining at the local level or even at the local-international level. In negotiations with the international also, indices have little or no positive value except for public relations purposes. Economic force and emotion, not statistics nor their interpretation, determine collective bargaining. . . .
>
> Statistical indices are useful toward your side of a controversy in two areas. In determining one's own course of action, you have to be honest with yourself and you must know the impact of your decisions on your company. You cannot afford to select an index because it makes you happy but only because it tells a true story. Second, there is the dubious use in attempting to persuade the public—a use which possibly should be banned.

a. Would you agree with Mr. Caples that statistics and economic data generally play no major role in affecting either party's decisions at the negotiating table?

b. Analyze the use and effectiveness of the presentation of data in the steel negotiations described above.

3. During the course of the 1956 steel negotiations, the Chamber of Commerce of the United States commented in its monthly publication, *Economic Intelligence:*

> The companies made an offer, prior to the strike, of a five-year contract with wage and benefit increases, estimated to equal about 65¢ per hour over the life of the contract. The union leaders pronounced this "too little, too late and too long."
>
> The union leaders only vaguely stated what they would settle for.
>
> Now, of course, if the steel companies go beyond their final prestrike offer, they are *putting a premium on future strikes.* Union leaders would say: "See what extra we got for you by striking."
>
> For this reason, it's important for American business management to discover in advance, before a strike occurs, what is fair, what is right, what is equitable and what is economically feasible. Then make an offer on that basis

and be sure that the facts and the reasons get through to the workers and the public.

If the union leaders or the workers can show that the judgment of management is wrong on equity or economic grounds, management, of course, should be ready to reconsider what it had thought of as its final offer.

But once management has made a decision as to what is fair and right, after having listened to all the arguments and all the evidence, it must stick to that final offer. Otherwise, if a strike then occurs, it puts a premium on future strikes. It helps to spread the strike fever.

On the other hand, Professor Sumner Slichter, in describing in his book *The Challenge of Industrial Relations* what steps the parties could take to improve the process of collective bargaining, suggested:

Be prepared to compromise. This means that each side should propose more changes than it expects to get. There has been much dispute over whether it is better for employers and unions to ask only what they are willing to fight for, or whether each side should propose considerably more than it would be willing, if necessary, to accept. If each side quite definitely regards its proposals as the minimum terms which it is willing to accept, this is in reality the equivalent of entering the conference with a closed mind. If negotiations are to be a process of exploring the problems of each side and of working out fair compromises, both unions and employers should suggest more than they might be willing to accept. This, of course, does not mean that their proposals should be extravagant or unrealistic. The proposals should be carefully considered before being offered and they should have real merit.

a. Compare the U.S. Chamber of Commerce position with General Electric's bargaining formula, described in Chapter 5. Are they in agreement?

b. Indicate the areas of disagreement between the Chamber's position and that of Professor Slichter.

c. Which of these two approaches would you expect to be more successful? In answering this question, first define what you mean by "successful."

4. With respect to the 1956 steel negotiations, reported above:

a. Itemize all the pressures upon each of the parties which contributed to the other's bargaining power.

b. What influence do you believe public opinion played in these negotiations?

c. List the various ways in which each of the parties sought to manipulate the bargaining power relationship to its advantage.

d. The Chamber of Commerce comment in question 3, above, suggests that the steel companies erred in their bargaining strategy by not adhering to their original offer. Do you agree?

e. In 1955 Benjamin Fairless, former president of United States Steel, was cited by the Duquesne University Chapter of the Society for the Advancement of Management for his success in achieving a high degree of union-management cooperation in his company. Assuming no radical change in the union-management relationship between then and June of 1956, would you conclude that the 1956 steel strike indicated that the 1955 award was undeserved or premature?

5. Analyze the Bethlehem collective-bargaining agreement reprinted in this chapter as follows:

a. Read the agreement quickly and examine its table of contents. Determine four categories or classifications under which most or all of the contract's provisions can best be classified. Classify all the provisions under these four headings.

b. On the strength of the above and assuming that the agreement adequately and accurately represents the members' wishes, what does the agreement tell you about the primary interests which workers seek to protect through their union?

c. Are you surprised at the inclusion or omission of any matters? If so, analyze the reasons for your surprise. Do they tell you anything about your own system of values and predispositions?

d. What provisions would you, as management, have most strenuously resisted?

e. For what provisions would you, as a union member, have most strenuously fought?

f. What provision would you, as a union official, have most vigorously sought?

g. Do your conclusions under (*d*), (*e*), and (*f*) above suggest differing systems of values and motivations of these three groups?

8: The Bargaining Unit

Collective bargaining takes place on behalf of a defined group of employees, and the collective agreement applies to the same defined group of employees. This "defined group" is known as the bargaining unit.

The definition of the bargaining unit may appear to be a relatively simple and uninteresting matter, but in actuality it is freighted with considerable drama and significance. Among the issues which it raises are whether large-scale ("industry-wide") units have deleterious economic effects, what kinds of units permit unions best to fulfill their representative functions, whether units should be defined in such a way as intentionally to improve the bargaining power of workers, how units once established may be stabilized.

Some of these issues we shall encounter in greater detail in later chapters. Because the National Labor Relations Board has been given the authority to determine the "appropriate" bargaining unit for purposes of conducting representation elections, there will be some further discussion of the unit in the next chapter. The employer argument that multi-employer and industry-wide bargaining are monopolistic devices which should be eliminated or controlled will also be developed in more detail in a later chapter, along with union counterarguments.

COLLECTIVE BARGAINING STRUCTURES: THE EMPLOYER BARGAINING UNIT

Bureau of Labor Statistics Report No. 1, 1953, pp. 1–2, prepared by Theodore W. Reedy, assisted by Gloria Johnson, in the Division of Wages and Industrial Relations

As collective bargaining developed through the years, many types of bargaining structures evolved. In most cases these structures developed gradually as employers and unions sought to adapt to changes in economic circumstances, relative bargaining power, and other conditions. Changes in bargaining structures generally reflect efforts to find the best possible bargaining arrangement for the parties, for both negotiation and contract administration.

On one side of the bargaining table, the employer unit may range from one employer with one or more plants to an association covering virtually an entire industry. On the other side, the employee unit may consist of an industrial or craft union, or various mixtures of these types with local, regional, or national representation, or a group of unions working together in a trades department or other special bargaining combination. The type and character of the units of bargaining vary among industries, among areas, and within industries and areas.

The purpose of this study is limited to an analysis of employer bargaining units. From the point of view of scope and jurisdiction, two broad types of employer bargaining units can be distinguished. The first, the single-employer unit, represents bargaining by single plants or by more than one plant under a common management. Thus, single-employer contracts range from the purely local agreements, negotiated for a single plant with one or more unions, to agreements covering all plants of a far-flung corporation.

The second broad type of bargaining unit, the multiemployer bargaining unit, provides several distinct kinds of contracts. Form contracts are identical agreements signed by different employers practically always at the request of the union. They are found most frequently where there are a large number of small competing business organizations, particularly within a metropolitan area. These agreements are classified as multiemployer principally because the terms of the contract are applied uniformly to employers who may not have participated in the actual negotiations. The trucking industry provides many examples.

Another type of multiemployer contract, found rather infrequently, is that in which employers jointly participate in contract negotiations, without, however, being members of any formal association. By far the most prevalent of all the types of multiemployer bargaining is association bargaining, which is carried on by groups of employers combining for the purpose of negotiating contracts with labor unions. The association may range from an organization which meets only during contract negotiations to an elaborate organization with a constitution, bylaws, and a regular staff of officers. Between these extremes are many variations in organization and procedure, which follow no fixed pattern by industry, region, or stage of collective bargaining development. Federations of associations are occasionally organized, usually in the same locality, to conduct negotiations on a correspondingly broader scale.

EXTENT OF MULTIEMPLOYER BARGAINING

Analysis of collective-bargaining agreements,[1] covering 8,410,000 workers, shows that one-third of the workers are under agreements signed by groups of employers or employer associations. The remaining two-thirds of the workers are covered by agreements negotiated by single employers. Railroad agree-

[1] A sample of 11,460 agreements, current in 1951, was used for this study. These agreements, on file in the Bureau of Labor Statistics, covered about 8,410,000 workers. Seventy percent of these agreements covering 66 percent of the workers were in manufacturing industries; the rest were in nonmanufacturing, excluding railroads. . . .

ments were not included in this analysis. In view of the practice of nationwide bargaining on wages in the railroad industry, and making allowances for agreements not accounted for, it appears probable that as many as 5 million workers are involved in multiemployer bargaining.

Of the agreements analyzed, approximately five-sixths, covering about 5,750,-000 workers (68 percent), were negotiated on the basis of single-employer units, whereas one-sixth, covering 2,660,000 workers (32 percent), were negotiated on a multiemployer basis. Thus, it is clear that agreements with single employers remain the predominant type.

EMPLOYER ASSOCIATIONS

State of New York, Department of Labor, Division of Research and Statistics, Publication Number B-71, New York 13, N.Y., November, 1953, pp. 3–5

EMPLOYER ASSOCIATIONS ENGAGED IN COLLECTIVE BARGAINING IN NEW YORK STATE

Questionnaires were mailed by the Division of Research and Statistics of the New York State Department of Labor in the first quarter of 1953 to all employer associations in New York State that were believed to engage in collective bargaining. Information obtained in the course of the survey indicates that the 561 employer associations listed in this directory engage, or were engaged within the past two years, in collective bargaining affecting workers in New York State.

Altogether approximately 1,000,000 workers in New York State are covered by association-union contracts. These represent 20 per cent of all private nonfarm workers in the State, and 30 per cent of all union workers outside of agriculture and government. The manufacturing industry having the largest proportion of workers under association agreements is apparel (78 per cent), while the smallest proportion (1 per cent) is in machinery and in professional and scientific apparatus, ignoring those industries in which there is no association bargaining at all. Outside of manufacturing, the industry with the smallest proportion of employees covered by association agreements is wholesale and retail trade (7 per cent), and the highest proportion is in construction (73 per cent).

Of union workers in the State, 30 per cent in manufacturing and 37 per cent in nonmanufacturing are under association agreements. Over four-fifths of the organized workers in the apparel and construction industries and over half of those in real estate (primarily building service and maintenance), in transportation (excluding railroads), in services, and in lumber manufacturing are covered by union contracts negotiated with employer associations. On the other hand, relatively few of the organized workers in the industries making machinery and fabricated metal products are under such agreements.

The following description is based on reports from 476 employer associations. These associations reported in the spring of 1953 that they were parties to 691 union agreements. The agreements covered over 882,000 workers and involved over 38,850 of the 42,000 firms that were members of the associations.

SIZE OF ASSOCIATIONS

Employer associations engaging in collective bargaining in New York State range in size from 2 to 2,500 member firms. Associations with at least 10 but fewer than 20 members are about a fourth of all those studied; but almost one-half have 40 or more members. Most associations with 50 or more members are in apparel manufacturing, construction, services, transportation (excluding railroads), and wholesale and retail trade. All of the five associations reporting 1,000 members or more are in nonmanufacturing industries—real estate, wholesale and retail trade, and transportation (excluding railroads). . . .

BEGINNING OF COLLECTIVE BARGAINING

The year in which collective bargaining began was reported by 446 associations. Seventeen associations had a record of over 50 years of negotiations with unions. Fourteen of these are in the construction industry. A few reported a history of over 65 years of collective bargaining.

Fifteen per cent of the associations first began to negotiate with unions during the period 1932-1936. In the next five years, another 27 per cent entered into collective bargaining relations with unions. Altogether, 63 per cent of the associations started to bargain collectively after 1937. About 3 per cent had bargained collectively for one year or less preceding the time of survey.

LOCAL BARGAINING

Anglo-American Council on Productivity, Industrial Engineering, London, 1954, pp. 72–73

Contrary to U.K. practice, in the U.S. collective bargaining on a national basis is rare. Wage increases are negotiated generally on a plant or, in some instances, a district basis and, moreover, by the local branch of the union concerned, whose autonomy is far greater than that of the local union branch in Britain. . . . Local negotiation of wages and conditions adds to the interest taken by employees in the activities of their own company, since their trade union's success in wage negotiation is closely related to the success of the company. This outlook is natural where one trade union includes all employees in a firm within its ranks, irrespective of their trades.

From National Association of Manufacturers, Industry Believes, New York, 1951, p. 25

RESOLUTION, CONGRESS OF AMERICAN INDUSTRY, DECEMBER, 1947

Where collective bargaining exists as the result of the voluntary and free choice of employees, the Congress of American Industry urges that, in accordance with public policy, such collective bargaining should be carried on at the plant and company level in order to assure maximum production and industrial peace.

INDUSTRY-WIDE BARGAINING

Statement of A. P. Richards, Vice President and Treasurer, The Ohio Can & Crown Co., Massillon, Ohio, in Taft-Hartley Act Revisions, hearings before the Senate Committee on Labor and Public Welfare, 83d Cong., 1st Sess., 1953, part 2, pp. 792–793

Our basic business is the can business. In the can industry upward of 75 percent of all cans are manufactured by two large corporations, and the remainder by some 50 or 60 smaller companies of varying size. We are one of the smallest. The larger can companies with unlimited financial resources are in a position to and do to a certain extent offset increased labor cost by installation of labor-saving equipment. For instance there is available, to those with the money to buy it, equipment which will save one-half the labor of printing the labels on cans. There is equipment available to cut the labor of stamping tops and bottoms of cans by more than one-half, and many other labor-saving devices available to those in our industry where money is no problem. But, those of us who do not have access to unlimited capital must live with a labor disadvantage when compared to the large corporations.

Now, it is very apparent that if through industrywide bargaining we are required to pay the industry rate, that it is only a matter of time until we must close our plant. But you say, aren't the workers in your plant entitled to make as much money as the workers in the plants of the big corporation? That seems like a reasonable question. But the real question is, Would our workers be better off at what we can afford to pay them, or being without a job? There is no doubt about how our employees would answer that.

We do not hear too much complaint from the large corporation about industrywide bargaining. I think that the reason is obvious, as it is evidently very much to their advantage to know that all companies in the industry must pay the same labor rates, giving to the large companies whatever advantage they can have and do obtain through more modern and labor-saving equipment.

There can be no question that industrywide bargaining, if allowed to continue, will eventually mean the end of all small and even medium-sized companies who do not have the unlimited capital resources possessed by dominant industry corporations.

Testimony of Matt Triggs, Assistant Legislative Director, American Farm Bureau Federation, in Taft-Hartley Act Revisions, hearings before the Senate Committee on Labor and Public Welfare, 83d Cong., 1st Sess., 1953, part 1, pp. 209–211

SENATOR DOUGLAS: When you say you are opposed to industrywide bargaining, are you opposed to regional bargaining?

MR. TRIGGS: Yes, sir. I would hesitate to define just what I mean by "industrywide bargaining." Fundamentally, however, we believe that the right place for bargaining is between an employer and his employees. There may be some exceptions to that which could be justified.

SENATOR DOUGLAS: I do not want to cause you trouble, but what would you do in the collective agreements between these pools of dairy farmers and the city distributors of milk, where you have an agreement which applies to a milkshed for the city as a whole?

For instance, in my city, Chicago, the milkshed extends up beyond Madison, Wis., and south beyond Peoria. There is an agreement which fixes the price of milk for all producers, arrived at by collective bargaining between the representatives of the Pure Milk Association and the representatives of the city distributors. That is a regional agreement. If you are to be consistent, then you would have to outlaw that.

MR. TRIGGS: Let me say first, sir, I am not familiar with the particular local situation you mention.

SENATOR DOUGLAS: I think the facts are approximately correct as I have stated them.

MR. TRIGGS: Most of these situations are operated under the Federal Marketing Agreement Act. Is that true in this case?

SENATOR DOUGLAS: That is true, but principles of justice should apply across the board for agriculture as well as for industry.

MR. TRIGGS: Again let me say that I do not believe in general that there is any interference with the entry of a person into the market, and that the best that the agreement can do is to stabilize the price over a long period of time. Otherwise, they result in the production of surpluses.

SENATOR DOUGLAS: May I say that labor will give exactly the same defense. They will say that industrywide agreements will stabilize wage rates over a region, at least, and result in a more stable long-run condition.

What I am puzzled about is why what is sauce for the gander should not be sauce for the goose as well.

MR. TRIGGS: Let me say I am not at all sure that if a lot of these problems were presented to our people, they would not feel something should be done about them. I am not capable of analyzing the problem in each of these cases, because I am not familiar with them.

SENATOR DOUGLAS: But in the old days where the city distributors dealt with each dairyman individually, the result was that they would play one dairyman off against the other, and the dairymen were consequently in very bad shape. So they combined together in their federations, which are really marketing unions, and drove as good a bargain as they could with the city distributors. Obviously they needed organization for their protection. As a matter of fact, in some cases they resorted to strikes, and they dumped the milk on the highways and carried out destruction of property. It was really pretty rough. I can remember days in Wisconsin when it was really pretty rough.

MR. TRIGGS: In my own State of California, it is always true that a new dairyman can enter the market. He may or may not join the association. Many do, and many do not.

SENATOR DOUGLAS: In many cities they cannot get access to the urban market unless they are a member of the dairymen's marketing association, which in some cases does partial processing.

MR. TRIGGS: Of course, that subject, as I understand it, is now before some committee of Congress investigating the local situation.

SENATOR DOUGLAS: Do you intend to appear before that other committee and urge that these agreements be voided?

MR. TRIGGS: Not that I know of, sir.

SENATOR TAFT: I might suggest to you that even the strongest advocates of abolishing nationwide bargaining do admit regional bargaining so far as I know. In the coal field it would be impossible to do it without breaking it down to regions. In the field of building trades and also printers I think they admit the fact that citywide or countywide bargaining must be permitted. So that is not quite so much out of line with the milk as if you did not take such an extreme position on it.

MR. TRIGGS: I don't mean to take an extreme position, sir. You will notice I used the word "primarily" and that is intended to recognize the fact that there may be some circumstances just as you have described, where long experience has demonstrated that it is a sound way of doing it and there is no apparent harm done to the general interest.

SENATOR TAFT: Of course, that is one of the difficulties of writing any law that limits nationwide bargaining, to undertake to define the extent to which regions can do it. If you arbitrarily divide up the coal region into 6 regions or 10 regions, that is one of the troubles in it. But everybody agrees that you have to do that if you do ban nationwide bargaining.

From Federal Labor Relations Act of 1947, minority views of Senator Thomas, Senate Committee on Labor and Public Welfare, 80th Cong., 1st Sess., Report 105, 1947, part 2, pp. 6–8

INDUSTRY-WIDE COLLECTIVE BARGAINING

Provisions specifically prohibiting area-wide and industry-wide collective bargaining were rejected by the committee for inclusion in the bill as reported. We approve this action by the committee but, in view of announcements by some members of the committee that they intend to reinsert such provisions through amendments offered on the floor of the Senate, we have set forth below the considerations which motivated us in supporting the striking of such provisions from the bill.

The Bureau of Labor Statistics estimates that more than 4,000,000 workers in American industry are covered by contracts between a union and more than one employer. Some of these are industry-wide; most are regional or citywide in character. A ban on such bargaining would disrupt existing relationships in these industries and make it necessary to renegotiate contracts covering 4,000,000 workers. Instead of negotiations resulting in a relative handful of agreements, which cover thousands of employers as a group, the result would be piecemeal negotiations with thousands of individual employers, over a prolonged period of time, with thousands of individual agreements splintering the uniform standards previously achieved through industry bargaining.

Industry-wide bargaining is a logical development of present-day industrial organization. Employers are organized on an industry-wide scale; first in Nation-wide corporations, and second in trade associations. Competition is Nation-wide in character.

We should like to indicate what would be the effect of a ban on industry-wide bargaining on present-day industrial relations.

Any attempt to ban actions by employers to form voluntary associations for the purpose of collective bargaining would deny this group the protection accorded employee organizations. In many trades and industries, employers have joined together to bargain with unions representing their employees. In such industries as longshoring and building construction—where workers change employers from day to day or week to week—bargaining through employers' associations is the only practical method for establishing uniform wages and working conditions and eliminating cutthroat competition. Almon E. Roth, President of the National Federation of American Shipping, in a statement before the committee, warned that a ban against industry-wide bargaining would result in a diversity of wage rates and working conditions among ships operated from the same coast, plying between the same ports, tying at the same docks, and employing, in turn, the same men:

Such a condition leads to the playing off of one steamship company against another by the unions, to extreme labor unrest, and eventually to the disruption of steamship operation.

Many employers prefer industry-wide or association bargaining. Mr. Vincent P. Ahearn, executive secretary of the National Sand and Gravel Association, testified before the committee:

Some employers believe that if they could not bargain on an industry-wide basis, unions could simply isolate one employer after another and force capitulation to their demands.

This would create a situation where the weakest member of an industry would set the standard for the others.

Because numerous employers are covered by a single collective-bargaining agreement, less time is lost in the bargaining process. Settlements are made simultaneously for these employers rather than on an individual employer-by-employer basis. Industrial peace is achieved in one step, rather than over a prolonged period of time. Bargaining with hundreds of individual firms for the same things is both wasteful and unfair to both sides.

Many small employers lack the skill in bargaining and research facilities available to unions. A ban on association of employers combining for the purpose of pooling their knowledge and resources in collective-bargaining negotiations would impair the bargaining power of employers.

Industry-wide agreement on wages protects wage standards from being undercut by lower-wage areas and lower-wage employers. By the same token, industry-wide bargaining may save individual employers from being singled out as wage leaders in their respective industries. A ban on such agreements would result in separate agreements with individual locals. Many firms control or own subsidiary plants in districts outside an immediate geographic area. Such firms would have to negotiate agreements with numerous local unions in widely scattered localities—a task that would unavoidably become snarled up in wage differentials and eventually would revive the old cutthroat competition and the law of the jungle between company and company, between area and area.

Barring joint activities of local unions and reducing the functions of international unions to that of an advisory body should, in fairness, require the same treatment for corporations with plants scattered widely over the country.

The charge is made that industry-wide bargaining leads to industry-wide strikes which threaten the public welfare. We should like to emphasize that it is not the character of the bargaining which brings about major strikes, but the organized joint refusal of that industry's employers to meet the union's demands. Under company-by-company bargaining, employers would try to drive standards down to the level of the lowest in the industry, and unions would seek to attain the level of the highest, and the result would be an epidemic of strikes throughout the various units of the industry.

A ban on industry-wide bargaining would minimize the role of the international union and prohibit it from exercising its authority to intervene in strikes of its affiliates; and prevent it from employing its prestige in its own industry for moderation and restraining counsel.

In order for the Senate to fully realize the potential impact of a ban on industry-wide bargaining by large geographical areas, we call attention to a study recently prepared by the Bureau of Labor Statistics, which shows the extent of bargaining in specific industries with associations and groups of employers. A careful examination of these industry groupings must of necessity uphold the committee's action in deleting that part of the bill which would seek to disrupt existing collective-bargaining practices which have developed in the past decades.

Testimony of Morton J. Baum, President, Clothing Manufacturers Association, in Taft-Hartley Revisions, hearings before the Senate Committee on Labor and Public Welfare, 83d Cong., 1st Sess., 1953, part 4, pp. 2174–2177

The Clothing Manufacturers Association of the United States of America has a membership of approximately 850 manufacturers, who produce about 90 percent of all the men's and boys' tailored clothing in this country. Our members are located in most States of the Union, from New York to California, and from Maine to the deep South. We are the national association of our industry. Local associations of clothing manufacturers that are affiliated with us are the Philadelphia Clothing Manufacturers, New York Clothing Manufacturers Exchange, Rochester Clothier's Exchange, and the New England Clothing Manufacturers Association.

Our board of directors consists of 31 manufacturers who represent all of the clothing markets, and these directors are elected by the respective markets. On our board of directors we have representatives of large firms and small firms, and various types of manufacturers, such as those who sell direct to the consumer and those who sell their product to thousands of retailers throughout

Area Coverage of Group Bargaining Showing Area of Bargaining with Associations or Groups of Employers, by Industry

Bargaining on a national or industry-wide scale	Bargaining by geographic (regional) areas	Bargaining within a city, county, or metropolitan area
Coal mining	Canning and preserving	Baking
Elevator installation	foods [1]	Beverages, nonalcoholic
and repair	Dyeing and finishing	Book and job printing and publishing
Glass and glassware	textiles [1]	Building service and maintenance
Installation of	Fishing	Clothing, men's [2]
automatic sprinklers	Hosiery	Clothing, women's [2]
Pottery and related	Leather (tanned, cur-	Confectionery products
products	ried, and finished) [1]	Construction
Stoves	Longshoring [1]	Cotton textiles
Wallpaper	Lumber	Dairy products
	Maritime	Furniture [2]
	Metal mining	Hotel and restaurant
	Nonferrous metals	Jewelry and silverware
	and products,	Knit goods
	except jewelry and	Laundry and cleaning and dyeing
	silverware [1]	Leather products, other
	Paper and pulp	Malt liquors
	Shoes, cut stock and	Meat packing
	findings [1]	Newspaper printing and publishing
		Paper products, except wallpaper
		Silk and rayon textiles
		Steel products, except stoves [2]
		Tobacco
		Trade [2]
		Trucking and warehousing [2]

[1] There also is some bargaining on a city, county, and/or metropolitan-area basis.
[2] There also is some bargaining on a regional and/or industry-wide basis.

the country. Therefore, it can be seen that our board is modeled after the pattern used by the Federal Government to establish industry advisory committees, and is truly representative of the entire men's and boys' clothing industry of the United States.

Prior to 1937 collective bargaining was on the regional or individual firm basis. This was highly unsatisfactory, both to the union and to the industry. We found that there was a constant shifting of factories from one locality to another in a desperate race to seek lower wage levels, with the consequent loss of job security for workers and utter chaos at the industry level. This trend encouraged competition on the basis of shaving labor costs rather than on the basis of increased efficiency and progressive methods of merchandising and selling.

It was the considered judgment of our manufacturers that industry-wide bargaining was of definite advantage to the industry whose members were located in various regions of this country and were competing nationally in selling their products. It was the experience of our industry, at the time when we bargained on a regional or individual basis, that the union sought out the manufacturer or region that was most able, in the opinion of labor, to pay the highest possible wage increase, and the union then reached an agreement with that manufacturer or that region. Once a regional or individual agreement had been completed and announced, particularly if it was with a nationally known company, an industry pattern was set, and the other members of the industry found the wage demands of the union were "frozen" and further collective bargaining hampered or made impossible because of the wage increase already announced.

The position of manufacturers in the other markets thus was weakened. The union benefited considerably in regional bargaining since it could call a strike in the factory of one manufacturer or a group of manufacturers located in a market which did not grant a wage increase, and permit manufacturers located in other markets to operate. Thus great competitive pressure was exerted upon those manufacturers whose plants were closed. If the struck plants did not settle quickly, their competitors would take away the customers of the firm that was unable to deliver merchandise.

Despite this seeming advantage, the union found that regional or individual bargaining was detrimental to the functioning of orderly collective bargaining for the industry as a whole.

Recognizing that collective bargaining on a regional basis was highly unsatisfactory, both labor and management determined that industrywide bargaining was preferable. Accordingly, in 1937, the first collective bargaining contract on an industrywide basis was signed.

SENATOR TAFT: Mr. Baum, that was with the Amalgamated Clothing Workers?

MR. BAUM: That is correct, Senator Taft.

SENATOR TAFT: That is the union run by Mr. Potofsky?

MR. BAUM: By Mr. Potofsky, that is right.

Since that date, there have been periodic meetings between the national association and the union on matters subject to bargaining collectively, such as hours, wages, vacations, holidays, fringe payments, and so forth. Only recently we completed our industrywide negotiations, which had been going on for several months, granting a wage increase of 12½ cents an hour effective May 25, 1953. This is the first wage increase in our industry since November 1950, due to the fact that the industry had overproduced and was in a depressed market. Each clothing market and each type of manufacturer was represented on the association's labor committee, so that the views of all industry segments were known and fully voiced.

I wish to point out that our industrywide bargaining does not cover the problems that ordinarily arise in local markets due to local conditions and local traditions. The local member organizations that are affiliated with our association handle such matters on a day-to-day basis.

We bargain on an industrywide basis only on matters that are industry-wide; we bargain locally on local labor matters.

As a result of industrywide bargaining, we find that competition which resulted from undercutting of the wage scales has practically stopped, and that greater efficiency in factory operations and progressive merchandising methods have become the important factors in determining the success of a clothing business.

I wish to stress that competition is probably stronger among the manufacturers than it has ever been. The profits of the industry are certainly no greater than they have been in the past. However, competition now is on a socially desirable level. It is not based upon lowering wages, but rather upon efficiency and merchandising skill. . . .

Now, opponents of industrywide bargaining have said, "The industry meets with the union, agrees upon a wage increase, and then manufacturers uniformly raise prices at the expense of the consumer." Obviously, such a situation is entirely fantastic as far as the clothing industry is concerned. We have about 900 manufacturers in our industry, located in all parts of the United States, and general agreement to increase prices would not merely be illegal but physically impossible. Let me stress, labor, usually representing well over 30 percent of the wholesale price, is merely one of the many components entering into the cost of the garment. In fact, the cost of the piece goods and trimmings totals over 45 percent of the wholesale price. These three are the principal items of cost. Gentlemen, I cannot emphasize too strongly that ability to purchase desirable fabric well styled and at the right price, innate skill to design a well-fitting and attractive garment, experience in producing that garment efficiently, and a lifetime knowledge of selling, promoting, and advertising the garment are the outstanding reasons for the success of any men's clothing manufacturer. Strong and active competition is the lifeblood of our industry, but not at the expense of the workers.

As a result of constructive industrywide bargaining, we have had no stoppage or strike during this period, and there has been constant recognition on the part of labor and management that it is most desirable that both cooperate so that we have a healthy industry and satisfied employees.

From Business Week, July 2, 1955

FORD SUGGESTS INDUSTRY-WIDE BARGAINING

There was some consternation in the business community at Henry Ford II's decision to give the CIO auto union a contract that Walter Reuther could hail as a great victory in his union's fight for the guaranteed annual wage. Close analysis of that contract has now convinced many in industry that the

Ford Motor Co. got itself a pretty good deal and that much of what Reuther claims is a considerable exaggeration.

Now Henry Ford has jolted businessmen again. In an interview published in the Detroit News, he declared, "I am very much in favor of industry-wide bargaining." This is a shocker. For even longer than they have been attacking GAW, business spokesmen and business organizations have been inveighing against industry-wide bargaining as an unmitigated evil. As a matter of fact, employer opposition in principle to industry-wide bargaining has existed for so long that it is taken for granted to the point where the merits and de-merits of the issue are rarely, if at all, discussed in business circles.

Employers formulated their position on industry-wide bargaining in a period when unions were much weaker than they are now. With only a part of an industry organized, the unions pressed for industry-wide negotiations as a device for imposing their wage bargains and contract conditions on un-organized firms. Employers resisted this successfully and adhered to a theory of bargaining under which each individual firm would be free to make the most advantageous contract it could.

When powerful unions spreadeagled the steel, auto, and other mass produc-tion industries, the situation changed. Now, the union makes a key bargain with the one company best suited to its bargaining purposes. Thus, in the steel industry, the steel union made its first pension contract with Bethlehem be-cause, for historic reasons, that company was less resistant on the pension issue. For reasons equally cogent, it makes its key wage bargains with U.S. Steel. In every case, however, that key bargain becomes, in effect, a master contract which the rest of the industry adopts.

In autos, the situation is even bleaker. There, the union has been concerned to have the contract termination dates for GM, Ford, and Chrysler come at spaced intervals. Its standard tactic is to whipsaw one against the other; getting, for example, a package worth X from one company, then bargaining with the second, not on the basis of its expiring contract but on the new X base, to come out with X + 1. It ends up with X + 2 from the third company, then starts the round over again.

Ford has just been through a rugged experience in which the union was able to win what it did by keeping the employers separated and coolly picking Ford as its target. Many employers, remote from the pressures that were put on Ford, complained about the result. Now Ford has a suggestion which, by making it impossible for the union to play one employer off against another might affect such results. It is not without significance that Reuther responded by stating that "the UAW is opposed to industry-wide bargaining," and by declaring that, "the UAW won't accept it."

The Ford proposal just won't make sense in many industries, and he made it clear when he offered it that he was only talking about his own. Within that context, and in other industries where the very big and powerful unions operate, it is worth more than rejection without consideration simply because it doesn't fit what may now be an obsolete business shibboleth.

From Business Week, June 16, 1956

A STEP FORWARD IN STEEL BARGAINING

Just as the auto industry resents the suggestion that its Supplementary Un-employment Benefit programs are in the genus Guaranteed Annual Wage, so the steel industry bridles when the technique it is using in current labor negotiations is described as industrywide bargaining. Yet what the steel com-panies are doing now is certainly a change from what they have done in the past and a change in the unmistakable direction of industrywide bargaining.

Tandem bargaining is perhaps the best quick description of how steel dealt with its union up until this month's new contract negotiations got under way. One company—U.S. Steel, except for one year when Bethlehem took the slot—did all the haggling with the union. If an agreement wasn't reached peacefully, the whole industry was struck, and it waited passively until the one company found settlement terms. Then, all the other producers signed for the identical terms that the one company had accepted. Invariably there was growling from other managements at what the "big fellows" had settled for, but the system continued year after year.

Tandem bargaining has, from the employer's point of interest, all of the major disadvantages of industrywide bargaining and none of its advantages. There is some real value to employers, if one wage contract is going to blanket them all, to have the marginal companies represented at the bargain-ing table. The less prosperous firms are then in a position to exercise a veto power over a bargain that is just too rich for them to take. Individual bar-gaining is, of course, more realistic and greatly preferable, but the steel in-dustry has never tried it and apparently won't in the discernible future.

This year, John Stephens for U.S. Steel is only one among three equals who represent U.S., Bethlehem, and Republic in negotiating the fateful 1956 contract. It would be better, we think, if all the basic steel producers who will sign the contract ultimately written were represented at the bargaining table—that is, as long as individual bargaining isn't going to be tried. But what is happening this year makes more sense than what prevailed in the past. We hope that it augurs a peaceful, satisfactory settlement.

WHERE SHOULD BARGAINING TAKE PLACE?

One industry in which the parties have been particularly contentious over the definition of the bargaining unit has been the telephone industry, or more accurately the American Telephone and Telegraph Company's portion of that industry. The A.T. and T. wholly owned operating sub-sidiaries historically have negotiated local agreements with their em-ployees, but the union has maintained that this leads to "shadow" bar-gaining since the subsidiaries' policies are made by A.T. and T. head-quarters (or by "195 Broadway," as the head office is often referred to, after its New York address), with which the union is not in a direct bar-

gaining relationship. The company has denied that it exercises such a control.

In 1950, following several telephone strikes, a special subcommittee of the Senate Committee on Labor and Public Welfare conducted hearings on industrial relations in the Bell System, at which representatives of the parties testified. Majority and minority reports and recommendations were subsequently issued by the subcommittee. The following excerpts relate to the question of the "unit"—whether negotiations should be conducted by the individual subsidiaries or on a systemwide basis. These committee reports were reprinted in later committee hearings.

Excerpts from Taft-Hartley Act Revisions, 83d Cong., 1st Sess., 1953, part 3, pp. 1576–1577, 1599–1600

LABOR-MANAGEMENT RELATIONS IN THE BELL TELEPHONE SYSTEM

From the majority report

. . . Any description of the local associated Bell companies as autonomous corporations is theoretical and can only be justified in the strictest legal sense, for, as the summary of the evidence that follows will show, these companies function as parts in a closely integrated corporate system completely and directly controlled by the A.T. & T. management. This A.T. & T. control flows from its stock ownership of most of the associated companies, from license contracts which it has with all the operating associated companies in the system, and from the long, continued control which A.T. & T. executives have exercised through the years over promotions and salary increases of administrative officers in the associated companies. This latter type of control has gradually built up within the Bell System a Nation-wide administrative staff which is highly responsive to the suggestions and advice on policies and practices emanating from the A.T. & T. management staff. . . .

This controlling influence of A.T. & T., as the evidence shows, has had a direct effect upon the course of labor relations in the system. . . . Much of this effect, under present bargaining conditions, is disruptive. For instance, there have developed among the various Bell companies uniform bargaining strategies and approaches which have slowed and thwarted the collective bargaining process on the local company level, until bargaining has steadily become less and less effective, and strikes and threats of strikes, throughout the system are becoming more and more common. . . .

The integrated wage structure that has been established in the system is another factor resulting from this closely coordinated control which has complicated collective bargaining at the local company level and engendered poor labor-management relations. Management insists that Bell System wage rates are based on the prevailing wage rates in each community, and that, therefore, bargaining on wage increases is a purely local matter which must take place on the local company level. But the evidence shows that the closely woven Bell System reflects itself in a wage policy extending beyond the local labor

market areas in which the telephone exchanges exist, and as a means of
maintaining stability to the system's wage structure, wage differentials have
been established between the various Bell companies, as well as between the
different wage areas within each company. These differentials are therefore
factors for consideration in any bargaining on wage changes, and this fact
prompted the national telephone panel, in applying the wage-stabilization
policy of World War II to the telephone industry, to conclude that "any
realistic application of wage policy to the telephone industry must take into
account the existence of the Bell System itself." [1] . . .

The coordinating influence of the A.T. & T., and its concomitant effect on
the collective bargaining process, is even more apparent in the case of the
pension plans of the Bell companies. These plans are uniform throughout the
system and provide for the interchange of benefit credits of employees trans-
ferring from company to company. The plans are merged, through this interchange arrangement, into one general system plan, which makes it impracticable for the unions to bargain with respect to changes in the plan
at the local company level, because a change in any one company's plan would
disrupt the general plan. The futility of bargaining on pensions under these
conditions becomes even more evident when the union doing the bargaining
represents the employees of only one department of a single company. The
evidence shows no attempt on the part of the Bell System management to
correct this situation, although the Bell companies say they recognize that
pensions are a proper subject matter for bargaining. . . . In fact, the companies have refused to do any real bargaining on pensions and have made
uniform unilateral changes in the plan from time to time. . . . The repeatedly
unsuccessful attempt of the various unions throughout the system to bargain
on pension changes over the last several years has materially worsened labor-
management relations in the system. . . .

The basic cause for the bad labor-management relations in the Bell System
revolves around the collective-bargaining process, and the inability of the
unions to bargain at a level of management which possesses the responsibility
and authority to make final decisions. We have seen that in this closely integrated system matters such as wages and pensions cannot be adequately
dealt with at a local management level, where only a part of the problem can
be considered. The subcommittee believes very definitely that A.T. & T. cannot
expect to contain collective bargaining within small segments throughout the
system while it makes system-wide decisions for piecemeal application to those
segments. When A.T. & T. has bargained with CWA [Communication Workers
of America] on system-wide issues, negotiations have been successful.

The subcommittee is not impressed with the claims of management that

[1] The national telephone panel was a tripartite body established by the War Labor
Board in 1944 for the purpose of settling labor disputes in the telephone industry
under the national economic stabilization program. The panel was composed of six
members, of whom two represented the public, two represented labor, and two represented industry, one of whom was from the Bell System (H. 313, subcommittee
exhibit B, p. 4).

bargaining can be more effective on the departmental level. The Southern
Co. covers 9 whole States with 11 different wage areas and 600 different communities; yet, bargaining for the whole company is done at one table where
negotiations are carried on to cover the entire 9-State area. And, in the long-
lines department of A.T. & T., which operates throughout 41 different States
and the District of Columbia, bargaining is coordinated for all five of its
major departments by only one chief negotiator.

Some of the unions in the alliance * have urged that this subcommittee find
some way in which the Bell System can be required to bargain on the local
associated company level. But in view of the closely integrated nature of the
system itself and the controlling influence of A.T. & T., the subcommittee believes that it is utterly unrealistic to expect the parent A.T. & T. to relax the
control which it has by the economic fact of stock ownership and by the
political fact of the election of company boards of directors and the selection
of company officers. The subcommittee strongly believes that A.T. & T. should
do the bargaining with the unions on national issues such as wages and
pensions which extend beyond any departmental or associated company bargaining unit. With this view, even some of the unions within the alliance
appear to agree.

Minority views of Mr. Taft, Mr. Smith of New Jersey, and Mr. Nixon

The majority of the committee conclude that—
The Bell System cannot expect to contain collective bargaining within
small segments throughout the system while it makes system-wide decisions for piecemeal application to those segments. When A.T. & T. has
bargained with CWA on systemwide issues, negotiations have been successful. . . . The subcommittee strongly believes that A.T. & T. should
do the bargaining with the unions on national issues such as wages and
pensions. . . .

We recognize that the power of the American Telephone and Telegraph
Co. to control the labor policy of its affiliated companies does present a problem
and some justification for requiring the company to bargain on a system-wide
unit. But this condition is not unique as applied to employers. Of equal concern
is the fact that international unions such as the steel workers and the auto
workers and the truck drivers not only have the power to, but frequently do,
dictate the terms and conditions of every collective bargaining contract entered into by their affiliated locals with many completely independent small
businesses. This fact was established by abundant evidence presented to the
Senate Committee on Labor and Public Welfare and other Senate committees
in the Eightieth and Eighty-first Congresses. The steel workers union in

---

* Editor's note: The Alliance of Independent Telephone Unions, an association of
small unions, represents employees in perhaps one-third of the fractionalized units of
the Bell System. It is opposed by the Communication Workers of America, AFL-CIO,
the largest union in the telephone industry, representing about half the bargaining
units in the Bell System. CWA would prefer a system-wide unit, while most of the
Alliance unions prefer the present arrangement of local departmental units.

particular forbade any local to settle for less than a national wage pattern decreed for the steel industry, even though the members of the local were employed in another industry having no relation to the steel industry. . . .

If CWA were to obtain the right to represent nationally in a single unit all employees in the Bell System the effect inevitably would be to freeze out all of the other unions which now represent at least 40 per cent of the employees. Employees now represented by non-CWA unions have repeatedly refused CWA affiliation in spite of extensive and costly organizing campaigns conducted among them. Furthermore, while these hearings were in progress, the National Labor Relations Board conducted an election among the traffic employees of the New England Telephone & Telegraph Co. (90 NLRB No. 102 (1950)). The CWA lost the election to an independent union by an overwhelming margin (H. 483). If a national unit were to be established, the interests of such competing unions would be sacrificed and the wishes of thousands of employees overridden. It is significant that Edward J. Moynahan, on behalf of the Alliance of Independent Telephone Unions, representing about 100,000 telephone workers in unaffiliated unions, testified (H. 257):

> It is the position, too, of the Alliance that so-called *Bell System-wide bargaining would be completely improper* since the largest portion of the Bell System is not represented by any one union. In fact, any recommendation by this committee for system-wide bargaining would fly in the face of the rights that have been assured to the large number of collective bargaining agents throughout the Bell System which have been freely chosen by groups of employees outside of any national union set-up. [Italics added]

A 1949 NLRB proceeding in Ohio demonstrated in miniature what the majority recommendation would accomplish on a Nation-wide basis. The CWA desired a unit comprising all of the employees of the Ohio Bell Telephone Co. The Board ordered an election on that basis which was won by the CWA. Wiped out entirely in the process was the Southwestern Ohio Telephone Workers, which for many years had represented the employer's plant department in the southwestern part of the State and which had an unexpired contract in effect at the time of the election. This union, having no membership in other parts of the State, could not compete with the CWA in a State-wide election. (See Ohio Bell Telephone Co., 87 NLRB No. 161 (1949).)

The results of the present system of representation do not warrant the freezing out of freely chosen unions by the institution of a system of Nation-wide bargaining. Collective bargaining throughout the period 1940-50 has resulted in substantial wage improvement for telephone workers. The CWA in 1950 issued a pamphlet entitled "Then and Now" which points to the gains made by telephone workers not only as to wages, but as to pensions, vacations, sick leave payments, etc., as a "record to be proud of." The union claims credit for the "good wages and working conditions employees enjoy today." . . .

This pamphlet is also evidence that wage and working conditions of telephone workers throughout the United States have not been placed in a strait jacket of uniformity. Increased living costs prevailing in large metropolitan cities are shown to be offset by wage differentials. Other regional and sectional differences are likewise revealed. The need for such variations to meet local conditions would be overlooked or become subordinated if bargaining were conducted on a national basis under the threat of Nation-wide interruption of an essential service. . . .

A Nation-wide bargaining unit, on the other hand, would give one labor organization control over all employees in this vital communications industry, a power not unlike that possessed by the United Mine Workers in the coal industry and the railroad brotherhoods in rail transportation. The United Mine Workers, by strike action almost each year since the war, has cut off or limited the national supply of coal. Railroad strikes, in recent years, prevented only by Federal seizure, have threatened economic paralysis. The demand for industry-wide bargaining in the telephone industry means entrusting to the hands of a few union leaders the power to strangle the voice communication lines of economic life in the United States.

If industrywide bargaining is extended to the telephone industry, the American people must face the prospect of frequent and paralyzing interruptions of service called by union leaders, who in 1949-50 advocated both strike action, against the desires of their membership, and "jamming" or other forms of sabotage to "completely choke telephone communications in this country" (H. 564). Complete cessation of telephone communications cannot be tolerated. No union today has achieved such a position of power as to enable it to bring about a complete interruption of telephone service or to risk the consequences of such an attempt. It would be shortsighted and foolish for the Government to assist the ambition of the CWA to seize such power.

UNIT INTERESTS OF CRAFT AND INDUSTRIAL UNIONS

The structure of the unions and the structure of the bargaining units in which they appear as representative agents have some relationship. Although craft unions sometimes appear as the bargaining agent in comprehensive units, and industrial unions have—somewhat less frequently— been certified as the bargaining representative of craft units, in general craft unions show up in craft units, and industrial unions predominate in comprehensive units.

The larger comprehensive units are always subject to possible disintegration, however. Composed of workers of many different occupations and degrees of skill, they are likely to include special-interest groups which have become disgruntled because they feel their interests have not been adequately taken care of but have been lost in the "general" interest. This is likely to be especially true if there are groups of skilled workers in a unit where the majority are unskilled and semiskilled. Sometimes the union tries to assure the stability of such a unit, encompassing diverse interests, by providing for the direct representation of the special-interest group on the bargaining committee.

The reverse situation is also possible—that small, special-interest craft groups may come to feel that they would improve their bargaining position by casting their lot with a larger group in a comprehensive unit. This is likely to be true where the importance of the skill involved is diminishing, perhaps by virtue of some technological change which makes that skill less necessary than it once was.

This possibility of the disintegration of a comprehensive unit or of the absorption of a craft unit provides the basis for the long-standing feud between craft-oriented and industry-oriented unions. Each type of union seeks to guard its bargaining units from raids by rival unions, through special devices. Something of this issue comes out in the two statements which follow. There is additional pertinent material in the next chapter, since the National Labor Relations Board also gets involved in this matter.

Statement by William Schoenberg, General President, United Cement, Lime and Gypsum Workers International Union, in Labor Relations, hearings before the Senate Committee on Labor and Public Welfare, 81st Cong., 1st Sess., 1949, part 6, pp. 3482–3484

(The) amalgamation of cement, lime and gypsum Federal labor unions was a natural occurrence due to the close similarity of operating equipment, production methods, and processes existent in the three industries. Therefore, when the international charter for this group of workers was issued by the A. F. of L. in 1939, it expressly provided for jurisdiction over workers engaged in the manufacture, production, and processing of cement, lime, and gypsum, including the quarrying of material that is used exclusively in the production, processing, or manufacturing of cement, lime, and gypsum.

Industrial unionism and single-plant collective bargaining units for the workers of these industries came into being through a definite and clear-cut need and was carefully designed to meet the prevailing conditions. From the beginning, those "old-timers" with many years' service in the cement industry realized that effective unionization of cement plants could be accomplished only if all workers in each establishment came under and comprised a "plant-wide" bargaining unit and operated through a single union group, the same as in coal mines. These "old-timers" well knew that unionization along so-called craft lines could not succeed for numerous reasons attributable to obvious natural conditions, a few of which being as follows:

Most cement plants are well removed from the main industrial areas, being located in small rural communities in order to be near the quarries and mines that supply raw material, with these small towns and communities having virtually grown up with the cement mill. Previous to unionization by the cement workers, almost universally no type or kind of labor union existed in these localities. The craft unions seldom indicated any interest whatsoever in the problems of the cement workers, for it was obvious, first, that there were only on the average of about 20 to 25 cement-plant employees who could be considered for recruitment as members of the 10 or 12 craft unions who might claim jurisdiction, and, second, none of the cement workers were true craftsmen, for it has long been customary in the industry to train and develop from ordinary laborers a type of mechanic able to perform the required work for many of the skills of the real craftsmen are not needed to a measurable degree in a cement mill. Thus, the condition gradually developed of practically all these types of workers in a cement plant being so-called home-made mechanics who, although they had never served an apprenticeship of a trade, were well qualified and fitted for the work available.

A further condition made impractical the unionization of cement workers on a craft basis—a normal condition of the cement-plant work requirements not being sufficient to utilize the services of a journeyman craftsman on a full-time basis. Thus, organization by crafts would result in confinement of the craftsman to his particular type of work, and since it would not be full time, a condition would immediately arise which was intolerable in a small community where generally the cement mill afforded the principal source of employment. Economical operation of a cement mill can hardly be adapted to inflexible craft working groups. The working crew must be flexible and interchangeable, adaptable to continuous operations, for cement mills can operate economically only on a continuous, round-the-clock basis. An experienced cement worker must be able to perform several kinds of work about the mill, and his rate of pay is governed by the type of work performed—his various skills are compensable only when utilized. The union-wage-rate schedules and working conditions are so arranged as to prohibit discrimination, favoritism, or unjust consideration.

As an illustration of the foregoing, let us consider that a cement kiln must be relined with firebrick from time to time. Such work demands considerable knowledge and skill with this particular type of work, and then it is usually done under the direct supervision of the plant engineering department, yet it does not require the services of a journeyman bricklayer. Nor would this particular work alone provide even half-time employment for one person. Therefore, the actual kiln-relining work is usually done by a "burner" (kiln operator) or some other full-time operating employee who has acquired the necessary know-how down through the years.

Lastly, the working relationship environment and peculiarities of the cement workers are not at all conducive to organization by crafts. In a cement mill you find a compact, closely related and historically interchangeable group of workers, who, due to the circumstances of small communities, virtually work and live together. Their working conditions, habits, and temperament are governed exclusively by a group complex—separate their working conditions and team spirit into strictly regulated, isolated groups and you completely disrupt their harmony and effectiveness. The success of the organized cement workers is almost wholly attributable to their "all for one and one for all" philosophy. . . .

Congress should . . . make clear that all employees of a given plant, mill, mine, factory or other industrial establishment, have an undeniable and inalienable equity in the determination of an "appropriate collective-bargaining unit" affecting them and, further, that no minority group, of themselves,

should be permitted to divide or separate a plant-wide or employer-wide unit
into a craft unit or group.

*From the report of UAW President Walter P. Reuther to the 16th Constitu-
tional Convention, 1957, in the United Automobile Worker for April, 1957*

NEW TOOLS, TACTICS, TECHNIQUES FOR COLLECTIVE BARGAINING

During the twenty-odd years of the history of the UAW, we have learned
that we were able to make progress only as we were able to unite workers and
to pool their collective strength and determination at the bargaining table.
The complete failure of craft unions to protect and advance the interest of
workers in the mass production industries and the success of the industrial
unions in this respect offers conclusive proof that workers in these basic industries, whether production, skilled trades, office workers, technicians or
engineers, can best solve their problems and advance their common individual
interests only as they stand and act together through the instrument of a
single powerful industrial union.

In the early period of the UAW, all of the workers stood together in the
elementary struggle to win recognition of the right to bargain. Our first collective bargaining agreements were simple one-page documents, limited essentially
to the recognition of our right to bargain. During the past 20 years collective
bargaining has become more complex and our collective bargaining agreements
now cover many phases of industrial relations.

Collective bargaining will continue to be more complex as the technology in our industries becomes more complex. Our Union has the
responsibility of finding new and effective tools, tactics and techniques
for dealing with these new and increasingly complex problems. The
Union is a living body and collective bargaining is a living process.
Nothing is static and progress is possible only in terms of change. What
represented an effective approach to collective bargaining at the beginning
of our Union is no longer realistic or effective for new approaches must
be made to new problems.

Without in any way weakening or compromising the principles of industrial
unionism, which is the source of the strength and the solidarity of our Union,
we must find ways to refine the principle of industrial unionism in order to
meet new problems, to meet the problems common to all the workers in our
Union and yet at the same time to be able to deal satisfactorily with special
problems within our Union. No member of our Union has a right to special
privilege, but every member of our Union, who may have a special problem
because of the nature of his work, has a right to have this special problem
dealt with effectively.

STRONGER BARGAINING POSITION

To achieve this balanced approach to our problems, the International Executive Board is recommending certain refinements in the collective bargaining
policies of our Union which will put us in a stronger position at the bargain-

ing table and enable us to better advance the interest of all our members and, at the same time, deal with certain special problems. This approach which further refines the principle of industrial unionism enables our Union to take to the bargaining table the combined collective power of all the workers while providing the Union with special leverage which will improve and strengthen our bargaining position.

I have personally participated in most of the major negotiations in our Union during the past 21 years, and I know as a matter of practical experience that the policy that we are recommending will put us in a stronger position to enable us to do a better job for all the members of our Union. This policy will further unite and solidify the ranks of our Union and represents an application of a refinement and a maturing of the industrial union principle in our kind of basic industry.

DIRECT REPRESENTATION

In essence, our policy suggests that we make provisions in the structure of our collective bargaining machinery to assure that skilled trades groups, office workers, technicians and engineers, in plants in which there are sizable groups of workers in these classifications, be permitted direct representation in the negotiation and administration of our bargaining agreements and with the negotiation of supplementary agreements dealing with their special problems on which they have the right to act.

This policy would not be applied mechanically. It would be carried out only in those local unions where there are sufficient numbers of workers in these categories to make it workable and practicable.

This policy, in addition to giving us the basis for solidifying our ranks and mobilizing maximum solidarity at the bargaining table, will also enable the Union to meet the problem of raids by craft unions under the current policies of the National Labor Relations Board and also will enable the Union to carry out more effectively the task of organizing unorganized workers, the white collar and clerical field and the thousands of technicians and engineers working in industries under our jurisdiction.

I am confident that in practice the new collective bargaining tools, tactics and techniques that our policy makes possible will further strengthen the structure of our industrial Union and will make possible greater collective bargaining gains for all of our members.

The strength of an industrial union is always to be in a position to utilize its full advantage in whatever section of the industry that advantage may be. This is the superiority in a mass production industry of the industrial union form of organization over the separated efforts of various groups which have never been and can never be successful.

In order to increase the effectiveness of our Union and to mobilize the full efforts of the apprenticeable skilled trades and related groups in behalf of themselves and the remaining members of the Union, and looking toward the very real advances which can be won for all UAW members in 1958, the International Executive Board advanced the following program for consideration by the 1957 Convention for incorporation in the demands of 1958:

1. That the merit spreads as they now exist in the tool-die, maintenance and other related skilled trades classifications be eliminated and that the present maximum rates of these classifications be considered the starting point of negotiations. There shall be a demand that added to this old maximum rate shall be a very substantial wage increase taking into account the tremendous forward progress of the industry and with particular reference to the inequities and disparities which now exist in such magnitude in the various skilled trades classifications. This demand would not be at the expense of the remaining members of the Union, but consistent with the efforts the Union must make for major economic advances in wage and other matters for all of our people. The new rates then established as a result of the demands and the negotiations would be a minimum rate guaranteed to all in the classification and beyond which advances could be made but with no maximum limit.

2. In order to fully mobilize apprenticeable skilled trades and related groups for themselves and to the common objectives which will be formulated for all, we urge that upon application to and approval of the International Union with regard to any specific location the following become a matter of constitutional right:

a. Apprenticeable skilled trades and related workers, members of our Union, shall be permitted separate voting on matters pertaining only to their trades and classifications. They would continue to vote in the general unit on matters common to all of the workers. In similar fashion, production workers, office workers, engineers and technicians would decide those questions which affected only themselves.

b. Since employers quite often are not influenced simply by voting, it is also necessary to provide that under prescribed circumstances skilled trades workers be permitted the right to strike action in accordance with constitutional provision and the approval of the International Union.

3. In order to make meaningful the rights expressed in paragraph 2, it will be necessary to provide that skilled trades workers shall have direct representation of their own choosing as part of all local shop bargaining committees and of all national bargaining committees. Provision must be made that these representatives are elected to and from the appropriate skilled trades groups. . . .

FOR DISCUSSION AND ANALYSIS

1. Although employers have been most active in seeking legislative limitations on or an actual ban of industry-wide bargaining, there is one school of thought which maintains that to outlaw industry-wide bargaining would—in some instances at least—actually increase the union's bargaining power. Under what circumstances might this be true?

2. Why is it that employers may differ among themselves as to the preferable size of the bargaining unit? Is it because their aspirations

differ (are the goals of a small businessman the same as those of the management of a large corporation?) or because they find themselves in different economic circumstances?

3. If the international union retains the power of disapproving locally negotiated agreements, what difference does it make to management whether the bargaining unit is company-wide or industry-wide?

4. A graduate student making an investigation of the collective bargaining relationship between the New York local of the Brotherhood of Painters and the master painting contractors association found that *both* parties said they could get a better contract for their members by associational (multiemployer) bargaining than would be possible on a single-employer basis. How could this be true for *both* parties?

5. What significance may the size of the bargaining unit have (*a*) on the government of a union, (*b*) on the management of a company?

6. Assume for the sake of argument that the charge of the Communication Workers of America and the conclusion of the majority subcommittee report on the Bell System was valid, and that A.T. and T. did in fact control the policy of its subsidiary operating companies, while insisting that the union bargain only with those subsidiaries. Under this assumption, the union has no opportunity to bargain directly with the management people who actually make the decisions. To what extent may this be considered a legitimate device of the company to increase its bargaining power relative to the union, a method of manipulating bargaining power to its advantage no different from the union's effort to improve its bargaining position by securing a system-wide unit? Or to what extent may it be considered a device which is used to thwart the processes of collective bargaining, to frustrate genuine interchange between the two parties? What criteria do you use in deciding what may be legitimate manipulation of the bargaining power relationship, not designed to scuttle that relationship, on the one hand, and on the other hand attempts at destroying the relationship itself?

7. The minority report of the special subcommittee investigating labor relations in the Bell System opposed a system-wide bargaining unit, among other reasons on the ground that if the Communication Workers of America won such an election it would freeze out the numerous small independent unions now bargaining for particular groups of employees, who presumably prefer their own small union as their representative to an over-all industry-wide union, in the control of which they would have a smaller voice.

In the very notion of unions as representatives of all the employees in a bargaining unit is implicit the notion that the majority wish of employees shall be respected. If a majority of employees in a single company choose one union rather than another, the members of the second union are "frozen out" so far as having their "own" representative is concerned. If a comprehensive union is established, blanketing in all the employees of a company, craft groups are denied their own separate representation. In these instances, however, we do not usually argue that the fact that such small groups have lost their right to a separate representation necessarily means that the comprehensive unit is undesirable. We recognize that as soon as we adopt a representative process, necessarily some minority individuals or groups will be represented by people or agents who are chosen by a majority. This fact, however, is not itself somehow determinative of the size of the bargaining unit, since such minority problems occur in any representative process.

Can you develop any principles defining under what circumstances a small segment of workers should be allowed to have the right to name their own special representative and when they may legitimately be required to throw in their lot with a larger bargaining unit, desired by some majority?

8. A comprehensive or industrial unit contains diverse groups—some workers more skilled than others, or occupationally differentiated, or even spatially distinct from the others. Such groups may splinter the larger bargaining unit by seeking to establish their own separate bargaining unit. What considerations might affect the decision of such a group either to remain in the comprehensive unit or to seek to leave it?

9: The National Labor Relations Board and Representation Elections

The functions of the National Labor Relations Board established by the Wagner Act of 1935 were not much modified by the Labor Management Relations (Taft-Hartley) Act of 1947, although the structure of the Board was considerably altered. As the Act itself declares, in the sections reprinted below, the Board is principally concerned with two functions: (1) the conduct of representation elections, to determine whether a majority of employees wishes to be represented by some specified union, within a bargaining unit which has been defined by the Board; and (2) the determination of whether employer or union has engaged in "unfair labor practices," which are spelled out in the Act and which, on the whole, seek to eliminate hindrances to the collective-bargaining process without intervening in the actual collective-bargaining settlement.

In this and the next two chapters the Board's role will be examined. Chapter 9 contains the portions of the Labor Management Relations Act which relate to the Board's functions as well as materials dealing with representation elections. Chapter 10 considers unfair labor practices chargeable to employers, while Chapter 11 is concerned with union unfair labor practices, concluding with a few over-all impressions of whether the Act and the Board's administration of it have impinged adversely on the unions.

LEGAL DEFINITION OF NLRB FUNCTIONS

Portions of Labor Management Relations Act of 1947 Relating to the National Labor Relations Board, as amended by Public Law 189 of 1951 *

NATIONAL LABOR RELATIONS BOARD

Sec. 3. (*a*) The National Labor Relations Board (hereinafter called the "Board") created by this Act prior to its amendment by the Labor Management Relations Act, 1947, is hereby continued as an agency of the United States, except that the Board shall consist of five instead of three members, appointed

* Portions of the original act of 1947 which were eliminated by the 1951 amendment are enclosed in brackets. Provisions which were added are shown in italics.

by the President by and with the advice and consent of the Senate. Of the two additional members so provided for, one shall be appointed for a term of five years and the other for a term of two years. Their successors, and the successors of the other members, shall be appointed for terms of five years each, excepting that any individual chosen to fill a vacancy shall be appointed only for the unexpired term of the member whom he shall succeed. The President shall designate one member to serve as Chairman of the Board. Any member of the Board may be removed by the President, upon notice and hearing, for neglect of duty or malfeasance in office, but for no other cause.

(b) The Board is authorized to delegate to any group of three or more members any or all of the powers which it may itself exercise. A vacancy in the Board shall not impair the right of the remaining members to exercise all of the powers of the Board, and three members of the Board shall, at all times, constitute a quorum of the Board, except that two members shall constitute a quorum of any group designated pursuant to the first sentence hereof. The Board shall have an official seal which shall be judicially noticed.

(c) The Board shall at the close of each fiscal year make a report in writing to Congress and to the President stating in detail the cases it has heard, the decisions it has rendered, the names, salaries, and duties of all employees and officers in the employ or under the supervision of the Board, and an account of all moneys it has disbursed.

(d) There shall be a General Counsel of the Board who shall be appointed by the President, by and with the advice and consent of the Senate, for a term of four years. The General Counsel of the Board shall exercise general supervision over all attorneys employed by the Board (other than trial examiners and legal assistants to Board members) and over the officers and employees in the regional offices. He shall have final authority, on behalf of the Board, in respect of the investigation of charges and issuance of complaints under section 10, and in respect of the prosecution of such complaints before the Board, and shall have such other duties as the Board may prescribe or as may be provided by law.

Sec. 4. (a) Each member of the Board and the General Counsel of the Board shall receive a salary of $12,000 a year, shall be eligible for reappointment, and shall not engage in any other business, vocation, or employment. The Board shall appoint an executive secretary, and such attorneys, examiners, and regional directors, and such other employees as it may from time to time find necessary for the proper performance of its duties. The Board may not employ any attorneys for the purpose of reviewing transcripts of hearings or preparing drafts of opinions except that any attorney employed for assignment as a legal assistant to any Board member may for such Board member review such transcripts and prepare such drafts. No trial examiner's report shall be reviewed, either before or after its publication, by any person other than a member of the Board or his legal assistant, and no trial examiner shall advise or consult with the Board with respect to exceptions taken to his findings, rulings, or recommendations. The Board may establish or utilize such regional, local, or other agencies, and utilize such voluntary and uncompensated services, as may from time to time be needed. Attorneys appointed under this section may, at the direction of the Board, appear for and represent the Board in any case in court. Nothing in this Act shall be construed to authorize the Board to appoint individuals for the purpose of conciliation or mediation, or for economic analysis.

(*b*) All of the expenses of the Board, including all necessary traveling and subsistence expenses outside the District of Columbia incurred by the members or employees of the Board under its orders, shall be allowed and paid on the presentation of itemized vouchers therefor approved by the Board or by any individual it designates for that purpose.

Sec. 5. The principal office of the Board shall be in the District of Columbia, but it may meet and exercise any or all of its powers at any other place. The Board may, by one or more of its members or by such agents or agencies as it may designate, prosecute any inquiry necessary to its functions in any part of the United States. A member who participates in such an inquiry shall not be disqualified from subsequently participating in a decision of the Board in the same case.

Sec. 6. The Board shall have authority from time to time to make, amend, and rescind, in the manner prescribed by the Administrative Procedure Act, such rules and regulations as may be necessary to carry out the provisions of this Act.

RIGHTS OF EMPLOYEES

Sec. 7. Employees shall have the right to self-organization, to form, join, or assist labor organizations, to bargain collectively through representatives of their own choosing, and to engage in other concerted activities for the purpose of collective bargaining or other mutual aid or protection, and shall also have the right to refrain from any or all of such activities except to the extent that such right may be affected by an agreement requiring membership in a labor organization as a condition of employment as authorized in section 8 (*a*) (3).

UNFAIR LABOR PRACTICES

Sec. 8. (*a*) It shall be an unfair labor practice for an employer—

(1) to interfere with, restrain, or coerce employees in the exercise of the rights guaranteed in section 7;

(2) to dominate or interfere with the formation or administration of any labor organization or contribute financial or other support to it: *Provided,* That subject to rules and regulations made and published by the Board pursuant to section 6, an employer shall not be prohibited from permitting employees to confer with him during working hours without loss of time or pay;

(3) by discrimination in regard to hire or tenure of employment or any term or condition of employment to encourage or discourage membership in any labor organization: *Provided,* That nothing in this Act, or in any other statute of the United States, shall preclude an employer from making an agreement with a labor organization (not established, maintained, or assisted

by any action defined in section 8 (*a*) of this Act as an unfair labor practice) to require as a condition of employment membership therein on or after the thirtieth day following the beginning of such employment or the effective date of such agreement, whichever is the later, (i) if such labor organization is the representative of the employees as provided in section 9 (*a*), in the appropriate collective-bargaining unit covered by such agreement when made; [and (ii) if, following the most recent election held as provided in section 9 (*e*) the Board shall have certified that at least a majority of the employees eligible to vote in such election have voted to authorize such labor organization to make such an agreement:] *and has at the time the agreement was made or within the preceding twelve months received from the Board a notice of compliance with Sections 9 (f), (g), (h), and* (ii) *unless following an election held as provided in section 9 (e) within one year preceding the effective date of such agreement, the Board shall have certified that at least a majority of the employees eligible to vote in such an election have voted to rescind the authority of such labor organization to make such an agreement: Provided further,* That no employer shall justify any discrimination against an employee for nonmembership in a labor organization (A) if he has reasonable grounds for believing that such membership was not available to the employee on the same terms and conditions generally applicable to other members, or (B) if he has reasonable grounds for believing that membership was denied or terminated for reasons other than the failure of the employee to tender the periodic dues and the initiation fees uniformly required as a condition of acquiring or retaining membership;

(4) to discharge or otherwise discriminate against an employee because he has filed charges or given testimony under this Act;

(5) to refuse to bargain collectively with the representatives of his employees, subject to the provisions of section 9 (*a*).

(*b*) It shall be an unfair labor practice for a labor organization or its agents—

(1) to restrain or coerce (A) employees in the exercise of the rights guaranteed in section 7: *Provided,* That this paragraph shall not impair the right of a labor organization to prescribe its own rules with respect to the acquisition or retention of membership therein; or (B) an employer in the selection of his representatives for the purposes of collective bargaining or the adjustment of grievances;

(2) to cause or attempt to cause an employer to discriminate against an employee in violation of subsection (*a*) (3) or to discriminate against an employee with respect to whom membership in such organization has been denied or terminated on some ground other than his failure to tender the periodic dues and the initiation fees uniformly required as a condition of acquiring or retaining membership;

(3) to refuse to bargain collectively with an employer, provided it is the representative of his employees subject to the provisions of section 9 (*a*);

(4) to engage in, or to induce or encourage the employees of any employer to engage in, a strike or a concerted refusal in the course of their

employment to use, manufacture, process, transport, or otherwise handle or work on any goods, articles, materials, or commodities or to perform any services, where an object thereof is: (A) forcing or requiring any employer or self-employed person to join any labor or employer organization or any employer or other person to cease using, selling, handling, transporting, or otherwise dealing in the products of any other producer, processor, or manufacturer, or to cease doing business with any other person; (B) forcing or requiring any other employer to recognize or bargain with a labor organization as the representative of his employees unless such labor organization has been certified as the representative of such employees under the provisions of section 9; (C) forcing or requiring any employer to recognize or bargain with a particular labor organization as the representative of his employees if another labor organization has been certified as the representative of such employees under the provisions of section 9; (D) forcing or requiring any employer to assign particular work to employees in a particular labor organization or in a particular trade, craft, or class rather than to employees in another labor organization or in another trade, craft, or class, unless such employer is failing to conform to an order or certification of the Board determining the bargaining representative for employees performing such work: *Provided,* That nothing contained in this subsection (b) shall be construed to make unlawful a refusal by any person to enter upon the premises of any employer (other than his own employer), if the employees of such employer are engaged in a strike ratified or approved by a representative of such employees whom such employer is required to recognize under this Act;

(5) to require of employees covered by an agreement authorized under subsection (a) (3) the payment, as a condition precedent to becoming a member of such organization, of a fee in an amount which the Board finds excessive or discriminatory under all the circumstances. In making such a finding, the Board shall consider, among other relevant factors, the practices and customs of labor organizations in the particular industry, and the wages currently paid to the employees affected; and

(6) to cause or attempt to cause an employer to pay or deliver or agree to pay or deliver any money or other thing of value, in the nature of an exaction, for services which are not performed or not to be performed.

(c) The expressing of any views, argument, or opinion, or the dissemination thereof, whether in written, printed, graphic, or visual form, shall not constitute or be evidence of an unfair labor practice under any of the provisions of this Act, if such expression contains no threat of reprisal or force or promise of benefit.

(d) For the purposes of this section, to bargain collectively is the performance of the mutual obligation of the employer and the representative of the employees to meet at reasonable times and confer in good faith with respect to wages, hours, and other terms and conditions of employment, or the negotiation of an agreement, or any question arising thereunder, and the execution of a written contract incorporating any agreement reached if requested by either

party, but such obligation does not compel either party to agree to a proposal
or require the making of a concession: *Provided,* That where there is in effect a
collective-bargaining contract covering employees in an industry affecting commerce, the duty to bargain collectively shall also mean that no party to such
contract shall terminate or modify such contract, unless the party desiring
such termination or modification—

(1) serves a written notice upon the other party to the contract of the
proposed termination or modification sixty days prior to the expiration date
thereof, or in the event such contract contains no expiration date, sixty days
prior to the time it is proposed to make such termination or modification;

(2) offers to meet and confer with the other party for the purpose of
negotiating a new contract or a contract containing the proposed modifications;

(3) notifies the Federal Mediation and Conciliation Service within thirty
days after such notice of the existence of a dispute, and simultaneously therewith notifies any State or Territorial agency established to mediate and
conciliate disputes within the State or Territory where the dispute occurred,
provided no agreement has been reached by that time; and

(4) continues in full force and effect, without resorting to strike or lock-
out, all the terms and conditions of the existing contract for a period of
sixty days after such notice is given or until the expiration date of such
contract, whichever occurs later:

The duties imposed upon employers, employees, and labor organizations by
paragraphs (2), (3), and (4) shall become inapplicable upon an intervening
certification of the Board, under which the labor organization or individual,
which is a party to the contract, has been superseded as or ceased to be the
representative of the employees subject to the provisions of section 9 (*a*), and
the duties so imposed shall not be construed as requiring either party to discuss
or agree to any modification of the terms and conditions contained in a contract
for a fixed period, if such modification is to become effective before such terms
and conditions can be reopened under the provisions of the contract. Any employee who engages in a strike within the sixty-day period specified in this subsection shall lose his status as an employee of the employer engaged in the
particular labor dispute, for the purposes of sections 8, 9, and 10 of this Act,
as amended, but such loss of status for such employee shall terminate if and
when he is reemployed by such employer.

REPRESENTATIVES AND ELECTIONS

Sec. 9. (*a*) Representatives designated or selected for the purposes of collective bargaining by the majority of the employees in a unit appropriate for
such purposes, shall be the exclusive representatives of all the employees in
such unit for the purposes of collective bargaining in respect to rates of pay,
wages, hours of employment, or other conditions of employment: *Provided,*
That any individual employee or a group of employees shall have the right at
any time to present grievances to their employer and to have such grievances
adjusted, without the intervention of the bargaining representative, as long as

the adjustment is not inconsistent with the terms of a collective-bargaining contract or agreement then in effect: *Provided further,* That the bargaining representative has been given opportunity to be present at such adjustment.

(*b*) The Board shall decide in each case whether, in order to assure to employees the fullest freedom in exercising the rights guaranteed by this Act, the unit appropriate for the purposes of collective bargaining shall be the employer unit, craft unit, plant unit, or subdivision thereof: *Provided,* That the Board shall not (1) decide that any unit is appropriate for such purposes if such unit includes both professional employees and employees who are not professional employees unless a majority of such professional employees vote for inclusion in such unit; or (2) decide that any craft unit is inappropriate for such purposes on the ground that a different unit has been established by a prior Board determination, unless a majority of the employees in the proposed craft unit vote against separate representation or (3) decide that any unit is appropriate for such purposes if it includes, together with other employees, any individual employed as a guard to enforce against employees and other persons rules to protect property of the employer or to protect the safety of persons on the employer's premises; but no labor organization shall be certified as the representative of employees in a bargaining unit of guards if such organization admits to membership, or is affiliated directly or indirectly with an organization which admits to membership, employees other than guards.

(*c*) (1) Whenever a petition shall have been filed, in accordance with such regulations as may be prescribed by the Board—

(*A*) by an employee or group of employees or any individual or labor organization acting in their behalf alleging that a substantial number of employees (i) wish to be represented for collective bargaining and that their employer declines to recognize their representative as the representative defined in section 9 (*a*), or (ii) assert that the individual or labor organization, which has been certified or is being currently recognized by their employer as the bargaining representative, is no longer a representative as defined in section 9 (*a*); or

(*B*) by an employer, alleging that one or more individuals or labor organizations have presented to him a claim to be recognized as the representative defined in section 9 (*a*);

the Board shall investigate such petition and if it has reasonable cause to believe that a question of representation affecting commerce exists shall provide for an appropriate hearing upon due notice. Such hearing may be conducted by an officer or employee of the regional office, who shall not make any recommendations with respect thereto. If the Board finds upon the record of such hearing that such a question of representation exists, it shall direct an election by secret ballot and shall certify the results thereof.

(2) In determining whether or not a question of representation affecting commerce exists, the same regulations and rules of decision shall apply irrespective of the identity of the persons filing the petition or the kind of relief sought and in no case shall the Board deny a labor organization a place on the ballot

by reason of an order with respect to such labor organization or its predecessor not issued in conformity with section 10 (c).

(3) No election shall be directed in any bargaining unit or any subdivision within which, in the preceding twelve-month period, a valid election shall have been held. Employees on strike who are not entitled to reinstatement shall not be eligible to vote. In any election where none of the choices on the ballot receives a majority, a run-off shall be conducted, the ballot providing for a selection between the two choices receiving the largest and second largest number of valid votes cast in the election.

(4) Nothing in this section shall be construed to prohibit the waiving of hearings by stipulation for the purpose of a consent election in conformity with regulations and rules of decision of the Board.

(5) In determining whether a unit is appropriate for the purposes specified in subsection (b) the extent to which the employees have organized shall not be controlling.

(d) Whenever an order of the Board made pursuant to section 10 (c) is based in whole or in part upon facts certified following an investigation pursuant to subsection (c) of this section and there is a petition for the enforcement or review of such order, such certification and the record of such investigation shall be included in the transcript of the entire record required to be filed under section 10 (e) or 10 (f), and thereupon the decree of the court enforcing, modifying, or setting aside in whole or in part the order of the Board shall be made and entered upon the pleadings, testimony, and proceedings set forth in such transcript.

(e) [(1) Upon the filing with the Board by a labor organization, which is the representative of employees as provided in section 9 (a), of a petition alleging that 30 per centum or more of the employees within a unit claimed to be appropriate for such purposes desire to authorize such labor organization to make an agreement with the employer of such employees requiring membership in such labor organization as a condition of employment in such unit, upon an appropriate showing thereof the Board shall, if no question of representation exists, take a secret ballot of such employees, and shall certify the results thereof to such labor organization and to the employer.

(2) Upon the filing with the Board, by 30 per centum or more of the employees in a bargaining unit covered by an agreement between their employer and a labor organization made pursuant to section 8 (a) (3) (ii), of a petition alleging they desire that such authority be rescinded, the Board shall take a secret ballot of the employees in such unit, and shall certify the results thereof to such labor organization and to the employer.]

(1) *Upon the filing with the Board, by 30 per centum or more of the employees in a bargaining unit covered by an agreement between their employer and a labor organization made pursuant to section 8 (a) (3), of a petition alleging they desire that such authority be rescinded, the Board shall take a secret ballot of the employees in such a unit and certify the results thereof to such labor organization and to the employer.*

[(3)] (2) No election shall be conducted pursuant to this subsection in any bargaining unit or any subdivision within which, in the preceding twelve-month period, a valid election shall have been held.

(f) No investigation shall be made by the Board of any question affecting commerce concerning the representation of employees, raised by a labor organization under subsection (c) of this section [no petition under section 9 (e) (1) shall be entertained], and no complaint shall be issued pursuant to a charge made by a labor organization under subsection (b) of section 10, unless such labor organization and any national or international labor organization of which such labor organization is an affiliate or constituent unit (A) shall have prior thereto filed with the Secretary of Labor copies of its constitution and bylaws and a report, in such form as the Secretary may prescribe, showing—

(1) the name of such labor organization and the address of its principal place of business;

(2) the names, titles, and compensation and allowances of its three principal officers and of any of its other officers or agents whose aggregate compensation and allowances for the preceding year exceeded $5,000, and the amount of the compensation and allowances paid to each such officer or agent during such year;

(3) the manner in which the officers and agents referred to in clause (2) were elected, appointed, or otherwise selected;

(4) the initiation fee or fees which new members are required to pay on becoming members of such labor organization;

(5) the regular dues or fees which members are required to pay in order to remain members in good standing of such labor organization;

(6) a detailed statement of, or reference to provisions of its constitution and bylaws showing the procedure followed with respect to, (a) qualification for or restrictions on membership, (b) election of officers and stewards, (c) calling of regular and special meetings, (d) levying of assessments, (e) imposition of fines, (f) authorization for bargaining demands, (g) ratification of contract terms, (h) authorization for strikes, (i) authorization for disbursement of union funds, (j) audit of union financial transactions, (k) participation in insurance or other benefit plans, and (l) expulsion of members and the grounds therefor;
and (B) can show that prior thereto it has—

(1) filed with the Secretary of Labor, in such form as the Secretary may prescribe, a report showing all of (a) its receipts of any kind and the sources of such receipts, (b) its total assets and liabilities as of the end of its last fiscal year, (c) the disbursements made by it during such fiscal year, including the purposes for which made; and

(2) furnished to all of the members of such labor organization copies of the financial report required by paragraph (1) hereof to be filed with the Secretary of Labor.

(g) It shall be the obligation of all labor organizations to file annually with the Secretary of Labor, in such form as the Secretary of Labor may prescribe, reports bringing up to date the information required to be supplied in the initial filing by subsection (f) (A) of this section, and to file with the Secretary of

Labor and furnish to its members annually financial reports in the form and manner prescribed in subsection (f) (B). No labor organization shall be eligible for certification under this section as the representative of any employees [no petition under section 9 (e) (1) shall be entertained], and no complaint shall issue under section 10 with respect to a charge filed by a labor organization unless it can show that it and any national or international labor organization of which it is an affiliate or constituent unit has complied with its obligation under this subsection.

(h) No investigation shall be made by the Board of any question affecting commerce concerning the representation of employees, raised by a labor organization under subsection (c) of this section [no petition under section 9 (e) (1) shall be entertained] and no complaint shall be issued pursuant to a charge made by a labor organization under subsection (b) of section 10, unless there is on file with the Board an affidavit executed contemporaneously or within the preceding twelve-month period by each officer of such labor organization and the officers of any national or international labor organization of which it is an affiliate or constituent unit that he is not a member of the Communist Party or affiliated with such party, and that he does not believe in, and is not a member of or supports any organization that believes in or teaches, the overthrow of the United States Government by force or by any illegal or unconstitutional methods. The provisions of section 35 A of the Criminal Code shall be applicable in respect to such affidavits.

PREVENTION OF UNFAIR LABOR PRACTICES

Sec. 10. (a) The Board is empowered, as hereinafter provided, to prevent any person from engaging in any unfair labor practice (listed in section 8) affecting commerce. This power shall not be affected by any other means of adjustment or prevention that has been or may be established by agreement, law, or otherwise: Provided, That the Board is empowered by agreement with any agency of any State or Territory to cede to such agency jurisdiction over any cases in any industry (other than mining, manufacturing, communications, and transportation except where predominantly local in character) even though such cases may involve labor disputes affecting commerce, unless the provision of the State or Territorial statute applicable to the determination of such cases by such agency is inconsistent with the corresponding provision of this Act or has received a construction inconsistent therewith.

(b) Whenever it is charged that any person has engaged in or is engaging in any such unfair labor practice, the Board, or any agent or agency designated by the Board for such purposes, shall have power to issue and cause to be served upon such person a complaint stating the charges in that respect, and containing a notice of hearing before the Board or a member thereof, or before a designated agent or agency, at a place therein fixed, not less than five days after the serving of said complaint: Provided, That no complaint shall issue based upon any unfair labor practice occurring more than six months prior to the filing of the charge with the Board and the service of a copy thereof upon the person against whom such charge is made, unless the person aggrieved thereby was prevented from filing such charge by reason of service in the armed forces, in which event the six-month period shall be computed from the day of his discharge. Any such complaint may be amended by the member, agent, or agency conducting the hearing or the Board in its discretion at any time prior to the issuance of an order based thereon. The person so complained of shall have the right to file an answer to the original or amended complaint and to appear in person or otherwise and give testimony at the place and time fixed in the complaint. In the discretion of the member, agent, or agency conducting the hearing or the Board, any other person may be allowed to intervene in the said proceeding and to present testimony. Any such proceeding shall, so far as practicable, be conducted in accordance with the rules of evidence applicable in the district courts of the United States under the rules of civil procedure for the district courts of the United States, adopted by the Supreme Court of the United States pursuant to the Act of June 19, 1934 (U. S. C., title 28, secs. 723–B, 723–C).

(c) The testimony taken by such member, agent, or agency or the Board shall be reduced to writing and filed with the Board. Thereafter, in its discretion, the Board upon notice may take further testimony or hear argument. If upon the preponderance of the testimony taken the Board shall be of the opinion that any person named in the complaint has engaged in or is engaging in any such unfair labor practice, then the Board shall state its findings of fact and shall issue and cause to be served on such person an order requiring such person to cease and desist from such unfair labor practice, and to take such affirmative action including reinstatement of employees with or without back pay, as will effectuate the policies of this Act: *Provided,* That where an order directs reinstatement of an employee, back pay may be required of the employer or labor organization, as the case may be, responsible for the discrimination suffered by him: *And provided further,* That in determining whether a complaint shall issue alleging a violation of section 8 (a) (1) or section 8 (a) (2), and in deciding such cases, the same regulations and rules of decision shall apply irrespective of whether or not the labor organization affected is affiliated with a labor organization national or international in scope. Such order may further require such person to make reports from time to time showing the extent to which it has complied with the order. If upon the preponderance of the testimony taken the Board shall not be of the opinion that the person named in the complaint has engaged in or is engaging in any such unfair labor practice, then the Board shall state its findings of fact and shall issue an order dismissing the said complaint. No order of the Board shall require the reinstatement of any individual as an employee who has been suspended or discharged, or the payment to him of any back pay, if such individual was suspended or discharged for cause. In case the evidence is presented before a member of the Board, or before an examiner or examiners thereof, such member, or such examiner or examiners, as the case may be, shall issue and cause to be served on the parties to the proceeding a proposed report, together with a recommended order, which shall be filed with the Board, and if no exceptions are filed within twenty days after service thereof upon such parties, or within such further period as the Board may authorize, such recommended order shall become the order of the Board and become effective as therein prescribed.

(*d*) Until a transcript of the record in a case shall have been filed in a court, as hereinafter provided, the Board may at any time, upon reasonable notice and in such manner as it shall deem proper, modify or set aside, in whole or in part, any finding or order made or issued by it.

(*e*) The Board shall have power to petition any circuit court of appeals of the United States (including the United States Court of Appeals for the District of Columbia), or if all the circuit courts of appeals to which application may be made are in vacation, any district court of the United States (including the District Court of the United States for the District of Columbia), within any circuit or district, respectively, wherein the unfair labor practice in question occurred or wherein such person resides or transacts business, for the enforcement of such order and for appropriate temporary relief or restraining order, and shall certify and file in the court a transcript of the entire record in the proceedings, including the pleadings and testimony upon which such order was entered and the findings and order of the Board. Upon such filing, the court shall cause notice thereof to be served upon such person, and thereupon shall have jurisdiction of the proceeding and of the question determined therein, and shall have power to grant such temporary relief or restraining order as it deems just and proper, and to make and enter upon the pleadings, testimony, and proceedings set forth in such transcript a decree enforcing, modifying, and enforcing as so modified, or setting aside in whole or in part the order of the Board. No objection that has not been urged before the Board, its member, agent, or agency, shall be considered by the court, unless the failure or neglect to urge such objection shall be excused because of extraordinary circumstances. The findings of the Board with respect to questions of fact if supported by substantial evidence on the record considered as a whole shall be conclusive. If either party shall apply to the court for leave to adduce additional evidence and shall show to the satisfaction of the court that such additional evidence is material and that there were reasonable grounds for the failure to adduce such evidence in the hearing before the Board, its member, agent, or agency, the court may order such additional evidence to be taken before the Board, its members, agent, or agency, and to be made a part of the transcript. The Board may modify its findings as to the facts, or make new findings, by reason of additional evidence so taken and filed, and it shall file such modified or new findings, which findings with respect to questions of fact if supported by substantial evidence on the record considered as a whole shall be conclusive, and shall file its recommendations, if any, for the modification or setting aside of its original order. The jurisdiction of the court shall be exclusive and its judgment and decree shall be final, except that the same shall be subject to review by the appropriate circuit court of appeals if application was made to the district court as hereinabove provided, and by the Supreme Court of the United States upon writ of certiorari or certification as provided in sections 239 and 240 of the Judicial Code, as amended (U.S.C., title 28, secs. 346 and 347).

(f) Any person aggrieved by a final order of the Board granting or denying in whole or in part the relief sought may obtain a review of such order in any circuit court of appeals of the United States in the circuit wherein the unfair labor practice in question was alleged to have been engaged in or wherein such person resides or transacts business, or in the United States Court of Appeals for the District of Columbia, by filing in such court a written petition praying that the order of the Board be modified or set aside. A copy of such petition shall be forthwith served upon the Board, and thereupon the aggrieved party shall file in the court a transcript of the entire record in the proceeding, certified by the Board, including the pleading and testimony upon which the order complained of was entered, and the findings and order of the Board. Upon such filing, the court shall proceed in the same manner as in the case of an application by the Board under subsection (e), and shall have the same exclusive jurisdiction to grant to the Board such temporary relief or restraining order as it deems just and proper, and in like manner to make and enter a decree enforcing, modifying, and enforcing as so modified, or setting aside in whole or in part the order of the Board; the findings of the Board with respect to questions of fact if supported by substantial evidence on the record considered as a whole shall in like manner be conclusive.

(g) The commencement of proceedings under subsection (e) or (f) of this section shall not, unless specifically ordered by the court, operate as a stay of the Board's order.

(h) When granting appropriate temporary relief or a restraining order, or making and entering a decree enforcing, modifying and enforcing as so modified, or setting aside in whole or in part an order on the Board, as provided in this section, the jurisdiction of courts sitting in equity shall not be limited by the Act entitled 'An Act to amend the Judicial Code and to define and limit the jurisdiction of courts sitting in equity, and for other purposes', approved March 23, 1932 (U.S.C., Supp. VII, title 29, secs. 101–115).

(i) Petitions filed under this Act shall be heard expeditiously, and if possible within ten days after they have been docketed.

(j) The Board shall have power, upon issuance of a complaint as provided in subsection (b) charging that any person has engaged in or is engaging in an unfair labor practice, to petition any district court of the United States (including the District Court of the United States for the District of Columbia), within any district wherein the unfair labor practice in question is alleged to have occurred or wherein such person resides or transacts business, for appropriate temporary relief or restraining order. Upon the filing of any such petition the court shall cause notice thereof to be served upon such person, and thereupon shall have jurisdiction to grant to the Board such temporary relief or restraining order as it deems just and proper.

(k) Whenever it is charged that any person has engaged in an unfair labor practice within the meaning of paragraph (4) (D) of section 8 (b), the

Board is empowered and directed to hear and determine the dispute out of which such unfair labor practice shall have arisen, unless, within ten days after notice that such charge has been filed, the parties to such dispute submit to the Board satisfactory evidence that they have adjusted, or agreed upon methods for the voluntary adjustment of, the dispute. Upon compliance by the parties to the dispute with the decision of the Board or upon such voluntary adjustment of the dispute, such charge shall be dismissed.

(*l*) Whenever it is charged that any person has engaged in an unfair labor practice within the meaning of paragraph (4) (*A*), (*B*), or (*C*) of section 8 (*b*), the preliminary investigation of such charge shall be made forthwith and given priority over all other cases except cases of like character in the office where it is filed or to which it is referred. If, after such investigation, the officer or regional attorney to whom the matter may be referred has reasonable cause to believe such charge is true and that a complaint should issue, he shall, on behalf of the Board, petition any district court of the United States (including the District Court of the United States for the District of Columbia) within any district where the unfair labor practice in question has occurred, is alleged to have occurred, or wherein such person resides or transacts business, for appropriate injunctive relief pending the final adjudication of the Board with respect to such matter. Upon the filing of any such petition the district court shall have jurisdiction to grant such injunctive relief or temporary restraining order as it deems just and proper, notwithstanding any other provision of law: *Provided further,* That no temporary restraining order shall be issued without notice unless a petition alleges that substantial and irreparable injury to the charging party will be unavoidable and such temporary restraining order shall be effective for no longer than five days and will become void at the expiration of such period. Upon filing of any such petition the courts shall cause notice thereof to be served upon any person involved in the charge and such person, including the charging party, shall be given an opportunity to appear by counsel and present any relevant testimony: *Provided further,* That for the purposes of this subsection district courts shall be deemed to have jurisdiction of a labor organization (1) in the district in which such organization maintains its principal office, or (2) in any district in which its duly authorized officers or agents are engaged in promoting or protecting the interests of employee members. The service of legal process upon such officer or agent shall constitute service upon the labor organization and make such organization a party to the suit. In situations where such relief is appropriate the procedure specified herein shall apply to charges with respect to section 8 (*b*) (4) (*D*).

INVESTIGATORY POWERS

Sec. 11. For the purpose of all hearings and investigations, which, in the opinion of the Board, are necessary and proper for the exercise of the powers vested in it by section 9 and section 10—

(1) The Board, or its duly authorized agents or agencies, shall at all reason-

able times have access to, for the purpose of examination, and the right to copy any evidence of any person being investigated or proceeded against that relates to any matter under investigation or in question. The Board, or any member thereof, shall upon application of any party to such proceedings, forthwith issue to such party subpenas requiring the attendance and testimony of witnesses or the production of any evidence in such proceeding or investigation requested in such application. Within five days after the service of a subpena on any person requiring the production of any evidence in his possession or under his control, such person may petition the Board to revoke, and the Board shall revoke, such subpena if in its opinion the evidence whose production is required does not relate to any matter under investigation, or any matter in question in such proceedings, or if in its opinion such subpena does not describe with sufficient particularity the evidence whose production is required. Any member of the Board, or any agent or agency designated by the Board for such purposes, may administer oaths and affirmations, examine witnesses, and receive evidence. Such attendance of witnesses and the production of such evidence may be required from any place in the United States or any Territory or possession thereof, at any designated place of hearing.

(2) In case of contumacy or refusal to obey a subpena issued to any person, any district court of the United States or the United States courts of any Territory or possession, or the District Court of the United States for the District of Columbia, within the jurisdiction of which the inquiry is carried on or within the jurisdiction of which said person guilty of contumacy or refusal to obey is found or resides or transacts business, upon application by the Board shall have jurisdiction to issue to such person an order requiring such person to appear before the Board, its member, agent, or agency, there to produce evidence if so ordered, or there to give testimony touching the matter under investigation or in question; and any failure to obey such order of the court may be punished by said court as a contempt thereof.

(3) No person shall be excused from attending and testifying or from producing books, records, correspondence, documents, or other evidence in obedience to the subpena of the Board, on the ground that the testimony or evidence required of him may tend to incriminate him or subject him to a penalty or forfeiture; but no individual shall be prosecuted or subjected to any penalty or forfeiture for or on account of any transaction, matter, or thing concerning which he is compelled, after having claimed his privilege against self-incrimination, to testify or produce evidence, except that such individual so testifying shall not be exempt from prosecution and punishment for perjury committed in so testifying.

(4) Complaints, orders, and other process and papers of the Board, its member, agent, or agency, may be served either personally or by registered mail or by telegraph or by leaving a copy thereof at the principal office or place of business of the person required to be served. The verified return by the individual so serving the same setting forth the manner of such service shall be proof of the same, and the return post office receipt or telegraph receipt

therefor when registered and mailed or telegraphed as aforesaid shall be proof of service of the same. Witnesses summoned before the Board, its member, agent, or agency, shall be paid the same fees and mileage that are paid witnesses in the courts of the United States, and witnesses whose depositions are taken and the persons taking the same shall severally be entitled to the same fees as are paid for like services in the courts of the United States.

(5) All process of any court to which application may be made under this Act may be served in the judicial district wherein the defendant or other person required to be served resides or may be found.

(6) The several departments and agencies of the Government, when directed by the President, shall furnish the Board, upon its request, all records, papers, and information in their possession relating to any matter before the Board.

Sec. 12. Any person who shall willfully resist, prevent, impede, or interfere with any member of the Board or any of its agents or agencies in the performance of duties pursuant to this Act shall be punished by a fine of not more than $5,000 or by imprisonment for not more than one year, or both.

LIMITATIONS

Sec. 13. Nothing in this Act, except as specifically provided for herein, shall be construed so as either to interfere with or impede or diminish in any way the right to strike, or to affect the limitations or qualifications on that right.

Sec. 14. (a) Nothing herein shall prohibit any individual employed as a supervisor from becoming or remaining a member of a labor organization, but no employer subject to this Act shall be compelled to deem individuals defined herein as supervisors as employees for the purpose of any law, either national or local, relating to collective bargaining.

(b) Nothing in this Act shall be construed as authorizing the execution or application of agreements requiring membership in a labor organization as a condition of employment in any State or Territory in which such execution or application is prohibited by State or Territorial law.

Sec. 15. Wherever the application of the provisions of section 272 of chapter 10 of the Act entitled 'An Act to establish a uniform system of bankruptcy throughout the United States', approved July 1, 1898, and Acts amendatory thereof and supplementary thereto (U.S.C., title 11, sec. 672), conflicts with the application of the provisions of this Act, this Act shall prevail: *Provided,* That in any situation where the provisions of this Act cannot be validly enforced, the provisions of such other Acts shall remain in full force and effect.

Sec. 16. If any provision of this Act, or the application of such provision to any person or circumstances, shall be held invalid, the remainder of this Act, or the application of such provision to persons or circumstances other than those as to which it is held invalid, shall not be affected thereby.

Representation elections involve a number of issues, such as whether there is an adequate showing of employee interest in having a union represent them, whether a contract already negotiated by one union at some time in the past bars another union from claiming to represent either a part or the whole of the employees in question, whether the unit requested is an appropriate one for holding an election, what employees are eligible to vote, and other matters. Since we cannot cover all such issues we have concentrated on the question of whether a union may split a group of employees off from a larger unit already represented by another union.

In the first case below, the Machinists had sought to represent a group of employees already represented by the Printing Pressmen. If the Board had decided in favor of the petitioning union it would have ordered an election among the employees involved to ascertain whether in fact they wanted the Machinists as their agent. In this instance, however, the Board rejected the petition for the reason stated in its opinion.

REPRESENTATION MATTERS

Federal Paper Board Co., National Folding Box Co. Division, and International Association of Machinists, AFL-CIO, 117 NLRB No. 79, 1957

DECISION AND ORDER

Upon a petition duly filed under Section 9 (c) of the National Labor Relations Act, a hearing was held before George A. Sweeney, hearing officer. The hearing officer's rulings made at the hearing are free from prejudicial error and are hereby affirmed.

Upon the entire record in this case, the Board finds:

1. The Employer is engaged in commerce within the meaning of the Act.

2. The labor organizations involved claim to represent employees of the Employer.[1]

3. No question affecting commerce exists concerning the representation of employees of the Employer within the meaning of Section 9 (c) (1) and Section 2 (6) and (7) of the Act, for the following reasons:

The Employer is engaged in the manufacture of paper board and paper boxes at its board mill and box plant, located on contiguous property in New Haven, Connecticut. The Employer contends that the unit sought by the Petitioner, consisting of machinists, millwrights, electricians, welders and other employees in the mechanical maintenance department of the Board mill, is inappropriate and, in substance, asserts that the only appropriate unit is the unit now represented by the Printing Pressmen[2] combining production em-

---

[1] The United Paper Workers, Local 463, AFL-CIO, was permitted to intervene on the basis of a possible interest in the unit alleged as appropriate.

[2] The Printing Specialties & Paper Products Union No. 508, International Printing Pressmen & Assistants' Union of North America, AFL-CIO.

ployees at the box plant and all of the Employer's maintenance employees.[3] The Intervenor does not dispute the appropriateness of the unit sought by the Petitioner but objects to the inclusion therein of certain employees whom it represents.[4]

The record shows that in 1944, as a result of a consent election the Printing Pressmen were certified as exclusive bargaining representative for the production employees in the box plant and all of the Employer's maintenance department employees. Since its 1944 certification, the Printing Pressmen has continued to represent all of these employees in a single unit. Prior to 1955, the maintenance department employees had serviced both the box plant and board mill. However, in 1955, the Employer divided its central maintenance force into 2 crews, assigning one permanently to the box plant and the other permanently to the board mill. Although it appears that as a result of this change the crews are now separately supervised, the record shows that the nature of the work performed by the maintenance employees remains unchanged and their seniority rights and fringe benefits unaltered. Furthermore, the record shows that in filling maintenance vacancies that may occur in the future preference will be given to present maintenance employees, regardless of their present assignment. Thus, in view of these factors affecting the essentials of the employer-employee relationship herein and reflecting a continuation of past working conditions and personnel practices, we are not persuaded that a mere administrative change of the type in question is sufficient to overcome the controlling effect of the 13-year history of bargaining covering the combined box plant production and multiplant maintenance unit represented by the Printing Pressmen.[5] Accordingly, in view of the long history of collective bargaining and the community of interest between the board mill and box plant maintenance employees arising from common duties, identical fringe benefits, their department-wide seniority and their assured preference in bidding for maintenance department job openings, we find that only a single unit of all the Employer's maintenance department employees combined with the box plant production employees, the unit currently represented by the Printing Pressmen, is at this time appropriate. Accordingly, as the Petitioner seeks in effect to sever from the existing production and maintenance unit represented by the Printing

[3] As the contract has now expired, we deem it unnecessary to consider the Employer's further contention that its contract with the Printing Pressmen, executed January 3, 1955, to expire December 30, 1956, is a bar.

[4] On October 11, 1956, the Board issued a Notice of Show Cause in this proceeding to determine whether or not the Printing Pressmen had been representing all the employees in the unit for which it had been certified. We are satisfied from the responses to the Order to Show Cause that the Printing Pressmen has been representing the employees in question. Under the circumstances, our decision herein is predicated solely upon a resolution of the issues raised in the original hearing and the briefs submitted by the parties.

[5] E.g., see *Waldensian Hosiery Mills, Inc.*, 85 NLRB 758. Cf. *Manhattan Coil Corporation*, 98 NLRB 1246; see also *Pioneer Division, The Flinthote Company*, 109 NLRB 1273, 1276.

Pressmen a multicraft unit of maintenance employees in the board mill, and the severance of such a unit is contrary to Board policy,[6] we shall dismiss the petition.[7]

IT IS HEREBY ORDERED that the petition filed herein be, and it hereby is, dismissed.

THE AMERICAN POTASH DOCTRINE

107 NLRB No. 290, 1954

The plaguing question of the circumstances under which craft groups might be allowed to separate themselves out from a larger comprehensive bargaining unit was given its most recent answer in the American Potash case. There the Board ruled that craft units would be allowed to separate whenever two conditions were met: (1) that the group of employees petitioning for separate representation constitute a genuine craft group, with characteristics distinguishable from other workers (apprenticeship in a trade is considered one hallmark of a craft, for example), or that the group of employees constitute a departmental unit with craftlike characteristics, who have traditionally bargained as a unit (such as employees in a power-house), and (2) that the union seeking representation rights has traditionally represented such a group.

Of the newly adopted craft severance rule, the Board majority said:

In adopting our new rule, we wish to make it clear that the requirement that the unit sought to be severed must be a true craft group will be rigidly enforced in cases where severance is sought on that basis. We propose to exercise great care in making certain that in the administration of this rule only groups exercising genuine craft skills will be embraced within the ambit of the rule, and that the requirements will not be relaxed over a period of time.

As to the craftlike department units encompassed in the opinion, the Board said: ". . . we shall require strict proof (1) that the departmental group is functionally distinct and separate and (2) that the petitioner is a union which has traditionally devoted itself to serving the special interest of the employees in question."

F. L. Jacobs Co., Danville Division, 108 NLRB No. 85, 1954

Board dismisses petition filed by Lodge 710, IAM, AFL, which sought to represent as a separate craft unit tool and die makers, concluding:

[6] E.g., see *Fort Die Casting Corp.*, 115 NLRB 1749; *North American Rayon Corp.*, 111 NLRB 963.

[7] Nor is our determination affected by the fact that the Printing Pressmen prior to the hearing advised the Board that it desires to relinquish jurisdiction over the board mill maintenance employees. It is clear that there has been no cessation of representation of the board mill maintenance employees and that the Printing Pressmen will continue to represent them under their existing certification.

. . . It seems clear . . . (1) that the employees classified as tool and die makers whom the Petitioner would sever as a craft unit do not have the high degree of skills associated with this craft, and (2) that the work available at the plant is not such as to require a high degree of skill or furnish opportunities for the exercise of tool and die precision on any substantial or broad craft basis. Under these circumstances, and in accord with our recently declared policy, we dismiss the petition, finding that the proposed unit for the Employer's tool and die makers is not appropriate for severance at this time.

American Can Co., 108 NLRB No. 234, 1954

Board dismisses petition filed by Chauffeurs, Teamsters & Helpers "General" Local Union No. 200, which sought to sever a unit of truck drivers from an existing production and maintenance unit currently represented by the intervenor, Steelworkers, CIO.

In dismissing the petition, a majority of the Board—Members Murdock, Peterson, Rodgers and Beeson—concluded:

. . . we find that the facts of this case do not warrant the severance of the truck drivers from the existing production and maintenance unit. Of particular significance is the fact that most of these employees are *not* hired as drivers, and are to a large extent throughout much of the year, shifted back to nondriving jobs, thus performing production work inside the plant along with other production and maintenance employees. Because of these circumstances it does not appear that they constitute a craft or a functionally distinct departmental group with special interests essentially different from those of the employer's other employees under the test as enunciated in the *American Potash* decision.

Rayonier, Inc., 114 NLRB No. 6, 1954

Board dismisses petition filed by IBEW Loc. 1924, which sought to sever an alleged craft group of instrument men and a departmental group of powerhouse employees from an existing unit of production and maintenance employees represented since Sept. 16, 1954, by Locals 395, 610, and 877 of Pulp & Paper Mill Workers, AFL, intervenor. The Board concluded:

. . . As the . . . facts show, none of the instrument men or powerhouse employees herein sought to engage in electrical work to any substantial degree, and by far the greater portion of the activity of both groups is concerned with work on materials which have nothing to do with electricity or its applications. Under these circumstances, we are satisfied that the petitioner does not meet the requirement of the *Potash* rule (107 NLRB 1418). Therefore, assuming, without deciding that the employer's instrument men constitute, for purposes of severance, an appropriate craft group and that its powerhouse employees constitute an appropriate departmental group, we are nevertheless convinced that the Petitioner does not historically and traditionally represent crafts or departments of this type. Accordingly, we shall dismiss the petitions in both cases.

MULTIPLE CRAFT SEVERANCE

Koppers Co., Chemical Division, Williams Plant, and Local 390, International Brotherhood of Electrical Workers; United Association of Journeymen and Apprentices of the Plumbing and Pipe Fitting Industry; Lodge 823, International Association of Machinists; and Local 66, Office Employees International Union, 117 NLRB No. 64, 1957

DECISION AND DIRECTION OF ELECTIONS

Upon separate petitions duly filed under Section 9 (c) of the National Labor Relations Act, a consolidated hearing was held before Lewis T. Roebuck, hearing officer. The hearing officer's rulings made at the hearing are free from prejudicial error and are hereby affirmed.

Upon the entire record in these cases, the Board finds:

1. The Employer is engaged in commerce within the meaning of the Act.

2. The labor organizations involved claim to represent certain employees of the Employer.

3. Questions affecting commerce exist concerning the representation of employees of the Employer within the meaning of Section 9 (c) (1) and Section 2 (6) and (7) of the Act.

4. The appropriate units.

The Petitioner in Case No. 39-RC-1086, Local Union No. 390 of the International Brotherhood of Electrical Workers, AFL-CIO, herein called the IBEW, seeks to sever a craft unit of all maintenance electricians classified as electricians 1st class and electricians 2nd class, and all maintenance instrument men classified as instrument mechanics 1st class and instrument mechanics 2nd class, from a production and maintenance unit at the Employer's Williams plant in Port Arthur, Texas, which is currently represented by the Intervenor, International Chemical Workers Union, Local 557, AFL-CIO.[1] The Petitioner in Case No. 39-RC-1087, United Association of Journeymen and Apprentices of the Plumbing and Pipe Fitting Industry of the United States and Canada, AFL-CIO, herein called the Plumbers, requests severance of a craft unit of all pipe fitter-welders 1st class and pipe fitter-welders 2nd class from the existing production and maintenance unit. The Petitioner in Case No. 39-RC-1097, Lodge 823 of District 31, International Association of Machinists, AFL-CIO, herein called the IAM, seeks to sever a craft unit of all inside and outside machinists and apprentices from the production and maintenance unit. The Petitioner in Case No. 39-RC-1092, Local 66, Office Employees International Union, AFL-CIO, herein called Local 66, seeks to represent a unit of office

---

[1] The Intervenor, which was certified by the Board in 1953 as bargaining agent for all production, maintenance and service employees, excluding all office clerical and plant clerical employees, guards, cadet engineers, professional employees, and all supervisors, has represented this unit under a contract with the Employer which is not here asserted as a bar.

clerical employees who are currently unrepresented and for whom there is no history of collective bargaining.[2]

The Employer and the Intervenor moved to dismiss the petitions in Case Nos. 39-RC-1086, 39-RC-1087, and 39-RC-1097 on the ground that the employees sought are not craftsmen exercising the skills of their respective crafts. In Case No. 39-RC-1092, the Employer moved to dismiss the petition on the ground that the requested office clerical unit was inappropriate because it includes employees who the Employer asserts are confidential employees.[3]

The Employer is engaged in the production of polyethylene and ethylbenzene at its Williams plant in Port Arthur, Texas, where it commenced production operations in 1953. In the production of polyethylene, ethylene gas is brought into the Williams plant under pressure and is then compressed and reacted into polyethylene. In producing ethylbenzene, benzene and ethylene are reacted and styled into the final product.

In addition to various production buildings and office structures where the office clericals sought by Local 66 are housed, the Employer has a maintenance shop in which the maintenance department is located. It is in this department that the electricians and instrument men, pipe fitter-welders, and inside and outside machinists whom the IBEW, Plumbers, and IAM, respectively, seek to represent on a craft basis, are located.

A. *Maintenance electricians and instrument mechanics unit*
(Case No. 39-RC-1086)

The IBEW seeks to sever a craft unit of all maintenance electricians classified as electricians 1st class and electricians 2nd class, and all maintenance instrument men classified as instrument mechanics 1st class and instrument mechanics 2nd class at the Williams plant from the existing production and maintenance unit. The Employer contends that the petition in this case should be dismissed on the ground that the employees sought are not craftsmen. The Intervenor urges that the Board deny craft severance to the IBEW on the ground that the unit is not sufficiently large to justify severance.

There are three maintenance electricians 1st class and five instrument mechanics 1st class in the maintenance department who work under the immediate supervision of a maintenance foreman who formerly was a 1st class electrician.[4] Both classifications of employees have separate work benches and

---

[2] On January 4, 1957, Local 66 moved to sever its case from the other cases herein for decisional purposes, asserting that the issues presented in its case were divorced from those presented in the craft severance cases and should be decided separately to expedite a decision thereon. However, in view of our decision to direct elections in the craft severance cases herein, as well as in Case No. 39-RC-1092 filed by Local 66, we find that it will best effectuate the policies of the Act to direct that simultaneous elections be held. The motion to sever filed by Local 66 is therefore denied.

[3] The Intervenor did not intervene in Case No. 39-RC-1092 and took no position with respect to Local 66's unit request in that case.

[4] Except when required to work overtime or on emergencies, no other foremen supervise these employees.

storage lockers where tools and test instruments customarily used by electricians and instrument mechanics are kept. Both classifications report to these areas at the beginning and the end of their work day. Time cards for both classifications are kept solely by their foreman.

The Employer purchases its current at a voltage of 69,000 volts from a local utility. This voltage is fed into two transformers on the Employer's premises where it is reduced to 2300 volts. From there, the current is transmitted to various substations around the plant where the voltage is further reduced to 440 volts and 110 volts, and is directly transmitted to appropriate motors in the plant. The electricians cut into or work on these high voltage lines without cutting off the power and, in doing so, utilize the special protective equipment and tools employed by the electrical craft. When work must be performed in the power substations, only the services of electricians are utilized.

In addition to servicing the foregoing high voltage equipment, the maintenance electricians perform trouble-shooting on electrical equipment, install various electrical motors, maintain space heaters and freon gas in the air conditioning system, and repair the Employer's refrigeration equipment.

The five instrument mechanics 1st class install, maintain, and repair temperature and pressure gauges, flow records and controllers, thermometers, relief valves, sight glasses, and all allied equipment necessary for controlling the chemical processes in which the Employer is engaged. In checking instruments in the plant, which are operated both electrically and by air pressure, the instrument mechanics utilize specialized equipment located at their work bench which are not used by any other classifications of employees.

The Employer asserts that, although the electricians and instrument mechanics exercise skills and utilize tools customarily associated with their respective crafts, they lack the qualities of craftsmen because the Employer maintains no apprenticeship or formalized training program by which they can acquire craft skills, because 1st class jobs are acquired by competitive bidding for vacancies, and because these employees perform work outside of their respective crafts. The record discloses that, in hiring electricians and instrument mechanics, the Employer investigates the applicant's past experience in his trade. Of the electricians and instrument mechanics who were called to testify in this proceeding, all had extensive experience in their trade. Thus, one electrician had approximately 20 years of experience as an electrician and had been rated as a journeyman. Another electrician had in excess of 2 years experience as a 1st class electrician before his employment by the Employer and acquired a 1st class rating with the Employer after 3 years of experience in a helpers' pool. One instrument mechanic testified that he had approximately 10 years previous experience as an instrument mechanic in addition to training he received at a vocational training school.

Pursuant to the contract between the Employer and the Intervenor, 1st class ratings are acquired by bidding for posted job vacancies. When electricians and instrument mechanics with prior experience are hired and no vacancies in the 1st class ratings exist, they are placed in a helpers' pool. When a 1st class rating is vacant, the job is filled by bids. In selecting a candidate for the position, the

Employer assesses the skills and qualifications of the candidate. The Employer's maintenance department foreman testified that no employee attains a first class rating without possessing the requisite qualifications acquired through training either at the Employer's plant or elsewhere.

The record discloses that there are no transfers between electricians and instrument mechanics and the other job classifications. Because the Employer does not employ carpenters, masons, or operating engineers, the electricians and instrument mechanics perform the work of these classifications but only to the extent that such work is necessary for the completion of their own electrical or instrument duties.

On the basis of the foregoing, and the entire record, we are satisfied that, despite the absence of an apprenticeship or formalized training policy, the 1st class electricians and instrument mechanics make use of all the skills usually associated with their respective crafts. We therefore find, contrary to the Employer's contention, that these employees constitute an identifiable skilled and homogeneous craft group which may, if they so desire, be separately represented.[5] Moreover, we find without merit the Intervenor's contention that the petition herein should be dismissed because the unit sought is too small to warrant severance.[6] As the IBEW has traditionally devoted itself to the representation of such employees, we find that the criteria for craft severance have been met.

Accordingly, we find that the Employer's maintenance electricians 1st class and instrument mechanics 1st class employed at its Williams plant in Port Arthur, Texas, excluding all other employees, professional employees, guards, watchmen, and all supervisors as defined in the Act may constitute an appropriate unit within the meaning of Section 9 (b) of the Act, if they so desire.

B. Pipe fitter-welders unit (Case No. 39-RC-1087)

The Pipefitters in Case No. 39-RC-1087 seek to sever a unit of all pipe fitter-welders 1st class and pipe fitter-welders 2nd class from the existing production and maintenance unit on the ground that they constitute a severable craft group. The Employer and the Intervenor moved to dismiss the petition in this case, contending that the unit sought is inappropriate because it is not composed of craftsmen.

There are 9 pipe fitter-welders in the requested unit who are supervised by 2 foremen who also supervise the machinists in the maintenance department. All the pipe fitter-welders possess 1st class job classifications. The duties of the pipe fitter-welders consist of repairing and replacing all types of pipe, including cast iron, concrete, steel, stainless steel, and masterlode; replacing valves; maintaining pipe in pump and cooling drains; and, performing welding operations

---

[5] See *East Texas Pulp & Paper Company*, 113 NLRB 539, 544–45; *Universal Watch Corporation*, 116 NLRB No. 188; *American Tobacco Company, Incorporated*, 115 NLRB 218, 219. As the Employer does not employ any 2nd class electricians or instrument mechanics, we shall not include such classifications in the unit description.

[6] See *American Tobacco Company, Incorporated, supra*.

in connection with the foregoing duties.[7] In the performance of their duties, the pipe fitter-welders utilize such tools as pipe machines, cutting torches, wrenches, and welding machines.

Like the electricians sought by the IBEW, the pipe fitter-welders indicated their past experience in that trade on their application forms at the time of their employment. In addition, these employees underwent welding tests to establish their proficiency in that field. The record discloses that pipe fitter-welders who are not initially hired to fill 1st class openings are placed in a helpers' pool until vacancies in such classifications arise, at which time they are selected for such openings provided that they possess the requisite skill. One of the pipe fitter-welders who was initially hired as a 1st class pipe fitter-welder had, previous to his employment with the Employer, served an apprenticeship and had attained a journeyman pipefitter rating.

Pipe fitter-welders do not interchange with any other employees at this plant. Except in cases of emergency, or when overtime work is required, pipe fitter-welders do not perform work outside their trade. Because the Employer does not employ all of the gamut of crafts at its plant, pipe fitter-welders, like the electricians, may perform some carpentry or masonry duties but only insofar as these duties facilitate or are necessary for the performance of their pipe fitting-welding work.

Although the Employer maintains no apprenticeship or formalized training program for pipe fitter-welders, we are satisfied on the record that these employees utilize the skills and equipment generally identified with the pipe fitting craft. Accordingly, we find that the pipe fitter-welders constitute a craft group which is entitled to separate craft representation if the employees so desire.[8] As the Plumbers have traditionally represented such craft groups, the criteria for craft severance have been satisfied.

We find that all pipe fitter-welders 1st class [9] at the Employer's Williams plant in Port Arthur, Texas, excluding all other employees, professional employees, guards, watchmen, and all supervisors as defined in the Act, may constitute an appropriate unit within the meaning of Section 9 (b) of the Act.

C. Inside and outside machinists unit (Case No. 39-RC-1097)

The IAM requests severance of a craft unit of all inside and outside machinists and apprentices from the production and maintenance unit. The Employer and the Intervenor oppose severance of these employees on the ground that they are not craftsmen.

The Employer employs 10 1st class inside and outside machinists in its maintenance department. Their duties consist of repairing pumps, packing, making shafts, fitting bearings, refacing and reseating valves, stems and plugs, running engine lathes, and turning shafts during which they work to close

[7] All welding for structural steel is performed by the boilermakers in the maintenance department.

[8] See American Tobacco Company, Incorporated, 108 NLRB 1211, 1213.

[9] The Employer does not employ any pipe fitter-welders 2nd class. We shall therefore omit this classification from the unit description.

tolerances. In addition, the machinists make small shafts and bushings and remove pipes on pumps up to the first joint, from where the pipe fitter-welders take over. In the performance of their duties, the machinists use such tools as lathes, shapers, Do-all saws, and drill presses. No other employees in the department operate these tools.

The record discloses that machinists possess and exercise the skills of journeymen machinists and that there is no interchange between machinists and other classifications of employees. While some of the machinists perform such work as crating machinery, building scaffolds, and putting forms in concrete, it seems clear that the normal duties of these employees during regular working hours are those performed by machinists.

Although the Employer does not maintain an apprenticeship or formalized training program for the inside and outside machinists, we are satisfied that the machinists here sought possess and exercise the skills normally associated with the machinists' craft and that they are craftsmen.[10] Accordingly, as the IAM has traditionally represented units of these craft employees, we find that the inside and outside machinists may, if they so desire, choose to be separately represented by the IAM for the purposes of collective bargaining.

We find that all inside and outside 1st class machinists [11] at the Employer's Williams plant in Port Arthur, Texas, excluding all other employees, professional employees, guards, watchmen, and all supervisors as defined in the Act, may constitute an appropriate unit within the meaning of Section 9 (b) of the Act.

D. Office clerical unit (Case No. 39-RC-1092)

In Case No. 39-RC-1092, Local 66 seeks a unit of all office clerical employees at the Employer's Williams plant in Port Arthur, Texas, excluding all production and maintenance employees, guards, watchmen, and all supervisors as defined in the Act. The Employer asserts that the requested unit is inappropriate for the reason that it would include employees who are confidential employees, and contends that the petition should, for this reason, be dismissed.

There are 16 office clerical employees at this plant who are currently unrepresented. The Employer asserts that the secretary to the plant manager, the stenographer-clerk who works for both the plant manager and the assistant plant manager, and the two stenographer-clerks who work for the personnel manager, are confidential employees. The record discloses that the plant manager, assistant plant manager, and the personnel manager formulate, determine and effectuate all labor relations policies for the Employer in that they draw up contract proposals, participate in contract negotiations with labor organizations, and execute negotiated labor agreements on behalf of the Employer. In addition, they process grievances arising under collective bargaining contracts. The secretary and stenographer-clerks in question take dictation and type up the

[10] See *Ketchikan Pulp Company*, 115 NLRB 279, 282.

[11] As the Employer does not now employ inside and outside machinists' apprentices whom the IAM seeks in its petition, we shall exclude such classifications from the unit description.

Employer's contract proposals before they are submitted to labor organizations, take minutes of grievance discussions and type up grievance replies, and receive, route, and file confidential advisories from the Employer's labor relations attorney relating to suggested labor relations policies.

On the basis of the foregoing, we find that the secretary to the plant manager, the stenographer-clerk who works for both the plant and assistant plant managers, and the stenographer-clerks who work for the personnel manager, assist and act in a confidential capacity to persons who formulate, determine and effectuate management policies in the field of labor relations. We therefore find that they are confidential employees.[12] The fact that Local 66 seeks to represent confidential employees who may not properly be part of an otherwise appropriate bargaining unit of office clerical employees does not, as the Board has frequently ruled, require dismissal of its petition.[13] The Employer's motion to dismiss the petition herein is therefore denied.

Accordingly, we find that a unit of office clerical employees at the Employer's Williams plant in Port Arthur, Texas, excluding the secretary to the plant manager, the stenographer-clerk who works for both the plant and assistant plant managers, the stenographer-clerks who work for the personnel manager, all other employees, professional employees, guards, watchmen, and all supervisors as defined in the Act, constitute a unit appropriate for the purposes of collective bargaining within the meaning of Section 9 (b) of the Act.

In view of the foregoing, we shall direct that elections be conducted in the following unit (A) and voting groups (B), (C), and (D) of employees at the Employer's Williams plant in Port Arthur, Texas:

(A) All office clerical employees, excluding the secretary to the plant manager, the stenographer-clerk who works for both the plant and assistant plant managers, the stenographer-clerks who work for the personnel manager, all other employees, professional employees, guards, watchmen, and all supervisors as defined in the Act.

(B) All maintenance electricians 1st class and instrument mechanics 1st class, excluding all other employees, professional employees, guards, watchmen, and all supervisors as defined in the Act.

(C) All pipe fitter-welders 1st class, excluding all other employees, professional employees, guards, watchmen, and all supervisors as defined in the Act.

(D) All inside and outside machinists 1st class, excluding all other employees, guards, watchmen, and all supervisors as defined in the Act.

If a majority of employees in voting groups (B), (C), or (D) select a union seeking to represent them separately, those employees will be taken to have indicated their desire to constitute a separate bargaining unit and the Regional Director conducting the election is instructed to issue a Certification of Representatives to the labor organization selected by the employees in each group for such unit, which the Board in such circumstances, finds to be appropriate for purposes of collective bargaining. On the other hand, if a majority of the

[12] See *The B. F. Goodrich Company*, 115 NLRB 722, 724.

[13] E.g., *Plankinton Packing Company (Division of Swift & Co.)*, 116 NLRB No. 160 at page 2.

employees in any of voting groups (B), (C), or (D) do not vote for a union which is seeking to represent them in a separate unit, these employees shall remain part of the existing unit and the Regional Director will issue a Certification of Results to such effect.

DIRECTION OF ELECTIONS

As part of the investigation to ascertain representatives for the purposes of collective bargaining with the Employer, elections by secret ballot shall be conducted as early as possible, but not later than 30 days from the date of this Direction, under the direction and supervision of the Regional Director for the Region in which this case was heard, and subject to Sections 102.61 and 102.62 of National Labor Relations Board Rules and Regulations, among the employees in the unit and voting groups described in paragraph numbered 4, above, who were employed during the pay-roll period immediately preceding the date of this Direction of Elections, including employees who did not work during said pay-roll period because they were ill or on vacation or temporarily laid off, and employees in the military services of the United States who appear in person at the polls, but excluding those employees who have since quit or been discharged for cause and have not been rehired or reinstated prior to the date of the elections, and also excluding employees on strike who are not entitled to reinstatement, to determine whether they desire to be represented, for purposes of collective bargaining, in unit (A) by Local 66, Office Employees International Union, AFL-CIO, or by no union; in voting group (B) by Local Union No. 390 of the International Brotherhood of Electrical Workers, AFL-CIO, or by International Chemical Workers Union, Local 557, AFL-CIO; in voting group (C) by United Association of Journeymen and Apprentices of the Plumbing and Pipe Fitting Industry of the United States and Canada, AFL-CIO, or by International Chemical Workers Union, Local 557, AFL-CIO; and, in voting group (D) by Lodge 823 of District 31, International Association of Machinists, AFL-CIO, or by International Chemical Workers Union, Local 557, AFL-CIO.

The representation election can be an exciting contest. Although the vote is to determine whether or not the workers wish to be represented by a union, popularly such an election is viewed as a contest between union and company. If the union is rejected, it is often said that the company "wins."

Needless to say, unions enter such contests with every determination to come out ahead. In part it is a matter of prestige—the more victories it can win at the NLRB polls, the easier it is to persuade other workers that they too should join up. In part it is a matter of recovering an investment—organizing can be an expensive undertaking, and the return on such an investment comes only with the per capita payments to the national office. This does not mean that unions organize workers with an eye to how much they can get back in dues on their original investment, but it does mean that unions, like other organizations, must have an income that balances their outgo in order to survive.

PREPARING FOR THE NLRB ELECTION

From Ernest Calloway, Some Notes for Trade Union Organizers, part 6, St. Louis Teamsters' Research Bulletin, April 15, 1955

In most cases an organizing campaign will reach its highest point of interest and intensity in an election conducted by the National Labor Relations Board to determine the legal collective bargaining agency for the employees in question.

To invoke the services of the board in a representation case, it is necessary to obtain signed authorization cards from at least 30 percent of the employees in the bargaining unit. However, an organizer should be extremely careful in invoking the board's services until he has at least 60 to 70 percent of the employees signed up. The prerogatives of management under the present administration of the Taft-Hartley law are many, and their traditional weapons of intimidation and coercion have been sanctified by a series of new administrative decisions from the board. To over-come these hurdles, the organizer should only consider NLRB services after he has been successful in obtaining authorization cards from an overwhelming majority of the workers in the shop or plant. If the election is lost, it will require another year before a new one is permitted under NLRB rules.

So the first task of an organizer in invoking the services of the Board is to determine the extent and depth of union sentiment in the shop. If he is uncertain, it's better to wait until the situation improves. Hasty decisions in this matter of seeking the services of the board in representation cases have torpedoed far too many organizing efforts.

The representation election is the first initial test of unity among the new union members. It is also a test for the organizer and his efforts. The date has been set.

The nature of the campaign during this pre-election period is quite different from the initial and middle stages of the drive. The only thing that counts in an election is an 'X' in the square for the Union. Every move and all strategy should be in the direction of getting at least 51 percent of the employees to pencil an 'X' in the proper square. The early stages of the campaign moved at a slow pace. This phase of the campaign must move at a high intense tempo.

The primary object during this period of the campaign is that of holding together and creating a solid front among the employees who *have* signed authorization cards. While this does not exclude the task of obtaining additional authorization cards, it does mean that a great deal of attention must be given to the task of holding the *committed* group together for the election. This short campaign must be an enthusiastic, inspiring one. It is during this period that the employer will concentrate on defeating the Union, and nothing should be left un-done to over-come any and all efforts of the employer. All meetings, speeches, home calls, leaflet distributions, etc. should be planned in the direction of holding your committed group together.

THE LEAFLET CAMPAIGN

During this period leaflets should be distributed daily. A great number of the leaflets should be around the positive advantages of sticking together. How to Vote leaflets should be distributed as often as possible. Where to mark the X is one of the most practical leaflets during this period. In many cases, satire leaflets on the activities of the employer and his supervisor have been effective. It helps to wean workers away from the psychological influences of the employer.

If possible, a Leaflet Distribution Committee should be created among the members. This has certain definite advantages. Workers in the shop distributing leaflets before going to work will obtain greater reception, and more important it builds the spirit of determination and unity.

ACTIVE CARD FILE

An active card file on general attitude toward the Union should be set up for each individual employee who has signed an authorization card. If possible, non-signers of cards should also be included in this file. The card should include name, address, phone number, wage rate, department, years of employment, classification and space for organizer's notes on the individual. This file should be kept confidential and used only by the organizer. The file should be separated into three sections, namely: Weak, Strong, and Tend to Waver. This should aid the organizer in determining his points of concentration for additional work during the pre-election period.

HOME CALLS

If possible, a Home Call Committee should also be created among those who have signed authorization cards. Any work that can be given to the rank and file employees during the pre-election period will certainly add to the spirit to win. Cards for home calls should be broken down according to streets and neighborhoods, and each member of the committee made responsible for a particular area of the town. Reports on calls should be made as often as possible. Information from these reports should be added to the active card file.

ESTABLISHING A NEGOTIATING COMMITTEE

During the pre-election period, the organizer could very well establish a Negotiating Committee to prepare the group for the task ahead after certification has been granted by the National Labor Relations Board. This has certain psychological advantages during the pre-election period. It creates an atmosphere of eventual victory and serves as a form of positive encouragement for the group.

USING COMMUNITY LEADERS

In smaller communities, the organizer should attempt to hold a series of meetings in which pro-labor community leaders could be invited to urge the workers to vote for the Union. These leaders also could be used for special radio or television programs during this period. The key operation of this period is that of building a sustained enthusiasm and reducing the area of fear of the employer among the employees. The use of outstanding community leaders contributes a great deal to this aspect of the program.

MOCK ELECTION, THE NIGHT BEFORE

The night before the election is the big night. Every effort should be made to have maximum attendance at this meeting. If necessary, door prizes should be given. The meeting should be kept an enthusiastic one. Use rank and file members as much as possible. They should tell why they are voting for the Union. Don't leave any of the employer's arguments un-answered. In many campaigns, mock elections have been conducted on the night before. Pass out sample ballots and have each one vote. Count the ballots and announce the vote. This is good training on how to mark ballots. Finally, elect the individuals who will serve as observers for the Union.

RIVAL UNIONS

When two or more unions are contending in an NLRB election, the campaigning can get heated. In 1954 the International Union of Electrical, Radio and Machine Workers (IUE) challenged the representation rights of the independent union at the Tung-Sol Co., in New Jersey. The IUE accused the independent of intentions of affiliating with the United Electrical, Radio and Machine Workers (UE). The IUE and UE have been bitterly antagonistic since the latter was expelled from the CIO in 1950 on charges of being Communist dominated. Below are reproduced leaflets circulated to employees in the bargaining unit during the period of campaigning prior to the election.

THE MEANING OF THE SECRET BALLOT

Today we vote. The election is being held in an atmosphere of violence and coercion. Threats are the order of the day from the independent.

But we don't have to be the victims of intimidation. For we have the SECRET BALLOT—the greatest gift of our American heritage.

It was the SECRET BALLOT that defeated Boss Hague.

It was the SECRET BALLOT that defeated Boss Crump.

It was the SECRET BALLOT that defeated Boss Pendergast.

It was the SECRET BALLOT that defeated crooked Tammany Hall.

It was the SECRET BALLOT that always defeated the crooked Politicians.

Now, today, YOU can defeat the company union and outside interference in your affairs. Your weapon is the SECRET BALLOT. It protects you because nobody will ever know how you vote.

Win a clean, decent American Trade Union—the only Union on the ballot—the IUE-CIO.

VOTE IUE-CIO

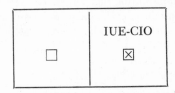

$15 ᴀssᴇssᴍᴇɴᴛ ᴛᴏ ᴘᴀʏ $25,000 ᴅᴇʙᴛ

If the independent wins the election, every Tung-Sol worker will be assessed *$15 and up* to pay the $25,000 debt of the independents. And the debt is still going up as they run up bigger campaign bills.

With the independents in the saddle, Tung-Sol workers will face:

1. $15 and up out of everyone's paycheck to pay other people's bills.

2. Loss of the $30,000 in the local treasury to National UE. This is the result of the deal pulled off between the independent and National UE. But this is ʏᴏᴜʀ money. It belongs to ʏᴏᴜ the members.

3. No right to vote on election of officers. Present officers are to be appointed to continue indefinitely.

IUE-CIO Stands for Immediate Elections of all Officers by Voting Machines in the Plant

VOTE IUE-CIO

ʏᴏᴜ'ʟʟ ʀᴇɢʀᴇᴛ ɪᴛ ɪꜰ ʏᴏᴜ ᴅᴏɴ'ᴛ ᴠᴏᴛᴇ ɪɴᴅᴇᴘᴇɴᴅᴇɴᴛ ᴏɴ ᴛᴜᴇs., ɴᴏᴠ. 9ᴛʜ

The ɪɴᴅᴇᴘᴇɴᴅᴇɴᴛs have presented to you, a program far superior to the IUE's or any other labor organization. It is a program for the people of Tung-Sol, a program that you ᴍᴜsᴛ support because it means a victory to better all conditions for the workers of Tung-Sol.

ꜰᴏʀ ᴛʜᴏsᴇ ᴏꜰ ʏᴏᴜ ᴡʜᴏ ʜᴀᴠᴇ ᴅᴇᴠᴏᴜʀᴇᴅ ᴛʜᴇ ᴠɪᴄɪᴏᴜs ʟɪᴇs, ᴄʜᴀʀᴀᴄᴛᴇʀ ᴀssᴀssɪɴᴀᴛɪᴏɴs, ꜰʟɪᴘ-ꜰʟᴏᴘᴘᴇʀs, ᴀɴᴅ ᴀᴄᴄᴜsᴀᴛɪᴏɴs ᴏꜰ ᴛʜᴇ IUE. ʏᴏᴜ ᴛᴏᴏ, ᴡɪʟʟ ʀᴇɢʀᴇᴛ ᴛʜᴀᴛ ʏᴏᴜ ᴅɪᴅ ɴᴏᴛ ᴠᴏᴛᴇ ɪɴᴅᴇᴘᴇɴᴅᴇɴᴛ.

A malicious, whispering campaign started because you refused to take or read the IUE's leaflets. IUE has become more than desperate. They ʜᴀᴠᴇ ʙᴇᴄᴏᴍᴇ ɪɴsᴀɴᴇ.

The organizers admit that they are just paid to give out leaflets. They cannot answer your questions so, they resort to lies and defamation of character to make you forget your program and what your officers have done and sacrificed for the workers in Tung-Sol. The IUE claims all the lies they have told come from the workers in Tung-Sol. Are you too, Liars? . . .

ᴀʟʟ ᴏꜰ ᴛʜᴇɪʀ ʙʟᴏᴡs ʜᴀᴠᴇ ʙᴇᴇɴ ʙᴏᴏsᴛs.

Your officers are known to you, have fought for you, have fought for trade unionism and a democratic principle. Your officers have presented the truth to you through-out this long, bitter campaign. Your officers have settled grievances for you to the best of their ability and limited circumstances—they have demonstrated their ability, capability and unity under great pressure. The only thoughts the INDEPENDENTS have had in the campaign have been a better program, better wages and better working conditions for their co-workers.

YOU'LL REGRET IT IF YOU DON'T WHOLEHEARTEDLY UNITE TO SUPPORT THE INDEPENDENTS AND THEIR PROGRAM. Without unity, you cannot have a strong union, strong contract and strong leadership.

IUE in all of their plants have portrayed a beautiful picture of disunity, deplorable working conditions, high initiations, high dues payments, assessments, poor selected leadership and STRIKE FANATICS, while at the same time no support is given to the workers. THEY want numbers in people and money from you to further their raids in peaceful plants.

The IUE will print lies about your program and working conditions but, not about your officers. Should they print falsehoods about your officers and members, naming them, they know court action can be taken. BEWARE OF THEIR (IUE) LAST MINUTE WHISPERING CAMPAIGN TO WHICH THEY WILL STOP AT NOTHING IN THEIR FINAL MOMENTS OF DESPERATION.

Have No Regrets After Election Day. Your Affiliation Will Be

WITH INDEPENDENT ONLY

VOTE INDEPENDENT, LOCAL 433 on Tuesday, November 9th

LOCAL 433

INDEPENDENT

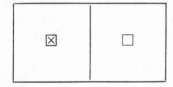

Flash!! IUE Monroe Settlement—   .1¼ Cents—Lost Holiday—No Seniority

LOW TACTICS—SURE DEFEAT

The IUE has shown that it is out for personal gain and power only. They don't give a rap about the Tung-Sol workers including the people that are being fooled by their glib tongues.

It's real funny to see the holier-than-thou attitude of the IUE concerning the money spent by the Independent in this campaign. What we're wondering is— who's going to pick up the $100,000 tab the IUE spent to try to win this plant?

Don't forget they have many more raids planned for others and, more raids mean more assessments from workers.

The IUE's main objective, as stated in the papers, is to wreck the UE, not to fight for better conditions for their members. Isn't that some admission for a so-called union to make?

VOTE INDEPENDENT, LOCAL 433

Issued by Members and Workers of Local 433, Independent

FOR DISCUSSION AND ANALYSIS

1. Suppose a group of employees decided they would like to form a union. What steps would they have to follow in order to have a union certified as a bargaining agent by the NLRB?

2. What issues of *public* policy are involved in the question of whether craft groups should be allowed to split off from comprehensive bargaining units?

3. The representation election procedure is designed to allow employees to select a bargaining agent of their own choosing. One professed objective of the AFL-CIO is to determine *in advance of an election* what union should have the jurisdictional claim to any group of employees, avoiding jurisdictional disputes. Do you see any conflict between these two policies? If so, how do you believe it should be resolved?

4. The NLRB has the authority to set aside an election if it believes that under the circumstances "the free and untrammeled expression of choice by the employees" was impaired.

Suppose a union during the course of a representation campaign made claims to having won wage rates at other plants higher than was actually the case, as a means of inducing employees to vote for it in the coming election. Would you consider this sufficient ground for voiding the election? Suppose it claimed to have won high wage rates at a fictitious plant? On the basis of what criteria would you determine whether in any case the campaign allegations of union or management had made a "free" choice of representative impossible?

(The student might wish to consult the Gummed Products Co. case, 112 NLRB No. 141, and the Otis Elevator Co. case, 114 NLRB No. 234.)

5. Employer statements no less than union statements may void an election. Here are excerpts from two letters circulated by different companies a day or two before the election was held. Would you consider that either or both constituted an interference with the free choice of a bargaining representative by the employees involved?

a. The letter, after urging employees to vote, answering statements appearing in union leaflets, and reminding employees of how well they had fared with respect to wages and other employee benefits without a union, continued in the following vein:

We value the fine personal relationship which has always existed between us. Up to now you have been free to come to us about any matter whatever. If the union wins we will no longer be able to adjust questions of wages, hours and working conditions with you as individual. Also if the union wins it will bargain for all production and maintenance employees whether or not they join the union. This does not mean that we would penalize you or be unfriendly to you. It does mean that we might have to cease dealing with all of you as we have up to now, personally and individually. *We would like to continue, and be able to improve, these relations. We hope you feel the same way about it.*

If you wish this personal relationship to continue mark your ballot with an X in the square designated for a NO vote. [Italics supplied]

b. This letter contained the following statements, under the heading "What can you expect from *any* Union?":

3. To have wage increases, insurance and other benefits held up. For example—Ashland Telechron employees now represented by UE are being prevented *right now* from enjoying your recent wage increase and insurance benefits. You'd have an improved pension plan now too if both UE and CIO were not today making it impossible for us to give it to you and other Telechron employees. This improved pension plan would provide a minimum pension of $100 to $125 per month to people with 25 years of service.

(Note: You may wish to check your own conclusion against that of the Board in General Electric Co. and UE, 92 NLRB No. 160, and Telechron and UE, 92 NLRB No. 113.)

6. There are numbers of workers below the age of twenty-one, and even many below the age of eighteen. In a representation election, would you impose any age limit on a worker's right to vote? In one case, an official of the Board ruled that workers above the age of eleven were entitled to vote. By talking to the child actors who were involved, he concluded that below that age they had no comprehension of the issues involved, but above that age they seemed to have a reasonable understanding of what the election was all about. Would you accept this ruling? Should the principles underlying an age limit for voting in union representation elections be the same as those applying to civil elections?

10: Taft-Hartley Unfair Labor Practices on the Part of Employers

The restraints on employers which were set forth in the Wagner Act have been retained in the Taft-Hartley Act. Certain labor practices are branded "unfair," and employers engaging in them may be brought before the National Labor Relations Board and ordered to "cease and desist" from such behavior. The philosophy behind this part of the law is that the decision by workers as to whether or not they wish to be represented by a union should be left to them; threats of reprisal for joining a union constitute an unwarranted denial of the worker's right to designate an agent. Moreover, refusal by an employer to recognize and bargain with a majority union is likewise viewed in the law as a denial of the worker's right to be represented by an agent. The cases below illustrate the NLRB's effort to define, through individual decisions, the line of conduct which an employer should not follow in labor matters.

SECTION 8(a)(3) DISCRIMINATION AGAINST EMPLOYEES FOR UNION ACTIVITY

Old King Cole, Inc., and United Automobile Workers, 117 NLRB No. 48, 1957

FINDINGS OF FACT

I. THE BUSINESS OF THE RESPONDENT

The complaint alleges, the Respondent admitted, and the undersigned finds that Old King Cole, Inc., is and has been at all times material herein, a corporation duly organized under and existing by virtue of the laws of the State of Ohio. At all times material herein, the Respondent has maintained its principal office and place of business in Louisville, Ohio, where it is now and has been continuously engaged in the design, manufacture and sale of displays and fuel cell mandrels. In the course and conduct of its business operations, the Respondent annually causes and has continuously caused its products, said products having a total value in excess of $100,000, to be sold, transported, and delivered in interstate commerce to and through States of the United States other than the State of Ohio, from its Louisville, Ohio, plant.

Respondent is, and was at all times material herein, engaged in commerce within the meaning of the Act.

II. THE LABOR ORGANIZATION INVOLVED

International Union, United Automobile, Aircraft & Agricultural Implement Workers of America, AFL-CIO, is a labor organization admitting to membership employees of the Respondent.

III. THE UNFAIR LABOR PRACTICES

A. *The facts*

In November 1954, the Respondent opened a new plant known as Plant 3 in Louisville, Ohio, located about 1½ blocks from its Plant 1 where the Respondent manufactured displays and its main office is located. During the period in question here about 70 employees were employed manufacturing fuel cell mandrels for airplanes in Plant 3 under Paul Streby as plant superintendent, Herman Valentine as foreman of the tank building and shipping departments and Clayton Gregory as foreman of the finishing department. Neither plant was organized by any union.

For reasons only hinted at in this record, the employees of Plant 3 began thinking about joining a labor organization sometime in early June 1955.[1] At the request of some of the employees, employee Julia Capaldi through her husband, a union member employed at the Canton Ford Plant, got in touch with David Sherwood, UAW representative, who called on her at her home and explained union organization to her about June 8, 1955. Union organization had begun.

On June 16, employees Capaldi, Nettie Heddleson and Angeline Borger signed union application and authorization cards and 4 days thereafter Jack Griffiths and his mother, Beatrice, did likewise. During the period involved here approximately six union meetings were held at employee Ada Manse's house or at Eagle's Hall in Louisville which were attended by as many as 25 or 30 employees from the plant, including those mentioned above, at which time more union cards were signed. At one of these union meetings Sherwood told the employees that they should wear union buttons at the plant openly as a protection against being discharged. A number of the employees including all those aforementioned began to wear UAW and CIO buttons in the plant during working hours. These same employees and others began soliciting the other employees to attend union meetings and to join the Union. This solicitation was carried on both during working hours as well as during the rest periods and off hours. Certain of the other employees began reporting to their foremen and other supervisors about these solicitations so that the Respondent was soon aware of the union activity and convinced that some 9 employees, including Capaldi, Heddleson and the 2 Griffiths, were responsible for it.

Although Herman Valentine spent all his time among the employees of his department and Streby testified that he spent at least 7 of the 8 hours of his

[1] All dates herein are in the year 1955 unless otherwise specified.

day among the employees of Plant 3, the testimony of these two witnesses for the Respondent indicated that during this whole period until August 8, they personally heard employees talking about the Union during working hours on only one or two occasions. Nor did either of them notice any undue amount of visiting and talking among the employees during working hours until they began to receive reports from employees that they had been solicited to join the Union. Indeed, after receiving such reports, neither personally noted any unusual changes in the work habits of the employees of the plant.[2]

Perhaps this is not to be wondered at for the testimony of the Respondent's witnesses fully confirmed the evidence given by the General Counsel's witnesses that there were no plant rules against talking, chatting or visiting during working hours and that "everybody" indulged in these pastimes at will. In fact one of the Respondent's witnesses, Angeline Borger, who was prone to almost unlimited exaggeration, testified that "everybody, mostly all of the employees" took as long as "45-minute rest periods." In addition various and sundry employees, including the wife of Foreman Valentine, solicited the plant employees to purchase practically any type of merchandise one can imagine in the plant during working hours. The list of goods for sale in the plant by employees included plastics, work pants, clothes, shoes, cosmetics, shawls, household goods, linens, salt and pepper shakers, and chances on punchboards. Vice President Mike Valentine and his brother Foreman Herman Valentine sold chances for a couple of Catholic funds and athletic events in the plant. In addition there were biweekly check pools held in the plant where the money was collected and distributed during working hours to the lucky holder

---

[2] Streby testified on direct examination that the only employee he ever spoke to about being away from his work was Jack Griffiths on one occasion 3 or 4 weeks before his discharge. Later, however, when asked the same question by the Trial Examiner, Streby suddenly recalled that he had warned Griffiths no less than four times about wandering around the plant too much, the last time being on the Monday before the Thursday of Griffiths' discharge. Herman Valentine, on the other hand, after testifying that he had warned Griffiths in all seven or eight times about being away from his work, suddenly testified that, as Jack Griffiths was away from his work every 5 or 10 minutes during the last 2 weeks of his employment, he had had to warn Griffiths about twice a day. However, Valentine testified further that Griffiths had not become "radical" about leaving his work until these last 2 weeks of employment. In his testimony Valentine attempted to give the impression that Jack Griffiths had no business in the shipping department or elsewhere in the plant but the facts showed that it was Griffiths' duty to pick up carts from the shipping department and materials from other parts of the plant. In other regards also the testimony of both Streby and Valentine was at least equally self-contradictory, exaggerated and unreliable. Capaldi, Heddleson and the two Griffiths all denied that either Streby or Valentine had ever warned them about spending too much time from their work or about talking about the Union on company time. In view of the unsatisfactory nature of the testimony of both Streby and Valentine, as well as the straightforward nature of the testimony of the four above-mentioned employees, the undersigned credits their denials of having received any such warnings.

of the paycheck containing the best poker hand among the numbers printed on the check. Foreman Herman Valentine also participated in these.[3] Obviously the Respondent's plant was operated in a very friendly, social atmosphere without the strict adherence to rules of behavior so common in larger plants. In fact there were no posted or published rules of any kind in the plant until August 1, 1955.

As noted the Respondent was cognizant of union organizational efforts soon after its commencement.

The Respondent announced and put into effect as of July 5 a new, and presumably higher, scale of wages.

On July 5 [4] President Jackson had the employees of Plant 3 assembled about 15 minutes before the lunch hour break. After all the employees had assembled, the start of the meeting being held up for a period because some of the employees were slow arriving, Jackson made the following prepared statement:

Old King Cole has always felt that what was best for all employees was best for Old King Cole. Up to the present time it has never been necessary for Old King Cole employees to deal with management through a 3rd party in an effort to make the employees wants known. However, if the majority of the employees now feel that a third party is necessary to represent them, then Old King Cole management is willing and ready to work with the third party of the employees choice. There are several things you should know and understand before you decide.

1. Once you decide to have a third party represent you, you cannot change your mind if you don't like it. Once you're in, you're in.

2. Once you have a third party representing you, the third party and only the third party discusses and settles all questions regarding employment.

3. Wages, Old King Cole has all ways felt that we would have the best

---

[3] Herman Valentine admitted participating in these check pools only once and would only say that his wife's and his own selling activities among the employees were limited to "our own time." There is credible evidence to the contrary. Due to the admitted participation of both Mike Valentine, Herman Valentine and his wife in these activities in the plant and on company time, the undersigned was not favorably impressed by the Respondent's expressed "surprise" at learning at the hearing of these things "for the first time" being "carried on behind management's back" in the plant. Nor was the undersigned impressed by the Respondent's claim that these activities were restricted to a period from November 1954 to February 1955, for the uncontradicted evidence shows that the practice was continuing as late as Christmas time 1955.

[4] Although President Jackson, Vice President Worthington, Streby and Foreman Valentine all testified that they believed this speech was made on June 20 or June 30 instead of July 5 as the witnesses for the General Counsel had testified, it was clearly established that the speech was made in fact on July 5 when Respondent's witness Menendez testified that he had gone on his vacation on July 4, had not heard the speech but had heard about it upon his return to the plant on July 11. However, the actual date of the speech is relatively unimportant.

and happiest employees by paying the highest possible wages. This we have done in the past and will continue to do in the future.

4. Seniority at the present time, seniority is based on length of service to the company.

I would like to meet with a smaller representative group to discuss further, any complaints you may have. Please select such a group and I will meet with them on Wednesday, July 6th. In order that I may know the opinion of the majority of you, would you advise your foreman of how you feel, so that he may report to me.

Apparently while waiting for the few straggling employees to arrive, Jackson told those present that he had heard something which made him "very unhappy," i.e., that the employees were trying to organize a union, that he did not believe that the employees needed a third party to negotiate for them, but, if they thought they did, he knew a man in Akron who could get them a union.[5]

Later that same day Jackson repeated this speech almost identically to the employees of Plant 1 except that he changed the last paragraph to read:

In order that I may know the opinions of the majority, would you please take a slip of paper and mark it yes if in favor of a third party and no if not in favor.

Also later that day Foreman Valentine with paper and pencil took a poll of each employee in Plant 3 requiring a "yes or no" answer as to whether the individual wanted a union. Of the four employees involved here, all answered the question "yes" except Jack Griffiths who informed Valentine that after Jackson's speech he did not know how he stood on the question. When employee Mary Santee refused to vote, Valentine left but returned later to tell her that Jackson wanted the department to elect two women and a man to the committee which was to find out what it was that the employees wanted and meet with him later.

That same evening just before quitting time the employees of Plant 3 gathered at the clock preparatory to punching out and elected two women and a man to the committee. Mary Santee, Nan Kessler and Howard Adams who were elected to this committee were all wearing union buttons. Valentine was sitting at his desk 50 feet away during this so-called election.

Pursuant to instructions these three committee members conferred with their fellow employees during the lunch hour on July 6 and learned what grievances and what demands the employees had in preparation for the scheduled meeting with Jackson that day.

About 2:30 that afternoon Foreman Valentine informed Mary Santee that it was time for her to go in with the committee to see Jackson in his office. Jackson who was accompanied by Streby and Gregory at the meeting, told the committees from Plants 1 and 3 that he wanted to know what the employees wanted. He then went around the room from one committeeman to the next, having each explain what grievances or requests their fellow em-

[5] Jackson denied having made the above-found statements "in his speech" as did other of Respondent's officials and employees. With one exception he did not deny having made such statements while awaiting the arrival of the last employees.

ployees had made. After the members of the committee had each explained what their constituents wanted, Santee asked Jackson to announce which requests Respondent would grant as the employees wanted to know the results but Jackson announced that he was going on a vacation for 2 weeks but would announce his decision upon the seven requested items upon his return. During the meeting Santee stated that the employees were not satisfied with the nonsecret poll Valentine had taken and would like to vote again at a secret election. Jackson said that the employees could have a secret vote if they wanted but "I have got the vote right here and I am satisfied." As he concluded the meeting Jackson stated: "If you went on with this union, . . . you won't meet with me again." [6]

In a speech given to the assembled employees and confirmed in an almost identical letter dated July 25 and sent to each employee, Jackson answered the requests made by the committee as follows on July 20:

On Wednesday, July 6, Mr. Streby, Mr. Gregory and myself met with a group of employees to discuss various conditions of employment which have led to some dissatisfaction in the past. These conditions as related to us by the group were as follows:

1. A dust condition in the grinding room of the finishing department.
2. Pay for 6 holidays.
3. Maintenance man for fuel cell plant.
4. A hard and fast seniority rule based on date of original employment.
5. Insurance.
6. Automatic pay increase until top pay is reached.
7. ½ days pay for employees sent home without working at least ½ day.

On July 6, we advised the group that we would report back to you in two weeks giving our answers to each of the above requests. Those answers are as follows:

1. Dust conditions: We have ordered additional equipment, the installation and proper usage of which should solve the problem.
2. Paid Holidays: We will pay 8 hours for Labor Day, Christmas Day, New Years Day, Thanksgiving Day, Decoration Day, and July 4th, provided the employee works the last scheduled 8 hours before the holiday and the first scheduled 8 hours after the holiday on his shift.
3. Maintenance: We are endeavoring to hire additional maintenance men as soon as we are able to find satisfactory men, we will assign as many as required to the fuel cell plant.
4. Seniority: We will establish at once a hard and fast seniority list based on date of original employment.
5. Insurance: For a number of months we have been investigating various kinds and costs of insurance and we will establish an insurance plan for all employees.
6. Pay Increases: We will set up a schedule of automatic pay increases until top pay is reached.

[6] The Committee never again met with Jackson.

7. We will pay ½ day's pay to employees sent home without working at least ½ day.

Those are the things the group asked for, we have agreed without question to comply with all of your requests, and in addition, we are setting up for the benefit of all employees a profit sharing plan, the nature of which is still in the planning stage. We have been considering this for some time and I don't know yet just how it is going to work. I don't know any of the financial details, except this, it will be based on the profits of Old King Cole, Inc., and those figures will be taken from the financial statements which we are required by law to make each year to the Department of Internal Revenue, and which are audited by Certified Public Accountants.

At the July 6th meeting one of the group raised the question: "How do we know you will do these things if we don't have a contract?" That is a good question which I can answer in this way, we have been in business for over nine years and have provided continuous steady employment during that time. From time to time we have posted various plant rules on the bulletin boards and we have followed those rules without any contract. From time to time we have agreed to give wage increases and vacation benefits, all of these things have been done without a contract. Incidentally, wages have almost doubled in the last nine years. By the same token we will, just as soon as possible write up a detailed statement of the things which we have agreed to do in this letter and that statement will be posted on all the bulletin boards. It will be a matter of company policy and it will be followed in all respects. I should point out to you, however, that after the profit sharing is worked out it must be approved by the Department of Internal Revenue before it can go into effect. We will attempt to obtain that approval as quickly as possible after the plan is worked out.

Promptly after this speech had been given employee Angeline Borger removed the union button which she had been wearing because, as she put it, she "agreed" with everything Jackson offered. As she removed her button, Beatrice Griffiths told her not to be "a fool" and do just what Jackson wanted but to keep on wearing her union button as protection against being discharged.

Borger reported this episode to Foreman Valentine on company time along with the fact that she claimed that Beatrice Griffiths had threatened "to beat hell out of her" if she did not wear her button and that Griffiths had threatened "bloodshed" if the Union did not succeed in the plant. Herman Valentine was so unimpressed with the report that he instructed Borger: "Well, just pass it off and go back to your work." [7] Borger also reported to the Respondent that

_____

[7] According to Herman Valentine's testimony, he immediately went to Griffiths and "warned" her that there should be no "bloodshed" but Griffiths denied to him ever having made the remarks reported, even as she did on the witness stand. The undersigned must credit the denial. This is the only evidence of any warning being given to any employee allegedly having made a threat to be found in this report.

Griffiths had threatened that she, Borger, could no longer ride in their car pool if she did not wear her union button. The fact is that Borger continued in the Griffiths' car pool until the Griffiths were discharged despite the fact that there is no showing that she ever wore her union button after Jackson's speech of July 20.[8]

Also after Jackson's July 20 speech shipping clerk Menendez testified that he reported during working hours in turn to Foreman Valentine, Plant Superintendent Streby and later to President Jackson that Jack Griffiths had again solicited employees Haidet, Seaman and himself in the restroom to join the Union and that, after the three shipping department employees had affirmed the fact that they were not interested in the Union as they considered Jackson's offer a very fair one, Griffiths had stated: "The hell with Mr. Jackson," that he was going to do what the Union said, that they were going to get a union in the plant or else somebody was going to get "punched in the nose."

At the hearing Menendez testified that he reported this restroom incident to Valentine and Streby the day it occurred and to Jackson "a few days" later. On July 28, however, both Menendez and employee Haidet gave signed statements to Respondent's labor relations consultant Rector in which both gave the date of the incident as July 27. Menendez was incorrect one time or the other.

Furthermore the written statement of July 28 related exclusively to Griffiths' having "solicited" Menendez and one or two other employees three times in the month of July during working hours either to join the Union or to attend union meetings. While the statement refers to the restroom incident as being "an argument about us joining the union," the statement makes no reference at all to "punching noses," "bloodshed" or "beating Menendez up" such as came out in the oral testimony of Menendez and Jackson as well as other supervisors. If Menendez' oral testimony is correct, this is a strange omission to have been made by Respondent's labor consultant who was preparing the statements for the express purpose of justifying a discharge. Especially is this so as the statement which refers to only three instances of solicitation between July 6 and July 27 contains such sentences as: "He has *continuously pressured* me, Richard Haidet and Kenneth Seaman to join the union during working hours" and "he has *continuously bothered* me at my work by arguing and coercing me in this manner" [italics added] so that it is clear that the writer of the statement was not given to understatement. On the stand Menendez testified that Jack Griffiths had approached him about the union in all "three or four times, possibly five." However, Menendez explained that he "was getting tired of [Griffiths'] getting around trying to coax me into joining the

[8] As a witness Borger indicated an almost pathological determination to mouth all sorts of accusations against the dischargees in broad generalizations. She brooked no interference from the rules of evidence, the Trial Examiner, counsel, or indeed, spectators in the courtroom in carrying out her determination. She displayed an equal determination in refusing all efforts to make her become specific as to statements, times, persons and places. Her bland generalizations and obvious exaggerations were not conducive to belief in the honesty and sincerity of her testimony.

Union when I wasn't interested" and that he reiterated the same restroom incident to President Jackson because he [Menendez] "thought [Jackson] was the man who run the company. I thought I should tell him so if Mr. Streby did not do something about it, maybe Mr. Jackson would."

About July 26, after receiving reports that the two Griffiths, Capaldi and Heddleson were continuing their activities on behalf of the Union on company time, Jackson in consultation with Streby decided to discharge all four of the aforementioned employees.

On July 28, Jackson called in his labor relations expert, Harvey B. Rector of Akron, told him of the reported incidents and that he, Jackson, thought "we should discharge the people because there was nothing we could do to change their minds and to get them back to work" and asked Rector for his advice on the situation. Rector's advice "was that we should get these people who had made complaints to me to put them in writing, which we did." Upon receipt of this advice Jackson had five employees, including Menendez, report to his office on July 28 where Rector spent the rest of the day taking statements from them regarding any union activities engaged in by the four in question here including both that engaged in on working time and on the employees' own time. The employee who gave Rector the longest statement was shipping clerk Menendez whose statement accused Griffiths of "continuously pressuring" the three shipping department employees to join the Union and "continuously bothering me at my work, by arguing and coercing me in this manner." [9]

At the end of the working day of July 28, Foreman Valentine sent Jack Griffiths to Streby's office where Streby told Griffiths that he was discharging Griffiths and handed him his paychecks and a dismissal slip stating the cause of discharge as: "Union activities on company time." When Streby could only tell Griffiths that he was being discharged for "union activities," Griffiths asked if he could go see Jackson. [10]

Following his discharge Griffiths and his car pool, including Angeline Borger, did in fact go over to Plant 1 where, on his way to Jackson's office, Griffiths met up with Menendez with the result that a fight between them ensued in the course of which Menendez was hit by Griffiths' fist in the nose

[9] It must also be noted here that, while Menendez testified that Griffiths threatened to punch somebody in the nose and while Jackson testified that he checked alleged threats by the Griffiths to "beat up" Menendez and found them to be correct from Menendez, the statement of Menendez taken by Rector on July 28 contained not one single word about any threats. Nor does this statement contain one single fact which would justify the use of the word "coerce" despite Menendez' oral testimony to the contrary. If Menendez' oral testimony was correct, it is hard to believe that a labor relations expert preparing a statement to justify the discharge of an employee would deliberately omit such facts.

[10] Streby's account of this meeting differs in that, according to Streby, after having been told that he was discharged for union activities on company time, Griffiths stated that he "knew the rat that had turned him in," "a big, one-eyed Spaniard" and that "he'd get him." The denial by Griffiths of this testimony is credited for reasons appearing throughout this report.

and eye drawing blood and Griffiths received a bump on the head. When they were separated, Griffiths continued on to Jackson's office where Jackson refused to speak with him and ordered him out of the plant.[11]

Griffiths and his car pool then repaired to the police station where Griffiths started to file a charge of assault against Menendez but was advised against it by the policeman on the desk on the ground that he would have little chance of winning if Menendez had been cut and bled. Griffiths left the station without filing the charge.

At the end of work on July 29, Foreman Valentine called Julia Capaldi to his office where he handed her a discharge notice stating the reason for the discharge to be: "Union activities on company time." Capaldi inquired if he had proof which Valentine said he had. As Capaldi stated that Valentine would have to prove it, Streby walked into the room and Capaldi asked if she was being discharged on account of her work, to which Streby answered: "No, your work is okay." [12]

Although, according to the testimony of the Respondent, it had been determined to discharge all four individuals here involved on or about July 26, Jackson explained that the discharge of Capaldi was postponed a day because he did not have "satisfactory proof of her activities" until July 29. The "proof" which Jackson secured the following day was a statement from one Mary

[11] Jackson testified at the hearing that he called Menendez to his office at about 2:45 p.m. on July 28 and kept him there until 3:40 (10 minutes after quitting time) specifically so as to keep Menendez from harm because he, Jackson, had heard reports whose accuracy he had checked with Menendez to the effect that Jack and Beatrice Griffiths had threatened to "beat up" Menendez. As previously noted none of these alleged threats are even mentioned in the statement taken by Rector from Menendez dated July 28. If Jackson's testimony is true, this seems a strange oversight. Moreover it was on July 28, the same day as the fight, that Menendez was giving his statement to Rector in Jackson's office. It, therefore, seems more logical that Menendez happened to be in Jackson's office on the afternoon of July 28 in order to give his statement rather than for the reason advanced by Jackson.

Furthermore as Menendez was the shipping clerk stationed in Plant 3 as Griffiths well knew, it would appear more logical that Griffiths would have looked for him at his place of work in Plant 3, if he had been in fact looking for Menendez, rather than at Plant 1 for there is not one iota of testimony that Griffiths had any idea that Menendez was not at his regular place of work.

[12] Valentine's testimony differs in that he testified that he told Capaldi that he had to let her go because she was "leaving your job too much and you are throwing the burden on your partner" whereupon Capaldi swore at him saying that she ought to slap his face. On the contrary, however, Streby who spent ⅞ of the day among the employees of Plant 3 testified positively that he had never seen Capaldi, Beatrice Griffiths or Heddleson ever leave their work to go to another employee's mold during working hours. It is thus a bit difficult to accept Valentine's testimony over that of Streby—especially as it is undenied that Streby told Capaldi in Valentine's presence that her work had been "okay." Furthermore, confidence in the reliability of Herman Valentine was not enhanced by his testimony of having received reports on the union activities of the dischargees here from one Pearl Treadway who, by stipulation, was proved not even to have been employed during the period in question.

Masterana, who did not appear as a witness at the hearing, to the effect that on July 6, Capaldi came to her place of work, handed her an application card and asked her to join the Union during working hours.[13]

On August 8, Streby handed Beatrice Griffiths and Nettie Heddleson their dismissal notices giving the usual reason for the discharge: "Union activities on company time." To Heddleson, Streby stated: "I don't like to fire anyone but I only work here. . . . I don't know [why Heddleson was being discharged] unless you have been talking union on company time," that her work had been good but that she would "have to let the Company and the Union fight it out." To Griffiths, Streby stated: "I don't like to do this . . . but I have to. . . . It's my orders." When Griffiths inquired if she had not been giving a good day's work, Streby answered: "It isn't that. That is not why you are being fired. I would just as leave you work for me as anyone out there." [14]

On August 1 between the two sets of discharges the Respondent posted its first and only set of plant rules which were divided into three classifications depending on the seriousness of the offense, (1) "minor," (2) "major," and (3) "intolerable." Although counsel for the Respondent disclaimed the fact that these rules played any part in the discharges of Beatrice Griffiths or Heddleson, President Jackson stated that the only rules which either of them could have broken were the following:

Major

3. Unnecessary conversations away from respective work stations are prohibitive [sic].

6. Interfering with fellow employees on the premises at any time, such as threats, intimidation, coercion, etc. Violation of a major rule shall result in a 3-day layoff.

Despite the announced penalty, Beatrice Griffiths and Nettie Heddleson were discharged.

Either between the discharges of July 28 and 29 and those of August 8 or after all four discharges, Streby made the following announcement to the assembled employees of Plant 3:

I just called you people together to have a little talk with you. I am not a speaker so bear with me a little while will you, because what I have

---

[13] This incident is mentioned in one of the other statements obtained by the Respondent on July 28.

[14] Streby did not deny making these statements. In fact he corroborated that opinion when he testified positively that the only one of the employees he ever spoke to about being away from work was Jack Griffiths and that he only spoke to Jack once about 3 or 4 weeks before the discharge. However, Streby was highly inconsistent in his testimony. For instance, he testified at page 304 of the record regarding the women dischargees: "Well it is about the same, I mean, they were wandering back and forth from mold to mold and talking to people" whereas 4 pages later in the record, at page 308, he testified positively by the single word "no" that he had never seen any of the three women involved here go over to another employee's mold. It is difficult to put much, if any, reliance in a witness as inconsistent as that.

to say will not take long. Management and myself think we have a good group of people working in our plant, and we want to keep all of you working for us. So I am asking you to stop union activity on company time. If you continue union activity on company time I will be forced to discharge you, as you know we have already discharged some. I don't want to do that so please don't force the issue. What you do outside of the building is up to you, so let's not have any more union activity on company time.

None of the four discharged employees have been reinstated.

B. CONCLUSIONS

1. Interference, restraint and coercion

In its brief the Respondent argued that it was not guilty of interfering with, restraining, or coercing its employees in violation of Section 8 (*a*) (1) of the Act because: (1) Jackson's speech of July 5 [15] was a noncoercive speech and thus protected under the so-called free speech section of the Act, Section 8 (*c*); and (2) there was nothing "coercive" about the poll taken for the Respondent by Foreman Valentine on July 5 at which the foreman required each of the employees to vote "yes or no" on the question whether he was in favor of union representation or not.

As to Jackson's speech of July 5 it may be conceded that the speech was "noncoercive" in the sense that there were no threats of reprisal. However, Section 8 (*c*) of the Act protects an employer in the expression of his "views, arguments, or opinion" etc. regarding unions to his employees only so long as those expressions contain "no threats of reprisal or force or promise of benefits." The last three quoted words are important also. Speaking in the background of the new wage rates whch went into effect that very same day, Jackson in effect told the employees that it was not necessary for them to be represented by a third person and suggested his meeting with a smaller representative group to discuss their complaints the next afternoon. Jackson admitted that the purpose of his making this speech was to find out what was wrong in the plant which created this desire for union representation and what the employees wanted from the Respondent. Although not spelled out in the speech placed in evidence, the committeemen and the employees were informed that it was the duty of the committeemen to find out what grievances their constituents had and what they wanted, a duty performed by their meeting with the employees at noon on July 6. Both the committeemen and the

[15] Respondent's brief refers only to a single speech which from the description was that of July 5 as it was in this speech that Jackson offered to deal with "third parties" if the employees desired and also requested a smaller representative committee to meet with him the following day, July 6. The brief makes no mention of Jackson's second speech on July 20 when he announced the granting by the Respondent of all the employees' demands and, in addition, that the Respondent was instituting a profit-sharing plan. He ended this last speech by stating that these concessions would not be embodied "in a contract" but would be posted in the plant "as a matter of company policy."

employees recognized the Respondent's implied promise of benefits to be granted to them through the suggested committee. It is significant that the committee requested an immediate answer from Jackson at the end of the meeting on the grounds that the employees would want to know the results. Jackson's promise was that implicit in the speech of July 5.

Jackson himself recognized the promise of benefit implicit in his July 5 speech by announcing on July 20 not only the granting of all the demands made on behalf of the employees by the Committee but also the granting of a new profit-sharing plan for the employees which had not even been suggested by the employees. Furthermore on July 20 Jackson made the *quid pro quo* for the benefits he had just announced crystal clear when he stated that these promised benefits would not be embodied in "a contract" but would only be "a matter of company policy" posted on the company bulletin board unilaterally by the Respondent. Hence, in order to obtain these promised benefits, the employees would have to renounce their right to union representation and their right to have their working conditions embodied in a union contract. What Jackson was stating in effect was: "These benefits the Company will unilaterally give you on condition that you employees renounce your right to union representation and to have your working conditions embodied in a union contract." Respondent's witness Borger recognized this *quid pro quo* by promptly removing her union button because, as she put it, "I thought everything he offered was all right"—and so she removed her union button in recognition of Jackson's condition. However, the two Griffiths, Capaldi and Heddleson refused to accept this illegal condition, expressed that refusal by word and deed, all of which were duly reported to the Respondent, and were discharged for their pains. It is significant that the statements taken by Rector refer exclusively to union activities occurring subsequent to the speech of July 5.

The speeches of July 5 and July 20 were integral parts of a single act: an offer of economic benefits in return for the renunciation of the right to union representation. As such these speeches do not qualify as an expression of any "views, argument, or opinion" etc. Therefore Section 8 (c) of the Act does not protect the Respondent in this regard either. A verbal act is not protected under Section 8 (c). These promised benefits conditioned as they were upon illegal restrictions on the rights of employees guaranteed by the Act amount to interference, restraint and coercion of the employees in violation of Section 8 (a) (1) of the Act. The undersigned so finds.[16]

Likewise in its brief the Respondent professed to see nothing "coercive" in having its Foreman Valentine require each and every employee in Plant 3 to vote "yes or no" on whether the individual was in favor of union representation, recording that vote (but not the name of the voter, according to the Respondent's evidence) on a pad of paper. Respondent appears to lay considerable stress upon the fact that no names were recorded by Valentine.

[16] The Respondent's July 5 profession of willingness to deal with "third parties" if the employees so desired, becomes pure pro forma lip service to the Act in the light of all the facts.

The employees themselves protested because the poll was not taken by secret ballot. Even Foreman Valentine testified that there had been no need for Jackson to tell him why he was ordered not to record names for he himself could figure out how such a vote "would be used against a person" if the names were recorded on paper.[17] If such a poll could "be used against a person" when recorded on paper, it could also "be used against a person" when recorded in the memory of a supervisor. Requiring an employee to disclose to a company supervisor a desire contrary to that just previously expressed by the employer must necessarily be coercive and an interference with the employee's freedom of choice. If the supervisor conducting the poll can recognize the danger, how much more must the employee who is required to cast the ballot. . . .

In fact in the instant case the poll was an integral part, together with Jackson's speeches of July 5 and July 20, of Respondent's offer to confer benefits on the employees in return for their repudiation of union representation. The purpose of the poll was the same as the purpose of the benefits conferred, i.e., to secure the renunciation of union representation by the employees. Thus the purpose of the poll, like the speeches and the benefits conferred, was to interfere with the right of the employees to bargain collectively through "representatives of their own choosing" and, thus, is a violation of Section 8 (a) (1) of the Act. The undersigned so finds.

2. The discharges

The Respondent's admission, contained both on the dismissal notices and in Streby's speech, require the conclusion that each of the four dischargees was discharged by the Respondent because of its belief that each of them had been engaging in "union activities," a cause for discharge prohibited by Section 8 (a) (3) of the Act. The *Radio Officers* case [18] makes it clear that discharge for such a cause necessarily "discourages" membership in a labor organization and violates Section 8 (a) (3) of the Act. But here, due to the dismissal notices and Streby's speech, Respondent's intention to discourage union activities was made patent to all employees.

As noted, the dismissal notices state the cause of discharge in each case to be "union activities on company time." At the opening of the hearing Respondent maintained only that the stress should be laid on the phrase "on company time." During oral argument Respondent changed its position when it argued:

Now actually the union activity was more or less incidental. The important thing was that the employees were engaging in something which interfered with production and that was the reason they were discharged.

This change of position hardly jibes with Streby's speech—nor with the admitted purpose behind Jackson's two speeches which was to find out what

[17] Apparently the later poll in Plant 1 was taken by recording the names of the employees under headings "For" or "Against" which may well account for the fact that Jackson testified that few, if any, of the employees in Plant 1 voted in favor of union representation.
[18] 347 U.S. 17.

grievances the employees had and what they wanted without even so much as mentioning any alleged decline in production in the plant. Jackson recognized that "all was not right" in the plant and that there were existing grievances at the time he made his first speech. It was the union organizational drive which bothered Jackson—not the alleged decline in production which had not bothered him while it continued from late April through May nor until it became clear that the employees were organizing.

While it is quite true that an employer has a perfect right to establish reasonable rules regarding union activity on company time and property so long as such rules are not in themselves discriminatory against such activity, the Respondent's change in emphasis at the end of the hearing was necessitated by the fact, well established in the evidence, that any rule which this Respondent attempted to enforce against these four employees for engaging in "union activities on company time" must of necessity have been discriminatory in fact because the Respondent not only countenanced, but engaged in through its own official family, solicitations on company time and property for practically any other cause one can conceive: charities, personal merchandising, gambling, and even idle social conversation, athletics and personal pleasure. In fact the Respondent itself did not hesitate to use company time and property for antiunion solicitation. In order not to have created a discriminatory no-union-solicitation rule, the Respondent would have had to change its whole lax and friendly policy of operation in the plant. This the Respondent failed to do, except insofar as union solicitation by these four employees was concerned. None of the other activities being carried on on company time and property were stopped.[19]

As, therefore, the Respondent's making a rule against union solicitation on company time without also including in that rule all the other solicitations which were also occurring on company time and property would necessarily have been discriminatory and illegal, Respondent's position by force of those circumstances changed to the contention put forth in oral argument that the union activities on company time "interfered with production." However, Jackson as a witness testified that for some undisclosed reason these other activities occurring on company time and property somehow did not interfere with production. Jackson was unable to explain this phenomenon.

But be that as it may, in order to prove that this union solicitation interfered with the production of Plant 3, the Respondent produced a graph of what it called the daily "production efficiency" of Plant 3. Jackson arrived at these daily "production efficiency" figures by dividing the "market value" of the fuel cells produced at the plant during the day by the direct labor payroll of the plant for that same day. Jackson acknowledged the crudeness of this computation. An economist might well object to the very bases thereof.

According to Jackson's testimony, his long experience with this method had

---

[19] Foreman Valentine testified that he stopped such other activities if and when he saw them. However, the evidence is undenied that such activities continued, despite Valentine's testimony, at least until Christmas 1955.

proved that if this problem in division resulted in a figure of 227, then production for the plant was "normal," any higher figure indicated above normal production and anything lower showed below normal production for the plant. Jackson's claim of 227 as "normal production" was not substantiated by the chart in evidence which, however, commenced only as of March 1955, when the Respondent started to retain these figures as permanent records, one result of a Board field examiner's investigation of this case.

A comparison of the facts and figures for 2 individual days selected at random, one of very low "production efficiency" and the other of very high "production efficiency" when some 50-odd tanks were manufactured on the first day and only 30-odd on the second day disclosed the interesting fact that when cells for B-42 aircraft were being manufactured, "production efficiency" tended always to be higher than on those days when no B-42 mandrels were being manufactured. Thus it became apparent that "plant production efficiency" depended greatly on what orders were being filled for apparently B-42 tanks were high in "market value." One need not be a trained economist to perceive other fallacies and shortcomings in this admittedly crude yardstick on which Jackson relied in his operation of Plant 3.

However, this graph with all its obvious shortcomings would still give some indication of the production of the plant. But the graph in evidence, even if taken at full face value, fails to prove the Respondent's contention. This graph showed "production efficiency" of Plant 3 to be:

(1) April 28–June 28 (with 2 single days excepted): below normal;

(2) June 28–July 15: approximately normal, a few days above and a few days below;

(3) July 15–August 2: steadily above normal efficiency;

(4) August 3–August 20: steadily below normal;

(5) August 21–January 19, 1956: relatively normal both above and below;

(6) January 20, 1956, and thereafter: steadily above normal.

According to the Respondent's testimony, about the last of June upon his return from his vacation, Jackson, noting the decline in production efficiency which began late in April, called in Streby and Foreman Valentine and requested them to find out the cause of this so-called decline. After checking the usual causes of such a thing, i.e., bad materials, absenteeism, etc., neither Streby nor Valentine was able to locate a cause for the phenomenon. Thereafter, according to this same testimony, Streby and Valentine began receiving reports from employees of being solicited to join the Union on company time and property.[20] Therefore, according to the Respondent's argument, there being no other discernible cause, the decline must have been, and was, therefore, caused by this union activity. Or, as stated in the Respondent's brief, "the best answer to this is that something was interfering with production efficiency

[20] It appears strange that these two supervisors were personally unable to discern such activities although purportedly looking for the cause of the production efficiency decline until after these reports were received if there had been any substantial amount of such solicitation.

and there is not even a hint of any other source of interference [other than the union solicitations reported].[21]

The trouble with this argument, of course, is that the slump in production began on April 28 but union solicitation did not commence until after June 8. Chronology alone proves that the slump was not caused by union solicitations. Respondent's attorney candidly admitted at oral argument: "Now no one can say what caused it [the fall in production efficiency] in early May." Counsel is only partially correct for Jackson knew that the employees were dissatisfied with their existing working conditions but did nothing about it until he announced the new wage rates to be effective as of July 5. The responsibility for this dissatisfaction rests upon Respondent.

Despite Respondent's admission that no one could say what caused the April slump, it then went on to argue:

> . . . But we do know that the production efficiency started going down in May. There could have been a dip for a while which wouldn't have been of any great consequence, but that didn't come back up. It stayed in the red. And there was absolutely no explanation of it unless it was this [union] solicitation on company time.

In addition to the speculative quality of this argument, it is also subject to two fallacies: (1) the unknown causes of the original slump still remained unresolved so that the union solicitation which began on June 8 could have been only another possible cause for the continuation of the decline; and— much more important—(2) on June 28 Respondent's graph shows that production efficiency in Plant 3 became and remained normal or above until August 2. Thus for a solid month prior to the discharges of Jack Griffiths and Capaldi allegedly for interfering with production by their union activities production was in fact normal or above for the first time since April 28, a period of 2 months. Obviously, therefore, the union activities engaged in were not interfering with production. The graph proves that Streby was correct in telling the dischargees here that they were not being discharged because of their work. Accordingly the undersigned must find that the union activities engaged in by the four involved here did not interfere with the production efficiency of

---

[21] Although the Respondent professed to know of "no other cause" for this decline in production efficiency, the record here indicated an almost innumerable number of other possible causes: (1) Jackson knew of the existence of a number of unresolved grievances in the plant and, indeed, had announced a pay increase effective as of July 5; (2) on July 6, Jackson discovered at least seven other instances of unsatisfactory working conditions existent in the plant; (3) according to Foreman Valentine, the plant was never busy during the first hour of the day; (4) according to the Respondent's witness, Angeline Borger, "everybody" was given to taking "45-minute rest periods"; (5) according to the testimony of other of the Respondent's witnesses, "all the employees" stood around their machines engaged in idle chatting; (6) the evidence disclosed unmistakably, albeit supposedly to the Respondent's "surprise," the existence of a number of individual enterprises being carried on during working hours having nothing to do with the Respondent's work; (7) supervisors and others were engaging even in athletic practice on company time.

Plant 3 and also that Respondent did not discharge them, or any of them, on account of any such alleged interference.

Furthermore Respondent's graph rather conclusively establishes the fact that Respondent's witnesses patently exaggerated the extent and the effect of the union activities of the dischargees. It is to be recalled that Foreman Valentine testified vividly to the effect that, during his last two weeks of employment, Jack Griffiths became "radical," left his work every "five or ten minutes," could not be found "half the time" and had to be "warned" once or twice a day or more. Yet the graph proves that during this same two week period described by Valentine as Griffiths' "radical" period, production efficiency at Plant 3 was steadily above normal and climbing higher. Ironically enough July 28, the day of Jack Griffiths' discharge, proved to be the day of highest production efficiency with one exception until January 1956. In view of the reliance placed on the graph of Jackson in running his plant, the undersigned must accept the evidence of the graph over the oral testimony of Valentine and others. . . .

The Respondent was not excited about activities "on company time" for all the above noted extracurricular activities in the plant on company time continued unabated with the supervisors even practicing for the company horseshoe team during working hours. The social chatting at work continued. The merchandising continued. The check pools continued.

But the evidence clearly demonstrates that Jackson was worried about the threatened advent of a "third party" as exemplified by his speech of July 5. Admittedly he wanted to find out what grievances his employees had and what they wanted and thus forestall organization of the plant by granting benefits which could be posted in the plant "as a matter of company policy" but not embodied in "a union contract." The benefits granted on July 20, as recognized by Angeline Borger in removing her union button, were conditioned upon the renunciation of representation by a labor organization by the employees. Hence the benefits were granted in return for the employees' abandoning representation by a union organization.

But through reports received from employees Menendez, Isue and Borger, Jackson discovered that even after his speech of July 20, Jack Griffiths had said "to hell with Jackson's offer," he was continuing his efforts for union organization; that Beatrice Griffiths had told Borger not to be a fool and take off her union button for that was just what Jackson wanted; and that both Capaldi and Heddleson had continued their efforts to organize the Union after July 6. Thus it became clear to Jackson that his promised benefits had not succeeded in causing these four employees to renounce their efforts to obtain union representation. Hence even though Respondent's production efficiency was either normal or above for the first time in months and even though Streby found no fault with the work of any of the four, Jackson chose to discharge these four employees for continuing their activities on behalf of the Union despite the benefits he had granted them conditioned upon the abandonment of such efforts. Streby's speech confirms this finding.

Accordingly, the undersigned is convinced and, therefore, finds that the

Respondent discriminatorily discharged Jack Griffiths on July 28, Julia Capaldi on July 29, and Beatrice Griffiths and Nettie Heddleson on August 8, because of their activities on behalf of the Union and in order to discourage membership therein in violation of Section 8 (a) (3) and (1) of the Act.

IV. THE EFFECT OF THE UNFAIR LABOR PRACTICES UPON COMMERCE

The activities of the Respondent set forth in Section III, above, occurring in connection with the operations of the Respondent described in Section I, have a close, intimate, and substantial relation to trade, traffic, and commerce among the several States, and tend to lead to labor disputes burdening and obstructing commerce and the free flow of commerce.

V. THE REMEDY

Having found that the Respondent has engaged in certain unfair labor practices it will be recommended that it cease and desist therefrom and that it take certain affirmative action designed to effectuate the policies of the Act.

It having been found that the Respondent discriminated in regard to the hire and tenure of employment of Jack Griffiths, Julia Capaldi, Beatrice Griffiths, and Nettie Heddleson, by discharging them, the undersigned will recommend that the Respondent offer to each of them immediate and full reinstatement to his former, or substantially equivalent positions, without prejudice to his seniority or other rights and privileges, and make each whole for any loss of pay he may have suffered by reason of said discrimination by payment to each of them of a sum of money equal to that which he would have earned as wages from the date of the discrimination against him to the date of the offer of reinstatement less his net earnings during such period, in accordance with the formula set forth in F. W. Woolworth Company, 90 NLRB 289.

In the opinion of the undersigned, the unfair labor practices committed by the Respondent in the instant case are such as to indicate an attitude of opposition to the purposes of the Act generally. In order, therefore, to make effective the interdependent guarantees of Section 7 of the Act, thereby minimizing industrial strife which burdens and obstructs commerce, and thus effectuate the policies of the Act, it will be recommended that the Respondent cease and desist from infringing in any manner upon the rights guaranteed in Section 7 of the Act.

Upon the basis of the foregoing findings of fact and upon the entire record, the undersigned makes the following:

CONCLUSIONS OF LAW

1. International Union, United Automobile, Aircraft & Agricultural Implement Workers of America, AFL-CIO, is a labor organization within the meaning of Section 2 (5) of the Act.

2. By discharging Jack Griffiths on July 28, 1955, Julia Capaldi on July 29, 1955, and Beatrice Griffiths and Nettie Heddleson on August 8, 1955, thus discriminating in regard to their hire and tenure of employment and thereby

discouraging membership in International Union, United Automobile, Aircraft & Agricultural Implement Workers of America, AFL-CIO, the Respondent has engaged in and is engaging in unfair labor practices within the meaning of Section 8 (a) (3) and (1) of the Act.

3. By offering promises of benefits to employees to induce them to renounce their right to union representation and by polling their employees as to their union affiliations and sympathies; and by interfering with, restraining, and coercing its employees in the exercise of the rights guaranteed in Section 7 of the Act, the Respondent has engaged in and is engaging in unfair labor practices within the meaning of Section 8 (a) (1) of the Act.

4. The aforesaid unfair labor practices are unfair labor practices affecting commerce within the meaning of Section 2 (6) and (7) of the Act.

RECOMMENDATIONS

Upon the basis of the foregoing findings of fact and conclusions of law, and upon the entire record in the case, the undersigned recommends that Old King Cole, Inc., Louisville, Ohio, its officers, agents, successors, and assigns, shall:

1. Cease and desist from:

a. Discouraging membership in International Union, United Automobile, Aircraft & Agricultural Implement Workers of America, AFL-CIO, or any other labor organization, by discriminating in regard to their hire and tenure of employment or any term or condition of employment or in any other manner;

b. Polling its employees concerning their union affiliations and sympathies; promising employees benefits in order to induce them to renounce their right to union representation;

c. In any other manner interfering with, restraining, or coercing its employees in the exercise of their right to self-organization, to form labor organizations, or to join or assist International Union, United Automobile, Aircraft & Agricultural Implement Workers of America, AFL-CIO, or any other labor organization, to bargain collectively through representatives of their own choosing, and to engage in concerted activities for the purpose of collective bargaining or other mutual aid or protection, or to refrain from any such activities except to the extent that such right may be affected by an agreement requiring membership in a labor organization as a condition of employment as authorized in Section 8 (a) (3) of the Act.

2. Take the following affirmative which the undersigned finds necessary to effectuate the policies of the Act:

a. Offer to Jack Griffiths, Julia Capaldi, Beatrice Griffiths, and Nettie Heddleson immediate and full reinstatement to his former or substantially equivalent position, without prejudice to his seniority or other rights and privileges and make each whole, in the manner set forth in the section above entitled "The remedy," for any loss of pay each may have suffered by reason of the Respondent's discrimination against him;

b. Preserve and make available to the Board or its agents upon request, for examination and copying, all payroll records, social-security payment records, timecards, personnel records and reports, and all other records necessary to analyze the amount of back pay due and the rights of employment under the terms of this recommendation;

c. Post in conspicuous places at the Respondent's Plants 1 and 3 in Louisville, Ohio, including all places where notices to employees are customarily posted, copies of the notice attached hereto as Appendix A. Copies of said notice to be furnished by the Regional Director for the Eighth Region, shall, upon being duly signed by the Respondent's representatives, be posted by it, as aforesaid, immediately upon receipt thereof, and maintained for at least sixty (60) consecutive days thereafter. Reasonable steps shall be taken by the Respondent to insure that said notices are not altered, defaced, or covered by any other material;

d. File with the Regional Director for the Eighth Region, within twenty (20) days from the receipt of this Intermediate Report, a report in writing setting forth in detail the steps which the Respondent has taken to comply herewith.

The Board adopted the trial examiner's report and recommendations.

THE FREE SPEECH ISSUE

One issue which has excited controversy has been the extent to which employers are free to fight attempted organization by counterpropaganda. In the early days of the Board, under the Wagner Act, an employer's expressed opposition to unionization or to a particular union attempting organization might, in the context of a program of antiunion conduct, be viewed as interference with the employees' right to organize. In a context of antiunionism, an employer's statements opposing unionization were construed as carrying a threat.

This interpretation was bitterly opposed by employers, who contended that it deprived them of their constitutional right to freedom of speech. In the Taft-Hartley Act, Section 8 (c) was designed to answer their objections. It declared that any employer statement respecting unionization was privileged providing it did not carry any threat of penalty to employees if they did not conform to the views expressed, or promise of reward on condition that they did conform.

The preceding case contains actions which relate to this issue. For example, the July 5 and 20 speeches of President Jackson in the Old King Cole *case were found to contain promise of benefits if employees rejected the union, hence violative of Section 8 (a) (1) and unprotected by Section 8 (c).*

Union officials have quite generally maintained, however, that the NLRB's application of Section 8 (c) has allowed employers to make statements during organizational campaigns which, while free of threat or promise on their face, contain such threat or promise by virtue of the authority of those who make them. The decision below was one of the early decisions on this issue made by the Board following passage of the

Taft-Hartley Act. In it the trial examiner found that statements of an employer were coercive in the context of his antiunion conduct, carrying an implicit threat to employees who supported the union. The Board, however, overruled the trial examiner's findings, holding that there was no actual threat contained in the employer's remarks, hence they were protected by Section 8 (c).

Mylan-Sparta Co. and United Construction Workers, UMW 78 NLRB No. 161, 1948, from the intermediate report of the trial examiner

FINDINGS OF FACT

I. THE BUSINESS OF THE RESPONDENT

Mylan-Sparta Company, Inc., is a Tennessee corporation with its manufacturing plant, office and place of business at Sparta, Tennessee,[1] where it is engaged in the manufacture, sale, and distribution of men's and boys' shirts. It annually purchases and causes to be transported in interstate commerce to its plant at Sparta in excess of $1,000,000 in materials, and annually sells and causes to be transported in interstate commerce in excess of $1,000,000 in finished products.[2]

II. THE ORGANIZATION INVOLVED

United Construction Workers, UMWA, A.F. of L., is a labor organization admitting to membership employees of the Respondent.

III. THE UNFAIR LABOR PRACTICES

A. Background and sequence

In early March 1946, a hearing was held in Sparta, Tennessee, before a Trial Examiner of the National Labor Relations Board upon a complaint (based upon a charge filed by the Union) issued against Charles C. Bassine and certain other individuals and trustees doing business under the name of Mylan Manufacturing Company, Mylan Manufacturing Co., Inc., and Mylan-Sparta Co., Inc. (the present Respondent),[3] the Sparta-White County Chamber of Commerce, and certain Sparta citizens, alleging violation of Section 8 (1) and (3) of the Act. On April 5, 1946, the Trial Examiner issued his Intermediate Report in the above proceeding, finding that all the parties named as respondent in said complaint had engaged in and were engaging in certain unfair labor practices and recommending that they cease and desist therefrom and take certain affirmative action including the publishing of a cease and desist notice in the local newspaper, the Sparta Expositor. On August 26, 1946, the Board sustained the Trial Examiner's findings in part as to unfair labor practices committed by the respondent partnership, above described Mylan-Sparta Co., Inc.,

[1] The main business office is located in Nashville, Tennessee.

[2] Findings based on the pleadings and a stipulation on commerce in the record.

[3] Although Mylan-Sparta Co., Inc., is the title used in the previous case it is obvious and the undersigned finds that the Mylan-Sparta Co., Inc., and the Mylan-Sparta Company, Inc., has reference to the identical corporation.

Mylan Manufacturing Co., Inc.,[4] and M. C. Wallace, but dismissed as to the local chamber of commerce and certain other individual respondents. The Board's decision provided for the conventional posting of a cease and desist notice, but did not require that said notice be published in the local newspaper. On September 12, 1946, the Union filed a petition for certification of representatives in a unit consisting of the maintenance and production employees of the Respondent, excluding office workers and supervisory employees, and the Board ordered a pre-hearing election which was set for November 1, 1946. However, prior to the election date and on October 28, 1946, the Board granted the Union's request for leave to withdraw the petition for certification and no election has been held.

The allegations of unfair labor practices in the present complaint cover a period beginning in March after the conclusion of the previous hearing and continuing on and until the withdrawal of the representation proceeding in late October 1946. . . .

B. Activities during the representation proceeding

As heretofore found, the Union on September 12, 1946, filed a representation petition covering the maintenance and production employees, and as a result the Board ordered a pre-hearing election to be held among such employees on November 1. Toward the end of the election campaign, on October 24, the Respondent caused to be published in the Sparta Expositor a full page advertisement entitled "Just Facts." [5] The first sentence of this published statement, in bold type was as follows:

The United Mine Workers Union is again in Sparta to try to collect yearly dues of about $15,000 from our employees. That money is the beginning and the end of what they are after and they will promise anything to get it.

The article then continued:

"This is the same union that came up to the mines on the mountain several years ago" and "promised the miners the whole world . . . ," "nobody believed it but the mines closed up and they have stayed closed to this day . . . honest men were out of work . . . families went hungry and where was the union? The union packed up its wonderful promises and went away but left behind a ruined business and a ruined people. THE UNION WAS GONE!"

It next stated:

A few years later another union came by to show the silk mill [6] how to run their business. . . . Again a business was closed down and again people were out of work. After that Sparta was left without any industry. Condi-

[4] Mylan Manufacturing Co., Inc., apparently is no longer functioning as one of the successors to the partnership and as indicated in the previous Board decision.

[5] As heretofore found, this as well as other published statements of the Respondent and Bassine, its president, were also mailed by the Respondent to all persons whose names appeared in the White County telephone directory.

[6] Welwood Sparta Silk Mill which occupied part of the Respondent's present site. See previous Board's decision [70 NLRB 592].

tions became very bad. The railroad was about to pull its tracks out of the County—and not a single union organizer was in sight with even the smallest kind of a little promise. THE UNION WAS GONE!
The statement proceeded,

Now once more the unions are back with us. They weren't here when we built our business; they weren't here when we worked day and night, borrowing money, selling goods or getting 1000 people jobs. They weren't here when we started shipping car loads over the railroads and kept the tracks running into our town. They weren't here to build our town, help our poor and give our good citizens jobs. No sir, they are here now with those same old promises all shined up to look like new. The union wants to get paid for those promises and the price is about $15,000 a year. Our employees are the people who are asked to do the paying and it is up to our employees to say whether they will or not.

TO OUR EMPLOYEES

Our relations have always been most pleasant. Sure, we've had our ups and downs but we always were able to straighten them out to every one's complete satisfaction, weren't we? Things haven't changed. We're the same happy family, all striving to contribute our part—management by every possible benefit to you—you by your good production effort. No outside element is necessary for the continued happiness and security of our employees, town and county. A union can't help! It can only hurt!

MYLAN-SPARTA CO., INC.[7]

On October 28, 1946, the Respondent caused to be published in the local newspaper another full page statement headed "UNIONS ARE OBJECTIONABLE." Excerpts from the article follow:

Unions cause . . . strikes . . . when unions cause slow downs, wages go down. When unions strike, wages disappear. . . . Unions never gave anyone in White County a job. Our history shows that unions caused our people to lose jobs. . . . The union is telling you that if you don't join the union you won't have a job. That is not true. Our history shows just the opposite. When our people joined unions in the past that is when there were no jobs. . . . the union is telling you that no matter what may happen we cannot close our factory—that is not true. We have the right for good business reasons to close . . . entirely or in part at any time. It's just the same as if we were running a farm or a grocery store or a gasoline station. Ask any of them if they can close. Ask the mines if they could close. Ask the silk mill if they could close.

TO OUR EMPLOYEES

You will shortly be asked to vote by secret ballot for or against the union. You may have already signed a union card. THIS DOES NOT LEGALLY RE- QUIRE YOU TO VOTE FOR THE UNION, YOU CAN CHANGE YOUR MIND, THE

[7] Full text of the article is attached as Appendix B. [Here omitted.]

BALLOT IS WHAT COUNTS AND THAT BALLOT IS SECRET. NO ONE WILL EVER
KNOW HOW YOU VOTED. The Company wishes to impress upon you the
importance of voting at the proper time. Every one is urged to vote. The
Company has every confidence in your intelligence and good will. We
look forward to many happy years of future benefits and accomplishments
together.

MYLAN-SPARTA CO., INC.[8]

On October 28, as heretofore found, the Union's request was granted for
leave to withdraw the representation petition. On October 31, Respondent published another full-page statement in the local newspaper wherein it congratulated its employees because the "Union and the National Labor Relations
Board have called off the election." [9]

CONCLUSIONS AS TO INTERFERENCE, RESTRAINT, AND COERCION

The Respondent's acts and statements during the employees' organizational
activities of 1946 must be viewed against the background of unfair labor practices heretofore found by the Board during the union activities of 1945, particularly the condoning by the Respondent's predecessors (including President
Bassine) of a speech by a local business man in a mill meeting that the coal
mines and the silk mill had been closed because they were organized by a
union and warning the employees that the Mylan plant would also close in the
event that the Union organized it. The published statement of the Respondent
issued in April 1946, shortly after the receipt of the Trial Examiner's Intermediate Report in the previous case to the effect that the Respondent had the
"right" among other things "for business reasons . . . to expand operations,
to reduce operations, or to cease operations altogether and we fully intend to
exercise that right," was certainly not compliance with the recommendations
in the previous case. Standing alone, it could be construed as a statement on
the part of Bassine and the Respondent that they disagreed with the findings in
that Report, as they certainly had a perfect right to do. However, the use of
the language above quoted, that the Respondent had a right to cease operations, and that it fully intended to exercise that right, publicly announced during the revival of the union campaign and when employees were being told
that President Bassine and Plant Manager Feinstein would close the plant if
the Union came in had the effect of confirming, instead of repudiating, in the
minds of the employees the rumors spread by Floorlady Qualls that the mill
would close in Sparta if the employees organized.

If there was any doubt in the minds of the employees or the townspeople in
the spring of 1946 that the Respondent was threatening to remove the mill if

[8] Full text of the statement is attached to Appendix C. [Here omitted.]

[9] On another full-page of the same issue of the Expositor, the Respondent published
a speech President Bassine had delivered before the local Rotary club on October 28
and before the local Civitan club on October 29. The speech so published was a
diatribe against the Act, the Board, and the Board's personnel, as well as against
"aggressive union organization." It stated flatly, "We will not abide by its [the
Board's] decision."

the employees organized, that doubt must have been removed (after the Union had filed a petition seeking representation and a date had been set to permit the employees by an election to decide for themselves whether they wanted collective bargaining representation by the Union), when the Respondent published its "Just Facts" statement of October 24 wherein it stated, "This is the same Union" that organized the mines a few years ago and "the mines closed . . . a union tried to show the silk mills how to run their business . . . again a business was closed down and again people were out of work." "Now once more the Unions are back with us . . . with the same old promises . . ."; and when it published "Unions are Objectionable" on October 28, wherein Respondent said, "Unions never gave anyone in White County a job. Our history shows that Unions caused our people to lose jobs. When people joined unions in the past that is when there were no jobs." "The Union is telling you that no matter what may happen we cannot close our factory . . . that is not true. We have the right for good business reasons to close . . . at any time." "Ask the mines if they could close. Ask the silk mill if they could close." . . .

DECISION OF THE BOARD, PASSING ON THE TRIAL EXAMINER'S REPORT (ABOVE)

. . . (a) The published statements of the Respondent, in substance, recited the history of a local mill and a mine, each of which had closed after being organized, and declared that the Respondent could close its plant at any time for good business reasons despite assertions to the contrary by the Union. The Trial Examiner found these statements coercive when viewed against a background of previous unfair labor practices.[10] The statements, however, contain no threat of coercion, and they do not acquire a coercive character because the Respondent had on another occasion committed unfair labor practices.[11] A prophecy that unionization will ultimately lead to loss of employment is not coercive where there is no threat that the Respondent will use its economic power to make its prophecy come true.[12] Furthermore, the Employer's statements were apparently factually correct, and the remarks about the closing the plant were made in reply to allegations by the Union that the Employer could not close its plant without violating the Act. . . .[13]

Accordingly we find that the Respondent has not interfered with, restrained,

[10] *Matter of Mylan Manufacturing Company,* 70 N.L.R.B. 574, enf'd. as mod., Feb. 10, 1948 (C.C.A. 6), 21 L.R.R.M. 2368.

[11] *Matter of Tygart Sportswear Company,* 77 N.L.R.B. No. 98.

[12] *Matter of Electric Steel Foundry,* 74 N.L.R.B. 129.

[13] This case is distinguishable from *Matter of Lafayette National Bank of Brooklyn,* 77 N.L.R.B., No. 195, where the Board majority found that the employer's statements contained a clearly implied threat to blacklist union members. In the present case, the Respondent refers to undesirable results which have followed union organization in certain instances, but does not suggest that such results will be brought about through the exercise of the Employer's influence. Member Murdock does not concur in distinguishing the instant case from the *Lafayette* case, having dissented in that case because of his view that there as here, the employer's remarks did not suggest that the employer's own influence would be used to bring about detrimental results to those who joined the Union.

or coerced its employees in the exercise of the rights guaranteed in the Act. The complaint will therefore be dismissed in its entirety.

Testimony of Joseph A. Beirne, President, Communications Workers of America, CIO, in Taft-Hartley Act Revisions, hearings before the Senate Committee on Labor and Public Welfare, 83d Cong., 1st Sess., 1953, part 3, pp. 1552–1553

I cannot do a legal analysis of the section of the act, 8 (c), which deals with the so-called free-speech provision. However, I can express a fundamental with relation to this provision—as Americans we unionists believe as staunchly as any group in the right of free expression. The Bill of Rights lives as vividly with union people as it does with all other segments of our people.

We are also believers in fair play and it is on that aspect of this provision of Taft-Hartley that we draw back to gain our perspective. Our experience with this provision has given us definite proof that some management has believed in and practiced the art of stretching the free-speech provision far beyond anything contemplated by Congress. Too many employers consider that section 8 (c) grants them the right to make anti-union statements. They do not differentiate between unfair labor practices and representation cases. They only understand that their expression should not contain "threat of reprisal or force or promise of benefit" whatever the occasion might be.

The phrase free speech is a misnomer when it is used to describe a right or permission under law for an employer to use his power as an employer to influence the thinking and action of his employees on matters affecting unions and their activities.

It is a coined phrase which misleads. Such free speech is a license for employers to use the privilege of their position and their economic strength to influence and to control activities of their employees and the unions to which they belong.

This is not free speech in the traditional sense, but rather it is the use of full economic weight and position to influence and affect the rights and privileges of employees.

Rights guaranteed to employees under section 7 of the act—those rights of self-organization and concerted activities for purposes of collective bargaining, and other mutual aid or protection—were sired in the conditions which were found to exist as a burden upon interstate commerce at the time of enactment of the Wagner Act. These conditions were restated in part as the basis for the Taft-Hartley Act. They are well known and need not be repeated at this time.

The point is simply this—the use of a catch phrase such as free speech should not be the basis for causing a return to conditions which existed prior to the Wagner Act.

For example: Employers should be neutral at a time when collective bargaining representatives are being chosen. They should not be allowed to use either dominant position as employers to influence—on company premises and during work hours—the choice by employees of their collective bargaining representatives.

There should be no limitation on the use of speech as evidence of an unfair labor practice simply because such speech does not express or imply any threat or reprisal or promise of benefit, as such. Any expression, whether written or oral, whose purpose is to influence employees should be considered, especially where it involves company premises, time, and money.

Where does free speech stop and "threat of reprisal or force or promise of benefit" begin when job threats are made to people whose occupations give them particular skills which cannot be used in other industries?

We in CWA are faced with such occupational problems because it is a well-known fact that work in the telephone industry builds skills but not the kind that can be utilized in other fields.

We can cite cases in which the free speech provision has been abused without conscience in captive audiences where employees have been directly threatened with their jobs if they observe picket lines and in other instances where there has been play on sectionalism and suggestions against minorities.

Employers, through the write-in of the so-called free speech provision, have been led to believe they are free to express themselves in any manner to their employees.

Employers, under the guise of free speech should not be allowed to use their positions as employers, their economic strength, and their control of employees during working time to release a flood of communications to such employees designed to interfere with the choice of collective bargaining representatives or to restrain, coerce, or interfere with lawful activities of their employees and their union.

8 (a) (5) REFUSAL TO BARGAIN

Southern Saddlery Co. and Local 109, United Leather Workers, 90 NLRB No. 176, 1950

DECISION AND ORDER

On October 10, 1949, Trial Examiner George A. Downing issued his Intermediate Report in the above-entitled proceeding, finding that the Respondent had engaged in and was engaging in certain unfair labor practices within the meaning of Section 8 (a) (5) and (1) of the Act, and recommending that it cease and desist therefrom and take certain affirmative action, as set forth in the copy of the Intermediate Report attached hereto. Thereafter, the Respondent filed exceptions to the Intermediate Report and a supporting brief.

The Board [1] has reviewed the rulings made by the Trial Examiner at the hearing and finds that no prejudicial errors were committed. The rulings are hereby affirmed. The Board has considered the Intermediate Report, the Respondent's exceptions and brief, and the entire record in the case, and hereby adopts the findings, conclusions, and recommendations of the Trial Examiner with the following additions and modifications:

[1] Board Member Paul L. Styles has disqualified himself from participating in this case, because the complaint herein was originally issued under his signature as Regional Director of the Tenth Region.

We agree with the Trial Examiner that the Respondent did not fulfill its obligations under the Act of bargaining in good faith with Local 109, United Leather Workers International Union, A.F.L., herein called the Union, as the representative of its employees. The essential facts in this case are not in dispute. Since 1943, the Respondent has recognized the Union as the representative of its employees. Thereafter, from time to time, the parties executed collective bargaining agreements which continued in effect, as to wage rates, until April 1948. In February 1948, the Union advised the Respondent that it wished to reopen the wage agreement at the expiration of its term in April 1948 and, in the latter month, the parties commenced negotiations. About 10 meetings were held between April 1948 and March 1949, when bargaining between the parties was abandoned.

The Respondent willingly met with the Union at all times. Negotiations centered almost exclusively upon the Union's request for a wage increase. Although negotiations were commenced in April 1948, it was not until October that the Union made a specific demand for an across-the-board increase of 30 cents an hour. In a later conference held on February 5, 1949, the Union reduced its demand to 10 cents an hour. Both demands were rejected by the Employer. At the final conference, held on March 4, 1949, the Respondent rejected a suggestion that it grant the employees a token increase of 5 cents an hour.

At the very outset of the negotiations, the Respondent opposed the Union's demands on the ground that it was financially unable to grant any wage increase. Throughout the bargaining period, the Respondent persisted in its contention that, because of poor business conditions, it could not afford to raise wages. Finally, the Union, at the last three conferences, requested the Respondent to furnish information substantiating its claim of financial inability to grant a wage increase. The Respondent, however, refused to furnish any information relating to its financial condition on the ground that it was contrary to its policy to divulge such information to anyone.

The fact that the Respondent met willingly and conferred at length with the Union does not necessarily establish that it had been bargaining in good faith. Mere participation in meetings with the Union and protestations of willingness to bargain do not alone fulfill the requirements of Section 8 (a) (5) and 8 (d) of the Act, for these are only the surface indicia of bargaining. Bargaining in good faith is a duty on both sides to enter into discussions with an open and fair mind and a sincere purpose to find a basis for agreement touching wages and hours and conditions of labor.[2] In applying this definition of good faith bargaining to any situation, the Board examines the Respondent's conduct as a whole for a clear indication as to whether the latter has refused to bargain in good faith, and the Board usually does not rely upon any one factor as conclusive evidence that the Respondent did not genuinely try to reach an agreement.

[2] *Globe Cotton Mills* v. *N.L.R.B.*, 103 F. 2d 91, 94 (C.A. 5, 1939).

In this case, there was one principal subject for negotiation, namely, the Union's request for an increase in wages. Although the Union progressively reduced the amount by which it demanded the employees' wages be increased, the Respondent steadfastly maintained that it was financially unable to raise wages. The Respondent offered no counterproposals[3] nor did it make other efforts to compromise the controversy. Thereupon, the Union requested the Respondent to substantiate its contention. In so doing, the Union, pointing to the fact that the Respondent had consistently paid dividends to its stockholders, requested information relating to the Respondent's record of dividend payments, the amount of dividends paid, and the rate of dividends in relation to the Respondent's capitalization. The Respondent informed the Union that dividend payments during the past 10 years had been small, but refused to divulge any further information. The Union then suggested that the Respondent substantiate its claim by submitting a financial statement. This suggestion was rejected. Lastly, the Union asked the Respondent to furnish in dollars and cents a breakdown of manufacturing costs. This request was also rejected. At this point, after 11 months of negotiations, further conferences between the parties were discontinued.

The Respondent argues that it was under no obligation to substantiate its position by communicating to the Union any facts relating to its financial condition. We believe, however, that, if the Respondent was unwilling to modify its initial opposition to the Union's demands for a wage increase, it should, at the very least, have made a genuine and sincere effort to persuade the Union to accept its position. Here, the validity of the Respondent's position depended upon the existence of facts peculiarly within its knowledge. The Respondent, therefore, in our opinion, was obliged to furnish the Union with sufficient information to enable the latter to understand and discuss intelligently the issues raised by the Respondent in opposition to the Union's demands. The extent and nature of such information depends upon the bargaining which takes place in any particular case. The Respondent, by maintaining the intransigeant position that it was financially unable to raise wages and, at the same time, by refusing to make any reasonable efforts to support or justify its position, erected an insurmountable barrier to successful conclusion of the bargaining. We believe that such conduct does not meet the test of good faith bargaining. Accordingly, we find that, under the circumstances, the Respondent has failed to discharge its duty to bargain collectively with the Union and thereby has violated Section 8 (a) (5) and 8 (a) (1) of the Act.

[3] We do not find that, in this case, the Respondent's failure to make any counterproposals is by itself a persuasive indication that the Respondent was not bargaining in good faith. Under some circumstances, a Respondent's failure to offer any counterproposals during negotiations, while at the same time refusing to retreat from its original bargaining position, is indicative of a lack of good faith in bargaining. However, a counterproposal is not indispensable to bargaining when, from their discussions, it is apparent that what one party would offer is wholly unacceptable to the other and that a counterproposal would be an obviously futile gesture. *Globe Cotton Mills v. N.L.R.B., supra.*

THE REMEDY

After issuance of the Intermediate Report, the Respondent advised the Board that it had signed a collective bargaining agreement with the Union and moved to dismiss the complaint herein on the ground that the case had become moot by reason of the execution of this agreement.[4] It is unnecessary for us to consider the content of this agreement in order to decide the motion.[5] Regardless of the provisions of the contract or its effect upon further collective bargaining between the Respondent and the Union, we find no merit in the Respondent's contention. It is well established that the issues raised by filing charges alleging a refusal to bargain do not become moot by reason of the subsequent execution of a collective bargaining agreement.[6] The record in this case reveals that the Respondent has shown a disregard of its duty to bargain collectively with the representative of its employees. Accordingly, we are convinced that the policies of the Act can best be effectuated by an order requiring the Respondent to take the remedial action hereinafter set forth.

ORDER

Upon the entire record in the case, and pursuant to Section 10 (c) of the National Labor Relations Act, as amended, the National Labor Relations Board hereby orders that Southern Saddlery Company, Chattanooga, Tennessee, its officers, agents, successors, and assigns, shall:

1. Cease and desist from:

a. Refusing to bargain collectively with Local 109, United Leather Workers International Union, A.F.L., as the exclusive representative of all its employees at its Chattanooga, Tennessee, plant, excluding office clerical employees, watchmen and guards, professional employees, and supervisors as defined in the Act;

b. Interfering in any other manner with the efforts of Local 109, United Leather Workers International Union, A.F.L., to bargain collectively with it on behalf of the employees in the aforesaid appropriate unit.

2. Take the following affirmative action which the Board finds will effectuate the policies of the Act:

a. Upon request, bargain collectively with Local 109, United Leather Workers International Union, A.F.L., as the exclusive bargaining agent of all its employees in the appropriate unit described above with respect to rates of pay, wages, hours of employment, and other conditions of employment;

[4] The Respondent's request for oral argument of its motion is hereby denied because the notice of motion and affidavit and exhibit in support thereof and the record in this case, in our opinion, adequately present the issues.

[5] Of course, neither the contract itself nor any evidence as to the circumstances surrounding its negotiation are before us as part of the record made at the hearing in this case.

[6] *Yawman & Erbe Manufacturing Company*, 89 NLRB No. 108; *American National Insurance Company*, 89 NLRB No. 19; *American Radio Association*, 82 NLRB 1344; *Pacific Molded Products Company*, 76 NLRB 1140; *Augusta Broadcasting Company*, 58 NLRB 1493; *J. I. Case Company* v. *N.L.R.B.*, 321 U.S. 322.

b. Post at its Chattanooga, Tennessee, plant, copies of the notice attached hereto as an Appendix.[7] Copies of said notice to be furnished by the Regional Director for the Tenth Region shall, after being duly signed by the Respondent's representative, be posted by the Respondent immediately upon receipt thereof and maintained by it for sixty (60) consecutive days thereafter in conspicuous places, including all places where notices to employees are customarily posted. Reasonable steps shall be taken by Respondent to insure that said notices are not altered, defaced, or covered by any other material;

c. Notify the Regional Director for the Tenth Region (Atlanta, Georgia), in writing, within ten (10) days from the date of receipt of this Order, what steps the Respondent has taken to comply herewith.

APPENDIX A

NOTICE TO ALL EMPLOYEES
PURSUANT TO
A DECISION AND ORDER

of the National Labor Relations Board and in order to effectuate the policies of the National Labor Relations Act, as amended, we hereby notify our employees that:

WE WILL bargain collectively, upon request, with LOCAL 109, UNITED LEATHER WORKERS INTERNATIONAL UNION, A.F.L., as the exclusive representative of all our employees in the bargaining unit described below with respect to rates of pay, wages, hours of employment, and other conditions of employment.

The bargaining unit is:

All employees at our Chattanooga, Tennessee, plant, excluding office clerical employees, watchmen and guards, professional employees, and supervisors, as defined in the Act.

WE WILL NOT in any manner interfere with the efforts of the above-named union to bargain with us, or refuse to bargain collectively with said union as the exclusive representative of the employees in the bargaining unit set forth above.

SOUTHERN SADDLERY COMPANY
_____
(*Employer*)

Dated _____   By _____
(*Representative*)   (*Title*)

This notice must remain posted for 60 days from the date hereof, and must not be altered, defaced, or covered by any other material.

[7] In the event this Order is enforced by decree of a United States Court of Appeals, there shall be inserted in the notice before the words, "A Decision and Order" the words, "A Decree of the United States Court of Appeals Enforcing."

Taylor Forge and Pipe Works and Forge and Machine Workers, 113 NLRB No. 65, 1955, as summarized in Board press release

Board orders company to furnish, upon request, to Forge and Machine Workers Industrial Union, Ind., the "degree" or point evaluation assigned by company to each of the factors evaluated in each of its hourly rated jobs in determining the point range for such jobs of company's employees; and post compliance notices for 60 days.

A majority of the Board—Members Murdock, Peterson and Leedom—stated in part:

. . . We believe that the evidence clearly establishes the relevancy and essential necessity for the substantiating data requested by the union. Thus, it is undisputed that the substantiating data is part of the Respondent's job evaluation system. Further evidence of relevancy is the fact that the Respondent has agreed to supply such information on any particular job if the Union should process a grievance on that job.

We can see no essential difference in the need for wage data information requested, as here, on an overall basis and the need for such piecemeal information, the furnishing of which is agreed to by the Respondent. Thus, it is clear that, if the data is relevant and necessary in the case of individual grievances, it is equally relevant and necessary where the object of the negotiation is to establish broad pay formulas which will eliminate the necessity of filing individual grievances . . .

In a separate dissenting opinion, Chairman Farmer and Member Rodgers stated in part:

We believe that the majority's conclusion in this case establishes a broadside principle for every issue even remotely resembling a wage information situation. . . .

We do not view the recognized duty of an employer to furnish wage information of the usual variety as an open sesame which requires an employer to furnish a union with all the minutiae leading to its subconclusions, which in turn, are the bases for the ultimate bargainable fact —the rate of pay an employer offers for each particular job. Where the information line is to be drawn cannot be stated as a precise rule; each fact situation must be scrutinized to determine the extent of an employer's obligation. The facts of this case show that the Respondent has fulfilled its duty of disclosure. . . .

In any event we see nothing in the statute which imposes upon an employer the obligation to reveal, upon blanket request and with no pretense of any showing of need or relevance, such remote "information" or "facts" as are involved in this case. We believe rather, that argument whether certain work involves light, or sustained, or considerable, or continuous physical effort, for example, involves the language of the bargaining conference, and it properly belongs there. The Respondent here gave the Union all the facts about job classifications and descriptions, wage rates, individual earnings, and the total point score equivalent to each employee's wage scale. It even offered, if a dispute arose over any particular job to reveal detailed reasons—shown in the various designations for the 11 factors decided upon by its experts—for the wage rate on the job. Under such circumstances, we find it impossible to decide that the Respondent breached his obligation to bargain collectively, which is all that under the statute it was obligated to do.

FOR DISCUSSION AND ANALYSIS

1. Suppose that John Jones was one of the most active employees in attempts to organize a union. He had been responsible for signing up a large number of fellow workers; he had allowed his home to be used as a union meeting place; he had been responsible for making initial contacts with a national union to secure support. Then suddenly John Jones is fired. He goes down to the regional office of the NLRB and tells his story, fills out a form charging that his employer has violated the Act by discharging him for his union activity. The Board investigates the matter and processes the charge.

At the hearing before the trial examiner, the employer claims that Jones's union activity had nothing whatever to do with his discharge. Jones was fired, he says, because he had come in late that morning for the third time within a month, and because the quality of his work had deteriorated, indicating that he wasn't paying as much attention to his job as he should, and what's more he wasn't producing quantity, either—on the piece-rate job at which he had been employed he had been making only a little more than the base rate, when it was expected that an average employee would be able to make 25 per cent above base, and on top of that he had talked back to a foreman when the foreman had told him to stop talking to another employee and get back to his job. There was plenty of reason to let him go without the union matter.

In the face of Jones's charge and the employer's denial, how can the Board make a determination as to whether or not Jones had been discharged for union activity?

2. Employees who participate in a strike for higher wages and other demands are entitled to reinstatement after the strike is over, in the absence of any serious misconduct on their part during the strike (such as violence on the picket line). However, a striker always runs the risk of being replaced; there is nothing that prevents an employer from hiring other workers to take the places of the strikers. And strikers who are permanently replaced do not have any special rights. Permanently replaced strikers, according to the Board, "merely have the right not to be penalized for their concerted activity, and are not entitled to preferential status in hiring." The Board has always emphasized, however, that this does not mean that a striker may be discharged before he is replaced.

Rationalize this policy in the light of Section 8 (*a*) (3) of the Act.

3. In the Old King Cole case, one of the unionists advised a wavering member not to remove her union button but to keep on wearing it "as protection against being discharged." In the light of pre-NLRB days, when the wearing of a union button was more likely to cause discharge than to protect against it, how can you explain this unionist's advice?

4. Union leaders have maintained that employer comments and speeches during a representation campaign can never be wholly free of a coercive power. Just by virtue of his managerial authority, his power to discharge and discipline and to reward by promotion or special favor, what an employer asks his employees to do—such as to vote against a union—must necessarily carry a special force behind it. The conclusion of those who hold this view is that employers should stay on the sidelines during a representation election; an election, they maintain, is the business of the workers and should be free of any employer interference, whether or not explicitly of a threatening or inducing nature. Do you agree?

5. In the *Southern Saddlery* case, reported above, a majority of the Board found that the employer had failed to bargain in good faith because it had "stubbornly" refused to reveal the factual basis on which it had concluded that it could not afford a wage increase. Suppose that the company, without referring to its financial ability to grant a wage increase, had simply refused to make any concession to the union. (*a*) Do you believe that good-faith bargaining requires an employer to *explain* his reason for refusal? (*b*) Must the employer support such an explanation by whatever relevant factual information he may have? Must there be a *full* disclosure of information by him? (*c*) May withholding of factual data under some circumstances be considered a legitimate method of manipulating relative bargaining powers to the employer's advantage? Under what circumstances? What is the dividing line between using economic data as a legitimate bargaining weapon and failing to use economic data as an unlawful attempt to evade the obligation to bargain in good faith?

11: Taft-Hartley Unfair Labor Practices on the Part of Unions

SECTION 8(b)(1): COERCION OF EMPLOYEES

In the period of the Wagner Act, 1935–1937, Federal law imposed no proscriptions on labor unions in their dealings with their members or with employers. The National Labor Relations Board, it is true, by administrative interpretation gradually moved toward establishing certain "good faith" obligations on the union if they were to gain admittance to the Board's processes. A union seeking representation rights on behalf of a body of employees could not (at least openly) discriminate against certain of them by denying membership on grounds of color, for example. A union not itself bargaining in good faith could not press charges that an employer refused to bargain. These somewhat uncertain and occasional constraints on union behavior were expanded and made uniform on all unions operating in interstate commerce by provisions of the Taft-Hartley Act. Behavior which deprived workers of free determination of whether or not they wished a union to represent them, and which coerced employers into conforming to union wishes by tactics defined as unfair, came under the same ban as employer unfair labor practices. The cases that follow are examples of the Board's efforts to interpret what union conduct is proscribed under the law.

National Labor Relations Board release for morning papers, Monday, October 25, 1948

N.L.R.B. MAKES FIRST RULINGS ON STRIKE ACTIVITIES UNDER L.M.R.A.

The National Labor Relations Board today issued its first rulings on strike activities under the Labor Management Relations Act, 1947.

The five-man Board unanimously ruled:

1. A local union restrained and coerced employees under the law by engaging in "mass picketing" which had the effect of "forcibly blocking" the entry of employees' automobiles onto plant property.

2. A local union intimidated employees when strikers and their companions in cars pursued strikebreakers for a considerable distance from the plant.

3. Pickets were not engaging in intimidatory conduct under the law when they "vilified and verbally abused as scabs" those employees who deserted the strikers' ranks. In making this ruling the Board unanimously stated: "Insofar as the abuse of the strikebreakers amounted only to name calling and . . . vocally vented resentment, we do not find that it was within the purview of Section 8 (b) (1) (A) (which makes it an unfair labor practice for a union or its agents to restrain or coerce employees in their right to join or not to join a labor organization). Such a finding is expressly precluded by Section 8 (c) of the Act which provides:

> The expressing of any views, argument, or opinion, or the dissemination thereof, whether in written, printed, graphic, or visual form, shall not constitute or be evidence of an unfair labor practice under any of the provisions of this Act, if such expression contains no threat of reprisal or force or promise of benefit."

Today's rulings were made in a case which arose out of a strike called by Local 6 of the International Longshoremen's and Warehousemen's Union (C.I.O.), at the Sunset Line and Twine Company, Petaluma, California. The unanimous Board reversed the Intermediate Report of Trial Examiner C. W. Whittemore, who had held that the Union's activities were not "coercive" within the meaning of the amended Act. . . .

In accordance with the majority decision, the Board ordered both the International and Local unions to cease restraining and coercing employees of Sunset Line and Twine Company and to post notices in both Petaluma and San Francisco union offices announcing that it will cease such activities.

The unions were also ordered to notify the N.L.R.B. Regional Director at San Francisco within 10 days as to what steps they have taken to comply. If the unions do not comply with the Board's decision, the Board will seek enforcement of its order in the United States Court of Appeals.

Specific acts which the unanimous Board found constituted illegal activities included:

1. a group of pickets and union officials in a number of automobiles trailing an automobile in which non-strikers were driving home;

2. blocking of the driveway to a plant parking lot with a line of pickets and a union official calling upon the pickets to "pull" the non-strikers out of a car;

3. 200 or 300 pickets and sympathizers blocking ingress to the plant; and

4. following a non-striker by car and then threatening him with physical punishment.

Discussing two incidents in which the pickets lined up across a driveway to the plant and refused to move aside to let the cars of non-strikers pass, the Board said:

> The car drivers were faced with the choice of running down the pickets, at the risk of inflicting serious injury, or driving away. This interposition of passive force to prevent employees from going to work is, we believe, a form of restraint proscribed by Section 8 (b) (1) (A).

As to the incidents in which pickets and union officials followed the cars of non-strikers, the Board said:

> The conduct of the strikers and their companions, quite apart from the words they used, in trailing the greatly outnumbered little group of strike-breakers for a considerable distance through the town was clearly intimidatory. This pursuit away from the plant by an inimical superior force clearly conveyed the unspoken threat that the strikebreakers might well be subjected to bodily harm. As such it was hardly less coercive within the meaning of Section 8 (b) (1) than an express threat of physical violence.

The Board said further:

> It is immaterial that this conduct failed to deter the non-striking employees from returning to work. It was reasonably calculated to accomplish that end, and its inefficacy in this particular instance is no defense to the charge that it was violative of the Act.

The "mass picketing"—in which a crowd of 200 or 300 composed of strikers, fellow union members and other apparent sympathizers gathered around the main plant entrance in an effort to shut the plant down completely—"patently involved restraint and coercion of employees attempting to go to work, and we so find," the Board said. The crowd massed so closely around the driveway that some cars of non-strikers were turned back, the Board found.

National Labor Relations Board, release for morning papers, Thursday, April 14, 1949

N.L.R.B. HOLDS UNION ORGANIZER VIOLATED L.M.R.A. BY THREATS IN SPEECH

In a case involving consolidated charges of unfair labor practice against both a union and an employer, the National Labor Relations Board today found a labor union organizer guilty of coercion against employees in violation of the Labor Management Relations Act when she told a meeting of employees that "those who do not join the union will eventually lose their jobs."

A majority of the Board also ruled that it was a violation of the Act when she told an employee member of the audience that "we have ways of handling people like you that argue against the Union."

The statements were made by Mavis Lane, organizer for the International Ladies Garment Workers Union (A.F.L.), at a meeting held in McAlester, Oklahoma, December 6, 1947, for the purpose of organizing employees of Seamprufe, Inc., lingerie manufacturer.

In a companion case heard and decided at the same time, the Board found that the Seamprufe company violated three sections of the Act by:

1. discharging two employees for union activities;
2. granting wage increases and paid holidays and vacations timed to defeat free organization of employees;
3. questioning employees about their union affiliations, and
4. contributing support to the formation of the Seamprufe Employees Asso-

ciation by allowing it to hold meetings in the plant and conditioning wage increases on the success of the Association.

The Board dismissed a charge that the company had dominated the Association. . . .

The Board ordered both the company and Miss Lane to cease their illegal activities. In addition, it ordered the company to reinstate the two illegally discharged employees with back pay, and to cease contributing support to the Association or "any other labor organization."

The decisions and orders in the two cases were signed by all five Members of the Board. However, Chairman Paul M. Herzog and Member John M. Houston expressed disagreement with the finding that Miss Lane's two statements violated the Act. They said they could find nothing "coercive" in the union organizer's statements, but were writing no formal dissent because they considered themselves bound by a previous majority decision on the same subject in the *Smith Cabinet Company* case. . . .

In today's decision, the majority found that both of Miss Lane's statements exceeded the bounds permitted by the "free speech" provision of the Act. About 30 Seamprufe employees were at the meeting.

Of Miss Lane's statements, the Board said:

Both statements, taken together, give an impression of a fixed determination by an organized group, represented by Lane, to take punitive action against anyone who opposed, or did not support, its program. Such statements would in our opinion be reasonably calculated to coerce anti-union or non-union members of Lane's audience in the exercise of their right, under the amended Act, to refrain from joining the Union. Accordingly, we find, contrary to the Trial Examiner, that both the statements quoted above from Lane's speech violated Section 8 (*b*) (1) (A) of the Act.

(Section 8 (*b*) (1) (A) prohibits a labor organization or its agents from restraining or coercing employees in the exercise of their rights to self-organization as guaranteed by the Act.)

SECONDARY BOYCOTTS

National Labor Relations Board, release for afternoon papers, Tuesday, March 29, 1949

N.L.R.B. RULES "PRODUCT" PICKETING VIOLATES BOYCOTT BAN

The National Labor Relations Board today ruled unanimously that a union violated the secondary-boycott ban of the Labor Management Relations Act by having its pickets "follow the products" of a struck employer to the premises of other employers.

The ruling was made in a case involving the Printing Specialties and Paper Converters Union, Local 388, A.F.L. Charges against the union were brought by Sealright Pacific, Ltd., Los Angeles, a manufacturer of paper food containers and milk bottle caps.

In "following" Sealright goods, union pickets followed trucks bearing Sealright merchandise to the loading platforms of Los Angeles Seattle Motor Express, Inc., a truck line, and picketed the trucks there. They also picketed the docks of West Coast Terminals Company, where paper for Sealright was being unloaded from a steamship.

The Board held that this picketing violated the secondary-boycott ban, on the ground that it constituted inducement and encouragement of employees of the two shipping concerns to refuse to handle Sealright goods with an object of compelling their employers to cease doing business with Sealright. . . .

The Board ordered the union to cease encouraging employees of the two firms "or any other employer, by picketing or by related conduct" to engage in a strike or concerted refusal to perform services with an object of compelling their employers to cease doing business with Sealright. It also ordered the union to post a notice announcing that it will cease its unlawful activities.

The Board's decision said in part:

It is clear from the record in the instant case that the pickets were authorized by the Respondent [Union] to follow trucks carrying Sealright products to other plants. Indeed, as the Trial Examiner found, the Respondent regarded such conduct as an extension of its primary picket line at the Sealright plant.

Moreover, it is established by the testimony of both Walter J. Turner, secretary-treasurer, and Patrick J. Morgan, business representative of the Respondent, that these officials knew of and took an active part in all picketing operations relating to Sealright products. Turner himself warned R. C. Lacey, president of Los Angeles Motor Express, Inc., that his business would be picketed unless Lacey declined to handle Sealright products. On several occasions Morgan accompanied the pickets and spoke to employees on the Los Angeles Seattle docks. The evidence in the record is persuasive that the Respondent and its pickets were in full agreement that products destined to and from the Sealright plant should be picketed, wherever found. We find therefore that the pickets were acting within the scope of their authority as agents of the Respondent in establishing a picket line on the docks of the West Coast Terminals Co. and Los Angeles Seattle Motor Express, Inc. . . .

The union called the strike at Sealright October 27, 1947, after the parties had been unable to reach agreement on terms of a new contract. Approximately 78 production employees were involved.

International Brotherhood of Teamsters vs. Schultz Refrigerated Service, 87 NLRB No. 82, 1949

DECISION AND ORDER

THE FACTS

The facts with regard to this allegation of the complaint are as follows: Schultz, engaged in the business of transporting perishable goods by truck between several States and particularly, within the metropolitan area of New York City, is the employer directly involved in a labor dispute with the Respondent. For some 12 years before August 31, 1948, the termination date of its last contract with Schultz, members of the Respondent union in their capacity as truck drivers were employed by Schultz to make deliveries to and pick-ups from various business concerns located in New York City. The dispute between the Respondent and Schultz arose when Schultz removed its New York City terminal to Slackwood, New Jersey, on August 28, 1948 [1] and thereafter refused to negotiate a new contract for the future employment of Respondent's members. Schultz, however, continued to operate its transportation business in New York City. For that purpose it employed members of a New Jersey local [2] to perform the driving duties previously performed there by members of the Respondent.

The Respondent thereupon resorted to the picketing activities alleged in the complaint to be violative of the Act. During the month of September 1948, following the termination of its contract with Schultz, it picketed Schultz' trucks operating on or in front of the premises of Manhattan Refrigerating Company, United Dressed Beef Company, Meadow Provision Company, Inc., and other customers and consignees of Schultz located in New York City. The nature of the picketing is undisputed. As soon as the replacement drivers prepared to load or unload their produce, the pickets began walking *around Schultz' trucks*, announcing by means of printed signs that truck driving members of the Respondent, employees of Schultz, had been locked out of their jobs. The picketing was at all times peacefully conducted. There was no picketing at consignee's premises except as incidental to the picketing of Schultz' trucks.

THE ALLEGED VIOLATION OF SECTION 8 (*b*) (4) (A)

It is the contention of the General Counsel that the Respondent's picketing of Schultz' trucks at the premises of its customers and consignees had as its objective the illegal inducement or encouragement of a secondary boycott within the meaning of Section 8 (*b*) (4) (A). The Trial Examiner, relying upon the literal language of that Section, without regard to its legislative history, or the paramount right of a labor organization to engage in a *primary* strike for lawful objectives, found that such picketing, although constituting peaceful "primary" picketing against a primary employer (Schultz) at his only place of business that could be located in New York City, was nevertheless violative of Section 8 (*b*) (4) (A).

We find it impossible to reconcile the Trial Examiner's preliminary finding that the Respondent engaged only in primary picketing with the conclusion that it thereby violated the Act. As we have frequently held, the legislative history

---

[1] On August 27, 1948, Schultz informed the Respondent by letter that the New York terminal would be closed on August 28, but that Respondent's members who were willing to work from the New Jersey terminal, would be assigned work until the expiration of the existing contract on August 31.

[2] Schultz entered into a closed-shop contract with Local 469, the Slackwood, New Jersey local of the International Brotherhood of Teamsters, Chauffeurs, Warehousemen and Helpers of America, AFL, on August 27 or 28, 1948. This date is incorrectly given in the Intermediate Report as July 27, 1948.

of Section 8 (b) (4) (A) reveals that this Section of the amended Act was directed against *secondary* boycotts and *secondary* strike activities.[3] Certainly, it was not the intent of Congress, nor has the Board so construed the language of Section 8 (b) (4) (A), to proscribe *primary* action by striking employees, who are engaged in a legitimate labor dispute with their own employer.[4] Thus, the language of Section 8 (b) (4) (A), forbidding labor organizations to induce or encourage strikes for the purpose of forcing any employer to cease doing business with any other person, must be read with the implicit condition that such inducement or encouragement be accomplished by secondary, but not primary means. Within the area of primary conduct a union may lawfully persuade all persons, including in this case the employees of Schultz' customers and consignees, to cease doing business with the struck employer. Little indeed would be left of the right to strike, reaffirmed by Congress in Section 13 of the Act,[5] if the striking employees were denied the concomitant right of peacefully picketing the immediate business of their employer. The lawfulness of such conduct has been recognized by a unanimous Board in the recent *Pure Oil* case,[6] where we said:

> The fact that the Union's primary pressure on Standard Oil may have also had a secondary effect, namely inducing or encouraging employees of other employers to cease doing business on Standard Oil premises, does not, in our opinion, convert lawful primary action into unlawful secondary action within the meaning of Section 8 (b) (4) (A). To hold otherwise might well outlaw virtually every effective strike, for a consequence of all strikes is some interference with business relationships between the struck employer and others.

[3] Pertinent comments to this effect by Senator Taft, a cosponsor of the Act, appear in *United Brotherhood of Carpenters and Joiners of America, District Council of Kansas City, Missouri, and Vicinity, A.F. of L.,* and *Walter A. Said, as Agent for United Brotherhood of Carpenters and Joiners of America, District Council of Kansas City, Missouri, and Vicinity, A.F. of L.* (*Wadsworth Building Company, Inc., and Klassen & Hodgson, Inc.*), 81 NLRB No. 127. During the course of Congressional debate Senator Taft stated:

> This provision [Section 8 (b) (4) (A)] makes it unlawful to resort to a secondary boycott to injure the business of a third person who is wholly unconcerned in the disagreement between an employer and his employees.

93 Cong. Rec. 4323 (April 29, 1947). The test set forth in the *Wadsworth* case and recited by the Trial Examiner in the Intermediate Report is applicable therefore only in the event the union's picketing activities are found to be in furtherance of a *secondary boycott.*

[4] *Oil Workers International Union, Local Union 346 (CIO), (The Pure Oil Company),* 84 NLRB No. 38; *United Electrical, Radio and Machine Workers of America and Local 813 of the United Electrical, Radio and Machine Workers of America (Ryan Construction Company),* 85 NLRB No. 76.

[5] This Section provides:

> Nothing in this Act, except as specifically provided for herein, shall be construed so as either to interfere with or impede or diminish in any way the right to strike, or to affect the limitations or qualifications on that right.

[6] *Supra.*

The sole issue in this case therefore is the validity of the General Counsel's theory that the nature of the Respondent's picketing was secondary rather than primary.[7]

Plainly, the object of all picketing at all times is to influence third persons to withhold their business or services from the struck employer. In this respect there is no distinction between lawful primary picketing and unlawful secondary picketing proscribed by Section 8 (b) (4) (A). Necessarily then, one important test of the lawfulness of a union's picketing activities in the course of its dispute with an employer is the identification of such picketing with the actual functioning of the primary employer's business at the *situs* of the labor dispute.

Admittedly, the application of the above test in this case poses a special problem. Heretofore, in cases involving an interpretation of the restrictions contained in Section 8 (b) (4) (A), the primary employer and, generally, the secondary employer, conducted their operations at fixed geographical locations. Thus, in the *Wadsworth* [8] and *Sealright* [9] cases, it was clear that the immediate vicinity of the struck plant, the situs of the primary employer's business, constituted the area of lawful, primary strike activity. Under these circumstances, the union by extending its picket line to the premise of other employers and thus abandoning the scene of its actual dispute with the primary employer, went beyond the protected area of primary picketing. Its picket line so extended was no longer local in point of contact to the primary employer's manufacturing operations, the only business directly involved in the labor dispute. Such picketing, a majority of the Board there held, was secondary conduct violative of Section 8 (b) (4) (A).[10]

In this case the primary employer's only geographical premises are a terminal in New Jersey, removed from all contact with its customers and consignees, and a dispatcher's office in New York City. But the business with which we are concerned is not confined to these specific localities. Here a fleet of commercial trucks, transporting products over a wide area in New York City, are the necessary instruments of the primary employer's operations. Clearly, therefore, in view of the roving nature of its business, the only effective means of bringing direct pressure on Schultz was the type of picketing engaged in by the Respondent. It would have been pointless, indeed, of the Respondent to estab-

---

[7] It is noteworthy that neither the General Counsel nor the charging party has excepted to the Trial Examiner's finding that the Respondent's picketing activities amounted only to "primary" picketing of a primary employer.

[8] *Supra.*

[9] *Printing Specialties and Paper Converters Union, Local 388, A.F.L.* (*Sealright Pacific, Ltd.*), 82 NLRB No. 36.

[10] See also, *Denver Building and Construction Trades Council etc.* (*Earl C. Gould and John C. Preisner, d/b/a Gould & Preisner*), 82 NLRB No. 137, involving a general contractor and a non-union subcontractor operating on the same construction project. There the Board held that the union had directed its picketing activities at the general contractor, a secondary employer. Thus identified, the union's conduct was found to be violative of Section 8 (b) (4) (A). A similar factual situation was presented in *International Brotherhood of Electric Workers, Local 501, A.F. of L., and William Patterson* (*Samuel Langer*), 62 NLRB No. 132.

lish a picket line at the New Jersey terminal and yet allow Schultz to carry on its extensive business activities in New York City, unhampered by the Respondent's protesting voice at the very scene of their labor dispute. Section 8 (b) (4) (A) does not, in our opinion, require that the Respondent limit its appeal to the public in so drastic a manner.

In their dissenting opinion the minority argue that Schultz' employees were engaged in a secondary boycott by picketing at the premises of Schultz' customers. We are at a loss to understand the criteria employed by the minority, other than a strong conviction that they have correctly interpreted "the rules for legality as set down by Congress," to reach their conclusion. The minority evidently regard as insignificant the facts: (1) that Respondent's picketing was limited strictly in time and area to *Schultz' trucks*; (2) that the employees involved in the labor dispute were employed by Schultz as truck drivers in New York City; (3) that Schultz, at the time of the picketing, was engaged in his normal business of transportation in that city. We think these factors most important.

It would seem clear that the truck drivers employed on Schultz' trucks are directly concerned only with the business of driving those trucks in New York City. Whatever their interest in the New Jersey terminal, that interest results from their employee interest in the transportation aspect of Schultz' business, not the reverse, as in the *Sealright* case,[11] where a union of production employees picketed the trucks of an independent operator at a scene remote from the situs of the labor dispute. The Respondent union was free within the bounds of *primary* action to publish to the world the facts of its dispute with Schultz and thereby enlist public support for its cause. Concededly, in selecting a forum to air its grievance, it chose those locations and occasions most likely to advise Schultz' customers and their employees in New York City that the replacement drivers, about to load or unload produce for Schultz, were taking the jobs of the regular truck drivers who had been locked out by their employer. But the forum so selected was *within the immediate vicinity of Schultz' own trucking operations and the aggrieved employees' own employment*.[12]

Indeed, as the Trial Examiner found, there was no other place in New York City where the Respondent could give adequate notice of its dispute with Schultz.[13] It therefore selected the struck vehicles as the most appropriate ob-

---

[11] *Supra.*

[12] Citing the *Northland Greyhound* case, 80 NLRB No. 60, the minority contend that Schultz' trucks are not the truck drivers' place of employment. In the cited case the Board, faced with a problem of conflict of State laws, held that the law of the State in which the employer's headquarters was located should determine the place of employment of bus drivers for the purpose of holding a union-authorization election. The *Greyhound* case does not determine the location of an employer's business or of truck drivers' employment for the purpose of defining primary picketing.

[13] We do not find it necessary, however, to accept the Trial Examiner's finding that the location of Schultz' trucks on the premises of its customers and consignees constituted the former's "place of business" in New York City. It is sufficient, in our view, that the trucks were the main instrumentality of Schultz' mobile business

jects of primary pressure. In so doing the Respondent was acting in a manner traditional to employees in all other industries, who choose to stand before their place of employment and point out their replacements to the interested public as strike-breakers, and their employer as unfair. Such picketing, virtually synonymous with the right to strike, is an exercise of a historic right thought necessary to the effectiveness of a strike. We do not believe that the truck-driving employees in this case should be denied substantially the same right to advertise their grievance in the most effective manner possible, through a picket line around their peripatetic employer's trucks, which comprise that employer's own business in New York City at the point of direct contact with the patronage of its customers and consignees.[14]

In our opinion Respondent's picketing was directed solely at the continued functioning of Schultz' business while its employees, some of whom had been employed on the picketed trucks from 6 to 13 years, were locked out of their jobs. Viewed in this context, we cannot regard the incidental interference with the business of other employers as sufficient to convert the Respondent's otherwise lawful primary picketing into unlawful secondary conduct.[15] Significantly, those employers are not before this Board complaining of any interference with their business. Rather, the available evidence indicates that the secondary

---

activities in that city, without adopting terminology commonly used with reference to fixed geographical premises.

Schultz, in fact, did not occupy a "place of business" in New York City. The retained dispatcher's office on 17th Street was used only to receive and relay telephone calls. Apparently it was the practice of Schultz' drivers to contact the dispatcher either by telephone or by stopping there to receive instructions. Customers did not come into physical contact with this office, nor does the evidence indicate that the drivers were required to do so.

[14] Our dissenting colleagues argue that the application of this reasoning to the transportation industry "removes from the protection of Section 8 (b) (4) (A) all employers doing business with truckers. . . ." We contemplate no such sweeping consequences from our decision that the facts in this case establish the primary nature of Respondent's picketing activities. The fact that the secondary employers in this case, as in the *Ryan* and *Pure Oil* cases, *supra*, were incidentally affected by the primary pressure exerted against a primary employer does not *per se* change the primary nature of the picketing. A different case would be presented had Respondent failed to confine its picketing to Schultz' trucks or had it otherwise employed secondary pressure against Schultz' customers.

[15] Our dissenting colleagues ascribe to our opinion "the application of the test of effectiveness" in determining the legality of Respondent's conduct. "The right to strike," they assert, "is not equivalent to the right to conduct an effective strike." Nowhere in our decision do we find that the right to strike encompasses all forms of effective picketing. We had thought it clear that our decision rests squarely on the proposition that Respondent, by picketing Schultz' business at the situs of the labor dispute, had engaged in primary, rather than secondary, activity. It would seem self-evident that effective *primary* picketing is a common incident of a lawful strike without which the phrase "right to strike" would lose much of its meaning. This type of picketing, we have held, is not a violation of the Act, whether or not it happens to be effective.

employers in this case adopted a strict hands-off policy toward Schultz in the latter's dispute with the Respondent. William Haughton, superintendent of consignee Manhattan Refrigerating Company, testified credibly, contrary to the testimony of Louis J. Schultz, that the Respondent at no time threatened to picket the premises of that company or to induce its employees to engage in a strike against their employer. Both Haughton and Joseph K. Storer,[16] vice president of Manhattan Refrigerating Co., testified that their employees, in fact, were not requested and therefore did not refuse to handle products on the picketed vehicles.[17]

CONCLUSION

We conclude, on the basis of all the facts in the case, that the Respondent has engaged only in primary picketing of a primary employer and that such picketing is not violative of Section 8 (*b*) (4) (*A*). Accordingly, we shall dismiss the complaint in its entirety.

JAMES J. REYNOLDS, JR., AND J. COPELAND GRAY, MEMBERS, DISSENTING

The facts of this case relative to the picketing are simple. Upon entering New York City, Schultz' trucks were trailed by the Respondent's members in automobiles. When a Schultz truck reached a consignee's premises it was either parked in front of such premises or driven on the premises to a loading dock. The Respondent's members then left their vehicles and formed a picket line around the truck, either on or in front of the consignee's premises, depending upon the location of the truck. When Schultz' truck left the particular consignee's premises, the picketing of the premises ceased. No attempt was made to picket Schultz' terminal in New Jersey, or his New York City office even though on a number of occasions and for hours at a time Schultz' trucks stopped there.

The Respondent was involved in a labor dispute with Schultz. It was not engaged in a labor dispute with any of Schultz' New York City customers or consignees. Schultz is therefore the primary employer, while his New York City customers and consignees are secondary employers. The question before this Board is whether or not the Respondent Union's picketing on or in front of the premises of the secondary employers, as above described, is prohibited by Section 8 (*b*) (4) (*A*) of the Act.

There is no controversy over the fact that Respondent's pickets were on or in front of the premises of secondary employers while carrying on their picketing. Nor can there be any doubt that they had as an objective the inducement and encouragement of the employees of the secondary employers to refuse to perform their duties in order to force the secondary employers to cease doing business with Schultz. At the hearing in this matter counsel for the Respondents stated: "We did not want to picket in Trenton where it does no good. We want to picket where it will be effective." Again he stated: "Of course we hoped

---

[16] The name of this official is incorrectly designated as "Joseph K. Stover" in the Intermediate Report.

[17] Haughton's testimony to this effect appears in the Intermediate Report.

that the men [employees of Schultz' customers] wouldn't unload the trucks in front of the picket line. That was the only way we could be effective. Of course we hoped that." In the *Gould and Preisner* case, footnote 10, *supra*, where, as here, the picketing occurred at a secondary employer's premises during the presence thereon of employees of the primary employer, this Board found a violation of the Act. In that case, significantly, the Board's decision rested in part on admissions of the respondent as to its motives including a statement in its brief to the effect that "the only way in which it was feasible for the unions to exert economic pressure on Gould and Preisner was to withhold their labor on projects where Gould and Preisner men were employed."

The majority here differentiates this case from the previous ones, including *Gould and Preisner,* involving the violation of the same Section of the Act by establishing two new doctrines: (1) In the trucking industry the *trucks* of the employer are both his place of business and the situs of employment of his employees, and (2) the right to strike is equated with the right to conduct an *effective* strike. We are unable to concur with either of these doctrines.

The establishment of this type of mobile labor dispute has manifold defects. Among other things this reasoning ignores our decisions in other cases, among them the *Northland Greyhound* case,[18] in which we were faced with the problem of ascertaining the place of employment of bus drivers for the purposes of conducting a union-authorization election. We held that the focal point of the employment relationship of the bus drivers was their headquarters, that is, the place where they reported to work, received their instructions, and were paid. We believe the same tests are applicable to the truck drivers here. If, however, the test used by the majority for the Teamsters in this case is followed in the future, the situs of the labor dispute, the place of employment of the drivers, and the picketing may be found in any places which the trucks visit. Application of today's decision to other businesses in which an employee works *from* rather than *in* an office or factory, if consistency were our criterion, points to the conclusion that a sample bag, a tool kit, or a brief case is the place of employment of a salesman, a craftsman, or an insurance agent respectively, and the right of a union to picket in a dispute involving such employees will be determined by the location of the sample bag, tool kit, or brief case.

More particularly, the application of this doctrine removes from the protection of Section 8 (*b*) (4) (*A*) all employers doing business with truckers, for it is their premises that become the primary premises of the trucker at least while his trucks are loading or unloading there. This we consider to be an unwarranted limitation of the intent of Congress to protect neutral third party employers at their own places of business from the discord resulting from a labor dispute between a primary employer and his employees. In this connection we find no significance in the Respondent's limitation of its picketing to that area of a secondary employer's premises around Schultz' trucks or to a time limited to when Schultz' trucks were on the secondary employer's premises. There is no requirement in the Act that the striking union set its secondary

---

[18] *Northland Greyhound Lines, Inc.,* 80 NLRB No. 60.

boycott aim at completely disrupting the operations of the secondary employer but only that he ultimately be brought, by the failure or refusal of his employees to perform services, to the point of ceasing to do business with the primary employer. The limited picketing here was obviously and admittedly aimed at this proscribed result. It follows therefore that the facts of this case are completely dissimilar to those of the *Pure Oil* case, *supra*, cited and quoted by our colleagues, because there the picketing was limited to the premises of the primary employer.

The second theory advanced and relied on by the majority of our colleagues and with which we cannot agree is the justification of the actions of the Respondent on the grounds that it was "the only effective means of bringing pressure on Schultz. . . ." This conclusion is followed by the observation that "it would have been unrealistic, indeed, of the Respondent to establish a picket line at the New Jersey Terminal and yet allow Schultz to carry on its extensive business activities in New York City, unhampered by the Respondent's protesting voice at the very scene of the labor dispute."

The application of a rule of effectiveness in reaching a determination as to whether or not there has been a violation of the statute is novel to us. We had heretofore assumed that the Congress intended to prohibit certain types of activities to labor organizations. The secondary boycott is one of these activities. We do not deny that the activities of labor organizations prohibited by the amendment of the Act are effective. It was this very effectiveness which led to their proscription when the Congress determined that such activities were inimical to the public welfare. To now determine that one of the tests of the legality of the activity here in question is that the forum chosen was the only effective one open to the Respondents injects, in our opinion, an irrelevant consideration into our deliberations. The right to strike is not equivalent to the right to conduct an *effective* strike. Congress has seen fit to limit the areas in which industrial conflict may be carried on and it should not be our function to find otherwise. The Court of Appeals for the Ninth Circuit stated:

> Congress has now undertaken, in the exercise of its power under the Commerce Clause, to prohibit altogether or sharply to curtail the use by labor organizations of certain economic weapons which they have heretofore freely employed. In an effort to narrow the area of industrial strife, and thus to safeguard the national interest in the free flow of commerce, it has in effect banned picketing when utilized to conscript in a given struggle the employees of an employer who is not himself a party to the dispute.[19]

Finally, we fail to see the significance attached by the majority to the fact that the secondary employers herein did not file charges with this Board. This novel test of violation of the Act has no bearing whatever on the factual issue before us. In cases without number the fact that all possible complainants were not before us had not weighed our judgment. For instance, to cite one of the many cases available, we found a violation in a matter closely analogous to

[19] *Printing Specialties and Converters Union, et al.* v. *Le Baron*, 171 F. 2d 331 (C.A. 9).

this one in the *Sealright* case, *supra*, where the secondary employers had not complained of the violation.

By way of conclusion and recapitulation we again must express our disapproval of the majority's enunciation of the doctrine of a roving situs and place of employment in the case of the trucking industry and the correlative theory that this industry creates a special problem deserving of special treatment. We know of no precedent for the first of these two theories and forecast that consistent application of this doctrine will largely vitiate the provisions of Section 8 (*b*) (4) (A) as to all employers using transportation in their business. Nor do we find sanction in the Act or precedent in the body of the law for designating one group of labor organizations for unique treatment when on its face the applicable statute makes no such exemption. The majority has further condoned the actions of the Teamsters by finding that the picketing it conducted was the only *effective* means at its command. We are confounded by the application of the test of effectiveness to the legality of the Respondent's activities. We find no mandate upon us to guarantee a labor organization the right to conduct an effective strike as opposed to an abortive one. The sole test which we are deputized to apply is whether or not the activity in question is conducted within the rules for legality as set down by Congress. Our colleagues also advert to the fact that the pickets marched closely around Schultz' trucks and departed when the trucks departed. Disagreeing as we do with the roving situs theory of the majority we find no significance in this behavior. Even were we to grant the validity of this theory the air of legality with which the majority clothes the Respondent's activities was completely wafted away at the hearing in this matter when counsel for the Respondent repeatedly admitted the object of the picketing to be the inducement of the employees of the secondary employer to refuse to perform their duties with the object of forcing the secondary employer to cease doing business with Schultz.

As we do not believe that the cab of a truck is a place of employment or that the truck itself is the place of business of Schultz, or that the Respondent is entitled to the most effective place to advertise its labor dispute without regard to the proscriptions of the law, we must therefore conclude that by carrying their labor dispute to the premises of secondary employers for admittedly unlawful purposes the Respondent herein has violated Section 8 (*b*) (4) (A) of the Act.

International Brotherhood of Teamsters and Sterling Beverages, 90 NLRB No. 75, 1950

DECISION AND ORDER

In the recent *Schultz* case,[1] we had occasion to consider whether a labor organization had violated Section 8 (*b*) (4) (A) of the Act by picketing the trucks upon which its members were employed at the situs of a labor dispute with an employer, who was engaged in the business of transportation. As the

[1] *Schultz Refrigerated Service, Inc.*, 87 NLRB No. 82.

Trial Examiner in the instant case observed, the dividing line between primary and secondary picketing is not susceptible of the application of a rigid formula, but must turn upon a careful analysis of the relevant facts in each case. In the *Schultz* case a majority of the Board found that the picketing complained of was primary picketing and therefore not violative of the Act. It was particularly important in that case, as here, to examine the means whereby the respondent union sought to bring pressure against the primary employer Schultz, because in both cases the picketing occurred in front of the premises of a secondary employer, who was a neutral party to the labor dispute. Under the circumstances of the *Schultz* case, the majority was persuaded that the respondent had clearly identified its picketing with the actual functioning of the primary employer's business at the scene of their labor dispute. The record in that case disclosed that the pickets had paraded in a U-shaped manner around Schultz' trucks. Pointing to this fact as evidence of the primary nature of the union's conduct, the majority's decision emphasized "that Respondent's picketing was limited strictly in time and area to *Schultz' trucks.*" In a *caveat* to its decision the Board elsewhere stated: "A different case would be presented had Respondent failed to confine its picketing to Schultz' trucks or had it otherwise employed secondary pressure against Schultz' customers."

The record in the instant case reveals that on at least two occasions the Respondent Union placed pickets at the entrance to Ruppert's brewery in anticipation of the arrival and during and after the presence inside the plant of trucks belonging to Sterling, the primary Employer with whom the Respondent Union had a labor dispute. Because the loading platforms here were located inside the plant area, rather than abutting on a public street as in the *Schultz* case, the pickets could not picket around the trucks themselves while they were being unloaded. Of necessity they were limited to picketing the *Ruppert plant entrances* through which the trucks had passed. The placards carried by the pickets stated that the Union's dispute was with Sterling. Nevertheless, the picketing constituted inducement or encouragement of the employees of Ruppert, the secondary employer, to cease handling products on Sterling trucks. As we have previously held,[2] such picketing comes within the proscription of Section 8 (b) (4) (A), unless we were to agree with the Trial Examiner that the picketing was "direct primary labor activity aimed immediately at the employer involved in the principal dispute" and only incidentally affecting the secondary employer.[3] On the basis of the facts in this case we cannot so agree.

The record in this case discloses that pickets of the Respondent paraded in front of the secondary employer's premises when Sterling's trucks were not physically present at Ruppert's plant and failed to establish that direct and immediate relationship between the picketing and the object picketed necessary to a finding of purely primary picketing. Thus a driver for Sterling testified,

[2] *Wadsworth Building Company, Inc.*, and *Klassen & Hodgson, Inc.*, 81 NLRB 802; *Sealright Pacific, Ltd.*, 82 NLRB 271.

[3] *The Pure Oil Company*, 84 NLRB No. 38; *Ryan Construction Corporation*, 85 NLRB No. 76; *Schultz Refrigerated Service, Inc., supra*.

without contradiction, that when his truck approached the Ruppert brewery, Respondent's picket was already patrolling the entrance to the plant. On another occasion, when a Sterling truck had entered the Ruppert driveway, a picket appeared and continued to patrol in front of Ruppert's premises for at least 15 and possibly more minutes after all of Sterling's trucks had left the secondary employer's plant. In our opinion, such picketing, unlike that in the *Schultz* case which was directed solely at Schultz' trucks, was not confined to the primary Employer's *trucks,* but extended directly to the secondary employer's own premises.[4] The line must be drawn somewhere, and this is where we draw it.

We therefore find, contrary to the Trial Examiner, that the Respondent Union has violated Section 8 (*b*) (4) (A) of the amended Act by picketing the premises of Jacob Ruppert.

JOHN M. HOUSTON, MEMBER, DISSENTING

In my judgment, the determination of my colleagues that the Respondent violated Section 8 (*b*) (4) (A) by picketing cannot be supported on the facts of this case. Their decision today appears to be inconsistent with the sound principles enunciated only a few months ago by a majority of the Board in the *Schultz* case.[5]

After most careful and thorough consideration, we specifically stated in the *Schultz* case that, in determining whether picketing is protected as primary action, an "important test is the identification of such picketing with the actual functioning of the primary employer's business at the *situs* of the labor dispute" (emphasis contained in original decision). We found in that case that the test was met by substantial evidence that the labor dispute related to the drivers of Schultz' truck, and that the picketing at the operations of other employers was *identified* with Schultz' business because it occurred in the area of the latter's trucks and because the placards used disclosed Schultz as the struck employer.

In the case before us now, the sole dispute between the Respondent and Sterling related to the conduct of Sterling's terminal operations at Ruppert's plant. The picketing by the Respondent was *strictly* confined to the entrances

---

[4] This distinction, in the opinion of Board Member Murdock, is emphasized by the fact that Sterling's trucks, which the Respondent was allegedly picketing, were at all times beyond the ambulatory range of the patrolling picket. In the *Schultz* case the proximity of the picketing to Schultz' trucks made incidental its effect on the secondary employer's business. Here, the physical situation was such that the Respondent could not relate its picketing at Ruppert's plant directly and immediately to its alleged objective. Conceding that the Respondent may have found itself in a difficult position, Member Murdock does not believe that the doctrine of the *Schultz* case should be extended further to make picketing in front of a secondary employer's premises lawful, where the nexus between the. picketing and the truck allegedly picketed is as tenuous as it is in this case. The attempt in the dissenting opinion to harmonize the facts of the two cases serves only to accentuate their distinction.

[5] *Schultz Refrigerated Service, Inc.,* 87 NLRB No. 82.

to Ruppert's unloading platforms [6] *at times* when Sterling's trucks and employees were present or immediately expected. And the placards similarly referred to Sterling alone as the struck Employer.[7] Yet, despite this positive identification of the picketing with Sterling's business at the very situs of the labor dispute, the majority in this case reaches a directly opposite conclusion and finds that the picketing was not primary but secondary action and therefore illegal.

. . . Chairman Herzog and Member Murdock, in an apparent attempt to distinguish the two cases, attach overriding significance to the fact that, on two occasions, picketing was conducted when Sterling's trucks were not on Ruppert's premises. Member Murdock relies, in addition, on the circumstance that the picketing here occurred on the public thoroughfare at the entrance to Ruppert's unloading platforms, rather than around the trucks themselves. Upon analysis, however, I find these distinctions are not substantial or persuasive.[8]

With respect to the picketing at times when Sterling's trucks were not present, my two colleagues refer only to the testimony of driver St. Laurent, to the effect, that when he arrived at the entrance to the unloading platform on March 28, he "saw" a picket there, and to the testimony of Sterling's treasurer, Faria, that on March 29, picketing continued for 15 minutes after one of Sterling's trucks had left the unloading platform. The triviality of these instances, in the face of the overwhelming evidence that the Respondent's picketing was directed solely at Sterling's operations, I should have thought would be readily conceded. However, in any event, as to the March 28 incident, the record shows that Sterling's trucks were then operating on a well-established unloading schedule, concerning which the Respondent was undoubtedly fully apprised; and that late the next morning, when Sterling was proceeding on an off-schedule basis, no picketing whatsoever was commenced until *after* Sterling's truck had entered Ruppert's premises. Therefore, the only realistic conclusion justified by the record is that the arrival of the trucks on March 28 and the appearance of the picket were virtually coincidental. As to the March 29 incident, it is significant that during the 15 minutes found to be so critical by my colleagues, Sterling's treasurer, Faria, was still on the premises, and the picket was apparently unaware that Sterling's other three trucks, which were parked on the public street at some distance from the entrance, had been directed to leave the area. Any picketing during this interval of 15 minutes resulted solely from the misapprehension of the picket, induced by the con-

[6] These platforms were 50 feet or less from the plant entrances and were in open view.

[7] The alleged secondary employer in the present case is not before the Board complaining of any interference with its business, a factor also expressly mentioned as "significant" in the *Schultz* case.

[8] It may be observed that at the hearing in this proceeding, which occurred after the issuance of the Intermediate Report in the *Schultz* case, the General Counsel admitted that: "If there ever was a twin case, that [the *Schultz* case] is a twin case to this one."

tinued presence of Faria, that other Sterling trucks would immediately enter the premises.

As to the location of the pickets on the public thoroughfare, the necessary implication of Member Murdock's finding would seem to be that, in order to exercise its right to conduct lawful primary picketing in this very common situation, a union must first *unlawfully* trespass upon an employer's property. There is no warrant for such a holding either in the *Schultz* case or in any provision in the Act. The test, as I have already noted, is the identification of the picketing with the operations of the primary employer at the scene of the dispute. Here, the sole dispute related to the backing up or terminal operations conducted by Sterling on Ruppert's premises.[9] And identification of the picketing with Sterling's operations at this actual situs of the dispute was enhanced, rather than impaired, when the Respondent confined its picketing to those very platform entrances where Sterling's trucks unloaded.

Accordingly, as the Respondent's picketing was conducted at the situs of its labor dispute with Sterling and was unmistakably identified with the functioning of Sterling's business by virtue of: (*a*) the location of the pickets at the entrances where Sterling's trucks were about to be unloaded; (*b*) the strict limiting of the picketing to those times when Sterling's trucks and employees were present or immediately expected; and (*c*) the display of placards unequivocally identifying Sterling alone as the struck employer, I would find, under the authority of the *Schultz* case, that such picketing was protected primary activity. Consequently this complaint should be dismissed.

Excerpts from remarks of NLRB General Counsel Robert N. Denham before the American Trucking Association, Washington, D.C., January 30, 1950

You will recall that Section 8 (*b*) (4) of the law provides that it will be an unfair labor practice for a union "to engage in or to induce or encourage the *employees of any employer to engage in a strike or a concerted refusal, etc.*"

The key spot here is that the language I have just quoted applies solely to the encouragement or inducement of *employees* of any other employer to refuse to handle merchandise, etc., etc. There are many business men—probably many of you—who have the business agent of some union which may or may not represent your employees, come to you in the front office and say, in effect, "Mr. Boss, I represent Local 123 of the X Union, and we are having a little dispute and trouble with the ABC Company. As a matter of fact, we have struck the place and have a picket line there. Now we would appreciate it very much if you would just not buy any more merchandise from them, or send any of your trucks down to pick up merchandise, or deliver any merchandise to them as long as that situation lasts. I hope you will cooperate with us to that extent but, of course, if you don't care to, why, then, we may find that it is necessary to put a picket line in front of your place, too." I don't have to tell you that the answer of most merchants and manufacturers in busi-

---

[9] Member Murdock, by requiring the Respondent to invade Ruppert's premises to picket around the trucks, is shrivelling the situs of the dispute from the terminal operations to the trucks themselves.

ness would generally be, "Well, I don't want any trouble. I can get along without buying any of that fellow's stuff or selling anything to him until after he gets over this dispute. All right, I'll go along with you." And so the business agent has established his boycott, and you don't buy or sell any more merchandise to the fellow whose place is on strike. You don't know why the strike exists, or whether there is any merit in the dispute. You haven't any interest in it one way or another; all you do know is that he is a man with whom you normally would do business, and you do know that if you don't do what the union says, you will find a picket line in front of your place.

Well, the next move is that the ABC Company files a charge against the union, alleging a secondary boycott in violation of Section 8 (*b*) (4) (*A*) of the law. There's no question about this being a boycott of a very vicious sort, but because the business agent talked to the Boss and not to the employees, even though the end result is the same, there is absolutely no remedy provided in the National Labor Relations Act. In short, there's a secondary boycott that isn't a secondary boycott within the meaning of the law as presently written.

Statement of General Electric Co., in Taft-Hartley Act Revisions, hearings before the Senate Committee on Labor and Public Welfare, 83d Cong., 1st Sess., 1953, part 2, pp. 975–976

SECONDARY BOYCOTT—A CASE HISTORY

In the early morning hours of May 10, 1951, at a plant near Paterson, N. J., a truck of the Hoffman-Quinlan Transportation Co., driven by one L. Reyngoudt, set out with a truckload of steel upon a trip to the General Electric Co. plant at Schenectady, N. Y., a run of about 150 to 200 miles. Driver Reyngoudt was a member in good standing of his Paterson, N. J. local of the International Brotherhood of Teamsters, Chauffeurs, and Warehousemen (usually called the teamsters).

But the kingdom of the teamsters is, in some respects, not unlike mediaeval kingdoms, and is divided into duchies, or perhaps, baronies, with fixed and rigid territorial boundaries. And somewhere near Albany, N. Y., driver Reyngoudt's truck passed out of the Duchy of Paterson and into the Barony of Local 294 of the teamsters, which is ruled by its business agent, Peter Postma. The Barony of Postma, like many teamster domains, has a quaint native custom, under which all trucks entering its borders from other parts of the teamster kingdom must hire a local 294 driver. Of course, since trucks which enter the barony from outside eventually leave the barony to return to their place of origin, the "outside" driver does not normally step out of the truck at the changeover, but the local 294 driver merely steps into the truck and receives a pleasant ride, with pay, from Albany headquarters of the Barony of Postma to the truck's destination and back again.

Being aware of this charming custom of the area, driver Reyngoudt drove directly to local 294's headquarters in Albany (which is about 20 miles from Schenectady), with the anticipation of a half hour's pleasant companion on

the last lap of his trip. However, for reasons unknown, Reyngoudt was not
supplied with a native to occupy the featherbedded seat in his truck. So after
waiting 3 hours, he phoned his seniors at the Hoffman-Quinlan Co., and was
told that he might as well go on to the GE plant alone.

Although driver Reyngoudt had felt unnoticed and forsaken at Albany, his
lonely departure did not go unnoticed, for he had hardly come within sight
of the GE plant when the Baron of Postma imperiously ordered James Reid, an
official of the GE plant, not to unload Reyngoudt's truck. When Reid ventured
to inquire what would happen if the truck were unloaded, the Baron informed
him that all truck deliveries to and from the plant would stop.

Mr. Reid, being a brave man and unsympathetic with native customs which
waste money and retard progress, ordered the truck unloaded, and behold—
trucks of all sizes, makes, and colors owned by independent trucking firms
stopped and turned away from the gates of the GE plant.

But not all the trucks turned away, for the "Baron of Postma" and his advisers are not without guile, and they knew that they were doing something
which Congress had meant to condemn in the Taft-Hartley Act as a secondary
boycott. But they had noted that section 8 (b) (4) of that act had been written
to condemn secondary boycotts only in cases where employees were induced
or encouraged [not] to perform work. Consequently, the "Baron of Postma"
told a small unit of truck drivers of the GE plant, which unit was represented
by local 294, to continue to work and drive the GE trucks. But he had called
the truck owners in the Albany-Troy-Schenectady area, who do most of the
trucking in and out of the GE plant, and induced them, the employers, to call
their trucks away. Thus, since employers, rather than employees, had been induced to participate in a secondary boycott, local 294 could not be guilty of
an unfair labor practice under section 8 (b) (4), or be sued for damages under
section 303. The NLRB and a Federal court of appeals have so held (*Conway's
Express* (87 N.L.R.B. 972); *NLRB v. Conway's Express* (195 F (2d) 906),
in both of which cases the "Baron of Postma" also was involved).

Now, the truck owners in the Albany-Troy-Schenectady area did not call off
their trucks because of any affection for the Baron, or any disaffection for
GE. As they plaintively explained it to two GE representatives, they were
subject to the Baron's will, and could not hope to continue in business if they
offended him in any way. They were sympathetic with GE's problem, and
they hated to lose the GE plant business, but they had to bow the knee
when the Baron clapped his sword and bellowed.

*Testimony of Arthur J. Goldberg, General Counsel, Congress of Industrial
Organizations, in Taft-Hartley Act Revisions, hearings before the Senate Committee on Labor and Public Welfare, 83d Cong., 1st Sess., 1953, part 1, pp.
581–584*

I would like to make this general observation about this [secondary boycott]
provision: This provision involves the very difficult question of to what extent
boycotts and strikes and other activities in connection with boycotts are to be

permitted and to what extent they are to be prohibited by provisions of law.

This section as written practically makes illegal all of the traditional types of boycott operations that unions engaged in and have felt it was necessary for them to engage in in order for them to protect their legitimate interests. I note with considerable satisfaction, Senator Taft, your amendment now proposing to liberalize this section in part, which is contained on page 24 of the committee print, and which reads:

That nothing in (A) of this section shall be construed to make it an unfair labor practice for a labor organization to induce or encourage employees to engage in a concerted refusal to perform work which because of a current labor dispute between another employer and his employees is, for the duration of such dispute, no longer being performed by the employees of such other employer.

Your amendment then would—

SENATOR TAFT: We have met a lot of criticism from that, I must say—at least I have—from the other side, from the employers.

MR. GOLDBERG: I would assume that there would be criticism from that source, and yet it seems to me—

SENATOR TAFT: And there is some proper criticism. Certainly it has to be more clearly defined.

MR. GOLDBERG: The difficulty in this field in general is always the question of how to define what you are attempting to make legal, and to render illegal. But I say the basic principle of that amendment which protects the right of employees not to work on struck goods is certainly a sound provision. This is something that labor people regard to be immoral, something that they regard to be an unjustified prohibition on their legitimate activity.

SENATOR TAFT: However, the provision was intended to cover the case where a plant is operating and when the strike comes they transfer their work to some other plant. It was certainly not intended to authorize the case of refusal, for example, if you were building a house, to accept millwork from a firm manufacturing millwork, which is an entirely different line of operation. I do not know that it does. I only raise that question. I certainly did not intend to authorize the general theory that just because goods were coming from a plant where there was no union, or even where there was a strike, that the union could refuse to handle those goods in subsequent manufacture into something else. I certainly did not intend that. It has been criticized as perhaps being able to be construed to that effect.

MR. GOLDBERG: Of course, I had hoped that the Senator covered that.

SENATOR TAFT: I think I explained the purpose of it when I introduced it in 1949. I do not think it is fair for a firm which is having a strike to transfer the job to some other place and then make the men work on it there.

MR. GOLDBERG: I agree with that entirely.

SENATOR TAFT: I think that is the main feature. Just how far beyond that it ought to go, that is what we are trying to determine.

MR. GOLDBERG: My own view, the position we have taken before and which we reassert now, is that if you are going to have labor activity that is meaningful in a competitive society, you have got to give the labor organizations the opportunity not only to conduct the boycott that you have defined in the limited way that you have now defined it, but you have got to extend that to a broader area if we really are going to believe in competition between labor and industry in the protection of standards.

SENATOR TAFT: I do not agree to that at all. Fundamentally, the secondary boycott provision is this: It is not a dispute between the employer and his employees. The whole idea is to protect some third party who is not involved in that dispute, who is conducting his business as he sees fit to do it, from being injured by a secondary boycott by the employees, the labor union. . . . This is solely the question of third parties not being injured because of a dispute in which they are in no way involved.

MR. GOLDBERG: Are they not necessarily involved in the dispute when they are handling the goods of a party that is involved in the dispute?

SENATOR TAFT: I do not think they ought to be in any way involved. The answer is "No."

MR. GOLDBERG: Let me put to you, then, again, the case I think I put to you in 1949, which I think still is the classical case, and that is the *Duplex* v. *Deering* case that we discussed in 1949. I looked at it again last night just to refresh my recollection of it.

How can it be said from the facts of that case that this party is a neutral party? Let me recall again what the facts were.

The machinists' union had organized three firms that made presses. They had contracts with those 3 firms to grant the 8-hour day, to establish a minimum wage scale, and to comply with other wage standards. The Duplex Co. refused to do this. It was the fourth firm that made presses. They were the four firms in the United States that made presses. The Duplex Co. operated on a 10-hour day. It refused to establish the minimum wage scale. It disregarded other standards that at least now, by the experience of the times, we would regard to be minimum wage standards.

The machinists' union was then approached by the 3 employers in the industry that they had organized, and the 3 employers in the industry said to the machinists' union, "If you are unable to maintain the standards of this industry, we are going to have to go back on the 8-hour day that we gave you, we are going to have to establish a 10-hour day; we are going to have to establish a contract that contains no minimum wage standard, and we are going to have to abrogate the provisions of our contract with you that provide for fairly tolerable working conditions in the plants."

Faced with that situation, the machinists' union, back in the 1920's then went out and declared a boycott of Duplex products.

SENATOR TAFT: Absolutely unjustifiable; absolutely unjustifiable. Your argument leads to the conclusion that the Government must fix wages in all the plants; that they must see that there is no variation in this scale set up by the unions in agreement. Oh, yes; absolutely. You say that although the Government cannot do that, we will let all the people, by indirect pressure on all their customers, force them to do what these other three people have agreed to do.

No; I think this is an absolute denial of the entire theory of free collective bargaining and free business in the United States.

Incidentally, in this committee, there was not any legitimate objection to outlawing secondary boycotts when we had these hearings in 1947. The committee agreed, I think 13 to 2, that really there was practically no defense against it.

I remember Senator Morse and Senator Ives trying to devise special methods to stop this, which is recognized as an outrage in the labor field. That is the field of secondary boycotts.

I just cannot see any argument for supporting secondary boycotts.

MR. GOLDBERG: I would like to make the argument, I would say that under the facts as I gave them to you, it is not a question of Government fixing wage standards at all. It is a question of allowing people to use economic power against economic power, and by that competition to try to arrive at an adjustment of conflicting interests.

SENATOR TAFT: There was some argument for secondary boycotts when you had no Wagner Act at all, but today if you want to organize a plant you have a method of going in and persuading the employees that there ought to be a union. If you cannot persuade them, then there ought not to be a union and there ought not to be any indirect pressure on their products and their work to make them unionized. . . .

On your same theory, this one case, you could put on a boycott of every nonunion plant in the United States that is not organized, even though they are paying wages higher than your wages, even though there are no sweatshop conditions.

We have a minimum wage law to prevent sweatshop conditions.

MR. GOLDBERG: I think you and I would agree that the minimum wage law we have does not adequately protect against sweatshop conditions, and that it ought to be improved.

SENATOR TAFT: I think it perhaps is not wide enough, but as far as the rate is concerned for the minimum wage, it is all right. Of course, it is not what you would call a standard wage.

MR. GOLDBERG: I hope that this committee will take under consideration the question of improving the minimum wage, but the point I am making is that I think the jungle prevails, not in the way that you indicated, but the jungle prevails when an employer can upset the established labor standards of an industry in the way that Duplex attempted to upset it and was successful in part—

SENATOR TAFT: By persuading men to work for them and refusing to be unionized. The men were satisfied thereby, presumably, because the majority of them did not want to organize a union.

MR. GOLDBERG: But this was a perfectly peaceful appeal. It did not involve violence. This was an appeal by a union to its membership handling this product not to handle a product which they deemed to be unfair to things which the union was striving for.

SENATOR TAFT: What union?

MR. GOLDBERG: The machinists. This was their own membership. That is the point I am making. This would apply under Taft-Hartley.

SENATOR TAFT: They were not making them, because their own members were not in that plant.

MR. GOLDBERG: This was a case of installing the presses. The machinists also represented the installers of the presses, and what they were appealing to were members of their own organization.

SENATOR TAFT: So you can organize the thing on a vertical basis, as the teamsters try to organize the warehouse employees. You can work a secondary boycott to organize industries that are not even organized at all.

MR. GOLDBERG: That assumes, you know, that it is a light thing for a union to declare a secondary boycott situation. It is never a light thing for a union to appeal to its own people to refrain from working, because there is a very great economic inhibition against that. Union people cannot just appeal to people to carry on a boycott. When we say a boycott, we mean that people are asked to strike. That is not the easiest thing for union people to get other people to do.

THE IMPACT OF TAFT-HARTLEY ON THE UNIONS

Testimony of John L. Lewis, President, United Mine Workers of America, in Taft-Hartley Revisions, hearings before the Senate Committee on Labor and Public Welfare, 83d Cong., 1st Sess., 1953, part 4, pp. 1909, 1915

LAISSEZ FAIRE IN LABOR

Let the mine workers make a proposal to this committee and to the Congress. It is this: Since management has cried out so sorely against the Wagner Act and all the manifold injustices alleged to be contained therein, let them now join us in repealing the Taft-Hartley Act in toto, lock, stock, and barrel; hoof, hind, horns, and hide; horse, foot, and dragoon, including the Wagner Act itself upon which the Taft-Hartley is founded. This would give to this country, its employers, and employees an opportunity (in light of our joint experiences under both Wagner and Taft-Hartley) to practice for a season true, free, and genuine collective bargaining without governmental interference, free from the brooding shadows which presently hover over all bargaining tables. This proposal is seriously made.

The ever-rising tide of industrial strife in recent years and the repeated governmental interferences, both past and present, under existing law, and the bitterness engendered thereby in all segments of our population, justify the Congress in stripping the statute books of both the Wagner and Taft-Hartley Acts. Leave the Norris-LaGuardia and the Clayton Acts as the Federal rule and guide in the field of labor-management relations. Let it be tried for a period of time and then the voice of experience can dictate to a future Congress what, if any, legislation is needed in this field, or which may be indicated in the public interest.

. . . The first step that the Congress should take and the administration should join, would be to make the voluntary, unincorporated associations of workers in this country, entitled "labor unions", free to bargain with their employers in the American way. Restore again that ancient privilege in the market place: the right to sell or not to sell, the right to buy or not to buy, a rule just as old as civilized man. How long not to buy? That is modified by the requirements, by the needs of the potential buyer. He will make the decision. How long to withhold and not to sell? Again that is determined by the seller. The restraints that are upon him will always regulate his contact and he will always sell before he will starve and the buyer will always buy at whatever price before he will starve.

It is that basic and elemental. The human equation is there. You cannot, by fiat, regulate the bargaining in the market places. You know they tried it in ancient Rome. You know it was tried in ancient Cathay. Down through the pages of history it has been proven not expedient and not practical, and it has been impossible to maintain social, economic, or political tranquillity and stability by legislative, executive, governmental, or royal fiat.

That is what the Taft-Hartley Act is. It is a fiat from the throne of the predatory interests of this country acting through their manservants, who have seduced Congress and beguiled Congress, in anger and in haste, to commit this crime and atrocity on free America. So we say: Away with it! Let reason prevail for a time. We say away with it. Let us repeal this thing, put everybody on equality, and then the Congress can study and observers can observe and the pseudo economists can put on their slide rules and we can take a look at the result when needs must and wisdom indicates. What's the matter with that? What's the matter with it? Congress is lost in an intellectual and legislative morass on this question. It is confusion compounded! Forty bills on this question! Amendments galore and manifold. Who knows what? When will it be simplified in the American way?

Reply by George Meany, President American Federation of Labor, in Taft-Hartley Revisions, hearings before the Senate Committee on Labor and Public Welfare, 83d Cong., 1st Sess., 1953

SENATOR GRISWOLD: I am wondering if you would like to express an opinion on the suggestion made here last week by Mr. John L. Lewis that it would be better if we repealed the Taft-Hartley law and repealed the Wagner Act, I mean repealed the whole Labor-Management Relations Act, set up a good Conciliation and Mediation Service, and then let management and labor meet across the bargaining table and really argue things out.

MR. MEANY: No; I would be very much opposed to that. Of course, from the viewpoint of the well-organized unions like my own particular union and like Mr. Lewis' union, that is all right, that is fine. But from the viewpoint of the poorer-paid industries that need unionization, that is not all right.

Textile Workers of America, CIO, April, 1953, in Taft-Hartley Act Revisions, hearings before the Senate Committee on Labor and Public Welfare, 83d Cong., 1st Sess., 1953, part 3, pp. 1523–1529, 1536–1537

TAFT-HARTLEYISM IN TEXTILES, WITH SPECIAL REFERENCE TO CONDITIONS IN THE SOUTHERN BRANCH OF THE INDUSTRY

It has been said by defenders of the Taft-Hartley Act that the law cannot be so bad; that, after all, unions are still operating; they are still winning wage increases; they are still able to win strikes.

These things are true. But they do not mean that the Taft-Hartley Act is not so bad. They simply mean that the big, well-established unions, which have organized most of the workers in their jurisdiction, have so far been able to escape the worst effects of the law.

What defenders of Taft-Hartley do not mention is that in the last 5 years, new organization has been stopped dead in its tracks.

Let me show you how it has affected our own operations.

Our union represents approximately 400,000 textile workers—about one-third of the basic textile industry in the United States. About 100,000 others are organized into various splinter unions. The great majority of textile workers —some 700,000—are not organized at all, and most of these are in the Southeastern States.

We believe that industrial peace and a sound, healthy economy can be brought about in the textile industry only through the growth of union organization, especially in the South. Most of our income is spent on organizing campaigns in that area.

On pages 12 and 13 of the blue book you will find a summary of the results during the last 11 years—5½ years before the Taft-Hartley Act and 5½ years since.

The first striking fact you will notice from table 3, on page 12, is the sharp drop in the number of elections held since the act was passed. I can assure you this was not due to any reduction in our efforts. On the whole, we had more organizers on the staff, and spent more money, in the last 5½ years than

Table III. Representation Elections Lost and Won by TWUA in the South, 1942–52, Comparison of 5½ Years before with 5½ Years after Taft-Hartley

Totals	All elections		Elections won		Elections lost		Percent won	
	Number	Number employees	Number	Number employees	Number	Number employees	Number	Number employees
Before Taft-Hartley....	260	145,816	150	67,747	110	78,069	58	46
After Taft-Hartley.....	150	85,408	56	14,906	94	70,502	37	17
Total for 10-year period............	410	231,224	206	82,653	204	148,571	50	36

in the earlier period. These figures show that in most of our campaigns we were not even able to reach the point of asking for an election with any reasonable chance of winning.

THE CHAIRMAN: You mean elections for representation?

MR. RIEVE: That is right, Senator.

You will see that in the 5½ years before Taft-Hartley, we engaged in 260 representation elections in the South. We won 150, or 58 percent, involving 67,747 workers. I admit that this was not a prounion landslide; organizing in the South is not easy under any circumstances.

But look at what has happened since Taft-Hartley. In the last 5½ years we were able to engage in only 150 elections. We won 56, or 37 percent, involving only 14,906 workers.

And this is only part of the story. On page 13 you will see what took place after the elections were won.

Table IV

Of 56 NLRB elections TWUA won in the South during 5½ years (August 22, 1947 to December 31, 1952) after Taft-Hartley, the results were:

In 24 situations (43 percent) agreements were signed and companies appear to be bargaining and negotiating. (In some cases history is too short to judge.)

In 10 situations (18 percent) companies signed first agreements or stipulations but have refused to negotiate renewals, are stalling, etc., and doing all they can to eliminate the union and collective bargaining.

In 22 situations (39 percent) no agreements have been signed at all and the local unions have been wiped out.

Of 150 elections TWUA won in the South during 5½ years (January 1, 1942 to August 22, 1947) before Taft-Hartley, the results were:

In 115 situations (77 percent) agreements were signed and collective bargaining made some headway.

In 10 situations (7 percent) first agreements were signed, but companies thwarted further collective bargaining.

In 25 situations (17 percent) no agreement was signed (including at least 5 situations where plants went out of business).

In the 150 mills where elections were won before the act was passed, we have established successful and continuing collective bargaining relationships in 116 cases, or 77 percent.

In 10 cases, first agreements were negotiated but never renewed. These include some mills where elections were won during the war, and where the National War Labor Board compelled the employer to sign a reasonable contract. As soon as the War Labor Board went out of business, the employer provoked a strike and destroyed the union.

In 24 cases, or 16 percent, no agreement was ever signed. Five of these mills have been liquidated—not because of the union, but because they were marginal operations which were ready to fold up anyway.

Now let me call your attention to what has taken place in the 56 mills where we won elections after the Taft-Hartley Act.

In 24 of them, or 43 percent, contracts have been signed and a continuing relationship appears to be established. A few of these are too recent for us to be sure about them.

In 10 mills, or 18 percent first contracts or stipulations were signed, but the employers refused to deal with the union after they expired. Some of these 1-year agreements were signed by the employers to escape the possibility of contempt of court proceedings for refusing to bargain.

In 22 cases, or 39 percent, no contract has ever been signed and the local union has been wiped out.

In short, during 5½ years of the Taft-Hartley Act, we have actually established collective bargaining in a total of 24 southern mills, employing 7,364 workers. More than half the time the workers could not get a union even after they voted for one.

This tells you what has happened. It does not tell you why it happened. That is a much longer story. . . .

Let me describe, in a general way, the course of a typical organizing campaign at a typical textile mill in the South.

In the first place, let me say that we do not pick the name of a mill out of a hat, and open up a campaign. In every case we have reason to believe that the workers want and need a union. Most of the time they have told us so themselves. Once in a great while we act only on the knowledge that wages and working conditions are so far below standard that there must be a desire among the workers for a remedy.

I am making this point because it has been said by Senator Taft, among others, that we have failed in the South because the workers do not want a union. I assure you that we do not start a campaign unless we are reasonably certain of a good reception from the workers.

A campaign begins with the assignment of a single staff member—an organizer—to the project. He gets in touch with the workers who have already indicated their interest in the union. They bring him up to date on conditions in the mill; they supply him with additional names and addresses; they agree to help spread the union message to other workers.

This preliminary work is carried on, as much as possible, in secret. We all know the law forbids an employer to discharge workers for union activity. Probably the southern mill owners know it, too, but they do not let their knowledge bother them. In many mills, saying a good word for the CIO is a sure way to be fired.

If these preliminary activities indicate there is a real interest among the workers, an open campaign is begun. Additional organizers are assigned to the campaign. Leaflets are prepared and distributed at the gates. Committees of workers are organized, even though there is still a risk that they will lose their jobs.

During this period, as often as not, the employer is quiet. Of course, on some occasions the union organizers have been run out of town as soon as they appeared, by self-appointed vigilantes or even by local police. At other times union representatives have been refused accommodations at local hotels or rooming houses, and have been denied the right to rent a place for union meetings. And as I have indicated now and then there have been dismissals of pro-union workers even this early in the campaign.

But these are not typical, and it is a typical campaign I am attempting to describe. Usually the employer waits until the union asks for recognition, and files a petition for an election with the National Labor Relations Board. A union is permitted to file for an election by showing that 30 percent of the eligible workers have signed cards. But as a matter of practice our union never files for an election until more than 50 percent have signed.

As soon as a petition is filed the fun begins.

Leaders of the union movement may be fired out of hand, and if the company has a mill village, they may be evicted from their homes. . . .

Union organizers and prounion workers may be followed day and night by local police, mill supervisors, or both. . . .

SENATOR PURTELL: May I ask a question, Mr. Chairman?

THE CHAIRMAN: Senator Purtell.

SENATOR PURTELL: I noticed that when you were describing some conditions here, you said these are not typical, and it is a typical campaign that you are going to describe now. Are you now describing a typical campaign and not an unusual one?

MR. RIEVE: That is correct, Senator.

The union may be refused the right to buy advertising space in the local newspaper, or time on the local radio station. As far as the newspapers are concerned, there is no remedy at all; as for radio, the Federal Communications Commission cannot or does not provide a swift or complete remedy. . . .

Agents of the employer—agents in every sense but the terms of the Taft-Hartley Act—may conduct a violent antiunion drive, using tactics which would be illegal for the employer himself, even under the present law, and using to the fullest extent the press and radio facilities which have been denied to the union. These agents may be the chamber of commerce, or a so-called citizens' committee or even clergymen. This development is almost routine; we are surprised when it does not happen. . . .

The employer himself is sure to send out at least one antiunion letter—playing on fear, prejudice and in general the baser instincts of man. The employer may also conduct "captive audience" meetings of workers in the mill on company time. We have, over the years, presented so many cases of this kind that I will not belabor the point. I think you all know these things happen. Actually, I think it is fair to say that under the Taft-Hartley Act they are supposed to happen. At least they are encouraged to happen by the so-called free speech provision.

The result of all of these activities, in a large number of cases, is that the union withdraws its petition for an election. As you have seen when we do feel able to go through with a vote, we lose more often than we win. A majority of the workers have been convinced that it just is not healthy to vote for the union.

Several questions may have occurred to you while I have been describing this typical organizing campaign. You may be thinking that some of these employer activities are illegal, even under the Taft-Hartley Act—in particular, the firing of prounion workers. That is true. But the law has little effect, since the only penalty for such a violation is a slap on the wrist. Since the NLRB simply says, in effect, "go and sin no more," I must repeat what I have said before: The penalty for firing prounion workers is nothing more than a license fee for union-haters. . . .

You may also have in mind the fact that the final step in any organizing campaign is a secret ballot election, and therefore the workers cannot really be prevented from expressing their true feelings. Unfortunately the single safeguard of a secret vote is not enough to make up for all these antiunion activities. For one thing, we cannot convince workers we cannot reach; and in addition, the Government's guarantee of a free choice looks very weak compared to what is happening right on the scene.

Another question you may be considering is that many of these antiunion activities were also carried on under the Wagner Act. That is correct, though they were not so numerous, and the chances of obtaining a remedy from the NLRB were much better. . . .

Let us suppose that in spite of all the opposition I have described, the workers in a southern mill do in fact vote for a union. The figures I gave you at the beginning of my testimony showed that more than half the time they cannot get what they voted for.

A number of the cases in our brief, and a number of others we presented in 1950, will tell you the reasons. I will give you a summary of only one of them—the story of Aldora Mills in Barnesville, Ga. . . . This mill, I might say, is a subsidiary of the General Tire & Rubber Co.

We won an election in this mill on April 8, 1946. About a week later we wrote to the company asking for a conference. As you will see from the full record, union representatives made at least 10 efforts to arrange a meeting, using letters, telegrams, and telephone calls. But the first face-to-face contact of any kind did not take place until July 17, more than 3 months later, and this was only a meeting with the plant manager on grievances.

The first actual negotiations took place on August 27. In the next 5 months, 9 other meetings were held. The employer spokesmen spent most of their time telling the union representatives that they did not really represent the workers. This was after an election had been held.

At this point a Federal conciliator entered the case. From January 29 to March 20 there were seven more conferences. No progress was made. On March 24 and 25, a NLRB hearing was held on the union's charge of refusal to bargain. On August 23, 1948—2 years, 4 months, and 15 days after the election—the Labor Board issued an order directing the employer to bargain, and to reinstate 4 workers who had been fired for union activity.

But did this bring justice to the workers or to their union? Look at the rest of the story.

The company appealed the Board's decision to the courts. One year, 8 months, and 6 days later—April 29, 1950—the Fifth Circuit Court of Appeals upheld the Board.

SENATOR DOUGLAS: That was about 4 years after the election.

MR. RIEVE: That is right.

Even then the company found excuses not to meet until June 25. Two months elapsed until the second meeting, held August 25. The succeeding dates were September 27, October 31, November 14, and December 13. This was the final meeting; the company refused to meet again.

Since the company's refusal to obey either the Board or the court was so flagrant, one more legal weapon remained—contempt of court. The union urged the Board to undertake such a case in July 1951, when it became apparent that the company would not sit down with us at all.

A contempt action was filed by the Board in January 1952. But on June 6, 1952, the Fifth Circuit Court refused to consider the action because a decertification petition had been filed, and therefore, according to the court, the employer had "reasonable" grounds for refusing to meet with the union.

SENATOR DOUGLAS: That was over 6 years after the original election?

MR. RIEVE: That is correct. But that is not the full story yet, Senator.

The Board has refused to act on the petition, on the grounds—the very sound grounds—that if the union could be decertified, the cause was the employer's illegal refusal to recognize the union as bargaining agent. And there the matter rests, apparently forever. The court refuses to act, because there is a decertification election pending, and the Board refuses to act because it takes the position that the union should not be decertified after the company refused to deal with it.

This is not an unusual case. I am just citing it as an example.

There, gentlemen, you have these "powerful unions" you have been hearing about. As I said 3 years ago, the NLRB does not give decisions in these cases —it performs autopsies.

True, we have a second alternative. We do not have to seek justice through the NLRB. If the workers are aroused, and if they insist, they can also go out on strike.

I want to take note, at this point, of the fact that in our union, as in other democratic unions, strikes are not "called"—they are voted by the workers who are going to do the striking. We who have been given the responsibilities of leadership are not very enthusiastic about strikes unless they are unavoidable. Strikes are always a risk; and they are always expensive.

But suppose the workers, in a case such as I have described, insisted upon a strike?

The company would immediately obtain from the State courts an injunction placing severe limitation on all strike activities. These injunctions usually are so broad and so vague that the strikers often cannot tell what is legal and what is not—until they are arrested. Meanwhile, company supervisors are under no restriction whatever in their efforts to threaten or bribe the strikers, or bring strikebreakers into the plant.

Whether the strikebreakers who soon appear—mostly at wages and working conditions much better than the employer had offered before—actually produce any cloth is not important. The fact that they go in and out every day, and draw regular wages, has a very discouraging effect on the strikers.

I am not going to belabor the point about strikebreakers having the right to vote while strikers do not, in case there is an election while a strike is in progress. From what I have read in the newspapers, I get the impression that everyone now realizes this is ridiculous. As our union said, as a sort of grim joke, if such a ruling is to continue, there should also be a law to the effect that only strikers may become strikebreakers—no outsiders allowed. This would narrow down the contest to those who were really involved.

Let us look briefly at what is happening to the strikers who have not been arrested for violating the injunction. I am not speaking of those who have been arrested.

They soon find they no longer have credit anywhere in the community—not even with their landlords. They may have been carried for months during a layoff, but as strikers they have suddenly become outcasts. If the plant is in a mill village, they may be evicted from their homes. They must put cash on the line for everything they need—food, rent, utilities, car payments, even hospital care. And in addition, of course, they are abused in the press and over the radio, they are snubbed on the streets, they are threatened and cursed and arrested. Is it any wonder that southern strikes are often lost?

And even if the strikers give up, if they vote to go back, they often fail to regain their old status. The leaders of the union movement are told that they have been "replaced"; and they find a cold reception elsewhere. If any of you think the blacklist has gone from American industry, I advise you to talk to some of these former strikers. . . .

THE CHAIRMAN: Thank you, Mr. Rieve. I want to ask you 1 or 2 questions that occurred to me as you gave your testimony.

I do not think any of us, certainly not myself, would disagree with you at all in deploring, as you do, the conditions in the South. There you have a situation where there is a strong antiunion sentiment. That is not a result of the Taft-Hartley Act. It is merely a situation in a certain section of the country with regard to unionism in general. The attempt to unionize there has caused some of the difficulties. It is a legitimate attempt and we have encouraged it by legislation, setting up labor unions, and as you say, the collective bargaining principle.

I cannot see anything in your testimony which proves that the Taft-Hartley Act is to blame for the outrages you are discussing. I cannot see where you have made suggestions here that will solve the question of atmosphere. It seems to me that the question of atmosphere you are discussing has nothing to do with the law, but the education of the people in the area. It is a different question than just the amendment of legislation. . . .

The question of atmosphere, which is a large part of your debate, is something that is inherent in a certain part of the country where there is resistance to unionism. I have been as eager as you have been to see how we could get at that. I do not think it is fair to say that the Taft-Hartley law suddenly came up and made these conditions. These conditions existed long before the Taft-Hartley law and the Wagner Act, and I am wondering how to get at it.

MR. RIEVE: Senator, . . . I cited to you our experience during the last 11 years—5½ years under the old Wagner Act, and 5½ years under the Taft-Hartley Act, and I showed you the difference. I showed you what organization progress was made during the first 5½ years—and it was not phenomenal; I am not trying to imply that, because I admit that prejudices and what have you existed—and I showed you what had happened in 5½ years under the Taft-Hartley law. I cannot help but reach the conclusion that the Taft-Hartley law created an atmosphere and gave employers certain legal rights they did not possess under the Wagner Act and that that is responsible for what has happened during the last 5½ years.

I think I gave you figures as to how many people we took into our union during the 5½-year period under the Wagner Act, how many contracts we signed, what happened to them, and I also gave you figures showing what happened under the Taft-Hartley law. There is a great contrast between the two periods. I cannot help but reach the conclusion that the Taft-Hartley law has much to do with the situation, although I don't minimize the problem of education, and what have you.

Senator, like in all things in life, I believe in education to its fullest extent. I think government has to help in the educational processes and one way to do so is to create the type of atmosphere that will permit that type of thing.

POLITICS AND THE NLRB

From Fortune, October, 1956 *

Is the NLRB anti-labor? The Democratic platform says that it is; specifically, the charge is that the Eisenhower Administration is "administratively amending Taft-Hartley into a more intensely anti-labor weapon by stacking the National Labor Relations Board with biased pro-management personnel who transformed the act into a management weapon by administrative decision." This charge was the culmination of a long series of labor and Democratic thrusts at the NLRB. The most vigorous assailant has been Senator Wayne Morse, but Governor Harriman, Adlai Stevenson, and Estes Kefauver have all charged the board with bias. The board is plainly to be a major campaign issue.

The opening salvo in the campaign against the board was delivered by Senator Morse last March in a speech that occupies thirty-five pages in the

* Reprinted by special permission from the October, 1956, issue of *Fortune;* © 1956 by Time, Inc.

Congressional Record. Most of the speech was prepared for Morse by Mozart Ratner, who was an assistant general counsel for the board during the Truman Administration. The speech charged that only Republican members had been appointed by the Administration; that a wave of firings had "driven the morale of the agency to a frighteningly low level"; and that the decisions of the board had been consistently pro-management. Morse has stuck to these basic charges, though a lengthy rebuttal (fourteen pages) by Senator Smith of New Jersey pointed to a number of distortions in the original speech—some of the decisions Morse complained about, for example, had actually been made by Truman appointees.

Five new men

Here are the five men who have been named to the board by this Administration:

Guy Farmer, nominally an independent, though actually a strong supporter of Eisenhower in 1952, is a political conservative and strong advocate of state's rights. Farmer, who was chairman of the board during his stay in office (July, 1953, to August, 1955), was greeted by labor with a chorus of dismay when he was first appointed. But as chairman he often voted with the Truman appointees, once at least on a major case—a decision that broadened the wage data employers are required to submit in collective bargaining. Farmer has retired to private law practice.

Philip Ray Rodgers, appointed in August, 1953, had been a staff member of the Senate Labor Committee. A conservative Republican, he had been close to Senator Taft, and it was Taft, in effect, who sponsored him for the board. When Farmer left the board, Rodgers was made temporary chairman, and it was considered likely that he would be named permanent chairman. But Rodgers did not get the top job. (It is almost universally believed at the NLRB that he was "vetoed" by Secretary of Labor James Mitchell—precisely because of the Taft connection.)

Albert Beeson was appointed in February, 1954, to fill out the term of a resigning member, and was not reappointed when that term expired. His appointment was attacked by labor; he was a management man—he had been industrial-relations director of a California firm, Food Machinery & Chemical Corp.—and he approached his assignment with public assertions that the board had previously been pro-labor. In his short term on the board Beeson was consistently pro-management.

Judge Boyd Leedom had little background in labor law at the time of his appointment in February, 1955. He was picked after the Administration, dismayed at the Beeson imbroglio, demanded that Mitchell find a noncontroversial man for the next opening. Mitchell suggested to his subordinates in the Labor Department that the state judiciary might be a logical place to look, and an assistant solicitor in the department, who knew Leedom, suggested the Judge. Leedom was called by his friend, was told the job was available, and was given just a day to decide whether he would take it. Several months after his appointment, he was named permanent chairman, to the dismay of

Rodgers' backers. Leedom is a Republican, but he is identified with no particular wing of the party.

Stephen Bean, who was named to the board in November, 1955, is a Republican and a former Mayor of Woburn, Massachusetts. From 1950 until his appointment, he had been a trial examiner at the board, and had generally been regarded as middle-of-the-road. He was sponsored for the job by Secretary of Commerce Weeks. And he was approved by Mitchell, who has what amounts to a veto over all board appointments.

It all depends

It is apparent that the Eisenhower appointees have indeed been Republican and/or conservative, as Senator Morse charges. It is perhaps worth noting, however, that Truman's appointees were virtually all Democratic and/or "liberal." At the time that the Republicans came into office, the board chairman, Paul Herzog, was a Democrat; one member was a former Democratic Congressman from Kansas; another was a former Democratic Senator from Utah; another was a former trade-union official from Alabama; and the fifth was a political independent who had been administrative assistant to Senator Morse. . . .

There is not much question that, so far as ground-breaking cases are concerned, the Eisenhower board has tilted noticeably in the direction of management. It has removed the protection of the federal labor laws from employees of many small firms. (The same decision, it should be noted, also strips protection from the small employer, e.g., a repair shop besieged by the Machinists Union.) The board has narrowed the area of legality for secondary boycotts. It has augmented the "free speech" rights of employers. It has increasingly tended to find that smaller bargaining units are "appropriate" under the law. (Though here again it is a bit uncertain whether the decision helps labor or management more.) . . .

In his influence on the pro-management tilt of the Eisenhower board, the general counsel has played as large a role as the new members. It is the counsel who determines which cases to prosecute initially, and which to appeal in the courts. Peterson, whose term as a board member expired in August, and who was not reappointed, commented sourly to Fortune on the record of the Republican general counsel, "To my knowledge, no new cases have been initiated seeking to test any principle where labor was apt to get an advantage. The areas selected for testing have been those in which established labor rights may be overthrown."

Like Chairman Farmer before him, Judge Leedom insists that the Eisenhower board is as fair as it can be; that it has no ideological predispositions when it confronts major policy cases. But a lot of Republicans are making another defense of this board. They are arguing that its pro-management bias is simply a correction of many years of pro-labor bias by Democratic boards.

Behind these campaign arguments there is the simple fact that the board is an important prize. In practical terms, many labor people feel that the most important benefit they could derive from a Democratic Administration would be control of the board.

FOR DISCUSSION AND ANALYSIS

1. In one case the NLRB ruled that a union-organized slowdown during the course of negotiations was a violation of Section 8 (*b*) (3), as it constituted a refusal to bargain in good faith. The union had also resorted to such harassing tactics as refusing to work overtime and extending rest periods beyond their normal limits on its own authority, with the consequence that the employer was unable to make production plans for delivery commitments. The Board maintained that the union was exercising its bargaining *powers* to thwart or impair the bargaining *process*. The Supreme Court overruled the Board, however, holding that the employer could, if he chose, close down his shop rather than subject himself to such harassments, but that as long as he maintained operations there was nothing in the law which made these concerted activities of the union any less legal than a strike. Like a strike, they were an exercise of bargaining power designed to win demands. Do you agree with the Board or the Court, and as a matter of law or of principle?

2. Analyze the majority and dissenting opinions in the Schultz case. Identify the basis for disagreement among the members of the Board. Do you agree with the majority opinion or the dissent? State the grounds for your agreeing with one and disagreeing with the other.

3. Labor unions have argued that Section 8 (*c*), the "free speech" clause in the Taft-Hartley Act, should protect them in their appeal to employees of secondary employers not to work on "hot" goods (that is, goods made by an employer with whom the union has a dispute). Such appeals, they have argued, contain no threat of reprisal or promise of benefit. They should be treated no differently from the appeals of an employer to his employees to vote against a union in a representation election. Do you agree?

4. Take any of the NLRB cases reported in this and the preceding two chapters. Referring to the provisions of the Labor Management Relations Act, describe the successive steps that case went through before being decided as it was. Are there any further steps which a losing party can take after the NLRB has rendered its decision?

5. Some labor relations experts have argued that the National Labor Relations Board now intervenes in union-management affairs much more than is desirable in a society which prides itself on the right of individual discretion. It has sometimes been suggested that all that is really necessary is the representation election procedure, with the provision that neither employer nor union may seek to determine the election outcome by resort to threats or bribes. Everything else would be left to the parties to work out for themselves, on the strength of their relative bargaining powers.

Look over the cases in this and the two preceding chapters and determine which ones would still have fallen within the purview of the Board under this limited scope of its authority, and which ones would have been outside its jurisdiction. Would you be willing to accept this restriction on the role of the NLRB?

6. Do you accept the conclusion which Mr. Rieve draws from the evidence he presented, in the statement given in this chapter? What other evidence might you want before arriving at a conclusion?

12: Union Security

For almost as long as unions have existed in this country the issue of the closed shop (or some variation of it, such as the union shop) has been a live one. Whether employees may be obligated to join a union as a condition of employment, and if so under what conditions, has been an issue before legislatures and courts for 150 years. In the earliest recorded conspiracy cases, dating back to the early nineteenth century, judicial opinion tended towards the view that unions could not force membership on unwilling workers. The Massachusetts case of Commonwealth v. Hunt in 1842 suggested there were certain circumstances, however, under which workers might decide that they would not work alongside anyone who was not a member of their organization.

At the turn of the century, however, unionism was faced with a counteroffensive from the employers in the form of the "American plan" or "open shop," which technically admitted union and nonunion employees alike to employment, but which in actuality was usually operated to exclude any but nonunion men. This approach was formalized in the form of the "yellow dog" contract, the obverse of union security, under which employees agree not to join a union, as a condition of employment. The first materials in this chapter relate to such yellow-dog contracts.

The yellow-dog contract was made unenforceable by the Norris-LaGuardia Act of 1932. In the period of rapid unionization of the 1930s and early 1940s, unions once again strove to achieve union security provisions. Although the Taft-Hartley Act put an end to union efforts to secure the closed shop (in interstate commerce), it permitted the union shop with certain restrictions. That the controversy is still unresolved, however, is indicated by the continued agitation of employers to eliminate even the restricted union shop and to secure state action outlawing all forms of union security, as permitted by the Taft-Hartley law, and by the opposition of the unions to this employer offensive coupled with efforts to make legal once again the closed shop, at least in certain industries.

546

UNION OPPOSITION TO "YELLOW-DOG" CONTRACTS

Statement of John P. Frey, President, Ohio Federation of Labor, in hearings by the Committee on Labor of the Senate of the 87th General Assembly of Ohio, on Senate Bill No. 30 [voiding "yellow-dog" contracts], 1927 (mimeo.), pp. 69, 70–72

The employers for a number of years have employed the ablest attorneys that they can secure in order to find ways and means by which the American Trades Union Movement can be strangled, apparently under the guise of human liberty, and they are the ones who invented this so-called "Yellow Dog" or individual contract. . . .

The employers began—and they have done this nationally, because it is as much a Massachusetts, Connecticut, Pennsylvania, Wisconsin, Nevada, Colorado, California—problem as it is an Ohio one—simple contracts in which the employee merely had to pledge himself that he would take no collective action with his fellow employees in any matter connected with wages or shop conditions. They got away with that. Then they added that he would not become a member of any trades union while he remained in the firm's employ, and, getting away with that, they became a little bolder and they added that he would not while in the employ of the company, talk over the question of unionism with any member of the union, and having gotten away with that, feeling quite satisfied over it, they went a little further and they compelled the man, as the price of securing a job, or retaining his position, to sign a contract which pledged him that after he left the firm's employ, he would never again talk to any of the firm's employees on the question of trades unionism or endeavor to prevail upon them to join a union.

We could submit to the Committee a mass of evidence which they would have no time to read to substantiate what I have just said. The Contracts, Mr. Chairman of the Committee, that have already been presented to you, convey the full evidence of what I have just said.

Then the employers in some States, and notably in Ohio, due to the workings of the attorneys whom they employed for the purpose of making trades unionism impossible, for the purpose of destroying collective bargaining, and making labor absolutely helpless, went one step farther. They went to their employees and compelled them as the price of retaining their job, to sign a contract such as is being considered this evening, and then after that coercion had been applied, they wrote letters to the unions—and I want to read one or two of these to the Committee so that they will be informed of how carefully the representatives of the anti-union employers' associations are endeavoring to protect the rights of their non-union employees. Here is a letter written by the law firm of Tuttle and Ross of Cincinnati. It is directed to the Secretary of the National Union of which I have the honor of being an officer.

Dear Sir: It has been called to our attention that an effort is being made to persuade and induce the employees of the John B. Morris Foundry Company of Cincinnati to become members of the International Iron

Moulders Union of North America and you as one of its officers are engaged in this effort.

The purpose of this letter is to notify you that all of the employees of this company have accepted employment under written contract and agreement with the company; that the shop is being operated and will continue to be operated upon a non-union basis, and as non-union, that the employer will not recognize or have dealings with the labor union; that the employee is not a member of any labor union and that while employed by said company that the employee will not become a member of any labor union and will have no dealings, communications or interviews with the officers, agents or members of any labor union in relation to membership by the employee in a labor union or in any relation to the employees employment.

In the recent decision of the United States Supreme Court, in the case of the Hitchman Coal & Coke Company versus Mitchell, it is said that an employer who conducts his business on a non-union basis may legally have a contract with his employees that they are non-union and will so continue while in his employment, and that the officers and the agents of labor unions, having knowledge of such an arrangement, may be enjoined from soliciting any employees for membership in the union and from interfering with such arrangement. In other words, an employer has a right to employ only those who are non-union and who agree to continue non-union while in his employment and the employer is entitled to have union interference with this arrangement enjoined.

If, as has been reported, you have been engaged in any way, directly, or indirectly, in endeavoring to persuade the employees of the John B. Morris Foundry Company to join a union and thus violate their contract, you fall within this decision and unless you discontinue such action the company may proceed to protect its legal rights as outlined in the case referred to.

ADAIR *v.* UNITED STATES

Supreme Court of the United States, 208 U.S. 161 (1908)

MR. JUSTICE HARLAN, OPINION OF THE COURT

This case involves the constitutionality of certain provisions of the act of Congress of June 1, 1898, 30 Stat. 424, c. 370, concerning carriers engaged in interstate commerce and their employés. . . .

The 10th section, upon which the present prosecution is based, is in these words:

That any employer subject to the provisions of this act and any officer, agent, or receiver of such employer, who shall require any employé, or any person seeking employment, as a condition of such employment, to enter into an agreement, either written or verbal, not to become or remain a member of any labor corporation, association, or organization; or shall threaten any employee with loss of employment, or shall unjustly discriminate against any employee because of his membership in such labor corporation, association, or organization; or who shall require any employee or any person seeking employment, as a condition of such employment, to enter into a contract whereby such employee or applicant for employment shall agree to contribute to any fund for charitable, social, or beneficial purposes; to release such employer from legal liability for any personal injury by reason of any benefit received from such fund beyond the proportion of the benefit arising from the employer's contribution to such fund; or who shall, after having discharged an employee, attempt or conspire to prevent such employee from obtaining employment, or who shall, after the quitting of an employee, attempt or conspire to prevent such employee from obtaining employment, is hereby declared to be guilty of a misdemeanor, and upon conviction thereof in any court of the United States of competent jurisdiction in the district in which such offense was committed, shall be punished for each offense by a fine of not less than one hundred dollars and not more than one thousand dollars.

It may be observed in passing that while that section makes it a crime against the United States to unjustly discriminate against an employee of an interstate carrier because of his being a member of a labor organization, it does not make it a crime to unjustly discriminate against an employee of the carrier because of his not being a member of such an organization.

The present indictment was in the District Court of the United States for the Eastern District of Kentucky against the defendant Adair.

It thus appears that the criminal offense charged in the count of the indictment upon which the defendant was convicted was, in substance and effect, that being an agent of a railroad company engaged in interstate commerce and subject to the provisions of the above act of June 1, 1898, he discharged one Coppage from its service *because of his membership in a labor organization—* no other ground for such discharge being alleged.

May Congress make it a criminal offense against the United States—as by the tenth section of the act of 1898 it does—for an agent or officer of an interstate carrier, having full authority in the premises from the carrier, to discharge an employee from service simply because of his membership in a labor organization?

This question is admittedly one of importance, and has been examined with care and deliberation. And the court has reached a conclusion which, in its judgment, is consistent with both the words and spirit of the Constitution and is sustained as well by sound reason.

The first inquiry is whether the part of the tenth section of the act of 1898 upon which the first count of the indictment was based is repugnant to the Fifth Amendment of the Constitution declaring that no person shall be deprived of liberty or property without due process of law. In our opinion that section, in the particular mentioned, is an invasion of the personal liberty, as well as of the right of property, guaranteed by that Amendment. Such liberty and right embraces the right to make contracts for the purchase of the labor of others and equally the right to make contracts for the sale of one's own labor; each right, however, being subject to the fundamental condition that no contract, whatever its subject matter, can be sustained which the law, upon reasonable grounds, forbids as inconsistent with the public interests or as hurtful to the public order or as detrimental to the common good. This court has said that "in every well ordered society, charged with the order of conserving the safety of its members, the rights of the individual in respect of his liberty may, at times, under the pressure of great dangers, be subjected to such restraint, to be enforced by reasonable regulations, as the safety of the general public may demand." *Jacobson v. Massachusetts*, 197 U.S. 11, 29, and authorities there cited. Without stopping to consider what would have been the rights of the railroad company under the Fifth Amendment, had it been indicted under the act of Congress, it is sufficient in this case to say that as agent of the railroad company and as such responsible for the conduct of the business of one of its departments, it was the defendant Adair's right—and that right inhered in his personal liberty, and was also a right of property—to serve his employer as best he could, so long as he did nothing that was reasonably forbidden by law as injurious to the public interests. It was the right of the defendant to prescribe the terms upon which the services of Coppage would be accepted, and it was the right of Coppage to become or not, as he chose, an employee of the railroad company upon the terms offered to him. Mr. Cooley, in his treatise on Torts, p. 278, well says: "It is a part of every man's civil rights that he be left at liberty to refuse business relations with any person whomsoever, whether the refusal rests upon reason, or is the result of whim, caprice, prejudice or malice. With his reasons neither the public nor third persons have any legal concern. It is also his right to have business relations with any one with whom he can make contracts, and if he is wrongfully deprived of this right by others, he is entitled to redress." . . .

While, as already suggested, the rights of liberty and property guaranteed by the Constitution against deprivation without due process of law, is subject to such reasonable restraints as the common good or the general welfare may require, it is not within the functions of government—at least in the absence of contract between the parties—to compel any person in the course of his business and against his will to accept or retain the personal services of another, or to compel any person, against his will, to perform personal services for another. The right of a person to sell his labor upon such terms as he deems proper is, in its essence, the same as the right of the purchaser of labor to prescribe the conditions upon which he will accept such labor from the person offering to sell it. So the right of the employee to quit the service of the employer, for whatever reason, is the same as the right of the employer, for whatever reason, to dispense with the services of such employee. It was the legal right of the defendant Adair—however unwise such a course might have been—to discharge Coppage because of his being a member of a labor organization, as it was the legal rights of Coppage, if he saw fit to do so—however unwise such a course on his part might have been—to quit the service in which he was engaged, because the defendant employed some persons who were not members of a labor organization. In all such particulars the employer and the employee have equality of right, and any legislation that disturbs that equality is an arbitrary interference with the liberty of contract which no government can legally justify in a free land. These views find support in adjudged cases, some of which are cited in the margin. Of course, if the parties by contract fix the period of service, and prescribe the conditions upon which the contract may be terminated, such contract would control the rights of the parties as between themselves, and for any violation of those provisions the party wronged would have his appropriate civil action.

MR. JUSTICE HOLMES, DISSENTING

Where there is, or generally is believed to be, an important ground of public policy for restraint the Constitution does not forbid it, whether this court agrees or disagrees with the policy pursued. It cannot be doubted that to prevent strikes, and, so far as possible, to foster its scheme of arbitration, might be deemed by Congress an important point of policy, and I think it impossible to say that Congress might not reasonably think that the provision in question would help a good deal to carry its policy along. But suppose the only effect really were to tend to bring about the complete unionizing of such railroad laborers as Congress can deal with, I think that object alone would justify the act. I quite agree that the question what and how much good labor unions do, is one on which intelligent people may differ,—I think that laboring men sometimes attribute to them advantages, as many attribute to combinations of capital disadvantages, that really are due to economic conditions of a far wider and deeper kind—but I could not pronounce it unwarranted if Congress should decide that to foster a strong union was for the best interest, not only of the men, but of the railroads and the country at large.

HITCHMAN COAL CO. *v.* MITCHELL

Supreme Court of the United States, 245 U.S. 229 (1917)

About the 1st of June a self-appointed committee of employees called upon plaintiff's president, stated in substance that they could not remain longer on strike because they were not receiving benefits from the Union, and asked upon what terms they could return to work. They were told that they could come back, but not as members of the United Mine Workers of America; that thenceforward the mine would be run non-union, and the company would deal with each man individually. They assented to this, and returned to work on a nonunion basis. Mr. Pickett, the mine superintendent, had charge of employing the men, then and afterwards, and to each one who applied for employment he explained the conditions, which were that while the company paid the wages demanded by the Union and as much as anybody else, the mine was run nonunion and would continue so to run; that the company would not recognize the United Mine Workers of America; that if any man wanted to become a member of that union he was at liberty to do so; but he could not be a member of it and remain in the employ of the Hitchman Company; that if he worked for the company he would have to work as a non-union man. To this each man employed gave his assent, understanding that while he worked for the company he must keep out of the Union.

Since January, 1908 (after the commencement of the suit), in addition to having this verbal understanding, each man has been required to sign an employment card expressing in substance the same terms. This has neither enlarged nor diminished plaintiff's rights, the agreement not being such as is required by law to be in writing. . . .

That the plaintiff was acting within its lawful rights in employing its men only upon terms of continuing non-membership in the United Mine Workers of America is not open to question. Plaintiff's repeated costly experiences of strikes and other interferences while attempting to "run union" were a sufficient explanation of its resolve to run "non-union," if any were needed. But neither explanation nor justification is needed. Whatever may be the advantages of "collective bargaining," it is not bargaining at all, in any just sense, unless it is voluntary on both sides. The same liberty which enables men to form unions, and through the union to enter into agreements with employers willing to agree, entitles other men to remain independent of the union and other employers to agree with them to employ no man who owes any allegiance or obligation to the union. In the latter case, as in the former, the parties are entitled to be protected by the law in the enjoyment of the benefits of any lawful agreement they may make. This court repeatedly has held that the employer is as free to make non-membership in a union a condition of employment, as the working man is free to join the union, and that this is a part of the constitutional rights of personal liberty and private property, not to be taken away even by legislation, unless through some proper exercise of the paramount police power. *Adair v. United States*, 208 U.S. 161, 174; *Coppage v. Kansas*, 236 U.S. 1, 14. In the present case, needless to say, there is no act of legislation to which defendants may resort for justification. . . .

Upon all the facts, we are constrained to hold that the purpose entertained by defendants to bring about a strike at plaintiff's mine in order to compel plaintiff, through fear of financial loss, to consent to the unionization of the mine as the lesser evil, was an unlawful purpose, and that the methods resorted to by Hughes [a UMW organizer]—the inducing of employees to unite with the Union in an effort to subvert the system of employment at the mine by concerted breaches of the contracts of employment known to be in force there, not to mention misrepresentation, deceptive statements, and threats of pecuniary loss communicated by Hughes to the men—were unlawful and malicious methods, and not to be justified as a fair exercise of the right to increase the membership of the Union.

THE NORRIS-LAGUARDIA ACT ON "YELLOW-DOG" CONTRACTS

Act of March 23, 1932, 47 U.S. Stat. 70, c. 90

Sec. 2. In the interpretation of this Act and in determining the jurisdiction and authority of the courts of the United States, as such jurisdiction and authority are herein defined and limited, the public policy of the United States is hereby declared as follows:

Whereas under prevailing economic conditions, developed with the aid of governmental authority for owners of property to organize in the corporate and other forms of ownership association, the individual unorganized worker is commonly helpless to exercise actual liberty of contract and to protect his freedom of labor, and thereby to obtain acceptable terms and conditions of employment, wherefore, though he should be free to decline to associate with his fellows, it is necessary that he have full freedom of association, self-organization, and designation of representatives of his own choosing, to negotiate the terms and conditions of his employment, and that he shall be free from the interference, restraint, or coercion of employers of labor, or their agents, in the designation of such representatives or in self-organization or in other concerted activities for the purpose of collective bargaining or other mutual aid or protection; therefore, the following definitions of, and limitations upon, the jurisdiction, and authority of the courts of the United States are hereby enacted.

Sec. 3. Any undertaking or promise, such as is described in this section, or any other undertaking or promise in conflict with the public policy declared in section 2 of this Act, is hereby declared to be contrary to the public policy of the United States, shall not be enforceable in any court of the United States and shall not afford any basis for the granting of legal or equitable relief by any such court, including specifically the following:

Every undertaking or promise hereafter made, whether written or oral, expressed or implied, constituting or contained in any contract or agreement or hiring or employment between any individual, firm, company, association, or corporation, and any employee or prospective employee of the same, whereby

(*a*) Either party to such contract or agreement undertakes or promises not to join, become, or remain a member of any labor organization or of any employer organization; or

(*b*) Either party to such contract or agreement undertakes or promises that he will withdraw from an employment relation in the event that he joins, becomes, or remains a member of any labor organization or of any employer organization.

GENERAL MOTORS ON UNION SECURITY

Charles E. Wilson, President, General Motors Corporation, in Labor Relations Program, hearings before the Senate Committee on Labor and Public Welfare, 80th Cong., 1st Sess., 1947, part 1, p. 464

Do not misunderstand me. I am not in favor of the "yellow dog" contract. I never had one. I never would have had one because I do not believe in those kinds of things.

Likewise, I would not have a closed shop, either. I am never going to sign one. When it gets around to that, it will make a farmer out of me.

UAW HAS UNION SHOP SPLURGE

From Business Week, October 8, 1955

In less than four months, nearly 600,000 additional UAW members have come under union shop contracts. Of the union's 1,389,091 dues-paying members (Aug. 31 estimate), some 1,215,455, or 87.5%, are covered by straight union shop agreements. New agreements already negotiated but not yet recorded will increase the percentage. Out of 1,583 contracts on file in union headquarters, 989 now provide the union shop.

Tracing this sudden change in the UAW's union security efforts is simple. You have only to go back to June 12, 1955, the date of the new three-year contract between General Motors Corp. and the UAW. That contract provided for the first time at giant GM, the full union shop.

Signing of that agreement broke the log jam that had been piling up for years. In rapid succession, UAW negotiated the union shop at Chrysler, International Harvester, Deere & Co., and in Detroit automotive tool and die shops, among others.

Facts of Life—Why did GM give in this year after resisting the union shop since its initial UAW agreement in 1939? Basically, GM believed that the "principle" had become a pretty shopworn item over the years.

In 1950, it had given UAW a "modified" union shop, under which new employees were required to join UAW but could drop out if they chose at the end of one year of employment. During the five-year contract—from 1950 to 1955—GM hired 600,000 new employees. Of these, only 600 elected to withdraw from UAW after a year's time.

And GM knew this year that UAW was determined to end the modified shop and win full coverage. In the light of practical facts of life, GM believed it would be a pretty small issue over which to take a strike.

Few Objectors—When the end came, GM had some 16,000 employees who were not UAW members. A polite letter went out to all of those, informing them that the new contract required them to join UAW by Aug. 26 or face discharge.

The only resistance popped up in Indianapolis where a non-member unsuccessfully took the case to court. After the deadline passed, there were about 100 employees who objected to unionization on religious principles; the union is investigating each individual case. Less than a dozen—those who simply refused to join the union—were discharged.

UNION-SECURITY PROVISIONS IN AGREEMENTS, 1954

By Rose Theodore, Division of Wages and Industrial Relations, U.S. Bureau of Labor Statistics, from the Monthly Labor Review, vol. 78, 1955, pp. 649–658

Federal labor legislation since 1935 has safeguarded the right of a majority of the employees in a given unit to choose representatives for collective bargaining purposes who would speak for all employees. Through collective bargaining union members have traditionally sought more specific guarantees of the status of their unions by the negotiation of clauses requiring that all employees should be or become union members. Federal and some State statutes currently in effect, however, restrict the degree to which union membership may be established by employers and unions as a condition of employment.

The union-shop clause usually requires employees already on the payroll to become union members and new employees to join within a specified time after hiring. It is the principal type of union-security provision now found in labor-management contracts, according to an analysis made by the Bureau of Labor Statistics of 1,716 collective bargaining agreements in effect during all or part of 1954. Nearly two-thirds contained union-shop clauses.[1] Of the 7,405,000 workers covered by the agreements studied, 64 percent were employed under union-shop provisions.

Maintenance-of-membership clauses, which do not require employees to join the union but to maintain membership once acquired, appeared in 14 percent of the agreements. The remainder of the agreements studied (21 percent) contained sole-bargaining clauses which recognize the union as the exclusive bargaining agent, but do not specify membership requirements. In the South, where the union-shop and maintenance-of-membership provisions are prohibited in a number of States under so-called "right to work" laws, union status in two-thirds of the contracts examined was limited to sole-bargaining clauses.

Three-fourths of the agreements had checkoff provisions under which employers agreed to deduct union dues from employees' pay for transfer to the union.

Most of the agreements analyzed for this study covered 1,000 or more workers.[2] No attempt was made to balance the distribution of agreements studied between those affected by the union-security regulations of the Labor Management Relations (Taft-Hartley) Act of 1947 (LMRA) and those not covered by that act. The act applies to establishments engaged in industries affecting interstate commerce, excepting railroads and airlines.[3]

A comparison of results of the present study with the Bureau's 1952 report [4]

[1] Some excluded certain groups of workers from the membership requirement. Provisions which required union membership before the date of employment (commonly referred to as "closed-shop" clauses) were included in the union-shop category.

[2] This selection of agreements represents an incomplete transition from samples used in earlier studies, which were comprised of agreements covering both small and large groups of workers, to a new basis for agreement analysis limited to all agreements covering 1,000 or more workers. The collection and analysis techniques used in the agreement analysis program are described in the Monthly Labor Review, June 1955 (p. 673).

[3] Railroad and airline agreements are not collected by the Bureau and, therefore, were not included in this study. Workers in these industries come under the provisions of the Railway Labor Act, which was amended in 1951 to permit negotiation of union-shop agreements.

[4] See Union-Status Provisions in Collective Agreements, 1952, Monthly Labor Review, April 1953 (p. 383). For earlier studies, see Union Status Under Collective Agreements, 1950–51, Monthly Labor Review, November 1951 (p. 552); Union-Security Provisions in Agreements, 1949–50, Monthly Labor Review, August 1950

reveals little change in the prevalence of the union shop. To some extent, this may be a reflection of the increased use of long-term agreements in recent years, which tended to stabilize certain aspects of collective bargaining.

Since 1952, 5 additional States have adopted legislation outlawing union-security provisions,[5] bringing the total with such laws to 18 as of March 1955. However, passage of these five new statutes had little effect on the results of the present study, since agreements in these States represented a relatively small proportion of the agreements studied. Moreover, enactment of the State laws did not affect agreements already in existence.

THE UNION SHOP

When an employer negotiates a union-shop provision, he agrees to require, as one of the conditions of employment, that all, or nearly all, employees must join the union within a specified time and must remain members in good standing.[6] The development of harmonious relationships between management and labor is often advanced as one of the benefits to be gained from such arrangements. One contract phrased this attitude as follows:

   a. Both the company and the union feel that the greatest amount of harmony will exist, that better labor relations will prevail, and that employee interests will be more adequately represented and better served if all eligible employees become members of the union.

   b. Accordingly it is agreed that all eligible employees should within 30 days from their hiring date become and remain members of the union in good standing. . . .

Types of Provisions. Provisions for a union shop were found in 1,122 or nearly two-thirds of the 1,716 agreements examined. . . . A similar proportion of the workers were covered by the union-shop provisions, which were of several types. The type most common (60 percent of the union-shop agreements) required that all present employees be or become union members within a specified time [7] and that all newly hired employees join within a specified time after starting work. Under such agreements there is no limitation on the employer in the selection of new workers, either in terms of hiring only union members or of giving preference or consideration to union members. For example, one company guaranteed the union that it would require:

(p. 224); and Extent of Collective Bargaining and Union Recognition, 1946, Bureau of Labor Statistics Bull. 909, June 1947 (11 pp.).

   [5] The 5 States are: Alabama, Louisiana, Mississippi, South Carolina, and Utah.

   [6] National Labor Relations Board decisions have emphasized that union membership requirements under the LMRA may be fulfilled simply by the tender of initiation fees, where required, and periodic dues.

   [7] The time allowed was generally 30 days, which is the minimum specified by the LMRA. A few agreements merely provided for a union shop "to the extent permitted by law," as in the national anthracite and bituminous coal-mining agreements, which read in part: ". . . It is further agreed that as a condition of employment all employees should be or become members of the United Mine Workers of America, to the extent and in the manner permitted by law. . . ."

(1) All present employees who are members of the union, as a condition of continued employment, to maintain their membership in the union during the life of this agreement through payments to the union of uniformly required initiation fees and dues, and (2) all other present and future employees who, during the life of this agreement, are members of the bargaining unit but who are not members of the union, as a condition of continued employment, to join the union 30 days after the date of their employment or the effective date of this agreement, whichever is later, and thereafter maintain their membership in the union through payments to the union of uniformly required initiation fees and dues.

Exemption from the membership requirement was granted to certain groups in the bargaining unit (commonly designated as a modified union shop) in 204, or 18 percent, of the 1,122 contracts. In most instances, employees who were not union members when the agreements became effective were not required to join the union. A few contracts exempted only employees with relatively long service; a few others required a specific proportion of new employees (e. g., 9 out of every 10) to become union members within a specified time.

An escape period after 1 year, during which new employees were permitted to withdraw from the union, was provided in 42 agreements. . . .

The closed shop, which is the strongest form of union security agreed to by employers in collective bargaining, usually requires that only union members may be hired; however, if no union members are available, other workers may be taken on provided that they join the union prior to or shortly after starting work. The closed shop is forbidden in industries subject to the LMRA, but it is still found in establishments not covered by the act or by State bans. In the present study, 87 agreements, concentrated largely in local trade and service industries, contained closed-shop provisions. These accounted for less than 8 percent of the union-shop agreements.

a. All employees, steady or extra, covered by this agreement, shall be hired only through the office of that union having jurisdiction over the particular employee. Such employees shall be and remain in good standing in the union and must obtain a work slip from the union before going to work. If within a reasonable time, under the circumstances, the union is unable to supply satisfactory help to the employer upon request, then the employer may hire outside of the union, provided such employee so hired shall obtain a work slip from the union before going to work except in cases of emergency, then the employee so hired shall obtain a work slip within 72 hours, and further provided that such employee makes application to become a member of the union within 15 days after his employment and completes the application within 30 days from date of employment.

b. In the event an employee neglects, fails, or refuses to comply with the provisions of section (*a*), the employer agrees upon demand to remove any employee from the job who is on the job in violation of section (*a*). . . .

MAINTENANCE OF MEMBERSHIP

Under a maintenance-of-membership provision, the employee is not required to join the union, but if he is a member when the clause becomes effective or later chooses to become a member, he must thereafter maintain his membership as a condition of employment. Usually, however, such provisions provide for an escape period immediately after signing of the agreement to permit withdrawals from the union. After this period, maintenance of membership is generally required for the duration of the contract.

All employees who, 15 days after the date of certification by the NLRB that all of the provisions of the LMRA have been complied with by the union, and that the union has been authorized pursuant to the provisions of such act to enter into a maintenance-of-membership agreement, or who, 15 days after the date upon which it becomes legal to enter into a maintenance-of-membership agreement without such certification, are members of the union in good standing in accordance with the constitution and bylaws of the union, and all employees who thereafter become members of the union, shall as a condition of employment, remain members of the union in good standing for the duration of this agreement.

Any employee who wishes to withdraw from membership in the union during the above 15-day period may do so by written notification by registered letter to the union.

Some contracts permit withdrawal from the union during an escape period beginning 1 year from the effective date of the contract. If the employee does not resign then, he is required to maintain his membership for the duration of the agreement. . . .

The prevalence of membership-maintenance clauses has declined since World War II. The Bureau estimated in 1946 that 25 percent of all workers under agreement were covered by such clauses; by contrast, 17 percent of the workers under the agreements examined in 1954 were similarly covered (chart 1). Widely used in the major steel agreements, this type of union security covered nearly three-fourths of the workers in the primary metal industries.

SOLE BARGAINING

All agreements, by their nature, assure sole-bargaining rights to the union.[8] In most agreements, as already indicated, the union's status is further protected by requirements that employees acquire or retain union membership as a condition of employment. However, in 21 percent of the agreements in this study,

---

[8] Direct reference to the status of unions as exclusive bargaining representatives is found in section 9 (*a*) of the LMRA, as follows: "Representatives designated or selected for the purposes of collective bargaining by the majority of the employees in a unit appropriate for such purposes, shall be the exclusive representatives of all the employees in such unit for the purposes of collective bargaining in respects to rates of pay, wages, hours of employment, or other conditions of employment."

The union and the employer may voluntarily agree on exclusive recognition or may request an NLRB election (under section 9 (*c*) of LMRA) to determine the issue.

Chart 1. Union-Security Provisions in Collective Bargaining Agreements, 1946, 1949–50, and 1954 [1]

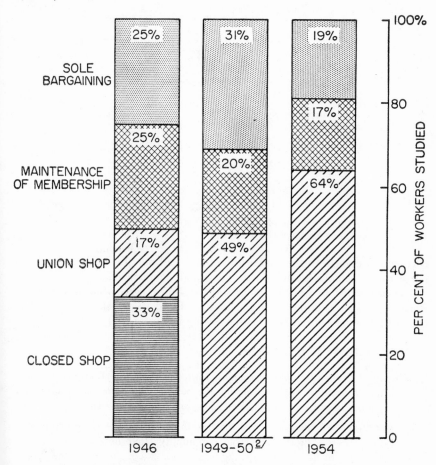

UNITED STATES DEPARTMENT OF LABOR
BUREAU OF LABOR STATISTICS

[1] The 1946 estimates relate to the proportion of all workers under agreement covered by each type of union status. Closed and union shop clauses are not shown separately for 1949–50 and 1954. Bureau reports issued since passage of the Labor Management Relations Act have classified closed shop as a type of union shop.

[2] Adjusted figures, reflecting inclusion of anthracite and bituminous coal-mining and Ford Motor Co. union shop agreements excluded from data in the published 1949–50 study.

Chart 2. Union-Security and Checkoff Provisions in Collective
Bargaining Agreements, 1954

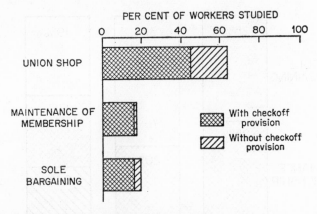

PER CENT OF WORKERS STUDIED

UNITED STATES DEPARTMENT OF LABOR
BUREAU OF LABOR STATISTICS

covering 19 percent of the workers, the union had only the exclusive right to
bargain for all employees in the unit, union and nonunion alike. . . .

The proportion of workers under sole-bargaining agreements has dropped
from 25 percent, as estimated in the 1946 study, to 19 percent of the workers
covered by agreements analyzed in the present study (chart 1).

INDIVIDUALISM vs. UNIONISM

*Testimony of Walter Reuther, President, United Automobile Workers, in Taft-
Hartley Act Revisions, hearings before the Senate Committee on Labor and
Public Welfare, 83d Cong., 1st Sess., 1953, part 1, pp. 409–418*

MR. REUTHER: We think, you see, that the union is an attempt to extend the
democratic processes in the industrial community; that organized society is
based upon the principle that within the framework of a given society the people
who make up that society have to work out rules and regulations to govern the
relationship of one to the other.

Collective bargaining through the union is an attempt to extend that principle into the industrial community. People have rights and privileges and
obligations in the community as a whole, but within industry they had no rights
in the past. Collective bargaining is an attempt to establish their rights as
economic citizens within the industrial community.

Obviously, in order to do that, they have to work out rules and regulations.
They have to have the machinery of self-government. The union represents
that kind of machinery.

The union performs some very important and essential functions. We handle
grievances. We handle the grievances of all the workers. We have umpire

machinery. The unions pay for the umpire machinery. When he hands down a decision, all the workers get the benefits. We have legal services. All the workers get the benefit of the cases we may process in unemployment compensation. All the workers get the benefit because we establish precedents; we work out basic policies. We have a medical department. We work on health problems. We work on occupational diseases. All the workers get the benefit of these.

Since all the workers in the industrial community get the benefits of these services performed by the union, made possible by the union, we believe that since all the workers share in the services all the workers ought to share in the cost of providing those services.

THE CHAIRMAN: Might I say this: I have had some independent union representatives wait upon me recently, and they think the solution is proportional representation. They do not see why they should be compelled to accept a union that may have 51 percent of the votes. They think if they have 49 percent or if it is divided into 3 or 4 different groups, there should be proportional representation in the bargaining agreement.

Would that appeal to you, or do you think that is unsound?

MR. REUTHER: That is the French system, and that is the shortest road to chaos you can travel, because then you get a competition of irresponsibility, seeing who can outbid the other fellow to try to capture a few more percent.

THE CHAIRMAN: It seems to me what you are arguing for is definitely a government within the government. If you are going to set up a government within the government, we are going to be compelled to police certain internal affairs of the unions.

MR. REUTHER: It is government by majority rule, and what is wrong with that? We fought the Revolutionary War around a very fundamental principle, and we were right: Around the idea of taxation without representation.

This is the other side of that coin. This is the matter of representation without taxation. One principle is as sound as the other, because if it is wrong to be taxed without representation, it is wrong to have representation without taxation.

Since all the workers in the industrial community have a right to vote democratically in determining whether our union is going to be the bargaining agency, we cannot get sole bargaining rights unless a majority of the workers support us at the National Labor Relations Board. So having gotten majority support, we then represent the machinery by which the workers in the industrial community govern themselves and have their work done. They all get the benefits of that machinery; they ought all to pay the taxes which make that machinery possible.

That is all we are asking. It seems to me that is a very sound thing.

The only test ought to be, No. 1, Is the government within the industrial community, represented by the union, established by democratic majority decision? No. 2, is its membership open to all the people who have a right to participate in that industrial government?

SENATOR DOUGLAS: You mean is the union open?

MR. REUTHER: That is right. No. 1, is it democratic decision by majority rule? No. 2, is it open membership? Those are the limitations.

SENATOR DOUGLAS: On that very point, I would like to ask some questions. I think your argument is overwhelming and convincing on the question of the union shop. But when you move from the union shop, where the employer has the initiative in hiring and the men after being hired join the union, to the closed shop, where the men must join the union before they can be hired, then you get into an initial difficulty. It is just this: suppose the union is a closed union, whether by absolute prohibition of entrance or by excessive initiation fees or by unduly prolonged apprenticeship periods, or what not. Then you may be giving privileges to those inside the union, but certainly those who are outside and who, if they could come in, would be good union men, suffer.

What would you say on that question if you have a closed shop? Is there a legal obligation upon us to see that the union should be an open union? . . .

MR. REUTHER: . . . I personally think that it is wrong for a union to have a closed membership in which they attempt to build a labor monopoly in order to exploit the advantages of a monopoly. I think that is morally wrong, I think it is economically wrong.

SENATOR DOUGLAS: Do you think that problem should be attacked through governmental legislation?

MR. REUTHER: I think you ought to try to correct the abuses where there are specific abuses.

SENATOR DOUGLAS: By legislation?

MR. REUTHER: I think the labor unions ought to do it themselves.

SENATOR DOUGLAS: But if they do not?

MR. REUTHER: If they do not, then I think if you are going to permit the closed shop to be applied, then I think there ought to be safeguards. . . .

SENATOR PURTELL: Mr. Reuther, I am intrigued by your answer to Senator Douglas. In other words, where these abuses exist, you say what we ought to do is threaten, "and if you aren't a good boy we will pass legislation."

I would assume, therefore, that until such time as we do say that, we can expect a continuation of these abuses? If they are bad and they should be corrected and are not being corrected, is not the answer legislation?

MR. REUTHER: The point is that I think you ought to put the first responsibility on the unions themselves to correct the abuses where they exist, but you ought to do it under circumstances that will not deny the application of principles by those unions who are not abusing them. Taft-Hartley just blankets the thing and just says nobody can do this. You try to rationalize the justification for that by getting into this whole discussion about the right to work.

I think that that idea also has been greatly misunderstood, because I think we all recognize that what we are trying to preserve in the world is human freedom. We are trying to broaden it and strengthen it and give more people the rights to enjoy it.

But human freedom is not an absolute value; it is a relative value. You can exercise what we call human freedom in a given society only in your relationship to other people, both in the local community, in the State community, in the

ational community, and ultimately in the world community. You have no
uman freedom excepting in your relationship to other people. All of these
ings we call our basic human freedoms are relative values. They are not
bsolute values.

Take freedom of speech. That is not an absolute thing. It is a relative thing.
ou have a right to exercise freedom of speech, but it is curtailed in certain
situations. You cannot stand up in a crowded theater and yell "Fire," because
that takes you beyond the framework in which you can exercise the right of
freedom of speech. You can drive your car, but we have traffic laws. You have
o do it a certain way. As a matter of fact, the laws do not make it harder to
drive. Without traffic laws you could not drive a car at all.

That is the way with the right to work. It also can be a qualified basic right.
The qualification ought to be that within the framework of this democratic industrial community, through the union, with open membership and the democratic right to say what is right and what is wrong, it seems to me at the point
where you have a democratic union and every worker has access to membership, every worker has an equal voice in determining what the policies and
program of that union are, who its leadership will be, at that point any curtailment of the right to work within the framework of that kind of democratic
structure, is no more or greater curtailment of your basic rights than the way
freedom of speech is curtailed.

It seems to me that we get our ideas all mixed up in this field. This right to
work seems like a sacred thing that is being violated. It is not being violated. It
is being worked out within the democratic framework of the union machinery. . . .

SENATOR GOLDWATER: Mr. Chairman.

I am very much interested in Mr. Reuther's development of the closed shop
and the union shop. There is only one question in this whole field in my mind.
What about the man who just does not want to belong to a union?

MR. REUTHER: Well, if a fellow works in a General Motors plant and does
not want to belong to a union, he does not have to work there.

SENATOR GOLDWATER: But suppose he wants to work there?

MR. REUTHER: If you want to live in a certain community and you want the
benefits of the work of that community, you have to pay taxes in that community. If you do not, you do not have to live in that community. That is the
freedom of choice. The only check is that it has to be a democratic choice,
decision; it has to be a majority democratic decision.

Inside of the industrial community, General Motors has 400,000 employees.
How can a complex industrial society like ours work out machinery within this
industrial community to meet these problems unless it can be done by a democratic decision of the people involved?

SENATOR GOLDWATER: I get down to the individual who does not want to
belong to a union. Let us extend your thinking a little bit further. Take the
matter of churches. Certainly churches benefit everybody. Yet we all do not
support churches. Should we include laws to tax everybody to support churches
in the community? Whether all of us agree or not, organizations like the

Chamber of Commerce, for instance, do a lot of good for the people who liv
in the community, but I do not have to belong to the Chamber of Commerc
and neither do you. Yet, because I am a member and pay my dues, I feel prett
much like you, as a union man, feels about the man who will not join your union
but I recognize the right of that competitor of mine or any other friend to say
"yes" or "no" to membership in an organization that he will admit benefits him

It gets down to that, and that is, in my mind, the only question: What abou
the individual?

MR. REUTHER: The UAW-CIO, for example, to use a specific case, are
certified as the sole collective bargaining agent. We represent every General
Motor worker in our units. No church represents all the people in the community. You are dealing with an entirely different kind of thing. The church is a
fraternal religious organization that you can choose to belong to or choose not to
belong to; but our unions are the sole bargaining agent under the law. We represent every General Motors worker. When we process a grievance, every General Motors worker gets the benefit of that. If we have a case that goes to the
court on some workmen's compensation case, that sets a principle, and every
GM worker gets the benefit of that protection that we want. If we have our
doctors go in and check on the dust in a foundry or the fumes in a factory plant
and we take corrective steps to protect the health of the workers, every worker
in that plant gets the benefit of that.

The church does not perform that kind of function in the community. The
church deals with the spiritual values. You can either choose to get them or you
can choose not to get them.

But we are by law the agency by which all workers in a given factory take
care of their industrial problems. In other words, we really are like a government within that factory, within that industrial community. If you are going
to have a government within the industrial community, you have a right to
insist that it is a democratic government; you have a right to insist that the
workers who make up the industrial citizens in that industrial community have
a right to elect their officers democratically, have a right to make democratic
majority decisions. But having made the democratic majority decisions, the
people in the minority are obligated to go along with the majority just as they
are when you vote taxes for schools in your community. What is the difference?
It is the same principle.

SENATOR GOLDWATER: I do not agree with you there. I see what you are
getting at, and I think we could probably spend a whole year arguing about
that point.

I keep getting back to the one question: Suppose a man does not want to
belong to a union? You are not a government. The dues to the union cannot be
compared to taxes. They do not bring all the benefits that taxes bring. I merely
inject that.

MR. REUTHER: They do in the industrial community.

SENATOR GOLDWATER: I wanted to get your thinking on what about the individual, because it all gets down, as you say, to the freedom of the individual,
his desire to belong to a union or not, his desire to—let us forget churches—his

.esire to belong to the Chamber of Commerce or not, or to any other organiza-
ion that might be helpful, to support the Red Cross or not, the Community
Chest or not.

MR. REUTHER: You go out to the Ford plant. I worked for 6 years in the Ford
plant under the old system before we had a union. You talk to the workers out
there. When they voted 88,000 to 1,000, that was an expression that they had
found a new freedom. The union has given them greater freedom than we ever
had, freedom from terror, and intimidation, and insecurity.

SENATOR GOLDWATER: I do not disagree with you. I agree with you. I think
the unions have done wonderfully. But there are still a thousand men who do
not want to belong to the union. You see what I am getting at. To my mind,
you are tampering with the basic freedom that this Government is set up to
give the people.

SENATOR GRISWOLD: It seems to me, Mr. Reuther, in the field of civil rights,
you do not believe that because 51 percent of the people make a decision one
way, that they should force their opinion upon the other 49 percent. We are
talking about the rights of minorities, and a great deal of our Constitution and
a great deal of the Bill of Rights is to protect the minority against the excessive
demands on the part of, say, 51 percent of the people to force their will upon
the minority. I do not altogether believe that 51 percent of the people in any
community or in any economic group have a right to force their rights upon
the other 49 percent. There might be a situation in a State where they force
everyone to belong to the Democratic Party or the Republican Party just
because a majority voted that they wanted the Democratic Party or the Republican Party to represent them in the field of government, but certainly you
would say that was contrary to the rights of human beings.

MR. REUTHER: I am opposed to the majority taking away the rights of the
minority. We are not talking about that. We are talking about the question of
whether they ought to belong and pay their taxes in an industrial union. They
do not take away their rights. As a matter of fact, it facilitates their rights.

SENATOR GRISWOLD: In some ways it does take away their rights, to some
extent, to work there without belonging to the union. That is a minority right.

MR. REUTHER: I am never able to understand this, Mr. Chairman: The
American Medical Association has taken the closed shop principle and applied
it with a vengeance. In the average city, if you do not belong to their setup,
worked out by their quota system and everything, you cannot get a hospital bed.
It is quite all right for the American Medical Association to apply the principle
of the closed shop to their profession, but when a group of workers try to
protect their interests by applying that same principle, it suddenly becomes un-
American and a violation of all the basic values.

SENATOR GRISWOLD: You should apply the rule you referred to in answer to
Senator Douglas. You had better work out the wrongs in the situation and not
use that as an argument to prove that you are right in your situation.

MR. REUTHER: The principle is sound. . . .

SENATOR DOUGLAS: . . . may I offer a suggestion which might clear up
some of this very real difficulty. I do not know that it will effectively do it.

There is an inevitable conflict in a few cases between effective collective actio and individual conscience. There is no doubt about that. I am wondering if th provisions which are made in some unions and mass industries could not gen erally be followed out: namely, that where a man's religion or his conscienc really restrain him from joining the union, if he pays the equivalent of unio dues and thus bears his share of the cost of the benefits which he receive without being an active participant, could that not be regarded as satisfactory even if he does not become a formal union member.

MR. REUTHER: Senator Douglas, we do that every day of the week. There are certain religious groups who, for reasons of conscience, feel that they cannot participate. We have worked those out. We have worked it out with the Seventh Day Adventists, the Brethrens, and other groups. We have had no difficulty, because that is a matter of being sensible and reasonable. But that is something quite different from a worker who just does not want to belong to a union because he says it violates his principles.

SENATOR DOUGLAS: I understand. I mean, could not some such arrangement as that meet, say, 99 percent of the real conflict, not the artificially engendered conflict?

MR. REUTHER: I think it could. I do not think you would have any trouble working it out where it is a matter of conscience. You will find the unions are willing and have been willing and are doing it, working out such practical problems.

SENATOR DOUGLAS: Would you be willing to have some such provision as that put in the law?

MR. REUTHER: Certainly. We would not object to formalizing what we are doing in practice.

COMPULSORY UNIONISM

Statement of Herman W. Steinkraus, on behalf of the Chamber of Commerce of the United States, regarding proposed National Labor Law Revision, in Labor Relations, hearings before the Senate Committee on Labor and Public Welfare, 81st Cong., 1st Sess., 1949, part 5, pp. 2462–2464

It would be appropriate at this point to mention the closed shop. The Wagner Act made it an unfair labor practice for an employer to discriminate against employees by reason of union membership or lack of it, but permitted unions to make a closed-shop contract with an employer whereby he could avoid that prohibition, in part, by discriminating for union members. In other words, it was wrong for an employer to discriminate but all right for a union to do so or force the employer to do so. The result is illogical. If compulsion is wrongful conduct for an employer, it is equally wrongful for a union. If a monopoly is wrongful conduct for an employer, it is equally wrongful for a union. There is no subtle change from wrong to right merely because of the character of the person perpetuating the wrong.

The chamber has long contended that compulsory unionism interferes with the free and uncoerced choice of employees with respect to collective bargaining. Employees should be free to join or not to join a labor organization. Their right to work should never be dependent on union membership.

If unions cannot recruit and hold members on their merits, they should not be allowed to force employees into membership. If I am unable to persuade a customer to buy my product, I am not allowed to sell it to him by compulsion. Why should any different rule apply to unions?

Moreover, this compulsion at times works another way. A qualified employee may want to work and be willing to join the union which holds a closed-shop contract. If the union, however, won't admit him to membership he is denied employment opportunity. This, too, is wrong. It is unjustifiable monopoly of a basic and cherished right: the right to earn a living. The closed shop, coupled with a closed union, has been too common a device for abusing the rights of employees for Congress simply to close its eyes to it.

A compulsory unionism contract restricts the plant management in an unwarranted and disadvantageous manner in the selection and retention of suitable employees. Under such a contract, the employer would be able to hire only persons who are willing to become members of the recognized labor organization if they are not already members. Other persons who have good and sufficient reasons of their own for either preferring membership in a different labor organization, or in none at all, would either refuse to work for the employer, although they might be highly desirable and useful employees from every standpoint, or they would have to pay additional initiation fees and double dues, if they want to retain membership in another union of their choice.

Under a compulsory unionism contract, the employers would be compelled to discharge any employee, no matter how long his period of employment or how satisfactory, if such employee is unwilling for some reason of his own, to be a member of the recognized labor organization or is unwilling to pay dues to it. This might easily cause serious interference with the efficient operation of the plant.

The closed or union shop involves mandatory dues payments. This deprives the union members of their democratic control of their organization. The members lose their right to resign and stop paying dues, which is their most effective means of preventing arbitrary or unscrupulous action, or even racketeering, by their leaders. It permits the union leader to be a dictator and destroys the principle of majority rule. It forces a member of the union to quit his job as the only escape from supporting an organization which may have become wholly unsatisfactory to him.

Compulsory membership in a particular union violates the basic principle that employees should not be required by the employer to take part in any organization or activity or enroll in any benefit plan in order to secure or keep a job. It is a sound principle that all such participation should be strictly voluntary.

The attempt of the unions to eliminate "free riders" through the closed shop is unfair to the minority group. No one ever heard about "free riders" until the unions started to collect "fares" in the form of initiation fees, dues, and assessments. This restriction on freedom of choice of the worker (who, many times, cannot afford to leave his job and community in search of another) is like compelling Republicans in a county or town which has voted Democratic to contribute to the support of the Democratic Party or leave the locality. All must pay their assessed taxes for public services. But taxes cannot be collected to maintain the party treasury.

Compulsory unionism is harmful to the rights of the unorganized worker, the worker who does not want to join a union. Recent Supreme Court decisions have indicated that legislation which protects the rights of the unorganized worker may be enacted by the States where they feel it necessary to correct a situation which is inimical to the public welfare. Denial of the right to work of a worker who happens not to sympathize with the union is denial of a fundamental right. It is said that a worker who cannot get a job because of closed-shop restrictions can go to a nonunionized area to get a job. Far from a defense of compulsory unionism, that statement is a strong argument for outlawing it.

An employee should have the right to continue to live in the place where he may have lived all his life. He should not be arbitrarily forced to spend his savings and disrupt his family life. No, this argument shows most clearly one of the basic failings of the closed shop and why it should not be legalized.

These types of abuses, multiplied many times, were what led Congress to outlaw the closed shop. The arguments against it have not lost their cogency at all. Basic limitations on workers' personal liberty are involved in any closed-shop contract. Restraint, often amounting to absolute, arbitrary monopoly, on an employer's control of his business, of his right to hire employees he considers most suitable for his organization, of his communication lines with his employees, exists under any closed-shop contract. The basic principle of the right to work is flagrantly disregarded. Nor are such practices made less of an evil by calling them union security measures, rather than compulsory unionism.

UNIONS ASPIRE TO GOVERNMENTAL POWER

Statement of General Electric Co. in Taft-Hartley Act Revisions, hearings before the Senate Committee on Labor and Public Welfare, 83d Cong., 1st Sess., 1953, part 2, p. 964

To say that compulsory unionism and its consequence, the industrial community, is no more than the application of the principle of majority rule is obviously untrue. The specious nature of such argument may be demonstrated by merely recalling that many of us have in our own neighborhood communities, voluntary neighborhood organizations. These neighborhood organizations are also run on the principle of majority rule. They do much to represent the interest of the neighborhood in civic matters; their activities protect and enhance property values, in general they promote the common interests and welfare of all within the neighborhood community. How surprised and resentful each of us would be, however, if we were told that merely because we were a part of that neighborhood community, we had no choice but to join its organization, abide by its rules and regulations, and to pay dues, any amount of money which the majority determined was necessary to support its projects. How particularly surprised and resentful most of us would be if we found that while being compelled to join and support this neighborhood community, the officers of the organization were using its funds and our dues to promote and support political candidates, we opposed, or to promote and support measures which we considered would lead to the ultimate socialization of the Nation.

The very fact that union officials admit their aspirations ultimately to be the governing officials of the so-called industrial community discloses the extent of the power they seek. In brief, they believe that unions, as the governing mechanism of this industrial community should exercise many of the powers of a sovereign state with reference to that community.

We venture to suggest that no idea involving a more radical departure from our American constitutional traditions has ever been urged upon the Supreme Court or suggested to a congressional committee. Until so startling a thesis is officially accepted, there will continue to be only two categories of circumstances in which an American citizen need consider himself subject to the taxes, laws and penalties prescribed by officials he disapproves merely because they have been prescribed and established under the principle of majority rule. The first such category is where the individual voluntarily joins an organization and voluntarily elects to remain in it. The second category, of course, is where the individual's residence and citizenship naturally subjects him to the sovereign authority of a Federal or State Government or some branch thereof. It is our opinion that unions obviously belong in the first category and should not be given the right to exercise any of the compulsory sovereign powers which rightfully belong only in the second category.

FREEDOM OF ASSOCIATION AND MAJORITY RIGHTS

Testimony of Robert B. Watts, Vice President and General Counsel, Consolidated Vultee Aircraft Corp., San Diego, Calif., in Taft-Hartley Act Revisions, hearings before the Senate Committee on Labor and Public Welfare, 83d Cong., 1st Sess., 1953, part 2, pp. 716–717

On the subject of compulsory unionism, we go all the way. We say that the proviso of section 8 (a) (3) should be taken out. We think that you come to grips at this point with the basic concept of individual freedom. We think that the only reason and justification for the present Federal toleration of the union shop is the so-called free rider argument. And we say, in response to that, that when the statute enunciates as the policy of the United States, that there should be a freedom of workers to associate, it means what it says; and that there is equally a freedom on the part of those who do not wish to join unions but to remain by themselves and to amass, if they please, their own financial resources, in order to combat the union at a later election. Indeed we think that the suggestion that the unions have now become so much endowed with sovereignty as to refer to themselves as government, as they have before this committee, indicates the unconscious degree to which these labor leaders have been led in their acquisition of power.

We say, gentlemen, that freedom of association is at the root of this act. There is nothing in this act which guarantees the development and creation of labor unions. This act guarantees the freedom of employees to organize and to choose whomever they wish to represent them. They can choose a movie actor if they wish. This act guarantees that, having organized themselves and having selected a representative, their representative is entitled to bargain freely with the employer.

SENATOR TAFT: That sounds like an easy thing, but we really took the step right there to limit freedom. Because we say that if a majority want X as a bargaining agent, the right of the other people to bargain themselves or to choose their own bargaining agent is destroyed.

MR. WATTS: I agree with that, sir.

SENATOR TAFT: So that really the fundamental concept of the whole business of enforcing collective bargaining is far more restrictive of individual liberty than the union shop, in my opinion, because they cannot bargain; those people are deprived of the right to bargain. Now, that we have accepted, and so, when you go on the union shop theory and say that you have to join the union, it does not seem to me to be nearly as important a deprivation as that which takes place at the very basis of the Wagner Act.

MR. WATTS: Except that I suggest, Senator, that it is not as unrealistic to protect the right of those individuals who represent the then minority, and who, perforce, have to be represented in bargaining by the majority.

SENATOR TAFT: You say you have got to let X bargain for you. I do not know why you should not say you have to pay X to bargain for you. I do not see the difference.

MR. WATTS: What I am suggesting is that you ought to have the right, as the minority, to oppose X on the next occasion of an election.

SENATOR TAFT: Oh, yes. You have the right to do that. You can vote the union out.

MR. WATTS: Well, I think I have indicated my point here, which is that we believe that there isn't any halfway business on this compulsory union membership.

SENATOR TAFT: I think I would dispute that entirely. I think the union shop is entirely a different thing from the closed shop, fundamentally different.

Do you have many union shops in the industry?

MR. WATTS: No; we don't have many. We have some. And those have been brought about very much against our will and under the circumstances of bargaining which I have described earlier, under the aegis of governmental representatives.

SENATOR TAFT: Well, the essential difference is very clear. One is that under the union shop the employer reserves the right to put anybody to work he wants to put to work. Under the union shop anybody who wants to get a job can get a job without the consent of the union. Those are the essential freedoms that are maintained, which maintains freedom of transfer in the whole labor field and gives them the right to go into the industry which they want to. In other words, the closed shop does eliminate most of the freedom which we want to preserve. The union shop, though, does not seriously infringe upon it.

IS THE CLOSED SHOP DEMOCRATIC?

By Leonard John Turner, in The Painter and Decorator, June, 1953

Would we say that those who come from other lands and work and enjoy the fruits of our country should not be subject to the laws and taxes which our Government imposes for the welfare of all? Should we allow them to impose their own way of life on ours? Should we have to change our laws to suit those who have come from decadent and "foreign" lands, merely because they are not used to prosperity as we know it? It would be a fine kettle of fish if only the dutiful and patriotic citizens of Our Country were made punishable under the law and taxable.

"Oh, I didn't take out citizenship papers, so you can't punish me for breaking the law," would be quite logical under open-shop citizenship. "I don't need to pay this State tax because I only took out papers for another State." It sounds pretty silly, doesn't it, when put this way; but that is the argument the supporters of the open-shop are handing Our People. But that is how some non-Unionists and some anti-Unionists are thinking. Enough to make a Judge sputter and fume to hear such silliness. . . .

Some men object to being "forced" to join a Union and stand on their constitutional rights to contract with their employers on an individual contract basis. Have we the right to deny him that privilege? You will note that I am stating the arguments as the "opposition" expresses them. Let the non-Union man look at the matter in another way, I plead.

Just as when the frontiers of land were closed we were no longer a pioneer country, so have the frontiers of Industry closed. Whereas in the early settlements there was little if any law enforcement and might was right, so in the early days of Industry might was right and the man who was in the strongest position was a law unto himself. But today law enforcement has come to Industry in the form of Labor Unions and Brotherhoods. Standards of conduct are established democratically and are democratically controlled by organizations of majorities of workmen in the various industries. All workmen in America have benefited from the struggle and work of Unions. Better standards of living, improved working conditions and wages have been gained for all in industries through the *levelling upwards* of the unionized workingman.

"But," you may say, "in this third grouping of forces we have to respect the minority right." That is true—in part.

The minority right extends only to the right to express dissent in Local Meetings, in District or State Council Meetings or in the National Conferences of a Union or Brotherhood. The minority also has the privilege of staying away from meetings and withholding its vote. That is the right of every individual in a Democracy.

But the rights of an individual do not extend to the right of non-payment of taxes. All workingmen owe it to themselves and to their country to join a Brotherhood or Union and to pay dues willingly. They also owe it to their fellow workers to become self-governed and to obey the Industrial laws which they themselves have set up.

The Constitution of the United States and the British North America Act have set a precedent for us to show how we may delegate various phases of Our sovereignty to several Governments. Our Federal rights we delegate to Washington—or Ottawa—and our State or Provincial rights to State or Provincial Government. Our civic rights are in the control of City Officials and Our working rights are delegated to Our Union Locals and Federations.

"If you are afraid that you will lose your personality and just be lost in the mob if you join a Union, then you are planning your careers under a delusion," I recently told a group of technical school students. No one in America has ever lost his or her individuality by becoming a citizen and by exercising the citizen's right to act in the voting booth or to speak his mind on a platform. How much are you or I going to lose of our precious little personality by bringing it down to the Local meeting and testing it out on the floor of the meeting? Life is a friction with one's fellow beings. Activity in the life of your Local is living as it is planned in the democratic way.

LEAVING FREE CHOICE TO THE INDIVIDUAL

Testimony of Frederick G. Atkinson, Vice President for Personnel, R. H. Macy & Co., New York, appearing on behalf of the American Retail Federation, in Taft-Hartley Act Revisions, hearings before the Senate Committee on Labor and Public Welfare, 83d Cong., 1st Sess., 1953, part 2, pp. 1095–1098

We believe that unions deserve and are entitled only to the support which they earn but not to support, financial and otherwise, which they obtain by the coercion of union shop or in other forms of compulsory union membership. . . .

THE CHAIRMAN: In a plant which we will say is organized, where union X is voted to be the bargaining agent, where you get a vote of, say, 51 percent or 52 percent or something like that to support union X, you admit that union is the bargaining agent?

MR. ATKINSON: For representation purposes, yes, sir.

THE CHAIRMAN: For representation. And even the 49 percent, which you say should not be compelled to join the union, are represented by that bargaining unit. Now, does your thinking contemplate any way by which the 49 percent that may be benefited by that bargaining would pay their share of the freight, or do you think that is not necessary?

MR. ATKINSON: There is traditionally an imputed benefit to those who are not members of the union. The argument on this, which has been persuasive in my mind, is this: We all benefit to a greater or lesser degree from things to which we do not directly pay. We benefit from the work of the Red Cross, from that of the Boy Scouts of America, from that of hundreds of voluntary associations to which we may or may not subscribe. Because we contribute to the Red Cross one year is, to my mind, no reason why we should be compelled thereafter, under penalty of loss of our employment, to contribute every year in the future. Or because we enjoy some indirect benefit from what the Red Cross does is no reason why we should all be forced to contribute to it.

If you were to carry to its logical conclusion the doctrine that every one must pay for every imputed benefit which he enjoys directly or indirectly, we would have no money left with which to buy our groceries.

I personally see no reason why we should have a legal compulsion to pay for an imputed benefit, which in some cases the individual simply does not believe in, the one who does not want to join the union, or who does not want to subscribe to the Red Cross.

THE CHAIRMAN: I do not think that analogy is quite apt. I think in an industry where we have a recognition of the right of the employees in the industry to choose negotiators as their bargaining agents, and that has been legalized, where we recognize collective bargaining as the heart of the whole management-labor relationship—you would agree with that?

MR. ATKINSON: Quite so.

THE CHAIRMAN: If that is true, if you have provided a way to determine who will be the people to do the sole negotiating for the workers, I think it is a different case from your Red Cross analogy, or a different case from the chamber of commerce, by which we all benefit but to which we do not all contribute.

Now, I have difficulty in saying that those who benefit by that whole process have not some responsibility to it, although I am not arguing about compulsory unionism. I am not saying that is necessary. I want to find some alternative which recognizes the fact that there are some costs involved to the people in doing their bargaining and negotiating.

MR. ATKINSON: My answer to that would be that, one, we should set up as their representative the organization which represents the majority, and, secondly, they should be participants to the extent that they believe their own best interests dictate. They should not be participants by reason of any form of compulsion which says, "You must pay this tax because somebody else says you enjoy a benefit from it." That would be my answer, sir. . . .

The employee who does not wish to be a member of a union, which for bargaining purposes includes him in its representation, it seems to me, is entitled to join the union or stay out. He is not entitled to assert himself as a union official or a committee member if he is not a member of the union. But he should have the free choice to either leave it to this group to represent him, or to get in and undertake to instruct them. And if he wants to get in and undertake to instruct them, as many workers do, of their own free will, why then he obviously should place himself in good standing as a member. But if he chooses not to participate in this, if he thinks it is not to his best interest, and he prefers to disassociate himself from it, I think that also should be his right.

THE CHAIRMAN: Should he be compelled to strike in case the leaders decide there should be a strike and 51 percent are in the union that called the strike and 49 percent are not? Should the 49 percent then be compelled to participate in the strike?

MR. ATKINSON: You are raising a completely different question, sir. Except when there is violence, the decision among employees as to who goes out on strike very often is not consistent with union membership. . . .

THE CHAIRMAN: Let us suppose a secret ballot is taken in favor of a strike.

MR. ATKINSON: Yes?

THE CHAIRMAN: And that secret ballot, say, is 51 percent for and 49 percent against. That makes that strike legal.

MR. ATKINSON: It represents the will of the majority. That is correct.

THE CHAIRMAN: Now, then, you would say that the minority that were against the strike would not have to pay any attention to the vote for a strike?

MR. ATKINSON: Well, this is a more subtle matter. The decision whether to go out on strike is a function of too many different things. It may be a question of personal conviction or principle that one should never cross a picket line regardless of the merits of the dispute. There are others who feel that it is important to get this week's pay and, therefore, who do not want to be deprived of it, and put that ahead of some considerations of union action or principle. So that, in the absence of forceful prevention of the worker from going to work, these democratic votes that you describe as the strike issue do not tend to be controlling. They do not tend to deprive the man who wants to go to work of his right to do so—again I say, in the absence of violence or force that might keep him out of the plant. He may be in trouble with his union. They may say, "You have violated our picket line. You went to work when we said you shouldn't." But that is not a basis for losing his employment, because the act itself protects him as long as he pays his dues.

THE NONUNION MAN IS NOT A FREE RIDER

From "The Right to Work," an address of J. C. Gibson, Vice President, Atchison, Topeka and Santa Fe Railway Co., before the 1956 spring meeting of the Industrial Relations Research Association, Milwaukee, Wis., May 4, 1956

The unions complain about what they call free riders—those workers who do not belong to a union but are forced by law to have their wages, hours, and working conditions established by the union representing the workers in their craft or class. They argue that it is unfair to let any worker share in the results of union bargaining without bearing part of the expenses.

But the unions themselves asked Congress for the power to represent and bind all employees in the bargaining unit, including those not union members. They saw how valuable this power to speak for non-members would be to them. It removes all competition and cements their monopoly position. They sought this power, knowing what obligations it entails, and their present complaint that the immensely valuable privilege they obtained is actually a burden rings hollow indeed.

TAXATION WITHOUT MEMBERSHIP

Testimony of Walter P. Reuther, President, United Automobile Workers, CIO, in Labor-Management Relations, hearings before the House Committee on Education and Labor, 83d Cong., 1st Sess., 1953, part 3, pp. 1011–1012

CHAIRMAN MCCONNELL: Let us consider one angle of this payment of taxes for services and the free-rider argument. Suppose an employee who benefits from the activities of the union, and I can see where a citizen does receive tangible benefits from the activities of a union, but suppose he paid taxes or suppose he paid a fee for such services without joining the union. What do you think of that approach? As a union leader, I guess that approach would not suit you, but I am trying to answer your simile here with regard to a citizen paying taxes for services.

MR. REUTHER: If we were guilty of what the people who carry on the antiunion propaganda against the union shop and the closed shop claim and they charge we are guilty of, we would say to you that is a good arrangement. We will have a small union, but everybody outside will have to pay us tribute.

We are not interested in the building of dues-collecting agencies. Collective bargaining is an extension of the democratic processes into the industrial community, and we want to develop maximum industrial economic citizenship by participation in our unions. If we were just interested in money, I would say "Yes," but we are not. We think that collective bargaining in responsible unions is possible only if you have democratic participation of the membership.

HAVE UNION MEN THE RIGHT TO REFUSE TO WORK WITH NON-UNION MEN?

Statement of Gerhard P. Van Arkel, Counsel, International Typographical Union, in Labor Relations, hearings before the Senate Committee on Labor and Public Welfare, 81st Cong., 1st Sess., 1949, pp. 2812–2814

. . . The legal question, the real legal question is not: Shall we permit or deny the closed shop agreement? The question goes much deeper than that. The real question is: Have union men the right to refuse to work with non-union men?

Because the closed-shop agreement is no more than the symbol of the right of union men to refuse to work with competing nonunion men. . . .

THE CHAIRMAN: Mr. Van Arkel, may I break in there?

MR. VAN ARKEL: Yes, of course.

THE CHAIRMAN: Aren't you leading us down quite an alley there by that kind of argument for the closed shop and letting the closed shop rest on that sort of arrangement?

Does any workman have the right to say, "I am not going to work with an

Englishman or with a Chinaman or with a man who has red eyes or green eyes or a bald head?"

MR. VAN ARKEL: I think, Senator, he has exactly the same right that an employer has to say, "I am not going to hire an Englishman."

THE CHAIRMAN: Let us not get onto anyone else's right. Let us keep with the logic of your assertion.

Now I myself would feel in a very hazardous position in going onto the Senate floor and arguing the story of the closed shop on just that narrow basis, namely that every man has a right to decide with whom he is going to work. How in the wide world could you ever run a railway on that kind of theory?

MR. VAN ARKEL: I think it is done every day, Senator. People certainly quit their jobs because they don't like their fellow employees.

THE CHAIRMAN: I am not going to work because I don't like the conductor and I don't like the motorman and I don't like the kind of passengers they carry.

MR. VAN ARKEL: Senator, I am confident that happens every day in American industry, that all sorts of people quit their jobs because they object to fellow employees. They may object to them for any one of a variety of reasons.

THE CHAIRMAN: They quit their jobs as individuals.

MR. VAN ARKEL: That is true.

THE CHAIRMAN: And they lose their identity immediately because if a closed-shop group decides it shall not take a stand of that kind, why, then what is the individual to do? He either has to get out of the closed shop, which brings him to the horn of another dilemma, or he has to quit working altogether.

While I know that what you are saying is the commonest kind of argument used, I believe that if you think it through in its complexities in this extremely complex life we are leading—shall I take my money out of a bank because I don't like the bank president? I have the right. But what happens?

You see, when you argue a thing just from the standpoint of right, you bring society to an end, an absolute end.

It is like the very interesting story told to us the other day, that if you enter marriage on a basis of contract and the contract is so wide that you cover every detail of life, that is not satisfactory.

Now, I think it is all right for you to defend the closed shop—I am going to defend it, but I am not going to defend it just upon a man's right to decide with whom he is going to work, because society just stops if you stay in the realm of right, and there are no rights unless there are a few responsibilities and a few duties, and rights become important because they are entered into on the basis of some sort of sacrifice. That is, I give up something in order to have these rights. Democracy just ceases to exist the moment you take from it the idea of common consent, because then freedom becomes complete license and nothing is held together. Man in his very nature has to get along with other men, and of all the institutions which we have had which amount to anything—and the closed-shop idea is an awfully good idea and a good institution, I am not arguing that, but it is not based upon the theory of absolute right, absolute individual right, because it falls by the wayside.

You may be able to argue in that way in the law court where there are absolute justices and all the rest of it, but by getting the absolute justice they destroy justice, and that is the history of man—and you know it—therefore, I think that those of us who have to defend this proposition ought to be on the alert to detect a narrow view of what constitutes a right, knowing that to make it into an absolute, we would bring about the destruction of that which we are trying to defend. . . .

MR. VAN ARKEL: I am grateful for the admonition, but I would like to observe this; that I also feel in legislating and also in arguing law cases one is constantly facing the problem of the relative importance of rights.

THE CHAIRMAN: Now, you are talking sense; excuse me.

MR. VAN ARKEL: I would suppose that the right which we have considered most valuable and most sacred in this country and which we are least willing to infringe is the right of a man to quit his employment for any reason, no reason, bad reason, good reason. That is an important right in our democratic society.

THE CHAIRMAN: . . . There is no absolute right when once you recognize the existence of society. There just isn't an absolute right because you have a conflicting of rights in everything you do, and when you have a conflict of rights, the settlement comes in some hazy place up here in the realm of the highest kind of argument, not where society works, and I think you can never do a greater injustice, either to employers or to employees, than to lead them into that place where they stand for these absolutes which do not and cannot exist.

MR. VAN ARKEL: Very good, Senator, but if I can just point this out: One of the factors in this whole situation—let us get away now from talking of rights and I will get into the field where I shouldn't be; namely, the question of the practical problem of the closed shop, which I had hoped to avoid.

It is true that, for very good reasons historically, union men have felt their craft and their union is weakened if they consented to work in the company of nonunion men. It is an old tradition and it is a very strongly ingrained tradition.

Now, if we recognize that men have the right to leave their employment because they are exercising a tradition of which they are proud and which they hold for the best of reasons, then I suggest that we cannot, consistent with the Constitution and consistent with the right of a man to leave his employment, apart from the question of the engineer or the man flooding the mine, pass effective legislation which will compel men to remain at work in the company of nonunion men.

All I am attempting to say here is that as long as the constitutional guaranty against involuntary servitude persists that union men will de facto insist upon and maintain closed-shop conditions, closed-shop agreements or not.

CLOSED SHOP AND UNION SHOP

National Labor Relations Act of 1947, report from the Senate Committee on Labor and Public Welfare to accompany S. 1126, 80th Cong., 1st Sess., 1947, pp. 6–7

It is clear that the closed shop which requires preexisting union membership as a condition of obtaining employment creates too great a barrier to free employment to be longer tolerated. In the maritime industry and to a large extent in the construction industry union hiring halls now provide the only method of securing employment. This not only permits unions holding such monopolies over jobs to exact excessive fees but it deprives management of any real choice of the men it hires. Extension of this principle to licensed deck and engine officers has created the greatest problems in connection with the safety of American vessels at sea. (See testimony of Almon E. Roth, id., vol. 2, p. 612.)

Numerous examples were presented to the committee of the way union leaders have used closed-shop devices as a method of depriving employees of their jobs, and in some cases a means of securing a livelihood in their trade or calling, for purely capricious reasons. In one instance a union member was subpenaed to appear in court, having witnessed an assault upon his foreman by a fellow employee. Because he told the truth upon the witness stand, the union leadership brought about his expulsion with a consequent loss of his job since his employer was subject to a closed-shop contract. (See testimony of William L. McGrath, id., vol. 4, p. 1982.)

Numerous examples of equally glaring disregard for the rights of minority members of unions are contained in the exhibits received in evidence by the committee. (See testimony of Cecil B. DeMille, id., vol. 2, p. 797; see also, id., vol. 4, pp. 2063–2071.) If trade-unions were purely fraternal or social organizations, such instances would not be a matter of congressional concern, but since membership in such organizations in many trades or callings is essential to earning a living, Congress cannot ignore the existence of such power.

Under the amendments which the committee recommends, employers would still be permitted to enter into agreements requiring all the employees in a given bargaining unit to become members 30 days after being hired if a majority of such employees have shown their intent by secret ballot to confer authority to negotiate such an agreement upon their representatives.* But in order to safeguard the rights of employees after such a contract has been entered into, three additional safeguards are provided: (1) Membership in the union must be available to an employee on the same terms and conditions generally applicable to other members; (2) expulsion from a union cannot be a ground of compulsory discharge if the worker is not delinquent in paying his initiation fee or dues; (3) if a worker is denied membership or expelled from

* Editor's note: The requirement of such a secret-ballot authorization of a union to negotiate a union-shop provision was eliminated by the amendment of 1951.

the union because he exercises the right conferred on him by the act to work for the change of a bargaining representative at an appropriate time he cannot be discharged.

It seems to us that these amendments remedy the most serious abuses of compulsory union membership and yet give employers and unions who feel that such agreements promoted stability by eliminating "free riders" the right to continue such arrangements.

ADVANTAGES OF THE CLOSED SHOP

Testimony of J. J. O'Donnell, President, National Constructors Association, New York, N.Y., Taft-Hartley Act Revisions, hearings before the Senate Committee on Labor and Public Welfare, 83d Cong., 1st Sess., 1953, part 3, pp. 1344–1345

THE CONSTRUCTION INDUSTRY

The typical construction worker is not truly the employee of a specific employer; he is, rather, the employee of the industry, gaining employment from whatever contractor happens to be engaged in work in the area of his home. If construction activity is low in his home locality, he travels to nearby areas for work, and often to other States and regions. Historically, and largely because he cannot depend upon a single employer for his livelihood, the average or typical construction worker looks to his union for the security which other workers find in factory, shop, mine, or office.

The union in the construction industry, while primarily—and properly—serving its members, also serves the contractor employers. Consider the situation of a contractor who enters a locality, perhaps for the first time, to conduct a project. He has no long-term interest in the area or in the many workers of various and different skills whom he intends to employ. The careful recruiting and screening of prospective workers—standard practice for a manufacturing unit, for example—are impractical and almost meaningless to the construction contractor. His needs, rather, are of a different order. He requires some arrangements to assure him of a measure of stability and uniformity of labor rates and labor costs prior to commencement of work.

I might pause here for a moment to interject an example. We frequently move into areas, such as my particular company is doing now in North Dakota, where primarily there has been very little large industrial construction. My company is about to erect a very large refinery in that area. However, prior to bidding on the construction of that refinery, we had to know something about labor costs. . . .

It is not too easy to determine when you are bidding on a $20 or $30 million job what your costs will be, unless you have some way of determining the cost of the nonwage benefits. The cost of welfare funds alone is becoming an increasing problem in our industry. If we find out that a specific rate for a specific craftsman is X dollars, that does not mean our entire labor cost will be X dollars. It will be X dollars, plus the cost of these other benefits.

Furthermore, when we move into an area, we must have some method of quick recruitment—for relatively short employment periods—of experienced and skilled mechanics. The building trades unions can provide these needs.

As a matter of fact, in our industry the building trades unions have supplied us with skilled craftsmen for almost 50 years.

By negotiation with local employers, the local unions can establish uniform wage rates and working conditions which normally remain in effect for specific periods of time. Local unions can foresee employment needs, they can arrange, through transfer of men from project to project and through advertising their needs to neighboring localities and affiliated locals, to supply qualified men when and as they are needed.

Against this background, the present requirements and prohibitions of the act [which] relate to union security are inapplicable from a practical standpoint.

Testimony of John C. Stevenson, Attorney, Los Angeles, Calif., on behalf of the Los Angeles Joint Council of Teamsters, No. 42, in Taft-Hartley Act Revisions, hearings before the Senate Committee on Labor and Public Welfare, 83d Cong., 1st Sess., 1953, part 3, pp. 1698–1699

CANNING AND TRUCKING

With respect to the International Brotherhood of Teamsters, the casual employment problem, as I have said, is very similar to that in the building trades. We have it particularly in three divisions of our operations. The first is the canning industry. The bargaining in the canning industry is very similar to that in the construction industry. The workers are employed for very short periods, usually 2 to 6 weeks on any particular pack. The union is responsible in the canning areas for recruiting these workers for all packing plants where union contracts are in existence. The turnover in a given area is tremendous during the canning season. In 1 year it required more than 40,000 workers to fill 17,000 jobs because of the turnover. Many of the workers never complete a 30-day period at any particular plant. For this reason the 30-day restriction of the Taft-Hartley Act on union-security contracts is completely unworkable, as it is in the construction industry.

The union is the only agency that has a complete list of available workers who can be dispatched to any plant requiring help. The expense of listing and dispatching such workers is borne exclusively by the union, yet they are unable to secure union-shop contracts which require membership because of the extremely short working season and shifting of employees from plant to plant.

More important, the employers cannot secure accurate cost figures in advance of production if these negotiations for labor contracts are delayed until after the production season begins. The employers and unions in this industry are in complete agreement that the 30-day requirement of the Taft-Hartley Act should be eliminated in order that complete contract may be negotiated before work commences. . . .

A similar problem to this exists in casual labor for auto-freight lines. Here the casual labor is dispatched and works for only a few hours or at most 2 or 3 days for any one company.

As in the canneries, the union is the only source of available competent help. They are furnished on a few hours' notice. This problem exists in every large city in the Nation.

It would require perhaps a year or more for the average employee in this particular field to complete 30 days of actual employment for any one employer. Los Angeles unions alone spent $2,000 a month securing and dispatching this help to the employers.

I want to say in that connection that one practical experience perhaps will help the committee. We have there a dispatching hall and dispatch approximately 200 men a day to various casual jobs, usually in the evening. We have also a complete list where we keep the work reports of these men. We had some 4 or 5 men dispatched who were casual labor and who got into trouble, either through the fact that they drank or other reasons, and the employers rendered a report back to the so-called hiring hall. The result was that we took those men off the hiring lists of availability after 1 or 2 or 3 offenses.

They went down at night or sent down at night actually to apply for casual employment at the docks and the foreman there said, "We get our men from the union hall."

They filed charges before the National Labor Relations Board based on discrimination. The union refused to pay them anything at any time. However, the employers to keep from being harassed by a week or 10-day hearing and employing attorneys, having their foremen in attendance at these meetings, actually gave them anywhere from $25 to $150 apiece to dispose of their claims. At that time we told the Labor Board that if we were going to be harassed in that fashion, we would close the hiring hall and put a sign on it allowing the Labor Board to make the dispatches direct from there. That stopped the argument for the moment.

Now, the point I want to make is this, that it is impossible to get this help in any other fashion. Newspaper ads won't serve because 1 day a freight company will want 40 men, the next day 5, and there are such a variety of companies that they could not possibly secure them. In the old days they got them from skid row and that type of help. Today we have experienced, competent help that follow this field year in and year out, and we ask that they be eliminated from the terms of the act.

Statement of Joseph Curran, President, National Maritime Union, in Taft-Hartley Act Revisions, hearings before the Senate Committee on Labor and Public Welfare, 83d Cong., 1st Sess., 1953, part 4, p. 1889

WHY THE CLOSED SHOP IS IMPORTANT TO THE MARITIME UNION

A Coast Guard survey shows that the average turnover of a ship's personnel per voyage is 32 percent, actually 31.97 percent. Although the average voyage is less than 1 month, we will simplify our observation by using 32 percent as the average monthly turnover rate. This means that every month there are 32 separations for every 100 seamen employed aboard our ships. This is eight times the average monthly 4 percent turnover rate of all the United States manufacturing industries during 1952. In other words, every job aboard ship becomes open during an average 3-month period. It is little wonder that merchant seamen through their unions are vitally concerned with replacing open jobs with union members.

QUESTIONS IN APPLYING THE TAFT-HARTLEY ACT

Testimony of George J. Bott, General Counsel, National Labor Relations Board, in Taft-Hartley Act Revisions, hearings before the Senate Committee on Labor and Public Welfare, 83d Cong., 1st Sess., 1953, part 4, pp. 2136–2138

From the consideration Congress gave in 1947 to the subject of union security, and more particularly to the closed shop, we know that the amendments of that year were intended to eliminate arrangements whereby unions, through control of their memberships, were able also to control employment and work opportunities in certain industries. The enactment of section 8 (*b*) (2) and the amendment of the proviso to section 8 (*a*) (3) rendered the closed shop unlawful, and imposed restrictions upon lesser forms of union security. But controversy as to the impact of the law in this regard is one of the most difficult problems facing all of us.

Many difficult questions have arisen, for example, in connection with the use by employers of unions as sources of labor supply. In many industries, as you know, employers regularly obtain workers through union facilities. This appears to be the only method, as these industries are now operated, by which in many cases employers can be sure of obtaining the skilled or migratory or occasional help they need.

There is no doubt that unions, in responding to such calls by employers, cannot under the present law make union membership or activities a criterion of referring a man for the job. But what other conditions, apart from and unrelated to union membership or activities, may a union operating such an employment agency impose on individuals seeking jobs? May the union, by agreement with an employer, prevent the employment or secure the discharge of individuals who do not obtain work through its facilities? May it refuse to refer an applicant for a job because, pursuant to a seniority arrangement or rotation schedule by which priority is given to persons longest unemployed, the applicant is not yet entitled to referral? May it set up other controls such as experience or good behavior, or standards for journeymen, or residence in the locality?

Similar questions also arise where unions do not control the initial hiring of employees, but, nonetheless, thereafter seek to affect the tenure of their employment for reasons unrelated to union membership or activities.[1]

[1] For example, some people have thought that a union could not obtain an employee's discharge on the ground that the employee was a Communist, a dope peddler, or for some similar reason was a disruptive factor in the plant. In one case a charge

The questions which I have raised strike at the core of a subject that has always been critical in harmonious relations between employers and unions. Differences in treatment may perhaps be warranted, however, depending on the special problems and methods of operations of particular industries. Thus, the employment practices and economic conditions in industries characterized by casual employment, like the building and construction trades or the shipping trades, among others, have depended largely on the use of union facilities. Disruption of long-established employment procedures designed to fulfill the needs peculiar to those industries, can, of course, be accomplished only with much greater effort than in businesses which have experienced no need for union cooperation in maintaining an employment system. In making these comments, however, I mean to express no value judgments which, I think must be based on greater study than I have been able to give the subject.

THE CLOSED SHOP PREVENTS BUSINESS EFFICIENCY

Letter of Leland Hazard, Vice President and General Counsel, Pittsburgh Plate Glass Co., Pittsburgh, Pa., in Labor Relations, hearings before the Senate Committee on Labor and Public Welfare, 81st Cong., 1st Sess., 1949, part 6, pp. 3383–3385

February 10, 1949

Hon. Elbert D. Thomas
Chairman, Senate Committee on Labor and Public Welfare,
United States Senate, Washington, D. C.

Dear Mr. Chairman: The Senate Committee on Labor and Public Welfare is at present holding hearings on S. 249, a bill "to repeal the Labor-Management Relations Act, 1947, to reenact the National Labor Relations Act of 1935, and for other purposes." Despite the extension of the hearings, there may be limited opportunity for oral testimony. Therefore, may we express by this letter our opinion on the closed shop. We request that this letter be made a part of the record of the hearings.

Although we are opposed for numerous reasons to the enactment of S. 249

---

was filed with my office alleging the commission of an unfair labor practice because an employee was discharged, at the request of the union, because he had signed the Stockholm peace petition. I felt that the employer on his own initiative could have discharged the employee for this reason, since it did not pertain to union membership or activity, and therefore should be allowed to discharge him for the same reason even though at the request of the union. The request was not made pursuant to any union-security agreement, or on the ground that the employee had been expelled from the union. Accordingly, I refused to issue a complaint. But if Congress meant that the only discharges which an employer could properly make at the request or insistence of a union are those pursuant to a valid union-shop contract even though the reasons for the discharge have nothing to do with union membership, then I was wrong in not issuing a complaint in the Stockholm peace petition case.

as introduced, we presently emphasize our concern about the proposed repeal of section 8 (a) (3) of the National Labor Relations Act, as amended. This section prohibits the closed shop.

First, let us make it plain that in opposing the closed shop for this company and for companies similarly situated we are not opposing union security. Our record will bear this out.

As early as 1940, our company agreed with our glass workers' union upon a contract provision which gave the union 100 percent regular dues-paying membership. In this contract, we retained the right to select and hire new employees but agreed that after 30 to 60 days each employee was obligated to pay the prescribed union initiation fee and to maintain the payment of regular union dues. This did not include the payment of fines or assessments or subject the employee to discharge for bad standing in the union except for failure to pay regular union dues.

This form of union security has become established throughout our 30 plants and is now available to some 18,000 employees.

You will see that for 10 years we have practiced the form of union security which was sanctioned in the Labor-Management Relations Act, 1947. During this period, the CIO union in our glass plants, the AFL and District 50 unions in our paint and chemical plants have remained strong. In collective bargaining these unions have obtained wages, hours, and working conditions which place our employees in the top bracket of American industry.

Our decade of experience with the form of union security which the law now provides demonstrates that the closed shop is not necessary to union security.

Why, then, are we concerned about the proposal to repeal the prohibition against the closed shop? Primarily because of our sales branches and warehouses. We distribute the products of our 30 plants through more than 100 major distribution units. These units are located in most of the States of the country and in areas in which the closed shop of the building and construction trades was prevalent prior to 1947. These distribution units are service establishments for supply and installation of glass and the servicing of painting contractors' requirements. These establishments offer permanent employment for almost 4,000 hourly employees. In many of these establishments, unions had compelled us to grant the closed shop long prior to 1947. The power of these unions to impose the secondary boycott and to use other coercive measures was so great that no single establishment could resist and stay in business.

Section 8 (a) (3) neutralized this power. We immediately laid down a rigid policy. As labor contracts in our sales branches and warehouses expired, we refused to renew unless the closed shop provisions were eliminated. We refused to accept any of the so-called bootleg provisions to circumvent the closed shop prohibition.

We were able to negotiate, with the aid of the law, over 100 contracts without the closed shop. This was a major accomplishment which certainly could never have been attained without section 8 (a) (3).

If the closed shop prohibition is repealed outright as contemplated by S. 249, this company will have great difficulty in preventing, perhaps find it impossible to prevent, reestablishment of the closed shop in its sales branches and warehouses. The competition in the various building and construction areas in which our distribution units operate is of the keenest and as our competitors find themselves unable to resist union pressure for the closed shop it will be difficult for our company to resist and remain in business.

Now, why do we regard a return to the closed shop with such deep concern? Because the closed shop is a deterrent to efficiencies and lower costs. It stands to reason that if an employer is in a position to hire his own employees and to pick the best qualified for the job, efficiency and production will improve. On the other hand, if an employer must make a union his employment agency, as he must under the closed shop, he has no opportunity to use modern and efficient methods of employee selection.

Let us give the committee an illustration. We have a sales and warehouse branch which would provide permanent employment for about 50 glaziers. Under the closed shop, we were compelled to accept intermittent services of some 150 different individuals—3 men rotating on each job. The union would send us a glazier for a week, then take him away and send us another glazier for the same job. Perhaps 3 weeks later, we would get back the first glazier. And so it went.

The committee will readily see that under such conditions it would be impossible to develop group skill, employee morale, or the continuing relationship which benefits both employer and employee.

Multiply this condition by more than a hundred times for our sales branches and warehouses and then multiply it several hundred times for similar service establishments in many industries and trades and you will have an index to the magnitude of waste, inefficiency and cost to the public of the closed shop.

Given for a few years the relief from the closed shop which the law now provides, we should be able to increase services and lower the costs of services substantially. We should be able to supply more of our products to more people at lower prices.

The closed shop is not related to union security in a company which offers permanent employment. Rather, it is the usurpation by unions of the right to hire and fire. The closed shop deprives the employer of the right to hire the best qualified workers; it deprives workers of the opportunity of obtaining permanent employment on the basis of individual merit; it places upon the consumer the extra cost of inefficiency and featherbedding; it prevents ingenuity, progress, service and lower prices in the construction trades. And these benefits which the public rightfully demands can be had without harm to unions or workers. The closed shop is not necessary to a union's right to bargain for wages, hours, and working conditions. It is not necessary to the right to strike. It is not necessary to the union's financial security. In our industry it is an outmoded, antiquated device, as unsuited to modern industrial relations and personnel management as the yellow-dog contract.

We are aware that there may be employers, particularly those who offer only casual and intermittent employment, who raise no objection to the closed shop. Since such employers maintain no continuing relationship with workers, they may actually find it a convenience to designate the union as an employment agency. If the committee should become convinced that such employers are actually suffering from an absolute prohibition of the closed shop, then there is a method by which proper discrimination can be made between the need of employers who offer permanent employment and those who offer only casual or intermittent employment.

The absolute prohibition of the closed shop could be removed so that an employer who desires to agree with the union upon a closed shop would be free to do so. However, the revision in the law should make a strike to compel the closed shop an illegal strike as in the case of a secondary boycott (section 303 L.M.R.A. 1947) and an unfair practice under section 8 (*b*) (4) of NLRA, as amended.

This would enable small employers in countless small manufacturing, distribution and service establishments throughout the United States—employers who offer permanent employment, who need the right to select their employees, who need the opportunity to reduce costs and prices by the efficiencies of continuing employee relationships—it would enable such employers to resist the closed shop. It would enable this company to resist a reestablishment of the closed shop and to make its contribution toward lower costs of construction and housing.

Respectfully yours,
Leland Hazard

THE "RIGHT TO WORK" LAWS

The Labor-Management Relations Act of 1947, Section 8 (a) (3)*, outlawed the closed shop in interstate commerce and introduced certain restrictions on the union shop. In addition, Section 14* (b) *permitted states to pass more restrictive legislation, outlawing all forms of union security, if they so wished. Under this provision so-called "right to work" laws have been passed in a number of states making unlawful or unenforceable collective agreements which required membership or dues payment as a condition of employment. In other states employer committees have been formed to work for passage of such legislation. The materials which follow relate to these efforts.*

Excerpts from a publication of the Industrial Relations Division, National Association of Manufacturers, 1956

TWENTY QUESTIONS ABOUT THE RIGHT-TO-WORK

1

Q. What is the right-to-work controversy all about?

A. Because a number of states have sought to strengthen the basic rights of their citizens to work without having to join a union, organized labor has rolled its big guns into position to fight these laws.

Essentially these laws make it unlawful to deprive a person of a job because he does not belong to a union—or because he does belong. They also make it unlawful for an employer to enter into agreement with a union to make membership in such unions a condition of employment. In short, they insure the right to work *with* or *without* union membership.

The only issue at stake is whether employees are to be forced to join a union in order to hold a job.

2

Q. Why are union officials opposed to right-to-work laws?

A. One would think there could be no argument in a free society against a man's basic right to work without having to join a union. And yet union officers have announced that their #1 target is to eliminate state right-to-work laws.

This is a curious thing—the more so because all their objections do not succeed in hiding their one real fear—namely, that when unionism is placed on a voluntary basis they have to get their new members on the basis of *meriting* the employee's support.

This is the way every other organization in the country operates. You sell a man on the value of membership and then you keep him sold by performing a useful service.

It is therefore easy to see why union leaders are so wrought up. Over the years, closed shop and union shop contracts have made the organizer's job easy. The new employee has to accept union membership along with his new job. If he fails to pay dues, he is discharged. It's that simple!

It would seem that unions are afraid to test their value to employees by giving men and women the American right to refuse to join if they do not wish to. . . .

17

Q. How are employee relations affected where a union controls the work force in a plant through compulsory unionism?

A. Where a union has the power to compel membership—and can coerce the individual—it is tempted to use this power in many ways.

Knowing that they can control the entire work force in a plant, union officers are more prone to make bargaining demands on a take-it-or-leave-it basis and to use strike threats arbitrarily.

The employer may be obliged to discharge employees—even his most able and experienced employees—if they should fail to pay dues.

Members have no effective way to protest union activities of which they disapprove since they cannot resign from the union and remain on the payroll. This can lead to discontentment and frustration on the job.

For good employee relationships, individual employees should have freedom of expression, but under forced unionism, the voice of the individual is effectively drowned out. . . .

19

Q. Why is there a movement in other states for the enactment of right-to-work laws?

A. Because more and more people are becoming aware that without such laws, even in this free country, one's right to work may be conditional on the whims of a union organization and that it may be valid only as long as payments are made to that particular private organization.

The public more and more is recognizing the danger of this worsening situation and is seeking to correct it by enacting protections of a man's freedom to get and hold a job without the compulsion of joining a union or remaining a union member.

20

Q. *Why is compulsory unionism—in any form—a menace to America?*

A. Because it is one of the most basic issues of our times. After nearly two centuries of freedom in this nation we are now confronted with this fundamental question:

Must an American citizen belong to a private organization—called a labor union—in order to earn his living at his job?

Compulsory unionism denies free men the right to choose their own course of action—and this is the bedrock foundation on which America was built.

No argument for compulsory unionism—however persuasive—can possibly justify invasion of the right of individual choice.

For a society which is dedicated to the freedom and sanctity of the individual, it is tragic to realize that we have permitted compulsion by a single group— a total denial of the individual's freedom to act.

In 1955 the legislature of Kansas passed a "right-to-work" bill outlawing all forms of union security. On March 28, Governor Fred Hall vetoed that bill, in a message from which the following excerpts have been taken.

VETO MESSAGE OF HOUSE BILL NO. 30, BY GOVERNOR FRED HALL

The enactment of the "right-to-work" bill may be remembered as a dark hour in Kansas legislative history. I doubt that there has ever been a time that the people of Kansas, the members of the legislature and the governor have been subjected to a greater campaign of propaganda. House Bill 30 is a lobbyist bill. The words "right-to-work" have become a magic phrase, and, like magic, few really understand them.

The campaign to enact this law began several years ago and was instigated by a few men who would profit by such a law. They carried their propaganda campaign through every community in the state. They have used every method at their command including many respectable organizations to influence and crystallize public opinion in favor of this bill. We can only speculate how much money has been spent and is still being spent on radio, telegrams, and newspapers to influence the legislature and the governor in their judgment.

The legislative record of this bill is almost incredible. It has been proposed for several sessions beginning, I believe, in 1947. I recall that it was defeated in a committee of the house of representatives two years ago. It was referred to the legislative council and has been studied by the council the past two years. It was not recommended by the council to this legislature. Neither the house committee nor the senate committee of this legislature recommended the passage of the bill. The chairman of the house committee pleaded for consideration of the legislative council recommendations. The chairman of the senate committee declared the "right-to-work" bill does not cure any of the ills of labor or of management. The chairman of this committee also served as the chairman of the legislative council committee. The council committee investigated the claims of "Right-to-Work, Incorporated," the official lobby organization for the "right-to-work" bill. . . .

Under ordinary circumstances no bill could have survived this kind of history.

I have been deeply disturbed by the efforts of the proponents of House Bill No. 30 to turn the farmers of Kansas against labor in Kansas. In the senate debate a senator said, "Farmers are more interested in this bill than any other group. One thing that has disturbed farmers is a statement of Walter Reuther of the CIO that labor is raising a fund of $25 million to get the guaranteed annual wage."

The senator added, "This means if you guarantee wages for the working man you must guarantee profits for the groceryman and it can only lead to a Socialistic Government."

This is not a sound argument. It has nothing to do with either the rights of individuals to work or not join a union. It does betray the real purpose of House Bill No. 30. It is not legislation for the problems of today but for the fears of tomorrow. This argument goes to the very foundations of America. America is essentially a classless country. Those who would pit one group of people against another to make it otherwise are doing their country a great disservice. The rights of all groups in America are entitled to equal consideration and protection.

President Eisenhower expressed the rightful place of labor when he said,

Today in America, unions have a secure place in our industrial life. Only a handful of unreconstructed reactionaries harbor the ugly thought of breaking unions. Only a fool would try to deprive working men and working women of the right to join the union of their choice. I have no use for those, regardless of their political party, who hold some foolish dream of turning the clock back to days when unorganized labor was a huddled almost helpless mass. The right of men to leave their job is a test of freedom. Hitler suppressed strikes. The drafting of strikers into the Army would suppress strikes. But that also suppresses freedom. There are some things worse, much worse, than strikes—one of them is the loss of freedom.

I am aware of the fact that many states in the union have enacted laws similar to House Bill No. 30. In doing so I believe they have acted contrary to the great heritage and freedoms of America. Throughout the country this law has become a symbol to labor of its loss of freedom. We are not obliged to follow their lead. Many wrongs do not make a right and the hucksters tactics cannot make a wrong thing a right thing. It is time to face up to this issue and set an example for others to follow. The people of Kansas believe in the right of labor to organize and in the principle of collective bargaining. I will not approve any law which destroys this right and this principle. House Bill No. 30 will ultimately do both. It is not constructive, but punitive, legislation. It is clearly contrary to the best interests of all the people of Kansas.

It is with great personal regret that I must differ with you on the merits of this bill. I am hopeful that on further reflection you will agree with me. This is not an easy decision to make. I have no alternative. It would be wrong for this bill to become law in Kansas. As the Governor it is my duty to say so and to act accordingly.

From a speech, "Trends in Labor Relations for 1957," by Herbert R. Northrup, Vice President, Penn-Texas Corporation, given at the Ninth Annual New England Congress, National Metal Trades Association, Providence, R.I., April 9, 1957

"LOYAL EMPLOYEES" AND JOINERS

. . . The emotional reaction to shorter work weeks, automation and engineering problems all put together are mild compared to the feelings engendered by the union shop issue. When Indiana became the 18th state to pass the so-called "right-to-work" law, it became inevitable that the fight over this legislation which bans all forms of compulsory unionism would be extended. Indiana is the first really industrialized state to pass such a law. It is most significant that, although the demand for this legislation was pushed by some industry groups, notably the National Association of Manufacturers, it was actively opposed by large business in Indiana. According to TIME Magazine, executives of the Radio Corporation of America, Seagram's, the Allison Division of General Motors, and Cummings Engines were among those who opposed the enactment of this law. Support for the law, in terms of votes, came largely from farmer and small business-minded legislators.

I am no friend of compulsory unionism. It seems to me at best an anomaly that unions expect the employer to maintain employee union membership. One would expect that unions would be able to handle that themselves. Certainly compulsory unionism seems a strange bedfellow to a democratic state. Nevertheless, I think it is a real question whether management ought to be in the forefront of any activities on behalf of such legislation.

We oppose governmental intervention in labor disputes. Yet one effect of a right-to-work law is to deprive management of the right to negotiate about the union shop or other such forms of compulsory unionism. Such negotiations are sometimes valuable in obtaining desirable objectives. I frankly do not like to be deprived of this right to negotiate.

Those of us who hold this view are in the minority among business executives, but it is interesting to note that we do have some friends. For example, J. Irwin Miller, Chairman of the Board of the Cummings Engine Corporation, had this to say, and I quote:

The classic argument against the union shop is the right-to-work argument. The average American manager feels that there is a character known as the loyal employee, and this is the fellow who is supposed to figure that joining the union is a fate worse than death. Well, this man is in the same category in my opinion as the Easter Bunny and Santa Claus. I have never found him.

Actually, the really valuable man to management is not the fellow who stays out of the union, but rather the one who gets into the union, participates in the union organization and tries to bring to bear a factual point of view instead of an emotional one. In all the labor controversies that I have ever been involved in, the man who stayed out of the union and merely collected benefits was no help to management's cause.

FOR DISCUSSION AND ANALYSIS

1. The closed shop (or some variant of it) has been a thorny issue ever since labor unions made their appearance in the United States. In a succinct, analytical statement, explore why this issue has been so sharply and inconclusively debated.

2. Is there any dilemma involved in (a) giving maximum support to collective bargaining and (b) maximizing the personal freedom of the individual worker to decide whether or not to join a union?

3. Opponents of compulsory unionism have argued as follows:

If it is good to force people to join purely private outfits because some of us feel they would benefit, should we not also *force* people to join the church? If so, what church—one selected by an overwhelming majority in a "representation" election?

How would you answer the above questions?

4. The president of a large national union once remarked, "The union shop is no more compulsory than for an employer to say, 'If you want to remain at work in my shop, you must start to work at 8:00 A.M., you must not smoke on the job, etc.' Is that compulsory?"

Do you agree or disagree?

5. In a public session where a lawyer was attacking union-security provisions, a member of the audience raised this question: "I would like to ask the speaker whether or not he sees an analogy between the union drive for compulsory membership and the exclusivistic practices and high entrance requirements of the professional organizations, and whether or not he anticipates in the future a concern on the part of society for a right to work in those professions." Reference was clearly to the legal and medical professions. What basis, if any, is there for such a question, and what would be your reply?

6. A minister who is also a student of labor concluded, after an examination of the issues pro and con union-security clauses:

If I were a union member or officer I would oppose the union shop in most situations. I think unions will be stronger, in the long haul, when they have to win their membership on merit.

If I were an employer I would encourage employees to be active in the union, rather than in fighting the union shop. In fact, as an employer I would suspect the employee who wouldn't join a union. If he will shirk his obligation to his fellow workers, I wouldn't trust him to be honest to his employer.

In the light of union arguments for the union shop, and employer arguments against it, do you consider this a satisfactory resolution of the issue?

13: Management Rights

Corresponding to the issue of union security is the matter of management's right to manage. Although this issue, like union security, dates back for many, many years, it was particularly acute in the period following World War II, when unions—which had been restrained by the War Labor Board for four years—displayed their newly acquired strength in a number of demands which led a suspicious management to question whether it would all end in "socialism." Although the issue has not been so hotly debated in recent years, it still remains—and probably will always remain—a battleground for unions and managements.

MANAGEMENT'S RIGHT TO MANAGE

Statement of management and union members of Committee II of the President's National Labor-Management Conference, November 5–30, 1945

STATEMENT OF MANAGEMENT MEMBERS

Labor members of the Committee on Management's Right to Manage have been unwilling to agree on any listing of specific management functions. Management members of the committee conclude, therefore, that the labor members are convinced that the field of collective bargaining will, in all probability, continue to expand into the field of management.

The only possible end of such a philosophy would be joint management of enterprise. To this the management members naturally cannot agree. Management has functions that must not and cannot be compromised in the public interest. If labor disputes are to be minimized by "the genuine acceptance by organized labor of the functions and responsibilities of management to direct the operation of an enterprise," labor must agree that certain specific functions and responsibilities of management are not subject to collective bargaining.

In the absence of agreement, therefore, the management members of the committee herewith submit their report.

S. B. GROVE
C. R. HOOK
H. W. PRENTIS, JR.
E. J. ROBESON, JR.
C. O. SKINNER
C. E. WILSON

The Committee on Management's Right to Manage was charged with the consideration of the second topic on the agenda of the President's Labor-Management Conference which reads as follows:

"The extent to which industrial disputes can be minimized by full and genuine acceptance by organized labor of the inherent right and responsibilities of management to direct the operation of an enterprise."

The committee has interpreted the meaning of the assignment to be:

"The extent to which industrial disputes can be minimized by full and genuine acceptance by organized labor of the functions and responsibilities of management to direct the operation of an enterprise."

During the conference the executive committee gave this committee an additional assignment:

"The question of the unionization of foremen for collective bargaining."

The National Labor Relations Act requires collective bargaining "in respect to rates of pay, wages, hours of employment, or other conditions of employment," where "employes" have elected to bargain collectively. It is, therefore, an obligation of management to adhere strictly to the provisions of this act.

It likewise should be an obligation on the part of unions to recognize, and not encroach upon, the functions and responsibilities of management. Failure to accept this obligation has increased labor disputes. Even today, efforts are continuing on the part of certain unions to extend the scope of collective bargaining to include matters and functions which are clearly the responsibility of management. The functions of management must be preserved if American business is to continue progressive and efficient, create more good jobs and further raise the general standard of living. Management must always exercise its functions with due regard to its social responsibility.

FUNCTIONS AND RESPONSIBILITIES OF MANAGEMENT

In order to clarify this problem, the committee has discussed many of the important functions of management involved in operating a business. The management members have classified some of them for the purpose of avoiding misunderstandings and minimizing industrial disputes. We have placed them in two classifications:

The first comprises those matters which are clearly the functions and responsibility of management and are not subject to collective bargaining.

The second comprises matters in respect to which it is the function and responsibility of management to make prompt initial decisions in order to insure the effective operation of the enterprise, but where the consequences of such actions or decisions are properly subject to review when they involve issues of alleged discrimination, affect wages, hours, working conditions, or agreed-upon management-labor practices. Such matters should be handled promptly under grievance procedures mutually agreed to as being appropriate for each specific item. Illustrative of items which we believe belong in the first classification and which are not subject to collective bargaining are:

The determination of products to be manufactured or services to be rendered to customers by the enterprise; and the location of the business, including the establishment of new units and the relocation or closing of old units. (When it becomes necessary to relocate a unit or close an old unit or transfer major operations between plants, management should give careful consideration to the impact of such moves on the employes involved, and discuss with them or their accredited representatives possible solutions for the resulting problems.)

The determination of the layout and equipment to be used in the business; the processes, techniques, methods and means of manufacture and distribution; the materials to be used (subject to proper health and safety measures where dangerous materials are utilized) and the size and character of inventories.

The determination of financial policies; general accounting procedures—particularly the internal accounting necessary to make reports to the owners of the business and to Government bodies requiring financial reports; prices of goods sold or services rendered to customers; and customer relations.

The determination of the management organization of each producing or distributing unit; and the selection of employes for promotion to supervisory and other managerial positions.

The determination of job content (this refers to establishing the duties required in the performance of any given job and not to wages); the determination of the size of the work force; the allocation and assignment of work to workers; determination of policies affecting the selection of employes; establishment of quality standards and judgment of workmanship required; and the maintenance of discipline and control and use of the plant property, the scheduling of operations and the number of shifts.

The determination of safety, health and property protection measures, where legal responsibility of the employer is involved.

The second classification comprises matters in respect to which it is the function and responsibility of management to make prompt initial decisions in order to insure the effective operation of the enterprise, but where the consequence of such actions or decisions are properly subject to review by grievance procedures mutually agreed to as being appropriate for each specific item. Among items illustrative of this classification are:

Discharge of employes for cause; the application of seniority provisions of contracts; penalties imposed as the result of disciplinary action, and such other matters as may be mutually agreed upon.

The management members of the committee recognize that the items listed in each of these classifications above do not include all of the subjects that may arise in connection with the negotiation or administration of any given collective bargaining contract. We believe, however, that genuine acceptance on labor's part of the above classification of these items would do much to define with reasonable accuracy an area of responsibility which must be left to management, if management is to function effectively in the interest of labor, the investor and the consuming public alike.

UNIONIZATION OF FOREMEN

The management members of the committee recognize that various crafts, such as the building and printing trades, among others, have established prac-

Sourcebook on Labor

tices over a long period of years which permit inclusion of foremen in collective bargaining units in accordance with union constitutions, and the following recommendations are not designed to alter such long-standing practices.

However, in any report on management functions, the term "management" must be defined to include all levels of managerial and supervisory personnel and not confined to top ranking executive and administrative officials. Executive management cannot properly function and discharge its responsibilities without adequate assistance. It is therefore fundamental that there be no unionization of any part of management.

As a practical matter, supervisors organized for collective bargaining purposes would of necessity be faced with the problem of whether a particular decision or action would be serving the objectives of the union or carrying out the policies of management. The supervisors cannot properly function in a position of dual obligation.

To the foreman is delegated the ultimate responsibility of directing the workmen at the point where they are actually engaged in production. Since the foreman exercises managerial authority, he must be solely and exclusively responsible to higher management.

Furthermore, under collective bargaining agreements, the foreman usually makes the first management disposition of all grievances. With union foremen having supervision of union workmen, the foremen could not receive and act on grievances for the management, since it would mean the unions had taken over both sides of the bargaining table.

In requiring that employers bargain with foremen's unions whose members are the direct representatives and an integral part of management, either the National Labor Relations Board is misinterpreting the Wagner Act or the act itself is inconsistent and contradictory.

The management members of the committee therefore urgently recommend that the term "employe" in the Wagner Act should be clearly defined, either by the National Labor Relations Board or by Congress, to exclude all persons holding full-time managerial and supervisory positions.

Concluding this report, the management members of the committee desire to express their appreciation for the candid, forthright and friendly attitude displayed by the labor members throughout the committee's deliberations.

STATEMENT OF LABOR MEMBERS

AFL: Duffy, Durkin, Spradling.
CIO: Carey, Golden, Townsend.

The committee on management's right to manage is charged with the consideration of the second topic on the agenda of the President's Labor-Management Conference which reads as follows:

"The extent to which industrial disputes can be minimized by full and genuine acceptance by organized labor of the inherent right and responsibilities of management to direct the operation of an enterprise."

The committee interprets the topic to be as follows:

The extent to which industrial disputes can be minimized by full and genuine acceptance by organized labor of the functions and responsibilities of management to direct the operation of an enterprise.

The National Labor Relations Act requires collective bargaining "in respect to rates of pay, wages, hours of employment, or other conditions of employment," where employes have elected to bargain collectively. It is, therefore, an obligation of management to adhere strictly to the provisions of this act. . . .

The extensive exploratory discussions of the committee have brought forth the wide variety of traditions, customs and practices that have grown out of relationships between unions and management in various industries over a long period of time.

Because of the complexities of these relationships the labor members of the committee think it unwise to specify and classify the functions and responsibilities of management. Because of the insistence by management for such specification the committee was unable to agree upon a joint report. To do so might well restrict the flexibility so necessary to efficient operation.

It would be extremely unwise to build a fence around the rights and responsibilities of management on the one hand and the unions on the other. The experience of many years shows that with the growth of mutual understanding the responsibilities of one of the parties today may well become the joint responsibility of both parties tomorrow.

We cannot have one sharply delimited area designated as management prerogatives and another equally sharply defined area of union prerogatives without either side constantly attempting to invade the forbidden territory, thus creating much unnecessary strife.

The labor members of the committee believe there is need for a more widespread realization and thorough understanding of the significance and importance of the management function in modern industry. In the main this will follow, rather than precede, the development of sound industrial relationships.

In our American political democracy the tradition is well established that government operates best when it enjoys the confidence and consent of the governed. In the same American tradition both labor and management must come to a realization that both can function most effectively when each enjoys the confidence and has the consent of the other.

The labor members of the committee believe that as acceptance of the role of labor organizations in our economic society progresses so will come both clearer understanding and recognition of the importance of the management function together with a greater appreciation on the part of union members, investor-owners and the whole managerial and supervisory organizations of the large responsibilities that go along with it.

Management and labor are both vitally concerned with full, regular and efficient production. Each has functions to perform in the attainment of that common objective.

The labor members believe that we shall move forward toward the achievement of greater goals of national well-being to the degree that we concern ourselves with the education and broader understanding of both labor and management regarding the complexities of industrial and human relationships.

During the conference, the Executive Committee gave this committee an additional assignment:

"The question of the unionization of foremen for collective bargaining."

The labor members of the committee feel that it would be inappropriate for the committee to make any recommendations on the matter of unionization of foremen while cases involving this issue are pending before the National Labor Relations Board.

It is the opinion of the labor members of the committee that if the representatives of management and labor in each industry would confer on the functions of management and labor in the same friendly spirit as the committee approached the subject assigned, industrial disputes would be minimized, production increased and the public interest well served.

MANAGEMENT *MUST* MANAGE!

From "A Steelmaker Discusses the Issues," a radio address by Admiral Ben Moreell, Chairman of the Board and President, Jones & Laughlin Steel Corp., January 11, 1952

. . . Under our system of free enterprise and mass production, we obtain a division of labor by a process of natural selection. Each person gravitates to the place where his talents are best employed. The process is not infallible but, by and large, the people in management are there because that is where their abilities can be used the best. This process of natural selection has given us the best industrial management and the highest standard of living the world has ever seen. We believe, therefore, that *management* should continue to *manage*—because it can do the job better than anyone else.

People—including employers!—have become accustomed to the phenomenon of unions bargaining concerning wages and hours. But at times we encounter situations where management's discretion on matters considerably removed from wages and hours appears to be limited by the union-negotiated collective agreement. In the arbitration decisions of grievance matters which follow, issues are raised by the union which most managements would instinctively presume should fall within their sole purview.

THE RIGHT TO SUBCONTRACT

Weber Aircraft Corporation and International Association of Machinists, Lodge 727, 24 LA 821, 1955

EDGAR A. JONES, ARBITRATOR

The following questions were determined by the parties at the hearing to be a mutually acceptable formulation of the issues to be decided by the arbitrator.

1. Are the layoffs of Freda M. Quinn, Ira A. Stadalman, Ben Westman, and William A. Wright proper subject matters for grievance within the provisions of the current collective bargaining agreement between the Company and the Union dated October 20, 1954?

2. If the answer to (1) is "yes," were the individuals named laid off for just cause by the Company on April 4, 1955?

3. If the answer to (2) is "no," what award does the arbitrator make?

Statement of facts

In 1951, Weber Aircraft Corporation, a subsidiary of Weber Showcase and Fixture Co., acquired from Airquipment Company, a subsidiary of Lockheed Aircraft Corporation, the assets of the business presently operated by the Company. When Airquipment Company was formed in 1946 out of a division of Lockheed, IAM Lodge 727 was certified as collective bargaining representative of the new corporation's employees.

Shortly before the Weber acquisition, the Airquipment management decided to contract out part of the plant maintenance work. The decision was carried through by the incoming Weber management. Accordingly, in June, 1951, an independent contractor whom we shall refer to as the XYZ Co., was engaged to do the outside window washing on an office building. Eventually, some time prior to the present grievance, the XYZ contract had been broadened to cover the washing of inside and outside windows on the Company's two office buildings and its production office.

Weber employees wear a distinctive yellow badge at all times inside the plant. It is required to be readily visible. The XYZ window washers have always worn a differently colored badge denoting nonemployees, either white or green, but never yellow. Weber janitors, members of the bargaining unit, some of whom are grievants here, worked in and around the same areas as did XYZ janitors when the latter were washing inside windows.

In November, 1954, in the midst of a decline in its business, the Company undertook a study of the feasibility of contracting out all of its janitorial work. On March 22, 1955, and again on March 28, the vice-president in charge of manufacturing, Mr. Johnson, telephoned the business representative of the Union, Mr. Foote, and informed him that the Company had decided, first, to "sub-contract" all of its janitorial work to an outside firm, which we shall refer to as the ABC Co., on or about April 1, 1955, and, second, to lay off its seven janitors on that date. The Union objected, indicated that it was unaware of the XYZ janitorial contract, and, upon consummation of the Company's decision, processed the grievances of the four employees involved here.

Neither the ABC Co. nor the XYZ Co. are related to Weber Aircraft other than as independent contractors.

Relevant contractual provisions

The Company relies on Article I, Section 6, "Right to Manage Plant":

Except as abridged, delegated, granted or modified by this Agreement, or any supplementary agreements that may hereafter be made, all of the rights, powers and authority the Company had prior to the signing of this Agreement are retained by the Company, and remain exclusively and without limitation within the rights of management.

The Union relies on Article I, Section 2, "Exclusive Representation"; Section 3, "Period of Agreement"; Section 5, "Scope of Agreement"; Section 8, "Union Security"; Article II, Section 1, "Strikes and Lockouts"; Article III, Section 4 (3), "Arbitration"; Article IV, Section 1, "Basis of Seniority"; Article VI, "Employee Privileges"; Exhibit A, "Factory Occupations," listing the "Classification" and "Rate" of "Janitor" at "1.63". Article I, Section 2A, "Exclusive Representation," is as follows:

For the period of this Agreement the Company recognizes and accepts the Union as the exclusive representative of all the employees of the Company, except those listed in Subsection (B), for the purpose of collective bargaining in respect to rates of pay, wages, hours of employment, or other conditions of employment.

Subsection (B) of Article I, Section 2 does not except the classification of "Janitor" from the bargaining unit. Article I, Section 8, "Union Security," establishes a union shop.

Union position

The substance of the Union's position is that the Agreement, read as a whole, precludes outside contracting despite absence of explicit prohibition. It notes first that the Company refers to its outside contracting for janitorial service as a "sub-contract." This, the Union says, is inaccurate. The arrangement is not in fact a sub-contract in the accepted sense of the word, the sense in which the Union sought in 1954 to negotiate a new provision in this Agreement limiting the Company's right to subcontract. The distinction, the Union feels, is important and not merely a matter of semantics. It turns on whether the Company in good faith sends work out of the plant to be performed elsewhere or, instead, displaces its Union employees with another employer's personnel who then perform the same work on Company premises as did the displaced Company employees. The former may be allowable under the Agreement, but the latter, this case, is not.

The Union cites the Recognition provision [Article I, Section 2] wherein Lodge 727 is recognized as the exclusive representative of all Weber employees including the janitors. It asserts that "the only legal time for excluding of employees from the bargaining unit to be brought up is during negotiations. Where a job is in the bargaining unit and in existence, the Company cannot unilaterally exclude it from the unit. . . . [I]n past negotations, classifications have been by mutual agreement excluded from the bargaining unit. . . . [as] was that of the Industrial Nurse." (Union Rebuttal Brief, p. 4) The reference is to the 1952 handling by the Company and the Union of the removal from the bargaining unit of the Industrial Nurse job classification. That was negotiated; this was not; that was good labor-management relations; this was not.

In addition, the provision establishing the term of the Agreement [Article I,

Section 3] is cited by the Union, together with the denomination and rate of pay of the "Janitor" classification [Agreement, Exhibit A, p. 48], as establishing "the right of job security to work so long as work remains available to him within the plant. The work of these Janitors is still available to them in the plant." [Union Rebuttal Brief, p. 5] Furthermore, the parties contemplated that the Union would represent employees whose work "transpires on the Company's premises at their present plant." [Union Rebuttal Brief, p. 5]

Again, the Union Security provision [Article I, Section 8] insures the Union against layoffs of this nature because, "if the practice perpetrated by the Company in this case was expanded to the other job classifications existing under the Union Agreement, we would see the spectacle of a plant full of people working and the Union not having a single, solitary member among them due to the fact that said employees would be working for agencies which we do not represent." [Union Rebuttal Brief, p. 5]

The Seniority Article [Article IV], the Union urges, is also set to naught by the Company's layoff which renders "the entire concept and provisions of this article completely meaningless." How shall this appear to other Weber hourly-paid employees if it be upheld? "If it is legal for the Company to do what they have done in these cases, then it would evidently be legal for them to delete the entire bargaining unit the same way, by doing the same thing to every employee on the payroll." This is "very unwholesome" since it could lead to the ousting of employees "regardless of how many years they had spent building up the Company by their years of service and seniority." [Union Rebuttal Brief, p. 7] It is an economy, true, but, "We venture to say that if the Company did delete the entire bargaining unit en masse by this procedure with one stroke of their unilateral pen, the arbitrator would unquestionably rule against them. The Union's position is therefore relatively simple: If it is illegal to kill 500 people by massacre, then it is also illegal to kill off four people the same way. The magnitude of the killing should not make it any more legal one way or the other." [Union Rebuttal Brief, p. 7] "The Company attempted to show . . . by various documents how much money per hour they would be saving by doing what they did. These savings referred to, of course, are achieved at the expense of our Union Janitors who are covered by our Union Agreement. . . . Whether this was accomplished with good faith or with bad faith is immaterial. The net result was the same: Our Union Janitors suffered loss of their jobs." [Union Rebuttal Brief, pp. 9–10]

Finally, with reference to arbitration decisions on this point,[1] the Union observes that, "there have been decisions both ways on cases of this kind. . . . [T]he arbitrator will have to reach his own conclusions, securing such ideas as he might be able to come up with through study of these . . . cases," noting nevertheless that "many of the cases listed by the Company refer to the sending out of work to other manufacturing concerns for the other . . . concerns to do

---

[1] The Union cites the following cases: Magnolia Petroleum Co., 21 L.A. 267 (Larson); Stockholders Pub. Co., 16 L.A. 644 (Aaron); Bethlehem Steel Co., 16 L.A. 111 (Killingsworth); Parke Davis & Co., 15 L.A. 111 (Scheiber); Celanese Corp. of America, 14 L.A. 31 (Wolff).

in their own plant." (Union Rebuttal Brief, p. 12) The Union concludes: "In view of the generous statement and suggestion to the arbitrator contained in the Company's . . . brief [see Company Position, infra], the Union, too, wishes to make a generous statement and suggestion to the arbitrator: Inasmuch as the Union is merely trying to get simple justice for the Janitors, and not trying to unmercifully crucify the Company, we suggest to the arbitrator that we think a fair ruling from him would be to restore the jobs of the Janitors to them with full back pay *minus* any earnings or any unemployment compensation obtained by the Janitors while they were in a state of layoff from Weber Aircraft Corporation." (Union Rebuttal Brief, pp. 12–13)

Company position

The Company's layoff action was premised on its interpretation of the management prerogative clause [Article I, Section 6, supra] of the Agreement. This section reserves to the Company "exclusively and without limitation" all rights not "abridged . . . by this Agreement." The Company points to the lack of any express prohibition of outside contracting and concludes that the Agreement leaves its subcontracting power undiminished, at least in this instance. This interpretation is bolstered, it argues, by the fact that the Union in negotiations preliminary to this Agreement proposed but did not press (at least, did not secure) an express bar on the subcontracting "of any work that could normally be performed by our people so long as there are any people on the recall list for said work." (Company Exhibit # 3)

The Company notes that "good faith is an important element in these outside contractor cases." It then denies emphatically any intent or desire to sap the strength of the Union as the representative of its employees. It cites its policy of bringing back into the plant types of work previously subcontracted by Airquipment, thereby augmenting the Union's strength. It interprets the Union's concern to be that this action of the Company, if upheld here, "may be used as a precedent to undermine the bargaining unit through contracting out substantial portions of the work normally performed by employees in the unit." It therefore advances the following statement: "Should the arbitrator wish to reassure the Union, in the event this arbitration is decided in favor of the Company, that the decision cannot be used as a precedent for any further outside contracting but that each case must stand on its own facts in light of the overall principle that the Company must use good faith in respect to the bargaining unit, the Company certainly has no objection to such a statement." (Company Brief, p. 12) The good faith of the Company, it argues, is demonstrated, first, by the fact that this outside janitorial contract is just a projection of a long standing practice not hitherto challenged by the Union, and, second, by the economies dictating the action. These latter may be digested from the memorandum (Company Exhibit #1) prepared and on February 7, 1955, submitted by the Plant Maintenance supervisor to the vice-president in charge of manufacturing.

Further, the Company emphasizes that the ABC Co. is in fact an independent contractor, that Weber has no direct supervisory control over ABC employees

Weber Janitorial Costs [1]

	1953	1954	1955 (est.)
Labor [2]...........................	$22,738.10	$35,363.96	$25,200.00
Supplies.........................	8,027.87	9,165.38	7,200.00
Total........................	30,765.97	44,529.34	36,720.00
Contract bid [3]_..................	27,564.00	27,564.00	27,564.00
Realizable savings................	3,201.97	16,965.34	9,156.00

[1] The memorandum estimated that improved janitorial service to be received from ABC Co. would require, to duplicate it, a capital investment by Weber of $1600.00 for equipment.

[2] Including fringe benefits at $4,320.00 in 1953 ($.20 per hour), $5,400.00 in 1954 ($.25 per hour) and $4,320.00 in 1955 ($.30 per hour). " . . . 1954 janitorial labor costs for Company employees embraced some 21,600 hours as indicated by the statistics on fringe benefits. Under [ABC] maintenance two employees working 40 hours a week for 52 weeks produced 4,160 hours of work. For the afternoon crew, assuming that 12 employees worked 3 hours each, 5 days a week, 52 weeks a year, these hours total 9,360 or total overall hours of 13,520 or almost 8,000 hours less than for Company employees in the janitorial field." (Company Brief, p. 7)

[3] $2,297 per month was the lowest of five (5) bids, including all but a few supplies.

but, on the contrary, under the terms of the ABC contract must present any complaints it may have to the ABC foreman to whose directions alone the ABC janitors must respond.

Finally, the Company distinguishes the cases relied upon by the Union, advances its own authorities,[2] notes that the trend of decisions supports the Company's position, and concludes thus:

[I]n all recent cases the issue of outside contracting has been decided in favor of the company. In each instance the arbitrators have stressed the factors present in this case, namely, good faith on the part of the Company and the absence of a contract prohibition against the outside contract work. Here . . . good faith . . . is bolstered not only by past practice in outside contracting but by unusually strong contract provisions as construed by the Union itself in contract negotiations. (Company Brief, p. 11)

[2] Re Berger, 78 N.Y.S. 2d 528, 9 L.A. 1045 (1948); B. F. Curry, Inc. v. Reddeck, 86 N.Y.S. 2d 674 (1954); Carbide & Carbon Chemical Co., 24 L.A. 158 (Kelliher); Vickers, Inc., 24 L.A. 121 (Haughton); Dalmo Victor Co., 24 L.A. 33 (Kagel); Washington Post Co., 23 L.A. 728 (Healy); Allegheny Ludlum Steel Corp., 23 L.A. 171 (Blair); Tungsten Mining Corp., 19 L.A. 503 (Maggs); Appalachian Electric Cooperative, 19 L.A. 815 (Holly); National Tube Co., 17 L.A. 790 (Garrett); Youngstown Sheet & Tube Co., 14 L.A. 645 (Blair); International Harvester Co., 12 L.A. 707 (McCoy); Amoskeag Mills Inc., 8 L.A. 990 (Copelof); Cords Ltd., Inc., 7 L.A. 474 (Stein); Electro-Physical Labs, 7 L.A. 474 (Kaplan).

Discussion

This kind of case is difficult to decide. Strong policies are at loggerheads. The concern of the parties quite understandably reflects the grave import to their respective operations of, on the one hand, the Company's power to subcontract and, on the other, the Union's protection both of the seniority benefits of its members and its own bargaining-unit strength. A clash of conflicting interests in such a vital area can generate a good deal of friction harmful to the continued maturing of the bargaining relationship. These parties are therefore to be commended for the restraint and good will which each has evidenced in the presentation of this case.

It is not unusual, of course, that diverse viewpoints should be reflected among arbitration awards. Here however, there is apparent a tendency even among experienced arbitrators to be dogmatic in quite general terms. Thus, for instance, one arbitrator concludes that arbitrators are "virtually unanimous in holding that a Company may not unilaterally remove a job from the bargaining unit, even where there is no express limitation to that effect in the agreement or when there is a management rights clause." [3] Yet another, in contrary vein, declares that, "The arbitration decisions are unanimously to the effect that the Company has the right to subcontract work unless the contract specifically restricts that right." [4] More accurately, a third finds the cases cut down the middle and concludes, "In summary, previous decisions form no sure guide. There is no long line of decisions supporting the reasoning of either side . . . no sure and guiding light." [5]

A reading of a substantial cross-section of the reported decisions indicates that the only unanimity reflected in the cases is that of diversity. Each is a law unto itself. Collectively, they point up the delusiveness of generalizing about the content of arbitration awards. Cases supporting Company action stress the retention of management of the right to subcontract work where there is no express prohibition in the agreement.[6] Cases upholding Union grievances give paramount emphasis to the effect, collectively or individually, of the Recognition, Seniority, Wage, and Fringe Benefits clauses of the agreement [7] and the

[3] Bethlehem Steel Co., 16 L.A. at 113 (Killingsworth).

[4] International Harvester Co., 12 L.A. 707 at 709 (McCoy). Accord: Carbide & Carbon Chemicals Co., 24 L.A. 158 (Kelliher); Elkouri, How Arbitration Works 237 (1952).

[5] A. D. Juilliard Co., Inc., 21 L.A. 713 at 723 (Hogan).

[6] See, for example, Appalachian Electric Corp., 19 L.A. 815 (Holly); Allegheny Ludlum Steel Corp., 23 L.A. 171 (Blair); Amoskeag Mills, Inc., 8 L.A. 990 (Copelof); Ashland Oil & Refining Co., 8 L.A. 465 (Wardlaw); Cords Ltd., Inc., 7 L.A. 748 (Stein); Dalmo Victor Co., 24 L.A. 33 (Kagel); International Harvester Co., 12 L.A. 707 (McCoy); National Sugar Refining Co., 13 L.A. 991 (Feinberg). Of course this can involve interpretation of differently worded clauses. See Washington Post Co., 23 L.A. 728 (Healy).

[7] See, for example, Bridgeport Brass Co., 15 L.A. 559 (Donnelly); Celanese Corp. of America, 14 L.A. 31 (Wolff); A. D. Juilliard Co., Inc., 21 L.A. 713 (Hogan); New Britain Machine Co., 8 L.A. 720 (Wallen); Parke Davis & Co., 15 L.A. 111 (Scheiber). But see Dalmo Victor Co., 24 L.A. 33 (Kagel).

stability of the bargaining unit.[8] Past practice in which either party has acquiesced has been given decisive weight in some cases.[9] In others, the location of the work subcontracted, whether on the premises of the Company or those of the independent contractor, has been accorded significance.[10] Whether or not union employees are displaced has been deemed important.[11] Finally, the existence of good faith has been required of the Company [12] which is to say, an effort by the Company to subvert the express terms of the Agreement or to undermine the strength of the Union will not be upheld.[13]

A survey of judicial decisions may indicate how a court in a given jurisdiction may be expected to resolve a similar fact complex if the court conforms to the doctrine of *stare decisis*. A survey of arbitrations may also establish a pattern of past judgment. But its effect on future decisions depends on the relative sense of reasonableness it may evoke in a particular arbitrator. It is still a misnomer to use the rather pretentious phrase, "industrial jurisprudence", with reference to arbitration. It is possible, of course, to cumulate groups of "Company" and "Union" decisions on either side of a given point.[14] But, aside from a rough consensus of commonsense, as yet there is no interior logic flowing from interrelated principles characteristic of jurisprudence. Nor is there apt to be so long as courts refrain from imposing (and parties refrain from seeking) judicial review of arbitration awards in much the same ratio as prevails today.[15]

In the instant case, there are two significant factors with opposite pulls on the judgment of the arbitrator.

First is the fact underscored by the Union that the economy sought by the Company at the expense of the janitors involved no more than bringing non-union janitors into the plant to do the work hitherto done by union janitors. To argue that economies are thereby affected does not conclude the case. It is as

---

[8] See, for example, Stockholders Publishing Co., 16 L.A. 644 (Aaron).

[9] See, for example, Allegheny Ludlum Steel Corp., 23 L.A. 171 (Blair); Tungsten Mingni Corp., 19 L.A. 503 (Maggs); Vickers, Inc., 24 L.A. 121 (Haughton); Youngstown Sheet & Tube Co., 14 L.A. 645 (Blair).

[10] See, for example, Magnolia Petroleum Co., 21 L.A. 267 (Larson); Celanese Corp. of America, 14 L.A. 31 (Wolff). But cf. Stockholders Publishing Co., 16 L.A. 644 at 649 (Aaron).

[11] See, for example, Carbide & Carbon Chemicals Co., 24 L.A. 158 (Kelliher); Electro-Physical Laboratories, Inc., 7 L.A. 474 (Kaplan); Tungsten Mining Corp., 19 L.A. 503 (Maggs).

[12] See, for example, Carbide & Carbon Chemicals Co., 24 L.A. 158 (Kelliher); Cords, Ltd., Inc., 7 L.A. 748 (Stein); Swift & Co., 10 L.A. 842 (Healy); Vickers, Inc., 24 L.A. 121 (Haughton).

[13] See, for example, Bethlehem Steel Co., 16 L.A. 111 (Killingsworth); Dalmo Victor Co., 24 L.A. 33 (Kagel); Magnolia Petroleum Co., 21 L.A. 267 (Larson).

[14] See, for example, Elkouri, How Collective Bargaining Works (1952).

[15] I do not mean to discount the effect of the unfortunate tendency to judicial preemption of arbitration which perhaps is observable currently. See, for example, Black v. Cutter Laboratories, — Cal. 2d —, 278 P. 2d 905, 23 L.A. 715 (1955); Summers, Judicial Review of Labor Arbitration, 2 Buffalo L. Rev. 1 (1952).

accurate (and obvious) to observe that a completely nonunion Weber plant would be a good deal less costly than the one in which union wage scale and fringe benefits now prevail. A cursory reading of this or any collective bargaining agreement will readily demonstrate that the collective bargaining process inevitably entails the sacrifice by the Company of many potential dollar economies in the interest of the welfare of its employees.

The Union sought a bar to subcontracting in the 1954 negotiations. But it assertedly dropped its proposal when the Company made evident to it the indispensability of subcontracting in the airframe industry and, more particularly, to Weber Aircraft. It is clear from the Union proposal (see Company Position, supra) that it contemplated the situation where work was sent outside the plant and remained outside while union members were on layoff for lack of work inside the plant. Thus the unaccepted proposal then advanced cannot now be said to have foreclosed the Union's present position concerning the bringing in of an outside firm to do work on plant premises with the consequent layoff and, presumably, eventual discharge of the grievant janitors.

This brings us to the second and converse point. Since 1951 the Company has been doing on a limited scale exactly what the Union complains of in this case. It brought in an independent contractor to wash office windows, work on the premises which the Union janitors certainly could have done. Indeed, for a while the XYZ janitors washed the outside panes and the Weber janitors the inside panes. Eventually, the XYZ janitors did both. This is the past practice exception that has been thought sufficient in some cases to render subcontracting proper which otherwise might be improper under a collective agreement.[16] If there were no more to this case than that, the decision would be less difficult.

But the Union denies categorically that it collectively, or its shop stewards individually, had any actual knowledge of the window washing arrangement. The only means of distinguishing between the Weber and the XYZ janitors was the differently colored identification badges worn by employees and nonemployees of Weber. No uniform was worn by the outside janitors. Their truck was even unmarked. Further, the testimony of Company witnesses indicated that the company had not notified the Union of the 1951 XYZ contract until March, 1955, and then in connection with this dispute. The Union business representative testified that the first he knew of the XYZ window washers was on March 28, 1955, when the Company vice-president in charge of manufacturing informed him of it by telephone in the course of announcing the impending company action which gave rise to these grievances.

All this seems to boil down to the necessity of a decision by the Arbitrator whether or not the ostensible ignorance on the part of the Union of the status of the XYZ janitors is so incredible as to be beyond belief or, if not, is nonetheless so negligent as to mean that the Union cannot fairly rely now upon its actual lack of knowledge.

[16] See note 12 supra.

The Arbitrator accepts the Union's disclaimer of knowledge. Perhaps it is a source of embarrassment to the Union that its people did not recognize that XYZ rather than Weber janitors were polishing up the windows on the big front door. The Company, after all, is not alleged to have made any effort to camouflage the XYZ janitors or their tall ladders on the outside walls of the office buildings. Yet it remains true that the Company at no time previous to this controversy made known to the Union the existence of its contractual arrangement with the XYZ Co.

The Arbitrator can see no reasonable basis for imposing upon the Union the affirmative duty of ascertaining the unit status of each Weber employee. Indeed, he doubts very much if it would advance the relationship of the parties were his decision to force Union stewards to become snoopers that they might ferret out employment relationships which might otherwise remain unknown to the Union at the peril of an adverse ruling on this issue of past practice in some future arbitration. That would certainly be the effect of upholding the Company's position on the past practice issue here. The Arbitrator therefore concludes as follows: so long as the Company does not inform the Union of the presence on the premises of nonunion employees doing work allotted by the Agreement to union employees, and so long as the Union officials in the plant are in fact unaware of their presence, awareness of the nonunion employees ought not to be imputed to the Union irrespective of actual knowledge.

This conclusion, it should be emphasized, is limited to the issue of past practice raised in this case. It should also be added as a caution that it does not mean that shop stewards can ignore completely the union or nonunion status of employees with whom they come into contact. Circumstances are readily conceivable where this or another Arbitrator might feel required to find actual knowledge to be the fact despite disavowal by the Union, and this simply because it would be too incredible to believe otherwise. This case has seemed to the Arbitrator, on balance, to fall just short of that incredibility.

The unresolved area of dispute is then reduced to the question of whether the Company retained the power under this Agreement to lay off its janitors in order to bring onto the premises an independent contractor to take over the balance of the Company's janitorial work. It is useless to attempt to decide that question by framing general propositions which make up in forcefulness what they lack in precision. The power to subcontract exists, it is important, but it is not unqualified. This is acknowledged explicitly in the arguments of both parties.

The Company is legitimately concerned lest resolution of this dispute in favor of the Union unduly constrict its use of the subcontracting device in an industry where it is indispensable to business success. The Company's suggestion that the Arbitrator explicitly confine the precedent scope of this Award recognizes the equally legitimate concern of the Union that a decision for the Company could render the Union vulnerable to a process of whittling away of its strength in the unit by subcontracting arrangements.

Mindful of these factors, the Arbitrator adopts the case-by-case approach suggested by the Company and applies it to the resolution of this dispute as follows: it was an unreasonable exercise of its subcontracting power for the Company, while subject to this Agreement, to effectuate an unnegotiated reduction of the bargaining unit by laying off its union janitors and replacing them with nonunion janitors of another employer in order to gain economies in the conduct of janitorial work on its premises.

AWARD

The answers to the questions submitted for decision are accordingly as follows: (1) Yes; (2) No; (3) The janitors laid off shall be restored without loss of benefits to the "active payroll" status they possessed before their layoff. They shall receive back pay, less earnings or unemployment compensation received by them during their layoff, but only for the periods of their layoff when they were ready and able to perform the duties of their classification.

Hertner Electric Co. and United Electrical, Radio & Machine Workers, 25 LA 286, 1955

BOARD OF ARBITRATION: S. S. KATES, CHAIRMAN; FRANK H. INGRAM, COMPANY-APPOINTED, AND MARIE J. REED, UNION-APPOINTED, THE LATTER DISSENTING

Statement of the case

The grievance in this case (No. 181) reads as follows:

Letting job 151 [Sweeper-Office] go outside the bargaining unit while people are layed [sic] off. Union requests back pay while people outside of the bargaining unit are doing the job.

Although the facts complained of by the Union in this grievance originated during the 1953–54 collective bargaining agreement, the parties expressly agreed that this grievance "shall be governed by the substantive provisions of the present [1954–55] contract."

The agreed "Authority of the Arbitrators" further provides:

The authority of the panel in adjudicating the issues placed before it in these grievances is to apply the express language of the contract to the situations involved, functioning in a judicial and not a legislative capacity. The panel may not amend, vary or change the terms of the contract. It is not the intention of the parties that the panel shall go beyond the intent as expressed in the language of the contract. Any issue which the panel is unable to resolve by a determination based upon the express language of the contract is to be referred back to the parties for negotiation.

Paragraph 63 of the 1954–55 contract provides that:

(63) A grievance is defined for the purpose of this contract as a claim that the Employer or the Union has violated some express provision of this contract, or failed to perform some obligation expressly assumed under this contract.

I have found from the evidence in this case the following facts.

For many years the cleaning of offices and washrooms at the Cleveland plant was done by the "Sweeper–Office", who during the period relevant to this grievance was Julia Toth. During the same period window cleaning was being done under contract with a window cleaning company except for a short time in 1947 when Company employees did the window cleaning.

On June 7, 1954 Mrs. Toth went on sick leave, and for a while during her illness her work was done on a temporary basis by another employee. When this temporary employee quit the job, the work was done on a temporary basis by a janitor or shop laborers.

During the July vacation period an independent cleaning contractor was brought into the plant to do an annual office and washroom clean-up job. This cleaning contractor was thereafter retained on a trial basis to do the daily office and washroom cleaning until August 2, 1954, at which time a one-year contract was entered into with the same cleaning contractor for regular daily office and washroom cleaning.

Thereafter, the cleaning contractor supplied two employees evenings, for about four hours each, using power equipment, to do the same general work formerly done during daytime eight-hour shifts by Mrs. Toth mostly with hand equipment. (The Company at the arbitration hearing refused to comply with an order of a majority of the arbitration board to produce its contract with the cleaning contractor, by reason whereof I am inferring that the contract if produced would have shown the fact as claimed by the Union, namely a lower hourly wage rate for the cleaning contractor's employees than Mrs. Toth had been receiving.)

During the entire time the cleaning contractor was doing this work, Rebecca McManus, a laid-off employee entitled to demand this job by reason of her seniority status, was ready and willing to do this work, although neither she nor the Union made any demand on the Company with respect thereto.

Beginning in June, 1954, negotiations for the new 1954–55 collective bargaining agreement between the parties were under way. In June, 1954, the Union had made a series of demands for the new contract, including a request for a "No moving clause (New)" to provide as follows:

> For the duration of this agreement the company agrees not to move all or part of its present operations covered by this contract unless by agreement with the Union.

No work will be subcontracted while regular employees are laid off.

This clause was refused by the Company, and neither this nor any other language specifically referring to moving or subcontracting was included in the 1954–55 contract.

At the arbitration hearings the parties were in sharp disagreement as to whether this Union proposal was intended merely to limit so-called "runaway shops" and subcontracting to be done outside the plant, or whether it was intended to include all subcontracting, both inside or outside the plant. It is my conclusion from all the evidence that when the Union submitted this demand it did not contemplate the possibility that an issue as to the subcontracting of regular repetitive continuing operations within the plant would arise, and that only the matters of "runaway shops" and subcontracting of operations outside the plant were sought to be covered thereby.

Likewise, in the early stages of the negotiations, and before the cleaning contractor was employed, the Company had submitted a new job list, containing fewer designations than the pre-existing one, and including a designation with respect to "Job 19B. Janitress Class B." Paragraph 99 of the 1954–55 contract, signed August 18, 1955, reads as follows with respect thereto:

99. The Employer has installed a job evaluation plan. The Union is not a party to the job evaluation plan. The rates of pay, job titles and other details of such plan are herein established in the contract. . . .

The job description prepared by the Company with respect to "Job 19B. Janitress Class B", under date of July 15, 1954, states, under "Principal Duties", as follows:

Clean office, toilet and washroom areas. Mop and wax floors, dust, empty waste baskets, and vacuum clean.

The Union has at all times contended that the job descriptions prepared by the Company with respect to these jobs are not binding upon it, but only the job titles and wage rates.

On August 3, 1955, while negotiations with the Company concerning the new contract were being carried on in New York by the Union including the chairman of the plant union and the Union's international representative, the shop committee met with the Company's plant superintendent in Cleveland to discuss the Union's oral complaint as to the Company's contracting of the office cleaning work. At this meeting the company categorically claimed that it had the right to subcontract this work.

Thereafter, on August 10, 1954, the shop committee, including shop chairman Folley, who had temporarily returned from the New York contract negotiations, signed grievance 181 in Cleveland reading as first quoted above. Mr. Folley returned to New York on August 11, 1955 for further contract negotiations, at which time he told Mr. Hirschberg, the Union's international representative, of this grievance.

Nevertheless, after further negotiations in New York, in which this grievance apparently was never specifically mentioned in the discussions of the Union's previously requested subcontracting clause, the new 1954–55 contract was signed on August 18, 1955, without the inclusion of any language specifically referring to subcontracting of any kind.

The written grievance dated August 10, 1955, which had been orally discussed on August 3, 1955, was formally filed with the Company on August 23, 1955, and was initialled by the Company superintendent at that time as being "timely under the terms of the contract."

I find from the evidence that the Company acted in good faith, for reasons of plant improvement and efficiency and under a claim of right, in entering into the cleaning contractor arrangements, and not for the purpose of harming, undermining or cutting the size of the Union.

Position of the parties

Disregarding several contentions of the parties which I deem immaterial to this case, the parties in substance contend as follows.

Union Position. The Union contends that the intent of the express language of the contract is to prohibit the Company from unilaterally employing an independent contractor to do the work within the plant covered by the "Janitress Class B" job, formerly known as "Sweeper—Office"; the preamble and recognition paragraphs of the contract (paragraphs 1 and 3) show that all employees in the particular plant, with certain exceptions not including the "Janitress Class B", are included in the bargaining unit; that the inclusion of this Job 19B in the job titles, which were specifically made a part of the 1954–55 contract by paragraph 99, shows that this job was covered by the collective bargaining contract and could not be taken away from the Union's jurisdiction by any unilateral action of the Company; that paragraph 33, making seniority the controlling influence in all cases of layoff and rehiring of employees, prohibits the indirect hiring of employees without seniority through an independent cleaning contractor; that paragraph 121, providing that the contract supersedes all previous written or verbal agreements between the parties and concludes all collective bargaining negotiations on all subjects, precludes the Company from relying on any past practice as a precedent in this case; and that the management rights clause of the contract is of no aid to the Company as to this grievance because the contracting of the cleaning work was discriminatory as to Mrs. Toth.

Company Position. The Company contends that under the arbitration board's authority, it must find express contract language specifically prohibiting the contracting of cleaning work in the plant before it may say that such contracting is prohibited; that the paragraphs relied on by the Union do not prohibit such contracting; that the management rights clause, paragraph 103, reserves to the Company the exclusive right and power to manage its plant, including contracting, and that such right with respect to contracting has not been relinquished or affected by any other clauses of the contract; that no discrimination existed here; that since the issue of contracting the cleaning work had been specifically raised between the Company and Union in Cleveland and was known in New York during the contract negotiations, and since the Company had entered into a cleaning contract under a claim of right during the contract negotiations, and since the Union had requested a specific clause prohibiting all "subcontracting" in the collective bargaining negotiations, and since the new collective bargaining contract which was thereafter signed contained no prohibition of subcontracting either within or outside the plant, no such prohibition may now be read into the contract; that since the Company had the right to contract the cleaning work, the seniority clauses had no bearing, being applicable only to jobs held by Company employees who are members of the bargaining unit; that the inclusion of the Janitress Class B job in the list of job titles is irrelevant to the present controversy, since there are many unfilled jobs in the job title list, and the list was intended merely to provide a system to classify Company employees so that they might be properly paid in relation to the skill and the effort they would use in performing tasks assigned to them by the Company; that paragraph 121 makes the express provisions of the contract controlling, and precludes the Union from claiming any prohibition of subcontracting which was not specifically stated in the contract.

Discussion

Although perhaps an oversimplification, I believe that the controlling logic of the present case may be stated in semi-syllogistic form as follows:

A. An employer's right in good faith to control plant operations, including the subcontracting of operations, is limited only by statutory or other valid governmental restriction, or by voluntary relinquishment, as by contract.

B. No statutory or other governmental restriction against subcontracting appears in this case.

C. During the period of the negotiations for the 1954–55 contract, the Company, in oral discusions of the present grievance, had specifically claimed the right to subcontract the in-plant cleaning work now in controversy.

D. Thereafter, the 1954–55 contract was signed without any specific prohibition of, or reference to, subcontracting of cleaning work.

E. Therefore, it cannot be said, under the circumstances of this case, that the Company voluntarily relinquished its right to subcontract this particular cleaning work. . . .

Effect of Including Job Title and Rate in Contract. The Union contends, most earnestly, that the Company nevertheless expressly relinquished its right to subcontract the cleaning work by including the Janitress Class B job title and job rate in the job list which was made a part of the new contract. Thereby, says the Union, and by reason of the Union Shop provisions of the contract, the Company agreed that that job, and all persons filling that job, were to be included in the bargaining unit and within the jurisdiction of the Union; and since the cleaning company employees did the same general work which this job title and the Company's description of the particular job required, the Company had no right unilaterally to take the job, and the employees filling the job, away from the Union's jurisdiction. I can not agree with this contention.

The fact that this job title and its accompanying wage rate were included in the wage schedule merely means that if the job were filled by an employee of the Company he would be entitled to the particular wage rate specified. I do not find that the "intent of the express language" of the contractual references to the job titles and corresponding wage rates, or of the job list itself, is that the Company may not subcontract work falling under such job references. Nor can it be said, in my opinion, that the job list was intended to specify who was to be covered by the collective bargaining agreement. That already had been fully covered in the recognition clause—paragraph 3—in all-inclusive terms.

Moreover, since the Company, at the time the contract was signed, had been specifically denying any relinquishment of its right to subcontract the cleaning work, we cannot overcome such specific denial by an inferential admission to the contrary through the adoption of the job list.

Also to be borne in mind is the fact that the job list had been submitted long before the cleaning subcontracting issue had ever arisen; and, as already indicated, the specific situation as to the latter bears more strongly on the problem than the general implications of the former. . . .

Under all the circumstances and the evidence in this case, I have concluded that the Company did not violate its obligations under the 1954–55 contract to the Union or any of its members by subcontracting the cleaning work in controversy. . . .

THE NLRB AND MANAGEMENT RIGHTS

The issue of managerial prerogatives enters in still another way. The Taft-Hartley Act, carrying over provisions from the Wagner Act, requires employers to bargain with the union concerning wages, hours, and conditions of employment. At times, however, employers have refused to negotiate with unions concerning some matter which, it is claimed, falls outside these boundaries and involves a management right. If the union alleges a refusal to bargain, it is then up to the Board to determine—subject to court review—whether the employer must bargain on the issue. That is to say, the Board must decide whether the subject is an appropriate one for collective bargaining. The materials below all deal with this matter.

NLRB v. Phoenix Mutual Life Insurance Company, 167 F. 2d 983 (C.A. 7), May 7, 1948, certiorari denied 335 U.S. 845–73 NLRB 1463

ON PETITION TO ENFORCE BOARD ORDER

BEFORE MAJOR AND MINTON, CIRCUIT JUDGES, AND DUFFY, DISTRICT JUDGE

. . . About September 1, 1944, Mr. Herbig, the manager of the Chicago-LaSalle Office, called a meeting of the salesmen and announced the resignation of the cashier, telling them selection of a successor was under consideration by the home office and that the new appointee probably would be transferred from another branch office. The impending change loomed important to the salesmen by reason of their dependence upon the cashier's department for information and assistance affecting their earnings. During the two weeks after the announcement the salesmen discussed the matter of the cashier's successor at some length.

On the morning of September 11, and again at lunch on that day, the salesmen met and expressed their dissatisfaction with the fact that they had suffered inconvenience and loss of time due to the "breaking in" of four different cashiers during the last few years. The salesmen discussed the advisability of making a recommendation to respondent and all of them agreed that the assistant cashier was well qualified to fill the vacancy, and that they would prefer her to an outsider; but as to whether the salesmen should recommend the appointment of any specific person there was some disagreement. Salesman Davis was designated by the group to write a letter which, if approved and signed by all ten of the salesmen, was to be sent to the home office. Davis, with the assistance of Johnson and Goldberg, prepared a tentative draft of such a letter, which was discussed and revised at a subsequent luncheon meeting of the salesmen.

Before the final draft had been agreed upon the manager learned of the proposed letter and questioned salesman Goldberg, who explained that the final draft had not been completed and that he therefore did not know just what the contents would be. The manager thereupon advised him not to sign it.

On September 15, before Davis had an opportunity to put the letter in final form, he and Johnson received notices from the respondent terminating their agency contracts. The letters were almost identical. Each stated:

> Your recent action and involvement in the resignations and new appointment affecting our Cashier's Department have been so far beyond the premise of your responsibility, and so completely unpleasant that in full agreement with the Home Office we are cancelling your Agent's Contract, effective thirty days from today.

The letters further instructed Davis and Johnson to turn in their supplies and rate books, to have their desks cleaned out, and their agency affairs closed by noon of the following day.

Section 7 of the act provides that "employees shall have the right . . . to engage in . . . concerted activities, for the purpose of collective bargaining *or* other mutual aid or protection." By incorporating this language, Congress must have intended to include within the act what the usual meaning of these unambiguous words conveys. A proper construction is that the employees shall have the right to engage in concerted activities for their mutual aid or protection even though no union activity be involved, or collective bargaining be contemplated. Here Davis and Johnson and other salesmen were properly concerned with the identity and capability of the new cashier. Conceding they had no authority to appoint a new cashier or even recommend anyone for the appointment, they had a legitimate interest in acting concertedly in making known their views to management without being discharged for that interest. The moderate conduct of Davis and Johnson and the others bore a reasonable relation to conditions of their employment. It was, therefore, an unfair labor practice for respondent to interfere with the exercise of the right of Davis and Johnson and the other salesmen to engage in concerted activities for their mutual aid or protection. The findings of the Board that Davis and Johnson were discharged because they engaged in concerted activities for their mutual aid or protection is supported by substantial evidence on the record as a whole. . . .

MAJOR, CIRCUIT JUDGE, DISSENTING

I would deny enforcement of the Board's order for the reason that the "concerted activities" in which respondent's insurance salesmen engaged, as found by the Board, were not for their "mutual aid or protection," as contemplated by Sec. 7 of the Act. In my judgment, both the stated purposes of the Act and a reasonable interpretation thereof required a holding that it was never contemplated by Congress that such activities should form the basis for an unfair labor practice. It must be remembered that no labor dispute or labor union, or the right to form, join or assist a labor organization, or any right on the part of the salesmen, or refusal on the part of the respondent to bargain collectively, as those terms are defined by the Act and many times construed by the courts, are involved. Neither is there any grievance concerning wages, rates of pay, hours of employment or conditions of work. In fact, the grievance is not only petty but personal and private in nature.

The grievance concerns the selection by respondent of a cashier, which was wholly the prerogative of management. To put it bluntly, their grievance was directed at a matter which was none of their business or concern. The opinion of the majority on this aspect of the case has the effect of enlarging the jurisdiction of the Board beyond all intendments and penalizes an employer for discharging an employee who busies himself in concert with fellow employees about matters which are none of their concern, all under the guise that it is for their "mutual aid or protection." I would suppose under the holding of the majority that the salesmen would also be protected if they engaged in "concerted activities" regarding respondent's president, its board of directors, its attorneys, the location of its office, or the form and contents of the policies issued by respondent which the salesmen are authorized to sell, this notwithstanding that respondent would be under no obligation to bargain with them concerning these and other matters wholly within the realm of the managerial orbit, all under the pretext that they had a "legitimate interest" in such matters.

Inland Steel Company v. NLRB; United Steel Workers of America, CIO et al. v. NLRB; 170 F. 2d 247 (C.A. 7), September 23, 1948, certiorari granted 335 U.S. 910 (United Steel Workers), certiorari denied 336 U.S. 960 (Inland Steel Company)—77 NLRB 1

BARGAINING ON PENSIONS

The Company's refusal to bargain concerning a retirement and pension plan is based solely on its contention that it is not required to do so under the terms of the Act. . . .

The Company relates in lengthy detail the complicated nature of its retirement and pension plan, for the purpose, as we understand, of showing that it is impossible, or at any rate highly impractical, for it to bargain relative thereto with the multiplicity of bargaining units which the Board has established in its plant. It states in its brief:

Retirement and pension plans such as the petitioner's cannot be dealt with through the processes of compulsory collective bargaining required by the National Labor Relations Act, which entail bargaining within the units of the character established by Section 9 (a) and (b) of that Act.

The Company concedes that "Congress could have established a requirement of compulsory collective bargaining upon any subject which a representative of the employees chose to present for that purpose," and we understand from some parts of its argument that it tacitly concedes that some retirement and pension plans may be within the scope of the bargaining requirement. However, we find in the Company's reply brief, in response to the Board's argument, what appears to be the inconsistent statement that "Congress intended to exclude from the compulsory bargaining requirement of the Act all industrial retirement and pension plans. The law is a law for all and it is the same law." We agree, of course, with the last sentence of this quotation. We also are of the view that the bargaining requirements of the Act include all retirement and pension plans or none. Otherwise, as the Board points out "some employers would have to bargain about pensions and some would not, depending entirely upon the unit structure in the plant and the nature of the pension plan the employer has established or desires to establish." Such a holding as the Act's requirements would supply the incentive for an employer to devise a plan or system which would be sufficiently comprehensive and difficult to remove it from the ambit of the statute, and success of such an effort would depend upon the ingenuity of the formulator of the plan. We are satisfied no such construction of the Act can reasonably be made.

It is, therefore, our view that the Company's retirement and pension plan, complicated as it is asserted to be, must be treated and considered the same as any other such plan. It follows that the issue for decision is, as the Board asserts, whether pension and retirement plans are part of the subject matter of compulsory collective bargaining within the meaning of the Act. The contention which we have just discussed has been treated first, and perhaps somewhat out of order, so as to obviate the necessity for a lengthy and detailed statement of the Company's plan.

Briefly, the plan as originally initiated on January 1, 1936, provided for the establishment of a contributory plan for the payment of retirement annuities pursuant to a contract between the Company and the Equitable Life Assurance Society. Only employees with earnings of $250.00 or more per month were eligible to participate. Effective December 31, 1943, the plan was extended to cover all employees regardless of the amount of their earnings, provided they had attained the age of 30 and had five years of service. The plan from the beginning was optional with the employee, who could drop out at any time, with rights upon retirement fixed as of that date. On December 28, 1945, the Company entered into an agreement with the First National Bank of Chicago, wherein the Company established a pension trust, the purpose of which was to augment the Company's pension program by making annuities available to employees whose period of service had occurred largely during years prior to the time when participation in the retirement plan was available to them. These were employees whose retirement date would occur so soon after the establishment of the plan that it would not afford them adequate retirement annuity benefits. The employees eligible to participate in the pension trust were not required to contribute thereto, but such fund was created by the Company's contributions.

An integral and it is asserted an essential part of the plan from the beginning was that employees be compulsorily retired at the age of 65. (There are some exceptions to this requirement which are not material here.)

The Company's plan had been in effect for five and one-half years when, because of the increased demands for production and with a shortage of manpower occasioned by the war, it was compelled to suspend the retirement of its employees as provided by its established program. In consequence there were no retirements for age at either of the plants involved in the instant proceeding from August 26, 1941 to April 1, 1946. This temporary suspension of the compulsory retirement rule was abrogated, and it was determined by the Company that no retirements should be deferred beyond June 30, 1946. By April 1, 1946, all of the Company's employees, some 224 in number, who had reached the age of 65, had been retired. Thereupon, the Union filed with the Company a grievance protesting its action in the automatic retirement of employees at the age of 65. The Company refused to discuss this grievance with the Union, taking the position that it was not required under the Act to do so or to bargain concerning its retirement and pension plan, and particularly concerning the compulsory retirement feature thereof. Whereupon, the instant proceeding was instituted before the Board, with the result already noted.

This brings us to the particular language in controversy. Sec. 8 (5) of the Act requires an employer "to bargain collectively with the representative of his employees, subject to the provisions of Sec. 9 (a)," and the latter section provides that the duly selected representative of the employees in an appropriate unit shall be their exclusive representative "for the purposes of collective bargaining *in respect to rates of pay, wages, hours of employment, or other conditions of employment. . . .*" [Italics supplied.] The instant controversy has to do with the construction to be given or the meaning to be attached to the italicized words; in fact, the controversy is narrowed to the meaning to be attached to the term "wages" or "other conditions of employment."

The Board found and concluded that the benefits accruing to an employee by reason of a retirement or pension plan are encompassed in both categories. As to the former it stated in its decision:

> With due regard for the aims and purposes of the Act and the evils which it sought to correct, we are convinced and find that the term 'wages' as used in Section 9 (a) must be construed to include emoluments of value, like pension and insurance benefits, which may accrue to employees out of their employment relationship. . . . Realistically viewed, this type of wage enhancement or increase, no less than any other, becomes an integral part of the entire wage structure, and the

character of the employee representative's interest in it, and the terms of its grant, is no different than in any other case where a change in the wage structure is effected.

The Board also found and concluded that in any event a retirement and pension plan is included in "conditions of employment" and is a matter for collective bargaining. After a careful study of the well written briefs with which we have been favored, we find ourselves in agreement with the Board's conclusion. In fact, we are convinced that the language employed by Congress, considered in connection with the purpose of the Act, so clearly includes a retirement and pension plan as to leave little, if any, room for construction. While, as the Company has demonstrated, a reasonable argument can be made that the benefits flowing from such a plan are not "wages," we think the better and more logical argument is on the other side, and certainly there is, in our opinion, no sound basis for an argument that such a plan is not clearly included in the phrase, "other conditions of employment." The language employed, when viewed in connection with the stated purpose of the Act, leads irresistibly to such a conclusion. And we find nothing in the numerous authorities called to our attention or in the legislative history so strongly relied upon which demonstrates a contrary intent and purpose on the part of Congress.

The opening sentence in the Company's argument is as follows: "Section 8 (5) and 9 (a) of the Act do not refer to industrial retirement and pension plans, such as that of the petitioner, *in haec verba*." Of course not, and this is equally true as to the myriad matters arising from the employer-employee relationship which are recognized as included in the bargaining requirements of the Act but which are not specifically referred to. Illustrative are the numerous matters concerning which the Company and the Union have bargained and agreed, as embodied in their contract of April 30, 1945. A few of such matters are: a provision agreeing to bargain concerning nondiscriminatory discharges; a provision concerning seniority rights, with its far reaching effect upon promotions and demotions; a provision for the benefit of employees inducted into the military service; a provision determining vacation periods with pay; a provision concerning the safety and health of employees, including clinic facilities; a provision for in-plant feeding, and a provision binding the Company and the Union to bargain, in conformity with a Directive Order of the National War Labor Board concerning dismissal or severance pay for employees displaced as the result of the closing of plants or the reductions in the working force following the termination of the war. None of these matters and many others which could be mentioned are referred to in the Act "*in haec verba*," yet we think they are recognized generally, and they have been specifically recognized by the Company in the instant case as proper matters for bargaining and, as a result, have been included in a contract with the Union. Some of the benefits thus conferred could properly be designated as "wages," and they are all "conditions of employment." We think no common sense view would permit a distinction to be made as to the benefits inuring to the employees by reason of a retirement and pension plan.

Richfield Oil Corp., petitioner, v. NLRB, respondent, United States Court of Appeals for the District of Columbia, No. 12483, January 16, 1956

BARGAINING ON A STOCK PURCHASE PLAN

DANAHER, CIRCUIT JUDGE

Petitioner "Richfield" asks us to review and set aside, and the Board seeks enforcement of, the Board's order issued against Richfield October 18, 1954. The Board had found that Richfield violated §8 (*a*) (5) and (1) of the National Labor Relations Act [1] by refusing to bargain with Oil Workers International Union, CIO, with respect to an employee stock purchase plan which the company had unilaterally put into effect as of July 1, 1953.

Richfield produces, refines and sells petroleum products in interstate and foreign commerce and employs about 5,000 employees. The company engages in collective bargaining with some 11 labor organizations. Since April 1945, and at all times material to the issue raised here, Oil Workers Union has been the exclusive collective bargaining representative of about 2,000 production, construction and maintenance Richfield employees.

On April 14, 1953, Richfield announced to its employees a voluntary "Stock Purchase Plan" of the deferred distribution type. The Plan had not previously been discussed with the Oil Workers Union, although there was then in full force and effect a collective bargaining agreement with that Union. The latter thereupon wrote as of April 2, 1953, expressing its desire "to meet with the Richfield Oil Corporation for the purpose of negotiations on the proposed 'Stock Purchase Plan.'" Richfield declined such negotiations, insisted that the Plan had been "finally adopted" subject only to clearance with the Commissioner of Internal Revenue, but expressed willingness to meet with the Union "for the purpose of explaining the Plan." Meetings were accordingly held on May 7, 1953, and again on May 13, 1953, when the Union proposed certain modifications embodied in a "Plan" it submitted, purposed "to encourage employees to provide additional security for their retirement through systematic savings." The Union sought to establish the plan by *contract* to be ratified by the Union, to enlarge the group of eligibles, to protect Union members while in authorized leave status, to prescribe certain safeguards in the event of strike or lockout, to relate various types of "service" time to certain situations otherwise covered in the outstanding collective bargaining agreement, and in other respects to vary the Richfield plan. After Richfield flatly advised that it "did not consider the Stock Purchase Plan to be a proper subject of collective bargaining," the Union charged Richfield with unfair labor practices.

The complaint recited that "the Union requested the Respondent to bargain collectively with it in respect to the Respondent's unilaterally promulgated

---

[1] Act of July 5, 1935, 49 Stat. 452, as amended 1947, 61 Stat. 140, 29 U.S.C. § 158 (1952).

Stock Purchase Plan as exclusive bargaining representative" of the employees[2] in its unit, and Richfield's refusal so to bargain. Unfair labor practices accordingly were alleged.

The facts were stipulated for the purposes of the hearing. Attached as exhibits were the exclusive bargaining agreement then in force,[3] certain amendments thereto, Richfield's announcement, the Plan, a retirement plan and a retirement annuity plan concluded by agreement in 1944, and various other documents or correspondence. The retirement plan benefits were provided by a group annuity contract, paid for by Richfield, and were in addition to those provided under an "Employees Group Insurance Plan" and by the Social Security Act. The retirement annuity plan for Richfield employees was paid for by joint contributions of Richfield and its employees, with participation optional with each eligible employee.

Adequate details of the Stock Purchase Plan can be gleaned from the findings, included in the Board's "Decision and Order." [4]

One member dissenting, the Board majority concluded on the record as a whole that the Plan represents a mandatory subject of collective bargaining. The opinion said, in part:

We think that a common sense, nontechnical view of the Plan, including its manifest purpose, its unmistakable emphasis upon the long term accumulation of stock for future needs rather than upon stock ownership as such, its requirement that participants be employees, and its provision for benefits which are related to the employees' length of service and amount of wages while participating, compels the conclusion that benefits accruing to employees thereunder represent a part of the compensation or remuneration received by the employees for their labor, differing from their weekly wages only in form and time of payment.

The Board found that the term "wages" comprehends emoluments of value flowing from the employment relationship. In like manner, the Plan, in its objectives and in its operation, was said to affect "conditions of employment." On both predicates the Board overruled Richfield's contention that the Plan is not the subject of compulsory collective bargaining.

Richfield in its brief argues that "no employer can be compelled by law to provide for the acquisition of its own shares by its employees, and the law gives neither to the employer nor to a trade union any right to compel employees without their consent, to buy the corporate shares of their employer, however needy that employer may be." The Company has offered, of its own

---

[2] By December 1, 1953, 2,547 out of 3,318 eligible employees had become participants in the Plan, including 820 of the 1,340 eligibles represented by the Union.

[3] The agreement dealt in detail with many employment problems including transportation and travel time, holidays, vacations, sick leave, and leaves of absence. Under the heading "Benefits," we read: "This agreement shall in no wise affect the status of employees on whose behalf it is made with respect to benefits derived or to be derived by employees as a whole from membership in any group insurance, stock purchasing plans or pension funds."

[4] 110 N.L.R.B. 356 (1954).

volition, a plan by which employees will be assisted by Richfield in the purchase of the latter's shares. No one, so far as we can see, has asserted that Richfield can be compelled by law to provide for the purchase of its shares. No one has sought to compel employees, without their consent, to buy Richfield's shares. As a matter of fact, employees who enter upon the plan, under its terms, may even withdraw from the purchase program at any time. The Plan in its every aspect was conceived and formulated by Richfield itself. We are offered by the language quoted a strange interpretation of the issue as we see it, yet the statement finds counterpart in other arguments offered in the Richfield brief.

For example, "Richfield's plan is offered as something separate from the wage agreement, to afford (as the plan states), an opportunity for employees to invest in the Company's stock, and thereby to promote a close and continuing association with the Company's business. As analysis discloses, *the plan is nothing more than that*" [emphasis added], we are told.

Since analysis is invited we look more closely at the terms proposed.

A Richfield employee having been employed for more than one year and being between the ages of 30 and 65, may at stated dates contribute through regular payroll deductions up to 5 per cent of his normal wage, but not less than $5 per month. Richfield then promises to contribute regularly an amount equal to one-half of the employee's monthly contribution. "The Company will make an annual contribution of a sum based upon the ratio of its profits to invested capital which will adjust the total monthly contributions made by the Company to the following schedule." Then, having specified that "profits" shall mean the Company's net income after taxes for the preceding calendar year, Richfield in its schedule shows that its annual contribution will run from 50 per cent to 75 per cent. No cash or stock is to be distributed to anyone while a member of the Plan, but at or after age 55 a man may receive all cash and stock credited to his own member account, representing his contributions, and to a "trusteed" account, representing the Company contributions. If upon *termination of service* of less than 10 years, a man withdraws before age 55 except because of death or defined disability, he may receive all cash and stock credited to his "member" account, but only a reduced percentage of the same credited to his trusteed account, prorated according to a schedule of service. If he withdraws from the Plan *while remaining an employee*, an employee may receive only the cash and stock credited to his own member account, and, irrespective of age, or years of membership in the Plan, he will not be entitled to any part of the cash or stock in his trusteed account. There are other details which we need not now mention except that the Plan defines "service." That term shall mean the continuous period of time he is an employee of the Company "in accordance with its established policy." The Plan says: "Its continuity shall not be deemed broken during any period of authorized leave of absence or during any layoff period not exceeding the consecutive days prescribed by the Company's policy when the layoff occurs. Its continuity shall be immediately broken by discharge, resignation or layoff exceeding the prescribed period."

Enough has been said on this point to demonstrate that the Plan is some thing "more than that" argued to us. Certainly "continuity" of uninterrupte service means that each participating employee will receive from the Compan an emolument equal to at least 50 per cent of his own contributions if th Company's net earnings reach only 11 per cent per annum, while his emolu ment for each additional per cent of net profits increases 5 per cent up t a maximum of 75 per cent of the employee's contributions. If that is no tantamount to a wage incentive program for uninterrupted service, it should a a minimum, cause any employee, all eligible participating employees, sub stantial concern as to what happens should there be a strike. The Plan i silent on the point. If 68 per cent of the Company's eligible employees ar participating in the Plan, and they are, they might readily consider themselve ill-advised to take any steps which would disentitle them to receive Compan contributions reaching to a possible 75 per cent of their own contribution over the period of participating years.

Perhaps on the foregoing account, the Union sought an agreement that th Plan was not to be impaired or abrogated "as a result of, or solely by reaso of, any strike or lockout." In that context the Union proposed a definit understanding that "the effect of any strike or lockout shall be limited to th effect of suspension of contributions by both Company and participants durin the periods of strikes or lockouts." The Union, too, asked firm agreemen that "Participation by an employee who is granted a Union leave of absenc shall not be terminated during such leave but allotments shall be suspende in accordance with the suspension provisions of the 'Stock Purchase Plan.' The Union suggested further that the Plan run concurrently with its collectiv bargaining contract, the provisions of the Plan accordingly not be "subject t change as to Employees or Participants represented by the Union," and other wise as proposed. Apart from clarification of the status of its members in suc particulars, it is possible the Union also had in mind the impairment of it status in the eyes of its members as well as other Company employees when despite its having been chosen as the bargaining representative of its unit wit a valid contract in full force and effect, Richfield nonetheless unilaterally an without notice to the Union, announced the Plan. The bland assertion tha Richfield contemplated merely an opportunity for employees to invest in th Company's stock would seem to fall short of its conclusion that "The Pla is nothing more than that." (supra.)

Richfield argues that bargaining as ordered by the Board "interferes with it legitimate rights under the law, and its exclusive right to control of manage ment." Counsel argues that "There are certain matters concerning which th law does not permit, much less compel, collective bargaining, even when suc matters are terms or conditions of employment." There is no provision of th Act which precludes collective bargaining on a deferred payment stock pur chase plan such as we have before us. It is difficult to understand that voluntary agreement to bargain on such a subject can be said to be a matte "which the law does not permit." The parties expressly stipulated before th Board:

Certain corporations in the oil industry have in the past several years bargained with unions representing their employees with regard to plans under which the employees may engage in stock purchase programs whereby they acquire stock in their corporate employer at terms more favorable than those available to the public generally because of employer contributions proportionate to the employees' contributions to such stock purchase program. Neither Counsel for the General Counsel nor the Charging Party will offer or rely upon the foregoing fact as showing a practice, either in industry generally or in the oil industry of bargaining with respect to such plans; General Counsel and the Charging Party will offer the said fact and rely thereon, for the sole purpose of showing that there is precedent for such bargaining. (J.A. 14–15)

Richfield does not limit its argument to what the law will "permit," to be sure. As to what the law will "compel" and to illustrate its point concerning non-bargainable proposals, Richfield cites situations involving closed shop provisions not in conformity with requirements of the Act, welfare and retirement fund proposals which unlawfully discriminate, demands for excessive union membership fees and certain featherbedding provisions. The quick answer is that what the Union sought to discuss was none of these things, and nothing like any of them. Of course employers will be protected in their legitimate rights, indeed the Board makes clear that the statutory representative cannot act, and the employer need not bargain with it, except as the representative of the employees as such. Moreover, if the Board should enter and thereafter seek enforcement of an improvident order, except as to a permitted bargainable issue, the courts are still here.[5]

There is involved no threat to Richfield's "maintaining the integrity of its own business ownership, the control of its own management and its own representatives free from union interference." Nor is there substance to the claim that the situation "necessarily and inevitably involves bargaining about the conditions and prerogatives of ownership." Richfield in support of such contentions tells us, and cites cases [6] to prove its point, that when Congress classified supervisors as a part of management, management itself and all management representatives were already beyond a bargaining duty imposed by the Act. On that premise the Board is assailed for its failure to assure management immunity from union interference. Somehow, the claim falls as short of reality as the cases cited fail to deal with the issue here.

Richfield says that the Board's order will result in violation of the fundamental requirements of the Act and its basic policy by dividing the loyalty of the union between the duty of ownership on the one hand and to employees on

[5] Compare Labor Board v. Express Pub Co., 312 U.S. 426, 437 (1941); May Stores Co. v. Labor Board, 326 U.S. 376, 388, 389 n. 10 (1945); Labor Board v. Warren Company, 350 U.S. 107, 112 (1955).

[6] Packard Co. v. Labor Board, 330 U.S. 485 (1947); Texas Co. v. National Labor Relations Board, 198 F. 2d 540, 542 (9th Cir. 1952); National Labor Relations Board v. Retail Clerks Inter. Ass'n, 211 F. 2d 759 (9th Cir. 1954), cert. denied, 348 U.S. 939 (1954).

the other. Richfield sees conflicting representations between ownership and employee interests, between stockholder employees and non-stockholder employees and between those employees who aspire to be investors and shareholders and those who do not. It is to be doubted that there are such basic conflicts as Richfield envisions, but if there are, what are we to say in the light of its claim that its own, indeed its whole, purpose in offering the plan is to provide "an opportunity for employees to invest in the Company's stock"? Richfield here relies upon the *Bausch & Lomb Optical Co.* case, 108 N.L.R.B. 213. A mere reading of the case will disclose that it is totally inapposite to our problem. There, the union had set up a competing business with that of the company for whose employees it proposed to speak. It can scarcely be said that employees as stockholders are analogous to employees as competitors from a bargaining point of view. Where only stockholders are to have the right to be heard, the Union shall have no voice whatever as a statutory representative, the Board emphasized.

In any event, the Union has asked nothing concerning managerial functions. The Plan is limited to open market share purchase. The maximum rate of employee contributions is 5 per cent of salary, yet there are some 4,000,000 shares outstanding, we are told. The bargaining the Union sought involves, not control of the Company, but the status of the offer and of the employees who rely upon it. Richfield invites its employees to become stockholders whether they belong to this Union or not, and seeks to keep them as stockholders by withholding their deferred benefit of Company contributions until as to each employee, all conditions of the Plan shall have been met. To the extent that the Board may rely upon such provisions as stating a "condition of employment" and hence may establish one of the bases upon which its order rests, we think it is correct. Equally Richfield's fears are ill-founded, we suggest, if the Company is correct in its representations to us that "Richfield may terminate the entire plan at will." Section X, if it be controlling, and on this point we do not rule, in part expressly provides: "The Board of Directors of the Company reserves the right to amend or terminate this PLAN at any time."

Richfield seeks to pitch its argument on yet additional grounds which may be briefly noted. We are told that the duty to bargain collectively could not have been intended by Congress to cover a "field as significant as that of stock acquisition and ownership." Aside from the fact that Congress never forbade such bargaining, the Company's point is not of the essence of the issue before us. Our question is far more narrowly limited since Congress expressly *has* provided for collective bargaining with respect to wages and conditions of employment. To the Board has been left the determination as to what facts and circumstances spell out "wages" or what situations involve other "conditions of employment." We will presently reach consideration of the case in those very terms.

Meanwhile we note the Company's further claim that the Board's order violates constitutional rights:

1. by "depriving the employer of freedom and liberty of contract con-

cerning the disposition of its property" in contravention of the Fifth Amendment [7];

2. by superseding the individual employee's freedom of contract by binding employees to purchase stock with funds already earned and owned by them [8]; and

3. by transcending the authority delegated to the Board because as so exercised, the Board's power may be "so broad as to include the ownership of corporate employers," all without "understandable limitations on its scope"; and besides, the Act as so interpreted, may "invade the field of legislation reserved to the States." [9]

It requires no citation of authority to support the obvious, that in designating bargaining representative, employees make their choice "for the purpose of negotiating the terms and conditions of their employment." [10] The Union here ought to speak only for its own bargaining unit, as the Act authorizes with respect to "rates of pay, wages, hours of employment, or other conditions of employment." Under the Plan, only a limited, defined class of employees will be eligible to participate, but they must be employees. Their chance to receive from their employment an emolument to be contributed by the Company depends, not only upon their continued service in an employee status over a prescribed number of years, but upon their own contributions up to 5 per cent of their wages or salary. So what is "service" within the meaning of the Plan, how "wages" shall be determined upon which to base the percentage of

[7] But the stock is to be bought in the open market, hence from individual willing sellers, and otherwise the terms of the offer have been fixed by the Company itself.

[8] But participation in the Plan is entirely voluntary and optional with the employee, just as is participation in the Retirement Annuity Plan, long since established by the Company.

[9] But neither the Union's proposed "Memorandum of Understanding" nor its proposed modifications in the Plan looked to "ownership" of Richfield. The Board's order went no farther than the Richfield "Cease and desist from refusing to bargain collectively with Oil Workers International Union, CIO, as the exclusive bargaining representative of its employees in the appropriate unit with respect to its 'Stock Purchase Plan.'" Moreover, in its opinion the Board said:
At the bargaining table, therefore, the statutory representative cannot act, and the employer need not bargain with it, except as the representative of employees as such, and only with respect to "rates of pay, wages, hours of employment, or other conditions of employment." And, even in these areas it may be appropriate to point out to those who are inclined to equate an employer's obligation to bargain with a complete and abject submission to every union proposal, the Act, in the words of the Supreme Court, "does not compel any agreement whatsoever between employees and employers." [Citing N.L.R.B. v. American Nat. Ins. Co., 343 U.S. 395] On the occasion of stockholder meetings, corporate elections, or any other matter in which only stockholders have the right to be heard, the union has no voice whatever as a statutory representative. 110 N.L.R.B. at 363. And see § 8(d): ". . . but such obligation does not compel either party to agree to proposal or require the making of a concession." 29 U.S.C. § 158(d) (1952).

[10] § 101, 61 Stat. 136 (1947), 29 U.S.C. § 151 (1952).

possible contributions, or how continuity of status is to be ascertained and preserved, or what effect there may be upon the employees' rights to participate in future benefits in the event of strikes or lockouts, or whether a Union
man on Union business may be on leave of absence, or whether "Company
policy," undefined, shall solely govern the effect of lay-offs upon the employees'
right to future benefits, or what relationship the "Company policy" in such
matters shall bear to similar bargainable issues previously resolved in the outstanding collective bargaining agreement with the Union, and comparable
problems, may become of great importance in cementing harmonious industrial
relations between the Company and its employees. To achieve the purposes of
the Act, resolution of issues on any such subject may well further the objectives
Congress sought, although we do not decide, in the absence of a record on a
particular point, that any special problem inevitably gives rise to a necessity
for bargaining. The result in any such situation will depend upon the outcome
of bargaining with reference to it, and complete agreement may follow negotiations.

The very fact that Congress has not defined "wages" or "terms" or "other
conditions of employment" makes it clear that the Board is to deal within its
own competence and expertise with the multiple variance of differing aspects
of the problems arising in these fields. Then the courts will review and determine ultimately whether or not the Board has acted permissibly and correctly.
Thus, we have no difficulty in appreciating the observations of Circuit Judge
Woodbury:

> At least, without attempting to mark the outer boundaries of the word
> "wages" as used in the Act, or attempting to enunciate a generalizing prin-
> ciple for the decision of future cases (generalization must await the
> accumulation of a body of decided cases pricking out the line between
> subject matters within the Act and subject matters outside its scope) we
> think it can safely be said that the word "wages" in §9 (a) of the Act
> embraces within its meaning direct and immediate economic benefits
> flowing from the employment relationship. And this is as far as we need go,
> for so construed the word covers a group insurance program for the reason
> that such a program provides a financial cushion in the event of illness or
> injury arising outside the scope of employment at less cost than such a
> cushion could be obtained through contracts of insurance negotiated
> individually. [11]

So, too, we can here see that the deferred distribution program as outlined in
the Plan offers emoluments of value comprehended within the term "wages,"
and accrued from the employment relationship.[12]

Likewise, we agree with the Board opinion that the Plan comes within the

[11] W. W. Cross & Co. v. National Labor Relations Board, 174 F. 2d 875, 878 (1st
Cir. 1949).

[12] See "Collective Bargaining on Stock Purchase Plans," Sobernheim and Brown,
55 *Colum. L. Rev.* 1000 (1955); Comments, 43 *Geo. L.J.* 309 (1955); 23 *Geo. Wash.
L. Rev.* 609 (1955); "Compensating the Corporate Executive," Washington and
Rothschild, Ch. 6 and 7 (Rev. Ed. 1951).

"conditions of employment" category. It would add nothing to go beyond the views expressed by the Seventh Circuit:

> Suppose that a person seeking employment was offered a job by each of two companies equal in all respects except that one had a retirement and pension plan and that the other did not. We think it reasonable to assume an acceptance of the job with the company which had such plan. Of course, that might be described merely as the inducement which caused the job to be accepted, but on acceptance it would become, so we think, one of the "conditions of employment." Every day that such an employee worked his financial status would be enhanced to the extent that his pension benefits increased, and his labor would be performed under a pledge from the company that certain specified monetary benefits would be his upon reaching the designated age. It surely cannot be seriously disputed but that such a pledge on the part of the company forms a part of the consideration for work performed, and we see no reason why an employee entitled to the benefit of the plan could not upon the refusal of the company to pay, sue and recover such benefits. In this view, the pension thus promised would appear to be as much a part of his "wages" as the money paid him at the time of the rendition of his services. But again we say that in any event such a plan is one of the "conditions of employment." [13]

Richfield's petition for review will be denied and the Board's order for enforcement will be granted as prayed for in its answer to the petition.

Let an order enter accordingly.

WILBUR K. MILLER, CIRCUIT JUDGE, DISSENTING

I dissent because, in my opinion, the stock purchase plan is not a subject concerning which the Act requires collective bargaining. Cf. Board Member Beeson's dissenting opinion in this case, 110 N.L.R.B. at 366 (1954).

The dissenting opinion of Board Member Beeson, referred to above, reads in part as follows:

I cannot agree with the majority in finding the Respondent guilty of a refusal to bargain regarding its stock purchase plan. The majority's determination that such plan is a proper subject for compulsory bargaining between a corporation and the representative of its employees is not supported by the language of the Act and contravenes both the intent and the basic purposes of the Statute. To so find seems to me an utterly unrealistic and dangerous expansion of the usual area of collective bargaining. It is in my opinion not in the interests of the public much less the true interests of the parties.

[13] Inland Steel Co. v. National Labor Relations Board, 170 F. 2d 247, 253 (7th Cir. 1948), *cert. denied* on this issue, 336 U.S. 960 (1949); and see National Labor Relations Board v. J. H. Allison Co., 165 F. 2d 766 (6th Cir. 1948), *cert. denied*, 335 U.S. 814 (1948); cf. National Labor Relations Board v. Black-Clawson Co., 210 F. 2d 523 (6th Cir. 1954).

Section 8 (*a*) (5) and 8 (*d*), insofar as pertinent, requires bargaining as to "wages" and "other terms and conditions of employment." Admittedly, the Courts in cases like *Inland Steel* and *W. W. Cross* have held that such matters as pensions and insurance coverage, which guarantee to the employees definite immediate or future benefit, are encompassed by the above provisions. However, the stock purchase plan here involved, unlike those matters, affords *no* certainty whatsoever of either present or future emolument to any employee. The plan is merely designed to encourage employees to become *co-entrepreneurs*, sharing in a future potentially profitable investment, subject to all the risks faced by the other stockholders. The Company's contribution under the plan has no immediate value to the employee. Its future value is purely speculative, depending on business conditions, the success of management, and the fortunes of the market place. The employee's own investment is equally speculative and is subject to neither an assured return or a guarantee of principal or dividend.

To find an offer to employees of co-ownership with an indefinite, speculative possibility of capital enhancement, to constitute a wage or term or condition of employment, strips those phrases of their ordinary meaning. Merely because the plan is offered *to* employees does not, of course, convert it to a mandatory bargaining issue. . . .

Apart from the fact that stock purchase plans fall outside the traditional meaning of "wages" and "other terms and conditions of employment," I believe other sections of the Act as well as its basic policies establish beyond doubt that Congress not only never intended the quoted language to include stock purchase plans, but on the contrary intended to exclude such matters from the scope of compulsory bargaining. . . .

FOR DISCUSSION AND ANALYSIS

1. Professor Slichter has suggested that one way by which employers can contribute to the improvement of the collective bargaining relationship is to: "Consult the union representatives before putting into effect new policies or rules which affect the employees. Invite criticisms of the proposals and suggestions for improving them from the union representatives."

Many management people would fear that to follow this advice would be to encourage the intervention of unions in management decisions, leading ultimately into a kind of "joint management." Is this a reasonable fear? Or, to the contrary, would following Professor Slichter's advice be likely to forestall the unions' making demands on management, as some have suggested?

2. Refer to the Management Functions clause, Section 13, of the Bethlehem–Steelworkers agreement, in Chapter 7. Of what value to management is such a clause?

3. The following case was one prepared by Professor Harry Shulman when he was teaching industrial relations at the Yale Law School.

One of the demands served upon Peerless Company by Unity Lodge in their negotiations for a new agreement was for a provision stating in substance that "the company will not let to an outside contractor any of the work of maintenance of plant and equipment which the company could do with its own force of maintenance employees." The Company steadfastly refused to make any such commitment or to limit in any way its power to decide whether to do particular maintenance work itself or let it out to independent contractors. The Company maintained that it must be free to choose its course in this respect on the basis of its own appraisal of efficiency, economy, business needs, and other factors. The negotiators were deadlocked on this issue for two weeks after all other issues had been tentatively agreed upon. Finally, after a continuous session of 42 hours, the new agreement was signed. On the issue in question the agreement provided as follows:

> The Company does not intend to let any of its maintenance work to
> outside contractors unless it is work which cannot be done with its
> own employees and equipment, or cannot so be done as efficiently or
> economically as by an outside contractor, or in time to meet the need.
> The Company reserves, however, the sole right to decide whether to
> do the work itself or let it to an outside contractor.

The agreement was signed on May 10. In July the Company let a contract for maintenance work. In August it let another. On each occasion the Union protested that the work could be done by the Company with its own employees and equipment in time to meet the need. The Company replied that it found that contracting out in each instance was more economical. The Union requested the data upon which this judgment was made, particularly the bids and contracts of the outside contractors. It asked that it be consulted and given the relevant information before the contract is finally let. The Company refused this request. It refused to show the bids or contracts on the specific ground, among others, that it let the contracts after soliciting and receiving sealed bids, that disclosure to the Union would result in the bids becoming known to the trade, and that the Company's future solicitation of bids would thereby be prejudiced. The Company insisted that it was under no obligation to disclose to the Union the date on which it made its decision to let the contracts.

Draft a brief arguing either (a) the union's right to a review of the relevant data, or (b) the company's right to make its decision free of any disclosure of data to the union.

4. J. B. S. Hardman, a long-time participant in and student of the labor movement, has said:

> Power accumulated by an organized group cannot remain inactive,
> static. It must be put to certain uses as a result of which it spends itself

and simultaneously generates new, greater power. The possession of power by an organized group compels action in the interest of further expansion, or doom is the inevitable alternative. Trade unions which possess no power do not have to decide not to lead a vigorous, expanding life. They could not do so if they would. Trade unions which possess power cannot conveniently rest on their laurels. They are obliged to set out for greater stakes and cannot avoid transgressing the bounds of their immediate objectives.

(*a*) Explain this statement. (*b*) Do you agree with it?

5. Should the responsibility for defining the "appropriate" subject matter for collective bargaining be left to the NLRB, which makes its determinations on a case by case basis, or should this be a matter which is left to the parties themselves to determine, on the basis of their relative bargaining strengths, free of governmental intervention?

14: The Grievance Procedure

The grievance procedure is to most unionists the heart of collective bargaining. The day-to-day applications of the terms of the agreement determine whether a person receives the wage rate to which he is entitled, is given first refusal of a job opening to which his seniority gives him claim, is not laid off out of turn, can call his foreman to account for discriminatory treatment or unwarranted discipline. Any "gripe" over his treatment can have its outlet in a recognized process in which his union representative takes the matter up with his supervisor. If the issue is unresolved at this stage and if the union believes his complaint is well founded, management people at several higher levels can be required to reexamine the matter in conferences with union officials. If these bilateral discussions fail to produce agreement on whether the employee has been fairly treated, the union may demand arbitration. For John Jones, the man at the bench, the grievance process is the subject's right to dispute the king; it is the means by which management's exercise of power can be made reasonable and responsible. The cases that follow illustrate how this process operates.

GRIEVANCE AND ARBITRATION PROVISIONS

From Collective Bargaining Provisions, Bulletin No. 908–16 of the U.S. Bureau of Labor Statistics, 1950, pp. 1–4

In the day-to-day operations of a plant, involving hundreds and sometimes thousands of workers, problems are bound to arise which affect labor-management relations and the application or interpretation of the terms of the union agreement. They may deal with the procedure of making time studies, the assignment of jobs, disciplinary action, the fairness of transfers and promotions, and other matters involving individual workers or groups and whole departments. Sometimes situations develop which were not foreseen when the agreement was negotiated and for which the agreement has made no provision; occasionally the terms themselves are ambiguous. There are, in fact, few matters contained in labor agreements, and few aspects of the employer-employee relationship which may not, at one time or another, provide the basis for a controversy.

631

Because of the wide range of potential misunderstandings, practically all collective bargaining agreements set up some sort of grievance adjustment machinery to insure smooth and uninterrupted operations of the plant under the agreement. The grievance machinery exists to interpret and apply the agreement clauses and give realistic and practical significance to many of its provisions. It is the medium through which employees may protest any alleged or real injustices caused by management in exercising its functions.

The grievance machinery has variable functions, depending on the scope and limitations on its use prescribed in the agreement. Its function may be restricted to fact finding in those instances where the dispute centers about the presence or absence of certain facts. Was the discharge for a justified cause? Is an employee qualified to fill a certain position? Was the job done in a workmanlike manner?

It may have a judicial or interpretive function particularly when the dispute arises from the agreement itself and involves the interpretation, application, or enforcement of the agreement terms. Does the seniority clause provide for plant-wide, or departmental seniority? When overtime is permitted "in an emergency," do rush orders constitute emergencies? The line between fact finding and interpretation is not always clear and, even where clear, both aspects may be involved in a dispute.

Insofar as the grievance procedure results in the creation of rules and regulations to cover a situation not foreseen by the parties at the time the agreement was negotiated, its function is also legislative or law-creating. There is a legislative implication in the joint preparation of rules and regulations which are provided for in some agreements, to implement and make workable certain provisions accepted in principle by both parties, but not sufficiently amplified for application.

Grievance procedures are essentially devices for maintaining peace and orderly operations in the plant. They constitute explicit recognition by labor and management of the need for replacing unrest and dissatisfaction, which may arise during the life of the contract, with an agreed upon framework for handling and disposing of problems arising in the day-to-day relationships between the management and workers.

As experience in most plants has proven, the most important element in the successful adjustment of plant problems is a wholesome attitude of the parties to the agreement and to each other—good faith and confidence in each other, a cooperative spirit, and mutual respect. Nevertheless, the procedure itself is an important factor in the maintenance of harmonious relations and a safeguard against possible work disruptions. A good procedure promotes the development of good relations even though it does not in itself insure successful adjustment. A poor procedure is a stumbling block in the way of good relations, since it focuses disagreement over the procedure itself rather than over the problem.

The method of using the procedure is that of presenting an issue to successively higher levels of management until it is adjusted, is referred to arbitration, or settled by some other means. It is understood, or explicitly stated, that strikes and lock-outs are to be used only after all other steps provided for the adjustment of the dispute have failed.

Except for a few industries or trades which have developed their own unique practices, there exists a basic pattern underlying the procedure for adjusting disputes in most plants.

The first stage in the adjustment process is the crystallization of a specific grievance and its presentation to a representative of the employer. There are several alternative methods by which the complaint may be presented—by the aggrieved worker himself, by a union representative working in the plant who has this specific assignment, or by a union representative not employed in the plant, as for example, the union business agent. The first-stage representative of the company in almost every case is the foreman.

The second stage, if the complaint has not been satisfactorily adjusted in the first instance, consists of one or more negotiations on the part of union representatives with successively higher levels of management. In those agreements made between a union and an association of employers, rather than an individual company, the hierarchy of appeals usually includes negotiations with officers of the association.

A succeeding stage is mediation. Some agreements provide that on the failure of the parties to reach a settlement by direct negotiations, an outside agency, such as the Federal Mediation and Conciliation Service, shall be requested to mediate the dispute.

The last stage is arbitration by an impartial arbitrator or arbitrators (or a bipartisan board with an impartial chairman).

Depending upon the character of the industry, as well as the bargaining tradition of the union, appeal of a foreman's decision on a grievance to the higher company officials may be handled by the officers of the local union with or without the active participation of regional or international union officers in the final stages of negotiations. Locals organized on a city-wide basis, or including many small shops or work places in a given area, ordinarily settle their grievances without reference to their international officers, the business agents dealing with the designated officials of the companies.

On the other hand, unions bargaining with large industrial corporations often delegate the higher stages of grievance appeals to their regional or international representatives in order to take advantage of the more skillful bargaining ability of the higher union officials. Also, when a grievance case reaches the highest company officials, the decision may involve an important principle of union-management relations, applicable to more locals than the one originally involved in the dispute.

The employee's immediate supervisor is ordinarily the first representative of management to whom a grievance is presented. In small establishments, the owner himself may handle the initial complaint; in large individual concerns the foreman, the department superintendent, division superintendent, and the plant manager may take their turn in dealing with the union. Personnel or labor relations officers, where these are employed, usually take an active part when appeal is taken beyond the foreman, although in some instances the personnel officer is involved only after negotiations with the departmental officials have failed to secure a settlement.

In a number of industries, agreements are made with associations of employers which are city-wide, regional, or Nation-wide in scope. Although these associations at times serve solely for the purpose of negotiating new agreements, they may also act as enforcement agencies, in which case the association officials help to settle disputes which arise between the union and any employer who is a member of the association.

Establishment of any grievance procedure entails agreement on the following basic points:

1. *Definition of Grievance.* Some contracts open the machinery to any dispute, while others limit it to interpretations and applications of the agreement.

2. *Representation on Grievances.* This includes the step in the procedure at which the employee may call on the union to represent him, the manner of initiating a grievance, the method of selecting representatives, the functions of such representatives, limitations on the number of union representatives who are permitted to handle grievances, limitations on their activity, special protection and privileges for representatives, and compensation for grievance work.

3. *Appeals Procedure.* This includes the establishment of the procedures to be followed in case the grievance is not disposed of at the first instance; identification of the union and management representatives involved in each step; and the setting of time limits at the various steps, including a limitation of the retroactive date beyond which grievance adjustments shall be inapplicable.

4. *Arbitration.* Included are definitions of the scope of arbitration, which is sometimes narrower than the area covered by the rest of the grievance machinery; the method of invoking arbitration; the selection of the arbitrator; reference to a permanent arbitrator if the parties agree to have one; the rules of arbitration procedure; and the expenses of arbitration.

THE GRIEVANCE PROCESS

Excerpts from Making Grievance Procedure Work Successfully, handbook of District 50, United Mine Workers, 1945

We have watched three different types of grievance committees. One is the blustering, threatening type that goes in with an obvious chip on its shoulder and immediately antagonizes the management. Very often its attitude forces the management into a fight, even though the case is reasonable.

Another is the timid, fearful type which presents its case as though it were begging some favor from the supervisor. Its meetings with management are reminiscent of the days of the employee representation plans and the other company unions. Fearful of incurring the displeasure of the management, it accepts the company's answer without question or argument.

The third type is polite but firm. It presents its case courteously and calmly. It neither cowers before the superintendent nor does it threaten to throw him out the window. It doesn't beg favors but asks for justice. It has an air about it of knowing that it is right and it lets the superintendent know that it intends to fight the case until justice is done.

Which type of Committee do you think is most likely to be successful? Which type do you think wins the respect of management? Which type is practicing real collective bargaining? Which type represents your Local Union?

YOUR AGREEMENT

Before you can interpret your agreement or know whether a proper grievance exists, you must know your contract. Become thoroughly familiar with it; know what your rights and what your limitations are. Print or mimeograph enough copies for a full distribution to the membership. Every officer, shop steward, and member of the grievance committee, at least, should have a copy.

There is no such thing as a standard contract for all our diversified industries. Each agreement has been negotiated with a view toward obtaining as much as possible for the workers in their own field. One feature in our contracts is, however, standard: the section on adjusting disputes and grievances. Since this is the section which concerns us, we are printing it here:

ADJUSTMENT OF GRIEVANCES

Should any difference arise between the Company and the Union, or its members, as to the meaning and application of this agreement, or should any local trouble of any kind arise in any plant, there shall be no suspension of work on account of such differences but an earnest effort shall be made to settle such differences immediately in the following manner:

First, between the aggrieved employee and the foreman of the department involved. The department steward may accompany the aggrieved employee;

Second, between a member or members of the Grievance Committee, designated by the Union, and the foreman or superintendent of the department;

Third, between a member or members of the Grievance Committee, designated by the Union, and the general superintendent or manager of the work or his designated assistant;

Fourth, between the representatives of the National organization of the Union and the representatives of the executives of the Company; and

Fifth, in the event the dispute shall not have been satisfactorily settled, the matter shall then be appealed to an impartial umpire to be appointed by mutual agreement of the parties hereto. The decision of the umpire shall be final. The expenses and salary incident to the services of the umpire shall be paid jointly by the Company and the Union.

The need for following each step set forth in your agreement must be stressed. Skipping a single step may prove costly. Although technical interpretations of the letter of the agreement are troublesome and undesirable because they lead only to frequent friction between the company and the union, nevertheless there are certain parts of the contract which must be carefully followed.

The steps for adjustment of grievances is such a part of the contract because all remedies must be exhausted under the provisions of the agreement before further action can be taken.

GRIEVANCE MACHINERY

We suggest that your grievance machinery consist of shop stewards and the general grievance committee.

Shop Steward. The shop steward is elected by the workers in the department, division, or job. In addition to assisting with grievances, he should be responsible for the collection of dues in the particular department which he serves as steward. It is his duty to try to settle disputes which arise on the job when a worker is unable to reach a satisfactory agreement with his foreman. All grievances presented to him for adjustment must be written out in full on the grievance report. If he is unable to secure a settlement of the grievance, he should report it to the general grievance committee for further action.

General Grievance Committee. The general grievance committee usually consists of four members with the president of the local union serving ex-officio. The general grievance committee and the company's representatives should hold regular meetings. The local union should present its facts by means of the record on the grievance report and its witnesses. Both sides should be permitted to ask questions. If an agreement can be reached, it should be reduced to writing and signed by both parties.

If no agreement can be reached, the general grievance committee and the union membership should carefully consider the question of whether or not to appeal to an impartial umpire. This step should only be taken if the committee and membership feel confident that the grievance is right and just and the union's case is sufficiently strong to outweigh the arguments advanced by the company. In such case, consult your regional director of District 50 and ask that a field representative be assigned to the case.

Impartial Umpire. If it is decided to appeal the case to an impartial umpire, great care must be taken to secure the fairest possible arbitrator. Care should be taken to secure a person who will judge the case according to logic and justice and not according to technicalities. Judges and lawyers, even though noted for liberal opinions, too often will base their opinions on legal interpretations of the agreement and not necessarily according to what is fair to the aggrieved employee. Make sure, that the person selected has no connections with the company.

A mediator from the United States Department of Labor can usually be depended upon for an honest decision.

One of this country's truly outstanding arbitrators was Harry Shulman, Sterling Professor of Law and later Dean of the Law School, Yale University, who died in 1955. For 12 years he had served as umpire in the Ford-UAW relationship. There follow excerpts from his Preface to Opinions of the Umpire *(collected decisions for the period 1943–1946) and five opinions in cases decided by him, expressing a philosophy of labor relations and grievance proceedings.*

THE ROLE OF ARBITRATION IN GRIEVANCE DISPUTES

From the Preface to Opinions of the Umpire, by Harry Shulman, 1946

Contract is a primary mechanism in the functioning of our economic organization; and faith in the performance of contracts is fundamental to our economic order. While the occasion for resort to courts for redress against breach of contract is relatively rare, contracts generally are made on the underlying assumption that their enforcement can be assured by judicial remedy.

Faith in substantial performance is no less essential in the case of collective labor agreements than it is in commercial or financial transactions. But enforcement through the courts is an unreliable assumption upon which to base collective labor agreements and an impractical remedy for breach of them. This is due in some measure to the judicial analyses of the nature of such agreements and the resulting obstacles to their legal enforcement which are not found in the case of commercial contracts. But the major difficulty is that court procedures are simply unsuited to the enforcement of collective labor agreements. The nature of the parties' relationship requires continuous performance and daily adjustments. Litigation would tend to interfere with the realization of this requirement. The expense involved is too great for many—perhaps most— of the disputes. The time required to secure final adjudication is intolerably long, prolonging the parties' disputes when what is sought is harmony. The seeming technicality of the law, the requirement of professional legal representation, and the remoteness of the courts from the shop, both physically and in habits of thought and procedures, are further serious obstacles.

Accordingly, collective labor agreements require continuous collective bargaining by the parties; and provision is made for the joint disposal of disputes through so-called grievance procedures. But even in wholly mature and completely stable enterprises, the parties may find some disputes under the contract which cannot be resolved in their bargaining conferences. Increasingly, arbitration has been resorted to as a means of resolving such disputes, that is, disputes as to the meaning of their existing and binding contract as distinguished from negotiations for a new contract or amendments. . . . .

The collective agreement is a means to a greater end. Like the marriage vow, it only launches the parties' life as joint enterprisers. The success of the enterprise, like the success of a marriage, depends upon the satisfactory adjustment of the conflicts and frictions in the day-to-day life of the parties. These adjustments must be made by the parties themselves and require daily cooperation in tolerant and generous consideration of each other's needs and complaints. And it is only by their own honest and daily cooperation that the parties can achieve the greater end—an efficient enterprise operating with justice for those engaged in it and for the public welfare. That, indeed, is the ultimate justification for both private enterprise and labor unions.

THE CASE OF A WILDCAT STRIKE

Ford Motor Company and UAW–CIO, Opinion A–151, 1944

HARRY SHULMAN, UMPIRE

The Chairman of the Flat Rock Plant Committee was given a disciplinary layoff of two weeks. As soon as this became known, a stoppage of work shut the plant down on September 20, 1944. Efforts to persuade the men to return to work proved unavailing. As a final means of effecting a resumption of work, the parties agreed to waive the several steps of the grievance procedure and to bring directly to the Umpire the case of the Plant Chairman and the other employee who was involved in the incident. A hearing at the Umpire's office was scheduled for October 3rd. But on September 30th, the plant went down again for a reason related to the Chairman's disciplinary penalty. The plant was still down on October 3rd when the parties appeared for the hearing, and is still down now.

The Company objected to the holding of the hearing while the employees were on strike. It objected, further, to the consideration of the case at all in the expedited manner. It urged that the special agreement to waive the prior steps of the grievance procedure was made for the purpose of restoring production in the plant; that in stopping work on September 30th and continuing the stoppage thereafter, the men destroyed the consideration for the agreement and abandoned the scheduled procedure.

These positions must be sustained. The current stoppage, like its predecessor, is, of course, completely unauthorized, in defiance of the Union's regularly constituted leadership, in violation of the Constitution and By-laws of both the International and the Local, and in disregard of the no-strike pledge. These features should surely condemn the stoppage in the mind of any thinking worker. But the feature bearing more closely upon the Umpire's function is the fact that the stoppage is an outright breach of the parties' Agreement.

When a Union enters a plant, one of its very first concerns is the establishment of a grievance procedure. For the grievance procedure is fundamental in civilized collective bargaining. A Union and its members can choose, if they like, to settle each day to day dispute by strike action. They could stop work every time a supervisor or other representative of management did something that they deemed improper. But union men long ago recognized that this method of protest would destroy the Union and their own economy. For this method would necessitate a stoppage nearly every day. Now workers live by production. Strikes are costly to workers as they are to management. In normal times an occasional, deliberate test of strength by strikes on matters of major importance may be necessary and desirable. The anticipated victory is then deemed to be worthy of the cost. But wanton and needless use of the strike weapon weakens the weapon itself, casts undue burden on the workers, and threatens to destroy their organization.

The workers who shed their blood and whose families suffered the pain of hunger and privation in order to establish the right of collective bargaining, those workers saw these dangers and rejected this anarchistic method. They asked for a just and civilized reign of order, the collective agreement which states the rights and obligations of the parties for its duration and establishes a regular procedure for their enforcement. They cherished the strike weapon for effective use in crises, when, for example, negotiations for a new contract failed. Even then they sought to preserve the strength of that weapon by permitting its use only after deliberate consideration and decision made by the Union in prescribed ways. Provisions of union constitutions and by-laws state in careful detail how and when authorized strike action is to be taken.

The Ford contract is true to this tradition. It established a grievance procedure which insures final determination in an impartial manner. And it provides that, during its term, the grievance procedure, not strikes or interruptions of production, shall be employed for the adjustment of grievances. This is the rule of order for which generations of working men have struggled. They understood and appreciated it. It should be clearly understood and appreciated now.

It is, of course, entirely obvious that when parties sign a collective agreement, they fully expect that disputes will arise as to its interpretation and application from day to day. That is precisely why the grievance procedure was established. It is the orderly, economic procedure prescribed for those situations in which a violation of agreement is alleged. The obligation to employ this procedure rather than the work stoppage is a solemn contractual obligation which law and honor require to be observed. To employ the stoppage when the grievance procedure is available is to abandon the contract. In no case is the grievance procedure more effective and adequate than in the case of an allegedly improper disciplinary penalty. The aggrieved employee can be fully compensated; and no other employee need suffer any loss. There is no reason for imposing an economic loss on hundreds of employees for the purpose of securing illegally to one of them that which he can get in an orderly, legal manner without loss to any employee.

ROLE OF THE UNION COMMITTEEMAN

Ford Motor Company and UAW–CIO, Opinion A–116, 1944

HARRY SHULMAN, UMPIRE

No committeeman or other union officer is entitled to instruct employees to disobey Supervision's orders, no matter how strongly he may believe that the orders are in violation of agreement. If he believes that an improper order has been issued, his course is to take the matter up with Supervision and seek to effect an adjustment. Failing to effect an adjustment, he may file a grievance. But he may not tell the employee to disregard the order.

The employee himself must also normally obey the order, even though he thinks it improper. His remedy is prescribed in the grievance procedure. He may not take it on himself to disobey. To be sure, one can conceive of improper orders which need not be obeyed. An employee is not expected to obey an order to do that which would be criminal or otherwise unlawful. He may refuse to obey an improper order which involves an unusual health hazard or other serious sacrifice. But in the absence of such justifying factors, he may not refuse to obey merely because the order violates some right of his under the Contract. The remedy under the Contract for violation of right lies in the grievance procedure and only in the grievance procedure. To refuse obedience because of a claimed contract violation would be to substitute individual action for collective bargaining and to replace the grievance procedure with extra-contractual methods. And such must be the advice of the committeeman, if he gives advice to employees. His advice must be that the safe and proper method is to obey Supervision's instructions and to seek correction and redress through the grievance procedure.

Some men apparently think that when a violation of contract seems clear, the employee may refuse to obey and thus resort to self-help rather than the grievance procedure. That is an erroneous point of view. In the first place, what appears to one party to be a clear violation may not seem so at all to the other party. Neither party can be the final judge as to whether the Contract has been violated. The determination of that issue rests in collective negotiation through the grievance procedure. But in the second place, and more important, the grievance procedure is prescribed in the Contract precisely because the parties anticipated that there would be claims of violations which would require adjustment. That procedure is prescribed for all grievances, not merely for doubtful ones. Nothing in the Contract even suggests the idea that only doubtful violations need be processed through the grievance procedure and that clear violations can be resisted through individual self-help. The only difference between a "clear" violation and a "doubtful" one is that the former makes a clear grievance and the latter a doubtful one. But both must be handled in the regular prescribed manner.

Some men apparently think also that the problems here involved are evils incident to private profit enterprise. That, too, is a totally mistaken view, as a moment's reflection will show. The problems of adjustment with which we are concerned under the Contract are problems which arise and require adjustment in the management of an enterprise under any form of economic or social organization. Any enterprise—whether it be a privately owned plant, a governmentally operated unit, a consumer's cooperative, a social club, or a trade union—any enterprise in a capitalist or a socialist economy, requires persons with authority and responsibility to keep the enterprise running. In any such enterprise there is need for equality of treatment, regularity of procedure, and adjustment of conflicting claims of individuals. In any industrial plant, whatever may be the form of the political or economic organization in which it exists, problems are bound to arise as to the method of making promotions, the assignment of tasks to individuals, the choice of shifts, the maintenance of discipline, the rates of production and remuneration, and the various other matters which are handled through the grievance procedure.

These are not incidents peculiar to private enterprise. They are incidents of human organization in any form of society. On a lesser scale, similar problems exist in every family: who shall do the dishes, who shall mow the lawn, where to go on a Sunday, what movie to see, what is a reasonable spending allowance for husband or daughter, how much to pay for a new hat, and so on. The operation of the Union itself presents problems requiring adjustment quite similar to those involved in the operation of the Company—problems not only in the relations of the Union to its own employees but also in the relations between the members of the Union. Anyone familiar with seniority problems knows that the conflict of desires within the Union are quite comparable to those between the Union and the Company. And any active member of Local 600 knows that the frictions and conflicts within a large Union may be as numerous and difficult as those between the Union and the Company. Such "disputes" are not necessarily evils. They are the normal characteristics of human society which both arise from, and create the occasion for, the exercise of human intelligence. And the grievance procedure is the orderly, effective and democratic way of adjusting such disputes within the framework of the collective labor agreement. It is the substitute of civilized collective bargaining for jungle warfare.

But an industrial plant is not a debating society. Its object is production. When a controversy arises, production cannot wait for exhaustion of the grievance procedure. While that procedure is being pursued, production must go on. And some one must have the authority to direct the manner in which it is to go on until the controversy is settled. That authority is vested in Supervision. It must be vested there because the responsibility for production is also vested there; and responsibility must be accompanied by authority. It is fairly vested there because the grievance procedure is capable of adequately recompensing employees for abuse of authority by Supervision.

It should be definitely understood, then, that a committeeman has no authority to direct or advise an employee to disobey Supervision's instructions; that his authority is expressed in the duty to take the matter up with Supervision and seek an adjustment through negotiations and the grievance procedure; that an employee must obey Supervision's instructions pending the negotiations or the processing of his grievance, except only in the rare case where obedience would involve an unusual health hazard or similar sacrifice; and that disobedience by the employee, or counsel of disobedience by a committeeman, is proper cause for disciplinary penalty. . . .

PROTESTED ASSIGNMENT OF WORK

Ford Motor Company and UAW–CIO, Opinion A–71, 1944

HARRY SHULMAN, UMPIRE

This case was specially submitted to me for prompt decision in view of what was regarded by the parties as the emergency character of the dispute.

The Structural Iron Workers at Rouge belong to the Maintenance Unit. They have two shifts only. They do not have now, nor have they had for some time, a midnight shift. Some days ago Management decided to erect some iron work in the Production Foundry. The job was estimated to require about three days' work for a gang of six iron workers. The job could not be done on the iron workers' regular shifts because the equipment at the site of the proposed construction operates during those shifts and makes the construction work unduly hazardous. In Management's opinion, the job could also not be done efficiently or economically on one or more Sundays. Accordingly, Management directed an established gang of six iron workers who normally work in the area of the Production Foundry to come in at midnight rather than on their regular shifts for the three days required to complete the construction. The men refused to do so, were supported in their refusal by the Unit officers, and the serious situation developed which led to the submission of the dispute to me. . . .

The sole issue here involved is the right of the Company to assign the men on sporadic occasions to work during irregular hours for temporary, short periods.

I hold that the Company has the right and that the employees must accept the assignment. Any question as to the rate of payment which must be made to the employees is then a matter to be raised through the regular grievance procedure.

It must be pointed out again that in providing a grievance procedure, the Contract creates responsibilities as well as rights. Disputes as to rights under the Contract must be handled through the grievance procedure—not through coercion or insubordination. Particularly when that procedure includes an Umpire with power to make final and binding decisions and power to make retroactive financial adjustment, there can be no warrant for ignoring that procedure and resorting to power methods.

The purpose of all the relations between the parties is to produce material. The parties are not engaged in the enterprise for any other object. The accomplishment of that object—production—should not be delayed by disputes as to the manner of payment or other incidents. The parties have set down their rights and obligations in written agreements. They have provided a good grievance procedure with an Umpire for the final determination of disputes under their Agreements. And they have solemnly pledged individually and collectively that, particularly in matters on which the Umpire is empowered to rule, there shall be no "curtailment of work, restriction of production, interference with work, strike, stoppage" and so forth.

Management obviously has the initial responsibility to assign and direct the work of the plant. The employees and the Union may, of course, believe that rights or privileges granted to them are involved, which the assignment or direction endangers or violates. It is precisely for the purpose of providing protection for such rights and privileges that the grievance procedure was created. That procedure is the prescribed method. Refusal to take the assignment or obey the direction is the very thing for which the grievance procedure is the prescribed substitute. Without a grievance procedure an employee or a Union may well feel that he can and must refuse the assignment or direction and have it out with the employer first, because otherwise there would be no other remedy for vindicating the claimed right. But that is just the thing that a grievance procedure is designed to avoid. It is the remedy for the vindication of the right.

The situation would become intolerable if every employee or committeeman could hold up work, as was done in this case, until the dispute as to the work is decided. That is anarchy, not order. That is indicative of a lack of adequate procedure or lack of confidence in the procedure. Given a grievance procedure in which the parties have confidence, then the work must go on and the disputes as to it processed through that procedure. Employees and committeemen must recognize this as the way of order and the way required by the Contract. It is hardly necessary to point out, by way of caution, that I am not speaking of a case in which a particular employee refuses an assignment because of a valid reason peculiar to him, such as, for example, a health condition to which he alone is subject, distinguishing him from other employees on that job.

My award, then, is that the Company's assignment in this case must be obeyed. Any question as to the payment for the work done should be raised by a grievance in regular course. Should such a grievance be filed in this case, I shall, in the light of the situation, be ready to hear it on short notice.

Ford Motor Company and UAW, Opinion A–278, 1952

HARRY SHULMAN, UMPIRE

The regular method for determining the propriety of a protested assignment is not by refusal to do the work, but by invoking the grievance procedure or by special submission to the Umpire. That is the method always safe and always proper. It is the required method in the usual run of cases. . . .

It may be objected that to require employees to do the work as assigned pending determination of the propriety of the assignment through the contractual provisions is to enable the employer to enforce what may be an improper assignment for the period that the case is pending,—and that may be a long time. The grievance procedure, may, of course, provide appropriate redress for loss unjustly suffered in that period. And the time need not always be long; the procedure for special submission provides means of expedition when necessary. But to the extent that some time is necessarily required, the answer is that the result is inevitable and must have been contemplated and accepted by the parties when they entered their collective Agreement. Business enterprise, whether private or public, requires management. And management requires administrative initiative, one important phase of which, as expressly recognized in Article IV, Section 1, is the assignment of work. The whole idea of establishing a grievance procedure is based on the assumption that Management will act and that its action may be in violation of the Agreement. And it is precisely for such alleged violations that the Agreement prescribes its procedures and prohibits resort to work stoppage. Of course, these procedures, and the whole Agreement, can work effectively for the accomplishment of their goals only if both parties act in good faith, with a modicum of good sense, and with respect for each other and for their commitments. Acting in this way, an employer will rarely make blatantly improper assignments. . . .

THE CASE OF THE LADY IN RED SLACKS

Ford Motor Company and UAW–CIO, Opinion A–117, 1944

HARRY SHULMAN, UMPIRE

A, a Highland Park employee, was reprimanded and docked one half hour because she wore slacks described as bright red in color. The objection was to the color, not to the slacks; the girls are required to wear slacks. And the objection is based on the safety and production hazards that would be created by the tendency of the bright color to distract the attention of employees, particularly that of the male sex.

Protection of employees against safety hazards by the publication and an enforcement of safety rules is an accepted duty of Management which Management must discharge however distasteful the task may be to it or to the employees. If Management determined upon investigation that certain forms of attire tended to distract the attention of employees in a "co-ed" plant with resulting safety hazards and interference with production, and if it published rules prohibiting such forms of attire, it probably could not then be said that such rules were unreasonable or beyond the proper scope of Management's duties.

But such is not the case here. Neither the Company nor the Plant Management promulgated or published any rules as to the color of employees' clothing. The claimed general understanding that bright colors were "taboo" is no more definite than that. What color was proper and what color was "taboo" was apparently a matter depending entirely on the spot reactions of individual Counsellors of Labor Relations officers to particular slacks as they appeared on the scene. And the claimed understanding was the product, not of the publication of a rule, but of alleged repetition by word of mouth and by diverse unspecified persons. Apparently bright green slacks were tolerated. And there was no effort at specification of other articles of clothing, or the fit thereof, which might be equally seductive of employees' attention. Yet it is common knowledge that wolves, unlike bulls, may be attracted by colors other than red and by various other enticements in the art and fit of female attire.

It is clear that there was here no effort to survey the field and to prescribe knowable and enforceable rules. The matter was left largely to idiosyncrasy of circumstance and of persons in authority. That is not the way to prescribe or enforce rules of conduct.

A's reprimand is to be expunged from the record and she is to be reimbursed for the half hour lost in the Labor Relations office.

A QUESTION OF DEMOTION FOR INCOMPETENCE

Standard Oil Company (Indiana) and Central States Petroleum Union, Local 117, Independent, 25 LA 32, 1955

EDWARD C. BURRIS, ARBITRATOR

This is a proceeding instituted by Local No. 117 of the Central States Petroleum Union under the final step of the grievance procedure of the Union's collective bargaining agreement with the Company. In accordance with the provisions of Article II, Section 7, the parties requested the Federal Mediation and Conciliation Service to submit a panel of arbitrators, and from this panel, Edward C. Burris was selected to serve in this case.

On April 16, 1955, a hearing was held in the Company offices of the Neodesha, Kansas, Refinery, with opportunity for presentation by both parties of their positions and with opportunity to present witnesses and to cross-examine the witnesses of the other. At the conclusion of the hearing, the parties requested the opportunity to present briefs in support of their positions, such briefs to be postmarked not later than May 26, 1955. Rebuttal briefs were, by agreement, to be postmarked not later than June 3, 1955. A transcript of the proceedings of the hearing was taken by a court reporter and made available to both parties and to the arbitrator.

Issue

The issue for determination is submitted by stipulation of the Union and the Company as follows: Whether or not the Company's action of demoting C. E. Hawthorne from the classification of Machinist Second Year to the classification of Laborer was justified.

Case history

The Neodesha Refinery of the Standard Oil Company (Indiana) is engaged in the refining of crude oil into gasoline and related petroleum products. The Company consists of two principal divisions—the Process Division and the Mechanical Division. This case is concerned with the Mechanical Division.

Mr. C. E. Hawthorne is 43 years of age. Prior to his employment as a Laborer by the Standard Oil Company (Indiana) on January 2, 1951, he had had previous experience as a bus driver and as a salesman. In March, 1951, he became a Watchman; on August 5, 1951, a Storehouse Helper; and on February 2, 1953, he became a Machinist First Year under the Company's Progressive Plan. On February 2, 1954, he became a Machinist Second Year.

In a letter dated November 16, 1954, the Union was informed that Mr. Hawthorne was to be demoted to the classification of Laborer, effective November 22, 1954. The letter stated:

This action is being taken because of Mr. Hawthorne's lack of ability to acquire a satisfactory degree of skill as a Machinist.

Mr. Hawthorne entered a grievance, and this grievance was processed through the steps of the grievance procedure and ultimately to arbitration. . . .

Position of the Union

The Union contends that the demotion of Mr. Hawthorne is unjustified for the following reasons:

1. The demotion is but the culmination of a series of acts of discrimination against him because of his assertion of his contractual and union rights.

2. Even if the acts complained of were true and constituted an adequate

ground for demotion, the Company is precluded from now asserting them because:

A. They occurred prior to Hawthorne's last promotion and were known at that time.

B. Hawthorne was given no warning that his work was not entirely satisfactory.

C. The list of complaints was not presented during the grievance procedure.

3. The complaints against Hawthorne are not valid and do not constitute a sufficient ground for permanent demotion.

4. Hawthorne's demotion is violative of past practice, no other employee in the Progressive Plan having been permanently demoted.

Position of the Company

The Company contends that:

1. No written rules have been violated.

2. The arbitrator may not substitute his judgment for that of the Company in determining employee ability.

3. Mr. Hawthorne does not have the ability satisfactorily to perform Machinist work.

4. Mr. Hawthorne was offered ample time, and sufficient opportunity to acquire the knowledge and skill necessary satisfactorily to perform assigned work.

5. The Company did not act contrary to any practice or policy established by its own actions or by acquiescing in a course of conduct carried on over a long period of time.

6. In demoting Mr. Hawthorne, the Company acted in good faith and not arbitrarily nor with ulterior purpose.

Discussion of the issue

What evidence was disclosed at the hearing concerning the ability or lack of ability of Mr. Hawthorne to do Machinist work?

Mr. W. A. Mason, a Machinist who has been with the Standard Oil Company since 1932 and was with the predecessor company for seven years before that, testified that Mr. Hawthorne was his Helper for approximately three months. Mr. Mason testified that Mr. Hawthorne was polite and courteous, that he was never insubordinate; and when asked to compare him with other people who had been serving him as a Helper, he replied that Mr. Hawthorne "was just as good as any of them." (Record, page 74)

Mr. Charles Eaton, a No. 1 Pumper who has been with the Standard Oil Company and its predecessor refinery since 1917, stated that Mr. Hawthorne had done a good job of maintaining the pumps and that he frequently was able to diagnose pump difficulties and solve them on his own initiative and that he frequently made suggestions as to potential difficulties with other pumps which enabled Mr. Eaton to write out a work order for repairs on these pumps. Mr. Eaton was asked this question: "Then, on the basis of your experience with other mechanics and procedure and effectiveness of other people who came in to work on these particular pumps, could you judge Mr. Hawthorne's ability?" Mr. Eaton's answer was: "I would say it was as good as the average as the other machinists." (Record, page 106)

Mr. Bill Holper, who has been with Standard Oil Company of Indiana for nine years, the last five of which have been at the Neodesha Refinery, stated that Hawthorne's repairs of pumps are "as good as any other Machinist's."

On the other hand, Mr. Robert H. Colwell, Superintendent of the Mechanical Division, did not agree with the opinions of the above witnesses.

Likewise, Mr. John A. Brewer, Assistant Superintendent of the Mechanical Division, stated that Hawthorne visited too much with fellow workers, on occasions was found sitting in windows rather than working, and on other occasions was simply doing nothing.

It should be pointed out, however, that in the very nature of things Mr. Colwell and Mr. Brewer had limited opportunities for personal observation of Mr. Hawthorne's work, and that from their own testimony many of their criticisms of Hawthorne and his work were criticisms which had been passed on to them by Mr. Harold Brown, Machine Shop Foreman. Furthermore, there was considerable uncertainty in the testimony of Mr. Colwell and Mr. Brewer concerning specific times and places, and an admission on occasions that (for example, in the plating up of soaker drums) trouble with leaks on soaker drums was not an uncommon thing and that the Company had been plagued by this type of problem both before Mr. Hawthorne became a Machinist and since his demotion to Laborer.

There were two or three deficiencies in Mr. Hawthorne's work which apparently have some substance. It appears from the testimony that Mr. Hawthorne did have some dislike for climbing ladders or working from high scaffolds; but he testified (Record, page 239) that this fear was no longer present, and neither Mr. Colwell nor Mr. Brewer could cite comparatively recent instances where this had been a problem.

The Company charged Mr. Hawthorne with "lack of success in maintaining tools and equipment while working in the tool room." In cross-examination, Mr. Brewer agreed that this pertained largely to a group of shovels with broken handles. The Company did not contradict Mr. Hawthorne's testimony that while he was working in the tool room it was not his duty to repair shovels, but rather to saw off the handle so they could not be used as salvage. In fact, this entire criticism would be a criticism of his work before he entered his duties as a Machinist.

Mr. Brewer testified that one of Mr. Hawthorne's shortcomings was "an excessive amount of time required to accomplish given jobs." But Mr. Brewer acknowledged that his comments were based upon very casual observations. Indeed, no incidents of this were testified to positively as having occurred since February 3, 1954, the beginning date of Mr. Hawthorne's service as a Machinist Second Year.

Another charge leveled against Mr. Hawthorne was that of "damaged bolts due to the use of nuts having different thread than that on bolts." Apparently this referred to one instance in which one bolt of a group of 24 bolts on a particular plate was so damaged.

The Company charged Mr. Hawthorne with "frequent requests for help when working alone." Yet Mr. Brewer testified that the Machinist who worked on the pump usually had a Helper "the majority of the time" (Record, page 205). Mr. Brewer was not particularly helpful in clarifying this complaint against Mr. Hawthorne.

The Company charged Mr. Hawthorne with "wearing gloves while attempting to do Machinist work." Mr. Hawthorne testified that he had worn gloves on some occasions during the earlier part of his service as a Machinist due to an allergy which had been cured for some time.

Mr. Hawthorne was likewise charged with a lack of initiative. Yet testimony of both Company and Union witnesses was that Mr. Harold Brown did not like for his employees to do things differently from the way that he told them or to attempt to make repairs according to their own diagnosis. Mr. Hawthorne's testimony indicated that on at least one occasion he made a suggestion that steel rings be replaced by hydraulic packing rings and that this had been done with presumably some saving to the Company since the latter type of rings seem to last a longer period of time.

The Union criticized the Company for the lack of an adequate training program for Machinists. Yet it is true that presumably Mr. Hawthorne had the same opportunities for training as did other Machinists. Testimony by two or three Union witnesses indicated that responsible Company representatives stated that it was the Company's responsibility to train the individual and that if the results were not satisfactory, it is the fault of the Company, not the individual. Most of the Company training is in the nature of on-the-job training without specific collateral training.

The over-all picture of Mr. Hawthorne's ability or lack of ability as gleaned from the hearing is that his work, while not outstanding, was reasonably satisfactory. If such were not the case, testimony by Mr. Howard Brown, Mr. Hawthorne's immediate supervisor, would have been very helpful. Judging from the hearsay evidence concerning Mr. Brown's opinion of Mr. Hawthorne's ability, Mr. Brown was somewhat unfavorably impressed. If such opinion is Mr. Brown's evaluation of Mr. Hawthorne's ability, it is quite possible that his attitude may have been influenced by an incident just prior to Mr. Hawthorne's beginning as a Machinist First Year on February 2, 1953. On the occasion in question, Mr. Hawthorne apparently indicated to his Foreman that he wanted to discuss with a higher official, Mr. R. H. Colwell, Superintendent, Mechanical Division, the reason for his not being placed on the Progressive Plan. While assenting to Mr. Hawthorne's doing this, Mr. Hawthorne felt that Mr. Brown was displeased at this action. Following this incident, Mr. Hawthorne was assigned to a somewhat disagreeable task of cleaning all of the ten machines in the machine shop with oil and sandpapering them down. Testimony of several witnesses indicated that this was an unusual procedure and that it was in the nature of a retaliation or punishment for Mr. Hawthorne. Indeed, on his own initiative, Mr. Pfeifer, the Union Steward in the machine shop, requested a hearing with Mr. U. M. Clerkin, Personnel Supervisor, to discuss the matter.

The treatment of Mr. Hawthorne following the accident of August, 1954, in which it was necessary for the first joint of the index finger to be amputated surgically, is another incident which tends to raise a question in the mind of any unprejudiced person concerning the attitude of Mr. Brown toward Mr. Hawthorne.

Findings of fact and conclusions

Considering the testimony of all the witnesses for both Company and Union, the arbitrator must find that while there were some deficiencies in Mr. Hawthorne's work, his work was reasonably satisfactory. The arbitrator finds that the recommendation that Mr. Hawthorne be demoted from Machinist Second Year to Laborer was based to a great degree upon the recommendation of Mr. Brown, his Foreman, whose opinions could easily have been colored by his personal feeling toward Mr. Hawthorne.

The arbitrator finds that the judgments of Mr. Colwell and Mr. Brewer concerning Mr. Hawthorne's ability or lack of it were reflections very largely of the opinion of Mr. Brown and that, in the nature of things, this would be expected, and that, therefore, the action in "going along with" Mr. Brown's recommendation should not be construed as criticism of them.

Although the record indicates that on occasions the quality of Mr. Hawthorne's work was discussed with him by his Foreman, Mr. Hawthorne was apparently never given a warning notice for the alleged poor quality of his work during the twenty months he worked in a Machinist classification.

In North American Aviation, Inc., 17 LA 784, a demotion was held to be improper because an employee had received no warning notice during his four years of work.

In Hiram Walker and Sons, Inc., 19 LA 447, a demotion for incompetence was set aside because, among other reasons, the employee had never been given a specific individual warning.

The case for the demotion of Mr. Hawthorne would have been much clearer, had there been convincing evidence that on one or more occasions his Foreman had warned him that failure to improve the quality of his work would lead to demotion.

The Company has no precise standards regarding the quantity or quality of work expected of a Machinist Second Year. Thus, its judgment is based entirely upon the subjective evaluation of the supervisors who worked with Hawthorne. Neither Mr. Colwell nor Mr. Brewer, by their own testimony, were in a position to evaluate the day-to-day work performance of Hawthorne. For reasons unknown to the arbitrator, the Company chose not to place in evidence at the hearing the evaluation of Hawthorne's work by using his Foreman, Mr. Harold Brown, as a witness. Thus, the arbitrator was deprived of the testimony of Mr. Brown who should have been in a superior position to evaluate Mr. Hawthorne's work.

The arbitrator finds that the Company's action in demoting Mr. C. E. Hawthorne from the classification of Machinist Second Year to the classification of Laborer was not justified and that this error should be corrected by the placement of Mr. Hawthorne again into the Machinist Second Year classification with retroactive compensation at regular straight time hourly rates for the period since his demotion to the time when he shall have been returned to Machinist Second Year classification, less, of course, earnings which he has received at regular straight time rates in his employment with the Company in the interim.

DISCHARGE FOR HORSEPLAY

United States Rubber Co. and United Textile Workers, 25 LA 723, 1955

A. R. MARSHALL, ARBITRATOR

A Board of Arbitration heard a dispute involving the discharge by the Company of an employee indulging in horseplay in Winnsboro, South Carolina on December 1, 1955. The Board consisted of the following: F. C. Phillips, Company Arbitrator; W. M. Hall, Union Arbitrator; and A. R. Marshall, Impartial Arbitrator and Chairman of the Board of Arbitration, selected by the Company and Union Arbitrators and appointed by the Federal Mediation and Conciliation Service. The Board of Arbitration could not reach a unanimous decision so in accordance with the provisions of the contract the award is being rendered by the Chairman.

The Company's case was presented by N. E. Williams, Industrial Relations Manager; while the Union's case was handled by Joseph Petigo, International Representative. Witnesses for the Company were: D. D. Rice, Overseer of Weaving; George Osborne, Shift Supervisor; and DeWitt Cothran, Shift Supervisor. Union witnesses were the following: Lawrence Walters, Grievant and former Loom Fixer; Steve Talbert, Weaving Department; Berlie Miller, Cloth Hand in Weaving Department; Henry Baughman, Weaving Department; Raymond Moore, Weaving Department; Z. L. Brown, Fixer in Weaving Department; Sam Hungerpiller, Weaving Department; E. M. Hunter, Weaving Department; and W. M. Hall, President and Business Agent of Local 1800.

The issue

The Union's grievance concerning the discharge of Lawrence Walters is dated September 15, 1955, and reads as follows:

On Friday Sept. 9/55, Mr. Rice the overseer of cloth weaving saw Lawrence Walters playfully kick another employee. Mr. Rice called him into the office and ask him why he kicked the other employee, Mr. Rice ask if he were mad or had the other employee done any thing to him. Mr. Walters told Mr. Rice that he was not mad and the other employee had not done anything to him, that he just kicked him playing. Mr. Rice then told Mr. Walters that he was discharging him for horseplaying. The union contends that this disciplinary action taken by the company is unjust, as other employees in this department has violated the rules by horse-playing in the mill, and were only warned. We further contend that the action taken was arbitrary, discriminatory, and unreasonable. We ask that Mr. Lawrence Walters be put back on his regular job, with all his seniority, and be paid for all time lost as the result of this discharge. This grievance is brought under sections #5 and #7 of the current agreement.

The kicking incident

There is no substantial disagreement between the parties with reference to the facts in the so-called kicking incident on September 9, 1955, that led to the discharge of Lawrence Walters, a Loom Fixer in the Cloth Weaving Department.

The Union's Statement: "On Friday, September 9th, 1955, Lawrence Walters, Sam Hungerpiller and Steve Talbert were engaged in a brief conversation near Talbert's work bench in the weaving department. When this conversation was concluded, at approximately 6:10 A.M., Hungerpiller and Walters turned and started to walk away. When Talbert turned his back on Walters, Walters lightly and playfully kicked Talbert with the flat side of his foot. This action was observed by Mr. D. D. Rice, the Weave Room overseer. Shortly thereafter Walters was called to the office by Rice and discharged."

The Company's Statement: "At about 6:30 A.M. on Friday, September 9, Mr. D. D. Rice, overseer of the Cloth Weaving Department, observed Mr. Lawrence E. Walters, a loom fixer in the department, approach Steve Talbert, who had his back toward Walters (Talbert was talking with another employee) and saw Walters kick Talbert with apparent force. Talbert immediately turned toward Walters following the kick and he and Walters, apparently at the same time, observed Mr. Rice approaching. Walters turned and walked toward his work area and Talbert returned to his job. Mr. Rice went to the department office and sent for Mr. Walters. When Mr. Walters arrived at the office, Mr. Rice asked him why he had kicked Mr. Talbert. Mr. Walters replied, 'No reason.' Mr. Walters was asked if Mr. Talbert had done anything to him and Mr. Walters replied that he had not."

Union's position

The Union contends that the penalty in this case is much greater than it should have been. The penalty in this and other disciplinary cases should bear some relationship to the offense, and the Union thinks that the Company was wrong in discharging Walters. It appears to the Union that the Company has singled out a single man and penalized him for what all the other men in the department, with few exceptions, have been guilty of. The penalty of discharge has not worked out well, argues the Union, for workers in this department are still continuing to kick each other; the disciplinary action inflicted upon Walters did not prevent further horseplay.

The Union also points out that while horseplay is generally frowned upon and discouraged with varying degrees of intensity by various employers, it still

exists to some extent in every industrial plant. "There is generally a direct relationship between the monotony of the work or the relationship between the
employees and their immediate supervisor as to the degree to which this type
of emotional outlet is exercised."

The Union thinks that there is a very poor relationship between the Company's supervisors and the employees in the weaving department, pointing out
that a very large number of employees in this department have either quit their
jobs or have been discharged for one reason or another. Not only production employees but also supervisors have been included in this turnover, according to
the Union.

The one warning which Walters has received is discounted by the Union
as being of little significance and not an example of horseplay as is present in
the instant case. The reprimand referred to was for an alleged infraction of the
safety rules, for sliding a quill across the floor in the direction of another employee in order to attract the latter's attention that the "dope wagon" (refresh-
ments) was in the vicinity. In the opinion of the Union the reprimand was not
a proper one for a large number of other quills were already on the floor at
the time.

As justification for the position it has taken in this case the Union cites the
following arbitration case: Rock Hill Printing and Finishing Company (16 LA
722); and Forbes Trucking Company (17 LA 110).

As noted above one of the main points of argument made by the Union is
its contention that kicking each other was (and is) customary in the department
and was (and is) practiced by all the workers with few exceptions. It is urged,
therefore, that the Company should not have disciplined so severely the one
employee who was caught doing something that almost all of them did almost
all the time.

Seven Union witnesses testified in great detail as to the facts about kicking
noted above. They testified that the employees made a practice of kicking each
other. The kicking that was done was said to be devoid of any pain and no one
ever got hurt by it. One witness testified that in a few seconds on one occasion
he got kicked four or five times. In addition to the testimony about kicking,
there was also testimony that sometimes tool boxes have been nailed down and
balls of waste have been thrown around the room.

The Union does not think that Walters' past record of employment should
be held against him in this case. The Union made this argument when the
Company brought out the facts of Walters' employment record upon cross-
examination of the latter.

Company's position

The Company contends that it was justified in discharging Walters for engaging in horse-play as this sort of act on the part of an employee is very serious,
is against a long-standing rule of the Company, and is disruptive of production.

The Safety Handbook of the Company, which is given to every employee
emphasizes the importance of safety to the employees and to the Company.
This Handbook provides in part as follows: "The following acts on the part of

an employee are UNSAFE and will not be permitted on Company property AT ANY TIME (a) Indulgence in horse play. . . ."

Walters is said to have known about the Company's rules, as does every other employee, and knew that he was in violation of the rule against horseplay. Some time previous to the incident related above which caused the Company to discharge Walters (October 15, 1954) he was observed "throwing a quill along the floor in the direction of another employee." The Company's representative stated that Walters was warned about this matter and told that he would be discharged if he violated a plant rule against horseplay in the future.

The Company thinks that the fact that no one was hurt in the present incident does not minimize the potential danger that can result from horseplay. In this connection the Company points out that employers are liable under the South Carolina law where injuries to employees occur as a result of horseplay, citations being made as follows: Allsep v. Daniel Construction Company (216 S.C. 268; 57 S.E., 2nd 427); and McCoy v. Easley (Woodside) Cotton Mills (218 S.C. 350; 62 S.E., 2nd, 772).

"A Company has a responsibility to promulgate and enforce rules in the interest of the safety and protection of its employees, and would be derelict in its duty if it failed to establish penalties for violation of these rules that in management's judgment were required for their proper enforcement." The Company further contends that the Board of Arbitration should not substitute its judgment for that of management as to what is the proper penalty for violation of the rule against horseplay for to do so "would make it extremely difficult, if not impossible, for supervision to carry out its responsibility to maintain discipline and provide a safe work place for its employees."

The Company finds it difficult to believe that horseplay in the form of employees kicking each other is as prevalent as the Union witnesses say it is; if it is, then the Company thinks it must have been kept very secret. But in any event, argues the Company, the fact that employees do engage in horseplay without the knowledge of the Company does not make the practice any less serious and subject to disciplinary action.

By means of cross-examination when Walters was testifying at the hearing the following information was revealed concerning the employment record of Walters with the Company. He was first hired on October 25, 1943, but subsequently discharged because he gave his age as being a year older than he really was. He was later hired again and discharged for refusing to run his job. He was brought back for a third time and discharged again in April, 1945. He was rehired in the same department and again discharged for not running his job and smoking in a restricted area. He was rehired again in 1950 after being out for five years but quit his job when reprimanded by his supervisor. His last date of employment dates from October 25, 1954, and his last discharge about eleven months later for engaging in horse-play as noted above.

Discussion

The facts in this very unusual case are not contradictory. The dispute is unusual in that the witnesses for the Union insist that they and other employees make a habit of kicking each other and by this information seek to prove that the Company by disciplinary action to an employee who engages in this type of horse play is acting in a discriminatory manner. This argument cannot be accepted. There is no evidence that this pastime of impetuous teen-age youths was known by the Company to exist to an appreciable extent or at all among its adult employees, otherwise it would undoubtedly have disciplined other workers who were guilty of such horseplay.

The arbitrator is impressed with the fact that the witnesses for the Union testified in such great detail as to the prevalence of the "kicking game" among the employees of the Cloth Weaving Department with no visible indication of chagrin in taking part in an activity which is certainly not becoming to adults who are being paid to engage in productive effort. It goes without saying that the Company has a right to expect that the employees will understand that this kind of horseplay should immediately come to an end and that the Company has a right and an obligation to take proper disciplinary action against future offenders. It is apparent that the morale of employees who think they are justified in playing tricks on each other and in kicking each other with the flat of the foot needs to be improved; and the first step seems to be in a self-evaluation of their responsibilities to the Company and to themselves. What the Company can do to increase this morale is not known, but it is desirable that a study be made to ascertain the causes of unrest so that something may be done to remedy the situation. It is to be regretted if the men engage in this childish form of recreation to the extent that was indicated at the hearing, although the undersigned and others should be aware of the fact that a relation of this type is in some cases not as bad as at first it might appear to be.

In spite of rejection of the Union's defense that the Company has been discriminatory the undersigned agrees with the Union that the penalty of discharge is too severe in this case. Walters was discharged for the single offense of kicking another employee, plus the fact that he had previously been warned in connection with another incident almost a year previously. The two incidents do not constitute flagrant violations of the rules of the Company to the extent that discharge is justified, but some lesser penalty would have been proper. It is not intended that the above statement be interpreted to mean that horseplay should be tolerated by the Company or that proper disciplinary action to bring it to an end is not desirable. It is just that the penalty of discharge does not fit Walters' playful action, although a disciplinary layoff would have been appropriate. Walters should be reinstated to his former job with full seniority rights but with no back pay for time missed. In returning to his job he should realize that the Company has a right to expect him to behave himself, to engage in no further frivolous conduct, to attend to his production duties.

Walters has a very poor employment record with the Company. He has been discharged and rehired a number of times since he first began working with the Company in 1943. No claim has been made that Walters' several dismissals by the Company should be considered in making an award in this case but since his bad record has been introduced as testimony some statement should be made on what influence it has had on the decision that has been reached. No consideration has been given to this acknowledgely bad record of employment for the reason that when the Company last hired Walters the latter had a right to expect that he would receive the same consideration as would other employees. It should be noted in this connection that although Walters was discharged and quit several times, the Company has rehired him the same number of times, and as far as is known it was under no obligation to give him further employment on any of these occasions.

AWARD

After careful consideration of the arguments and evidence as presented by the parties, I make the following award:

The Union's grievance dated September 15, 1955, concerning the discharge of Lawrence Walters on September 9, 1955, is sustained in part. Walters shall be reinstated to his former job without loss of seniority rights but with no back pay.

DISCHARGE OF A UNION STEWARD

Green River Steel Corporation and United Steelworkers, Local 4959, 25 LA 774, 1955

JOHN F. SEMBROWER, ARBITRATOR

Submission

The discharge on Sept. 9, 1955, of Joseph C. Holland, at that time a second helper on furnace No. 4 working the 12 midnight to 8 A.M. shift, under an accusation of violating Article XIII, the no-strike clause of the Agreement entered into by the parties on Oct. 1, 1954, and still in full force and effect, came before the undersigned as sole arbitrator pursuant to Step 5 of the Grievance Procedure, Article VIII, Sec. 3.

The arbitrator conducted a hearing on Dec. 9, 1955, at Owensboro, Ky., with Keith C. Reese, Esq., representing the Union, and Frank A. Logan, Esq.; Fred B. Redwine, Esq. and Jack A. Keenan, secretary and personnel director, representing the Company.

Facts

Although there is no sharp disagreement between the parties as to the physical occurrences surrounding the discharge of Joseph C. Holland, about the only fact on which there is no dispute whatever is that he was discharged on Sept. 9, 1955, terminating an employment which had begun on July 6, 1953, and was without reprimands or other blemishes on his employment record. It is necessary for the arbitrator to make a number of findings of fact as to the collateral matters, based upon listening to and observing the demeanor of the witnesses as they gave testimony which was recorded in shorthand and transcribed.

There was tension in the plant on the night of Sept. 8–9, 1955. Several unauthorized strikes had occurred in the recent past (Tr. 39)[*], and the foreman, known in this plant as a melter, one Len Norcia, was so apprehensive that at 1 A.M. he had telephoned the general superintendent, Robert Spence, that trouble was brewing (Tr. 29). An employee, Paul Lott, a motor inspector, early in the shift had exchanged sharp words with Norcia when the latter told him to leave the chemical laboratory, to which it appeared that employees frequently repaired during breaks in their work (Tr. 3). Lott had filed a grievance against Norcia (Tr. 36). Soon after the grievant, Holland, reported to work, a fellow employee, Farmer, told him of the incident involving Lott (Tr. 3), and asked him what he was going to do about it. Holland told Farmer that he was going to "stay out of it," since he had "enough trouble of his own" and Lott was not in his department.

Holland testified (Tr. 5) that Farmer told him at 1 or 1:15 A.M. that "the guys were fed up with how things had been going and that a strike would be in order" (Tr. 4). Holland related that he stuck to his job (Tr. 4) which was interrupted when his glove caught fire, and he went for another. Upon his return he was confronted by Norcia, who asked him where he had been and, by implication at least, criticized him.

At 6:20 A.M., according to Holland's testimony, the "heat" in his furnace had been completed, and as he went for a drink of water, four employees gathered at No. 3 Furnace—Bratcher, Umbreit, Royal and Keller—called him over (Tr. 5) and asked him if he had heard the "rumors" of an impending strike. They asked Holland what he thought of it (Tr. 4), and Holland testified: "I told them all I knew was what Farmer had told me—that I had been busy all night." Holland testified on direct and cross examination that Royal spoke so loudly and animatedly that he could not get in any other remarks (Tr. 5, 10). He was aware that if the men walked out they would be violating the terms of the contract (Tr. 10), and he testified that he did not agree with them (Tr. 10), but on the other hand he didn't feel that he had the opportunity to raise his voice against it (Tr. 10).

Holland felt that Norcia was "watching him like a hawk" (Tr. 10), and he testified that Norcia passed by the group at No. 3 Furnace and said something he did not hear (Tr. 5). Then Norcia returned at 6:30 A.M. and said to Holland: "I am sending you home, and he didn't say why" (Tr. 5). Holland's first impulse was to follow Norcia into the office for a talk (Tr. 5), but instead he went to his furnace, picked up his lunch bucket, and headed for the clocks. He heard Norcia call after him (Tr. 5), "Where are you going?" To the answer, "Home; you sent me home," Norcia replied: "Can't a guy get hot once in a while? How about coming back to work?" Holland replied, "No, you sent me home so I am going home" (Tr. 5).

Holland clocked out and walked to his automobile (Tr. 6), and looked back as he drove away, seeing the four other employees walking out after him. He paused at a parking lot near the mill, and the others caught up. Holland testified on direct examination that, "I didn't say much because due to my trouble, my mind was a bit hazy as to the best action for them to take."

[*] Editor's note: References are to the verbatim transcript of the hearings.

At about 7:15 A.M., the little group saw the automobile of Robert Washburn, Union representative, and Local President Savu, coming over the hill as they hurried to the scene after receiving a telephone call from the plant superintendent. "Mr. Washburn told me to direct the guys in to work," Holland testified (Tr. 7), and he did so, urging the employees arriving for the 8 A.M. shift to go on in.

A striking aspect of Norcia's version of the incident was his testimony that during the rumors of a strike, and at one time when the whole crew was at No. 3 Furnace and he (Norcia) "told Holland and Farmer that Lott had a grievance filed against me (Norcia) and to let it go to see how it came out, Holland kept quiet." (Tr. 36) On cross examination he elaborated: "I said I didn't hear him (Holland) say a word. He wouldn't talk to me."

Norcia was suspicious of Holland: "Since I knew a strike was coming on, I figured he might be in it." (Tr. 39) Asked why he thought so when he had not heard Holland say a word, Norcia testified, "Holland had a better record on my turn, and I figure he felt if he could get rid of me and get together the melters, the slate would be clean." By way of explanation as to why he pursued Holland and asked him to return to the job, Norcia testified: "Well as Washburn said before that I was an awful mean fellow up there. He has had everybody trying to believe it and I was trying to eliminate that idea." (Tr. 38) Norcia also testified that Holland "hollered to the fellows, 'let's go,' and motioned his arm." (Tr. 37)

This incident also was described by two of the men in the cluster at No. 3 Furnace. Roland Umbreit, first helper and a candid witness who testified that he did not believe in walkout strikes and had told Farmer that he could not leave his furnace charged with steel, related that Farmer, not Holland, was the instigator and that he and the others were trying "to get Farmer not to walk out" (Tr. 20). He testified that Holland's contribution to the discussion was to "relate the story of the glove" (Tr. 20, 22), and "that was all." Clyde Ford, who was discharged after the walkout and no longer works for the Company, said Farmer was the instigator. Neither Ford nor Umbreit saw Holland make any signs or say anything beckoning the others to follow him. (Tr. 23, 24)

As to the reason for the discharge of Holland, Norcia testified (Tr. 39) that he sent him home because: "I figured . . . he wasn't working and because he was instigating the strike. I could kill two birds with one stone." But Jack A. Keenan, the personnel director, answered categorically (Tr. 44) that Holland was discharged because he had violated Article 13. He testified (Tr. 45) that Norcia "didn't state the reason for sending Mr. Holland home was for agitating a strike," but "for not performing his duties." However, Mr. Keenan left no doubt whatever that the reason for Holland's discharge was the alleged violation of Article 13. (Tr. 45)

There was considerable confusion over whether Holland was, in fact, the steward on the shift. Under direct questioning (Tr. 17), Holland testified that, although he appeared on the list of Stewards for D turn, he was not the steward on that particular shift. On cross examination, he acknowledged that there was no other steward on duty and that the one who would have so functioned, one Garner, had not been on duty for upwards of four months. Holland indicated clearly that he thought of himself as a steward: "I did my duty as a member of the union and an employee of Green River Steel to try to settle things before real trouble started." (Tr. 18) He agreed (Tr. 9) that certain employees in his department or area were to tell him about any difficulty.

On direct examination, Holland described a steward's duties: "A shop steward's duty is to take the grief and headache off supervision; to try to work out little troubles before they amount to something big; to more or less help the company run a smooth operation." (Tr. 9) On cross examination he was asked: "You know as a shop steward they recognized you knew that" (i.e. a walkout would be violating the terms of the contract)? (Tr. 10) He did not deny then that he was a steward, but answered: "I suppose so. I was busy working a heat and you have to stay there and work it and you can't be running off unless it is important."

Farmer, in relating Lott's trouble with Norcia to Holland, appeared to regard Holland as steward, and Holland corrected him only to say that Lott was under the jurisdiction of a steward in another department. Umbreit testified (Tr. 23): "Well, I thought Holland was a steward," although he did say that matters often were taken up with Richardson, the Union vice-president, and that "We weren't putting too much faith in a steward at that time." (Tr. 23) Norcia thought Holland was a steward; "I thought he was and everybody else thought he was." (Tr. 41) Tony Brown, the assistant personnel director, acknowledged that Holland was listed on a memorandum of Aug. 29, 1955, from the Union to the Company (Joint Exhibit #2) as steward on D turn, whereas Garner was steward on C turn of which Norcia was the foreman. But he testified (Tr. 48) that the Company regarded the men listed as stewards and union officials.

Pertinent contract clause

The following is the only citation from the Agreement made by either party:

ARTICLE XIII—STRIKES PROHIBITED

The employees, the Union, its officers, agents and members agree that so long as this Agreement is in effect, there shall be no strikes, sitdowns, slow-downs, stoppages of work or other interruption or impeding of production, and they will not otherwise permit, engage in, countenance, authorize, instigate, aid or condone such acts. The Company reserves the right to provisional discharge of any employee or employees who violate the provisions of this Article, and agrees that upon such discharge of such employee or employees, it will provide to a Union representative a list of names, check numbers and addresses of employees whom the Company has so discharged.

Discussion

In view of the foregoing summary of the testimony, the following facts emerge:

Holland was discharged, not for failure to do his work, as some of the foreman's testimony seems to indicate, but clearly because of an alleged violation of Article XIII. This was the ground assigned by the Company and carried through Step 4 of the Grievance Procedure, although the personnel manager admits (Tr. 45) that the foreman himself never assigned this ground, and Norcia himself testified that in sending Holland home he was killing "two birds with one stone." (Tr. 39)

Holland's errors, if errors they were, were of omission rather than commission. An employee with a clean record theretofore, he seemed to have determined to try to stay clear of the difficulty swirling around him. His fellow employees were tugging at him on the one hand, and his foreman on the other. The foreman was overwrought, perhaps entirely justifiably, by a gnawing anxiety that there was a covert gathering of forces against him. This undoubtedly was heightened by his consciousness of past criticism of his leadership (Tr. 38). Norcia probably did "watch Holland like a hawk," as Holland testified, and alternatingly he tried to be stern, as when he made issues of Holland's absence from his furnace, and solicitous, as when he almost pleaded with Holland to intervene on his behalf with the men and to let the Lott grievance take its course, and then urged Holland to disregard his go-home order and to return to the job. Indeed, it was Holland's very silence and refusal to intervene that seemed to disturb his foreman most. This does not make out a case for discharge unless something is added by way of a duty upon Holland to act affirmatively rather than passively. Only Norcia's uncorroborated testimony says that Holland tried to lead the men out with him.

It may not be seriously argued that since the foreman asked Holland to return to the job, Holland never actually was sent home. An order from one's supervisor is not to be taken lightly, and had Holland refused to go home in the first place, he would have been insubordinate and in violation of the Contract. Holland had the right to take the order to go home at face value.

But the crucial question remains whether Holland was, in fact, the steward on this shift, and if so, whether this imposed affirmative duties upon him. As to the first issue, it seems clear that ostensibly he was the steward. Technically Holland may not have been the steward on this particular shift, but he had color of being so by virtue of his presence on the list of stewards, the lack of clear-cut understanding as to where stewards were qualified as such or just for shifts, plus the fact that no other steward was on the job at the time. Holland's own testimony is illuminating on this point. He talked like the steward; in his job he did nothing to inform others that he was not the steward or to point out who was the Union's representative in the plant that night if he was not. To all intents and purposes, it appears that he was the steward and we must so regard him.

Having crossed that bridge, we now may inquire whether, as steward, Holland had a status which made mere inaction culpable in itself. In the development of labor relations the post of steward has become one of recognized importance, dignity and responsibility. "Moreover, the occurrence of a work stoppage, whether sanctioned, or directed or not, imposes an affirmative obligation on the part of the Union (through its officers) to see that the employees involved go back to work," said the arbitrator in 18 L.A. 919, Canadian Gen. Electric Co. Such views are frequently expressed by arbitrators, and increasingly so.

Here the Union fully recognized this responsibility, as amply indicated by Messrs. Washburn and Savu literally jumping from their beds in the dawn and rushing to the scene, their only complaint being that the plant superintendent had not apprised them of the situation sooner. ("I felt they had let it go on all night without calling us then instead of waiting until morning." Mr. Washburn (Tr. 29).) Mr. Washburn testified (Tr. 34) that after he arrived, "We definitely told Holland and Lott in no uncertain terms they were jeopardizing the jobs of the other men and themselves and we directed the boys to see that they reported for work."

To Holland's credit, perhaps, he did so without demurrer, when Washburn showed him the course to follow. But in contrast with the decisive action of his union officials, Holland's shortcomings are all too apparent. Apparently at first he tried to ignore the situation entirely. According to Umbreit, in his testimony on behalf of Holland, he and the other employees at No. 3 Furnace were trying to dissuade Farmer from walking out when they called Holland over. What did he contribute but to tell of his own recent unpleasant experience with the foreman over his flaming glove, which hardly was oil to spread on the troubled water? Holland complained that he did not "have the opportunity" to counter the arguments of Royal, who was urging a walkout, so while he opposed it he did so silently. Finally, after he had been sent home and was across the road with the men who had walked off the job, Holland testified that "I didn't say much because due to my trouble my mind was a bit hazy as to the best action for them to take." It took Mr. Washburn to show him the way; that it was to urge the men to the job and back to work, which to be sure, he then followed. Holland gave an acceptable definition of the steward's role (Tr. 9), but he failed to back it up with action.

In mitigation of Holland's conduct, it may be said that he may have been distracted by harassment which preoccupied him with "his own troubles." The foreman had a vague idea of what he might expect from a steward in helping to hold the situation in line, but he never really presented it squarely and forthrightly to Holland. Finally, the foreman hopelessly confused the issue by ordering Holland home for an offense of not doing his work, which was discarded as the basis for the discharge in favor of a charge of violation of Article XIII. In all kindness, it may be pointed out that neither the foreman nor the steward precipitated into this tense situation that was fraught with so many serious consequences was a man of long experience in his particular role.

Discharge is the capital penalty of employer-employee relations, and it is fundamental to all legal systems that such charges must be specific and precise. The case for discharge is not made out here, but on the other hand, Holland is not blameless. He has lost wages which may be considered a penalty and a hard-earned lesson. As an employee with a theretofore unblemished record and a union officer who knew the definition of his role if not their application, he deserves the chance of a restoration of his job with full seniority, but without back pay.

AWARD

Accordingly, the Award is that Joseph C. Holland is to be restored immediately to his job as a second helper with full seniority rights including the period of his discharge, and he is not to receive back pay.

DISCIPLINE FOR INSUBORDINATION

Magor Car Corporation and International Association of Machinists, Lodge No. 1733, 26 LA 832, 1956

ROBERT R. FRANCE, ARBITRATOR

Through the Federal Mediation and Conciliation Service, The Magor Car Corporation, hereafter referred to as the Company, and the International Association of Machinists, Clifton Car Lodge No. 1733 of District 161, hereafter referred to as the Union, submitted the following dispute to the undersigned for a final and binding award:

Was the issuance of warning slips on or about March 6, 1956 to R. E. Muller #1164, B. Ferrante #1173, Adrian Silverstein #1167, and Al Zaorski, #1289 justified? If not to what relief are they entitled?

Hearings were held on April 23 at the Company's offices in Clifton, N.J. Both parties were present and had full opportunity to argue their cases. Appearing for the Company were H. W. Muni, Assistant to the Vice President; T. M. Zollo, Personnel Director; J. J. McCarthy, General Foreman; Vincent Scordato, Welding Foreman, and J. R. Kortvellessy, Superintendent. For the Union, John B. MacKenzie, Business Representative; Harold Philips, President; Nicholas Julino, Shop Chairman; Robert E. Jones and Al Vasquez, Committeemen; Nicholas Sawczyn, Steward; and Robert Muller and Al Zaorski, grievers appeared.

The Union requested permission to file a post-hearing brief. The Company decided not to file a brief but reserved the right to comment on the Union's brief.

The workers involved are employed at fitting and tacking box car doors. They are paid on an incentive basis with a daily quota of 12 doors. On March 5, 1956 a discussion arose concerning whether or not these men should attempt to finish their twelfth door before quitting time. On March 6, 1956, the Company issued warning slips, charging that the men had refused to obey orders of their foreman. Because the warning slip issued to Ferrante was his second, he was given a day's suspension without pay.

The Company's position

Mr. Scordato, the Welding Foreman, testified that at about 3:45 P.M., Muller approached him and told him that because of a crane break-down earlier in the day, the welding crew would not be able to finish the twelfth door. Muller argued that the crew should receive an hours day-rate time and that the foreman should issue passes for the crew to leave after the eleventh door was finished. Scordato and Muller proceeded directly to the work area. Scordato places the arrival there at about 3:50. At that time, Zaorski was removing gages from the burning outfit indicating the crew was preparing to stop work. Silverstein and Ferrante were finishing up the eleventh door.

Scordato decided that they should try to make the twelfth door. He told the men to start on it. However Muller and Zaorski continued to argue with him. In a few minutes Silverstein finished his work on the eleventh door and joined the argument. Ferrante finished the eleventh door in a few more minutes —according to Scordato's estimation, about 4:00 P.M.,—and then he, too, joined the discussion. Scordato testified that the argument continued and that during it he told the men several times to get started on the twelfth door. At about 4:10 P.M. he broke off the argument and left. No work had been done on the twelfth door then.

Mr. Kortvellessy, the superintendent, testified that about 3:45 P.M. he noticed that the welders had stopped welding on the doors in the first position. He told them to go back to work or the company would take disciplinary action. Then he went to check with the foreman, Scordato, whom he found talking to Muller. He told the foreman that no passes would be issued for the men and that he should get them back to work. At 4:15 P.M. he checked back on the situation and noticed that there was still no work being done.

The Company argues that the men were clearly told to start work on the twelfth door by both their foreman and the superintendent. When they failed to do so, the company was justified in taking disciplinary action in the form of issuing warning slips. If the men felt that they had a grievance concerning the time lost because of the crane breakdown and that they should not have been asked to start on the twelfth door, they could take up their case through the grievance procedure provided in the contract. However, they were required to carry out the orders of their supervisors.

The Union's position

The Union contends that the welding crew members had a justifiable grievance which they were discussing with the foreman and that no refusal to obey orders was involved. The Union claims that because of the breakdown of the crane the men felt that they could not finish the twelfth door. They therefore wanted the foreman to give them credit for the hour they lost because of the crane failure and to issue passes as had been done in the past in similar situations.

Muller testified that no direct orders to return to work were given by the foreman. Rather, he continued to discuss the merits of the case with Muller.

The other Union witnesses also denied that direct orders had been given to them.

The Union also disagrees with the Company's version of the times involved. Muller and Sawczyn, the steward, testified that it was after 3:50 p.m. when they started to walk towards the work place. After Muller had started to talk to Scordato, the Superintendent entered the discussion for a while, then Muller called in the steward and they proceeded to the work place.

The Union witnesses claim that the discussion in the work-place between Muller, Sawczyn, and Scordato continued for quite a while before Silverstein and Ferrante finished the eleventh door. Zaorski testified that he finished taking off the gages and joined the discussion at about 4:10 and that Silverstein and Ferrante were still working them. Sawczyn testified that Silverstein joined the discussion for only a moment and then returned to help Ferrante finish the eleventh door. Sawczyn further stated that as he left the work-place he walked past a clock in a nearby department and noticed it read 4:16 p.m. At that point he heard the crane signal given to lift the eleventh door, indicating that it had been finished only a few minutes previously.

Opinion

It is first necessary to make a finding of fact concerning the timing of the incidents involved since the parties' versions were in conflict. In the arbitrator's opinion this is important with reference to the case of Ferrante and Silverstein. In general, the arbitrator is inclined to accept the Union's version of the timing. It would seem that the discussions involved would have taken more time than indicated by the Company's testimony. In addition, the Company witnesses were estimating the times since they had no reason to be checking their watches during the argument. One Union witness, the steward, did have a definite point of time for the completion of the eleventh door, at approximately 4:15 p.m.

In as much as the contract provides that the men are to wash up at 4:20 p.m., it does not seem to the arbitrator that Silverstein and Ferrante should have been given warning slips for not carrying out the Foreman's orders to start on the twelfth door. During most of the time when he was directing that work be begun on the twelfth door, they were working on the eleventh.

In the case of Zaorski, there is no reason why he could not have obeyed the foreman's directions. In fact, his activity in removing the gages was clearly to stop work rather than to complete any activity. Although in Zaorski's opinion he was never given a direct order to work on the twelfth door, it seems reasonable to interpret the foreman's remark to him: "Let's go on the twelfth door" as an order.

In the case of Muller another aspect must be considered. When Muller first approached the foreman, he was certainly legitimately taking up a grievance with his supervisor as he had every right to do under the contract. The question then arises as to how long a worker can continue to argue his case after the foreman has made a decision and told him to return to work. On the one hand, the private employment situation is not one of militaristic discipline in which the superior's word is carried out without question. On the other, it is possible for a worker to be obstructive, and through continued argumentation, after his supervisor has heard his complaint and reached a decision, to frustrate the efforts of management to direct the work force.

It is likely that Muller felt strongly that the foreman was being unfair in insisting that the twelfth door be started. He therefore was unwilling to accept the foreman's decision without further attempts to change his mind. But to permit a worker to continue to argue with his foreman after a reasonable length of time could result in disruption of the work process and an undermining of the foreman's authority.

The contract provides a grievance procedure to protect workers from unfair decisions by supervisors. The grievance procedure also is instituted to settle differences of opinion without disrupting operations. If Muller felt the foreman's decision was unfair, he still should have obeyed it, and then obtained redress by submitting a formal grievance. Instead he continued to press his case for what, in the opinion of the arbitrator, was an unreasonable length of time. In the process he thwarted the foreman's attempt to get work started on the twelfth door.

AWARD

The issuance of warning slips on or about March 6, 1956 to R. E. Muller #1164 and Al Zaorski #1289 was justified. The issuance of warning slips to B. Ferrante #1173 and Adrian Silverstein #1167 was not justified and the slips shall be removed from their records. In addition, Ferrante shall be paid for the loss of a day's pay resulting from his suspension in connection with the warning slip.

FOR DISCUSSION AND ANALYSIS

1. There are two points of view as to the function of a union steward. One approach says that the steward should himself be satisfied that a member's grievance is legitimate before he processes it. Thus one union advises its steward that if the contract does not appear to have been violated, or if the company has not acted unfairly, or if the worker's safety or health has not been endangered, the steward should not be afraid "to tell the worker that his complaint is not justified. There is double danger in trying to make a grievance out of it: the workers are led to expect impossible results, and the company gets a chance to attack the union. The union's position is then damaged both with its membership and with management."

But other union leaders have taken exception to this approach. They have argued that the union "must defend the claimed right of the worker whether his case be good or bad. . . . The union is required to act as attorney in the case. It is not the function of any attorney to judge his client; he is required by the rules of our society to defend him." It is argued that if the union does not perform this function, then the individual worker does not truly have representation in his individual relationships with management.

Which of these points of view would you defend?

2. It has sometimes been argued that an effective grievance procedure can be set up by a management for its employees, even in the absence of a union. Outline on paper a grievance procedure for an unorganized plant which attempts to do just that. Compare your procedure with the typical procedure in an organized plant. How do the two compare, as to points of strength and weakness?

3. The problem in the following case was stipulated by the parties as whether X was discharged by the company on May 14 for just cause. The matter was heard before a committee of three of the Connecticut Board of Mediation and Arbitration, consisting of Joseph F. Donnelly, Warren L. Mottram, and Samuel F. Curry. The statement of the case is given, without decision. What would have been your answer to the question posed?

Company position

On either May 10 or 11 [1956], it came to the attention of the Plant Superintendent that X, who had worked for the Company since 1951, had been discharged from Peck, Stow and Wilcox on October 10, 1951, for stealing. This information was reported to the President of the Company, and the Application for Employment form filled out by X was reviewed. Although requested to indicate past employment, the form contained no indication of any period of employment at Peck, Stow and Wilcox. The application stated that for two years prior to his employment by the Company in 1951, he worked for his brother in a nursery.

The Company checked these charges with Peck, Stow and Wilcox on May 14, and confirmed that X had been discharged on October 11, 1951, for stealing two pipe wrenches. On the grounds that he had falsified his Application for Employment, the Company discharged him on May 14, 1956.

Union position

The Union states that it was common knowledge among employees of the Company that X had been discharged for stealing at Peck, Stow and Wilcox. His foreman was aware of it, as was the general foreman. In fact, he had secured this job through the intervention of a foreman of the Company who promised to speak to the Superintendent for him. The Union claims that the Superintendent knew of his discharge, and most probably knew of the reason of his discharge.

The Union claims that the Company has used this incident only as a pretext for getting rid of X. In fact, last April, during the discussion of a grievance involving X, the President of the Company, in the presence of the Union Committee, stated that the Company did not want X around any longer.

Discussion

Falsification of records by an employee is generally looked upon in industrial relations as an offense deserving of severe discipline. Here the fact of such falsification is not in dispute, but is admitted by the employee. Accordingly there rests no burden upon the Company to prove that X has been guilty of wrongdoing; to the contrary the Union has the burden of proving that the penalty, in view of all the circumstances, was too severe.

A discharge for falsification of records, following as it does a prior discharge for stealing, would greatly limit, if not terminate, the employment opportunities of X in industry. Because of such almost fatal results, the Board has weighed with extreme care all the circumstances of this matter. . . .

4. Arbitrator Ralph Seward heard the following case, dealing with a discharge for participating in a plant fight. The statement of the case is from his opinion. Write a decision stating your grounds for sustaining, modifying, or overturning the discharge.

This grievance presents the question of whether or not Management was justified in discharging James W. Daniels, the grievant, for participating in a fight with Carl Snow, another employee. The fight took place on February 14, 1955. Both men admitted participation in it, and each alleged that he was the victim of an unprovoked assault by the other. No supervisory employee witnessed the fight, and while other employees saw both men fighting, no one other than Daniels and Snow, themselves, admitted to a knowledge of how the altercation began.

Company policy

It is the Company's general policy, when two employees have a fight in the plant, to discharge both participants. In accordance with this policy, after completion of the various proceedings required by Article XII of the Agreement, both Daniels and Snow were discharged. Though the Union represented both employees at their discharge hearings, it now claims that Snow was the aggressor and the sole individual at fault and that Daniels did nothing more than defend himself against two unprovoked attacks.

Snow did not testify at the Umpire hearing. As no representatives of Management or Supervision saw the fight, all the testimony concerning it comes from Daniels and from two employees who testified on his behalf. On the basis of their testimony, the facts appear to be as follows.

Testimony of witnesses

On February 14, 1955, Daniels who was a Chipper and Shop Steward in the Billet Yard Department, reported for work on the afternoon shift. Shortly after he entered the General Welfare Building to punch his time card, some of the employees complained to him that Carl Snow had unfairly persuaded the

Foreman to assign him for three consecutive days to the chipping of 7⅝ inch bars—an assignment which offered exceptionally high incentive earning opportunities. As there had been an understanding that the assignments to this work would be rotated daily, Daniels—as a Steward in the Department—decided to speak to Snow about this complaint.

Daniels then went to the Welfare Building of the Billet Preparation Yard, saw Snow in the locker room and asked him why he was assigned to the 7⅝ inch bars for three consecutive days. Daniels testified that Snow quickly became angry, accused him of lying, swore at him and hit him in the mouth, causing it to bleed. The two locked in a brief struggle and then, when they broke apart, Snow swung at Daniels with a scarfing torch, swearing that he would kill him. This attack was broken up by other employees. Shortly after the two had finished changing their clothes, Snow suggested that they go to see Foreman Wrenn. Both men left the Welfare Room and went towards the Foreman's office in an adjacent building. When they arrived there, however, Snow refused to enter the office and made remarks which he said were designed to get Daniels to fight him. Daniels, nevertheless, turned away to go to work. As soon as his back was turned, Daniels states, a piece of tie plate—apparently thrown by Snow—struck the wall just above his head. Daniels turned around and saw Snow running toward him. A scuffle ensued, during which Snow attempted to get hold of the tie plate again, and Daniels tried to prevent him from reaching it. Finally Snow broke free, picked up the tie plate and hit Daniels on the head and shoulders with it several times. The men were separated by other employees. Daniels then went to the Foreman's office, to the clinic for medical attention and to the Plant Police Department where he voluntarily made out a statement as to what happened. Following this he went home and on the following day entered the hospital where he remained for several weeks.

Conflicting statement

This account of the affair, of course, is based on the testimony of Daniels and two of the employees who helped break up the fight in the locker room. In his written statement to the Plant Police and in his testimony at his discharge hearing, Snow accused Daniels of pulling a knife on him twice—once in the locker room and once outside of the Foreman's office—and alleged that all he was doing was trying to protect himself. Snow was not available for cross examination on these statements, however, and under the circumstances his written statements cannot be given weight equal to the oral testimony of Daniels and his supporting witnesses. It may be noted that these witnesses denied that Daniels had a knife in his hand at any time during the altercation in the locker room.

5. The following case involving a discharge for alleged insubordination was heard before Arbitrator Robert G. Howlett. The statement of the case is his, but his decision has been omitted. Had you been arbitrator, how would you have decided the matter?

Background facts

The Hastings Manufacturing Company operates a plant in Hastings, Michigan, where approximately 365 production employees are employed. At the Hastings plant, the Company manufactures automotive piston rings, spark plugs and oil filter cartridges. The Union has represented the production and maintenance employees for a number of years.

The grievant, S. was employed as an operator of two Splitters, machines used for splitting tubular iron castings approximately three and three-quarters inches tall (known as "pot castings") into rings for subsequent machining into piston rings.[1] The castings are brought to the Splitters in gondolas on wheeled dollies or trucks with rubber tired wheels. Generally there were two or three gondolas at grievant's machines. When one gondola had been emptied of castings, another gondola was moved into position next to the machines. It was often necessary to move one gondola of newly split rings out of the way in order that a gondola of pot castings could be brought into the proper position for the splitting operation.

The testimony, while somewhat vague, tended to prove that grievant was dissatisfied because the gondolas of pot castings were so parked that he had to move one gondola out of the way in order to pull or push another gondola in for use at the Splitters. At about 9:30 A.M. on Wednesday, February 8, 1956, grievant, while working at his Splitters, "hollered" to one of his supervisors, Assistant Foreman Gerald Smelker, and (in the words of Mr. Smelker) "told me to move a single 'gon' of rings, castings, I should say, out of his way". Assistant Foreman Smelker was attending to other duties and did not move the gondola or arrange to have it moved. About fifteen minutes later, grievant called to another of his supervisors, Foreman Vern Allerding, and (as Mr. Allerding testified) "wanted to know if there couldn't something be done about the placing of the gons at his operation".[2] Foreman Allerding told grievant that he was "busy right now, but that I will talk (to the Assistant Foreman) and see if we can't arrange it some way so the gons can be placed as they should be". At about 10:00 o'clock on the same morning, Mr. Smelker walked in an aisle near to grievant's Splitters. Grievant thereupon, in an angry manner, shook his finger under the Assistant Foreman's nose and said, "You damned——, I am all through with you. You can —— — ——. I will get this done somewhere else."[3]

The assistant foreman made no comment. He walked to the foreman's office approximately "50 or 100 feet" from grievant's Splitters to inform the foreman of the occurrence. While he was relating the incident to the foreman, grievant appeared in the foreman's office and with face flushed, again shook his

---

[1] There are ten Splitters in the area, eight of which (manned by a total of four employees) were in operation when the incident here involved occurred.

[2] The fact that grievant was on incentive may have been the reason for his particular interest in having the gondolas so placed that no time would be lost in the Splitter operations.

[3] Witness Smelker repeated the last sentence as "I'll get this taken care of somewhere else."

finger under the assistant foreman's nose and designated him as the same receptacle as previously.

Foreman Allerding ordered grievant to return to his machine which, after a few seconds of hesitation, he did. At about 10:30 the foreman went to grievant's machine and told him that he and the assistant foreman had decided to turn in a report of his actions to the Personnel Office. Grievant retorted, "Well, that's all right, but I am not going to have anything more to do with him."

The foreman thereupon prepared a written report of the incident and turned it in to the Personnel Office. On February 10, 1956, grievant was given a disciplinary lay-off reading as follows:

You are hereby laid off for one week, the week commencing February 13, 1956. This layoff is for misconduct in the profanity directed toward, and names called, a foreman on Wednesday morning February 8.

You are to report for work at the regular time Monday morning February 20, 1956.

The grievant admitted his action but, both he and the Union disagree with the penalty imposed.

Position of Company and Union

The Union does not condone grievant's action but contends that his offense is covered by Rule 23 promulgated by the Company,[4] which reads as follows:

Conduct unbecoming to an employee and the uttering of vile, obscene, and provocative remarks. First offense—warning; second offense—three days off; third offense—one week off; fourth offense—discharge.

The Company contends that Rule 23 is not applicable because (1) it applies only to the relationship between employee and employee (i.e. employees within the bargaining unit) and not between employee and foreman; and (2) grievant's offense was more serious than the uttering of "vile, obscene and provocative remarks," his conduct amounting to insubordination.

The Company urges that it has the power to impose the disciplinary layoff under the management functions and other provisions of the contract; as well as the inherent right to impose discipline for breaches of conduct, even though there is no regulation or contract provision specifically detailing an offense or the punishment therefor.

The management functions clause (Article XII), of the contract provides that "The Management of the plant and the direction of the working force and the affairs of the Company, including the right to hire, to suspend and discharge for cause . . . and the right to release employees for due cause and for lack of work or for other legitimate reasons are vested exclusively in the Company, subject to the terms of this Agreement."

Article XIII of the Agreement sets forth the procedure with respect to disciplinary action and one section provides that "Any employee violating any term of this Agreement shall be subject to disciplinary action, including discharge."

[4] The rules are established by the Company. They are not bargained rules.

Discussion

The Company, in contending that grievant was guilty of insubordination, urges that the words used showed contempt for the assistant foreman and hence were more than the vile, obscene and provocative language described in Rule 23. The Company also lays considerable stress upon the statement of grievant that he would have nothing more to do with his assistant foreman. These words, says the Company, were "words of defiance of supervision" and hence their utterance was insubordination.

The grievant is not charged with a refusal to obey any direction of the foreman or assistant foreman; and except for a few seconds of hesitation when the foreman ordered him to return to his machine (after he followed the assistant foreman into the foreman's office) there is nothing in the record to disclose any refusal to obey any order of supervision.

15: Seniority

Seniority is the device by which the allocation of scarce opportunities is made among workers—who gets the remaining jobs when some have to be laid off, who receives the promotion when numbers of individuals would like to have it, who is called back to work when operations resume after a shutdown, who has first chance to work overtime when there are more people than can be used who would like this opportunity to earn extra income, and so on. Seniority is based on length of service in the defined seniority unit.

In general, workers prefer that scarce opportunities be rationed on this basis, whereas many managers would prefer that scarce opportunities be allocated on the basis of superior ability. But even among workers there are often conflicting views as to how seniority should operate—within what units, for example.

A UNION VIEW OF SENIORITY

From Making Grievance Procedure Work Successfully, handbook of District 50, United Mine Workers, 1945

Job security is one of the prime objectives of workers in mass production industries which restrict chances for advancement. The most successful way to prevent favoritism, discrimination, or unfair treatment so far as hiring, advancement, layoff and rehiring after layoff are concerned has been the seniority system.

Seniority means that the worker with longest record of continuous service as the senior employee is entitled to preference. It is written into the contract for the purpose of giving to the employees an equitable measure of security based on the simple and just standard of length of continuous service.

Wherever possible plant-wide seniority is preferable and should be the basis of a seniority system. THIS MEANS THAT THE MEMBERS HAVING LONGEST SENIORITY IN THE ENTIRE PLANT HAVE PREFERENCE IN ANY DEPARTMENT ON THE WORK THAT THEY ARE CAPABLE OF PERFORMING. Older men are entitled to such preference:—

First—Because they have demonstrated their skill for the longest period of time.

Second—Because the management has a responsibility toward men who have given their energy, intelligence, and best years in making profits for the company.

Third—It sets up a single standard capable of being understood by all and easily applied.

Fourth—It prevents the introduction of more and more divisions by the company with the increased possibility of competition within the units of the plants and against the best interests of the union.

Fifth—It is a check against the speed-up by eliminating arbitrary discharge and rehiring since success of the speed-up depends on the worker's constant fear of losing his job at first sign of slackening speed.

Sixth—It is a safeguard against the speed-up system in so far as the standard of production is not set by the youngest workers.

Seventh—It is a defense against discriminatory firing whether based on personal prejudice or antiunionism.

Eighth—Where the system is automatic and simple to understand, it is an important factor in reducing the number of grievances based upon the difficult problems of layoffs, rehiring after layoffs, and promotions.

The commonly stated argument of the company that straight seniority does away with initiative and efficiency is purely without foundation. The seniority systems of the United Mine Workers of America and District 50 are of sufficiently long standing to prove otherwise.

Furthermore, the company's right to discharge inefficient workers has never been taken away. Where the company claims that certain employees with less seniority are exceptionally qualified for specific jobs, the union takes the position that such employees may be retained where advisable, provided a fixed percentage of such employees is agreed upon.

Wherever possible, shop committeemen should be placed at the head of the seniority list during their period of office in order to insure the continuity of responsibility which such an office requires.

Where there are many different departments, each requiring special skill and knowledge, it is often impossible to establish plant-wide seniority or fix arbitrary rules which will apply to all equally. The question of which seniority system shall prevail in your plant is a serious and important one. It should be the subject of careful consideration before a final decision is reached.

Make the seniority rule simple and workable so that it will be clearly understood by the entire plant. Although skill, knowledge, ability, and other intangible factors may be part of your seniority clause, remember that these should and must be only incidental to what seniority really means, namely, continuous length of service.

Your contract may read, "ability and efficiency being equal, seniority shall govern." Since absolute equality is never found, interpret the rule to mean that only striking differences in competency or ability or efficiency warrant a departure from the true meaning of seniority.

Under the union principle of the greatest good for the greatest number, younger men should be protected by providing rules for spreading work during slack periods. This should not be considered as violating the rule of seniority.

THE EMPLOYER'S VIEW OF SENIORITY

Excerpts from Information Bulletin No. 20, Employee Relations Division, National Association of Manufacturers, 1955

Length of service is sometimes used as the sole determinant for granting preference under the seniority principle—it is then known as "straight" or "strict" seniority. In the interest of managerial efficiency, as well as for the best long-range good of employees, many companies modify seniority by making other occupational factors (such as ability, job performance, etc.) of paramount importance, giving weight to length of service only when all other factors are relatively equal.

The question of whether or not seniority is to be the controlling factor in layoffs and other personnel actions looms large in current labor-management negotiations. Labor leaders are becoming more and more insistent that seniority should be the sole determinant in such actions.

This trend is not confined to demands during contract negotiations. Many companies report that although their contracts permit them to maintain well-balanced work forces by utilizing "qualified" seniority, they are under pressure to revert to the use of length of service alone when layoffs become necessary during the life of the contract. In this situation most employers have maintained that management freedom to operate efficiently is best for the employees in the long run. Further, they hold that the principle of the sanctity of the contract is jeopardized by yielding to such demands. . . .

Seniority as the sole criterion in such actions serves neither the best interests of the employer nor the employee. Used this way, it reduces all employees to a common level where no recognition or reward for difference in abilities or performance is possible. Thus, it blocks the advancement of able individuals and destroys their incentive to grow and improve. Straight seniority also penalizes young or new employees because the only way in which they can attain job security, or the opportunity for advancement, is through long service on the job.

The factor of ability is the most generally used and the most important limitation on the length-of-service criterion. Of course, other qualifications such as skill, performance, merit, job knowledge, training, etc., may be taken into consideration.

It is vital to the development and maintenance of good human relationships that the factors used to qualify length of service be measured in as objective and equitable manner as possible. To do so, management should develop adequate techniques, including the best use of:

employee records
job descriptions
merit rating plans
supervisory appraisal ability.

Management not only has the responsibility for developing an accurate, reliable and fair method for evaluating employee skill and ability—one which supervisors understand, accept and cooperate in—but day-to-day actions must support it. For example, if—despite the existence of a policy which gives weight to ability—supervisors follow the path of least resistance and, in the hope of avoiding grievances and union problems, promote strictly in accordance with seniority, the real objective will have been thwarted.

Further, the principle of basing seniority on skill and ability can be made to work only if action is taken with respect to unsatisfactory work performance at the time it is first recognized. It is too late to wait until a layoff is imminent and then suddenly "discover" that a person is not doing a qualified job. This is particularly true if a supervisor has tolerated the alleged unqualified work for a period of time.

The time to tell the employee that he is not doing a qualified job is when the supervisor first discovers it—not when a curtailment looms. To do otherwise is to invite a breakdown of the seniority system, and to disrupt morale. . . .

A major problem in extensive layoffs is "bumping" which may result in job transfers for the greater part of the retained work force. Such situations may be alleviated . . . by restrictions on the number of "bumps" that may result from any one layoff, and by specifying certain occupational groups which cannot be bumped.

Such companies consider that a certain amount of "bumping" is desirable because it protects a company's older employees. It gives employees who have been with the company a long time the opportunity of dropping back to a lower classified job, rather than go "out the door."

The problem of "bumping" in temporary layoffs of relatively short duration can be completely avoided by establishing a separate procedure for such situations, under which layoffs are made without regard to seniority. However, if the layoff is extended beyond a specified number of days at any time, or in a year, then the usual seniority procedure takes effect. . . .

Many managements insist on the exemption of certain employees from the seniority system so as to (1) protect and retain exceptional employees and supervisors, and (2) to insure that during employment cut-backs an adequate work force with the proper proportion of needed skills will be maintained.

In general, these exceptions are handled in labor agreements by:

1. Listing jobs or occupational groups to be exempt or

2. By provisions permitting management to retain—without regard to their seniority—a certain percentage of the work force whose special skills or training, or whose work, is vital to the efficient operation of the plant. . . .

The ability of management to freely select or reject candidates for promotion is a matter of extreme importance.

Only management has the knowledge requisite for matching the candidate's abilities to the requirements of the job. The success of the company reflects the ability of its people—it is vital that each job be filled by the best man available.

Promotion on an objective and equitable basis is basic in sound human relations. Competent management, of course, adheres to this principle but is well aware of the possibility that some of its employees may feel that only the "fair-haired boys" are promoted to the more desirable and better-paying jobs. To eliminate any possibility of this morale-destroying impression among employees, employers give weight to length of service in making selections for promotions.

Union negotiators press for promotions solely on the basis of seniority, provided that the employee wants the job. Experience has shown this to be an undesirable procedure. There is constant agitation to promote the senior employee and give him a trial period to ascertain whether he has the necessary ability. If it develops that he has even the bare minimum qualifications, he usually stays on the job even though employees of greater ability and potentialities, but with less seniority, are available.

The most satisfactory procedure, from the viewpoint of both employee and employer, is to give weight to length of service only when in the opinion of management the qualifications of the candidates are relatively equal.

MANAGEMENT, ON THE IMPORTANCE OF ABILITY IN PROMOTIONS

Comments by personnel and industrial relations directors, collected by Norman J. Pentecost in the preparation of a paper for submission to a research seminar at the Graduate School of Business, Columbia University, 1957

Ability is always an important factor in considering promotions but is more important in some jobs than in others. Where there is a seniority clause, contract language has definite influence on decisions concerning promotions. Arbitration decisions in recent years have made it necessary to balance ability with seniority, meaning that it has not always been possible to promote the best qualified individual. This tends to drive the alert, aggressive short service employee to seek employment elsewhere or to satisfy his ambition in other directions, such as holding Union office.

Seniority clauses greatly influence decisions concerning promotion. By and large, ability becomes an issue only on the higher rated and skilled jobs, and here only where there is a clearly demonstrable difference in *relative* ability as between the applicants.

In our lower grades, seniority governs promotions. The man need only demonstrate during a trial period that he can do the job to the satisfaction of management, subject, of course, to grievance. Regardless of labor grade, the same rule applies to promotions to jobs in higher labor grades within the department. Outside the department in the higher labor grades, we select the man we judge to be the best suited to the job, and ability is the principal factor governing selection.

While it is true that seniority had some bearing on promotions when we had no labor contract, we were not restricted and, as a result, some promotions had the appearance of discrimination which to some extent could be true. Labor contract or no labor contract, no supervisor or manager can help but feel the impact of intangible or subjective influences such as attitude toward the job and company, the ability to get along with people, etc. When not restricted by the terms of a contract, a supervisor will in many cases make selections for promotion with these respective factors in mind, and I believe that our supervisors would not be exceptions.

We always consider ability as an important factor in decisions concerning promotion. Our contract provides that for promotion to any classification above that of helper a man must possess the necessary ability to progress within a reasonable time to the next higher classification in the particular line of work and to ultimately progress to the classification of journeyman. Considering this provision in the contract we do not differentiate between certain types of jobs concerning the importance of ability. Seniority clauses very definitely have had an influence on our decisions concerning promotions. Our contract provides that competency being sufficient, seniority shall prevail. In cases where the margin is very narrow in determining whether a man possesses sufficient competency, I am sure that seniority many times influences our decisions.

Normally, we stress ability more on the skilled jobs. However, if there is a great difference in the abilities of the men concerned, even in the semi-skilled jobs, we introduce aggressiveness, attitude on the job and ability in order to get the best man on the job.

Ability is of less importance in unskilled and semi-skilled occupations as compared to skilled occupations. Seniority clauses have caused us to be more objective in measuring ability and more careful in our decisions. We are occasionally forced to promote employees less desirable because of attitude, cooperativeness, willingness and moral character because of lack of an objective measure and proof of the difference. We include those characteristics in ability, the Union usually does not.

Ability is always a factor in the decisions concerning promotions, the importance of this factor increasing as the skill requirements of the job increase. Where ability and other qualifications are relatively equal seniority governs the selection.

In all promotions, ability to do the job to which promoted is a very important factor. In promotions to higher hourly paid jobs relative ability becomes important, since it is from these higher jobs that future salaried foremen must be selected. Obviously, where supervisory qualifications are required, mere ability to perform a job is not enough. Consequently, it will be noted in the seniority section of our Labor Agreement that when promotions are to be made to the highest hourly paid jobs relative ability becomes a consideration along with seniority. Our feeling is that even in the absence of a labor agreement we would still give some weight to seniority in making promotions. Our Company has a long history of promoting from within, and naturally tries to favor its older employees consistent with getting the required job properly done.

Certainly ability is an important factor in decisions concerning promotion. I think that potential ability or "capability" is also of considerable importance. In instances where we can make value judgments without the pressure from the union to compromise an issue on a "political" basis we could make better decisions. This is based on the realistic assumption that management is better off getting the best man for the job into the job irrespective of seniority.

The individual as well as the union regard seniority as the controlling factor; we insist on ability as governing. There is a distinction between seniority entitling a man to a preferred job and seniority entitling him to consideration for a preferred job. Seniority without regard to the other factors (ability and physical fitness) gears everything to the level of the less efficient, penalizes the good worker for initiative, and eventually brings to a lower level the overall efficiency of the entire group.

Greater consideration is given ability in more skilled jobs. More consideration is given to seniority than was given before our contractual agreements. However, seniority has always been given a great deal of consideration in this Company, in cases where more than one man was qualified for the job.

As the company grew from 5,000 to 30,000 people, it became impossible for supervisors to adequately judge people's ability. There were many claims that via favoritism, relatives and friends were being promoted. We gave in to the pressure and instituted a straight seniority system. I don't think ability matters much in the first five labor grades. The skill needs get stiffer above that though and it's at these higher levels that we sometimes by-pass a senior man. For example, if a job requires some imagination and ingenuity the supervisor is in the best position to judge whether or not the senior man has it. If he picks a junior man and the senior man "hollers," then we must give it to the senior man on a trial basis. Most of the time the supervisor is right. How do we judge imaginativeness? In a lower ranking job, did the man innovate new tools or procedures? It is safe to say that ability is more important in the higher skilled jobs.

My philosophy is that ability and merit should be the sole basis for promotions. It's completely unfair to be unable to reward a young fellow with ability, initiative and ambition because he faces an overwhelming seniority roster. I'm not even convinced that the majority of union members really want it. It's been my experience that it's the unskilled employees who shout the most for a seniority system and not the higher levels of semi-skilled and skilled. This is because they possess no skill or ability qualities to protect them in promotions. I think the skilled and semi-skilled workers prefer to get along without it and get ahead on their ability.

I'll admit that I believe there is a high correlation between seniority and ability on the unskilled and lower semi-skilled levels. The average fellow has the ability and desire to learn the next higher job. We are so advanced technologically today that much of the skill involved has been taken over by the machine. Even though this is true, there still are a few "deadheads" who can't or won't learn the next higher job properly, so the company needs some protection against being forced to promote on seniority even on the lower job levels.

THE PRACTICE OF SENIORITY IN SOUTHERN PULP MILLS

By George W. Brooks and Sara Gamm, Department of Research and Education, International Brotherhood of Pulp, Sulphite and Paper Mill Workers, Monthly Labor Review, vol. 78, 1955, pp. 757–765

The seniority system in southern sulphate pulp mills includes within itself many different elements that are found elsewhere in the pulp and paper industry, but the system is necessarily distinguished from other branches of the industry and from other industries as well. The language of the collective bargaining agreements in the southern mills, like other plants in the pulp and paper industry, gives barely a clue to the operation and significance of the seniority arrangements they provide. Nevertheless, each man in the mills understands how the system operates and where he stands.

Basically, a worker's position depends on the line of progression in which he works, because it defines the steps through which a man must move up, from one job to another. The line is determined in part by the nature of the industrial process, but there is some room for choice on the part of the companies and the union. The decision may be to include a large number of different jobs and different operations in one line, or it may be to set up many different lines which are administered independently of each other. This choice has important effects both for management and for the workers.

The system, once defined, is operated through a set of rosters which make it workable. The primary roster is based on the line of progression. It is used, together with considerations of ability, for all promotions, and together with plant or departmental seniority, for purposes of layoffs.

BASIS OF THE SYSTEM

The subject of seniority, even confined to the pulp and paper industry, has such varied meanings that any generalizations are of very limited value, principally because differences in industrial processes alone, apart from differences in size and complexity of establishment, require differentiation in practice. Seniority is therefore examined within the context of only one branch of the pulp and paper industry, the southern kraft or sulphate pulp mill. This is the type of mill operated extensively throughout the Southern States, usually in conjunction with a paper mill and sometimes with corrugated-box or bagmaking facilities.

Agreement Provisions. Normally, the first step in studying seniority would be to examine the collective bargaining agreement. Unfortunately, an examination of hundreds of agreements in the pulp and paper industry showed that either the agreement is too general to have any specific meaning, or the terms used do not mean what they seem to say.

One of the clearest and most concise provisions in the southern sulphate industry begins with the statement: "The principles of seniority shall govern in promotions, layoffs, demotions, filling vacancies, transfers, and rehiring, provided the employee has the necessary qualifications." The agreement goes on to define three types of seniority, "job seniority, departmental seniority, and mill seniority." Job seniority is defined as length of service on a given job within a line of progression. Departmental seniority is defined as "length of service in line of progression." In practice, it should be noted, "lines of progression" are not coincident with administrative "departments," so that the meaning of the term "departmental seniority" under this agreement is not the meaning normally ascribed to the words. This agreement continues with some general descriptions of how the different types of seniority are applied and lays down elaborate steps for handling grievances which arise. Although the agreement is well written and reasonably clear, it does not begin to explain how seniority works in practice.

Other agreements are far less specific and exact than the one cited. Yet, an examination of practice in the plants discloses a systematic (even rigid) attention to length of service in promotions, transfers, layoffs, and rehiring; and the meaning of seniority *in practice* is clear and generally understood.

Nature of Mill Operations. Since seniority gets its meaning from technology, a study of seniority in southern pulp mills begins with a brief examination of the operations in this type of mill.

1. The logs come into a *woodyard* where the bark is removed.

2. The logs then travel on conveyors to the *woodroom* where large machines equipped with knives cut the logs into pieces small enough to be cooked in the digesters.

3. The chips travel on conveyors to the *digesters*, the large tanks in which the wood chips are "cooked" with steam and chemicals, under pressure, until the lignin has been dissolved and the cellulose can be separated.

4. When the cooking is done, the digesters are emptied, and the pulp travels to the *wet room* to be washed several times and screened of impurities.

5. The liquor that has been used for the cooking then goes to the *recovery* process where it is burned and treated to permit recovery of the chemicals for use again.

6. The pulp may then go to the *bleach plant* for whitening before it is dried on a pulp machine (if it is going to be shipped) or sent in liquid form to the paper-machine room for use.

The mill operates 24 hours a day, 7 days a week. Therefore, there are 4 separate crews for every operation, working different shifts during the week. Three of the shifts work on any given day during the week; the fourth is the swing shift, necessary because each man works 40 hours for 3 weeks and 48 the fourth week. Thus, there is a minimum of 4 men on each job. Sometimes a crew includes more than 1 man at a given job classification, so that the full number for the classification may be 4, 8, 16, or some other multiple of 4. Shifts are rotated each week.

Job Skills. The operations described above can be grouped roughly into 5 separate parts: the handling of the wood, the cooking of the pulp, the cleaning and refining of the pulp, the recovery of the chemicals, and the bleaching. In addition, there is a maintenance crew. The operations require work forces of varying size and composition with respect to skill and job responsibility.

Within any one operation the jobs are so organized that one man has a very large degree of specialized skill and responsibility, with other men of less skill helping him. Thus, the digester cook, one of the highest paid men in the sulphate pulp mill, is in charge of a crew which does most of the work of filling the digesters, capping them, checking on the progress of the cook, emptying the digesters, and so on. When a man starts to work on the digesters he is a capper, without any skill. As he becomes familiar with the equipment and the process, he moves up from one job to another, each time acquiring more responsibility than he had on the job below. At the top of this ladder is the cook who has a thorough knowledge of the equipment and general responsibility for the whole operation.

The standard practice in sulphate pulp mills is to do all training on the job. Each man learns how to operate the equipment by working first at a very simple job, then at a more difficult and more responsible job, and so on up the line.

THE "LINE OF PROGRESSION"

Within this framework the meaning of seniority becomes clear. A man acquires his experience and his position in the mill—meaning his seniority—by working on a number of different jobs, progressing from the easiest and least responsible up a ladder, step by step, until he has acquired the necessary knowledge and skill for the top job.

The technological requirements of the plant limit the way in which a seniority system can operate, but within these requirements there is considerable area for choice. The choice is exercised in the definition of the lines of progression. There may be numerous separate lines for different operations, or a group of related operations may be combined into a single line, but the single line represents an extreme choice among the many alternatives. For example, in a typical southern mill, it is possible to have either a single line or separate lines of progression for the digesters and the diffusers and washers. In practice, these are two separate but closely connected operations. The stock that is used in the second operation comes directly from the digesters, and the two operations are interdependent. The alternatives are diagrammed in chart 1.

To a considerable extent this same choice exists with respect to the whole pulp mill. It is possible to set up separate lines representing different operations in the mill or to combine operations. Over the years there has been considerable experimentation. The tendency has been in the direction of combining different operations, until today the largest southern producer has one single line of progression for the entire pulp mill. The bleach plant, which is relatively new in the southern industry, is an exception and has its own line. The mechanical crews are also in a separate line.

Chart 2 shows how this single line works. A man starts in 1 of the 4 bottom jobs and from here he moves up, step by step, weaving back and forth from one

Chart 1. Alternative Lines of Progression (Two Operations in a Typical Mill)

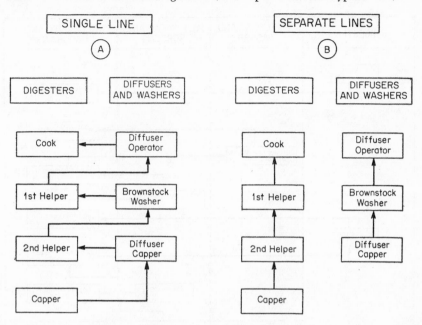

operation to another. By the time a worker reaches the top job of cook in the digester room he has mastered all operations in the mill. At two steps of the ladder, where there are alternative jobs for the worker, the company may require him to work some time at each job for their convenience.

This single line represents an extreme choice. At the opposite extreme would be four separate lines of progression. If there were four such lines in the plant diagrammed in chart 2, a man would have to make a choice about where he wanted to work and then go into the bottom job in that operation. If he wanted to work on the digesters, he would begin as digester capper and then move up the digester line, first to liquor runner, then to 1st helper, and finally to cook. A man who started at the bottom of the recovery and evaporators line would move up from caustic 2d helper to recovery 2d helper, to precipitator man, to slacker room man, and so on through the jobs in that column on the chart. There would be no movement across the broken lines which separate the four operations.

In practice, there are many different combinations of lines which tend to approach the single line, but remain somewhere between the two extreme cases. The limits upon choice, in the final analysis, are practical ones, based upon the need for on-the-job training to meet technical requirements.

Lines of progression tend to become institutionalized. Generally speaking, experience in bargaining in one mill will be carried over to newly organized mills, although some variations arise because of technological differences. Lines of progression also tend to be modified in a number of ways, sometimes to serve

Chart 2. A Single Line of Progression in a Southern Pulp Mill

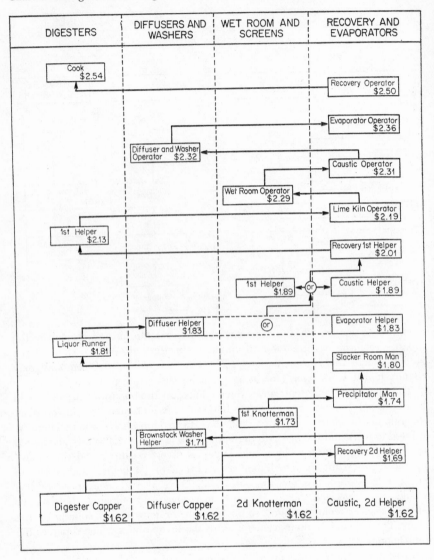

DIGESTERS	DIFFUSERS AND WASHERS	WET ROOM AND SCREENS	RECOVERY AND EVAPORATORS

special purposes. The lines can be used, for example, to differentiate the opportunities for white and Negro employees. Frequently the lines are modified to avoid "dead end" jobs.

Comparison of Alternative Lines. Certain advantages and disadvantages are implicit in the different types of progression. From the standpoint of the company, the single line offers a number of advantages. The company gets a relatively flexible work force. All of the men on top jobs have had experience throughout the pulp mill and are, therefore, able to substitute for each other or on other jobs in emergency. Even the men lower in the line have some experience in other parts of the mill.

This advantage is particularly useful in developing supervisory staff. Supervisors are typically taken from the top operator jobs, so that the company gets men who have a wide experience throughout the mill and are thus better able to deal with the problems which arise. On the other hand, the personnel process is considerably complicated under a single line of progression. At least one change must be made for every job classification when a vacancy occurs in a top job. Thus, in the pulp mill described, there would be about 15 job changes if a cook left the mill under a single line of progression, but only 4 under a separate line for the digesters.

From the standpoint of the union, alternative lines also offer certain advantages and disadvantages. If the union is interested in creating the maximum number of opportunities for the older men, taken as a group, the single line is preferable. For any particular worker, the relative advantage of the alternative lines depends upon where he happens to work and what happens in the operation or line in which he is located. For example, if there are 4 or 5 different lines, each with a relatively small number of jobs, a young man at the bottom of 1 line may be better off when vacancies arise in his line than he would be if there were 1 single line for the whole mill. But, for the membership as a whole, the security of the older workers as a group is promoted by the single line.

On the other hand, if there is a single line, each man must learn a large number of jobs, unattractive as well as good ones. With separate lines of promotion, a man can choose to work in a line that he likes, a line that includes work which is fairly attractive to him and excludes some of the dirtier and disagreeable jobs in another operation. The men may want this choice.

In individual circumstances, the issues become complicated by many other considerations. Once a set of lines has been established, it is difficult to change them if there are very real and substantial conflicts of interest among the men in the work force, quite apart from how management feels. Nevertheless, changes are negotiated from year to year, as the companies and the union attempt to correct inadequacies in existing arrangements.

THE SYSTEM IN OPERATION

Any system of seniority requires two things for its administration. The first is a definition of the system itself. Under lines of progression, the worker's seniority rights are defined in terms of his position in the line and his length of service there. For some purposes, as described below, his seniority also depends upon how long he has been in the plant or how long he has been in his line of progression.

Secondly, the operation of this system, like any other, requires a mechanism which permits easy, day-to-day administration. This is provided by a set of rosters which contain the names of all employees arranged according to their length of service as defined by the system. In the typical sulphate pulp mill, the rosters are comprised of several parts. The basic roster depends upon job service in the line of progression, but in addition, there are rosters based upon plant service or departmental service which are used for special purposes.

The construction and use of rosters in a simplified pulp mill can be illustrated by reference to chart 3. Unlike an actual mill, the sample mill has 3 men on each shift job instead of 4. There is a bank of digesters manned by a crew of 4, a bleach plant with a crew of 3, and a screen room with a crew of 3. There is a labor pool and a small maintenance crew. For each job are listed the men on

Chart 3. Illustrative Plant Setup

OPERATION A	OPERATION B	OPERATION C
Digesters	Bleach Plant	Screen Room

COOK Rate $2.40

	Hired	Job
Dimaggio	1926	1934
Berra	1921	1936
Dark	1925	1935

BLEACHERMAN Rate $2.25

	Hired	Job
Altrock	1919	1932
Boudreau	1922	1934
Appling	1920	1940

SCREEN TENDER Rate $2.00

	Hired	Job
Coleman	1924	1936
Ferrell	1929	1937
Embre	1927	1935

1st HELPER Rate $2.20

	Hired	Job
Johnson	1938	1939
Noren	1945	1949
Groth	1932	1948

LIQUOR MAKER Rate $2.10

	Hired	Job
Jackson	1937	1943
Evers	1928	1944
Lopat	1942	1947

SCREEN HELPER Rate $1.90

	Hired	Job
Gowdy	1931	1938
Hornsby	1934	1940
Kinder	1940	1947

2d HELPER Rate $1.95

	Hired	Job
Ingersoll	1935	1940
Lazzeri	1941	1949
Newsom	1946	1950

BLEACH HELPER Rate $1.85

	Hired	Job
Kennedy	1939	1946
Ostrowski	1947	1948
Mantle	1944	1950

RIFFLER MAN Rate $1.70

	Hired	Job
Cobb	1923	1941
Irving	1936	1942
Furillo	1930	1940

BLOWPIT MAN Rate $1.75

	Hired	Job
Mack	1943	1949
Robinson	1951	1951
Quillan	1950	1952

D—MAINTENANCE

MECHANIC CLASS A Rate $2.30

	Hired	Job
Parnell	1949	1949

LABOR POOL Rate $1.60

	Hired
Paige	1948
Ruth	1952
Thomson	1952

HELPER, A Rate $2.10

Hermanski	1933	1940

HELPER, B Rate $1.80

Snider	1952	1952

the job, the dates they were hired, and the dates they began working on their present jobs.

Although highly simplified, this plant presents a realistic picture of how any given plant might look. Thus, a few men have attained relatively high positions, although they came into the plant much later than other men who are still in relatively low-paying jobs. This situation is not characteristic, but it does happen in actual practice and is, therefore, reflected in the sample plant.

Promotions. Promotions in southern pulp mills are based upon the lines of progression in the mills. Men can move up only in fixed sequences and in no other way. Whether a man moves up to a vacant job above him depends upon his seniority and also his ability to take the higher rated job. Normally, a man can expect to be promoted when the job next above his becomes vacant and he has longer service on his own job than any other man in the same job. This expectation is based on the fact that the line itself is an expression of training requirements of the job. In addition, it provides security of opportunity for the men in the line in the sense that there is a predictable reward for reliable performance. Furthermore, under this procedure a large measure of the diffi-

Chart 4. Alternative Lines of Progression for the Sample Mill

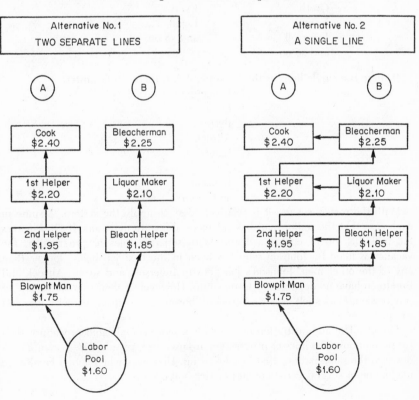

culty which frequently arises around the issue of "ability" is eliminated because the line of progression enables the company to test the capacities of the men as they move from one job to another.

The operation of the system cannot be examined without reference to a specific line of progression. The roster cannot be constructed without it. For purposes of illustration, two alternatives are set up for the simplified pulp mill, with the same fictitious rates indicated on the plant setup.

The alternatives are diagrammed in chart 4. Alternative No. 1 provides for separate lines in operations A and B. Alternative No. 2 combines these operations into a single line.

The roster follows the line of progression. If operations A and B are in separate lines, there are two separate rosters for these operations. They are the lists of the men who work in each operation arranged according to their jobs and their length of service on their jobs. The rosters would look like this:

Roster for operation A	Roster for operation B
Dimaggio	Altrock
Dark	Boudreau
Berra	Appling
Johnson	Jackson
Groth	Evers
Noren	Lopat
Ingersoll	and so on
and so on	

If there is a single line for the two operations, there is one roster:

Dimaggio
Dark
Berra
Altrock
Boudreau
Appling
Johnson
and so on

With the rosters set up, it is relatively easy to apply the system. Assume in each case that the senior man has sufficient ability to move up. If Dark leaves the mill, his job of cook is vacant. With separate lines of progression, the vacancy is filled by Johnson who has been in the next job below longer than any of the other men. Johnson's job goes to Ingersoll, and so on. Altrock and Boudreau have no opportunity to move up. However, if there is a single line of progression, Dark's job goes to Altrock, Johnson moves up to Altrock's job, and so on.

Layoffs. The administration of layoffs is a more complicated procedure than for promotions. The lines of progression are used in reverse order. A man moves down in the same pattern that he moved up. However, when actual layoffs are made, one of several variations in practice will occur.

Layoffs may be made on the basis of plant service, with certain restrictions based on position in the line of progression. Men are laid off from jobs at the bottom of the line first, so that a man who stands high in the line of progression is protected even though his plant service is shorter than that of other men lower in the line. (Normally a man's plant service corresponds to his position in the line, but there are exceptional cases.) Sometimes layoffs are made entirely upon the basis of the line of progression, but more commonly, workers affected by a reduction in force can exercise their plant seniority to "bump" other men in lower jobs. In exceptional cases, layoffs are made on the basis of departmental seniority in the usual sense of the term, combined with the line of progression.

The administration of layoffs under the system most common in the southern mills—use of the line of progression and plantwide seniority—is outlined below.

Assume that the company decided to close its bleach plant because the market for bleached pulp has contracted. The company would lay off 9 men, corresponding to the 3 jobs in chart 3, each with 3 men for the different shifts. The layoffs would be made on the basis of the *plant* roster which lists all employees according to date hired. For the simplified pulp mill, this roster would list 36 names, beginning with Altrock, who was hired in 1919, and ending with Ruth, Snider, and Thomson, all hired in 1952.

The plant roster, in combination with the progression rosters, would determine which nine men shall be laid off. If a man is above the bottom job in his line of progression, he is protected from layoff until all men below him have been laid off, without regard to date hired. He has no protection if he is at the bottom of the line, however, and in the labor pool. Layoffs are made, beginning at the bottom of the plant roster, and in our example, the nine men at the bottom are:

Thomson
Snider
Ruth
Robinson
Quillan
Parnell
Paige
Ostrowski
Newsom

Of the 9 men, 2 are protected by virtue of their positions in the line of progression. They are Parnell, who is a top mechanic, and Newsom, who is a 2d helper on the digesters. The other 7 men are laid off, including 1 man in the bleach plant. The next two on the roster are Noren who is in a protected position, and Mantle who is not. He is laid off. The next man is Mack, not protected. He makes the ninth man to be laid off.

There are 7 men from the bleach plant who have not been laid off: the bleachermen, the liquor makers, and 1 bleach helper. They now can bump down their line of progression, taking the best available jobs for which they are qualified.

If alternative No. 1 is the line of progression, with separate lines for the digesters and bleach plant, Altrock, Boudreau, and Appling, the men at the top of their line, will be able to go into the jobs of blowpit man at the bottom of the digesters line, or one of them would take the B helper job in the maintenance crew if he could qualify for it. The other men would have to go into the labor pool.

Under alternative No. 2 (a single line for the two operations), Altrock, Boudreau, and Appling would bump the 1st helpers on the digesters, who in turn would bump the 2d helpers. The liquor makers who had been displaced (Jackson, Evers, and Lopat) would take the jobs of blowpit man or B helper in maintenance. The 2d helpers on the digesters, at the bottom of the progression roster, would go into the labor pool.

In actual practice there are many variations. But the basic element in any system is the line of progression which defines the path of movement, both upward and down. The definition of the line determines in any plant how often a man in any given operation will have an opportunity to advance. Furthermore, this line will determine to some extent the amount of protection he has against layoff and demotion in the event of a reduction in force. However, in addition to his position in the line, his plant service or departmental service will influence his fate in the event of layoff.

LAYOFFS AND SENIORITY

International Paper Co., Southern Kraft Division, and International Brotherhood of Pulp, Sulphite and Paper Mill Workers, Locals 385 and 609, 23 LA 497, 1954

BOARD OF ARBITRATION: PAUL M. HEBERT, CHAIRMAN; MAX HARRISON, EMPLOYER-APPOINTED; AND GEORGE W. BROOKS, UNION-APPOINTED, DISSENTING

This grievance involves an interpretation and application of the seniority provisions of the contract between the parties. There is no dispute as to the facts out of which the grievance arose. On February 13, 1954 the Company curtailed operations by closing down one of its paper machines at the Springhill, Louisiana mill. This shutdown, occasioned by lack of orders, in turn affected the need for Kraft pulp and it became necessary for management to lay off, in addition to the crew of the machine involved, a number of other employees in jobs affected in the Kraft pulp mill. The laid off employees were recalled to work when operations on a full-scale basis resumed on February 28, 1954.

Local Union 385 of the International Brotherhood of Pulp, Sulphite and Paper Mill Workers, under date of February 17, 1954, filed a grievance on behalf of the laid off employees in the Kraft Pulp Mill, complaining that the employees were incorrectly and unjustly laid off and claiming pay for these employees for the time lost between the date of lay-off and the resumption of work. The grievance does not contest the necessity for the curtailment of production but protests the method of the lay-off in the Kraft Pulp Mill. It is conceded that the lay-offs were not made in the reverse order of the employees' seniority. It is established from the evidence that some employees with long seniority were laid off, while employees with junior status within certain job classifications were retained. This resulted from the method of layoff under which the junior men in each affected job classification were laid off regardless of their company seniority.

Position of the Union

The Union contends that the lay-offs under the method employed constituted a contract violation as the lay-offs were conceded to have ignored seniority except for the concession that the youngest man in each classification on each shift was selected for lay-off. It is the Union's position that the junior man in each classification should not have been laid off but should have been permitted to exercise his seniority to the job next below in the line of progression. In other words, the Union's position is that in making the force reduction, employees should have been demoted down into other jobs in accordance with their job seniority and departmental seniority and the lay-offs then made in the reverse order of seniority. The Union strenuously urges that all employees have seniority rights at all times in all lay-off situations. Pointing to the contract provisions (Section VI, on Seniority, and particularly to Section VI, A (1) (a) and Section VI, B (5) (b) of the contract) the Union argues that the principle of seniority is inherently applicable to the lay-offs here involved. The Union also contends that the lay-offs constituted a "reduction of forces" within the meaning of the contract and also that the curtailment of production was "extended" as that term is used in the agreement.

Position of the Company

The Company relies on Paragraph (G) (1) of Section VI, contending it is the contract provision that governs the dispute and the Company argues that it was completely within its rights, under the contract, in carrying out the lay-off in the manner in which it was actually done. The cited contract provision reads:

> In cases of reduction of forces or extended curtailment of production, employees will be demoted in the reverse order of their promotion and laid off in the reverse order of their seniority. (Paragraph G (1) of Section VI of the Collective Bargaining Agreement.)

It is the position of the Company that lay-off on the basis of seniority is required only in cases of "reduction in forces or extended curtailment of production" and that the two-weeks shut-down here was neither a "reduction of forces" nor an "extended" curtailment of production as contemplated by the contract. The Company contends that the contract was so drawn to avert the necessity of demotions and retraining on short shut-downs.

The contract

It is to be noted that the contract in effect at the time this dispute arose is an agreement between the Company and three international unions: The International Brotherhood of Paper Makers, the International Brotherhood of

Pulp, Sulphite and Paper Mill Workers and the International Brotherhood of Electrical Workers, effective date June 1, 1953 with anniversary date of June 1, 1954. The two other Unions, not parties to this arbitration proceeding, have not presented any grievance affecting their members with respect to the lay-off here involved. The following provisions of the contract are pertinent:

A. Types of Seniority:

1. For the purposes of this Agreement there shall be three (3) types of Seniority: Job Seniority, Department Seniority and Company or Division Seniority.

a. Job Seniority is defined as the length of service on a job within a line of progression. All jobs on the same level within a line of progression shall be considered as one job for purposes of promotion. It is understood, however, that the Company has the right to rotate men on various jobs carrying the same rate in the line of progression if, in Management's opinion, experience on more than one job is desirable for promotion to the next higher rate.

b. Department Seniority is defined as the length of service in a line of progression.

c. Company or Division Seniority is defined as the length of service in the mills and facilities of the Company now identified as the Southern Kraft Division.

B. 1. In the consideration of seniority in promotions first preference shall be given to Job Seniority. Where Job Seniority is equal Department Seniority shall prevail. If Job and Department Seniority are both equal, then Company or Division Seniority shall determine the promotion. Exceptions to this order of preference may only be made by mutual consent of the Company and the Local Union involved.

2. Seniority will operate according to lines of progression agreed upon between the Local Unions and the Mill Manager. Such lines of progression shall be subject to change only by mutual agreement of the two parties.

3. When it is necessary to fill the bottom job in a line of progression other than by hiring from the outside, Management will take into consideration seniority and ability and when all the factors which constitute ability are relatively equal, then seniority will determine the promotion.

4. In filling subsequent vacancies in the line of progression up to, but not including those classifications listed below in Paragraph (B-6), the senior qualified Employee will be promoted. Should a question arise as to whether or not the senior Employee is qualified, and it cannot be resolved by agreement between the Union and Management, the senior Employee will be given a reasonable trial period on the job in question. If, after a reasonable trial, it is found that the Employee is not performing satisfactorily the functions of the job, he will be returned to his former position and will become junior to the two (2) next oldest men. The job will then be filled by the senior qualified man.

5. a. It is understood and agreed that no step in the line of progression,

the training in which is necessary to the next step, will be completely blocked by men who are unable or unwilling to progress further. Should such a situation appear to be developing, Management and the Union involved will discuss remedial measures.

b. When an Employee is promoted around a job and/or job level in a line of progression, he shall begin the accumulation of Job Seniority on all by-passed classifications at the same time he begins to accumulate seniority on the job to which he is promoted. . . .

G. 1. In cases of reduction in forces or extended curtailment of production, Employees will be demoted in the reverse order of their promotion and laid off in the reverse order of their seniority. . . .

SECTION VII—ADJUSTMENT OF COMPLAINTS

E. 4. The Board of Arbitration shall have no power to add to or subtract from or modify any of the terms of this Agreement or any Agreement made supplementary hereto nor to establish or change any wage.

Discussion and findings

It is a fundamental that seniority carries rights only to the extent that the contract so requires. Whatever seniority rights employees have exist only by virtue of and to the extent specified in the collective bargaining agreement. A strict and literal interpretation of contract seniority provisions should not be applied where such application would defeat the whole spirit and purpose of the seniority system. Normally, however, the details of the seniority system are matters for the bargaining table and a Board of Arbitration is not at liberty to re-write the contract to correct injustices if the meaning of the contract is clear from its wording.

The contract, above quoted, contains no general provision, similar to that contained in many agreements, that seniority shall govern in all lay-offs where ability and skill are equal. During the period from 1939–1948 the labor agreements in effect at the plant did contain a clause requiring the management to take into consideration seniority and ability if employees were "to be promoted or laid off" and further provided that when all of the factors that constitute ability are relatively equal, then seniority will prevail. The change in phraseology of the contract to that above quoted in the light of the omission of the general clause making seniority a major consideration in lay-offs is of itself significant. In the opinion of the majority of the Board, this, in itself, reflects a lack of intention of the parties to require the application of the seniority principle to lay-offs generally and affirmatively shows an intention that the exercise of seniority rights are to be limited to the specific situations in which the parties have defined its applicability in the contract.

Union's Views.—The Union urges, however, that in interpreting the contract the Board must take into consideration that seniority is in a stage of transition to a system established in 1952 under which there is now a single unbroken line of progression in the Kraft Pulp Mill from the lowest paid job to the highest. In this connection, the Union relies upon the seniority section as a

whole to imply that "the principles of seniority shall apply in . . . layoff"—
though the contract does not expressly so provide. More specifically, the Union
urges that Section VI, (A) (1) (a) defining "job seniority" when considered
with Section VI, (B) (5) (b) implies that seniority is to control in the
movement of personnel both upward and downward the line of progression.
In its excellent brief, the Union urges that the last cited contract provision,
under which an employee begins to accumulate job seniority on by-passed
classifications at the same time he accumulates seniority on the job to which he
is promoted, means that lines of progression are to be observed in a downward
movement of personnel. Unless movements down the line are held to be
governed by seniority, the clause referred to, says the Union, would be
meaningless.

The Board has carefully studied the contract and has considered the able
arguments that have been made both orally and by brief, in support of this
construction. A majority of the Board cannot, however, accept that interpretation of the contract. There is nothing in Section VI (A) (1) (a) which defines
three kinds of seniority from which an obligation to follow seniority in a line
of progression in making all lay-offs is to be implied. Section VI (B) (5) (b),
in providing for the accumulation of job seniority on all by-passed classifications
at the same time the employee begins to accumulate seniority on the job to
which he is promoted does not mean that the seniority principle shall govern
all lay-offs. This provision may be given effect by recognizing its applicability to
those lay-offs that are found to be protected by seniority in the contract. The
specifically cited portion of the contract is in the part dealing with promotions
and cannot be construed by implication to have the broad results contended
for by the Union of supplying a provision by implication for the express
provision for seniority on all lay-offs when the parties themselves have left
such broad phraseology out of the contract. For similar reasons the Board does
not construe Section B (2), also in the part dealing with promotions, as
meaning that seniority shall apply to all lay-offs.

Applicable Section.—If the job protection contended for by the Union is
found to exist under the contract it must be by virtue of the specific section
dealing with seniority on reduction in forces. Section G (1) reads:

> In cases of reduction in forces or extended curtailment of production,
> Employees will be demoted in reverse order of their promotion and laid
> off in the reverse order of their seniority.

From a study of the provision it seems clear that two types of lay-offs are
covered by the contract by specific provision and that seniority shall control
in those two situations only. They are "reduction in forces" or "extended
curtailment of production." It is a well-settled canon of statutory and contract
interpretation that the expressed enumeration will exclude that which is not
enumerated. In the light of the expressed provision that employees will be laid
off in the reverse order of their seniority in cases of "reduction in forces or
extended curtailment of production" this Board must so construe the contract
as to give effect to that clause. This Board is without power to add to the
contract by applying the seniority principle to layoffs which do not fall within

these two enumerated classifications. When the parties provided in their contract that seniority should apply to an "*extended* curtailment of production" they certainly must have meant, by the logical inference from that language that not *all* curtailments of production giving rise to lay-offs were to be on the basis of seniority. In other words a curtailment of production that is not "*extended*" which gives rise to a lay-off is not within the meaning of the contract. Because of the limiting language used, the Board is of the opinion that the term "reduction in forces" as used in the contract necessarily means something different from an "extended curtailment of production" but does not encompass lay-offs due to temporary as distinguished from "extended" curtailments of production. If the term "reduction in forces" were interpreted to include any lay-off, regardless of its character, cause or duration, the succeeding clause which enumerates "extended curtailment" of production would have been completely unnecessary and entirely superfluous. Such an interpretation would virtually re-write the clause by reading it out of the contract. Had the parties intended broadly to include all lay-offs, permanent, extended and temporary, it would have been relatively simple to so provide in the contract. The Dictionary of Labor Law Terms (CCH 1953) defines the term "layoff" to mean a "temporary, prolonged, or final separation from employment as a result of lack of work." It is significant that the parties have avoided the use of the term "lay-off" in this broad sense but have chosen instead of that term, *which was in previous contracts*, the two specific occasions for the exercise of seniority, namely, "reduction in forces" or "extended curtailment of production." The Board must consider that this change in the contract terms was intended to have a meaning and the only logical interpretation is that the language is not as broad as the term "layoff" in its usual meaning but encompasses only lay-offs which are either due to an extended curtailment of production or a reduction in forces, but not including reduction in forces due to a temporary curtailment of production.

Memorandum of Understanding.—A majority of the Board is of the opinion, therefore, that a layoff due to a temporary curtailment of production is not within the protection of the seniority provisions of the contract. The construction placed on the contract by a majority of the Board finds added support in a memorandum of understanding prepared by the Company and circulated to all mill managers setting forth agreements as to contract interpretations reached at a conference on November 11, 1953 between representatives of the Company and the international officers and international representatives of the three unions that are parties to the contract. This memorandum was introduced in evidence by the Union. The memorandum tends to establish that at that time the parties apparently were in agreement that demotions down the line of progression would be called for *in a reduction of forces for an extended period of time*. The pertinent portion referred to reads:

Demotions

In cases of demotions brought about by a reduction in forces for an extended period of time, employees are to be demoted in the reverse order of Job Seniority, step by step down the line of progression. For the purposes of making such demotions, an employee's Job Seniority on a given job is computed as the length of time he spend (sic spent) on that job plus his length of service on all higher jobs in the line of progression. When an employee bumping down the line of progression reaches a job level in which all employees on that level have greater Job Seniority than he has on that and all higher jobs, he must then bump down around that level to a lower level. Upon reaching the base rate, employees are to be laid off in the reverse order of their Company seniority.

The parties were obviously then considering that the requirement of demotions was not applicable to short lay-offs.

Meaning of "Extended"—It is true that the contract contains no definite period of time beyond which the curtailment of production resulting in the lay-off will be deemed to be "extended" or not temporary as has been done in some collective bargaining contracts, including some in the paper industry. The absence of such a provision may lead to differences between the parties in instances of curtailed production. Such differences may call for interpretation and application of the contract to specific facts and circumstances. But this difficulty does not mean that the plain import of the contract is to be ignored. The Company's contention that it is beyond the power of a Board of Arbitration to review the Company's judgment as to whether a particular curtailment is "extended" is not correct. Necessarily, in a given case, the arbitrators must determine whether the curtailment of production was "extended" or temporary. That determination would not be one applicable to every case, and an addition to the contract but would constitute a review of whether the Company had deviated from the contract in a case which should, under the circumstances, be properly characterized as "an extended curtailment of production." The Company at the time of the shutdown must exercise a reasonable judgment as to whether the curtailment will be "extended" or temporary in its nature. This Board will not, however, attempt to define any specific period of time which would make the curtailment "extended." To do so would be to supply a provision which the parties should themselves supply if it is to be part of the contract. Such exact definition of duration must come from the bargaining table.

We turn to our specific case. A majority of the Board concludes that a *reduction in forces* was not here involved. It is clear that it was never intended that the lay-offs would be permanent. The lay-offs were caused by an economic condition within the industry, a lack of orders, which was expected to be of temporary duration though the exact duration was not known. A Company representative testified that when the machines were shut down on February 13th, the Company expected that full-scale operations would be resumed about March 1st. This was not, therefore, in the opinion of the Board a "reduction in forces" as that term must be understood in the instant contract.

Was it "an extended curtailment of production" within the meaning of the contract? The shut-down of the machine and consequent lay-offs took place on February 13, 1954 and the lay-off continued until operations resumed on February 28, 1954. At the time that the shut-down occurred the exact duration of the lay-offs was not known though the Company hoped to resume operations by March 1. The notice to the employees was indefinite as to the time of resumption of operations but did state "all personnel connected with this machine will be notified when the machine will start up." Testimony was adduced that the Company moved immediately to contact its New York Sales Department to see to what extent the loss of production could be absorbed in the other mills of the Company to avert a situation in which this would be an "extended" lay-off. Moreover, it was testified to that the Company knew that it had March orders to fill so the curtailment was not expected to extend into March. But the mere indefinite character of the lay-off does not prevent the lay-off from being temporary. The significant fact is that the Company hoped and expected it to be of not longer than 16 days duration and it acted to realize this expectation. It was established by the evidence that on or about February 20th the Company was able to assure the Union that operations would actually be resumed on February 28th. The Board finds that under the facts here presented this specific lay-off of 15 days cannot be said to be an "extended curtailment of production" when resumption of full scale operations took place immediately after that period, and when 7 days after the shut-down, assurances were given to the Union that operations would be resumed in eight days. The Company was justified, in the opinion of the Board, in determining that lay-offs would not be of extended duration and in treating the curtailment of production as one of a temporary nature. This is not to say that every curtailment of production of 15 days or less necessarily falls short of being an extended curtailment of production as there may be some circumstances in which it would be unreasonable for the Company to conclude that the curtailment when made would not be extended. A series of recurring short shut-downs under some circumstances could constitute an extended curtailment of production. If a lay-off initially thought to be temporary should ripen into an extended curtailment of production, there would then arise a duty to call back the employees and to make demotions along the line of progression in accordance with seniority. The Board is limited to deciding on the facts before us, that the shut down here involved was not an extended curtailment of production within the meaning of the contract.

Hardship Cases—In the consideration of this matter the Board was much impressed with the evidence adduced by the Union as to specific cases in which it alleges there was the undesirable and unjust result of laying off a number of persons with many years of service while others with fewer years of service were retained.[1] There is no denying of the equity that is inherent in the

[1] For example, F. M. Cobb, with 12 years of seniority had advanced to the position of 1st helper in the Digester Room which was the position he held on February 13, 1954. The four youngest helpers in the Digester Room had to be laid off and as he was one of the 4 junior helpers he was laid off. Had he not been promoted he might not have been laid off due to his senior status in the job classifications below his in the line of progression; J. B. Delafield, with fourteen and one-half years of seniority was laid off as he was a junior employee in the job classification of 1st Helper Recovery Room; De Otis Bradley, whose total company service was 29 years was laid off because of his junior status in his job classification.

Union's argumentative inquiry and statement: "How capricious the layoff must have seemed to a man who last week was promoted (no doubt to his considerable satisfaction) to a higher rated job! Had he refused the promotion, or had it been offered a week later, he would have retained his job during the lay-off, and some other man would have been laid off in his place" (at page 15 of Union's Brief).

This Board, however, is not a court of equity with a roving mandate to re-write the contract in the interest of justice but must apply the provisions of the contract as the parties have made it where the meaning is reasonably clear. Any injustices or inequities in the contract as written must be corrected at the bargaining table. Especially is this so in the instant case in which the Company may also properly point to the equities on its side of the problem and to the administrative difficulties, expense, inefficiency of operation and problem of retraining that would be involved in reshuffling a large number of employees in production curtailments of relatively short duration. It may be added that efforts were made by the Company to minimize individual hardship by otherwise utilizing or placing employees on vacation to avoid loss of time. At the hearing the Company's representatives stated that a moral obligation to senior employees is recognized and a willingness was expressed to negotiate a feasible plan to cover future instances of the type involved in this grievance.

Other Awards—A long list of decisions of other arbitrators have been reviewed to determine what light they throw on the instant problem. Though there are a few decisions to the contrary, a number of decisions have been found which support the position that seniority must be applied to all lay-offs, regardless of duration, despite the contention of management that short lay-offs are not within the intendment of the seniority provisions. However, where the contracts have been so interpreted there has generally been an absence of any language in the contract making a distinction between lay-offs of long and short duration or they contained broad provisions expressly making seniority applicable to all lay-offs. No case has been found on all fours with the one before us. Here we hold that the line of arbitration awards above referred to are not applicable because the contract here involved unmistakably evidences an intention to distinguish between lay-offs of an extended character and those due to temporary curtailment of production.

Finally careful consideration has been given to the Union's contention that to deny this grievance means that the Union has moved backward in the matter of job protection and seniority rights while normally progress is in the direction of strengthening seniority rights. With this contention the majority of the Board cannot agree. In the bargaining the Union has gained recognition of seniority rights on lay-offs that are reductions in forces or extended curtailments of production, which may well be considered to be more substantial job protection than that afforded by the vagueness of the clause in effect prior to 1949. Prior to the present Section VI, G (1) the company was required to give consideration to seniority in all lay-offs, but its judgment (subject to challenge in the grievance procedure) on the question of whether the factors that constitute ability were relatively equal might well be controlling. We cannot ignore the fact that change in the seniority clause, according to the testimony, was requested by the Union. There is substantial reason why the Company would agree to make demotions down the line of progression in lay-offs of an extended nature but would be unwilling to so contract for lay-offs due to temporary curtailment of production. All parties to the agreement, including the negotiating unions, were apparently willing to see some gain in the present contract provision. It is significant in this connection that there is no evidence that the parties have altered their contract in this respect in the subsequent bargaining at anniversary date in 1954—and this despite the pendency of the instant grievance.

For the reasons assigned the following award is made:

AWARD

The grievance of the Union arising out of certain lay-offs at the Springhill plant during the period from February 13 to February 28, 1954 is denied. No contract violation took place in the manner in which the lay-offs were made.

The foregoing award, when signed by a majority of the Board, shall be operative as the disposition of the dispute.

DISSENTING OPINION OF UNION ARBITRATOR, BROOKS

I am unable to concur with my colleagues. There are several points at which their decision does violence to the language of the agreement and to the facts. Two of these seem to me to be central:

1. The majority opinion rests upon a proposition which they describe as follows:

When the parties provided in their contract that seniority should apply to an "extended curtailment of production" they certainly must have meant, by the logical inference from that language that not all curtailments of production giving rise to lay-offs were to be on the basis of seniority. In other words a curtailment of production that is not "extended" which gives rise to a lay-off is not within the meaning of the contract.

Contract construction

Although the majority state that a board of arbitration has no authority to change the terms of the agreement, they have done exactly that by this decision. They have assumed, to begin with, that Section VI (G) 1 is the controlling statement with respect to lay-offs and that all other parts of the seniority section are subordinate to it. I cannot find anything in the agreement nor in the history of the section which lends any support to this view. But, more seriously, they have also in effect added to the agreement the following clause:

Unless a lay-off is for an "extended" period (a month or more, according to the Company) the selection of employees to be laid off is entirely within the discretion of the Company, without *any regard whatsoever for seniority.*

The only basis I can find for this view is that it is the negative of Section VI (G) 1. I cannot find a trace of evidence that the parties ever intended to say anything like this; yet this is exactly what the majority affirm to be the meaning of this agreement.

I think that another interpretation is the only one which is consistent with the language of the agreement. It seems clear that the parties intended to make an *absolute* rule for the application of seniority in "extended curtailment" while leaving a greater degree of flexibility for lay-offs of a shorter period of time. The rule enunciated by the majority leaves the company free to lay off the senior digester cook for a month and to retain the man most recently hired at the bottom of the entire line of progression. If the company does not in fact do this, it is restrained only by its whims or its own judgments about its "moral obligation." There is nothing in the contract, say the majority, to inhibit such an action. This is fantasy.

Meaning of "extended"

2. The conclusion of the majority that the curtailment was not "extended" is based upon the curious assumption that "extended" is an antonym of "temporary." After stating (and I agree) that the Board of Arbitration should review the company's judgment as to whether a particular curtailment is "extended," the majority say

> Necessarily, in a given case, the arbitrators must determine whether the curtailment of production was "extended" or temporary. That determination would not be one applicable to every case, and an addition to the contract but would constitute a review of whether the Company had deviated from the contract in a case which should, under the circumstances, be properly characterized as "an extended curtailment of production. . . ."

Later on the majority say "It is clear that it was never intended that the lay-offs would be permanent."

The majority have thus equated "extended" with "permanent," an identification which tortures the English language and is not encouraged by the language of the contract. An extended lay-off can also be temporary. If the company had told the employees when they were laid off on February 13 that they were to return to work on a specific date, much later (say July 1), the lay-off would be temporary. According to the decision of the majority, it would therefore not be "extended," and the company would have a completely free hand in deciding whom to lay off.

I cannot believe that such a possibility ever entered the minds of the parties to this agreement.

PROMOTION AND THE DETERMINATION OF ABILITY

Kuhlman Electric Co. and United Automobile Workers, Local 778, 26 LA 885, 1956

ROBERT G. HOWLETT, ARBITRATOR

Grievance No. 6002

In January, 1956, the Company posted a notice of openings in the second class electrical maintenance classification. Among the employees who applied were Aloysius Piesik, whose seniority dates from May 23, 1944, and Jack Dean, with seniority from September 30, 1947. Both employees were working as second class electrical testers, a classification having a lower wage rate than the job of second class electrical maintenance.

The Company chose Jack Dean, the employee with the lesser seniority, in preference to Aloysius Piesik.[1] Mr. Piesik thereupon filed a grievance reading as follows:

I, the undersigned, with equal ability and more seniority protest the appointment of Jack Dean to the Electrical Maintenance opening. I request the appointment with full rights of seniority credits.

The Company replied as follows:

Selection of the man chosen for the Electrical Maintenance opening was based on ability as determined through interview, interview with department supervisor, evaluation of educational background, problem solving ability, electrical knowledge, continuation of education, and potential for growth in the department. In our judgment the man selected rated the highest on the combination of these factors.

The parties have stipulated that the question for the arbitrator is:

Has the Company complied with the provisions of the Agreement between the parties in the selection of Jack Dean over Aloysius Piesik for a posted opening on Second Class Electrical Maintenance?

The rules pertaining to the promotion of employees are found in Section 9 of Article IV of the agreement:

Where new jobs or vacancies occur, they will be posted on the bulletin boards by Management. Employees having ability for same may make application to the Personnel Manager for these jobs.

In cases of promotion to higher job classifications within the bargaining unit, the factors to be considered shall be ability and seniority. Where the ability of the employees under consideration for the promotion is substantially equal, then seniority shall govern. The Company shall give the Union the reason for the selection of an applicant under this section if the Union so desires. . . .

Prior to selecting the particular employees for the vacancies, the Company gave each applicant two examinations. One consisted of the Wonderlic Personnel Test, a twelve minute examination prepared for use in industry as a selection instrument in employment and placement, and as an indicator of future possibilities. The test shows general ability rather than aptitude for a specific job. The second test, written by the Company, was designed to show the applicants' knowledge of work in the Electrical Maintenance Department.

The Company had never previously used written examinations of this scope, although short tests containing three questions had been, on some occasions, used in the past. The Personnel Manager testified that the weight given to each test was "about fifty-fifty."

[1] There was a dispute concerning other employees, but it was resolved by the parties prior to the submission of Grievance No. 6002 to the arbitrator.

Out of a possible twenty-one, Dean scored fifteen on the electrical knowledge test, whereas Piesik scored seventeen.

On the Wonderlic test, Dean scored twenty-six which, according to the author of the test, places him one point above the level of foreman, production control man, job analysis and time study man, and eight points above the minimum for skilled mechanic, which, the Company says, is the type of work involved in the second class electrical maintenance classification. Grievant scored fourteen, which, according to the author of the test, is one point below the minimum for general factory help and four points below the minimum for skilled mechanics.

In addition to the tests, the Company also considered (1) the educational background of the two applicants, (2) the continuation of their education, (3) age and physical condition, and (4) attitude.

Dean had completed the eleventh grade and passed the United States Armed Forces Institute General Education Development Test at the high school level. Piesik had completed the eighth grade.

Dean was engaged in formal home study courses in radio and television for the past year and a half. The Company reported that the courses consisted of one hundred eighteen regular lessons, eighteen mathematics, algebra and trigonometry lessons and fifteen experiment kits. Dean had completed one hundred one lessons.

Piesik had done outside reading in trade journals and publications concerning electronic controls, time controls, heating ovens and other electrical fields. He had performed service work on television sets and radios.

Dean is twenty-six; Piesik is forty-three.

While both employees are "in apparent good health" a question was raised as to a foot injury suffered by grievant in a foundry prior to his employment by the Company and also as to an impairment of vision.

Dean is described by management as "Quiet type of person, appears eager to learn, tries hard to please and is co-operative." He is said to have "a sincere desire to get ahead and work his way into a more responsible position" and he "has a record of being dependable." Grievant is said to have "a tendency to be somewhat loud and outspoken and not as co-operative as is desirable in helping achieve departmental goals."

Position of the parties

The Union vigorously objects to the use of the two written tests as one basis for selecting an employee for a vacancy. The Union has no objection to the use of written tests, as such, but urges that they may not be instituted by unilateral action of the Company, as the Union Committee is entitled to know the type of questions and the weight to be given the tests before written examinations may be used as a basis for promotion. The Company, says the Union, had not used written examinations in the past, and the institution of this method of testing is an alteration of the intent and purpose of Section 9 of Article IV. Past practice, it is urged, must be continued until changed by agreement of the parties. The Union also contends:

1. Grievant has had practical experience on the job for which he applied on Saturdays, when other employees have been absent, and during inventory periods.

2. The Company is seeking to promote the "best qualified man" which is not the test established by the contract. The Union says that some of the questions asked on the Electrical Maintenance Department examination were of first class potential, whereas, the job to be filled was in the second class category.

3. Grievant passed the portion of the examination covering electrical knowledge and experience with a higher rate than Dean.

4. Grievant has worked in the Electrical Maintenance Department without supervision.

5. With respect to grievant's impairment of vision, his present job has a higher visual point evaluation than the second class electrical maintenance job.[2]

The Company contends that its sole motivation in selecting an employee for a job "is to pick the best qualified employee with the understanding that if two or more applicants have substantially equal qualifications, then seniority shall be used as the tie-breaker." "The selection," says management, "was based on employee interviews, interviews with the supervisors, evaluation of their educational background, problem solving ability and general elementary electrical knowledge as measured by brief tests, continuation of education and potential for growth in the department." The Company contends that it is continually searching for a better method of exercising its managerial responsibility of promotion and that it may adopt written examinations unless there is a contract prohibition against their use.

Management further contends that the parties have agreed on a job definition wherein there is required "the use of complicated drawings and specifications, advanced shop mathematics and book formulas, wide variety of precision measuring instruments, broad shop knowledge."[3] Because of this, the Company contends, a high school education is a definite advantage over an eighth grade education. The Company further contends that the written tests were only part of the selection procedure, and that the selection was also made because (1) Dean had a better education than Piesik, (2) his age (the maintenance foreman stated he was looking for employees with a potential for future upgrading), (3) his greater interest in further education, (4) his attitude toward his fellow employees, and (5) the performance of the two employees.

---

[2] The Company has an evaluation plan for all jobs. "Frequent mental/visual attention" has an evaluation of 20 points for second class electric maintenance and an evaluation of 30 points for second class electrical tester, grievant's present job. No distinction is made as to the "mental" and "visual" portion of this particular attribute. Second class electrical maintenance has 628 evaluation points, whereas second class electrical tester has 590. Jobs in the plant range from 328 to 710.

[3] This statement is made in the Company brief, and while the statement was not denied by the Union, the job description for the job submitted in evidence, does not express such a high educational requirement.

Discussion

Seniority clauses generally (and perhaps of necessity) are founded (or founder) on abstractions, as draftsmen seek to limit length of service as the criterion for promotion and other aspects of job security and job movement. The concepts of "ability," "aptitude," "fitness," "skill," "capability," "merit," and "qualifications," not to mention the appending of adjectives ("required ability," "satisfactory experience," "necessary qualifications") renders difficult the task of the arbitrator. The plaintive cry of one arbitrator speaks for the profession:

If the parties to collective bargaining agreements do not set up a more specific standard of reference than that contained in the abstract word "ability," then it seems to me that the most they can expect from themselves and their arbitrators are sincere but inexact personal judgments as to the comparative standing of various employees.[4]

Prior to the advent of collective bargaining agreements, management had the power, and the legal right, to promote (and to demote, lay-off and recall) at will. Employees were generally moved from job to job, or in and out of the factory, as productive efficiency required. The unions, often charging favoritism, sought job security for senior employees. Thus there developed limitations on management's freedom to move employees. To say that the contest between seniority and ability results in a head-on collision between job security and productive efficiency is an over-simplification, but these conflicting viewpoints are always in evidence in both collective bargaining and arbitration where seniority is involved.[5]

Promotion clauses (other than the infrequent ones based solely on seniority *or* competence) are generally divided into four categories: [6]

1. *Seniority the Primary Factor.* The senior employee is promoted provided he is able to perform a specified requirement of the job, such as "minimum," "normal," "average" or "sufficient." [7]

---

[4] Gabriel N. Alexander in "Factor of Ability in Labor Relations," published in *Arbitration Today,* Bureau of National Affairs, 1955, pages 60, 61. See also, Douglas Aircraft Co., Inc., 25 LA 600, 603 (1955); Public Service Electric & Gas Co., 12 LA 317, 321 (1949); and Elkouri, *How Arbitration Works,* Bureau of National Affairs, 1952, pages 241–251.

[5] Of course, if length of service, as the sole basis for advancement, should result in a wholesale promotion of inefficient employees, workers would lose their job security, for the enterprise would fail. Perhaps the issue of seniority vs. ability is not as great as the arguments of management and union make it appear. It has been suggested that seniority *may* be as good a guide to future performance as ability. See James J. Healey and Jean T. McKelvey in "The Factor of Ability in Labor Relations," published in *Arbitration Today,* Bureau of National Affairs, 1955, page 45, et seq.

[6] Some arbitrators have suggested there are two types of seniority clauses. See Pittsburgh Steel Co., 21 LA 565, 567 (1953).

[7] International Harvester Company, 11 LA 1190 (1948); North American Cement Corporation, 11 LA 1109 (1949); Aviation Maintenance Corporation, 13 LA 677

2. *Seniority and Other Qualification Equal.* Seniority and another requirement are both factors, but there is no reference as to the weight to be given to
each, i.e. "due regard to length of service and ability," and "promotion shall be
based upon seniority and capability." [8]

3. *Seniority the Secondary Factor.* Ability or other qualification is the
primary factor unless equal, in which event, seniority will prevail.[9]

4. *Ability Limited by an Additional Factor.* Ability or other qualification is
stated to be the primary factor, but is limited by a qualifying word—usually
"relatively" or "substantially." An additional factor is added to type (3), thus
creating a penumbra area in which ability may be superseded by seniority.[10]

The Kuhlman Electric Company promotion clause falls within type (4). The
senior employee receives the promotion if his ability is "*substantially*" equal to
that of the junior employee. Thus, a senior employee may be preferred, even
though his ability is less than that of some junior employee, but the exact line
between employees is difficult to draw. The problem is well stated by Arbitrator
Whitley P. McCoy, former Director of the Federal Mediation & Conciliation
Service:

> The term "substantially equal" has a meaning obviously different from
> the unmodified word "equal." "Equal" might conceivably be construed as
> meaning "substantially equal," but "substantially equal" could not possibly
> be construed as meaning "exactly equal." The parties, in writing this sec-
> tion, quite apparently contemplated a situation where one applicant
> would be slightly better qualified than another, but not substantially so,
> in which case seniority should be the controlling factor. So they provided
> that where the qualifications are *substantially* equal seniority should
> govern. This provision means that the superiority of one over the other
> must be by a substantial margin, not so slight as to cause doubt or to leave
> room for reasonable question. This seems so clear as not to require elabora-
> tion.[11]

(1949); United States Rubber Company, 18 LA 834 (1952); West Virginia Pulp and
Paper Co., 20 LA 385 (1953). A trial period is frequently required for the employee
promoted under this type of clause.

[8] Standard Oil Company, 11 LA 810 (1948); Pennsylvania Salt Manufacturing
Company, 14 LA 12 (1949); International Harvester Company, 21 LA 183 (1953);
Callite Tungsten Company, 11 LA 743 (1948); Shell Oil Company, Inc., 4 LA 13
(1946). Trial periods are sometimes required in clauses of this type.

[9] Dewey & Almy Chemical Company, 25 LA 316 (1955); Ford Motor Company,
2 LA 374 (1945); Chrysler Corporation, 14 LA 143 (1950).

[10] Examples of "substantially equal" are Douglas Aircraft Company, Inc., 25 LA
601 (1955); Connecticut Power Company, 13 LA 459 (1949); Southern Bell Telephone & Telegraph Company, 16 LA 1 (1951); Marlin-Rockwell Corporation, 17 LA
254 (1951). Examples of "relatively equal" are Acme Steel Co., 9 LA 432 (1944)
("relatively equal" seems to mean the same as "equal"); Hercules Powder Company,
10 LA 624 (1948); Seagrave Corporation, 16 LA 410 (1951); Bethlehem Steel Company, 24 LA 820 (1955).

[11] Southern Bell Telephone & Telegraph Company, 16 LA 1, 10 (1951). Should
"substantially" or "relatively" ever be used as modifying "equal"? Are not two persons

The word seems to be used in the subject contract as meaning "about" or "approximately." [12]

Of importance in this arbitration is the fact that Section 9 does not refer to general ability or native ability, but ability "for the promotion"—ability to perform the particular job sought. This is emphasized by the first portion of Section 9, which states that when new jobs or vacancies are posted on the bulletin boards "employees having ability for same (the new job or vacancy) may make application therefor." It is therefore necessary to relate each employee's qualifications to the job to be filled in making the decision to promote or not to promote.[13]

Management in its testimony and argument stressed the importance of securing the "best qualified" or "highest qualified" employee, the employee with the "greatest ability" or "most ability," or with "potential for upgrading." The Union, on the other hand, tried to create a type (1) seniority clause out of Section 9. It contended that under past practice seniority prevailed if the employee could "do the job," but no evidence was presented to substantiate this theory. Neither theory is correct under the type (4) clause (Section 9) which is the subject matter of this discussion.

The Company's interest in securing the best qualified employee for promotion is understandable. Management is interested in the success of its enterprise and one aspect of successful operation is competent employees. Possibly the Union should have as great an interest in general competence and ability, for the success of the business will redound to the benefit of all employees. However, the contract language must control unless and until changed.

A job description of second class electric maintenance was adopted as of September 23, 1953:

> Under general supervision, perform routine electrical maintenance operations, such as replacement of burned out bulbs and tubes, cleaning electrical fixtures, regular routine lubrication and inspection of motors, replacement of fuses: replacement or repair of switches, portable tools, extension cords, run conduit or wire according to sketch or diagram or detailed instructions; assist in trouble shooting; repair an installation of electrical and connected mechanical equipment.

Dean and Piesik must be compared with respect to the factors used by the Company in promoting Dean, in order to determine whether the two are *substantially* equal—or, in the alternative, whether Dean is *substantially* superior to Piesik. The arbitrator is convinced that Dean is *superior* and that under a type (1) clause Dean would be entitled to the promotion. But is he suffi-

---

or things either equal or *not* equal? We may take comfort in the use by the framers of our Constitution of "more perfect union."

[12] It has been held that "relatively" cannot mean "about" or "approximately," but means that applicants must be compared, thus making the phrase "relatively equal" mean "equal." Acme Steel Company, 9 LA 432, 435 (1947).

[13] Douglas Aircraft Company, 25 LA 600, 603 (1955).

ciently superior (i.e. "substantially superior") to justify a disregard of Piesik's seniority? [14]

Educational Background. While formal education is not a guarantee of success in any job, it is a factor to be considered. Dean is superior to Piesik, in this regard.

Continuation of Education. The Company stresses the fact that Dean has taken formal home study courses, while Piesik's study has been confined to informal reading. The Union seeks to minimize Dean's efforts on the ground that Dean's study of radios and television is not of assistance in the job sought because the Company does not manufacture these products, and algebra and trigonometry are not used in the second class electrical maintenance job. It seems evident that any study in the field of electricity and electronics will benefit an employee at the Kuhlman plant and that such study should be encouraged. While the testimony with respect to Dean's work was hearsay and Piesik's testimony was general, it appears that both these employees have displayed interest in study which will be helpful to them as employees of the Kuhlman Electric Company.

Health. Both employees appear to enjoy good health, except for Piesik's eyes. He testified that he does not need to wear glasses, and that he can see moving objects from the side, although he does not see them clearly. In further support of his physical ability, he pointed out that he had been performing his present job in a satisfactory manner, and that since 1951 he has done part time work as a second class electrical maintenance employee. The arbitrator must take note of the fact that the mental and visual demand for the second class electrical maintenance classification is less than that for second class electrical tester, the present classification of both Piesik and Dean. No evidence was submitted by the Company with respect to Piesik's alleged foot ailment; and he testified that it did not bother him, and he could climb if the job required it. The fact that Dean, at twenty-seven, is several years younger than Piesik, who is forty-three, is not an advantage insofar as this job is concerned. It would appear that Dean may be slightly superior to Piesik with respect to health.

Attitude. "Attitude" is difficult to determine, although the particular attribute is important—the degree thereof depends on the job to be performed. No persuasive testimony was presented by either Company or Union with respect to the attitudes of the two employees. The Electrical Testing Department foreman, who might be expected to know more about the attitude of both Dean and Piesik than any other supervisor, was not called to testify. The Company laid stress on an "interview" between Piesik and Guzdzial, the Maintenance Department foreman. The Union contends this was not a "formal" interview. A conversation did take place, although it is patent that there was no exhaustive treatment of Piesik's ability to fill the vacancy. The foreman testified that he asked Piesik whether he had done anything since his last interview which

---

[14] Some arbitrators give weight to the difference in the seniority of applicants for a job, but such a comparison is not pertinent under the clause here involved. International Harvester Company, 21 LA 183 (1953).

should be added. Piesik replied in the negative, but no testimony was offered with respect to the prior interview. The Company stated that "all applicants were interviewed" but there is no testimony with respect to the results of the interview with Dean.

While the strict rules of evidence do not apply in arbitrations, the arbitrator must hold that there has been no evidence on the issue to support the Company's allegation with respect to Dean's superiority in "attitude" as compared with Piesik.

The Examinations. In some respects this arbitration was presented as though the issue were the right of the Company to require written examinations rather than Dean vs. Piesik.[15]

The Union urges that before the Company may require written tests, it must be consulted in order that the Union committee may know the types of questions which will be asked and the weight which will be given to them.

The Company urges that it is attempting continuously to develop the best method of finding the best qualified men for promotion, that promotion of employees is a management responsibility and that unless the contract prohibits the use of written examinations, the Company may require applicants to submit to them.

The Company is correct up to a point. It is not bound by established practice in its method of determining "ability."[16] The Company may not, however, unilaterally change the qualifications of a job. Thus, in Pennsylvania Salt Manufacturing Company, 14 LA 12 (1949), a Board of Arbitration held that a Company did not have the right to require a high school education and high school chemistry or equivalent where these requirements had not existed before. An examination might be of such difficulty that it would, in fact, result in a change in the qualifications.[17]

The electrical knowledge test is specifically related to the job sought by Dean and Piesik. The Wonderlic Test is related only generally to promotion to second class electrical maintenance. The Company's testimony and argument were directed primarily toward showing the importance of the Wonderlic test as a measurement of general ability and potential of the employees examined. As the Personnel Manager said, the Company is seeking employees to promote

[15] The exhibits disclose that a grievance raising this general issue had been filed by the Union, and that arbitration was contemplated; but subsequently a determination was made not to submit this issue to arbitration.

[16] Mr. Guzdzial testified that prior to the filling of the present vacancy (1) applicants were tried out, (2) selections were ordinarily made from the Electrical Testing Department, (3) it was hoped that people interested in the Electrical Maintenance Department would take formal training, but there were no written tests, (4) it was felt that the method in use was not adequate, (5) the past practice had been satisfactory in line with those who had applied for the jobs, and (6) the Company was looking for people with potential.

[17] See also Standard Oil Company, 11 LA 810 (1948); International Harvester Company, 21 LA 183 (1953). See American Can Company, 10 LA 613 (1948) for an excellent discussion of the use of aptitude tests. There was no limiting contract language which prevented the employer from giving considerably more weight to the tests than is possible here.

"not just for the moment but for promotion in the department." Meritorious as this idea may be it is not within the contemplation of Section 9, which limits "ability" to "*the* promotion" which the employees under consideration are seeking to secure. While the Wonderlic test is not an examination which, if required as a condition to being considered for a job, changes the qualifications of the job (and hence is contrary to the existing requirements), the Company has given it greater weight than the contract language justifies. Dean may be a man who, after service as a second class electrical employee, will be well qualified for promotion to first class, while Piesik may reach his ultimate peak as a second class. This, however, is not the contract basis for promoting the junior employee over the senior employee, if their abilities to fill the second class electrical maintenance job ("ability . . . for the promotion") are *substantially* (or about) equal.

Experience. In neither brief nor testimony did the Company make much of the respective experience of the two employees within the plant. The Union sought to give the impression that the work performed by Piesik in the Maintenance Department was almost constant; and it was not until the arbitrator asked just how long Piesik had worked on various second class electrical maintenance operations that it appeared that this work was confined to three or four days in each of the years 1953, 1954 and 1955, although considerably more extensive in 1951 and 1952. Piesik testified that he worked, at times, without supervision.

Mr. Guzdzial testified that when Piesik worked in the Maintenance Department, he was usually used to clean motors, overhead cranes and ventilator fans and for pulling wires. He also said that Piesik was called in primarily because he was acquainted with stock and that he was called in to "help, not to take the place of a second class man." He had told Piesik, during the interview, that he believed he would have no trouble in passing the electrical test.

Dean had never performed any work in the Maintenance Department.

Satisfactory performance of an employee in operations of the vacant job is a factor in determining "ability." Other things being equal, the man who has had some experience on a job can become a competent employee in the classification faster than a man who has had no such experience. The testimony disclosed that in previous promotions, experience has been considered.

The job descriptions disclosed that the second class electrical maintenance job is a more difficult job than second class electrical tester, but the tester job is good preparation for the maintenance job.

A reference to "job rate data sheet" for second class electrical maintenance discloses that the attribute of "education" (112 points) requires "knowledge of electricity and electronics, use of measuring instruments, such as meters and gauges." From the testimony, including the electrical knowledge test, it appears that both Dean and Piesik are reasonably qualified for this second class maintenance job. The job (under the attribute of "experience," with 132 points), according to the data sheet, requires approximately one year to learn. Dean may have the ability to learn more rapidly, but Piesik already knows some of the operations. From the Wonderlic test, it appears that Dean is probably superior in the ability under "Initiative and Ingenuity" to "plan and perform sequence operations," and to "make general decisions as to quality and tolerances"; this attribute being evaluated at 84 points out of a total of 628.

In summary, Dean and Piesik rated approximately as follows:

Educational Background: Dean is superior.

Continuation of Education: Dean may have a slight advantage over Piesik.

Physical Condition: Dean may have a slight advantage over Piesik. Age is not a factor for the vacant job.

Attitude: The testimony was inconclusive with respect to either of the men.

Electrical Knowledge: Piesik has a slight advantage over Dean.

Problem-Solving Ability: (Wonderlic Test) Dean is substantially superior to Piesik, but this test is primarily directed toward general ability and not qualifications for the specific job here involved.

Experence on the Job: Piesik is superior to Dean. There was no testimony as to which employee is superior as a second class electrical tester.

The two employees are within the area of substantial equality for the job of second class electrical maintenance, hence Piesik, the senior employee, rather than Dean, should have been selected for the promotion.

The grievance made no request for retroactive pay in the event it were held that Piesik was entitled to the promotion; and the Union spokesman stated that the Union was "not interested" in back pay. Consequently, none is awarded.

FOR DISCUSSION AND ANALYSIS

1. Examine the seniority provisions in the Bethlehem-Steelworkers contract in Chapter 7. Prepare a summary statement of how seniority affects layoffs, rehiring, and promotions. Obviously such provisions restrict but do not eliminate management's discretion in these areas of personnel policy. In what respects, if any, would you say that these provisions run counter to policies management would have adopted if left to its own interests? If you were a personnel director of one of these companies, what policies would you advocate to minimize the effect of any aspects of these provisions which you consider unfavorable to management's interests?

2. A collective bargaining agreement calls for promotions on the basis of seniority, where ability is relatively equal. A job falls open, and a number of employees "bid" for it. The company selects X, who is junior to several other bidders, justifying its choice on the ground that its observation of the several applicants has led it to believe that X has ability superior to the others.

   a. Would you consider that management was justified in making this selection, on the basis it asserts?

   b. Would you consider that the senior employees (and the union) would have any ground for protest?

3. How great a difference in ability do you think should be established before a junior employee is chosen over a senior man? *Any* difference whatsoever? How much of a difference becomes significant, in other words?

4. A vacancy occurred and a number of employees applied to fill it. In an arbitration award the senior applicant was rejected on grounds of unfitness for the job, which was then awarded to a junior employee. Some time later another employee, junior to the rejected applicant but senior to the one accepted, filed a grievance claiming a right to the job. The company urged that the first arbitration settled the matter, but the union contended that it had settled the matter only so far as the most senior applicant was concerned. After his rejection, others next on the seniority roster might protest the appointment of a junior man over them.

How would you decide this issue? Do you see any way in which a management might protect itself from endless arbitrations if it reached down the seniority list to promote some exceptional young person?

5. Select any of the cases reported in this chapter. Summarize union and management views. Outline the logic by which the arbitrator arrived at his conclusion. Recognizing that there are at least two sides to most such issues, write a dissenting opinion designed to justify a conclusion different from that at which the arbitrator arrived.

16: Union Influence on Productivity

There is little question that the union's organized efforts to reduce rates of operation, to force the use of extra men, and to protect its members from punishment for failure to perform according to management's standards have had—other things being equal—an effect of reducing productivity. The questions which can less readily be answered, however, are (1) whether there has been justification for such efforts (and by what—or whose—norms justification proceeds), and (2) whether the union has offset these adverse effects on productivity with favorable effects, perhaps attributable to improved worker morale or to an added stimulus to managerial efficiency, with the result that there has been no net reduction in productivity attributable to the unions, and perhaps, indeed, even some improvement.

SPEEDUP

From the report of Walter P. Reuther, President, United Automobile Workers, to the 16th Constitutional Convention, 1957, pp. 53–57

To the UAW, collective bargaining is a year-round activity embracing far more than the periodic negotiation of new contracts. It is a daily struggle to win for each worker in his plant a measure of dignity on the job, a voice in the matters that affect his welfare and protection against being forced by his company to work at a pace injurious to his health and well-being. Ever since the birth of our Union, the fight against speedup has occupied a central place in this daily struggle and in the attention of both the local unions and the International Union.

The UAW was born out of the early struggles against the immorality and inhumanity of the speedup system for which the automotive industry was notorious and which exploited workers, endangered their health and safety, and shortened their lives in the corporations' selfish drive for more production and greater profits.

Workers in our plants are faced constantly by management pressure for increased production based on intensified human effort. Prosperous firms maintain the pressure out of greed for larger profits than those they already enjoy. Firms in a shaky financial position use that fact as an excuse to demand that the workers produce more than they properly should. Firms in difficulties because of inefficient management or obsolete equipment attempt to impose speedup on the workers to make up for managerial deficiencies.

With the intensification of the competitive struggle among the corporations in our industries, financial and managerial weaknesses become more clearly apparent and the speedup problem is aggravated. We have therefore had occasion frequently since the last Convention to apply the policy of speedup spelled out by the International Executive Board on April 28, 1949, in the following language:

The UAW is unalterably opposed to and will fight against any attempt by employers to endanger the health and safety of workers by forcing them to perform an unreasonable workload. One of the major reasons that our Union came into existence was the revolt of workers against the inhuman speedup that existed in the automobile industry before it was organized.

New model changes in the automobile industries have historically created disputes over the question of production standards. These problems have been further complicated by efforts on the part of certain corporations and plants to improve their competitive position by trying to cut costs at the expense of the workers.

The UAW fully recognizes and supports the idea that the standard of living of the people can be raised only by reducing unit costs and making available more goods at lower prices.

However, we insist that reductions in the unit cost of production must be made possible by improved technology and production processes and by efficient engineering and management, and not by placing an unfair workload on workers. While supporting efforts to reduce unit costs on the sound and legitimate basis of technological advances, we stand uncompromisingly opposed to, and will resist with all our strength, any efforts on the part of management to reduce costs and expand profits by speeding up the workers.

It is our policy to authorize strike action in any plant, large or small, big corporation or small shop, when the facts show that an employer is attempting to drive his workers to make them produce more than a fair day's work.

The readiness of the International Executive Board to authorize strike action in production standard disputes when requested by any local union membership through the democratic channels provided by the UAW Constitution has, in itself, acted as a restraining influence on corporations tempted to increase their profits by speeding up their workers. On many occasions, however, it has been necessary for local unions to go through the process of taking strike votes before management could be persuaded to abandon its efforts to increase profits through speedup. Where the strike votes alone were insufficient pressure to bring about satisfactory settlements of production standard disputes, the International Executive Board has not hesitated to authorize strikes and to give them effective support when they occurred.

Official authorization of a strike by the International Executive Board serves in effect as the Union's last warning to the company involved that if it fails to work out fair and acceptable production standards it will face strike action.

During the past year, thousands of production standard disputes have been worked out through day-to-day collective bargaining at the plant level. The International Union has, based upon local union membership requests, authorized 74 strikes on production standard disputes, of which 17 were in GM plants, five in Chrysler plants, and one in a Ford plant. Many additional requests for authorization were made by local memberships, but the issues were settled without the need for authorization. In accordance with the established policies of the International Union, strike authorization is always granted whenever the membership, through secret democratic vote, as provided for in the Constitution of the UAW, requests such strike authorization and the issues in dispute on production standards are not resolved satisfactorily. Not one single strike authorization request, made as a result of a secret democratic rank-and-file vote, has been denied by the International Union where the production standards in dispute were not worked out satisfactorily.

The International Union's policy with respect to strike authorization in production standard disputes has, of course, been uniformly applied in both large and small companies. Our Union is one of the few unions that insist on retaining the right of workers to strike even during the life of the contract on matters such as production standards which could not be properly arbitrated. We do not accept the view that an arbitrator, even if he had the wisdom of a thousand Solomons, can in our complex industry establish a sound basis for determining how hard any worker should work on his job.

The policy of the UAW relating to the right to strike on production standards is based upon the broad concept that workers should receive a fair day's pay for performing a fair day's work. The policy provides that the decision as to how hard a worker should be required to work for his wage is not a matter that can be decided arbitrarily by either an engineer with a stop watch, or an official of the corporation, or of the Union. What constitutes a fair day's work is a matter to be worked out through collective bargaining at the plant level by the people directly involved.

To make this policy effective, the engineers on the staff of the Research and Engineering Department devote a major part of their efforts to educational activities designed to equip the local union leadership to protect the rank and file against the varied speedup tactics of the so-called "scientific management" experts employed by the corporations. Our Union has always recognized that the fight against speedup is one that requires constant vigilance and an alert and active membership supported by the local and International leadership. The educational efforts of the International Union in this field are designed to maintain that vigilance and to prepare the local union leadership to take aggressive action whenever the threat of speedup appears.

Such vigilance and aggressiveness at the plant level are the key elements in the fight against speedup. The International Union, as such, has no means of detecting speedup where it occurs and of initiating action against it. The initiative must come from the local union level. The militancy and solidarity of the membership must be mobilized in the defense of the workers directly victimized by the speedup. With that solidarity expressed in strike votes taken under the machinery provided in the Constitution, full support of the International Union is assured. The International Union has never hesitated to provide all the support and assistance in its power to bring about satisfactory settlement of speedup disputes.

The leadership of the International Union shall continue to cooperate with the leadership and membership of the local unions in carrying out this realistic and effective policy on the basis of firmness and militancy so that we can protect our workers against speedup in any and all forms.

SLOWDOWN

In the matter of reinstating J. Puckett and C. H. Walters, with pay for lost time; Chrysler-UAW Appeal Board, Case No. 878, 1952

DAVID A. WOLFF, CHAIRMAN

"The Union requests immediate reinstatement of J. Puckett 99–2132 and C. H. Walters 99–3112 who were discharged for allegedly refusing to meet production standards. The Union also requests back pay for all lost time."

Statement

The final Company answer to the grievance, prior to the Appeal Board step, was the Statement of Director of Labor Relations. It read:

In this grievance the Union requests the reinstatement of J. Puckett, 99–2132 and C. H. Walters, 99–3112 with back pay for all time lost. Puckett and Walters were discharged for refusing to meet production standards after having been warned that they would be discharged if they continued to slow down production by failing to do a fair day's work.

Puckett and Walters formed one of several teams working on the Zig Zag seat cushion assembly in the Trim Department at the Dodge Main Plant. They and other employees working on this operation were not meeting production standards. Management examined the job to determine if there were any mechanical or other difficulties in connection with it to prevent the employees from meeting the standards and found there were none. Supervision talked to each employee on the job on several occasions and warned them that they were expected to produce according to the standards.

On July 11, 1951, all of the trim operators on this job were again informed that management expected them to trim cushions according to the standards and warned them that failure to do so would be grounds for a penalty. The requested production was not obtained and warning tickets were issued against the first team consisting of J. Puckett and C. Walters because the quantity of work of the entire group is controlled by the first team.

On July 12, 1951, all the Zig Zag operators were again told of management's request for standard production. J. Puckett and C. Walters, the first team, still refused to meet production and were sent home for the balance of the day. The other operators in the group were warned about their failure to meet production whereupon the entire group struck and walked off the job.

On July 18, 1951, J. Puckett and C. Walters again failed to meet production and being the lead team their failure to meet production again affected the production of other employees so they were disciplined for the balance of that day and the next day.

On Friday, July 20, 1951, all the operators were again warned that management expected them to meet production but Puckett and Walters continued their slowdown to such an extent that they rode the conveyor beyond the location where their job should have been completed thus forcing other operations out of their normal work locations. Their actions necessitated stopping the line on three different occasions in order to get the workers back into normal working position. At 3:20 P.M., on this same day the first team, consisting of two employees other than Puckett and Walters, started to perform their work in a manner that was closer to the standards. Puckett walked over and spoke to them after which this team started stalling. When the foreman instructed the first team to keep working to 3:45 P.M. (quitting time), Walters berated the foreman. When the foreman told Walters that he was talking to the first team, Walters remarked "It concerns me as well as them." J. Puckett stated "Nineteen is all I am going to do."

On July 23, 1951, when J. Puckett and C. Walters again failed to meet the requested production they were told they would be discharged if they continued to loaf on the job. They continued to loaf on the job and were discharged.

J. Puckett and C. Walters were both given many opportunities to meet production standards. Each one not only refused to produce the required production but also, by their words and deeds, discouraged other employees from doing so. J. Puckett and C. Walters were properly warned, disciplined and informed that if they continued to fail to produce, their loafing would result in their discharge. They failed to conform to the production standards required and were discharged.

The grievance is denied.

The Statement of Labor Relations Supervisor, given during the grievance procedure included the following language:

The following day, July 12, the operators were again advised as to the production expected and during the morning no improvement was made. Employees Puckett and Walters were also warned about using 80 instead of 40 hog rings per job and refused to follow instructions to use only the required amount (40).

The Union Statement of Facts read:

On July 23, 1951, J. Puckett, Badge No. 99–2132 seniority August 25,

1948, and C. H. Walters, Badge No. 99–3112, seniority date July 24, 1948, were discharged for allegedly failing to meet production standards. Puckett and Walters were employed in the Dodge Main Trim Shop, Group 22, and were working on the seat cushion operation. The seat cushion operation is performed on a suspended oval conveyor system consisting of what is known as "bucks" which hang from the conveyor. There are approximately twenty of these "bucks" and the line moves clockwise. The seat cushion springs, the cushion covering and the air foam rubber wadding, among other types of equipment, are placed on the "bucks", from which the operators working in teams of two build up the seat cushion to completion.

On Wednesday, July 11, 1951, the total number of operators on the seat cushion line was composed of nine two-man teams. These operators were building five jobs per hour. The Dodge Main Plant Management had instituted a campaign in the Trim Shop, as a whole, to get more production from employees on various jobs, including the seat cushion job, even though production on the seat cushions had been five jobs per hour since the start of the model, which was approximately November, 1950. Management informed the operators on the seat cushion job that they expected them to raise their production from five jobs per hour to nine jobs per hour. However, the production remained at five jobs.

On Wednesday, July 11, 1951, at approximately 2:00 P.M., William Stevens, foreman over the seat cushion job returned from a meeting of the plant supervision and stopped the seat cushion conveyor line, and walked over to the point on the line where the teams of operators ordinarily start their particular operation. Puckett and Walters happened to be at that point on the line, making preparation to start their designated seat cushion job. Foreman Stevens told them that they were expected to raise production and that failure to do so could result in a penalty. Production was not increased by Puckett and Walters or by any of the other teams, and warning tickets were issued to Puckett and Walters.

On Thursday, July 12, 1951, all of the operators on the seat cushion line were again told of Management's request for more production and warned that failure to meet production could result in a penalty. At 3:15 P.M., Puckett and Walters were disciplined by the foreman for the remainder of the day. None of the other operators were either disciplined or given tickets, even though they had performed their operations in the same manner as Puckett and Walters and had produced at the rate of five jobs per hour.

On Friday, July 13, 1951, Puckett and Walters did not report for work. However, production remained at five jobs per hour.

On Monday, July 16, 1951, Puckett and Walters reported for work and production remained at five jobs per hour. No one was disciplined or ticketed.

On Tuesday, July 17, 1951, Puckett and Walters reported for work.

still were out; a mass meeting was held at Keworth Stadium at Hamtramck at 9:00 A.M.; several thousand were present; both of the Assistant Chrysler Directors of the Union spoke to the people, said their action constituted an unauthorized strike and, told them to go back to work; although certain employees urged the group to stay away the Assistant Chrysler Directors prevailed and a motion to return to work was passed; however, at the suggestion of an employee the motion was amended to provide that no employee should raise production; this was an indication of the tremendous pressure not to increase production placed, not only on the Trim Shop and on the Zig-Zag seat cushion line but even more particularly, on Puckett and Walters, whose disciplining had precipitated the walkout; on July 20th all the people went back to work; after Puckett and Walters were discharged on July 23rd the Trim Shop went out at noon on July 24th, necessitating the closing of the plant; during the morning of the 24th, prior to the walkout, production remained at five pieces per hour; on July 25th the employees came to work at 7:15 and again walked out at 8:15; during this period production on the Zig-Zag seat cushion assembly line remained at five; the employees stayed out July 26th and July 27th; another mass meeting was held on July 29th; this meeting was addressed by the Union's Chrysler Director and by the International Vice-President who urged the people to return to work; the employees returned to work on Monday, July 30th; production remained at five for a week or ten days thereafter; it then was increased to six; around the last of August it was increased to seven; it has remained at that figure since that time. . . .

The Statement on Behalf of Chrysler Corporation follows:

On July 23, 1951, J. Puckett 99–2132 and C. H. Walters 99–3112 were discharged for refusing to meet production standards, as well as acting in an insubordinate manner toward their foreman on several occasions.

Puckett and Walters formed one of several teams working on the Zig-Zag seat cushion assembly in the Trim Department at the Dodge Main Plant. Puckett and Walters were not meeting production standards, but rather were engaged in a restriction of production. They limited their production to five (5) jobs per hour or less, whereas at the beginning of the 1951 model they were turning out six (6) jobs per hour under identical conditions. At the present time the trimmers are producing at the rate of seven (7) jobs per hour per team. The Time Study figure of 8.9 jobs per hour per team has been disputed by the Union for some time. The employees in this group and the Union representatives have never resorted to the orderly procedure as outlined in Section 2 of Article IV, 'Rates of Production' in the event of such a dispute, but rather have committed coercive acts, prohibited by Article I, Section 6 of the Corporation-Union Agreement.

On July 11, 1951, an attempt was made to obtain a fair days' production on this operation. The supervisor of the Zig-Zag Trim Group stopped the conveyor line at 2:15 P.M. in order to inform all the trimmers that the rate of production expected on this job was eight (8) per hour per team.

1948, and C. H. Walters, Badge No. 99–3112, seniority date July 24, 1948, were discharged for allegedly failing to meet production standards. Puckett and Walters were employed in the Dodge Main Trim Shop, Group 22, and were working on the seat cushion operation. The seat cushion operation is performed on a suspended oval conveyor system consisting of what is known as "bucks" which hang from the conveyor. There are approximately twenty of these "bucks" and the line moves clockwise. The seat cushion springs, the cushion covering and the air foam rubber wadding, among other types of equipment, are placed on the "bucks", from which the operators working in teams of two build up the seat cushion to completion.

On Wednesday, July 11, 1951, the total number of operators on the seat cushion line was composed of nine two-man teams. These operators were building five jobs per hour. The Dodge Main Plant Management had instituted a campaign in the Trim Shop, as a whole, to get more production from employees on various jobs, including the seat cushion job, even though production on the seat cushions had been five jobs per hour since the start of the model, which was approximately November, 1950. Management informed the operators on the seat cushion job that they expected them to raise their production from five jobs per hour to nine jobs per hour. However, the production remained at five jobs.

On Wednesday, July 11, 1951, at approximately 2:00 P.M., William Stevens, foreman over the seat cushion job returned from a meeting of the plant supervision and stopped the seat cushion conveyor line, and walked over to the point on the line where the teams of operators ordinarily start their particular operation. Puckett and Walters happened to be at that point on the line, making preparation to start their designated seat cushion job. Foreman Stevens told them that they were expected to raise production and that failure to do so could result in a penalty. Production was not increased by Puckett and Walters or by any of the other teams, and warning tickets were issued to Puckett and Walters.

On Thursday, July 12, 1951, all of the operators on the seat cushion line were again told of Management's request for more production and warned that failure to meet production could result in a penalty. At 3:15 P.M., Puckett and Walters were disciplined by the foreman for the remainder of the day. None of the other operators were either disciplined or given tickets, even though they had performed their operations in the same manner as Puckett and Walters and had produced at the rate of five jobs per hour.

On Friday, July 13, 1951, Puckett and Walters did not report for work. However, production remained at five jobs per hour.

On Monday, July 16, 1951, Puckett and Walters reported for work and production remained at five jobs per hour. No one was disciplined or ticketed.

On Tuesday, July 17, 1951, Puckett and Walters reported for work.

Production remained at five jobs per hour and no action was taken by Management.

On Wednesday, July 18, 1951, production still remained at five jobs per hour and Puckett and Walters were disciplined by Foreman Stevens for the remainder of the day (approximately two hours) and for the following day, Thursday, July 19, 1951.

On Friday, July 20, 1951, production still remained at five jobs per hour. No one was disciplined or ticketed.

On Monday, July 23, 1951, Puckett and Walters were warned that unless they raised their production, at least to eight jobs per hour they would be discharged. No warning was given other operators. The production of all operators remained at five jobs per hour. At 2:55 p.m., Foreman Stevens discharged Puckett and Walters.

The Union contends that Puckett and Walters were the victims of discriminatory action by the Dodge Main Management in that they did not conduct themselves any differently than any other team of operators on the seat cushion job at any time during the entire controversy over production standards. They performed five jobs per hour consistently and did no more or no less than the other eight teams. The foreman stopped the line on July 11, 1951, and selected these two employees solely on the basis of chance and only because they were stationed in the first location on the line at the time the line was stopped. It could just as easily have been any one of the other eight teams.

After that time, the foreman concentrated his entire efforts to get more production on these two employees, ignoring all of the other operators throughout the entire controversy. Even though Puckett and Walters were given written tickets, disciplined on two occasions, and eventually discharged, the other operators were given nothing more than verbal instructions to do more production.

The Union feels that the discharge of these two employees is too severe and very discriminatory because of the fact that they conducted themselves in no different manner than the other operators on the line and should not have been dealt with any differently.

Puckett's and Walters' records with the Company are very good. Neither employee has been in any kind of trouble prior to this dispute. Neither has ever been disciplined or ticketed before.

Without prejudice to its position that these two employees be reinstated with full back pay and seniority, the Union requests that in the event it is determined that grounds for disciplinary action did exist the Chairman should modify the penalty because of the very good past records of these two employees and because of the discriminatory method used by the Management in selecting them for discipline.

The Union said: the Company was, and for a considerable time had been, carrying on an overall effort to increase production in the plant; this was particularly so with regard to the Trim Shop, and especially as to the Zig-Zag seat cushion assembly; during the long period of the entire controversy in the Trim Shop there were several work stoppages; in the past in similar situations the parties jointly worked out production problems; however, here the Company took an arbitrary position, saying it would settle for nothing less than the time study figures; since the model started production on it had been five per team per hour and the increase to nine jobs would have been almost a one hundred percent increase, which was a big jump; it is difficult to time study most Trim Shop operations; this is particularly true of the considered work; no two jobs are exactly the same; the inherent nature of the material used, and its lack of uniformity causes difficulties; it was for this reason that the parties previously had jointly worked out the requirements of a normal day's work, regardless of time study; the Company's position, particularly in this case, created a general fear that it was attempting an overall speed up, and a belief that if the employees made the increased production requirements, production requirements would be further increased generally; the employees felt that if the Company was successful in obtaining production equal to that set by time studies, it would institute a Company-wide campaign for greater production; as a result of the aforesaid, the entire plant was in a turmoil over the Company's efforts to speed up; the impression might be gotten from the Company's statements that Puckett and Walters had jobs different from those of the other teams on the Zig-Zag seat cushion assembly line; as a matter of fact, their jobs were exactly the same as those of other teams; the first team starting each day was called the lead-off team; the groups rotated, each team, unless absent, being the lead-off team on the day their turn came up; if a team was absent when it would have been the lead-off team, the next team took over; since there were nine teams in regular operation, with no absences, a team would be the lead-off team every ninth working day; as a result, it is obvious that Puckett and Walters could not have been the lead-off team on each occasion when the Company described them as such in some of its statements; as a matter of fact, Puckett and Walters absented themselves on July 13th because that was the day when they would have been the lead-off team and they were fearful that were they present the Company would single them out for not meeting the requested standards; the set up of lead-off men resulted by an arrangement of the employees themselves; as the lead-off team was the first to start, it could be the first to finish, thus permitting the men on it to have a little extra time at the end of the shift; this was the only reason for the arrangement of rotating teams; after the operation began there was no difference in the work of any of the teams; the lead-off team lost its identity as soon as one round had been completed; the "bucks" on the line were numbered and, as a result, each team could tell the one on which it was to work; if and when the line was speeded up, it became necessary for the men to finish up their work beyond the normal finishing point; it would be impossible for one team to work on any more jobs per day than any other team; any team could slow down all the other teams; in the instant situation no team could be pointed out as having any greater responsibility than any other team for the non-increase of production; when Puckett and Walters were disciplined on July 18th the other employees walked out; on July 19th they still were out; a mass meeting was held at Keworth Stadium at Hamtramck at 9:00 A.M.; several thousand were present; both of the Assistant Chrysler Directors of the Union spoke to the people, said their action constituted an unauthorized strike and, told them to go back to work; although certain employees urged the group to stay away the Assistant Chrysler Directors prevailed and a motion to return to work was passed; however, at the suggestion of an employee the motion was amended to provide that no employee should raise production; this was an indication of the tremendous pressure not to increase production placed, not only on the Trim Shop and on the Zig-Zag seat cushion line but even more particularly, on Puckett and Walters, whose disciplining had precipitated the walkout; on July 20th all the people went back to work; after Puckett and Walters were discharged on July 23rd the Trim Shop went out at noon on July 24th, necessitating the closing of the plant; during the morning of the 24th, prior to the walkout, production remained at five pieces per hour; on July 25th the employees came to work at 7:15 and again walked out at 8:15; during this period production on the Zig-Zag seat cushion assembly line remained at five; the employees stayed out July 26th and July 27th; another mass meeting was held on July 29th; this meeting was addressed by the Union's Chrysler Director and by the International Vice-President who urged the people to return to work; the employees returned to work on Monday, July 30th; production remained at five for a week or ten days thereafter; it then was increased to six; around the last of August it was increased to seven; it has remained at that figure since that time. . . .

The Statement on Behalf of Chrysler Corporation follows:

On July 23, 1951, J. Puckett 99–2132 and C. H. Walters 99–3112 were discharged for refusing to meet production standards, as well as acting in an insubordinate manner toward their foreman on several occasions.

Puckett and Walters formed one of several teams working on the Zig-Zag seat cushion assembly in the Trim Department at the Dodge Main Plant. Puckett and Walters were not meeting production standards, but rather were engaged in a restriction of production. They limited their production to five (5) jobs per hour or less, whereas at the beginning of the 1951 model they were turning out six (6) jobs per hour under identical conditions. At the present time the trimmers are producing at the rate of seven (7) jobs per hour per team. The Time Study figure of 8.9 jobs per hour per team has been disputed by the Union for some time. The employees in this group and the Union representatives have never resorted to the orderly procedure as outlined in Section 2 of Article IV, 'Rates of Production' in the event of such a dispute, but rather have committed coercive acts, prohibited by Article I, Section 6 of the Corporation-Union Agreement.

On July 11, 1951, an attempt was made to obtain a fair days' production on this operation. The supervisor of the Zig-Zag Trim Group stopped the conveyor line at 2:15 P.M. in order to inform all the trimmers that the rate of production expected on this job was eight (8) per hour per team.

Puckett and Walters were the first team to start off at this rate. However, as the job progressed, they made no effort to obtain a higher rate of production than their previous rate of five (5) per hour per team. As a result of their failure to finish their job at the proper place, where the finished cushion is taken off the conveyor, they continued to work on the cushion, thereby disrupting other operations. This necessitated stopping the conveyor line on several occasions during the first hour. Furthermore, it is clear that Puckett and Walters were deliberately stalling. This is evident from the fact that they took eight (8) minutes to complete the first two cushions but on the third, fourth and fifth cushions they took 11, 12 and 16 minutes respectively. For their conduct, they were placed on written notice, at approximately 3:15 p.m., that unless they met the required production they would be disciplined.

The following day, July 12, 1951, supervision again attempted to gain the cooperative effort of the employees in this group in raising production from five (5) to eight (8) jobs per hour. Instead of cooperating, however, Puckett and Walters, along with others in the group, had to be warned by the foreman that they were using an excessive amount of hog rings on the cushions (75% to 100% more than needed). Again the warnings went unheeded, and at 3:10 p.m., Walters and Puckett were sent home for the remainder of the day because of their failure to follow instructions (insubordination) and obtain the required production. As soon as they were disciplined, the remaining employees walked off their jobs, in violation of Article I, Section 6 of the contract.

No further attempt was made by management to obtain a fair days' work until the following Wednesday, July 18, 1951, at which time the group was again requested by their foreman to meet the required production of eight (8) cushions per team per hour. Soon afterwards, the lead-off team consisting of Puckett and Walters was again observed by their foreman stalling on their job, performing their tasks in such a manner that they would still be working on their cushion after it had passed the finish line. This action caused other employees such as stuffers, conveyor loaders, and assemblers to work out of position and again required stopping the line several times. Finally, at 1:35 p.m. when it was apparent that Puckett and Walters would in no way cooperate but instead intended to counteract every attempt to increase production to a reasonable rate, they were again disciplined. They were sent home for the remainder of that day, and the following day as well. As Walters and Puckett were leaving the department, the balance of the employees stopped work and followed them out, which again was in violation of the contract. All were put on written notice of this fact.

On Friday, July 20, 1951, after the lunch period all of the trimmers were again warned that management expected them to meet the required production. After an hour's work all of the teams except Puckett and Walters had stepped up their rates of production to 6 jobs per hour. Puckett and Walters however continued their slowdown (approximately

4½ cushions per hour which was a lower rate of production than their rate for 7–11–51) to such an extent that they rode the conveyor beyond the location where their cushion should have been completed thus forcing other operations out of their normal work locations. Their subsequent actions necessitated stopping the line on three different occasions in order to get the assemblers back into normal working positions.

Throughout all of these interruptions in production, Puckett and Walters were warned that if they continued in their slowdown tactics, they might be discharged.

Shortly after 3:20 P.M., the lead-off team started on their twentieth cushion (for the afternoon) which was one (1) in excess of their usual production. Puckett at this time left his job and was observed as well as heard by the foreman advising the lead-off team to slow down since management would want more production next week if they were to give any additional jobs this week. Immediately thereafter this team began stalling. The foreman, seeing this, instructed the lead-off team to keep working. At this point Walters spoke up and said, "Why in hell don't you get off our backs? You've been riding us all day." The foreman replied that he was speaking to the lead team to which Walters retorted, "It concerns me as well as them."

The following Monday, July 23, 1951, Puckett and Walters continued their restrictive measures after they had been warned of the consequences of their insubordinate acts, for which they were properly discharged.

The following day all of the employees in the Trim Department walked off their jobs which stopped all assembly operations. Similar work stoppages occurred on succeeding days up to July 30, 1951, resulting at Dodge Main alone in a loss of 2,256 cars and 430,400 man hours.

Both J. Puckett and C. Walters were given many opportunities to increase their production up to the standard which they failed to do but rather retrogressed from approximately 5 on July 11, to 4½ on July 20, 1951, while some of their co-workers in spite of the restrictive efforts expended were able to increase their production from 5 to 6 cushions per hour.

Puckett and Walters not only failed to increase their production but also by their words and deeds, which in themselves were insubordinate, discouraged other employees from doing so. Both employees were properly warned as required by the Impartial Chairman in Appeal Board Case No. 528. A number of warnings and disciplinary action short of discharge resulted only in a more non-cooperative and belligerent attitude, on the part of Puckett and Walters, the final penalty of discharge was imposed as a last resort.

The Union representatives at the Appeal Board step have agreed that there were ample and justifiable grounds for discipline, but that the way the discipline was executed against only two individuals in the group was of a discriminatory nature and therefore should be rescinded.

In answer to this argument, it should be clear from the above facts that these two employees were more involved than the others in the group in that they were responsible, by their stalling actions on the line, for influencing and deterring to a great extent their fellow employees from increasing production as requested. Furthermore, since Puckett and Walters were the only two disciplined in the group, which discipline the Union did not contest as being improper or discriminatory, it is not now proper for the Union to complain of the latest discipline assessed for the same offense.

Because of their loafing, stalling, slowdown, and insubordinate actions Puckett and Walters were properly discharged after previous warnings and discipline.

The grievance should be dismissed.

In support of this Statement the Company introduced a statement by William Stephens, foreman, Department No. 99, which statement was based on notes taken by him at the time the events referred to occurred. Stephens handles two merry-go-rounds. On the occasions under consideration he was the only foreman present. His statement follows:

Ever since February 19, 1951 when employees in my group cut back their production from 6 to 5 jobs per hour, I have continually requested them for more production. They responded in every case by increasing their time for each cushion from the regular 5–7 minutes to 12 minutes per job, which amounted to a slowdown.

On July 11, 1951 at 2:15 P.M. I stopped the zig-zag conveyor line and informed all the trim operators that the required rate of production that management expected them to perform was 8 jobs per hour per team. I then set the line speed for this amount. Puckett and Walters were the first team to start off and as they approached the finish line I noticed that they had not completed their job. They continued working on their cushion until it interfered with employees on other operations such as stuffers, conveyor unloaders, cover stretchers, and assemblers, at which time I stopped the line.

I then warned them about working out of position and started the line up again. As time went on they continued to stall and take more time for each job,

> 1st job in 8 minutes
> 2nd job in 8 minutes
> 3rd job in 11 minutes
> 4th job in 12 minutes
> 5th job in 16 minutes.

The above time for each job was in excess of what other trimmers took to complete their jobs. I had to stop the line several times. At 3:15 P.M. I placed Walters and Puckett on written notice that they had failed to get the required production and warned them that they would be disciplined. . . .

On July 18, 1951 I had asked the group to increase production at 1:15 P.M. they made no effort to do more than 5 jobs per hour. The group was warned and Puckett and Walters were again sent home for 1½ days since they were riding the line down further than the other employees. Puckett and Walters were also warned that a continuance of this action would result in more severe discipline to the possible extent of discharge.

On July 20, 1951 at 12:00 noon I again requested the group to increase their rate to 8 jobs. As I was instructing the employees as to the rate of production, J. Puckett spoke up and said "If they told you to jump out the window, you'd do it." I then told the men to go back to work and increase their production. All of the teams had 6 jobs out at 1:00 P.M. except the team of Puckett and Walters which had after an hour's work, less than 5 jobs done. About this time I saw J. Puckett go over to the lead-off team and heard him tell them (J. Bonk and R. Colonna) that "If we give them a half job today they will want more tomorrow." After this remark the lead-off team started stalling. I then went over to them and told them to continue working until 3:45 (quitting time). C. Walters then spoke up and said "Why in Hell don't you get off our backs? You've been riding us all day."

I told him that I was speaking to J. Bonk and R. Colonna, not to him, to which he replied "It concerns me as well as them."

When Puckett and Walters on the following Monday, July 23, continued stalling production, they were discharged. Finally after refusing to leave my office until they had discussed their discharge with both the Chief Steward and Committeeman, they proceeded to the Superintendent's Office where they picked up their discharge slip. . . .

The Company said that efforts to increase production must be made some place, and that at the time of this situation the Company was first trying to increase production on the first shift rather than attempting an overall increase at one time; as a result, it had not then attempted to obtain greater production on the second shift. The Union commented that this supported its contention that the considered employees were being singled out. . . .

Findings

The Chairman recognizes the impropriety of Puckett's and Walters' acts and the propriety of the receipt of substantial discipline by them. At the same time, he believes that, viewed in the light of the surrounding circumstances, the discipline given was disproportionately great.

The problem of more production had been existent at the plant for a considerable time. Obviously the Company believed increased production should be forthcoming, while a considerable segment of the Union membership generally opposed a number of the particular increases which the Company felt to be proper. At the time of the incidents here under consideration, this was particularly so in the Trim Shop, and especially on the Zig-Zag seat cushion line. That production on the Zig-Zag seat cushion line could have been increased without detriment or hardship to the employees on that line is indicated by the present production on the operation. Whether the exact method used by the Company's representative in his attempt to increase production, was one most likely to accomplish the desired result, may be open

combination of skill, care, interest, and effort is something that should be going up all the time in the skill and care and interest, and should perhaps be going down as to physical effort, as we know how to take the work out of the work.

MR. BURKE: I understand. . . .

MR. BOULWARE: What we are saying here is that this is the way we can provide—I do not know, but maybe a 4-day week.

MR. BURKE: I understand that the theory of mass production is that the idea is to take the load off the man's back as much as possible.

Now, in writing a law, you would advocate, then, that that law provide that the setting of production standards shall not be subject to the process of collective bargaining?

MR. BOULWARE: Oh, no, indeed. What we are after here is this: You have a full day's work, by reasonable modern standards. That is the way we describe it, a full day's work content. And what we are after here is that you cannot come in and by force set up the situation where a fellow is going to do a half day's work just because of some power involved, when it is unfair, palpably unfair, to other people. There are plenty of irregularities in a day's work. You cannot regulate the machines that well.

MR. BURKE: But production standards can properly be subject to the processes of collective bargaining.

MR. BOULWARE: That is right.

WHAT IS FEATHERBEDDING?

Testimony of George W. Armstrong, Jr., Chairman, Industrial Relations Committee, National Association of Manufacturers, in Taft-Hartley Act Revisions, hearings before the Senate Committee on Labor and Public Welfare, 83d Cong., 1st Sess., 1953, part 1, pp. 257–258

MR. ARMSTRONG: It is recommended that the present featherbedding provision be strengthened by providing that it is an unfair labor practice to cause or attempt to cause an employer to pay for the hiring of employees who in his judgment are not required or for the performance of services which in his judgment need not be performed.

SENATOR TAFT: Mr. Armstrong, this matter, of course, was up particularly in the conference committee on the Taft-Hartley law in 1947. The difficulty we had was in determining who was going to determine whether this demand was a reasonable demand or not. We hesitated to give the Board power to go into every industry and decide how many men were needed and how many men were not needed. I see you put it entirely in the employer's judgment. That raises the question of the full-crew law. The union said, "To run a train safely we require five men." The employer said, "I want only four."

Are you going to be absolutely bound by the employer's decision on the question? You have the case of mine inspectors where the union says, "To be safe in this mine we insist on two inspectors." The employer said, "One is enough."

Do you propose that the union cannot demand two men under those cases, when the subject of making the demand or insisting upon it as a condition of the contract becomes an unfair labor practice? Do you think we should go that far?

MR. ARMSTRONG: I think the employer is about the only one who can judge as to the work to be performed and the people required to do that work.

SENATOR TAFT: In effect, what you say is that the union cannot say to the employer, "We want two mine inspectors," because if they do they are subjecting themselves to an unfair labor practice judgment.

That seems to be rather a radical position for us to take. If you do not do that, then you have to say somebody will determine, the Board presumably, whether it is a reasonable demand or not. Then you put the Board into the actual operation of a thousand industries about which they know very little and are hardly competent to decide.

MR. ARMSTRONG: I can see in cases where safety is involved, that there is considerable room for someone else aside from the employer to have a voice in that. But in these instances, there is no hazard here, no hazard question at all.

SENATOR TAFT: I mean the man might say, "We can't play decent music with 3 men, we have to have 5 in this theater. And we insist in order to show our proper professional capacity we must have 5 men."

Do you rule that out as an unfair labor practice if they demand 5 instead of 3 in the movie orchestras? I want to call your attention to the difficulties that we are up against as a method of trying to work up practical solutions to problems even if we agree on the principle.

LEAVE FEATHERBEDDING TO COLLECTIVE BARGAINING

Statement of Arthur J. Goldberg, General Counsel, Congress of Industrial Organizations, in Current Antitrust Problems, hearings before the House Antitrust Subcommittee, 84th Cong., 1st Sess., 1955, part 3, pp. 2149–2150

Union practices which employers denounce as featherbedding are the counterpart of employer practices which unions denounce as the "stretchout." If featherbedding may be defined as union insistence on pay for work that is not done, the stretchout may be defined as employer insistence that workers perform more work without corresponding additional pay.

If it is bad for a union to ask for pay for work which is not being done, it must be, from a balanced view, equally bad for an employer to require the union to agree to extra work without the employer paying for it. But we have not heard of anybody's recommending legislation which would make it an unfair labor practice for employers to require unions to agree to a stretchout provision.

Nor do we recommend such legislation. The issues involved in featherbedding and the stretchout are better left to collective bargaining.

Modern industry can have devastating consequences on the worker's livelihood and health unless the worker, through his union, makes some attempt to abate the impact so that the worker alone is not compelled to suffer the full consequences of the management drive for profit making. In the course of collective bargaining, therefore, management and labor have evolved working rules, which Professor Slichter, of Harvard, has put under the heading of industrial jurisprudence, to determine sensible ways of meeting the many problems of finding a mutually agreeable middle ground between workers being worked too hard and workers lying down on the job.

This is not to say that the stretchout or featherbedding is not in some situations carried to unsound extremes, but it is extremely doubtful whether a legislative rule can be devised which will automatically catch within its provisions only the unsound and leave undisturbed the sound practices.

In fact, the two legislative attempts to date to deal with featherbedding have both come to nothing. The first of these was the Lea Act, aimed at the American Federation of Musicians, while the second is the present section 8 (*b*) (6) of the Taft-Hartley Act. No charge of a violation of either act has ever been sustained by the courts. As a matter of fact, very few featherbedding charges have even been filed with the National Labor Relations Board, which is clear evidence that the problem has been much exaggerated.

In the summer of 1950 eighteen divinity students worked as laborers in Pittsburgh steel mills and factories while enrolled at the summer seminar of the Presbyterian Institute of Industrial Relations, of which Marshal Scott is dean. Students gathered to exchange and discuss experiences regularly over the three-month period.

WHAT MAKES A MAN WORK AND HOW HARD DO MEN WORK?

Excerpts from the Dean's Report on the results of this project

No subject was discussed more frequently from the evening of the first day on the job until Labor Day than that of efficiency on the job and the motivation to work. All the students appeared to go through the same cycles in their own experiences (possibly two of the men on one job did not follow the pattern closely).

On the first day or two of the job the going seemed rough. Quickly, however, the men got the impression that most men aren't working too hard and that there was plenty of opportunity for "goofing" on the job. At supper there was much joking about it. But as the summer wore on the grind got more and more wearisome and the men got more and more tired. There was little joking about goofing at work in the last month of the summer.

Toward the end of the summer one evening was spent in discussion of how men work and why. The experience of this group, recognizing its limitations (for instance, no man was on a mass production assembly line, no man had a skilled job), revealed several tendencies:

1. Not all idle time is loafing. Frequently the job of the man is to tend the machine and when his chore is done he must wait for the machine to act before he is needed again.

2. At some jobs the work pace is such that no man can keep it up for hours at a time and there must be rest periods on the job.

3. The supply of tools and its relation to work efficiency was one of the most surprising discoveries of the summer. In most of the mills and factories there was an inadequate supply of hand tools for laborers. In the steel mills it is common practice for one shift to hide the tools they have found so that the next two shifts can't find them. A lot of time is spent hunting tools. In one factory, which has an alert management, one student kept track of his time for a whole day. That day he spent more time hunting tools than in productive work. The tools needed could have been paid for by one man's pay check for one day.

4. Of much greater importance, however, in the mind of the students were two other factors. One is the attitude and the skill of the foreman. The foreman, it was found, needed to know his job but also must know how to handle men. In one plant there was a high level of work efficiency and the workers were happy. Yet the wage rate was lower than in most of the other plants. The reason seemed to lie with the management. The workers had a union and the management fully accepted it; the management had a foreman who was effective in dealing with men. If a worker had a rough job one day he was given an easier assignment another day. Thus men had a sense of being treated personally, and fairly. They had a sense of freedom from knowing that they could speak to the foreman or make suggestions and that they had the protection of the union, which would receive a fair hearing.

In other shops there were foremen who lacked the ability to plan work well and there were foremen who sought to boost their egos by taking every opportunity to deflate the men they supervised. In such shops it was sometimes almost a game for laborers to see how little they could do and get away with it.

The experience of the students of this project was that the foreman is the *most important* factor between good work and poor work—and his attitude toward persons is at least as important as his know-how about the productive process.

5. The other major factor is in some respects closely related. For many men—probably *most* men—the work motivation is not production of a product but is the desire to get the weekly pay check. If a man works only for a pay check then a minimum of effort and efficiency is sufficient. In many jobs there is little sense of importance to turning out a few more routine motions per hour or per day and opportunities for advancement by working harder are not very obvious to the worker. A lot of men feel and say "What's the use?" Again, the foreman, more than any other person, can give to the workers other satisfactions and other motives than the pay check—if he is skilled enough.

There was no evidence, within the experience of the group, that labor unions had curtailed the amount of work effort or work efficiency on the job. In the only shop where a union had been introduced recently it was reported that work efficiency had increased.

The group had very limited experience—too limited for drawing conclusions

—with economic incentives, such as bonuses, but all had the impression that management greatly over-rates economic incentives and that much greater benefits could come from more attention to better human relations—attitudes and feelings.

WHAT INDUSTRY EXPECTS FROM ORGANIZED LABOR

Excerpt from an address by Charles R. Sligh, Jr., President of the Board, National Association of Manufacturers, at the 60th Annual Congress of American Industry, New York City, December 9, 1955

. . . contract agreements which limit the amount of work which may be performed, or which require more people on the job than are necessary to perform the work, are destructive of labor's interest, as well as of management's. The cost of featherbedding must show up in the price of the product and cut down its market among consumers.

Limiting a brick layer to the number of bricks per shift that he could lay in half the time, or a tile setter to so many square feet of tile, only insures that less brickwork or tile will be used in architecture.

Gerald Strayer, a member of the Bricklayers' union of Toledo, developed a gadget to take the place of plumb lines. It enabled him to lay 1,000 bricks in the time it took other good bricklayers to lay just 800. His union officials told him to junk it. When he refused, he was fined $50. When he refused to pay the fine, he was suspended.

Management spends about $12,000 to provide plant and tools for each industrial worker. Limiting the use of these tools by slow-downs is an economic waste which can do no one any good.

Argumentation between union and management over the former's influence on industrial efficiency has most recently centered on the subject of "automation." The unions have been less enthusiastic about such technological developments than have managements because they have been concerned with the short-run impact on their members. Managements have tended to be more optimistic about the adjustive powers of the economy. Both are agreed, however, that the results will be beneficial in the long run.

AUTOMATION: PROMISE AND PROBLEMS

By Walter P. Reuther, from the American Flint, April, 1956

In the spread of automation and the prospective large-scale industrial use of atomic energy—and the possible practical utilization of solar energy, as well—we are faced with mighty forces whose impact on our economy can be vastly beneficial or vastly harmful, depending on whether we succeed or fail in achieving economic and social progress that will keep pace with changing technology.

We have been told so often that automation is going to bring on "the Second Industrial Revolution" that there is, perhaps, a danger we may dismiss the warning as a catch-phrase, and lose sight of the fact that, not only the technique, but the philosophy of automation is revolutionary, in the truest sense of the word.

Automation does not only produce changes in the methods of manufacturing, distribution, many clerical operations, and in the structure of business organization, but the impact of those changes on our economy and our whole society bids fair to prove quite as revolutionary as were those of the First Industrial Revolution.

The revolutionary change produced by automation is its tendency to displace the worker entirely from the direct operation of the machine, through the use of automatic control devices.

In other words, automation is a technique by which whole batteries of machines, in some cases, almost whole factories and offices, can be operated according to predetermined automatic controls. The raw material is automatically fed in, the machine automatically processes it, the product is automatically taken away, often to be fed automatically into still another machine that carries it automatically through a further process. In some cases, the machine is self-regulating—that is, it is set to turn out a product within certain tolerances as to size or other factors, and if those tolerances are exceeded, the machine itself detects the variation and automatically adjusts itself to correct it.

POTENTIAL BENEFITS

What is the attitude of the trade union movement to this new technology of automation?

First of all, we fully realize that the potential benefits of automation are great, if properly handled. If only a fraction of what technologists promise for the future is true, within a very few years automation can and should make possible a four-day work-week, longer vacation periods, opportunities for earlier retirement, as well as a vast increase in our material standards of living.

At the same time, automation can bring freedom from the monotonous drudgery of many jobs in which the worker today is no more than a servant of the machine. It can free workers from routine, repetitious tasks which the new machines can be taught to do, and can give to the workers who toil at those tasks the opportunity of developing higher skills.

But in looking ahead to the many benefits which automation can produce, we must not overlook or minimize the many problems which will inevitably arise in making the adjustment to the new technology—problems for individual workers and individual companies, problems for entire communities and regions, problems for the economy as a whole.

What should be done to help the worker who will be displaced from his job or the worker who will find that his highly specialized skill has been taken over by a machine? What about the businessman who lacks sufficient capital to automate his plant, yet has to face the competition of firms whose resources enable them to build whole new communities in some areas, while others are turned into ghost towns? How can we increase the market for goods and services sufficiently and quickly enough, to match greatly accelerated increases in productivity?

Obviously, there will be problems for the workers who are displaced from their jobs by automation. This is not merely a problem of finding a new job. By its very nature, automation will tend to eliminate unskilled and semi-skilled jobs, while the new jobs it creates will be at a much higher level of skill.

Another aspect of the same problem is that of the worker with a specialized skill who finds that his skill has been made valueless because a machine has taken over his job—such as the skilled machine operator displaced by a self-operating lathe or the bookkeeper whose job is taken over by an electronic "brain."

If automation is going to displace any substantial number of workers in either of these two ways, we will need a carefully organized retraining program to give them the opportunity of acquiring the skills they will need. Such a program must take into account the needs of the workers, the fact that most of them will be mature men and women to whom the learning of new skills may not come easily, and that they have to live and support their families while they are acquiring these skills. The program will require not merely training facilities and expert vocational guidance; it will have to include provision for training allowances to replace lost wages during the training period.

An alternative solution will have to be found in the case of older workers, not old enough for normal retirement, but too old to learn new skills or to adjust to the demands of the new technology. In some of our collective bargaining agreements, we have already laid the foundations for a system of early retirement which could help to meet such situations.

But in the very nature of most private pension plans, the problem cannot be solved through collective bargaining alone. Industrial pension plans are based on the assumption that the worker, when he retires, will also be eligible for social security benefits. Much as we have improved the level of private pensions in recent years, a worker who is forced to retire before the age of 65 would find it impossible to maintain a decent standard of living on his industrial pension alone. There is thus the need for earlier social security payments to workers who are forced into retirement before the age of 65 because technological changes have taken their jobs from them and their age makes it impossible for them to find other work.

The growth of automated factories can create problems of dislocation not only for individual workers but for the whole communities. It is often cheaper to build a new plant from the ground up, so that the whole design of the buildings can be related to the industrial process, than to attempt to remodel an existing plant.

In addition, corporations frequently seem to prefer to employ on automated processes workers who have had no experience with older methods. Thus, an employer whose only concern is his own profit, may decide that it is to his advantage to build a new plant in a new location, perhaps hundreds of miles away, without any consideration for the old community.

Even today, there are scores of distressed communities in our nation, where hundreds of thousands of workers have been left stranded by shutdown plants, industry migration, closed coal mines and curtailed operations of railroad repair shops. The impact of automation will possibly create additional pockets of substantial unemployment, even if high employment levels are maintained nationally.

Government assistance is required to aid in solving the pressing problems of such communities at present; government assistance has not yet been forthcoming, despite campaign promises made in the fall of 1952. Additional government aid will be needed in the future, as the new technology becomes widespread.

If the result of automation is that a large number of workers in a plant have to learn new skills, it is just as reasonable to expect the employer to pay the cost of retraining, including the payment of wages during the retraining period, as it is that he should pay the cost of building the new plant or installing the new equipment. When a plant is moved to a new locality, the employer has a responsibility not merely to retrain those workers who wish to move with the plant, but also to bear at least part of their cost of moving and new housing.

With the spread of automation, there will be a growing need for specialized semi-professional technicians, as well as for professional engineers and skilled workers. The education system of the nation should be preparing now to meet these requirements.

ADJUSTMENT PERIOD

From the viewpoint of the national economy, the greatest problem posed by automation is the threat of violent fluctuations in employment and production during the period of adjustment to the new technology. With the widespread introduction of automation speeding up the potential output of goods and services, there is the possibility that markets may not grow fast enough to sustain high employment levels. . . .

One of the fruits of automation which we should welcome is the opportunity it gives us to meet the present and growing social deficits in health, housing, schools, highways, natural resources, and other public services. Through increased productivity, our economy can meet the cost of these long-delayed measures without strain—and their achievement will help, by creating new jobs, to ease any necessary adjustments in employment.

It is within our power to see to it that these economic and social changes take place in an orderly and evolutionary manner—towards improved standards of living and social welfare, and extension of leisure and new horizons of individual opportunities for educational and cultural achievements. Such evolutionary changes in the coming decade will require forethought, planning and guidance. . . .

If we accept the challenge of the new technology, if we use foresight and act wisely and vigorously, we can help to usher in an age of abundance and freedom, the like of which the world has never known.

ATTITUDES TOWARDS AUTOMATION

Excerpts from an address by Malcolm P. Ferguson, President, Bendix Aviation Corporation, at the 3d International Conference of Manufacturers, New York City, November 29, 1956

"Wholehearted acceptance" of automation is most common among representatives of management. Many go so far as to say it is absolutely *essential* to attainment of national goals.

Ralph J. Cordiner, president of General Electric, testified at hearings held by the American Congress to explore automation and technological changes that the United States will require an estimated 40 per cent more goods and services by 1965 though it will have only 14 per cent more people in the labor force. Industry must be encouraged, he said, to invest in more productive machinery and methods. Faster progress in the newer field of automation seems to us to be the only available solution to this problem, Mr. Cordiner said, particularly in situations where we have exhausted the known economic possibilities in the more familiar field of simple mechanization.

George Meany, president of the AFL-CIO, recently expressed an attitude very close to "whole hearted acceptance" of automation. He was quoted as saying, in part, that "automation, coupled with atomic power, will change the lives of all of us" and "labor sees no reason to fear the time when factories will run virtually on an automatic basis, with machines operating machines." But he went on to say that there will still be plenty of work to be done by people and, "if it becomes possible to put into effect a shorter work week to *maintain full employment,* let us promptly accept this opportunity to lighten the burdens of the American people."

The attitude of "acceptance with reservations" is more common among labor leaders. They agree that automation is a good development, but some of them insist that planned intervention—either through government or through collective bargaining—is necessary to protect people against the alleged "bad side effects" of automation.

There is real danger that these fears about objectionable corollary effects may seriously slow down automation by imposing an additional cost upon production. If such burdens offset the savings from increased efficiency, the incentive for technological improvements may be impaired or destroyed. . . .

It is elementary that long-run improvements in national economic welfare can have no other basis than increases in productivity. During the two centuries since the beginning of the industrial revolution, the level of living in the Western World has been raised tremendously. The chief impact of automation will be to permit the continuation of this historical improvement of human welfare.

In discussing the impact of automation on employment, a distinction must be made between labor displacement through technological change and technological unemployment. To say that automation will cause labor displacement is by no means equivalent to saying that it will bring about unemployment.

If you were to go along with the statements of some labor spokesmen that automation holds out the fear of dislocation, distress, unemployment and misery, you would have to say that technological progress, in and of itself, destroys jobs and does not create new ones. This leaves one wondering how the United States could have advanced so far technologically without a continuous increase in unemployment and without the welfare measures certain American labor leaders advocate for the future.

Automation, actually, will create new jobs as well as new and higher skills. The industry itself must produce automation devices, controls and equipment of all kinds of which computers themselves will be a substantial product. There will be engineering, development, sales, servicing and maintenance of product and all of the other requirements of this new industry involving machines, mechanical and electrical devices, hydraulics and electronics.

In discussing attitudes toward automation—or what you might describe as the "politics" of the matter—here are some interesting points:

The record of economic growth in the United States makes it seem almost absurd to fear unemployment as a result of improved technology. Let's have a look at it: Since 1870 productivity in the American economy has quadrupled. In other words we are, on the average, able to do any given task with one-fourth as much labor as it took in 1870. Yet the number of persons employed by private business has increased from about 12 million in 1870 to about 60 million at present. Productivity has more than doubled since 1900, yet the rate of unemployment has actually declined slightly since then—it was 5.1 per cent of the civilian labor force in 1900, 4 per cent in 1955, and still lower in 1956. Our economy provides 67 million jobs, many of which would not exist if it were not for our advanced economy.

Thus the real problem involved in the relationship of automation to unemployment is the problem of labor displacement and the need for people to adapt themselves to new jobs and opportunities rather than the problem of mass unemployment.

People will shift from lines of work in which their services are no longer needed to other, often better jobs. There is no virtue in keeping more people at work making automobiles than are actually needed. To do so would be to cheat society of the services these people would be performing and to cheat the people themselves of new opportunities.

The great increases in agricultural productivity through mechanization would not have enriched our lives and the lives of our farmers if we had insisted on keeping *three-quarters of our population* on farms, as was the case in our grandfathers' time. It is by freeing labor for other tasks that agricultural progress has made one of its chief contributions to the rising standard of living for all of us.

Cases can be cited of whole industries that increased their total employment after the introduction of automation. The use of dial equipment by the telephone industry, beginning about 1920, is one such instance. Since 1920 the operating telephone companies have more than doubled their employment. The use of continuous-flow methods in the oil refining industry also began about 1920 and this industry's employment has about doubled, too. The reason for this outcome is the development of more and cheaper methods of producing telephone service and motor fuels, resulting in a greater expansion of their use.

Realistic estimates of the rate of labor displacement that may be anticipated from automation indicate that it will be very minor indeed compared to the rate of labor displacement that is going on all the time, from other causes. The U. S. labor force is in a continuous state of flux right now with about 6 million people entering it or leaving it each month.

It seems reasonable to hope that automation will result in jobs becoming more interesting, less tiring, and, in general, more personal. Muscular labor already has been largely eliminated by machine production, but some monotonous, repetitive jobs have been created. Automation will tend to alter this type of job.

Automation will probably offer opportunities for eliminating jobs which create special risks to health and safety. In some fields, it can reduce the likelihood of individuals coming into contact with dangerous or toxic substances. It may contribute to the productive power of older workers and open many opportunities where age handicaps are no longer important. Fatigue can be reduced because automation will tend to eliminate jobs where the operator is paced by the machine.

Management will, of course, play a big role in determining progress toward automation. But it will not only initiate automation. It will be in the midst of all the changes which the new technology will bring and *will have to adapt itself* to them. *We will need more management* . . . tighter control and coordination of every detail of the production process . . . and probably more individuals at every level making more decisions of a management type than they had previously.

AUTOMATION—FRIEND OR FOE?

Excerpts from the General Electric Employee Relations News Letter of April 8, 1955

WHY DOES—AND MUST—BUSINESS AUTOMATE AS FAST AS POSSIBLE?

The urge for survival, growth, strength, profit and usefulness—in the face of temperate and intemperate competition—is what spurs business to automate as fast as feasible. Technological advance gives the customer lower costs, higher quality, greater quantity and broader variety of products and services. The business which fails to keep in the front row of pioneers of such advances soon finds it has lost its customers and jobs to the one that does stay up front.

A recent article in the Lynn IUE-CIO newspaper scolded us for losing a big order. The union paper claimed we had not put in as much automatic labor-saving equipment as the midwestern competitor who got the business. If the editor's claim had been correct, his position would have been extremely well taken.

For the question is not whether a given *industry* or all industry will automate as far and as fast as feasible. The only question for its employees—as well as for all others concerned—is whether a given *company* will be among the leaders of the parade, or will try to follow, or will even earlier fall by the wayside.

WHAT MAY PEOPLE BE PERSUADED TO FEAR?

There has always been resistance to change, fear of the unknown. New machines have always been distrusted—until the favorable facts at last become widely known.

An 1830 propaganda cartoon on our office wall shows all the dire disasters to be expected from the introduction of steam power in factories. It even went so far as to recommend that mothers bear no more children since steam would take away any possibility of jobs for them.

At the turn of the century, the motor car was questioned by most sober people—and seemingly feared or hated by almost as many on both economic and moral grounds. The automobile now gives us the world's largest industry—and hundreds of times the jobs which the harness, coach, and buggy-whip factories supplied. We have even forgotten how we distrusted that great labor and accident saver, the self-starter, when it was introduced.

It would have been permissible for anyone to expect that the dial telephone was going to eliminate operators and cut telephone employment. Just the opposite has happened, of course, because the dial savings made it possible to increase the value and attractiveness of the service and to bring on the great expansion in the installation and use of phones that has occurred—so that in just the last ten years the number of telephone operators in this country has increased by 79 per cent.

THE SHORT-TERM FALSE ALARM

This is not to say that there *might* not occasionally be a relatively few *short-term* displacements here and there from the automation process itself—even though the gloomiest detractors of automation are finding it hard to uncover any really convincing evidence of such displacements.

The immediate result sought from the automation process is a reduction in relative cost and a resulting more attractive competitive offering to customers. The employer is likely to get more business as a result of the more attractive offering on the item automated—and hence retain or increase employment even though there are fewer employees per *new unit of output*.

On the other hand, his customers may not want more of this particular item but will apply their new savings to additional purchases of other kinds of goods from other makers. Then in the absence of sufficient natural attrition of the work force employed on that item, there may be temporary layoffs by this particular employer unless he has a large and varied local operation in which there are other openings as a result of the turnover or expansion in the rest of his lines there.

But, in any event, the employer must automate to stay alive and to keep all or the bulk of his jobs alive—and he can only automate if he gets his costs down appropriately. If he tries to keep on the payroll people he does not need, his costs are too likely to prevent him from meeting competition and from supplying *any* jobs at all. So it is imperative to the rest of his employees—as well as to him and all others concerned—that he remove from his payroll any substantial surplus of employees not needed.

Fortunately, there are two alternatives for any such few that might be temporarily displaced.

The first is that—as history shows—any such displacements can normally expect to be quickly absorbed in the new jobs created as the new savings go into added purchases. Incidentally, job opportunities have grown fastest in industries like ours where technological progress has gone forward the fastest.

Second—if the times are such that some general unemployment interferes temporarily with this reemployment—the employer has provided out of his funds alone an unemployment compensation which is set at the proportion of the employee pay that is judged appropriate by the citizens in each state through their legislatures there. For those employees at the lower end of the earning scale—these being the ones most likely to experience the few displacements that may occur—the benefits tend to go up to around 65 per cent of their normal take-home pay and to last as long as a half year.

The point is that there is no royal road to technological progress and, if we want to continue to see our level of living go up, some risks by *all* are inescapable. Since it is no longer a question of whether industry in general will automate, but only whether a *given company* will be a leader or fall behind, anybody who is temporarily displaced by improvements in that company would lose his job anyhow—along with all the other employees in that company losing their jobs—if it should fall back in the parade.

DESPITE CHAMBER OF COMMERCE COMMERCIALS, LABOR DOES NOT OPPOSE AUTOMATION

From the Oil, Chemical and Atomic Union News, April 4, 1955

Some leaders in American business and industry are now hard at work building up the idea that the American worker is afraid of progress.

Specifically, the charge is that labor is opposed to the introduction of automation in the fear that it will produce mass unemployment.

On the contrary, all the evidence available indicates that organized labor is NOT opposed to automation as such but wants to make sure that its impact on the economy is cushioned and that the worker will get his share of its benefits.

In addition, there are strong signs that the "myth" of labor opposition to automation actually will be used to fight against such labor demands as the guaranteed annual wage and similar benefits.

Within recent weeks, "Washington Report," published by the U. S. Chamber of Commerce, has been devoting itself to what it calls "the attack on automatic machines" with organized labor as its obvious target.

Recently, it published an old 19th Century handbill calling upon the people of Philadelphia to keep the Camden and Amboy railroad out of the city. The appeal of the handbill, addressed to "artizans, mechanics, citizens," was based on the dangers of a railroad running through the city's streets, the ruin of trade and the annihilation of the prosperity and comfort of Philadelphia.

"Washington Report," published the handbill under the head, "*The Fearful Always Attempt To Halt Progress*," and declares that it is in the tradition of those who are afraid that automatic machines will create mass unemployment and may create a depression.

Later, "Washington Report" returned to the battle with an article headed "Attack on Machine Called 'Vicious Propaganda' by Ben Fairless."

"Washington Report" chimed in with its declaration that "the attack on automatic machines continues unabated."

Significantly, it then remarks, "general belief in such propaganda would hamper the development and the use of machines. For instance, a guaranteed wage to prevent technological unemployment could be a major roadblock to technical progress."

Now, in reality, what has been the attitude of today's labor leadership toward automation?

We have a number of examples showing clearly that American labor leadership is NOT fighting the introduction of automatic machinery, but that it does see grave cause for concern that automation will be introduced without the slightest regard for the workers displaced and without the slightest planning for the social and economic consequences that will follow.

Past experience has taught American labor leaders that the workingman is the chief one left to "pick up the pieces" when there are great technological changes made in the economy.

Thus they have been pounding away on the theme that while business and industry are holding out bright hopes for an increase in jobs as a result of automation, business and industry are saying little and doing less about jobs during the period of transition.

Writing in a current issue of the magazine *Fortune*, AFL Pres. George Meany declared flatly that "*the trade union movement does* NOT *oppose technological change.*" He added that "*the answer lies in cushioning the shocks that attend it.*"

CIO Pres. Walter P. Reuther appeared before the Joint Congressional Committee on the Economic Report to comment on President Eisenhower's recent Economic Report. Outlining the tremendous potential of the automatic factory, Reuther spoke of productivity increases in the days ahead "which may well be tremendous, making possible the creation of abundance in terms undreamed of before."

"These growth potentials," he said, "will make possible vast improvements in the living conditions of the American people. They can be a major asset in developing both national strength and power and stability of the free world."

But he declared, "from the Administration we have received no analysis of this potential, no guideposts for future economic growth, no discussion of the probable temporary dislocations arising from automation, no preparation of the Congress and of the people to meet the new technology and to use it for the benefit of the nation."

Thus organized labor has clearly stated that it is NOT fighting automation. Instead, it sees just as great a potential in automation for the future well-being of the nation as does industry.

But American labor has expressed determination that the dislocations inevitably caused by automation shall be cushioned and, further, that automation will serve not merely to increase profits, but to give workers a better life.

FOR DISCUSSION AND ANALYSIS

1. Can you see any reasons why one benefit of increasing productivity should not be a reduction in the amount of worker effort required on any operation?

2. Several of the employers' statements on automation emphasize the worker's fear of change. Yet it is well known that many people enjoy change—variety—for its own sake. What are the characteristics of change which at least some people might be expected to fear, and what are the characteristics of change which those same people might be expected to welcome? Are there any ways of reducing the less desired aspects of change and emphasizing the pleasing aspects, as means of lessening resistance to technological innovation?

3. Is resistance to technological change something characteristic of workers but not of management people? Are there any types of feather-bedding in which members of management engage? If so, why do these not receive the same publicity as worker actions?

4. What fundamental issue is raised in the exchanges between Mr. Boulware of General Electric and Representative Burke, and between Senator Taft and Mr. Armstrong of NAM, reproduced in this chapter? How do you think this issue can best be resolved?

5. How should the fruits of productivity increases ideally be shared?

17: Strikes

The one aspect of collective bargaining of which the public is more conscious than any other is probably strikes. In many minds the word "strike" would be freely associated with the word "union."

In the first item of this chapter, the Bureau of Labor Statistics reports on strikes for the year 1956—how many of them occurred, how many workers were involved, and how many man-days of employment were lost in consequence. Because interest generally centers on the major strikes, however, it has appended a compilation of all strikes involving 10,000 or more workers during the year.

REVIEW OF LABOR-MANAGEMENT DISPUTES, 1956

Bureau of Labor Statistics News Release, December 28, 1956

Work stoppages beginning in 1956 idled fewer workers than in any year since 1942 with the exception of 1954, according to preliminary estimates released today by the Labor Department's Bureau of Labor Statistics. The number of strikes beginning in 1956 and the total man-days of idleness resulting from all work stoppages in effect during the year also were below a majority of the post-war years. Almost half of all 1956 idleness was accounted for by the nationwide steel strike in July and the continuation of the Westinghouse stoppage that had begun in 1955.

An estimated 3,800 stoppages began in 1956 compared with 4,320 in 1955. These stoppages involved approximately 1,900,000 workers as against 2,650,-000 workers in 1955. Idleness resulting from all strikes in effect in 1956 was estimated at 33.0 million man-days; the corresponding total in 1955 was 28.2 million man-days.

Twelve stoppages, each directly idling at least 10,000 workers, began during the year. Most of these lasted less than a month but four continued for longer periods. In addition to the steel stoppage, which continued into early August, these strikes included the 112-day Republic Aviation strike on Long Island, the 98-day strike at U.S. Steel's Tennessee Coal and Iron Division in Alabama, and the 71-day construction strike in the New Orleans area.

Disputes over wages and related issues were a major cause of 9 of the year's 12 large strikes. The construction and the primary metals industries (steel and aluminum) each experienced 3 major stoppages. One stoppage of

740

10,000 or more was recorded in aircraft, meatpacking, glass container manufacturing, farm equipment, tire manufacturing, and longshoring.

See accompanying tables for detailed statistics:

Table 1. Work Stoppages, 1946–1956 [1]

Period	Stoppages beginning in year			Man-days idle during year (all stoppages)		
	Number	Workers involved		Number (thou- sands)	Percent of estimated working time	Per worker involved
		Number (thou- sands)	Percent of total employed			
1956 [2]........	3,800	1,900	4.3	33,000	0.3	17.4
1955..........	4,320	2,650	6.2	28,200	.3	10.7
1954..........	3,468	1,530	3.7	22,600	.2	14.7
1953..........	5,091	2,400	5.6	28,300	.3	11.8
1952	5,117	3,540	8.8	59,100	.6	16.7
1951..........	4,737	2,220	5.5	22,900	.2	10.3
1950..........	4,843	2,410	6.9	38,800	.4	16.1
1949..........	3,606	3,030	9.0	50,500	.6	16.7
1948..........	3,419	1,960	5.5	34,100	.4	17.4
1947..........	3,693	2,170	6.5	34,600	.4	15.9
1946..........	4,985	4,600	14.5	116,000	1.4	25.2

[1] All work stoppages known to the Bureau of Labor Statistics and its various co-operating agencies, involving six or more workers and lasting a full day or shift or longer, are included in this report. Figures on "workers involved" and "man-days idle" cover all workers made idle for as long as one shift in establishments directly involved in a stoppage. They do not measure the indirect or secondary effects on other establishments or industries whose employees are made idle as a result of material or service shortages.

[2] Preliminary estimates.

Since the public is generally not concerned with the several thousand small strikes which occur in any year, but may become irritated and inconvenienced by a few major strikes, it is the latter which governments— both state and Federal—have sought to control in some manner. The wave of strikes which broke over the nation following the ending of wage controls after World War II aroused public resentment from consumers who had for four war years been waiting to buy automobiles and refrigerators and houses which—at the moment when fulfillment seemed

Table 2. Work Stoppages Beginning in 1956 in Which 10,000 or More Workers Were Involved (Based on Preliminary Information)

Beginning date	Approximate duration (calendar days) [1]	Establishment(s) and location	Union(s) involved [2]	Approximate number of workers involved [2]
Feb. 20	112	Republic Aviation Corp., 4 plants—Long Island, N.Y. area	Int'l Ass'n of Machinists; Int'l Bro. of Electrical Workers; and Int'l Union of Operating Engineers	12,000
April 28	98	Tennessee Coal, Iron and Railroad Division, U.S. Steel Corp., Birmingham, Ala.	Bro. of Locomotive Firemen and Enginemen (Ind.) [3]	21,000
May 1	27	Construction industry, Northeastern Ohio (including Cleveland area)	Building Trades Unions	30,000
May 1	71	Construction industry, New Orleans area, Louisiana	Int'l Ass'n of Bridge, Structural and Ornamental Iron Workers	10,000
July 1	36 [4]	Steel industry, nationwide	United Steelworkers	500,000
July 7	12	Construction industry, San Francisco area, California	United Bro. of Carpenters and Joiners	13,000
August 1	25 [5]	Aluminum Company of America and Reynolds Metals Co., 13 States	United Steelworkers	27,000
Sept. 1	28 [6]	Members of Glass Container Manufacturers' Institute; National Association of Pressed and Blown Glassware; and some independent companies, 16 States	American Flint Glass Workers Union	47,000
Sept. 20	10	Swift and Company, 26 States	Amalgamated Meatcutters and United Packinghouse Workers	25,000

Beginning date	Approximate duration (calendar days) [1]	Establishment(s) and location	Union(s) involved [2]	Approximate number of workers involved[2]
ct. 2	3	Caterpillar Tractor Co., East Peoria, Ill.	United Automobile Workers	19,000
ov. 1	18	Firestone Tire and Rubber Co., 7 States: Calif., Ind., Iowa, Mass., Ohio, Pa., and Tenn.	United Rubber Workers	21,000
ov. 16	9	Shipping industry, Port of New York and other East and Gulf Coast ports	Int'l Longshoremen's Ass'n (Ind.)	60,000

[1] Includes nonwork days, such as Saturdays, Sundays, and established holidays.

[2] The unions listed are those directly involved in the dispute. In union rivalry or risdictional disputes all the unions involved are listed although one or more may t actually participate in the strike. The number of workers involved may include embers of other unions or nonunion workers idled by the dispute in the same tablishment.

"Workers involved" is the maximum number made idle for one shift or longer in ablishments directly involved in a stoppage. (In those instances in which idleness ctuates during the strike, the actual number of workers idle on varying dates used in computing the man-days of idleness.) This figure does not measure the irect or secondary effects on other establishments or industries whose employees made idle as a result of material or service shortages.

[3] Until July 1 plant workers were idled by dispute of the Firemen and Enginemen. that date plant workers, represented by the United Steelworkers, also struck upon e expiration of their contract.

[4] On July 27 the United Steelworkers and 12 major steel producers signed a mem- ndum of agreement incorporating the provisions of a 3-year contract. Workers gan returning to work as soon as individual contracts were signed, and by August ll of the major steel producers had signed new agreements.

[5] Aluminum Company of America reached agreement on August 9, and Reynolds etals Co. on August 25.

[6] Glass Container Manufacturers' Institute reached agreement on September 9, tional Association of Pressed and Blown Glassware on September 28.

*imminent—these work stoppages were now denying them. One conse-
quence of this widespread exasperation was the writing into the Taft-
Hartley Act of Title II, giving the government certain specific powers in
strike situations which threatened public health and safety. And in nine
states legislation was passed giving state governments powers of intervention in certain types of walkouts.*

*As the materials reproduced here will indicate, however, there has been
continuing disagreement over the effectiveness and desirability of strike-
control procedures. On the one hand, there are some—principally in the
business community—who are satisfied to leave the present provisions
untouched. There are numerous others, however, who regard the emergency-strike procedures as relatively ineffective and undesirable—some
because they do not go far enough and others because they go too far.*

THE TAFT-HARTLEY ACT ON NATIONAL EMERGENCY STRIKES

TITLE II—CONCILIATION OF LABOR DISPUTES IN INDUSTRIES AFFECTING COM-
MERCE; NATIONAL EMERGENCIES

Sec. 201. That it is the policy of the United States that—

(a) sound and stable industrial peace and the advancement of the general
welfare, health, and safety of the Nation and of the best interests of employers
and employees can most satisfactorily be secured by the settlement of issues
between employers and employees through the processes of conference and
collective bargaining between employers and the representatives of their
employees;

(b) the settlement of issues between employers and employees through
collective bargaining may be advanced by making available full and adequate
governmental facilities for conciliation, mediation, and voluntary arbitration
to aid and encourage employers and the representatives of their employees to
reach and maintain agreements concerning rates of pay, hours, and working
conditions, and to make all reasonable efforts to settle their differences by
mutual agreement reached through conferences and collective bargaining or
by such methods as may be provided for in any applicable agreement for the
settlement of disputes; and

(c) certain controversies which arise between parties to collective-bargaining agreements may be avoided or minimized by making available full and
adequate governmental facilities for furnishing assistance to employers and
the representatives of their employees in formulating for inclusion within such
agreements provision for adequate notice of any proposed changes in the
terms of such agreements, for the final adjustment of grievances or questions
regarding the application or interpretation of such agreements, and other
provisions designed to prevent. the subsequent arising of such controversies.

Sec. 202. (a) There is hereby created an independent agency to be known
as the Federal Mediation and Conciliation Service (herein referred to as the

"Service," except that for sixty days after the date of the enactment of this Act such term shall refer to the Conciliation Service of the Department of Labor). The Service shall be under the direction of a Federal Mediation and Conciliation Director (hereinafter referred to as the "Director"), who shall be appointed by the President by and with the advice and consent of the Senate. The Director shall receive compensation at the rate of $12,000 per annum. The Director shall not engage in any other business, vocation, or employment. . . .

(c) The principal office of the Service shall be in the District of Columbia, but the Director may establish regional offices convenient to localities in which labor controversies are likely to arise. The Director may by order, subject to revocation at any time, delegate any authority and discretion conferred upon him by this Act to any regional director, or other officer or employee of the Service. The Director may establish suitable procedures for cooperation with State and local mediation agencies. The Director shall make an annual report in writing to Congress at the end of the fiscal year. . . .

FUNCTIONS OF THE SERVICE

Sec. 203. (a) It shall be the duty of the Service, in order to prevent or minimize interruptions of the free flow of commerce growing out of labor disputes, to assist parties to labor disputes in industries affecting commerce to settle such disputes through conciliation and mediation.

(b) The Service may proffer its services in any labor dispute in any industry affecting commerce, either upon its own motion or upon the request of one or more of the parties to the dispute, whenever in its judgment such dispute threatens to cause a substantial interruption of commerce. The Director and the Service are directed to avoid attempting to mediate disputes which would have only a minor effect on interstate commerce if State or other conciliation services are available to the parties. Whenever the Service does proffer its services in any dispute, it shall be the duty of the Service promptly to put itself in communication with the parties and to use its best efforts, by mediation and conciliation, to bring them to agreement.

(c) If the Director is not able to bring the parties to agreement by conciliation within a reasonable time, he shall seek to induce the parties voluntarily to seek other means of settling the dispute without resort to strike, lock-out, or other coercion, including submission to the employees in the bargaining unit of the employer's last offer of settlement for approval or rejection in a secret ballot. The failure or refusal of either party to agree to any procedure suggested by the Director shall not be deemed a violation of any duty or obligation imposed by this Act.

(d) Final adjustment by a method agreed upon by the parties is hereby declared to be the desirable method for settlement of grievance disputes arising over the application or interpretation of an existing collective-bargaining agreement. The Service is directed to make its conciliation and mediation services available in the settlement of such grievance disputes only as a last resort and in exceptional cases.

Sec. 204. (a) In order to prevent or minimize interruptions of the free flow of commerce growing out of labor disputes, employers and employees and their representatives, in any industry affecting commerce, shall—

(1) exert every reasonable effort to make and maintain agreements concerning rates of pay, hours, and working conditions, including provision for adequate notice of any proposed change in the terms of such agreements;

(2) whenever a dispute arises over the terms or application of a collective-bargaining agreement and a conference is requested by a party or prospective party thereto, arrange promptly for such a conference to be held and endeavor in such conference to settle such dispute expeditiously; and

(3) in case such dispute is not settled by conference, participate fully and promptly in such meetings as may be undertaken by the Service under this Act for the purpose of aiding in a settlement of the dispute.

Sec. 205. (a) There is hereby created a National Labor-Management Panel which shall be composed of twelve members appointed by the President, six of whom shall be selected from among persons outstanding in the field of management and six of whom shall be selected from among persons outstanding in the field of labor. Each member shall hold office for a term of three years, except that any member appointed to fill a vacancy occurring prior to the expiration of the term for which his predecessor was appointed shall be appointed for the remainder of such term, and the terms of office of the members first taking office shall expire, as designated by the President at the time of appointment, four at the end of the first year, four at the end of the second year, and four at the end of the third year after the date of appointment. Members of the panel, when serving on business of the panel, shall be paid compensation at the rate of $25 per day, and shall also be entitled to receive an allowance for actual and necessary travel and subsistence expenses while so serving away from their places of residence.

(b) It shall be the duty of the panel, at the request of the Director, to advise in the avoidance of industrial controversies and the manner in which mediation and voluntary adjustment shall be administered, particularly with reference to controversies affecting the general welfare of the country.

NATIONAL EMERGENCIES

Sec. 206. Whenever in the opinion of the President of the United States, a threatened or actual strike or lock-out affecting an entire industry or a substantial part thereof engaged in trade, commerce, transportation, transmission, or communication among the several States or with foreign nations, or engaged in the production of goods for commerce, will, if permitted to occur or to continue, imperil the national health or safety, he may appoint a board of inquiry to inquire into the issues involved in the dispute and to make a written report to him within such time as he shall prescribe. Such report shall include a statement of the facts with respect to the dispute, including each party's statement of its position but shall not contain any recommendations. The President shall file a copy of such report with the Service and shall make its contents available to the public.

Sec. 207. (a) A board of inquiry shall be composed of a chairman and such other members as the President shall determine, and shall have power to sit and act in any place within the United States and to conduct such hearings either in public or in private, as it may deem necessary or proper, to ascertain the facts with respect to the causes and circumstances of the dispute.

(b) Members of a board of inquiry shall receive compensation at the rate of $50 for each day actually spent by them in the work of the board, together with necessary travel and subsistence expenses.

(c) For the purpose of any hearing or inquiry conducted by any board appointed under this title, the provisions of sections 9 and 10 (relating to the attendance of witnesses and the production of books, papers, and documents) of the Federal Trade Commission Act of September 16, 1914, as amended (U. S. C. 19, title 15, secs. 49 and 50, as amended), are hereby made applicable to the powers and duties of such board.

Sec. 208. (a) Upon receiving a report from a board of inquiry the President may direct the Attorney General to petition any district court of the United States having jurisdiction of the parties to enjoin such strike or lock-out or the continuing thereof, and if the court finds that such threatened or actual strike or lock-out—

(i) affects an entire industry or a substantial part thereof engaged in trade, commerce, transportation, transmission, or communication among the several States or with foreign nations, or engaged in the production of goods for commerce; and

(ii) if permitted to occur or to continue, will imperil the national health or safety, it shall have jurisdiction to enjoin any such strike or lock-out, or the continuing thereof, and to make such other orders as may be appropriate.

(b) In any case, the provisions of the Act of March 23, 1932, entitled "An Act to amend the Judicial Code and to define and limit the jurisdiction of courts sitting in equity, and for other purposes," shall not be applicable.

(c) The order or orders of the court shall be subject to review by the appropriate circuit court of appeals and by the Supreme Court upon writ of certiorari or certification as provided in sections 239 and 240 of the Judicial Code, as amended (U. S. C., title 29, secs. 346 and 347).

Sec. 209. (a) Whenever a district court has issued an order under section 208 enjoining acts or practices which imperil or threaten to imperil the national health or safety, it shall be the duty of the parties to the labor dispute giving rise to such order to make every effort to adjust and settle their differences, with the assistance of the Service created by this Act. Neither party shall be under any duty to accept, in whole or in part, any proposal of settlement made by the Service.

(b) Upon the issuance of such order, the President shall reconvene the board of inquiry which has previously reported with respect to the dispute. At the end of a sixty-day period (unless the dispute has been settled by that time), the board of inquiry shall report to the President the current position of the parties and the efforts which have been made for settlement, and shall include a statement by each party of its position and a statement of the employer's last offer of settlement. The President shall make such report available to the public.

The National Labor Relations Board, within the succeeding fifteen days, shall take a secret ballot of the employees of each employer involved in the dispute on the question of whether they wish to accept the final offer of settlement made by their employer as stated by him and shall certify the results thereof to the Attorney General within five days thereafter.

Sec. 210. Upon the certification of the results of such ballot or upon a settlement being reached, whichever happens sooner, the Attorney General shall move the court to discharge the injunction, which motion shall then be granted and the injunction discharged. When such motion is granted, the President shall submit to the Congress a full and comprehensive report of the proceedings, including the findings of the board of inquiry and the ballot taken by the National Labor Relations Board, together with such recommendations as he may see fit to make the consideration and appropriate action.

NATIONAL EMERGENCY DISPUTES *

From the First Annual Report of the Federal Mediation and Conciliation Service, 1948, pp. 55–58

Boards of Inquiry. The current provisions of the act (sec. 208 (a)) make the submission of a report by a statutory board of inquiry a condition precedent to the President requesting the Attorney General to apply for an injunction. If the dispute threatens a national stoppage of critical proportions, it becomes necessary for the President to appoint the board a sufficient period of time in advance of the deadline date in order to afford it an opportunity to convene, to investigate, to hold hearings, to prepare and submit its report, and to give the Attorney General a reasonable opportunity to apply to the courts for an injunction in anticipation of a stoppage. Experience under the current provisions demonstrates that approximately 10 days to 2 weeks is required, as a minimum, to enable boards of inquiry satisfactorily to perform their statutory duties in most national emergency situations.

The Service has found that appointment of a board of inquiry in advance of a stoppage deadline and the scheduling of hearings before such a board, has the effect of interfering with the collective bargaining of the parties, particularly in relationships in which it is traditional not to reach a settlement until the eleventh hour. Mediation cannot be performed effectively when either the representatives of the Service or of the parties are before a board of inquiry, or when the parties await the report of the investigations of such a board. Further, the record will disclose that the relatively short period of time afforded to such boards to investigate the facts relevant to a dispute has exposed them to criticism and has afforded them insufficient time to operate at maximum efficiency and effectiveness.

Experience has also demonstrated that despite the great national importance of several disputes, relatively little publicity was given to, or public notice

* This account does not undertake a critical evaluation of the basic structure and merits of the national emergency dispute provisions in the act. It does attempt to set forth the special experience of the Service with particular provisions thereof.

taken of, the reports of boards of inquiry. This may have been due to the fact that these boards were forbidden to make recommendations which might reasonably be expected to be given wide publicity, and restricted themselves to an exposition of the issues in controversy and the positions of the parties thereon. Although the facts relevant to a dispute may not have been known in the detail in which they were set forth in the reports of the boards of inquiry, it is believed that they were generally matters of public knowledge. Apparently the Congress required board of inquiry reports to be submitted and made public because of the desirability of mobilizing public opinion behind a settlement of the controversy. This desire has not been fulfilled to a satisfactory degree.

It should also be observed that under current provisions of law, if the Federal Mediation and Conciliation Service does not make a public recommendation of settlement (a procedure it will normally refrain from adopting because nonacceptance of its recommendation might destroy its future usefulness to the parties) a dispute might well run the 60-day period prior to the deadline date and the 80-day period of the injunction—a period of 20 weeks—without any public recommendation of settlement calculated to bring public opinion to bear on the parties.

Use of the Injunction. It is the experience of the Service that in some of the national emergency disputes occurring in the last year the issuance of an injunctive order did much to forestall a national crisis and to assist in achieving a peaceful settlement. Similar claims for the utility of injunctions, such as are provided in current law, as a means of protecting the national welfare, cannot be made in respect of other national emergency disputes. Indeed, the final report of the board of inquiry in the maritime dispute involving the Pacific coast longshoremen's union observed that the employers and unions in that dispute regarded the injunction period as a "warming up" rather than a "cooling off" period (p. 27). National emergency disputes vary widely in their facts and circumstances, and it is unlikely that any machinery can be devised that will guarantee satisfactory handling in all situations.

One of the conclusions which the Service is undoubtedly justified in drawing from its experience of the last year is that provision for an 80-day period of continued operations, under injunctive order of a court, tends to delay rather than facilitate settlement of a dispute. Parties unable to resolve the issues facing them before a deadline date, when subject to an injunction order, tend to lose a sense of urgency and to relax their efforts to reach a settlement. They wait for the next deadline date (the date of discharge of the injunction) to spur them to renewed efforts. In most instances efforts of the Service to encourage the parties to bargain during the injunction period, with a view to early settlement, falls on deaf ears. Further, the public appears to be lulled into a sense of false security by a relatively long period of industrial peace by injunction and does not give evidence of being aware of a threat to the common welfare which would produce a climate of public opinion favorable to settlement. Whether this experience dictates the desirability of a shorter injunction period or an injunction period of indefinite duration the Service expresses no opinion at this time.

Last Offer Ballots (sec. 209 (b)). In every national emergency dispute to date the results of a ballot conducted by the National Labor Relations Board pursuant to section 209 (b) of the act have been overwhelmingly for rejection of the employer's last offer. For reasons which need not be elaborated here it is fair to assume that the likelihood of any ballot in the future having a contrary result, is small and remote. These ballots are expensive to conduct, and the experience of a year demonstrates that they do nothing to promote settlement of a dispute. To the contrary, they are a disrupting influence in collective bargaining and mediation. The last or final offer of an employer which the National Labor Relations Board is under an obligation to submit to ballot, is not likely to be the ultimate offer in fact, on the basis of which a settlement will be reached. Most decidedly this was the case in the disputes involving the Oak Ridge National Laboratories, the West coast maritime and longshoremen's unions and the Atlantic coast longshoremen's union. Unions and their membership appear to regard such last offers as counteroffers in bargaining which, if accepted, mean a repudiation of union leadership. Experience with the strike ballots required by the War Labor Disputes Act as well as the Labor Management Relations Act, 1947, discloses that workers are not likely to repudiate their representatives in the course of contract negotiations.

A vote turning down an employer's last offer places additional obstacles and difficulties in the way of a settlement. Union representatives must necessarily accept the vote as a mandate from the rank and file of workers that they may regard as practicable and possible bases of settlement only those offers of employers substantially more favorable than the one rejected. With foreknowledge of this consequence, employers tend to keep in reserve, and not to represent as a last offer which may be submitted to ballot, concessions which might result in a settlement. Union leadership and employees, aware that employers assess the situation in this manner, act accordingly. Thus, the mandatory last offer ballot sets into action a cycle of tactical operations by both parties which cancel each other out and delay serious efforts to arrive at a prompt resolution of their differences.

The national emergency dispute provisions discussed above (sec. 209 (b)) require the National Labor Relations Board to conduct a ballot of employees on the last offer of their employers. Section 203 (b) directs the Service in the generality of cases within its jurisdiction to suggest to the parties that they agree to submit the last offer of the employer to a secret ballot of the employees. The experience of the Service with this provision has not been such as to justify the conclusion that it has contributed materially to the settlement of disputes.

PRESIDENT TRUMAN IN THE 1952 STEEL STRIKE

In 1952, to avert a shutdown of the nation's steel mills during the period of the Korean conflict, President Truman "seized" the steel mills and continued to operate them in the name of the Federal government. He was reluctant to invoke a Taft-Hartley emergency injunction in view of the fact that the Steelworkers had already refrained from striking at his request for a longer period than such an injunction would have required. Steel management sued in the Federal courts, however, and the Supreme Court ruled that the President's action was unconstitutional. Thereupon the mills reverted to private ownership and the Steelworkers immediately struck.

From President Truman's address to Congress, June 10, asking legislative sanction to validate the action which he recommended

I should like to report to the Congress on certain events that have happened in connection with the current dispute in the steel industry since I last communicated with the Congress on that subject.

On April 9, I informed the Congress that I had taken action to provide for temporary operation of the steel mills by the Government. At that time, I indicated the reasons that had impelled me to take that action.

I pointed out that the Congress might wish to take action providing for a different solution of the grave problem confronting the nation as a result of the steel dispute. I also said that, if the Congress did not act, I would continue to do everything in my power to keep the steel industry operating and to bring about a settlement of the dispute.

The Congress took no action.

Accordingly, Government operation of the mills continued and intensive efforts were made to bring the parties into agreement. Meetings between the parties were held from April 9 to April 15, and on May 3 and May 4. But their differences on a number of issues were so great that no settlement could be reached.

Meanwhile, some of the steel companies had instituted court proceedings for the purpose of challenging the President's power to keep the steel mills in operation. This case reached the Supreme Court, and on Monday, June 2, a majority of that court decided that the President did not have the power, in this instance, to operate the mills. I immediately ordered that Government possession of the mills be relinquished.

On the same day, a strike was called and most of the steel industry was shut down. Thus, the situation that I had sought to avoid was brought about. I had managed to keep steel production going from the end of December to the second of June—a period of more than 150 days—even though the companies and the union had no collective bargaining contract. Now it had been made impossible for me to prevent a break in production.

Very shortly thereafter I was informed there was a reasonable prospect that the parties might be able to reach a settlement of their dispute if they could be brought together again to negotiate.

I have said repeatedly that the ultimate and proper settlement of this matter can be achieved only by agreement between the parties. Consequently, I have sought at every opportunity to help bring about such an agreement.

That, obviously, was the step that was called for in the circumstances prevailing last week. Moreover, it seemed essential that the negotiations be given every possible chance to succeed—that no other action be taken which would be likely to make either party unwilling or unable to negotiate in good faith.

That is the course that was followed. The parties were called back into negotiations. They met from Thursday, June 5, until Monday, June 9. Although they made some progress, they were not able to reach a final agreement. We are now, therefore, faced with the necessity of using some other means for getting the steel mills back into production.

When the negotiations were broken off, last night, representatives of the parties indicated that they would "cooperate in assuring production of military requirements essential to our forces engaged in combating Communist aggressors."

This morning, I have instructed Dr. Steelman, Acting Director of Defense Mobilization, and Mr. Lovett, the Secretary of Defense, to arrange with the companies and the union to meet as many of our urgent military requirements as possible under this pledge.

It is impossible to determine at this time just how much steel can be obtained in this manner. We should be able to meet our most critical military needs. But, at the same time, we cannot expect to get enough steel in this way to meet all the essential needs of the defense program.

The fact is that we need steel, not just for immediate combat requirements, but also for equipping all our armed forces—and to help equip those of our Allies. We need steel for constructing defense plants and new atomic energy installations.

There are vital industrial requirements for steel—for such items as power generating equipment, freight cars, and oil producing equipment. These needs are very urgent and must not be indefinitely delayed by a steel shutdown.

Our national security depends upon our total economic strength, and steel is the basic element in that strength.

Consequently, we are faced with the imperative need for getting most, if not all, of the nation's steel mills back into production very promptly.

There are several possible courses of action that might be followed. However, I believe there are two main possibilities.

One of these is Government operation of the steel mills.

The other is the use of a labor injunction of the type authorized by the Taft-Hartley law.

The Congress can choose either of these two courses. I cannot. I could only use the Taft-Hartley approach. In my judgment, that is by far the worse of the two approaches.

Consequently, I feel that I should put the facts before the Congress, recommend the course of action I deem best, and call upon the Congress—which has the power to do so—to make the choice.

I believe the Congress should make its choice with a view of bringing about three objectives:

First, to secure essential steel production; second, to assure fair treatment to both parties, in accordance with sound price and wage stabilization policies;

third, to encourage the parties to settle their differences through collective bargaining.

Each of these objectives is important to the national interest, and the Congress should act to serve all of them.

I believe the course which is most likely to achieve these objectives is to enact legislation authorizing the Government to take over the steel plants and to operate them temporarily until the parties reach a settlement. This is the course I recommend.

A seizure law, if properly drafted, can achieve the objectives of assuring steel production, treating both parties fairly, and encouraging collective bargaining. The key requirement of such a law, if it is to accomplish these ends, is to provide for fair and just compensation to the owners for the use of their property during a seizure, and fair and just compensation for the work of the employes.

The Constitution protects the owners of property during a period of Government operation by requiring that they be given just compensation—and they can appeal to the courts to enforce that requirement. The law should give similar protection to wage-earners.

This means that changes in wages and working conditions during seizure should not be prevented by law. If they were, the seizure would mean that workers would be compelled to work indefinitely without a change in wages, no matter how much a change might be justified. This is obviously not equal justice under the law.

In order to be fair, the law must provide for a method of determining just compensation for the owners and the workers during the period of Government operation. This can be done by the establishment of special boards to work out specific proposals for the purpose, within the general framework of the Government's stabilization policies. In this way, the legislation can assure continued steel production, and fair treatment for both parties during Government operation.

Seizure should not, of course, be regarded as a means of determining the issues in dispute between management and the union. Those issues will have to be settled by the parties through their own collective bargaining. Legislation providing for Government operation will not prevent collective bargaining.

As a matter of fact, the type of legislation I have described will undoubtedly increase the incentives for the parties to settle their differences through bargaining.

The companies will face the possibility of receiving something less than their normal profits as just compensation. And the workers will face the prospect of getting less than they think they are entitled to. Indeed, I made this plain on May 3, when I informed the parties that Government changes in wages and working conditions would not be satisfactory to either side.

I therefore recommend that the Congress promptly enact seizure legislation such as I have described, which will restore full-scale steel production, provide fair treatment for all concerned and maintain incentives for both parties to reach agreement on the disputed issues through collective bargaining.

There is another course which the Congress could follow. That would be to enact legislation authorizing and directing the President to seek an injunction of the type authorized under the Taft-Hartley Act, but without going through the formality of appointing a board of inquiry and waiting for its report.

I do not recommend that the Congress adopt the Taft-Hartley approach. I think it would be unwise, unfair, and quite possibly ineffective.

The nation has already had the benefit of whatever could be gained by action under the Taft-Hartley Act. That act provides for two main things. It provides for a fact-finding board to investigate and report on the issues in dispute. In the steel case, we have already had the facts fully determined and reported by the Wage Stabilization Board.

The Taft-Hartley Act also provides for injunctions against a shutdown for a total of eighty days. In the steel case, the union already, even before April 8, had voluntarily postponed strike action for ninety-nine days. In so far as fact-finding and delay are concerned, therefore, the practical effects of the Taft-Hartley Act were achieved in this case some time ago.

Over and above these facts, however, there are other compelling reasons for not using an injunction of the Taft-Hartley type in the steel case. Its effect would be to require the workers to continue working for another long period without change in their wages and working conditions. This would be grossly unfair.

The Wage Stabilization Board, the Government agency charged with the responsibility for these matters, has found—and the companies have admitted—that the workers are entitled to improvements in wages and working conditions. The union members stayed at work, at the Government request, during the period the case was being considered by the Wage Board, and later during the period of Government operation from April 8 to June 2.

In these respects, the union and its members have cooperated fully with the Government in the public interest.

And yet the effect of a Taft-Hartley labor injunction would be to penalize the workers and to give the advantage to the steel companies.

I want to make it very plain to the Congress that the result of using a Taft-Hartley type injunction in this dispute would be to take sides with the companies and against the workers.

Furthermore, a Taft-Hartley injunction would take away management's incentive to bargain and to work out the issues in dispute. The companies would have nothing to lose and everything to gain by delaying an agreement for as long as the injunction was in effect. Thus a Taft-Hartley injunction in this case would not only be unfair, it would hamper, rather than help, the collective bargaining negotiations.

Moreover, use of the Taft-Hartley law would not guarantee a restoration of full-scale steel production, which should be our primary objective. Nothing in the act can restore steel production immediately or automatically.

As the Congress knows, the first step that must be taken under that act is to appoint a board of inquiry to investigate and report the facts of the matter.

Previous experience indicates that it could take as much as a week or ten days for such a board to complete its task.

If such a board were appointed and made its report, and the Attorney General were directed to seek an injunction against a strike, the question would arise whether a court of equity would grant the Attorney General's request, in view of the union's previous voluntary ninety-nine-day postponement.

Furthermore, even if an injunction were granted, there is no assurance that it would get the steel mills back in operation. I call the attention of the Congress to the fact that such an injunction did not get the coal mines back in operation in 1950.

If, however, the judgment of the Congress, contrary to mine, is that an injunction of the Taft-Hartley type should be used, there is a quicker way to do so than by appointing a board of inquiry under the Taft-Hartley Act. That would be for the Congress to enact legislation authorizing and directing the President to seek an injunction, without waiting for any board to be appointed and to report.

I do not want to be misunderstood. I believe the Taft-Hartley procedure would be unfair, harmful and futile—futile at least in helping to bring about a settlement, and perhaps also in restoring production. I hope very much that the Congress will decide that the Taft-Hartley type of injunction should not be used at all and that seizure legislation should be enacted instead.

In any event, I hope the Congress will act quickly. The issue of peace or war hangs in the balance, and steel is a vital element in that outcome.

We are engaged, with other free countries, in a mighty effort to build up the military defenses of the free world. We must build up this military strength if we are to have a reasonable chance of preventing World War III. But we cannot do it without steel, for steel is the backbone of our defense production, and, indeed, of our whole industrial society.

Every action I have taken in the dispute in the steel industry, beginning last December, has been based on the paramount necessity for maintaining the production of essential steel products in the present defense emergency.

When I took the extraordinary step of seizure in the absence of specific statutory authority, I pointed out that "with American troops facing the enemy on the field of battle, I would not be living up to my oath of office if I failed to do whatever is required to provide them with the weapons and ammunition they need for their survival."

Now a majority of the Supreme Court have declared that I cannot take the action I believe necessary. But they have said very clearly that the Congress can take that action.

Whatever may have been the intention of the court's majority in setting limits on the President's power, there can be no question of their view that the Congress can enact legislation to avoid a crippling work stoppage in the steel industry.

Mr. Justice Black said the Congress "can authorize the taking of private property for public use. It can make laws regulating the relationships between employers and employes, prescribing rules designed to settle labor disputes, and fixing wages and working conditions. . . ."

Mr. Justice Frankfurter said that by enacting the Taft-Hartley Act the Congress in effect decided "the only recourse for preventing a shutdown in any basic industry, after failure of mediation, is the Congress."

Mr. Justice Jackson referred to "the ease, the expedition, the safety with which Congress can grant" emergency powers of the type needed to handle this crisis.

The issue is squarely up to you gentlemen of the Congress. I hope the Congress will meet it by enacting fair and effective legislation.

AN ALTERNATIVE STRIKE PROCEDURE

Statement of Richard A. Lester, Professor of Economics, Princeton University, in Taft-Hartley Act Revisions, hearings before the Senate Committee on Labor and Public Welfare, 83d Cong., 1st Sess., 1953, part 4, pp. 2447–2448

STRENGTHEN THE PRESIDENT'S HAND

It is difficult to conceive of a more unsatisfactory procedure than that for national-emergency disputes contained in title II of the act. Cyrus Ching, director of the Federal Mediation and Conciliation Service, explained the patent defects in his first report for the year ending June 30, 1948. By then that title had been used in six disputes, so that his conclusions were based on considerable experience.

The emergency provisions of the act actually hinder disputes settlement in the following ways: (1) The President is faced with the dilemma of premature intervention or perilous delay, especially in continuous process industries like steel and aluminum. The dilemma arises out of the fact that between 4 and 14 days have been consumed from the time a board of inquiry is named until its initial report was prepared, which in turn forms the basis for a request for an injunction. Appointment and inquiry by the board well in advance of the date set for the strike, though necessary for timely application of an injunction under the awkward board procedure, interferes with collective bargaining, occupies the parties with the board's activities rather than with collective bargaining, and crystallizes the parties' positions early because the board has to ascertain them and then publicity is given to the stated positions.

(2) The possibility or certainty of an injunction and the absence of any other specified course of Government action affect the strategy of collective bargaining by taking the pressure from management and tending to lull the public. No assurance is provided for retroactivity of the terms finally accepted or for prevention of strike preparation, such as stockpiling, during the injunction period.

(3) The secret ballot on the employer's "last" offer is a most unfortunate arrangement because the workers always vote to reject, which solidifies differences just before the injunction is lifted and renders subsequent compromise more difficult. Strike votes are really a ritual to indicate union solidarity and

confidence in the leadership, designed to impress management and the public. Experience with the Smith-Connally Act and since under Taft-Hartley had demonstrated beyond a doubt that the idea of a "last offer" vote is based on the false premise that union members will repudiate their leadership and vote to accept less than they are likely to get if they vote to reject knowing that the Government cannot permit the strike to continue.

The final step, submission of the dispute to Congress, is certain to put it squarely into partisan politics and to subject it to political maneuvering. Congress is hardly the appropriate body to decide the merits of a dozen or two dozen issues in a labor dispute, including such matters as incentive methods of payment, seniority, and work rules. With bargaining in terms of "whole-package deals," most of the agreement may be in dispute and slight variations in working can make a significant difference. It is difficult to think of a more inappropriate body to which to submit a labor dispute for final adjudication than the Congress.

There is no excuse for further delay in replacing the emergency disputes procedure in title II with one that will serve to encourage self-settlement by the parties themselves, deter resort to Government intervention, and provide sufficient flexibility to adapt to changes in the international situation and to the existence or nonexistence of wage control.

The arrangements I recommend are based on the following assumptions:

1. The goal should be preservation of, and maximum reliance on, collective bargaining.

2. The strike performs the function of penalizing both parties, thus encouraging compromise and voluntary settlement.

3. Strike situations differ and military and other needs change, so that it is not possible to state in advance the industries or companies in which a strike can create a national emergency.

4. With such variation in the circumstances surrounding each case, Government intervention is bound to be an art. It should have available a number of types or methods of intervention and not [be] hamstrung by a single rigid procedure.

5. By such means as uncertainty of Government action, public explanation by the parties of their inability to agree, and levy of financial penalties on both sides, some of the pressures of the strike may be created in cases where work stoppage cannot be permitted to run its course.

6. Methods of Government intervention tend to acquire a certain magic or disrespect with usage. Frequency of use and failure of a national administration to support Board recommendations (as occurred in railroad disputes in 1941 and 1943) may destroy much of their usefulness, at least temporarily.

7. Trust must be placed in the President, as representative of all the people, to select the proper method or methods of intervention and to apply it or them as seems best suited in any particular case to achieve the goal of maximum reliance on collective bargaining.

8. To minimize Federal intervention and permit State experimentation with various methods, real emergency disputes whose impact is without significant

military implications and is confined chiefly to one locality (namely, local electric, natural-gas, or transportation strikes) should by amendment of the act be made subject to State or municipal intervention, with the Federal Government's power to intervene kept in reserve should the situation alter so as to threaten national health or safety.

The Taft-Hartley Act should be revised to give the President by legislation the power, in case of a genuine national emergency dispute, to utilize any one or a combination of the following:

1. Appoint an ad hoc board to hold a hearing at which the parties are to explain why they have been unable to settle their dispute by collective bargaining and to show cause why they should not accept voluntary arbitration.

2. Appoint an ad hoc fact-finding board with power to make unenforceable recommendations.

3. Apply for a court injunction that could run for a stipulated or unspecified period of time.

4. Seize the property with the power to make it costly for both parties to have the dispute continue during seizure.

Item 4 is designed especially to make Government intervention distasteful to both sides, to induce the parties to settle their own troubles. . . .

If collective bargaining is to be maintained, the Federal Government should be in a position to exert real pressure on both parties in order to break a deadlock and induce an agreement. As I explained in an article in the New Republic for June 16, 1952, the Virginia Public Utilities Labor Act, first passed in 1947 and revised in 1952, exerts such financial pressures during State seizure in a labor dispute. Under that law, the State takes 15 percent of the net revenues of the business as a fee for its operating services during the seizure period and the pre-existing terms of employment remain frozen, with discontinuance of the checkoff of union dues.

Undoubtedly the imposition of such a two-edged penalty raises certain legal and practical problems. The company may be operating at a loss or the courts may not allow the full 15-percent fee. If a company's labor costs are much larger than its net profit, the avoidance of, say, a 10-percent wage increase in exchange for 15 percent of the company's current profits might seem a profitable transaction, providing one disregards adverse effects on labor morale and other concomitant disadvantages to the company's industrial relations, but no sensible management would do that. Although theoretically it would be desirable to have the financial pressure on both parties well balanced and relatively equal, strike experience indicates that a significant amount of pressure on each side is usually all that is necessary. Also, this method is suggested as only one alternative available to the President and not as a cure-all.

It may be objected that this four-way procedure gives the President too much power and discretion. Experience would seem to indicate, however, that some such legislation is needed to deal effectively with real national emergency disputes. If the President of the United States cannot be trusted to use such powers, who can? And the protection of the courts would remain available to parties in case they believed their constitutional rights had been invaded.

Testimony of Walter P. Reuther, President, United Automobile Workers, in Taft-Hartley Act Revisions, hearings before the Senate Committee on Labor and Public Welfare, 83d Cong., 1st Sess., 1953, part 1, pp. 393–406

PLACE THE RESPONSIBILITY ON CONGRESS

MR. REUTHER: . . . Going on now to the national emergency provisions, we recognize the fact that, if and when the welfare, the safety, and the security of our Nation are in jeopardy, as the result of a labor dispute, that the Government, as the agency of all the people has an obligation to act in order to protect the public good. Nobody can argue against that point of view. Certainly, the public interest transcends the narrower interest of the parties in any labor dispute. We recognize that obviously, if you cannot defend the whole of our free society, then we as free labor or free management can't enjoy rights within that free society. So that we do not argue as to the right of the Government to interfere. But we believe that Government interventions ought to be only in those situations where you actually have an emergency.

SENATOR IVES: Who is going to determine that?

MR. REUTHER: I think in the first case it ought to be determined by the President, and that the remedies ought to be worked out by the Congress. That is what I suggest. We believe that under Taft-Hartley with all the steps predetermined by law, a great deal of the pressures which make collective bargaining work are removed from the collective-bargaining table. And because of that, issues that might normally be resolved by the give and take of collective bargaining are not resolved and, therefore, you get a dispute. We believe that if you could wipe out the predetermined steps in Taft-Hartley that deal with national emergencies, and say to the parties, "It is your baby; it is your responsibility. You step up to it," and let the Government intervene only in the event of an emergency that does actually jeopardize the public safety and the public welfare in each specific situation on a tailor-made basis by specific acts of Congress, then the parties would not know what was going to happen, and that would give them a sense of urgency to sit down and bargain.

SENATOR IVES: That is exactly what I have tried to do in a couple of bills I introduced.

MR. REUTHER: That is right. And we think that the bills you have introduced embody this same basic approach and we think it is sound. I have sat in a lot of bargaining situations. I have sat down with corporations having as many as 400,000 employees covered by a contract. I know from practical experience that you do more collective bargaining an hour or two before the deadline than you do in 2 months before that time, because that is the nature of the animal. Everybody figures "We will see what the other fellow is going to do."

You wait, and you maneuver, and you try to get yourself in the position where you can get the best bargain out of it. So you wait until the last minute before you begin to yield and make concessions and begin to put everything on the table.

THE CHAIRMAN: Would you approve, Mr. Reuther, if we attempted to get the mediation service into the picture earlier than we do today? Would that help?

MR. REUTHER: Sometimes mediation helps. If the parties don't understand each other, mediation helps them to get some of the misunderstandings out of the way and get a better clarification of the areas of dispute. But if the parties are merely holding back for the purpose of maintaining the strongest bargaining position, then conciliation won't change that, because the problem there is not misunderstanding. They understand each other too well. And that is why they are not moving. But the point is—and this is a practical matter, this is not theory; you know, you get from theory to practice in collective bargaining very abruptly; this is the practice of collective bargaining. You are sitting there on two sides of the table, and the fellows say, "We have 2 weeks yet. There is no hurry." Then they have 1 week and then they have a couple of hours and then they get down to brass tacks. If Taft-Hartley says there is an 80-day injunction hanging out here, and industry feels "Well, this is going to be big enough, this will create a big enough emergency so that we can get a Taft-Hartley injunction," when they have 1 hour, they really haven't 1 hour; they have 1 hour plus 80 days. The result is that there is no pressure, there is no urgency. The weight of responsibility on the parties is not there. And without the pressure of responsibilities on the parties at the collective-bargaining table, collective bargaining won't work. . . .

There are a number of real advantages not to bargain if you think the Government will come in and bail you out for 80 days. First of all, you will not put your offer on the table, because if, out of Taft-Hartley intervention the Government sets up a fact-finding board, and supposing the company was really willing to give 10 cents and they lay 10 cents on the table, they figure well the fact-finding board will start with 10 cents and will compromise the thing with the 10 cents toward the union position. But if you don't put any figure on the table, then the fact-finding board will start with zero and maybe they will compromise at 10 cents instead of 10 cents plus. So there is every incentive not to bargain, there is every incentive not to lay anything on the table. Then, also, when you are dealing with large corporations and large industries—for example we used to say back in General Motors that 1 penny was worth $6 million. Well, if you can withhold a few pennies for a few months, that runs into many, many millions of dollars. Therefore, the 80-day injunction thing may delay a settlement for a period, retroactive wage increases may not be granted, and the company can save many millions of dollars by the simple process of delay. We believe, and I say this very sincerely, based upon the practical experience that we have had in collective bargaining, that any Government machinery that tends to lessen the sense of urgency, that tends to minimize the full weight of the responsibilities on the parties at the bargaining table, will discourage and weaken collective bargaining and will increase the possibilities of greater areas of disputes, and therefore, create the need for greater Government intervention in the long pull.

SENATOR DOUGLAS: Mr. Chairman, may I ask another question at this point?

THE CHAIRMAN: Senator Douglas.

SENATOR DOUGLAS: Does not the requirement that toward the end of the 80-day period the workers must vote on the last offer of the employer, tend to restrain the employers, at least in the early stages of negotiation, from really offering as much as they might later give under free collective bargaining?

MR. REUTHER: Our whole experience, Senator Douglas, has been that the minute we get involved in the 80-day period, there is less collective bargaining than at any other time. If you will get the statement of Mr. David Cole, who was the head of the Federal Mediation and Conciliation Service, and get Mr. Ching's statement when he headed that agency, they will tell you that their experience has been in practical situations where they went in and tried to mediate and conciliate, that there was no give and take whatever during the 80-day period; the situation was just rigidly frozen there, everybody waiting for the thing to get out of the way so they could get back to collective bargaining, the corporation obviously taking care of the 80-day because every day they didn't have to make a wage adjustment they were saving money.

SENATOR HILL: I was just going to say this, in line with the statement you are making, I suppose you are going to comment on the effect that the injunction has on labor's position. The injunction is only against labor, not against management and labor. What does that do to weaken labor's position or what does that do to encourage management not to bargain collectively? Are you going to comment on that?

MR. REUTHER: Workers having exhausted the efforts to arrive at a reasonable and satisfactory settlement of the issues in dispute through collective bargaining have as their final recourse the withholding of their labor power. That is the only thing they have to sell in the free market so they decide to withhold it and not sell it. Workers threaten the use of that economic weapon only as an effort to change the status quo. The status quo is not satisfactory. The injunction is using the power of the Government and the courts to maintain the status quo. Obviously the use of the injunction is always on the side of management. There is no such thing as the impartial intervention of Government. If Government intervenes through the process of the issuance of an injunction, it is intervening on management's side of the argument, because it is maintaining the status quo which the workers want to change. There is no such thing as an impartial intervention. The Government intervenes to maintain the status quo and that is exactly what the company wants to maintain, the status quo. The status quo is unsatisfactory and that is why the workers want to change it. That is obviously why we object to the use of the injunction because the injunction is a weapon used to maintain the status quo and bolster the position of the employer in opposition to the position of the workers.

THE CHAIRMAN: That wouldn't be true, would it, if you had your ultimate settlement retroactive to the beginning of the dispute. You would simply maintain the status quo until you get the final decision. If you make it retroactive, I think that will meet the argument you are making now, that the workers are necessarily damaged by the injunction.

MR. REUTHER: Many times, you see, collective bargaining is a very complex process. The ability of a group of workers to make a good bargain as of one calendar date may not be the same at a later calendar date. You may not be able to overcome that by any retroactive adjustment. You must also remember that when you work out a retroactive adjustment, that has an impact on the total economic package in other respects. So you can never recapture or re-create the elements in a given collective bargaining situation at a later date, because you are dealing here with a living, dynamic kind of process that changes.

Now, if you say you go back to the period before the 80 days began, you can't re-create the thing. There may be situations in the industry where the seasonal aspect of the production cycle may have a great bearing upon the ability of workers to get what they consider to be a satisfactory arrangement. Eighty days later, maybe, the pressure in the industry has tapered off a great deal and the employer can coast for a while. So the minute the Government intervenes to interfere with the give and take of free collective bargaining and the free play of economic forces, the Government automatically, by the nature of the problem, intervenes on the employers' side.

SENATOR IVES: Mr. Chairman?

THE CHAIRMAN: Senator Ives.

SENATOR IVES: I think there is one thing that all of us have kind of ignored in our conversation on this subject. Of course we want justice, equity, fairness and all of those things, where labor is concerned and where management is concerned. But in this particular instance we are dealing with a national emergency, and you yourself stated that the President is the one who should determine what constitutes a national emergency and when it occurs. The national emergency of the type we are talking about requires production. How are we going to get production during all of this period of time when the controversy exists and which, of itself, seems to be causing a work stoppage? That is the big question. It is the public interest that is involved which overshadows some of these other things while this period exists. What is your answer there?

MR. REUTHER: Well, to begin with the number of situations in which we did really have the kind of national emergency which threatens safety and the welfare of the whole Nation, the community, the number of those kind of situations are very few.

SENATOR IVES: Well, it occurred in the steel dispute, for example, last year.

MR. REUTHER: They are very few. That is one of the bad features of Taft-Hartley. Every time some management has a bellyache, they get a Taft-Hartley injunction. Every time there is some slight inconvenience, they get a national emergency Taft-Hartley injunction. . . .

When you have an emergency, then the Government has an obligation to move. But we believe that you should let the parties in collective bargaining carry on their work under the full pressures of the responsibilities and the urgencies of given collective-bargaining situations. If industry makes a fair offer to labor, the labor people have to think that over, they have to say to themselves, "Is this a reasonable proposition? Do we take it back to the men and try to nail the thing down and settle it?" If it is a reasonable provision, you will find that the labor leaders will take it back to the men involved and they will nail it down, the thing will be settled. On the other hand, if the labor people offer management a reasonable proposition, they have to think, are they going to risk a strike? the loss of production? the loss of their profits? and if that is reasonable, I think that they will, under circumstances where the weight of the responsibilities is on the parties, they will find an area of agreement. But if both of them figure, "Why should we try to work it out? The Government is going to take over for 80 days," then you transfer the responsibility. Under Taft-Hartley industry knows precisely what will happen. Under the proposal that we suggest, having the thing wide open, with the Government, through the President in the first instance, certifying a national emergency, and then having Congress make a tailormade answer to that problem, we believe that both parties then would feel, "Well, we better work it out ourselves because we don't know what those people in Washington are going to do to us."

SENATOR IVES: I follow you until you talk about Congress making a tailormade answer to the problem. How is Congress going to make that tailormade answer? That is the thing that has been bothering me no end. If you can tell me how they are going to do it, I wish you would. I think somewhere, in the area I have tried to cover in my two bills, an area you are talking about, is the answer to what we are seeking. But that is the question. How is Congress going to make a tailormade answer to the problem?

MR. REUTHER: I think the tailormade answer must reflect the elements of a given situation. If you are dealing with one type of situation, you may come up with one type of answer. In another situation, you would vary your answer.

SENATOR IVES: I tried to approach it this way, by steps, so that Congress could be apprised of the situation in time. And the tailormade answer that you are talking about might possibly be evolved under those conditions. I don't think there is any sureness that it would be, but I gathered from your prepared testimony here that you do not like the steps that I suggest. You want to slash right in, "The President declares a national emergency. Congress acts." You know what happened in 1946 when Congress contemplated drafting strikers, at least an effort was made to draft everybody that wouldn't go to work under certain conditions. I would not dare leave the thing like that without preliminary effort in the hands of the Congress.

MR. REUTHER: First of all, I can envision the possibility of a national emergency arising only in a very limited area of this total problem. And certainly, it wouldn't be something that came out of the clear blue sky. The administration would know, the Congress would know, that this was coming up. If at the last minute labor and management were able to resolve it, everybody could say, "Thank God, that is behind us." On the other hand, having been apprised of the situations in the course of its development, then you could meet it. In other words, if the situation is so urgent as to take away from men the right to act as freemen, it is also of such urgency as to require the Congress to sit down and do something about it in terms of that specific problem.

SENATOR IVES: You want to make sure that when the Congress sits down to act on it that it does the right thing and nothing else. How best can you arrive at what would be the best thing?

MR. REUTHER: I would run a chance of having Congress do the right thing in specific national emergencies rather than have a law that does the wrong thing in all situations.

SENATOR IVES: I am not talking about the law. What criticism have you regarding the bills, either one or both, that I have introduced, in which I tried to make that approach, intelligently and by comprehensive steps?

MR. REUTHER: Let me try to answer that. We are in agreement on the basic approach. We agree that it is an attempt to minimize the area of intervention and to maximize the responsibility on the parties at the bargaining table. We are together.

SENATOR IVES: That is correct.

MR. REUTHER: Now, the difference between our approach and yours is that you provide some intermediate machinery to go into effect—a sort of a fact-finding board and so forth for the 30- and 60-day period, as I understand.

SENATOR IVES: No 30-day period. Just a 60-day in one, no limit in the other, no period at all.

MR. REUTHER: Our difference there is that we believe that even that amount of machinery will tend—although not to the extent that Taft-Hartley does—your bill is a much more realistic approach than Taft-Hartley. But we believe that the number of national-emergency situations will be so infrequent that if the President could certify them, he could have the Conciliation Department working on them, and all the information would be gathered without this intermediate machinery. That would tend to maximize the pressure and the responsibility at the bargaining table. Your bill is better than the present Taft-Hartley machinery; there is no question about that in our mind. But we believe that having no machinery at all but having the machinery and the solution tailor-made in each situation is the most effective way to deal with this problem.

SENATOR IVES: We at last arrive together again. I say tailormade. That is what I am trying to have, something that will be tailormade when the Congress does act. But I don't follow you in reaching to that tailormade proposal.

MR. REUTHER: We don't want anything to detract from the pressures of the bargaining table until they really are in trouble. Then you can move fast. As I say, this is not something that is going to come out of the blue sky. You are going to know about it. The President can certify it. In certifying it, he could make recommendations. He could say "I think under this situation you ought to do thus and so" to meet the problem quickly. Then Congress can sit down.

SENATOR IVES: I think I get your point. You think it is up to the President to advise the Congress as to the action which should be taken, that Congress should act upon his proposal?

MR. REUTHER: I think he ought to certify to you the character of the emergency requiring your action, and he could say to you, I think, that this and this ought to be the approach. And you could either accept his recommendations or you could not.

SENATOR IVES: Suppose the Congress should not accept them?

MR. REUTHER: Then you make your own.

SENATOR IVES: Under conditions at a time when the Congress might not be fully acquainted with all the facts. How about that?

MR. REUTHER: That is why you have machinery in Congress to get the facts. You take the auto industry. I just do not see how we can create a national emergency, unless all the production of the auto industry were on defense work.

SENATOR IVES: I do not think you could. But you certainly could do it in steel, as was shown last year, and it could be done in coal as was demonstrated a couple of years prior to that time.

MR. REUTHER: In any situation where a national emergency could be created, you would know about that. There are only a handful of those possibilities, you would know about them. I say it gets back to this fundamental question, that when you take away from freemen the right to withhold their labor power, that is a very basic step, and it is one that you should not do as a blanket proposition, it is one that you ought to do only when there are situations of a compelling enough nature to justify that kind of a drastic step. I would put that full responsibility on the Congress, because when Congress does that, I don't think it will do it lightly. I think that you will have to have a real emergency before Congress will do that.

SENATOR IVES: You will have to have a real emergency, but you want to make sure that the Congress is sufficiently acquainted with conditions and is able to act intelligently when they do occur.

MR. REUTHER: You see, if you had a situation, if an industry that was dragging its feet in a given collective-bargaining situation felt it could 'get an 80-day injunction, it will say "Why should we settle? We can get an 80-day injunction." Under Taft-Hartley they drag their feet. But if that same industry feels "Maybe they will seize the property, and maybe they will establish right away that any wage adjustments would be retroactive. They may do a lot of things that industry does not like," maybe that will exert greater pressure upon industry to do something about it. On the other hand, labor would not know what would happen to them. They wouldn't know whether they would be put through the wringer on it. Maybe we better sit down. At the point where there is a great deal of uncertainty as to what the Government will do when it intervenes, you will get a greater sense of urgency at the bargaining table to settle than you will when the parties know in advance what is going to happen, because it is already predetermined. We think that any steps that are predetermined by law tend to minimize the pressure at the bargaining table, and anything that minimizes the pressure makes for inability to get together. . . .

SENATOR LEHMAN: May I ask a question? It is not quite clear to me at what point you advocate that Congress may intervene in a strike or threatened strike. Would you recommend that the intervention of Congress can be had only on the issuance of a proclamation by the President certifying to an emergency, or would you give Congress the discretion to intervene on its own responsibility in advance of the issuance of a proclamation?

I ask that because I was wondering whether you had in mind that Congress should be given the right to bring pressure to bear on the two disputants in the hope of compelling a reasonable and fair settlement. I am not quite clear what you have in mind.

MR. REUTHER: I think as a normal procedure it would be the responsibility of the executive branch of the Government to be in close contact with the developing situation and make recommendations. That would not preclude, however, under our understanding, the right of Congress to intervene without having the matter referred by the executive branch of the Government. Congress certainly has the right, and if in its judgment it felt it was justified in intervening without having the matter referred by the executive branch of the Government, you could intervene directly.

SENATOR LEHMAN: The reason I ask that, as I interpret your testimony it is to the effect that if both sides to a dispute are uncertain in respect to what action Congress might take or recommend, pressure could be brought to bear to cause a settlement to be made, is that correct?

MR. REUTHER: That is right.

SENATOR GRISWOLD: Mr. Chairman.

It seems to me there has been no discussion about how you are going to put into effect or enforce this tailormade decision that Congress might make. Really what you are talking about doing is making Congress the top-level wage board, and then what are they going to do? What if Congress comes out with a tailormade decision saying, "We will retain the status quo indefinitely," and then what if the men refuse to work? What happens?

MR. REUTHER: The point is, I think you have to work on the assumption that both labor and management have some sense of responsibility in that kind of emergency situation. If people are going to defy the decision of the appropriate Government agencies, you have a state of insurrection.

I ask you, what would happen if, having the Taft-Hartley 80-day emergency provision, every labor union in a situation that was a potential national emergency said, "Let's just set our time schedule 80 days ahead. We will drift through the 80-day injunction period and then we will strike at the end of it." What would you do then? You would have to meet and act upon that kind of emergency. You would have to meet that emergency. So what we say is, meet that same responsibility that you have at the end of the 80 days without the use of the 80 days, and get the full benefit of the pressures at the collective bargaining table.

SENATOR GRISWOLD: I do not quite understand how that 80-day provision is of particular damage to either side as long as the decision that comes out at the end of the 80 days is retroactive. Most strikes are for economic benefits, and if they are retroactive, just as Senator Smith pointed out, I do not see where you have been damaged any, and in the meantime the public interest has been protected. At least, that is the theory.

The point I make is, what if Congress comes out with a tailormade decision and says, "We will retain the status quo for 90 days or 120 days or 6 months, and then the decision at the end of that time will be retroactive." What if an organization, either of managers or of labor, say, "We refuse to operate on that basis"? Are you not going to have to go into the courts and have injunctions, bring a mandamus and a lot of other legal actions, and throw the whole force of Government into really the maintenance of the decision that Congress may have made?

MR. REUTHER: Obviously, if Congress made a tailormade decision to meet a certain emergency situation and either party to the dispute defied Congress and the emergency continued, then in order to protect the welfare you would have to use the full power of the Government, in court action, et cetera. You would have to do that because the public good must be protected.

SENATOR GRISWOLD: That is the theory back of the Taft-Hartley law, is it not? . . .

MR. REUTHER: Senator, the point we are making is that the uncertainty in the situation creates greater pressure on the parties and a greater sense of urgency to settle. But under Taft-Hartley, where you have the treaty type of thing, they know exactly what is going to happen, so the pressure is not there.

SENATOR GRISWOLD: If we adopted that plan and had a tailormade decision, do you approve of putting strong clauses in there to provide for the enforcement of the decision that Congress may make, using all the processes of Government to put it into effect? You would not disapprove of the most stringent provisions in the act if it was a tailormade decision for that particular case? Do I understand you correctly?

MR. REUTHER: Our proposal obviously contains within it the idea that if the Government is going to tailormake a decision, then the Government obviously has to exercise its authority in the implementation of that decision. Otherwise, it is an academic exercise.

SENATOR GRISWOLD: If Congress in its decision decided instead of them making the tailormade decision, to set up a board that would make a tailormade decision, what is the difference? What if Congress decided, instead of our trying to judge all of these economic and social matters that are involved in a labor dispute, we will set up a board of experts which will in each case make a tailormade decision? Then could not Congress put strong provisions in that act to make that decision effective? That is the normal way that the Government operates. This whole executive department that you speak of is really a product of the executive branch of Government, is it not? The Constitution provides for a President, but it does not say what duties the Department of Labor will have or anything, so it is just a matter of congressional act as to what the National Labor Relations Board shall do, and the General Counsel can do. All these things that are discussed here are really congressional decisions.

MR. REUTHER: This gets back to the fundamental problem in the world between our free society and the totalitarian part of the world. If we cannot find the social mechanisms by which we can resolve the areas of economic conflict between labor, management, and other economic groups, and if we have to rely upon Government by creating machinery, then we are in trouble.

We want to put the maximum reliance upon the voluntary processes by having the parties not be able to look to Government for the use of predetermined machinery. We want to minimize that in order to maximize the voluntary process.

However, in those isolated and remote cases where the voluntary process creates a national emergency of the size and proportions that jeopardize the public safety and welfare, then the Government, as the agency of all the people, has an overriding obligation to intervene. But the intervention is not predetermined, nor is the particular type of intervention predetermined. It is that uncertainty that puts the greatest amount of pressure on the voluntary process and encourages it to operate.

In our kind of world there is no substitute for the voluntary process. That is the whole concept of a free society, to try to find a way to maximize the voluntary process, that people will participate in the voluntary process out of a sense of moral and social responsibility. The minute you predetermine Government intervention, you make it more difficult for the voluntary process to operate. That is the whole basic idea we are trying to advance.

SENATOR GRISWOLD: I can understand the viewpoint that you would like to make the decision voluntarily on both sides, but if Congress acts in the heat of emotion or perhaps because boys are being killed some place or men are being shot during a period of labor strife in Chicago, I do not believe the decision by Congress will be as fair to the public as it might be if the Congress in its wisdom set up a fair-minded board which would be ahead of the problem, which would see it coming a year ahead or 6 months or 3 months ahead and make their decision on the basis of long study of the details of the question. Certainly Government does not operate that way. That is why you set up departments of Government, the Federal Trade Commission, the Federal Power Commission, the Federal Communications Commission, so they, being theoretically experts in that particular field, can make a long study of the problem and arrive at a sound decision in the interest of the public. I do not believe that every time there is a dispute on the Fair Trade Act or pertaining to whether TV should go into an area or whether or not we should broadcast baseball games, Congress should suddenly be asked to make a tailormade decision to answer that particular question. I do not believe it will work.

MR. REUTHER: We have been working at this thing and we do think it will work. That is why we propose it. We think this is the way to get collective bargaining to work and to settle these things at the bargaining table, and that the number of areas in which the Government will have to intervene will be very limited.

If you intervene on this basis, we think that you will minimize the need for intervention. Where you have to intervene, it seems to me that Congress can act in a rational and intelligent manner and create machinery to try to bring about an adjustment that will reflect equities.

In the situation where the railroad workers were threatened with being put in the Army, Congress was not stampeded. Congress acted very sensibly and did the right thing in that situation. We have that much faith in Congress. We think the choice here—

SENATOR IVES: They came very near being stampeded, as I recall. If it had not been for Senator Taft, they might have been.

MR. REUTHER: Being very nearly stampeded is not as serious as being stampeded, you see.

SENATOR PURTELL: Does it not appear, Mr. Reuther, since we are talking about national emergency, since the Government will only intervene in a particular sense in the public interest, it would be timesaving if there were predetermined methods so we could handle this thing? Having exhausted or having given great thought and care to the method to be employed, we could apply it immediately and save the necessary time in the public interest to solve what is then a national emergency.

MR. REUTHER: You are choosing between two sets of values. You are choosing between: Do you want to have the machinery handy so you can bring it into play very quickly; and how much pressure does that detract from the bargaining table? Which is the more desirable? Do you want the maximum pressure at the bargaining table, or do you want convenient machinery handy?

We say that the advantages that make for maximum pressure at the bargaining table, that will encourage the voluntary process and strengthen that, that that is a more important value than the handy machinery. That is the difference here.

Testimony of A. J. Hayes, President, International Association of Machinists, in Taft-Hartley Revisions, hearings before the Senate Committee on Labor and Public Welfare, 83d Cong., 1st Sess., 1953, part 4, pp. 1806–1810

COMPULSORY ARBITRATION

. . . It is my considered judgment that real national emergency situations could be handled most fairly and effectively in the following manner:

1. The President of the United States be specifically empowered to decide whether a major labor-management dispute is a serious threat to our national security or welfare.

2. In such cases as the President determines a national emergency exists, he shall, within a prescribed time, appoint a tripartite emergency board consisting of an equal number of representatives from labor, industry, and neutrals.

3. Following the determination of the President and the appointment of the emergency board, the entire relationship between the parties in dispute shall remain in or revert to the status quo existing immediately before the dispute occurred.

4. This emergency board should be empowered, within a prescribed time limit, to conduct a full hearing and such other investigations as may be necessary.

As soon as possible, but not later than the last day in the prescribed time period, the board should submit to the parties either its unanimous or its majority recommendations.

5. The parties to the dispute should be allowed a prescribed time—probably 30 days—either to accept the emergency board's recommendations or to settle the dispute on some other mutually satisfactory basis.

6. In the event either or both parties fail or refuse to accept the recommendations and fail to agree upon a mutually satisfactory settlement within the 30-day period, the recommendations of the emergency board will become binding upon both parties, effective on or retroactive to the date determined by the board, and shall remain in effect for the period of time determined by the board which in no case shall be longer than 1 year.

SENATOR IVES: What you are defining there, Mr. Hayes, is more in the way of compulsory arbitration, which may have its place in certain circumstances. But what I am interested in here is this: How are you going to be sure that these people keep working?

The big difficulty in a national emergency such as you are citing here is the question of how to keep the workers working. That is why we are floundering around here. We have a provision, as you know, in the Taft-Hartley Act, which nobody is quite satisfied with, and we have all kinds of suggestions for substitutes. You are making one here, which I think has some merit under certain circumstances. But how are you going to keep them working? How are you going to keep production going in a situation of that kind? You do not answer that in your proposal here.

MR. HAYES: You mean: What is the machinery of compulsion?

SENATOR IVES: Yes. How are you going to see that they keep working?

MR. HAYES: I think that the law would provide for certain penalties for violation of it, like any other law that we have does.

SENATOR IVES: In other words, immediately after this emergency board is established, they have to keep working. Is that it? If they do not, they get penalized.

MR. HAYES: Or they are on strike, and they have to go back to work.

SENATOR IVES: They would have to go back to work. Otherwise they would be penalized.

MR. HAYES: And the employer would have to maintain the status quo also.

SENATOR IVES: Or he would be penalized.

MR. HAYES: Yes.

SENATOR IVES: Maybe you have something there. In other words, you would have a money penalty. You would have a penalty in dollars. You would not throw anybody in jail, would you?

MR. HAYES: No. You would have, I presume, a money penalty.

You see, Mr. Chairman, if I may be permitted: I do not think this is the ideal solution to industrial disputes. However, I think it is a better solution than any solution thus far established. From a labor standpoint at least, certainly it is better than the 80-day provision of the present act and the injunction which might follow. Because that provision merely issues an injunction against the labor union and forces the members of unions to work under conditions that are wholly unsatisfactory to them, without providing any machinery for solution at all. . . .

SENATOR IVES: What you are trying to do is to offer something here that makes sure work goes on and a settlement is finally reached, and you are going to do it by the process of compulsory arbitration. I cannot quite agree with you on the compulsory arbitration approval. I do not think we are going to need compulsory arbitration. Because if you insist that they keep working or get fined, I think that will take care of it, and they will quickly come to terms.

MR. HAYES: Of course, I am sorry I can't share that view. Our experience in the labor movement has been the other way. And that has not occurred. I mean, that certainly does not bring about an equitable settlement of the dispute.

SENATOR IVES: Well, certainly compulsory arbitration does not either.

MR. HAYES: Compulsory arbitration certainly does bring about a decision in the dispute.

SENATOR IVES: It brings about a decision, but not an equitable one many times.

MR. HAYES: Without a long delay. You see, the danger in any of these provisions that have been recommended, even giving the Congress carte blanche authority to make its own decision in the case of an industrial dispute, is that they all involve a great deal of delay, procrastination, whatever you might call it. And during this period of delay, the relationship between the workers and the company deteriorates and actually brings about a situation which will result in another labor dispute as soon as either party feels that they have an advantage. In other words, the thing crops out probably year after year. And what we are seeking to do, or what we should seek to do, in my opinion, under this act, is to improve industrial relations and human relations.

SENATOR IVES: I am not sure that your plan of compulsory arbitration would do that. That is why I would stay away from any solution of that nature, any solution at all. I would rather leave it, in each instance, to the Congress to pass ad hoc legislation. That might be compulsory arbitration under certain circumstances. It might be seizure. You cannot tell what it would be. It would depend on the conditions.

MR. HAYES: We would be very vigorously opposed to that, and I think it would be a very serious mistake to do that. Because there are many incidents that precede a situation that finally develops into a national emergency. The press, the radio, news commentators, are all involved, and they prejudice the public and they prejudice Congress one way or the other in situations of that kind. And I think that Congress, or many in Congress, might be unduly influenced by the kind of publicity that was given to the issues in the dispute, and also in some instances by political considerations, in making their decision with regard to the handling of an emergency dispute. . . .

SENATOR IVES: I think your remedy is worse than the disease. When you speak of the railroads, compulsory arbitration with them might be a very proper remedy. Or the utility companies, where the rates themselves are established by Government or at least by the agencies of Government. But when you get into a situation such as the steel situation last year, that was a national emergency if we ever had one, for the Government to set out and resolve the things by compulsory arbitration—and under the program you are suggesting here that is exactly the way it would have wound up, with compulsory arbitration—I am inclined to think that the Government would be exercising too much authority. It takes away the bargaining rights of everybody. Easily a Board of that kind could reach a conclusion which could wipe out a given industry, because it would be so unfair.

MR. HAYES: Of course, I have more confidence in the type of people that would be selected for that purpose, Mr. Chairman. And I might say that again it is necessary to stress that this proposal is based upon the alternatives that we have; not upon an ideal situation, which we know is impossible. But it is based upon the alternatives. And all of the alternatives that we, in the organized labor movement, have at the present time, in effect are injunctions which compel our people to work under conditions that are wholly unsatisfactory to them and do not give them a settlement of the dispute at all. And at best your proposal to permit Congress to act under those circumstances would hang a sword over the heads of our people.

STATE EMERGENCY DISPUTE LEGISLATION IN ACTION

A panel discussion from Proceedings of the Third Annual Conference of the Association of State Mediation Agencies, 1954, pp. 12–22

ROBERT STUTZ, CONNECTICUT, CHAIRMAN

Introductory remarks

The subject of emergency disputes legislation is of particular interest to me as a public member of the Connecticut State Board of Mediation and Arbitration for the reason that in the past year we seem to have had a rash of utility disputes and utility strikes. Whether or not they were emergencies, depends upon where you sit, I think, but they have engendered a certain amount of pressure and I think—I might also go so far as to say I fear that that pressure may develop in the form of some proposed legislation when our state legislature next meets.

That may tip my hand a little as to how I might feel towards some of the emergency legislation which has been in operation, and clarification of which I hope will develop as the discussion goes along. Certainly we can all agree that the question of how to deal with emergency disputes is a very vexing and perplexing one. We all know—and it has been well stated—that the best prophet of the future is the past, and so for the next hour and one-half we're going to look at the past and the present, at some of the experiments that have been carried out in the field of various states, in dealing with emergency disputes.

What we're going to ask the panel members to do, is present to us in as brief a form as possible a description of their experiences with emergency disputes legislation. . . .

ALLAN WEISENFELD, NEW JERSEY

New Jersey, as I think most of you know, was one of the first states in recent history which sought to cope with the problem of labor disputes in public utilities. Public utilities were singled out for treatment because an extended dispute, in a gas utility, for example, can have disastrous effects on life and property.

The New Jersey Legislature, in 1946, enacted a bill providing for gubernatorial seizure of a utility property involved in a labor dispute when said dispute represented a threat to the health and welfare of the people served by the utility.

This legislation was predicated on the philosophy that an informed citizenry would, in its own self-interest, so act as to minimize the threat of the loss of an essential service and thereby further the possibility of peaceful settlement of disputes. One year of experience was adequate to illustrate the fact that the statute did not operate to muster public opinion to the point that its influence in utility labor disputes could be noted.

In 1947, facing a strike of telephone workers, the law was amended to provide for compulsory arbitration following seizure.

Perhaps from lack of experience as much as for any other reason, the statute was over-utilized. The mere threat to strike in a major utility sufficed to induce gubernatorial seizure with consequent deleterious effects on collective bargaining.

As appreciation of the effect of this statute on bargaining grew, reliance on it diminished. A strike in a major electric utility was permitted to play its role for more than a week before the then-Chief Executive seized the property. The seizure order was issued only when information reached the State House that the operation might be substantially interfered with and a large segment of the population would be deprived of electricity if the law were not applied.

Subsequent to the U. S. Supreme Court decision in the Wisconsin case raising the issue of constitutionality of compulsory arbitration laws, the New Jersey statute was permitted to lie dormant. For example, the state tolerated an extended gas strike and, despite pressure from one of the factions to "do something," allowed the discipline of the strike to play its role.

The New Jersey administration does not regard the law with the same attitude as did the preceding administration. Governor Meyner, prior to his election argued that the law needed substantial change since it hindered rather than enhanced complete bargaining between the parties.

One of the first acts of the new administration was the appointment of a tripartite committee of nine to study the New Jersey and similar statutes. He directed this committee to make findings on the operation of the New Jersey Law and such recommendations as it deemed appropriate.

This committee explored the problem extensively and intensively. Its report was published September 9, 1954. The findings can be summarized as follows:

1. There is grave doubt as to the constitutionality of the New Jersey Law dealing with labor disputes in public utilities.

2. Regardless of constitutionality, compulsory arbitration statutes do violence to enunciated public policy favoring collective bargaining as a device to insure industrial peace.

The committee unanimously recommended that the present law be repealed in its entirety. With a single dissent, it recommended that the New Jersey

Legislature adopt a joint resolution holding that the keeping of industrial peace in public utilities rests essentially with the employers and the organizations of workers and not with government. The committee further urged more extensive utilization of the New Jersey State Board of Mediation for the settlement of utility disputes. The dissenting member of the committee felt that fact-finding rather than mediation should be the terminal point in the handling of these disputes.

These recommendations have been applauded by labor and utility employers, with few exceptions. The newspapers of the state have been less enthusiastic. Such editorial comments as I have read express the belief that enactment of the committee's recommendations would leave the people of the state without adequate protection in the event of an "emergency."

Whether one accepts or rejects this committee's recommendations depends in large measure on one's concept of what constitutes an "emergency." If we believe that a lack of public transportation service or inadequate pressure in the gas mains is the price we pay in a democratic society for the privilege of freely disagreeing with one another, then we are inclined to accept the committee's views. If, on the other hand, we feel that our society is of such a delicate and complex structure that its very fabric is threatened by a utility strike, then we would probably look askance at these recommendations.

There is considerable authority supporting the theory that many "emergencies" represent only varying degrees of inconvenience.

It is my own feeling that express statutory legislation is not really required to cope with actual authentic emergencies. Legislation, even when constitutional, merely gilds the lily. The inherent powers of the Executive Office appear to be ample to cope with the really serious problem. If legislative action is required for a particular situation, it is—in New Jersey, at least—a relatively simple matter to provide for a special session of the legislature.

As matters now stand, the Governor of New Jersey plans to discuss the problem of labor disputes in public utilities with his legislative leaders in the light of his committee's report. The final outcome of the committee's recommendations is anyone's guess.

HARRY L. HANSON, MINNESOTA

I am opposed to compulsory arbitration as a means of settling disputes. This statement hardly seems compatible, since we are discussing emergency dispute legislation, with my position as a representative of a state government charged with the responsibility to do everything possible to protect the public from the inconveniences and economic losses sustained through strikes and lockouts. Certainly I would be the last one who would want to see a hospital struck or a community without light or power. I can clearly visualize, as you can, the suffering and hardship that such a work stoppage could bring, but there is too much at stake to accept compulsory arbitration too readily.

I firmly believe that if our country is to continue economically stable with a rising standard of living, we are going to have to do all within our power to place the responsibility for proper labor relations with labor and management and not devise "gimmicks" which give them an opportunity to duck that responsibility.

In Minnesota, we have two regulations governing labor disputes involving emergencies.

First, we have the Charitable Hospital Act which prohibits strikes in charitable hospitals and provides for compulsory arbitration of minimum wages and maximum hours. Unless the parties can agree on an arbiter, the governor appoints one. A recent supreme court decision has interpreted minimum wages and maximum hours generally as all cost items, but excludes union security. This law was passed by our 1947 Legislature. Since that time, many hospital disputes have been arbitrated in accordance with the Statute. What disturbs me is this: I have seen negotiations take place with the aid of a conciliator when an honorable settlement could easily have been reached between the parties had they not been reluctant to assume their responsibilities. Administrators have said, "We think this is a fair settlement, but we are not going to take the responsibility," (and they mean "heat") "of forcing increased hospital costs and possible increased charges on the public."

When they take that position, they are fully aware that an arbitrator might make an award that is even higher than what would be accepted by the union. Where does the public come in if that happens? Management representatives in these situations are only shirking their responsibilities. I hold no brief for the union representative who takes a similar position in saying, "That is a fair settlement, but I am not going to take the 'heat' in either accepting it or recommending it to my membership; let it go to arbitration."

In these situations, neither the representative of management nor the representative of the union is doing his job. Such proceedings can lead only to either excessive cost to management or unfair wages and conditions to employees. If the parties in these situations were without the crutch of compulsory arbitration, would they assume and carry out their responsibilities? I think our unions and our employers, faced with the full responsibility, would accept it. . . .

Compulsory arbitration is nothing more or less than government dictatorship that will lead us down a dark road. There is little certainty of equity in contract arbitration (not that there is in direct negotiations either), but at least the terms are not dictated by an outsider. What about fixing responsibility?

Still, what of the sick and the injured? Can we take a chance with a life for the sake of theoretically better labor relations?

In this limited capacity, compulsory arbitration has been successful in Minnesota for our charitable hospitals. We had better stay with it. At the present time, the unions holding bargaining rights in our hospitals do not oppose arbitration.

We are desperately in need of more qualified arbiters. Much work needs to be done in the study of arbitration practices to be more certain of realistic awards.

Our second piece of legislation designed to take care of emergency labor disputes involves a fact-finding procedure. The Minnesota Labor Relations Act provides for the settlement of labor disputes through the medium of conciliation. All labor disputes, including public utilities, are handled in the same manner. All settlements are voluntary; there is no provision for compulsory arbitration in public utilities.

When it appears to the Labor Conciliator that a strike cannot be avoided in a dispute involving a public utility, he refers the dispute to the governor as being one involving the public interest. The governor may then appoint a fact-finding commission made up of one representative of labor, one representative of management, and one representative of the public, to study the dispute and report their findings to the governor. The referral to the governor of a dispute involving the public interest automatically stays the strike for thirty days.

This procedure has been successful in the majority of disputes. Only one strike has occurred in a public utility. In that situation, a commission was not appointed since the dispute was one affecting commerce and the state was without jurisdiction. However, the final settlement was accomplished through the efforts of state conciliation.

The most salient points of fact-finding under our state law are:

1. all settlements are voluntary
2. the responsibilities to manage and to lead are left with the prime parties and are not left to the whims or theories of outsiders; and
3. the fact finders are local people so that all phases of the dispute are worked out on a local level.

I repeat, we feel very strongly in Minnesota that the responsibility to manage must be left with management and labor and not to outsiders. Disinterestedness or neutrality does not necessarily mean equity. . . .

In the early years of the law, when the parties of the dispute felt that they would eventually end up in fact-finding procedures, they would "sit on their hands" and do very little negotiating for fear of jeopardizing their negotiating position. However, with experience, they have discarded that procedure and free collective bargaining takes place, even to such an extent that it is common to hear either party say, "Let's get down to business so we don't have to go to fact-finding."

During the war period, we were guilty of using our fact-finding procedures too freely in an effort to prevent strikes with the result that our fact-finding procedure lost some of its stature. We are now limiting our use of fact-finding procedure to disputes involving public utilities.

We feel very definitely that our state law does have the approval of all segments of our economy. We see no reason for any significant legislative change in our present labor relations act. We do admit that there is room for perhaps considerable improvement in our operations. Changes in procedures and policies are being made with the advice of labor and management, and surprisingly enough, they are for the most part in agreement as to where corrections should be made.

L. E. GOODING, WISCONSIN

While I believe in collective bargaining, I am not one of those who make a fetish of it. I do not believe that emergency legislation such as we have in

Wisconsin necessarily means that we are not going to have collective bargaining. We have not had enough experience with this type of legislation anywhere to definitely come to such a conclusion. It is true that in Wisconsin after the so-called Public Utility Act was adopted we had many threats of strikes. In spite of the law, we had some strikes. Concededly, labor unions were opposed to any limitation of their right to strike and were advised by counsel that the law was invalid and could not be enforced. Eventually, such was the holding of the United States Supreme Court. That Court held that the Wisconsin Public Utility Law was in conflict with the National Labor Relations Act and for that reason could not be applied to any utilities within the State of Wisconsin if their business brought them within the jurisdiction of the National Labor Relations Board. That, of course, took in practically every utility employer within the State of Wisconsin under the standards then being applied by the National Board. . . .

It is, of course, possible that the existence of this legislation in Wisconsin did affect free collective bargaining during the time that an attempt was made to enforce it. If it did affect collective bargaining, it was not for the reason usually given—that the parties wanted to wait for arbitration. I agree with Mr. Hanson's statement on the experience in Minnesota that the normal tendency of the parties would develop the desire to get down to the business of bargaining so they would not have to appear before one of those fact-finding boards in Minnesota, or an arbitration board in Wisconsin. In other words, my opinion is that, given ample opportunity to apply the law, the same thing would develop in Wisconsin that Mr. Hanson states developed in Minnesota in the minds of bargaining representatives. However, it is apparent that the New Jersey committee appointed to undertake a study came to an entirely different conclusion. Generally, neither labor nor management have any desire to have their collective bargaining problems finally settled by an outsider, who may be wholly unsatisfactory to either one or the other. Normally, they desire to dispose of them by attempting to arrive at an agreement in bargaining across the table. I am convinced that, if we had had sufficient experience under these emergency anti-strike laws, the parties would bargain more freely and more honestly than they bargain today. I say that in view of some of the things that I understood Mr. Weisenfeld to say. In collective bargaining, when the union is weak, the employer is in a position to dictate the terms of the agreement. On the other hand, if the union is in a strong position and able to shut down the operation of the business, it is in a position to do the dictating. It is always the public that has to pay.

A great many collective bargaining agreements between labor organizations and public utility employers today contain provisions providing for the arbitration of disputes arising during the negotiation of a new bargaining agreement. This agreement to arbitrate usually is not to take effect until the expiration of the present agreement. The parties have no idea of what the issues between them will be when such agreement is executed. It is somewhat difficult for me to see why the arbitration of terms and conditions to be included in the new agreement, when such arbitration is based upon the provisions of an expiring agreement, does not interfere with free collective bargaining to exactly the same extent that a statutory compulsory arbitration act would interfere.

My position basically is that we are in a new field. Our compulsory arbitration laws have been applied generally, and in Wisconsin, entirely, to situations which, if allowed to develop, would affect large segments of the community. We have not had enough experience in Wisconsin, nor in any of the other states which have adopted some type of legislation to attempt to control these emergencies, to make broad statements that they will not work. It is, of course, entirely possible that this type of legislation or something that might grow out of it would be beneficial to the general public and at the same time, in no way seriously harm the parties immediately involved in the dispute. One way that such a determination could be made would be by testing the efficiency of various types of emergency legislation, whether it included compulsory arbitration or not in the different states, hoping eventually that the experience gained would help solve some of the present difficulties.

DANIEL C. ROGERS, MISSOURI

Missouri has the so-called emergency legislation in the field of public utilities only. We have no other labor relations statute. The statute was enacted in 1947. It gives the State Board of Mediation jurisdiction in labor disputes of all public utilities including transportation, except railroads. Our Board is a tripartite board consisting of two management members, two labor members, and a public member. I am the public member and Chairman of the Board.

Our law is a simple one. It's divided into two divisions. One division establishes the State Board of Mediation and gives us general mediation authority in all labor disputes in public utilities. The parties do not invite us to come into their dispute. The statute puts us into their dispute from its inception.

Therefore, we have as many cases subject to our jurisdiction, as there are contracts negotiated every year in public utilities in the State of Missouri. Roughly, we have one hundred public utilities in Missouri. We have jurisdiction in any dispute between the employees and the utilities. Of course, we rarely have a dispute between the employees and the utility unless the employees are organized, so you may assume, therefore, that all our dispute experience is between unions and management. Each time a union or a utility under our statute gives the other sixty days notice of desire to make changes in the contract, it must specify those changes and file a copy with the State Board of Mediation. Upon receipt of requests for changes, we docket what we call a "case," and give the dispute a case number. In this manner approximately 100 cases are docketed as they come in during the year. Upon being docketed, it becomes the duty of the Board to watch those cases and see that negotiations are concluded in some manner or other. When I acknowledge receipt of every "case" that is docketed, I include the following paragraph in my letter:

> It is always the sincere hope of the members of the Missouri State Board of Mediation that labor agreements will be amicably and successfully negotiated between the parties in their own collective bargaining

conferences. Confidence is expressed that you will do so in this case. How-
ever, if a situation should arise requiring the mediation services of the
Missouri State Board of Mediation, under the provisions of Chapter 295,
RSMo 1949, it will be appreciated if either or both parties will advise this
Board promptly.

That paragraph is the key to our administration.

We keep educating the parties that it is their duty to settle their own disputes, in their own collective bargaining conferences. If, however, they should
reach an impasse, they report it to the Board. In that situation, the Chairman
in conference with them will, in most cases, be able to get the parties together.
I always want them to believe that even though I come to assist them it's really
a minor assistance, and that they themselves have successfully concluded the
negotiations.

Out of the 100 cases we docket, not more than 20 even become anything like
problem cases. The remaining 80 are removed from the docket by correspondence. In at least one-half of the 20 problem cases, I encourage the parties to go
back into negotiations to settle the dispute or I go to the place myself to work
with them to settle it. Out of the other ten, three, four, or five of them develop
into near strike situations each year.

That's about the way we handle mediation in public utilities in Missouri.

Our statutes also provide that should these efforts in mediation break down,
there shall be a public hearing panel. It's our policy to avoid public hearing
panels because we feel that it's in the interest of free collective bargaining to
keep panels out of it, and not to encourage the parties to depend upon the
services of the panel. We want them to do their own bargaining. But we do
have the so-called fact-finding panels and they are valuable if properly used.

These panels issue only recommendations. Their findings are not binding. A
few parties urge the use of panel services each year. When they use panels, we
request that they stipulate that the findings of the panel shall be final and
binding. In the majority of cases the parties so stipulate.

The second provision of the Act, is the provision for seizure by the governor.
The Act simply states that if the public interest, health and welfare become
jeopardized by reason of a strike or the threat of strike, the governor, upon so
finding, may seize the utility and operate it for the use and benefit of the State
of Missouri.

This seizure provision has not been litigated in our state to a conclusion
before our Supreme Court. We are not, however, the slightest uneasy concerning the legal validity of seizure as a principle under the police power. Our
statute may be poorly drafted, mechanically. But the principle of seizure is
sound. Seizure is sound, simply because it is based upon jeopardy to the public
interest, health and welfare. No one has a right to conduct a strike, however
meritorious, if it jeopardizes the public interest, health and welfare. And, in a
civilized society, we do not need to wait until we have an absolute catastrophe
before the public has a right to step in and say that there must be an end to a
strike or lockout. The people will not much longer sit by idly and let manage-

ment and labor jeopardize the public interest with strikes or lockouts in industries that are so essential to the public welfare.

In Missouri, a large measure of success, if I should claim that we are succeeding in administering our law, is due to the sympathetic understanding and the fearless stand that our governor always takes in the so-called public emergencies. In close cooperation with the State Board of Mediation, he will in each situation take some very positive public stand on the strike, whether actually in progress or scheduled to go in effect. His participation is by means of a telegram to the parties warning them of their public duty and demanding that their dispute shall continue in mediation until settled.

The public interest must be protected by the governor, because it's the public policy of the State of Missouri that every public utility must render its service safely, adequately, and continuously.

Therefore, where is there any inviolate "right" to strike? Where does a utility have any "right" to lock out under the law of the land?

Here's what the governor said in part in one particular case:

The traveling public is entitled to your transportation services continuously. The Company holds both a certificate of public convenience and necessity and an interstate permit from the public service commission of Missouri to operate as a common carrier of passengers for hire upon and over the public highways of Missouri. This authority to render a vital service to the public should no longer be violated. Therefore, I request and expect that you cooperate with the State Board of Mediation in an effort to restore transportation service upon the routes of the (company) in Missouri.

We have other communications of that kind here that the governor has sent to transit systems and to electric light and power systems.

It's strong language. But, it's the public interest that's threatened. Strange as it may seem to some people, the parties respect the seizure statute and the governor who stands by it.

Strikes or lockouts which jeopardize the public interest are not some sacred thing that the people should shrink from and say that we have no part in them. It's the people's business. Years ago the right of contract on the part of public utilities to fix their rates with the public was taken away from them. I don't say that we should take the right of collective bargaining decisions away from the disputing parties. Let them negotiate, but if they fail, rather than have the public interest jeopardized, I advocate with compulsory arbitration or even seizure. It's certainly far better than allowing a calamitous strike. People will not tolerate the calamitous situations caused by strikes or lockouts, at least not in public utilities, and perhaps not in some of the other industries.

We're just too far along in our social development to tolerate such things and I think our seizure law in Missouri is a good law. It's written approximately correct. There are some things that could be bettered in it, but if we administer it impartially and wisely, I think it will continue to have widespread endorsement of the people.

FOR DISCUSSION AND ANALYSIS

1. One labor expert has made the assertion, "People who talk about prohibiting strikes are really talking about prohibiting collective bargaining." Do you agree?

2. In the message accompanying his veto of the Taft-Hartley bill (a veto later overridden by Congress) President Truman made the following criticism of the "emergency-strike" provisions:

. . . a fundamental inequity runs through these provisions. The bill provides for injunctions to prohibit workers from striking, even against terms dictated by employers after contracts have expired. There is no provision assuring the protection of the rights of the employees during the period they are deprived of the right to protect themselves by economic action.

Appraise the validity and significance of this criticism.

3. It has been argued that an antistrike law or some form of strike control should apply only to cases of genuine emergency. (a) Do you concur? (b) If so, how would you define "genuine emergency"?

4. Compare and contrast the strike-control approaches of Mr. Reuther and Mr. Hayes in their testimony reproduced above. Itemize the advantages and disadvantages of each proposal. Which do you prefer?

5. The New Jersey Governor's Committee on Legislation Relating to Public Utility Disputes, in a questionnaire addressed to a number of labor and management people, asked this question:

"If you were drafting a law designed to promote peaceful industrial relations in public utilities consistent with protecting the tripartite interest involved, what features would you incorporate in such a law? And why would you include those particular features?"

How would you answer?

18: Wage Determination

The diversity of problems which may arise in the process of wage determination is such that only a few of the major issues can be dealt with in this chapter.

We start with the setting of the rate on individual jobs, a matter which is frequently done by the process of job evaluation.

Setting Individual Rates

In 1951 the Armstrong Rubber Co. of West Haven, Conn., sought to institute a system of job evaluation, but was opposed by the union, which called a strike on this and related matters. The company—believing its employees had been misled—undertook to educate them concerning the "full facts of job evaluation" and at the same time to acquaint the public with its position in the strike. Below are reproduced portions of two advertisements which appeared in the New Haven Register and were reprinted by the company for additional distribution.

HOW MUCH IS A JOB WORTH?

Men and women who work ask themselves not only—"How much am *I* worth?"

But, sooner or later, they begin to think about the work done by other people —people who work next to them, or in other departments of a company. It's human to make comparisons. Every day you hear people doing it. They use words like "Joe is a smarter fellow than Mike," or "Mary is better looking than Sally. . . ."

At Armstrong, we are planning to complete a *program* of job evaluation on which we have been working for a long time.

There are many reasons why we feel obligated to complete this program now. Here are some of the reasons that are important to every person who works at Armstrong, and in the community in which we all work.

1. We believe our average wages are among the highest in the New Haven area. *Our policy will always be to keep them there.* Job evaluation will make this possible on an unbiased, scientific basis. It will make it possible also to be

sure that each individual is rewarded *fairly* for the amount of skill, care, and effort required on his job.

2. Job evaluation means more *job satisfaction* for the individual through making sure that jobs and men are matched. We want people to be placed in the jobs they can do best—which means usually the job they will *most enjoy*. We cannot be sure this is accomplished, *no matter what else we may do*, until evaluation of every job in our plant has been completed.

3. We want to keep down the total *cost* of manufacturing our products without reducing anyone's pay. In fact, at the same time we are proposing to complete the job evaluation program we have offered to *increase* wages throughout the factory on an average of 11½ cents an hour.

4. With regard to *future* wage increases, completing our job evaluation program will make it possible for us to be sure that each individual employee gets his *fair share* of whatever the increase may be.

5. When we bid on government contracts, as our part in the new national defense program, the Government will ask: "How do you *know* your bid is fair in comparison with others?" *Job evaluation* will help us answer this question—in your interest and ours.

These are some of the reasons why we feel a job evaluation program is necessary *now*. These reasons apply not only at Armstrong, but in many other manufacturing plants that have job evaluation programs.

For thousands of plants *already* do have such programs, and many authorities believe that job evaluation has helped to make the average American worker the highest paid in the world.

Besides this, remember, every time you ask yourself:

What's *my* job worth?, or What's *his* job worth?

You are making a job evaluation.

THE ARMSTRONG RUBBER CO., WEST HAVEN, CONNECTICUT

HOW MUCH IS ANY JOB WORTH?

(And what "yardstick" would you use to measure it?)

This is the third of three simple questions. But the answer to them—and understanding the answer—is important to every American. The *American* answer is part of the truth we are defending everywhere.

Here are the three simple questions:

What is *my* job worth?

What is *his* job worth?

What is *any* job worth?

Under Communism, the answer to all three is . . . Nothing! Nothing, except what people *you do not choose* choose to decide.

In America, the answer to "what is *any* job worth," is

What *you* put into it, in skill, care and effort.

What *you* put into it, compared with what other people have to put into *their* jobs.

The *method* by which the skill, care and effort required of you are measured in relation to the amount required for other people's jobs, is called *job evaluation.*

Job evaluation is concerned only with accurate, unbiased measurement of the *comparative* amount of skill, care and effort your job requires as against other jobs in the same plant or the same industry. It has nothing to do with whether wages are high or low in the plant where you work.

In practice, this is decided (at Armstrong and in thousands of other plants in the United States) by *collective bargaining.*

In a Union Shop like Armstrong, only through collective bargaining can your wage level go up or down.

Job evaluation can decide only what your job is worth compared with other jobs in the plant.

Collective bargaining is a basic method for arriving at agreement on what people should be paid. We have accepted this idea at Armstrong, and continue to bargain even when agreement seems difficult. We believe in collective bargaining.

But when you ask yourself: "what is any *job* worth?" you have to consider some other things also . . . things that *must* be considered in any collective bargaining that is carried out in good faith on both sides.

You have to consider:

Are *costs* high or low in this company *and* industry in relation to the amount of money taken in from sales?

Is this company in "tough" or "easy" competition with other companies in the same industry?

Does this company make a "high" or "low" profit in relation to its total amount of sales?

Does this company provide "steady" or "unsteady" employment year after year?

Does the company maintain "high" or "low" wage rates in the community where it operates?

Back of all collective bargaining are questions like these.

They have to be taken into account in any collective bargaining worthy of the name.

And when they have been considered in good faith by both sides of the bargaining table, it is necessary to remember also

That what any job is worth is decided in the long run by:

1. The total wage bill a company can support if it is to keep its prices reasonable and make a reasonable profit.

2. *How much* a company can pay for *each* kind of job, without being unfair to the people who work on other jobs.

By considering and dealing with these two questions *together*, American industry has managed to pay its workers *better* than any other industry, *under any other system in the world.*

When these two questions are separated or ignored you get:

Bankruptcy *or Communism.*

In the long run, we believe, *these are the same thing!*

So, we are asking Armstrong workers, through the representatives of *their* choice to agree to a job evaluation program that will *help assure* the permanence of their own jobs and of the high wages we pay and are prepared to *increase now,* and as circumstances permit in the future.

THE ARMSTRONG RUBBER CO., WEST HAVEN, CONNECTICUT

JOB EVALUATION PLANS

Excerpts from What's Wrong with Job Evaluation?, International Association of Machinists, 1954, pp. 20–26, 51–63

There are four basic job evaluation plans in common use. Two of these are quantitative (*point rating* and *factor comparison*) and two are non-quantitative (*job ranking* and *classification or slotting*). By quantitative, we mean that an attempt is made to measure, through points or money, the quantity of each factor designated in the plan for each job. The most usual factors are skill, responsibility, effort, and working conditions. It is assumed that these factors are common to all jobs and that the amount or quantity of each factor can be accurately measured to determine the job's relative value. Those jobs given the greatest number of evaluated points are naturally the highest paid jobs, and those with the lesser number are the lowest paid jobs.

The non-quantitative plans view each job in its entirety, and do not attempt to single out and measure with an absolute point or money system the quantity of each factor in each job. Usually, the non-quantitative plans permit the consideration of influences external to the actual job itself; i.e., supply and demand of a particular skill, career prospects, area or industry wage patterns. Because of this, organized labor has found this type of plan to be the least objectionable. . . .

A. NON-QUANTITATIVE JOB EVALUATION PLANS

1. Job ranking

The most common of the non-quantitative job evaluation plans (one that doesn't attempt to measure each factor) is the job ranking method. It is by far the simplest and does not involve the complicated evaluation process that you find with the quantitative plans. In short, the title and brief description of each job is placed on a card of convenient size. The cards are then stacked according to their estimated relative importance, with the job warranting the highest compensation at the top of the stack and the card warranting the lowest compensation at the bottom. The procedure most usually followed when ranking jobs under this method is to have the union committee and the management rank the cards independently of each other. After each has completed this process, both committees compare their findings to note discrepancies. Disagreements should be settled by the give and take of collective bargaining. . . .

After ranking is agreed upon, a single money rate or rate range is then assigned to each job or each group of jobs, if jobs are grouped into labor grades.

The assignment of money rates to the evaluated jobs should be accomplished through the give and take of collective bargaining. . . .

2. The classification or slotting method

Another non-quantitative system of job evaluation is the Classification Method, which in some areas has also been known as the Slotting Method. This method is used by many employers.

The Classification or Slotting Method, like the Ranking Method, attempts to view and evaluate each job in its entirety. There is no attempt to break down, isolate, and measure each factor. Furthermore, consideration of external forces is sometimes permitted under this system. A list of predetermined labor grades with specific requirements is first established. The number of labor grades agreed upon will vary, depending upon the range of jobs to be evaluated. If the number of labor grades with the requirements has been established, each individual job is analyzed and compared to the requirements of each labor grade. A job will be placed in the labor grade which contains the requirements most comparable to those of the job. After each job is slotted or ranked in its proper labor grade, the parties will determine the rates of pay for each grade. Many times, however, the rates of pay assigned to each labor grade are determined prior to the evaluation of the job. In the former case, where they are assigned after the evaluation, there is a tendency, according to the job evaluation experts, for assignments to be unduly influenced by present rates. They claim that in all probability intraplant inequities will be continued.

B. QUANTITATIVE PLANS

1. The point rating method of job evaluation

The point rating method of job evaluation is perhaps the most commonly used method of formal job evaluation plans. When one refers to job evaluation plans they usually refer to this method. The basis of this method rests upon the assumption that each job in a particular shop or plant is composed of a given number of common factors. This number of factors may vary from four to forty depending upon the writers of the plan. The factors most commonly used are skill, responsibility, effort and job conditions. Each of these factors is broken down into subfactors. For example, skill is broken down into education, experience, initiative and ingenuity. Effort is broken down into physical and mental demands, etc. Each factor is given a range of points which is further broken down into a specific number of points for each subfactor. Furthermore, each subfactor may have various degrees as reflected in Table 1.

While some plans give a like number of points to each factor, there are others which weigh certain factors more heavily than others. These are known as weighted point rating job evaluation plans.

Following Table 2 you will note the definition of the "Complexity Factor," which was taken from a rather elaborate job evaluation plan. This factor is broken down into six degrees (see Table 2) with a range of points from 20 to 100. In this particular plan there are ten different factors each of which are

Table 1. The National Electrical Manufacturers Association Job Evaluation Plan

Factors	1st degree	2nd degree	3rd degree	4th degree	5th degree	Total points possible
Skill						
1. Education	14	28	42	56	70 ⎞	
2. Experience	22	44	66	88	110 ⎬	250
3. Initiative and ingenuity	14	28	42	56	70 ⎠	
Effort						
4. Physical demand	10	20	30	40	50 ⎞	
5. Mental or visual demand	5	10	15	20	25 ⎠	75
Responsibility						
6. Equipment or process	5	10	15	20	25 ⎞	
7. Material or product	5	10	15	20	25 ⎟	
8. Safety of others	5	10	15	20	25 ⎟	100
9. Work of others	5	..	15	..	25 ⎠	
Job Conditions						
10. Working conditions	10	20	30	40	50 ⎞	
11. Unavoidable hazards	5	10	15	20	25 ⎠	75

Southern California Aircraft Job Evaluation Plan

Factors	1st degree	2nd degree	3rd degree	4th degree	5th degree
Skill [1]	245	Minimum	400	Maximum	
Mentality	20	40	60	80	100
Responsibility for material and equipment	20	40	60	80	100
Mental application	10	20	30	40	50
Physical application	10	20	30	40	50
Job conditions	5	15	25	35	45
Unavoidable hazards	5	15	25	35	45

[1] Degrees not applicable to skill factor.

Table 2. Points Assigned to Each Degree of Each Factor of a Weighted Job Evaluation Plan

Degree	1 Complexity	2 Education	3 Experience	4 Maturity	5 Initiative	6 Errors	7 Contacts	8 Supervision	9 Physical demands	10 Working conditions
1	20	20	10	20	20	10	10	5	10	10
2	30	40	20	20	30	20	20	10	20	20
3	45	60	30	30	40	40	40	15	30	30
4	70	90	50	50	55	80	60	20		
5	85	130	70	70						
6	100	...	90							
7	...	...	120							
8	...	...	135							
9	...	...	150							

divided into from three to nine different degrees. Unlike the N.E.M.A. Plan, the factors are not broken down into subfactors. Each degree of each factor has a specific definition and a specific point value.

COMPLEXITY FACTOR

The diversity of job content and the degree to which judgment must be exercised are reflected in this factor. The complexity increases with the variety of different things covered by the position and the difficulty of using the necessary knowledge for successful job performance.

1. Simple, repetitive, routine duties. Little or no choice of action.

2. Routine duties involving different well-defined procedures. Work is easily understood and is performed in sequence established by instruction or precedent.

3. Routine duties within easily understood procedures. Minor decisions are required which may be related to procedure or precedent. Relating cases to precedent requires original thinking and quality of results may be affected.

4. Work is chiefly standard in nature, and generally covered by procedure or precedent. Choices of action are available which may considerably affect quality of work and effectiveness of results.

5. Duties require detailed knowledge of theory and principles of a major function. Procedures and techniques are generally established but interpretation of Company policy and application of principles of an established occupation or profession is regularly required.

6. Duties are complex and diverse requiring application of broad principles to problems not soluble by application of standard or precedent. Work to

definitely assigned goals, making necessary modifications to methods and approaches.

When evaluating a particular job under this plan, the job is analyzed in the light of the degrees of each factor and the corresponding point value of that degree most closely resembling the requirements embodied in that job is assigned to that job. For example, if the complexity factor in a "stenographer-general" job closely resembles the definition of the fourth degree of the complexity factor, that job would be assigned 70 points for that factor. After the job is evaluated for all factors and a point value is assigned for each, the points are then totaled to determine the total point value of the job. Table 3 reflects the breakdown or range of points for each job level or labor grade. (Job level, job group, or labor grade, are common terms used to define groups of similarly valued jobs.)

Table 3. Salary Evaluation Manual Points Assigned to Job Levels

Job level	Point range
1	Up to 160
2	165–200
3	205–240
4	245–280
5	285–320
6	325–360
7	365–400
8	405–440
9	445–480
10	485–520
11	525–560
12	565–Over

A job evaluated to 390 points would be placed in job level 7. To each job level in Table 3 is assigned a single rate or rate range, and all classifications or jobs falling within the point range opposite the job level will receive that rate. There is a definite relationship between the number of points assigned each classification and the wage rate that classification will receive. . . .

The plan outlined in Table 2 above is a weighted point rating plan. This means that the 9 of the 10 factors used in the plan have different point values and an increase or decrease of one factor will not have the same effect on the total evaluated points as another. The number of factors used, and the weight given to each factor, will be determined by the scope and nature of the unit to be evaluated. Because this plan was used to evaluate a technical and office unit in an airframe plant, the Physical Demand and Working Conditions Factors are weighted quite low. (4% each or a total of 8%.) As could be expected, most jobs are either routine office jobs or technical jobs; neither require strenuous physical exertion, nor are the working conditions particularly obnoxious. On the other hand, you will note that upon examination of the N.E.M.A. Plan, these factors total 20% of the total point value of the plan, and in the Southern California Aircraft Plan, these factors represent 25% of the total. The latter two plans were devised to evaluate jobs where the physical demands and working conditions factors would normally warrant a higher value. It is impossible to judge whether the 4%, 20% or 25% weights are fair determinations unless one actually examined the work performed in those plants where these plans are used. . . .

2. Factor comparison method of job evaluation

The factor comparison system of job evaluation is very similar to the point rating system in that it attempts to measure the quantity of each factor for each job designated in the plan. The principal difference, however, is that instead of attempting to assign a particular *point* value to each factor, the actual *money* value of each factor is assigned to that factor.

The first step when employing this method is to determine a number of key jobs ranging from the lowest to the highest skill. . . . After selecting eight or ten jobs (the number depends on the total number of jobs in the unit) the committee of union and management representatives (providing there is joint participation) will rank these jobs according to each factor, as shown in Table 5. That is, all jobs are ranked according to Mental Requirements, Skill, etc. Differences in opinion between the members of the committee can be averaged out.

Table 5. Average Rank Assigned Key Jobs (with fractions eliminated)

		Factors				
	Rate	Mental require-ments	Skill	Physical require-ments	Responsi-bility	Working condi-tions
Tool and diemaker............	2.20	1	1	6	2	7
Automatic screw machine set-up.	2.00	3	2	4	3	6
Engine lathe operator..........	1.90	2	3	8	1	8
Turret lathe operator..........	1.80	4	4	3	4	3
Milling machine operator.......	1.70	5	5	5	6	4
Assembler....................	1.60	7	7	1	7	1
Drill press operator............	1.50	6	6	7	5	5
Common laborer..............	1.40	8	8	2	8	2

You will note, that where one job might rank first in Mental Requirements, it may not necessarily rank first with the other factors.

The next step is to rank each job in terms of the money value for each factor. That is, if the present rate for tool and diemakers is 2.20 per hour, it is necessary to determine what part of the total rate is to be attributed to the skill factor, to the responsibility factor, etc. The total amount assigned to all factors cannot exceed the rate for that job. (See Table 6.)

Table 6. Money Value Distributed and Prior Ranking Assigned Key Jobs

| | | \multicolumn{10}{c}{Factors} |
| | Present rate | Mental require- ments | | Skill | | Physical require- ments | | Responsi- bility | | Working conditions | |
		MVD¹	R²	MVD	R	MVD	R	MVD	R	MVD	R
Tool and diemaker....	$2.20	$.562	1	$.728	1	$.324	4	$.360	2	$.226	6
Automatic screw machine set-up.....	2.00	.482	3	.690	2	.292	6	.324	4	.212	7
Engine lathe operator.	1.90	.550	2	.474	5	.134	8	.606	1	.136	8
Turret lathe operator..	1.80	.310	4	.490	3	.368	3	.332	3	.300	3
Milling machine operator..........	1.70	.302	5	.476	4	.316	5	.312	5	.294	4
Assembler.....	1.60	.224	7	.256	7	.496	1	.250	7	.374	1
Drill press operator...	1.50	.276	6	.384	6	.264	7	.310	6	.266	5
Common laborer......	1.40	.222	8	.172	8	.466	2	.194	8	.346	2

¹ MVD—Money Value Distributed.
² R—Prior Ranking.

After the assignment of money value for each factor for each job is completed it is necessary to compare the ranking of the factor in terms of money value to the prior ranking. If there are any discrepancies, that is if the two rankings do not agree, adjustments can be made by either party, or if no agreement is reached, it is necessary to *drop* these jobs from the list of key jobs.

After the jobs on which no agreement is reached have been dropped from the list a comparison scale is established to provide a measure for slotting all other jobs. In the comparison scale the key jobs are *ranked by factor* showing the cents value assigned that job for that factor. (See Table 7.)

You will note that the job of Carpenter's Helper is slotted between the Drill Press Operator and the Assembler for the Mental Requirement factor. This job evidently requires less mental effort than the Drill Press Operator and more than the Assembler. The opinion of the parties will determine whether this job is allocated 23 or 26¢ or another figure for the value of this factor. This process is repeated for all factors to obtain the rates for jobs other than the key jobs. . . .

ASSIGNMENT OF WAGE RATES TO EVALUATED JOBS

Before explaining the various methods used to assign values to evaluated jobs it is necessary to describe briefly the many variations of rate structures that

Table 7. Comparison Scale for Evaluating Job of Carpenter's Helper by Five Key Jobs

Mental requirements	CA [1]	Responsibility	CA
Engine lathe operator...........	.550	Engine lathe operator...........	.606
Turret lathe operator...........	.310	Turret lathe operator...........	.332
Drill press operator............	.276	Drill press operator............	.310
Carpenter's helper		*Carpenter's helper*	
Assembler....................	.224	Assembler....................	.250
Common laborer...............	.222	Common laborer...............	.194

Skill		Working conditions	
Engine lathe operator...........	.474	Assembler....................	.374
Turret lathe operator...........	.490	Common laborer...............	.346
Carpenter's helper		Turret lathe operator...........	.300
Drill press operator............	.384	*Carpenter's helper*	
Assembler....................	.256	Drill press operator............	.266
Common laborer...............	.172	Engine lathe operator...........	.136

Physical effort	
Assembler....................	.496
Common laborer...............	.466
Turret lathe operator...........	.368
Carpenter's helper	
Drill press operator............	.264
Engine lathe operator...........	.134

[1] (CA—cents assigned).

may be used when assigning money rates to evaluated jobs. The determination of the form to be used is separate and apart from the actual money rates assigned to each classification or to each labor grade. By form of rate structure, we mean one of the following:

a. Single rates for each classification with uniform differentials between rates (Fig. A, Chart I)

b. Single rates for each classification with varying differentials between rates (this differential can either be expressed centswise or percentagewise) (Fig. B, Chart I)

c. Rate ranges for each classification with a uniform spread for all rate ranges, and uniform differentials between rate ranges; they may or may not overlap (Fig. C, Chart I) and

d. Rate ranges for each classification with various spreads for each rate range and various differentials between rate ranges; they may or may not overlap. (Fig. D, Chart I)

Chart I

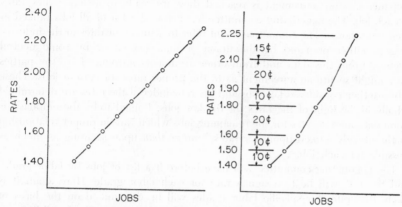

Fig. A. Single rates with uniform differentials between jobs, or groups of jobs. (Labor grades.)

Fig. B. Single rates with varying differentials between jobs, or groups of jobs. (Labor grades.)

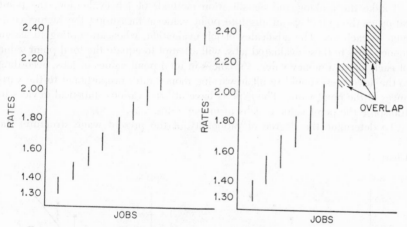

Fig. C. Rate ranges with uniform spread and uniform differentials between ranges.

Fig. D. Rate ranges with varying spreads and varying differentials between ranges. (Note overlapping.)

Assignment of money rates under the job ranking method

The assignment of money rates to evaluated jobs, when using the Ranking Method of job evaluation, *might appear* to the casual observer to be no different from what might occur in the give and take of everyday collective bargaining. As you will recall, the union and management committees decide independently

of each other the ranking of all jobs and then compare notes to resolve discrepancies. After agreement is reached they are ready to assign money rates
to each job. The negotiating committee has before it a list of all jobs ranked in
their importance. The committee might refer to a survey of rates in the industry
or area either prepared by the union or management or by some neutral
agency. From this data and from other arguments introduced by the parties
they might secure an agreement as to the proper rates for *certain* jobs. These
jobs are then considered key jobs and the remainder of the rates are determined
wholly in the light of the rates for the key jobs. Immediately, the emphasis is
upon determining rates for the remaining jobs which "are in proper relationship
to the already agreed upon key rates," *rather than* upon securing as much as
possible for each job. . . .

The negotiating committee will have before it a list of jobs by labor grades
and the task will be to assign a rate for each labor grade. Here again it is
likely that rates for specific labor grades will be determined on the basis of
area or industry wage surveys and through other arguments. These will become,
we might say, key labor grade rates and rates for the other grades will be
determined in light of those already agreed upon. . . .

Assigning rates under the point rating system

Unlike the ranking and classification methods of job evaluation, the point
rating method employs an absolute point value in measuring the factors common to each job. The advocates of job evaluation, when attempting to assign
money rates to these evaluated jobs, will attempt to equate the total point value
of each job to a money value. Variances in total point values of jobs, according
to the advocates, should result in varying money rates proportional to the variances of the point value. The experts have utilized various statistical devices to
transpose the point value of jobs to money rates. . . .

To determine the degree of rationality of the present wage structure, the

Chart II

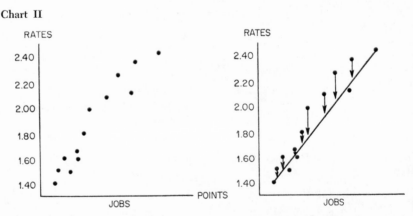

Fig. A. Scatter diagram.   Fig. B. Application of conversion
                                            line to scatter diagram.

job evaluation expert would plot the present money rate and point value of each job on a simple graph. The negotiated wage rate is expressed in cents per hour and is represented on the vertical axis, and the evaluation points are represented on the horizontal axis, as shown in Chart II, Fig. A. Each dot, as indicated in Fig. A, represents the job plotted according to evaluated points and the present rates. The job evaluation experts would hastily observe that the present wage structure is not a rational one, since the money rates of the job do not progress in accordance with the evaluated points for the jobs. He would then draw a line from the lowest to the highest paid job, as indicated in Chart II, Fig. B. This is commonly called a conversion line and is also referred to as the wage curve. To "bring all the other jobs in line" with their point value, the job evaluation expert would recommend that those jobs falling above the line should be reduced in pay, while those jobs falling beneath the line should be increased. The rates of those jobs remaining above the line would be red circled, i.e., the present incumbents would continue receiving the highest rate but upon leaving their jobs the new employees would receive the lower evaluated rate.

There are other methods of drawing a conversion line than the one mentioned above. Some management consultant firms use the "least squares" method and others may draw a line merely by "inspection". . . .

Just what are the job evaluation experts saying when they use this method to determine a wage structure? Essentially they are indicating that there should be a fixed money relationship between the various jobs. The wage curve can also be interpreted as a progression curve; that is, to measure the rate at which one has to move to ascend to the highest paid job. You will note in Chart III, that curve X represents a lesser rate of progression than curve Y. That is, if one were to move from point 1 to point 2, the rate increase would be 7¢ on curve X, while the rate increase would be 23¢ on curve Y. . . .

You will note in Chart IV, that by slightly raising the lowest paid job the entire wage structure will be altered. Also, that by slightly raising or lowering the highest paid job, the entire wage structure will likewise be changed. . . .

You will note in Chart V, Fig. A, that an across the board wage increase will slightly raise the wage curve. The slope of the curve will not change. If a percentage increase is granted however (Fig. B), you will note that the new wage curve is slightly upward sloping. A series of percentage increases given over a period of years, therefore, will radically alter the wage curve initially established. Essentially, if the highest paid job is increased more than the lowest paid job, then the curve will tend to slope upward. The relative value of the points will increase and thereby permit greater monetary and point changes in jobs than existed heretofore. Since the highest and lowest rates, according to the users of this method for determining a wage structure, form a skeleton upon which all other rates are hung, the greater the opportunity to raise the higher rate, the greater the opportunity to increase the spread between the highest and lowest rate.

Some plans have a mathematical formula which is applied to the Point Value of jobs to determine the wage rate for the job. Under this system the plant base

Chart III

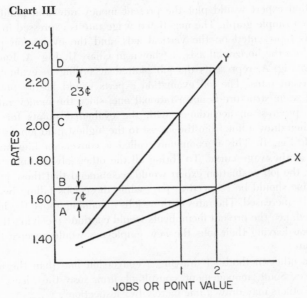

Wage increases resulting from point increases vary depending upon slope of wage curve.

Chart IV

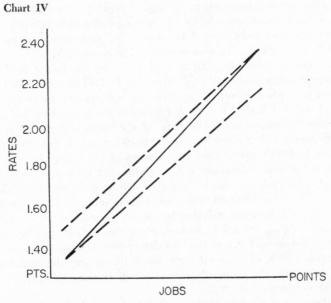

Effect of raising lowest rate and lowering highest rate when applying conversion line.

Chart V

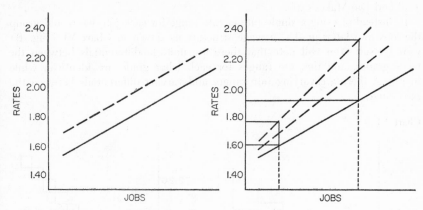

Fig. A. *Effect of across the board in-crease.*

Fig. B. *Effect of percentage wage in-crease.*

rate (usually laborer) that is negotiated is multiplied by the mathematical formula and would be applied in this manner:

Suppose the Laborer rate is $1.20.

Jobs with point values between	Multiply by wage rating factor	Job rate
215–235.............	1.20 × 1.0000	$1.20
240–260.............	1.20 × 1.0833	1.30
265–285.............	1.20 × 1.1333	1.36

The slope of the wage curve and the length of the wage curve reflect the wage structure of a given unit or plant. Actually, the curve is nothing more than a line drawn through the plotted rates of each job. The length of the curve will reflect the range from the lowest to the highest paid jobs, and the slope of the curve reflects the differentials between the rates of pay for each job and also reflects the money value of each point. It should be emphasized that the money value per point under most job evaluation plans is not constant. Only if the wage curve is on a true 45 degree angle will wage rates progress at exactly the same rate as the points are increased. 50 points to the Laborer's job usually has a higher value than 50 points to the Tool and Die Maker. For example, under most interpretations of the National Metal Trades Association Plan, the Laborer's job is evaluated to 150 points and the Tool and Die Maker's job to 350 points. If the Laborer's rate is $1.50 (a penny a point) the Tool and Die Maker's rate would be $3.50 using the one cent multiplier. As evidenced by those plants using the NMTA plan, very rarely do you find a rate this high for Tool and Die Maker's job.

If, instead of using a single rate or rate range for each job, we would group the jobs into labor grades, a wage structure as shown in Chart VI (Fig. B) would result. You will note that there are uniform differentials between the labor grades, and the rate ranges for each labor grade are identical, while in Fig. A there are varying rate ranges and varying differentials between the rate ranges.

Chart VI

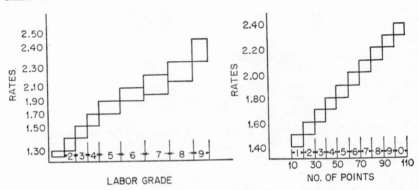

Fig. A. Labor grade wage structure with various rate range spreads and varying differentials between labor grades. (Note overlapping.)

Fig. B. Plant A—Labor grade wage structure with identical range spreads and uniform differential between labor grades.

"SCIENTIFIC" WAGE ADMINISTRATION

Excerpt from a speech by George W. Brooks, Director of Research and Education, International Brotherhood of Pulp, Sulphite and Paper Mill Workers, in McGill University Industrial Relations Centre, Sixth Annual Conference, Proceedings, 1954, pp. 78–79

One of the most disastrous developments of the last ten or fifteen years has been the tendency to introduce "scientific" methods into personnel administration. If I said "scientific" as though it were a nasty word, it is because I meant to. In personnel matters "scientific" means the application of mathematics to otherwise simple problems. Let me take the example of job analysis. This is the introduction of scientific determination to replace the old fashioned higgling and haggling. The impact on a union is serious. Before we had job analysis in some of our plants a typical grievance would go something like this. A mechanic would come to a steward and say, "These other monkeys are making five cents more than I am. What's the matter." "Come on," Bill the steward would say, "we'll go and see the foreman." So they would go off and see the foreman and argue with him. The foreman would explain that the jobs are different. "Besides," he would say, "you are not entitled to any step up yet." And then they would argue that he was doing the same job the others were doing and they go round and round and perhaps the answer would still be no. They would take it up to the next step and the answer might still be "No." But if he did not get his increase he would know exactly who said "No," he would know what happened to it.

Nowadays all this is changed. He goes to the steward and says, "Bill, I ought to get a raise. Everybody else is getting more than I am." Up to now the process is the same as before; however, at this point, the steward does not act natural. "Yeah," he says, "just as I thought. That's an analyzed job. I'll take care of it." Four months later the member goes to him again. "What happened to my wage increase?" "Oh," he says, "I sent it in." He waits a little longer and may send it in again. Pretty soon a couple of experts come from Blank City; this is a very fair and impartial process. One of these fellows is from management, the other is from the union. Both are experts. These are very, very smart fellows, they have slide rules, they have stop watches, they have charts, these guys are really equipped. They talk to this fellow and ask him a lot of questions. They put marks on a piece of paper, they talk to other fellows and make a "thorough investigation" as the saying goes. They go away and our employee says, "Hey, I want my nickel." "We haven't analyzed this job yet. Don't be so stupid. We're just taking data now." He waits a couple more months. Well, one day the call comes down for Joe to go up to the office and to bring Bill with him. The foreman doesn't handle this one. The personnel officer does.

The steward is wise by now. He knows that if they are going to say yes they do not call anyone up to explain it. The answer must be no but he doesn't say anything. They go to the personnel officer and he says, "Hello there, how do you do. Sit down here." They pass the time of day for a while. Then the personnel officer says, "All we want to do in this plant is give everyone just the right wage." This is a line borrowed from St. Thomas Aquinas but he doesn't know it. He gets a big piece of paper with a lot of marks and dots on it, some with red circles around them. He says, "Sit right up here, Joe, I want you to see this. Now, we want to give every man the right rate. On this chart we have all these jobs. If you divide this by that and multiply by this you find that this job turns out exactly on the line. You understand that, don't you?" Well the steward over there is nodding his head, and Joe is no dummy either so he says, "Yes, thank you, thank you." It will be about five years before he has courage enough to tell the personnel man what to do with his piece of paper.

These are serious matters. I think that most of you will agree with me that in our kind of political and economic society workingmen need to take part in the determination of their own affairs, not just because workingmen want to aggrandize themselves, as they undoubtedly do, but because they are a significant element in the community. We can frustrate the process if we want to. It is not as hard as companies used to think it was. What I am saying is that I think you ought to turn your back on that viewpoint insofar as your positions permit you to do so and take the view that the maximum participation of workingmen in affairs which affect their own lives should be encouraged;

it is not only the decent thing for the company to do but that it is in the company's own interest to see that the process takes place on a wide scale and as frequently and intelligently as it possibly can. Test everything you do by asking whether it is comprehensible to the men who are affected by it and reject it offhand if it is not. In our society we believe that people have to take part in the determination of their own affairs. We are not willing to entrust them to the wise people, to the good people or even to the elected people. We want everybody to take part. That may be just a matter of faith but it is a faith to which you ought to find it as easy to subscribe as I do.

Question addressed to and answered by Wayne T. Brooks, Director of Industrial Relations, Wheeling Steel Corporation, during a conference on Grievances and Arbitration, conducted at the University of West Virginia, 1956, pp. 36–37 of the Proceedings

QUESTION: I would like to address this to Mr. Brooks, from a student's point of view. How far do grievances usually go in the grievance procedure before they are settled?

MR. BROOKS: Normal grievance procedure, with a couple of exceptions which I will enumerate, should have its beginning at the point closest to where the event occurred. Now if it occurs in a crew of men with one supervisor, or if it occurs with a crew of 500 men and a supervisor, that is where the grievance should begin. If the grievance is settled at that point, obviously that is the end of it. If the grievance is not granted, it moves up the chain of command within the company. In most of the steel contracts we have a five-step grievance procedure. The fifth step being an arbitrator, the fourth step being the top of the company, the third step being at the plant, the second step the superintendent level, and the first step at the place where the grievance originated. However, if the origin of the grievance involved rates of pay or other matters which are ordinarily negotiated at a higher level, the grievance procedure would begin at a higher level.

There are those contracts which stop rate-of-pay grievances short of arbitration. I am not sympathetic with that approach at all. It is based on the strictly mechanical concept that a rate of pay is a mathematical certainty, and no one can disagree with it. I think that grievance procedure should admit that there may be honest disagreement among people and provide for a final man to make a decision. We should always try to reach our own settlement. But this idea of saying that a matter can't be arbitrated because it is a mathematical certainty omits too much of the human element.

THE UNION'S CRITICISM OF JOB EVALUATION

From What's Wrong with Job Evaluation?, published by the International Association of Machinists, 1954, pp. 8–10, 19

Job evaluation is consistently presented by employers as one phase of "scientific management." This concept came into being around the beginning of World War I and supposedly describes a particular approach to solving problems of personnel, production, and marketing within industry. Scientific management received its greatest impetus in the early '20's. It was at this time when the vicious open-shop campaign was inaugurated which was designed to cripple and destroy organized labor. Many employers at this time were under the mistaken impression that "scientific management" would solve all their personnel problems and ward off any attempt of organization upon the part of their employees. Briefly, scientific management attempts to apply the basic tenets of the various physical sciences to the human problems of industry. The early advocates (and also the later) believed that if one closely examined the cause and effects of certain personnel and production problems in industry one could soon form generalizations or formulas which, if adhered to, would solve the present problems and those of the future. Needless to say, the industrial engineer who was hired by the employer to lower his wage cost could not be expected to propose anything that would solve the human problems of industry, if the improvement meant a higher wage cost.

The very presence of organized labor is evidence of their empty recommendations. Because of the widespread promotion of job evaluation plans by management consultants, and its very frequent acceptance by employers, one should, by this very fact alone, be extremely dubious of its claimed accomplishments. It is rare indeed that an employer will pay thousands of dollars to a management consultant firm for establishing a job evaluation plan that will result in an overall higher wage bill for his firm.

It should be clearly understood that we do not believe that job evaluation is scientific in the true sense of the word. Employers and management consultants have attempted to label it as such, but have only done so to sell it to the union. As a rule the products of "scientific management," including job evaluation are designed to weaken the union; they essentially mistrust the collective action of the workers—and it is evident upon examination of most collective bargaining agreements today that they contain little or no evidence of being scientific.

Other phases of scientific management which are supposed to solve the production and wage problems in industry are incentive systems, bonus plans, profit sharing plans and time and motion studies. *It should be emphasized that these other fields of study, which are also products of scientific management, have no relation to job evaluation.* It is possible that they may be in existence in various degrees at the same time in any one plant, but they are entirely different and should not be confused or identified with one another.

An *incentive system* is a device through which employees are encouraged to produce more units at a work pace above normal in order to increase their earnings.

Motion study is a method to analyze, simplify, and standardize work processes and individual work operations.

Time study, on the other hand, is a technique used to establish the amount of time it would take an average qualified employee, working at a normal pace, to complete a given task. Time and motion studies are usually employed where incentive or piece rate systems of wage payments are used.

Bonus plans are usually initiated by the employer and provide for the payment of a lump sum of money at various intervals, in addition to the employees' regular compensation. Determination of the amount of the bonus and when it is to be paid usually lies solely with the company.

Profit sharing plans are also initiated by management and provide for the payment of a fixed percentage (usually in a lump sum) of profits *after* they have reached a certain level. The intent herein is to identify the worker with the profit status of the company, even though the individual worker has no control over the direction of the business.

Job evaluation is allegedly a systematic attempt to determine the relative value of each job. It seeks to answer the question, "What is each job worth in relation to other jobs in a plant or unit?" Methods of job evaluation differ to a considerable degree but all are common in that they seek to determine the relative ranking of jobs and thereby determine their relative wage rates. The object of job evaluation is allegedly to establish a more equitable wage structure than that existing beforehand.

Job evaluation differs from the old practical give and take collective bargaining that sought to secure as high a wage as possible for each job and each individual. This is contrary to the basic ideals of the I.A. of M. We have always felt that it was our primary obligation to secure as much as we possibly could for each job and each individual.

Job evaluation received its greatest impetus during World War II. It was during this period of frozen wages that employers substantiated intraplant wage increases on the "scientific findings" of these job evaluation plans. The War Labor Board approved these intraplant inequity increases based upon the reasons set forth by the parties and the job evaluation plans became more solidly entrenched in the employers' industrial relations tool box. By using the job evaluation plan to secure certain wage increases, otherwise prohibited by the War Labor Board's regulations, organized labor did not exercise its full strength in combatting its introduction. Unfortunately, their immediate gains were far offset by future losses. . . .

Just what is a "rational wage structure"? Are labor unions against "rational wage structures"? What is the difference between a "rational wage structure" and the one which is presently in effect? These questions are not as simple as they sound, and they demand attention.

According to the employer a "rational wage structure" is one in which jobs are ranked with their rates *according to his ideas*. The employer will attempt to show that the ranking is in accordance with the requirements of each job and that the differentials between the jobs reflect the differences in requirements.

The employer accomplishes a major victory when he can persuade the union to talk in terms of a "wage structure" rather than rates for particular classifications. When you speak in these terms you have already weakened your position since you cannot forcibly demand additional adjustments for particular classifications without *admittedly* disturbing the entire wage structure. The human mind is limited in this respect since we tend to perceive and comprehend things as they are associated with other things. If the employer can convince you to think "you will be disturbing a rational relationship if you seek a particular classification adjustment" he has won half the battle.

This is a subtle point, but a very important one. Since we commonly think in terms of things as they are associated with other things the employer has an easy task in conditioning the union to think in terms of wage relationships rather than individual rates. For many years we have conceived of our *own* relationships between jobs, but we never conceded that they were fixed or sacred. Job evaluation seeks to fix these relationships and make them sacred. Our conception of what a differential should be may change from year to year and we do not want to lose that opportunity to freely change our minds.

CHANGED WORK LOAD AND DEMAND FOR NEW CLASSIFICATION

Cameron Iron Works and International Association of Machinists, 24 LA 665, 1955

CLYDE EMERY, ARBITRATOR

Facts of the case

About November 1, 1954 a machinist in the classification Grinder-External & Internal was assigned the operation of two grinders simultaneously. Prior thereto employees in that classification had been assigned to only one machine. His production increased from approximately 28 pieces using one machine to approximately 48 pieces using two machines.

There is no provision in the Agreement for increased pay under these circumstances. Rates are not on a piece work basis. There are no job descriptions.

The Company made a time study of the operation. (The Union requested the opportunity to make a study, but was refused.) This showed that an operator of one grinder was idle 61% of his time, and that when operating two grinders he was still idle 42% of his time.

Opinion

The Union seeks an award that a new classification must be established for the operator of two grinders.

The Union's request is based on Article VII, Section 5 of the Agreement: Should it become *necessary or desirable* to create *new job classifications* during the term of this agreement, the *Company shall establish wage rates* that bear a fair and equitable relationship to the then existing wage schedule within the plant. The *Company will then notify the plant committee of the new job classification created and the wage rates* established for the new job classification . . . the *plant committee may initiate a grievance, alleging that the new wage rate* does not bear a fair and equitable relationship to other wage rates within the plant. . . . Pending determination of any grievance, the *job classification and wage rate established by the Company* may be placed into effect, subject to adjustment retroactively if determined to be erroneous (emphasis added).

The Union contends that it is necessary, or at least desirable, to create a new classification for the two-grinder machinists. Is the Company under a duty to establish a new classification when in fact that is "necessary" or "desirable"? Or does the Company have sole discretion as to whether, under those circumstances, to create a new classification or not?

The only mandatory language in the first quoted sentence is about the Company's establishing *wage rates*. Thus if a new classsification is in fact created, the Company must set wage rates for it. But must the Company create the classification if that is "desirable"?

It is arguable that the first clause means that. However, there is a strong management rights section, Article XI, Section 3, which states: ". . . all other *rights not herein expressly relinquished are vested exclusively in the Company. . . .*" (emphasis added). It is difficult to believe that the language "should it become necessary or desirable to create new job classifications" expressly relinquishes the freedom which the Company would otherwise have to establish them or not. It is more likely that the quoted clause means "if the Company creates a new classification," which it would do if it considered that to be necessary or desirable.

It will be noted that the Plant Committee's first entrance on the scene is after the Company has decided on classification and wage rates; the Company then notifies the Committee. This is accented by the last italicized phrase (quoted above), about the "job classification and wage rate established by the Company." It is further accented by the unrebutted Company testimony that at the last negotiations the Union sought orally, without success, to obtain a voice in establishing new classifications. In support of the reasoning in the preceding paragraph, the section says the committee may initiate a grievance about the *new wage rate;* there is no provision for a grievance about the Company's not creating the classification.

Altogether, it is believed the quoted sections do not put a duty on the Company to establish new classifications, or allow a grievance for its failure to do so. . . .

The Union has a strong case for a wage adjustment. Production, by using two grinders, has been almost doubled. Greater effort is required than with one machine. Responsibility is doubled. Machines are of different makes and have different controls; valves of different sizes are ground on the two machines, thus finishing at different times. All this requires much more thinking. However, the machinist is still a Grinder; his work is of the same type as formerly; merely having *more* work doesn't sound like a new classification. Frequently there is considerable variation within a classification from work station to work station, as to effort, responsibility, idle time, etc. Furthermore, some employees in seven classifications—including one instance in the present classification—have from three to six years been operating two (or more) machines. That fact has not changed those classifications. Also, the decisive first sentence of Article VII, Section 5 has been repeatedly renegotiated (it has been in the Agreement since 1944) after those instances of multiple machine assignment began. . . .

The Union is greatly concerned about the employee's added responsibility and his lessened ability to meet it. Of course he can be at the controls of only one machine at a time, and often is at neither, while traversing the 11 feet between machines. The Union fears that quality of work will lessen, more emery wheels will be broken, and the employee will be charged with both. It believes that presence at a machine can prevent excess loading and occasionally can lessen the damage caused by wheel breakage. It requested a statement from the Company relieving the operator from responsibility except for the machine whose controls are within his reach. The Company replied that it isn't practical to predetermine responsibility for mishaps.

The general foreman of the department testified that since the change, there has been no greater damage to parts or equipment and no greater breakage of wheels. Both parties testified that a machine, after finishing its grinding, can run a few minutes without damaging the part—giving the employee time to get back to that machine.

In any event, it seems clear that the Company cannot properly hold an employee responsible for an accident caused by his absence from a machine (because at the other machine, or on his way to or from it)—and it is believed the Company would not want to impose such responsibility.

Article IV, Section 2's time limit for the award was waived by the parties.

AWARD

For the above-stated reasons, the arbitrator does not have the power, under the Agreement, to direct the establishment of a new job classification.

Company Wage Level

In addition to the question of the rate for one job relative to other jobs within a company, there is the question of the general level of wages in one company compared to wages in other companies. This is what is involved when we speak of a company as being a "poor payer" or a "high wage company."

Among the issues pertinent to this topic is whether one company should be expected to follow a wage "pattern" set by another company, or whether "ability to pay" should affect relative wage levels.

MANAGEMENT'S RESPONSIBILITY

Excerpt from an address, "What Industry Expects from Organized Labor," by Charles R. Sligh, Jr., Chairman of the Board, National Association of Manufacturers, at the 60th Annual Congress of American Industry, New York City, December 9, 1955

. . . Industry expects that organized labor will recognize that in a free economic society industry and trade must compete to meet the needs and desires of consumers—and so must be guided by the market places as to prices, jobs and wages.

Unions may insist upon, and employers may agree to, a certain level of wages, but the consumer has the last say. If consumers refuse to buy the product at a price which will permit this wage level—or in sufficient quantity to keep the members of the union fully employed—it is an indication that the services of these workers have been priced out of the market. A collective bargaining agreement in these circumstances isn't worth the paper it is written on.

It is necessary, therefore, for union leadership to place some faith in management's judgment as to what wage scale and other labor cost provisions will best promote a thriving, growing business. Pattern bargaining often is harmful to an industry, and the calling of a strike to force what, in the final analysis, is an economic impossibility imposes hardship, suffering and loss on all concerned.

ABILITY TO PAY

Excerpt from Report of the Eight-hour Commission, Appendix VI, Railway Wage Schedules and Agreements, by William Z. Ripley, 1917, p. 346

Railroads differ widely from one another in at least three respects; namely, in financial ability, in traffic requirements on the commercial side, and in merely physical operating conditions. Of these, the arbitrations under Federal auspices in recent years have, without exception, sanctioned the elimination of all distinctions as to financial ability in the adjudication of wage disputes. The laborer is held to be worthy of his hire, regardless of the employer's status. The fallacy of the old doctrine that wages are a last charge upon industry is now generally conceded. As for private industry, data collected by the first Tariff Board have since been confirmed by the New York State Factory Investigating Commission, to prove the coexistence of competing establishments which continue indefinitely to pay widely variant wage scales—not infrequently differing by 50 per cent. Profits under such conditions do not arise from differential skill in management. They are in part extorted from labor. No such policy of making wages a last charge upon industry ought to be tolerated in public service employment; and, in fact, the principle concerning ability to pay has now received universal acceptance, not only in the railroad field but wherever arbitrations have occurred in the domain of public utilities.[1]

[1] The chapter opens in 1894 by the decision of Judge Colwell of the United States District Court, refusing to permit a reduction of wages on the Union Pacific because of the financial disability of the company. Even earlier than this, the London dock laborers' strike in 1890 had established the same principle, that profits ought not to enter into the determination of wages. The first railroad arbitration under Federal auspices, that of the eastern engineers in 1912, rather timidly accepted this view in the statement that statistics of compensation to capital led to so uncertain a conclusion that they should not be made a controlling factor in the award. The board announced that it would not deny an increase of wages merely upon the ground of hardship to the employing railroads. In substantially these words they proceeded to "eliminate the claim" of inability to pay. In the firemen's award the next year no reasoning was set forth, although the brief of the men deals repeatedly with the topic. The eastern conductors' arbitration, also in 1913, dismissed the matter by a quotation from the chairman of the general managers' committee (p. 2054), "All will, of course, agree that the first charge upon railway revenue must be fair payments to employees." In the western engineers' award of 1914-15, there is no reference to the argument either

Atlantic City Transportation Company and Division 1358, Amalgamated Association of Street, Electric Railway and Motor Coach Employes of America, 9 LA 580, 1948

DAVID L. COLE, CHAIRMAN OF THE BOARD OF ARBITRATION

Financial condition of Company

A further deterrent to too rapid a narrowing of wage differentials is the financial situation of the Company. In its fiscal year ending July 1947 it showed a profit of less than the cost of the improvements sought by the Union. If this Company were asked to pioneer in establishing high or unusual wages or other conditions, this would be a strong deterrent. While the chairman does not subscribe to the view that financial inability of an employer is of no consequence in determining wage rates, nonetheless the principle must be employed cautiously. Against an effort, as stated, to attain new levels or to make innovations it is a strong factor. Against improving substandard wages or eliminating clear inequities it is entitled to very slight consideration.[1] After all, basically the risk of profit or loss is management's, not the employees'.

ABILITY AND INABILITY TO PAY

From the transcript of an informal talk given by Clarence B. Randall, Vice President, Inland Steel Co., before the American Management Association meeting at the Palmer House, Chicago, on February 13, 1946, when on short notice Mr. Randall was asked to substitute for the scheduled speaker

I am going to try to put to you now a concept that I have never tried to express even in private. It is an idea that has been growing in my mind, and I hope it flowers here, but I offer you no encouragement.

---

way, although the dissenting members of the board seek to prove an ability to pay more wages than were allowed "without detriment." There is no evidence that the argument was given weight of any consequence.

As for public utilities, the Boston Elevated Railway arbitration award of January, 1914, declared that the board "attaches great weight to the argument that the men are entitled to fair and adequate wages so long as they are employed, and that it is for others to decide whether the company is to be gradually bankrupted, the passengers pay more, or the community as a whole come to the rescue of the situation." In the San Francisco Street Railway arbitration of 1903 it was the unanimous opinion of the board that the test of ability to pay would not be considered. The nearest to dissent from this view occurred in the Georgia-Florida Railway arbitration of 1914, in which case the United States Circuit Court overrules the appeal of the company from the award, it having averred that it could not afford to pay the rates allowed. The dissenting opinion in the Chicago switchmen's arbitration of 1910 is also in point. The only instance brought to our attention of a cut in wages awarded under arbitration because of the necessitous condition of the employer was the award of 1915 in the Vancouver Street Railway case.

[1] It is significant in this regard that the Trenton Transit Company granted a wage increase in 1947 from $1.12 to $1.30, to match the new Public Service rate, in spite of the fact that it is now being operated in receivership.

As I see it, there is a sharp difference between inability to pay and ability to pay in relevance on the labor problem. To spell it out, I go back a moment and ask, "Fundamentally, what is the obligation of the employer towards the employee in regards to wage?" Clearly, the employer must pay the going rate for the job in his area. And that going rate is determined by competitive forces in a free economy. And it is right that it should be so.

Another slogan that the C.I.O. is dropping, and that public opinion will compel them to drop, is "Equal pay for equal work." Incidentally and parenthetically, I point out that equal pay for equal work, which is the principal slogan that Lawson Stone and I heard about all through the steel case last year, is totally inconsistent with ability to pay. But, pass that. Equal pay for equal work throughout the country is the worst thing that can happen to the United States. It will mean that every factory in every small town will move to Chicago. If I had my way, as I have said often, the Association of Commerce in Chicago would devote its great talents not to bringing industry to Chicago but to persuading them not to come. The most wholesome economy we could have would be that in every little hamlet of one to five thousand throughout the country there would be agricultural background and an industry in that town to support the surplus labor.

That can only be true if, in those towns, the wage scale is equitable for the manufacturer. Otherwise the manufacturer cannot live. He must transport his materials out there and bring his goods back to the market. But it is better for a man to bring up his family in a small country town at a lower wage than to bring that family to the great city and have the discomforts of living among the great masses.

Now, competition exists always between the small town and the big city on just that point in a free economy. I am interested in iron mines in the Lake Superior district. We develop a machinist and pay him a rate way below what he can obtain if he goes to Detroit. But his brother went to Detroit and keeps writing him that it is a terrible place to live and bring up a family. And this fellow would rather take the lower rate and work at the iron mines than get the higher rate and live in Detroit. And whenever the disparity gets too great, he tells us to take a jump in the lake and goes to Detroit. And after we have been so long without a machinist, we bump the machinist's rate and he comes back from Detroit to us. And that is the way wages are determined. That competitive situation in a free economy fixes the area wage.

Now, I say, that is where inability to pay is a proper factor. When the employer, whether he be an exservice man just starting in business for himself or whether he be a marginal fellow for one reason or another, if he cannot pay that going rate and stay in business, it is perfectly proper for him to advance inability to pay to his employees as justification for a lower wage scale. And when he does that, the employees make their choice: do they want to go on living in that neighborhood and keep their homes and work at less than they could get in another factory; or do they want to walk out and close the plant? And, under those circumstances, inability to pay is, in my judgment, a proper subject of discussion between management and employees, namely, when the employer cannot meet the going wage in his area.

But, when the employer is successful and solvent, he discharges his obligation by meeting that going wage. And, then, if both intelligent and solvent and a good citizen, he tries to raise the standards of his workers by paying better than the going wage and lifting the area wage. But at no point beyond there does ability to pay have anything to do with it. When he has thus met his obligation to the worker, the profit that he makes beyond that is the reward for his enterprise and skill and is the incentive to management which lies at the basis of our entire free enterprise system. . . .

BARGAINING ON WAGES

From the text of a radio interview with Charles M. White, President, Republic Steel Co., by Harold Fleming, business-news correspondent of the Christian Science Monitor, over the ABC Network, December 10, 1945, during the course of negotiations between the steel industry and the Steelworkers

MR. FLEMING: As a president of a steel company, Mr. White, what's your understanding of genuine collective bargaining?

MR. WHITE: Well, Mr. Fleming . . . let's see . . . one of my men has defined it to me this way. "Genuine collective bargaining is finding out what the men want, and then trying to figure out how nearly you can meet it." And I guess I'll stand on that one. Find out what they want, and figure out what you can do about it.

MR. FLEMING: All right, why don't you open up your books to show how much money you're making?

MR. WHITE: There are many reasons, but the biggest one is that you can't tie wages to profits.

MR. FLEMING: Well, why not?

MR. WHITE: Well, in the first place, you can't tie wages to profits when there aren't any profits. In the second place, when management comes to consider a wage increase, they always have to take into account a host of other factors besides profits.

MR. FLEMING: What are those factors?

MR. WHITE: Well, there's the effect on prices, both of what we sell and what we buy. Then, there's the relationship of wages and prices in steel with wages and prices in a host of other industries. Then we have to consider the long-range outlook in competitive markets for steel.

GENERAL WAGE REDUCTION

Portland Woolen Mills and Textile Workers Union of America, 24 LA 38, 1955

BOARD OF ARBITRATION: PAUL L. KLEINSORGE, CHAIRMAN; WILLIAM E. ROBERTS, COMPANY-APPOINTED; AND LEO LEVENSON, UNION-APPOINTED, THE LATTER DISSENTING

The question presented to the Arbitrator was stated by the parties in their joint letter of December 21 as follows:

Whether there shall be a reduction in the hourly wage rates at Portland

Woolen Mills of 9½¢ per hour or any part thereof and whether the cost of living bonus present in the existing wage rates shall be frozen at 4¢ if at all, and/or discontinued.

The parties were unable to resolve their differences concerning this question, and resorted to arbitration as provided in Section IX of the collective bargaining agreement. Mr. Leo Levenson was selected as the Union representative on the arbitration panel, and Mr. William Roberts was chosen by the Company. Dr. Paul L. Kleinsorge of the University of Oregon was appointed as the chairman and impartial member. Hearings were held on the premises of the Portland Woolen Mills on January 4, 1955.

The Company's arguments

The Company is the moving party in this case, and requests a decrease of 9½¢ per hour in wage rates plus the elimination of the escalator clause with the freezing of the present cost of living bonus of 4¢ into the wage rates. The Company stated that in the past wages have been adjusted through negotiation and also through the application of the escalator clause which is based upon the Consumers Price Index published by the Bureau of Labor Statistics. Since the inauguration of the escalator clause, the cost of living bonus had increased gradually to 5¢ per hour, and then had fallen to 4¢. This is the 4¢ which the Company asks to be frozen into the wage rates. The 9½¢ figure was selected as the proper size of the proposed wage decrease, because that was the amount of the last wage increase granted by many mills in 1951 before conditions in the industry began to deteriorate.

Financial Position—Portland Woolen Mills' first argument involved its ability to maintain the present wage scale and still stay in business. The Company claims that the general business situation in the industry is bad. Many mills have closed. In some cases employees voluntarily have taken wage decreases in order to keep mills in operation. In other cases arbitration awards have resulted in decreases. The difficulties have not been confined to any one area, and the trend appears to be for mills to seek relief through reductions in wages. Portland Woolen Mills says it has suffered with the rest of the industry, and that the outlook for the Company is far from bright. The figures for 1954 undoubtedly will show a deficit. The Company is well established and is not insolvent yet, but unless it is given some relief, it may have to begin liquidation proceedings.

Portland Woolen Mills illustrated this point with exhibits showing its profits before and after taxes, its dividend payments, and its additions to (or deductions from) surplus for the period 1944–1954. The Company enjoyed profits from 1944 until 1950, and paid dividends on both its common and preferred stock. In 1950 its profits had fallen to the point where no dividends could be paid on the common stock, and most of the dividends on the preferred were paid out of surplus. The Company always has met its dividend obligations to the preferred stockholders, although these payments resulted in deductions from surplus in 1952 and 1954 as well as in 1950. Since 1949 the common stockholders have received only one dividend, which was paid in 1953. The preferred stock is a 6% cumulative preferred which was issued at a par value of $100 per share. It is now selling for about $90 per share. The common stock was issued at $5 per share, and is selling for about $3.

Total sales (less discounts) in terms of dollars have fluctuated, but not as much as the profit margin. The cost of doing business per dollar of sales has increased, and the profit margin has narrowed. In 1944, for instance, with total sales of $5,472,896.92, the cost of doing business was $4,781,526.83, and the profit before taxes was $691,370.09. In 1954, the estimated sales figure was $5,575,000.00 with a cost of doing business of $5,525,000.00 leaving a profit figure of only $50,000.00.

On the basis of such figures, the Company contends that its financial situation is worsening. This is a part of the general trend in the industry, which was relieved temporarily by the Korean War, but which is now continuing on its way downward. Portland Woolen Mills' rate of profit is at present less than 1% of sales. The rate of profit for the industry is less than the Bureau of Labor Statistics' figure for all "manufacturing."

The Company borrows some $2,000,000 per year to finance its customers. The banks are becoming concerned about the Company's condition, and are watching its financial position closely. Portland Woolen Mills is fearful that the banks will cancel its line of credit. This would be a death blow. If the line of credit is reduced, rather than canceled, production will have to be curtailed. The Company stated that curtailment to one shift would result in failure, and that a temporary shut-down (to wait for better times) would be impractical. The skilled workers would leave the community and could not be replaced, and during the shut-down the unused mill would deteriorate so rapidly that after a brief interval too much of an investment would be required to reopen it. At the present time the Company claims it needs additional working capital for technological improvements to reduce costs. But because of the deductions from surplus, it is losing capital rather than gaining it.

Therefore, the Company concludes that it must be granted the requested wage decrease if it is to remain in operation. If it is required to pay the present wage scale, its net earnings will be so low that it will be unable to meet its obligations and will be forced to liquidate. This will result in a permanent loss of jobs for its employees.

Competitive Situation—The Company's second argument was closely related to the first and involved the competitive situation in the industry. Competition is very keen because of the existence of excessive productive capacity and the rivalry of unorganized mills. The ending of the Korean conflict reduced the total demand for the Company's products, and in addition wool has had to meet the competition of synthetic fibers. The trend of man-hours worked at Portland Woolen Mills has been downward. This trend is not due to technological improvement, but rather to a decline in production. Because of price increases, the dollar sales figures do not indicate the decline in production, but the Company has been fighting a losing battle for its markets. Changes in style and the development of new fabrics sharply reduced the Company's sales of cloth for men's heavy, outerwear garments. The Company tried to switch to women's wear, but this change only partially recompensed for the loss of sales in men's wear. Sales of blankets also have tapered off because of the severe competition from mills in other areas, and the Company has difficulty competing in the eastern markets because of the freight advantage of the eastern mills.

Again the Company concludes that its wage scale must be reduced if it is to meet competition and stay in business. It claims that the wage reduction would not be used to swell profits, but rather to decrease prices in order to meet competition.

Wage Pattern—Portland Woolen Mills' third argument was that in the past it has followed a wage pattern which was established by such companies as the American Woolen Company, the largest firm in this branch of the industry. The Company claims that it followed this pattern when wage rates in the industry were rising and that it should be permitted to follow the same pattern when the wage rates are falling. The Company submitted exhibits to show that there has been a close correspondence between wage rates paid by Portland Woolen Mills and the American Woolen Company, with Portland Woolen Mills lagging somewhat behind when changes were made. The overall increases granted by the two companies since 1944 were within ½¢ per hour of each other. Then in 1954 American Woolen decreased wage rates by 9½¢ per hour and froze the 4¢ cost of living bonus into the wage rates. The American Woolen Company is organized by the same union as Portland Woolen Mills, and Portland Woolen Mills feels that it should receive the same treatment.

The Company stated that in the past the Union had used American Woolen as a criterion for wage increases. The Company cited a Union letter of March 15, 1951, which refers to "the settlement pattern established by the Union with the American Woolen Company," and cited also a Union strike bulletin which stated, "We will go to work when we get the American Woolen settlement."

The Company pointed out that other arbitration cases have resulted in wage decreases. In the Cheney Brothers case (Cheney Brothers and Textile Workers Union of America, September 14, 1953, 21 LA 159) the arbitrator awarded a 9¾¢ per hour wage decrease, and stated that 91 per cent of other northern textile manufacturers already had cancelled the general wage increases granted in 1951. He stated further that the parties traditionally have followed a pattern of wage adjustments. Other arbitration cases including Botany Mills, 22 LA 653, Berkshire Woolen Company, Marion Worsted Mills, and many more resulted in similar reductions in wage rates. Frequently these cases included the freezing of the 4¢ cost of living bonus, and its incorporation into the wage rates.

Portland Woolen Mills feels that the evidence proves the existence of pattern bargaining in the industry, and maintains that its request for a wage rate reduction is in accordance with the pattern and should be approved. The Company is aware that in some operations no reductions in wages have been requested, but it points out that many of these companies did not grant the 1951 increase which the pattern is now eliminating. These cases, therefore, do not represent an exception to the general trend. Also in other cases the contracts were not open for wage adjustments, and no decreases could be negotiated at this time. The Company stated that it does not want to place a wage decrease into effect, but it concludes that it must if it is to survive. In the future, if business conditions for the Company and for industry improve, undoubtedly the Union will press for a restoration of the higher scale and perhaps even for further improvements.

Employees' Earnings—The final argument presented by the Company was that its employees are well paid according to industry standards. Evidence was introduced to show that the straight time hourly earnings of the Company's employees are above those of textile workers in other areas. Even with a 9½¢ per hour decrease, the earnings would be above the average for the United States as computed in 1952 before many decreases were placed in effect. Portland Woolen Mills claims that since 1944, the percentage increase in its wage rates has been higher than the percentage increase in cost of living for the Portland area or for the United States as a whole. Even with a 9½¢ per hour decrease, the overall wage increase since 1944 will be greater percentagewise than the increase in cost of living.

The Union's arguments

Pattern Bargaining—The Union rejected the Company's request for a reduction in wage rates, and takes exception first to the Company's claim that it has followed general wage patterns in the industry and is, therefore, entitled to the same relief which has been obtained by other woolen and worsted firms. The Union maintains that the merits of each case must be considered separately, and that with regard to Portland Woolen Mills the circumstances do not warrant a reduction. In the Botany Mills case, for instance, the wage reductions were occasioned by the sharp recession in demand for certain fabrics, particularly worsteds. But the production of woolen apparel fabrics and blanketing (such as manufactured by Portland Woolen Mills) has increased markedly. A number of companies have determined that they did not need the relief that might be afforded by wage reductions, and voluntarily have maintained their wage levels. In the blanket field, with one exception, none of Portland Woolen Mills' TWUA-organized competitors has reduced wages. The one exception is the Beaver Brook Mill of the American Woolen Company which was included in the settlement following a strike of the company's twelve plants. The Union submitted the names of some forty-six woolen textile companies which have not reduced wages, including three West Coast mills which, with Portland Woolen Mills, comprise the bulk of the West Coast woolen and worsted industry.

Under these circumstances the Union feels that it is far-fetched to claim that a set pattern of wage reductions exists in the industry. Deviations were recognized in some instances during the period of wage increases when unions were insisting upon pattern wage increases from prosperous firms. Deviations are also noticeable on the downturn. In some cases the reductions are less than the "pattern," and in other instances there are no reductions at all.

Increased Productivity—The Union's second argument was that the employees have cooperated with the Company in its attempts to increase productivity. New machines and methods have been introduced which have displaced some workers and which have required those who remain to work harder than before. Work assignments have been increased. The Union contends that it is grossly unfair to add a wage cut to the larger burdens which the employees have accepted.

Inadequacy of Existing Wage Level—The Union's third argument was that the existing wage level is inadequate to meet the cost of living measured by the accepted American standard. A "City Worker's Family Budget" prepared by the Bureau of Labor Statistics requires a yearly income higher than that being earned by the average worker at Portland Woolen Mills. The Union finds that to bring the workers up to the "necessary minimum" standard of living, a wage increase of some 47¢ per hour is required. On this basis, a wage decrease is out of the question. In the United States, the breadwinner is typically the sole support of his family, but if his earnings are too low his wife and children must work to supplement his income. Such a situation is opposed to our national standards.

In addition the Union maintains that the wage adjustments negotiated by the parties since 1950 were based largely upon increases in the cost of living. In April, 1951, an escalator clause was agreed upon by the parties which provided an automatic means of adjusting wages to changes in the cost of living during the term of the agreement. In view of this arrangement, it would be a gross injustice to wipe out these past wage increases without a commensurate decline in living costs.

General Wage Trend—The Union's fourth argument was that the proposed reduction in wages is contrary to the general trend of wages in the United States. Workers in many other industries recently have received substantial wage increases. For instance, the lumber workers in the Northwest were granted 7½¢ per hour. Since 1950 the overall wage increases granted by other industries have exceeded those granted by Portland Woolen Mills. The Union concludes that in the face of this upward trend in wages throughout the nation, there is no reason for a wage reduction in the present case.

Company's Financial Position—Finally, the Union denied the Company's argument that it was unable to maintain the present wage scale and remain in operation. The Company has a history of profitable operation, and has built up a surplus which is more than adequate for it to meet the contingencies arising from the sharp recession suffered by the woolen industry in 1954. From the reports of the Federal Reserve Board and the trade press, the prospects for woolen textiles have greatly improved, and the large, growing California market should provide Portland Woolen Mills with an excellent outlet for its products. The Union paints a bright picture for the immediate future, and holds that the Company's financial resources are ample to carry the Company over the transitional difficulties of the textile recession, which is now coming to an end.

In any event, the Union questions whether it is the high cost of labor that has caused the difficulty. Undoubtedly style changes, the competition of synthetic fabrics, and the high cost of wool had something to do with it. A reduction of 9½¢ per hour in wages would not mean much of a reduction in cost per yard anyway. Labor cost is only about 27% of sales. Some mills may have moved to the South to take advantage of lower wages, but many of the mills that have closed down were antiquated operations that had opened temporarily to take advantage of the war demand. They were not organized and had never paid high wages. They should not be compared with Portland Woolen Mills which has proven over the years that it has the know-how to run a successful business.

Discussion

Ability to Pay as Factor—Much of the material presented by the Company in its plea for a reduction in wage rates had to do with its financial ability to maintain the present wage scale. If ability to pay is to be a controlling factor in this case, and if the Company is found to lack this financial ability, a wage reduction could be granted without consideration of the other arguments. The Chairman of the Arbitration Panel is convinced (in spite of the Union analysis) that the Company is in financial difficulties, and that its future is not bright. It is quite possible that the stockholders will find it to their advantage to close down the operation and to liquidate the assets before further losses are incurred so that they may retrieve as much as possible of their investment. There is no real proof that the recession in the textile industry has ended, and even though there may be some improvement in the woolen industry, Portland Woolen Mills appears still to be in difficulties.

The Chairman believes, however, that the ability to pay argument cannot be granted as controlling in arbitration cases. There are many precedents to this effect, and the point was established long ago. An employee is not a partner— he does not share in the profits and should not be expected to share in the losses. Wages of an employee cannot be made to depend upon profits—if they were, efficient employers would be penalized with high wages, while less efficient employers would be subsidized with low wages. The Company must pay standard rates for its equipment, tools, and fuel, and other costs such as electricity and telephone. It must pay the established rate of interest on its loan from the bank, and the established premiums on its insurance policies whether it is prosperous or suffering losses. The Chairman sees no reason for making an exception of wages. The Company should pay the standard wage rates regardless of its financial ability.

Situations may occur under which discretion would direct the employees to accept a wage reduction below the standard to help keep their employer in business and to maintain their jobs. But that is a decision for the workers to make. When the employer's plea is based solely on inability to pay, the reduction below standard should be a voluntary sacrifice, and not one forced upon the employees by an arbitrator. It is not the function of arbitration to require the workers to take less than a fair and reasonable return for their services.

What Is the "Standard" Wage Rate?—The problem, then, becomes one of determining what the standard wage rate is. If the Company's rates are above the standard, a reduction may be granted. If not, the request for a reduction must be denied. In the Chairman's opinion, the "standard" wage rates are the rates being paid to similar jobs elsewhere in the industry. Obviously there are many different rates being paid by many different companies, and if the data were available, a weighted average might be taken as the criterion. But in the case of the Portland Woolen Mills, there is a history of using the wage scale of the American Woolen Company as a standard. The Union denies that such a pattern exists, but the close similarity of the wage changes over a number of years indicates more than mere coincidence. The statements made in the past by the Union in letters and bulletins also substantiate the conclusion that the American Woolen Company scale has been used by the parties as a standard. On this basis, Portland Woolen Mills' request should be approved, since in 1954 the American Woolen Company decreased wage rates by 9½¢ per hour and froze the cost of living bonus into the wage rates.

It may be argued that one company, even a very large one like American Woolen, should not be taken as the standard. The Union pointed out that there are many woolen textile companies which have not reduced wage rates at all, and others which have made reductions of less than the 9½¢ requested by Portland Woolen Mills. The evidence indicates, however, that cancellation of the 1951 increases has been widespread in the textile industry. The Company contends that in most cases where reductions have not taken place the firm either did not grant an increase in 1951 or the contract is not yet open for wage adjustments.

Further study by the Arbitration Panel showed that some 6,698 of the 12,349 employees working for the forty-six companies listed by the Union as not reducing wages are non-union, that 1,500 are employed in a carpet mill, which is not a comparable business, and that 550 are employed by AFL mills which have a different wage structure. Thus less than 4,000 of the 12,349 who are maintaining their wage rates are comparable to the employees at Portland Woolen Mills. On the other hand, the National Association of Wool Manufacturers states that 35,188 employees (of whom 3,720 are non-union) have taken wage decreases. It appears, therefore, that wage decreases are the overwhelming rule, rather than the exception in the wool industry. Also the precedents of other arbitration cases lead the Chairman of the Panel to conclude that the 1951 increases would not have been granted if the industry had realized that a sharp recession was soon to follow. If the wage reductions are as widespread as the evidence indicates, it is likely that the wage rates at Portland Woolen Mills will be above the weighted average in the industry even if the requested reduction is placed in effect.

Increased Productivity—In addition to the arguments concerning ability to pay, pattern bargaining, and standard rates, the Union stated that the employees had cooperated with the Company to increase productivity, and that it would be grossly unfair to add a wage cut to the heavier burdens the employees have assumed. The Chairman feels that it is unfortunate and discouraging that increased work assignments and decreased wages should come at the same time. But it is always the duty of employees to be as productive as possible (consistent with their health and general welfare) just as it is the duty of the employers to provide the most efficient management possible. The secret of high wages is the high productivity of labor. Over the long run, it is to the advantage of labor, as well as of management, for the workers to strive to increase their productivity.

BLS Family Budget—The Union contended that according to a budget prepared by the Bureau of Labor Statistics, the workers are earning less than the "necessary minimum" standard of living. Such budgets are attempts to measure what workers should have, and they are useful for purposes of analysis. It will be a happy day when all workers earn the "necessary minimum," and that is a goal we should try to reach. But at present it appears that large groups of people (including many in the textile industry) will earn less than this for a long time to come. In addition, even though everyone earned at least the "necessary minimum," it is very doubtful that each wage earner would spend his earnings strictly in accordance with the provisions of the budget.

Prior Adjustments—The Union claimed that the wage adjustments in the past were placed in effect largely to compensate for increased cost of living, and that it would be unjust to cancel these increases without a commensurate decline in living costs. The Company denied that all of the increases were to compensate for the rising cost of living. In any event, the Company proved that percentagewise the wage increases had been greater than the cost of living increases, and that even with the proposed reduction in wages, the wage increases would still be greater than the rise in cost of living.

General Wage Trend—The Union also stated that the proposed reduction in wages is contrary to the general trend of wages in the United States. This is true. For a number of years, through 1954, the trend of wages has been upward. But there are indications that this trend is coming to an end unless the country once more becomes involved in an international conflict. Although in general 1954 was a year of wage increases, some decreases occurred in industries other than textiles. In view of the competitive and financial situation in the textile industry, it is not surprising that wage reductions should occur there.

Competitive Disadvantage—The Chairman of the Arbitration Panel has no way of estimating the extent of the financial relief that the requested wage adjustment will give the Company. The Company claims that its competitive position will be improved far more than the Union's argument would indicate. The Chairman does not believe that inefficient management should be subsidized by the employees through below standard wages. But in view of the widespread wage decreases in the woolen textile industry, he is convinced that Portland Woolen Mills' relatively high wage scale places it at a competitive disadvantage. He concludes that this wage scale is above standard and not in accord with the pattern established in the past. For this reason alone he approves the Company's request for a reduction to bring its wage rates closer to the standard prevailing in the industry.

DECISION

Although the Chairman of the Arbitration Panel did not agree with the Company that the proposed wage reduction of 9½¢ per hour and freezing of the 4¢ cost of living bonus should be permitted on the ground that the Company is financially unable to maintain the present wage scale, he did concur with the Company argument that the parties have engaged in pattern bargaining for wages in the past, and that the Company should not be required to pay wage rates above the pattern standard. The pattern standard is to eliminate the 1951 wage increases and to freeze into the wage rates the cost of living bonus. The Chairman concludes, therefore, that the Portland Woolen Mills shall be permitted to reduce wage rates by 9½¢ per hour, and to eliminate the escalator clause (Section XXIV of the collective bargaining agreement) with the freezing of the 4¢ cost of living bonus into the existing wage rates.

GENERAL WAGE INCREASE

Aerovox Corporation and International Brotherhood of Electrical Workers, *25 LA 23, 1955*

BOARD OF ARBITRATION: JOHN A. HOGAN, CHAIRMAN, APPOINTED BY THE PARTIES; ARTHUR WALKER, UNION-APPOINTED; AND WILLIAM KAMERON, EMPLOYER-APPOINTED

A hearing was held on the above entitled matter on February 18, 1955 in New Bedford, Massachusetts before the undersigned Board of Arbitrators. The Arbitration Board was appointed under the procedures of the contract between the parties dated April 14, 1954, and set forth in Article 1, Subsection 5. The Board consists of Arthur Walker, representing the Union, William Kameron, representing the Company, and John A. Hogan of Durham, New Hampshire, Third Arbitrator, appointed by the parties.

At the hearing the Union was represented by Francis X. Moore, International Representative, and James Powers, President of the Local Union. The Company was represented by Roger E. Titus, Esq., of the firm of Abramson, Titus & Levenson, New Bedford, Massachusetts, and Mr. Hyman L. Molrel, Director of Personnel.

Subsequent to the hearing and after studying the exhibits and testimony, the Arbitration Board met in Boston, Massachusetts on February 24, 1955. It was agreed that the Third Arbitrator should write this opinion and decision and send it to the other members of the Board for their signatures, with or without dissent.

The issue

At the hearing the parties stipulated to the following submission of the issue in arbitration:

Shall there be an adjustment in the straight time hourly wage rates of the employees covered by the Agreement dated April 14, 1954? If any adjustment is warranted, shall it be up or down; by how much and on which jobs?

Contract provisions

This dispute goes to arbitration under Article 9, Section 5, of the current agreement entered into by the parties and made effective on April 14, 1954. Section 5 of Article 9 reads in part as follows:

The Union shall have the right to reopen this Agreement once during the second six months of this Agreement for the sole purpose of considering adjustment of straight time hourly rates. If the Union elects to exercise this right of reopening, it shall do so by notifying the Company in writing. Notice may not be served prior to October 14, 1954. Upon failure to agree, either party may submit the matter to arbitration in accordance with Article 1 of this contract.

Background of the bargaining

The first contract between the parties was made effective in April 1952. At that time wages were controlled under the Wage Stabilization Board's program. No general increase was granted but it was stated that individual wage adjustments were made amounting to an average of approximately 4 cents per hour.

The contract contained an automatic cost of living clause and in 1953 the cost of living adjustments were incorporated into the rate structure. Also in the 1953 bargain the production bonus, which at that time was averaging approximately 8.8 per cent of wages, was also converted into the hourly rates of the employees.

In the April 1954 negotiations the Union asked for a substantial wage increase. The Company stated that it was not in a position at that time to grant any wage increase. The contract was ultimately signed providing for one extra paid holiday, making a total of 7 paid holidays; some improvement in vacation pay and the incorporation of a .8 cent cost of living adjustment into the rate.

In reaching agreement in the 1954 negotiations the parties incorporated into the contract a wage reopening clause providing for the right of the Union to reopen wages after six months. The reason behind the wage reopening and the purpose of including it in the contract was stated without contradiction, to be the following: the Company was not willing to agree to a wage increase in April 1954 because of its precarious financial position at that time. It was agreed, however, to allow the Union to reopen wages in the event that conditions improved over the six months subsequent to the signing of the contract and it was agreed that the Union would have the right to bargain the wage rate question at that time.

The Company manufactures and sells various types of capacitors. These are also known as fixed electrical condensers and are used in various types of electrical appliances and equipment. The Company also manufactures other electronic components and equipment.

About 100 employees are covered by the bargaining unit involved in this case. This unit for which the I.B.E.W. holds exclusive bargaining rights includes the maintenance employees. About two-thirds of the jobs are skilled, comprising such occupations as electrician, tool and die maker, machinist, mechanics, welders, pipers, millwrights, painters, carpenter. The rest involved are unskilled jobs such as laborers, and porters.

In addition to the bargaining unit which includes the maintenance employees there exists in this plant another Union made up of approximately 2000 production workers. This Union, known as the "Association," is unaffiliated.

In January of 1955 the Company granted a 2 per cent general wage increase to the production workers in the Association. This followed a similar increase granted in November 1954 by a near-by competitor, Cornell Dubilier. The Cornell Dubilier contract is a two-year contract expiring in October 1956.

Position of the Union

The Union's request for a general wage rate increase is justified for the following main reasons:

1. Wage increases granted elsewhere by companies producing similar products far exceed the wage adjustments granted at Aerovox over the past several years. Union Exhibit #1 shows that wage rate increases granted by competitor firms for similar skills as those involved at Aerovox far exceed the adjustment at Aerovox over the past five years. Compare for example the increases granted at Aerovox, Olean, New York plant, at Cornell Dubilier plant in New Bedford, Massachusetts, South Plainfield, New Jersey, Worcester, Massachusetts, Indianapolis, Indiana and for Automatic Manufacturing Company, Newark, New Jersey.

Actually, no general wage increases have been granted at Aerovox in New Bedford, Massachusetts over the entire bargaining history with the Union beginning in April 1952. The result is that Aerovox has lagged far behind its national competition over these years.

2. The existing wage rate structure at Aerovox is below that in the Boston area and is below that of competitors located elsewhere but producing similar products which require similar skills. Union Exhibit #2 indicates that a B.L.S. survey of the Boston area shows average rates by occupations consistently higher than at Aerovox. Similarly, the wage rate structure at the Cornell Dubilier plant in South Plainfield, New Jersey is far higher than that at Aerovox. The Arbitrators should also note the comparisons with Cornell Dubilier at its Worcester, Massachusetts plant.

Furthermore, a wage increase is needed to adjust upward the wage scale for many employees who actually earned less in 1954 than they did in previous years. (See Union Exhibit #6) It should also be noted that wage trends have been toward higher rates in the maintenance and skilled jobs, on a national basis, since 1946. This has been due to the need to reestablish the differentials between the skilled maintenance jobs and the unskilled jobs which were reduced during the war period when cents-per-hour general increases were granted rather than percentage increases.

3. The Company has the ability to pay wage increases at this time. The

latest financial statement, published in Moody's Manual of Investment, for the year ending December 1953, shows that the Company's financial position warrants a wage increase. Net income in 1953 was over $1 million as against $779,000 in 1951 and $302,000 in 1945.

The Union submits the statement of the president of Aerovox Company as reported in the New Bedford Standard-Times for January 20, 1955. The Union points out the optimistic nature of this statement. According to President W. Myron Owen the Company's earnings in November 1954 were better than for any preceding month in the year.

In summary, the evidence on past wage adjustments in comparison with competitors' past wage increases, the evidence on wage rate comparisons at the present time and the Company's capacity to pay justify the Union's demand for a wage increase at this time.

Position of the Company

No wage increase is justified at the present time for the following main reasons:

1. The Arbitration Board should be concerned only with what has happened since the last collective bargaining contract was agreed to on April 14, 1954. At that time the Union requested a substantial increase in wages but the Company pointed out that the economic outlook was not good and that its business and financial situation did not warrant a general wage increase. The Union eventually recognized this and it was agreed that although some improvements of the contract could be granted no general wage increase was in the picture. The parties recognized the possibility of an improvement in economic conditions and this was why a wage reopening clause was inserted into the contract. This clause gave the Union the right to reopen the wage question after six months. Thus, the background of the bargaining shows that unless it can be proved that business conditions have so changed since April 14, 1954 to warrant a wage increase none should be granted. The Company submits that the evidence shows that economic conditions have not improved and that the Board should rule against any increase in wages.

2. The financial and economic position of the Company has not improved since April 14, 1954 and the outlook for the remaining months of the contract does not warrant an increase in wages. Company Exhibits #1 through #6 show clearly that market conditions for its product have deteriorated and that the Company is caught in a squeeze between falling prices and rising costs of materials. The Company's backlog of orders shows no improvement (Company Exhibit #1), the volume of sales declined substantially between the years 1953 and 1954 (Company Exhibit #3), the prices of the Company's products have declined in an increasingly competitive market (Company Exhibit #5), between 1953 and 1954 the volume of production of radio and television capacitators declined 41 per cent (Company Exhibit #6) and, finally, the cost of raw materials has increased by an average of approximately 12 per cent since January 1954 (Company Exhibit #7).

Furthermore, the Company's production and sales has declined relative to the national market. As noted above, the volume of sales of radio and television capacitators in 1954 was 41 per cent less than in 1953 for this particular Company. For the country as a whole TV set production increased slightly from about 7,200,000 sets to 7,350,000. Radio production decreased from 13,370,000 sets to 10,400,000 sets. A TV set uses approximately five times as many of the Company's type of capacitators as does a radio set. Combining the figures, therefore, indicates that, on a national basis, the use of capacitators declined approximately 5 per cent between 1953 and 1954 as against a decline of 41 per cent in the Company's production.

3. The Company's wage structure is above that of its competitors in the area. Company Exhibit #9 shows that, on the whole, rates at Aerovox are above most of the wage rates for similar job classifications at Cornell Dubilier, its chief competitor located in the same labor market and they are above the rates of Sprague Electric plant located in North Adams, Massachusetts. These companies are the two competitors of Aerovox and they represent the companies for which comparisons should properly be made. The B.L.S. Wage Rate Survey submitted in evidence by the Union does not represent a proper comparison and should be disregarded by the Arbitration Board. The B.L.S. survey extends beyond the labor market and covers industries that are not comparable with electrical component parts. It is not proper, for example, to compare wage rates paid in aircraft or in steel fabrication to electrical products rates. And it is not proper to go to plants located in the high wage areas of New York and New Jersey and into the middle west for comparisons. The Company could use lower wage rate plants in the south but recognizes that only comparisons within the industry-area are relevant. These comparisons show that Aerovox pays the going rates and a little bit more than its direct competitors.

4. The Company suffered substantial losses due to Hurricane Carol and these losses mean that its current financial position has been further impaired. The losses suffered from Hurricane Carol, as calculated up to the present point, amount to over $1,400,000. Negotiations are in process with the insurance companies but it is clear that the Company will get substantially less than its actual losses in the form of damages. This Company was the hardest hit of any in the area. Break-downs are still occurring every day or so which may be attributed to the effect of the water damage caused by the hurricane. Such damage is likely to be a costly factor over many months and beyond the time when the Company could expect to receive damages through application of insurance policy.

5. In April 1954 the Company granted improvements in the contract which amounted to an over-all cost of about 1.5 per cent of the payroll for the workers involved. This is equal to 2.4 cents per hour. The slight wage increases granted by competitors of the Company in the area since April 14, 1954 do not justify the Union's demand. In November 1954 Cornell Dubilier granted an increase to the same Union of 3 cents an hour. The Arbitrator should note that this wage increase negotiated into a two-year contract which does not expire until October 1956. The other major competitor of the Company, Sprague Electric, granted an increase of only 2 cents an hour in December 1954. Considering the

over-all position of the Company, therefore, the Board should rule that the Company's wages are in line with its competitors and that its economic position does not warrant an increase.

6. The economic outlook for this Company does not justify an increase at the present time. The Board should remember that this contract expires in April 1955. The outlook for the Company's products and profits between now and the expiration date of the contract is not good.

The Union misinterprets the statements made by the President of Aerovox as reported in the New Bedford Standard-Times for January 20, 1955. Actually, this article shows that, for the present at least, the Company needs all the working capital that it can get. The article points out that the Company has had to suspend payments for two years on the presently outstanding loan from the Prudential Insurance Company and it has had to discontinue payment of cash dividends for two years. The planned expansion which it hopes will increase sales in the future will not take effect until the end of 1955 at the very earliest. Thus, the facts are clear that for the present and for the period over which this contract still is effective the Company is not in a financial or economic position to warrant a general increase in wages.

Discussion

Background of the Wage Reopening Clause—A fair evaluation of the respective claims of the parties requires that they keep clearly in mind the bargaining framework within which the Arbitration Board is operating. And it is important for the Board to keep this frame of reference in mind in order to insure a fair and reasonable exercise of its powers. The Board is operating under a wage reopening clause negotiated into the present contract in April 1954. Uncontradicted testimony reveals the following facts with respect to the collective bargaining background of the reopening clause.

In the 1954 contract negotiations the Union asked for a substantial increase in wage rates. The Company replied that it was not in an economic and financial position to grant the wage increases requested by the Union. The final settlement included contract improvements which amounted to approximately 1.5 per cent of the bargaining unit payroll. It was also recognized by the parties that conditions might change sufficiently to warrant an adjustment in wages prior to the termination date of the contract in April 1955. Therefore, the parties negotiated a wage reopening clause which allowed the Union to reopen the wage rate question after six months. The presumption was that if a showing could be made that business and economic conditions had so improved for the Company that a wage increase was warranted then such might be negotiated. The decision in this case, therefore, turns on whether or not anything has happened since the last bargain to warrant a wage adjustment and if so, how much should the wage adjustment be and in what direction.

What has happened since the last bargain to justify a wage adjustment?—In considering the above question, two factors warrant special appraisal. The first is the evidence with respect to wage increases granted by direct competitors of the Company and the second is the evidence with respect to financial and economic conditions and trends since the last bargain.

The relevant evidence with respect to wage increases granted since the last bargain reveals the following facts. In November 1954 an increase of 3 cents per hour in wage rates was agreed upon by the International Brotherhood of Electrical Workers and the management of the Cornell Dubilier plant located in New Bedford, Massachusetts. This means that a local of the same Union as that involved in this case and a direct competitor of the Company located in the same town reached agreement on a general wage increase of 3 cents per hour which was made retroactive to October 1954 and which was included in a two-year contract terminating in October 1956. Another direct competitor of the Company, Sprague Electric, granted an increase of 2 cents per hour in December 1954 at its North Adams, Massachusetts plant. These companies produce a product similar to that made at Aerovox and compete with Aerovox in the national market.

Subsequent to these wage increases granted by the Company's competitors, Aerovox, in January 1955, granted a wage increase of 2 percent to its production workers who are covered by a separate collective bargaining agreement and who are members of a different Union. This Union is not affiliated with the A. F. of L. or the C.I.O. On the basis of this evidence of what has happened since the last bargain, the Board concludes that the Union involved in this case is entitled to a general increase in wage rates of 2 percent. Such an increase should reestablish the general wage rate relationships as they existed after the last bargain on April 14, 1954 between the bargaining unit here involved, the production workers at Aerovox and employees at competitor plants. If the parties believe that certain individual wage rates are out of line they have the option of correcting these through collective bargaining. But in view of the background and purpose of the wage reopening clause and the evidence, which will shortly be discussed, with respect to economic conditions at Aerovox the proper general increase for the Board to order is that which the Company itself has granted to other employees and that which its direct competitors have granted to their employees since the last bargain.

The evidence on the financial condition of the Company, economic changes since the last bargain and market outlook for the remaining months of this contract do not justify the Board awarding an increase of more than 2 per cent at this time.—The uncontroverted facts submitted in evidence with respect to the financial position of the Company may be summarized briefly as follows:

Between 1953 and 1954 the volume of sales declined from $16.2 million to $13.4 million. Furthermore, for the last half of the year, July to December 1954, the most relevant period from the standpoint of the wage reopening question, the sales volume declined from slightly over $7 million to $6.3 million. On April 1, 1954 the Company's backlog of orders amounted to approximately $1,800,000. On February 1, 1955 the backlog of orders totaled approximately $1,738,000. (Company Exhibit No. 1.) Company Exhibit No. 5 shows that prices covering 90 per cent of the total dollar sales volume of the Company declined between 5 per cent and 20 per cent, depending upon the product involved, between February 1, 1954 and February 14, 1955. On about 50 per cent of the dollar value of raw materials purchased, costs rose by an average of approximately 12 per cent during the year 1954. (Company Exhibit No. 7.) The Company's output of radio and television capacitators declined by 41 per cent between the years 1953 and 1954.

It should be clear from the evidence on business trends for the Company since the last bargain that the Board cannot award a wage adjustment at this time of more than 2 per cent. The 2 per cent is justified on the basis of similar increases granted by competitors of the Company since the last bargain as well as by the Company itself to the production employees. But no evidence was produced to show that other companies in the area had granted wage increases of specific amounts which entitled the Aerovox workers to a wage increase of more than 2 per cent. In appraising the question of outlook for the Company, the Board must keep in mind the fact that the termination date of the present contract is April 14, 1955. Notice of termination has already been given. Thus, in approximately one month's time, the parties will be engaged in negotiating a new contract. The facts with respect to future outlook, such as they exist at the time of this bargaining, are a relevant bargaining consideration. But the facts with respect to the estimates of possible future expansion of the Company, if the Company is successful in developing a new product, are applicable to a time in the future too remote to be used by this Board as a relevant consideration in judging the justice of a wage increase under this wage reopening clause.

The statements made by Mr. W. Myron Owen, President of the Company, as reported in the New Bedford Standard-Times, dated January 20, 1955 do not warrant the Board's ordering more than a 2 per cent wage increase. These statements indicate that the Company is currently short of working capital in view of its short term needs. For this reason the Company decided to suspend cash dividend payments to stockholders for two years and to suspend payments on its outstanding loan from the Prudential Insurance Company for a period of two years. The Insurance Company agreed to the suspension of payments on the loan on the basis of the Company's agreement to suspend cash dividends payments. The later item will enable the Company to add about $1,500,000 to its working capital.

The Company hopes to market a new type of capacitator that may increase its sales volume by from $10,000,000 to $15,000,000 per year. But the earliest date suggested for mass production of the new product is the end of the year 1955. Thus the impact on the financial position of the Company will not take effect until 1956. This factor, obviously, becomes a matter for future bargaining of the parties in the event that the new product has an important effect on the Company's financial position. But in view of the long time span involved between the present plans for expansion and their actual execution and in view of the considerable amount of guess work and hazardous predictions necessarily included in the estimates, this Board cannot use such estimates for the distant future as a basis for ordering wage adjustments in this wage reopening clause.

The Board cannot re-bargain the wage terms of the contract on the basis of comparative wage data known to the parties when they reached their last agree-

ment.—This point relates to the first item considered in this discussion. At the time of the last bargain in April 1954 the parties were aware of comparative wage rates between Aerovox and other companies in the electronics industry located in the immediate area and elsewhere throughout the country. They reached an agreement at that time with full knowledge of the facts. This Board cannot go behind that agreement and re-bargain it in terms of wage rate comparisons between Aerovox and Cornell Dubilier in South Plainfield, New Jersey, or B.L.S. rates in the greater Boston area, or wage comparisons with other companies which existed at the time of the last bargain. In other words, the Board cannot substitute its judgment for the judgment of the parties, nor its decision for the collective bargain of the parties.

The relevant evidence is the evidence with respect to what has happened since the last bargain. This evidence has been discussed above in terms of wage increases granted by competitors since the last bargain and in terms of economic changes and trends as they affect Aerovox which have occurred since the last bargain. The evidence on these factors adds up to a justifiable increase of 2 per cent, no more, no less. This is the award in this case.

If the parties believe that this award results in inequities, or if new data indicates a different award is justifiable, they have their redress in the collective bargaining on the new contract which takes place next month. But on the evidence before this Board, and considering the collective bargaining framework within which the Board operates, the proper decision is that there shall be an upward adjustment of 2 per cent in the wage rates.

AWARD

There shall be an increase of 2 per cent in straight time hourly wage rates for all jobs covered by the agreement between the parties.

Wages in a Partly Unionized Economy

UNION RESPONSIBILITY FOR WAGE CHANGES

From Economic Intelligence, published by the United States Chamber of Commerce, December, 1953

Recent studies indicate that both the layman and some economists tend to exaggerate the extent to which labor unions can and in fact do raise wages. Such an error may undermine a balanced and sensible judgment about appropriate labor legislation and proper public labor policies.

UNION BATTLES NEWSWORTHY

Union wage battles are newsworthy. Under collective bargaining, wage rates tend to be fixed and rigid for a year or two. Then either with or without public fanfare wage rates go up 5% or 10%. The fact that the wage change is expressed as an accomplishment of the union, and the change is identified with a few definite personalities, makes for "personal" news. Forces that work themselves out slowly and unnoticeably in nonunionized companies suddenly come to a head in unionized plants. They must then be handled at a definite time and the consequences may appear dramatic and obvious.

Wage changes in union shops and in nonunionized plants are illustrated in the accompanying diagram. Wage changes in nonunionized companies operate without fanfare, impersonally and more or less steadily. So they tend to go unnoticed.

Wage Changes in Union and Non-Union Plants

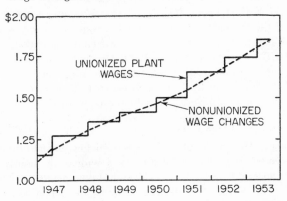

Many studies have been made to determine the effect of unions on wages. The evidence is conflicting, confusing and contradictory. But a growing number of economists are coming to the conclusion that by-and-large the same forces that permit and generate wage changes in nonunionized plants operate in roughly the same way in unionized plants.

100 YEARS HISTORY

Let us look at the period covering the last hundred years. In the 25-year period 1853 to 1878 hourly earnings rose 71% while the cost of living rose 25% —or, about one-third as fast as wages. Very few establishments were unionized then.

In the 50-year period 1853 to 1903, hourly earnings rose by 127%, while the cost of living rose only 38%. Only a very small fraction of our economy was unionized.

In the 75-year period 1853 to 1928, hourly earnings rose 569% while the cost of living rose 171%—or less than one-third as fast. Both money wages and real wages rose greatly. This three-quarters of a century was a period of few unions, except for the World War I period. Employers' rivalry in the labor market for scarce labor, and the competition in the goods market to sell goods, forced a free, unregulated, relatively nonunionized economy to spread the benefits of rising investment per worker and improved tools of production broadly among all.

In the last 20 years—a period of fabulous union growth—the share of the national income going to labor, while shifting a bit from year to year, has not changed perceptibly. In 1936, for example, compensation of employees, according to Department of Commerce figures, was 66% of our national income. In 1952 the figure was almost the same—66.3%. Yet during this period we have had the Wagner Act, minimum wage laws, political promotion of unions, and a terrific amount of labor turmoil, strikes and threats of strikes and enmity. Even if it were conceded that unions through one all-out effort could raise their members' share of the national income by 2% or 3%, this would be no more than the normal rise in productivity which occurs year by year.

In the World War II boom (say, 1939 to 1948) unorganized workers in some sectors of the economy had substantially greater wage increases than the unionized. For example, average annual fulltime earnings of domestic servants in 1948 were 272% of such earnings in 1939. The figure for nearly 100%-unionized auto workers was only 192%, while farm labor wage rates rose by 250%. In World War I wage rates in the nonunionized coal mines increased more than in the unionized in spite of feverish activity in the unionized sector.

AUTOMATIC WAGE INCREASES

Before General Motors adopted the cost-of-living escalator plus the 2½% annual improvement factor, a careful study was made of the hourly earnings in manufacturing generally, as well as in General Motors plants.

Had the General Motors formula been adopted by the American economy generally in 1940, the average hourly earnings in June 1951 (a year after Korean inflation began) would have been within 1 cent of the actual hourly earnings. The President of General Motors pointed out that if this had been done in 1940 we "would certainly have saved a lot of friction and strikes. . . ."

Indeed, if this formula had been generally adopted in 1910, more than 40 years ago, and adhered to throughout two world wars and a great depression, average hourly earnings would today be within a few cents of what they are in fact. Furthermore, the same would be true for the trend of actual hourly earnings based on this formula on a year-by-year basis. We are not arguing here for the General Motors formula, but merely trying to throw light on what governs wages.

In fact, there is good evidence that some unions have held wages down. This is partly attributable to the fact that contracts are ordinarily opened only once a year. It is also due to the fact that union leaders insist on getting credit for wage increases. Thus to cite the case of one farm implement company, in July 1952 when the contract expired the union made very extreme demands. Management offered a wage increase varying from 5¢ to 9¢ per hour. The offer was turned down and up to November 1953 employees have gotten no increase whatsoever.

A study of wage movements from 1909 to the present shows no systematic correlation with the percentage of workers unionized. Perhaps many workers are becoming aware of this. At any rate, since the mid-1940's the percentage of the labor force unionized has declined fairly steadily. Yet since 1945 average hourly earnings in manufacturing increased 74%, with roughly similar increases in other sectors of the economy, some of which are less unionized and some more unionized.

This brings us back to Taft-Hartley changes. Market forces account for basic wage changes—union and nonunion. A competitive free market economy *automatically* passes into the hands of workers the gains of rising productivity.

In fact, under competition there is no way for inventors, savers, stockholders or businessmen to keep the gains of technological progress to themselves.

This all has an important bearing on whether there is need for any relaxation of Taft-Hartley in terms of the economic progress and welfare of the American worker.

From the AFL News-Reporter, December 18, 1953

WAGE HIKES "FREE GIFT OF BOSSES," SAYS THE CHAMBER OF COMMERCE

Yes, dear wage earners of America, there is a Santa Claus. And you'd never recognize him behind those whiskers if it hadn't been for the sharp detective work of Dr. Emerson P. Schmidt, research director for the United States Chamber of Commerce.

Dum, ta, dum, tum. The good doctor went hunting through statistics in search of the facts, ma'am, with a veritable dragnet, and he came up with a great discovery. Briefly stated it is this: The great gains scored by you American workers in the past 16 years were not due to unionization, not won by struggle, but—get this!—the free gift of your bosses!

If it is a little difficult for you to picture your employer climbing down your chimney and stuffing your Christmas stockings with free and unsolicited wage increases, just listen to what Dr. Schmidt has to say in the latest issue of "Washington Report," published by the Chamber of Commerce:

"A competitive free market economy automatically passes into the hands of workers the gains of rising productivity."

AUTOMATICALLY, mind you.

What about the strikes, the picketing, the weary hours of negotiation to wrest higher wage rates and better working conditions from the employers?

All that is just sound and fury, signifying nothing, says Dr. Schmidt. His statistics SHOW that the percentage of national income going to wage earners in 1952 was no higher than in 1936.

What about these statistics? If you have always suspected that statistics are stranger than fiction, listen to what Boris Shishkin, AFL economist, has to say about Dr. Schmidt's.

In 1936, says Shishkin, average wages in manufacturing industries were only $21.78 a week. Now, with most of those factories unionized, the average has been raised to $71.91 a week. That's not all. The unions have improved working conditions, obtained vacations with pay, paid holidays, retirement pensions, health benefits and many other forms of security for the workers.

Before declaring a war of statistics between the clashing conclusions of the two economists, it should be pointed out that Dr. Schmidt failed to mention that 1952 was a year of unparalleled prosperity for business and rising profits took a greater share of the national income than in 1936. Farm income was also far higher. Therefore the percentage represented by personal income out of the whole kitty of national income is not, of itself, particularly significant. It is not representative.

But it is fruitless to try to answer statistics with other statistics. And those of you who have served on the firing line in the struggle of labor to improve its status should not allow your blood pressure to shoot up because of Dr. Schmidt's effort to disguise your employer as Santa Claus. After all, everyone knows it just ain't so.

Did you ever hear of a real Santa Claus who would fight against paying his helpers the legal minimum wage of 75 cents an hour, or $30 a week in these times of high living costs? Do you think Santa Claus would try to wipe out your Social Security fund, as the Chamber of Commerce is doing?

Dear wage earners of America, when you strip the false whiskers off Dr. Schmidt's Santa Claus it becomes obvious that he is an old phony.

THE NATIONAL WAGE BARGAIN

Presented before the Columbia University Seminar on Labor, 1952, by the late Arthur Meyer, former Chairman of the New York State Mediation Board, who was widely respected for his understanding of the labor scene

In our fractionalized wage bargains, economic analysis is largely devoted to wage comparisons and a comparison of wage increases. The use of macro-economics will be confined to cost of living data supplemented by a veneer of conflicting arguments as to how to increase demand and stabilize employment. Over the debate will hang an awareness of the power content of the situation and this awareness will color the calculations of the parties. A good agreement will fall within the area of their reasonable expectations. The settlement will not and cannot be concerned with its larger impact on real wages and the appropriate division of the national income. The objective of fractionalized collective bargaining is specific peace and not the general good.

Peace does not always come and, when it fails, the limiting point of the contest is trial by combat. The up-to-the-minute apology for the strike is that it brings a catharsis of hatred and anger and thus exorcises these evil emotions. If you can believe that you can believe anything. Would it not be more comforting and at least as reasonable to return to an older piety and say that the result of trial by combat represents the judgment of God?

But, since peace usually comes and the strike is exceptional, it is more important to ask whether peace is enough and whether other goods will somehow follow. I am not enough of a mystic to believe that. In classical economics we have a theory of self-regulation. Some people assume that the theory is sound and that its seeming shortcomings are due to departures from its simple prescription. You cannot, they say, expect self-regulation to function if you constantly inject discretionary regulation. Others assume that self-regulation has failed and that planned regulation must fortify its infirmities. Either view is consistent and people will presumably adopt the assumption that they consider valid.

There is, however, a third and bastard view which is very generally held. The third view is that self-regulation has failed but that we must strive to avoid planned regulation as far as possible and, in some important segments of the economy, avoid it altogether.

According to classical economics the labor market was supposed to be self-regulating and was related to the other factors of a self-regulating system. But the classical labor market was weighted against the worker. To adjust the balance of power it was supplanted by collective bargaining.

Collective bargaining on a case by case basis is the bargaining of two monopolists. It rests on the assertion of a peculiar power—the ability to abstain from closing an essential transaction. Market valuation is impossible, for the labor which is the subject of a collective bargain cannot ordinarily be bought or sold elsewhere. Nor is there any basic criterion of price, for the resort to comparative wages, to the extent that such a device is used, is like fixing the time by a mutual inspection of a number of separately questionable clocks. Free collective bargaining is not only not self-regulating; it has no definable organic relation to the economy of which it is a vital part.

And yet it is precisely here that the third point of view which I mentioned is most devoutly held. There must be no planning in respect to collective bargaining, no system of communication between the makers of national policy and the makers of discrete bargains: This is the religion whose devotees number the vast majority of trade unionists, industrialists and public men in the field of labor relations. No serious effort has been made to measure the effects of collective bargaining or to determine the limits of its usefulness. No cleansing scepticism questions its pretensions. It is an idol of contentious power which, at the best, may be placated, but which a strong taboo has sealed and sequestered from the help of supporting action or of systematic thought.

In opposition to this irrationalism, I would encourage the existing trends towards the integration of both labor and industry and the increase in the size of our bargaining units. Every step in that direcion will bring us nearer to a national labor bargain covering all of the major sections of industry. Long before we reach that point, the magnitude of labor agreements will impel the participation of government not merely as a mediator but rather as a recognized adviser. In accepting such a role, government would boldly undertake a task which it has already fugitively approached, a task directly related to its own fiscal and monetary policies and one of such importance that no lesser force can, without such assistance, appropriately perform it.

The difficulties to be overcome do not dissuade me. I think in terms of an evolutionary process in which each step, while bringing us nearer to a goal, may also at times be applied and tested. Nor is this evolution spun of vague hope. It has been going on for years and is now proceeding at an accelerated pace. Labor bargains are growing bigger and bigger, the public interest is growing greater and greater, the intrusion of government is becoming more and more frequent. Whether this evolution shall be encouraged or discouraged is an intensely practical problem. Those who see basic infirmities in the anarchy of formless bargaining will support an alternative which, though opposed by many, is clearly within the tenor of our way. The question is where are we going, and I discern in the national labor bargain a distant point towards which we are slowly moving, a destination already marked on the sign posts of our journeying. . . .

Pattern bargaining, as now practiced, is not a satisfactory alternative to a national labor bargain. It throws on one group, quite fortuitously, a responsibility which should be shared by all. To the extent that the pattern is followed, it is followed uncritically. It is solely a pattern of alteration and no consideration is given to the various garments which the alteration would affect.

The national bargain might make it possible to rationalize the wage structure. Inter-industry, as well as intra-industry and geographical differentials, could be pondered and either justified or amended. Inter-union competition, now damaging to both industry and labor, should be reduced to an appropriate debate. Furthermore, the increase in money wages, justified by the over-all increase in technological efficiency, could be applied on some generalized basis. . . .

The plan that I have suggested is subject to the doubt inherent in all planning. If there is grave danger in the irrationalism of discrete bargains, is there another and an equal danger in taxing reason beyond strength? Has our past experience been so fortunate as to justify the hope that industry and labor can, with the advice of government, reach appropriate solutions of large and complex problems? Such solutions would also appear to require the assistance of our social scientists. Can our economists help in respect to the application of the very theories on whose formulation they have failed to agree? These questions do more than suggest that any particular remedy is inappropriate. Stated as they usually are stated, they imply that our economic sickness is incurable.

For there is a weakness inherent in the very nature of our delicate and highly geared economy with its vast number of complex and variable determinants. We once hoped to escape the making of difficult adjustments, resting our expectations on an ingenious theory of self-regulation. When that failed, as most of us believe it has failed, some of us turned our thoughts to socialism and others to the atomization of production. Either of these opposites may be defended for both of them are, in this context, simplifying agents that reduce the number and complexity of the determinants.

I would prefer, however, to avoid either the socialization or the atomization of our economy. Though I do not hold that the maximization of production is the main end of the good life, it is an important consideration. And I see no reason to believe that any other system is likely to match the potential production of our own. Cured of the imperfections that impair its output and threaten its existence, a system of controlled competition might reach levels of production that would satisfy even the economic appetite that grows by what it feeds on.

Assuming that it will not be easy to retain the virtues of a competitive system and yet eradicate its defects, the attempt is still mandatory. The specific proposal I have made is supported by custom and caution. It suggests following a partly blazed trail by slow stages to a desirable destination. Merely pointing out that all traveling is hazardous is scarcely relevant criticism when our present station is fraught with gravest peril.

FOR DISCUSSION AND ANALYSIS

1. Explain whether, and if so how, a job-evaluation plan would in fact answer the two sets of questions raised by the Armstrong Rubber Co. in its ads, reproduced at the start of this chapter.

2. In the period following World War II, the Netherlands made use of interindustry (national) job evaluation as an instrument of national wage policy. What difficulties would be encountered in attempting to evaluate the worth of jobs by such a procedure across industry lines?

3. It is often argued that wages should not be based on the profitability of a company, that the worth of a worker should not be determined by whether the company employing him is making a profit or sustaining a loss. On the other hand, it is frequently asserted that intelligent workers should be willing to make some wage concession, accepting a pay cut or at least a wage increase less than that being granted in better-heeled companies, if their own employer is experiencing financial difficulty; to insist on being paid as much as comparable workers are receiving would only result in endangering their very jobs.

Are these two positions reconcilable?

4. Summarize the union and company arguments in either of the wage arbitrations reproduced in this chapter. Assume that you must choose between the union and the company, accepting one position or the other but being precluded from any compromise. Write a decision justifying your choice. Then write a supplementary decision in which you explain what your determination would have been, and why, had your discretion been unfettered.

5. If it is true, as Emerson Schmidt of the Chamber of Commerce suggests in the article from *Economic Intelligence* reproduced in this chapter, that it is market forces and not unionism which have accounted for rising wages, and that wage levels would be where they are now even in the absence of unions, then how would you answer the question which the AFL *News-Reporter* raises: "What about the strikes, the picketing, the weary hours of negotiation to wrest higher wage rates and better working conditions from the employers?"

6. Resolved: that the determination of wage rates by collective bargaining in more than 125,000 different bargaining units is anachronistic

and should be abandoned in favor of some more systematic and rational method of determining how much workers in their various jobs should receive relative to each other and relative to other income claimants.

a. Outline a case for the affirmative and the negative on the above proposition. Which do you think has the stronger arguments?

b. Why should wages be singled out for such treatment, in contrast to interest, for example?

19: Labor Monopoly

From their earliest days unions have been branded as monopolies operating at the expense of the community. It is also true that from their earliest days there have been those who have maintained whether rightly or wrongly that the degree of monopoly power exercised by unions is necessary if they are to secure favorable terms from employers. As Horace Greeley once expressed it, in the absence of such collective action wages would be forced downward "just as surely as water runs down hill."

The interesting question, then, is not whether unions are monopolies—the Taft-Hartley Act, which requires an employer to deal exclusively with the majority representative of his employees, obviously gives them a certain monopoly advantage (which may, however, be pallid alongside the employer's advantage as the "exclusive" employer of the union's membership). The more significant issues are how much monopoly power should be allowed to the unions and what forms it may take. Most of the materials which follow deal with these questions.

ORGANIZED LABOR

Report of the Attorney General's National Committee to Study the Antitrust Laws, Stanley N. Barnes and S. Chesterfield Oppenheim, cochairmen, March 31, 1955, pp. 293–306 *

At the outset, we emphasize that appraisal of the Nation's labor-management relations policy goes beyond this antitrust study. It follows that we assume, as Congress recently "declared," the "policy of the United States" to be elimination "of certain substantial obstructions to the free flow of commerce" by "encouraging . . . collective bargaining and by protecting . . . workers' . . . full freedom of association [and] self-organization . . . for the purpose of negotiating the terms and conditions of their employment or other mutual aid or protection." [1]

Accordingly, our inquiry considers only those union activities, not directed at such established union ends, but instead at direct restraints on commercial competition. This Committee believes that union actions aimed at directly fixing the kind or amount of products which may be used, produced or sold,

---

* Footnotes have here been renumbered for the convenience of the reader.
[1] 29 U. S. C. § 151 (1952).

their market price, the geographical area in which they may be used, produced or sold, or the number of firms which may engage in their production or distribution are contrary to antitrust policy. To the best of our knowledge, no national union flatly claims the right to engage in such activities. We believe that where the concession demanded from an employer as prerequisite to ordering the cessation of coercive action against him is participation in such a scheme for market control, this union conduct should be prohibited by some statute.

Within this scope of our inquiry, we consider, first, the extent to which judicial interpretations of the Clayton [2] and Norris-LaGuardia Acts [3] remove these labor practices from the Sherman Act. Second, we analyze whether these union restrictions, not reached by antitrust, were intended by Congress to be outlawed by the Labor-Management Relations Act of 1947.[4]

1. ANTITRUST COVERAGE

Some twenty years after the passage of the Sherman Act, the Supreme Court, in *Danbury Hatters*,[5] considered its application to union activities. There the union inspired a nationwide consumers' boycott of plaintiff's non-union-made hats. The result was a substantial drop in shipments of plaintiff's hats to out-of-state customers. The Supreme Court held this activity by the union a violation of the Sherman Act, apparently because the union sought to and did restrain interstate commerce in plaintiff's hats.

In apparent response, Sections 6 and 20 of the Clayton Act sought to exclude certain activities in the course of a "labor dispute" from the antitrust laws. Section 6 declares that "the labor of a human being is not a commodity or article of commerce." It further provides that "nothing contained in the antitrust laws shall be construed to forbid the existence and operation of labor . . . organizations, instituted for the purposes of mutual help, and not having capital stock or conducted for profits, or to forbid or restrain individual members of such organizations from lawfully carrying out the legitimate objects thereof; nor shall such organizations, or the members thereof, be held or construed to be illegal combinations or conspiracies in restraint of trade under the antitrust laws." Supplementing that provision, Section 20 barred issuance of Federal injunctions prohibiting activities such as strikes, boycotts or picketing "in any case between an employer and employees, or between employers and employees, or between employees, or between persons employed and persons seeking employment, involving, or growing out of, a dispute concerning terms or conditions of employment." Section 20 concludes with the broad language: "[N]or shall any of the acts specified in this paragraph be considered or held to be violations of any law of the United States."

The Supreme Court narrowed this exemption in the *Duplex* [6] and *Bedford*

[2] 15 U. S. C. §§ 12 *et seq.* (1952).
[3] 29 U. S. C. §§ 101–110, 113–115 (1952).
[4] 29 U. S. C. §§ 141–188 (1952).
[5] *Loewe* v. *Lawlor*, 208 U. S. 274 (1908).
[6] *Duplex Printing Press Co.* v. *Deering*, 254 U. S. 443 (1921).

Cut Stone [7] cases. There the scope of Section 20 was limited to disputes be-tween an employer and his own employees. Both these involved economic pressures created by concerted refusals to work on rather than to consume, as in *Danbury Hatters,* the plaintiff's product.

Thus in *Duplex,* members of the International Association of Machinists and other craft union members in New York refused to install plaintiff's presses manufactured in Michigan with non-union labor and shipped to out-of-state markets. This attempt to reduce the shipment of Duplex presses was held to violate the Sherman Act.

The *Bedford Cut Stone* case differed only in that the plaintiffs, an associa-tion of employers producing and shipping around 70 percent of the cut stone used throughout the country, had ceased recognition of the union and were threatening its very survival in the quarries. Members of the union employed by building contractors in various states refused to handle cut stone shipped by any of the plaintiffs; and the resulting cessations of stone shipment were declared to be restraints illegally caused by the union.

The immunity under Section 20 was also marked out in the *Coronado Coal* [8] cases. These involved no boycott but rather a mine shut-down caused in part by a concerted walkout and in part by wanton destruction of the mine's physical facilities. Obviously Section 20 of the Clayton Act did not immunize such acts of violence. Nevertheless, the Supreme Court found that the resulting stoppage had only an "indirect effect" on interstate commerce and, accordingly, held that there was no violation of the antitrust laws. However, when the plaintiff later showed that the union intended to keep the plaintiffs' non-union mined coal out of interstate markets, thus eliminating its competition with union mined coal, the Court held that this specific intent made the restraint "direct" and thus violative of the Sherman Act.[9]

A partial reaction to the *Duplex* [10] and *Bedford Cut Stone* [11] restrictions of Clayton Act Section 20, was the Norris-LaGuardia Act of 1932.[12] This aimed "to restore the broad purpose which Congress thought it had formulated in the Clayton Act but which was frustrated, so Congress believed, by unduly restric-tive judicial construction." [13] Accomplishing this end, "labor dispute" was there defined to include "any controversy concerning terms or conditions of employ-ment . . . regardless of whether or not the disputants stand in the proximate

[7] *Bedford Cut Stone Co.* v. *Journeymen Stone Cutter's Association,* 274 U. S. 37 (1927).

[8] *United Mine Workers of America* v. *Coronado Coal Co.,* 259 U. S. 344 (1922); *Coronado Coal Co.* v. *United Mine Workers of America,* 268 U. S. 295 (1925).

[9] This result was later confirmed, where the restraint was effected solely through the exercise of peaceful economic pressures. *Alco-Zander Co.* v. *Amalgamated Cloth-ing Workers,* 35 F. 2d 203 (E. D. Pa. 1929).

[10] *Duplex Printing Press Co.* v. *Deering,* 254 U. S. 443 (1921).

[11] *Bedford Cut Stone Co.* v. *Journeymen Stone Cutter's Association,* 274 U. S. 37 (1927).

[12] 29 U. S. C. §§ 101–110, 113–115 (1952).

[13] *United States* v. *Hutcheson,* 312 U. S. 219, 236 (1941).

relation of employer and employee." [14] In addition, Section 20 barred Federal injunction of enumerated union organizational and economic pressure activities.[15]

In *Apex Hosiery Co.* v. *Leader*,[16] the Court found it unnecessary to rely on Norris-LaGuardia in holding that an organizational strike, though interfering with interstate hosiery shipments, did not violate the Sherman Act. That Act, the Court noted, aimed at "restraints," like those this Committee now considers, "upon commercial competition in the marketing of goods or services." [17] In *Apex*, however, it was "plain that the. . . . [union] did not have as its purpose restraint upon competition in the market for petitioner's product. Its object was to compel petitioner to accede to the union demands" for organization.[18] From this decision there emerges a distinction, deemed essential by this Committee, between union activities aiming, on the one hand, at furthering rightful union objectives and, on the other, at directly "suppressing [commercial] competition or fixing prices" of commercial products.[19]

The antitrust impact of Norris-LaGuardia was first construed by the Supreme Court in *United States* v. *Hutcheson*.[20] There involved was a strike by one union against an employer who had assigned work to a competing union's members. Removing such conduct from the Sherman Act, the Court held that Congress, by the passage of the Norris-LaGuardia Act, had in effect overruled the *Duplex* construction of Section 20 of the Clayton Act. As a result, the Court concluded that all union self-help conduct specified in the concluding clause of Section 20, as well as Section 4 of Norris-LaGuardia, was now immunized from Sherman Act sanctions.

Hutcheson's rationale, however, was, in its own language, limited to "where a union acts in its own self-interest and does not combine with nonlabor groups,[21] . . ." While *Hutcheson* treated union pressure which fell short of coercing employer participation, *Allen-Bradley Company* v. *Local No. 3*,[22] decided some five years later, involved a consummated union-employer scheme. There, Local No. 3, comprised of electrical workers in the New York area, agreed with "contractors . . . to purchase equipment from none but local manufacturers who also had closed-shop agreements with Local No. 3," and with manufacturers "to confine their New York City sales to contractors employing the Local's members." [23] These contracts, the Court found, were "but one element in a far larger program in which contractors and manufacturers united . . . to monopolize all the business in New York City." [24] This fact of

[14] 29 U. S. C. § 113 (c) (1952).
[15] 29 U. S. C. § 104 (1952).
[16] 310 U. S. 469 (1940).
[17] *Id.* at 495.
[18] *Id.* at 501.
[19] *Ibid.*
[20] 312 U. S. 219 (1941).
[21] *Id.* at 232.
[22] 325 U. S. 797 (1945).
[23] *Id.* at 799.
[24] *Id.* at 809.

union-employer combination was held to distinguish *Allen-Bradley* from *Hutcheson* and, in turn, to subject Local No. 3 to the Sherman Act.[25]

It is not yet settled whether *Allen-Bradley* permits antitrust prohibition of an agreement between one union and one employer requiring conduct whose object is some direct market restraint. The majority there assumed, without deciding, that "such an agreement standing alone would not have violated the Sherman Act." [26] However, as the separate opinion emphasized, employer inspired agreements were not solely involved; instead some respondents were "individually coerced by the union's power to agree to its terms. It is, therefore, inaccurate," that opinion went on, "to say that the employers used the union to aid and abet them to restrain interstate commerce." [27] Accordingly, it may be that the employer connivance which *Allen-Bradley* requires might be inferred largely from a labor-management contract agreed to at union insistence.[28]

Even in the absence of such connivance, where the activity involved both aims, in the language of the *Apex* decision, at "suppressing [commercial] competition or fixing prices" [29] and is not sanctioned by the Labor-Management Relations Act, antitrust proceedings may not be foreclosed. In *Hawaiian Tuna Packers* v. *International Longshoremen and Warehousemen's Union,*[30] for example, fish canners sought treble damages from Local 150, made up of some crew members and boat owners who apparently were also crewmen. The complaint alleged that Local 150 demanded that the plaintiff canner contract to buy a season's catch at fixed rates per pound. Upon plaintiff's refusal, the union cut off its fish supply and, as part of its plan to coerce plaintiff to fix prices, agreed with fishermen in competing waters to boycott plaintiff. Upholding the complaint against the defendant's motion to dismiss, the court held that a demand to fix prices made by a combination of crewmen and owner crewmen brought the case within *Allen-Bradley.*[31]

Beyond connivance, however, that court held that the facts alleged failed to state a case involving or growing out of, as the Norris-LaGuardia Act re-

---

[25] Similarly note *Brotherhood of Carpenters* v. *United States*, 330 U. S. 395, 399–400 (1947); see also *Philadelphia Record Co.* v. *Manufacturing Photo-Engravers Ass'n. of Philadelphia*, 155 F. 2d 799 (3d Cir. 1946); but see *Albrecht* v. *Kinsella*, 119 F. 2d 1003 (7th Cir. 1941).

[26] 325 U. S. 797, 809 (1945); see also *id.* at 818.

[27] *Id.* at 814.

[28] In *Loews Inc.* v. *Basson*, 46 F. Supp. 66 (S. D. N. Y. 1942), a union comprising projectionists, deliverers and cutters sought to compel a movie producer-distributor to license only exhibitors who employed union projectionists. The producer-distributor objected, but the court held nonetheless its entry into the proposed contract would constitute an illegal "combination between a union and a nonlabor group" (*id.* at 72); cf. *Anderson-Friberg Inc.* v. *Justin R. Clary & Son*, 98 F. Supp. 75, 82 (S. D. N. Y. 1951); but see *Meier and Pohlmann Furniture Co.* v. *Gibbons*, 113 F. Supp. 409 (E. D. Mo. 1953).

[29] 310 U. S. 469, 501 (1939).

[30] 72 F. Supp. 562 (D. Hawaii 1947).

[31] *Id.* at 566.

quires, a "labor dispute." That Act, the court reasoned, "was not intended to
have application over the disputes over the sale of commodities . . . [or] to
include controversies upon which the employer-employee relationship has no
bearing." [32]

Supporting the suggestion that a dispute involving the object of direct
market control may not constitute a "labor dispute" within Norris-LaGuardia
are analogous decisions upholding state action restricting labor activities not
sanctioned by Taft-Hartley.[33] *Giboney* v. *Empire Storage Co.*,[34] for example,
involved picketing by union peddlers of an ice supply plant to bar ice sales to
nonunion peddlers. If Empire had agreed to stop selling ice to nonunion deliverers, the Supreme Court concluded that such conduct would have violated
the state antitrust statutes. Accordingly, since no question of conflict with the
Federal labor relations scheme was even raised,[35] the Court upheld application
of the state policy whose "purpose . . . is to secure competition and preclude
combinations which tend to defeat it." [36]

Summing up, our analysis of these "three 'interlacing statutes' " [37] suggests
that commercial restraints by unions may be vulnerable to antitrust proceedings:

(1) Where the union engages in fraud or violence and intends or achieves
some direct commercial restraint; [38]

(2) Where the union activity is not in the course of a labor dispute as defined
in the Norris-LaGuardia Act.[39] Construing this statute, the Supreme Court has
recognized "its responsibility to try to reconcile" two "declared Congressional
policies." The "one seeks to preserve a competitive business economy; the other

[32] *Id.* at 566; similarly, note *Columbia River Packers Ass'n.* v. *Hinton*, 315 U. S. 143
(1942); see also *Louisville & N. R. Co.* v. *Local Union No. 432*, 104 F. Supp. 748
(S. D. Ala. 1952); *Pacific Gamble Robinson Co.* v. *Minneapolis and St. Louis Ry. Co.*,
85 F. Supp. 65 (D. Minn. 1949).

[33] See, for example, *Giboney* v. *Empire Storage & Ice Co.*, 336 U. S. 490 (1949);
Whitaker v. *State of North Carolina*, 335 U. S. 525 (1949); *Lincoln Federal Labor
Union* v. *Northwestern Iron & Metal Co.*, 335 U. S. 525 (1949); *AFL* v. *American
Sash & Door Co.*, 335 U. S. 538 (1949).

[34] 336 U. S. 490 (1949).

[35] It was not necessary for the Court to consider there whether the union activity
involved ran afoul of the Taft-Hartley subsection 8 (b) (4) (A). Its legality under
that provision, however, seems open to question. Initially, it seems clear that "an
object" of the picketing was, as that section requires, to foreclose Empire from "doing
business with any other person." The primary issue would be whether the union
activity constituted, within the meaning of that provision, encouraging "the employees
of any employer to engage in a . . . concerted refusal in the course of their employment to . . . handle . . . any material . . . or to perform any services." Cf.
National Labor Relations Board v. *International Rice Milling Co.*, 341 U. S. 665, 670
(1951).

[36] *Giboney* v. *Empire Storage Co.*, 336 U. S. 490, 495 (1949).

[37] *Allen-Bradley Co.* v. *Local No. 3*, 325 U. S. 797, 806 (1945).

[38] Cf. *Apex Hosiery Co.* v. *Leader*, 310 U. S. 469, 501–504 (1940); 29 U. S. C.
§ 104 (i) (1952); *Coronado Coal Co.* v. *United Mine Workers of America*, 268 U. S.
295 (1925).

[39] See 29 U. S. C. § 113 (c) (1952).

to preserve the rights of labor to organize to better its conditions through an agency of collective bargaining." Accordingly, its task is in each case to determine "how far Congress intended activities under one of these policies to neutralize the results envisioned by the other." [40] Accomplishing this task may require giving content to the Norris-LaGuardia Act's general definition of "labor dispute." We have noted that recent decisions suggest that courts may infer Congressional intent to apply antitrust to those labor activities, not sanctioned by the Taft-Hartley Act, which aim at direct commercial restraint.[41]

(3) Where a union combines with some nonlabor group to effect some direct commercial restraint.[42] . . .

2. RELEVANT PROVISIONS OF THE LABOR-MANAGEMENT RELATIONS ACT OF 1947

Against this background of possible avenues for antitrust suits, Congress in 1947 considered amendments to the National Labor Relations Act. The bill passed by the House, the Conference Committee Report notes, "contained a provision amending the Clayton Act so as to withdraw the exemption of labor organizations under the antitrust laws when such organization engaged in combination or conspiracy in restraint of commerce where one of the purposes or a necessary effect of the combination or conspiracy was to join or combine with any person to fix prices, allocate costs, restrict production, distribution, or competition, or impose restrictions or conditions, upon the purchase, sale, or use of any product, material, machine, or equipment, or to engage in any unlawful concerted activity." [43] Explaining omission of such provisions from the enacted Bill, the Conference Report continued: "Since the matters dealt with in this Section have to a large measure been effectuated through the use of boycotts, and since the conference agreement contains effective provisions directly dealing with boycotts themselves, this provision is omitted from the conference agreement." [44]

The so-called boycott provisions provide in relevant part that "it shall be an unfair labor practice for a labor organization or its agents to engage in, or to induce or encourage the employees of any employer to engage in, a strike or a concerted refusal in the course of their employment to . . . handle or work on any . . . materials . . . or to perform any services, where an object thereof is (A) forcing or requiring . . . any employer or other person to cease using . . . or otherwise dealing in the products of any other producer . . . or to cease doing business with any other person . . ." or "(D) forcing or requiring any employer to assign particular work to employees in a particular labor organization or in a particular trade, craft, or class rather than to employees in another labor organization or in another trade, craft, or

[40] *Allen-Bradley Co.* v. *Local No. 3*, 325 U. S. 798, 806 (1945).

[41] See e.g., *Hawaiian Tuna Packers* v. *International Longshoremen & Warehousemen Union*, 72 F. Supp. 562 (D. Hawaii 1947); see also *Columbia River Packers Assoc.* v. *Hinton*, 315 U. S. 143 (1942); cf. *Giboney* v. *Empire Storage Co.*, 336 U. S. 490 (1949).

[42] See e.g., *Allen-Bradley Co.* v. *Local No. 3*, 325 U. S. 797 (1945).

[43] 93 Cong. Rec. 6380 (1947).

[44] *Ibid.*

class. . . ." [45] Moreover, it further provides that "Whoever shall be injured in his business or property by reason of any violation" of these provisions "may sue therefor . . . and shall recover the damages by him sustained and the cost of the suit." [46]

These provisions have been applied to enjoin certain union activities aimed [47] at restricting the use of competing products in a given area.[48] *United Brotherhood of Carpenters and Joiners of America* v. *Sperry*,[49] for example, involved union picketing and blacklisting of a builder using prefabricated building material. The court, granting an injunction pending hearing, found that such union actions "handicapped" the builder and "delayed [him] in carrying forward . . .

---

[45] 29 U. S. C. § 158 (1952). The language of subsection (*D*), incidentally, would in all probability encompass the union activities held not subject to antitrust coverage in *United States* v. *Hutcheson*, 312 U. S. 219 (1940). Similarly note *United States* v. *Carrozzo*, 37 F. Supp. 191 (N. D. Ill., 1941), *aff'd sub nom* 313 U. S. 539 (1941).

[46] 29 U. S. C. § 187 (*b*) (1952); see, e.g., *Longshoremen's and Warehousemen's Union* v. *Juneau Spruce Corp.*, 342 U. S. 237 (1952).

[47] Relevant here is a Supreme Court holding that "under this section it is not necessary to find that the *sole* object of the union activity was an illegal one." (See *National Labor Relations Board* v. *Denver Building and Construction Trades Council*, 341 U. S. 675, 689 [1951].)

[48] For cases ordering cessation of some union efforts to block use of more efficient products see *Joliet Contractors Association* v. *National Labor Relations Board*, 202 F. 2d 606 (7th Cir. 1953); *cert. denied* 346 U. S. 824 (1953); *National Labor Relations Board* v. *United Brotherhood of Carpenters and Joiners of America*, 184 F. 2d 60 (10th Cir. 1950).

Note also *In re Washington and Oregon Shingle Weavers Council*, 101 N. L. R. B. 1159 (1952) (Shingle Weavers Council order to "cease and desist from . . . encouraging their members to . . . strike" against a shingle company (*Id.* at 1163) as part of the union effort to eliminate "all unfair Canadian or other 'nonunion' shingles from the United States market." [*Id.* at 1168]), order enforced *National Labor Relations Board* v. *Washington-Oregon Shingle Weavers District Council*, 211 F. 2d 149 (9th Cir. 1954); *In re Bakery Drivers Local 276*, 100 N. L. R. B. 1092 (1952) (Bakery Drivers Union ordered to cease and desist from encouraging employees of various retail outlets to engage in a concerted refusal to handle bakery products of a company which the union was seeking to organize). Similarly, note *Construction and General Laborers Local 320*, 93 N. L. R. B. 751 (1951); *In re International Brotherhood of Teamsters, Chauffeurs, Warehousemen and Helpers of America, Local 87*, 87 N. L. R. B. 720 (1949), order enforced, *National Labor Relations Board* v. *Service Trade, Chauffeurs, Salesmen & Helpers, Local 145*, 191 F. 2d 65 (2d Cir. 1950). For cases where the Board has enjoined a union, as part of a scheme to pressure an employer of a plant already organized, from encouraging workers of a customer concertedly to refuse to handle the product of the employer involved in the dispute, see *In re Metal Polishers Local 171*, 86 N. L. R. B. 1243 (1949); *In re Wine, Liquor and Distillery Workers Union, Rectifying and Wine Workers International Union of America, A. F. of L. Local 1*, 78 N. L. R. B. 504 (1948), order enforced, *National Labor Relations Board* v. *Wine, Liquor and Distillery Workers Union, Rectifying and Wine Workers International Union of America, Local 1*, 178 F. 2d 584 (2d Cir 1949).

[49] 170 F. 2d 863–869 (10th Cir. 1948).

[his] program of purchasing and erecting" prefabricated houses.[50] These labor activities were later held by the Board to be an unfair labor practice and its order requiring their cessation was ordered enforced by a circuit court.[51]

Similarly, *Joliet Contractors Association* v. *National Labor Relations Board* [52] involved a union by-law which, one circuit court found left members with no "choice but to refuse to work when discovery was made that preglazed sash was being used." [53] The record there revealed, moreover, that in several instances glaziers on a job, in compliance with this by-law, walked off the job when preglazed sash was purchased. As to these instances of restraint, the circuit court affirmed the Board's order requiring a union to "desist from applying its bylaws . . . to induce and encourage . . . a strike or concerted refusal in the course of . . . employment . . . where an object thereof is to require their employer . . . or other person to cease doing business with any other employer or any person who uses or sells preglazed sash." [54]

As these two instances suggest, certain means for curbing union activities aimed directly at suppressing commercial competition may be proscribed by the boycott provisions of the Labor-Management Relations Act. However, only those activities " 'specifically provided for' in the Act" [55] are restricted. The result, in the language of the Court in the *Joliet Contractors* [56] case may be "numerous apparent incongruities." There, for example, "if two or more glaziers refuse to accept employment because of the use of preglazed sash there is no violation as they have not concertedly refused to work in the course of their employment. However, if they discover the use of preglazed sash after they are on the job and then refuse to work, it is a violation because they have done so in the course of their employment. At the same time, if there is only one glazier on each of several jobs and they each refuse to work, it is not a violation because their refusal is not concerted. These incongruities and others which could be mentioned are unavoidable because of the plain unambiguous language employed by Congress in enumerating the elements required to constitute a violation." [57]

[50] *Id.* at 867.

[51] See *United Brotherhood of Carpenters and Joiners of America* (Wadsworth), 81 N. L. R. B. 802 (1949), order enforced, *National Labor Relations Board* v. *United Brotherhood of Carpenters and Joiners of America*, 184 F. 2d 60 (10th Cir. 1950).

[52] 202 F. 2d 606 (7th Cir. 1953), *cert. denied* 346 U. S. 824 (1953).

[53] *Id.* at 612.

[54] *Id.* at 611. There the Board had held as an unfair labor practice the union's inducement of glaziers already on a job to cease installing preglazed sash (99 N. L. R. B. 1391, 1410, 1415 [1952]). However, the Board held not within the Act union inducement of its members, not yet on a job, not to work on preglazed sash (*Id.* at 1412–1413). The result, in the language of the court affirming this order, may be "numerous apparent incongruities," *Joliet Contractors Association* v. *National Labor Relations Board*, 202 F. 2d 606, 611 (7th Cir. 1953), *cert. denied* 346 U. S. 824 (1953), thus permitting certain union pressures against use of new products.

[55] *National Labor Relations Board* v. *International Rice Milling Co., Inc.*, 341 U. S. 365 (1951).

[56] 202 F. 2d 606, 611 (7th Cir. 1953); *cert. denied* 346 U. S. 824 (1953).

[57] *Id.* at 612.

3. CONCLUSIONS AND RECOMMENDATIONS

As the limitations of our inquiry require, no one of our conclusions or recommendations implies any change of labor's freedom under the antitrust laws to act in concert in order to promote union organization or bargain collectively over wages, hours, or other employment conditions. Reported cases indicate, however, that some unions have engaged in some practices aimed directly at commercial market restraints by fixing the kind or amount of products which may be sold in any area [58] or their market price.[59] Such activities run counter to our national antitrust policy.

Some means for carrying them out may be enjoined by the Labor-Management Relations Act,[60] whose enforcement, we note, is presently dependent on receipt of formal complaints. Moreover, such union activities are, to some but as yet unfixed extent, now subject to antitrust coverage. As a practical matter, these union restraints usually gain commercial significance to the extent that there is employer participation—either voluntary or coerced.[61] However, to repeat, we believe that where the concession demanded from an employer as prerequisite to ceasing coercive action against him is participation in or submission to such a scheme for market control or commercial restraints, this union conduct should be prohibited by statute. Accordingly, to the extent that such commercial restraints not effectively curbed by either antitrust or Labor-Management Relations Act exist, then we recommend appropriate legislation to prohibit these union efforts at outright market control.

Regarding such legislation, this Committee recommends:

a. It should cover only specific union activities which have as their direct object direct control of the market, such as fixing the kind or amount of products which may be used, produced or sold, their market price, the geographical area in which they may be sold, or the number of firms which may engage in their production or distribution. By "object" this Committee means only the immediate concession demanded from an employer as a condition precedent to halting coercive action against him. In drafting such legislation, greatest care should be given to protecting labor's "full freedom of association [and] self-organization . . . for the purpose of negotiating the terms and conditions of their employment or other mutual aid or protection" as now provided in 29 U. S. C. § 151 (1952).

[58] See e.g., *Allen-Bradley Co.* v. *Local No. 3*, 325 U. S. 797 (1945); *Joliet Contractors Association* v. *National Labor Relations Board*, 202 F. 2d 606–611 (7th Cir. 1953), *cert. denied* 346 U. S. 824 (1953); *United Brotherhood of Carpenters and Joiners of America* v. *Sperry*, 170 F. 2d 863 (10th Cir. 1948); cf. *United States* v. *American Federation of Musicians*, 47 F. Supp. 304 (N. D. Ill. 1942), *aff'd* 318 U. S. 741 (1943); *United States* v. *Carrozzo*, 37 F. Supp. 191 (N. D. Ill. 1941); *aff'd sub nom.* 313 U. S. 539 (1941).

[59] See e.g., *Columbia River Packers Association* v. *Hinton*, 315 U. S. 143 (1942) *Hawaiian Tuna Packers* v. *International Longshoremen and Warehousemen Union* 72 F. Supp. 562 (D. Hawaii, 1947).

[60] See cases n. 48, *supra.*

[61] Cf. *Allen-Bradley Co.* v. *Local No. 3*, 325 U. S. 797, 809 (1945).

b. Unlike the present Labor-Management Relations Act,[62] the Government should have power to proceed, on its own initiative, without formal complaints from others. A coerced employer, for example, might find it advantageous to acquiesce rather than complain. Thus, were the Government dependent upon formal complaints of others to initiate actions, some wrong to the public interest might go uncorrected.

c. Unlike the Sherman Act, such legislation should not contain provisions for private injunction. In the labor-management area, private injunctive remedies under the Sherman Act have in the past been subject to abuse. In any legislation, therefore, primary reliance should be on Government-initiated enforcement.

Walter Adams dissents from this majority report. In his words:

Should Congress find that union commercial restraints not curbed by antitrust or Taft-Hartley are widespread, the majority suggests a possible approach for halting them. This suggestion, however, is so general that its enactment would confuse rather than clarify existing law. Moreover, because of its vagueness, it might be construed—erroneously perhaps—as prohibiting some union activities generally regarded as normal and necessary.

Thus the majority suggestion aims at "specific union activities which have as their direct object control of the market." To the extent that the limits of challenged union conduct are defined in terms of "object" (i.e., intent), the proposal is subject to potential abuse. Unlike the Taft-Hartley Act, it does not pinpoint specific malpractices in terms of a clearly delineated course of conduct. Instead, it makes broad recommendations of an undefined and unknown impact.

In dissenting, I am not unmindful of the concern over allegedly widespread labor abuses. I believe, however, that corrective legislation—if, when and by whomsoever proposed—should be based on a careful and comprehensive investigation of all the facts within the context of market reality. Such legislation, if and when enacted, should become part of our labor-management code, and not part of the antitrust laws. Raymond Dickey joins in this dissent, but adds his view "that present Labor-Management Relations Act and antitrust provisions can effectively curb those commercial restraints by unions which concern the majority."

THE ECONOMIC POWER OF LABOR ORGANIZATIONS

From the statement of Admiral Ben Moreell, Chairman of the Board of Directors and President of Jones & Laughlin Steel Corporation, to the Senate Committee on Banking and Currency, August 24, 1949

At the outset, we should face one fact squarely. When two workers agree to stand together in their demands on the "boss" for certain pay and working con-

[62] 29 U. S. C. § 160 (*b*) (1952) provides that the Board may issue complaints and hold hearings apparently only "[w]henever it is charged that any person has engaged in or is engaging in any such unfair labor practice."

ditions, we have a restriction on competition for work and the beginning of a monopoly. When all of the workers in a shop band together, we have an extension of the restriction on competition. Over the years, the public has recognized that this kind of restraint of competition is beneficial and in the public interest.

As the organization of workers expands to all of the shops of one company, then to all of the companies in a single industry, and then when the same organization penetrates into other industries, some completely unrelated, the public interest demands that we stop and appraise our position.

Many labor organizations have thus grown into huge combinations, with the economic power—frequently exercised—to restrain trade and reduce competition in significant degrees. With such power, labor unions can and do affect prices, and quantities and qualities of production. Whether or not such unions are, in a strict sense, complete labor monopolies, is not important. Some are, in fact, complete monopolies. Others are so strategically placed in our economy that the end result of their actions is equivalent to complete monopoly power.

In the two industries in which I am now directly interested—steel and coal—the labor organizations exercise, in fact, almost a complete monopoly of the usable labor. There are other industries, such, for example, as automobiles, rubber, oil, electrical products, and the garment trades where similar conditions exist. The individual railroad brotherhoods are limited to specific employe functions, but a strike by any one brotherhood shuts down all railroad service. In the same manner, positions of great strategic power are held by the craft unions in the building trades—the teamsters, stationary engineers, and others.

The records of the hearings before this Committee recite many ways in which labor organizations have applied their economic power, and there is no dearth of examples where strikes and threats of strikes have slowed down and at times disrupted our entire economy. The public is well aware of these occurrences. In recent weeks the restriction on coal production imposed by the United Mine Workers has received wide publicity. If there should be a steel strike the entire country will feel its disastrous effects and the public will be keenly aware of it.

The price increases and restrictions on production which result from formal agreements between labor and management are not so clearly evident to the public. But the public pays the bill just the same. In the rising market of recent years, increases in wages in any industry, which have not been balanced by increases in production or reductions in other costs, have been passed on to the consuming public. When labor cost increases are not counterbalanced by increased production, it means that labor gets a bigger slice of the pie, and since the size of the pie remains the same, the rest of the public gets a smaller portion.

There is another important factor in the economic power of unions which should be noted. There is a truism that power tends to concentrate, to be drawn into the hands of fewer and fewer men. So it is with a large union. Regardless of written constitutions and by-laws, in practice, the power to impose a monopoly and restrict competition gravitates into the hands of a comparatively few leaders. There are few checks and balances. Direction by a

ingle man or by an oligarchy seems to be required by the nature of labor
inions' objectives. There is no question in my mind that more democratic
orms of union meetings, more frequent referendums and elections, greater
>olice protection to prevent intimidation and attacks, the use of a fair secret
>allot and more stringent quorum requirements for a vote on affirmative action
vould have desirable effects without interfering with the efficiency of operation
»f the unions. However, if we may judge the future by the past, I believe that
he actions taken and demands made by union leaders will, in most cases, be
onfirmed by a majority of the union members, just as the monopolistic activ-
ties of corporate managements were strongly supported by stockholder groups
>rior to 1890, and even thereafter, in spite of the antitrust laws. We should,
herefore, face the probability that the concentrations of economic power which
iow rest in the hands of a few men will not be dispersed by more democratic
mion procedures. If we are to have corrective action, it must be as a result
»f legislation.

Realism requires that we modify our claim that we have a free economy
vhose course is determined by competitive forces. Prices, quality, production
.nd plant improvements are, in many instances, significantly affected by the
legree of wisdom, integrity and concern for the public interest exercised by
iotent labor leaders. The ability to materially affect conditions in strategic
ndustries, such, for example, as transportation, steel and coal, places some
mion leaders in positions of strategic importance with respect to the course of
iur whole economy.

The concentration of economic power in the hands of labor leaders who are
iot responsible to the public and who are subject to little restraint by law is an
xtremely important development in our industrial life. I believe that we
annot safely accept this modification of our free economy in the hope that
vith the passage of time, the accumulation of experience, and the sobering
ffect of responsibility, this power will be tempered by benevolence and wis-
lom. All human experience discourages such belief. It teaches us that power is
orrosive. Union organizations seem to pass through three stages—(1) the
haotic period of organization; (2) the period of stabilization and cooperation
vith management; and (3) the period of entrenchment and self-perpetuation
y a powerful leadership. It is in this last stage that the corrosive effect of
ower makes itself felt. If this country is to have a controlled economy in spite
f the many disastrous examples which should steer us away from that course,
:t our economy be controlled at least by leaders who are responsible to all of
s, and not by those who represent special interests and who are responsible
nly to a small segment of the people.

As a result of their ability to shut down strategic industries and to impose
niform conditions upon an entire competitive field, labor leaders can exert
ompelling economic pressure on all of the public, as well as on individual
mployers. The pressure brought to bear on the public is often more effective
a gaining labor's objectives than would be the case if it were applied only to
pecific employers. The force of public opinion here comes into play. Alert labor
:aders are thoroughly aware of this and they play the game accordingly. If

the effects of a threatened steel strike could be confined only to the steel industry, many persons—workers and stockholders—would be injured; but their
percentage of the whole public would not be great. But the effects of a steel
strike cannot be so confined and, in fact, the effects will be felt by practically
everyone. Individually, and collectively as a nation, such a result cannot be
ignored.

It follows, therefore, that most labor demands and the frequent result of
unsatisfied demands—strikes—are, in effect, imposed on the public. The demands
of organized labor, which have been mounting each year, are buttressed by so
much economic power that employers have seldom refused some concessions.
Each year, wages, costs and prices have gone up. A depression might curb this
progression, but a depression is an exorbitant price to pay for something
which intelligence and courage should enable us to avert. Furthermore, the
power of organized labor will be exerted to maintain monetary wage rates even
when prices are falling and, as a result, real wages are rising. This will accentuate unemployment and retard recovery from the depression.

In the process described above, smaller enterprises have usually been injured
competitively more than the large companies because the demands of labor
have been geared to the paying abilities of the large mass producers who
operate with greater efficiency and at lower unit cost. It would be difficult for
industry-wide unions to proceed in any other manner. Industrial competition
is thus restrained to the detriment of the public interest, and more especially of
those localities where smaller industries may be located.

Plant improvement and increased mechanization have sometimes been
directly prevented by union mandate, but more frequently they have been prevented indirectly because increased labor costs have consumed financial
resources which would otherwise have been spent for improved equipment.
Thus increased labor costs have in many cases prevented the very thing which
would justify them, i.e., increased production. The incurring of debt by many
companies, particularly since the almost complete drying up of the equity
market, thus becomes mandatory to achieve increased efficiency as a counter-
balance to larger labor costs. Furthermore, because union contracts are of relatively short duration and prospective labor cost increases are unknown,
production stability over a long term is extremely difficult.

For many years the national economy has been under severe pressure to
return to labor a steadily increasing share of the national production. This
process has had some beneficial effect on the economy. Employers have been
stimulated to devise more productive procedures and labor expanding devices
But I believe that we are approaching the point of diminishing returns, if we
have not already reached it. It becomes more and more difficult to compensate
for increases in the cost of labor by means of technological improvements and
managerial skill, so that additional rewards to labor will have to be met in
whole or in large part through increased prices or a decreased return on investments, measures which are frequently impossible.

The extent to which we can continue to yield to demands for higher labor
costs without material injury to the nation cannot be foretold. But it is im-

ortant to note that there is now no law or other governmental or industrial authority upon which we can rely to insure that the power in the hands of labor organizations will be kept within the bounds of economic health.

Through the period of increasing labor power, organized labor has obtained short-range benefits. Monetary wages are at a new high, as are real wages. It is important to note that industry-wide unions operating over large areas of the country are generally more concerned with monetary wages than with real wages. In the many instances where price rises have absorbed much of the labor gains, the bill has largely been paid by unorganized labor and the general public. Whether there has been a fair division of benefits and burdens could only be determined by a more comprehensive study than any I have seen.

Certainly it is true that since industry-wide wages and working conditions have changed uniformly, this element of competition among industrial concerns has been eliminated. That is an apparent benefit to the larger industries and to the labor unions concerned. Its contribution to the public welfare is doubtful. In some cases, small groups of workmen in small plants by alliance with employes in other plants have undoubtedly been strengthened in their bargaining power with strongly financed and ruthless managements.

We must bear in mind, however, that "labor's gains" can be properly appraised only when we consider their long term effects. In the ultimate analysis, permanent gains for labor depend entirely on the stability of industry. Labor can be paid only out of the proceeds of production. I believe that while production per man-hour has increased, by far the larger part of this increase is due to improved equipment, rather than to increases in effort or skill of the workers. We then face the question—can industry continue to devise new tools, machinery and processes and find the capital necessary to finance them in order to offset the rising costs of labor by increasing production? If not, labor will have been shortsighted—and we will all suffer.

A number of other dangers have been created. In some industries, a uniform scale of wages has been established across the country. The differing conditions in plants and localities which have a distinct bearing on real wages have been ignored. Some plants have been forced to close and others have not been built because allowances have not been made or have been inadequately made for such differences. Raises in one strategic industry have been followed by similar raises in another and then by equivalent raises "across the board." Our price level has been on an upward spiral dictated in large measure by labor leaders. This sequence of wage cost increases is now described as a series of "rounds"—first, second and third. The present steel demands are recognized as starting a "fourth round" drive. Every person and every industry now has a stake in each opening negotiation. If we can still describe our economy as "free," the definition of the word has been changed.

Competition within industries has also been reduced. Uniform wage levels have been stabilized for the efficient, the inefficient, the large and the small. Wages are based less on skill and productivity and more on seniority and mass bargaining power. Industrial management is comforted by the assurance that competitors must pay the same labor rates. This has two undesirable effects:

first, there is no collective bargaining except between a few labor leaders and one or a few leaders in the industry, and second, it stifles competition in a most important field of costs. I believe that these conditions heralded the start many years ago of the British industrial decline. That was not noted in England until it was too late. Or, if noted, it seemed to give no cause for alarm. I trust that we will be more alert here. The lessening of competition for any reason seems to bring decay.

The best time to arrest decay is at the beginning. We must not drift into a static economy with a growing population. If we should permit this, it must result in a lowering of our standards of living. With no larger pie to share, and more with whom to share it, this is inevitable. We have already met the challenge of concentrations of financial and industrial power. It would be a pity to default to a concentration of similar economic power in the hands of labor leaders. New legislation is needed now.

The character of such legislation is a more difficult problem. The objective is clear—to avoid injury to the public interest from excessive concentration of economic power in the hands of labor leaders. At the same time, we must preserve the important social gains of collective bargaining. Only the evil must be eradicated.

As I see it, there are three courses open to us—first, we could so define the legitimate objectives of labor unions as to prohibit them from controlling production, preventing improvements, imposing any form of featherbedding (including "made work"), fixing prices, excluding prefabricated articles and items manufactured in other cities or by other groups of labor, limiting the use of labor-saving machines and similar unjustifiable practices which still exist and for which we pay dearly;—second, we could restrict the power of unions by limiting the size of unions, subjecting them generally to the antitrust laws and forbidding industry-wide bargaining; or, third, we could proceed along a combination of both lines of legislative restrictions.

The first step can and should be taken immediately. I can see no justification for restrictive labor practices which seek to control prices or production. I have a strong feeling of resentment when I learn that my clothes cost more because a union leader has limited the use of the most efficient cutting machines, fixed the cost of labor to be included (irrespective of actual cost) in the price of each grade of suits, and prevented the introduction of new and cheaper methods of manufacture. No American should be permitted to exact that tribute from another American. Economically, it is unwise for all. I can see disaster ahead if we permit one man to restrict by personal edict the coal production of the nation. I know that building costs could be reduced in many sections if restrictive building trade practices were stopped. These evils are violations of our social and economic codes. They are seriously detrimental to the public interest. They should be eliminated forthwith.

The legislative prohibition of specific restrictive and uneconomical labor practices is relatively easy to draft and will not interfere with labor's legitimate aims. It will free many industries to make available to the public the full benefit of technological improvements. Many costs, now sustained artificially by enforced waste, will fall. Many prices will be reduced. Some new industries will become practicable.

Some students of this problem think this obvious step will cure many of the evils which we now face. Although I believe such legislation is vital in the public interest, I am sure it is not the complete answer. While it will contain labor's great economic power within the bounds of legitimacy, it will have no effect on the present concentration and further growth of that power.

The second measure, the curbing of labor's power by restricting that power itself, is a more difficult problem. The principal suggestions for such legislation have been along the lines of strengthening and expanding our antitrust laws to treat labor unions and industry alike. There is, I think, a solid historical basis for trying to solve the problem along antitrust lines. I have been told by my counsel that the common law antitrust principles which really sired the English Statute of Monopolies and our Antitrust Laws were directed primarily at craft organizations. These common law and statutory principles broke up the ancient craftsmen guilds which in the fifteenth century dominated and restricted trade and competition. At that time, however, the artisan was an individual enterpriser and the restrictive regulations of the guilds had the color of labor and enterprise combinations in restraint of trade. I am told also that the inclusion of labor within the scope of our antitrust laws has been a subject of legislative discussion in the United States since the passage of the Sherman Antitrust Act in 1890.

The extension of the antitrust laws to industry and labor alike has an appeal to logic. It seems only fair and proper to treat all types of economic concentrations alike. We have learned from the experience of England that labor restrictions on competition can do just as much injury to the public as industry restrictions. At the same time, I believe in collective bargaining. Every union engaged in that activity restrains and, in fact, eliminates competition among some individual workers. A return to complete freedom of competition among workmen would destroy all unions. Such a backward step should not be considered. While we seem to have made some exceptions for labor in our thinking about restraints of competition, today competition on the labor side of our economic table is nonexistent. About the only labor competition we now have is the struggle of unions for extensions of their jurisdictions and the competition among leaders for prestige.

If we use the antitrust approach, the problem is to draw a satisfactory definition of the extent to which labor, as a whole, shall be permitted to restrain competition within its ranks. Frankly, I am not yet clear as to whether the antitrust approach is best and, if so, where the line is to be drawn. There are many facets of the problem which need further study. I am convinced that some legislative curbs on union power itself—in addition to outlawing the type of restrictive practices mentioned—are necessary, but I am not yet ready to advocate precisely what curbs will be most beneficial.

Any reasonable inclusion of labor unions within the scope of the antitrust laws will destroy industry-wide bargaining and will, at least, reduce the authority of the large international industrial unions. Those will be desirable results if industrial and labor power are to be fairly balanced and a reasonably free play of economic forces assured.

I realize that many industrial executives and all leaders of industry-wide unions claim that there are benefits to the public, to labor and to industry in industry-wide bargaining. Some industrial stability is assured, even though for relatively short periods and at the expense of competition. It is, of course, easier for an industrial company to negotiate with one union than many and to know that its competitors will be subjected to the same wages and conditions of labor. It is claimed that industry-wide unions have reduced wildcat strikes and introduced some discipline in the labor ranks. Union leaders find that industry-wide bargaining augments their economic power, facilitates their political appeal to government and the public, and permits them to use general criteria for a single industry instead of being forced to consider individual situations on their own merits.

Nevertheless, in my opinion, industry-wide unions and industry-wide bargaining will inevitably lead to compulsory arbitration. We may struggle against that undesired result. We may delay its coming, but if we cling to industry-wide bargaining, compulsory arbitration will come. Labor's compelling force in industry-wide bargaining is an industry-wide strike. Our present economic and social structures are so interwoven that industry-wide strikes of appreciable duration cannot be permitted, except in a few industries of the luxury type. Therefore, in all threats of industry-wide strikes the public must intervene and decide the issue. Compulsory arbitration is the only effective way for the public to act. . . .

The preservation of labor's bargaining power at a level at least equal to that of industrial management is, of course, most important. I have already expressed myself on that subject. In enterprises employing large numbers of employes, I have no doubt that an enterprise-wide union would preserve labor's bargaining power. For example, a union representing the approximately 36,000 J&L wage-earners would have a bargaining power well able to cope with the J&L management. If that were done, I think production and wages in the J&L plants would improve. Much as my softer nature is tempted by the ease of knowing that my competitors and I will have the same labor rates and conditions, I believe that the competitive incentive of standing on our own feet would spur me and other J&L employes to more dynamic efforts. That would bring about more production, more pay and more earnings—and a greater contribution to the national welfare. If unions would compete with each other for higher wages by increasing efficiency and productivity, it would greatly stimulate our national economic health. I believe also that in the large company adequate protection could be easily found to prevent company domination of any union. In fact, I think such protection already exists in our present labor statutes.

My greatest concern with this proposal is with respect to small companies with small groups of employes. I am not sure whether the proportionately reduced size of both management and labor will provide a balance. I have some concern, also, with some few industries like oil refineries and hydroelectric power where there are large aggregations of capital and relatively few employes. I have not been able to make an adequate study of that phase of the problem. I know that size limitations for unions representing the labor of two or more employers have been suggested. That might be satisfactory provided balanced bargaining strength can be obtained. I am quite certain that if we devote ourselves to an impartial investigation of this part of the problem in the light of the principles outlined, a satisfactory solution should not be too difficult.

One curb, however, could be immediately imposed on industrial unions. Industrial unions should, by legislation, be confined to a single industry. There is no economic or social justification for permitting the power of a single union leader to cover several industries. There is already an excessive concentration of power in the practical monopoly of coal mining labor by the United Mine Workers. It is clearly harmful for that union to extend into other industries as it now does through its District 50. The automobile field is enough for the United Automobile Workers, which now is in agricultural implements and other industries. The curb suggested, although directed at the scope of unions and thus at their economic power, cannot weaken the bargaining power needed to protect the workers. This is admittedly not a solution of the problem but it will help to prevent the situation from getting worse while the necessary studies are in progress.

Defining the role of the international industrial union in the future, if company-wide unions become the bargaining unit, also has its difficulties. The international industrial union, like every other economic instrumentality, must face the test of national welfare. If deemed desirable, such international unions might well perform functions in the labor field similar to those performed by industrial and trade associations. That would not be an inconsequential role to play. Its leaders would then operate on the policy level only.

The role of the craft union is even more of a problem. Some of our greatest national losses in waste and idleness have resulted from conflicts between the craft and industrial unions. This is another promising field for study. Should the craft unions be permitted in established companies whose employes can be adequately represented by industrial unions? Should craft unions be confined to the intermittent industries like the building trades? Should craft unions even in the intermittent fields be subjected to the antitrust laws? We know that their power to make work, control prices and limit efficiency and production must be ended. How much farther should we go? Here again I must confess that my studies and experiences have not progressed sufficiently for me to be specific.

To summarize briefly, the national economy is now subject, without any effective restraints, to the undue concentration of power in the hands of a comparatively few labor leaders. If our free economy is to be preserved, such labor power must be curbed. Power tends to corrupt and subjecting labor power to proper restraints is just as desirable as was the curbing of governmental, financial and industrial power.

Two necessary steps are clear. Labor leaders must be shorn immediately of their power to impose undesirable restrictions on industry—restrictions which directly control production, materials, prices and quality. Industrial unions should forthwith be confined to single industries and not allowed to cover several different industries. We must start on the elimination of industry-wide bargaining. Whether we should accomplish that by restricting the size of unions or by including unions within the scope of the antitrust laws or by some other means requires further study. Such study should be started promptly on a comprehensive and thorough basis if the basic structure of our incentive system of free enterprise is to be preserved.

MORE AUTONOMY FOR LOCAL UNIONS

Supplemental views of Senators Robert A. Taft, Joseph H. Ball, Forrest C. Donnell, and W. E. Jenner, in National Labor Relations Act of 1947, Senate Committee on Labor and Public Welfare, Report No. 105, 80th Cong., 1st Sess., 1947, p. 51

An amendment in three parts to restore to union locals autonomy in the exercise of their bargaining rights, and thus check the trend toward Nation-wide bargaining which threatens the public welfare by making possible the stoppage of an entire industry. These amendments require the Board to certify as bargaining agent unions containing only the employees of a single employer, or of different employers in the same metropolitan district or county, thus preventing the certification of a national or international union. Of course, the union certified may be affiliated with such a national or international union. The amendment further prevents the NLRB from treating industry-wide associations of employers as a single employer, and the employer unit becomes the largest unit permitted for collective bargaining purposes. The amendment further makes it an unfair labor practice for a national or international union to coerce any local union to sign or not to sign a proposed collective-bargaining agreement.

The amendment does not outlaw industry-wide or area-wide bargaining as does the House bill. It merely carries out the original intent of the Wagner Act and gives the employees of each employer the right to settle with their own employer. Thus Nation-wide bargaining may be authorized by the unions, say, in the coal fields, but if any local becomes dissatisfied it may withdraw and sign up with its own employer just as employers today may withdraw from an employers' association and sign up with their own employees. It seems essential to us that the trend toward Nation-wide bargaining be checked and that local employees be given some freedom from the arbitrary dictates of the leaders of national unions.

The committee in particular heard testimony with regard to the United Steel Workers, in which field it has been customary to certify the international union as bargaining agent. Hundreds of unnecessary strikes were called last year because the international union officers forbade any settlement at less than $2 a day increase until the union settled with the United States Steel Co. Strikes had to be called in many plants where the men were prepared to reach an agreement with their employers, even in industries far removed from the steel industry. We believe such an amendment is essential to restore to employees the collective bargaining rights guaranteed to them by the National Labor Relations Act, which, in too many instances, have been abrogated by the complete concentration of union power in the international union officers.

DEALING WITH INDUSTRY-WIDE BARGAINING

Statement of Raymond S. Smethurst, Counsel, National Association of Manufacturers, in Labor-Management Relations, hearings before the Joint Congressional Committee on Labor-Management Relations, 80th Cong., 2d Sess., 1948, part 1, pp. 157–159

A year ago, representatives of the National Association of Manufacturers urged committees of Congress then considering labor legislation to deal effectively with industry-wide collective bargaining, pointing out that:

Monopolistic practices in restraint of trade are inherently contrary to the public interest, and should be prohibited to labor unions as well as to employers. It is just as contrary to the public interest for a union or unions representing the employees of two or more employers to take joint wage action or engage in other monopolistic practices as it is for two or more employers to take joint price action or engage in other monopolistic practices.

That principle represents the association's position and belief today just as it did in 1946.

The association believed then that industry-wide bargaining should be outlawed, in the public interest, for the following reasons:

1. National industry-wide strikes, resulting from industry-wide bargaining, endanger the public by depriving it of the production of goods or the supplying of services.

2. National industry-wide strikes necessitate governmental intervention and a governmentally imposed settlement.

3. National industry-wide strikes give impetus to public demand for compulsory arbitration.

4. Compulsory arbitration would result in a denial of the right to strike and thus destroy free unionism. Likewise, by removing control over major elements of a business enterprise, compulsory arbitration would destroy free management. By destroying both free unionism and free management compulsory arbitration ultimately would mean the destruction of the free enterprise system.

5. Industry-wide bargaining results in uniformity of wage rates and other employment-cost factors which represent from 55 percent to 90 percent of the final cost of industrial products. Uniformity in the major element of product cost is conducive to uniformity in selling price with resultant stifling of healthy competition at the market place.

6. When employers combine for purposes of industry-wide bargaining for the fixing of uniform labor costs, there is a strong tendency to combine for other purposes such as indirect control of prices, allocation of markets, restric-

tion of output, slowing of technological advancements, and other practices encouraging monopoly or the accumulation of monopoly power.

7. When employers and unions combine for purposes of industry-wide bargaining there is also a strong tendency to combine for the purpose of preventing new businesses to enter the industry or the area where the combination functions. Industry-wide bargaining, therefore, discourages the healthful competition brought about by new producers coming into the field.

8. Our national labor policy is founded upon the principle that free collective bargaining between an employer and his employees will result in a peaceful settlement of their differences. When industry-wide bargaining replaces bargaining at the plant or company level, the fundamental purposes of collective bargaining are distorted and the free operation of local unions is obstructed by the need for carrying out decisions made elsewhere. The problems of the specific plant and of the employees of a specific company are neglected and the union becomes more of a political organization than a labor organization. Industry-wide bargaining, therefore, in and of itself is an impediment to the effectuation of national policy.

9. Union dictatorship flourishes under industry-wide bargaining since it requires strict obedience by local unions and their membership. The local union's traditional function of representing the interests of its members becomes secondary to the interests of the international organization and the individual member is subordinated to both. Industry-wide bargaining, therefore, by concentrating power in the hands of a few union officers adversely affects the rights and interests of the individual employee.

There is no need to labor the obvious by explaining that today industry-wide bargaining and industry-wide concerted action continues to be a national problem. Nation-wide strikes have made it abundantly clear that the problem transcends the direct interests of employers and organized employees. . . .

Congress should attack the causes and the results of industry-wide bargaining by prohibiting the practice, and by prohibiting the industry-wide strike.

If, however, for reasons which were felt to be controlling last year, Congress does not desire now to outlaw both the practice and result of industry-wide bargaining, I would like to suggest an alternative proposal:

(1) Continue to permit collective bargaining voluntarily on a group basis; (2) outlaw the industry-wide strike; and (3) subject any industry-wide agreements to the Sherman Antitrust Act. If no industry-wide agreement could be negotiated the law should then require negotiations to be resumed on a plant or company basis, free from collusion or concerted action between employers or local unions. As a further suggestion, it might be desirable to require that all industry-wide agreements contain no-strike clauses binding the labor organization against encouraging or supporting a strike or any other concerted activity during the term of the agreement.

I recognize that community and area bargaining is well established in some industries in certain sections of the country. In principle, these arrangements are just as bad as those of Nation-wide scope but it is the latter which presents a national problem. In the area or community situation, the States presumably are fully capable of protecting their citizens from any abuses resulting from community-wide strikes. That is the historic function of State governments.

Therefore, Congress might at this time concern itself solely with the problems presented by the type of national industry-wide strikes which affect substantially the entire Nation. However, in subjecting industry-wide or group agreements to the antitrust laws, area and community agreements should not be exempted insofar as they may result in a restraint of interstate commerce.

NATIONAL UNIONS ARE MONOPOLISTIC COMBINATIONS

Statement on behalf of the National Association of Manufacturers, filed with the Attorney General's National Committee to Study the Antitrust Laws, with specific reference to immunities accorded organized labor, in Current Antitrust Problems, hearings before Antitrust Subcommittee (Subcommittee No. 5) of the House Committee on the Judiciary, 84th Cong., 1st Sess., 1955, part 2, serial no. 3, pp. 1810–1812

. . . Organized labor is one of the strongest economic forces existing in the United States today. If citation be needed, mere reference to the many recent nationwide rail, coal, and steel strikes will demonstrate not only that monopoly power is possessed by some international labor organizations but also that such power is exercised for the purpose and with the effect of restraining, impeding, and preventing commerce.

This monopoly power is exercised, it should be stressed, by the international organization—a combination of unions—not by the local unions which are primarily concerned with negotiating mutually satisfactory terms and conditions of employment with an employer. It is achieved partly by constitutional provisions similar to article XVII of the United Steelworkers of America (CIO), which provides:

"Section 1. The international union shall be the contracting party in all collective-bargaining agreements and all such agreements shall be signed by the international officers. . . ."

As an indication of the effectiveness of such constitutional provisions, take the case of a small plant, Marvel Industries, which bargained with a local union and reached agreement calling for substantial wage increases. The contract was signed by the company, the bargaining committee, and the international representatives assigned to the case, then ratified by the employees. About a month after it was put into effect, the international union returned the contract, stating it must be redrafted to comply with requirements of international union policy and ordered a strike to enforce the increased demands. After 4 weeks the company, to save its business, capitulated to the international union (House labor hearings, 1953, pt. 6, p. 1886).

As indicated, it is the combination of labor organizations acting as a national or international union which poses antitrust analogies and which requires antitrust remedies and limitation. It is elementary that business concerns, acting alone, may lawfully do many things which if done in combination or concert would bring down the wrath of antitrust. No one would deny, for example, the clear right of an individual steel producer, acting independently, to curtail production or raise or lower prices for economic reasons. By the same token, no one would deny the right of the employees of an individual employer to strike, as a union, for more favorable working conditions. To repeat, it is when unions combine or agree or conspire together to take joint action, as in the recent nationwide strikes, that the antitrust philosophy against the exercise of monopoly power should apply. Certainly there can be no doubt today that the exercise of such monopoly power as has been witnessed in recent years is at least as damaging, if not more so, than the same tactics if undertaken by business organizations through combinations or conspiracy. Yet the one is prohibited while the other is freed of restraint and in fact encouraged.

An antitrust approach to the problem of labor monopoly need not necessarily attempt to itemize particular activities and conduct which should be considered violations of antitrust laws. Rather the problem should be attacked at its roots —the power and dominance of the national or international union over its local constituents.

Normally it is not the activities of an isolated local union dealing with one or more employers in a community which raises antitrust analogies; it is the combination, conspiracy, or agreement between several or all locals of an international union which result in actions adversely and unreasonably affecting the economy.

It should constantly be borne in mind that the antitrust laws are the laws of free commerce and trade; and that the labor laws are simply that, i.e. laws which are designed to establish the ground rules for the conduct of negotiations between employers and their employees for the single broad purpose of reaching an agreement on terms and conditions of employment. Thus it is entirely proper and appropriate for specific practices by labor organizations to be dealt with in the law of labor-management relations as a means to bring about a better atmosphere in which to conduct the negotiations looking toward mutually satisfactory agreement. Such specification of unwarranted labor conduct would be to the law of labor relations what the Clayton, Robinson-Patman, and Federal Trade Commission Acts are to the basic antitrust law. In other words the specific would complement the general in the public interest.

The broad philosophy of the Sherman Act, however, should and must deal with monopoly power, whether it be manifested in combinations of employers or in combinations of unions, since in either instance it is the free economy of the Nation, not merely relations between employers and employees which is threatened or adversely affected. Accordingly an approach to the problem of union monopoly power should be based on the philosophy of the Sherman Act.

This need not necessarily be accomplished, however, by attempting to apply its present provisions through appropriate amendments to the Clayton and Norris-LaGuardia Acts. Rather a new section or sections should be added to the Sherman Act. These should be so designed as to deal directly with the monopoly power of national or international unions. To use traditional antitrust language, for example, the proposed new provisions could embrace contracts, combinations, or conspiracies between local unions, whether or not affiliated where the purpose or necessary effect thereof is unreasonably to impair, diminish, impede, obstruct, or prevent the production or movement of goods for or in interstate commerce.

It may be contended that a Sherman Act approach to the problem, along the lines suggested above, would break up international and national unions. The short answer to that argument is that strong national unions existed prior to adoption of the nationwide stoppage techniques.

International unions are not unlike the modern business or trade association in structure. Moreover many of their present practices, and the "congressionally permitted" restraints imposed by them . . . are not unlike methods which some trade associations adopted in the early days of their growth. When trade associations engaged in monopolistic activities, the Sherman Act was not used to compel disbandment but to eliminate monopoly practices. This policy is consistent with our national traditions; it should guide us in dealing with the monopoly power of organized labor.

THE MONOPOLY POWERS OF UNIONS SHOULD BE CONFINED TO CERTAIN OBJECTIVES

Testimony of Thurman Arnold, Washington, D.C., in Economic Power of Labor Organizations, hearings before the Senate Committee on Banking and Currency, 81st Cong., 1st Sess., 1949, part 1, pp. 71–74

. . . The unions are, in my judgment, and should be in a peculiarly advantageous position. They are attempting, and in many industries are succeeding, in monopolizing the supply of labor, and I think that they are probably entitled to do.

I think that they probably need the strength, if they can get it without illegal means, of Nation-wide unions which control the production. At least that is the principle of even the Taft-Hartley Act, which is supposed to be a slave-labor bill, and I think that it would be idle to dispute that at this time. The water has run under that dam, so we have a situation where labor is exempt from the antitrust laws, is not treated the same way with business in one respect, and that is that labor by voluntary methods can monopolize the labor supply, or at least attempt to monopolize the labor supply, and every union in the United States, of course, is now attempting to do it, some with greater success, and some with less success. That is the set-up of the unions.

The unions having had that power, however, it is a very dangerous thing to subject them to no curbs whatever. . . .

If we are going to give them monopoly power, we must confine their use of that power to certain objectives.

Now, what are these objectives? I think that wages and hours is a legitimate union activity, anything that concerns wages and hours. . . .

When, however, this wages-and-hours becomes used as a pretext to restrict production, and achieve control over management and production, it then falls or should fall, it seems to me, upon the prohibitions of the Sherman Act as an illegitimate activity of labor.

Now, I recognize the fact that if there can be no very sharp line . . . they will always come before the court under the guise of a wage-and-hour controversy, but we must allow the court, I think, the power to determine whether in fact it is.

There is no possible way of tying down the antitrust laws to any definite formula. The court must have that fact-finding power. I think, in the case that we have got before us, it is perfectly clear that the purpose of the strike has nothing to do with health or recreation or real wages and hours.

I think, if you pass a law which made that purpose an illegitimate purpose, you would find close questions between what was a legitimate wage-and-hour demand and whether an employer's attempt to increase production came within what we call the speed-up system. You would have questions of fact which the court must decide, and yet I know of nowhere we can put that power except in our courts, and I think that the refusal of any group to allow such questions of fact to be decided among the courts is a dangerous thing. I don't say that the unions are any different from industry. I have been debating with Senator Capehart in a friendly way about the basing-point system. Certainly the matter of whether a basing-point system is used in restraint of trade or whether it isn't is a question of fact which can't be defined very precisely, yet I think that those matters should be left to the courts, and neither labor unions nor industry should have an escape of saying, "We might lose an unjust case, and this throws our activities into confusion; and, therefore, we want an exception from the antitrust law."

So, it seems to me your bill should do what the Taft-Hartley Act does not do at all, doesn't consider, and that is to define the legitimate purposes of labor unions.

Now, I would say that the legitimate purposes of labor unions could be roughly described as those having to do with wages and hours, health, safety, their legitimate activities in promoting the strength of the union, and perhaps you could spell out a number of others.

It would take some thought to draft such a bill; and, having done that, I think the bill should define a few of the outstanding practices and brand them as illegitimate, and those practices which I would brand as illegitimate objectives would be, and I will name them again: . . . A strike to erect a tariff wall around a locality; the exclusion of efficient methods from industry; the refusal of unions to allow independent firms to remain in existence; the activities of unions in imposing and maintaining artificial prices or restricted production of any form; and the make-work system.

THE SIZE OF UNIONS SHOULD BE LIMITED

Testimony of Rolla D. Campbell, Huntington, W.Va., in Economic Power of Labor Organizations, hearings before the Senate Committee on Banking and Currency, 81st Cong., 1st Sess., 1949, part 1, pp. 136–138

If I am correct in my statement that the core of the difficulty we now face is monopoly then the obvious cure of the disease would be to eradicate the monopoly.

I understand Mr. Thurman Arnold was on the stand here recently and that he suggested a little different approach. He said that unions are by nature monopolies and that that fact should be accepted and that the law should define certain legitimate activities in which the unions could engage and certain illegal activities which would be unlawful.

My difference with that approach is that, using again the medical analogy, it deals only with symptoms; it does not go to the core of the matter. In medical practice, if you have a fever, you may take a medicine which will reduce the fever, but then the disease may pop out again in some other form. The approach always is to try to find the cause, and once you have found it, to try to eradicate it. That is the approach I think this Congress should have in this particular case.

Now, this same subject was before the House and the Senate when the bills which later became the Labor Management Relations Act of 1947 were under consideration. In the Hartley bill which was originally introduced in the House, there was a definite formula which limited the size of a union to the employees of a single employer, and it forbade collaboration between them as to prices and wages, hours, et cetera. There was an exception for local metropolitan areas. The hearings in that case demonstrated to my mind the futility of attempting to work out a definitive formula. Too many exceptions can always be brought forth to indicate that the rule, while it looks fair on its face, might be unfair when applied to many situations where the public interest is really not involved.

So the approach here would seem to be primarily to permit unions to be as large as they want to be, up to the point where, if they use their full economic power, they can make war on the public, and there they should be stopped, at that point.

Now, I think that most employers today are not against the use of the right to strike. They believe that both employers and employees ought to be able to use their economic power to settle their disputes. The reason for that belief is that once you take away from either unions or employees the right to suspend work or suspend employment, as the case may be, when they cannot agree, then the public interest will demand that some other form or means of settling disputes be substituted, and that form can take only one method. That is, by public regulation, where you would fix wages and hours and working conditions, the same way as we fix railroad rates and tariffs now under the Interstate Commerce Act, or in the same way in which utilities are generally regulated. I think that everybody would regard such result as highly undesirable because it would take away from our industry the vitality which comes from the fact that we are engaged in a competitive economy. . . .

In looking over the statutes of the United States dealing with the subject, it seems to me that Congress could approach the problem best by an amendment to section 2 of the Sherman Act, making another section of section 2, to prohibit the monopolization by any labor organization of the supply or representation of labor in any industry in interstate commerce which might have the power to jeopardize the maintenance of the Nation's economy or any substantial segment thereof. . . .

If such legislation should be adopted, then labor organizations would be under rules which are precisely similar to those affecting business, except that the area in which unions could operate would be a little more clearly spelled out than is the case with the present antitrust laws in their effect upon business.

As I view such legislation, it would do no harm to collective bargaining. Acting under it, if a union got to a size where a strike by it could imperil the Nation or any substantial segment of the Nation, then it would become an unlawful union and the courts, proceeding under such an amendment, would do exactly as they do with respect to corporations. They would break the union up into segments, then prescribe the limits of the permissible co-operation between those segments. But the unions and business organizations would then be on a parity of treatment.

Now, probably the most effective argument that could be made against this approach is that the standard is too general, that the unions could not know when they were in violation and when they were not. Of course, the answer to that is that business has exactly the same problems and has had to live with even a more general standard since 1890. The way they live with it is by seeking advice of counsel on questions affecting antitrust laws. Their counsel are usually very cautious and resolve all questions of doubt against the client and say, "If you will not engage in any activity which could reasonably be construed as a violation, then you need not fear the antitrust laws. If you engage in doubtful activities, you incur risks, and if you want to do it, you have to take the risks."

THE SIZE OF BARGAINING UNITS SHOULD BE LIMITED

Statement of Theodore R. Iserman, attorney-at-law, New York, N.Y., in Labor-Management Relations, hearings before the Joint Congressional Committee on Labor-Management Relations, 80th Cong., 2d Sess., 1948, part 2, pp. 868–870, 876

I recommend that Congress:

Forbid the Labor Board to find appropriate for the purposes of collective bargaining a unit consisting of employees of two or more employers, unless the total number of employees in the unit shall regularly be less than, say, 500, and when their places of employment are, say, within 50 miles of each other.

Senator Ball's bill last year put a geographical limit on the multiple employer bargaining units. H.R. 3020 included a geographical limit and put a numerical limit of 100 upon the number of employees of any one employer that a union could represent, together with employees of other employers.

The bills last year limited multiple-employer units consisting of employees of "competing" employers. If Congress uses this term, it should define the term. I think it could do so easily enough, and with a great body of law to show what the definition means, by saying that employers are "competing" when a combination or conspiracy between them to fix prices, allocate customers, or otherwise restrain trade would violate the antitrust laws.

To eliminate even this relatively simple question, however, I would increase the numerical limit of 100, which the House approved last year, to 500, and apply it to all multiple-employer units, regardless of whether or not the employers were "competing."

Limiting the total number of employees of different employers, rather than the number of employees of each employer, who might compose a multiple-employer unit, has, I believe, a further advantage, in that it would enable unions and employers in the building, stevedoring, and tugboat industries, and in others like them, to adjust themselves to the new law.

The theory is that joint bargaining by 500 employees and their employers in a limited area rarely will affect our economy in a serious way. At the same time, by permitting one labor organization to represent 500 people, we avoid compelling the operating engineers, for example, to set up a separate local for its few members in each of a number of establishments. We avoid compelling the typographical union to set up a separate local for each small job shop in a city. Employers of more than 500 people ought to be able to handle their own bargaining without leaning on their competitors, and 500 workers constitute a fair-sized local.

MR. SHROYER: Your two limitations would be used in the sense of "or" rather than "and," would they not?

MR. ISERMAN: I would use both of them. Five hundred employees in an area, in a 50-mile area. Where you have 500 employees, probably the geographical limitation is not particularly important, because it would almost have to be fairly local.

MR. SHROYER: Let us take, for instance, Akron, Ohio, where you have the major rubber industries. There you would have them all within the geographical area?

MR. ISERMAN: That is right.

MR. SHROYER: The other provision would still limit it to one employer, I take it?

MR. ISERMAN: Unless there were two small rubber companies with 250 employees each, then those two could bargain together. If you do not have a numerical limitation all the rubber companies in Akron can get together and bargain; all automobile companies in Detroit can get together and bargain, and you have in effect industry-wide bargaining. I think the numerical limit is more important than the geographical limit.

SENATOR SMITH: Then the numerical limit only applies where there are two or more employers?

MR. ISERMAN: Yes, sir.

SENATOR SMITH: How about the United States Steel Co., for example?

MR. ISERMAN: One constituent part of the union could represent all of the employees of United States Steel. There could be one union to represent all the employees of General Motors, Chrysler, Ford, or Bethlehem.

SENATOR SMITH: You do not object to that?

MR. ISERMAN: No. I will put it this way: One union representing the employees of a big employer does not have any more monopolistic effect, probably, than the employer himself has, but being able to represent two competing employers gives the union twice the monopolistic effect that either one of the two employers has.

I would make the bargaining units as big, within any one company, as seem to be correct.

SENATOR SMITH: Thank you, sir.

MR. ISERMAN: Hand in hand with my first suggestion, I would (2) forbid the Board to certify any labor organization as the collective bargaining representative of the employees of two or more employers, unless those employees constitute a proper unit under my first suggestion.

These two call for amending the Wagner Act and also amending the definitions in the Wagner Act and a few technical drafting changes.

(3) Forbid employers to combine together to deal with their employees, unless the employees constitute a proper unit under my first suggestion.

The House last year amended H.R. 3020 on the floor so that, after forbidding unions to represent employees of competing employers, except in the circumstances I have mentioned, it made unlawful:

any conspiracy, collusion, or common arrangements between competing employers to fix or agree to terms or propose terms of employment of their employees, or to subject such terms of employment to common control or approval, not permitted as to their employees or as to the representatives of their employees, with respect to the collective bargaining, concerted activities, or terms of collective bargains or arrangements of such employees.

This language seems to be appropriate.

(4) Forbid employees of different employers and their representatives similarly to combine or conspire together, or to subject themselves to common control, or to strike in concert. I would not forbid simultaneous strikes, but I would forbid concerted strikes by employees of two or more employers.

Combinations between employers, and certainly between competing employers, or between representatives of their employees ought to be unlawful, and those who enter into such combinations ought to be liable for damages that result from the combination.

But the principal sufferer is the public. Consequently, the law should direct the Attorney General to sue to enjoin such combinations, or to prosecute parties to them, just as he now does under the antitrust laws.

Provisions such as I have described would not forbid employers to join associations that furnish to them information and advice on wages, hours, rulings of arbitrators and Government agencies and other labor matters, as many trade associations do now, so long as the association did not have a controlling voice in any employer's bargaining. It would not forbid international unions to furnish similar information and advice to their locals, or to pay benefits to strikers, as long as they did not dictate terms to the locals or lay down rules or policies that the locals had to follow.

It is not merely when competing employers or representatives of their employees combine together that we have restraints of trade that, if they occurred in any context other than collective bargaining, our laws would forbid.

When any employer agrees with a union (*a*) to maintain certain prices; (*b*) to include in his labor costs for pricing purposes false and fictitious items or amounts, as clothing manufacturers do; (*c*) to limit his output; (*d*) to restrict his sales to a certain area; (*e*) to restrict his sales to certain customers; or (*f*) to buy from certain sources; or (*g*) to restrict the purchase, sale, or use of products, materials, machines, or services for any of these purposes, trade is restrained, and the injury to the public is just as great as when the employer makes a similar agreement with anyone else.

Consequently, Congress ought to forbid employers and labor organizations to enter into such agreements with each other, or for one to cause the other to enter into such agreements, as I have just described.

The law now forbids unions to engage in boycotts. Sometimes employers agree, in their contracts with unions, that the unions need not handle struck work or "hot" goods. I think when an employer agrees to a boycott of another employer, he ought to be equally subject to the law with the union. I am not sure that the present law does not reach employers that enter into such agreements with unions. It may, but it does not do so as specifically and expressly as I think it should.

I would forbid unions to cause or attempt to cause employers to engage in practices of the kind that would be unlawful if they were done pursuant to an agreement.

There have been proposals that we write into the antitrust laws, in general terms, language forbidding labor unions to engage in "restraints of trade." I approve of this, but I think it important to specify, in clear terms, those particular restraints of trade that we know exist and that we know should be forbidden. Otherwise, we may be long years finding out what the general terms forbid.

I should make persons who violate these clauses subject to restraints and penalties of the antitrust laws. I should make the Norris-LaGuardia Act inapplicable to them. . . .

MR. LANDIS: On industry-wide bargaining, what is to interfere with an employer or one unit setting the pattern for the other industries?

MR. ISERMAN: Nothing is going to interfere with it as long as the bargaining is going on fairly currently. However, you do not necessarily get a complete pattern in bargaining. Take this situation in the automobile industry. The General Motors settlement laid down a kind of pattern, but it was one that the Chrysler people evidently did not like. They set themselves another pattern, and we have yet to see what Ford is going to do. We have yet to see what some of the big parts manufacturers are going to do. However, there is no way of controlling that that I know of, and I would not recommend trying to control this pattern business at this time, because I think that if we broke up the control that the international union has over the bargaining with all of the employers, the pattern in bargaining would be less important than it is now.

IS LABOR TO BE TREATED AS A COMMODITY?

Statement of Arthur J. Goldberg, General Counsel, Congress of Industrial Organizations, in Current Antitrust Problems, hearings before the Antitrust Subcommittee (Subcommittee No. 5) of the House Committee on the Judiciary, 84th Cong., 1st Sess., 1955, part 3, pp. 2146–2148

The chamber, the NAM, and the Farm Bureau all ask that Congress outlaw industrywide, or areawide, or pattern collective bargaining. Such bargaining is, in their view, the epitome of labor monopoly.

This charge that national or regional or pattern bargaining is "monopolistic" and "a restraint of trade" reverts, of course, to the basic fallacy that human labor is to be treated as a commodity, and that organizations of those who have nothing to sell but the use of their minds and bodies constitute "restraints of trade."

This approach . . . is a false one. The issue is not one of monopoly versus competition, and the use of antitrust phraseology in this context serves only to mislead. The purpose of the antitrust laws is to preserve competition; but surely no one is suggesting that unions should compete with each other to see who can supply human labor at the lowest price. And surely no one is suggesting that individual workers should compete with each other to work at the lowest wage.

There is some suggestion in the chamber's statement that industrywide bargaining, and regional and pattern bargaining, are destructive of competition among the employers of labor. I do not believe, however, that such a charge can be generally supported. Such industries as men's and women's clothing, glassware, hosiery, pottery, and the silk and rayon dyeing and finishing industry, in all of which there is a long history of national or regional bargaining, are highly competitive. Professors Lester and Robie of Princeton, after studying 7 industries in which national or regional bargaining had existed for more than 10 years, came to the conclusion that such bargaining has no tendency whatever toward increasing monopolistic, noncompetitive, price policies. See Lester and Robie, Wages Under National and Regional Collective Bargaining, Princeton University Press (1946).

It is, of course, true that industry or area or pattern bargaining tends to prevent employers from competing with each other by paying lower wages than their competitors. But it is neither socially nor economically desirable for employers to compete with each other by paying lower wages. Further, uniform wage scales among employers do not eliminate price competition in the sale

of the employers' products. As Lester and Robie state, "Indeed elimination of
wage cutting has tended to stress efficiency of management as the most important factor in competition."

The chamber statement asserts that "the excessive costs of pattern bargaining can force smaller firms out of business." And the statement adds . . . :

"Furthermore, giant unions have not hesitated to impose even tougher demands on small and middle-sized companies unable to resist the tremendous
economic power of the giant industry unions. The effect of such union tactics
obviously has been to reduce competition, violating at least the spirit of our
national antitrust policy."

At this point the chamber's viewing with alarm becomes self-contradictory.
The charge that unions "impose even tougher demands" on small and middle-
sized companies means, if it means anything, that the unions are deviating
from pattern bargaining, and that the chamber is complaining about the
deviation. The assertion is in any event quite unrelated to fact.

The real question is not preserving competition against monopoly but a
question of power as between workers and employers. The chamber objects
to industry or areawide bargaining, and the NAM to bargaining by national
unions, not because it reduces competition among the employers in the sale
of their products, or because there should be competition among employees
to supply labor cheaply, but because it gives greater bargaining power to
labor. That is the issue, and unrelated antitrust questions are brought in
simply to confuse it.

Does nationwide, or regional, or pattern bargaining give too much power
to labor? I think the answer to that question, as a general question, is un-
qualifiedly "No." There is no evidence that in any major industry the financial
strength or the bargaining power of a union is larger than the financial
strength or bargaining power of the employers. Can you compare the United
Steelworkers of America, with assets of approximately $20 million, with a
single corporation like the United States Steel Corp., with assets of $3 billion,
and say that the union has the overwhelming power? Of course not. Does this
committee really think that it is necessary to break up the Steelworkers Union
into fragments so that the Steel Corp. will not be overpowered by the union
during the current negotiations? Of course not.

In its prepared statement, the chamber of commerce asserts that . . . :
". . . industrywide bargaining . . . is a clear-cut illustration of the inequity
or double standard in our antitrust laws which prohibits monopolistic combinations on the employer side, but permits comparable power combinations on
the union side."

This assertion is sheer nonsense. If there is industrywide bargaining, the
industry is by definition acting as a unit, and there is no double standard.

The fact that we have defended industrywide or areawide or pattern bargaining may leave the impression that unions are solely responsible for the
establishment of these types of bargaining. However, that is not the case,
and we do not want to take credit that is not wholly due us.

Indeed, industrywide or areawide bargaining can never be the sole creation of the union. Under the doctrines of the National Labor Relations Board employers may in appropriate situations bargain jointly if they and the union both so elect. However, an individual employer always has the option to refuse to agree to joint bargaining in the first place; and the further option to withdraw from joint bargaining at appropriate times.

The situation is essentially the same as respects "pattern bargaining," where a leader in the industry negotiates an agreement with the union and the pattern thus established is followed by the other companies in the industry. Unions may have some influence in preserving or extending pattern bargaining, but its creation is essentially due to decisions of management, which, in turn, reflect the economic organization of the particular industry. Let me illustrate.

One industry which is always singled out as an example of pattern bargaining is the steel industry. That is an industry I happen to know something about, since I have the honor to be general counsel of the United Steelworkers of America as well as of the CIO.

The fact is that it was the steel industry, not the union, which initiated the practice of following a pattern in wage movements. The industry follows a pattern not only on wage movements, but on prices, and it has been doing so for many years. Indeed, a disinterested study on wage movements in the steel industry from 1913 to 1932 shows that these wage movements followed a pattern even during those years, long before the union appeared on the scene. This study was made by Mr. George Seltzer, at the University of Chicago, and was financed by a grant from the Rockefeller Foundation. In his study, entitled "Pattern Bargaining and the United Steelworkers," Mr. Seltzer reaches the following conclusions on wage movements during the period 1913–1932:

"They show general agreement in the timing and amount of wage changes throughout the industry. . . . The United States Steel Corp. took the lead in 11 of the 14 general wage changes during this period; no other basic-steel firm assumed the leadership role more than once."

Mr. Seltzer concluded:

"It seems clear that the USA-CIO did not initiate uniformity of wage behavior in the basic-steel industry. This uniformity is rooted in the product and labor market structure of the industry.

"The synchronization of the wage behavior of basic-steel firms is in part a reflection of the larger business strategy prevailing in the industry."

Mr. Seltzer, I should make it clear, was talking about the uniformity of wage movements, rather than about the uniformity of individual wages. While the movement of wages followed a pattern in the steel industry before the establishment of the union, it is also true that the union has substantially contributed to the establishment of wage uniformity—that is, to equal pay for equal work. In the days before the union, wage rates for the same job varied widely not only from plant to plant but within a single plant, and there was little attempt at scientific job evaluation. Now, job evaluation plans

jointly operated by the companies and the union seek to insure wage uniformity throughout the basic-steel industry.

Again, before the creation of the union there was a very substantial differential between northern and southern wage rates, and there were other
intermediate regional differentials. In successive collective-bargaining contracts
negotiated over the years, the union gradually succeeded in eliminating all of
these regional wage differentials.

Thus while the union was not responsible for establishing the pattern of
wage movements in the industry, it has contributed to establishing a more
uniform pattern of wage rates. Frankly, we are quite proud that we have
done so. We believe in equal pay for equal work. We believe that steelworkers in the South should receive the same pay as steelworkers in the North.
They do the same work, their living costs are the same, and the steel they
make sells for the same prices. We do not see why they should not receive
the same pay. Or, to go back to an antitrust formulation, we do not believe
that the Nation's economic well-being would be promoted by requiring
that these steelworkers compete with each other as to who will work more
cheaply.

I have no doubt that the same general picture is true of other industries
where pattern bargaining prevails. This type of bargaining exists primarily
in industries like steel, automobile, meat-packing, rubber, and oil, where one
or more large corporations dominate the industry. Long before there were
unions in these industries, the dominant corporations in the industry set the
pattern both for the prices of the industry's products and for the wages of
its employees. This following of a pattern came about as a matter of deliberate
choice by the corporations, or because of the structure of the industry, or
some mixture of the two. In any event it was not foisted by unions on an
unwilling industry.

Today strong national unions exist in nearly all of these industries. It is
fortunate that they do. For without them the giant corporations would have a
free hand in fixing wages as they saw fit. It is only the existence of powerful
unions that has enabled the workers in these industries to get higher wages,
secure decent living standards for themselves, and make their contribution to
maintaining national purchasing power.

I do not wish, however, to leave any impression that we believe that industrywide or area or pattern bargaining is the only proper type of bargaining,
or necessarily the best type in all situations. That is not the case. We are not
in favor of any of these types of bargaining, as a general proposition, any
more than we are in favor of companywide or of local plant bargaining, or of
craft bargaining, or of any of numerous other types or combinations. All of
these diverse types of bargaining have emerged as responses to the needs
and realities of particular situations. Presumably both industry and management have found them desirable and workable, and certainly there is no indication that any of these various types of collective bargaining has harmed the
public interest.

UNIONS ARE ALREADY RESTRICTED

Statement of Andrew J. Biemiller, Member, National Legislative Committee
American Federation of Labor, in Current Antitrust Problems, hearings before
Antitrust Subcommittee (Subcommittee No. 5) of the House Committee on the
Judiciary, 84th Cong., 1st Sess., 1955, part 3, pp. 2028–2033

The effort to extend antitrust laws to unions is spear-headed by continued references by industry to so-called monopolistic power of unions and to giant unions. This is simply part of a semantic campaign designed to delude some of the public into believing that it might make sense to apply the antitrust laws to union trusts.

It is true that union membership has increased during the past two decade and that the financial position of unions generally has improved. But an examination of union strength and growth must be kept in proper perspective.

The total financial resources of all unions combined has been liberally esti mated as perhaps as high as $1 billion. This is a rough estimate made by Prof Nathan Belfer in his examination of union finances in Trade Union Investment Policy, Industrial and Labor Relations Review, Cornell University, April 1953 But this figure, standing alone, is highly misleading. These financial resource are not under the direction or control of any one organization.

THE CHAIRMAN: Would the fact of the merger of the CIO and the AFL make any difference in your characterization?

MR. BIEMILLER: Not as we see the situation. I am coming right to that.

Organized labor in this country is not centrally controlled. Even when the merger of the American Federation of Labor and the Congress of Industrial Organizations will be completed, the new federation will be made up of more than 145 separate national and international unions which determine their own policies. They in turn are made up of more than 60,000 local unions which are largely autonomous.

The various unions never act as a single unit. Each controls its own finances.

The American Federation of Labor, for example, no more controls the treasuries of its affiliated organizations than the United States Chamber of Commerce controls the combined assets of its member corporations.

The federation itself, incidentally, had a financial balance of but $1.5 million at the end of its last fiscal year's operations. Its total receipts for a year to cover all its expenses came to but $5.5 million. This is less than, for example, the Government's expenditures for the management of its Fish and Wildlife Service and it amounts to less than a fifth of the budget for the Weather Bureau. . . .

. . . The strength of unions lies, not in relatively meager treasuries, but rather in their membership.

While a union needs certain income to function, its ability to improve worker living standards is rooted essentially in its members' willingness to

ict together and, if necessary to withhold their labor. If legislation is enacted
io eliminate or restrict the right of workers concertedly to withhold their labor
ind peacefully to persuade the public to withdraw its patronage from a par-
icular employer, the union's strength is effectively dissipated even if it has a
ubstantial treasury. . . .

Actually, it is in the absence of a union that there is a monopoly in the
employment relationship. Without a union, the workers can hardly increase
vages or improve conditions through individual efforts. The employer alone
lecides. He truly has monopoly power over unorganized workers. It is only
vith the establishment of a union that workers can take some effective part
n determining their conditions of work. . . .

The abuses of which antiunion employers complain, either are already the
ubject of congressional regulation or are not actually significant abuses.

Those who argue that unions should be brought under the antitrust laws
ind it easy to utilize such time-worn phrases as "labor monopoly," "racketeer-
ng," and "featherbedding." These individuals find it far more difficult to state
exactly what union activities constitute such a threat to the free enterprise
ystem that they need to be the subject of specific action by Congress.

We have examined most diligently the recent arguments of those who favor
olacing unions under the antitrust laws. Frankly, we have found very few
pecific complaints regarding union conduct and nothing that is at all new.

Among the alleged types of union activity which antilabor spokesmen have
mentioned as monopolistic in character are the following:

1. Various types of secondary boycotts.
2. Pressure for the hiring of unnecessary labor.
3. Jurisdictional disputes.
4. Price fixing and control of the market.
5. Opposition to technological improvement.
6. Industrywide bargaining.

What is the status of these issues today? First of all, it should be noted
:hat Congress has seen fit over the opposition of organized labor to write
nto the Taft-Hartley law a number of provisions dealing with some of these
ooints. The statute, for example, includes specific provisions against activities
ioted by points 1, 2, and 3.

Not only does the law include these provisions which declare certain union
ictivities to be unfair labor practices subject to Government prosecution
through the National Labor Relations Board, but in another section of the
law the Congress provided that an injured party could sue for damages from
any injuries received as a result of these activities.

Under each of these provisions, in the Taft-Hartley law, action has been
taken against unions and union officials. Yet, we find the United States
Chamber of Commerce appearing before this committee complaining that the
NLRB has not interpreted this law correctly and that Congress should therefore pass a different type of statute. If this were done, it would open the
way for certain types of union activity to be punished in three different ways,

prosecutions by the NLRB, civil suit for damages, and prosecution by the Department of Justice.

Let me merely point out that organized labor, too, is very dissatisfied with these provisions of the Taft-Hartley law and with the manner in which the NLRB has interpreted them. We, too, believe that Congress should act regarding this problem.

We believe that as the law is now written and interpreted it unfairly penalizes certain union activities. However, we believe that the proper forum in which to argue this is the debate over the merits of the Taft-Hartley law. Merely because the Taft-Hartley law has not operated to the satisfaction of the chamber of commerce is no reason why Congress should pass a completely new law assigning authority to act in these matters to another Government agency whose jurisdiction would overlap and conflict with the functions of the NLRB.

Point four in the campaign against unions concerns so-called price fixing and control of the market through joint action with employers. Organized labor does not advocate collusion of this sort between unions and employers. Instances of such activity are extremely rare. On this issue the Supreme Court has made it quite clear that a union which joins with an employer in collusive action completely loses its immunity to antitrust action. Thus, no further legislation of any sort is needed to bring this type of activity by any union under the antitrust laws.

MR. KEATING: Do you have a reference to a decision which covers that?

MR. BIEMILLER: It is the Allen-Bradley case . . .

The fifth point involves alleged union opposition to technological improvement. It would be difficult today to find a dispute which has arisen as a result of union opposition to technological change as such. The disputes which have arisen over technological improvement rather reflect the union concern over the lack of adequate consideration for workers who may be directly and adversely affected by technological innovations.

The A.F. of L.'s attitude is best expressed by a paragraph in a recent article by President Meany for *Fortune* magazine:

Certainly the trade-union movement does not oppose technological change. There can be no turning back to a negative or shortsighted policy of limiting progress. . . . The answer to technological change lies in smoothing its transitions and cushioning the shocks that attend it. This means, in the immediate sense, the establishment of severance pay, retraining of skills, reorganization of work schedules. These are social costs that industry will have to bear in order to avoid the wasting of human resources—and to avoid our calling on Government to bear these costs if industry fails to do so.

It would be an exceedingly dangerous precedent to give employers by law an absolute right to introduce technological changes regardless of the effect on their workers, with the workers forbidden to take action to protect their own job rights and livelihood.

We believe that careful consideration of the implications of such legislation will convince the Congress against any action to make illegal union efforts to gain severance pay, transfer rights, gradual change, or other measures to ease any adverse social impact on workers of technological innovations.

The sixth item in the list of alleged union abuses, industrywide bargaining, has received thorough discussion in recent years. This discussion has helped to clarify the fact that there are in the United States today very few instances of complete industrywide bargaining. Many cases of so-called industrywide bargaining turn out, upon examination, to involve bargaining for a single large company or for a group of firms in a particular locality or region.

It is often forgotten that both labor and management have to agree on the scope of the bargaining unit. Where bargaining is conducted on an industry basis, this development has been the result of mutual agreement after both parties have weighed its possible effect on all aspects of the bargaining relationship.

It is important to remember that Congress itself has given thorough consideration to the issues involved in industrywide bargaining. In 1947 during the discussion on the Taft-Hartley law by the 80th Congress, a specific proposal to ban industrywide bargaining was rejected.

The American Federation of Labor does not endorse any particular bargaining system. We believe that the national interest is best served if unions and employers are free to choose for themselves the type of bargaining unit that best fits their particular situation. Prohibiting industrywide bargaining by statute would inject the Federal Government further into the framework of collective bargaining and could only lead to disrupting peaceful labor-management relations.

Let me conclude with several summary observations.

Proposals to restrict certain union activities through application of the antitrust laws are not rooted in any demonstration of genuine need for such drastic legislative action. They are rather the reflection of a continuing effort of certain employer groups to use any means possible to carve out areas of union activity from the scope of legitimate activity. . . .

We do not believe the particular minor or occasional activities of unions which certain employers have complained of warrant legislative consideration. But even if they did, a remedy as broad as the application of the antitrust laws is much too far-reaching.

Extension of the antitrust laws to unions would place under a legal cloud many traditional and necessary union activities. In many instances it would undoubtedly cut off the only effective means unions have to protect and aid workers.

The national interest is best served, not by increasing the avenues of legal entanglement for unions, but by minimizing restrictions on unions, for union activity to protect and improve worker status is in the interest of society as a whole. Any possible gain to society from curbing union activities by applying the antitrust laws would be far outweighed by the loss incurred from the stifling of union efforts in behalf of workers.

FALSE PREMISES OF RESTRICTIVE PROPOSALS

Richard A. Lester, Professor of Economics, Princeton University, in Taft-Hartley Act Revisions, hearings before the Senate Committee on Labor and Public Welfare, 83d Cong., 1st Sess., 1953, part 4, pp. 2449–2550

A demand to break up national unions or to subject them fully to antitrust legislation occurs each time that labor-relations legislation is under consideration in the Congress.

The arguments offered in support of such proposals are generally based on certain false premises. These erroneous assumptions are:

1. That national and regional bargaining are chiefly responsible for crippling strikes. Actually the manufacturing industries with such bargaining arrangements like pottery, glassware, glass bottles, west coast pulp and paper, men's clothing, and full-fashioned hosiery have been practically strike free during the past 15 to 50 years. Crippling strikes can and do occur in one company—a utility or a railroad; a national emergency dispute could arise with a strike of Aluminum Co. of America, United States Steel, New York harbor, or, as did occur, one plant of the American Locomotive Co. Crippling strikes took place in the railroad and coal industries 50 years or more ago when bargaining was on a company-by-company basis, for strikes that start in one company can spread to others. . . .

3. That national and regional bargaining lead to unduly high wages through monopolistic pricing. Studies, such as my investigation of wages under national and regional collective bargaining in seven manufacturing industries reveal that wages have not increased faster in those industries than for manufacturing as a whole and that occupational wage rates are not particularly high in those industries compared with related industries located in the same areas.

4. That competition between unions is desirable. Union rivalry is an unstabilizing and inflationary influence. Studies reveal that rival unionism is a potent cause of strikes. (See, for example, A. M. Ross and D. Irwin, Strike Experience in Five Countries, 1927–1947: an Interpretation, Industrial and Labor Relations Review, April 1951, p. 337.)

When complaints are made against industry-wide bargaining, apparently what is meant is wage determination by bargaining with a wage leader, which the union then seeks to spread to the rest of the industry. When no bargain is made with the leader, the ensuing strike may affect the whole industry. Such wage leadership and pattern spreading have, for decades, been characteristic of the mass production industries like steel, autos, rubber, agricultural implements, and electrical equipment as well as meatpacking, paper, and textiles. For example, studies of Prof. John Dunlop and Dr. George Seltzer indicate that wage leadership with industry-wide wage movements has characterized the steel industry for the past 50 years and thus antedates effective unionization of steel by at least three decades.

Both writers point out that the uniformity in timing and amount of wage change in basic steel during the past half century has been related to price leadership and pricing methods in steel and that synchronization of the wage behavior is in part a reflection of the business strategy of large firms in that type of industry. Consequently, restrictions on the union would not eliminate wage leadership and pattern spreading. (See Dunlop, Allocation of the Labor Force, in Proceedings of the Conference on Industrywide Collective Bargaining, University of Pennsylvania Press, 1949, pp. 38–40; and Seltzer, Pattern Bargaining and the United Steelworkers, Journal of Political Economy, April 1951, pp. 322–323.)

Proposals to subject unions to antitrust legislation seem to overlook the following:

1. That competition and rivalry do not generally have beneficial results in labor relations, and that labor and management are not competitors in the sense that producers of the same commodity are.

2. That employers have not been subject to the antitrust laws with respect to the purchase of labor services, and so have been free to cooperate or collude on wages and hiring as they wished without legal restraint.

3. That the boycott provisions of the Taft-Hartley Act prevent a union from taking action against two or more employers whose cooperation to defeat the union's strike is not similarly proscribed under that act.

Whenever hearings on labor-relations legislation occur, Congress is urged by some groups to enact a law to enforce autonomous local or company unions by restricting both bargaining and union action or policy determination to a single company or a single locality.

Advocates of such a program seem unaware of the fact that it would mean the practical destruction of craft unionism, the transformation of the two hundred-odd national unions into ineffectual federations that would duplicate present AFL and CIO setups, the compulsory severance of longstanding institutional and personal loyalties, and the enforced isolation of the parts of a movement with 15 million members and 150 years of militant tradition. It is like proposing to carve up the Presbyterian or Catholic church into local units which shall remain separate and autonomous.

Such a proposal has, of course, revolutionary implications for the structure of industry and for labor relations as well as for the structure of labor unions. To be logical and defensible, the program would also have to provide for a thoroughgoing dissolution of large firms and employer associations and, likewise, enforce independence of the severed parts of the dismembered company and personnel organizations. And in slicing up industrial combinations, account would need to be taken of the appropriateness of each segment as jurisdiction for a union. It has repeatedly been emphasized by labor experts that little more reason exists for cutting unions up according to the odd assortment of activities in which many multiplant companies are presently engaged (or may become engaged) than there is for a company to be restricted in its operations to the jurisdiction of a particular union. To insist that the unit of organization of a company and of a union should be identical and continue to be identical regardless of economic change is to ignore the different needs and historical development of individual companies and unions. The most economical and effective unit for business purposes may be completely inappropriate and unsatisfactory for the activities of a labor organization. Neither institution should be structurally straitjacketed by the peculiar needs and developments of the other.

Attempt to force by legislative fiat this special type of company unionism would generate all sorts of industrial strife and raise problems of enforcement that stagger the imagination. By creating a fundamental threat to union existence, it would make union security a major issue throughout the economy for an indefinite period. Severance of long established institutional ties and enforced autonomy of the pieces would require artificial barriers to communication between union officials and Federal policing of the internal affairs of labor organizations.

Prof. Sumner Slichter of Harvard is certainly correct when he writes: "It would be a mistake for public policy to attempt to undermine the dominant position of the national union in the American trade union movement, or to attempt to convert the movement into a grass roots affair in which union officers have much less influence and the rank and file more influence than is now the case. The strong national union fits American conditions"—nationwide markets served, for the most part, by large business units and workers' lack of class consciousness and desire to rely heavily on full-time officials for the conduct of union affairs. The sovereignty of the national union in the American labor movement is deeply rooted by over a century of experience and is equivalent to the sovereignty of the national state in world affairs.

FREEDOM OF ASSOCIATION OR MONOPOLY?

Testimony of Walter P. Reuther, President, United Automobile Workers, in Labor-Management Relations, hearings before the House Committee on Education and Labor, 83d Cong., 1st Sess., 1953, part 3, pp. 1026–1029

MR. GWINN: I have never been able to see how you arrive at what a fair wage is in a monopolistic situation where you control completely the worker and the number of them.

MR. REUTHER: We do not control the workers at all, and I do not control a single worker in America. What do you mean about that?

MR. GWINN: What percentage of the General Motors workers are in your union? . . .

MR. REUTHER: I would say that in the plants under contract, probably 95 percent.

MR. GWINN: For all practical purposes, then, you are a monopoly, an absolute monopoly.

MR. REUTHER: Would a Congressman be a monopoly if 95 percent of the people in his district voted for him? Would that make you a monopoly?

MR. GWINN: I would like to have that experience, and I would not know what to say about it.

MR. REUTHER: We have had that experience, and we have had 95 percent of the General Motors workers vote for us, and that does not make us a monopoly.

MR. GWINN: What is a monopoly except control of the asset or the commodity or the service?

MR. REUTHER: But no one has control over anybody, I don't control a single General Motors worker. They have much more control over me than I have over them. I am obligated to do what they tell me to do, but they are not obligated to do what I tell them to do. . . .

MR. GWINN: It would not make any difference whether you personally were controlling them or whether the union was controlling them. It is obvious, is it not, Mr. Reuther, that when 95 percent of the workers in the automobile industry are united as one, that for all practical purposes, it is a monopoly of the service or the working forces in that industry?

MR. REUTHER: Well, the purpose of collective bargaining is to facilitate workers acting together. Obviously, if you have them all acting together, that is collective bargaining and that is not a monopoly. How else would you do it?

MR. GWINN: Well, it seems to me when you get to the point where you have 95 percent of all the workers operating as a unit to get what they want, that you have no free market left and, therefore, you have no free choice.

You talked a good deal about freedom this morning, and I was very much interested in your devotion to freedom. If you take 95 percent of the workers together, is the employer free to do anything except what those 95 percent operating together demand of him?

MR. REUTHER: He surely is free, and he is free to say, "No," and they often say "No."

MR. GWINN: Well, he certainly is not free to go into the market and find other workers, is he?

MR. REUTHER: Well, you see, labor is not a commodity which you go and shop for in the free market place. Labor is something different than a commodity, and if you want to give American labor the status of another commodity you can go out and shop for on the free market place, you have missed the whole point. We are trying to develop collective bargaining, to advance.

MR. GWINN: No; it seems to me it is quite offensive to have a monopoly of human flesh, and I think that they are different. When you have 95 percent of all the workers united together so that neither the employer can find any free market at all for other workers and the employer has no choice at all, nor the man who is not a member of the union has any choice but to wait on what the 95 percent do, then you have a tight, fierce, absolutely decisive monopoly in the situation. This free collective bargaining that you talk about under those circumstances cannot exist, can it?

MR. REUTHER: Well, the workers have a right through the democratic decisions which they make to withhold their labor power, and the management has a right to withhold their job opportunities.

They can say, "O.K., we won't operate the plant under your conditions, and you won't work under our conditions," and so you have got the free play of two economic forces. Now, the only substitute for that, and the only substitute for the free play of economic forces in those circumstances is to have the Government make the decision; and when we start traveling that road, we are on the way to the destruction of everything that we are trying to defend in the struggle against communism.

I say you cannot substitute a Government decision for a decision which of necessity ought to be a voluntary one made between two parties.

Now, the General Motors Corp. does not even have to talk to anybody. They have got a small board of directors, and they make a decision, and that is their decision. They are not divided, and it is not 95 percent. It is 100 percent. They make a decision to commit their economic force in the implementation of a certain policy decision, and the union challenges that through the decision of the workers. We are no more of a monopoly in the exercise of our power than they are, and they are not a monopoly in that sense.

The whole concept of monopoly is where you get into the field where you are carrying out practices which are unethical and which are deliberately directed toward the restraint of free trade and free competition. We are not doing that.

MR. GWINN: That is all that we are talking about now, and where is the free competition in this whole business?

MR. REUTHER: The competition is between the General Motors Corp. and its workers at the collective-bargaining table. That is where the competition is. And if you do not think that there is intense competition, you ought to sit down and try to get more out of these big corporations. I have had that experience, and it is not easy.

If you think they have abdicated their power, and if you think they have surrendered, if you think that they are easily pushed around in the face of this powerful force you are talking about, I wish we could get some of the magic you think we have got, because we could use it at times.

MR. GWINN: It seems to me by the very definition of the terms, you have eliminated all choice and all freedom when you unify all of your forces, and you certainly effect a monopoly situation on all the competitors of General Motors when you monopolize, in collective bargaining, the bargaining table, and also have in your force the total labor force under command. I do not see how you can see it differently.

MR. REUTHER: You just treat labor as a commodity, and labor is not a commodity. Labor is people.

MR. GWINN: I know; that is an old story, and I do not treat it as a commodity. I want to make it free, and I am talking about freemen and not a commodity. That is what we are trying to get at here, so that we will have some basis for arriving at what is a fair wage or what is a fair price. The public is interested in this.

MR. REUTHER: Sure. But before we had strong unions, Congressman, the employer by arbitrary decisions decided the level of wages, and he just said, "This is it," and the worker either took it or went hungry. It was only when we developed unions and we began to make collective bargaining work that the individual worker, in conjunction with his fellow worker, began to be able counteract the arbitrary economic decisions made by the employer. And at the point where the worker develops an economic strength comparable or at least sufficiently strong to begin to get a measure of justice, you come up and say, "It is a monopoly."

UNION COULD CONTROL PRODUCTION, MANUFACTURER SAYS

From the Hosiery Worker, published by the American Federation of Hosiery Workers, April, 1952

Reading, Pa.—The [American Federation of Hosiery Workers] can work effecively against the evil of overproduction if it is able to organize from 80 to 100 per cent of the industry, Samuel F. Rubin, President of the Full Fashioned Hosiery Manufacturers of America, Inc., said in his address to the Convention here this month.

Rubin pointed out that there is no legal way for manufacturers to control inventories and production. Any attempt by manufacturers to join together to accomplish this end is as illegal as collaboration to fix prices. But the Union in its contractual agreements with the manufacturers could control production if it were dominant in the industry and thus function to restore stability to this badly overproduced industry.

He hailed the relations between the American Federation of Hosiery Workers and the Full Fashioned Hosiery Manufacturers of America, Inc., as a triumph of peaceful collective bargaining. . . .

THE WAGE PROBLEM IN TEXTILES

From Textiles: Crisis for America—A Special Report, Textile Labor, vol. 17, September, 1956, pp. 21–22

. . . By what law of man or nature must a worker who sweeps lint be worth little more than half the pay of a worker who sweeps iron-filings?

The solution of the wage problem is so simple that we hesitate to put it down. Let's insist, first, that it has nothing to do with the nature of the textile industry or the profit-margins of the employers; nor does it concern the ferocious competition in the textile markets.

The wage problem can be solved by the simplest of all methods—union organization. And this, in turn, would help no end to cure the ills. . . . Here's why:

If textile workers were 100% unionized, or close to it, they'd submit the same basic proposals to all employers in each division. No employer could complain that he was being penalized unfairly.

Would this constitute a labor-management "conspiracy" against the consumer, as some intellectuals argue? Not at all. [Just 55¢ added to the price of a $50 man's suit would bring average pay of woolen and worsted workers up to 1.97 an hour, the national standard in manufacturing. What's inflationary about that? Only 25¢ added to the price of a $20 dress would raise the average hourly pay of cotton-rayon workers to the same $1.97 level. Is this too great a burden to place on the consumer?]

Would this eliminate competition? Not at all. Though basic wages would be uniform, there would be an endless variety of differences based upon manhour output, the use of new and better machinery and processes.

Would this hurt the employers? Not at all. It would help them. To put it as bluntly as possible, a mill margin of 2% on a unit cost of $1 is 2¢; a mill margin of 2% on a unit cost of $2 is 4¢. If textile wages are doubled, the employers would be better off and the consumer would hardly notice the difference.

But no one employer—even now—can himself establish a new and higher wage pattern. It can be done only if all employers separately agree to union proposals.

FOR DISCUSSION AND ANALYSIS

1. The secondary boycott is frequently cited by business spokesmen as an example of union monopolistic practices. What is the basis of this charge?

2. Employers have sometimes spoken of a union's "monopoly power" as constituting a power to dictate to employer and consumer. If this is so, then why should unions have to fall back on the strike at times in an effort to secure their demands? Or does the strike itself constitute a form of dictation? Is the strike of a powerful union always successful? What precise content can you give to the notion of a union's dictating terms to others?

3. Union spokesmen have traditionally adopted the view (expressed by Arthur Goldberg in the readings above) that "we do not believe that the Nation's economic well-being would be promoted by requiring that [these] Steelworkers compete with each other as to who will work more cheaply."

How does this statement compare with traditional economic (competitive) theory? What is there to be said, if anything, on both sides of this argument?

4. In the testimony of labor witnesses, reproduced above, if Mr. Biemiller is right in saying that the strength of unions is in their memberships rather than in their treasuries, then what is the significance of the comparison made by Mr. Goldberg of the relative assets of United States Steel and the United Steelworkers? What standard can you suggest for comparison of the relative economic power of labor unions and corporations?

5. In a statement, "The Church and Social Order," 1940, the Archbishops and Bishop of the Administrative Board of the National Catholic Welfare Conference included the following pronouncement:

If a business is prevented by unfair competition from paying a living wage and if such competition reduces prices to such a level that decent and just

ages cannot be paid, then those responsible are guilty of wrongdoing and sin
rievously against moral principles as well as against the common good. The
emedy lies first in the adequate organization of both employer and employees
in their own proper associations and in their joint action; secondly, in adequate
egulations and supervision by the State through proper legislative enactment.

a. In this context, how would you define "unfair competition"?

b. Do you see any dangers in the remedies proposed?

6. A student once wrote, on an examination paper, "The only check to
ncreased labor costs is competition, enforced through restricting collec-
ive bargaining to the local level."

a. Is this the only check?

b. May not increased labor costs through higher wages be justified?

c. Do you want competition among labor, and if so in what form?

d. Can you *avoid* competition among labor, even if you wanted to?

e. How would you enforce collective bargaining at the local level?

20: Minimum Wages

In April, 1955, hearings were held by a subcommittee (chaired by Senator Paul Douglas, former professor of economics at the University of Chicago) of the Senate Committee on Labor and Public Welfare, on the question of whether the Federal minimum wage should be increased, and if so by how much. The Republican administration recommended an increase from the then prevailing rate of 75 cents to one of 90 cents. In general, business groups were opposed to any increase, and in any event to any increase greater than that recommended by the administration. The labor unions were pressing for a rate of $1.25, and had some support from the Democratic-dominated Senate, and particularly from so-called Northern "Liberal" Democrats. The rate which was finally legislated was $1 an hour.

*There follow excerpts from the three volumes of hearings (*Amending the Fair Labor Standards Act of 1938, *84th Cong., 1st Sess., 1955).*

THE ADMINISTRATION RECOMMENDS 90 CENTS

Statement of Hon. James P. Mitchell, Secretary of Labor, pp. 49–51, 54–56

SENATOR DOUGLAS: I notice that you think that a 90-cent minimum can be absorbed by industry, but that a dollar an hour minimum cannot be. I wonder if you would go into further detail?

SECRETARY MITCHELL: Yes, sir. I believe you have or will have these studies. I have here a wage distribution for factory workers in April of 1954, and, as I said in my prepared statement, our opinion in the Department of Labor is that the impact of the 90 cents would be about the same in 1955 as the impact of the 75 cents was in 1950, and we have a table here which is a survey of the factory workers in all of the regions of the United States, and there are some very significant figures which I would like to point out in the South.

In considering a Federal minimum wage, it seems to me that you have to consider the total Nation, and some of the problems of the regions, and you also have to bear in mind that one of the two major objectives of the act is a minimum wage which will not curtail employment opportunities. . . .

May I continue and point out that in the South 20 percent of the now

882

covered workers are getting less than 90 cents, 28.2 percent are getting less than a dollar, and 50 percent are getting less than $1.25.

Now, this is only the factory workers. I would assume that the percentage would be as high—we do not have the figures—if all workers were to be included. For example, this table shows that of the factory workers nationwide getting less than $1.25, there are 2,823,000. If you include all of the workers, factory workers and others covered, there would be close to 5 million people out of the 24 million covered who are getting less than $1.25. There are over 1,282,000 nationwide who are getting less than $1, factory covered workers.

So in answer to your question, it seems that in taking into consideration the impact of an increase, the sound impact which can be borne by the industries most affected, would indicate that a 90-cent rate is the desirable rate.

SENATOR DOUGLAS: But if industry adjusted so well to 75 cents in 1950, might it not also have adjusted very well to 80 cents or 85 cents in 1950 and, therefore adjust to $1 or more in 1955 or 1956, as well as it might have adjusted to 80 or 85 cents in 1950?

SECRETARY MITCHELL: Of course, Senator, that is a matter of opinion. We are going on facts here as to the adjustment.

SENATOR DOUGLAS: Every act is a venture of faith, Mr. Secretary.

SECRETARY MITCHELL: We believe, as I said, based on the past experience, that 90 cents is the sound rate, which the President has recommended to Congress.

SENATOR DOUGLAS: Do you have at hand statistics indicating the average hourly rates of industry as a whole in 1939 as compared to the present?

SECRETARY MITCHELL: At hand here, no; but we will be happy to furnish them.

SENATOR DOUGLAS: If it should be found that the average hourly rate has increased at a greater rate than the minimum, wouldn't that eliminate your opposition to a rate higher than 90 cents?

SECRETARY MITCHELL: Not necessarily, because there are many elements in the average hourly rate, such as collective bargaining and all of the other elements.

As I have tried to indicate here, what we are considering is a minimum rate than can be absorbed without undue hardship in the economy. The average hourly rate has many elements in it, and the minimum rate is not a prevailing rate. I don't think, sir, and I am no economist, that the relationship is a true one.

SENATOR DOUGLAS: So you are really going on the experience of 1949?

SECRETARY MITCHELL: That is right.

SENATOR DOUGLAS: You say, roughly, the 1949 increase was absorbed, the 90 cents would be only a little bit higher than the 75 cents, and that therefore it could be absorbed, because the percentage now below 90 cents an hour is about the same as the percentage below 75 cents was then?

SECRETARY MITCHELL: In 1950, yes.

SENATOR DOUGLAS: How about the production per man-hour, hasn't that been going forward since 1949?

SECRETARY MITCHELL: Yes, sir.

SENATOR DOUGLAS: Hasn't that been increasing by more than 6 percent in the 5 years?

SECRETARY MITCHELL: Totally, I would think so.

SENATOR DOUGLAS: You provide a total increase of 6 percent in real earnings. Eighty-five cents is needed for the increase in the cost of living, and 5 cents is for the real increase in earnings. We have a yearly increase in productivity which is normally estimated on an hourly basis of somewhere between 3 and 4 percent a year in physical goods.

Now, there is every reason to believe that this is as true of the lower wage workers as of the average workers. And it is certainly true that there has been such an increase during these last 6 years.

In view of that increase in productivity which reduces labor costs per unit, wouldn't it be safe to go above 90 cents?

SECRETARY MITCHELL: Well, Senator, I do not think that it is reasonable to believe, as you stated, that the increased productivity of the low paid workers is as great as the average or as great as others. We have no figures which would so indicate. . . .

SENATOR DOUGLAS: Mr. Secretary, you are acquainted with the statements of family budgets which your Department publishes?

SECRETARY MITCHELL: Generally, yes.

SENATOR DOUGLAS: In the Monthly Labor Review for May 1952, there was an analysis of a modest but adequate budget for four-member urban families in 34 cities of the country, which shows that estimates ranged from $3,441 in New Orleans to $3,965 in Washington.

There has been no decrease in the cost of living since October 1951, the general price level has remained approximately stable, but there has been a slight increase in consumer prices since then, so these figures are slight understatements of the amounts that would be required at present.

If you would take your 90-cents-an-hour wage and multiply it by 2,000 hours, which would be a full-time year, 50 weeks at 40 hours a week, you would come to an income of $1,800. Now, that is only slightly over one-half of the minimum required in New Orleans. As a matter of fact, I would like to correct my statement. The figures I have quoted are simply for goods, rents, and services, and do not take into account other personal costs and taxes, so in practice the minimum amount for all items in New Orleans was $3,812, and in Washington $4,454, so that your $1,800-a-year figure would be less than half of the amount required in New Orleans and approximately only 40 percent or slightly less of the amount required in Washington. This is for a four-member family.

I wonder if you had anything to say on this point?

SECRETARY MITCHELL: Well, sir, I think that you have to bear in mind that the minimum wage, as I have stated in my statement, has another objective, that it should be installed so as not to cause any major loss of employment opportunities or business mortality, if I may paraphrase it. . . .

Now, at no time in the history of the act has the minimum wage established by Congress approached or even nearly approached this concept of providing a minimum for a family of four.

SENATOR DOUGLAS: Well, isn't it probable a male worker actually produces enough to support at least half of the family?

SENATOR SMITH: Mr. Chairman, I might suggest could the Secretary speak a little louder, please? . . .

SECRETARY MITCHELL: I shall endeavor to raise my voice for both the chairman and the committee.

SENATOR DOUGLAS: Well, it is not in anger that you are raising your voice, but merely in a desire to be helpful.

SECRETARY MITCHELL: Oh, certainly; never in anger.

SENATOR DOUGLAS: Go ahead, Mr. Secretary.

What about this? Isn't it probable that a man earns enough at least to support half the family?

SECRETARY MITCHELL: I don't understand, Senator, the point you are making, or what you are driving at.

SENATOR DOUGLAS: Well, if it cost $3,612 to support a family of four in New Orleans, La., in October 1951, and $4,454 for the same month in Washington, and you are only providing for $1,800, whereas a $1 wage would provide for $2,000, isn't it probable that a worker will at least support half a family? Or are you saying that he shouldn't be permitted to support half a family?

SECRETARY MITCHELL: No, of course.

SENATOR DOUGLAS: Or should not be helped to support half a family?

SECRETARY MITCHELL: What I am trying to say, Senator, and perhaps not too clearly, is that we must bear in mind, and apparently the Congress in the past has always borne in mind, that the ability to absorb an increased wage is a real limiting factor in the setting of the wage, and this is evident, very evident, in the action of some of the State minimum wage setting activities, and as I said before, the minimum wage is not a prevailing wage, it is not a substitute for collective bargaining, and should not be. It is a minimum floor below which an employer may not go; below which an employer may not go.

SENATOR DOUGLAS: Well, shouldn't a man be permitted to support at least half a family? Is that too excessive a request?

SECRETARY MITCHELL: Well, sir, with the average hourly . . .

SENATOR DOUGLAS: If he didn't support half a family where would the human race come from?

SECRETARY MITCHELL: Well, the evidence in this country seems to be that a man's average weekly wage as of today which is the highest we have had in factory employment of some $71 plus . . .

SENATOR DOUGLAS: Well, all that a dollar an hour will do is to provide a minimum wage of a little over half the average.

SECRETARY MITCHELL: But I still say you must bear in mind . . .

SENATOR DOUGLAS: You are keeping him at less than half of the average.

SECRETARY MITCHELL: But you must bear in mind the ability of the economy to absorb it.

SENATOR DOUGLAS: You don't think the economy can stand a minimum equal to half of the average, or slightly over half of the average, perhaps 55 percent of the average?

SECRETARY MITCHELL: The average of what?

SENATOR DOUGLAS: The average which you have just quoted to me, the average weekly earnings. I am just taking your terms, Mr. Secretary.

SECRETARY MITCHELL: I think you have to consider, Senator, the place you are at, which is 75 cents, and how far you can go at this time in raising that 75 cents without too great a dislocation in some areas of this country in employment opportunities, and that has been our consideration.

SENATOR DOUGLAS: Mr. Secretary, it is a truism that if some people fall below the average, others must be above the average; isn't that true?

SECRETARY MITCHELL: Yes, I suppose statistically you are correct.

SENATOR DOUGLAS: Of course, most believe that their golf game is always better than the average game, but there is an element of personal bias. If some people are getting only $30 a week, and the average is $72, then it follows that the maximum earnings of wage earners is very much higher than $72, and probably in many cases around $100.

What I am trying to get at is whether the heavens would fall in on us if we fixed a minimum of, say, 55 percent of the average, and 40 percent of the approximate maximum, not the absolute maximum?

SECRETARY MITCHELL: I am sorry, I must repeat myself, but it seems to me in setting a minimum wage the Congress should bear in mind the effect of whatever wage it sets on the various regions of this country, and in our opinion a wage higher than 90 cents minimum might be difficult, seriously difficult, for the South particularly to absorb.

SENATOR DOUGLAS: Weren't these same arguments used in 1938 against an initial 25-cent minimum wage, and against an increase to 30 cents after a year? I sat on the subcommittee in 1949. We heard the same arguments against the 75-cent minimum wage.

SECRETARY MITCHELL: We are proposing here the same impact that the 75-cent wage made.

SENATOR DOUGLAS: But my point here is, isn't your attitude characterized by very little faith in the productivity of the American worker, or the productivity of the American industry?

SECRETARY MITCHELL: No, sir; my attitude is not characterized by that. I have great faith in the productivity of the American worker, or American industry, but here we are setting a nationwide Federal minimum wage, and I confess that I do not see the relationship of that action to the average hourly earnings, the productivity factors, and faith in the American worker. I have great faith in the American worker.

PERCENTAGES OF PRODUCTION WORKERS IN MANUFACTURING EARNING LESS THAN SPECIFIED AMOUNTS PER HOUR,* APRIL 1954

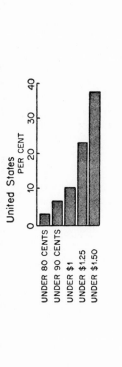

United States

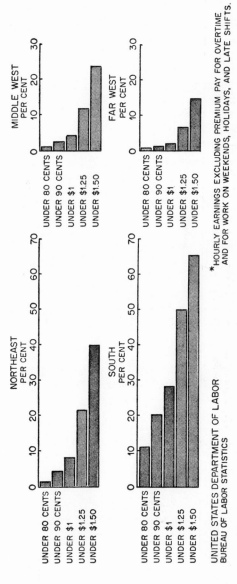

UNITED STATES DEPARTMENT OF LABOR
BUREAU OF LABOR STATISTICS

*HOURLY EARNINGS EXCLUDING PREMIUM PAY FOR OVERTIME AND FOR WORK ON WEEKENDS, HOLIDAYS, AND LATE SHIFTS.

Estimates of the Percent of Production Workers Earning Less than 85 Cents, 90 Cents, $1, and $1.25 an Hour, and the Percent Direct Increase in the Wage Bill Resulting from These Minimum-wage Rates, in Recently Surveyed Low-wage Industries, United States, April, 1954

Industry	Number of production workers at date of survey	Average straight-time hourly earnings	85 cents		90 cents		$1.00		$1.25	
			Percent of workers directly affected	Percentage increase in wage bill	Percent of workers directly affected	Percentage increase in wage bill	Percent of workers directly affected	Percentage increase in wage bill	Percent of workers directly affected	Percentage increase in wage bill
	Thousands									
Southern sawmills	171	$0.86	62	5	74	9	84	18	94	44
Work clothing	66	.96	41	3	51	5	67	11	88	32
Processed waste	6	1.10	18	1	30	2	41	5	73	18
Candy and other confectionery	47	1.20	6	(¹)	10	1	23	2	56	9
Men's and boys' dress shirts	89	1.09	26	2	33	3	46	7	74	20
Paddings and upholstery filling	6	1.42	2	(¹)	3	(¹)	9	1	25	3
Men's seamless hosiery	32	1.07	22	1	30	3	45	6	79	21
Jute goods	4	1.32	6	(¹)	7	1	23	2	42	8
Footwear	178	1.31	13	1	19	1	30	3	55	11
Cordage and twine	9	1.28	3	(¹)	5	(¹)	11	1	48	7
Cotton textiles	330	1.19	1	(¹)	4	(¹)	14	1	67	10
Structural clay products	56	1.57	5	(¹)	7	(¹)	10	1	22	4
Woolen and worsted	100	1.45	(¹)	(¹)	1	(¹)	2	(¹)	21	2
Synthetic textiles	56	1.22	1	(¹)	2	(¹)	8	(¹)	66	9
Converted paper products	189	1.46	2	(¹)	4	(¹)	10	1	33	4
Full-fashioned hosiery	55	1.48	7	(¹)	11	1	19	2	42	7

¹ Less than 0.5 of 1 percent.

Source: U. S. Department of Labor.

These earnings data derived from surveys made in recent years, have been adjusted to reflect significant changes in wage levels since the dates of the surveys. Employment data are as of the dates of the surveys.

WHY A 90-CENT MINIMUM?

Statement of Stuart Rothman, Solicitor, Department of Labor, pp. 88–91, 94–95

SENATOR DOUGLAS: . . . Now, what were some of these other industries that you thought were going to be adversely affected? . . .

MR. ROTHMAN: Work clothing is one.

SENATOR DOUGLAS: Work clothing. I don't believe I have the breakdown on work clothing, but would you give the figures?

MR. ROTHMAN: Yes, sir. Fifty-one percent of the employees in work clothing receive less than 90 cents an hour, and 67 percent in work clothing receive less than $1 an hour.

SENATOR DOUGLAS: What is the total coverage in work clothing?

MR. ROTHMAN: Sixty-six thousand production workers.

SENATOR DOUGLAS: Total. So you say 50 percent receive less than 90 cents?

MR. ROTHMAN: Fifty-one percent receive less than 90 cents.

SENATOR DOUGLAS: So that means approximately 34,000 are getting less than 90 cents and about 44,000 workers are getting less than a dollar?

MR. ROTHMAN: I think that is correct.

SENATOR DOUGLAS: And where are these factories located?

MR. ROTHMAN: Mainly in the South.

SENATOR DOUGLAS: Do you think it would deal a death blow to the South to raise the wages of 35,000 workers to $1 an hour?

MR. ROTHMAN: I think the impact of increasing the minimum wage, and the effect upon the particular industry, and the employees in that industry, is something that the subcommittee will have to determine. It is a matter of judgment.

SENATOR DOUGLAS: Well, I have a figure here from your own Department, Employment and Earnings, March 1955, which gives a figure for men's and boys' furnishings and work clothing, on page 30, average weekly earnings, $40.91, which would indicate at least $1 an hour. It is true that that includes men's and boys' furnishings as well as work clothing, but in the North are there many receiving less than 90 cents, or less than $1 an hour?

MR. ROTHMAN: . . . I am advised by one of the technicians, by an assistant administrator, Mr. Weiss, that there are, and I would suggest that Mr. Weiss answer that question directly.

SENATOR DOUGLAS: Mr. Weiss.

MR. WEISS: We find a fair number earning under a dollar.

SENATOR DOUGLAS: Your full name, please?

MR. WEISS: Harry Weiss, assistant wage administrator.

There are quite a fair number earning under a dollar in such things as cotton dresses and pajamas. There is quite an industry in rural Pennsylvania.

SENATOR DOUGLAS: Is that in the mining section?

MR. WEISS: Yes, in the anthracite section.

SENATOR DOUGLAS: There is a very large percentage of unemployment in that section?

MR. WEISS: In mining.

SENATOR DOUGLAS: And the families are in need?

MR. WEISS: I have no doubt that the families are in need.

SENATOR DOUGLAS: Well, I have been in the anthracite section and the situation there is very serious, and has been for some time. Families are desperate to earn anything that they can get. There is an idle pool of unemployed labor.

Might it not be in the public interest to raise the wages in these areas so that hard-pressed people would not be taken advantage of either in the North or the South?

MR. ROTHMAN: I think it is in the public interest to increase the minimum wage to the fullest extent possible.

SENATOR DOUGLAS: Well, I think it is certainly true in the North, as the witness has testified, and to a large degree I think it is true in the South, that you have this low wage in localities where there is a pool of idle labor, where the workers and their families are desperate, and where a hard bargain may be driven.

Now, I am not condemning these people, because if one person starts it, and undersells the others, it puts a very heavy strain upon the other employer. But isn't that a case where the State can step in and protect people against the bargains which their own necessities may drive them to? That is the theory of the minimum wage, that in the bargaining process worker and employer do not stand on an equal basis, and that the State, therefore, can properly use its powers to fix a minimum below which the needs of the individual cannot be met. That was the so-called difficulty with free cotton which many people have forgotten.

But isn't that possibly a case where we should remember it?

MR. ROTHMAN: I think those are all factors which the subcommittee will want to take into consideration.

SENATOR DOUGLAS: But, Mr. Rothman, we have summoned you here as an expert in this field to give us your advice. If we were to recommend a dollar it is quite possible that you might oppose the fixation of a dollar. Now we want to see how you feel about it and get your advice in the formation of the law, and not have it merely subject to criticism by you after such a minimum might have been fixed.

MR. ROTHMAN: I would suggest what the committee might want to do is determine the effect in these lower industries upon curtailing employment by setting this minimum wage. I am sure our interests are mutual in attempting to improve the economic and social and the human position of these persons of low income caught in the situation you describe of an unemployment area.

It may be, in our efforts to attempt to do that, you are dealing with the facts of a particular industry that would result in a curtailment of employment and not helping those persons. So we must be very careful, I am sure you will agree, that we don't do something that will hurt them.

SENATOR DOUGLAS: Might it not result in increasing the price of overalls and coveralls? If you fix this minimum wage below which the industry cannot go, and it raises costs, and assuming that would raise prices, it would increase the price of overalls and coveralls; isn't that true?

MR. ROTHMAN: I would think that an increase in labor costs may result in an increase in prices.

SENATOR DOUGLAS: Now, I don't think that this would increase the cost of living for bank presidents, because I believe their morning attire is different from overalls and coveralls. Therefore, complaints should not be made by representatives of that group. It would affect the cost of living of skilled workers and factory workers, but it so happens that the representatives of factory workers are here asking not for $1 an hour but for $1.25 an hour, and they have undoubtedly thought this over and have decided that they are willing to pay the price even though their overalls may cost a few cents more.

Now, are you going to say that you should protect them against themselves, Mr. Rothman?

MR. ROTHMAN: I think that the matter again gets down to the crux of the question of whether the industry can absorb the increase without curtailing the employment.

SENATOR DOUGLAS: We are asking for your assistance, Mr. Rothman. I didn't introduce the work-clothing issue, you introduced it, and now I am trying to follow this lead which you so kindly began.

MR. ROTHMAN: I think there are other factors besides increasing the price of the product that must be taken into consideration in determining the question.

SENATOR DOUGLAS: If the price of the product is increased, then the strain upon the employer is reduced, and if it is made uniform then you have an increase in price, do you not? Of course, there might be some shifting of industry.

MR. ROTHMAN: I couldn't answer that.

SENATOR DOUGLAS: Let us turn from work clothing to another low-wage industry. Is food one?

SENATOR SMITH: One question: When you refer to the possible increase in price, it occurs to me that the increase in price of the product might reduce the sales of the product and you might be back where you began. Is that true, or do you think that the product could stand an increase in price?

MR. ROTHMAN: I think your statement is true. As a matter of economics, increasing the price may result in reducing the sale of the product. I think among the factors, as far as the particular plant is concerned, it may have an adverse effect on that plant and not on others. I am not prepared to say what the effect of increasing the price of work clothing would be.

SENATOR DOUGLAS: I wonder if the staff would work out the percentage of labor cost in the production of overalls and work clothing, and calculate the increase in cost resulting from a minimum wage of $1 an hour. How much would this affect the retail price? That would be very interesting.

My offhand curbstone opinion is that an amount somewhere between a dime and a quarter would be a very liberal allowance, and I cannot imagine that the workmen of the country would greatly diminish their purchase of coveralls as a result of such an increase. I would not expect them to wear good suits to work because the price of coveralls has gone up. . . .

SENATOR DOUGLAS: We have taken sawmills, work clothing, men's and boys' dress shirts. Now, what else do you want to bring up?

MR. ROTHMAN: Whatever you may wish to inquire about.

SENATOR DOUGLAS: Well, candy and confectioneries lies up near the top. Forty-seven thousand production workers, at 90 cents, 10 percent affected; at $1, 23 percent affected; is that correct?

MR. ROTHMAN: Yes.

SENATOR DOUGLAS: Do you think a minimum of $1 an hour would hurt the candy industry? It would increase the wages bill by 2 percent; isn't that right?

MR. ROTHMAN: Yes, that is the figure.

SENATOR DOUGLAS: Do you think a 2 percent increase in the wages bill would greatly diminish the consumption of candy, or the number of boxes that a young man would give to his young lady?

MR. ROTHMAN: However, in the South the increase would be substantially more. . . . The increase in the South would be the difference between 3 percent and 9 percent, so there would be a difference between the country as a whole and the impact upon the part of the industry in the South.

SENATOR DOUGLAS: Is there anyone who is in the candy business here, or has a relative who is in the candy business?

Does anybody know about the markup of retail stores on candy?

I would be dubious whether it was any less than the 40 percent of wholesale price, or 67 percent of billing price.

If that is so—and I regret that I have not purchased as many boxes of candy for my wife recently as I might have, but I believe you can get a very good box of candy for $1.25 a pound—I wonder if manufacturing cost is more than half of that. Remember you are dealing with raw materials such as sugar, glucose, and other delectable items, and nuts. I doubt that the labor costs on these items exceeds 20 percent of the total, or, roughly, let us say, 25 cents for a pound. I think that is a very liberal estimate.

Now, you say there would be an increase of 2 percent for the country as a whole in labor costs; 2 percent of 25 cents is one-half cent. Do you think the addition in cost of one-half cent, or even a cent to $1.25 candy would be very appreciable, or if you come down into the lower figures, do you think that an increase of a fraction of a cent to a 5-cent bar of candy would deter the boy or girl from getting a candy bar after school hours? . . .

It looks on the surface if you only get an increase of 2 percent in labor costs in an industry where there is a big retail markup, where material costs are a major expense, where production as I have seen it in candy factories in Chicago —which make quite a lot of candy—I say where production is pretty well mechanized, it seems to me that this would be a very small increase in the cost of a pound of candy in terms of cents.

I don't think there would be much decrease in the demand for candy, and, hence, the employment in the candy industry.

MR. ROTHMAN: Perhaps Mr. Weiss, who is an economist, may have an additional contribution to this.

MR. WEISS: Well, Senator, I think perhaps the effort to highlight it has oversimplified the problem. The figures we are giving here are figures of the direct effects of bringing the workers under a particular rate to that rate. We are taking into account no indirect facts.

SENATOR DOUGLAS: You mean the relation of wages of workers affected by an increase in the minimum wage to the wages of other workers?

MR. WEISS: That is right.

SENATOR DOUGLAS: I am using the figures you have given me. You cannot ask me to be more critical of your figures than you are yourselves.

MR. WEISS: We can be quite critical of these figures in terms of telling the whole story.

I might also mention that, of course, there may be additional wage costs along the line before you get to the ultimate consumer with your candy, in the wholesale house, for example, and there may be a certain amount of pyramiding of costs and margins along the way, too, so it is pretty hard to start with an increase in labor costs at a factory and end up at the retail price level. It is just a difficult operation.

Stuart Rothman, Solicitor, Department of Labor, pp. 1512, 1519–1520

The maximum increase in the minimum wage that can be undertaken depends on the impact the increase would have on low-wage segments of industry where it must be paid. If the increase is too large to be absorbed without disruptive changes, the results are either unemployment in the affected firms or price increases. If the market will not take price increases, the low-paid workers whose jobs are at stake lose instead of gaining. If prices rise and the wage increase is paid through inflation the real cost is borne by low-paid workers outside the scope of Federal regulation and by pensioners and others in similar status.

Budget studies purporting to show what a minimum budget ought to be, changes in average wages for all manufacturing combined, and estimates of the trend in productivity for the whole economy are useful as background information and serve to suggest the need for reviewing the minimum wage. They do not offer an arithmetical formula for answering the question of how much it can be raised. . . .

The problem of the minimum wage is a problem of low-wage segments of industry and low-wage plants. To some extent it is expected that improvements in these industry segments and plants in management and organization, tools and equipment, and skills of the work force, will offset increases in wage cost resulting from an increase in the minimum wage. But no suitable data are available for measuring productivity in the affected industries and firms. It is obvious, and is mentioned here only for emphasis, that the gains from increased productivity in a steel mill or in an electronics plant, are not available to pay higher wages in a sawmill or a shirt factory. It is the sawmill and the shirt factory that must be studied to see what level of minimum wage is feasible.

SENATOR DOUGLAS: Now, just a minute, Mr. Rothman. The increased productivity in the steel-mill industry as a whole gives increased earnings to the workers in these industries; doesn't it? The workers with increased earnings will then be able to pay more for the shirts or for furniture and, therefore, you have an increase in the demand for these products, and a raise in their value, and hence a greater ability on the part of the industry to pay an increased wage?

If the theory of productivity means anything, it means that the gains in particular industries tend to be distributed over the economy as a whole.

MR. ROTHMAN: Senator, I think that you may be skipping a few steps with regard to the economics of selling and marketing shirts, and this question, I think, has come up before.

I would like to ask Mr. Weiss if he might want to elaborate upon the problem of marketing and competition in the shirt-manufacturing industry?

MR. WEISS: I wouldn't want to take issue with the chairman on his statements, and I think that it is no doubt true over the long run, but what we are facing here is a few months from now if the Congress imposes a minimum wage, what can the shirt plant do at that time? Twenty years later there might be the means for him to pay a high minimum wage, but it doesn't necessarily follow that he can pay it as of the time the Congress imposes it.

SENATOR DOUGLAS: Well, of course, there have been 6 years during which productivity has been increasing, and the real wages of the workers have been going up until 1953, I believe. During that time the workers purchase more shirts at higher prices. Therefore, the financial position of the shirt industry has improved because the general productivity of American industry has increased.

MR. ROTHMAN: Senator, you might be confronted with this problem: What you say may be true, and the steelworker, who isn't confronted with the problem of a 90-cent or $1 minimum wage because I believe they are making more than that, might pay more for a shirt, but as between two shirt manufacturers, one who now perhaps pays more than any minimum wage that is contemplated, and the one who doesn't, there is going to be a problem with respect to who they sell their shirts by the gross, to the jobber and the wholesaler, and it may very well be, and as this statement will point out as we approach this problem, we must think in terms of the competition within the particular industry, and the particular plants that are in competition with each other, and the difference of a few cents in the gross price of a product to the wholesaler may make the difference of who gets that sale, and I will come to that in a moment, if I may proceed.

The low-wage industries and segments of industries most significantly affected by any increase in the minimum wage are generally highly competitive and tend to operate on small-profit margins or at the break-even point. A cost increase imposed by a change in the law must be considered in terms of the operating margins of the affected segments and in terms of their competition in the market place. Sawmills compete in the sale of lumber, not of houses, and they compete with other sawmills. A factory making work pants does not sell over the retail counter. It competes with another pants factory in selling to expert buyers, and a difference of a few cents quoted at the factory can make or lose a sale. The extent to which the burden of a minimum-wage increase can be absorbed in the affected segments depends on a number of factors of internal plant operation, and the extent to which the burden can be shifted in the form of higher prices depends on the market position of the affected firms and industry segments.

In a number of instances where a higher rate would have substantial effects, the affected areas are segments of industries with a wide difference in wage structure. Some parts of the same industry would therefore have no added cost burden. In such a situation it would be particularly difficult, barring general inflationary trends, for the affected segments to raise their prices and maintain their market position at the higher price level.

Rebuttal by Solomon Barkin, Chairman, CIO Fair Labor Standards Committee, to the statement of the Solicitor of the United States Department of Labor, pp. 1547–1548

The solicitor is concerned with the impact of higher minimum wages on the low-wage segments of an industry, but he has expressed no solicitude for the economic security of establishments of fair employers in an industry whose economic security is undermined by the low-wage employers. He expresses no concern for the mills and plants which have closed by reason of this unfair competition. He is not alarmed at the migration of plants to low-wage areas. This indifference to the lot of the fair-minded employer is unmatched in the annals of the United States Department of Labor.

COMPETITION IS PREFERABLE TO LEGISLATION IN FIXING WAGES

Statement of Dr. Emerson P. Schmidt, for the United States Chamber of Commerce, pp. 713–714, 722, 724, 726–727, 729–731

MR. SCHMIDT: If there must be minimum wage fixing, the minimum should be fixed at a level which avoids the destruction of job opportunities and minimizes inflationary effects. We therefore oppose proposals to raise the minimum wage as unrealistic and self-defeating.

SENATOR SMITH: You are opposed to any raise at all?

MR. SCHMIDT: Yes. We doubt the wisdom of any increase at all for reasons which will become clear as we go along.

Even an increase to 90 cents would have disemploying effects, and raise costs and prices to consumers. Expanded coverage will greatly raise the cost of administration and be a further burden to the taxpayers, place new burdens on small employers, and further concentrate workers, who are barred by the law from jobs in covered employment, in the uncovered jobs and thereby depress wages there in the uncovered jobs.

Employers generally recognize the importance of paying good wages. This attracts good workers, reduces labor turnover, raises efficiency, improves industrial and community relations. Fixing minimum wages by law may benefit some workers, but at the same time it is likely to hurt other workers as consumers. It may have disruptive effects, and it tends to force concentration of workers with low productivity into the occupations not reached by the minimum wage law.

Everyone's income is always a cost to others. Every increase in one's income is an increased cost to others, unless such increase is offset by a rise in productivity.

SENATOR DOUGLAS: Mr. Schmidt, may I ask a question about the preceding paragraph?

You say that it will force the concentration of workers of low productivity into the occupations not reached by the minimum wage law. Many of those workers are not necessarily so much low-productivity as low-paid workers. Can you be certain it would have the same effect?

MR. SCHMIDT: I think as a generalization, Mr. Chairman, it would be correct to say that low-paid workers are low productivity workers unless they have very little in the way of ambition or aspiration. Some people are satisfied with a modest income. They may be secondary workers. They may be substandard workers. There are exceptions, but by and large I think given the American spirit to get ahead, there is a close correlation between low productivity and low wages.

If that were not the case it seems to me, employers, always looking for good labor, would attract these low-paid workers into their industries, and they would gradually move up.

SENATOR DOUGLAS: In other words, you would say that competitive bargaining for labor would tend to give to the workers that which they produce?

MR. SCHMIDT: By and large, I think that is what takes place, with some lags and frictions, to be sure. . . .

SENATOR DOUGLAS: I certainly would not deny that that factor is present, but I don't think we should reach the conclusion that every one therefore reaches that station in life to which his abilities entitle him.

MR. SCHMIDT: There is certainly a certain amount of luck and opportunity and timing.

SENATOR DOUGLAS: Not only luck, but some men operate under great disadvantages; others operate under great advantages.

MR. SCHMIDT: Some break through these disadvantages.

SENATOR DOUGLAS: That is right; an exceptionally energetic or able person, sometimes an exceptionally ruthless person, breaks through.

MR. SCHMIDT: That is right.

SENATOR DOUGLAS: I am saying this because I don't want to have spread on the record a lot of uncontested statements that poverty is exclusively the fault of the poor.

MR. SCHMIDT: I didn't say that, did I, Senator?

SENATOR DOUGLAS: That is the implication.

MR. SCHMIDT: No. I have lived among poor people a great many years. I have a farm in a very poor section of West Virginia, and I have studied those people very carefully, to see why the poverty persists, and why some break out, but this is not the place, I think, for a sociological discussion.

Unemployment and inflation could both be avoided if a higher minimum wage could be paid by reducing profit margins. Apparently many proponents of a higher minimum feel that this could easily be done. For example, it is sometimes said that most employers are responsible people and do pay decent wages, but that the law is necessary to protect workers employed by irresponsibles who keep in profits what they might be paying in higher wages.

But let us examine the situation as it really is. There is a natural tendency of a free-market economy to keep wages in line with productivity gains and preserve an equality of wage rates with productivity. In most industries, as we have noted, at least 25 to 30 percent of all employers make no profits. But a higher minimum wage may hit these marginal establishments, just as those above the margin.

It is true that these competitive forces do not always operate perfectly. Wage rates may occasionally lag behind general productivity gains temporarily. But the treatment of this situation should aim at the basic causes through providing a favorable climate for the operation of competitive forces, not at mere symptoms.

Somewhat related to the thesis that a minimum wage could be paid by reducing profit margins is the contention that a minimum wage increase stimulates improvements in productivity that would not otherwise take place; that is, it puts a premium on good management.

But this view implies that our economic system, profit and loss system, does not always provide such a premium. We can be sure that in a competitive economy any business which can operate more efficiently will do so. Legislation cannot do this job, but it can make it more attractive to the employer to disemploy workers by substituting capital for labor. . . .

The important point for your purposes here is that the absorption of a minimum wage increase through cutting profits or stimulating productivity is impossible on any significant scale. But wage costs will be affected by any new minimum. How, then, will they be absorbed?

It is apparent that the bulk of the impact of a minimum wage increase must be either (1) unemployment for workers with lowest productivity, or (2) price increases for the economy as a whole. The less price effects, the more serious the problem of unemployment. The less unemployment the more serious the problem of price increases. . . .

These considerations seem to have been evident to the President in his Economic Reports of the last 2 years. A year ago he recommended no increase, since it would have risked unemployment for workers with lowest productivity. This year, since the economy is moving upward, and average hourly earnings are rising anyway, the Economic Report recommends a 20 percent increase in the minimum because it will not have too serious effects.

In other words, these reports seem to imply that an increase is not good unless it is unnecessary; that is unless wage rates are increasing anyway. . . .

It is important to recognize that an increase in the minimum is translated into closely corresponding increases all along the wage scale.

On the day a higher minimum goes into effect, some of the pre-existing wage differentials above that will be reduced or eliminated. But these differentials are highly prized by workers and others. Furthermore, they perform essential economic functions as measures of productivity and incentives to attaining better skills.

In a speech before the Economic Club of New York on March 7, Secretary of Labor James P. Mitchell spoke forcefully of the "urgent need to raise the level of the skills of the American work force." There is no better way to promote the development of skills than by preserving these wage differentials.

Their eradication by minimum wage legislation is as impossible as it is undesirable. They can be counted on to reassert themselves as they have in the past—to induce upward adjustment of wage-rates even at levels not directly affected by the law.

Statistical evidence of this process at work in the past is available. Results of the Minimum Wage Increase of 1950, a study by the divisions of wage and hour and public contracts, shows the effects of pressure to preserve wage differentials in the industries for which the divisions had comprehensive data. These effects are already evident, even though the study was limited to a few months under the new minimum. The findings of this study are presented in the accompanying table:

Percentage Distribution of Wage Rates for Selected Industries, 1949–50 [1]

Hourly wage rates	Fertilizer		Men's dress shirts		Southern sawmills	
	March-April 1949	April-May 1950	August 1949	November 1950	October-December 1949	March 1950
Under 75¢.........	24	5	37	4	69	8
75 to 84.9¢......	19	34	15	27	15	66
85 to 94.9¢......	12	13	14	17	6	15
95 to 104.9¢.....	14	12	11	14	4	4
105 to 114.9¢.....	11	11	8	12	1	2
115 to 124.9¢......	8	8	5	8	1	1
125¢ and over.....	13	17	10	18	3	4

[1] Divisions of Wage and Hour and Public Contracts, Results of the Minimum Wage Increase 1950, pp. 21, 36, and 48.

Special attention should be paid to the summary figures in the next table, computed from the divisions statistics. These are estimates.

Relative Cost of Direct Wage Increases [1]

	Fertilizer	Men's dress shirts	Southern sawmills	Un-weighted average
Annual cost per 100 workers of—				
Raising wages up to 75¢ per hour...........	$3,800	$6,600	$12,200	$7,500
Raising wages above 75¢ per hour..........	3,400	14,600	3,400	7,100

[1] Divisions of Wage and Hour and Public Contracts, Results of the Minimum Wage Increase of 1950, pp. 21, 36, and 48.

LABOR'S REBUTTAL

Statement of Solomon Barkin, Chairman, CIO Fair Labor Standards Committee, concerning Dr. Schmidt's testimony, pp. 752–754

We have read Dr. Emerson P. Schmidt's testimony and find its argument without support in current research and knowledge. We supply the following as an answer to his statement.

Schmidt's major position is that he opposes raising minimum wages because they would be unrealistic and self-defeating. The first major reason is that it would destroy job opportunities; the second, that it would create inflationary effects; the third, that low-wage industries are low-profit industries and are, therefore, unable to pay higher wages; four, that the cost of the minimum should include not only the direct effect but also the increases required above the minimum; five, that if regional wage differentials are artificially reduced before capital has started to move . . . the region will be less attractive to investment; six, that it will burden taxpayers with the cost of administration; seven, that it will burden small employers; eight, that it will force workers into uncovered jobs and depress wages for them.

These conclusions are presented without supporting evidence and all of them fly in the face of current knowledge and past research. We shall examine these positions individually.

1. Dr. Schmidt maintains that no employer can, for long, pay less than any worker is worth. He alleges that the high degree of mobility and growing knowledge of job information through better information and communication assure such dissemination. The facts are very different. Numerous studies have been made in recent years of labor mobility which challenge Dr. Schmidt's conclusions. The fact is that there are many reasons for workers being immobile such as long-service employment; proximity to friends and families; unwillingness to move; dependence upon primary wage earners; desire for security. Professor Reynolds declares that "the value which most workers attach to security of employment can scarcely be overemphasized" (Lloyd G. Reynolds, The Structure of Labor Markets, 1951). Not only are there values in "staying put", but there are risks inherent in job changing. Even when a worker knows of a job for which he may apply, he runs the risk of finding that

the job has been filled; that he does not meet specifications, or that the job does not meet his standards. Also, he takes the risk of unemployment.

a. A summary of studies of "workers' reasons for job choices" makes abundantly clear that considerations outside the scope of neoclassical theory such as personal on-the-job relationships and family problems play an important role. Moreover, labor-market practices and conditions often act as barriers and discouragements to frequent and easy movement of workers in response to differences in conditions of employment. Chief among these are seniority provisions and the dangers of unemployment or of getting a poorer job which is inherent in job changing. (A. Bluestone, Major Studies of Workers' Reasons for Job Choice, Monthly Labor Review, March 1955, p. 301.)

b. Another erroneous conclusion of Dr. Schmidt is that "there is no way in which productivity gains can be kept away from the workers." Such a contention has no foundation even in classical economic theory. Wage levels are not determined by the rate of productivity advance. There are many other factors which control the wage level in an industry. The significant fact is that many industries in which productivity has risen strikingly have not granted comparable wage advances. We have already illustrated this fact in the textile industry. Man-hour productivity, as measured by the rise in yards woven per man-hour, rose from 1950 through 1954 by 23 percent, yet real average hourly earnings for this period have declined. . . .

We have similarly presented . . . an abundant array of information reflecting on the rise in productivity in such low-pay industries as seamless hosiery, canning and preserving, tobacco products, clay construction products, and confectionery. Data on the rise of productivity in the men's dress-shirt industry have also been submitted. The technological changes reported in recent years in the needle trades, canning and preserving, lumber, furniture, fertilizer manufacture, and processed foods are also set forth therein.

Despite impressive lists of advances the workers have not enjoyed improvements in earnings commensurate with the rise in productivity.

c. The third unfounded conclusion is that the businessman "divides his sales dollar" largely as a result of dictates of "market forces." Schmidt therefore concludes that there is no "justification for Government intervention in the relations between employers and workers."

However, we are not concerned merely with the distribution of the sales dollar. We are not averse to an increase in the sales dollar if necessary to pay decent wages. The American people have underwritten parity prices for the farmer to insure him a proper return for his labor and investment. A similar position is equally appropriate for the American worker.

But we must also recognize that there is another aspect to the productivity concept, that is, that improvements in productivity and efficiency frequently are stimulated by increases in wages. The range of opportunity for improvement is illustrated by the many examples . . . [of] "differences in productivity among plants in low-wage industries." Evidence is provided for the men's dress shirt, men's work shirt, processed food, seamless hosiery, women's and men's dress shoes, wood furniture, men's overalls and work jackets, and fertilizer industries. The data are derived from studies by the United States Bureau of Labor Statistics. The span of productivity between the low and the high producer is reassuring of the margin of improvement which is possible.

Adequate margins of profit are available and the absorption of the cost of the wage increase is entirely practical.

d. Unlike Dr. Schmidt, we believe that low wages are a result primarily of lack of bargaining power and disorganized competition within an industry. The basic remedy is the passage of minimum-wage legislation. Voluntary action cannot correct the present condition, since we have learned that the competitive pressure of the low-wage fringe group within an industry is capable of restraining the rest of the industry from raising wages.

e. The argument that inflation would be engendered by an adequate minimum is unjustified. First of all, the groups of industries likely to be affected are narrow. The major industries, particularly the large durable goods industries, will not be included, since their wages are considerably above the proposed minima.

Second, the industries and products likely to be affected include many which have, in recent years, not followed the same price trends as the general level of wholesale prices.

Therefore, price increases which may occur would only bring them more in line with general trends. To the extent that price increases will occur they will represent the removal of a subsidy of the American consumer by the low-wage earner. Moreover, the rises in productivity, both in the past and future, will offset some of the increased cost. . . .

f. The allegation is made that the rise in the minimum will also produce comparable increases above the minimum. Our experience in the past proves otherwise. We have already submitted evidence . . . accumulated by the United States Department of Labor, for the 1950 increase. We have evidence of the effect of the rise under the NIRA, the 75-cent minimum, the subsequent increases. The story runs, almost uniformly, that the industries most affected, which tended to be the unorganized or only partially unionized industries, increased wages primarily or almost exclusively of the employees at the minimum. The result of the adjustment is a clustering of the wages in low-pay plants at the minimum.

The experience during the thirties is most emphatic. The continued rise of minimum wages through the NIRA and the wage-and-hour law had resulted in the telescoping of the wage scale. During the war it was necessary for many companies to reevaluate their job rate differentials in order to attract proper persons for the higher skilled jobs. Job evaluation undertook, during the war and subsequently, to correct the concentration of rates which occurred as a result of management's failure to grant wage increases above the minimum comparable to the increases given to employees at the minimum.

The same condition will occur as a result of the pending legislation. The immediate effect of raising employees to the new minimum will not be to raise others. Only as the bargaining power and the economic circumstances favor, will there be forces generated to favor adjustments in the higher skilled jobs.

But in many of the low-paid industries, this adjustment does not occur since the employer's superior bargaining power tends to repress it. . . .

g. The concern for discouraging investment to the less developed regions is unfounded. First of all, these areas have developed strong economies. Second, many of the higher paid industries have already moved into these regions because of the market which now exists. Considerations other than low wages now govern the location of plants in these areas. . . . Finally, many of the higher paid regions have now become problem areas because of the scope and volume of migration. The significance of such mill closings from 1946–54 were described in the testimony of the Textile Workers Union of America. . . .

j. The workers in the low-wage industries are not likely to be forced out. If the employee is truly aged or handicapped, he can receive a specific exemption. As for the others, they may be expected to adapt themselves quickly and readily to such changes as the employer may introduce to meet the demands of higher wage levels.

THE "RATCHET" EFFECTS OF INCREASING STATUTORY RATES

Supplemental statement, prepared by the Research Department, National Association of Manufacturers, pp. 626–627

. . . If we assume purely for purposes of illustration that a minimum wage increase of 20 percent raises actual wages in the lower levels by an average of 12 percent and eventually all levels above that move up about 10 percent, then the total nonexempt payroll must be reckoned at least 10 percent higher. Thus unit labor costs move up at least 10 percent unless some new cost-saving factor is introduced. This move would wipe out profits in most companies unless prices could be increased accordingly without curtailing sales, production, and jobs. Hence, whether we slash profits or raise prices the results are undesirable and damaging to the economy. Moreover, it is important to recognize that as wage movements spread throughout the economy not only are direct wage costs involved but also the wages included in the costs of materials, parts, supplies, and services are affected. In the final analysis, labor costs add up to a very high proportion of total manufacturing costs and prices. Consequently, the impact of a rising basic wage structure is far greater on total costs and on prices than any available statistical data can reveal. Finally, if the rise in the wage structure is artificially induced and arbitrarily imposed and not based upon production and service, then we are merely indulging in a method of controlled inflation—a deliberate wage-price spiral which can only harm the economy and the people.

Statement of Peter T. Beardsley, Director, Law Department, American Trucking Associations, Inc., p. 658

If wages of relatively low-rated office employees, earning perhaps 85 cents an hour, were to be increased to $1.25 as a result of amendment of the wage-hour law, it necessarily follows that the higher-rated office employees would have to be given substantially the same increase to maintain recognized differentials in pay based on skill and experience. In addition, at the first opportunity after the $1.25 minimum wage became effective, employers covered by union contracts for other employees could expect a demand for new pay scales which would reinstate the differentials presently effective. There is customarily a definite wage relationship among all employees in the same company. Clerical workers, supervisory personnel and even top management are affected by a wage increase in the lowest rates. Differentials have to be maintained if an employer is to have a sound wage policy. The wartime wage stabilization policy recognized this customary interrelationship of wages and salaries by permitting the so-called "tandem" increases, whereby wage raises given initially to one group could be given to other groups which had customarily been granted the same increases as given the lead group.

HIGHER WAGES DO NOT NECESSARILY MEAN HIGHER COSTS

Statement of George Meany, President, American Federation of Labor, pp. 104–106

Underpayment of wages is an unfair competitive method. An employer should not profit because he can get away with substandard wages. A substantially higher minimum wage would help prevent this. It would also protect those companies which are willing to pay a decent minimum wage but do not do so for fear of being undercut by their competitors. . . .

Some have said that the minimum we are recommending would raise difficult problems for some industries with a significant proportion of low-paid workers. But past experience indicates that, if actually faced with the choice of meeting a decent minimum wage or going out of business, all but the most marginal firms will adjust to the higher minimum and continue to operate profitably. . . .

The costs of a substantially higher minimum wage can and will be met largely through increases in efficiency of management, labor, plant, and equipment. Low-wage companies will be forced to revise their managerial methods and to introduce greater efficiencies in their operations. The higher wages in themselves will help increase productivity, for they will improve morale, health, and efficiency.

It is difficult for many people to recognize or admit that higher wages do not automatically mean higher costs or prices. This is a fundamental fact of our economic system. The American experience is that higher wages stimulate increased productivity and efficiency. Competent management in this country consistently and successfully develops new methods and equipment to permit industry to function profitably with higher wage levels.

This is what distinguishes our industrial system. This Nation has refused to accept a static view. It has refused to be obsessed by the notion that wages could not be increased. It has responded to the challenge by developing increased efficiency to gain lower unit labor costs despite higher wages. It has therefore enjoyed greatly enriched living standards.

Statement of Walter P. Reuther, President, Congress of Industrial Organizations, pp. 325–326

SENATOR DOUGLAS: Mr. Reuther, may I ask a question: The advanced technology tends to be in the plants and industries which pay high wages. The plants which pay low wages tend to have antiquated machinery, in many cases, and poor management, and, in general, are at a lower level of efficiency; isn't that true?

MR. REUTHER: No, I don't think that is generally true. First of all high wages provide a tremendous constructive and dynamic force that stimulates technological progress. When the General Motors Corp. decides to spend a billion dollars to automate their plants, they are not only motivated by the desire to create higher technology, they are trying to displace high labor costs. That is the reason for the greater pressure toward technological progress. That is why in a contract where they pay coolie wages there is no real economic incentive for technical progress because human power is cheaper than machine power. I don't think you can make it a general statement that the low wage industries are the industries in which you cannot get greater technical progress. I think that greater technical progress is possible, and if you increase the wage levels of those industries you will find that that will provide a powerful economic incentive for management. I have tremendous faith in the ingenuity of American management within the framework of our free enterprise system.

You give them the economic incentives, and it is amazing what they will be able to do in the way of finding means of increasing labor productivity by better machinery and by reducing unit costs of production.

THE TEXTILE INDUSTRY CAN AFFORD HIGHER WAGES

Statement of Solomon Barkin, Director of Research, Textile Workers of America, pp. 487–488, 490–491

Unlike millions of workers in the other major industries, the textile workers have not shared in the great gains in our economy's productivity during the past 5 years. The wage gain negotiated by the union in the woolen and worsted and the New England cotton-synthetic branches of the industry in 1951 were given up because of the competitive pressure of unorganized low-wage mills. As a result, the employees have not received any improvement in their real wage standards since 1950.

Meanwhile, the productivity of the economy has made great strides. The joint committee on the economic report estimates that the output per man-hour rose in our private economy by some 15 percent from 1949 to 1953 (from $2.302 in 1949 to $2.641 in 1953, on a 1953 dollar basis). This represents an annual average rate of increase in productivity of 3¾ percent. This rate has undoubtedly been maintained since 1953, so that the total rise from 1949 through the first quarter of 1955 amounts to at least 20 percent.

The rate of increasing productivity in the textile industry has exceeded that of American industry as a whole in recent years. Most of the industry's vast expenditures on new plants and equipment has gone for improved machinery and technology. There has been a revolution in the types of machines on the floors of American industry. It is estimated that over 70 percent of the active machines are of postwar construction.

New equipment in all cases is faster and requires less manpower. Processes are telescoped so that entire operations have been eliminated. The machines have been made more automatic and packages have been made larger so that they run longer with fewer people to tend them. The surrounding working conditions have been improved so that yarn breaks occur less frequently. Automatic controls are being substituted for human inspection and supervision.

But these expenditures are only part of the reason for rising productivity. The textile industry is taking over the management technology of other industries. Centralized controls are being instituted over scheduling and production and systematic quality controls are being introduced. Plant layouts are being revamped for straight-line production. Materials handling is being reduced to a minimum, and where actually necessary, mechanical means are being substituted for labor. Technically trained supervisors and time study engineers are combining to tighten labor standards.

New fibres are challenging the older ones and in each instance the transfer of production is to plants with lower labor content per yard of output. This is indicated by the fact that whereas a worsted mill might require one-third of a manhour per yard of serge, a cotton mill would require less than one-tenth of a manhour per yard of cloth.

Moreover, we are on the threshold of further innovations. An industry accustomed to slow change is now being swamped by an avalanche of innovations originating both at home and abroad. The developments in other industries are truly revolutionizing it. What automation pretends to do for other industries, the current technical developments are already effecting in this industry.

The nature of the changes is suggested by the following rough calculation. Textile employment in January 1955 stood at 987,200 workers, which was 19 percent below the average employment level of 1947–49. According to the Federal Reserve Board, textile production for the month was actually 3 percent above the base period of 1947–49.

Another approximation is available from a comparison of employment trends and total textile woven yardage in the cotton, wool, silk, and synthetic fabric industry.

Another index of rising productivity is supplied in the annual report of a southern cotton textile mill, Graniteville Mills of South Carolina. It shows that for the 10-year period, from 1945 through 1954, it spent $18,028,000 on plant additions and replacements and the pounds of cloth produced per 1,000 manhours rose from 5,838 to 8,981, or 54 percent. In the last year alone, the pounds produced per 1,000 manhours rose by 10.84 percent, which is the largest productivity rise scored in any 1 year.

A comparison of the range of productivity at mills producing print cloth

	Production workers [1]		Production (millions of linear yards)				Yards per man-hour
	Employ-ment	Manhours	Total	Cotton	Silk and synthetic	Woolen and worsted	
	Thousands	Millions					
1947.....	768.7	1,589	12,371	9,817	2,039	515.8	7.8
1948.....	784.3	1,603	12,405	9,640	2,267	498	7.7
1949.....	680.9	1,322	10,923	8,406	2,086	414	8.3
1950.....	718.5	1,490	13,091	10,013	2,578	471	8.8
1951.....	707.9	1,438	12,887	10,136	2,350	375	9.0
1952.....	654.3	1,320	12,160	9,514	2,294	351	9.0
1953.....	645.1	1,313	12,946	10,203	2,410	338	9.9
1954.....	575.6	1,140	12,283	9,763	2,238	281	10.8

[1] Covers scouring and combing plants, yarn and thread mills and broad-woven fabric mills.

reflects on the growth in productivity. A most modern mill built in Greenwood, S. C. apparently requires 143 manhours per thousand pounds. A survey of five average mills by the United States Bureau of Labor Statistics shows that they require from 139 to 203 manhours per thousand pounds of print cloth. During a recent survey of another print cloth mill now operating in North Carolina, we found that it required 221 manhours per thousand pounds, a range of 70 percent between the lowest and highest producer. These differences indicate the potentials for higher productivity effected with the modernization of equipment, plant, and improved management.

The American Textile Machinery Association reports that a modernization program in a mill of 30,336 spindles would effect an increase in output per manhour from 4.9396 pounds to 9 pounds, or 82 percent. In another mill of 34,704 spindles, a modernization program of a modest type would increase its output from 4.720 pounds per manhour to 7.6316 pounds, or 62 percent. The same organization reports that the modernization of a mill in the production of combed broadcloth would effect a reduction in manhour per shift from 70 to 43 employees, or 63 percent.

The Whitin Machine Works, Inc., reports that the modernization of the production of a 20,000-spindle combed cotton knitting yarn mill would reduce costs by 36 percent, from 15.24 cents to 9.72 cents per pound. Most of the reduction would be effected through lower labor cost. This item would be cut from 14.3 cents to 6.2 cents per pound, or by 57 percent. The labor schedule, which required 217 employees before modernization, would be reduced to 124 persons, or by 43 percent. This company indicates that a reduction of 6.2 cents in labor cost and 0.08 cent in power will be offset by an increase of 0.2 cent in taxes and insurance and 0.6 cent in depreciation charges, so that the reduction in labor costs would have also to carry these larger tax and depreciation charges.

On the whole, a study of the information available to us from manufacturers shows that the rise in manhour productivity in the post-war years has been at the rate of at least 5 percent per annum. This is far in excess of the national average and the claims which are being made as to the likely effects of automation on the entire economy.

In the absence of wage increases by employers, enactment of a higher Federal minimum represents the only means available to textile workers for sharing in the great gains from increasing productivity in the industry and the economy.

In spite of the highly productive character of the textile industry and the big-business qualities of its ownership and operation, textile wages are near the bottom of the nation's manufacturing wage structure. Of the 33 industry groups covered by the act for which the Bureau of Labor Statistics reports average hourly earnings, only one (tobacco manufactures) had a lower straight-time average in January 1955 than textiles. The $1.34 average for textiles was far below the other major industries, with only two others within striking distance: apparel, $1.34, and leather and leather products, $1.36. The others were all over $1.50, with the average for manufacturing at $1.78. . . .

Of the 1,025,000 textile workers covered by the wage and hour provisions of the act as of April 1954, at most some 67,000 or 6.5 percent, were receiving less than $0.90 per hour. Wage increases necessary to bring these workers up to a minimum of $0.90 would amount to a maximum of $12 million a year, or 4/10 of 1 percent of the industry's covered payroll. Obviously this infinitesimal adjustment can be absorbed without difficulty.

A $1 minimum would require direct increases to a maximum of 150,000 covered textile workers, 14.6 percent of the total, and would increase covered payrolls by some $34 million a year, or 1.2 percent of the total. Inasmuch as payrolls represent approximately 25 percent of the textile sales dollar, the cost of a $1 minimum to the industry would be limited to 0.3 percent of its sales income (one-quarter of the percentage impact on payroll costs). Such a modest increase is clearly within the industry's capacity.

A $1.10 minimum would result in increases to a maximum of 310,000 workers in the industry, 30.2 percent of the total. The increase in annual payroll cost would amount to $80 million, or 2.9 percent of the total. Applying this increase to total sales income (with payrolls comprising 25 percent of sales) yields a total cost of the $1.10 minimum of 0.7 percent of sales, a cost well within the industry's ability to absorb without difficulty.

A $1.25 minimum would necessitate increases to a maximum of 512,000 covered textile workers, 49.9 percent of the total. Payrolls would increase by $203 million a year, or 7.4 percent of the total covered payroll. This represents an increase of 1.8 percent of sales income, surely not an insurmountable obstacle to the achievement of a decent wage standard for this industry. . . .

The effects of higher minima upon the textile industry in its two major regions . . . would be as follows:

In the Northeast, 16,000 workers, or 4.7 percent, would receive increases to the 90-cent minimum, raising covered payrolls by $2.8 million a year, or 0.3 percent. Adoption of a $1 minimum would result in increases to 30,000 workers, or 8.9 percent, amounting to $7.4 million a year, or 0.7 percent of covered payrolls. The $1.10 minimum would require increases to 58,000 workers, or 16.9 percent at a cost of $16.2 million annually, or 1.6 percent of payrolls. Enactment of the $1.25 minimum would yield wage increases to 113,000 northern textile workers, 33.1 percent of the total, and payrolls would increase by $41.6 million a year, or 4 percent.

In the South, the 42,000 workers who would receive increases under the 90-cent minimum comprise 7.8 percent of covered employment; payrolls would rise by $7.6 million, or 0.6 percent. The $1 minimum would require increases to 100,000 workers, or 18.6 percent, and payrolls would be advanced by $21.8 million, or 1.6 percent. The direct effects of a $1.10 minimum would be felt by 215,000 southern employees, 39.8 percent of the total, and payrolls would rise by $53.2 million, or 3.9 percent. Adoption of the $1.25 minimum would result in wage increases to 335,000 workers, 62.2 percent of the southern total, and payrolls would be augmented by $135.6 million, or 10.1 percent.

The effects of these adjustments on the industry's capacity to operate would be minimal as payroll costs represent only 25 percent of the total sales dollar. Thus the maximum effect of the $1.25 minimum on the industry in the Northeast would be to raise costs by 1 percent of sales, and, in the South, by 2.5 percent. The industry is quite capable of absorbing such increases in cost out of existing profit margin. Moreover, the increase in sales which would follow from the rise in buying power generated by an adequate minimum wage would further bolster the industry's capacity to adjust to the new minimum. . . .

The textile industry has not shared in the general prosperity of the American economy in recent years. Since the boom in demand for textiles generated by the Korean war came to an end early in 1951, the industry has experienced a decided slump in sales. The dollar volume of textile corporations fell from $14.7 billion in 1951 to $14.1 billion in 1952, $13 billion in 1953, and $11.5 billion in 1954. The Federal Reserve Board index of production for the textile mill products industry declined from an average of 107 in 1951 (1947–49 = 100) to 103 in 1952, rose to 104 in 1953, and declined to 95 in 1954. These declines occurred in the face of the growth in population, the boom in construction of new homes, and the generally high activity prevailing in the economy. They stem basically from the inadequacy of consumer incomes, particularly among the lower-income groups, to support a standard of living in which automobiles, television, and other hard goods have virtually become necessities, and at the same time to maintain decent standards of apparel.

The squeeze between rising fixed commitments to pay off installment and mortgage debt and the limited income of workers' families has resulted in a sharp decline in the proportion of the consumer's dollar going for clothing. From 9.5 percent in 1945, the proportion of consumer expenditures accounted for [by] apparel has declined steadily, reaching a low of 6.9 percent in 1954.

Consumer buying power, particularly of the lower-income families who have had to sacrifice their apparel standards to maintain the types of expenditures which have prior claims on limited income, is the key to the recovery of the textile industry. The average family with $1,500 a year income (which corresponds to an hourly rate of $0.75) spends $151 a year for clothing. An increase in income to $1,800 a year (equal to $0.90 an hour) would raise clothing expenditures to $183, or by 21 percent. Adoption of a $1 minimum would result in an increase in clothing expenditures for such a family to $205 a year, a rise of 36 percent. A minimum of $1.10 would yield annual clothing expenditures for this family of $227, an increase of 50 percent over the present level. Enactment of the $1.25 minimum would enable the typical family at this level to raise clothing expenditures to $260 a year, or 72 percent higher than at present.

The direct effects of an increase in the minimum wage would be to add the following amounts to the annual expenditures of affected families for clothing:

	Million
$0.90 minimum	$22
$1.00 minimum	54
$1.10 minimum	105
$1.25 minimum	225

The textile industry would also benefit from the many millions of dollars in increased expenditures for housefurnishings, automobile interiors and seat coverings, belting and other products made from textiles, which would flow directly from the adoption of a higher minimum wage. In addition, the indirect multiplier effects of the higher minimum would raise consumer expenditures for apparel and other textile products by several hundreds of millions of dollars a year. Thus, the adoption of an adequate minimum wage would offer a substantial stimulus to lagging textile sales and help appreciably in lifting the industry from its current slump.

INCREASING PRODUCTIVITY IS EXPENSIVE

Statement of Thomas O. Moore, Chairman, Industrial Relations Committee, National Association of Manufacturers, pp. 604–607

MR. MOORE: It is likely that an increase in the wage costs of some industries without a corresponding increase in productivity will necessitate some substantial work force reductions. The extent to which this might take place cannot be measured in advance, but it is fair to assume that a substantial minimum wage increase would bring about serious pressures in this direction and increase the risk of hurting the very people sought to be helped. Consideration must also be given to the danger that increases in production costs will create pressures for higher prices in goods and services. Such a development would nullify any gains which might be achieved for low-income workers by the increase in their minimum wage.

Senator, I would like to tell you this, that I know of my own experience, because you, as I, have a very high regard for the feelings of people, and in my home State I know of one company who had a stemming operation, and it was a question of whether they would keep several hundred people in that stemming operation or buy machinery which would do it automatically, and from a cost standpoint, which is what the stockholders look at, it was practically even in cost, so they, of course, kept the people to keep them in employment, but when the minimum wage was raised from 40 cents an hour to 75 cents an hour, then from a cost standpoint it became unfeasible, and they could not justify it to their stockholders, so they had to get automatic machinery to do that job. . . .

SENATOR DOUGLAS: Mr. Moore, we have had testimony that there has been an appreciable increase in productivity per man-hour in recent years, and that this increase has been especially marked in the case of the textile industry.

The January 1955 Economic Report of the President had charts which indicated that the average output per man-hour in manufacturing, and mining had risen by about 20 percent in the last 5 years, or an average increase of around 4 percent a year. . . .

We had figures submitted to us in which it was claimed that the increase in output per man-hour in the textile industry had been above this rate, that the number of spindles which workers were required to tend had increased; whether there was testimony that the speed per spindle had been raised, I cannot quite remember. But the argument was made that there had been an increase in output per man-hour in textiles of something over 5 percent a year for the last 4 or 5 years.

Do you have any comments to make on that?

MR. MOORE: Yes. I will thoroughly agree with you that there has been an increase in productivity. I think that figure is too high, but from the mills that I know of, and I visit a great many of them from time to time in my job, that has come about through an increase in the efficiency of the machinery more than an increase in worker efficiency.

For example, my company is comparatively small, as companies go, but we have spent a number of million dollars improving our textile machinery in the last 5 or 6 years, and practically all of the increases we have gotten in job efficiency have been through changes and modernization of machinery, and they are the mills that are going to suffer from an increase in the minimum, those little mills who have been running close to shore, sometimes in the red and sometimes a little in the black, who haven't had money enough to increase the efficiency of their machinery and by and large the greater companies with money to improve this machinery will not suffer from any increase, but these marginal mills located in smaller communities, and in most cases the lifeblood of that community will suffer.

SENATOR DOUGLAS: Of course, to the degree that there is an increase in output per man-hour, this helps to balance and in some cases more than offsets the increase in earnings per hour, because the test, I suppose, is the average labor cost per unit of output rather than the cost per man-hour.

MR. MOORE: The test in costing your product, sir, is the unit cost of labor in that product, that is right; but when you have to charge in what we call overhead or burden, the depreciation on the increased cost of this machinery which has become very expensive—for example, 30 years ago a cotton card would cost an average of $300 or $400. Now, it is between $3,000 and $4,000.

SENATOR DOUGLAS: In other words, the increased cost of machinery or capital per unit of output, has to be offset against the decrease in labor cost per unit?

MR. MOORE: Yes, and this machinery is very expensive.

AN INCREASE IN THE MINIMUM WILL HARM INDUSTRY

Statement of Alvin A. Voges, Secretary-Manager, American Veneer Package Association, Orlando, Fla., pp. 671–673

. . . we have tried to vividly portray the economic position of our industry today and as it would be if legislation is enacted to increase the present minimum hourly wage.

We have shown the mortality of the industry, 31.16 percent, at or about the time the minimum hourly wage was increased to 75 cents. We predict that if legislation is enacted to increase the minimum hourly wage to 90 cents, or higher, then in the succeeding 2-year period a similar percentage of our industry's establishments will discontinue operations.

This does not mean that our industry is opposed to paying higher wages, it simply means unless we increase our selling prices we cannot, as the exhibits show, increase the percentage of production labor cost to the value of the product, the 1952 percentage being 43.08 percent.

We have stated the industry would like to increase its selling prices but dares not, and that today's selling prices are at or below 1951 prices.

We have shown that our industry is rural in nature and able to employ unskilled labor and for these reasons are not comparable to low pay industries in metropolitan areas where the cost of living is considerably greater.

We have shown that our industry is composed of small business establishments—1952 average production employees per facility, 62.3—and Government has been stressing the need of helping small business. As a generalization, small business is less able to pay handsome wages than are the industrial giants. . . .

It is our considered opinion this industry cannot pay an increase in the minimum hourly wage rate without an increase in our selling prices.

If an increase in minimum wage is legislated it would be necessary to make a minimum increase in price in our products of 9 percent if minimum 90 cents and 14 percent if minimum $1. . . .

A farmer would then have to pay about 3 cents more for each bushel basket if minimum 90 cents and about 5 cents more if minimum $1.

All of the foregoing is calculated without giving acknowledgment to any increases in costs except the cost of our production labor. We think it obvious that all our costs will advance and the increase in selling prices would necessarily need to advance with them.

Sincerely believing we cannot successfully increase our prices, and sincerely believing it is not possible for us to pay the added expense if the minimum wage is increased, we are in a dilemma and see but one hope.

We previously evidenced our close association to agriculture and to the forest. We stated over 90 percent of our product is used to convey farm produce to market. We remarked that our industry is highly essential to the Nation in times of emergency and that it is necessary we be kept in productive position.

Therefore, if any of these bills to amend the Fair Labor Standards Act now before you for consideration do, in the final analysis, meet with your approval, we ask that the bill or bills approved be amended to exclude our industry from compliance.

Further, we asked that the committee vote "no" on a proposal for an increase in minimum hourly wage legislation at this time.

SENATOR MCNAMARA: Thanks for your fine presentation. I am sure it will be helpful to the committee.

Now, you mentioned in several places that you cannot successfully increase your price. Is that because of the competition of other materials in the packing business?

MR. VOGES: Paper relatively has such a low labor production cost in comparison with our industry, and paper mills generally are highly mechanized, so that they almost might be considered push-button factories that they are highly competitive with us and should we go above them our market would be lost.

SENATOR MCNAMARA: Of course, under the pending legislation the minimum wage would apply to them, but the point you make is that they are largely mechanized and you are not.

MR. VOGES: And such a small part of their increase would be labor that it wouldn't necessarily affect their selling price to any great extent.

AN INCREASE IN THE MINIMUM WILL HARM LABOR

Statement of Mose Gordon, Mose Gordon Lumber Co., Commerce, Ga., pp. 709–710

While a few members of our industry are well-financed and own enough land to assure them of a perpetual supply of timber, I want to emphasize again that the approximately twenty-one or twenty-two thousand operations which produce about 70 percent of the total production in the South are for the most part marginal operations, working on a shoe string. Particularly, the approximately 20,000 or more small portable mills, employing from 6 to 12 men each, are operated by men who in many cases perform some of the labor themselves. These men have the responsibility of paying their workers every Saturday, meeting the bills for supplies, equipment, repairs, fuel, etc., having what is left for themselves, and in many cases this is no more than some of their own workers receive.

It is my opinion that many Members of the Congress and leaders in our Government think only of the position of the few larger and more efficient manufacturers when considering legislation governing wages, hours, and other controls over the southern lumber industry. There is a natural reason for this; the larger operators are more conspicuous and are better known.

You seldom receive a letter from a constituent who is a peckerwood saw-mill-man primarily because usually he has no office, no typewriter, no clerical help, and the majority of them feel that they cannot express themselves well enough in a letter to describe their position to their Congressman and Senators.

If a minimum wage is fixed at a rate higher than the market would stand today, these marginal peckerwood operators will be hurt and many will simply have to shut down. There is no such thing as their operating at a loss, as they have no capital reserve.

Due to the high price of stumpage, labor, and other cost factors in the face of intense competition from other species of lumber and lumber substitutes, we have decreased our production roughly 50 percent of what it was during the 1940's.

We experienced an operating loss of 78 cents per thousand feet during 1954. Our labor cost under a 90-cent minimum wage would have resulted in a loss of $4.81 per thousand; and a $1 minimum wage would have produced a further operating deficit of $1.51 per thousand, or a loss during 1954 of $7.10 per thousand feet.

Because of competitive conditions and market potential existing during 1954, it would not have been possible to pass this increased cost on to the customer, because actual operating cost was not recovered during 1954.

Our company has invested about all we can in machinery and equipment, and it is doubtful that further cash outlay for increased mechanization would enable us to operate with some margin of profit under an increase in the statutory minimum wage. If such is feasible, it would involve dispensing with sufficient number of workers to justify this added expense. Since there is no other industry in the locality which might absorb these workers, they would be placed on the unemployment rolls and ultimately be obliged to seek work in an already overcrowded agricultural labor market.

It is not the intent of my company to continue operations for the purpose of liquidating its assets. Unless some general economic upheaval should occur, bringing on unprecedented inflation, we cannot foresee the possibility of continuing operations under a higher legislated wage. It is our policy, and we consider it good business, to pay the highest possible wages, but elementary economics dictates that these wages must be recovered in the sale of our products; and that does not seem possible at this time.

We have a deep sense of financial and moral responsibility to these heads of 367 families, all of whom we know personally. These people are mostly unskilled laborers. And it would be most difficult for them to secure adequate employment due to the economic conditions that now exist in our locality and would, therefore, work a much greater hardship on the greater percent of our employees than it would on us. As the farming industry is already overcrowded with mechanical devices to replace labor, and, too, the cotton acreage has been reduced to such a small amount that it would be impossible for the farming interest to absorb any overflow from another industry, we earnestly request that you give due and careful consideration to the welfare and continued betterment of these heads of families who are now happy and contented in the foothills of the Blue Ridge Mountains of north Georgia. Any increase in the minimum wage at this time, from our standpoint, will certainly work a hardship on the worker and not improve his lot.

INEFFICIENT MANAGEMENT IS THE CAUSE

Statement of A. F. Hartung, President, International Woodworkers of America, p. 1389

Operators cannot forever milk the benefits dry and leave nothing for the operation, the resource, or the worker, and this is exactly what has happened in the industry in the South for far too many years.

Most of the sawmills that would be affected by a $1.25 minimum are those which have continued to operate with obsolete equipment, by outmoded methods and in dilapidated buildings of nothing more than frame structure.

I might state that I have traveled extensively in the South. I have been in a lot of these mills that I am talking about, and the mills that are holding the wage level down are old-fashioned, and there has been no improvement made in them for a period of years.

They have been satisfied to make the profit that they are making and taking it out of the hides of the people who work for them.

SENATOR DOUGLAS: The lumber operators who appeared here referred to these mills as so-called peckerwood mills, the small mill which is moved from place to place, and which has only a few workers.

MR. HARTUNG: They use that expression, Senator. However, that is what we call movable mills, and they operate in other parts of the country very successfully and do pay a fair and reasonable rate. In such areas as in Colorado, Wyoming, Montana, you find many of those small portable mill operations, and my testimony will show later on that they do pay a much higher average than what we are asking for in the minimum rate.

Unlike the more progressive operators, who are a credit to the industry and their communities, they have not put any money back into their plants for improvement of equipment, or to provide safer or better working environment. Because of this, their production is low and costly.

MINIMUM WAGE AND LIVING COSTS

Statement of Thomas O. Moore, Chairman, Industrial Relations Committee, National Association of Manufacturers, pp. 611–613

SENATOR DOUGLAS: Mr. Moore, you now touch on an important point. It is frequently said in justification of the generally lower wage scale in the South that this is excusable on the ground that living costs are lower in the South. Do you think that is true?

MR. MOORE: Sir, I think that is too general to answer with a "yes" or "no," if I could be permitted to go further.

I would like to also say, now, that you have brought it up, Senator, that the lowest wages in our industry are not paid in the South. They are paid in certain other sections of the country. Now, we won't go into that. And statistics show that. But I think certainly in any rural community a man can live more cheaply than in a metropolitan community, and I would say generally, sir—of course there could be exceptions—that the cost of living in the South is lower than in other sections of the country because of climatic conditions, because our communities are usually rural rather than metropolitan, although we do have some fairly good-sized cities, and in those cities I couldn't say as to that.

SENATOR DOUGLAS: Of course, it is true that the fuel bill is lower in the South.

MR. MOORE: Yes, sir; and the clothing cost is lower because they don't have to wear as warm clothing, and other costs are lower; the type of construction of the houses, sir, is very different. We don't have to have storm windows, or so much insulation, or all of that down there.

SENATOR DOUGLAS: Of course, as you are aware, the Bureau of Labor Statistics takes an identical budget and prices this budget in different cities of the country so that you get the cost of an identical standard of living in various cities. I have a table before me which is drawn from the Bureau of Labor Statistic's City Worker's Family Budget and which shows the cost in New Orleans to be $3,812 for a family of four; in Jacksonville, Fla., $4,202; in Atlanta, Ga., $4,315. I am interested to notice that the cost in my city of Chicago, which has normally been regarded as a high-cost city, is $4,185 or less than the cost in Atlanta and slightly less than the cost in Jacksonville, Fla., though it is above the cost of New Orleans. The cost in Mobile, Ala., is $3,969, and in Richmond, Va., it is $4,338.

It is my impression that the regional differences in the cost of living are much, much less than commonly claimed, between cities of appreciable size, and as regards the difference between large and small cities I remember an investigation in Massachusetts which indicated that food costs in the smaller cities in Massachusetts were actually higher than in Boston because the food had to be shipped into Boston and shipped back from wholesale places to the smaller cities.

Now, in the smaller cities where you have garden plots that, of course, does decrease costs. I think that is now more widespread in the South than it was 40 years ago in the mill villages.

But it would seem to me that the so-called lower cost of living in the South was in large part not so much the lower cost of an identical standard of living, but the cost of a lowered standard of living.

MR. MOORE: Sir, with that I wouldn't agree. I could take you to certain sections in the North, or in the South, where the standard of living is not what you or I would like to see it, but I would say generally that the production worker in the South, everything considered, lives better than the production worker in the North that is crowded into these—I wouldn't call them tenements, I would say lower-cost apartments.

SENATOR DOUGLAS: Well, it is perfectly true the conditions in Lowell and Lawrence, New Bedford, Fall River, Paterson, Passaic, and some of the textile centers of the North, have been very bad. There is no doubt about that, and we are not proud of those conditions at all. That is perfectly true.

MR. MOORE: All I know, Senator is my own observation of that, and I don't know what factors were considered in that, but I would like to ask that man if he went to Saxapahaw, N.C., or Greenville, Miss., or places of that size, he would find a different situation. There has grown up in the South an industrial community combined with a rural community. We have the curb markets where vegetables and meat and good country hams can be bought much more cheaply than they can in those few areas you named, and all of those have a decided effect on the cost of living.

PROBLEMS OF SMALL BUSINESS MANAGEMENT

Statement of Gerald Bradford, Bradford Lumber Co., Grove Hill, Ala., pp. 703–705

I run a sawmill . . . I speak at the invitation of the Southern Pine Industry Committee, but I do not speak for them. I speak for myself, and I want to give you some facts with respect to my own company, and I speak for many others who actually fall into the same category in southern pine that I fall into myself.

I would like to tell you also, gentlemen, that if I were appearing here for labor in my section as their representative that I would not change a word that I am going to say to you this morning, because I believe very definitely that my appeal to you is as much or more—frankly, it could be of more— value to them, provided I made any impression on you. It could be of more value to them than it will be to me.

There is considerable question in my mind that even if you don't enact an increase and you let it stay where it is today—there is considerable question in my mind, gentlemen, that I will continue to exist as a small-mill operator.

I want to give you an example to prove that. Just last year, toward the end of the summer, I went in 1 day and my bookkeeper told me that we were out of money. Well, I thought I had a little credit down at the bank in Mobile. In fact, I was so confident of it I didn't even go down there to borrow the money. I just picked up the telephone and called up the bank and told them I needed some money. They just told me right back, and very quickly, that I didn't have any further credit down there. Well, I had a payroll coming up. It costs about, I would say, $6,500 to $8,500 a week in hard cash that I have to raise from somewhere every week to run this business. Well, naturally, that disturbed me. The only thing that I could do was shut my sawmill down. That is what I did. I shut it down, and I kept it down for 60 days through the winter months, through the bad operating period. Then this spring, when the sun started to shine again, we went down to—well, I paid all that I could, you understand, by shipping this inventory but I didn't do such a good job, and I didn't know just how I was going to come out—so I went down to Mobile and asked them if they would give me a stake and let me take a crack at it again. They extended me an additional credit of $29,000, which is a lot of money to me, but it doesn't last very long, based on the figures that I gave you a few minutes ago—that is, if you have a wet period, and you don't ship very much lumber.

We don't have a kiln. We put our lumber on the yard to air-dry it. If we have 2 weeks of rain, we might be in the hole $16,000. We don't have that much money in the bank.

I understand when I left down there that we were just about out of money again, and that we needed to borrow another $10,000. Now if we actually have to have it, I couldn't tell you exactly where it would come from, but I tell you this: That I will take a crack at getting it because we need to stay in business.

In the little town that I live in this is the only industry that we have. Most of the people that work there live in that area. A lot of them are farmers, and run a considerable farm in addition to working at the sawmill.

In giving consideration to the small operator in my class, and other small-business men, I would have to say, if there is a forgotten man in America— and I don't like the term very much, and I don't think there is one—I believe it would be the small-business man. I think that we are somewhat abused and browbeaten. We are ridiculed for paying low wages. You have heard the ridicule yourself right here. We are ridiculed for that, and we are hounded by Federal and State investigators. I have been, myself. Even though you make every effort that is within your power to follow the various Government regulations, it is a difficult proposition to do.

We are required to make Federal tax deductions from every employee we have. We have to fill out the social security reports, we make social security contributions ourselves, we make out personal income tax reports, we make severance tax reports, we make out State income tax reports, and we make a lot of others, gentlemen, that I couldn't even remember them all. Then when we get through with all of that, with our office force, and we are little business, then we give the rest of the time to attending to our own business.

I will tell you, these and other requirements that come down from legislation in Government are a terrible burden on a small-business man. There isn't anything we can do about it. We can't avoid them. . . .

To run a small business today, gentlemen, first you need to be a lawyer. . . .

I need to be a certified public accountant because these records have to be right or I might get in trouble with the income-tax department; I need to be a financier as a small business man so I can get the money to run my business on.

Senator, I need to be a sort of a business executive, too, and I need to be a personnel director, so that I could give the proper attention to my employees.

I am telling that to show you that big business can have an expert in every one of these lines. They can do these things. The things that you impose on us do not have the impact on big business they do on us, and, gentlemen, I think frankly we are destroying small business. Maybe that is good procedure. Maybe it is progress. Maybe it is what we ought to have, but that has been the basis of our economy, and we actually probably give employment to more people in the United States than does big business.

I am not against big business. I couldn't make automobiles and steel. I know that. I am for them. But I don't think that we ought to evolve our system in this country into one of big business alone. I think we ought to allow the small business to run also.

I just think this is true, that the return to a small business man today is not worth the effort, or the risk involved.

MINIMUM WAGES AS A DEFENSE AGAINST UNFAIR COMPETITION

Statement of David Dubinsky, President, International Ladies' Garment Workers' Union, pp. 224–225

An employer who pays a fair wage to his employees has little defense against unfair compensation grounded on the payment of substandard rates. As aptly stated some time ago by the president of Johnson & Johnson, Gen. Robert Wood Johnson: "There can be only one good reason for low wages, and that is the competitor who pays them." The existence of substandard conditions is a constant threat to the welfare of workers employed in competing establishments and to the companies themselves.

Take the case of a firm which manufactured knit underwear in Utica, N.Y., since 1874. During the war years it employed as many as 1,700 workers and as late as 1951 as many as 1,100. This was a fair employer, enjoying excellent relations with his workers and the union and thoroughly conscious of his responsibility to the community where the plant operated for so many years. Yet, this firm, which paid its workers at an average of $1.56 an hour, found that it was increasingly threatened by competition from low-wage areas. The firm's employment declined and it was losing business. In a desperate effort to balance out its costs, the firm decided to open a branch plant in a low-wage area. In this way it hoped to maintain its operations in Utica. Yet, even this measure proved futile in meeting the pressure of the rising unfair competition. Utica employment had to be reduced even further and by the end of 1953 the plant had to be shut down. Most of the employees, many with 30 years' standing, are jobless today, without prospect of other employment because the operations of other firms in Utica were similarly undermined by low-wage competition.

Not every employer, however, shows so much civic pride. Many others deliberately relocate their plants whenever they can find a competitive edge. Take the case of an old established company which employed about 400 people in its 2 Wisconsin factories and an equal number in its Alabama shop. However, it found greener fields elsewhere. Wisconsin production was gradually curtailed with the last of the workers laid off in December 1954.

Or take the case of an old established Philadelphia dress manufacturer, in business since 1906. When this plant was moved in 1953, its 215 workers lost their jobs. At all times Philadelphia operations had been profitable. The company preferred, however, to move to a community where local interests provided a plant at low cost and also assured a continued supply of cheap labor for whom the legal minimum was to be the maximum wage.

It is such cases that make a fair increase in the Federal minimum essential. Labor organizations are not always in the position to raise the wages and salaries of underpaid workers. Unscrupulous employers know this only too well. The local community pressures which they generate and exploit make the problem of improving the workers' conditions all the more difficult. Yet, the goods produced in such factories undermine the competitive standing of those firms who are doing their best to maintain fair labor standards. It is precisely in such cases, when the workers lack the protection of a union, that they need to be protected by law.

Unfair competition based on low wages is, of course, not confined to any one section of the country. Even in communities where high wages prevail, some workers are always found working for a pittance, reflecting the basic imperfection of the labor market. Workers do not always have the right information about the wage rates for their kind of work. They are frequently compelled to accept any work under the pressure of material needs. The adoption of a sound and going national minimum wage floor would go a long way toward remedying this situation, with a decided advantage to everyone. Economic growth, after all, is not conditioned on the existence of low wage levels. Thus, for example, between 1947 and 1954, the largest increase in nonagricultural employment occurred in the Far West, the region which pays the highest average wage in the Nation. The growth was 22 percent, as compared with the advance for the country as a whole of only 11 percent and in the Southern States of only 16 percent.

Statement of Marx Lewis, General Secretary-Treasurer, United Hatters, Cap, and Millinery Workers International Union, pp. 514–516

The key to an understanding of the economics of the headwear industries lies in an appreciation of the workings of competition carried to the uttermost limit. This situation, destructive as it is, is aggravated by two other factors: One of them is the labor costs, which . . . represent on an average 31 percent of the total operating costs. That was in 1939, but the percentage has not altered much in the intervening years. In a close competitive market these costs furnish a wide field in which competition can be conducted at the expense of the workers, and more particularly those who are not organized and, therefore, are in no position to prevent the competition from being conducted at their expense, and at the expense of those manufacturers who are for one reason or another trying to maintain a decent wage standard for their employees.

Another source of aggravation arises from the fact that the products, regardless of where they are produced, or whether they are produced under union or nonunion conditions, are sold in a national market, and retailers are fully aware that they can buy nonunion products, made by cheap labor, which will be comparable to those made in markets where higher wage standards and better working conditions prevail.

The fact that the manufacturers who enjoy an economic and competitive advantage by virtue of their lower labor costs are in a minority does not alter materially the damage which they cause. It requires no elaboration to prove that in industries such as ours, as highly competitive as ours are, even a small group can be a disruptive factor of substantial proportions.

As a result of this competition, based, as I have stated, on the lower wage scales in the unorganized markets, the standards which have been established in the union markets as a result of years of intensive effort, and great sacrifices, are gradually being undermined.

Illustrations from both the cap and men's hat industries will serve to demonstrate this point.

The cap industry had been organized, up until a few years ago, to the extent of about 80 percent. The organized workers had established wage standards and secured fringe benefits which were not extraordinary but which, with adequate employment, would provide them with a fairly decent standard of living. Wages for skilled workers ranged from $1.50 to $2 an hour. There were, in addition, employer contributions to health, welfare, and retirement funds which totaled another 7 percent.

In recent years business has drifted away from the established markets. The industry is now about 65 percent organized, and the nonunion workers are becoming more numerous each month, while the markets in which the higher standards prevailed are shrinking. During the past several years the organized workers have found it increasingly difficult to maintain their existing standards, and where they do it is at the expense of their employment opportunities. Economic improvement to which we feel they are legitimately entitled is out of the question.

What has happened is that factories have set themselves up in areas where, due to local conditions, the 75-cent national wage minimum is also the maximum. There are no fringe benefits of any kind. Organizing them is difficult, because of the hostility of the dominant economic forces in the community who want to keep these industries and attract others by assuring them that labor is docile and cheap. Intimidation and coercion are practiced freely by the employers, the National Labor Relations Board and the Labor-Management Relations Act to the contrary notwithstanding.

Unless these wages are raised by legislation to a point which would approach those that prevail in the rest of the industry, we are not now thinking of doing anything that would close the gap completely, we can do nothing to improve the standards of these workers or protect the rest of the industry against the destructive competition conducted at the expense of labor. . . .

The situation in our men's hat industry is not far different from what I have just stated to be the case in the cap industry. The men's hat industry has for many years been located in the North and East. The wage scales which were established enabled the workers, with adequate employment, to make a living. Recently some of the companies have begun to decentralize their operations because of the competition from the low-wage areas. Factories have been established in Tennessee and Missouri where the national minimum is also the maximum. I visited one of these factories several years ago, when we were engaged in trying to organize it, and with few exceptions the wage there was 75 cents an hour. The highest wage was $1.15 an hour, paid to just 1 worker out of 160.

Manufacturers in the higher wage areas claim that they cannot continue to compete indefinitely with employers who pay 75 cents an hour, while they must pay 2 or 2½ times that amount. They must, they say, either fold up entirely or go and do as others have done, find low-wage areas in which to operate.

We spent $2 million for a strike recently to defeat an attempt to create havoc for our industry and our workers by such removals. Had there been a reasonable attempt by legislation to prevent a gap between the higher wage and the lower wage areas that cannot be bridged by unionization because of the powerful forces arrayed against the labor movement in the low-wage areas we would not have had to endure this burden.

An increase in the national wage minimum from 75 cents an hour to $1.25 an hour will not, in our industries, close the gap. But it will narrow it to a point where it might be possible for those who want to deal legitimately with their employees and enable them to maintain an American standard of existence to do so. We would reduce the high mortality rate which now prevails in the headwear industries. In human terms, it would mean for the workers relief from the uncertainty and fear which forever haunt them.

Statement of the Northern Textile Association, p. 1232

The Northern Textile Association represents cotton and manmade fiber textile mills located predominantly in New England. The New England textile industry of which the cotton and manmade fiber textile mills constitute a significant portion, is the region's largest manufacturing employer with 173,000 workers.

The Northern Textile Association is in favor of a Federal minimum wage under the Fair Labor Standards Act of not less than $1 per hour. . . .

Wage disparities and inequities between New England and the southern States have plagued the cotton textile industry since the turn of the century. Wage differentials within the industry have been one of the most important causes of an employment drop of 160,000 persons in the New England cotton and manmade fiber textile industry since 1919. It is estimated that an equal number of related jobs have also been lost. In just the past 2 years 39 mills and 18,000 jobs have been lost in the industry in New England. . . .

LOW WAGES ARE A THREAT TO AMERICA

Statement of Solomon Barkin, Chairman, CIO Committee on Fair Labor Standards, pp. 356–357

The minimum wage law does not affect primarily or exclusively "the least skilled, least employable and the marginal workers in our economy." It applies to the lowest-paid workers. Low-paid and incompetent are by no means synonymous terms. The workers receiving less than $1.25 an hour are not paid low wages because they are unproductive or inefficient. Many of them are workers who have proved themselves indispensable to the industries in which they are employed. The trouble is that they are weak bargainers. They live and work in low-wage areas. They are immobile—they are heads of families, or wives, or young people, or older men and women. They suffer from racial or sex discrimination. Many possess skills that are not easily transferable. Many are victims of employer-controlled labor markets. For workers so completely dominated by circumstances which they do not control, the solution for the low-wage problem is an adequate legal minimum wage.

Low wages produce substandard citizens. For them, a diet adequate for health is out of the question. They suffer unduly from physical disabilities and longer illnesses. Draft rejections were highest among them. Life expectancy was shortest. They do not enjoy adequate medical facilities. Their educational opportunities tend to be limited. Their housing is poor.

Low wages are a threat to the future of the American family population and the nation. Children born or brought up in families with substandard incomes are handicapped from the beginning. They are undernourished and deprived of the opportunity for education and training that would enable them to rise above the economic level of their origin. We have a responsibility to improve the social conditions of which individuals are the helpless victims and for which they are not to blame.

The full cost of maintaining and reproducing workers' families should come out of industry, just as industry is expected to pay for the cost, maintenance and replacement of the machine which the worker operates. The realization of this basic principle means that the worker's wages must not only be such that he can buy the goods and services necessary for his support and that of his family, but he must be able, through taxes to contribute to the cost of educating his children, of protecting his home against fire, his person against assault and his property against theft.

To the extent to which the cost of his support must come from private or public relief instead of from wages, to the extent to which he must rely on medical care for which he cannot pay and toward which he has not contributed through taxes, to that extent is his employer being subsidized by the taxpayers and private charities. The consumer pays the full price for commodities in the market. It is unfair to compel him to add a subsidy to industry in the form of taxes to provide the necessities of life for industry's workers. A minimum wage law would relieve the taxpayer of at least a part of the burden that is rightly industry's obligation.

WHY UNIONS ARE INTERESTED IN STATUTORY MINIMUMS

Statement of David J. McDonald, President, United Steelworkers of America, pp. 453–454

Perhaps a few more facts with reference to the United Steelworkers of America would help the committee and the Congress to see our interest in the whole matter. Our union holds jurisdiction in basic steel and several allied industries. In the main, our total membership would be little affected directly by an increase in the statutory minimum wage to $1.25 an hour. In the steel industry, as noted, we have raised our minimum to $1.57 by collective bargaining. Our members work in what is generally regarded as a high-wage industry. Gross average hourly earnings for the most recent month were $2.27 according to the Bureau of Labor Statistics. Even our $1.57 minimum affects only 1 percent to 2 percent of the employees in the industry, and these are mostly janitors and sweepers. The labor jobs in the industry earn $1.62½ an hour or more.

We are proud of our collective bargaining gains in the wage field. We are firmly convinced that the attainment, through collective bargaining, of higher wages and higher standards of living and greater economic security will aid greatly in raising the wages, living standards, and security of the millions of unorganized and other low-paid workers in the United States. But this effort on behalf of workers with substandard conditions needs legislative assistance.

The interest of the Steelworkers Union in this fight to increase the statutory wage minimum to $1.25 and to increase coverage to persons now excluded from the present minimum is quite obvious. We are well aware that the steelworkers cannot be isolated in their economic progress. We know full well that the wage and other improvements which we can, and do, win by bargaining are forever threatened so long as there are millions of low-paid workers who do not earn enough wages to enjoy even a minimum standard of living.

One of the cardinal facts of our economy is that we must all move together on the wage front if we are to provide the purchasing power necessary to sustain the gains which we can make in our individual bargaining areas. This means that auto workers, electrical workers, textile workers, clothing workers, oil workers, communication workers, teamsters, machinists, and all other workers, organized and unorganized, North and South, must progress together if our Nation is to grow and prosper and if steelworkers are to grow and prosper. This is the reason for our interest in a decent minimum wage level.

THE BASIS FOR DECISION

Statement of M. W. Smith, Jr., Jackson, Ala., for Southern Pine Industry Committee, p. 689

The bills now before Congress to increase the minimum wage vary in the amount of increase from the lowest which would bring the minimum to 90 cents an hour to the highest which would bring the minimum to $1.35. Were these different amounts as proposed merely drawn out of thin air, based purely upon opinion? Or were they arrived at after careful study of their effects upon the Nation's business? Obviously such great differences must be derived from equally great differences in judgment as to consequences. If the motivating force back of these bills stems solely from a desire on the part of their sponsors to see worker incomes increased in order to enlarge consumer buying power then why stop at $1.35? Why not set the minimum at $50 per hour and increase consumer buying power even more? Plainly this would be absurd to us all. We enlarge the figure to absurdity merely to point out that before any increase in the minimum is voted Congress should know the answers to a lot of questions. Here are some of those questions:

1. What effect will a higher minimum have upon the Nation's entire wage structure? Will customary wage differentials continue to be maintained? (If so, then the total wage bill will be increased more than just the amount necessary to bring those workers below the new minimum up to it.)

2. What effect will a greater minimum have upon prices? Can the increase in the total wage bill be absorbed in some manner without raising prices to consumers?

3. A corollary to 2: Will a higher minimum cause prices of some goods to be raised to the point where consumers will shift their buying to substitute products?

4. Will an increase in the minimum wage discriminate against small businesses, injuring them to the extent of forcing them to shut down? (If so, then Congress will find itself inconsistently undoing with the left hand what it purports to do for small business with the right hand through the Small Business Administration program.)

5. Will a higher minimum stimulate further mechanization in industry causing unemployment?

6. Will a higher minimum work to the detriment of any particular region or regions?

7. Is a higher minimum wage the best way to help people with low incomes? Isn't there some better way?

8. What will be the effect of raising the minimum wage and at the same time lowering tariff barriers to admit goods produced by cheap foreign labor?

These and many other questions must be answered before a sensible decision can be reached on the problem of whether the legal minimum wage should be raised, and by how much: Whether to 90 cents, $1, $1.25, $1.50, $2, $5, $10, etc.

FOR DISCUSSION AND ANALYSIS

1. The Southern Pine Industry Committee polled its members in 1955 to discover how they were planning to meet the $1 minimum which was to go into effect the following March. The following are typical of the replies it received.

Increase our production by more mechanization and decrease the amount of hours worked.

Keep best workers. Lay off all others.

Either increase sale price or discontinue operations.

As our margin of profit is small, have no alternative other than to raise the price of our product.

That is the 64 dollar question—try to overcome via machinery and any other method that may come to mind.

Eliminate as many men as possible by changing operations.

Raise prices if possible and absorb what we have to.

Eliminate inefficient workers. Increase productivity of machines. Eliminate overtime.

If further inflation follows as seems inevitable it will be absorbed with increased prices.

Eliminate marginal workers, tighten production discipline, install more labor saving machinery.

Will have to absorb most of it, if not all and hope not to go broke.

Eliminate all overtime on hourly employees and continue trying for more efficiency. Endeavor to buy timber cheaper.

Hope for price increase to absorb some of extra cost—hope to reduce price of raw materials, if possible. Will install labor saving machinery—shutdown will be last resort after trying.

Will do our best to pass it on to consumer, but doubt that we can.

By economizing in every possible way, in all departments; by installing additional labor saving machinery, etc.; and reducing our working force accordingly. Even so, do not expect to be able to offset the full cost of the increase in wages, so will "try" to secure an increase in price for our product to compensate although this will depend on Supply & Demand.

Do the above replies seem to support the argument of those who are optimistic or pessimistic over the economic effects of an increase in the minimum rate?

2. Summarize all the arguments pro and con an increase in the minimum wage which you find in the testimony reproduced in this chapter. To what extent do you find that conflict is based on differences in beliefs as to the effects of a *specific* increase (that moving from a minimum of 75 cents to $1 will result in widespread unemployment, on the one hand, or that it will not result in widespread unemployment, on the other hand); and to what extent do you find that conflict results from a difference in views as to the over-all effects of *any* minimum wage?

3. Union officials have argued that "underpayment of wages is an unfair competitive method. An employer should not profit because he can get away with substandard wages."

Do you agree? How would you define "unfair" or "substandard" wages?

4. What should be the relationship between the minimum wage and a minimum family "standard of decency" budget?

5. What should be the relationship between an increase in the Federal minimum wage and an increase in national economic productivity?

21: Unions and Inflation

No issue has been more heatedly and inconclusively debated in recent years than union responsibility for inflation. Under conditions of full employment, are rising wages attributable to a boundless union appetite which businessmen are willing to try to satisfy, since price increases which are readily accepted by consumers supply the wherewithal? Or does full employment in its very nature create demand conditions which put upward pressure on prices, inducing businessmen to bid up wages to obtain needed labor in a lucrative market, and to meet the demands of unions in order to avoid interruptions to profitable production? Is it unions which initiate and propel inflationary pressures (on the supply side), or are they simply one of numerous interest groups which seek to "get theirs" when inflationary conditions, which would be present even in their absence, have been loosed by other forces (chiefly on the demand side)? Or may these different conceptions of the union role in the inflation process each be appropriate to particular circumstances?

PROSPECTS OF INFLATION

By Charles O. Hardy, Vice President, Federal Reserve Bank of Kansas City, in Prices, Wages, and Employment, Postwar Economic Studies No. 4, Board of Governors of the Federal Reserve System, Washington, 1946, pp. 23–24

. . . Even if wage increases are allowed only when no price increase is necessary, the net effect of collective bargaining under present standards is still inflationary. For stability of prices does not mean stability of all prices; it means that some prices rise and others fall. If the excessive profit margins that would otherwise lead to competitive price reductions are regularly absorbed in wage increases, the cases where prices rise for other than wage reasons are not offset in the general average by cases where they decline. In addition, higher prices in one industry often mean higher cost of materials in another, and higher wages in one industry create added pressures in others. Hence, unless the upward pressures are counteracted with anti-inflationary credit and fiscal policies, which reduce other prices to offset the cases where cost increases force higher prices, the price level steadily rises. . . .

The fact is that collective bargaining with strong unions, price stability, and full employment are incompatible. We can have any two of these, but not all

926

three. So long as union power is not dampened down by unemployment there is no apparent power in the state strong enough to check a parallel upward sweep of wages and prices.

The basic difficulty is that although the unions have a degree of monopoly power that is sufficient to make them irresistible in their respective fields, the bases are not broad enough to bring their specific interests into balance with the over-all consequences of their policies. The decision whether to demand wages so high as to force higher prices is made by each industrial union separately; the price consequences are spread over the whole community. No union's successful demands will raise its own members' living costs by nearly as much as it will increase their incomes. Even if each unionist believed that the effect of a series of wage increases in different industries would be nullified by the resulting inflation, it would still be good policy for each union to try to get its increases first and make them bigger than the average.

LABOR'S TRUE "MAGNA CHARTA"

From the Guaranty Survey, July, 1956, published by the Guaranty Trust Company of New York

As this is written, the nation faces the threat of a strike by 650,000 United Steelworkers. If the strike occurs, it will involve heavy losses, not only to the workers and their employers but to the whole economy. If long continued, it could assume the proportions of a national emergency and force governmental intervention. In any case, it will be the outcome of an attempt by the union to enforce an increase in wage rates and other labor costs estimated by management at 25 per cent, which far exceeds the rise in productivity by any possible standards of measurement.

THE "SPIRAL" AGAIN

Whether a strike occurs or not, any wage increase that may be won, if it exceeds the rise in productivity, will force a corresponding increase in prices of steel and its end products. This will be paid by consumers, including the steel workers themselves. Labor as a whole will gain little or nothing. The same experience will be repeated in many other industries before the year is out. The wage-price "spiral" will have been given another twist, one more in the long series of futile attempts to show that "labor is not a commodity" and that wages can be exempted from the market processes that determine the distribution of income.

This is a familiar pattern. Since the beginning of 1933 more than 630 million man-days of work have been lost as a direct result of work stoppages, with no account taken of the secondary idleness caused by the failure of struck industries to deliver their products or perform their services on time and by the decline in the purchasing power of striking workers.

What has labor to show for these losses? A rough idea can be gained from the Government's figures for manufacturing industries. The average hourly earnings of factory workers have more than quadrupled since 1932, but the increase has been offset by the rise in prices of finished goods. The ratio of earnings to prices, which measures the real ability of the worker to buy the product, has risen 76 per cent, while productivity (average output per man-hour) has increased 77 per cent. Thus, despite the sharp rise in money wages, the real gain to the worker has been limited to the increase in productivity, just as it was before the days of industry-wide unions and national-emergency strikes. In so far as unionization has tended to raise money wages faster than productivity has risen, the effect has not been to increase the real purchasing power of the workers but merely to cheapen the dollar. As far as wage rates in manufacturing industries are concerned, the gain to labor from its billions of dollars of lost pay due to strikes is precisely nothing.

THE SPECIAL EXEMPTION

This study in futility has come about mainly as a result of the persistent belief that the earnings of labor somehow can and should be exempted from the free-market processes by which prices, values, and distributive shares in general are determined in a competitive economy—a belief that is epitomized in the declaration that "labor is not a commodity." How did this expression originate, what does it really mean, and what does it imply?

Superficially, the statement that "labor is not a commodity" has a strong humanitarian appeal. It sounds like a sort of declaration of independence for labor, an assertion that the workingman is not a slave or chattel to be bought and sold in the market place. It was undoubtedly this aspect of the matter that led Pope Leo XIII in 1891 to issue his famous encyclical on the condition of labor, *Rerum Novarum,* a document that has done much to shape recent thinking on labor questions. The official English version contains these words:

"Religion teaches the rich man and the employer that their work-people are not their slaves . . . and that it is shameful and inhuman to treat men like chattels to make money by . . ."

No doubt it was likewise the humanitarian appeal, mixed perhaps with other considerations, that led Congress to declare in the Clayton act of 1914 that "the labor of a human being is not a commodity or article of commerce. Nothing contained in the anti-trust laws should be construed to forbid the existence and operation of labor, agricultural, or horticultural organizations, instituted for the purposes of mutual help, and not having capital stock or conducted for profits, or to forbid or restrain individual members of such organizations from lawfully carrying out the legitimate objects thereof; nor shall such organizations, or the members thereof, be held or construed to be illegal combinations or conspiracies in restraint of trade under the antitrust laws."

This provision was enthusiastically hailed as a "Magna Charta" of labor. Subsequent court decisions showed that its practical effects were much less important than had been thought, and Congress eventually found it necessary to pass the Norris-La Guardia act of 1932 in order to give labor unions the legal immunity that was deemed desirable. This, however, is beside the point. The point is that the majority in Congress, like many others, believed (1) that a legislative enactment could exempt labor from the normal competitive determination of its rates of pay, and (2) that labor would gain by such an exemption.

The same philosophy underlies the whole trend of recent governmental labor policy and labor legislation: the National Industrial Recovery Act of 1933, the Wagner act of 1935, the Fair Labor Standards Act of 1938, the Smith-Connally act of 1943, the Taft-Hartley act of 1947, and a multitude of other Federal and State laws. Some foreign countries still commonly called "free" have gone even further in regulating or influencing labor-management relations in general and wage rates in particular. Whatever the means may be, the underlying intent is the same: to "emancipate" the worker from the rule of the market, to prove that "labor is not a commodity."

WHAT IS A COMMODITY?

The statement that working people are not slaves or chattels and the declaration that their labor is not a commodity or article of commerce sound much alike, and this superficial similarity appears to have caused a great deal of confusion. Actually, not only are they two very different assertions, but in their final implications they are mutually contradictory. This becomes clear when a little consideration is given to the real economic position and significance of human labor.

The essential characteristics of a commodity or article of commerce are (1) that it is in demand and (2) that its supply is not unlimited. These two characteristics give it value, enable it to command a price in the market in exchange for other valuable things. The price is determined by the interaction of demand and supply—demand as affected by the commodity's price and usefulness, supply as affected by the price obtainable for it and the difficulty or cost of producing it.

Human labor possesses all these characteristics. It is in demand; its supply is limited; hence, it commands a price in the market. The demand for it arises from the fact that employers can use it profitably and is limited by the ability of employers so to use it. The supply arises from the need of workers to meet their personal wants and is limited by the number of workers and their preference for leisure, that is, for noneconomic pursuits.

Economists usually make a distinction between commodities and services, commodities being material articles and services consisting of useful actions. The distinction is not essential to the present purpose, because the basic economic characteristics of the two categories are the same. If labor is not a commodity in this sense, it is certainly a service, and from the economic standpoint it is, in every essential respect, a "commodity or article of commerce."

What does this mean to the individual worker? It means that he is the owner of a valuable commodity, his capacity to work, which other men are eager to buy and pay for. This commodity is inalienably his, and he is free to sell it in the most attractive market he can find. He can pick and choose, not only among pay offers but among occupations. He is, in a larger or smaller way, an independent proprietor, an entrepreneur. His opportunity to rise is limited only by his capacity to make himself useful to others through his ability, energy, and diligence. He is able to command an income from others, not by virtue of any authority or compulsion by a paternalistic state, not because of any protection or favor bestowed upon him by a public or private organization, but because others are ready to buy voluntarily, and in their own interest, what he has to sell. The fact that his labor is a commodity does not make him a slave or a chattel. On the contrary, it makes him, in the full sense of the phrase, a free man.

HOW WAGES ARE DETERMINED

To say that employers seek to "make money" by hiring workers is not to say that they are treating them like chattels. The employer does precisely what the worker does: he tries to employ his resources to the best advantage. In this endeavor, each party attempts to "make money" from the other; that is, each hopes and expects to profit by the employment contract, and each tries to make the best bargain he can. Only in this way can an economy of free enterprise function effectively. If it were not for the hope of "making money," there would be no employment and no enterprise. "Making money" is merely the form which the efficient use of resources takes in an enterprise economy. To read a sinister meaning into the phrase is to betray a lack of understanding of the whole economic process.

It is as pointless to criticize the employer for not paying more than he must as to blame the worker for refusing to work for less than he can get elsewhere. Each party obtains the best terms he can. The worker must work for a wage that will make it profitable for the employer to hire him in turning out a product at a price which consumers are able and willing to pay in a competitive market. The employer must pay a wage that will prevent the worker from being drawn away by other employers. In this way there is established a wage structure, a set of "going rates" for different occupations and grades of labor. These rates reflect the productivity of industry at the time, the quantity of goods and services produced in relation to the quantity of resources employed. If wage rates are not higher than they are, it is not because of the rapacity of employers but because the productivity of industry, while greater than ever before, is still limited.

The idea of a fair, just, or reasonable wage is very appealing. But what is fair, just, and reasonable under the conditions prevailing at a particular time? Since the dawn of history, buyers and sellers have had very different ideas regarding the concrete meaning of these words. How are such differences to be resolved? There is only one valid and objective criterion: the free market, which, under the consumer's whiplash (and the consumer means everyone), forces both buyers and sellers of labor to conform to the basic reality of the situation, the current level of productivity.

WHY LABOR IS FREE

In a free-enterprise, profit-and-loss economy, there is no escape from this basic reality. In the United States, powerful labor unions, developed under governmental protection and encouragement, may have been able to force money wages higher, but they have not been able to prevent prices from following, which means that they have not been able to lift real gains to workers above the rise in productivity. In some foreign countries where governments have exerted their powers even more directly for the supposed benefit of workers, those same governments now find themselves under the embarrassing necessity of restraining rather than encouraging the aspirations of workers for higher pay, because experience there, too, has shown that labor is a commodity after all, and that too rapid wage increases, instead of benefiting workers, merely produce inflation and disrupt balances of international payments by raising costs of production.

To abolish the market determination of wages—that is, the commodity character of labor—it would be necessary to destroy private enterprise and resort to socialism. Then the worker would really become a chattel. No longer would his wages depend upon his individual ability to make himself useful, as determined ultimately by the current state of industrial productivity, but upon the will of a political master, from whose decision there would be no appeal. No longer would he be free to choose his occupation, or even his place of residence; he would have to work at his assigned task, whatever and wherever it happened to be, at the bidding of the same political master.

The true "Magna Charta" of labor lies in the very fact that labor is "a commodity or article of commerce," not a pawn in a totalitarian game.

A NEW FORCE FOR INFLATION

National Association of Manufacturers, 1956, pp. 12–13

When an industrywide union, exercising monopoly control over the labor supply of an industry, demands wage increases which discount productivity gains far in advance, possible price reductions of mass-produced products are prevented and buying power is shifted unfairly from the public as a whole to the favored few who happen to work in the industry in question.

Furthermore, competition cannot act to restore the proper balance. Any new concern, attracted to the industry by growing demand, would have to submit to dictation by the same union and would not be permitted to establish labor costs which would reflect the true value of the services rendered in the economic situation then prevailing.

Thus, union monopoly power distorts economic rewards in favor of those who are under the umbrella of the monopoly, to the detriment of all other economic interests. In the situation which prevails today, where monopoly power over the labor supply is a reality in most of the nation's basic raw materials, manufacturing, transportation and communications industries, persistent inflation is a constant threat. . . .

The obvious remedy in the situation is to curtail the power of industrywide unions to engage in monopolistic practices and restore bargaining to the local level.

FIGHT AGAINST INFLATION

From the report of Walter P. Reuther, President, United Automobile Workers, to the 16th Constitutional Convention, 1956

Since they were first negotiated in 1948, the cost-of-living escalator clauses in UAW contracts have given most UAW members some degree of protection against rising prices. While these escalator provisions have kept the buying power of our wages from being washed away by inflation, they are only a partial and negative defense.

They cannot protect the savings of UAW members. They cannot defend the value of sickness and accident benefits, group life insurance policies, or pension benefits provided under our contracts.

In our fight against the ravages of inflation, moreover, we cannot afford to think of UAW members alone. The level of employment of our industries depends on the purchasing power of American consumers generally. The jobs of UAW members are threatened when the American public is robbed by unjustifiable price increases brought about by the greed of employers.

There is another basic reason why UAW's fight against rising prices has been waged on the broadest front. There has been a running campaign of distortion and misrepresentation regarding the causes of rising prices in this country since the end of the second World War.

Industry has charged that the major if not the sole cause of rising prices has been labor's wage demands. These charges have been circulated in most of the nation's press. And, since the coming of special-interest government to Washington, the assertion that wage earners themselves cause inflation has become the gospel of that government and, by inference, has been endorsed by the President of the United States.

UAW has challenged this malicious nonsense over the years and will continue to challenge it, not only in defense of the immediate interests of UAW members but in order that our whole economy may continue to expand.

MYTH MUST BE DESTROYED

Our surest defense against inflation—the loss of purchasing power, and the general decline in living standards that may follow our national failure to match an expanding productive power with expanding buying power—lies in a destruction of the "labor-causes-inflation" myth. It lies in public recognition that wages, prices, and profits are all parts of the equation that produces either abundance or depression, either good times or bad.

If wages, prices, and profits are out of balance—if employers get too much in the form of higher profits and prices and the great mass of consumers get too little in wages and other personal income, then we are in trouble. Purchasing power dries up, markets shrink, jobs become scarce and unemployment results.

Yet if wages, prices, and profits are to be kept in balance—in a dynamic balance of continuing expansion so that the expansion of production is equalled by an expansion in buying power—then the American public must know as much about what happens to profits and prices as it knows, or thinks it knows, about wages.

If wages, in other words, are public business (and they are), then prices and profits are public business too. And the way they fit into the pattern making for prosperity and abundance is public business.

The National Association of Manufacturers, individual employers, and a business-minded press have suppressed or distorted this vital relationship of wages, prices and profits. They have kept wages in the forefront of the public concern, while keeping industrial profits in the shadows. When corporate greed causes unwarranted price rises, the NAM has a ready story for public consumption and newspapers from coast to coast are standing by to peddle it. The story is that labor's demand for wage increases has forced the employer to put up the price of his product. The editorial wise men, who are always telling labor how to behave, never raise the fundamental question: Could the employer absorb the wage increase and still make a reasonable profit without raising prices? This question is never asked, except by the unions themselves, notably the UAW, and an occasional citizen of broad social vision.

Labor's wage demands are always assumed to be unjustified; management's price demands are always assumed to be proper. For over 10 years, now, UAW has sought to expose the scandal of this double standard.

Long before the present sharp upsurge in the cost of living, the UAW carried the campaign for higher purchasing power to the American people in the strike of the General Motors workers in the winter of 1945–46. Before that, during World War II, the UAW had supported price controls and had maintained in Washington a full-time consumer counsel to ride herd on government agencies and protect the price front against the inroads of profiteers.

The 113-day strike of GM workers after the war had been preceded by a carefully documented analysis of the corporation's ability to grant a wage increase without increasing the prices of GM products—and by a UAW offer to reduce the wage demand to whatever level might be shown to be necessary to avoid such a price increase.

UAW HAS ALERTED PUBLIC

At the time and throughout the postwar period whenever the auto, steel and other basic industries planned price increases, UAW has alerted the American public to corporation profits and pointed out how advancing technology and growing efficiency of production methods, particularly in the case of the automobiles, but also in American industry generally, has made it possible for industry to absorb wage increases out of phenomenal profits.

When the Korean War threatened an inflationary spurt in the summer of 1950, as the President of the UAW, I called upon President Truman and Congress, in behalf of UAW members and their families, to impose price controls.

Later in the same year, when the auto industry again contemplated price increases, a union analysis of auto industry profits demonstrated that they were so high that any further price increase would be unwarranted and a reckless aggravation of the inflationary threat.

In July, 1955, after the steel industry had raised prices and when price rises by Ford and General Motors were anticipated, the UAW Executive Board formally called for a thorough Congressional investigation of those inflationary moves of industry.

That was some time before the current sharp upward trend in prices began, but there were already signs that the trouble now upon us was brewing. There had been a creeping rise of industrial prices. These prices, however, were not being reflected in the over-all index because agricultural prices were falling and thus holding the general index down.

UAW understood then from the bitter experience of wage earners, however, that the storm would ultimately break if the responsibility of industry for inflation were not presented to the American people.

General Motors and Ford did raise prices in the fall of 1955. They defended their action, as usual, by attributing the rise to economic gains made by UAW members earlier in the year.

If the facts had been aired in the Congressional investigation for which UAW had called, they would have shown that the cost of our wage increases and other economic gains to these corporations amounted to about 20 cents an hour. They would have shown further that during the first nine months of 1955—before prices had been raised but after the gains of the workers had been largely in effect for four months—GM's profits before taxes came to $2.93 an hour for every hour worked in its plants by all its 400,000 U. S. factory workers, yielding a return on stockholder investment equal, on an annual basis, to 78.9 per cent. GM's rate of return after taxes would still have been fabulous: 36.5 per cent.

Such a Congressional investigation would have shown that in Ford's case hourly profits were $3.06—a rate of return on investment of 57.7 per cent before taxes and 26.1 per cent after taxes.

In a word, there was no excuse, economically or morally, for the price gouge of the fall of 1955. Yet it was this reckless greed of the automotive companies, combined with their headlong production race for the 1956 market, which piled up car inventories and produced the grave unemployment crisis of 1956 in the automobile centers.

Nor was this all. Auto companies again raised prices in 1956 despite the depressed market their own greed had caused, and despite widespread unemployment among auto workers.

UAW renewed its call for a Congressional investigation of the price gouge in March, 1956, publishing further data to show that high corporate profits proved the price boosts unnecessary.

PRESIDENT ASKED TO BACK PROBE

In November, 1956, after another rise in the Consumers Price Index had confirmed our worst earlier fears by kicking the cost of living to a record high,

I wrote directly to President Eisenhower. The President himself, in a press conference, had suggested that wage increases had caused the cost-of-living rise.

I asked President Eisenhower to support a sweeping investigation of the wage-price-profit relationship. I reviewed the history of UAW's concern for a dynamic economy, cited the facts regarding corporate price increases, and suggested that it was misleading to imply that labor and industry were equally guilty in causing inflation.

"We are of the firm belief that an objective analysis of all the economic factors relating to wages, prices and profits will furnish irrefutable proof that wage increases definitely cannot be blamed for recent price increases by major corporations in basic industries such as auto and steel," I wrote.

My letter to President Eisenhower also stated that a searching investigation would, in any case, enable the American public to inform itself and to fix responsibility where it belonged.

A reply from Presidential Assistant Sherman Adams on December 8, 1956, said that "Congressional investigations are the prerogative of the Congress, and I doubt that the President would wish to intrude in this field."

The Adams reply was a polite evasion. There is no constitutional obstacle in the way of the President's support of a Congressional action. President Eisenhower was not asked to investigate wages, prices, and profits himself; he was urged to lend the prestige of his office to a sober search for the truth rather than to a corporate public-relations campaign aimed at saddling the labor movement with the blame for inflation.

PROPOSAL BY UAW

The UAW, now as in the controversy with General Motors in 1945, stands by the policy of confining wage increases and other economic gains in "administered price" industries within the limits of the ability of an efficient firm, functioning under full-employment conditions, to pay such increases without a price increase.

In return for such a commitment, we suggest that every corporation which controls a strategic sector of its industry—perhaps 20 or 25 per cent of total sales—should give prior notification of its intention of raising prices to a governmental agency created for such purpose.

The corporation would then be required to disclose pertinent records indicating a need to make such a price increase. Such testimony would be made in open hearings and subject to cross-examination.

Full public disclosure of the facts would be made. The corporation involved would be free to pursue its price course. But the public would be alerted and informed, and would be able to judge for itself whether the price increase was justified.

Such a practice would impose no compulsion and would infringe no freedom. But it would minimize the abuse of freedom by men who today wield great economic power in industry, while they seek to evade their responsibility to the public.

INFLATION OR STABILIZATION?

From Steel and the National Economy, 1956, United Steelworkers of America, Pittsburgh, Pa., 1956, pp. 8–10

Contentions by management and by anti-labor spokesmen that all wage increases must result in price increases—that higher wages must lead to inflation —are without basis in theory, in practice and in fact. Rising wages and inflation are not part and parcel of a single phenomenon. Industry need not, and most employers do not, raise prices every time wages are increased. So much has been said and written proving that wages must rise relative to prices, that only economic isolationists in their remote-from-reality hideouts continue to prattle about higher wages causing inflation.

Contentions that wage rates can be increased without limit and still have no impact on prices are equally irresponsible. But, a healthy economy requires that wages and salaries must rise relative to prices and the only meaningful question is the degree to which wages can and must increase relative to prices.

Unions have never contended that higher wages could be paid without higher prices regardless of the size of the wage increase. Rather, labor has contended that the level of profits and changes in productivity should be taken into account in determining how much wages can be increased without increasing the general price level. On the other hand, those who steadfastly fight against wage increases attempt to propagate the view that every wage increase must result in a price increase.

It is unequivocally clear that unless wages and salaries increase somewhat more than prices, our economic growth will be halted. As our productive capacity and output of goods and services expand, there must be an increase in the real buying power of consumers. Except for inventory and investment booms which cause busts, our economy can grow no faster than the market for its products. The mainstay of that market is the purchasing power of our workers. . . . More than four-fifths of America's total output of goods and services, excluding what is bought by the Government, is purchased for personal consumption. It is the income of the wage and salary earners that accounts for the bulk of personal consumption. Rising real wages are an absolute prerequisite to economic prosperity and economic growth.

The history of our industrial development is a history of rising output per man-hour of work. The rate of change in productivity has varied from time to time, but the increase in efficiency—in production per man-hour—has been persistent and substantial. Workers can share in the benefits of rising productivity only through rising real wages. But even more important from the economic point of view is the continuing need for higher real wages as a basis for sustained high levels of production and income and employment.

Economists have long argued whether the benefits of rising productivity should be shared through constant prices and higher wages or through constant wages and lower prices, or a combination of the two. Most economists are at least dubious, if not firmly opposed, to a goal of declining prices. Falling prices tend to discourage investment and to retard economic expansion. Even if general price declines were desirable, it is doubtful that prices would actually be reduced by those industries which can best afford it—those whose firm grip on the market has permitted them to reap the profits by setting their prices high.

As the economy has grown, business enterprises have developed in size and scale and in organization, bringing much less price flexibility than was true in the past. Many objective analyses have been made demonstrating the growing stickiness of prices, especially for industrial products. Even when economic activity and productivity have risen relative to wages, there is little evidence of a readiness by the large industrial corporations to cut prices. Rather, our increasingly monopolistic industries tend to change their prices only in one direction, namely upward. If labor were to forego demands for higher wages and wait for employers to pass on the benefits of higher productivity through lower prices, we would surely experience short and intensive booms with tremendous profits and inadequate buying power, followed by severe depressions and mass unemployment. This is not a promising path to economic progress.

Labor often seeks wage increases that are proportionately higher than the rise in productivity, because wages have lagged in the past and profits have become exorbitant. Once labor's share is reasonable, increases should primarily take into consideration changes in productivity. In industries where productivity is rising at a lesser rate than for the total economy, wages should be increased in proportion to the over-all rate, even though some price increase might be necessary. In industries where productivity is increasing very rapidly, wages should rise more than in proportion to the national increase in productivity. This might well leave room for price declines.

The above policies would permit all workers to share in the improving productivity of the economy with extra benefits to workers in those industries where technological advancements are most rapid. It would result in only a slight upward trend in prices.

It should be noted that a percentage increase in wage rates proportionate with changes in productivity results in a sharing of the benefits of productivity between management, labor and investors. Not all the benefits of increased efficiency and mechanization are expected nor sought by labor.

History has demonstrated not only that wages can rise relative to prices, thus providing the increased purchasing power without which our economy would stagnate, but also that there can be substantial increases in wages with virtually no change in prices or living costs. The experiences of the immediate pre-Korea and post-Korea years are significant in this respect.

Since the end of World War II, there have been two periods of general price advances, both occasioned by factors other than higher wages. Also in this decade, there have been two longer periods of general price stability.

Prices rose sharply during the immediate postwar years of 1946 and 1947, following the removal of wartime price controls. This inflation reflected principally the release of accumulated demands for goods of all kinds following the removal of wartime restrictions on consumption and output. As shown in the following table, consumer prices increased 30 percent from January 1946 to January 1948. Wholesale prices for all commodities skyrocketed 50 percent. For all commodities other than farm and food items, the rise was 41.5 percent in these 24 months. Wages increased 30 percent during the same period, seriously lagging behind prices and barely providing workers with the same purchasing power per hour of work in January 1948 as in January 1946. Because of shortening of the work week, real buying power of weekly earnings declined markedly for a time following World War II.

Major Price and Wage Movements since the End of World War II (Index Numbers, 1947–49 = 100)

Period	Consumer prices	Wholesale prices		Hourly wages in manufac- turing [1]
		All com- modities	All except farm and food	
1. The immediate postwar boom:				
Jan. 1946................	77.8	69.6	72.1	75.0
Jan. 1948................	101.3	104.5	102.0	97.8
Percent change	+30.2	+50.2	+41.5	+30.4
2. Thirty months of stability:				
Jan. 1948................	101.3	104.5	102.0	97.8
June 1950...............	101.8	100.2	102.2	109.0
Percent change...........	+ 0.5	− 4.1	+ 0.2	+11.5
3. The Korean boom:				
June 1950...............	101.8	100.2	102.2	109.0
June 1951...............	110.8	115.1	116.2	118.8
Percent change...........	+ 8.8	+14.9	+13.7	+ 9.0
4. Five years of stability:				
June 1951...............	110.8	115.1	116.8	118.8
April 1956...............	114.9	113.7	121.7	146.0
Percent change..	+ 3.7	− 1.2	+ 4.2	+22.9

[1] Index of straight-time hourly earnings in manufacturing industries.
Source: United States Department of Labor.

The increase in personal consumption in 1946 and 1947 was made possible by spending the savings that had been accumulated during the war. Wage increases were not the cause of the inflation. Clearly, during these two years, wages were increased after prices were increased. Labor was on a treadmill trying to catch up with the galloping price level.

Inflation appeared again following the Korean outbreak in June 1950 largely because of speculation and scare buying. The rise in wholesale prices after Korea was, in fact, arrested by the end of January 1951 with the imposition of price controls, though living costs continued to advance for a few months longer. Again, as shown in the tabulation, wage rates barely kept pace with consumer prices. The figures show that between June 1950 and June 1951, both wage rates and retail prices increased 9 percent and wholesale prices of all commodities advanced almost 15 percent.

Between and after these periods of inflation, prices generally remained stable while wages continued to advance as labor productivity steadily improved. In the two and one-half years between January 1948 and June 1950 there was an 11.5 percent rise in hourly wages in all manufacturing industries while living costs advanced only one half of one percent and wholesale prices of all commodities actually declined. This decline was confined largely to farm products and food. Industrial wholesale prices showed little change over the period.

Most striking is the record of the years since the middle of 1951. During this interval of almost five years, wage rates in manufacturing industries rose 23 percent while living costs increased less than 4 percent and wholesale prices declined slightly. Again, food and farm prices dropped, whereas wholesale prices of industrial commodities rose a bit over 4 percent in the 58 months from June 1951 to April 1956. The increase occurred after the middle of 1955.

The rise in the last five years in the consumer price index took place largely in the second half of 1951 and in 1952 as a result of the spill-over of the inflationary impact of the Korean War. Consumer prices are today at practically the same level as they were four years ago. The rise in non-agricultural wholesale prices in the past nine months is difficult to justify. In the middle of 1955, prices of industrial goods were actually lower than at the beginning of 1951. Profits were already near an all-time peak in mid-1955 when the price advances were put into effect.

This picture covering the past decade, especially most of the last five years and the two and one-half years from the beginning of 1948 to mid-1950, clearly demonstrate that wages can be raised progressively without inflation. Not only have these wage increases during these years been associated with over-all price stabilization, but the fact is that in essence they have made our economic growth possible. There is no better way to generate the increase in consumer purchasing power needed to buy the products of our expanded economy than to raise real wages and salaries of workers.

The general pattern described above has not been characteristic of each and every industry nor of each and every employer. In many areas where prices are not truly free, such as the steel industry, but are subject to some degree of control—control by monopolistic firms—wage increases have been passed on in the form of higher prices, with consequent booming profits. . . . The data show that the absorption of wage increases over the past five years in most industries has not resulted in a "profitless prosperity." On the contrary, total profits have remained high and we seem to have experienced a general demonstration, with some exceptions, of the thesis that American business firms are interested in large volume at moderate margins. It is unfortunate that not all industries have revealed their belief in the practice of making more profits by producing and selling more and more goods with smaller margins rather than pushing prices and profit margins higher and higher, ignoring the general well-being of the over-all economy.

Some corporations try to justify their price gouging on the grounds that they need more profits to finance expansion. . . . Other companies frankly say that they seek to make all the profits they possibly can so that when depressions come they will be better able to weather the storm. This is truly a cynical and dangerous view because such behavior, if widespread, will induce depressions. We need wage and price policies based on confidence in America's future and on a sense of responsibility for the welfare of the entire nation. There are still too many employers who deviate from such policies.

INSTITUTIONALIZED INFLATION

From the 1955 annual report of United States Steel Corporation, pp. 26–29

Of great importance to industry and hence to U.S. Steel is the development of what appears to be a permanent and alarming peacetime trend of cost and price inflation. During the war period, 1940–1945, U.S. Steel's employment costs per employe hour increased at a rapid rate. . . . But in the ten years since 1945 there has been an uninterrupted and even greater rate of inflation in this cost. Over the whole period, 1940–1955, the average annual increase is 8.0 per cent compounded.

A paralleling employment cost inflation has been general throughout industry and Government. This has been reflected in greater taxes and mounting prices of things purchased by U.S. Steel. Thus U.S. Steel's costs other than employment costs have risen in step with its employment cost inflation. During the fifteen years since 1940 U.S. Steel's total of all costs per employe hour has increased an average of 8.7 per cent per annum compounded.

Since it is impossible for output per employe hour to be increased at anything like these rates it has been necessary from time to time—as competition permitted—to raise steel prices and thereby pass on to buyers of steel part of the underlying cost inflation. According to the Bureau of Labor Statistics the prices of steel mill products increased from 1940 to 1955 by 119 per cent. None of that increase has resulted in widening the percentage spread between costs and sales prices since U.S. Steel's income as a per cent of sales was less in 1955 than in 1940, despite 1955's higher operating rate.

Wartime inflation is characteristic of American history. Continuous peacetime inflation is not. In each of the decades immediately following the War of 1812, the Civil War and World War I, wholesale prices, according to the Bureau of Labor Statistics, receded to 46, 59 and 74 per cent, respectively, of the inflated level they averaged in the last war year. But in 1955 such wholesale prices had risen to 161 per cent of their average level in 1945. Prices in the tenth year after the War of 1812 were 68 per cent of those prevailing just before that war. The percentages for the Civil War and World War I were, respectively, 128 and 142. But prices in 1955 averaged 217 per cent of their 1939–1940 average. Something new has appeared in the American economy.

Two basic roots of the inflationary tendency are discernible. The first one is the institution of industry-wide labor unions, headed by leaders who, with power to bring about industry-wide strikes, seek always to outdo each other in elevating employment costs in their respective industries. The legislative and social framework within which they function compels them to compete in elevating this basic cost.

The other root is the Government's "full employment" policy under which the money supply must be inflated fast enough to accommodate the inflating employment cost, lest that mounting cost bring about its natural result of pricing some people out of their jobs, even though only temporarily. It takes ever more dollars to cover ever rising costs and prices if industry's full output is to be purchased. The money supply—people's bank deposits subject to check plus their pocket currency—was in 1955, on a per capita basis, 2.7 times what it was in 1940. This is equivalent to 6.8 per cent per annum compounded.

The abuse of labor monopoly privilege and the monetary policy that transfers to the public in higher prices the penalty of that abuse appear to be the main elements of institutionalized inflation. It would be most helpful in this regard if those responsible for determining wage costs and fiscal policies were constantly aware of the inflationary potentials of their decisions.

The possibility of steady cost-price inflation creates many complex problems of corporate adaptation thereto. But overriding them is the recurring tendency of the inflation to become spectacularly explosive. The checking of inflation by the monetary means available can and has resulted in business readjustment. If permitted to go unchecked, the eventual readjustment would no doubt be even more severe. Readjustment, as previously noted, has a multiplied impact on U.S. Steel. In mid-1953 U.S. Steel was operating at full capacity. By the summer of 1954 the rate had fallen below 65 per cent. By the end of 1955 operations were again near capacity. Thus capacity is made alternately to seem either excessive or inadequate. This is not an efficient long-time use by the nation of its capital invested in the tools of production. Hence great interest and importance attach to restraint of inflation which may be accomplished in part through monetary controls.

MONETARY CONTROLS

Monetary controls rest primarily with the Federal Reserve System, which includes the twelve regional Federal Reserve Banks and the Board of Governors in Washington. The Member Banks that serve the public are required by law to keep reserves on deposit with their respective Reserve Banks equal to a designated percentage of their own deposits. Through purchase or sale of Government securities (so-called "open market operations") the Reserve Banks have power to increase or decrease Member Bank reserves—to create "easy" or "tight" money conditions. When Member Bank reserves are increased beyond those required, the Member Banks are under pressure to use these excess reserves in loans, if possible, or in the purchase of securities. Such actions generally result in lower interest rates and an increase in Member Bank deposits. Since people's bank deposits constitute the principal part of the money supply, an increase therein is the process of inflating the money supply.

Conversely the Reserve Banks, by the reverse open market operation, may reduce the reserves of the Member Banks to the point where they are required to borrow from and pay an interest rate to the Reserve Banks in order to maintain their reserves at the legal requirement. Under this "tight money" circumstance pressure on the Member Banks to increase deposits through loan and investment expansion is replaced by the reverse pressure. This is the process of checking inflation or compelling deflation of the money supply.

CONFLICTING OBJECTIVES

The Reserve System's task of continuously maintaining money and credit conditions that will meet the needs of agriculture, commerce and industry without developing inflationary "boom" and reactionary "bust" is most difficult. The handicaps under which the System operates deserve more understanding than they are generally accorded. In wartime this general purpose, like other purposes, must be subordinated to the overriding "win the war" purpose. Money must be made "easy" so that the Government can sell great quantities of low-interest bonds to cover expenditures. This runs the risk of a dangerously inflated monetary and credit structure at the end of the war.

In peacetime, as previously noted, the general purpose is now partially subordinated to the policy of accommodating employment cost inflation. Moreover, there are many self-styled "liberals" who constantly, if shortsightedly, endorse "easy" money and protest any safeguarding tightening of money. It is a curious attitude because it is the "little folk" on fixed salary or pension and with savings deposits or bonds and life insurance who get "hurt" by decreasing buying power of the dollar. Thus $100 so invested ten years ago and cashed in today will buy less than 70 per cent of what it would have bought when it was invested.

In view of these handicaps the achievements of the Reserve System in recent years have been notable. By tightening money in 1952–1953 the post-Korea inflation that then threatened was checked. By easing money in mid-1953 the inventory readjustment was eased. By tightening money once again some months ago the prospect of renewed inflation was moderated. Although wholesale and consumer price indexes have been generally stable since 1953, there were inflationary advances in employment cost, construction cost, some industrial prices, and security prices in 1955.

The hope that serious inflation and reactionary collapse may be avoided in the future lies in a widening public understanding of the new institutionalized cost inflation and in public endorsement of the monetary restraints needed to keep it from becoming explosive. It is in those same developments that U.S. Steel's hope lies of more steadily and hence more economically utilizing its facilities and manpower in the enduring service of the nation.

AS WAGE INFLATION GOES . . .

From the 1956 annual report of United States Steel Corporation, pp. 25–29

For the last two decades U.S. Steel's operations have been conducted within a framework of unremitting cost inflation. This cost inflation is not unique with U.S. Steel—instead it is a matter of national concern. It has been the hope of many that the continuing cost inflation could be abated, even if complete stability could not be achieved. In this respect the year 1956 has been a disappointment. There is as yet no evidence of an abatement of cost inflation in the affairs of U.S. Steel.

. . . For the best part of two decades both U.S. Steel's employment cost per employe hour and its total of all costs per employe hour have advanced at rates, compounded annually, averaging 8.1 per cent and 8.8 per cent, respectively. These advances were fully sustained in 1956.

This current evidence supplements other reasons for believing that cost-price inflation is in danger of becoming a permanent feature of American life. Central to such conclusion is the fact that the vast power of industry-wide labor unions in compelling annual increases in employment costs far beyond increases in productivity is automatically compelling inflation. This is because, up and down the industrial production line, employment cost constitutes, directly or indirectly, the vast bulk of all costs. There is thus a natural sequence between the basic employment cost inflation and cost-covering price inflation since the latter is but the reflection of the former. To the extent that product price increases are eventually reflected in cost-of-living indexes, further employment cost increases are automatically generated by reason of so-called cost-of-living clauses in wage contracts. This starts the process all over again. Inflation is rapidly becoming automatic in America. Such inflation creates serious problems for business managements. These problems center around the finding of the additional dollars that are needed to finance the ever-increasing costs of doing business.

CAPITAL EXPENDITURES

Nowhere is the requirement for additional dollars more evident in U.S. Steel's affairs than in the purchase of facilities. Steel making requires heavy investment in long-term facilities. Since the close of World War II U.S. Steel has engaged in a huge modernization and expansion program. This program at the construction cost level prevailing at the end of the war would have required capital expenditures of $1.7 billion through 1956. But construction costs . . . have steadily risen at a rapid rate with the result that actual capital expenditures were $3.0 billion. The additional $1.3 billion, or about 75 per cent, is one measure in one area of the financing problem created by inflation. It represents additional dollars but not additional facilities.

INADEQUATE DEPRECIATION

Aggravating the problem of finding the additional dollars for expenditure for facilities is the serious inadequacy of the present Federal income tax formula for wear and exhaustion, often called depreciation. Recovery, through depreciation, of capital previously invested in facilities is essential if, through its re-expenditure, the supply and modernness of existing tools of production are to be maintained. Income tax law limits the total depreciation recoverable during the life of a facility to the number of dollars originally spent for it years ago. But with the value of the dollar steadily declining the buying power originally expended cannot possibly be recovered under this unrealistic limitation. Faster recovery, such as has been permitted under certificates of necessity, tends to reduce the inadequacy which would otherwise exist; but the only real basis of recovering purchasing power would be to adjust for the change in the dollar intervening between the year of capital expenditure and the year in which depreciation is taken. . . .

PRICES

The only continuing source of revenue that any company has with which to cover its costs and provide the income to justify its continuing existence is sales to customers. Since the basic employment cost inflation has far outstripped productivity increases, part of the cost increase has had to be passed on to customers in higher prices. U.S. Steel's employment cost per employe hour in 1956 was three and a half times that of 1940. Steel mill finished product prices in 1956, according to the Bureau of Labor Statistics, averaged less than two and a half times what they were in 1940. As basic costs continue to be forced upward, and as the depreciation deficiency widens, management's problem of finding the dollars required to maintain the business becomes more acute.

It is especially acute with respect to covering the depreciation deficiency because it takes two dollars, either from increased productivity or from customers in the prices they pay, to yield one dollar toward meeting the depreciation deficiency. This is because the tax authorities treat the two dollars as taxable income. To secure the additional dollars through increased productivity is most desirable, and every company competitively strives to increase productivity. To do so, however, requires heavy outlays for ever more modern and efficient equipment at the very time when equipment prices are rising and the depreciation source of funds to purchase it is undermined through taxation.

THE BROADER PROBLEM

While continuing inflation presents particular problems to managements, it presents broader problems to the nation as a whole. If the American people come to accept inflation as a way of life—however reluctantly or apathetically— it is inevitable that both individuals and business will come to compete in borrowing in order to buy now and pay off later in cheapened dollars. Such tendencies are already evidenced by unprecedented increases in both consumer and business indebtedness. Expectation of inflation induces something of a flight from money into goods. This, too, is evidenced by the increasing rapidity with which the nation's supply of money is turned over, by mounting inventories and by developing overcapacity in an increasing number of industries. Expectation of inflation stimulates the urge toward speculative spending at the expense of traditional forms of thrift through which productive capital is provided, thus unbalancing the economy.

Speculative overbuying—whether of commodities, stocks, real estate or other property—when financed through debt expanding more rapidly than income presents the historic framework out of which have come crisis and readjustment. No one wants to repeat that historic sequence, but the presence of wage inflation and resulting price inflation, together with widespread expectation that they will continue, augments the danger that it might be repeated. The means by which such a prospect may be avoided merit the most careful consideration of managements, of labor leaders, of legislators—in fact of all citizens.

STEEL PRICE INCREASES

From Facts on Steel: Profits, Productivity, Prices and Wages, 1956, United Steelworkers of America, Pittsburgh, Pa., 1956, pp. 31–39 and 29

For an extended period the Steel Industry has defended the Price increases it has levied by publicizing these claims:

1. Steel wage increases have forced higher Steel Prices;

2. A steel wage increase always results in higher Materials costs equal to the cost of the wage increase; and

3. Steel profit margins traditionally have been too low.

In recent years the Steel Industry has placed increasing emphasis on an additional *fourth* claim (really 2 claims) for higher Steel Prices—the alleged inadequacy of the charges permitted for Depreciation by the Federal Income Tax Law, and the "need" for larger Profits to finance the Industry's expansion of Steel capacity.

Each of these claims is examined in this section.

1—Steel wages in relation to steel prices

The Industry habitually refers to wage increases it has negotiated as "rounds" of increases but understandably is reticent about reviewing its Price increases.

In the 10 years from 1946 through 1955, Steelworkers negotiated wage increases in 8 years. In one year, 1949, there was *no* wage increase, but pension and insurance programs were negotiated. In 1951 there was *no* wage increase or other benefits of any sort.

In contrast, in the same 10-year period the Steel Industry generally raised its Prices as follows:

"General" Price Increases (on most products) ...... 12 times
Selected Price Increases (on some products) ...... 3 times
"Extras" (increases other than in base prices) ...... 3 times
Total "Rounds" of Price Increases .... 18 times

This means simply that the Industry has raised its Prices *twice* for each wage or "fringe" increase negotiated with its employees. . . .

The Bureau of Labor Statistics' Index of Wholesale Prices of Steel Mill Products shows a rise in Steel Prices (including "Extras" on some products) in more than 36 months during that 10-year period. . . .

The total hourly cost of all the wage and "fringe" settlements in that period was $1.318. . . .

. . . There were more than 1.3 billion manhours worked in 1955 by all employees in the Industry. Accordingly, the current annual "cost" of all of the wage and "fringe" benefits negotiated from 1946 through 1955 (based on 1955 manhours) equals slightly less than *$1.8 billion.*

The cumulative increase in the Price of Steel products from January, 1946, through December, 1955, has been $67.25 a ton. Finished Steel Shipments in 1955 totaled 84.7 million tons. Therefore, the current annual revenue gain (based on 1955 Shipments) from Steel Price increases since early 1946 is *$5.7 billion,* or *$3.9 billion* more than increased labor costs.

In short, since 1945, Steel Prices were increased by *$3.19* for each *$1.00* increase in total labor costs—a ratio of more than *3 to 1.* Labor costs measured from 1947 show an increase of *28.0%* vs. a Price increase of *78.2%* through March 1956—a *77.7%* average for the 1st quarter.

2—Steel materials costs in relation to steel prices

The cost of the Materials *purchased* by the Steel Industry has risen somewhat in the postwar period. But this rise has been moderate in relation to the rise in the Price of Steel products *sold* by the Industry.

The base period of the BLS Wholesale Price Indexes is 1947–49. From the base period to March, 1956 the Price of Steel Mill Products *sold* by the Industry has risen by 58.2%. This is equal to 78.2% on a 1947 basis.

This is far in excess of the price rise of the most important products *purchased* by the Steel Industry. Examples of the price increases of such products since 1947–49 include Scrap—22.3%, Bituminous Coal—7.0%, Petroleum and Products—16.8%, Gas—22.0%, Tin (pig)—10.4%, Oxygen—5.3%, Cement—38.5%, Sand, Gravel and Crushed Stone—22.4%, Electricity—a decline of 5.7%, Material Handling Equipment—48.1%—all of which have risen far less than *Steel* Prices.

The Annual Reports of the larger Steel Companies do not break out separately their Materials costs relating solely to Steel production. Accordingly, a precise estimate of such costs cannot be made. However, in testimony before the T.N.E.C., a United States Steel spokesman referred to the BLS Price Index of "All Commodities Other Than Farm and Food Products" (which the President's Council of Economic Advisors refers to as "industrial prices") as a close indicator of the movement of prices of the Materials purchased by the Corporation. That Index, from the year 1947 through the 1st quarter of 1956, rose by 26.7% (it was 27.6% by April). . . . The continued validity of that Index in relation to United States Steel's purchases is indicated by the fact that, from

1947, to 1955, U.S. Steel's total Materials costs (all materials) per ton of Steel products shipped increased by an almost identical amount—27.9%.

Thus, while Materials costs have risen about 28.0% since the year 1947, Steel Prices have been raised by 78.2%. Again Steel Prices have *exceeded* cost increases by a ratio of nearly 3 *to* 1.

An additional indication of the far more rapid rise of Steel Prices than of Steel's Materials costs since 1947 is the relationship of payments for Materials to the receipts from Sales. In 1947 Materials costs represented 45.2¢ out of each Sales Dollar, but by 1955 they had declined to 40.1¢.[1] U.S. Steel's Materials costs were 39.5¢ of each Sales Dollar in 1947, but only 33.1¢ in 1955.

All available data establish not only that Steel Prices have risen far more rapidly than the Industry's Materials costs, but also that there is no validity to the claim that increased labor costs somehow have a one-to-one relationship with increases in Materials costs.

The Industry's leading producer, United States Steel, demolished the Industry's own contention with a Table contained in the Corporation's 1952 Annual Report. It showed that the rise in average hourly employment costs had no fixed relationship to the rise in the average cost in Steel operations of purchased products and services (Materials) per ton of Steel Shipments. These comparisons from the Corporation's own 1952 Annual Report are shown in Table 18. . . .

Table 18. Comparative Changes in Materials and Employment Costs in U. S. Steel Corp.

Period covered	Increase as percent of 1940	
	Employment cost	Cost of materials
January, 1941—April, 1947............	56%	47%
April, 1947—July, 1948.............	16	42
July, 1948—November, 1949.........	14	18
November, 1949—December, 1950.....	19	3
December, 1950—July, 1952.........	23	24
July, 1952—December, 1952..........	27	4

It is apparent that the "formula" by which the Industry has attempted to justify Steel Price increases over a series of years—i.e., that the minimum amount by which Steel Prices must rise is *double* the cost of a wage increase (with no allowance for increased productivity) in order to offset future increased Materials costs—is a "formula" unrelated to reality.

[1] Based on the 9 of the 25 leading Companies for which Sales, Materials, and Wages and Salaries data are available for all years since 1939.

3—Steel profits in relation to price increases

The industry is not quite fair in using Net Profits as a measure of its profit margin in a labor cost dispute, since wage increases are paid out of Profits Before Taxes, but the facts on Net Profits only have been analyzed here, in order to meet the Industry's argument directly on the Industry's chosen ground.

The Net Profits of the Steel Industry (25 Companies) amounted to $126.4 million in 1939. The rate of Return on Net worth was 4.2%, a relatively modest return. By 1947 Net Profits more than tripled to $394.3 million, which was equivalent to a 10.5% Return on a 24% larger Net Worth—which is certainly a substantial Return.

Since 1947, despite an ever-larger demand for Steel, and a tremendously expanded capacity which enabled the Industry to meet this demand, the Steel Industry has persisted in a policy designed to widen already huge profit margins.

Thus, between 1947 and 1955 the Industry expanded its Net Profits from $394.3 million to more than a billion dollars ($1,019.4 million). Its rate of Return on Net Worth climbed from 10.5% in 1947 to *13.8%* in 1955. In the 1st quarter of 1956 Net Profits increased further to an annual rate of *$1,153.4 million,* and its rate of Return on Net Worth to *15.6%.* Increased Net Profits were achieved not only as a result of increased Sales, but by virtue of increased Profits per Dollar of Sales. Net Profits of 22 of the largest Steel Companies were equal to 6.2¢ per Dollar of Sales in 1947 and 7.9¢ in 1955. For U.S. Steel it was 6.0¢ in 1947, 9.0¢ in 1955, and 9.5¢ in the 1st quarter of 1956.

In this same period between 1947 and 1955 when the rate of Return on Net Worth in Steel *increased* from 10.5% to *13.8%* (and to *15.6%* in the 1st quarter of 1956), Net Profits in relation to Net Worth *declined* in All Manufacturing Industries from *15.1%* in 1947 to *12.3%* in 1955.[2] Net Profits per Dollar of Sales which were 5.7¢ in 1947 in All Manufacturing Corporations, *declined* to 4.1¢ in 1955 and to 4.3¢ in the 1st quarter of 1956.[3]

Since Net Profits in Steel have climbed by 706.5% from 1939 to 1955 (812.5% to 1956), by 158.5% from 1947 to 1955, and the rate of Return on Net Worth, as well as Net Profits per Dollar of Sales, has passed the average of All Manufacturing Industries, the Steel Industry understandably has reached for a new rationale for further Price increases.

4—Replacement and expansion needs as a basis for price increases

For the past few years, and especially in recent months, the Industry has rested its case for even higher Prices and greater Profits on a new theory. Steel Industry spokesmen are attempting to "sell" the proposition that (1) the Administration's refusal to revise the tax laws pertaining to Depreciation along the lines desired by the Steel Companies requires the Industry to raise its

[2] F.T.C.-S.E.C. Quarterly Industrial Financial Report Series for All Manufacturing Corporations. Data for 1st quarter 1956 were not available.

[3] U. S. Department of Commerce.

Prices again in order to have sufficient funds to maintain and replace its properties, and (2) Steel Prices must be higher so that Profits will be great enough to pay for the cost of *expanding* the Industry's capacity. . . .

This position of the Steel Industry on securing funds for maintaining facilities and for further capacity *expansion*—a position based on the Government's refusal to provide further special Depreciation allowances for the Industry—is an insistence that the public accept as a fair and equitable solution the proposition that the American consumers foot the bill in the form of higher Steel Prices. In addition, the American people are being told by the Steel Companies that a further boost in Steel Prices will be levied in order to pay for *new* Steel plants! Steel Companies' stockholders, under this plan, are to receive a gift—new Steel plants and enlarged facilities which will increase their equity in their Company, and, eventually, increase their Dividends—all at the expense of American consumers who will pay the costs by paying higher Prices for Steel products. Gone, apparently, is the concept of "risk" capital, of financing industrial expansion through flotation of stock or by means of borrowing on bond issues. Instead, the Steel Industry argues its right to collect "riskless" capital from unwilling consumers by forcing upon them higher Prices.

Lip service is given to the desirability of encouraging greater participation by the public in the ownership of the Industry. But the Steel Industry's actions have no such effect. The American people are to be given no opportunity to share in the Steel Industry's growth and prosperity. Raising funds for expansion through the sale of Common Stock to the public is rejected by the Steel Companies. The public is called upon to provide the funds, but it is shut out of participation in the Profits to be realized from the use of these funds.

As for the allied contention that higher Steel Prices were required to pay for the cost merely of maintaining the Steel Companies' existing properties (Depreciation), here again the Steel Companies' own financial reports demonstrate the falsity of the claim.

For example, from 1952 through most of 1955, prices in general, except for Steel Prices, were relatively stable—i.e., the cost of maintaining Steel facilities, replacing outworn and obsolete equipment, etc., was not appreciably different in 1953, 1954 and 1955. The financial reports of the Steel Companies to the Securities and Exchange Commission for the last 3 years demonstrate conclusively that additional revenue in the form of higher Steel Prices was *not* required to enable the Industry to replace obsolete facilities. The higher Prices charged in these three years, and the resulting increase in Profits, were forced consumer investments (without benefit of stock certificates) in the expansion of steel-making capacity, and were not necessary simply to replace and maintain existing facilities. . . .

Thus, in the 3 years from 1953 through 1955 the Steel Industry had $4.1 billion available for reinvestment in the Industry, of which only about 4% represented borrowed "outside" capital. In those 3 years the Industry accomplished the following:

1. Replaced obsolete capacity.

2. Expanded capacity by 10,815,620 ingot tons.[4]

3. Increased Dividends to stockholders by more than 30% (from $384 million in 1953 to $501 million in 1955).

4. Increased Working Capital by $1.5 billion.

The fact that all of the foregoing purposes were accomplished by the Industry without floating stock or borrowing more than a negligible amount of capital effectively disposes of the assertion that even higher Steel Prices are now required in order to yield sufficient funds for replacement. Instead of preparing for higher Prices the Steel Industry should be considering the extent of Steel Price *reductions* which it can and should put into effect.

Increases in productivity mean simply that unit labor requirements decline—that each ton of Steel is produced with less hours of labor. Even if the cost of each hour of labor is increased by wage rate increases proportionate to rising productivity, these increases can be *absorbed* out of the gains in productivity.

These productivity increases bluntly mean that the "real" earnings level of Steelworkers can rise significantly without increasing Steel costs or necessitating an increase in Steel Prices. Unfortunately the Steel Industry has been unwilling to set its Prices within the bounds of its costs but has, instead, insisted on raising its Prices to increase profit margins. This not only has caused inflation. It is inflation.

It is true that the Steelworkers' standard of living has risen during the last few years. But the increases received—and more—could have been met from the gains in productivity. Unwilling to accept this fact, however, the Industry has insisted on raising Prices—on receiving increases which have, in the main, added unwarranted increments to Profits.

Surely Steelworkers have every right to a fair share in the productivity gains which they have helped to achieve. This would permit stockholders and Steel users also to share in these gains. This is the fair way to divide up these gains. The Union has not asked for more. The Union has asked, as a basic floor, that Steelworkers' "real" wages increase as rapidly percentagewise as the "real" productivity increases in Steel. This, the Union has not been able to achieve. Consistently "real" productivity increases have outrun the increases in "real" wages. This is evident in the following moderately long range comparison which covers most of the period since the Union was founded:

	Increase in "real" productivity in steel	Increase in "real" straight time average hourly earnings in steel
1939–1956 (more than 16 years)....	68.8%	47.1%

[4] An annual rate of expansion greater than is projected by the Steel Industry for the next 5 years.

. . . In the past, the Union has often been forced to demand wage increases which in dollars and cents amount have exceeded the percentage increase in productivity. This has been forced on the Union because of the Industry's Price Policy which has caused inflation in Steel and has contributed greatly to it in the Economy and has, thereby, robbed the workers of the wages they were already receiving. They and their Union have been forced to pursue these rising prices—the cost of living—just to *maintain* their "real" wage position, i.e., their existing standard of living. This purely defensive role of a significant portion of many of the Union's wage proposals in recent years is generally unknown or overlooked.

If management, including Steel management, would refrain from insisting on its all too frequent, unnecessary, and inordinately large Price increases so that there could be price stability, there would be no need to catch up constantly with a rising cost of living, and increased money wages would then bring increased "real" wages. It would then be possible for labor to improve its wages, "fringes" and working conditions more nearly within the framework of rising productivity. Until management is willing to abandon its inflationary pricing policy, certainly, the Union has no choice but to insist on money wage increases greater in amount than the percentage productivity increases—if it is even to hold its own, let alone make any gains in "real" wages and in its standards of living.

EFFECT OF RECENT WAGE AND PRICE INCREASES IN STEEL

From Bulletin—Steel 1951–1955, A Comparison of Values, a memorandum issued by a stock brokerage firm, member of the New York Stock Exchange, July 7, 1955, p. 8

Last week steel wages were raised by 15¢ per hour on average and this was followed by price increases estimated to average $7.35 per ton. President C. F. Hood of U.S. Steel stated that the price increase was designed not only to compensate for the higher wage costs but also for "the steadily mounting costs of purchased goods and services, of state and local taxes, and of new construction." The excess of the price over the wage increase appears indeed to be substantial.

In 1954, average hourly earnings at U.S. Steel were $2.488 so that the wage increase was 6%. On the other hand the price rise amounted to 5.8%. In 1954 wages and salaries were 37.5% of U.S. Steel's sales volume but the wage rise will spread to other industries upon which the steel companies depend for raw materials and services. In the past, the cost of such products and services bought by U.S. Steel about equalled the company's wage costs, and it may be assumed that these costs will go up by about 50% of the wage rise.

On this basis it appears that the price increase exceeds the direct and indirect costs of the wage boost by about $2.00 to $2.50 per ton of steel shipped. If translated into earnings after taxes it can be estimated that the new prices will add about 40¢ per share to U.S. Steel's earnings this year, about $1.20 to the earnings of Bethlehem and corresponding amounts to the earnings of the other companies.

STEELS AFTER THE STRIKE

From a pamphlet issued August–September, 1956, by the same firm

The steel strike and the ensuing wage settlement and price increases have improved rather than impaired the investment position of the industry. Burdensome inventories have been absorbed and high capacity operations are likely to prevail during the rest of the year. Although the price increases have not quite come up to expectations they should more than offset the higher wage costs. In spite of recent moderate advances steel stocks continue to appraise existing capacity at only a fraction of reproduction costs, and the steel group remains the last major undervalued group in the market.

The main features of the new wage settlement in the steel industry are as follows:

1. Wage increases variously estimated to average between 20.3¢ and 25¢ per hour for the first year and between 45.6¢ and 55¢ for the next three years, depending on whether higher social security taxes, vacation payments, etc. are included.

2. A three-year non-reopenable contract as against two-year agreements in the past which could be reopened every year as to their wage clauses.

3. A 52-week supplementary unemployment benefit plan and a cost-of-living clause permitting wage increases twice a year tied to the cost-of-living index and practically applicable only on the upside.

To compensate for the higher costs the industry has posted price increases which range in the case of U.S. Steel from $7 to $21 and more per ton and reportedly average around $8.50 per ton or 6¼% of the prices existing before the strike.

In order to gauge the impact of wage settlement and price increases on the earnings of the steel industry the following factors have to be considered:

1. Assuming that about 20 man-hours are needed to produce one ton of finished steel, a 20¢ increase per hour in employment costs is equivalent to $4 per ton. It may be assumed further than the indirect effect of the wage rise on raw materials will over a period of time amount to another $2 per ton. Against this the increase in base prices is $8.50 per ton, so that the profit of the industry per ton of finished steel would be improved by about $2.50 per ton. While this subject is highly controversial, our estimate of the increment to profits is probably conservative as it may take less than 20 man-hours to produce a ton of steel, and besides this there has been a continuous increase of perhaps 3% per annum in productivity over the years and thus there is some compensation against wage increases. . . .

WAGE-PRICE RELATIONSHIPS

From Progress-sharing Can Mean Industrial Peace, by Charles E. Wilson, President, General Motors Corporation, published for General Motors men and women by the employee relations staff, GM Information Rack Service, 1952

Arrangements like ours for lifting and lowering wages in step with the cost of living are commonly called "escalator clauses." They are attacked by people who insist upon talking about "the wage-price spiral." I contend that we should not say "the *wage*-price spiral." We should say "the *price*-wage spiral." For it is not primarily wages that push up prices. It is primarily prices that *pull* up wages.

What makes prices? Basically prices are made by the volume of the supply of money as compared with the volume of goods and services available for purchase. This money supply includes cash in circulation, deposits in banks, private and governmental loans from banks. Governments are often the chief authors of rapid rises in prices. When governments, instead of balancing their budgets, borrow huge amounts from banks, they create an oversupply of money; much of this oversupply is used to bid for purchase of an undersupply of civilian goods; prices inevitably go up, and we have inflation. The working people did not make that inflation. They only want to catch up with it in order to be able to pay their grocery bills.

I contend that present high wages are more the result of fundamental inflationary money pressures than of unreasonable wage pressures by unions.

Consider the prices of many raw materials since the Korean War started. Certain of those materials rose by 25 percent and even by 200 percent in a few months. Did wages rise even 25 percent in those few months? Of course not. But many prices did.

I believe that if during this inflationary period there had been no unions and no labor contracts, average wages in the United States would have increased as much as they actually have. Why? Because they too would have reacted to supply-and-demand pressures and increased costs of living.

To guide our thinking in this matter, we of General Motors have taken the authoritative figures of the Bureau of Labor Statistics regarding consumers' prices for the last 30 years and the equally authoritative figures of the Federal Reserve System regarding the supply of money for the same period. The chart which displays these figures conclusively convinces us that:

"Changes in Consumers' Prices Have Followed the Money Supply."
"When the Money Supply Goes Up, Prices Go Up."
"When Prices Have Gone Up, Wages Have Gone Up."

RESPONSIBILITY FOR WAGE-PRICE RELATIONS

From "Wages and Economic Growth," an address by Lemuel R. Boulware, Vice President of Public and Employee Relations, General Electric Company, before the National Association of Manufacturers, New York City, December 6, 1956

While all of us businessmen have been remiss in many ways, I think all our fellow citizens have particular reason to be critical of those of us in the leading larger companies which have the most rapidly expanding technology and volume. I feel we have especially impeded, in two ways, the economy we have otherwise done so much to help.

First, I feel our wage and benefit settlements have been those which were most inflationary. And we have caused other pay increases to be more inflationary than they would have been without our example.

Second, I feel that the way we have distributed our cost savings—as between immediate pay raises on the one hand and, on the other, the price reduction, research expansion, and capital formation for faster progress—has been different from the way we Americans would all want it done if we had a common understanding of the course we must pursue to deserve and achieve the fastest possible progress for all.

We can't blame any miscarriage here on the unions. I think we larger employers have been almost entirely responsible, for we were paying the higher wages, giving the greater pay increases, and pioneering the high-cost benefits —long before unions were prominent in manufacturing. Only last year a veteran union official, when reminiscing with me about the factory organizing drives of the 1930's, said he and his associates went first to organize these same already highest paying plants and then had such pay levels to show when they went elsewhere. And Professor John Dunlop, of Harvard, has observed: "Wage leadership in the country has tended to be concentrated in industries in which productivity has been increasing more rapidly than the average. This tends to give an upward drift or prod to the wage level."

So I don't think we in the larger companies have any place to look—but at ourselves—for any misguided earlier unilateral action and for any later uncomplaining continuance of such misguided action in consort with the unions.

A CLASH OF OBJECTIVES

From the Guaranty Survey, January, 1957, published by the Guaranty Trust Company of New York

WAGES, STABLE MONEY AND EMPLOYMENT

The contradictions among the three objectives of rising wages, stable money, and continuous full or maximum employment are partly inherent in the objectives themselves and partly due to practical shortcomings which might conceivably be corrected if the goals were more intelligently pursued. There is no inherent reason, for example, why rising wages should exert upward pressure on prices; the difficulty arises when wage increases exceed gains in productivity and thus raise labor costs per unit of output.

Wage increases that are excessive in this sense may occur as a result of labor shortages (or overall employment), which cause employers to bid against one another for a labor supply which appears inadequate, or as a consequence of the power and inclination of labor organizations to demand and obtain increases in wage rates which exceed productivity gains. In a state of ideal economic equilibrium and human enlightenment, such things would not happen. In actual practice, however, they do happen.

Nor is there any inherent reason why wage increases should interfere with the full-employment objective. Here again, the difficulty arises from the tend-ency of wages to rise faster than productivity. In so far as employers are able to recover the higher costs by raising prices, full employment may be maintained, but only at the sacrifice of price stability. In so far as price increases are prevented, production becomes unprofitable, and price stability is maintained at the sacrifice of the full-employment objective.

At times of too rapid wage increases, therefore, monetary authorities face a painful choice. If they make enough money available to accommodate business at the higher price levels, they are acquiescing in inflation. If they do not, they are acquiescing in unemployment. The objectives of stable money and full employment are irreconcilable unless wage increases are limited to gains in productivity.

PROPOSED SOLUTIONS

Various solutions have been proposed. Some commentators are optimistic enough to believe that labor organizations can be "educated" to limit their wage demands to conform with productivity gains. There is little in the record to support this view. Union economists sometimes concede in their writings that there is a necessary correspondence between wage rates and productivity, but it is usually difficult to reconcile their words with the actions of officials at the bargaining table. Available measurements of productivity are rough estimates at best, and, even with the best will on both sides, there would still be room for wide disagreement between parties with large financial interests at stake in the outcome. Add to this the rivalry among union officials for the prestige that comes from having driven the shrewdest bargain, and it is difficult to believe that stable money will soon, if ever, outweigh dollars in the pocket in actual labor-management negotiations.

Others would hold wage increases in line with productivity gains by abolishing the right to strike and setting up a system of labor courts to adjudicate wage disputes. This solution would amount to direct governmental control of wages. It would mark the end of economic freedom for labor and management alike. Never, except possibly in time of war or supreme emergency, would or should the American people accept such regimentation. It would be a long first stride toward the destruction of free enterprise. Compulsory arbitration is an old proposal that has been consistently rejected by a people whose instincts warn them that in practice it would be but a step removed from slavery.

Short of this drastic solution, there have been numerous proposals aimed at limiting or curbing the power of organized labor. Some of these can be strongly defended on economic grounds. Their political feasibility, however, is another matter. For more than a generation, the legislative and administrative authority of government has been used, for the most part, to strengthen rather than weaken union power. It is difficult to envisage an early reversal of this trend.

CREEPING INFLATION

It is believed in some quarters that the aim of price stability should be abandoned and creeping inflation accepted as the least of the threatened evils.

This view is based on a recognition of what may fairly be called the inherent and inescapable contradiction between continuous full employment and stable money. The simultaneous realization of these two objectives would be possible only in an ideal society characterized by complete freedom, instant mobility, and infallible judgment and foresight, resulting in perfect equilibrium—such a society as never has existed and does not seem likely to exist on earth. As long as men are human, they will continue to make mistakes, and these will produce maladjustments causing some unemployment of productive resources, including labor.

Government cannot prevent the mistakes. It may, however, be able to conceal or minimize their unfavorable effects for a time by administering inflationary stimulants and thus keeping the economy under forced draft. This is what creeping inflation would be designed to do.

This abject surrender of the objective of stable money is objectionable on many grounds. It is morally offensive because it amounts to an advocacy of legalized robbery of millions of bank depositors, life-insurance policyholders, bondholders, pensioners, beneficiaries of trust funds, and others dependent upon fixed or sluggishly responsive incomes. It is politically offensive because inflation tends to undermine respect for a government that is systematically depriving its people of the benefit of their savings. It is socially offensive because monetary depreciation penalizes honest industry and thrift and places a premium on speculation and gambling. No one who has passed through or closely studied a real inflationary experience can suppose that the evils of inflation are economic alone. Stable character and government depend upon stable money.

"Creeping" is an insidious and misleading word when applied to monetary debasement. A depreciation of as little as 2 or 3 per cent a year, continued over the average duration of an individual's working career, would wipe out the greater part of the purchasing power of a life's savings. The cumulative effects of even a creeping inflation can be tremendous.

Creeping inflation, moreover, cannot be depended upon to creep. Prices do not rise uniformly. Distortions and maladjustments occur. These require correction, and the longer the correction is prevented by further inflation, the more serious the maladjustments become. Inflation has been aptly compared to the use of a drug, requiring larger and larger doses to produce the desired effect. The final outcome is an economic collapse, the exact form of which depends upon the amount of inflation administered.

The really fatal weakness of creeping inflation as a solution of the problem of conflicting economic objectives is not merely that it is an unsatisfactory solution but that, in the final analysis, it is no solution at all. No one denies that mass unemployment is a dire evil, and if it could be permanently prevented by creeping inflation, or even by galloping inflation, the choice of evils would be arguable. But neither experience nor common sense affords any support whatever for the view that the choice between creeping inflation and occasional unemployment is a real choice. The most that could be hoped for from creeping inflation would be a temporary respite, to be paid for, if experience means anything, by a truly disastrous collapse.

Adoption of the philosophy of creeping inflation would be especially dangerous at a time like the present, when inflation rather than deflation is the immediate problem, when more rather than less thrift is needed to meet the enormous demand for capital goods, and when central banking authorities are striving to preserve monetary stability in the face of political and popular pressure for easy money. Unless saving can be stimulated, inflationary pressure may, over a period of years, become even stronger than it is now. A systematic swelling of the money supply in an effort to prevent temporary readjustments would only intensify such pressure.

Political realities being what they are, the practical solution to the problem of conflicting objectives will probably be found in a compromise involving the partial achievement and the partial sacrifice of each. Such a solution will fully satisfy no one, but it is perhaps the best that can be expected in a situation where government is asked to be all things to all men.

INFLATION IS NOT THE WHOLE STORY

Testimony of Seymour E. Harris, Chairman, Department of Economics, Harvard University, in January, 1957, Economic Report of the President, hearings before the Joint Congressional Economic Committee, 85th Cong., 1st Sess., 1957, p. 496

CHAIRMAN PATMAN: I want to ask you to comment and to bring us up to date on a statement I think you made at one time, that although we had 50-cent dollars, we had almost 4 times as many to buy goods and services with.

MR. HARRIS: Yes.

CHAIRMAN PATMAN: And that meant that we were really about 100 percent better off.

MR. HARRIS: The point I was making there was—I could quote Secretary Humphrey, who makes this statement about once a month—namely, that you have a rise in the price level in the last 15 years and so forth, and he says that is terrible, every dollar is worth half as much. But he forgets about the rise of output that has come with the increase in the supply of money. Over the American history we have had an increase of supply of money of 3,500 times, but we also had an increase of income 400 times and relative stability of prices over that long period up until World War II. If you are trying to give the whole story you should not merely talk about the value of $1 but the question of how much is there available to be purchased with your dollars. Part of this rise of output is certainly associated with the rise in the supply of money. If you do not increase your money fast enough, you do not get an adequate increase of output.

REQUIREMENTS OF WAGE-PRICE POLICY

From "The Realities of Tight Money," an address by J. Cameron Thomson, Chairman of the Board, Northwest Bancorporation, and Vice President, Committee for Economic Development, before the 26th New England Bank Management Conference, Boston, 1956

The monetary authorities cannot be expected to do their job without the cooperation of both management and labor.

In our economy, prices and wages are free to move in response to changes in demand and supply conditions. If we are to have over-all price stability, some prices must of necessity go down while others go up.

Wage increases that are limited to about the average increase in productivity for all industries can be absorbed without forcing up the average level of prices. However, wage pressures tend to be the greatest in those industries that are advancing in productivity faster than the average increase in productivity.

If these wage pressures are fully satisfied, there will be no room for a reduction in prices in the rapidly expanding and more efficient industries. These wage increases will, in turn, tend to push up wages in other industries that are not enjoying rapid advances in productivity and the increased labor costs in these industries will tend to push their prices up. The general level of prices must go up under these conditions, since the least productive industries are increasing their prices, while the most productive industries are maintaining them at a constant level or even increasing them.

The existence of this "cost push" poses a most difficult problem for monetary policy. If the monetary authorities do not make available the money and credit necessary to support the inflationary push, unemployment is likely to be created. On the other hand, if they provide the necessary funds, the result will be inflation.

How can this problem be resolved?

There is, I think, no sure and easy answer. In our type of economy, the answer can only come from statesmanlike approaches by the heads of our major industries and the leaders of organized labor. The latter must avoid demands for wage increases which cannot be absorbed without price inflation. The former must find means of withstanding such demands when and if they are made.

Management must exercise restraint in their pricing policies as well. As I have already indicated, price stability requires price reductions in some industries as others are moving up. If pricing policies are set to exact the last dollar of profits in those industries which are expanding rapidly, the result will be the same as a price increase brought about by excessive wage increases. The enforcement of over-all price stability by monetary action alone will produce unemployment, whether the "cost push" comes from wages or profits.

Labor and industry share common objectives. They will both prosper under conditions of stable economic growth. They will both suffer if they make it impossible for the monetary authorities to pursue a stabilizing money and credit policy.

TIGHT MONEY POLICY HAS FAILED

From the AFL-CIO News, February 9, 1957

Miami Beach, Fla.—Calling on the Administration to "stop tilting with the windmills of inflation," the AFL-CIO Executive Council declared that the present "tight money" policy has "failed in its objectives" to head off price inflation, and that its "major achievement has been delay of worthwhile social programs."

The council declared that "real harm has resulted from the higher interest rates" of the tight-money policy, and that "important types of borrowers have suffered."

"Home buyers have had to face higher interest rates and fewer homes have been built," the monetary statement continued. "Farmers have found it more difficult to borrow enough to tide them over the planting and harvesting seasons. Small business has seen 1956 produce the highest rate of business failures since 1941.

"City and state governments have been forced to cut back or delay necessary improvements in schools, sewage, water, roads and other public works. Distressed areas have found it exceedingly difficult to secure the loans necessary to help them improve their economic situation."

THE RESPONSIBILITIES OF MANAGEMENT AND LABOR

From President Eisenhower's message on the State of the Union to Congress, January 10, 1957

Our economy is strong, expanding and fundamentally sound. But in any realistic appraisal, even the optimistic analyst will realize that in a prosperous period the principal threat to efficient functioning of a free enterprise system is inflation. We look back upon four years of prosperous activities during which prices, the cost of living, have been relatively stable—that is, inflation has been held in check.

But it is clear that the danger is always present, particularly if the Government might become profligate in its expenditures or private groups might ignore all the possible results on our economy of unwise struggles for immediate gain.

This danger requires a firm resolution that the Federal Government shall utilize only a prudent share of the nation's resources, that it shall live within its means, carefully measuring against need alternative proposals for expenditures.

For success, Government's efforts must be paralleled by the attitudes and actions of individual citizens.

The national interest must take precedence over temporary advantages which may be secured by particular groups at the expense of all the people.

In this regard I urge leaders in business and in labor to think well on their responsibility to all the American people. With all elements of our society, they owe the nation a vigilant guard against the inflationary tendencies that are always at work in a dynamic economy operating at today's high levels. They can powerfully help counteract or accentuate such tendencies by their wage and price policies.

Business in its pricing policies should avoid unnecessary price increases, especially at a time like the present, when demand in so many areas presses hard on short supplies. Of course, a reasonable profit is essential to the new investments that provide more jobs in an expanding economy.

But business leaders must, in the national interest, studiously avoid those price rises that are possible only because of vital or unusual needs of the whole nation.

And, if our economy is to remain healthy, increases in wages and other labor benefits, negotiated by labor and management, must be reasonably related to improvements in productivity. Such increases are beneficial, for they provide wage earners with greater purchasing power.

Except where necessary to correct obvious injustices, wage increases that outrun productivity, however, are an inflationary factor. They make for higher prices for the public generally and impose a particular hardship, not only on the active workmen, but on those whose welfare depends on the purchasing power of retirement income and savings. Wage negotiations should also take cognizance of the right of the public generally to share in the benefits of improvements in technology.

Freedom has been defined as the opportunity for self-discipline. This definition has a special application to the areas of wage and price policy in a free economy.

Should we persistently fail to discipline ourselves, eventually there will be increasing pressure on Government to redress the failure. By that process freedom will step by step disappear. No subject on the domestic scene should more attract the concern of the friends of American working men and women and of free business enterprise than the forces latent and active that threaten the depreciation of the value of our money.

The above theme was also contained in the Economic Report of the President, sent to Congress January 23, 1957, from which the following excerpt is taken.

A further responsibility of leaders of mangement and labor in a free economy derives from the fact that concentrations of power place in their hands the ability to take actions that, through the sensitive network of our economic system, significantly affect the nation as a whole.

Specifically, business and labor leadership have the responsibility to reach agreements on wages and other labor benefits that are fair to the rest of the community as well as to those persons immediately involved. Negotiated wage increases and benefits should be consistent with productivity prospects and with the maintenance of a stable dollar. And businesses must recognize the broad public interest in the prices set on their products and services.

The full burden of avoiding price inflation, which is an ever present hazard in an expanding economy operating close to capacity, cannot be successfully carried by fiscal and monetary restraints alone. To place this burden on them would invite the risk of producing effects on the structure and functioning of our economy which might, in the years ahead, impair the vitality of competitive enterprise. And failure to accept the responsibilities inherent in a free economy could lead to demands that they be assumed by Government, with the increasing intervention and loss of freedom that such an approach inevitably entails. The successful extension of prosperity with price stability must be a cooperative effort in which the policies of individuals and economic groups and of all levels of Government are consistent with one another and mutually reinforcing.

COMMENTS ON THE PRESIDENT'S RECOMMENDATIONS

Report of the Joint Economic Committee on the January, 1957, Economic Report of the President, 85th Cong., 1st Sess., 1957, Union Calendar No. 39, pp. 6–7

Hearings held during 1956 by the committee's Subcommittee on Economic Stabilization raised a number of questions with respect to the effectiveness of general credit controls in curbing inflation. The committee shares the President's concern over the uneven impact of monetary restraints, particularly as they affect school construction, residential construction, and the growth potentials of new and small businesses. The committee therefore urges a careful inquiry into the operation of the Nation's credit mechanisms and the institutional factors which determine the effectiveness of credit control. This study should give particular emphasis to the incidence of general credit controls and the manner in which the impact and burden of restraints may affect the attainment of continuing social and economic objectives, such as rising standards of educational and public health services and the encouragement of a vigorous and expanding small business population.[1]

---

[1] CHAIRMAN PATMAN: The concern which the committee report expresses over the uneven impact of present monetary restraints is certainly well taken. I would go even further. My impression is that we are today giving an exaggerated importance to monetary and credit powers of the Federal Reserve as instruments which can guarantee us stability and growth. Restrictive monetary policy, which makes for higher interest rates and adds to costs throughout the economy, carries with it a real risk of instability and stunted growth in the long run. The past year has, moreover, demonstrated its ineffectiveness in dampening a boom in plant and equipment expenditures. It has meanwhile proven all too effective in making credit unduly scarce and costly to small businesses, in curtailing efforts to improve the Nation's housing and to provide desperately needed public services, of which schools are perhaps the most conspicuous example. In short, the emphasis of recent years on monetary policy as a prime instrument in assuring stability gives danger of falling into an easy pattern of making high interest rates and tight credit a permanent habit in the United States.

Pioneer studies by our subcommittees in 1949–50 and 1951–52 contributed to widespread appreciation of the usefulness and limitations of monetary controls. The study which we now suggest should provide welcome and needed extension of our understanding in this important area of public policy.

We have given some study to the President's recommendation that leaders of business and labor assume greater responsibility in price policies and wage agreements for maintaining a stable dollar. This recommendation is in keeping with the declaration of policy of the Employment Act, which calls for cooperation of all public and private groups in seeking to achieve the objectives of the Act.

The President's recommendation stems from the caution expressed in the Economic Report that exclusive reliance on monetary and fiscal restraints to prevent rising prices raises serious obstacles to economic growth and stability. The testimony of several witnesses, including that of the Chairman of the Federal Reserve Board, however, questions this assumption.

It was pointed out during the hearings that this recommendation might frequently conflict with business and labor policies for obtaining the greatest gains from the use of available resources, the impetus upon which the successful operation of a free-enterprise economy depends.[2] In addition, it was suggested that carrying out this recommendation this year would involve widespread revision of existing wage contracts.

Numerous witnesses during the hearings referred to the most serious limitation on this proposal—the omission of workable machinery and standards which business and labor leaders might effectively use in accepting responsibility for maintaining a stable price level. We call to the President's attention the need for implementing this proposal if it is to be effective.

Exploratory study of this problem by the committee and staff during the past year suggests that carrying out the President's proposal will require, at a minimum, up-to-date and integrated statistics which show relationships among productivity, prices, wages, profits and other incomes. This involves bringing together data already available in or obtainable by Federal agencies. The executive branch should make these data, with interpretive analyses bearing directly on the problem of price stability, available as soon as possible. The committee considers the problem of achieving price stability one of the most urgent facing the country in both the short and long run. It will follow developments in this area very closely during the coming months.

The committee endorses the President's recommendations for strengthening Federal antitrust policy and urges even more vigorous action, based on the

[2] SENATOR WATKINS: The President's recommendation does not so much raise important questions with respect to the operation and effectiveness of the free-enterprise economy as it does to raise questions with respect to severe institutional interferences with the market mechanism which perhaps otherwise could more efficiently determine prices, incomes, and resource allocation. Implied rather is the need perhaps for more vigorous enforcement of the antitrust laws and other antimonopoly restraints which might better serve to produce prices, incomes, and resource allocations which a freer market mechanism would produce, if permitted to operate freely.

studies and recommendations of committees of Congress, to meet the Employment Act's objectives in this area.

The problems of small and new businesses in securing necessary financial
resources have been intensified in recent months by limited availability of
credit. The Small Business Administration and the Federal Reserve banks
(acting under the authority of sec. 13b of the Federal Reserve Act) should
keep in mind that these authorities were enacted by the Congress for the
express purpose of assuring small businesses, at all times, a fair share of the
limited supply of funds available for investment.

VOLUNTARY RESTRAINTS

*From Economic Intelligence, March, 1957, published by the United States
Chamber of Commerce*

Recently, the President has repeatedly called on business and labor to exercise restraint in their price and wage policies to help curb inflation. In his
Economic Report, he said: "Of particular importance in a prosperous economy
is the responsibility of leaders of business and labor to reach agreements on
wages and other labor benefits which are consistent with productivity prospects
and with the maintenance of a stable dollar." There have even been veiled
threats that direct price and wage controls might be necessary.

Are voluntary restraints possible?

In free markets voluntary restraints are ineffectual weapons against inflation.
Faced with changing market conditions, the individual businessman, no matter
how public-spirited, cannot substitute self-denial for self-interest. He must adjust
his output and prices to changing cost and market conditions.

Likewise, no individual union can be expected to exercise effective voluntary
restraints. The labor official must always strive to obtain, or appear to obtain,
for his own constituents as much as the market will bear, or at least as much
as other union bosses are getting for their members. Otherwise he may find
himself replaced by a subordinate who wants his job.

Furthermore, even with a stable general price level, some prices should
go up and others down. In individual cases, how are businesses and unions
to know what wage-price policies would be "consistent with the maintenance
of a stable dollar?"

Are voluntary restraints desirable?

That voluntary restraints are seriously proposed as anti-inflationary devices
is distressing evidence of how far we have departed from free market concepts. Voluntary restraints presuppose a degree of price jurisdiction which
generally does not exist. Businessmen can advance prices during inflation
mainly because excess demand bids them up. Even where there is some degree
of latitude in setting prices, customers still determine the sales volume at each
price.

More important, however, is the public misunderstanding and disregard of the economic role of the businessman and competition. In a market economy, we want the businessman to act as a businessman. We rely on him to strive to lower costs and to adjust his prices and output to obtain maximum profits. Unless he does, the market will not allocate resources efficiently and the composition of output will not conform to consumer wants and relative scarcities of resources. *Competition*, not voluntary restraint, should control pricing excesses.

Similarly, in wage determination, competition should operate to curb excessive demands. Powerful unions have been promoted by political protection, and government has encouraged monopolistic, industry-wide wage-fixing. It is hardly wise or realistic to rely on voluntary restraint by unions instead of on competitive markets. We can no more ask even a public-spirited labor leader not to behave as a labor leader than we should ask a businessman not to behave as a businessman.

What restraints are possible and desirable?

To reinforce general and impartial monetary and fiscal inflation controls, two kinds of restraints are possible and desirable.

First, public policy should seek to make markets work more efficiently. Competition must be maintained in all markets—for products, labor and financial capital. This involves vigorous enforcement of antitrust laws, long over-due regulation of labor monopolies, and removal of many harmful obstructions placed in free markets by governmental intervention.

Second, all members of the community—businessmen, labor officials, workers, consumers, writers, politicians, teachers and professional critics—should vigorously support those general monetary and fiscal measures needed to control inflation.

Especially, all groups must refrain from asking for special treatment to avoid credit restrictions, and they must refrain from demanding ever-increasing governmental services which add to the overload on the economy.

Exhortations for voluntary restraint may help make everybody more aware that inflation control is "everybody's business." Certainly, responsible public officials face an impossible task without strong public support.

A search for alibis and culprits, however, creates confusion. The issues should be made clear. In this matter, business and labor do have important responsibilities. But they are responsibilities shared in common with all citizens.

LIGHT ON CORPORATE PRICE POLICIES

Statement of Nat Weinberg, Director, Research Department, United Automobile Workers, in January, 1957, Economic Report of the President, hearings before the Joint Congressional Economic Committee, 85th Cong., 1st Sess., 1957, pp. 306–308

The very fact that exhortation is resorted to in order to restrain inflation points to the unique nature of current increases in the price level. They do not for the most part result from the blind and impersonal operation of market forces. They do not, on the whole, result from abnormally high demand or high production pressing against capacity limits. . . .

What these price increases do reflect in our opinion is the absence of price competition, and the operation of an "administered price" system. Under this system a few corporations furnishing "price leadership" to industries crucial to the national welfare hold the power to fix prices arbitrarily. They are not subject to the laws of the market place that inhibit the pricing practices of corporations in price-competitive industries. . . .

We hold strongly to the belief that the pressure of public opinion can minimize or at least reduce the extent of such abuse of pricing power. But the public can be mobilized to an effective expression of opinion only if it is equipped with the facts. General exhortation directed to all and sundry will not do the job. The specific and detailed facts of specific situations, leaving no room for doubt as to whether or not there has been abuse, can create a climate of public opinion which will induce self-restraint on the part of those who would otherwise be tempted to abuse that power. . . .

Specifically, we propose a statutory mechanism that would assure the public of an adequate flow of essential factual information concerning certain corporate price actions, without involving Government in the task of controlling prices. As we presently visualize it, legislation directed toward this objective would require advance notice and public justification of price increases proposed to be put into effect by any corporation which accounts for more than a specified percentage—perhaps 20 or 25 percent—of the total sales of its industry. Such a corporation would give notice of intention to raise prices to a governmental agency created for that purpose. The agency would thereupon conduct public hearings at which the corporation would be required to present detailed justification based upon its records of the need for the proposed price increase. Its testimony would be subject to cross-examination and its pertinent records open for inspection both by the agency and by representatives of organizations or groups opposing the proposed price increase, including other corporations which purchase goods produced by the firm proposing to raise its prices.

Following the hearing, the agency would promptly publish the contentions of the parties, and the facts as it had determined them. The hearings having been concluded, the notice period having expired, the corporation involved would then be entirely free to raise the price if it so chose. But the public would have the means to determine for itself whether or not the price increase was justified.

These proposals rest on the premise that an effective democracy must be an informed democracy. They impose no compulsion with respect to wage or price actions. They infringe no freedom. They are designed solely to minimize the abuse of freedom through the uninhibited exercise of economic power. They are aimed at encouraging responsibility in the exercise of economic power by removing the veil of secrecy that now conceals facts of vital public interest, and thus shelters the irresponsible.

PRODUCTIVITY, EARNINGS, COSTS AND PRICES

United States Bureau of Labor Statistics memorandum, May, 1957

PRODUCTIVITY, EARNINGS, COSTS AND PRICES IN THE PRIVATE NONAGRICULTURAL
SECTOR OF THE ECONOMY, 1947–56

At the request of the Joint Economic Committee, the Bureau of Labor Statistics has provided the Committee with data for inclusion in a study of wages, productivity, labor costs, profits and prices. Most of the information is based on series already published by the Bureau, and includes extensions of previously published estimates. Also included is a table, prepared at the request of the Committee, providing information on the relationship of earnings, productivity and prices for the total private nonagricultural economy during the postwar years 1947–1956. This statement is concerned with the data presented in the table, which is attached.

The data in the table are based for the most part on published statistics of the Office of Business Economics of the Department of Commerce, the Council of Economic Advisers, and the Bureau of Labor Statistics of the Department of Labor. However, included in the table is an estimate of total nonagricultural employee man-hours, prepared by the Bureau of Labor Statistics, which has not been previously published and is preliminary and subject to revision. The man-hours cover all wage and salary employees, including production workers, administrative employees, and executives.

These data are useful in providing factual background for studying the relationship between prices, wages, and productivity. Since they may be interpreted in various ways—and possibly misinterpreted—it is important to note certain statistical and conceptual limitations and qualifications.

The data refer to the total private nonagricultural sector of the economy and reflect the divergent movements of the various industries and industry groups such as manufacturing, mining, trade, construction, services, etc. which make up the total. However, the over-all trends are not necessarily representative of any individual industry or industry group. Thus, any conclusions that may be drawn as to the relationship of wages, productivity, and prices apply to the private nonagricultural sector as a whole and are not applicable to any particular component industry.

The estimates reflect not only the average of the changes in the various component industries but also the change in the relative importance of the components. The measure of real private nonagricultural product per hour, for example, is affected not only by the increase in productivity of the individual industries making up the total but also by changes in the relative importance of industries with differing levels of productivity (value added per man-hour). In a similar manner, the estimate of average hourly compensation is affected by shifts in employment from low to high earnings industries and vice versa. The index of employee compensation per dollar of real product (unit labor cost) is also influenced by changes in the relative importance of industries with different labor costs per dollar of real product. The trend in unit labor costs can also be affected by shifts between the corporate and non-corporate sectors of the economy.

Difficulties in interpretation caused by industry shifts is one of the reasons why the table is limited to the private nonagricultural sector of the economy. In the case of government, income payments consist entirely of wages and salaries, whereas, in the case of agriculture, labor compensation is relatively small compared to entrepreneurial income. Shifts in the relative importance of government and agriculture which have taken place in the last ten years might, on the more comprehensive basis, show changes in unit labor costs for the economy when in fact there may have been relatively little change for any of the component industries.

Another caution to be exercised in interpreting the data refers to the determination of cause and effect relationships. This is particularly true in determining the "cause" of price increases in a competitive economy. Prices are subject to numerous influences of changing market conditions and costs of production, and a change in price cannot be explained by reference to any single factor, even one as large as labor costs. Where the figures indicate that prices and unit labor costs showed about the same increase, or that one or the other showed a greater increase during a particular year or period of years, this should be taken as a description of what happened and not necessarily as an explanation of what "caused" the change. An increase in unit labor costs may lead to an increase in price, but conversely an increase in price can result in strong pressure for increases in wages.

There is moreover, a strong interaction between demand and costs. Rapidly rising demand for the product of an industry may lead to price increases and may also provide producers with the incentive to bid up wage rates in order to expand working force and production. In this event, it may turn out that labor costs rise as rapidly, or more rapidly, than prices. However, under these conditions, the basic initiating factor in the price increase is the rapid increase in demand, which leads to the bidding up of wage rates and a consequent rise in labor costs. The answer to the question of whether the wage increases cause the price increase or vice versa cannot be determined from the figures alone. There are many factors, including specific market conditions, which affect the wage and price structure. The figures are useful, however, in determining whether prices have increased more or less than one category of cost—unit labor costs. By inference, this relationship in turn helps explain changes in the proportion of labor versus non-labor payments.

Another general qualification is that although the figures given in the table probably represent the best estimates which can be made with available resources and data, they are not precise measures and too much significance should not be attached to relatively small differences between the various estimates.

Finally, it is emphasized that year-to-year changes in productivity, earnings, and prices, or in the relationship between these factors, are not uniform.

1. EARNINGS AND PRODUCTIVITY

Between 1947 and 1956, average hourly earnings of all employees (wages and salaries) increased by about 59 percent. If one adds to earnings the contributions of employers for social security, private health and insurance funds and similar supplemental payments, then total compensation per hour increased by slightly more than 61 percent.[1]

During the same period the Consumer Price Index—reflecting the prices of goods and services purchased with the income received by labor—increased by about 22 percent. If an adjustment is made to earnings for the increase in the Consumer Price Index, in order to convert money earnings to real earnings with constant purchasing power, then the increase in real earnings per hour was about 30 percent, including employer contributions, close to 33 percent.

At this point a comparison can be made between productivity and either of the two earnings estimates.

From the viewpoint of labor's share in the real gains in productivity achieved during the postwar period, the more appropriate comparison would be with earnings adjusted to reflect real purchasing power. On questions of changes in labor costs and other costs of production, the actual payments to labor in the current dollars of the given year should be used.

The table indicates that the increase in output per employee man-hour between 1947 and 1956 was about 26 percent, less than the increase in real earnings during the same period, regardless of the inclusion or exclusion of the supplements to wages and salaries. It is important to note, however, that between 1947 and 1952 real product per man-hour increased more than real hourly earnings (excluding supplements). By 1953 real earnings had about caught up with the increase in productivity, they remained in line through 1955, and it was not until 1956 that real earnings definitely exceeded productivity. Real earnings, including supplements, overtook productivity somewhat earlier and have remained ahead since 1954.

The increase in average hourly compensation in current dollars represents an increase in labor costs only to the extent that it exceeds the increase in productivity (real product per man-hour). This is true because unit labor costs are affected not only by the increase in compensation per hour but also by the number of man-hours required per unit. (Man-hours per unit is the reciprocal of productivity.) It is in this sense that productivity is a crucial element in the wage-cost-price relationship. It represents the margin within which wage increases can be granted without increasing production costs or curtailing the amount available for other income payments.

With this relationship as a background, the figures indicate that average hourly compensation in current dollars increased much more than productivity during the postwar period. The former increased by about 61 percent, the

[1] Both compensation and man-hours cover all private nonagricultural employees, including management, but excluding proprietors and unpaid family workers.

latter by 26 percent, leading to an increase in employee compensation per dollar of real product of about 28 percent.[2]

2. LABOR AND NON-LABOR COSTS AND PRICES

The price index used to compare with unit labor and non-labor costs, is derived for each year by dividing the actual dollar estimate of gross product in the private nonfarm sector of the economy by the constant dollar estimate (i.e., output in constant prices).[3]

This price index represents the change in price of all final goods and services produced by the private economy, minus the price of gross farm product. "Price" may be viewed as the sum of all the costs of production and distribution per unit—including labor, profits, depreciation, and other payments. Materials and intermediate services are not considered as separate cost elements in this concept of price (or cost) since the payments for labor, profits, etc., are cumulative, covering *all* stages of production and distribution, from raw materials to final product.

Having defined "price" as equal to the sum of the various costs per unit of output, it is relevant to compare the trend in labor payments per unit with total payment per unit (price) to determine (1) the extent to which labor costs per unit have gone up more or less than price; and (2) the change in the proportion of total income payments going to labor as distinguished from non-labor payments.

On the first point, the figures indicate that the increase of about 28 percent in employee compensation per dollar of real products was almost identical with the increase in price between 1947 and 1956. Inspection of the figures for individual years indicates that the price index was higher than the index for unit labor costs for every year prior to 1956, although the difference was very slight, and probably insignificant, in 1953 and 1954.

The close correspondence for the period as a whole between the price increase and the change in unit labor costs implies that total non-labor costs, which include depreciation, profits, entrepreneurial income, etc., must also have gone up by about the same amount during the period. This is so because price covers all income payments and not just labor compensation. In fact, labor compensation accounts for about 56 percent of the "price" of nonfarm gross private product. If non-labor payments per unit increased unit labor costs

[2] It should be noted that although the increase in unit labor costs represents the extent to which gains in hourly compensation exceed output per hour, the measure unit labor costs is independent of the particular measure of man-hours used in deriving the estimate. This is true because the same man-hour measure is used to obtain both the average hourly compensation and the output per man-hour figures. This points up the fact that unit labor costs can be obtained directly by dividing employee compensation by real product. The man-hours used in obtaining unit labor costs in the first method cancel out leaving total compensation divided by production. Thus the preliminary nature of the man-hour estimates used in the table will not affect the various comparisons.

[3] Both the current and constant dollar estimates are published by the National Income Division of the Department of Commerce.

Indexes of Labor and Non-labor Payments per Dollar of Real Product, Prices, Real Product per Man-hour, Employees Compensation per Hour in Current and Constant Dollars; Private Nonagricultural Sector of the Economy, 1947–56
(1947 = 100)

	1948	1949	1950	1951	1952	1953	1954	1955	1956 [1]
1. Private nonagricultural product (current dollars)	110.9	111.7	124.7	141.7	149.6	159.2	158.1	173.0	182.9
2. Employee compensation (current dollars)	110.3	108.6	119.7	137.5	147.6	158.9	157.4	170.7	183.5
3. Wages and salaries (current dollars)	110.5	108.5	118.7	135.8	145.9	156.9	154.9	167.7	180.3
4. Non-labor payments (current dollars)	111.7	115.8	131.0	147.3	152.3	159.7	159.0	176.0	182.1
5. Private nonagricultural real product (1956 constant prices)	104.1	103.8	114.4	121.9	125.8	131.6	128.7	139.4	143.4
6. Employee compensation per $ of real product	106.0	104.6	104.6	112.8	117.3	120.7	122.3	122.5	128.0
7. Wages and salaries per $ of real product	106.1	104.5	103.8	111.4	116.0	119.2	120.3	120.3	125.7
8. Non-labor payments per $ of real product	107.3	111.6	114.5	120.8	121.1	121.4	123.5	126.3	127.0
9. Implicit price change—private nonagriculture	106.5	107.7	108.9	116.3	119.0	120.9	122.8	124.1	127.6
10. Man-hours of employees	101.4	96.8	101.0	106.6	108.3	110.9	106.3	111.1	113.7
11. Real product per employee hour	102.7	107.2	113.3	114.4	116.2	118.7	121.1	125.5	126.1
12. Average hourly compensation	108.8	112.2	118.5	129.0	136.3	143.3	148.1	153.6	161.4
13. Average hourly wages and salaries	109.0	112.1	117.5	127.4	134.7	141.5	145.7	150.9	158.6
14. Consumer price index	107.6	106.6	107.6	116.2	118.8	119.8	120.2	119.9	121.7
15. Average hourly compensation in constant $	101.1	105.3	110.1	111.0	114.7	119.6	123.2	128.1	132.6
16. Average hourly wages and salaries in constant $	101.3	105.2	109.2	109.6	113.4	118.1	121.2	125.9	130.3

[1] Preliminary.

Department of Commerce and Council of Economic Advisers. Source: U.S. ... Report of the President, 1957, Table E–3, p. 126. Gross private nonfarm product in current prices. Source: U.S.

Line 2. Data for 1947–1955 from U.S. Department of Commerce, Survey of Current Business, National Income Number, July 1956, Table 14. Derived by subtracting compensation of farm and general government employees from total compensation. Includes employers' contributions to social security, private insurance and pension funds, compensation for injuries, and a few other minor items of income in addition to wages and salaries. The 1956 figure is a BLS estimate.

Line 3. Same source as line 2, Table 15. Wages and salaries include paid vacations, holidays, sick leave and other paid time off.

Line 4. Derived by subtracting employee compensation from total nonfarm gross private product. Includes corporate profits, capital consumption allowances, indirect taxes, net interest, income of unincorporated enterprises, net rental income and miscellaneous payments (including statistical discrepancy).

Line 5. Economic Report of the President, 1957, Table E–3, p. 126. Gross private nonfarm product in 1956 prices. Source: U.S. Department of Commerce and Council of Economic Advisers.

Line 6. Line 2 divided by line 5. Also equal to line 12 divided by line 11.
Line 7. Line 3 divided by line 5. Also equal to line 13 divided by line 11.
Line 8. Line 4 divided by line 5.
Line 9. Line 1 divided by line 5.
Line 10. Employee man-hours estimated by the Bureau of Labor Statistics. Covers the hours of all private nonfarm employees, including those employed by government enterprises. The man-hour estimates do not include the hours of proprietors and unpaid family workers. The hours contributed by the latter groups have been excluded in order to provide a more meaningful comparison between output per man-hour and compensation per hour.

An index of output per hour of *all* persons employed has been prepared and shows little difference from the index of output per employee hour shown in this table.

The employee man-hour estimate is based for the most part on the published series of the Bureau of Labor Statistics on employment and average weekly hours. The estimate of total hours covers paid hours, including paid holidays, vacation, illness. The BLS published estimates have been supplemented by the use of National Income and unpublished Census Labor Force data for those areas not covered by the BLS series. The man-hour estimates are preliminary and other estimates based on the man-hour indexes should also be considered as preliminary.

Line 11. Line 5 divided by line 10.
Line 12. Line 2 divided by line 10.
Line 13. Line 3 divided by line 10.
Line 14. Economic Report of the President, 1957, Table E–36, p. 164, converted to 1947 = 100. Source: Bureau of Labor Statistics.
Line 15. Line 12 divided by line 14.
Line 16. Line 13 divided by line 14.

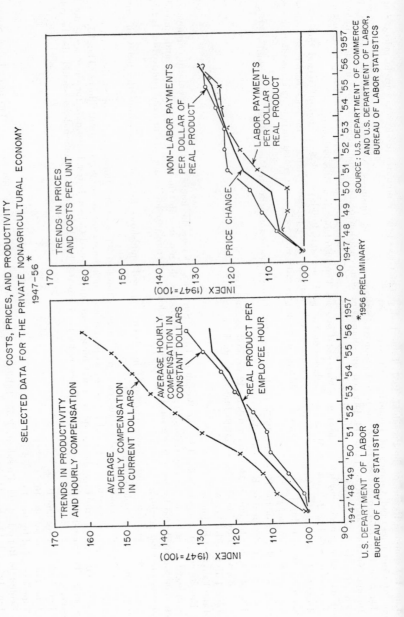

COSTS, PRICES, AND PRODUCTIVITY
SELECTED DATA FOR THE PRIVATE NONAGRICULTURAL ECONOMY
1947-56*

TRENDS IN PRICES
AND COSTS PER UNIT

NON-LABOR PAYMENTS
PER DOLLAR OF
REAL PRODUCT

LABOR PAYMENTS
PER DOLLAR OF
REAL PRODUCT

PRICE CHANGE

INDEX (1947=100)

1947 '48 '49 '50 '51 '52 '53 '54 '55 '56 1957

SOURCE: U.S. DEPARTMENT OF COMMERCE
AND U.S. DEPARTMENT OF LABOR,
BUREAU OF LABOR STATISTICS

*1956 PRELIMINARY

TRENDS IN PRODUCTIVITY
AND HOURLY COMPENSATION

AVERAGE
HOURLY COMPENSATION
IN CURRENT DOLLARS

AVERAGE HOURLY
COMPENSATION IN
CONSTANT DOLLARS

REAL PRODUCT PER
EMPLOYEE HOUR

INDEX (1947=100)

1947 '48 '49 '50 '51 '52 '53 '54 '55 '56 1957

U.S. DEPARTMENT OF LABOR
BUREAU OF LABOR STATISTICS

lone would have been about 16 percent, rather than the indicated increase of
bout 28 percent.

The implicit relative change in labor and non-labor payments is supported
y additional estimates, based for the most part on data published by the
Vational Income Division, Department of Commerce, supplemented by esti-
nates of the Bureau of Labor Statistics. These estimates indicate that labor
nd total non-labor costs per unit showed about the same increase (28 and 27
ercent respectively) from 1947 to 1956. Stated another way, the relative
hare of gross income going to labor and total non-labor categories was about
he same in 1956 as it was in 1947. This does not of course, imply that each
eparate category of non-labor costs remained unchanged.

CONTENDING FORCES

*'rom the statement by Frazar B. Wilde, Chairman, Research and Policy Com-
nittee, Committee for Economic Development,[1] and President, Connecticut
General Life Insurance Co., in January, 1957, Economic Report of the Presi-
'ent, hearings before the Joint Congressional Economic Committee, 85th
Cong., 1st Sess., 1957, p. 718*

. . . We know that some wage rates are pushed up faster than productivity,
nd some prices are raised in periods of high employment. There have been
ome periods when this seemed to be a general occurrence. But we do not
now whether this tends to happen on the average and most of the time if the
lemand for goods and services is not excessive. We know that there are strong
orces tending to make prices and wages rise. But there are also strong forces
ending to hold them down. Even in conditions of generally high employment
nd business activity, workers and management in particular firms and indus-
ries must reckon with the danger of pricing themselves out of their markets.
f labor unions and business really had the power, singly or together, to raise
rices and wages without limitation by the market, we could not explain why
rices are not much higher than they are.

FACING THE FUTURE

*'rom an address by Arthur F. Burns, Chairman, Council of Economic Advisers,
efore the National Federation of Financial Analysts Societies, Boston, May
1, 1956, in January, 1957, Economic Report of the President, hearings before
he Joint Congressional Economic Committee, 85th Cong., 1st Sess., 1957,
. 622*

The main uncertainties with regard to the future of the dollar are therefore,
rst, whether wages will tend to rise faster than industrial productivity; second,

[1] The Committee for Economic Development is a private, nonpolitical organization
f businessmen formed to study and report on the problems of achieving and main-
aining a high level of employment and production within a free economy. Its
esearch and policy committee issues from time to time statements on national policy
ontaining recommendations for action which, in the committee's judgment, will
ontribute to maintaining productive employment and a raising standard of living.

whether businessmen will give sufficient heed to the longer-range consequences of their pricing policies; third, whether the monetary and fiscal policies of Government will be sufficiently disciplined to keep in check such inflationary pressures as may from time to time develop. Experience since 1952, while favorable and encouraging on balance, is much too brief to be conclusive. It may be that our private or public policies will become reckless in later years. It may be that we will throw restraint to the winds. But it cannot be justly argued from the evidence so far available that a high-level economy is necessarily biased in an inflationary direction. It is a disservice both to truth and to social opportunity to describe our times as an age of inflation. We are living in an age that can be either one of inflation or of general price stability, depending on the courage and wisdom that private citizens and Government officials bring to their responsibilities.

FOR DISCUSSION AND ANALYSIS

1. In a reply to U.S. Steel's 1956 annual report, President McDonald of the Steelworkers maintained that "the facts are that productivity—output of steel per man hour—has more than offset the 'cost' of the Steelworker wage increase in recent years." Assuming this to be true, would this constitute an adequate defense to the charge that big unions like the Steelworkers have been responsible for inflationary pressures?

2. In the *Political Quarterly* of July–September, 1956, B. C. Roberts of the London School of Economics comments:

Post-war experience clearly establishes that no form of national wages policy which places the onus of responsibility on the unions by asking them to restrain their demands for higher incomes can work effectively if employers are free and willing to pay more in order to satisfy their labour requirements. . . . The most effective way of ensuring that wage incomes do not outstrip the availability of consumer goods is to see that the profits of employers are not so easily earned. Employers, as individuals, as well as in organizations, would then be compelled either to resist union wage demands more effectively, or to suffer a sharp cut in profit margins.

(*a*) Do you agree with this policy recommendation? (*b*) Whether or not you agree, how could this policy best be effectuated? (*c*) What alternative approach can you suggest?

3. Analyze the following statement of Nat Weinberg, economist for the UAW, made before the Joint Congressional Economic Committee in its hearings on the *January 1957 Economic Report of the President*, pp. 310–311:

We hear much advice these days to limit our wage demands to amount commensurate with increases in productivity. But surely those who offer this advice cannot, in good conscience refer to money wages. They must mean real wages. For, if applied to money wages in the face of rising prices this advice would mean constant declines in the living standards of workers and their families or, at the very least, a constantly diminishing share for workers in the increasing volume of goods and services that they produce. . . .

Therefore, if wage increases are to be compared to productivity increases for purposes of determining the influence of unions on the price level, the proper comparison is with real wages and not money wages. On this basis, it is clear beyond all possibility of doubt that the blame for price increases cannot be pinned on labor. It can be shown that the real economic gains of workers in the post-war period, including fringe benefits as well as wage increases, have not outpaced productivity, although it probably would have been desirable for them to do so.

4. Voluntary restraint by unions in making wage demands, and by managements in seeking price increases, was urged by President Eisenhower as a corrective to inflation. If you were a union president and anxious to comply with the President's wish, how would you translate this proposal into operational terms? If you were the president of a company and equally desirous of following the President's suggestion, how would this policy of voluntary restraint affect your pricing practices?

5. List all the various remedies proposed for inflationary pressures. Select the one which appears most promising to you and (a) build a case for it, (b) point out its weaknesses. Select the approach which strikes you as least promising and (a) prepare an analysis of its limitations and (b) indicate whatever advantages it may nevertheless possess.

22: Pensions

In a market society there are a number of circumstances under which a person who derives his income by working may find that income shut off. An accident may prevent his carrying on his customary work for the rest of his life. An illness may have the same effect temporarily. A layoff may relegate him to the ranks of the unemployed. Most certain of all, old age will ultimately remove him from the labor force. In all such instances the income which he normally derives from his employment ceases.

The twentieth century has been marked by an effort to alleviate these traumatic shocks which follow from a market economy, a form of economic organization which carries such advantages that our society is unwilling to abandon it but at the same time has become cognizant of the necessity of softening some of its harsher features. Consequently we have developed workmen's compensation and—on a lesser scale—disability insurance. Health insurance has been tentatively explored by governments and has become common on a group, voluntary basis or as a collectively bargained benefit. Unemployment compensation was introduced in the thirties, and private supplements to public compensation initiated in some industries in the fifties—a subject we shall deal with in the next chapter. Public old-age assistance and retirement benefits were made part of the basic Social Security law passed in 1935, and in the late forties public pensions were supplemented by private pensions. It is the pension movement which we shall consider in this chapter.

PENSION COVERAGE PRIOR TO 1937

From Pensions in the United States, a study prepared for the Joint Congressional Committee on the Economic Report by the National Planning Association, 82d Cong., 2d Sess., 1952, p. 10

The nearly universal coverage of current workers under retirement system is a very recent development. A little over 15 years ago there were only abou 6 million persons, less than 15 percent of those employed, with this protection Coverage was very uneven, ranging from virtually 100 percent in the communications industry to virtually nothing in retail trade or agriculture. Employer-sponsored plans, including railroads, covered about 3.7 million worker

976

nd the special systems for Government employees about 2 million. Around
00,000 nonprofit employees, such as clergymen and university and college
eachers, also had protection, and a few workers were covered by union-
ponsored plans.

Most employees of business and industry were protected under a retirement
rogram for the first time in 1937 when coverage under the Social Security Act
ecame effective.

OCIAL SECURITY OBJECTIVES AND ACHIEVEMENTS

*rom an article by Wilbur J. Cohen, Director, Division of Research and Statis-
cs, Office of the Commissioner, Social Security Administration, in Social
ecurity Bulletin, August, 1955, The Twentieth Anniversary Issue, pp. 2–3*

The Social Security Act of 1935 was designed to meet certain immediate
eeds and to help prevent future want and dependency such as engulfed the
ation at the time of its passage. Through the Federal-State partnership imple-
ented by Federal grants in aid, assistance soon became available under State
ws for needy persons in three groups of the population that, in good times as
ell as bad, have little or no capacity to earn their own living—the aged, the
lind, and children deprived of parental support or care through the death,
bsence from the home, or physical or mental incapacity of a parent. . . .

In 1939 the emphasis in old-age insurance was shifted from the individual to
ie family. Benefits were added for the aged wife and minor children of a
tired insured worker and for family dependents of insured workers who die
ther before or after retirement. The capacity of aid to dependent children to
feguard family life was strengthened in 1950, when Congress provided that
ederal grants could be used in payments that include the needs of the mother
r other relative who cares for the children as well as the children themselves.

In countless homes, therefore, insurance or assistance payments mean that an
ld couple can live out their remaining years together in a familiar setting, with
eir cherished possessions; that children in families broken by death or separa-
on or impoverished by the breadwinner's disability can continue to receive
eir mothers' care instead of being parceled out among relatives or left without
pervision or placed in foster homes while the mother takes outside work;
at families in which earned income has been cut down or cut off by misfor-
ne or old age have an assured income that they can use just as others in the
mmunity use their money, continuing to plan and manage their own affairs.

The dollars paid out under programs established under the Social Security
ct can be added, and so can the number of persons—old, young, and in the
orking ages—to whom these payments have gone. What cannot be computed
the peace of mind and self-respect made possible by these programs in homes
to which pay envelopes no longer come, the strain and worry and humiliation
verted from parents and from children whose lives otherwise might have been
arred by the anxieties of their elders or by separation from home and parents.
the midst of just concern about juvenile delinquency and other social
aladjustments in American homes, it is well to remember the far greater

number of homes where high traditions have been upheld in the face of adverse circumstances, frequently with the aid of the social security defenses created in the past 20 years. . . .

OLD AGE AND SURVIVORS INSURANCE AFTER TWENTY YEARS

By Victor Christgau, Director, Bureau of Old-age and Survivors Insurance, Social Security Administration, in Social Security Bulletin, August, 1955, pp. 12–17

The purpose of the old-age and survivors insurance program is to provide protection against economic insecurity for the worker and his family when the earnings upon which they have depended for support are cut off by his retirement or death. This basic purpose was reaffirmed by President Eisenhower in his social security message of January 1954. The President pointed out that the old-age and survivors insurance system had been developed in response to the need "arising from the complexities of our modern society. . . . The system is not intended as a substitute for private savings, pension plans, and insurance protection. It is, rather, intended as the foundation upon which these other forms of protection can be soundly built. Thus, the individual's own work, his planning and his thrift will bring him a higher standard of living upon his retirement, or his family a higher standard of living in the event of his death, than would otherwise be the case. Hence the system both encourages thrift and self-reliance, and helps to prevent destitution in our national life."

That the old-age and survivors insurance system, established by Congress in 1935, has moved toward its goal by relatively rapid stages is clear when the program's accomplishments are viewed against the backdrop of the years.

The old-age insurance program was designed as an expression of the Nation's conviction that older retired persons should have a continuing income, to which their rights would be established by law on the basis of their earnings and contributions and which would be available without a means test. The proportion of aged men and women in the Nation's population had been increasing. In the 1930's their plight had become particularly difficult. These were depression years, when even young persons found it increasingly hard to get or keep jobs and family savings evaporated.

Later, in 1939, survivor insurance provisions were added to the Social Security Act in recognition of the problem encountered by families when the breadwinner died. The resulting legislation was basically the old-age and survivors insurance program as it is today, although it has been expanded by the comprehensive amendments of 1950 and 1954.

The test of whether the new program was constitutional came early. This issue was resolved in 1937 by the U. S. Supreme Court in an 8-to-1 decision in which Justice Cardozo wrote:

Needs that were narrow or parochial a century ago may be interwoven in our day with the well-being of the Nation. What is critical or urgent changes with the times. . . . Congress did not improvise a judgment when it found that the award of old-age benefits would be conducive to the general welfare. . . . The number of persons in the United States 65 years of age and over is increasing proportionately as well as absolutely. What is even more important the number of such persons unable to take care of themselves is growing at a threatening pace. . . . The problem is plainly national in area and dimensions.

Ten years after the program's adoption, some 46 million workers were in jobs covered by the system and 1.3 million beneficiaries were receiving about $24 million in monthly benefits.

In 1952 the Director of the Bureau of Old-Age and Survivors Insurance pointed out that the 15 years of the program's operations "have demonstrated that social insurance can be successfully applied to meet American needs for protection against the economic risks of death and old-age retirement in modern life." By then, 60 million persons were working in covered jobs and some 4.3 million men, women, and children were getting benefits amounting to $152 million monthly.

Today, on the twentieth anniversary of the adoption of the Social Security Act, the Bureau of Old-Age and Survivors Insurance again looks back at the record of administrative and program accomplishment. An estimated 69 million workers will be in covered jobs this year and about 7.5 million beneficiaries are receiving checks totaling about $385 million each month.

Nearly 60 percent of the 14 million men and women in the United States now aged 65 and over either are getting old-age and survivors insurance benefits or are working and have acquired or are acquiring protection. About 70½ million have worked long enough in covered employment to be insured under the program, and nearly 30 million of them are permanently insured; whether or not they continue to work in covered employment, they will be eligible for benefits when they reach age 65 and retire, and their families have survivor protection. Nine out of 10 of the young mothers and children in the country have survivorship protection that will enable them to draw monthly benefits today if the breadwinner dies.

In 1953, at the invitation of Mrs. Oveta Culp Hobby, Secretary of Health, Education, and Welfare, a group of men and women from business, labor, agriculture, education, and professional organizations took a look at the question of extending the program's coverage. They recommended that coverage be made as universal as possible. Congressional committees later held public hearings at which representatives of organizations reflecting a cross section of American life presented their views on what changes should be made in the program.

The 1954 amendments, strengthening the principle of a contributory system with benefits varying according to past earnings and paid without a test of financial need, grew out of these deliberations. The revisions were in many respects the most significant since the 1939 amendments. They provided almost universal coverage, increased benefits, and provided for protecting the benefit rights of individuals out of work for extended periods because of physical or mental disability.

Maturity for the old-age and survivors insurance program is by no means an accomplished fact. No worker has yet been under the system for a full working lifetime, and beneficiary rolls are smaller than they will be in the future, when practically everyone who works will have had the opportunity to gain protection under the program.

COVERAGE

Questions of coverage were particularly troublesome for the architects of old-age insurance 20 years ago. Was it possible from an administrative standpoint to include in the program every type of employment? Could self-employment be covered? Could a workable system of tax collection and a sound method of reporting earnings be devised for all sorts of employment? Progress was destined to come gradually. At first, coverage was limited to employment in commerce and industry in the continental United States, Alaska, and Hawaii, where accurate and relatively simple wage reporting could be adapted to employers' regular bookkeeping practices.

In the 1950 amendments the barrier against coverage of other workers was removed for the first time. Categories of work for which coverage of old-age and survivors insurance had appeared too difficult in the beginning were included under the system.

Until then all coverage had been on a compulsory basis. Under a system permitting individual voluntary coverage, those who choose to participate are likely to be primarily those in the older age groups who can expect a large return for their contributions and those who can most easily spare the money. Persons with low incomes, although concerned about the loss of earnings upon retirement and the effect on their families in case of death, are likely to delay getting the protection they need because of the problem of meeting the day-by-day costs of the basic essentials of living.

The 1950 amendments continued in general to apply the principle of compulsory coverage, but elective coverage on a group basis was provided for employees of State and local government units and of nonprofit organizations. Constitutional barriers generally preclude the Federal Government from imposing an old-age and survivors insurance employer contribution tax upon State and local governments, and, traditionally, certain nonprofit institutions have been tax-exempt. These groups were therefore brought into coverage on elective bases.

Coverage on a compulsory basis was extended at the same time to nonfarm self-employed persons, many of the Federal employees not covered by the civil-service retirement system, and regularly employed farm and domestic workers. The 1950 law also extended coverage to Puerto Rico and the Virgin Islands and to Americans working abroad for American employers.

Congress extended coverage in 1954 to still more groups, including farm owners and some of the professional self-employed formerly excluded, additional farm workers and domestic employees and, on a voluntary basis, clergymen. It is significant that, although proposals for coverage on an individual election basis were made in connection with several other groups—such as farm operators and self-employed professional persons—clergymen were the only group for which this basis for coverage was acceptable to Congress.

In its report, the Committee on Finance in the Senate stated:

A provision for coverage on an individual election basis, while not generally desirable, is considered by your committee to be justified in this area because of the special circumstances. Many churches have expressed the fear that their participation in the old-age and survivors insurance program as employers of ministers might interfere with the well-established principle of separation of church and state. Many church representatives also believe that individual ministers who do not wish to be covered on grounds of conscience should not be required to participate in the program.

The 1954 amendments also removed the restriction against coverage of most State and local government groups with retirement systems of their own. Congress was careful, however, to express the policy that this extension of coverage was not intended to impair the protection such groups might already have under their own programs.

Thus today most of the gaps in coverage have been closed. About 90 percent of all paid jobs are covered by old-age and survivors insurance. As a result of amendments to the Railroad Retirement Act in 1946 and 1951, the railroad retirement and old-age and survivors insurance programs are so closely coordinated that railroad employment can be considered to be covered by old-age and survivors insurance.

The bulk of those still not included are Federal employees covered by Federal employee retirement systems, both civilian and military. Others not covered by the program are self-employed physicians, lawyers, dentists, naturopaths, osteopaths, chiropractors, veterinarians, and optometrists, as well as domestic and farm workers earning less than a specified amount and self-employed persons with net earnings of less than $400 a year.

BENEFITS

During the 1940's, when the Nation's attention was focused on the war, old-age and survivors insurance benefits failed to keep pace with prices and earnings levels, which had increased dramatically. The industrial employee who in 1939 earned $100 a month was earning an average of $249 in 1950. The cost of living had risen 73 percent. Benefits, however, continued to be determined by the formula established under the 1939 amendments and within the $3,000 annual wage ceiling in effect since the program's start. As a result, maximum monthly benefits in 1950 were $45.60 for the retired worker and $68.40 for an aged couple. During the 1940's many States had higher average old-age assistance grants than the maximum benefit that could be paid to a retired worker under old-age and survivors insurance, and more of the aged population were drawing old-age assistance payments than insurance benefits.

To remain effective, the old-age and survivors insurance program must keep pace with the social and economic changes that take place in a dynamic society like that of the United States. In 1950, benefits were increased in recognition of the rise in living costs and the increase in wage levels. The 1950 benefit formula resulted in maximum monthly benefits of $80 for the retired worker and $120 for the aged retired couple. These amounts represented substantial percentage increases from the maximum possible under the 1939 law. In 1952 the maximums were raised to $85 and $127.50 through adoption of a formula providing 55 percent of the first $100 of average monthly earnings and 15 percent of the next $200.

In her testimony before congressional committees during their consideration of the 1954 amendments, the Secretary of Health, Education, and Welfare said:

> Old-age and survivors insurance benefit levels were originally fixed in the mid-1930's, during a depression economy. Benefit increases enacted by Congress since then have done little more than keep pace with the inflationary trend our Nation has heretofore experienced. In my opinion, a readjustment of benefits to take into account the improved standard of the basic elements of living for the American worker is necessary. . . .
>
> These old-age and survivors insurance benefits are too low, under today's conditions, for old-age and survivors insurance to fulfill its purpose of providing basic retirement and survivorship protection and reducing the need for public assistance to the lowest possible level.

The new 1954 benefit formula kept the percentage of the first step at 55 but increased to $110 the amount of average monthly earnings to which it applied. At the same time, the second step of the formula was raised from 15 percent to 20 percent. Since annual earnings to be considered under old-age and survivors insurance were increased to $4,200 beginning with 1955, this new percentage applied to the next $240 of average monthly earnings.

The top benefit for a retired worker under the 1954 revisions ($108.50) is equal to 31 percent of $350, the maximum monthly earnings that can be counted. The first step of the benefit formula, however, calls for 55 percent of the first $110 of earnings. The program has thus continued to recognize that the lower-paid worker needs a higher percentage replacement of his previous earnings than do men and women with higher earnings.

When in 1951 coverage was extended by the 1950 amendments to about 10 million additional workers, these workers faced at retirement the prospect of having 14 years (1937 through 1950) during which they had no covered earnings included in computing their average monthly earnings for benefit purposes. To avoid this result, provision was made for a new "starting date" that put the newly covered workers in the same position as those first covered in 1937. The amendments specified that if a worker has 1 quarter of coverage (whenever earned) for each 2 calendar quarters elapsing after 1950 up to the time he reaches age 65 or dies, he is insured, provided he has worked at least 6 calendar quarters in covered employment. Any worker who has 6 quarters of coverage after 1950 can have his average wage figured by using only years after 1950. While this action was taken primarily for the newly covered workers, it also was advantageous for workers who had entered coverage in

1937 and continued to work after 1950. For them, the provision meant that their benefits could be based on relatively current earnings and did not have to include earnings in the years preceding the rapid rise in wages during the war.

When another 10 million persons were brought into the system by the 1954 changes, provision was made to eliminate, in calculating their benefits, the 4 or 5 years of lowest or no earnings. This provision was of particular help to the newly covered, who could drop out the 4 years (1951–54) when the opportunity for coverage was not open to them. For those workers who are already covered short periods of unemployment, sickness, or absence from work for other reasons will not reduce the average.

One of the principal causes of low average monthly earnings is long periods out of work because of extended disability. A section of the 1952 amendments would have preserved the old-age and survivors insurance rights of those who became totally and permanently disabled before reaching retirement age. That provision expired before it could become effective, and in 1954 the present "disability freeze" provision was adopted. Under it, periods of time during which a worker or self-employed person is out of work because of extended disability may be eliminated in computing benefits. This provision will also bring to the attention of State vocational rehabilitation agencies disabled men and women who might be restored to gainful work.

As an outgrowth of these changes, low benefit payments in the future will generally reflect the earnings of men and women who are part-time or intermittent workers—only marginally a part of the Nation's working population and not primarily dependent on their earnings for their support.

RETIREMENT TEST

Since 1940, when benefits first were paid on a monthly basis, the Social Security Act has prescribed the test to be used in determining when an individual is retired—that is, substantially out of gainful employment. The test has been revised with the changing times through which the program has passed since 1935. From 1940 through August 1950, benefits were intended to be paid only when the beneficiary was for all practical purposes completely retired from covered employment, and the law therefore provided that earnings of $15 or more in a month in covered employment would result in benefit suspension for that month. By 1950 a new philosophy was emerging: that it would be better if the older worker were able to retire more gradually and that therefore he should be able to receive his monthly benefits while engaging in some intermittent or part-time work. The 1950 amendments took cognizance of this philosophy. The revisions increased the permitted earnings amount to $50 monthly for beneficiaries under age 75 who worked in covered jobs and allowed earnings of $600 annually for those who had covered self-employment. In 1952, these amounts were raised to $75 and $900 respectively.

Today, under the 1954 amendments, beneficiaries are subject to a test based on earnings over the period of a year. Effective January 1955, they may earn $1,200 annually without loss of benefits. One month's benefit is suspended for each $80 above that amount, except that no benefit is suspended for any month in which the beneficiary does not do substantial work in self-employment or earn wages that exceed $80. With almost universal coverage, it became administratively feasible as well as logical to apply the earnings test to noncovered as well as covered employment.

In recognition of the fact that some persons covered by the system might work throughout their lifetime, never retiring to a degree sufficient to make possible receipt of monthly benefits toward which they had contributed, payments were authorized in 1950 to beneficiaries aged 75 or older regardless of the extent of their current employment. The 1954 amendments reduced the age to 72.

Payment of benefits as annuities at age 65 regardless of earnings has been consistently rejected as too expensive for the program to support. The purpose of old-age and survivors insurance benefits is to help prevent dependency by providing a regular income to breadwinners and their families when wages or self-employment income stops at retirement or death. If there were no retirement test, benefits would be payable not only to those who had retired but also to those older workers who are still employed and have substantial earnings. The additional benefits that would be paid out to employed workers and their dependents would add substantially to the cost of the system and would not increase the security of the beneficiaries unable to work or unable to find employment.

FINANCING THE PROGRAM

Money to pay benefits comes from taxes paid by employees, their employers, and the self-employed men and women covered by the program. Congress has made clear its intent that the old-age and survivors insurance program be self-supporting and actuarially sound. The tax schedule for the program is designed to accomplish this purpose.

From 1937 through 1949 the tax for employees and employers was 1 percent each on taxable earnings. In 1950 the rate went up to 1½ percent. The rate for the self-employed, who were first covered in 1951, was set at one and one-half times the employee rate. The rates increased in 1954 to 2 percent for employees and employers and 3 percent for the self-employed. Tax rates are scheduled to increase gradually until 1975, when they will be 4 percent each for employees and employers and 6 percent for the self-employed.

All taxes collected under the program go into the Federal old-age and survivors insurance trust fund, a special fund in the U.S. Treasury. Money in the fund can be used only to pay benefits and the costs of administering the program. Amounts not required for current expenditures are invested in interest-bearing U. S. Government bonds.

RELATIONSHIP TO OLD-AGE ASSISTANCE

Program growth during the past 2 decades is reflected in the relationship of old-age and survivors insurance to old-age assistance. From the beginning, old-age and survivors insurance was intended to maintain a basic income for retired workers and thereby reduce the need for public assistance. During the early years of program operation, more aged persons received old-age assistance than insurance. By January 1955, however, more than twice as many aged persons were receiving insurance—5.5 million—as were receiving assistance —2.5 million. The turning point was reached when the requirements for insured status were liberalized and benefits increased by the 1950 amendments.

BUREAU ADMINISTRATION

After every legislative change in the old-age and survivors insurance program comes the administrative challenge of making it work in daily operation. The rapid handling of applications for benefits and their prompt payment each month are major responsibilities of the Bureau of Old-Age and Survivors Insurance. So, too, is the accurate maintenance of the earnings records that are the basis for figuring the amount of each benefit.

Since the start of the program the Bureau has balanced the need for huge mechanized operations in keeping records and paying benefits against the necessity for serving people—treating each account-number holder and beneficiary as an individual.

The Bureau has the world's largest centralized unit of business machines. It is expected that in each 3-month period during 1955 the Division of Accounting Operations will record the opening of about 1 million new social security accounts, credit to individual records 53 million wage items received from 4 million employers and 1.2 million earnings reports from the self-employed, and compute 525,000 benefits on the basis of the earnings records of covered workers. During the same period, Bureau representatives in district offices will probably be seeing more people in the course of business than are seen by employees of any other Government agency except the Post Office Department and the Internal Revenue Service.

The policy of personal contact with each claimant began very early in the Bureau's history, for reasons that remain as forceful today as they were in 1937. When individuals come in to apply for benefits, they are usually facing a critical period in their lives emotionally and economically—for the worker, retirement or disability; for his family, the death of the husband and father. Not unnaturally, their ability to cope with formal, impersonal instructions is at a low ebb. Yet they must understand instructions about responsibility for reporting events that would terminate their benefits or suspend them. The Bureau has found, as well, that beneficiaries get payments faster when there has been face-to-face discussion to obtain the facts necessary to support a claim.

Today, every individual in the continental United States, Alaska, Hawaii, Puerto Rico, and the Virgin Islands can get in touch with an old-age and survivors insurance representative. If he is unable to reach one of the 532 district offices, he may transact his business with Bureau representatives who make regularly scheduled visits to about 3,400 other communities. The Division of Field Operations, one of the Bureau's four operating divisions, today supervises district offices through regional representatives in the nine regional offices of the Department of Health, Education, and Welfare. At first the district offices were little more than information centers and, for a time, registration centers. Since 1940, when payment of monthly benefits as authorized by the 1939 amendments began, claims operations have become the offices' major activity.

For a time, all decisions about eligibility for benefits were made centrally. In September 1942, as soon as procedures and guides were stabilized, this function was decentralized to the district offices.

As benefit rolls grew from 220,000 at the end of 1940 to the present 7.5 million, the local offices undertook the job of answering inquiries and helping beneficiaries report such events as changes of address or their return to work so that necessary action might be taken to deliver or suspend their benefits. District office work in providing this assistance to beneficiaries is now a substantial and growing part of the workload.

From the outset, every attempt was made to inform people about their rights under the program, urging them to get in touch with their local old-age and survivors insurance representative. This function too was largely centralized at the beginning, but today each district office, working from general guides, is responsible for getting information to the residents of the area it serves—a "grass roots" approach. Its success confirms the practicality of this policy.

Recordkeeping.—In contrast to this highly decentralized operation of the district offices, the recordkeeping activity is centralized in Baltimore in the Division of Accounting Operations. Social security account numbers are issued in the district offices. The application form and a duplicate of the social security card are promptly forwarded to the Division of Accounting Operations, where 113 million individual accounts have been established since the program began.

Each calendar quarter, employers covered by the program send to the Internal Revenue Service a tax return containing employee names, social security account numbers, and amounts of wages paid during the 3-month period. After an Internal Revenue audit to verify the amount of tax due, the return reaches the Division of Accounting Operations. Since the nonfarm self-employed were brought under the program in 1951, their reports of earnings, made annually on income-tax returns, follow the same route; the reports of the farm self-employed will also follow this route.

Beneficiaries need the proceeds of their checks to live on; they need to receive them on time and in the right amount. Within the Bureau, the responsibility for getting beneficiaries placed on the rolls and certifying the amounts of payment to the Treasury Department disbursing office that writes the checks falls to six area offices.

Area offices are also responsible for keeping the beneficiary rolls up-to-date. With 7.5 million beneficiaries, a lot can happen in the course of a month; the area office therefore certifies each month to the appropriate Treasury Department disbursing office the amount of the payment. This month-by-month action is necessary to remove from the benefit list the name of a beneficiary who dies or whose payment is discontinued for other reasons. He may also return to work and earn more than the retirement test specifies with the result that his benefit is suspended. In any 1 month, thousands of beneficiaries may change their addresses, which means at the least that in such instances corrected addressograph plates must be prepared so that the monthly checks will reach their proper destination.

All checks had been written by the Treasury Department after notification by the Bureau of the benefit amount, but in 1955 the Bureau passed a new administrative milestone when the area office in Birmingham took over the actual check writing from the Treasury Department disbursing office in the same city. Significant savings are anticipated. If they materialize, the process will probably also be used in the other five area offices.

Disability-freeze Operations. Late in 1954, a fourth operating division—the Division of Disability Operations—was created within the Bureau. The disability-freeze operation brought a new element into Bureau administration, involving a Federal-State partnership. Under the terms of the 1954 amendments, a State may designate one of its agencies to make determinations of disability on applications taken by old-age and survivors insurance district offices. Agreements for this purpose are worked out between the State agency and the Department of Health, Education, and Welfare. The Bureau's newest division has four major tasks—laying the groundwork for negotiations with the State agencies, reviewing State agency decisions on disability, making original decisions for those cases not covered by State agreements, and establishing standards and procedures for paying the State agencies, as well as developing medical guides, policies, and training materials for use by Bureau personnel and the State agencies.

Staff Services. In Baltimore there are, in addition to the operating divisions, the central headquarters staff. There about 500 employees provide personnel and administrative management services for the entire Bureau, train new employees and conduct refresher courses for older employees, prepare informational material, and develop policy to assure uniformity in the decisions made in applying program provisions to specific situations. There, too, the Bureau's research program is conducted to see how well the program is serving the people.

Systematic Planning. Careful and precise planning is a keystone of Bureau administration. A Bureau-wide system of work planning is one tool that is used.

The budget process is another planning tool. By 1942 the Bureau had moved into performance budgeting—where estimated costs and the activities planned for are brought together.

Administrative costs have been kept to a minimum by constant attention to improving ways of doing business, in small procedural details and in large-scale changes alike. Since 1941 the volume of the Bureau's work has increased about four times; the staff required to handle it has increased less than one-fourth as much as the workload. The administrative cost of about $112 million for this fiscal year will be about 1.8 percent of the income during the year to the old-age and survivors insurance trust fund. This percentage can be taken as a crude index of operational effectiveness. When the program was established, it was estimated that administrative costs would run to about 10 percent of trust fund income in the early years of the program and then drop to about 5 percent. Costs actually have never exceeded 3.6 percent since passage of the 1939 amendments.

SUMMARY

Old-age and survivors insurance over the years has provided an increasing measure of protection for the individual and his family against destitution and want resulting from loss of income when the breadwinner retires or dies. To the extent that the individual has been protected, society and the Nation's economy as a whole have been strengthened. The program has become identified with the economic welfare of the country within the framework outlined in 1948 by the Advisory Council in its report to the Senate Committee on Finance:

In the last analysis the security of the individual depends on the success of industry and agriculture in producing an increasing flow of goods and services. However, the very success of the economy in making progress, while creating opportunities, also increases risks. Hence, the more progressive the economy, the greater is the need for protection against economic hazards. This protection should be made available on terms which reinforce the interest of the individual in helping himself. A properly designed social-security system will reinforce the drive of the individual toward greater production and greater efficiency, and will make for an environment conducive to the maximum of economic progress.

Old-age and survivors insurance is not a static program. Having met many of the challenges of the past, it must constantly turn its attention to the future. For, as President Eisenhower has said, "To help individuals provide for . . . security—to reduce both the fear and the incidence of destitution to the minimum—to promote the confidence of every individual in the future—these are proper aims of all levels of government, including the Federal Government."

PUBLIC WELFARE AND THE INCENTIVE STATE

An address by Jarle Leirfallom, Director of Social Welfare, State of Minnesota, published in Public Aid in Illinois, November, 1949, and reproduced in Analysis of the Social Security System, hearings before a subcommittee of the House Committee on Ways and Means, 83d Cong., 1st Sess., 1954, Appendix 2, pp. 1212–1216

Public welfare functions today under a set of noble and praiseworthy concepts. These concepts, taught in our schools of social· work and proclaimed by our professional organizations, have in fact become so much a part of us that we do our work under their guidance. I am thinking of such concepts as respect for individual rights, a nonjudgmental approach to human situations, equal treatment for all persons, respect for democratic processes. As a social worker I am proud of these concepts, and without them the high character of the profession would be greatly diminished. These concepts must be preserved.

I believe, however, that there is need to develop certain additional concepts equally praiseworthy and important. In the absence of these as yet undeveloped concepts, I believe social work has failed to contribute to American life some things which it alone can contribute. I believe it is time for the solid citizens of the traditional American type who are in social work to take the leadership in adding to social-work credos some basic concepts consistent with the American way of life, born of good public policy. I am thinking of concepts regarding subjects such as these: "What is real social welfare?" "How can individual initiative, resourcefulness, and independence be retained?" "What about the welfare state?"

IN SUPPORT OF FREE ENTERPRISE

One of my pet peeves is that social work as a profession has been very watery in its support of our free enterprise system, our economy based on individual initiative. I have never heard a social worker get up on his two feet and defend our free enterprise system as one of the priceless advantages of American life, to be maintained at all costs. I have heard many social workers talk on the other side of the question or talk around it as though their convictions lay elsewhere. This gives social work a bad name. And worse than that, I believe such a position is wrong. It should not take much reflection to realize that materially, at least, the key to social welfare is high production— high production with a well-developed social conscience. Our relief standards in this country are higher than the wage standards in many other countries. Without high production and wealth that comes from labor and work, social welfare is an empty and meaningless thing. Certainly point No. 1 in any social-welfare program should be the maintenance of an economic and social system which yields high production and makes material resources available with which to work.

Our incentive economy is not only important for the material benefits which it yields, but also for the spiritual and personal benefits inherent in the system. Under our system you aspire to anything your little heart desires. You can aspire to be a lawyer, farmer, banker, teacher, millionaire, even a welfare worker if you want to, in accordance with your ability and circumstances, many of them under your own control. This opportunity of economic choice is so closely linked with personal freedom that to threaten the economic phases of this system strikes at the very roots of the social and personal phases. Therefore, purely from the point of view of emphasizing the rich benefits that come to the individual from living in a free society, social workers should be the first to step up and defend it, and doubly so when they consider that it yields not only this great personal satisfaction but also the greatest material benefits with which social workers work. It parallels George Bernard Shaw's great compliment to marriage, in which he explained why marriage is so popular and wonderful. He said, "Marriage is such a wonderful thing because it combines a maximum of temptation with maximum opportunity."

I have construed an "Incentive State" to mean our traditional American way of life, our free enterprise economy. I understand it to mean that an individual can choose a line of work in which he is interested and apply as much energy, initiative, and resourcefulness as he is willing and able and enjoy the benefits of his labors above and beyond the benefits enjoyed by his neighbor who does not make so great a contribution. In business he is entitled to enjoy the rewards of taking wise risks in the development of enterprises and the investment of his capital and labor.

FEAR IS A VERY VALUABLE THING

Perhaps one of the reasons social work has been so lukewarm on this subject is the fact that our free-enterprise economy is based on a system of rewards and punishments wherein fear plays a large part as an incentive to work and produce. Fear has been greatly maligned and abused. Someone made it public enemy No. 1 in our vocabulary. Fear of consequences and a system of rewards and punishments have been considered cruel and antisocial, and great efforts have been made to get around the hard facts of life by the promise of complete security, complete care of all, in order that all might abandon fear and punishment due to circumstances within their control as well as those outside their control.

Fear plays a great part in my life, and I consider it a very valuable thing to me and my family. We live at a lake. Fear that my children may drown or be harmed causes me to spend my time watching them carefully when they play on the lakeshore. They enjoy splashing in the water, and my wife and I get tremendous satisfaction out of their laughter and joviality when they do so, and it hurts us to deprive them of this joy. Yet fear causes us to expend our energy watching them and detracts from their pleasure many hours of the day when they might be allowed to play in the water but are not permitted to do so lest they be harmed. Or I might point out that there are many things that I would like to buy for my wife and children which we cannot afford; yet we spend three or four hundred dollars a year for life insurance, again impelled by the fear that the breadwinner might be killed and we would want our children to be provided for. Parenthetically, this concept is being increasingly ridiculed as a silly viewpoint in view of the adequacy of aid to dependent children and old-age assistance grants.

Perhaps the thought underlying all this would be more palatable if it were to be called, instead of fear, concern for the future. Let's call it concern for the future. Actually, concern for the future is one of the most valuable things of which man is capable, because it not only creates the desire to work and produce and do many fine things but it also gives man the vision to think, not only of himself, but of generations ahead. I am sure that many of the greatest things of life have grown out of a concern for the future, and it is indeed unfortunate that social work has had such a large part in abusing the concept of fear and concern for the future as an incentive in life, together with a system of rewards and punishments which is inherent in a free economy and a free society.

THE WELFARE STATE: AN ILLUSION

Today, there is much chaos in the thinking about the welfare state. The public is greatly concerned about this matter and would be grateful for clarification of the issues involved. These issues should be sufficiently clarified to make possible intelligent choices about the welfare state rather than have government slide along in the direction of greatest pressure.

It is my opinion that social work should announce itself, stand up and be counted on this important subject. I believe social workers, better than anyone else, can state that the concept of the welfare state is an illusion, a very dangerous one. The welfare state can well be compared to the mirage which a thirsty man chases across an unwatered desert. The harder he chases it, the sooner will come his end. Work, production, application, the desire to contribute lie at the root of genuine welfare; not a concoction of schemes as to how to get something for nothing. If each individual thinks of his government mainly in terms of what government can do for him and how much he can get from it, government soon becomes a giant cow whom everyone is attempting to milk. My group milks the cow in the afternoon, having spent the morning feeding the cow while someone else milked her.

One writer has put the proposition this way:

Our society and economy is divided roughly into two groups. One is the producing incentive group, the other is the nonproductive consuming group. Today more and more burden is falling on the producing group to support and pay for the nonproducing group. For example pensioneering movements, such as those which flourish so vigorously on the Pacific coast, aimed far beyond the normal obligations of the paying members of society to the nonpaying. Their central aim is to get as much as possible for the largest possible group, in the shortest possible time. Productive workers are expected to support the nonproductive groups with increasing liberality, which means a steadily increasing burden on production. This can go on for a while, but in the end it must mean the impoverishment of the whole nation. A society which progressively penalizes its producers for the benefit of its nonproducers is headed for trouble.

THE URGENT SEARCH FOR A REVERSE GEAR

The second law of thermodynamics is a hypothesis which has not yet been disproven, and until disproven will stand as a fact of life. It states that all forms of physical energy tend to level off and become unavailable for use, and no reverse process has been found to stop this leveling off and this gradual deterioration of physical energy. Some day the world will be cold, motionless, and dead unless the reverse process is found.

There is, in my opinion, a striking relationship between this law of physical energy and the concept of the welfare state as a leveling off of social and personal energy and resourcefulness. Just as physicists have strained every brain cell to find a reverse process to stop the leveling off of physical energy, so also social workers should in our society strain every effort to find a reverse process to stop the leveling off and dissipation of personal and individual energy and initiative.

The first step in that process, in my opinion, is to label frankly the welfare state as much of an illusion as the illusion of full employment which two neighbors might dream up by agreeing to pile rocks in one another's yards. The one man piles rocks in his neighbor's yard in the morning and picks them out of his yard in the afternoon where the other man piled them during the morning.

TWO BIBLICAL ADMONITIONS—AND SOCIAL WORK

The second step in finding a reverse process against the welfare state is to resort to the Biblical admonition to "feed the hungry, clothe the naked, take care of the poor." Social work should continue to do as it has so ably done in the past: We should make known to our people the need of dependent children, the needs of the aged, the need for rehabilitative mental hospitals, the best methods of taking care of the unemployed. About this we should continue to be adamant. We should, however, read the corresponding portion of the Biblical admonition which says that "by the sweat of thy brow shalt thou eat thy bread." Every ablebodied man should be expected to work with a minimum of foolishness about his ego and his libido and the open-end frame of reference. Individuals should be expected to use their own resources to the limit. Social workers should state equally flatly that the "pension" and "grab bag" concept of government, using government as a tool, which seems to be so popular today is a desecration of the American way of life which should not be permitted, and which if followed to its logical conclusion by every group that has access to government, will soon be like the mirage which causes a man to chase across the desert to an early end.

In this connection I would like to call your attention to the words of Chancellor Deane Mallot, of the University of Kansas, who says in part:

If one protests that people lean too much on Government, he is likely to be dismissed as a dark reactionary who favors the most medieval forms of laissez-faire. Would he deny benefits to the disabled veteran? Would he abolish unemployment insurance? Does he believe that Government has no responsibility for the welfare of its citizens? The questions are sharply barbed with accusations. They're designed to wither the most insensitive souls. And of course, they miss the point entirely. The point is that no people can prosper and enjoy the good things of life by living off Government. The way to a greater abundance does not lie through the Government at all; it lies only through production.

I'll wager to say that there is not a single social worker who does not know that in the selfish grab, which special groups make, the crumbs fall to dependent children, mentally incompetent persons, juvenile delinquents, and the weakest members of society. One of the high callings, therefore, of social workers, is to defend the weaker members whom they represent, by fighting to the utmost the tendency of pressure groups to make selfish raids upon public funds.

THE VISTA OF TOMORROW

Now let me ask a question about the vista of tomorrow. What should be the attitude of social work toward Government? Should social workers also seek to become a more effective pressure group, or should they make an effort to stop the trend in that direction, realizing that government by pressure groups is a cheap concept of democracy. Representative democratic government faces a crisis. I have come to that conclusion after having observed several legislatures at close hand, and noting how laws are passed. Groups use special skill in organizing themselves for the purpose of putting pressure upon government through elected representatives. Government becomes a trading post for these groups. It gets to be the tool rather than the arbiter in the large affairs of men. It seems that all representative government can do is to vote more and more benefits to each group that comes along. There must be an end some time. Old-age assistance recipients come in with pressure on their representative and he cannot turn them down. Veterans come in, and they cannot be turned down. Dentists come, and they can't be refused. Teachers have a powerful lobby, and there is no stopping them.

I have before me an article entitled "Don't Be a Monkey," and it says: "One way to catch a monkey, it is said, is to tempt the creature with bait placed in a small-mouthed bottle. The eager monk can slip his arm through the opening when his hand is empty, but once he has grasped the bait he can't pull free. So intent is he on getting the bait he won't let go, and therefore stays stuck." The same bait can be used to make monkeys out of men. Call the bait Government subsidies, and the bottle Government control. Call the monkey any one of the growing number of members of labor, farm, and professional groups who delude themselves that they can snatch the bait without being stuck with the bottle.

When an individual sets out to achieve the good life, he cannot find it solely in one place. That is, he cannot find it in work alone nor in recreation alone. Basically, and I am probably oversimplifying this, he finds the good life in his home, in the church, in the economy, and in good government. The contribution of the home and the church are obvious. The contribution of the economy and government should be equally obvious. The economy provides him with material things, and the opportunity to work and produce. Good government should safeguard his possessions, and protect him and his home, and should set up the necessary rules to keep individuals from infringing on one another's freedoms. Society is in a bad way when it begins to mix the functions of the economy and that of government. We are all acquainted with the separation of church and state, and countless men will go into a furious rage at the thought of mixing these two. These two powerful forces have been kept apart through the centuries, even though existing side by side. This has been possible because there has been no confusion about the two. Such is not the case so far as government and our economy is concerned. These two are becoming hopelessly mixed, and I believe the average citizen is very fuzzy in his thinking on the separation of the two. In fact, many citizens want the two to become more and more mixed and confused. Therein lies the great danger of the welfare state—the fact that there is no clear consciousness of the need to keep our economy and our government separate; rather, a will on the part of large groups in our population to mix the two even more can be disastrous to the country.

Government should be the arbiter in the large affairs of men, laying down democratically agreed upon rules for individuals and groups, pursuing their social and economic functions. Government, being a referee in the social and economic game, should not step in and play the game. Like a sports association or a referee of a football game, government should stay out of the field of play just as much as we expect a referee to refrain from picking up the ball and running with it.

I used to live on a farm. On the farm we had horses, cows, sheep, a dog, and various other odds and ends. Sometimes on Sundays after church when we were not required or permitted to work, we thought up a lot of funny things to do. Occasionally we would see if we could ride a pig, harness a dog, or even milk a horse. When we rode the pig we would get dumped in the mud, when we harnessed the dog he would get himself tangled up in the rope and would go nowhere, and when we tried to milk the horse we would have to dodge his hoofs. Imagine a farmer so stupid that he would try to make a living by milking his horses, riding his pigs, and hitching up his cows? Yet that is precisely what we are doing today in government so far as the welfare state is concerned. And there are many people so unenlightened (and I should say stupid) that they are trying to make their living off government, but the sad fact is that government cannot produce a living for individuals except in a completely socialistic or communistic state, and the end result of seeking a living from government is to achieve a socialistic or communistic state. In fact, you must start out with that assumption to begin with. In communism government owns all resources, all means of production, all items produced, and distributes them to the people. In Russia for instance, the government also controls the church and the home, being all inclusive. At least in that respect we are a long way from communism because before communism can prevail these independent elements must be swallowed up by government rather than kept separate as they are in this country. But can any intelligent person mistake the trend for what it is when government is increasingly swallowing up and controlling our economy?

OPTIMISM STILL POSSIBLE—IF

It seems that representative government has no reverse gear. Today the medical profession believes it is on the brink of a precipice, the doctors feel that government without reverse gear is going to push them over the brink with irreparable damage to a system which it believes is inherently valuable. Some of us feel that government without a reverse gear is pushing toward a welfare state which, when supposedly achieved, will be an illusion purchased by a great loss of personal freedom.

Do you not agree that we have many serious things to think and talk about? I do, and I am optimistic. I feel very much like Agnes Meyer does, speaking at the University of Minnesota:

I have no doubt that we shall be able to conquer every dangerous social trend at home and abroad, and invite mankind toward its destiny of truth and goodness, if we only continue to love liberty more than all else in the world, but liberty demands self-discipline of mind and character, perpetual effort, and a willingness to sacrifice a lesser to a greater good. Millions of people the world over have bartered their freedom for the specious security of dictatorship because it is the easiest thing to do.

CREDO WITH RESPECT TO SOCIAL SECURITY

From the testimony of Arthur J. Altmeyer, one of the original members of the three-man Social Security Board appointed to administer the Act, and first Commissioner for Social Security when that office was established in 1946, given before a subcommittee of the House Committee on Ways and Means, 83d Cong., 1st Sess., 1953, and appearing in the committee print, Analysis of the Social Security System, part 6, pp. 954–955

. . . In the consideration of the development of a social security program, we ought to proceed upon the assumption that we want to develop a social security system based upon a free enterprise system, and designed so as to promote all of the values inherent in a free enterprise system.

May I also say that we must proceed upon the assumption that every effort will be made to make this free enterprise system as productive as possible and as just as possible to the participants thereof.

I believe that a social security system ought to be designed to provide a minimum basic protection upon which the individual may build a further degree of protection as desired by him and his family. I do not look upon that minimum basic protection as simply an animal level of subsistence. I look upon it as a level that permits some degree of gracious living to all of the American people, and I believe that there is no fixed amount that should be established as the limit of a decent, humane, minimum basic protection for all of the American people.

I believe that a system of social security ought to protect all of the people against all of the major economic hazards which lead to destitution. I believe that a contributory social insurance system enabling people to help pay for their own protection ought to be the first line of defense against destitution, and the major element in any system of social security.

I believe that benefits should be related to income loss under this contributory social insurance system.

I believe that we must preserve both the principle of individual equity and the principle of social adequacy.

I believe that we should have a safe system of financing that looks to the future as well as the present and makes certain that we know where we are going and have set up an automatic system of financing so that these benefits that are provided as a matter of statutory right by the Congress of the United States may be preserved and protected and paid when due.

I believe that public assistance should be retained as the second line of defense against destitution.

I believe that every effort should be made to prevent the hazards causing destitution. I believe that there should be industrial accident prevention, that there should be employment offices to reduce the amount of unemployment to a minimum, that we ought to have hiring and firing practices that would permit persons in their fifties and sixties and seventies to continue to work if they want to and are able to do so. I think it is tragic and inhuman to throw them on the scrap heap just when they reach an arbitrary age limit, whether it is 65 or whether it is any other, and I believe that we should have rehabilitation programs of all sorts to enable people to continue to be productive, to restore their productive capacity if it has been lost or impaired.

PERSONAL RESPONSIBILITY FOR OLD AGE

Testimony of Hyman Blumberg, Executive Vice President, Amalgamated Clothing Workers of America, in Labor-Management Relations, hearings before the Joint Congressional Committee on Labor-Management Relations, 80th Cong., 2d Sess., 1948, part 1, pp. 415–420

[REPRESENTATIVE] HOFFMAN: Did you ever have any experience in business in a small city?

MR. BLUMBERG: Do you mean by that whether I was ever in business; I would say "No." I went into a shop, as I told you, at the age of 12.

MR. HOFFMAN: I only have a short time this morning, so I would like to have an answer to my questions.

MR. BLUMBERG: I have had experience in small communities, I have had experience in large cities in talking over with businessmen the problems of both business and labor.

MR. HOFFMAN: How many years have you been in business, either as an employer or as an employee?

MR. BLUMBERG: To be exact, 50 years.

MR. HOFFMAN: In your early experience, if you were in smaller communities, did you not find that it was true that the average citizen could provide for his own old-age security?

MR. BLUMBERG: Never in the experience of any workingman in this country has a workingman been able to accumulate sufficient funds to take care of himself in his old age.

MR. HOFFMAN: You make that as a statement of fact with reference to smaller communities?

MR. BLUMBERG: I make that as a statement of fact, with my experience in working with men and women in small communities, and in large communities, that no one has ever been able to accumulate enough from savings, from wages, to take care of himself and his wife when they reach old age.

MR. HOFFMAN: Then I will enlarge your information and say that on the street where I live, three brothers, Germans, coming from Germany and working in a furniture factory at $12 a week were enabled to buy their own homes, purchase their own insurance, and so forth, and their names were Schuman, and they live in the same block as I.

MR. BLUMBERG: I may enlighten you on this, that my mother, on wages of my father at $8 a week, bought her own home, but that meant that we kids did not eat.

MR. HOFFMAN: Do you mean that the Government should provide sufficient payments so that every individual who had not provided for his own security should be given enough to live "adequately," as we use that word today?

MR. BLUMBERG: I think the Government should provide for men who work for a living, when they reach the age of 65, or reach the age of 60, a sum that would keep body and soul together under present-day conditions.

What I mean by that is, have sufficient shelter and sufficient food.

MR. HOFFMAN: Then would you write into the law any provision which would affect the amount of that payment, any requirement that an individual in order to get those payments should have worked a certain proportion of the time and in accordance with his physical ability to work?

MR. BLUMBERG: Well, you will find that in the overwhelming majority of cases workingmen take work when they can get it. Loafers among workingmen are much more of a rarity than they are among the classes that have money.

You might find loafers but by and large a workingman, who has dependents takes work whenever he can get it and never refuses it.

MR. HOFFMAN: Undoubtedly that is true, but take this situation: Mr. Landis and I are working in the same factory on the same kind of job. He works whenever he is able. I like to hunt and fish, and whenever there is an excuse and I can get away with it I do that. We reach the age of 60, we lose our jobs for some physical defect, and we are not responsible.

Should I receive the same amount as Mr. Landis?

MR. BLUMBERG: You would not because under your present law you do not.

MR. HOFFMAN: Now, you are talking about where the contributions are made by the workers, but I am talking about citizens generally who have reached the age of 60, and who may not have been employed in industry. Perhaps he may have been a businessman.

MR. BLUMBERG: If I know industry at all, I know this, that no man ever holds his job by going fishing 3 days a week.

MR. HOFFMAN: No, but you do realize, do you not, that we do not all work with the same degree of energy, we are not equally as attentive to our work, and do not arrive as soon in the morning.

MR. BLUMBERG: I am a great believer in each person doing his best. That is the reason we have piecework in our industry. I have worked in shops where I could produce 40 a day and workers beside me did their best and went as high as 20 and 22 a day. That is natural ability and speed.

MR. HOFFMAN: Let us take the case of the businessman who is not in a factory. You said, as I understood you, that every person who reaches a certain age should be taken care of by a payment from the Federal Government. In the case of two merchants, one may attend to business, getting there at 7 in the morning and working until 7 at night. When those people get to a certain age should they be treated the same way as to payments and receive the same amount?

MR. BLUMBERG: When we speak of millions you always find a rule where there is room for exception. You are speaking of two men, whether laborers or employers. The employer who does not attend to his business usually goes out of business and you will find him, then, as one of the disgruntled fellows.

MR. HOFFMAN: When he reaches 60 he still gets the same payments?

MR. BLUMBERG: When he reaches 60, what would you do with him? If a minimum requirement to keep a man alive is $50, what would you do with him?

MR. HOFFMAN: I would certainly give him enough to keep him alive, if you are asking me a question; I would certainly do that. I would not let him starve, but I would not give him cake and pie, and I would see that he did not get the same amount as the fellow who worked all his life. . . .

MR. BLUMBERG: People make contributions to society to the best of their ability. For example a sharecropper down in Arkansas or in Arizona is doing the best he can. Perhaps his income is only $300 a year, or $400 a year. It is no fault of his.

MR. HOFFMAN: You would establish a system, then, where everyone is assured of an adequate living when he reaches a certain age, or when he has been employed so long? Would that not have a tendency to destroy thrift? If I am assured that I will get certain payments when I attain a certain age, regardless of what I do or say, will not the tendency be on my part to spend my money and not invest it in savings? . . .

MR. BLUMBERG: I do not believe that that has any bearing at all.

MR. HOFFMAN: You do not?

MR. BLUMBERG: No person who thinks ahead when he reaches the age of 65, who may get $45 a month, would think in terms that that $45 a month for the next 40 years would allow him to loaf. I do not think that has any bearing on it. . . .

MR. HOFFMAN: . . . If I know that after a certain time I am going to get a fixed sum, would not the tendency be for me to not take so much forethought, not cramp myself and not save quite so much, and not purchase for myself an annuity or bonds, or whatever I want?

MR. BLUMBERG: I do not believe it would have any bearing on that at all.

MR. HOFFMAN: As I understand your testimony, those who are participants in your insurance scheme get larger benefits for less money than they would in ordinary insurance?

MR. BLUMBERG: I would say yes; that is true.

MR. HOFFMAN: The cost of those benefits comes from the consumer, does it not? If the employer pays it all, as you say, he must of necessity add it to the cost of the product?

MR. BLUMBERG: Anything that goes into the cost of a product is usually met by the consumer. Sometimes unnecessary costs may be attached on. I do not believe any man is worth a quarter of a million a year, but there are a lot of them getting that.

MR. HOFFMAN: And the benefits that the employee gets are ultimately paid by the consumer, of course?

MR. BLUMBERG: Of course.

MR. HOFFMAN: So the net result is that, for instance, those in your industry, or in the coal mining industry, get those extra benefits at the cost of the public, generally, do they not?

MR. BLUMBERG: As a rule, yes.

MR. HOFFMAN: Do you know of any reason, for example, why the dairymen should not organize and add a cent or two to each pound of butter and each quart of milk, or the poultrymen should not add so much to each dozen eggs, and put it into an insurance fund? Is there anything in logic or reasoning why they should not do that? . . .

MR. BLUMBERG: You are putting a hypothetical question that should not be brought about in reality. Yet when you speak of consumers, bear in mind that the coal miners are consumers, the steel workers are consumers, the clothing workers are consumers, the white-collar workers are consumers, and the great population of this country are consumers, and their well-being adds to the prosperity of the farmer. You know what happened to the farmer in 1932.

MR. HOFFMAN: I asked you if there is anything morally wrong in any farmer or any other producer or handler in following the course of Mr. Lewis and some others in adding a certain percentage for a particular welfare fund.

MR. BLUMBERG: There is nothing morally wrong in the farmer saying, "I am going to divert 3 percent or 5 percent of my income for insurance," and I think he would be a smart man if he did it.

MR. HOFFMAN: Would there be anything wrong to adding that to his price?

MR. BLUMBERG: Any price he charges—when wheat went up in the last 4 years, from $1.50 to $3 a bushel, I would not say the farmer got it all, but any time the price goes up there is an addition to him.

MR. HOFFMAN: Then if each industry followed that course ultimately we would have here various groups, all the innumerable groups arrayed against each other, trying to get a special benefit.

MR. BLUMBERG: In order to do away with that why not have the Government take over the whole thing.

MR. HOFFMAN: Is that your theory?

MR. BLUMBERG: What is wrong with it?

PENSIONS IN OUR SOCIETY

Excerpt from "Economic Factors of Collective Bargaining," a talk by C. E. Wilson, President, General Motors Corporation, before the Chicago Executives Club, January 6, 1950

. . . It is clear to me that the reason for this strong demand for pensions and what is called old age security arises from a change from an agricultural to an industrial society. This is true not only in our country but also in Europe, in fact in all places where the people have come from the land into industry— from the country into the city.

On a farm, when a man was young, maybe he milked twenty cows a day. When he got old, say sixty-five, maybe he could only milk twelve; and when he got to be eighty, if he was still in good health, maybe he just fed the cows, but he still had at least a part-time job.

In a modern plant, with progressive manufacturing and conveyor assembly lines, a man who can't keep up his part of the work must be taken off that job. He can't do sixty percent of it as he gets older because that would reduce the whole production down to sixty percent. And if we did that in consideration for the old men, reducing the production for everybody in the group to their level, the whole country's production would be slowed down, costs and prices would go up, prosperity would be lost, and all of us, including the old men, would not get along very well.

The feeling of insecurity on the part of the industrial worker in the city which has led to the public approval of pension plans merely points up the desire on the part of all for some similar economic security in old age. Men of good will in all countries, whether they be politicians, labor leaders, industrial executives, professional men or workmen, recognize the same desirable objective; namely, a stable society with a continuing improvement in the welfare of all the people. But there is a terrific difference of opinion as to the best means of achieving this desirable objective and in how to measure the progress that is or is not being made. Apparently, these same differences of opinion exist regarding ways to take care of the aged. However, the desire for economic security in old age in one form or another is generally looked upon as one of the normal desires of enlightened human beings.

To properly appraise this problem of old age security or social security it is necessary to realize that such plans or programs in our country now rest upon five grounds:

1. The basic and normal desire on the part of all citizens for such economic security. This was recognized in private pension plans and savings plans long before there was any Federal plan or any great insistence on the part of unions for such plans.

2. The fact that the cost of caring for the old, the unemployed and the sick on at least a minimum subsistence basis must fall upon the economy in some form or other. They must be cared for in some way, and the problem really is how this can best be done and how this burden should be distributed.

3. In our prosperous nation men and women who have been gainfully employed and have had a standard of living much beyond a subsistence level are not satisfied in their old age to drop down to a mere subsistence level. They are willing to work and pay for some old age security, and the question is what portion of their current earnings are they willing to divert for this purpose.

4. Pensions have now been determined to be matters for collective bargain-

ing. Under these circumstances any plans which are developed by collective bargaining must be integrated with the Federal plan, whatever that is.

5. Since we have elected to have a Federal plan it should cover as many citizens as possible with the ultimate objective of covering on a minimum basis all those who are gainfully employed—the self-employed as well as those who work for others.

The problem would seem to be how to provide pensions at a tolerable cost without destroying self-reliance, without reducing effort on the part of the individual, without tying a man to his job and without destroying the initiative of the millions on which the prosperity of our country depends. If an important part of a workman's pension depends upon employment with a particular employer, all employers both large and small will have a great deal of difficulty in regard to employe separations which involve loss of pensions. Employers will hesitate to employ middle-aged workers who may be out of work, and other middle-aged workers will hesitate to take better jobs with other employers when such opportunities occur, for fear of losing an important part of their pensions. Such inflexibility in the working force would interfere with necessary production and business adjustments and would retard progress. Furthermore, private pension plans cannot effectively meet the situation in industries with inherently heavy labor turnover among numerous small employers, of which the construction industry is the best example.

Adequate Federal pensions financed on a sound basis would seem to be the real answer to the problem. Such Federal pensions must give more consideration to the requirements of skilled and semi-skilled workers and white collar workers than the proposed changes now before Congress would provide. Unless the benefits for higher paid workmen are made more nearly proportionate to their contributions and those of their employers the problem of making up the discrepancy will create an extremely difficult situation for many, if not most, businesses. Even those businesses which can meet this added burden will still be paying twice for the same pension, that is, once for the Federal plan and again to make up for its deficiencies for their better paid men. However, Federal pensions must not be too big or the cost will be too great. With this limitation, Federal pensions will not meet the demand in all cases, especially in high production industries where wages are high and employes are accustomed to a higher standard of living. In many cases such industries and their employes are located in the larger cities where the cost of living in retirement is also much higher.

I do not consider that federal pensions fully paid for by employer and employe are in any sense contrary to free enterprise but amount to an extension of the principle of group insurance. The federal old-age assistance program on a hand-out and political basis is much more likely to get us into difficulty. To reduce and ultimately liquidate the federal old-age assistance program should be the ultimate objective. This is why it is so necessary to extend coverage under the federal pension plan to the maximum number possible and ultimately have it cover all people who are or will be gainfully employed. It would seem that assistance on a need basis could well be left to the states and local communities. If you are not familiar with the federal old-age assistance program, you should familiarize yourself with it.

If the people of our country who are gainfully employed are taxed as a group through their employers and through payroll deductions so that in total pensions paid do not exceed collections under the plan, it is hard for me to see how the hope of receiving a pension some day on the part of those who have contributed will undermine their spirit of independence, confidence or self-reliance or cause them to lose their dignity, self-respect or moral stature. I think we should keep in mind that we are talking about some measure of economic security in old age for the millions of our fellow citizens who are the real producers of the nation and who are willing to work for the things they would like to have, among which is an old-age pension. We have millions of salesmen abroad in our country trying to persuade these same people to spend the last dollar they can get their hands on. We have radio, television and all forms of advertising programs designed to entice them to spend their money, and with the best of intentions they are likely to arrive at their old age without on their own initiative having accumulated adequate personal savings. They are also subject to the individual hazards of life which at various periods may use up such savings as they have been able to accumulate. This is why these same people are in favor of some form of insurance which they are also willing to pay for, and thus minimize their individual hazards. The popularity of industrial group insurance is evidence of this.

Improved technology and our American genius for organizing production and distribution have made it possible to reduce the workweek from sixty hours fifty years ago to forty hours now and at the same time raise the average standard of living. Efficient business administration and ever-improving technology, if not interfered with, will make it possible in the next ten years to underwrite minimum pensions without increasing current working hours or decreasing the purchasing power of an hour's labor.

It is my hope that the Congress will work out a sound federal pension plan that will greatly reduce the problem of individual businessmen, unions and employes and that those of you who have unions to deal with regarding this matter will find your union leaders willing to wait to see what the federal plan is going to be before pressing demands for immediate settlement of the pension issue.

PENSIONS IN THE UNITED STATES

Summary of the report, Pensions in the United States, prepared for the Joint Congressional Committee on the Economic Report by the National Planning Association, 82d Cong., 2d Sess., 1952, pp. 73–75, 77

Great progress has been made in the United States in the last 15 years toward solving the problem of income maintenance in old age. . . .

Even so, much remains to be done. The situation of the present aged is quite unsatisfactory. Benefits are low, on the average considerably below subistence except for those few, some 350,000, who are drawing pensions under both old-age and survivors insurance and private plans. The situation of aged widows is particularly unsatisfactory. While public retirement plans are at present paying about two-thirds of the retired men and their wives, and single and divorced women, less than one-fourth of the nonworking widows over 65 are drawing such benefits. Private plans pay benefits to not quite 10 percent of the first group and to very few of the second group. Another group for whom present arrangements are particularly inadequate is made up of those who were prematurely retired because of permanent and total disabilities.

There seems to be little reason for thinking that present pension commitments are too high for us as a nation. Pension payments to those 65 years of age and over now represent slightly less than 1 percent of the national income and, with greatly expanded coverage and liberalizations sufficient to keep up with increases in productivity, they would represent about 3.7 percent of the national income in 1975. The retired aged now make up about 10 percent of the nonproducers and by 1975 will represent about 13 percent, but other non-working groups are expected to stay the same or decline slightly so that the ratio of the gainfully employed to the nongainfully employed will be about the same in 1975 as now or even somewhat improved.

It is likely that under pension arrangements the burden of supporting the aged will be less than it would be in the absence of such arrangements. It is important, however, to continue to employ as large a proportion as possible of those aged who can and want to work both to reduce pension costs and to increase the total volume of goods and services available for all consumers. In this connection, pension plans should be designed so that they do not interfere with the employment of older workers or unduly inhibit the mobility of the labor force, since these results would reduce the total production of the economy.

The problems of fund accumulation need further study. There is some doubt as to whether interest-earning reserves are a very satisfactory way of meeting a major part of the long-run costs of retirement systems. The accumulation of these funds contributes to the productivity of the economy, but because they are largely invested in bonds their income does not increase as the productivity of the economy increases. Yet it is likely that the realistic liability of retirement systems must be measured in terms of the standard of living current at the time pensions are payable. As productivity increases and wages increase over the long run, people will expect bigger pensions. In such a situation funding is not as effective a way of financing as it is frequently assumed to be. . . .

In spite of disagreement on some points there is widespread agreement among business, labor and expert opinion in the United States concerning the broad pattern which should be followed in meeting the income maintenance needs of the aged. The pattern is this: employment for those aged who can and want to work, and for those who retire a universally available system of publicly administered old-age and survivors insurance, contributory in nature and wage related, plus supplementary retirement systems which take into account the protection afforded by old-age and survivors insurance but give additional benefits. The desirability of additional savings which the individual accomplishes on his own according to his ability and inclination is taken for granted. There is also support for public assistance available for those who even with full coverage by retirement systems will not have income sufficient to meet their minimum needs in old age. . . .

The provision of an assured retirement income is a prerequisite for satisfactory living in old age, but it is by no means a guaranty. Retirement income is necessary to give freedom from a sense of insecurity and freedom from feeling one is a burden on others. These are important freedoms, but the provision of income in old age should do even more; it should provide the economic base for a good life. Whether it does so in fact, depends not only on the amount of the income but on the capacity of the individual to adjust to his new life of retirement and on the opportunities open to him to make his new life rewarding.

The needs of the aged are as varied and as important as those of any other group. The aged cannot be given a pittance and then put off in a corner of community life and forgotten. Today, hundreds of thousands of pensioners are living out their lives friendless and alone—often in ill health, unoccupied, and without purpose. With many years of life yet ahead they are already awaiting death. The payment of a pension simply to keep them alive is not enough. The aged must be given the chance to participate in a variety of activities. They must have opportunity for recreation, for creative activity, for making friendships. They must have the opportunity to secure satisfactory living arrangements and satisfactory health care.

For those who throughout life have learned to adjust to changing conditions, retirement on a reasonably adequate income holds real promise. It does not need to be retirement from something; for increasing age can mean not only the loss of powers, but growth. Older people can and want to learn. Old age can be, and has for many been, a time of creative activity and rich rewards.

It would be difficult to overstate the role of assured money income in making retirement a new opportunity rather than a waiting for death. The improvement of income maintenance arrangements is, therefore, perhaps the most important single aspect of the movement to make life worth living for the retired aged.

THE GROWTH, COMPLEXITIES, AND SCOPE OF WELFARE AND PENSION PLANS

From Welfare and Pension Plans Investigation, final report of the Senate Committee on Labor and Public Welfare, 84th Cong., 2d Sess., 1956, pp. 11–14

In many ways the unparalleled development of private employee welfare and pension plans is a testimonial to the genius and managerial ability of industry and labor.

These plans had their first beginnings many decades ago. However, the greatest growth has occurred since 1940, and more especially since 1945. For the most part, these systems grew up like Topsy. Within the last 10 years they have mushroomed with amazing speed and with almost no regulations and safeguards. It is surprising, in a system of such magnitude and complexity, that the abuses and weaknesses discovered by the subcommittee are not greater.

Welfare plans provide life-insurance or death benefits, disability insurance or payments during periods of disability, and hospital, surgical and medical insurance or direct provision of health services as required. They are a joint enterprise of the worker and his employer, and spread the losses incident to these contingencies over the group. They may take the form of a commercial insurance policy, self-insurance, or Blue Cross, Blue Shield, or similar nonprofit prepayment plans.

Pension plans provide benefits upon retirement due to old age or permanent disability.

Today, these programs provide in some degree various insurance coverages or retirement pensions for 75 million persons—29 million workers and their 46 million dependents. Thus, almost one-half the total population is affected by these plans. Their risk-spreading efforts have been cast in a framework of hundreds of thousands of collective-bargaining contracts, employer-employee arrangements, insurance policies, and trust agreements formulated by such diverse groups as union officials, corporate officers, insurance executives, bankers, and uncounted and uncountable mixtures and interplays of these plans.

At the end of 1954, the number of employees and their dependents covered under these plans, for the various types of benefits, were as follows:

Number of Persons Covered

Type of benefit	Employ-ees	Depend-ents	Total	Employees covered as percent of all employees
	Millions	Millions	Millions	Percent
Welfare:				
Life insurance and death benefits.	29.5	1.1	30.6	55.0
Accidental death and dismember-ment......................	14.0	...	14.0	...
Temporary disability benefits.....	23.2	...	23.2	43.6
Hospitalization................	31.3	44.3	75.6	59.0
Surgical.....................	28.3	39.0	67.3	53.0
Medical......................	17.3	21.4	38.7	32.0
Pensions.....................	12.5	...	...	23.0

Approximately 60 percent of the workers who are covered for pension benefits and about 40 percent of those covered by the various welfare programs are under programs which are collectively bargained.

In 1954, total estimated employer-employee contributions to these programs amounted to $6,846,200,000, of which employer contributions were $4,537,-900,000 and employee contributions, $2,308,300,000.

The payments into these programs are an investment in a sound national economy and continued prosperity. They are an investment in labor-management cooperation. The benefits flow to both groups.

A. FACTORS CONTRIBUTING TO GROWTH

The underlying factors responsible for the development of these benefit plans and their phenomenal growth in recent years have been the same as those responsible for the development of the various governmental insurance programs. These include the human desire for protection against income loss and other costs arising from illness, unemployment, disability, old age and death, and the fact that such protection can be obtained more economically on a group rather than an individual basis. Other important factors which have encouraged the development of these private employee welfare and pension programs have been:

1. High corporation taxes during and since World War II, coupled with the allowance of tax deductions for contributions to these programs, thus permitting their establishment at a low net cost;

2. Wage stabilization programs during and since World War II and the Korean conflict, which froze wage rates but permitted increased employee compensation in the form of these "fringe" benefits;

3. Court decisions in the years 1948–50 which made welfare and pension matters a bargainable issue; and

4. Since 1948, the drive of labor unions to obtain welfare and pension programs. Labor spokesmen state that another reason for the development of these programs has been the inadequacy of benefits under the governmental programs.

The development of health benefit programs has also been spurred by the advances in medical science which, while increasing the efficacy of medical care, have also increased its costs and make it difficult for individuals to meet those costs except on a spread-the-risk basis. Similarly, the development of private pension programs has been due, in part, to an increased interest in providing for old-age security.

B. GROWTH OF PROGRAMS

An indication of the phenomenal growth of these various benefit programs in recent years is the increase of group life insurance coverage from approximately 9 million in 1949 to 29 million persons as of the end of 1954; the increase in persons covered by insurance companies under group hospital expense policies from 38,000 in 1935 to 35 million; the growth of the Blue Cross plans from 214,000 participants in 1935 to 44 million; and the increase in persons covered by pension programs from 3.7 million in 1940 to 12.5 million in 1954. . . .

C. TYPES OF ADMINISTRATION AND CONTROL

Generally, there are four types of welfare and pension plans, considered from
the standpoint of their administration and control:
1. Single employer administered plan;
2. Single employer—jointly (employer-union) administered fund;
3. Multiemployer—jointly (employer-union) administered fund;
4. Wholly union administered plan.

Virtually all plans fall into one or another of these classifications. The subcommittee roughly estimates that the proportions of workers covered under
welfare and pension plans through each of these four arrangements are as
follows: [1]

	Welfare plans	Pension plans
	Percent	Percent
Total, all types of plans.	100	100
Single employer administered plan	92.0	86.0
Single employer—jointly (employer-union) administered fund.	.5	.5
Multiemployer—jointly (employer-union) administered fund.	7.0	13.0
Wholly union-administered plan	.5	.5

PENSION PLANS—DESCRIPTION AND PROBLEMS

*From Welfare and Pension Plans Investigation, final report of the Senate Com-
mittee on Labor and Public Welfare, 84th Cong., 2d Sess., 1956, pp. 47–49,
50–51*

Pension plans have at least two features which differentiate them from welfare plans and which warrant separate discussion. One of these features is that,
unlike welfare plans which deal with short-term risks, pension programs deal
with long-term future contingencies. If a welfare program is unsoundly de-

[1] A recent survey in New York State found that of all employees who were covered
under health and welfare plans approximately 71 percent were covered under single
employer plans and 29 percent under multiemployer plans. In New York City the
proportion of the workers covered under multiemployer plans was approximately 40
percent; in upstate New York 9.5 percent. It is believed that the situation in upstate
New York would be more characteristic of the country as a whole than New York
City. Hence, it may be estimated that of the 29.5 million employees in the country
who are covered for life insurance and death benefits, not more than 9.5 percent,
or 2.8 million, would be covered through multiemployer jointly managed funds. The
subcommittee's own study of insured welfare funds, i.e., of insurance policies written
in which a welfare fund is the policy holder, found that the total premiums under all
such policies amounted in 1953 to $98 million. This is about 5 percent of the total
premiums on all group insurance written by insurance companies that year.

signed in that income is insufficient to meet benefit costs, that fact comes to light almost immediately and steps can easily be taken to bring the two into balance. However, in the case of a pension program which is inadequately funded, the inability of the program to provide the pensions which have been promised will not come to light for a considerable period of years, and by that time any correction of the program so as to prevent a defaulting on pension obligations will be most difficult, if not impossible.

The second feature of pension programs which necessitates separate treatment is that, in general, these plans require the accumulation of large reserves which must be invested and the income from which becomes an important source of future pension payments. These reserves, which are growing rapidly in volume, and which are largely in the hands of insurance companies, banks and other trustees, create a whole series of problems. One of the most significant of these is to assure that the funds are wisely and prudently invested and that the equities of the beneficiaries are protected.

DESCRIPTION OF PENSION PROGRAMS

There are no firm figures as to the total number of pension plans in this country, inasmuch as some plans are quite informal in character.

There are known to be some 17,280 so-called insured plans—i.e., plans insured or administered by insurance companies [1]—and there are estimated to be approximately 4,000 so-called trusteed plans, in which the pension fund is administered and invested by a bank or other trustee. In addition to these there are several thousand profit-sharing plans with retirement features, and probably many thousands of formal and informal pay-as-you-go plans. [2]

Of the 17,280 insured plans at the end of 1954, 11,550 were individual policy pension trusts, 3,410 were deferred group annuity plans, 760 were deposit administration group annuities, and 1,560 were combinations or variations of these types of plans. Of the 3,915,000 employees covered under all "insured" plans, almost two-thirds—2,350,000—were covered under the deferred group annuity plans, and 835,000 were covered under deposit administration plans. In the case of all of these plans, other than deposit administration, annuities on an individual or group basis are purchased from an insurance

---

[1] The Life Insurance Institute of America obtains reports annually from all insurance companies as to volume of group insurance written. These surveys cover pension and retirement plans insured or administered by insurance companies, and provide data on persons covered under such plans, total premiums paid, and reserves. Data for 1954 are reported in the Tally of Life Insurance Statistics, May 1955.

[2] The Internal Revenue Service up to the end of 1954 had "qualified" 28,307 employee pension, profit-sharing, and stock-bonus trusts, as meeting the requirements for tax exemption under sec. 401 of the Internal Revenue Code of 1954, and had issued 1,734 rulings on termination of trusts, leaving some 26,573 such trusts qualified at that time. The Service estimated that at the end of 1955 there were approximately 30,000 "qualified" trusts. A study by the IRS in 1946 found that approximately 70 percent of the qualified trusts were pension plans, and 30 percent were profit-sharing trusts; stock-bonus plans constituted a negligible proportion.

company and the insurance company guarantees the payment of pensions or annuities in question. In the case of deposit administration, amounts estimated to suffice to meet future pension obligations are deposited with an insurance company which holds and invests these funds; however, the insurance company does not guarantee that the funds so deposited will be adequate for meeting future pension costs.

Under the so-called trusteed plans, the employer or other entity establishing the plan, makes contributions into a pension fund. These contributions are of two sorts, those estimated to be required to fund pension obligations currently being earned by employees, and those required to fund the so-called past-service pension obligations. Some 80 to 90 percent of all pension plans of this type use a bank as corporate trustee to hold and invest the funds in accordance with a trust agreement. In most other cases a committee appointed by the employer performs this function. In some cases—a minority—the bank merely serves as custodian of the fund's securities or other holdings and has no discretion as to investments, the employer directing all investments. At the other extreme, the bank may have sole discretion as to investments. There are all variations in between these two poles, such as those in which the bank has investment discretion subject to such direction as the employer may from time to time wish to make, or in which the purchase of certain classes of securities or assets is specifically directed or specifically prohibited.

Under pay-as-you-go plans no pension fund is accumulated. The employer or other entity simply pays pensions out of current income as employees retire. The characteristic of such plans is that the costs are light in the initial years of the program, but then, other things being equal, increase progressively year by year as additional employees retire. Under these programs, employees have no security for future pensions other than the continued prosperity of the concern or entity operating the plan.

It is estimated that, at the end of 1954, approximately 12,500,000 employees were covered under all types of pension plans. About 7 million of these are covered under collectively bargained programs. Of the 12,500,000 covered employees, 3,915,000 were under insured plans, about 1 million were under pay-as-you-go plans, and the remainder, 7,585,000, under funded trusteed plans.

Total reserves of all insured plans at the end of 1954 were $9,800 million; total assets of all trusteed funds at the end of 1954 were probably about $12 billion [3] at book value, and possibly close to $13 billion at market value. Total reserves of all plans are, therefore, about $21.8 billion at book value.

Corporate pension and retirement trusts have been growing rapidly—from $6,356 million at the end of 1951 to $11,250 million at the end of 1954.

[3] The Securities and Exchange Commission, in its study of corporate pension funds, 1954 (release of October 12, 1955), found that these pension-trust funds had total assets at the end of 1954 of $11,250 million. This study covered all corporations exclusive of banks, railroads, and nonprofit organizations. The pension-trust funds of banks, nonprofit organizations, and of jointly managed and union administered plans might bring the total close to $12 billion at book values.

In 1954, total contributions to insured plans were $1,325 million; total contributions to trusteed plans were approximately $1,868 million; and total contributions, i.e., benefits paid, under pay-as-you-go plans, about $100 million.[4] The grand total of contributions to all plans were $3,293 million, of which approximately $2,866 million are estimated to be employer contributions and $427 million employee contributions.

The vast majority of all pension plans are established and administrated by employers and cover the workers of a single corporation or such a corporation and its affiliates. In some employer-administered plans representatives of the employees participate in the administration of the program. Frequently, this is restricted to passing on applications for benefits; generally, it is the employer who really controls and manages the program.

Since 1946 a considerable number of multiemployer jointly managed plans have developed, i.e., plans established under an agreement between a union and a number of employers and jointly managed by trustees representing the union and the employers. Among the principal plans of this type are the United Mine Workers welfare and retirement fund, the pension plans of the International Ladies' Garment Workers Union, the Amalgamated Clothing Workers of America, the International Brotherhood of Electrical Workers, and the recently formed Teamsters Central States, Southeast and Southwest areas pension fund. In addition, there are a small number of plans which are wholly administered by labor unions. These two types of plans together cover possibly 2 million workers, of which the great majority are covered under the jointly managed plans. Total contributions to these plans in 1954 are estimated at about $140 million, of which $120 million were employer contributions and the remainder employee contributions. . . .

SOME OF THE PROBLEMS

Without question the long-range nature of pension plans makes the manner in which these plans are financed of the highest significance. Basically, as already pointed out, there are three methods of financing pension plans.

Pay-as-you-go plans present the greatest element of uncertainty. While such a plan may be adequate in that it can be expected to meet the benefit payments, the foundation of such a plan is only as strong as its sponsor. If he is in an expanding industry whose products can be expected to remain in demand and if he can be expected to remain in business indefinitely, then the employees covered by it need have no fear that their retirement benefits will one day be discontinued. However, only a very unique enterprise can be sure to remain prosperous in perpetuity. In fact, the industrywide pension plan in the anthracite coal industry reduced its scale of benefits simply because of the economic plight of the industry. This illustration is not intended to reflect on the character of pay-as-you-go plans. Under certain circumstances such a plan may be highly desirable. It is important, however, in any formalized pay-as-you-go

---

[4] The pension program of the United Mine Workers welfare and retirement fund, which paid benefits of $70 million in 1954–55, is included here as a pay-as-you-go plan.

pension plan that all those concerned with it are aware of its limitations. If they desire, they can then make their own arrangements to supplement the plan. Disclosure of the financial experience of such plans would keep interested parties informed.

The great distinction between pay-as-you-go plans and funded plans, whether trusteed or insured, is that in the latter funds in the nature of deferred wages are currently set aside to meet future pension obligations to employees who qualify for benefits under the terms of the plan. If the pay-as-you-go plan is terminated, there is no such reserve.

Self-insured funded plans, usually trusteed, present a far stronger element of certainty of payment of benefits. The more fully funded they are, the more certain the benefits. In these plans the manner and extent of funding are the responsibility of their sponsors, even where banks are used as trustees. Sometimes such plans at the outset spend more than is warranted by the moneys available in an effort to secure more liberal benefits. With experience, careful administration, and competent actuarial advice, the plan's finances can be adjusted to the point where it will become adequately funded. The long-range nature of pension plans lends itself to such adjustment. Here again, the plan is as good as its sponsors. Whether or not a plan should be fully funded, or whether a plan must be fully funded in order to be adequately funded, is beyond the scope of this subcommittee. The subcommittee is convinced, however, that the manner of funding presents many problems and that proper funding is essential for the safeguarding of the employees covered by the plan. Employees get little security out of a pension plan that is discontinued. The manner of funding is so important that all interested parties should be kept fully informed as to the plan's experience, especially with respect to matters revealing the plan's ability to meet its commitments. This is as true in insured plans as in trusteed plans, particularly as the moneys used to fund the plan are in the nature of employee compensation.

Investment of the assets of trusteed plans presents other problems. Usually this is performed by corporate trustees and is their primary function. Sometimes they have full discretion in the selection of investments; sometimes by the trust agreement their discretion is limited. The investment earnings of the assets of a pension plan are most important. The higher the earnings, the lower the cost of the plan. The problem here is one of achieving the highest yield without sacrificing safety.

The corporate trustee's functions do not include those of determining the liabilities of the funds. It should be clearly understood that banks or other corporate trustees in selling the features of the trusteed type of plan, such as higher income return on investment, do not have the responsibility for the actuarial soundness of the plan. These functions remain with the sponsor or sponsors of the plan and are usually performed by an actuary retained for this purpose.

In insured pension plans generally the insurance carrier assumes the responsibility for the determination of the liability of the sponsor for the investment and safety of the funds. In other words, the insurance company guarantees the payment of certain benefits dependent upon the premium paid. It follows that under these circumstances the assumptions used by insurance companies would naturally be more conservative than would be typical of trusteed plans. The continuity of premium payments of course is a necessary prerequisite to an adequate funding of the insurance plan. Moreover, as the insurance company assumes the responsibility for evaluating the plan's liability, it reserves the right to make periodic reevaluations with a view to adjustment of premium.

In deposit administration plans, however, the problems are similar to those found in self-insured or trusteed plans.

PENSION PLANS IN SEVERAL INDUSTRIES

From Welfare and Pension Plans Investigation, final report of the Senate Committee on Labor and Public Welfare, 84th Cong., 2d Sess., 1956, pp. 89–90, 98–101, 124–126, 167–170, 175–177, 188–190

THE STEEL INDUSTRY

The pension benefits of most plans in the basic steel industry amount to 1 percent of the average monthly wage in the 120 months preceding retirement, multiplied by the number of years' service, less a fixed allowance of $85 for social security benefits. This pension is payable at age 65 to employees with at least 15 years' continuous service. The minimum company-provided pension for those over 65 cannot be less than $2 multiplied by the number of years' service up to a maximum of 30 years less $5. In other words, employees having 30 years' service or more receive a minimum of $55 a month from the employer with this amount being reduced by $2 per month for each year by which service is less than 30 years, down to a minimum of $25 per month for employees having only 15 years of service.

As originally negotiated in 1949, the plan provided a minimum pension of $100 a month including social security for an employee with 25 years of service or more. This could mean, for example, that $35 of the pension came from social security and the remaining $65 from the employer. When the social security benefits were increased, the effect was to progressively reduce the pensions payable by employers. Accordingly, a fixed allowance of $85 for social security benefits was established in subsequent negotiations, and was to remain constant irrespective of any subsequent modification in social security levels.

The typical pension plan also provides benefits for employees under 65 who are retired for disability causes and cannot engage in any gainful occupation. The minimum benefit is $75 a month until age 65 after which time the regular benefit applies.

The main variation from this typical pension benefit for normal retirement is an arrangement common to a number of plans by which the pension is determined solely on the number of years' service rather than through the 1 percent formula method.

Some plans provide simply for a flat benefit amount, while in others the benefits are graduated on the basis of years of service without reference to earnings. Generally, there are no disability benefit provisions in the smaller company plans, particularly those outside the basic steel industry.

The cost of these pension plans is borne entirely by the employers. Some plans are insured; some use banks as trustees and investment agencies; others are administered through separate corporate trusts established by the employers, and still others are on a pay-as-you-go basis.

Some agreements require the employer to deposit or earmark sufficient funds to meet pension costs of those employees retiring during the term of the contract—terminal funding, so-called. Some require the employer to fund in relation to the actuarial requirements of the program. In others the method of funding and providing pension benefits is left entirely to the employer. There are some pension plans, therefore, which are completely unfunded, with retirement benefits being provided by the employers from their current earnings on a pay-as-you-go basis.

The administration of all pension plans in steel is performed unilaterally by the employers; the union plays no part in this function. In each such plan, however, the agreement provides for a joint employer-employee committee to receive annual reports from the employing company and to review the operation of the program insofar as it affects individuals represented by the union.

At the present, none of the pension plans have any vesting provisions. The employees have no equity in the trust funds until such time as they become eligible for retirement. Even at that time, their actual retirement benefit is contingent upon the terms of the agreement then in effect between the employer and the union.

THE AUTOMOBILE INDUSTRY

Collectively bargained pension plans for hourly paid workers in the automobile industry were in many instances preceded by retirement programs for salaried employees and in some cases for hourly paid employees. Beginning in 1949, the UAW began to press for the incorporation of pension benefits in its collective bargaining agreements. In 1950, the union incorporated pension benefits in its contracts with the Big Three. It was decided that these pension plans should be on a fully funded basis; the union conducted a 105-day strike against Chrysler Corp. to make the company agree to fund its pension program.

At the present time, the union has bargained for some 260 pension plans covering over 1,100,000 workers. Statistics and estimates have not been compiled as to the aggregate annual amount of employer contributions required to finance pensions or current assets of pension plans, but it is clear that large sums of money are involved. The largest fund, General Motors, has assets exceeding $350 million, and the fund is currently increasing at the rate of $70 million a year.

About 80 percent of the UAW membership is covered by pension benefits, though less than 20 percent of the plants organized by the UAW have pension plans. Negotiations are resulting in the establishment by smaller concerns, of their own pension plans, and in the establishment of multiemployer plans, the largest being the aforementioned plan of the Automotive Tool and Die Manufacturers Association in Detroit. It involves 82 companies and covers some 8,500 workers. Three plans are financed by employers in diverse industries, namely, a plan in Toledo covering 2,000 workers in 27 plants; a plan in Detroit covering 600 workers in 6 plants; and a plan at Long Island covering an unspecified number of workers in 5 plants.

A. CHARACTERISTICS OF PRESENT PENSION PLANS

The majority of the pension plans for hourly paid employees are noncontributory; the employer pays all costs.

Almost all of the plans provide benefits without regard to the level of earnings of the employee, the monthly benefit being a specified amount times the number of years of service. Most of the plans provide for voluntary retirement at the normal retirement age of 65 and compulsory retirement at 68.

Virtually all of the plans negotiated by the union provide benefits for employees who become permanently and totally disabled before reaching retirement age. Eligibility for these benefits is conditional upon the employees having reached a specified age or having had a minimum number of years of service, or both.

Until 1955, very few of the plans provided for vesting. In the 1955 negotiations with the Big Three, the union won a measure of vesting in the plans of these companies and is striving for similar provisions in plans of smaller companies.

Most of the plans are "funded" plans. The majority, especially the larger plans, provide that the company pay into a fund the full current cost of benefits earned and, in addition, meet the initial past service liability over a period not exceeding a stated number of years. A somewhat lesser number provide that the company contribute into a fund a certain number of cents per employee-hour worked, this amount having been determined sufficient on the basis of an initial actuarial study to meet the cost of the specified benefits. The employer's obligations toward the program are fulfilled by the contributions made. A small minority of trusteed plans are terminal funded. A few— about 10 percent—of the total number of plans negotiated by the union are of the insured type.

Since the Big Three companies employ so high a proportion of all workers in the industry, and since their plans tend to set a pattern for the other companies, the pension plans of these companies will be described in more detail.

The plans of these companies provide a monthly pension on retirement at age 65 of $2.25 times years of service. (Hence, an employee with, say, 30 years of service would receive a pension of $67.50 a month, exclusive of social security benefits.) Pensions are payable only to employees who have had at least 10 years of service. Retirement between 60 and 65 is permitted but at actuarially reduced rates. Retirement at age 68 is compulsory.

Monthly benefits are payable for total and permanent disability, providing the employee is at least 50 and has had not less than 15 years of service with the company, in an amount equal to $4.50 times years of service. When the disabled employee reaches 65, and is eligible for old-age benefits under social security, his disability benefits are reduced to the normal retirement payments. The contracts of the Big Three contain a provision that if permanent and total disability should be provided under the Federal systems, the disability benefits payable by the company would be reduced by the amount of the disability benefit which the worker would receive from the Federal Government.

Vesting is provided for an employee who leaves the company's service after age 40 with at least 10 years of service. He becomes eligible for a deferred pension, payable at age 65, equal to $2.25 a month times his years of service after attainment of age 30.

The Big Three contracts provide that the company establish a pension fund and contribute annually to this fund an amount sufficient to fund both the pension rights earned during that year and the past service obligation over a 30-year period. The amount is determined by a qualified actuary. The company furnishes the union each year with a statement certified by the actuary as to the contribution determined to be necessary to meet the actuarial liability.

Each of the companies has entered into an agreement with a bank (in the case of General Motors it is seven banks) to hold and invest the pension fund and to pay pension benefits to persons authorized to receive them.

The employee's record of service is generally kept at the plants. At each plant there is a pension committee of an equal number of company and union representatives which reviews applications and decides whether the employee is eligible, and the amount of his disability or pension benefit. In each company there is also a central board, again composed of equal numbers of company and union representatives, which hears and settles cases which cannot be settled at the plant level.

Apart from its role of authorizing pensions, the union does not participate in the administration. It has no voice in the selection of the bank trustee, the terms of the trust agreement, or the investment of the pension fund. One of its past demands has been for some voice in investments. The Chrysler Corp. furnishes the union with a copy of the annual report of the bank trustee listing the investments of the fund, and the actuary's annual valuation report. General Motors does not give the union the actuary's valuation report but does provide a certification as to the contribution required to meet the actuarial liability, plus information as to the number of and amounts paid to pensioners and the number and age distribution of employees and past service credits. General Motors does not disclose the investments of the pension fund, but the total book value of the fund is a matter of public record, being set forth in the company's annual report to its stockholders. Ford provides the bipartite board of administration with annual information on the assets of the pension fund together with data as to the age, sex, and service record of employees covered by the plan, the number of pensioners, and amount of retirement benefits. The union is provided directly with an actuary's certification that the company's funding obligations have been met.

THE ELECTRICAL INDUSTRY

Some companies, such as General Electric, had voluntarily established pension programs prior to 1950. However, beginning in that year, the IUE and the electrical manufacturers established noncontributory pension programs through collective bargaining. These programs are negotiated on a benefits basis, the employer agreeing to provide specified retirement benefits and handling the entire administration of the program. The pension is usually computed at a fixed sum multiplied by years of service. Two such plans, for example, provide a monthly pension of $1.50 times the number of years' credited service not to exceed 35, a maximum of $52.50 a month, in other words. These pension benefits are paid regardless of any social security benefits to which the employee may be entitled.

With very few exceptions IUE plans are unilaterally administered by the employers. Each program provides for a joint labor-management committee, however, which reviews the operation of the program insofar as it affects IUE members. This committee has no function in the administration nor any voice in such matters as investment of the pension trust, nor does it as a general rule receive any information concerning such matters.

The IUE is involved in a few pension plans which are jointly administered by employer-employee representatives. One such plan, for example, covers 900 workers employed by a single New York manufacturer.

There are some 27 different plans established in negotiations between the IUE and electrical manufacturers which provide profit-sharing, severance pay, or combinations of both these features. Under such plans the employer sets aside a percentage of his profits each year, distributes a portion to the employees and deposits the remainder in a trust fund for the payment of severance and/or pension benefits. Most of these plans have vesting provisions. They are administered by the employers although joint labor-management committees review their operation and receive reports from the employers on such matters as investments and financial operations.

The IBEW established its own pension plan in 1928 which was financed by monthly assessments against participating members. Originally, each participant paid 37 cents a month into the pension fund which amount was increased from time to time to the present $1.60 a month. The plan originally provided for a monthly pension of $40 to participants with 20 years' continuous standing in the union and who were 65 years old. The pension was increased to $50 in 1946. This fund is administered and controlled by the IBEW itself and is known as the pension benefit fund.

It is important to note that the IBEW has two classes of members, designated as "class A" and "class BA." Only the class A members participate in the pension benefit fund plan through monthly assessment of $1.60. There are approximately 300,000 such members. The remaining 300,000 class BA members pay a monthly per capita tax of 70 cents to the international and do not participate in the pension plan.

On October 1, 1946, the IBEW and the National Electrical Contractors Association (NECA) entered into an employees' benefit agreement creating a retirement program for IBEW class A members to which the contractors would contribute. The plan commenced operation on May 5, 1947, following approval by Internal Revenue. The agreement created a national employees' benefit board consisting of 15 members, 7 from the IBEW, 7 from NECA, and

1 public member. It provided that each electrical contractor employing IBEW members would pay 1 percent of gross payroll to a local board. (Local boards, also created in the agreement, were to consist of 7 members, 3 from IBEW locals, 3 from NECA, and 1 public member, and were to be established in every locality in which a NECA chapter exists or where a collective bargaining agreement existed between NECA and IBEW locals.) The local board was to remit the 1 percent payroll assessments to the national board each month. The national board, in turn, was to pay a lump sum from these assessments to a board of trustees which amount was to match the contributions of all participating IBEW class A members to the pension benefit fund. These payments were to be made to the trustees on a quarterly basis and deposited to the pension benefit fund.

When this plan first commenced operation on May 5, 1947, both the IBEW class A member contributions and the matching employer contributions were deposited to the union's pension benefit fund. In the same year, the Labor Management Relations Act became law and prohibited commingling of employer and union funds. Accordingly, a separate fund was created by agreement and is designated as the "pension benefit trust fund." This fund was to be jointly administered by 1 IBEW and 1 NECA trustee and was henceforth to receive that portion of the employer contributions which matched those of IBEW class A members.

It should be noted that the 1 percent gross payroll contributions always exceed the amounts which are remitted quarterly to the pension benefit trust fund to match the IBEW member contributions. The surplus, according to a NECA official, is also turned over to the trustees of this same fund for investment purposes.

NECA has a membership of some 3,300 employer-contractors who contribute to the IBEW plan. There are some 7,800 non-NECA contractors who also contribute to the plan, making a total of about 11,000 employer-contributors.

Of the 300,000 IBEW class A members covered by the plan, only 123,000 are actually employed by electrical contractors who contribute to it. The remaining 177,000 are engaged in utilities, railroads, radio and television, Government work, and manufacturing. Thus, the contractors, in matching the $1.60 per month contributions of 300,000 class A IBEW members, are actually funding pension benefits for 177,000 additional participants who have no claim on them as employers.

The plan presently provides a monthly pension of $30 for a member 65 years of age and 20 years' union standing; $40 a month for 25 years' standing, and $50 a month with 30 years' standing.

At the present time, there are some 5,589 IBEW pensioners. Their pensions are all being paid from the pension benefit trust fund (to which matching employer contributions are deposited) while the moneys in the IBEW pension benefit fund (into which the $1.60 per month assessments from 300,000 class A members are deposited) are being allowed to accumulate and earn interest through investment. The trustees anticipate that future pension obligations will increase to the point that both funds will be needed to meet the demand.

Full disclosure is made of the operation of this plan to both the beneficiaries and employer-contributors through periodic reports and pamphlets. Annual audits are conducted, the results of which are incorporated in these reports.

Class BA members of the IBEW who do not participate in this plan are covered in some instances under separate pension agreements negotiated by their IBEW locals or under employer pension plans; however, unless they are so covered, or unless they elect to transfer to class A membership after a prescribed period and pay the required monthly assessments, such members receive no pension benefits.

THE BITUMINOUS COAL INDUSTRY

President John L. Lewis of the UMW had long been convinced of the need for a welfare and pension program for miners. He first put forward a demand for a welfare fund in the 1945 wage negotiations. The operators refused. Mr. Lewis did not press it that year, but in the following year it was the principal demand of the union. All of the union's demands were refused by the operators; no settlement was reached and coal production ceased. After a strike, from April 1 to May 22, 1946, the Government seized the mines under the War Labor Disputes (Smith-Connally) Act. On May 29, Secretary of the Interior Krug and the union entered into what became known as the Krug-Lewis agreement. This agreement, among other matters, provided for a welfare and retirement fund to be financed by 5 cents a ton contribution on coal produced for use or sale.

The agreement also provided for a comprehensive survey to be made by the Government of hospital, medical, sanitary and housing conditions in coal-mining areas to determine the improvements necessary to bring these up to "recognized American standards." Rear Adm. Joel T. Boone of the United States Navy was asked by the Department of the Interior to direct this survey. The report of the survey, A Medical Survey of the Bituminous Coal Industry, released in March 1947, made it plain that in many respects the existing medical facilities and services for coal miners were grossly inadequate.

In October 1946 Mr. Lewis charged that the Government was making certain unilateral interpretations of the agreement which in his view breached the contract. Unable to reach a settlement with the Government, the union terminated the agreement on November 20, and coal mining ceased. Secretary Krug held that the United Mine Workers had no right to terminate the agreement and asked for an injunction against the union under the Smith-Connally Act, which forbade strikes against the Government. Despite a restraining order the strike continued, and on December 3 United States District Judge T. Alan Goldsborough found the United Mine Workers guilty of contempt of court and fined the union $3.5 million and Mr. Lewis $10,000. The miners returned to work. Lewis appealed the case to the Supreme Court, which upheld the Goldsborough decision, fixed the [fine] at $10,000 on Lewis but reduced the fine on the union to $700,000.

During this period the fund has been inoperative largely because the Government, as administrator of the coal mines, and the union could not agree upon a neutral trustee. The Centralia mine explosion on March 25, 1947, in which 111 miners lost their lives, stimulated agreement on a neutral trustee, and Thomas E. Murray was so named. On April 18 the trustees—Capt. N. H. Collisson, the Administrator of the mines for the Government, John L. Lewis for the union, and the neutral trustee—met and as their first act authorized payment of death benefits of $1,000 to the survivors of the miners who had died in the Centralia disaster.

On June 30, 1947 the Smith-Connally Act expired and the mines were returned to the operators. A few days later they entered into an agreement with the union under which they agreed to the welfare fund and to increasing the royalty payments to 10 cents a ton. At that time, Ezra Van Horn became trustee for the operators, replacing the Government Administrator, Captain Collisson.

Up to this time, all benefit expenditures from the fund had been limited to payments of death benefits and to distress benefits, i.e., mainly provision of relief in disaster cases. Payment of pensions had not been initiated because the trustees were unable to agree on the amount of pensions or the nature of a pension program—one of the issues being whether the pension plan should be funded or operated on a pay-as-you-go basis. On January 17, 1948, Mr. Murray resigned as the neutral trustee. Mr. Lewis took the position that the refusal of the operators' trustee to agree to any proposals to activate the pension program amounted to refusal of the coal operators to honor their agreement and on March 15, 1948, the miners again stopped work. Subsequently, Mr. Van Horn filed several suits to prevent operation of the fund.

Failure of mediation efforts to end the work stoppage led President Truman to invoke the Taft-Hartley Act. A factfinding board charged that Lewis' circular letter of March 12 to the membership informing them that the welfare fund was unable to function had "induced the miners to stop work," and on April 13 President Truman ordered the Attorney General to seek an injunction against Mr. Lewis and the UMW to restrain them from continuing the strike. Judge Goldsborough issued a restraining order and scheduled a hearing, directing Mr. Lewis and the UMW to show why they should not be held in contempt because of the miners' refusal to return to work.

A few days later, on April 10, the stalemate over the naming of a third trustee for the fund was ended when Lewis and Van Horn agreed on Senator Styles Bridges of New Hampshire. On the day of the contempt hearing, April 12, the trustees met and voted to start pension payments. Lewis informed all local unions of the action and the agreement was honored. Judge Goldsborough held that the miners' return to work at this time did not constitute satisfactory compliance with his order. He proceeded with the contempt case and on April 20 found the union and Mr. Lewis guilty of civil and criminal contempt of court. The union was then fined $1.4 million and Mr. Lewis $20,000.

The trustees had agreed on pensions of $100 a month to men who were at least 62 years old, who had 20 years' service in the industry, and who had retired after May 29, 1946, the date of the Krug-Lewis agreement. The actual payment of pensions was held up because of various suits which had been filed by Mr. Van Horn. With the welfare program still in abeyance the union moved into the 1948 contract negotiations. Shortly after a settlement had been reached, Judge Goldsborough rejected Mr. Van Horn's third suit which had challenged the plan. Holding the Bridges-Lewis pension plan "a business-like" proposal, Judge Goldsborough's decision said—

There seems to be nothing that shocks the mind at the idea that the members of the United Mine Workers who have worked for 20 years under the ground and are 62 years old should get $100 a month pension. Of course, if the fund won't stand it, they will have to change it, but it is meager. It is just enough to keep them from being objects of charity in their old age; it is just enough to give them a little dignity. The court does not think that there is any justification in law or in sound reason for this complaint.

With the reaching of the 1948 wage settlement the operators removed the last legal roadblock to the operation of the welfare fund by instructing Mr. Van Horn to drop his remaining legal suit. The agreement provided for increasing the fund royalty payments to 20 cents per ton. In September 1948 the fund issued its first pension check.

At about the same time the medical program began operation. In July 1947, Dr. R. R. Sayers, formerly head of the Bureau of Mines, and previously with the United States Public Health Service, had been appointed chairman of the newly created medical advisory board for the fund. The trustees asked the board to study the types and standards of medical and hospital service to be furnished to miners in their communities, to suggest policies for physical rehabilitation, and to develop plans for carrying out the recommendations in Admiral Boone's medical survey of the industry. Dr. Sayers appointed a number of staff people and began developing plans for a medical program.

The first goal of the medical program was the rehabilitation of some of the worst cases of disabled miners, including many paraplegics. These cases were sought out and sent to various rehabilitation centers.

In April 1948, Miss Josephine Roche, a former coal operator and at one time Assistant Secretary of the Treasury, was appointed director of the fund. In September 1948, Dr. Warren F. Draper, a former Deputy Surgeon General of the United States Public Health Service, was appointed executive medical officer of the medical, health and hospital service. Shortly thereafter the medical program became operational; it consisted of (1) hospital care and physician's service in the hospital, office or home for miners who had been disabled for 6 months or more and for their families; (2) hospital and inhospital medical care for working miners and their dependents; and (3) a program of public health and preventive medicine.

It was decided that the fund should itself administer the medical benefits. Ten area medical offices, each under the direction of a doctor, were established. The facilities and physicians available in the coal-fields were employed but it was decided to make extensive use of medical centers for difficult cases.

Service for the miners was purchased from physicians and hospitals on a fee-for-service, free-choice basis. The area medical officers worked out the necessary arrangements with doctors and hospitals in their areas on the basis of reasonable charges for authorized services rendered to miners and their families.

The trustees announced on April 8, 1949 that thereafter pensions would be made available at age 60 instead of 62. However, other difficulties were ahead. The 1948 agreement expired on June 30, 1949, with the union and operators unable to reach an agreement. The union authorized the miners to work only 3 days a week. As a consequence, many of the operators stopped their royalty payments, and in September 1949 the trustees were forced to order a temporary suspension of fund benefits.

The miners began to stop work in protest against nonpayment of royalties and a series of off-again-on-again strikes and work interruptions ensued. Finally in March 1950 the operators and union reached an agreement which became the National Bituminous Coal Wage Agreement of 1950. In addition to a wage increase this provided for an increase of 10 cents a ton in royalties (bringing them to 30 cents a ton), and that the welfare fund would have as its trustees Mr. Lewis as chairman, Miss Josephine Roche, the fund director, as neutral trustee, and Charles Owen of New York as operator trustee. The operators agreed to pay up the royalties which were then in default.

In the fall of 1950 the operators created the Bituminous Coal Operators Association with authority to represent them in dealings with the union. Leaders in this move were the captive mines' interests who were desirous of continuous and stable production in the industry.

With the end of the dispute, the welfare fund reorganized and on June 1 pension payments were resumed. Hospitalization and medical services became available on July 1, but were limited thereafter to hospital care and physicians' services in the hospital for both disabled and working miners. (The provision of physicians' service in the office and home to disabled miners and their families had proved very expensive, subject to abuse, and was abandoned.) On October 12 the trustees announced a new program of maintenance benefits for disabled miners and dependents, and a new program of maintenance benefits for widows and dependent children, including their eligibility for medical and hospitalization services.

Effective October 1, 1952, the bituminous coal wage agreement of 1950 was amended to provide an increase in the royalty to 40 cents per ton. . . .

A. PENSIONS

The fund pays pensions of $100 a month to retired miners. The present major eligibility provisions are that the applicant must (1) be 60 years of age or over at the time of filing his application; (2) have completed 20 years of service in a classified job, i.e., a job subject to the collective bargaining agreement in the coal industry, during the 30 years immediately preceding his date of application; (3) have retired after May 29, 1946, the date the first fund was established, following regular employment in a classified job in the mine of an operator signatory to the agreement, and (4) have been regularly employed in a classified job in the coal industry immediately prior to the date the first fund was established. As of June 30, 1955, these pension payments were being received by 59,482 retired miners. Pensioners and their dependents are also eligible for hospital and medical care benefits.

An applicant may file for a pension either through his local union or directly at the Washington office of the fund. The information required of an applicant is extensive. The record of employment in the mines prior to 1937 [1] must be validated by certificates of miners who worked with the applicant during the time shown or by affidavits of employers.

The application blank contains a space for certification by officials of the local union that the applicant is a member of the local and also a space for certification by an authorized representative of the UMW district that the applicant is a member in good standing of the union. However, applications may be filed directly with the fund by miners not members of the union, and fund personnel state that applications are acted upon without reference to current union status.

In the past, various cases have come before the National Labor Relations Board against the United Mine Workers, charging that the welfare and retirement plan was being administered solely for the benefit of UMW members in good standing, in violation of sections 8 (b) (1) and 8 (b) (2) of the Labor-Management Relations Act of 1947. Substantially all of these charges have been disposed of at the NLRB regional office level, either by dismissal, withdrawal, or settlement. Only one resulted in an unfair labor practice complaint proceedings. This case was thereafter closed upon voluntary compliance by the union. In this case, it was agreed that the contract executed March 5, 1950, provided for the consideration of applications for fund benefits regardless of whether or not the applicant was a union member.

Applications for pensions and for all other benefits are processed at the Washington office. If necessary, extensive investigations, including field visits, are made to determine whether or not the applicant meets the eligibility conditions set up by the board of trustees.

Applications which present close questions of eligibility, or for which required evidence has been unobtainable through correspondence, are taken up with the assistant to the director by the supervisor of the examining unit for joint review. If further consideration of the applicant's eligibility status is required, the assistant to the director then presents the application and entire file to a special review committee. The assistant to the director and an assistant comptroller serve on each of these special review committees, and one or more supervisors and senior examiners from the examining units, other than those previously examining the application, are assigned for service on these committees. If the special review committee, after full review of the application, reaches a unanimous decision as to the eligibility status of the applicant, action on it is taken accordingly.

During the fiscal year ending June 30, 1955, 7,061 applications for pensions

[1] Post-1947 data available from Bureau of Old-Age and Survivors Insurance.

were received. In the same year there were 6,778 authorizations of pensions and 1,182 denials. Denials amounted to 16.7 percent of the number of applications received.[2] The chief reasons for denial of pensions in this fiscal year were (1) the applicant furnished no proof of 20 years of classified service out of the last 30 years (406 cases); (2) there was no proof of classified employment immediately prior to May 1946 (384 cases); (3) the requested evidence was not submitted; (4) the applicant furnished no proof of age; and (5) the applicant was presently employed in the coal industry.

The subcommittee staff members reviewed illustrative cases of pension applications which had been approved or denied and a small random sample of cases approved for pensions. They were impressed with the businesslike way in which these applications were handled and by the care taken to see that applications were acted upon in accordance with fund eligibility requirements.

The subcommittee either directly or through referral from Senators had received over the past year some some dozen letters from miners who were aggrieved because their applications for pensions had been denied. These cases were reviewed in detail with fund personnel. In every instance the denial of a pension was found to be in accordance with the eligibility requirements.

The eligibility conditions for pensions have been changed a number of times. An important change was made in 1953. Prior to this time, the essential eligibility conditions were that (1) the miner must be 60 years of age or older; (2) have retired after May 29, 1946; (3) have been employed in the industry in a classified job for a year preceding retirement; and (4) have had 20 years of service in classified jobs in the industry. In 1953 these conditions were changed to require that the 20 years of service must have been within the 30 years preceding retirement, and that the applicant must have been regularly employed in a classified job immediately prior to May 29, 1946.

These changes have caused a considerable number of persons to be denied pensions who would otherwise have been eligible under the former requirements. (As indicated above approximately a third of all denials in the 1955 fiscal year were on the ground that the applicant had not been employed in the industry immediately prior to inception of the fund.) The main reasons for these changes were that the fund was finding that many individuals who had retired or had left the industry prior to May 29, 1946, were obtaining temporary employment as miners only to qualify for pensions, and the mounting costs of the pension program required some tightening up of eligibility conditions.[3]

[2] Denials and applications do not add up to number of applications received since applications are not necessarily acted upon in the fiscal year in which they are received.

[3] The letters received by the subcommittee by some miners indicate a feeling on their part that there is some inequity involved in a situation in which a man may have worked the greater part of his life in the mines and yet be denied a pension because he had not been employed in the industry immediately prior to inception of the program or failed by a few months to have accumulated 20 years of service.

Once a pension has been authorized, the pensioner continues to receive it each month until death, or until he resumes employment in the coal industry; its continuance is not affected by subsequent changes in eligibility conditions, and fund personnel state it is in no way contingent upon the pensioner retaining his membership in the United Mine Workers. However, pensioners as a group have no equity in the fund and their pensions could be reduced or eliminated if the financial condition of the fund necessitated.[4]

The pension program is on a pay-as-you-go basis; there is no funding of benefits. The trustees representing the coal operators have on a number of occasions in the past voiced the opinion that the benefits should be funded, but Lewis and Miss Roche have thought otherwise.

Expenditures for pension benefits have increased steadily in the past 5 fiscal years, . . . going from $42,473,000 in 1951 to $69,896,155 in 1955. Inasmuch as the program is relatively young, it may be expected that pension costs will continue to increase for a number of years before leveling off.[5]

The total administrative costs allocable to the pension program are calculated by the subcommittee staff to be approximately 1.7 percent of total pension benefits paid. . . .

It was not possible for the staff to interview the coal operator's fund trustee, Mr. Charles A. Owen. However, his views were briefly ascertained by telephone. He said that there was no question as to the integrity and honesty of the fund. He thought the program was very well run. He said that in recent years all trustee resolutions have been unanimous and that his views on the program would echo those of Mr. Lewis and Miss Roche.

Mr. Owen was invited to testify at the hearings but was unable to do so. He did, however, send a letter which appears in the record of the hearings, and which affirms the above expressed views. He wrote, in part:

There is absolutely no question in my mind as to the integrity of the fund's administration, or the ability, honesty, and devotion of the principal administrative officers and employees of the organization. . . .

The producers have been kept currently informed of the fund's operations, with the result today that most of our more responsible people not only accept the fund but express themselves as satisfied with its performance. The trust's achievement of orderly retirement of over 60,000 miners is a noteworthy one and the exceptional hospital and medical care

---

[4] The UMW welfare and retirement fund for the anthracite coal industry, which is set up on the same basis as the bituminous fund, reduced all pensions in 1954 from $100 to $50 a month. The shrinking income of the fund, due to the declining demand for anthracite, was unable to finance the payment of pensions at the former level.

[5] It should be made clear that the fund is, in effect, a unit. There is no real separation of fund income or assets for pensions and for other benefits. The requirement in section 302 (c) of the Labor Management Relations Act, 1947, that moneys intended for payment of pensions shall be paid to a separate trust is met through the fund placing in a separate account from time to time amounts out of which pensions will be paid. Amounts withdrawn from this account may be used for payment of pensions and no other purposes.

afforded the miners and their dependents is commented on favorably both within and outside the coal industry.

Mr. Harry M. Moses, president of the Bituminous Coal Operators Association, which represents 65 percent of the tonnage of the organized part of the industry, told the staff that in his opinion the fund has been managed with absolute honesty and great competence. He did not see how the program could have been better managed. He has high regard for those who administer the program. He thought the fund is meticulous in granting or withholding pensions in accordance with the eligibility conditions. He said that in the early days of the fund, it had been less meticulous in this regard, and sometimes shaded requirements a bit in order to make pensions available to people who did not meet the eligibility conditions 100 percent. However, procedures have been tightened up, and there can be no present complaint in this regard.

The only complaints of the industry with the program are its costs. He thought that the operators felt that it would be better if the miners had some equity in the fund and the pension program was funded in some way; however, this might be very costly.

Mr. Moses gave a very brief statement at the hearings. Among other things he stated:

Following acceptance of the principle of the fund, the industry has taken considerable interest in making it work. From time to time, through the industry trustee, Mr. Owen, the industry has made and will continue to make suggestions for its improvement. We hope some day to establish confidence in this area so that some of these may be accepted and all receive consideration.

Since all must have the greatest respect for the low administration cost of the fund, and the meticulous honesty and integrity of the present trustees, most of the industry's suggestions have dealt with long-range programs to insure a balance between present and future costs limited by the economics of a highly competitive industry.

Mr. Joseph E. Moody, president of the Southern Coal Producers Association, which represents about 25 percent of the tonnage of the industry, when interviewed by the staff said that his association was not in favor of the fund. He felt that while the industry should provide complete care and compensation for miners injured in work accidents, there was no legitimate reason why it should be called upon to provide pensions for miners, or general medical care for miners and their families.

He felt that the union was using the welfare fund to discipline union members and to maintain its membership. He said that the applications for hospitalization benefits and pensions must contain a certification that the applicant is a paid-up union member. He thought this was tantamount to requiring union membership as a condition of eligibility and is illegal.

He thought that the 40 cent royalty was a burden too great for the industry to bear, that it had helped to raise the price of coal, and had lost markets for the industry.

ABUSES IN THE ADMINISTRATION OF PENSION PROGRAMS

From Welfare and Pension Plans Investigation, final report of the Senate Committee on Labor and Public Welfare, 84th Cong., 2d Sess., 1956, pp. 24–25

The contributions for benefits in jointly administered single or multiemployer plans set up in conformance with the provisions of the Labor Management Relations Act, 1947, flow into a trust fund from which either premiums for insurance benefits are paid or the benefits are provided through self-insurance. Many abuses and problems have been found in this type of plan. A great deal of this subcommittee's and other Federal and State governmental committees' attention has been given to this type of plan, which covers less than 10 percent of employees receiving group benefits under all types of plans.

Reported scandals in these jointly administered plans first focused attention on the lack of control surrounding the employee welfare program administration. Frequently, a characteristic weakness of this type of plan, particularly in the multiemployer plan, is diffusion of responsibility. Employers typically agree to contribute on a cents-per-hour or percentage-of-payroll basis and then too often take the position that their responsibility is ended, which permits unscrupulous trustees and others to control the fund.

This type of plan in conformity with requirement of the Labor Management Relations Act, 1947, must have an equal number of employer and employee trustees. Theoretically, this should give a balance of control between management and labor. It is probably, in part, because of this joint representation that wrongdoing has been brought to light in many cases, since in the unilateral plan the administrator himself is the only source of complaint.

Some excellently operated jointly managed multiemployer plans have been reviewed by the subcommittee. Where there is conscientious, reasonable, and intelligent application to the administration of such plans, both by employer and employee representatives, the operation has been found to be exemplary.

1. Malfeasance and nonfeasance

Many of the abuses in welfare funds have at their source the failure of trustees to be true to their trust. Union trustees have often used their trusteeships to serve personal gain. Employer trustees have sometimes connived with union trustees in such instances and at other times have closed their eyes. It was frequently found that employer trustees of joint funds completely abdicated their responsibilities. The subcommittee found instances of plans in which there had not been a meeting of the trustees for several years. In some instances, employer representatives took no interest whatever in the operation of the fund. In others, employer representatives designedly gave full control to the union in the hope that the union would eventually be discredited. On the other hand, employer representatives in some cases were subjected to coercion.

The LWIU welfare fund case presents a good example of nonfeasance on the part of the trustees. Though the trustees in that case did not engage in all of the practices criticized in the paragraph above, they at least were remiss in certain of their responsibilities to the detriment of the beneficiaries of the fund. They appointed a broker as their agent to handle insurance premiums without making arrangements to review his activities; the broker subsequently embezzled some $900,000 of these premiums, part of which was kicked back to an official of the Laundry Workers International Union. They permitted moneys secured through a discount in premium to be paid to welfare deputies appointed by the union without requiring any accounting for the expenditures by these deputies. Though they had certified public accountants to audit the fund, they did not see that a reconciliation was made with the insurance company. This case is discussed at length in the subcommittee's July 20, 1955, interim report.

2. Employer failure to make contributions

Another problem which has arisen in the multiemployer jointly managed type of plan is the failure of some employers to make their agreed-upon contributions. The United Mine Workers report that they generally have about 30 suits pending to collect delinquent payments and that as of August 1954, they were suing some 15 delinquent coal operators to collect over $300,000 due in royalty payments. In a Philadelphia fund reviewed by the staff, 75 percent of 140 employers were more than 2 months delinquent in their contributions.

3. Favored treatment to certain employers

An offspring of the delinquent-payment problem is favored treatment of contributing employers. The examination of a Pennsylvania multiemployer welfare fund showed that some employers made no contributions. The fund records showed that more than 100 (or over 20 percent) of the contributing employers were delinquent in payments. In some plans examined there were indications that the business agents of the union may have made off-the-record settlements with the delinquent employers. This is a serious abuse.

FOR DISCUSSION AND ANALYSIS

1. Comment on the address by Jarle Leirfallom, reproduced in this chapter.

2. It is sometimes said that a pension plan is of no benefit to an employer, and that an employer should not be expected to make payments to an employee when he is performing no useful service.

   a. Do you agree that a pension plan has no benefits to an employer which help to offset its costs?

   b. Build as effective a case as you can for the position that an employer should not be called on to pay an employee who is not working. Then make a case for the contrary view. Which of your arguments do you find more persuasive?

3. What is the advantage to the United Mine Workers of calculating payments to the Welfare and Pension Fund on a royalty basis (so much per ton of coal) rather than on employment basis (so many cents per man-hour worked)?

It has sometimes been charged that this royalty arrangement constitutes an excise tax imposed by the union on consumers, for its own benefit, and in this respect is unfair to workers in other industries whose unions have not similarly been able to impose a royalty or excise on the products or services which they produce. Do you agree?

4. A panel of management representatives which was discussing private pension plans argued that:

> Defects and flaws in these plans are born at the collective bargaining table. Programs involve actuarial assumptions which can be taken on either a conservative or liberal basis, and long-term judgment is applied to figures which are as debatable as the assumptions are debatable. Bargaining about that type of variable can lead to trouble.

For these reasons, this panel concluded that welfare and pension plans should not properly be a subject of bargaining.

Comment on this conclusion.

5. In negotiating for a pension (or welfare) plan, do you believe it would be preferable to bargain about benefits or costs?

23: Unemployment Compensation and Supplementary Benefits

The Social Security Act of 1935, which established public old-age insurance in the United States, also established a system of unemployment compensation—benefits paid for a limited duration to individuals who had previously been employed, who were now unemployed through no fault of their own, and who were seeking employment but could find none. Payments were made by employers in the form of a tax on payroll.

In the early years of the build-up of insurance funds (the first payments by most states were made in 1939), there was vigorous debate on whether funds should be pooled or held to an employer's account, on whether a tax on payroll would discourage new hiring, on whether an employer's tax contributions should be reduced on account of a favorable record in stabilizing employment ("experience rating"), and so on. In the intervening years new problems have joined or taken the place of the old ones. There has been increasing concern as to the adequacy of benefits, for example, and a continuing question as to whether it would be desirable to seek greater uniformity among the states in their amount and duration.

The problem of securing income to unemployed workers has been given a new dimension by the development in recent years of collectively bargained supplements to unemployment compensation, something which grew out of the unions' drive in the post-World War II period for a guaranteed annual wage.

WHAT IS UNEMPLOYMENT INSURANCE?

From the Employment Security Review, August, 1955, p. 1

What is unemployment insurance? Why do we have it? Who benefits from it? We who work in the program take it for granted that everyone knows the answers to these questions. Not everyone does. Certainly not everyone did 20 years ago when the program was started.

Briefly stated, unemployment insurance is an income maintenance program; it is insurance against a portion of wage loss when workers lose their jobs. Funds are built up by taxes on wages during periods of employment so that weekly benefits can be paid to workers during periods of unemployment.

In the United States, the program, up to June 30, 1955, had collected $20 billion for the payment of benefits; had paid out over $14 billion; and, with over $2 billion of interest on the funds, started the new fiscal year with a balance of $8 billion available for benefits.

Like any insurance, unemployment insurance provides for pooling resources to meet a widespread hazard. In the United States unemployment insurance spreads the cost of unemployment over all the geographical areas and industries within a State, some of which are more vulnerable than others to the hazard of unemployment. It spreads the cost over periods of time, in that taxes are collected in both good years and bad years and benefits are paid in varying amounts as needed, when economic conditions change from year to year.

SOCIAL INSURANCE

Unemployment is one of the most serious risks which wage earners in a dynamic industrial economy face—the risk of losing their jobs and their income. It is also one of the greatest risks to a community and to the Nation—the risk of losing the buying power of large numbers of people. Individual initiative and private enterprise alone cannot cope with such a risk.

For these reasons unemployment insurance is social insurance, fostered and administered by governments, rather than private insurance. Unemployment insurance is even more completely social insurance than such other wage-loss-compensation programs as old-age insurance, disability insurance, or workmen's compensation. Workers or employers can buy retirement insurance, health and accident insurance, or workmen's compensation insurance from private insurance carriers but no private insurance carrier sells unemployment insurance because of the unpredictable character of the risk of unemployment.

Unemployment insurance is not a general program to take care of all the unemployed. Its benefits are paid only to workers who normally depend for their livelihood on their earnings in covered employment and only when they are involuntarily unemployed and are able and willing to work. These benefits are paid as a matter of right to claimants who qualify as insured workers by reason of their past employment in jobs subject to the law and by reason of the circumstances of their unemployment.

Unemployment insurance has characteristics which distinguish it from other income maintenance programs, such as public assistance. There is no means test. Benefit amounts and duration are defined by law so that workers can know in advance what benefits they will be entitled to if they are unemployed and eligible under the terms of the law. The benefits are financed, not from general taxation but from contributions based on the workers' earnings; in most States all contributions are paid by employers.

THE NUMBER OF UNEMPLOYED

The American Workers' Fact Book, 1956, U.S. Department of Labor, pp. 84–89

The study of employment and unemployment trends is now so fully accepted that we sometimes forget that not too many years ago we had no count of un-

Unemployment Compensation and Supplementary Benefits 1031

employment at all. There were many guesses. And there were many opinions regarding who should be considered as unemployed.

Now we have monthly unemployment estimates made by the Bureau of the Census, which surveys a sampling of households around the country. This supplies the accepted count of national unemployment. For estimates of State and local unemployment other methods are used. Then again there are monthly and weekly data on the number of insured unemployed, that is, the number of people who file for unemployment insurance.

Month-by-month, year-by-year, the number of unemployed changes. It rises and falls with some regularity during certain seasons. It rises and falls with

Table 1. Annual Average Unemployment and Ratio of Unemployment to the Civilian Labor Force, 1929–55

Year	Unemployed (thousands)	Percent of labor force
1929	1,550	3.2
1930	4,340	8.7
1931	8,020	15.9
1932	12,060	23.6
1933	12,830	24.9
1934	11,340	21.7
1935	10,610	20.1
1936	9,030	16.9
1937	7,700	14.3
1938	10,390	19.0
1939	9,480	17.2
1940	8,120	14.6
1941	5,560	9.9
1942	2,660	4.4
1943	1,070	1.9
1944	670	1.2
1945	1,040	1.9
1946	2,270	3.9
1947	2,142	3.6
1948	2,064	3.4
1949	3,395	5.5
1950	3,142	5.0
1951	1,879	3.0
1952	1,673	2.7
1953	1,602	2.5
1954	3,230	5.0
1955	2,654	4.0

Source: U.S. Labor Department's Bureau of Labor Statistics for 1929–39; Bureau of Census, U.S. Department of Commerce, thereafter.

the fortunes of one or several of our large industries; with greater or less emphasis on defense production; with general business conditions.

The number of unemployed becomes a more meaningful measure when it is related to the total labor force. By getting the ratio of the unemployed to the labor force, we know what proportion of the persons who want jobs do not have them. This is generally stated as a percentage; it shows the number of unemployed for every hundred persons in the noninstitutional civilian labor force (Table 1). . . .

Many people, of course, do find jobs readily when they become unemployed. In the 9 postwar years (1947 through 1955) roughly about half the persons seeking jobs had been unemployed for no more than 4 weeks (Table 2). The percentage with 4 weeks or less of unemployment ranged from a low of 40 in 1954 to a high of 57 in 1953.

Table 2. Percent Distribution of Unemployment by Duration of Unemployment, 1947–55

Year	Total	4 weeks or less	5–14 weeks	15–26 weeks	Over 26 weeks
1947	100.0	48.6	32.9	10.9	7.7
1948	100.0	52.6	32.4	9.3	5.6
1949	100.0	44.7	35.2	12.6	7.5
1950	100.0	41.6	33.6	13.5	11.4
1951	100.0	53.4	30.5	8.8	7.3
1952	100.0	55.3	30.9	8.8	5.0
1953	100.0	56.8	30.1	8.2	4.9
1954	100.0	40.4	34.5	15.3	9.8
1955	100.0	42.9	30.4	13.8	12.7

Source: Bureau of the Census, U.S. Department of Commerce.

Some years were worse than others in terms of duration of unemployment. For example, in 1950, 1954, and 1955, from 25 to 26 out of every 100 unemployed persons were seeking jobs for 15 weeks or more, compared with the 9-year average of 19 out of 100. On the other hand, in 1953, only 13 out of every 100 job seekers were unemployed for 15 weeks or more.

STATE UNEMPLOYMENT INSURANCE BENEFIT PROVISIONS

Adapted from U.S. Department of Labor, Bureau of Employment Security, UIPL No. 445, November 1, 1956

As of December 1945, 98 percent of the covered workers were concentrated in States which provided for maximums ranging between $15 and $22 (excluding dependents' allowances). By December 1954, such maximums ranged

Unemployment Compensation and Supplementary Benefits   1033

between $20 and $35 with 10 States providing for $25 maximums and 17 States, with 57 percent of all covered workers, providing for a maximum of $30 per week. During the 1955 legislative sessions the upper limits on weekly benefits were increased in 32 States, and in 1956 they were increased in 4 additional States. Increases in basic maximums enacted during these two years ranged from $1 in Illinois to $10 in 7 States, with 9 States enacting increases of $3. The increase in the basic maximum in Illinois was accompanied by a higher maximum for claimants with dependents and with specified earnings. As a result of these changes, State unemployment compensation laws now provide for maximums (exclusive of dependents' allowances) ranging between $25 and $45 with the largest proportion of workers—40.6 percent—employed in States with maximums of $30 to $33. An additional 35.6 percent of the Nation's covered workers are subject to basic maximums of $35 or $36, while in Alaska the basic maximum is now $45.

Basic maximum weekly benefit	Percentage distribution of covered employment			
	Dec. 1939	Dec. 1945	Dec. 1954	Oct. 1956
Total......................	100.0	100.0	100.0	100.0
$15......................	77.0	7.5	....	....
16 to 19..................	23.0	16.4	....	....
20 to 24..................	....	74.3	11.2	....
25 to 29..................	....	1.8	29.6	23.7
30 to 34..................	....	....	59.1	40.6
35 and over..............	....	....	.1	35.7

[We may also relate] the maximum weekly benefit amounts enacted as of December 1954 and October 1956 to the average weekly wages of covered workers. Nationally, the average weekly wages of these workers increased from $74.52 for 1954 to $78.12 for 1955. Increases were experienced in every State except Alaska where a slight decline was reported. Because of higher earnings, the ratio of the maximum benefit of weekly wages declined in each of the 14 States where maximums remained unchanged since 1954. A decrease in the ratio is also noted in Illinois where the basic maximum was increased by only $1.

In general, however, the ratios have increased because of the higher maximum weekly benefits enacted in about three-fourths of the States.

As indicated above, maximum weekly benefit amounts represented 50 percent or more of average weekly wages in all but 2 States in 1939; in almost two-thirds of the States the ratio exceeded 60 percent. By the close of 1954, the gap between statutory maximums and weekly wages had widened so much that in only 2 States did the ratios equal 50 percent or more. The increases in

Maximum as percent of average weekly wages	Number of states		
	Dec. 1939	Dec. 1954	Oct. 1956
Total......................	51	51	51
Less than 40.0%...........	..	34	19
40.00–49.99...............	2	15	27
50.00–59.99...............	17	2	5
60.00 and over............	32	..	..

benefit maximums since that date are reflected in the fact that current statutory maximums represent 40 percent or more of average weekly wages in all but 19 States, although in only 5 States does the ratio exceed 50 percent.

In 2 of these 5—Hawaii (58.4%) and Mississippi (56.1%)—and in Massachusetts (49.5%), earnings somewhat higher than those represented by the 1955 average weekly wages are required to receive the basic maximum weekly benefit. In Mississippi, for example, high quarter earnings of $754.01 (a weekly average of over $58) are required for the $30 maximum. Claimants with earnings equivalent to the 1955 State average of $53.47 would be eligible for only $27. Consequently, claimants receiving the maximum in these 3 States are compensated for a smaller proportion of wage loss than that indicated by these ratios.

The effects of the increases in earnings and in maximum weekly benefits as well as other changes in the formula used for determining weekly benefits are reflected in the [following statistics:] the weekly benefit for total unemployment (including dependents' allowances) averaged $25.05 for the fiscal year 1955 with State averages ranging from $17.06 in North Carolina to $32.27 in Alaska. A total of 15 States paid benefits averaging $25 or more during that year. During the fiscal year 1956, weekly benefits averaged $26.33, primarily as the result of the increases in maximum weekly benefits discussed above. During that year a total of 25 States reported average payments of $25 or more. The effect of the statutory changes is more clearly discernible if we consider separately the experience in those States which enacted higher maximums during 1955. [Table on p. 1035.]

Nationally, the average weekly benefit for total unemployment represented about one-third of average weekly wages for fiscal year 1956—almost identical with the previous year's experience. Thus, the higher ratios of benefits to wages in such States as Arizona, Delaware, Ohio, and Washington and in the District of Columbia were more than offset by States where weekly wages rose at a more rapid rate than average weekly benefits.

The effect of raising the upper limit on weekly benefits is also noted in . . . the percentage of insured claimants who were eligible for the respective maximums. Nationally, about half of all insured claimants were eligible for the

Item	Average weekly benefit	
	April–June 1955	April–June 1956
Average for 34 States with higher max. wba enacted in 1955.......	$25.38	$28.14
Average for 17 States with no change in maximum...........	21.54	21.17

maximum in 1956 as compared with 59 percent during the preceding fiscal year. The greatest decreases were in Hawaii (where the maximum was increased from $25 to $35), New York ($30 to $36), Pennsylvania ($30 to $35), South Carolina ($20 to $26), and Vermont ($24 to $28).

The percentages [of claimants who exhausted their benefit rights during each of the last 2 fiscal years] are commonly referred to as "exhaustion ratios" and are useful as rough indicators of the relative incidence of the exhaustion of benefit rights among the various States. The general improvement in business conditions and increased opportunities for reemployment are revealed by the sharp decrease in exhaustions from 1955 to 1956. The exhaustion ratio for the latter year indicates that about 1 out of every 4 beneficiaries drew his full potential benefits. This experience was comparable to that of 1951:

Fiscal year	Exhaustions	
	Number (in 000's)	Ratio [1]
1949...................	1,277	27.0
1950...................	2,383	32.0
1951...................	1,060	24.2
1952...................	901	20.1
1953...................	785	18.8
1954...................	1,177	22.3
1955...................	1,774	29.4
1956...................	1,025	23.1

[1] Percent of first payments for 12-month period ended in March.

While trends in the number of exhaustions are indicative of changes in economic conditions, they also reflect statutory changes in the unemployment insurance program, particularly in the duration provisions of State laws. Thus, the lower 1956 exhaustion ratios in such States as Arizona, Arkansas, South Carolina, and Vermont reflect the longer duration of benefits provided by 1955 legislative amendments as well as the general improvement in the economy.

Changes since 1954 in the maximum duration provisions and in the basic formulas by which potential duration is computed [may be briefly] summarized. . . . Considering these amendments, about one-fourth of the covered work force is employed in States which provide for uniform duration of 26 weeks or 30 weeks (Pennsylvania). An additional 48 percent of the work force are covered by variable duration provisions with a maximum of 26 or 26½ weeks (Wisconsin). The remaining 27 percent of employment is subject to lower potential duration:

Uniform duration (weeks)	Percent of covered employment	Maximum variable duration (weeks)	Percent of covered employment
Total, 14 States	30.2	Total, 37 States	69.8
20	3.1 [1]	16	1.6
22	1.6	18	2.4
23	.5	20	7.7 [2]
24	.9	22	.9
26	15.9	24	8.7
30	8.2	26	46.4
		26.5	2.1

[1] Includes Georgia where claimants whose base-period earnings are equivalent to 4 times high-quarter wages are eligible for 22 weeks of benefits.

[2] Includes Colorado where claimants with specified employment experience may be eligible for 26 weeks of benefits.

TIME FOR ACTION!

From Economic Outlook, published by the CIO, April, 1955, p. 27

Unemployment insurance is woefully inadequate in spite of labor's determined efforts to improve it. The average benefit is now $25 a week. State maximums, with few exceptions, are still less than half of average wages of covered workers, even after 1955 amendments. Duration is too short, and many unemployed workers are deprived of payments by inexcusable disqualification clauses designed to save employers money.

We believe the time is ripe for action. The United States cannot afford to have millions of workers unemployed and billions of possible wealth not produced if we are to win the worldwide struggle against poverty and Communism.

GUARANTEED ANNUAL WAGE

From a resolution adopted by the 14th Constitutional Convention of the United Automobile Workers, Atlantic City, N.J., 1953

Workers and their families live by the year, a biological need which they share with stockholders and corporation officials. Corporations also live by the year. Interest rates, depreciation charges, taxes, executive salaries—all these items in the cost of keeping corporations alive are computed as annual costs.

The time has come to consider labor costs as annual costs also, because to the workers they are annual costs. Workers must provide for their needs every day in the year. They cannot meet those needs when they are left without jobs or earnings for weeks or months at a time. But little will be done to insure that they have jobs throughout the year until employers are given a greater financial responsibility in stabilizing employment.

The guaranteed annual wage is not a cure-all for our economic problems, but it can be the beginning, and the focal point, of a general attack on the basic problem of maintaining full employment in peacetime.

We have seen repeatedly how financial responsibility can convert management to social responsibility. A sound guaranteed annual wage plan will arouse management's social conscience and stimulate its social ingenuity by putting pressure on its pocketbook nerve. The guaranteed annual wage will compel management to take steps in its plants to end the instability of employment for which it is directly responsible. It will lead management to cooperate more readily in developing national economic measures designed to maintain full employment and full production by eliminating the causes of instability over which individual plant managements have no control. Industry will have cause to welcome rather than to oppose improved legislation to maintain the incomes and living standards of unemployed workers and their families.

Above all, the guaranteed annual wage will mark an end to irresponsible actions of employers which create needless unemployment, dislocation and hardship. It will end, for example, irresponsible decentralization of production and movement of plants which, though profitable to the employer, are costly to the workers and to the community in disrupted lives and weakened local economies.

No management in its right mind will pay to keep some of its workers in idleness while it hires others to do their work at new locations. The guaranteed annual wage will compel management to plan the extension or movement of its plants into new areas on a socially and economically sound basis by gearing decentralization to the expansion of markets and plant relocation to the orderly and gradual absorption of its existing work forces into other employment.

Adapted from an explanation of the UAW Annual Wage Study Committee's Proposed Plan for Guaranteed Employment in Industries in the Jurisdiction of the UAW, prepared for the delegates to the 6th International UAW Education Conference, April 8–11, 1954

PREPARING A GUARANTEED EMPLOYMENT PLAN THAT FITS UAW MEMBERS LIKE A GLOVE

WHAT THE UAW-CIO HAS BEEN DOING ABOUT THE GUARANTEED ANNUAL WAGE

After eighteen months of study in 1951 and 1952, the UAW Guaranteed Annual Wage Study Committee came to two basic conclusions:

1. . . . that *none* of the *existing* Guaranteed Wage plans meet the needs of workers in our industries—either they are not applicable to the economic conditions of our industries or they contain one or more features which are totally unacceptable to the UAW-CIO;

2. . . . that any Guaranteed Wage program developed for UAW members must have these objectives:

To provide the strongest practical incentives to employers to plan for regular, full-time, year-round employment for all seniority workers.

To provide regular income to those seniority workers when the employers fail to provide such employment.

With these goals in mind, the UAW Guaranteed Wage Study Committee began developing a Guaranteed Wage plan.

When the basic outline of the plan had taken shape, it was turned over to a subcommittee which was responsible for checking the plan against the provisions of our collective bargaining contracts. This subcommittee found no conflict between the plan and the contracts. It made several recommendations for modifications in the plan and for improvements in certain contractual provisions so that each would reinforce the other.

Principles of the plan

It became apparent as the committee's work proceeded that certain principles were essential to any plan that would meet the objectives which the Committee had set.

The committee reported to the International Executive Board which approved the following six principles which were subsequently endorsed by the 1953 UAW-CIO Convention:

1. The primary goal of a Guaranteed Annual Wage plan should be to stimulate management to provide steady full-time employment, week by week, the year round.

2. Guaranteed Annual Wage payments should be made to workers for whom management fails to provide work, in amounts sufficient to insure take-home pay adequate to maintain the living standards which the worker and his family enjoyed while fully employed.

3. All workers should be guaranteed employment or guarantee payments from the time they acquire seniority. The guarantee should assure protection

against a full year of layoff for all eligible workers and for shorter periods on a graduated basis for those who have not worked the minimum qualifying period.

4. Guarantee payments should be integrated with state unemployment compensation benefits so that employers can reduce their liabilities by effectively working toward the improvement of state laws.

5. The plan should be administered by a Joint Board of Administration having equal representation from the Union and from management, with an impartial chairman to break deadlocks. Decisions of the Joint Board with respect to eligibility and disqualification should be made independently of decisions made by state agencies with regard to unemployment compensation.

6. Financing should combine pay-as-you-go, to provide employers with incentives to stabilize employment, with a reserve trust fund to meet abnormal costs. Provision should be made for reinsurance to reduce the size of required reserves and to spread the risks of abnormal unemployment over the widest possible area of the economy. . . .

A content outline of the proposed plan

Note: The main features of the Plan worked out by the Study Committee are set forth in this section. Details have been omitted in this presentation of the basic framework of the plan in order to focus attention on its most important aspects.

I. THE GUARANTEE

A. Guarantee

The worker is guaranteed a full week's work. This is a defense against short work-weeks.

This part of the guarantee is like call-in pay. Call-in pay usually provides for four hours pay. The Guaranteed Wage contract clause will cover a full week. Its purpose is to induce management to schedule production so as to provide every worker with a full week of work every week he is called in to work. Scheduling of work for a week in advance is almost fully within management's control.

This guarantee will put an end to management's scheduling short work-weeks that yield the worker just enough to deprive him of his unemployment compensation benefits. It will assure the worker of the ability to plan ahead at least a week at a time. He will know whether there will be work for him next week at his regular job or whether he should look for other work.

[There is also a] guarantee against full weeks of layoff. It covers workers idled by total plant shutdowns as well as those affected by layoffs of a part of the total work force. It assures the laid-off workers that layoffs will not affect their ability to provide for the needs of their families.

They will be able to live on the same level when laid off as when they are fully employed. They will be able to meet payments on their homes, their furniture, their cars, and their household appliances, and will be able to continue as fully active consumers and to contribute their share to the stream of purchasing power needed to support the economy.

B. Coverage

All seniority workers are covered by the guarantee against full-week layoffs because all need the protection of the guarantee: low-seniority workers bear the brunt of the hardships imposed by the ups and downs in employment; high-seniority workers suffer along with those who have the least seniority when the entire plant is shut down whether temporarily or permanently. During the summer of 1953 for example, several of the Nash plants were shut down for ten weeks, throwing out on the streets the highest as well as the lowest seniority workers. In Hudson, even high-seniority workers got only ten days of work in all of January, 1954, and six days work in all of February.

In addition, the older workers face the greatest difficulties in finding new jobs if their plants move or close down permanently for other reasons. The abandonment of the Ford Iron Mountain plant meant permanent loss of jobs for workers some of whom had more than thirty years seniority. The Study Committee's plan therefore provides protection for both low and high seniority workers and for all those in between.

A plan which would provide security for one group of workers . . . would intensify insecurity for those not covered. If the guarantee covered only high-seniority workers, an employer who thought that he might not have sufficient work for the entire work force in the plant, might lay off more low-seniority workers than necessary in order to save the available work for the group covered by the guarantee.

High-seniority workers could also suffer under a limited coverage plan. In addition to laying off low-seniority workers when declining orders were foreseen, the employer would be tempted to find reasons to discharge workers whose seniority was approaching the minimum required for coverage under the plan.

Coverage for full-week layoffs cannot be extended to probationary workers for two reasons. First, they are on trial as to their suitability for their jobs. Second, employers would seek excuses to terminate rather than lay off and recall probationary workers if required to make guarantee payments to them when they are laid off.

The 40-hour guarantee can be applied to probationary as well as seniority workers because it is essentially an extension of call-in pay which applies to probationers under our present agreements.

C. Duration of guarantee payments

All workers are protected against short work-weeks every week in the year, regardless of what they may have drawn previously in guarantee payments.

The period in which guarantee payments may be received under the Study Committee's plan [for full-week layoffs] begins with the date of the layoff.

A fully eligible worker can always look forward to 52 weeks of security if he should be laid off. This feature distinguishes the UAW plan from those plans in which the guarantee is on a calendar year or fixed 12-month period basis. Under such plans, the employer has an incentive to reduce his potential liabilities by laying off a part of his work force at the end of the year. Under this type of plan the amount of security a worker can look forward to constantly diminishes as the end of the 12-month period or calendar year approaches. By the 51st week of the year, the worker has security for only one week ahead. The Study Committee's plan provides for the full duration of the guarantee following the date of layoff.

There is a limit to the degree of protection that a guaranteed annual wage can provide for low seniority workers without risk of drying up the job opportunities available for new workers, particularly younger workers.

If an employer were required to guarantee 52 weeks pay to any new worker from the date of hire, the employer would avoid hiring new workers if there was any uncertainty at all about the amount of work available in the year ahead. Employers might turn down orders or work their existing labor force excessive overtime, rather than take risks involved in hiring additional workers. Formation of new businesses would be made too risky because of the heavy possible guarantee liabilities, and the number of job opportunities in the economy would tend to diminish.

Graduation of the guarantee for the low-seniority workers provides security for new workers without destroying opportunity for them. This is particularly important to avoid turning young workers against the labor movement.

The proposed UAW-CIO plan is designed to provide for the maximum possible security consistent with the maximum job opportunity. It will leave the door wide open for new workers to be hired and will protect their living standards for as long as it is practicable to do so if they are laid off after acquisition of seniority.

Graduation will apply only to the workers with low seniority except after recall from a layoff. The number of weeks each such worker is guaranteed, will be directly related to the number of weeks he had worked since acquiring seniority. For example, a worker who worked 20 weeks after acquiring seniority would be entitled to twice as many weeks after acquiring seniority as a person who had worked only 10 weeks.

Just as the graduation of the number of weeks of guarantee is necessary to avoid discouraging employers from hiring new workers, graduation is also important to avoid discouraging recall of laid-off workers. Suppose, for example, a worker had been laid off long enough to have used up 49 of his 52 weeks of guarantee. A plan that gave him another 52 weeks guarantee from the minute he returns to work would discourage the employer from recalling him, unless there was absolute assurance of many months of work ahead following his recall. The employer might prefer to turn down orders or to work those still on the payroll excessive overtime, rather than take the risk of recalling laid-off workers.

To illustrate how the guarantee would build up for recalled workers, we may take the example of a worker who was laid off 20 weeks out of the 52 weeks guaranteed him at the time of his layoff. If he should be laid off again soon after his recall to work, he still has the remaining 32 weeks of guarantee payment plus any additional weeks he has accumulated. Thus, if following his recall, he works long enough to pick up an additional 10 weeks of guarantee rights, he will have 42 weeks of guarantee payments when laid off again. He can again build up rights to guarantee payments for a full 52 weeks.

D. Unemployment compensation

The employer's liability for guarantee payments to any worker for any week will be reduced by an amount equal to the basic state unemployment compensation benefit which the worker is entitled to receive for that week. Special provision will be made with respect to the dependents allowances paid under some state laws.

E. Availability for other work

1. Unless otherwise directed by the employer, a worker laid off for a full week will be required to register with the State Employment Service and to accept suitable employment.

2. Standards of "suitability" will be specified by the agreement, without regard to any standards that may be provided in the state unemployment compensation laws, in order to protect workers against pressure to accept jobs paying substandard wages, having substandard working conditions, etc.

3. If a laid-off worker who takes a suitable job with another employer fails in any week to earn an amount equal to his regular earnings with the guaranteeing employer, the latter will make up the difference.

4. A laid-off worker who takes a suitable job with another employer will remain eligible to receive guarantee payments, if and when again unemployed, for a period of time beyond the time when his guarantee payments would have ceased if he had not found other employment.

II. FINANCING

A. Cost of short work-weeks

Costs arising out of short work-weeks, or failure to notify workers in advance of a full-week layoff, will be met by the employer on a pay-as-you-go basis and will not be credited against his maximum liability.

B. Cost of full-week layoffs

Costs of payments for full weeks of layoff will be met·by the employer on a pay-as-you-go basis up to a specified maximum percentage of his current payroll.

C. Reserve trust fund

1. The employer will be required to make contributions to establish and maintain a reserve trust fund to meet costs of full-week layoffs in excess of the percentage of his current payroll specified in II, B above.

2. The employer will be required to build the reserve trust fund up to and

to maintain it at a specified percentage of his "base payroll." (The "base payroll" will be the highest number of manhours worked in the bargaining unit during any of a specified number of calendar years immediately preceding the annual review of the fund multiplied by the current average straight-time hourly wage rate.)

3. A "contribution rate" will be specified, in terms of a fixed percentage of "base payroll" sufficient to bring the reserve up to the required level within a specified period.

4. The employer's maximum liability, for current (pay-as-you-go) payments for full-week layoffs plus contributions to the trust fund, will be limited to the percentage of his current payroll specified in II, B above. The cost of current guarantee payments will be the first charge against this percentage, with the trust fund, if contributions are due it, getting the remainder up to the "contribution rate" or the amount due, whichever is less.

5. After the reserve reaches the required level, further contributions will be required to be made into the trust fund only (a) to replace withdrawals from the fund, (b) to adjust to increases in the "base payroll" resulting from increases in employment, or wage rates, or both, and (c) to adjust to unemployment compensation law amendments or changes in the terms of reinsurance which would have the effect of increasing the potential liabilities of the reserve fund. Such further contributions will be made at the "contribution rate."

6. Provision will be made for reducing the required size of the reserve fund below the originally specified level based on (a) decreases in the "base payroll," (b) increases in unemployment compensation benefits and duration, or both, and (c) increases in amounts available under reinsurance.

7. Reduction of the actual reserve, when warranted, will be accomplished by temporarily reducing the maximum percentage of current payroll specified under II, B above. Excess monies in the trust fund, above the amount required, will also be permitted to be used to pay reinsurance premiums.

8. The adequacy of the reserve will be reviewed annually by the Joint Board of Administration in the light of specified factors.

9. The employer will be permitted, at his option, to make additional contributions to the trust fund reserve over and above the "contribution rate" for the purpose of anticipating or averaging over good and bad years his pay-as-you-go liabilities for full-week layoffs. Such additional contributions will be earmarked for use in meeting pay-as-you-go liabilities only and will not be considered in the annual review of the adequacy of the fund.

III. ADMINISTRATION

A. *Joint board and committees*

1. The guarantee will be administered by a Joint Board of Administration composed of employer and union representatives in equal numbers plus an impartial chairman to break deadlocks.

2. Joint plant and regional committees, composed of employer and union

representatives only, will be established in multi-plant corporations and under pooled plans, to the extent necessary.

B. Functions of joint board

In addition to its other functions, the Joint Board of Administration will interpret the guarantee agreement and will decide all questions involving eligibility for guarantee payments, including the amount and duration of the payments due any worker, whether work offered him is suitable work, etc. The Board will make its own independent determinations in accordance with the provisions of the guarantee agreement and will not be bound by any determination or finding made under state unemployment compensation laws.

WHAT THE PLAN WILL NOT DO

Before developing the plan described in this pamphlet, the Study Committee carefully examined objections which had been raised at various times to guaranteed annual wage plans, actual and proposed, both by industry spokesmen and by professional economists.

The Study Committee found that objections to guaranteed wage plans are of two general types. The first consists of those which are merely expressions of prejudice against the idea of guaranteeing wages for workers. These objections will be raised by the same people to any guaranteed wage plan—or, in fact, to any improvement in the life of workers—that is proposed. They do not deserve to be taken seriously.

The second type of objection is raised by people who are honestly concerned about the effects of ill-considered guaranteed wage plans on an industry or on the economy as a whole. A plan poorly designed to meet the problems of an industry could do serious damage to the industry and to the workers employed in it. Similarly, widespread adoption of ill-conceived guaranteed wage plans could damage the economy as a whole by contributing to instability rather than stability, by cutting off job opportunities for young workers, or by stifling economic expansion and progress. Objections to guaranteed wage plans that arise out of such considerations require serious examination by responsible trade unionists concerned with the welfare both of their own membership and of the population as a whole.

The Study Committee gave earnest consideration to all objections which appeared to spring from honest concern with the effects of wage guarantees. Some of these objections the Committee found to be without real foundation in fact or based on misconception.

The remainder, which were both honest in their inspiration and based on real problems, formed the starting point for the Study Committee's work. The Committee's goal was to develop a plan which would provide genuine security for workers in industries under jurisdiction of the UAW-CIO, and be good for the economy as a whole.

Some of the problems that the Study Committee's plan is designed to meet have been dealt with in the preceding pages; others are discussed in the remaining pages of this pamphlet.

COSTS HAVE TO BE CONSIDERED

First there is the problem of costs. Frequently it has been argued that a wage guarantee in the industries under our Union's jurisdiction would be so costly as to result in the bankruptcy of the corporations.

If this were so, it would be a most serious matter. No plan would be acceptable which did not provide a substantial measure of security to the workers. On the other hand, costs must be realistic, for it would be suicidal to lead the members of our Union into a struggle for a demand whose cost was so high as to make it impractical or unobtainable in collective bargaining.

Furthermore, the costs of the guarantee plan must leave room for other economic gains in collective bargaining. Along with the guarantee, we must win advances in wages, improvements in our retirement and health security programs, and make progress in other areas where progress is called for by the needs and legitimate aspirations of the membership.

This means that the guarantee plan must be so framed as to avoid all costs not essential to its basic purpose. Furthermore, the plan must include a system of financing that will keep costs within bounds in a major recession when employers would be least able to meet high costs.

Costs will be a big issue with employers in negotiations. By examining the experience of the past, it is possible to determine whether or not the cost of any given plan, under conditions likely to occur, is realistically within the range of collective bargaining possibilities. The UAW-CIO Study Committee has tested out its proposed plan in terms of what it would cost under various circumstances. The cost, even under highly unfavorable economic conditions, has been found to be realistic in terms of reasonable collective bargaining expectations.

Estimates based on past experience, of course, do not make any allowance for savings resulting from management's response to the stimulus of the guarantee plan. Under the proposed plan, management will be able to reduce costs in four separate ways:

First, by stabilizing employment;

Second, by helping to achieve higher employment compensation benefits paid for longer periods;

Third, by helping to secure the creation of a sound reinsurance system; and

Fourth, by supporting national economic policies designed to maintain full employment.

If management takes effective advantage of these four cost reducing opportunities, the guarantee could ultimately be costless, or practically so. That would be the ideal situation as far as our Union is concerned because, as we have said repeatedly, it is work we want and not pay for idleness.

In the early stages of the plan, however, there would unavoidably be certain costs. First, there would be the cost of the creation of the reserve trust fund, and second, costs might arise during the period when management was learning how to stabilize employment.

As management succeeds in stabilizing employment, the savings from stability may actually outweigh the costs of the guarantee. For one thing, if peaks and valleys in production are avoided, it will not be necessary to maintain excessive investment in floor space and machinery that is actually used only to meet peak production loads. For another thing, the costs of labor turnover will be reduced. It is expensive to train new workers. Yet when companies hire to meet peak seasonal requirements and lay off at the end of the season, they must train a large number of new workers in every seasonal upswing. Training costs would also be reduced because the security provided by the guarantee would reduce the number of workers who quit their jobs.

The security of the guarantee would lift a heavy load of worry from the minds of the workers, and unworried workers are, obviously, more efficient workers than those who live constantly in the shadow of fear that their incomes may be cut off at any moment.

ABOUT "ECONOMIC FLEXIBILITY" . . .

Despite management hypocrisy on the subject of "flexibility," change is desirable if the economy is to progress. The process of change means that some companies and some industries expand while others contract. Therefore, a sound guarantee plan should not freeze workers to any company or industry; should not freeze employment levels in any segment of the economy; and should not discourage increased employment in expanding industries or in periods of recovery from recession.

This means that a guarantee plan (a) should not impose an immediate heavy liability when the employer adds new workers to his payroll; and (b) should not prevent movement of workers among employers or industries in a situation where some are expanding and others contracting. At the same time workers should not have to bear the entire cost of providing the necessary flexibility in the economy.

The UAW program avoids discouraging employers from hiring workers by materially adding to costs not when workers are hired but when they are laid off. The UAW program does not block movement of workers from one company or industry to another, first, because it requires laid-off workers to accept suitable employment offered to them and, second, because there is a limit on the period during which the worker may draw guarantee payments.

TECHNOLOGICAL PROGRESS CAN BE GOOD FOR ALL OF US

Our Union has never opposed technological progress. It has fought instead to win for workers the largest possible share in the fruits of technological advance. Consistent with this approach, a UAW guaranteed employment program should place no obstacles in the way of technological progress so that the way may remain open to continue the fight for ever higher living standards.

The benefits of advancing technology, however, are shared by the whole community. No one group of workers should be forced to suffer hardships in order that the whole community may enjoy the benefits of improved production methods.

The Committee's guaranteed employment program reconciles the dual objectives of technological progress and security for workers. Profits from installation of improved machinery will still be available to the employer. In most cases the guarantee plan will have no effect at all on such profits.

The normal turnover in the labor force from such factors as quits, deaths, retirements, etc., would usually be enough to absorb the impact of more efficient equipment even if there were no change in the amount of goods produced. If improved production methods are reflected, as they should be, in lower prices and increased output, even major technological changes could often be absorbed without layoffs. In the rare case where a major technological development results in a sudden and drastic reduction of labor requirements the guarantee payments made to the laid-off workers would give them time to make an orderly adjustment. They would not be forced, as they frequently are now, to grasp at any job that comes along, no matter how unsuitable or low paid.

The community as a whole would benefit because the employment of trained workers on jobs using less than their highest skills and abilities is wasteful. If laid-off workers are enabled to make an orderly search for jobs that will make the fullest use of their skills and abilities, the pool of goods and services available to all of us will be larger than it would be otherwise.

Where a technological change was of such a major nature as to cause the displacement of a substantial number of workers, the employer's savings would, within a short time, reimburse him for the guarantee costs involved in permitting the displaced workers time to adjust on an orderly basis.

In any case, the existence of the guarantee would provide an incentive for employers to plan the introduction of more efficient equipment for periods in which no workers, or the minimum number of workers, would be laid off.

ECONOMIC EXPANSION IS NOT DISCOURAGED BY GUARANTEED EMPLOYMENT PLAN

Similarly, a guaranteed employment plan must not discourage economic expansion. To support a growing population and a progressively rising standard of living, new plants must be built and new machinery installed. Such expansion may take place either within existing companies or by the formation of new companies. No guaranteed employment plan would be sound if it discouraged either type of expansion.

New investment, whether by existing or new companies, would be discouraged if the employer incurred a heavy and immediate liability for every new worker he hired. On the other hand, workers employed in new companies, or in new plants of existing companies, have as much right to security as other workers.

A sound guarantee plan must provide the maximum possible security for workers in new or expanding companies without discouraging expansion.

The UAW-CIO program accomplishes this by graduating the maximum number of weeks for which a laid-off worker may draw guarantee payments on the basis of the length of his previous employment.

While employment was expanding there would be no cost to a new company under the guaranteed plan, except the cost involved in building up a reserve trust fund. This cost is no different in effect than the cost of an increase in wage rates. Even this cost could be greatly reduced if reinsurance were available since in that case the required reserves would be smaller.

If expansion should be interrupted by layoffs, employer guarantee liabilities would be small because of the graduation of weeks of guarantee payments based on length of employment.

The expanding employer's workers would consist of a relatively large proportion of recently hired workers. Because the duration of guarantee payments to short-service workers is graduated, the costs of an extended layoff in a new company would be less than in an established competitor.

Moreover, payroll costs are not fixed costs under the UAW-CIO program. The employer's maximum liability will be a percentage of his payroll. This means that the cost of the guarantee will move up and down as employment fluctuates.

In this respect, also, the effect of the cost of the guarantee is like that of a wage increase. We have seen, in recent years, that rising wages and economic expansion can go hand-in-hand. In fact, they must go hand-in-hand in order to provide outlets for the increased production resulting from expansion.

Because guarantee costs fluctuate with payroll, their effects on expansion will be totally unlike the effect of such fixed costs as interest, property taxes, depreciation and other costs that are incurred in the course of creating a new business or expanding an old one.

More arguments ahead

We can expect that objections will be raised against our guaranteed wage plan in the months ahead. As our Union's drive for guaranteed wage agreements continues these objections will be answered. It is enough for the present to note that all known objections were explored by the Study Committee in its own deliberations and in meetings with the Public Advisory Committee. The Study Committee is confident that legitimate objections that have been raised to guaranteed wages in general or to certain other guaranteed wage plans have been met successfully in the proposed UAW plan. If any new ones should be raised in the future, the proposed plan will be re-examined and, if necessary, modified.

We are open-minded

If corporations with which our Union bargains find anything in the foregoing description of the plan which they consider unworkable or harmful, they will have the opportunity to explore the matter with the Union in joint study committees. Pride of authorship will not be permitted to stand in the way of changes in the plan which would make it a better and more effective plan from the standpoint of UAW members, or the economy as a whole.

As stated in the resolution of our Fourteenth Constitutional Convention, the UAW-CIO "remains flexible as to means for implementing the objective of the guaranteed annual wage. It is completely inflexible and totally committed as to the objective itself."

JOBS? OR JOBLESS PAY?

The Real Issue behind the New Guaranteed Wage Proposals, by the United States Chamber of Commerce, 1954, pp. 5, 7, 18, 20, 44, 48, 50, 52, 54, 66, 68, 89

JOBS—OR IDLE PAY?

The CIO's GAW plans being pushed today are almost entirely devoted to HOW MUCH, HOW LONG, and HOW to pay people NOT AT WORK.

They ask that an eligible worker be paid for a full year *even if he is not working.*

The few successful private guarantee plans operating today stress ways of keeping men *on the job and on the payroll.*

The union's plan for a "guaranteed wage" would become effective only *after* a man is laid off.

This is not "job security" but *pay for idleness.*

YEAR'S PAY FOR NO WORK!

CIO leaders want jobless benefits—payments to those not working—boosted to match or approach wages while on the job!

That is what CIO unions now seek when they talk of "Guaranteed Annual Wage."

This demand may be modified in bargaining but the policy is clearly set forth: Nearly full base pay guaranteed for one year after workers are laid-off or employment terminated.

No "easy way" out

A blunt admission that the "price tag" appeal has been hung on UC-GAW [Unemployment Compensation plus Guaranteed Annual Wage] comes from the United Steelworkers: "And this brings us to the second-named factor in the Steelworkers' proposals for the GAW—one that provides a sound answer to another typical objection, which is the cry of management that they 'can't afford it.'

"For it is to forestall this objection and to face realistically the fact that 'money makes the mare go' that the Steelworkers propose that the wage guarantee made by the company shall be geared into the existing unemployment compensation system.

"What this means, in practice, is that the company would only have to put enough money into the GAW trust fund so that the fund could make up the difference in weekly benefits between what the laid-off worker receives as state-federal unemployment compensation and what he is guaranteed under the plan."—(*Steel Labor*, February, 1944.)

This approach completely ignores the important question: "Who pays for unemployment compensation?"

The reserve-ratio formula

State Unemployment Compensation funds are maintained by payroll taxes on industries covered. Company tax rates, up to a maximum, are determined by benefits paid out.

In 30 states[1] the "reserve-ratio" formula is used. (Also in District of Columbia and Hawaii, making 32 such systems.) Each employer's record shows his payroll, how much he pays in, and how much is paid out to his workers getting jobless benefits. He must maintain a "reserve" in his account in a certain ratio to his payroll. If his reserve goes down, his tax goes up.

To illustrate what Mr. Jones [a hypothetical employer] found, the rating schedule of the Wisconsin law is used. (There are minor variations in other states, but the principle is the same.) Mr. Jones' yearly payroll is assumed to remain at $100,000. At the start of 1952, he had paid in $60,000 over the past years and payments against his account had been $50,000. His reserve therefore was $10,000, or 10 percent of his payroll, deemed sufficient by the State law. The table shows what happens to his tax rate if certain payments are made against his fund:

For the year	These jobless benefits were paid	Making total accumulated charges of	While his contributions total	And his reserve shows	Or % of payroll of	Making his tax rate in Wisconsin	And his tax payments
1952	$2,100	$52,100	$60,000	$7,900	7.5%	1.5%	$1,500
1953	2,500	54,600	61,500	6,900	6.9	2	2,000
1954	400	55,000	63,500	8,500	8.5	1	1,000
1955	600	55,600	64,500	8,900	8.9	1	1,000
1956	400	56,000	65,500	9,500	9.5	0.5	500
1957	0	56,000	66,000	10,000	10.0	0	0
Six year totals:	$6,000						$6,000

He can either pay the tax as levied, or he can, at the end of each year, pay directly into the State Fund the deficit in his reserve—say $500 or $1,000. In either case, the State fund has paid out $6,000 against his account and he has paid in $6,000 in the example shown above.

Thus, under this example, it makes no difference to Mr. Jones whether the "jobless benefits" are paid from the State Fund or by him directly to the

[1] Reserve Ratio states are: Arizona, Arkansas, California, Colorado, Georgia, Idaho, Indiana, Iowa, Kansas, Kentucky, Louisiana, Maine, Massachusetts, Missouri, Nebraska, Nevada, New Hampshire, New Jersey, New Mexico, New York, North Carolina, North Dakota, Ohio, Oregon, Pennsylvania, South Carolina, South Dakota, Tennessee, West Virginia and Wisconsin.

workers. "Supplementation" would cost him the same as a direct "GAW" plan. (In some states that have a minimum tax rate, it may appear that an employer would save this amount by using UC, but in practice, if lay-offs came, the minimum would doubtless be drained by claims of newly laid-off workers not even covered by his GAW.)

"Limitation" is not indefinite

It cannot be forecast what contribution figure for an Unemployment Trust Fund would be acceptable to a union that won acceptance for the UC-GAW idea. Nor can it be forecast how this figure might change from year to year.

In the Steelworkers' proposal to ALCOA, the union said: "The company shall pay into a trust fund, for each hour worked by an employee . . . ten (10) cents . . . The company's liability shall be limited to payment of the specified contribution . . ."

In IUE's proposal to Westinghouse, it is asked that "the payments to fulfill the guarantee shall be financed from a fund equal to 5% of the payroll."

In 1952, Murray Latimer for the United Steelworkers estimated the employer-financed fund could be supported by company contributions of about seven cents per hour worked by employees.

Steel Labor, February, 1954, said: "The steelworkers' proposal for the GAW does not demand of industry a 'blank check' of unlimited obligations and unknown quantity but . . . fixes the amount of the company's contribution on a per-hour basis, with this amount subject to reduction (but not to increase) in relation to the way the plan actually operates . . ."

Since UC-GAW would be part of the union contract, terms of the guaranteed pay provision would be subject for renegotiation at the expiration of the contract—usually one year.

The United Mine Workers Welfare Fund, inaugurated by the government in 1946 when in control of the coal mines, is of course an outstanding example of how contributions to a negotiated fund can zoom up. Bituminous coal mine operators are now assessed EIGHT TIMES as much as the original five-cent-a-ton levy of EIGHT YEARS ago and anthracite mine operators pay TEN times as much.

Extent of genuine liability

This is another field in which the unions are vague.

The Steelworkers say: "The company's liability . . . shall be limited to payment of the specified contribution to the trust fund."

The Electrical Workers say: "Labor proposes . . . that the obligation of management be limited to the contributions required to be made to a Trust Fund. . . ."

The "limited" liability concept develops an interesting contractual paradox: In the one clause, the company "guarantees" jobless benefits for a period of 52 weeks. In another clause, the union absolves the company of responsibility for fulfilling the "guarantee" beyond a certain maximum contribution.

The concept ignores moral and public opinion pressures that would build up among the workers and other members of the community if the company, which had agreed to a GAW, were to announce it could no longer make the promised payments.

Pay cut for some workers

Employer contributions to a GAW fund would be part of wage costs. Currently there is the suggestion that the GAW fund be established in lieu of an increase in pay (though many unions, of course, may seek GAW *and* other benefits).

Say the Steelworkers: "It should be ever borne in mind that a ten-cent (or whatever it might be) contribution to a GAW trust fund costs a company not one cent more than a similar increase in wage rates."

Assuming a 10-cent contribution per hour worked, this would mean, in most cases, that the bulk of workers in a plant would have to give up $4.00 a week in pay.

Many workers with long tenure and job security would have to forego a wage boost, assuming one is due, for GAW. Other workers, who leave their jobs to take a different one, would have given up such a pay increase and got no benefit. Under the Steelworkers plan, a new worker would have to take less pay than he might otherwise have drawn for three years before he would even qualify for GAW.

Also, there would be many who might qualify for GAW as far as seniority is concerned but could not draw payments for other reasons, such as refusing new work because he or she is out of the job market or leaving work for "no good cause." All these would have been taking less pay than they might have been otherwise.

Assuming many would forego a wage increase for company contributions to GAW, the present day situation raises the question of whether any rise in payroll costs are warranted. If not, would these workers give up 10 cents an hour of their present rates to finance GAW?

Payments out discriminate

Establishment of GAW would open up serious questions concerning seniority rights. There need be no assumption that GAW advocates do not aim for genuine job security or for protection of wages in cases of job losses. However, in reality, major problems would arise in connection with temporary lay-offs or seasonal partial shut-downs.

The Electrical Workers touch the surface of the problem in discussing GAW's effect on clauses of present contracts: "Most obvious is the seniority clause, including lay-off, recall, rehire, transfer, promotion and probationary period before acquiring seniority. The lay-off clause might provide that an employee has the *right to take a lay-off* in lieu of a transfer to a lower rate or less desirable job without losing his seniority."

(Here it is recognized that a "lay-off" might become a "right" to be exercised by employees.)

"Some contracts provide that the work be reduced to 36 hours or 32 hours before any lay-offs took place," the IUE continues. "If, however, the GAW provided 40 hours work for 52 weeks, some revision in the basic contractual provision would be required."

The Steelworkers' proposal would provide that there would be no reduction in the work-week for workers with one year or more seniority until workers with a year or less of seniority—not covered by GAW—had been laid off. Thus, those protected by GAW would be doubly protected in discrimination against employees *in the same plant* who are not eligible for the jobless pay.

Unfair to those drawing GAW

In any discussion of GAW, you have to assume conditions under which benefits are paid. The following example greatly simplifies just one of the problems of fairness to workers that could arise. Let us assume:

A company with 500 employees earning $80 each for a 40-hour week agrees for one year to contribute 10 cents an hour into a GAW Fund and to pay laid-off workers for 30 hours, or $60 a week each, from the fund.

All goes well for the first 26 weeks of the contract and the company pays into the GAW Fund 10 cents per hour or $2,000 weekly for a 26-week total of $52,000.

Now, a 10 percent lay-off is necessary for 13 weeks, meaning 50 men drawing $60 weekly or $3,000 a week from the GAW Fund for a 13-week total of $39,000.

Meanwhile, 13 more weeks of GAW contributions for 450 men at 40 hours a week or 18,000 hours would bring in $1,800 weekly or a 13-week total of $23,400.

Thus, at the end of 39 weeks, contributions total $75,400 and benefits paid out of the Fund total $39,000, bringing the Fund's balance to $36,400.

Now, another 10 percent lay-off for 13 weeks raises the prospect of paying 95 men at $60 a week or a weekly total of $5,700. Contributions for 405 workers will bring in $1,620 weekly, while the remaining $4,080 weekly would have to come out of the Fund's balance of $36,400. Simple division shows the Fund would last not quite nine more weeks, at which time there would be left only the $1,620 in weekly contributions to be divided among 95 workers or about $17 a week each.

The first 50 laid-off workers would have received 22 weeks of GAW pay at $60 per week, while the next group of 45 would have got only NINE weeks at $60. Neither group has any prospect of drawing $60 per week for 52 weeks as the "guarantee" promises. Would the Fund now stop payments to the first 50 until the next 45 were even with them? Or would payments be pro-rated? Or what?

Recognition by at least one union of this problem came in April with the IUE demands on Westinghouse. The electrical workers suggest no payments be made until the fund has accumulated for 52 weeks. Also, IUE proposed the Trust Fund be divided into three parts—one for employees with less than three years service; a second for those with three years to five years seniority; and a third for those with more than five years. Analysis shows the net effect of this division is to create at least three new problems in the place of one.

Foot in the door

One prominent feature of UC-GAW is joint administration of the proposed Unemployment Benefit Trust Fund to be financed by the company. This would open up opportunities for unions to get a greater voice in management responsibilities.

Administration of the funds, their investment, their possible use in "make-work" projects, and measures that might ease the drain on the funds are all fields in which management decisions would be questioned, scrutinized and perhaps reviewed by unions participating in the Fund administration.

Negotiations on amounts to be paid into the fund could require extensive probing into company plans and programs for the future. If such plans are to become joint activities of company and union, joint management will have arrived.

In its 1951 convention, the CIO demanded an equal union voice in such matters as pricing, production levels, rate of expansion, technological changes, size and location of new plants. The CIO's booklet, "Guaranteed Wages the Year Round," speaks of GAW: "If one company or even one industry cannot act alone, labor-management councils on an industry-wide or inter-industry basis should tackle the problem . . ."

Some economists warn of industry-union controls over pricing, marketing and production that would lead to cartelization in this country, presumably with some kind of government sanction and regulation.

As Dr. J. M. Clark commented in The Latimer Report (Page 467): "In any case the question opens vistas too broad for adequate consideration here."

Toward government controls

Many unions as well as professional economists foresee more Federal planning and controls resulting from guaranteed wage plans.

The Shipyard Worker, publication of the Industrial Union of Shipbuilding Workers, said (April 9, 1945): "The guaranteed annual wage plans cannot be established on a nation-wide basis without establishing a planned economy in America . . . Unplanned production, unrestrained competition are two conditions under which it would be impossible to guarantee job security of American wage earners."

The problem is also defined by A. D. H. Kaplan: "The fact that the program to put an industry under an annual wage may start out with short steps does not relieve us from the necessity of seeing what the cumulative effects may be of programming toward a widening coverage of guaranteed wages . . . If a generalized guarantee of annual wages is successfully promoted with the thought that the guarantee can be progressively expanded without contracting and radically modifying our present system of competitive private enterprise—then we are confronted with a dream that is destined to end only in disillusionment."—(*Guarantee of Annual Wages*, Brookings Institution, 1947, pp. 210–11.)

K. C. Adams, while editor of the *United Mine Workers Journal*, in *Forbes Magazine*, May 1, 1945, stated: "The whole /GAW/ program presages the junking of the American way of life and the forfeiture of our industrial liberties in return for a promised security which cannot be guaranteed—a bureaucratic rule over our whole scheme of life."

George Meany, President, American Federation of Labor, in *U. S. News and World Report*, November 6, 1953, said: ". . . It's almost an impossibility under our economic system to have a guaranteed annual wage in certain types of business."

SUMMARY

In facing up to today's problem of job stabilization and income security for workers, we must seek solutions in forward-looking practices which will not shackle our dynamic economy that makes jobs and progress possible.

It is one thing to see that there is a problem and to be willing to grapple with it. But it is quite another matter to be forced into accepting a so-called solution that won't prove out. We should not hesitate to reject—and condemn—suggested solutions that would be ineffectual in, if not damaging to, our economy. Neither wage earners nor business owners and managements will gain by sacrificing economic and, perhaps, political freedom for proposals that will not assure security but may assuredly upset our economy as we know it.

Current union proposals for a "guaranteed annual wage" are advanced as solutions to the problem of job stabilization and income security. We have seen they actually call for drastic modifications in our unemployment compensation system and laws. More than that, they would discourage, rather than encourage, incentives. In many instances, the result would be a bonus for idleness and a penalty for working. The UC-GAW proposals furthermore could lead to a situation in which one employer shifts part of the cost of his private "guarantee" plan to other employers and in which one group of workers reaps extra benefits at the expense of other groups of workers. Worst of all, perhaps, is that the promises of security held out by such plans could prove illusory.

The fact that UC-GAW does not provide the answer to our problem should not deter individual companies from serious study of steps they can take to provide more job stabilization and income security. Rejecting panaceas does not mean doing nothing else. Recognizing that there are many unpredictable and uncontrollable economic factors influencing employment and business conditions, we have examined, briefly, courses taken by some companies that have made progress in dealing with the problem of personal security in their plants. These actions have resulted frequently not only in more security for workers but in more profitable business operations.

Here, then, is a key to the problem. Insofar as measures to provide job and income security are part of sound business practices, then both workers and management will profit.

THE FORD SUPPLEMENTAL UNEMPLOYMENT BENEFIT PLAN

A general description prepared by the Ford Motor Company, June, 1955

THE PLAN

Ford Motor Company's newly-established Supplemental Unemployment Benefit Plan was conceived by staff executives who have had long experience in the fields of finance, law and industrial relations.

Founded on the twin principles of limited liability and predictable maximum costs, the Plan is compatible with and complementary to the free and competitive economy of the United States.

PURPOSE OF THE PLAN

The purpose of the Plan is to supplement, by private means, the State Unemployment Compensation payments received by hourly-rated Ford men and women during layoffs. The Company believed that a decision to supplement state benefits would be particularly justified with respect to short-term layoffs, when the employe's opportunity to find other work is relatively limited.

Basically, the Plan is intended to assist eligible employes in weathering layoffs. Benefits paid under the Plan will not be so high, however, as to discourage a worker from seeking other employment, particularly when his layoff is of long duration.

The Company has always paid the full cost of State Unemployment Compensation benefits received by its employes when they are temporarily out of work through no fault of their own. By adding to these benefits, Ford is simply extending and enlarging upon a concept which has long been firmly established in the laws of the 48 States.

UNDERSTANDING THE PLAN

A knowledge of the mechanics of the Plan is essential to understanding the principles underlying it and the management philosophy which will govern its operation.

Under the carefully-drawn provisions of the Plan, an eligible employe could receive cash benefits ranging up to a maximum of $25 a week. Eventually, these payments could extend to a maximum of 26 weeks during any one layoff. The number of weeks for which benefits may be paid will depend on the amount of money available in the applicable Trust Fund and the employe's individual status under the Plan.

ELIGIBILITY

Employes will become eligible to participate in the Plan only when they have acquired one year of seniority. Benefit payments will be made only when an employe is laid off through no fault of his own, as in the case of a reduction in force, discontinuance of a plant or operation, or because of a temporary suspension or curtailment of work. However, for certain lay-offs—such as those caused by labor disputes involving Company employes or property, or by acts of God, enemy action or sabotage—no benefits will be paid.

SPECIAL AND REGULAR BENEFITS

Within the limitation of the $25 maximum, the benefits—when added to State Unemployment Compensation—could give an eligible employe an amount equal to 65% of his weekly after-tax Ford wages for each of the first four weeks of a layoff, after an annual "waiting week." These 65% benefits are called "Special Benefits." There is a maximum of four Special Benefit payments in a calendar year until the applicable Trust Fund is approximately one-half funded, after which the maximum becomes eight per year.

After the Special Benefits are exhausted, the amount of the weekly benefit would be reduced. An eligible laid-off employe would then begin receiving "Regular Benefits" which could last for a maximum of 22 additional weeks. Regular Benefits, when added to State Unemployment Compensation payments, could equal 60% of the worker's weekly after-tax Ford wages.

In determining all benefits, the weekly wage will be computed on straight-time earnings (highest base rate during the last 30 days the employe worked plus cost of living allowance) for a forty-hour week.

It should be emphasized that the Company did not determine the benefit levels it would agree to on the basis of what the available funds would support, but rather on the merits of the levels as such.

CONTRIBUTIONS TO TRUST FUNDS

Benefit payments will be made only from two Trust Funds established by Ford Motor Company. The General Fund will cover employes engaged in the regular production activities of the Company. The Defense Fund will cover those in defense work.

The establishment of a separate fund for defense work recognizes that the risks of a layoff in connection with such work are inherently different from those involved in the Company's regular commercial operations. Sufficient flexibility is retained by the Company to assure that such segregation need be made only when it is administratively feasible and when a significant number of employes is involved.

CONTRIBUTIONS SOLE LIABILITY

The Company's contributions to these Funds constitute its sole liability under the Plan. Ford's financial obligation under the Plan is fixed at and limited to the contribution of five cents for each hour for which covered employes receive pay. However, no contributions to a Trust Fund are to be made when it is fully funded. Contributions based on pay received by defense employes are to be made to the Defense Fund; all others go to the General Fund. These are not contributions in behalf of particular employes, but represent a reasonable and suitable measure of the Company's financial commitment which will vary with the level of its activities.

MAXIMUM FUNDING

A limitation, called the "Maximum Funding," also has been placed on the total amount of money to be built up in the Funds. Based on current employment levels—140,000 hourly-rated workers—the Maximum Funding of the two Funds was set at $55 million on June 1, 1955. Every month, a new Maximum Funding amount will be computed. It will vary upward or downward in proportion to increases or decreases in the number of hourly-rated employes.

The initial amount of the Maximum Funding was based on the conservative assumption of a $25 average weekly benefit amount, which is the maximum. This conservatism was justified on the basis that the actual average cannot be precisely predicted, and that any deviations in the early stages of the Plan should be in the direction of building up the Fund more rapidly. Beginning in 1958, the Maximum Funding figure will be varied in relation to experience as to the actual amount of the average weekly benefit paid.

Thus, the total sum toward which the Company will make its contributions will be affected (within the over-all cents per hour limit) by the number of people covered by the Plan and the amounts actually paid in benefits.

TRUST FUND POSITION

Each month a "Trust Fund Position" of the two Funds also will be computed. The Trust Fund Position will show the market value of assets held in a Fund as a percentage of the current Maximum Funding for that Fund.

When the Trust Fund Position of a Fund reaches 100%—that is, when the market value of the Fund's assets equals the established Maximum Funding figure—the Company's contributions to that Fund will cease. Further contributions, at the rate of five cents for each hour worked by hourly employes, will be made only as necessary to bring the Trust Fund Position to 100% or to maintain it at that level. Subject to certain termination provisions, the Company's overall obligation to make contributions extends for the length of the three-year collective bargaining agreement signed in June 1955 with the UAW-CIO.

To enable the Funds to build up in the initial stages of the Plan, no benefit payments will be made for the first year of operation, or until June 1, 1956.

CREDIT UNIT SYSTEM

Employes having the required seniority will become eligible to participate in benefits through a system of acquiring "Credit Units" for weeks actually worked. A Credit Unit has no fixed value in terms of either time or money. It is simply a medium for translating employe service into benefit eligibility and duration under the Plan.

From June 1, 1955, through May 31, 1957, employes with less than ten years' seniority will acquire one-quarter (.25) Credit Unit for each week in which they work at least 32 hours. During the same period, employes with ten or more years' seniority will acquire one-half (.5) Credit Unit for each week in which they work at least 32 hours.

Beginning June 1, 1957, all employes will acquire one-half (.5) Credit Unit for each week in which they work at least 32 hours.

Non-working hours for which an employe is paid—such as vacation time and holidays—will count as working hours for the purpose of acquiring Credit Units.

In the event of layoff, the employe will obtain benefit payments from the Trust Fund in return for Credit Units he has accumulated. The maximum number of Credit Units he can acquire is 26. The number of Credit Units he actually has at the time of layoff will depend, of course, upon his own employment experience prior to layoff, his seniority and the extent to which he may have used previously-accumulated Credit Units to obtain benefits during earlier layoffs.

BENEFIT DURATION VARIES

The duration of benefit payments—that is, the number of weekly benefits an employe may receive—depends on the Trust Fund Position at the time of layoff and the number of Credit Units the individual employe has acquired through weeks worked.

When the Plan was formulated, it became obvious that fixed amounts of benefits could not be paid for fixed maximum periods without subjecting either the Company or the Trust Funds to unknown liability.

It was determined, then, that this risk could be avoided if either the benefit amount or the benefit duration were variable. The Company found that if benefit duration were variable, rather than the benefit amount, the average employe would not be adversely affected during most layoffs. The course of variable duration was adopted, therefore, and was accomplished by relating the number of Credit Units required for one weekly benefit to the current Trust Fund Position.

When the Trust Fund Position is 85% or more, only one Credit Unit will be required in exchange for one week's benefit. When the Trust Fund Position is at lower levels—as it will be during the early stages of the Plan, and as may happen thereafter because of heavy layoff experience—the exchange rate for Credit Units is less favorable. For example, when the Trust Fund Position is between 13% and 21.99%, an employe with less than five years' seniority would have to surrender five Credit Units for one benefit.

High-seniority employes have an advantage over their fellow workers with lower seniority in the exchange of Credit Units for benefits from the Funds. If the Trust Fund Position is between 40% and 48.99%, for instance, a 25-year employe will be able to obtain one benefit for one Credit Unit, while an employe with less than five years' service would need two Credit Units to obtain one benefit.

The rate of exchange for all employes is the same only when the Trust Fund Position is 85% or more. When the Trust Fund Position falls below that level, the rate of exchange becomes increasingly favorable to higher-seniority employes compared with the lower seniority group. This arrangement is a safeguard against the possibility that the Funds might be depleted or exhausted by payments to lower seniority employes during the early stages of a layoff, with little or no benefits left for higher seniority workers who might be laid-off later.

The table [given on this page] shows how the number of Credit Units required to receive the weekly supplemental benefit will vary with changes in the Trust Fund Position. It also demonstrates how the interests of long-service employes are protected by a sliding conversion scale which operates in their favor.

MARGINS OF SAFETY

The concept of the Maximum Funding and Trust Fund Position was adopted primarily to provide a "margin of safety" for the protection of employes—particularly higher seniority employes—in the event of heavy layoffs, whether repeated or prolonged. The adequacy of the Trust Fund cannot be measured simply by calculating the effects a single heavy layoff would have upon it, since it cannot be assumed that additional layoffs would not follow within a relatively short time.

If the Trust Fund position applicable to the week for which such benefit is paid is:	And if the seniority of the person to whom such benefit is paid is:					
	1 to 5 years	5 to 10 years	10 to 15 years	15 to 20 years	20 to 25 years	25 years and over
	The credit units canceled for such benefit shall be:					
85% or over.........	1.00	1.00	1.00	1.00	1.00	1.00
76—84.99%.........	1.11	1.00	1.00	1.00	1.00	1.00
67—75.99%.........	1.25	1.11	1.00	1.00	1.00	1.00
58—66.99%.........	1.43	1.25	1.11	1.00	1.00	1.00
49—57.99%.........	1.67	1.43	1.25	1.11	1.00	1.00
40—48.99%.........	2.00	1.67	1.43	1.25	1.11	1.00
31—39.99%.........	2.50	2.00	1.67	1.43	1.25	1.11
22—30.99%.........	3.33	2.50	2.00	1.67	1.43	1.25
13—21.99%.........	5.00	3.33	2.50	2.00	1.67	1.43
4—12.99%.........	10.00	5.00	3.33	2.50	2.00	1.67
Under 4%.	_____No benefit payable_____					

The effect of relating duration of benefits (through the device of varying Credit Unit cancellation rates) to the relative size of the Fund is to preserve comparable "Margins of Safety" and relative equities as among various seniority groups of employes at all levels of the Fund. For example, if the Fund is just below the half-way mark, the Plan in effect is a 13-week plan for the low seniority employe, assuming moderate layoffs, rather than a 26-week plan. The relative chances of such employes to enjoy the full 13 weeks' protection are comparable to their relative chances to enjoy 26 weeks' protection if the Plan is fully funded. The lower the relative size of the Fund, the more protection is weighted in favor of the higher seniority groups.

Thus, the Plan automatically accommodates itself to any reasonable level of contributions which may be agreed upon, as well as to the volume of layoffs actually experienced.

APPLY FOR BENEFITS WEEKLY

Specific application for benefits will have to be made by eligible employes each week. Benefits will become payable after one waiting week per year, in accordance with normal State Unemployment Compensation practices.

The cash amount of a weekly benefit will not normally be affected by the Trust Fund Position. However, should the Trust Fund Position fall below 13%, there would be a 20% reduction in all benefits paid, except that such reduction would not bring a benefit below $5 and would not apply to benefits already below $5. Should the Trust Fund Position fall below 4%, no benefits would be paid until the market value of the assets held by the applicable Fund had risen above 4% of the Maximum Funding.

The maximum benefit to be paid under the Plan will be $25. If the employe would be eligible for a benefit of less than $2, no benefit will be paid. The actual amount of the Supplemental Unemployment Benefit an employe receives will depend on the amount of his State Unemployment Compensation payment, his after-tax earnings, and whether he is receiving Special Benefits or Regular Benefits.

Take the case of a Detroit area employe with a wife and one child. Assume this employe currently is earning $100 weekly straight-time pay before taxes and $87.02 after taxes. He would be eligible under the 1955 bill amending the Michigan act for a State Unemployment Compensation benefit of $42 a week. Assuming, for example, no prior layoffs in that calendar year, an eligible employe would receive in the first four weeks of a layoff (subject to the waiting week provisions) an additional $14.56 under the Ford Supplemental Unemployment Benefit Plan, making his total income $56.56 a week or 65% of his take-home pay.

After the first four weeks of such a layoff, he would receive a Regular Benefit of $10.21 a week, bringing his total income to $52.21 or 60% of his take-home pay.

STATE PAYMENTS VARY

Unemployment Compensation benefits vary in the different states. By comparison with the Michigan employe, take the case of a Buffalo, N. Y., Ford employe with a wife and one child. Assume he is earning, like his fellow worker in Detroit, $100 weekly before taxes and $87.02 after taxes. He is eligible under New York laws for Unemployment Compensation of $36 a week. During the first four weeks of such a layoff, after the waiting week, he would receive an additional $20.56 under the Plan, making his total income $56.56 a week.

After the first four weeks of such a layoff, the Buffalo employe would receive a Regular Benefit of $16.21 a week, bringing his total income to $52.21.

Both cases assume the employe has sufficient credits to receive benefits.

In some cases, an employe can work part of a week and still receive benefits. The agreement provides that if an employe is afforded so few hours of work in a week that, even after working them, he still is eligible under his state's laws to receive Unemployment Compensation, then he also may draw benefits from the Fund.

The amount he can receive from the Fund will be the difference between the 65% or 60% maximum, whichever then is applicable to him, and the total of his Unemployment Compensation benefits plus any pay he received from the Company that week for time worked.

Take again the case of a $100-a-week Ford employe in the Detroit area whose usual weekly take-home pay is $87.02 and who would be eligible under the 1955 bill amending the Michigan act for an Unemployment Compensation benefit of $42 a week.

Under Michigan law, a worker who earns in a week less than half the state benefit to which he is entitled, may draw the full state benefit. Therefore, if the Detroit-area employe worked, say, four hours in one week, he could collect his full $42 state benefit in addition to the $10 (four hours at $2.50 an hour) he received from the Company in wages.

He then could apply to the Fund for a benefit representing the difference between $52 ($42 Unemployment Compensation plus $10 earnings) and $56.56 (65% of his take-home pay of $87.02). The supplemental benefit would be $4.56.

STATE INTEGRATION ESSENTIAL

Integration with State Unemployment Compensation systems is an essential condition to the effectiveness of the Ford Supplemental Unemployment Benefit Plan. Before the benefit payments can start, rulings must be obtained in states in which the Company has two-thirds of its hourly working force that simultaneous payment of a Plan benefit shall not reduce or eliminate the State Unemployment Compensation benefit for the same week.

If favorable rulings are not obtained by June 1, 1956, commencement of benefit payments will be delayed beyond that date.

Ford has 56% of its hourly-rated employes in Michigan, 11% in Ohio, and substantial employment in Illinois, New York, Missouri, California and New Jersey.

If appropriate rulings are not obtained from the home states of two-thirds of the employes before June 1, 1957, the Plan will be terminated as of that date.

If the Plan terminates prior to June 1, 1958, Company contributions to the Funds will cease and assets left in the Funds will be used for administration expenses and for payments to eligible employes in the form of benefits until the Funds are exhausted. In the meantime, steps will be taken to negotiate with the union on disposition of the five cents an hour which the Company will no longer pay into the Funds. If no agreement on disposition is reached during 60 days of such negotiations, the Company automatically will grant a five-cents-an-hour general wage increase to all hourly employes represented by the UAW-CIO.

Except in a few cases when state benefits run out before Company benefits, a benefit payment under the Plan will be made only upon proof that a state benefit has been paid for the same week, thus simplifying administration and avoiding duplication or review of state determinations as to eligibility and qualification.

The Plan also provides for discontinuance in any state when specified criteria indicate that the state program is doing a substantially equivalent job. Specifically, it provides for discontinuance of the Plan—on or after June 1, 1958—in states where fewer than 25% of employes with sufficient Credit Units for full benefits would be entitled to Special Benefits of $2 or more if they were laid off. Payment of Regular Benefits would also be discontinued in states where fewer than such number of employes would be entitled to Regular Benefits of $2. However, the Plan could become operative again in such states if an annual review showed that the cause for discontinuance no longer existed.

NON-INTEGRATED STATES

In the event the necessary rulings are obtained in the home states of two-thirds of the Company's employes, but similar rulings are not forthcoming in one or more of the remaining states, a special set of conditions governing payments from the Plan will take effect for the benefit of Ford employes in such non-integrated states, starting June 1, 1957.

Instead of Regular Benefits or Special Benefits, "Substitute Supplemental Benefits" will become payable to eligible employes in the non-integrated states. After an eligible employe who has been laid off receives State Unemployment Compensation benefits for two weeks after the waiting week, he may apply for a Substitute Supplemental Benefit under the Plan. To do this, of course, he would be obliged to forego the state benefit in that week.

The Substitute Supplemental Benefit, under these conditions, would be an amount equal to the Regular or Special Supplemental Benefit to which he would have been entitled for that week if supplementation were permitted, multiplied by three. The number of Credit Units to be canceled upon payment of a Substitute Supplemental Benefit for any week will be the number of Credit Units that would have been required to receive a Regular or Special benefit for the week in question, multiplied by three. If he so chooses, the employe may elect to take a benefit of four times his weekly benefit amount every four weeks, instead of the three week rotation.

ESTABLISHMENT OF TRUSTS

Both the General Fund and the Defense Fund will be established with banks or trust companies selected by and under agreements with the Company. The Company's contributions will be made directly to the Funds and will be held by the Trustees in cash or invested in obligations of the United States Government.

Expenses incurred in the administration of the Plan are chargeable against the funds.

BOARD OF ADMINISTRATION

Although the Company retains complete control over the selection of the Trustees for the Funds and the Union will have no voice in the investment of the Company's contributions, a Board of Administration will be formed consisting of three Company members, three Union members and an impartial chairman.

The Board by majority vote will render final decisions on appeals made by benefit claimants, authorizing benefit payments where appeals are granted, and will perform certain other duties of an administrative nature. It will not, however, have any power to decide questions which properly should be decided by State Unemployment Compensation agencies, or to review any determination made under State Unemployment Compensation laws. It will not have any separate staff or facilities of its own. . . .

AN ANALYSIS OF THE FORD-TYPE PLAN FOR SUPPLEMENTAL UNEMPLOYMENT COMPENSATION

Excerpts from a pamphlet published by the National Association of Manufacturers, 1955

THE IMPACT OF THE PLAN ON EMPLOYEES

From the standpoint of the individual employee, the outstanding fact under the Plan is that 5¢ per hour, which otherwise would be going into his pay envelope, is being paid instead into a pooled fund set up by private agreement between his employer and his union leaders. In order to benefit from this fund, he must be laid off.

Looked at superficially, this seems to be in the nature of insurance against unemployment, but the logic on which the usual insurance arrangement is based is lacking. Insurance is predicated on the theory that the last thing a policy-holder wishes to do is collect. A man must lose his life for his heirs to benefit from his life insurance. He will not normally court injury in an accident in order to collect accident insurance, nor develop a serious illness because he has hospitalization insurance. If he burns his house down for the sake of putting in a claim under a fire insurance policy, he goes to jail.

But, if he is insured against unemployment to the extent he suffers little or no loss of income, the more often he is laid off and the longer the layoffs last, the better off he is. It is not logical for people to work when they can have the same or nearly the same income by not working.

Furthermore, insurance is based on the payment of premiums proportionate to risk. The only circumstances under which the same flat premium is paid by everyone is where the risk is presumed to be the same for everyone. According to a survey by Opinion Research Corporation taken early in 1955, only 44% of manufacturing employees have ever collected state unemployment benefits. On the basis of this finding, 56% of the employees covered by the Ford-GM Plan may never be in a position to collect, yet the cost to them is the same as for the minority who are most likely to benefit.

Thus, the Plan is more like a social program than an insurance arrangement. It favors the short-term or occasional worker at the expense of the long-service employee, whose chance of being laid off usually is remote.

Furthermore, the man with family responsibilities is discriminated against in the amount of benefits he may draw in comparison with the single man. Also the employee who lives in a state where unemployment compensation benefits are high can draw only a minor percentage of the benefits permitted to a person who lives in a state with low unemployment compensation payments.

INEQUITIES IN THE AMOUNT OF BENEFITS

A table prepared by Unemployment Benefits Advisors, Inc., of Washington, D. C. (Reproduced below), shows some interesting comparisons. A man with an average size family (wife and two children) living in Michigan, where the majority of the Ford-GM employees are located, would draw $7.76 in Special Benefits for the first four weeks under the Plan and $3.94 in Regular Benefits for the next 22 weeks, assuming of course he had the necessary credit units and the fund position was high enough to permit full benefits.

On the other hand, a single man with no dependents would draw $15.20 in Special Benefits for the first four weeks and $11.72 in Regular Benefits for the next 22 weeks. If both are laid off for the full 26 weeks and are able to draw full benefits, the single man has a total potential of $318.64 while the family man can draw only a total of $117.72, or slightly more than one-third as much. A Michigan man with a wife and only one child does not fare even this well. His total potential benefits for the full 26 weeks amount to $80.62.

The extent to which Michigan employees with family responsibilities are subsidizing the income security of single men is even more marked when comparisons are made with other states. In Illinois the single man has a total potential benefit from the Fund of $370.64; in Missouri it goes up to $448.64; and in Texas it rises to $584.40.

These figures are based on an hourly rate of $2.10 for 40 hours, or a base wage of $84 a week. For highly skilled workers drawing more than $2.10 an hour, the payments would be greater in all these cases but the comparative differences would remain, short of the point where all employees were receiving the $25 maximum the Plan provides.

How long the union members themselves will permit such inequities is one of the unanswered questions surrounding the Plan. Most industrial employees are pretty effective with a pencil and paper when it comes to figuring out their own financial interests. The fact will not long escape them that $104 per year is going into the fund for each man and that before long $400 per individual will be piled up which he otherwise could have had to buy a new refrigerator, or TV set, or pay off some debts.

In view of the above it is probable the union is a long way from being out of the woods in winning enthusiastic support for the Plan among the rank-and-file members. Although the Plan was ratified when put to a vote, it is significant

State and Supplemental Unemployment Compensation Payments to Claimant with $84 Basic Weekly Wage Rate [1] under New Ford-GM Plans, in Illinois, Missouri, & Michigan

State and family class	Take-home pay	State U. C. 24-26 wks.	Ford-GM Plan		Total—Ford-GM plan plus state U. C.	
			First 4 wks.	5th to 26th wk.	First 4 wks.	5th to 26th wk.
(1)	(2)	(3)	(4)	(5)	(6)	(7)
Illinois						
Single.....................	$69.54	$28.00	$17.20	$13.72	$45.20	$41.72
Wife or 1 child...........	71.88	31.00	15.72	12.13	46.72	43.13
Wife and 1 child.........	74.22	31.00	17.24	13.53	48.24	44.53
Wife and 2 children......	76.56	34.00	15.76	11.94	49.76	45.94
Wife and 3 children......	78.90	37.00	14.29	10.34	51.29	47.34
Wife and 4 children......	81.24	40.00	12.81	8.74	52.81	48.74
Missouri						
Single.....................	$69.54	$25.00	$20.20	$16.72	$45.20	$41.72
Wife or 1 child...........	71.88	25.00	21.72	18.13	46.72	43.13
Wife and 1 child.........	74.22	25.00	23.24	19.53	48.24	44.53
Wife and 2 children......	76.56	25.00	24.76	20.94	49.76	45.94
Wife and 3 children......	78.90	25.00	25.00	22.34	50.00	47.34
Wife and 4 children......	81.24	25.00	25.00	23.74	50.00	48.74
Michigan						
Single.....................	$69.54	$30.00	$15.20	$11.72	$45.20	$41.72
Wife only..............	71.88	33.00	13.72	10.13	46.72	43.13
1 child only............	71.88	37.00	9.72	6.13	46.72	43.13
Wife and 1 child.........	74.22	42.00	6.24	2.53	48.24	44.53
Wife and 2 children......	76.56	42.00	7.76	3.94	49.76	45.94
Wife and 3 children......	78.90	43.00	8.29	4.34	51.29	47.34
Wife and 4 children......	81.24	43.00	9.81	5.74	52.81	48.74

[1] The basic weekly wage of $84 corresponds to an average hourly rate of $2.10 for 40 hours.

that one-third of the membership of the largest Ford local—Local 600 at the Rouge Plant—voted against acceptance of the Plan and the contract.

EFFECT OF THE PLAN ON THE INCENTIVE TO WORK

While it is argued there still remains reasonable financial incentive for a laid-off employee to seek work rather than draw state payments and plan benefits, it hardly can be denied that this incentive is not as effective as it would be without the Plan.

Those most likely to receive benefits from the Plan are the very employees who most need a financial incentive to induce them to work regularly—those with less family responsibilities, and those who make a practice of working only long enough to establish eligibility for unemployment benefits.

The impact of relatively high payments for idleness on the morale of those employees who are not laid off but have to work just as hard as ever for their money cannot be dismissed lightly. Many of these also probably would enjoy a vacation, even at 65% or 60% of take-home pay. It may be that some of the longer service employees will demand that their seniority be effective in reverse and that they be the ones to enjoy a layoff while the newcomers to the payroll are kept working.

EFFECT ON WILLINGNESS TO SEEK PART TIME OR NEW EMPLOYMENT

The effect of the Plan on the willingness of a laid off employee to make gainful use of his time or to find a new job quickly is best illustrated by setting up a hypothetical case.

Employee A, living in a state which provides a maximum of $30 a week unemployment compensation, is laid off. He goes to the employment office of his state system and collects his $30 and then goes to his private employer and gets a supplemental payment which brings the total up to 65%, and after four weeks 60%, of his former take-home pay. For this he does no work whatever.

Employee B, laid off from the same company, has an opportunity to pick up two days work at odd jobs for which he earns $30. But by choosing to work he is worse off than Employee A. The $30 he earns rules him out as far as the state payment is concerned and makes him ineligible for the supplemental payment from his company. His total weekly income is $30 for working while Employee A receives $50 or more for doing nothing.

Let us assume both have been permanently laid off due to a reduction in force at their company. The eagerness with which they read want ad columns and haunt employment offices will be affected by the fact they are assured of 65% of take-home pay for four weeks and 60% for an additional 22 weeks.

A man having family responsibilities cannot meet his needs very well on this curtailed income and will be under strong compulsion to get back to work quickly. But the person without family responsibilities may find 60% of his former pay adequate for his needs and therefore may be in no rush to resume gainful employment. Thus the stable citizen with his roots in the community is discriminated against in favor of the footloose and carefree roamer or drifter.

THE IMPACT ON STATE UNEMPLOYMENT COMPENSATION SYSTEMS

Public policy in the area of unemployment compensation, as developed in Federal law and in the laws of the various states, is based on the following principles:

1. Authentic members of the active labor force whose employment is interrupted through no fault of their own and who are available for other jobs should be eligible for cash benefits;

2. This eligibility should not be extended to casual or intermittent workers who for personal or other reasons occasionally seek jobs for short periods;

3. The amount of benefits paid to eligible people should be sufficiently below the going wage in an area so that it will be more profitable to work than to draw benefits;

4. The duration of benefits should be limited as the system is intended to cover only short-term unemployment and not to encourage waiting around indefinitely to be called back to jobs which may no longer exist;

5. Efforts on the part of employers to provide steady work should be encouraged by making the benefits a charge on production, paid by employers in the form of a payroll tax.

In addition to the above, the legislatures of all states have followed the principle that the amount of tax an employer is required to pay should be related to the degree to which his employees or former employees draw upon the state's unemployment compensation funds. If he lays few people off his tax payments can be reduced, or be eliminated altogether in some states once he has built up a reserve in his state account equal to a certain percentage of his payroll.

This is called experience rating. It stimulates efforts to stabilize employment and avoids the unfairness of making one employer pay for another's job fluctuations.

One other principle has been adopted by some states. This is a recognition of the need for a higher floor of protection for people according to the number of dependents they have. Michigan and Illinois have adopted special benefit schedules under which maximum benefits depend upon both the earnings of the applicant and the size of his family. These schedules are designed to relate benefits more closely to take-home pay after taxes.

In most states the maximum tax rate in the law is 2.7% of payroll, but employers with favorable experience pay lower rates. Many of the laws provide for an upward shifting of these lower schedules whenever the amount of money in the state unemployment reserve fund is depleted.

This is the basic structure and public policy of the state unemployment compensation system. Being a state system, it is readily adaptable to local conditions and needs and is constantly being revised state by state to meet changing circumstances. Such changes are carefully considered and exhaustively debated before being written into law, with all elements of the economy and the population within the state being given an opportunity to offer their views.

NULLIFYING STATE LAWS BY PRIVATE AGREEMENTS

An aspect of private plans for supplemental unemployment benefits which concerns all employers, and indeed all the people of a state, is the extent to which a plan of this nature nullifies public policy. The contracting parties to such a plan say, in effect, that the level and duration of benefits fixed by state legislatures are wrong and may be raised or extended as private interests may determine, thus taking into their own hands the law-making power which is a fundamental right of the whole people.

Were these private interests the only ones affected, financial or otherwise, by such an arrangement, it would be a matter of concern only to themselves. It is obvious, however, that supplemental benefits tied in with the state system could not be confined for long to certain groups of workers. A demand for equality of treatment for all people is sure to arise and either force similar supplemental plans on employers who may not be able to afford them or whose businesses may not be suited to them, or cause states to raise their benefits to a level where all employees fare alike. An example of how the Ford-GM Plan would operate in three important industrial states to change the intent and purpose of the legislatures as to benefit levels for various family classes is shown by the [preceding] table prepared by Unemployment Benefits Advisors, Inc. . . .

THE COMPARISON WITH SUPPLEMENTATION IN THE FIELD OF OASI

In its original argument for the guaranteed annual wage, the union stressed that the theory of private supplementation was not new but had been thoroughly tested in relation to old-age and survivors insurance. Privately financed pensions were negotiated in this area to bring total payments to people retiring on social security up to a bargained level. The union contended that private supplementation had worked with pensions and there was no reason to doubt its soundness in the field of unemployment compensation.

There is a basic fallacy in this argument which needs to be understood. An OASI beneficiary has departed from the labor market. His working days are over and he is considered in retired status. No matter what benefits his employer chooses to provide in addition to his social security pension, he will not become 65 a day earlier. The private benefit can be put at whatever level the competitive situation of the company can stand and still be of no consequence to other employers or to the public, outside of increasing the pressure for more pensions generally.

It is different with unemployment compensation. Private payments, either supplementing or extending state benefits, have an immediate effect on the individual's willingness to remain at work or to seek new work if laid off. The higher the total benefit or the longer the duration the more the incentive to work is undermined.

If supplementation became general, it might have a serious influence on the availability of labor. The nation might witness the economically ridiculous spectacle of jobs going begging while people who are being supported in idleness by unemployment benefits contrive in every way possible to avoid taking them.

THE IMPACT ON THE NATIONAL ECONOMY

THE IMPLICATIONS FOR THE FUTURE

The situation which is developing presents grave and perhaps insurmountable obstacles to the functioning of a free economy. Progress in our society is the result of enterprise—such as starting new businesses and expanding old ones. The financial burden of guaranteeing the wages of virtually all employees will reduce the eagerness of individuals to enter business or invest in enterprise and will undermine the drive of established companies to grow. Few people will be willing to risk their savings in new ventures if it means guaranteeing wages to employees, even when not working.

Furthermore, the personal incentives which have led employees to seek jobs which will utilize their highest skills and yield the greatest return in money and personal satisfaction will be further impaired. Guaranteed pay will become another factor tending to freeze people to their present jobs and their present employers. Rather than give up seniority and guaranteed pay to seek new opportunities or strike out for themselves, they will be inclined to stay where they are. They will have less urge to drive ahead—to shift from dead or dying lines to up-and-coming industries where opportunities would be greater. Ambitious newcomers will find their way upward blocked by people sitting in all the choice spots, their position frozen and supported by guarantees.

THE ECONOMIC ERROR WHICH UNDERLIES DEMANDS FOR WAGE GUARANTEES

Guaranteed wage demands are based on the theory that employment is man's natural state and that when unemployment occurs employers should be held responsible. Actually, people cannot be employed until someone takes positive action which results in the creation of jobs.

Simple logic would indicate, therefore, that it would be more constructive to foster and encourage conditions which lead to employment than to discourage job creation by schemes to saddle on employers the burden of guaranteeing wages when there is no work to be performed.

The acid test of supplemental unemployment compensation, and its further extension to the full guaranteed annual wage, is whether it will stimulate or discourage job making. In this regard the union claims that guaranteed wages will promote and sustain a high level of economic activity and thereby create jobs because people whose incomes are assured will spend more freely and continue to spend even when laid off. This argument ignores the fact that before people can spend at all or be in a position to collect guaranteed wages when laid off, they first must acquire jobs. It falls of its own weight if, because of wage guarantees, the job creating process is blocked.

THE EFFECT OF WAGE GUARANTEES ON JOB CREATION

Inasmuch as the process of job creation in a free, competitive economy depends on the willingness of individuals to risk their own capital or that of others, it follows that the more burdensome this risk becomes, the fewer jobs will be created.

The obstacles to the formation of new enterprises or the expansion of existing ones, even aside from the hazards of the competitive market, already are quite formidable. The high cost of government at all levels, and the excessive tax rates which are the result, make difficult the accumulation of capital by individuals. The incentive to risk hard-won capital in new enterprises or in expansion is already considerably diluted by the high premium the tax system exacts from earnings if the business is successful. So, with capital hard to come by and the rewards to be gained by risking it subject to tax rates which are discouragingly progressive, the creation of the new jobs which a growing population needs already is a problem.

Aggravating this problem by requiring employers to guarantee wages may have serious consequences by creating a steadily deepening job famine.

As far as existing enterprises go, simple logic indicates that wage guarantees will compel employers to keep a strict rein on new hiring. The inclination will be to get along with as few employees as possible, even when demand is on the rise, and not to take on new people until events prove a higher level of steady employment can be sustained. As a result, production always will lag several notches behind what it should be. The available quantity of goods and services and the standard of living will be proportionately lower.

THE EFFECT ON COSTS OF PRODUCTION AND PRICES

Wage guarantees will cost money and the consumer probably will pay the bill. Some companies may seek to avoid raising prices through greater productive efficiency, but productivity increases already are pretty well discounted in advance by annual wage increases and/or the annual improvement factor in union contracts. In an effort to overcome these handicaps, there may be efforts to develop and install more automatic machinery but, even so, the consumer will be paying because he will not benefit from reductions in price which otherwise would have been possible.

In the final analysis, the only way in which a portion of the population can be supported in idleness by wage guarantees is for those who are working and producing to forego, through paying prices higher than they otherwise would have to pay, a part of the standard of living they otherwise could enjoy.

THE EFFECT ON THE PRESENT PATTERN OF MANUFACTURING

In the American industrial economy, hardly a manufacturing company of reasonable size exists which does not buy from outside sources some things it could make itself if necessary. In fact, most small manufacturers exist as suppliers or sub-contractors to larger companies. Many of the latter find it more efficient to buy parts of sub-assemblies from outside than to fabricate everything in their own plants. Some of the giants of American industry do business with as many as ten to fifteen thousand small suppliers, who depend on this work for their very existence. Many of these are located in small towns and supply most of the jobs available to local people.

Wide application of wage guarantees could have the effect of seriously dislocating this pattern with distressing effect on small communities. If large companies are required to pay their employees even when there is no work for them to do, the tendency will be, whenever a pinch comes, for these companies to take into their own plants work now being done by outside suppliers. Thus, fluctuations in employment would be shifted to small employers who can least afford to pay wage guarantees and have the least flexibility in seeking other markets for their output. Many would be put out of business.

As an alternative, large companies dealing with small suppliers could force the burden of expansion on the latter whenever demand justified by farming out the manufacture of more components instead of increasing their own employment rolls. Then if a contraction in output became necessary, these smaller employers would be obligated to pay the guaranteed wages.

THE EFFECT ON BANKING AND FINANCE

The immediate effect of guaranteed wage plans is to begin piling up money in trust funds. As such plans spread, the amount of money tied up in these funds will become enormous. To the extent this money can be invested only in government bonds, as under the Ford-GM Plans, such capital becomes sterile and cannot be used by industry to finance economic activity or growth. Large sums which otherwise could be available to industry for research, the development of new products, the building of factories or the purchase of machinery, will be drained away. Already immense sums are tied up in pension and welfare funds, and these grow larger every day. The more money put aside in this fashion, the greater the danger of a venture capital famine as well as of a job famine.

Furthermore, much business activity is financed through borrowing from banks or insurance companies or through the underwriting of securities by investment bankers. The terms upon which such financing is obtainable and the readiness of institutions and bankers to invest are vitally affected by the obligations and financial commitments of the enterprise seeking to borrow.

In many cases, particularly involving small business, an otherwise attractive bank loan may be rendered unsound in the opinion of the lending institution by the existence of an obligation to pay wage guarantees. A borrowing concern which signs a contract involving such a guarantee may expect to have its financial status reviewed and perhaps the terms under which the loan was made may be modified.

THE EFFECT ON LABOR MOBILITY

Under the Ford-GM Plans, an employee who quits to take a better job loses all credit units and all possibility of receiving any benefits under the Plan. Thus, he is to some extent a captive of his present job. The closer such a plan comes to a full guaranteed annual wage, the more an employee will be inclined to stay where he is rather than move on to a better opportunity.

In a free, competitive economy it is important that industrial activity respond readily to changes in public demand. We progress by moving ahead, by continually creating something newer or better to satisfy the needs and tastes of the public. This process is slowed down and the national economy and standard of living suffer when employees are reluctant to shift from outmoded industries or declining companies to newer, more dynamic, more progressive outfits. The readiness to change, to shift, to move into newer and higher ground has been a fundamental aspect of our industrial development and the rise of our standard of living to its present point.

THE REAL ROAD TO JOB AND INCOME SECURITY

In pointing out the dangers of such devices as supplementary unemployment compensation and the guaranteed annual wage, American industry does not deny or dispute the need of industrial workers for steady jobs and steady pay. Every employer strives to create the greatest possible demand for his product and thus more jobs. It is good business for him to keep his employees at work steadily, all year round.

For more than fifteen years, the National Association of Manufacturers has pioneered in urging employers to take all possible steps to stabilize jobs throughout the year and in spreading concrete information as to techniques which have proved successful in overcoming fluctuations in employment due to seasonal demand and other factors.

Recently, the Association published a new booklet, entitled "Toward Steadier Work and Pay," which brings up to date the experience in this field. This booklet has been widely distributed to employers and is available to anyone interested in the problems of providing steady employment.

Job and income security in a free society can be achieved only by adhering to sound economic principles and practices. True security cannot be negotiated over the bargaining table nor created by a signature on a contract.

Peoples in other lands, who have been led to endure socialism or communism under promises of job or income security, have found the price of such security to be longer hours, harder work, lower wages and living standards and, above all, loss of freedom.

The only true road to the security we all seek is the broad highway of dynamic economic growth. The future it leads to is one of unlimited opportunities, more and better jobs, greater abundance and higher living standards.

This road may not always be smooth, to be sure, because human beings are not infallible and the best laid plans sometimes go awry. But the greatest mistake we could make would be to sacrifice progress on the altar of security —to forego any part of the magnificent future which lies before us by trying to guarantee ourselves what we have now.

FACING THE GUARANTEED ANNUAL WAGE

An editorial from Business Week of June 18, 1955, p. 200

Now that agreement has been reached in Detroit, the guaranteed annual wage has lost, at the very least, that fearsomeness it had because no one knew what form it would take or how expensive it would be. But the impact of this new phenomenon remains highly speculative.

The United Auto Workers did not get a guaranteed annual wage. Instead, it got a program that will provide workers with unemployment benefits in addition to those provided by the states. This falls far short of a full-fledged GAW. But whatever it is called and however limited, it is a form of wage guarantee.

IN THE PATTERN

As such, it is a further step in that evolutionary development—basic in America—that has provided greater security and stability within a dynamic enterprise economy. It is in the pattern established when industry set up its own pension funds to supplement federal social security. As the Detroit plan spreads, it is bound to accelerate changes, economic and social, that are already under way.

Over the past decade, the once sharp distinctions that set off the factory worker from the white collar worker have gradually faded. Differences in living standards have been erased. With employment high and wages rising, hourly workers have had what amount to assured incomes. Factory workers have, in fact, become part of the middle-class consumer market.

Accordingly, they have assumed heavy financial obligations, just like that portion of the population that receives regular salaries. And when workers took on mortgages and consumer credit obligations, it was inevitable that they should seek first to raise, and then to regularize their incomes.

A POWERFUL PROP

Although the insuring of workers' incomes cannot by itself produce permanent prosperity, it should be another substantial stabilizing factor in our economy. If a general business decline occurs, it will serve as a powerful prop. It might not prove effective in countering a major depression, but the other so-called economic stabilizers are not guaranteed to work, either.

The negotiators in Detroit were not thinking in depression terms. The negotiations were possible only because the industry has enjoyed a consistently high level of employment. And it was the vigorous competition between General Motors and Ford that led to agreement without strikes.

By any reckoning, the settlement is expensive. But it is not an incalculable price. Ford's John Bugas flatly stated that "this plan has a definitely predictable cost." He did not underestimate the problems it posed, but he expressed confidence that Ford, at least, will be able to live with it while maintaining prosperous growth. GM, too, feels the same way.

Many businessmen take a different view. They feel that though the increase in stability is desirable, it will cripple the dynamism of industry (BW—Jun.11'55,p29). They claim that businessmen who are confronted with increased costs brought by the need to set up insurance funds may become standpat and conservative, fearful of enlarging their labor force, unwilling to expand.

Some companies may adopt this approach, but experience shows that the most successful companies have been able to accommodate themselves to higher costs. Higher wage costs, in particular, have generally led to regularizing production and more mechanization. This has not meant any over-all rise in unemployment. On the contrary, the demand for labor has increased along with the increase in productivity.

INCENTIVE TO EXPANSION

If the past is any guide, then, the introduction of private insurance, with its increase in labor costs, should be an incentive to greater production and expansion. Certainly it is true in the case of Ford, which this week announced it was going ahead with plans to build a new engine plant in Lima, Ohio.

This project is only the first of a series that will be carried out in Ford's long term expansion program.

The costs of insuring workers may prove a heavy burden, especially to inefficient companies. But this is inherent in our free competitive system, where inefficiency is synonymous with red ink. Increased costs have always been an acid test of management efficiency. Those firms that face failure because of their inefficiency cannot place all the blame on the costs of such things as insurance funds. These will expose the weakness of an already weak firm and accelerate its decline, but they will not be the basic cause of failure.

TEST FOR MANAGEMENT

Business will have to face up to the fact that what has been established in Detroit will become a pattern in the fabric of our economy. Whether it comes in the UAW form or through improving the unemployment compensation system, it will cost money.

Nevertheless, increasing workers' security is a challenge that industry must meet. Its great record for achieving rising productivity and output, is once more put to the test. Prosperity—and profits—depend on management's ability to maintain stability as it expands. This will require all the dynamic qualities that American industry can command.

THE PITTSBURGH PLATE GLASS COMPANY SECURITY BENEFIT PLAN

By Donald J. Sherbondy, Director of Industrial Relations, Pittsburgh Plate Glass Company, from an article in American Economic Security, published by the United States Chamber of Commerce, December, 1955

On September 3, 1955, the Pittsburgh Plate Glass Company and the Libbey-Owens-Ford Glass Company signed a contract with the United Glass and Ceramic Workers of North America, CIO-CCL, providing for the establishment by each company of a so-called "Security Benefit Plan" for employees represented by the Union. A few salient facts with respect to the background out of which this plan originated may contribute to a better understanding of the purpose of the plan and the method for effectuating that purpose.

The bargaining unit of the Pittsburgh Plate Glass Company which is covered by the plan is composed of approximately 11,000 production and maintenance employees in eight plants at which flat glass is produced and fabricated. The similar bargaining unit of the Libbey-Owens-Ford Glass Company is of approximately the same size. Thus the two companies have a total of about 22,000 glass employees under the Security Benefit Plan.

For eighteen years the Pittsburgh Plate Glass Company and the Libbey-Owens-Ford Glass Company have bargained jointly with this Union. The two companies sign practically identical labor contracts.

In May 1954, the parties negotiated one-year labor contracts expiring on May 15, 1955. In those negotiations the Union requested a discussion of the guaranteed annual wage, but nothing of any significance developed with respect to the issue at that time. Late in 1954, however, the companies were advised that the Union intended to get a guaranteed annual wage agreement from the companies in the May 1955 negotiations.

Early in 1955, national representatives of the Union began holding mass meetings of their members at the various plant locations of the two companies to explain the plan already proposed in outline form by the United Automobile Workers and called by that Union the "guaranteed employment plan." The UAW proposal requested weekly guarantee payments in amounts sufficient to enable a laid-off employee to maintain the same living standards as when fully employed, and also provided for a 40-hour guaranteed work week.

The companies were strongly opposed to such a proposal. The immediate question was how to make that position and the reasons for it clear to the employees. During the period of the Union mass meetings on the subject, the Pittsburgh Plate Glass Company was receiving inquiries from foremen and other supervisory personnel in its glass plants for information with respect to the "guaranteed employment plan" and the position of the company on the issue. Rather than communicate directly with the hourly employees on the subject, the company decided to explain its position to all management personnel in the glass plants.

The company had established more than a year earlier an extensive supervisory training program in its glass plants under which each supervisor has at least an hour a week in conference training groups of about fifteen or twenty persons. A brief written statement of the company's views on the "guaranteed employment plan" was distributed and fully discussed in these conference training groups. The memorandum to management personnel pointed out that the "guaranteed employment plan" could not be effective in compelling the stabilization of employment as contended by the UAW. The company simply did not have the power to further stabilize production, and thus also to stabilize employment, as had been done by a few other companies such as Procter and Gamble in soap, Nunn-Bush in shoes, and Hormel in meat packing. The flat glass industry is a service industry, engaged primarily in manufacturing glass for customers in the automobile, construction and furniture industries. We have no control over any of these activities—no power to change the demand for automobiles, houses or furniture. We have no significant power to produce for inventory for later use in any of these industries even if we could handle and store the glass required. The requirements of customers as to shapes, sizes, thicknesses and qualities change so fast and are so unpredictable that much of the advance production would be unsuitable and therefore lost.

We also pointed out the ruinous costs that could result from such a guarantee. To attempt to finance a guarantee would involve either prohibitive price increases or depriving all employees of the possibilities of improvement in wage or fringe benefits.

In our glass plants the "guaranteed employment plan" could benefit only a minority of the employees. It would do nothing for the great majority. It was indeed a plan in support of "juniority" rather than seniority. The situation during the previous year of 1954 was an example in point. The passenger car production of our largest purchaser of automobile glass had dropped more than 40% in 1954 from 1953. Demand for our glass was quite low in the first half of the year and quite strong in the second half. 1954 was an abnormal year—a year of rather violent fluctuation. Even in that year, however, approximately 64% of our glass employees were not laid off for a single day.

Through this memorandum and the training conferences, management personnel were better prepared to discuss the issue in an informed manner in the various plant communities.

At the negotiations which began on May 2, 1955, the Union, as in previous negotiations, was represented by a bargaining committee of approximately 70 persons elected by the members of the various local unions. Under the Union constitution an agreement cannot be consummated without concurrence of the International President and the entire International Wage Committee. The expiration date of the two labor contracts was May 15, 1955, approximately two weeks before the expiration of the Ford and General Motors contracts. The major issue in the negotiations was the "guaranteed employment plan" and the bargaining on that issue was strenuous and determined. But when the chips were down the bargaining committee apparently did not believe there were sufficient advantages for all the employees in the "guaranteed employment plan" to justify a strike. We believe that the most persuasive argument against the proposal was the fact that it would benefit only a minority of our employees.

The parties agreed to a one-year contract, expiring May 15, 1956, with certain increases in wages and in the companies' contributions to the hospital and surgical insurance programs. The companies also indicated that they would cooperate with the Union in establishing joint labor-management committees to study the problems of stable employment and maximum production, and programs then in existence or negotiated in the near future in other companies with respect to such problems.

Early in the summer of 1955, after the Ford and General Motors negotiations were concluded, representatives of the two companies met with representatives of the Union to discuss the establishment of the study committees. In the course of that discussion the idea of a plan with a separate account for each employee was suggested. After considerable exploration it was decided that the idea was sufficiently meritorious for the companies to develop a detailed plan and submit it to the bargaining committee for possible approval.

Such a meeting of the bargaining committee was held in Cleveland, Ohio, during the week beginning August 29, and resulted in an agreement providing for the Security Benefit Plan and extending the labor contracts until September 25, 1958.

The provisions of the Security Benefit Plan, which is relatively simple, are as follows:

The company will enter into an agreement with a trustee, selected by the company, establishing a separate trust, referred to as a "Security Benefit Account" for each eligible employee in the bargaining unit. The company will contribute to each such account five cents for every hour actually worked by the employee on and after September 25, 1955. No part of the contributions may be recovered by the company.

Funds in the individual Security Benefit Accounts may be commingled by the trustee and treated as a consolidated fund for investment purposes. Investments by the trustees are limited to United States Government Bonds or equivalent securities to assure that the assets of the trust will be constantly of a safe and liquid character to meet any demands for large withdrawals. At the end of each year all earnings are credited to the Accounts in proportion to the balance in each Account. All costs of administration are paid by the company. During the discussions between the parties some consideration was given to paying the costs of administration out of the earnings, but the companies decided that it would contribute substantially to employee support of the plan if all earnings were retained exclusively for the employees.

The company does not begin making contributions into the Account for an employee until he has completed his probationary period and thereby becomes a regular employee. The contributions at five cents for each hour worked by the employee are then paid into his Account retroactive to his seniority date, which is normally his beginning date of employment.

No benefits will be payable to an employee from his Security Benefit Account . . . during the first year of his employment. Thereafter, for each full pay period (a pay period covers seven calendar days) that an employee is laid-off, or is absent from work because of injury or sickness, he may, in his discretion, withdraw from his Account a payment in an amount not to exceed 10% of the balance in his Account or $30.00, whichever is smaller. The minimum payment is $15.00 or the balance in his Account, whichever is smaller. Within these limits the employee may specify the amount of the periodic payments he desires. Payments during periods of absence for injury or sickness are not payable until the employee has been absent for two consecutive pay periods. Written forms will be provided to be used by employees in making requests for payments.

If employment is terminated for any reason, including retirement, the employee will receive the full amount in his Account. Upon an employee's death, payment will be made to the beneficiary designated by him or to his estate.

Company contributions to a Security Benefit Account cease after the Account attains a balance of $600 and are not resumed until the balance falls below $600. During such a period, when the company is not contributing into the Account of the employee, the company will credit an amount equal to the five cents for each hour actually worked by such employee toward additional vacation pay for the employee. The additional vacation pay will be paid to the employee when he receives his next succeeding vacation check, under the terms of the labor agreement between the company and the Union.

The trustee will have the right to use employees of the company as agents. Early in each calendar year the trustee will furnish each employee with a statement of the balance in his Security Benefit Account as of the end of the preceding year.

installment buying could exist if fifty million wage earners knew that whenever they were laid off or disabled their income would completely stop? Have you ever asked yourself why retail sales and construction declined almost not at all in early 1954 in spite of a substantial increase in unemployment?

We are building up a consumer economy which rests on the fundamental assumption of regularity of income of consumers; and yet, paradoxically, the very businessmen whose prosperity depends on this regularity of income are all too often found fighting improvements in the very systems that have made some regularity possible: workmen's compensation, unemployment insurance, disability insurance and social security.

Never in history has there been such a widespread interest in long-range economic projections among businessmen. Tremendous sums are being poured into research designed to anticipate economic conditions in future years. I only wish that some small part of this exertion could be channeled into an impartial fresh analysis of the part that will be played in future business prosperity by the various public systems that provide regularity of some income in periods of wage-loss. If the business community would only once approach this question as a matter of cold analytical long-term self-interest, business would become the staunchest advocate in the country of improvements in all these systems.

The corresponding private issue, of course, is concerned with the various features of collectively bargained contracts addressed to regularity and security of income. We all know that, in recent years, the outstanding development in labor-management relations has been the new preoccupation with regularity and security, rather than merely size, of income. This trend will undoubtedly persist. Most so-called fringe benefits are in this category. Supplementary old-age pensions; income in case of death of the breadwinner; supplementary workmen's compensation; disability cash benefits; supplementary unemployment benefits—and, in a sense, hospital and medical benefits—all are concerned with tempering the effect of interruption of regular income. Other trends, which will probably continue, also reflect concern for security and regularity: the increase in long-term agreements; the increasing prevalence of specific provisions on adjustments to technological change and on work assignments; automatic adjustments over a long-term period, such as escalator clauses, annual improvement factors, and deferred wage increases; increase in employment guarantees, weekly, monthly, and annually; and the movement for shorter hours per day and per week, with the object, among other things, of spreading the work and adding to the probability of regular employment.

The pattern is clear. American working people want and expect all these things because they are themselves typical Americans, because they want and expect to live as typical Americans live, and because they can only live this way if they can look forward to the kind of reasonable regularity of income that our way of life presupposes. One of the most important movements in the next twenty years, then, will be the movement toward this kind of regularity of income, as the result of both public and private measures.

FOR DISCUSSION AND ANALYSIS

1. Professor Slichter has commented: "One of the surprising things to me as an economist is that American businessmen have not taken the lead in insisting that Congress protect their markets and protect their investments by giving the country a truly adequate system of unemployment compensation."

How would you explain the lack of business support for something which, according to Professor Slichter, would be to business's interest?

2. How much unemployment compensation do you believe the "typical" worker might receive, and for how long, without impairing his incentive to work for an income?

3. It has been said that in certain industries where wage guarantees might be more feasible than in others, because of continuous demand or stabilized employment, guarantees are not needed. In companies subject to cyclical declines (where they are most needed) they are not feasible, since no one can foretell future business developments.

To what extent do you agree with this view?

4. The NAM has argued:

No business man, facing a decline in demand for his product, would meet the problem by raising his prices—nor would he exact new obligations from his customers. He would try to make his product cheaper and easier to buy, in every way possible.

But certain labor proposals would have the effect of making the services of labor more expensive—especially the guaranteed wage proposal. The guarantee would impose a new labor cost on the employer and require him to assume a new element of risk when he hired employees.

Thus the guarantee might restrict the market for labor and hence increase unemployment.

Comment on this view.

5. What significant differences do you observe between the GAW plan proposed by the UAW and the plan finally adopted in the automobile industry, which was largely drafted by Ford? Do you agree with Walter Reuther, UAW president, that "the essential features of the plan worked out in Ford negotiations conform remarkably closely to those we proposed"?

6. Reuther wrote in his presidential report to the UAW's 16th Annual Constitutional Convention: "In years to come, historians of the labor movement may well consider the winning of SUB agreements and the establishment of the GAW in our 1955 negotiations one of the most important collective bargaining achievements of all time."

(*a*) What reasons can you adduce for Reuther's making this assertion?

(*b*) Do you agree with him?

7. To what extent would effective full-employment planning eliminate the need for (*a*) unemployment compensation and (*b*) a guaranteed annual wage?

24: The Role of Unions in Society

What is the role of labor unions in American society?

This question is not one which can ever be conclusively answered—any more than we could conclusively answer the question: What is the role of the large corporation in America, or of political parties, or of farm bureaus, or of universities? Institutions—as long as they live—are always in the process of becoming. What they have been in the past influences what they are today and what they may become tomorrow. Changes in the unions' environment—in the business institutions with which they deal, for example—evoke new responses. The "needs" of the situation, as interpreted by union members and leaders and by those whom the unions in their operations affect, will motivate modification of direction.

Nevertheless, from an informed examination of the past and present we can derive some judgments about the developing future, and whether we like (or would like to change) the foreseen development.

At the Second Annual Conference on Industrial Relations, sponsored jointly by the Department of Industrial Relations and the Department of Psychology of the University of Buffalo, among the papers presented were one by a management representative and another by a union representative expressing opposed conceptions of the role of unions in American society. They are reproduced below from the Proceedings of the Conference, pp. 54-72.

ROADBLOCKS TO GOOD EMPLOYEE RELATIONS AND COLLECTIVE BARGAINING

By Leo Teplow, Associate Director, Industrial Relations Division, National Association of Manufacturers

Today, as never before in the history of our country, we are in desperate need of unity—unity of purpose, the kind of unity growing out of mutual confidence, national unity. It is not enough that we be united in our opposition to communism. The strength we need is the strength of constructive unity to attain positive goals. The unity we need cannot be created by fiat. It is not to be found in extensive legislative devices which may be regarded as a victory for one group or another and may serve to create further division among us. The unity we seek is the unity of the voluntary cooperation of free men who work together because they believe that their goal is right not only for themselves, but for the world as well and who have faith that their fellow citizens are working for the same goal. Our free and democratic society has demonstrated the miracle of production that we can accomplish when our forces are united, when we work toward a common goal. Today, unfortunately, we find such a pulling and hauling of special interests, each interested only in its own group, that we are most divided when there is the greatest need for unity. . . .

Fundamentally, our people are divided because we have not reached agreement upon our fundamental goals. Almost all of us give at least lip service to the concept of maximum individual freedom—but pressure groups demand compulsion be exerted on other groups or the public. All Americans believe in the dignity of the individual and in maximizing the individual's freedom of choice—but many of us seek the illusory palliative of top-heavy, all-powerful government to perform this or that service for us or to intervene in this or that activity. Most of us believe that the greatest good for the greatest number can be brought about by a system of free competitive enterprise in a democratic society—but there are many among us who directly or indirectly seek to promote socialism and impose the heavy hand of government regulation on all economic activities.

In this conflict of goals, the labor movement has a tremendously important part to play. Indeed, the labor movement may well play the decisive role. One may well ask, what is the ultimate goal of the labor movement? It is no longer enough to say as did Samuel Gompers thirty years ago that the aim of the labor movement can be expressed in one word "more." Today, it appears that the labor movement is veering away from its traditional business unionism, in the direction of a political movement, a movement based on an ideology departing from traditional American freedoms, a movement dedicated to compulsion over the individual rather than seeking greater freedom of the individual. Who can speak for the labor movement and define its ideology and goals?

On the one hand, we have the American Federation of Labor which predominantly favors a system of private competitive enterprise and the freedoms which only that system can provide. For example, a typical comment by William Green, President of the AFL follows:

> We in the American Federation of Labor are determined that free enterprise shall survive in America, because it has brought to the people of our country a higher standard of living than is enjoyed by any other nation on earth.[1]

So far as concerns the CIO, no such forthright endorsement can be expected. Many of the legislative programs espoused by the CIO, when assembled, can lead only to the conclusion that the CIO endorses a planned economy as a stepping stone to socialism. The acceptance of competitive enterprise on the

[1] American Federationist Weekly News Service, May 11, 1948.

part of the CIO is of a highly tentative nature. For example, Mr. L. S. Buckmaster, President of the United Rubber Workers, CIO recently stated:

The labor organizations of this country as democratic institutions are not wedded to any particular kind of economic system . . . we recognize and appreciate the great success which American industry has had under capitalism and we are ready and willing to try and make it work.

More to the point, Mr. Buckmaster says:

Occasionally, that solution (to employee problems) involves some trespassing on management's ideas of economic theory or their cherished notions of an individual's obligation to himself. We have what might be called a "problem-oriented" approach and we believe it to be socially and economically healthy.[2]

On the other hand, we have the statement of Mr. David J. McDonald, Secretary-Treasurer of the United Steelworkers of America who said:

And while we strive for lasting peace, we can, I think, at the same time demonstrate that the democratic way of life—to which we all adhere —is the very best way of life for all mankind; that free, competitive, democratic capitalism can provide a solution for the problems of mankind, and that by the very findings of that solution, demonstrate to all doubters that it is really the soundest, the finest, and the best way of life.[3]

To the same effect, recently, the CIO's Utility Workers Union of America issued a strong statement of policy opposing government expansion in the field of generation and distribution of electric power. The statement reads as follows in part:

Approximately one-fifth of the power generated in America today is distributed and sold by government agencies. We believe that further encroachment of government into the utility industry should be discouraged except in cases of national emergency. It is our firm belief that the best interests of all of the people of this nation can best be served and secured through collective bargaining in investor owned public utility corporations. We further recommend as a matter of policy that the National Officers, the Local Officers and members use every means available to prevent further nationalization of the utility industry.[4]

But the situation is not at all clear. It is urgent that organized labor make up its mind about the direction in which it would go, for by its actions, by its demands, by the utilization of its growing influence, it can either contribute to national unity if it decides in favor of democratic capitalism; or it can contribute toward irreconcilable internal conflict if it moves in the direction of a planned economy and government compulsion.

Organized labor has at least as much at stake in a free competitive economy as any other element of our economy. The freedom of organized labor to

[2] "Union Philosophy on Pensions" by L. S. Buckmaster, NICB Pension Conference, November 22, 1949.

[3] Speech at meeting of ILO Iron and Steel Committee, Cleveland, Ohio, April 23 to 29, 1946, quoted in "Your Human Relations," Volume 1, No. 2, Page 71.

[4] Daily Labor Report No. 86, May 3, 1950, pages A-6 and A-7.

organize, to negotiate, to invoke the processes and protection of government, to strike, and to deal on a basis of equality with management depends upon the existence of a free competitive society. Free collective bargaining can be carried on only between free managements and free labor unions having the capacity to commit themselves to abide by negotiated agreements. As Secretary of Labor, Maurice J. Tobin has stated:

I believe we must continue to maintain free unions and free collective bargaining in this country in order to preserve our democratic processes and free competitive enterprise.[5]

The converse of that statement is equally true. Democratic processes and free competitive enterprise are essential for the maintenance of free unions and free collective bargaining. In a socialized state, there is no free management and there can be no free unions. When the sole employer is the government, bargaining with the government is the only kind of collective bargain possible. Such bargaining is not and cannot be free. The stoppage of government services in case of strike comes too close to civil insurrection, particularly where the function involved is an essential one, for any government to tolerate it for long. Compulsions are necessarily brought into play and the freedom of unions must soon become circumscribed. It is to be noted that since the end of the war, it is not in capitalistic United States, but in socialist England that troops have been called in to break strikes.

On the side of management, while many labor leaders either do not recognize it or do not admit it, recognition of collective bargaining as a means of determining wages, hours and working conditions has received overwhelming acceptance. Employers in general have concluded that if their employees want to be represented by a union for collective bargaining purposes, it is only good management and good business to make collective bargaining work. Since unions have now developed a strength of over 15 million members, management realizes that unreasoning opposition to recognition of unions must inevitably result in government determination of wages, hours and working conditions. Consequently, during the past 15 years, a managerial revolution has taken place and management's spokesmen are among the foremost defenders of free collective bargaining where that is the choice of the employees.

But what is free collective bargaining? Is collective bargaining free if it results in the imposition of compulsion upon individual employees? Is collective bargaining free when the collective strength of labor unions is utilized for political purposes? Is collective bargaining free if employers and representatives of their employees are not free to determine their own working conditions? It seems to me that it is well worth reviewing the major roadblocks to free collective bargaining, for these are also the roadblocks that interfere with the achievement of national unity. These major roadblocks to free collective bargaining are:

1. Compulsion;
2. Industry-wide bargaining;

[5] Address by Secretary Tobin before group from Labor Department before taking oath of office, AFL Weekly News Service, August 17, 1948.

3. Diversion of organized labor's efforts into political fields; and

4. Recklessness in sowing dissension between management and employees.

There was a time when the American labor movement was devoted to the ideal of voluntarism in carrying out its program. For example, the December 1949 issue of the American Federationist reprints a speech by Samuel Gompers in which he stated:

So long as we have held fast to voluntary principles and have been actuated and inspired by the spirit of service, we have sustained our forward progress and we have made our labor movement something to be respected and accorded a place in the councils of our Republic. Where we have blundered into trying to force a policy or a decision, even though wise and right, we have impeded, if not interrupted, the realization of our aims.

. . . as one who . . . with singleness of purpose has tried to serve the labor movement honorably and in a spirit of consecration to the cause of humanity, I want to urge devotion to the fundamentals of human liberty —the principles of voluntarism.

No lasting gain has ever come from compulsion . . .

I want to say to you, men and women of the American labor movement, do not reject the cornerstone upon which labor's structure has been builded, but base your all upon voluntary principles . . .

How different is the situation today. It took an act of Congress to eliminate the compulsion of the closed shop from the industrial scene—and that enactment was bitterly opposed by labor leaders at the time of its enactment and ever since. In fact, it was only a few days ago that a New York court ruled that a newspaper delivery union could not maintain both a closed shop and a closed union. In this particular case, the union limited its membership to the sons of members of the union and insisted that employees who had been taken on during the war to meet the labor shortage be discharged later because the union had a closed shop contract and would not admit these employees to union membership.

The concept of compulsion in place of voluntarism extends throughout the gamut of labor philosophy. Instead of defending the rights of the individual employee, labor unions are increasingly adopting the concept that strong central unions must be able to exercise authority not only over individual employees, but over local unions as well.

Industry-wide bargaining is a natural concomitant of the concept of authoritarian unionism directing the lives and future of both individual members and local unions. Industry-wide bargaining prevents individual companies and local unions from reaching amicable agreement on conditions of employment satisfactory to them. The fate of the individual company and its employees is of little moment in the eyes of international union leaders who are concerned with overall national policies. It was no accident that during the 1949 steel strike Philip Murray, President of the Steelworkers Union said that a company which could not meet the union's pension demands did not deserve to remain in business. I wonder whether the employees of these companies would reach the same conclusion. It is no accident that during the nation-wide steel strike of 1946 when the international union would not let any of its locals settle for anything less than the national pattern, an appreciable number of union locals were forced to sever their affiliation with the international union in order to enable these locals to resume production on terms mutually satisfactory to the companies involved and their employees.

Let me cite a specific example of the manner in which national union control reacts to the disadvantage of both industry and employees of individual companies. During the 1949 steel strike, employees of many companies were called out on strike without regard to the relationship between the employees and the particular company. Some companies already had pension programs in operation which were far better than the pension program demanded by the union. One of these was Inland Steel which had had a pension program for 12 years— a program much more liberal than that demanded from U.S. Steel and other companies, although it was a contributory program. Under the Inland Steel program, employees received much more liberal benefits, their right to a pension vested after five years' service in the company so that employees could take their pension benefits with them if they left the company; and pension benefits were also available to survivors of Inland employees who died during employment.

Nevertheless, Inland employees were also called out on strike—a totally unnecessary and wasteful strike. Following this strike, Inland employees were given an opportunity to elect whether they would take the non-contributory pensions of the type agreed to by Bethlehem and other companies, or whether they would prefer the Inland pension program with its increased benefits. Both types of plans were explained to each employee by management and union. The election showed that 74% of employees elected the kind of program they had had before the international union called them out on strike.

It is only under industry-wide bargaining or under domination of local unions by the international union that such a departure from the theory of voluntarism is likely to take place. It is the stress and pressure of industry-wide bargaining which has seriously shaken public confidence in the theory and practice of collective bargaining. Not only does industry-wide bargaining entirely prevent public access to the products of the particular industry involved in case of a strike, but it is responsible for an increasing proportion of the man-hours lost because of strikes. In the year 1949, two industry-wide strikes alone—those in coal and steel—were responsible for 60% of all of the man-hours lost in strikes during the year.

Public impatience with strikes of that kind or the current strike on the railroads is bound to result in an increasing measure of government intervention, until free collective bargaining will become a thing of the past. Reliance upon compulsion and devotion to the theory of industry-wide bargaining are two of the major roadblocks to free collective bargaining. A third is the current addiction of organized labor for political mechanisms for achieving its economic aims.

Our private competitive enterprise economy operating in a democratic political system has resulted in so profound a devotion to individual freedom that we have achieved a fluid society in which men can rise as high as their ability and contributions warrant. Ours is a fluid society in which class consciousness is almost unknown. Even a decade ago, after the most ruthless depression we have ever known, there was little class consciousness among us. A survey announced by *Fortune* in February, 1940, showed that in response to the question: "What word would you use to describe the class to which you belong?"—47% of those replying—and they came from all walks of life—said that they belonged to the middle class. With these should be included the 2% that said that they belonged to the businessman or executive class. Only 15% admitted to being in the lower class, while some 3% were under the delusion that they belonged to an upper class. 27% of all the people questioned had not given the matter enough thought to be able to decide which class they belonged to. This is a result which would be possible in no other country in the world. This indeed is ample evidence that while the communists talk about a classless society, we have achieved it.

Industry-wide bargaining and political activity by labor unions are both bound to bring class consciousness to the fore. Industry-wide bargaining means that negotiation of local problems, comparatively simple at the local level, will be transformed into ideological differences at the national level, encouraging people to take sides on the basis of ideology. Political activity by labor unions is bound to have the same effect. The concept of labor solidarity developed in an effort to win economic demands will be transformed into a political weapon. Efforts will be made to get union members to vote not as citizens of a democracy, but as members of the union. Nothing is more likely to bring about a division of our society into classes. And what will be the direction of labor's effort in the political field? Wherever a labor party has been formed, it has been a socialist party. And the difference between communism and socialism is not a difference in the end product—it is only a difference concerning the means used to achieve the final goal of the authoritarian state and the death of individual freedom.

We have already gone a long way in the direction of politicalizing the labor movement. Listen to the words of warning of Donald R. Richberg, former Chairman of the National Recovery Administration Board:

Gompers fought bitterly and successfully the continuing effort of partisan socialists to convert trade unionists to their economic and political theories. Years later I came to understand two things. One, is that socialist guides will always lead the labor unions away from an economic program into a political program, which, in the forceful words of Samuel Gompers, is "economically unsound, socially wrong and industrially impossible." The other thing I have learned, which Gompers accurately foresaw, is that any political labor party will be dominated by socialists and that a socialist government will eventually destroy those very liberties, comforts and securities which labor unions are organized to gain, or to preserve, for industrial workers.

When labor unions go beyond economic pressures and appeal to reason, when they seek to compel all workers to join them, and all other community interests to be subservient to theirs, no theory of political action will justify their compulsory rule and their destruction of individual liberty and rights of property, except the socialist dogmas that support the creation of an all powerful, tyrannical state.

The industrial workers, long educated to resent dependence on an employer for jobs and the improvement of living standards, have been more easily persuaded to accept dependence on government officials for economic security, particularly when they felt that through their own labor organizations they would be able to regulate their official regulators.

In fact real collective bargaining, as the peaceful adjustment of conflicting minor interests in the light of common major interests, has practically disappeared in the relations of big labor and big business. Now we have political bargaining to produce a temporary coercive settlement in a permanent conflict, a dictated peace intended to last only until resources can be organized for the next battle in a never ending war.

This bargaining is for political ends, in which existing political power is called upon to help the contestants, with a clear warning that the labor movement is now primarily a political movement aiming at ultimate political control of government and that every politician should chart his course so that he will be counted either for or against the on-marching labor party.[6]

That is not a very optimistic picture. Additional grounds for pessimism exist in the mechanism which organized labor is increasingly utilizing in achieving its goals. I refer to the fourth roadblock: organized labor's recklessness in hurling charges or maledictions upon management and government—a process that Walter Gordon Merritt recently referred to as "constant infusion of venom."

Organized labor and the entire economy has much to gain from labor-management peace and harmony. But there seems to be an increasing tendency for the leaders of organized labor to resort to such preposterous vilification as to make industrial peace hardly likely. Let me give a few examples of what I mean. Here are a few words culled from a recent statement of that past master of Shakespearean English, John L. Lewis, taken from his communication to the President of the United States refusing his invitation to participate in hearings before a Presidential fact-finding board:

They (the miners) serve a harsh and brutal industry. Its toll of broken men and human flesh are without parallel in modern history. Their employers are, in a controlling sense, greedy, grasping and devoid of ordinary compassion . . . For eight months, Mr. President, they (the operators) have boasted that the abomination, known as the Taft-Hartley Act, rendered it unnecessary to concede anything, and that in the end your high office, wielding Taft's club, would beat the miners into submission . . . The mine workers know that any rejection of your agents' findings, after issuance, would cause them to face the oppressive legal sanctions

[6] U. S. Chamber of Commerce Pension Conference, Cincinnati, Ohio, March 29, 1950.

of Taft's bill of attainder against labor unions. The mine workers know also, Mr. President, that the heavy hand of government would not be laid concurrently on the shoulders of the coal operators as they make wassail in the privacy of their exclusive clubs . . . It is a travesty of justice that they (the coal miners) should now be slugged by a legal blackjack to satisfy the overweening avarice of their reactionary employers . . . To use the power of the state to drive men into the mines, on the terms and for the profit of private employers, is involuntary servitude . . .

Other less rounded but equally vindictive statements are to be found punctuating many of the major labor disputes. For example, during the hearings before the Presidential fact-finding board in the steel industry, Mr. Murray digressed from his testimony to make personal attacks on Mr. Voorhees of U. S. Steel, in one of which he referred to him as a "fat, sassy and very opulent man."[7]

On an earlier occasion before the same board, Mr. Murray referred to the management of the steel industry as "the most sanctimonious band of professional racketeers in this country." [8] A full page advertisement by the UAW-CIO upon the conclusion of the 100-day Chrysler strike contains in the headline a reference to "Chrysler Corporation's blind selfishness."[9]

These are only a few examples of this kind of thing on a national scale. Probably even more destructive of democratic government is the reckless statement made by Jim Carey, Secretary-Treasurer of the CIO, as reported in the press last November:

Your Chairman is not going to pay the least little bit of attention to any of these injunctions. The courts are being used in this situation by people who want to destroy the courts, and it is high time that the officers and locals of this organization take steps to defy these irresponsible actions by irresponsible, confused and ignorant judges.[10]

Mr. Carey was talking about injunctions obtained by his old union, the United Electrical Workers against the recently formed International Union of Electrical Workers. Mr. Carey was fighting communism in the CIO. Ironically, it would be hard to find a published communist statement more likely to undermine democratic government than this statement attributed to Mr. Carey.

All of these major roadblocks to collective bargaining can serve only to divide and confuse our people at a time when voluntary cooperation and unity are needed as never before. Whether we view the problem from the narrower focus of preservation of free collective bargaining or whether we view it from the larger aspect of the strengthening of the one democracy in which the hopes of the world are centered, we ought to take steps to eliminate compulsion, industry-wide bargaining, union political activity and reckless re-

[7] New York Times, August 27, 1949.
[8] New York Times, July 29, 1949.
[9] New York Times, May 7, 1950.
[10] New York Times, November 3, 1949.

crimination between management and labor from our current industrial scene. The progress to be made by organized labor in removing these obstacles will be a test of its devotion to both free collective bargaining and a democracy of free men.

PROBLEMS IN LABOR-MANAGEMENT RELATIONS

By Victor G. Reuther, Director of Education, United Automobile, Aircraft, Agricultural Implement Workers of America, CIO

What I have to say this afternoon will have to deal with the very practical problems that arise in the field of management-labor relations and in the whole area in which those activities relate to the total community. Even at the expense of adding further to the reputation which labor spokesmen have in the minds of Mr. Teplow, I shall not speak of "peace" and "unity" and "free enterprise" as though they were objectives or goals within themselves, for they are not. For peace has no virtue unless it is peace with justice. They had peace in the Soviet Union; I know for I worked there for two years. They had peace of a sort under Hitler, but it was peace without justice. They had a kind of unity, also, but not the kind which one would expect to achieve in the framework of a democratic society. Free enterprise is but a man-made mechanism. Unless it can help us achieve political and economic democracy like other man-made institutions, it must give way to more efficient means to achieve the desirable goals which are security, abundance and the highest degree of individual liberty.

Of course, I realize that peace has many definitions depending on who offers them and for what reasons. So has unity and so has free enterprise. William Green's or Philip Murray's definition of free enterprise may differ a great deal from the definition of that same term given by a spokesman of the Association of National Manufacturers. But what have we accomplished in merely the defining of terms, when what we ought to be doing is setting up these positive goals that Mr. Teplow referred to, toward which society as a whole should be moving, and then discussing the tools and the mechanisms that are required to achieve them and judging the available tools in terms of the extent to which they help us to reach the goals. Any other approach will defeat the purpose which I think the vast majority of Americans have in mind when they cooperate in the collective bargaining process or when they participate as citizens in election activities.

We have had a system of voluntarism for a long, long time. I am afraid that those who were in positions of leadership and responsibility by virtue of the tremendous economic power which they wielded apparently were unaware of the importance of voluntarism because they were very, very slow in stepping forward in providing answers or practical solutions to concrete economic and political problems that arose. As long ago as 1854 a writer by the name of Dickens, described a group of employers in a community which he called Coketown. He said—and I am quoting verbatim from Dickens, not from the CIO or Phil Murray or anyone else—

Surely there never was such fragile chinaware as that of which the millers of Coketown were made. Handle them never so lightly and they fell to pieces with such ease that you might suspect them of having been flawed before. They were ruined when they were required to send laboring children to school; they were ruined, when inspectors were appointed to look into their works; they were ruined when such inspectors considered it doubtful whether they were quite justified in chopping people up with their machinery; they were utterly undone when it was hinted that perhaps they need not always make quite so much smoke. . . . Whenever a Coketowner felt he was ill used—that is to say, whenever he was not left entirely alone, and it was proposed to hold him accountable for the consequences of any of his acts—he was sure to come out with the awful menace, that he would "sooner pitch his property into the Atlantic." This had terrified the Home Secretary within an inch of his life on several occasions. However, the Coketowners were so patriotic after all, that they never had pitched their property into the Atlantic yet, but on the contrary had been kind enough to take mighty good care of it.

That was a long time ago, and yet at this mid-century point there is great resistance and great reluctance on the part of those who are free to utilize this thing called voluntarism to come forward and propose solutions to our problem of unemployment and housing for the great mass of our people in this the richest and most productive country in the world who still lives in slums, in sub-standard housing conditions. They have yet to come forward with a voluntary proposal in the health field that will bring today's modern medical care within the reach of millions who want it and need it.

I believe in voluntarism, but a voluntarism that has a social responsibility and that expresses itself not in words alone but in deed. Our economic system and our democratic way of life will be judged not by Fourth of July speeches but by the extent to which it can translate its great productive wealth and its human resources into a life of abundance and security. At this mid-century point, the people in the United States, with about eight per cent of the world's population, have fifty per cent of the world's productive ability. We have not found the simple, easy solution of housing our people properly, clothing them properly, providing them with decent educational facilities. Our school system is pitifully inadequate for a nation with the resources that we have. We have not found the answer to our problem of unemployment or our health needs. Employers and industrialists, by virtue of their strategic positions of ownership in our economy, cannot escape their responsibility in utilizing voluntary channels if they prefer it that way to meet these problems. And our failure to meet them constitutes the greatest single threat to our democratic society.

I am sure that you will agree that in Italy, where I spent considerable time, and in France today, the communist threat is more real than in any of the western countries of Europe. And it is real precisely because the standards of living are lowest there and mass unemployment throws the entire economy into convulsions. In socialist Britain and socialist Scandinavia, if you wish to label them that way, they have done something about health, housing and full employment. There the communist parties are weakest of all. There democratic elections still exist, you understand, but the communists get a pitifully small vote. Why? Because the whole climate in which the people live is more wholesome and the corruption of a democratic society that ignores the social and economic ills just does not exist, or at least it is minimized to the extent that the communists and the fascists and others do not find fertile soil in which to plant their seeds.

But to suggest that we might do something to stop these problems in the United States does not mean that we have to barter our individual liberty and freedom in exchange for a greater measure of security and abundance. For who has proposed bartering or exchanging one's individual rights to speak or say what he wishes in exchange for a greater amount of economic goods? Labor leaders would be the last to propose that kind of a barter. They have been far more vigilant in the fight for freedom than any other segment of the community that I know of and have been far more vigilant in defending the rights even of opponents and minorities in a community which crushed minority groups. They are not unconcerned with the problem of individual freedom and individual liberty.

But these things are not normally accomplished by speech making, and nothing that I may have to say this afternoon itself will strengthen the cause of freedom and liberty. It is done in the shop and in the mills. I have no defense to make for labor's new-found interests in political action and I have no apologies for it. One need not apologize for an activity which urges people to exercise a responsibility which people admittedly should have in a democracy and to participate actively in legislative and political matters. But if we learned that lesson from anyone, we learned it from those who first organized for effective political action when employer associations were first active in seeking legislation which they considered advantageous to them, long before the CIO Political Action Committee came along.

Long before trade unions established nation-wide or corporation-wide industrial organizations, there had to be a corporation-wide structure. If all that we have done was to adapt our trade union structure to fit into a pattern that was already there, and if it is wrong in principle for trade unionists to band together within a corporation (if indeed we are talking about principles) then is it not just as wrong for employers to band together to form a huge corporation with headquarters in Wilmington, Delaware, to direct over one hundred General Motors plants in the United States and others scattered abroad? I took part in the early organization of General Motors, and I know how long we tried to settle some grievances on a local basis while we had an international structure in existence. There were many matters that we were free to discuss locally with local management. But the Corporation was quick to realize, indeed most corporations were quick to realize, that a decision or a concession made in one plant becomes known in others, and so the Corporation was quick to take away the authority of local plant managers to settle matters of that kind. They lodged it in a central labor relations office, not as a result of pressure from the trade unions but because they knew in terms of the corporation's own economic interests that they could protect their own position much better if they centralized it. If there is anything wrong, it does not come from centralization; if there is anything weak about the organization, it does not come from the fact that the union and the company are organized on a national basis throughout the country. What is wrong is not the bigness of industry or the bigness of government. The difficulty is that these three are not publicly permitted to seek the same basic republican goals and are not willing to justify their individual acts in relation to these total community goals.

I might cite some specific examples. I am sure all of you will admit that we have had a problem in this country in terms of those who have reached the twilight years of their lives needing a greater measure of security. There is need for a pension program. Now if a voluntary method is the best way of doing it, industry should have stepped forward with such voluntary proposals. It did not. It resisted it from the beginning just as it resisted unemployment compensation, as it resisted legislation on the question of child labor, as it has resisted virtually every single proposal that has been made of a general social character that would advance the well-being of the community at large, either at the industry or the legislative levels. It took great political pressure to get the United States government to begin even a modest, meager program in the direction of social security legislation, (and you have been told that after some twelve or fifteen years, the average worker is entitled to somewhere between $25 or $27 a month). I saw no voluntary programs coming forth, though we sought to get management cooperation to increase those benefits. They resisted it through organized political effort in Washington. And since we don't like to do everything through government, we thought we would go directly to industry and ask their cooperation. We were told that these things were really bad, that they undermine individual initiative, that the worker ought to be able to save for himself, that he ought to have the incentive to save and that they really undermine the free enterprise system and the American way of life.

We will not advance the community's interest by double talk and double standards, for honesty and frankness are essential in any democratic process whether it be bargaining or out in the general legislative field. When employers who sat across the table said they had principle objections to pension programs, that they would undermine the free enterprise system, would destroy individual initiative and would open the door to socialism (and that certainly a non-contributory program was worst of all) for those employers to say that at the very moment they themselves were enjoying the benefits of a very substantial pension program paid out of corporate earnings on a non-contributory basis, indicated that they were advocating a double standard of pensions for those who needed it least and who could afford it best and to deny it to those who need it most but could least afford it. If insecurity of the aged is a problem, it is best that it be attacked through the voluntary way.

Where is the initiative and leadership from industry to share some of its fantastic profits today to help meet that problem? Industry admits a responsibility to set aside funds to replace worn out machinery, to set aside funds to maintain plant facilities during periods of idleness, but on a principle basis, because of the threat of socialism and so on, industry relieves itself of any moral responsibility to set aside out of its earnings funds to help supplement the meager benefits under a federal program. On that issue, as a great many other issues, there are double standards and there is double talk.

We speak a great deal about the rights of the individual and say that trade unionism today is an oppressive force seeking to deny individual liberties to workers in the shop. The union shop or closed shop provisions are cited as a specific example of this. The union shop principle, the obligation of every worker in the unionized factory who enjoys the benefits of trade unionism to help assume the cost of it and the moral responsibility of participating in it, is a logical and very democratic extension of our political concepts of democracy. For any of you who move into a community and enjoy the facilities of city government—fire protection, school facilities, sewage disposal, road repair and so on—you may complain about them, you may consider them inadequate, you may hate the mayor and the chief of police who are helping to administer them, but you pay your taxes or your property will be taken from you and you would characterize a neighbor who would refuse to pay his taxes as a slacker and a hitchhiker.

Yet trade unions are established by as democratic a process, or even a more democratic process, as our city governments because by and large a percentage as large as 98 participates in the election which first establishes our union under secret government election sponsored by the NLRB. No such high majority of eligible voters participate in city, state or national elections, so who can say that this is not a democratic choice and when people who are democratically chosen in that manner set up rules and regulations which become a part of signed agreement and signed contracts that provide for economic gain, which aren't limited just to those who pay their dues. No union, as far as I know, has stepped forward and said that the raise will go only to those who pay their dues or are members of the union or that the pension provision will apply only to those who are in good standing. The unions have consistently said that the benefits shall go to all of those who work within the jurisdiction of the union in the contract.

This all stems not from the fact of disagreement about methods and so on, but rather stems basically from the fact that trade unions and collective bargaining as such have not in fact been accepted by very substantial parts of American industry. They have accepted a limited mechanism which would concern itself solely with wages, hours, and working conditions but would try to restrict and deny trade unionists participation in a broader field of the economy which is as fundamental to their well-being as the mere setting of wages. I refer specifically to the objection of industry in this country to concede to organized labor a right to inquire about the prices and policies of industry as if labor had no concern and didn't pay the price. What right has the corporation in a democracy—mind you, where we are talking about the concern of the whole community in very general terms—what right has one segment in the community, whether it be the employers or anyone else, to say that it alone has the arbitrary right to set prices without regard to the interests of the consumer or the wage earners or anyone else, and to say that the law of supply and demand of its own will adjust prices today?

With General Motors in one year getting a net profit after all taxes of some $650,000,000, can anyone say that there should not have been a price reduction or a more substantial increase in wages? How shall we arrive at a democratic decision in the economic field without giving others who are affected an opportunity to participate in the decision? This is a distortion of the democratic process. It is a denial of it to a tremendous portion of our community that has a very great stake in it. I could give you a detailed breakdown which would indicate that the General Motors Corporation, based upon its profits last year (and its profits for the first quarter of this year are even exceeding those fantastic figures), made more money in profit per Chevrolet produced than the total cost of all the hourly and salary wages and earnings of company executives combined that went into the production of that car! They made a profit of 19.5% or $198 for each unit produced while the total labor costs that went into the manufacturing of that car were $175. And I will tell you that the dealer in the automobile industry makes on the average a 25% cut for turning over the title and the key as compared to about 17.1% that goes for the total labor costs in the manufacturing of the car. I wouldn't want to start a personal fight or organized campaign against the dealers as such, but certainly we have a right as participants in an economy that professes to be democratic to inquire as to whether or not there is a fair distribution among wage earners as against the employers and as against the consumers.

Now there are a number of ways of doing this. You can continue this narrow concept of collective bargaining which says free enterprise means each guy, each group looks after himself and to hell with the rest, and you can fight it out according to the laws of the jungle. You can try to deprive the trade unions of factual data about profits and unit costs, telling them it is none of their business, that this is secret information, and that they have no right even to inquire into it. Then we can battle it out according to the laws of the jungle. Or there is another approach: the labor boys can sit down and join in the conspiracy with management to gouge the consumer. As a trade unionist, I have been invited on numerous occasions to keep my mouth shut about prices. Particularly before price controls were lifted on automobiles, our union was invited to go to Washington and join in a conspiracy with the automobile manufacturers association in an effort to break the price ceiling on cars, so we can get ours, they can get theirs and who cares if the consumer gets a gouging. I have great admiration for John L. Lewis in terms of the contribution he has made to the guys who go down in the pit and work under miserable conditions. While I disagree with him in his republican economic theory, I have respect for the contribution he has made. But one suspects that John Lewis has succumbed to an invitation on the part of the operators —the invitation came from them repeatedly—to join in a conspiracy to raise the price of a ton of coal and pass it on to the consumers. There is growing resentment not only in the community but in the ranks of labor for that kind of narrow, selfish, dog-eat-dog approach to collective bargaining and we will have no part of it. We insist on our democratic rights to inquire not alone about wages, but prices and profits and that is why on numerous occasions we said that we would give up our wage demands, if the corporations could prove that they could not pay them without raising the price of the automobile. We were not taken up on it.

It is because we wanted pensions, not alone for our members but for the whole community that we deliberately, knowingly and willfully made our job tougher in getting them by tying the pension program to the federal social security legislation. And let me tell you what happened as a result of that. The whole climate changed. Employers who had principle objections to pensions, who said they were socialistic, suddenly said, "Well, boys, it's silly to battle it out at the factory gate, you ought to get it down in Washington, so you won't have 76 varieties of pension plan." We asked where they had been these fifteen years. But something even more fundamental happened. The minute the Ford pension was signed, that very day people who have been as opposed to pension programs as C. E. Wilson suddenly came out for an increase in the federal benefits because our pension program said that the company would pay the difference between what the workers get in Washington and $100.

They began figuring it out. If they increased the payments in Washington, they would pay less out of the company funds. All of our appeals to logic and to reason and to community interest and to the need of those who have reached the retirement age had fallen on deaf ears. But when we touched that most sensitive nerve of all that runs from here to the pocketbook, they responded. And so, suddenly now, employers have joined us in Washington asking for an increase in federal pensions. That is good news no matter what led to it, but the truth of the matter is, voluntarism did not do it. Unfortunately one of the weaknesses we have to face is that those who have, want to hang on to it, and those who have not, want to get what they consider a more just share.

It is inherent in the democratic process, you know, that you do not declare peace and you do not declare national unity until you have some degree of economic and social justice that will form a healthy foundation upon which we can build. If those who have come before us have felt that peace and national unity were in themselves the sole, final, ultimate objective, there would have been no struggle and no effort to strengthen our democracy, to broaden and expand it and to meet the injustices and the insecurities that appear. This is a democratic struggle, which I hope we can minimize by voluntarily agreeing that this whole economic area involves more than just management and labor but embraces the whole community and by beginning to make collective bargaining as fundamentally democratic and as broad as our industrial society. Many of the things we deal with cannot be solved at the factory gate, and should not be solved with the view in mind of merely submitting to individual pressures, whether they come from management or labor, in the interest of patching it up and getting peace because we can get peace all right but a peace of injustice, of insecurity which would be an invitation to totalitarianism or an invitation to solve some of our unemployment problems by another shooting war with the expanded artificial employment that comes out of that.

It is because the American trade unionists have such a vital faith in the democratic way that they take so seriously their immediate role in it, and if we really want labor to grow out of the narrow concept where they are concerned only with their own gain, if we really want them to take into consideration the well being of the whole community (as we are reminded so often in full page ads), then all of us ought to go along with this new trend of labor's relating its economic demands to the total needs of the community and we ought to go along with labor's demand that we discuss wages not in a vacuum but in the light of all the facts that are available for the whole community and in the light of the relationship of wages to prices and profits. If we really want the community view to have precedence over the pressure group interests, then we ought to broaden the collective bargaining process so that our actions will give weight to our words.

THE EVOLUTION OF MANAGERIAL IDEAS IN INDUSTRIAL RELATIONS

Professor Edwin E. Witte, a former president of the American Economic Association and the Industrial Relations Research Association, is one of the best loved and best recognized students of industrial relations in the United States. Below he sets out his observations on the present state of union-management relations.

An address by Edwin E. Witte, reproduced by the New York State School of Industrial Relations at Cornell, 1954, pp. 20–22

It is now forty-five years since I first became a student of industrial relations problems. In the intervening years, I have often had a more active role in industrial relations than that of a mere student and observer. I have often been a participant in an in-between position, as a public employee or official connected with adjustment agencies and policy-making boards, or as a private arbitrator and occasional consultant. I have had a good opportunity to observe what has been going on in industrial relations in the United States.

The predominant impression I have formed is that great progress has been made toward improved industrial relations. The time when management could afford to be indifferent to industrial relations is long past. Few managements today resort to or believe proper the tough, ruthless policies and practices toward labor which were common in this country as late as the 1920's. Violence and lawlessness in labor disputes have greatly diminished. Most important is the recognition on both sides that production in modern industry necessarily must be a cooperative effort. The foremost problem of management in relation to labor is that of enlisting its wholehearted cooperation. Management has come to recognize that such wholehearted cooperation is most likely, when all workers are treated with dignity, consideration, fairness, and equality. The growth of unionism still poses a difficult problem for many managements. Considering the recency of this situation in many companies, the progress made in genuine collective bargaining has been most gratifying.

We have by no means attained the millennium. There is probably no firm which cannot improve its practices and much remains to be done to bring all industry into line with the generally recognized best policies.

But the reality of the progress which has been made cannot be doubted whatever tests are applied. Not only are there relatively fewer strikes but the bitterness produced by labor disputes has greatly diminished. Production has not reached possible maximums and the much-desired full cooperation of labor has not fully been realized. But per capita production is far greater in the United States than anywhere else and is still increasing at a satisfying rate. And just about everybody has benefited—the production and the clerical employees, the supervisors and the executives, and, yes, also the investors. More products and better products are available to the consumers and at prices which have increased far less than average incomes.

For the progress made much of the credit belongs to enlightened management. None of the ideas and practices in industrial relations which have been acclaimed, successively, in management circles has proven the complete solution hoped for by early enthusiasts. At least most of them, however, have left their imprint upon present-day practices and policies and have current, and not merely historical, significance.

The record of industrial relations in the United States reflects credit upon our nation and the managerial society we have developed. It is a basic American idea that continuous progress is possible and necessary. I, for one, believe that we will continue to make progress toward even more satisfactory industrial relations than we have attained.

FOR DISCUSSION AND ANALYSIS

1. The following statement appears in *The Challenge of Industrial Relations,* by Professor Sumner Slichter, published by Cornell University Press in 1947:

The rise of unions constitutes an epoch-making change in the economy—quite comparable to such institutional changes as the rise of the modern credit system or of the corporation. Unions are no longer simply organizations which put workers in a moderately better bargaining position in dealing with employers. They are seats of great power—of the greatest private economic power in the community. Their policies from now on will be a major determinant of the prosperity of the country. If their policies are farsighted, if unions see their stake in the prosperity of the community as a whole, unions will make a major contribution toward building a greater civilization in America. If unions are narrow, uninformed, and shortsighted in their policies, they will be as great a problem for the community as was the parochialism of the towns and small principalities in the later Middle Ages.

The literature of industrial relations has taken little account of the changed status of unions. The literature still treats unions as underdogs and ignores almost completely both the great problems and the great opportunities created by the power of unions.

Do you agree with Professor Slichter that unions are seats of the greatest private economic power in the community? To pinpoint the matter, do you believe that the fifty largest unions are more influential than the fifty largest corporations?

2. What changes would you like to see made in union-management relations in the United States to improve them? To what extent would you hold unions and to what extent managements responsible for the initiative necessary to bring about such changes?

3. If collective bargaining were to be scrapped altogether, what values, if any, would be lost to our society?

4. Two problems which face an industrialized nation such as the United States are (a) providing the manpower which industry will need if we are to enjoy a rising standard of living, on the one hand, and (b) finding jobs for an expanding labor force in the face of increased productivity, on the other hand. These problems are from one point of view antithetical—if men are needed to turn out more goods and services, then there is no need to worry about jobs for new workers. But labor demand and labor supply are seldom nicely correlated, and it is possible for a nation to fail to achieve one or both of these objectives.

Examples of conflicting views as to which of these two problems is likely to be more serious in the future are offered in the two statements reproduced below, one from the president of a large union, the other from the president of a large corporation.

After reading these statements, try to make estimates (drawing on data presented in the foregoing readings or on published data of the Bureau of Labor Statistics and the Bureau of the Census) which will allow you to answer these questions:

a. How large a labor force will be needed in 1975 to produce the goods and services which will give us as a nation a standard of living which has increased at the same rate as we have experienced in the past? (For this purpose you will have to make some informed estimate of likely increases in productivity.)

b. How large will the labor force be in 1975, on the basis of current estimates? (For this purpose the student may wish to consult the Census Bureau's *Current Population Reports: Labor Force*, Series P-50, No. 69,

October, 1956, "Projections of the Labor Force in the United States, 1955 to 1975.")

Statement of Walter Reuther, President, United Automobile Workers, in Automation and Technological Change, hearings before the Joint Congressional Committee on the Economic Report, 84th Cong., 1st Sess., 1955, pp. 106–108

Our economic needs will be rising in the years ahead. The population, it is expected, will increase from approximately 165 million at present to about 190 million 10 years from now. The number of households will rise from about 48 million now to an estimated 56 million in 1965. . . . But economic expansion does not arise simply because we desire it. Economic growth is the product of expanding markets that make possible the profitable utilization and further expansion of productive capacity. . . .

Productivity is already increasing at a faster pace than in the long-run past. In commenting on recent productivity increases in manufacturing, the August 1955 issue of the Federal Reserve Bulletin states that "output per man-hour has risen somewhat more rapidly over the past 2 years of recession and recovery than the average postwar rate of about 4 percent a year."

In other words, man-hour output in manufacturing industries, which had been rising at an average annual rate of about 3 percent in the long-run past before World War II, rose to an average yearly rate of approximately 4 percent after the war and to somewhat more than 4 percent in the past 2 years.

As a result of the sharp productivity increases of the past 2 years, employment has lagged considerably behind the improvements in general economic conditions. This is particularly true in manufacturing. In September 1955, there were 600,000 fewer wage and salary workers employed in manufacturing industries than in September 1953 (17.5 million 2 years ago in September 1953, by comparison with 16.9 million in September 1955).

Automation—in addition to the more conventional improvements in machines and work flow—will be increasing the rate of the national economy's rising man-hour output still further. Instead of average annual productivity increases of some 3 to 4 percent, the annual rate of rising man-hour output in the national economy may reach 5 to 6 percent or more.

With a civilian labor force of 70 million, 5 to 6 percent annual increases in the economy's man-hour output would make it necessary to add about 3½ million job opportunities each year, merely to absorb the possible displacement effect of rising productivity. Another way of stating it is that annual productivity increases of 5 to 6 percent in the coming decade will be capable of displacing about 3½ million or more employees each year, if the national economy fails to expand, along with the rapid improvements in productive efficiency. . . .

The problem grows still greater when we consider that the labor force will be increasing at an accelerating rate in the period ahead. And the accelerating growth of the labor force will require the addition of yet more new job opportunities each year, if high levels of employment are to be maintained.

Statement of Don G. Mitchell, President, Sylvania Electric Products, Inc., from the same hearings, pp. 182–183

I not only do not even remotely fear that mechanization or automation will cause long-term unemployment, but I am concerned about the strong possibility of a labor shortage in the years ahead, unless the rate of mechanization is increased.

The past gives us a good clue to the future. As reported by the Joint Committee on the Economic Report, and the United States Department of Labor, at year end 1947, some 44 million persons were employed in industry; in 1954, 50 million were employed. If production techniques had not progressed between 1947 and 1954, 58 million persons would have been required to produce the goods and services actually demanded in 1954. The American population simply could not have furnished that working force. Without increased mechanization, without laborsaving devices, and overall greater production efficiency, the public's needs simply would not have been met.

Now, let us look at the future. I recently read a survey in Factory Management and Maintenance magazine in which a gross national product of $850 billion was predicted for 1975 . . . Now, unless you buy the fact that it is possible to have that gross national product of $850 billion by 1975, then the rest of my argument is specious, but I believe that a high gross national product of that magnitude is possible, and I believe we will have it.

Our gross national product will be this year about $382 billion. Factory Management and Maintenance also predicted a working force in 1975 of 82 million people against 64 million people today. They point out if the present rate of automation continues, every available worker will have to be putting in 40 hours per week, in order to keep raising our standard of living at the rate it is being increased now. The entire Nation's long-term goal of a shorter workweek would be impossible. If Mr. Reuther wants the 32-hour workweek, which he says he does as quoted in yesterday's newspaper, then we had better get on the ball and speed up automation because if we don't, he cannot have it. A 32-hour workweek, for example, would require an estimated 105 million persons, and that large a force will not exist.

There is no question but that the rate of mechanization will have to be increased if we are to realize its ambitions of both a steadily rising standard of living and a shorter workweek.

On the strength of your findings as to the probable supply of and demand for labor in 1975, what conclusions do you draw as to the possibility or desirability of a shorter work week?

5. If prosperity and full employment continue indefinitely in the future, marred at most by minor downturns in business activity, how do you think unions will be affected? Will they be stronger, in a situation which would appear to enhance their bargaining power, or weaker, in a situation which would appear to make them less necessary to workers?